# MICROSOFT®
# WORD
## 2013

FILE    INSERT    DESIGN    PAGE LAYOUT    REFERENCES

## Nita Rutkosky

## Audrey Roggenkamp

Pierce College at Puyallup, Puyallup, Washington

Paradigm PUBLISHING

St. Paul

**Director of Editorial:** Christine Hurney
**Director of Production:** Timothy W. Larson
**Senior Editor:** Cheryl Drivdahl
**Production Editor:** Lori Michelle Ryan
**Assistant Production Editor:** Katherine Lee
**Cover and Text Designer:** Leslie Anderson
**Senior Design and Production Specialists:**
Jaana Bykonich and Jack Ross

**Design and Production Specialists:** Valerie King and
Sara Schmidt Boldon
**Copy Editor:** Susan Freese
**Indexer:** Ina Gravitz
**Testers:** Pat Jarvis and Jeff Johnson
**VP and Director of Digital Projects:** Chuck Bratton
**Digital Projects Manager:** Tom Modl

Care has been taken to verify the accuracy of information presented in this book. However, the authors, editors, and publisher cannot accept responsibility for Web, email, newsgroup, or chat room subject matter or content, or for consequences from application of the information in this book, and make no warranty, expressed or implied, with respect to its content.

**Trademarks:** Microsoft is a trademark or registered trademark of Microsoft Corporation in the United States and/ or other countries. Some of the product names and company names included in this book have been used for identification purposes only and may be trademarks or registered trade names of their respective manufacturers and sellers. The authors, editors, and publisher disclaim any affiliation, association, or connection with, or sponsorship or endorsement by, such owners.

**Acknowledgments:** The authors and editors are grateful to the many individuals who contributed to various aspects of this project. The following individuals reviewed the previous version of this book and offered valuable suggestions for Signature Word 2013: Paula Belmonte, MA, Union County College, Cranford, New Jersey; Dawn L. Dias, North Central Texas College, Corinth, Texas; Janel C. Doyle, Southcentral Kentucky Community and Technical College— KATI Campus, Bowling Green, Kentucky; Pat Jarvis, Truckee Meadows Community College, Reno, Nevada; Barb Kaufman, Portland Community College, Sylvania Campus, Portland, Oregon; Lisa Mears, MEd, Palm Beach State College, Lake Worth, Florida; Carol Thomas Merchant, MS, Tarrant County College, Fort Worth, Texas; Daniel Mondshein, MBA, MSIT, PhD candidate, Eastern Florida State College, Cocoa, Florida; Carol Schlievert, Conestoga College Institute of Technology and Advanced Learning, Kitchener, Ontario; Kristie Theis, Terra Community College, Fremont, Ohio. The following individuals also made significant contributions to the program: Ann Mills, Ivy Tech Community College; Ian Rutkosky, Pierce College at Puyallup; Brienna McWade; Trever Anderson.

We have made every effort to trace the ownership of all copyrighted material and to secure permission from copyright holders. In the event of any question arising as to the use of any material, we will be pleased to make the necessary corrections in future printings. Thanks are due to the aforementioned authors, publishers, and agents for permission to use the materials indicated.

Paradigm Publishing is independent from Microsoft Corporation, and not affiliated with Microsoft in any manner. While this publication may be used in assisting individuals to prepare for a Microsoft Office Specialist (core-level or expert-level) certification exam, Microsoft, its designated program administrator, and Paradigm Publishing do not warrant that use of this publication will ensure passing a Microsoft Office Specialist (core-level or expert-level) certification exam.

ISBN 978-0-76385-195-8 (text)
ISBN 978-0-76385-199-6 (text & disc)

© 2014 by Paradigm Publishing, Inc.
875 Montreal Way
St. Paul, MN 55102
Email: educate@emcp.com
Website: www.paradigmcollege.net

Printed in the United States of America

22  21  20  19  18  17  16  15  14  13        2  3  4  5  6  7  8  9  10

# Brief Contents

# Contents

# Preface

To prepare for a successful business career, students need to become proficient at word processing, which is the use of computer software to create documents such as letters, contracts, group mailings, newsletters, and brochures. Students will also find word processing helpful in creating and maintaining personal letters and records, documents that support home-based businesses and academic papers and reports.

*Signature Series: Microsoft® Word 2013* offers a clear, comprehensive approach to mastering Microsoft's popular word processing program, Word 2013. The textbook is designed to be used by students with or without prior knowledge of word processing and is well-suited for beginning, intermediate, and advanced word processing classes. After successfully completing a course using this textbook, students will be able to

- Create and edit memos, letters, and reports of varying complexity
- Plan, research, write, revise, and publish documents to meet specific information needs
- Format and customize a wide range of document types and styles
- Add and modify graphics and other visual elements to enhance written communication
- Organize content into tables, lists, and other structures that promote reader understanding
- Link and embed files from other Microsoft applications, and copy macros between documents
- Open and edit PDF files in Word
- Save files to SkyDrive and other remote locations
- Manage the process of editing and reviewing documents efficiently in a collaborative work environment

Well-designed textbook pedagogy is important, but students learn technology skills best through practice and problem solving. Technology provides opportunities for interactive learning as well as excellent ways to quickly and accurately assess performance. To that end, this textbook is supported by SNAP, Paradigm Publishing's web-based training and assessment system. Details about SNAP as well as additional student and instructor resources are found on pages xii and xiii.

## Textbook Features

*Signature Word 2013* is divided into six units that gradually lead students from a basic understanding to advanced proficiency. The following visual tour illustrates how each feature in the textbook contributes to a successful learning environment.

## Unit openers list chapters and unit assessments.

Each unit consists of five **chapters** that provide a well-balanced combination of theory and practical applicaton.

Each unit ends with a set of **Performance Assessments** that allow students to determine what they have learned and to apply their new skills in creative situations.

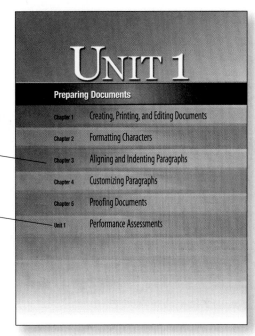

## Each chapter opens with a brief overview of the material covered in the chapter.

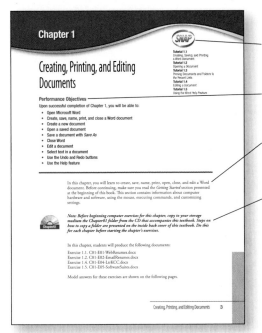

The SNAP logo identifies **interactive tutorials** that support the skills taught in the chapter.

A list of **Performance Objectives** identifies the specific learning goals of the chapter.

Introductory material provides an **overview of the new features and skills** covered in the chapter.

A helpful note gives simple **instructions for accessing the student data files** used in the chapter and is followed by a list of the files that students will need for the chapter exercises.

**Model answers** presented at the beginning of the chapter show students what they will create for each exercise in the chapter.

## Throughout the chapter, concepts are presented sequentially to build knowledge and skill.

**Bold headings** and **clear, concise text** describe new concepts and features.

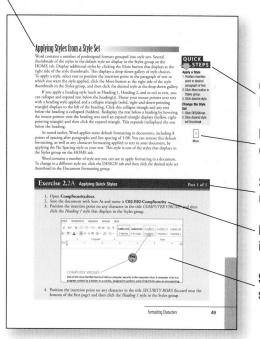

**Quick Steps** in the margin summarize the method for accomplishing key tasks covered in the text.

**Images** in the margin help students quickly locate the features described in the text.

Step-by-step **exercises** give students the opportunity to practice using the features they have just read about.

**Bold formatting** highlights the names of the student data files used in exercises and assessments.

**Screen captures** provide visual cues to guide students through the steps in the exercises.

## End-of-chapter materials provide opportunities for students to review and reinforce what they have learned.

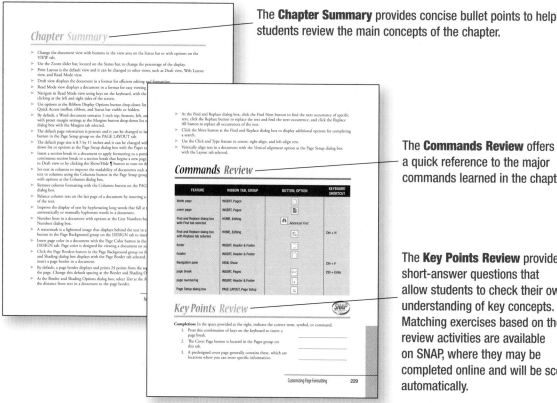

The **Chapter Summary** provides concise bullet points to help students review the main concepts of the chapter.

The **Commands Review** offers a quick reference to the major commands learned in the chapter.

The **Key Points Review** provides short-answer questions that allow students to check their own understanding of key concepts. Matching exercises based on these review activities are available on SNAP, where they may be completed online and will be scored automatically.

# Chapter Assessments offer graduated levels of performance-based exercises that students can complete without step-by-step guidance.

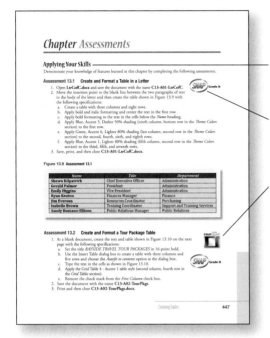

**Applying Your Skills** assessments allow students to demonstrate their knowledge of the skills taught in the chapter.

Versions of activities marked with a **SNAP Grade It** icon are available in SNAP, where they may be completed online, live in the Office application, and will be scored automatically.

**Start-from-Scratch** icons indicate exercises and assessments that give students practice in opening a new, blank Word document and then typing and formatting the content that they create.

**Achieving Signature Status** assessments challenge students to apply what they have learned while solving unique problems

**Expanding Your Skills** assessments prompt students to explore new features and learn additional skills.

**Bold formatting** and **magenta color** highlight text that students are to type into a document.

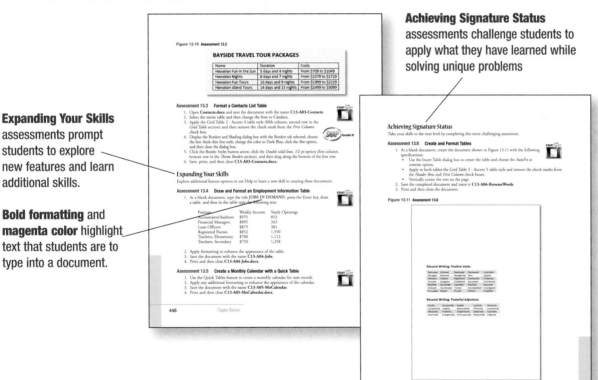

**End-of-unit Performance Assessments present unique situations for students to assess and apply their new skills.**

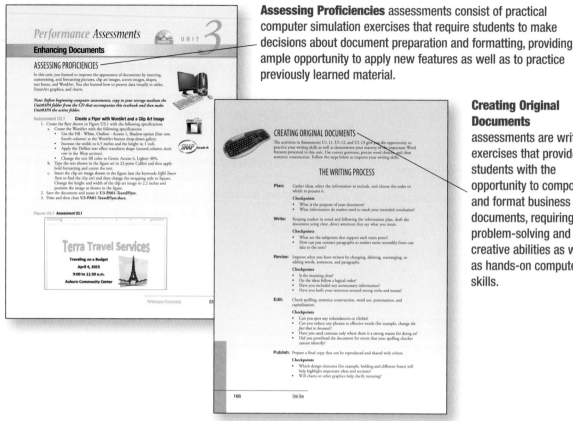

**Assessing Proficiencies** assessments consist of practical computer simulation exercises that require students to make decisions about document preparation and formatting, providing ample opportunity to apply new features as well as to practice previously learned material.

**Creating Original Documents** assessments are writing exercises that provide students with the opportunity to compose and format business documents, requiring problem-solving and creative abilities as well as hands-on computer skills.

# SNAP Web-Based Training and Assessment

Available at snap2013.emcp.com, SNAP is a web-based program offering an interactive venue for learning Microsoft Office 2013. SNAP includes a learning management system with an online grade book, multimedia tutorials, performance skill items, live-in-the-Office-application Performance Evaluations and Grade It Chapter Assessments, Key Points Review matching activities, a concepts test bank, and a set of course planning tools.

# Student Resources

**Student Resources Disc** Each textbook includes a Student Resources Disc that contains typed documents and files required for completing exercises and assessments. The first page of each chapter in the textbook provides instructions for accessing student data files from a specific folder on the Student Resources Disc. The student will need to copy this folder of files from the disc to a storage medium before beginning the section activities. ***Note: See the inside back cover of this textbook for instructions on copying a folder.***

**Internet Resource Center for Students** Additional material for students preparing to work in a business office is provided at the book-specific website at www.ParadigmCollege.net/SignatureWord13. Here, students will find the same resources that are on the Student Resources disc along with study tools, online quizzes, web links, and other information useful in education and work settings.

**SNAP Tutorials Disc** The SNAP tutorials are also provided on disc for use without the full SNAP program. These interactive tutorials teach the basics of Word and include self-check exercises that provide instant feedback.

**Online eBook** For students who prefer studying with an eBook, *Signature Word 2013* is available in electronic form. The web-based, password-protected eBook features dynamic navigation tools, including bookmarking, a linked table of contents, and the ability to jump to a specific page. The eBook format also supports helpful study tools, such as highlighting and note taking.

# Instructor Resources

### Instructor's Guide and Instructor Resources Disc
Instructor support for this text includes the printed Instructor's Guide packaged with the Instructor Resources Disc. The print and electronic resources include planning information, such as a course syllabus and lesson plans with teaching hints; presentation resources, such as PowerPoint presentations with lecture notes; and assessment resources, such as an overview of available assessment venues, live model answers for chapter exercises, live and PDF model answers and grading rubrics for chapter and unit assessments; and annotated model answers for selected assessments.

### Internet Resource Center for Instructors
The contents of the Instructor's Guide and Instructor Resources Disc package are available on the instructor's password-protected section of the Internet Resource Center for this title at www.ParadigmCollege.net/SignatureWord13.

### Computerized Test Generator
Instructors can use the multiple-choice question banks in the ExamView® Assessment Suite to create customized web-based or print tests for this textbook. The ExamView® Assessment Suite and question banks are provided on the Instructor Resources Disc.

### Blackboard Cartridge
This set of files allows instructors to create a personalized Blackboard website for their courses and provides course content, tests, and the mechanisms for establishing communication via e-discussions and online group conferences. Available content includes a syllabus, test banks, PowerPoint presentations, and supplementary course materials. Upon request, the files can be available within 24–48 hours. Hosting the site is the responsibility of the educational institution.

Blackboard

# Microsoft Office Specialist Certification: Core and Expert Levels

Earning the Microsoft Office Specialist (MOS) certification for Word demonstrates that you have acquired the expertise you need to get the most out of Microsoft Word and are prepared to move forward in your career or increase your productivity on the job, at school, or in your personal life. With the release of Office 2013, Microsoft developed a new set of objectives for the MOS certification exams. This textbook has been validated and approved by ProCert Labs (www.procert.com) as courseware covering both the core- and expert-level objectives in the MOS certification exams. Tables listing those objectives and a correlation showing where this textbook covers each objective are available at www.ParadigmCollege.net/SignatureWord13.

# System Requirements

This textbook is designed for the student to complete exercises and assessments on a computer running a standard installation of Microsoft Office Professional Plus 2013 and the Microsoft Windows 8 operating system. (***Note: Office 2013 will also operate on computers running the Windows 7 operating system.***) To effectively run Office 2013 and Windows 8, the computer should be outfitted with the following hardware and software:

- 1 gigahertz (GHz) processor or higher; 1 gigabyte (GB) of RAM (32 bit) or 2 GB of RAM (64 bit)
- 3 GB of available hard-disk space
- .NET version 3.5, 4.0, or 4.5
- DirectX 10 graphics card
- Minimum 1024 × 576 screen resolution monitor (or 1366 × 768 to use Windows Snap feature)
- Computer mouse, multi-touch device, or other compatible pointing device

Screen captures in this book were created using a screen resolution display setting of 1600 × 900. Refer to the Customizing Settings section of the Getting Started section that follows this Preface for instructions on changing your monitor's resolution. Figure G.9 on page xxv shows the Microsoft Office Word ribbon at three resolutions for comparison purposes. Choose the resolution that best matches your computer; however, be aware that using a resolution other than 1600 × 900 means that your screens may not match the illustrations in this book.

# About the Authors

**Nita Rutkosky** began teaching business education courses at Pierce College in Puyallup, Washington, in 1978. Since then, she has taught a variety of software applications to students in postsecondary Information Technology certificate and degree programs. In addition to this textbook, she has co-authored *Benchmark Series: Microsoft® Office 2013, 2010, 2007,* and *2003; Marquee Series: Microsoft® Office 2013, 2010, 2007,* and *2003; Using Computers in the Medical Office: Microsoft® Word, Excel,* and *PowerPoint 2013, 2010, 2007* and *2003;* and *Computer and Internet Essentials: Preparing for IC³.* She has also authored textbooks on keyboarding, WordPerfect, desktop publishing, and voice recognition for Paradigm Publishing, Inc.

**Audrey Roggenkamp** has been teaching courses in the Business Information Technology department at Pierce College in Puyallup since 2005. Her courses have included keyboarding, skill building, and Microsoft Office program training. In addition to this title, she has co-authored *Benchmark Series: Microsoft® Office 2013, 2010,* and *2007; Marquee Series: Microsoft® Office 2013, 2010,* and *2007; Using Computers in the Medical Office: Microsoft® Word, Excel, and PowerPoint 2013, 2010, 2007,* and *2003; Signature Series: Advanced Microsoft(R) Word 2013: Desktop Publishing; Paradigm Keyboarding and Applications I: Using Microsoft Word 2013, Sixth Edition, Sessions 1–60* and *Sessions 61–120;* and *Computer and Internet Essentials: Preparing for IC³,* all for Paradigm Publishing, Inc.

As you work your way through this textbook, you will learn functions and commands for Microsoft Word 2013, one of the applications included in the Microsoft Office 2013 suite. Word 2013 is a word processing program and you will need access to a microcomputer system to operate it.

## Identifying Computer Hardware

The computer equipment you will use to operate Word 2013 is referred to as *hardware*. You will need access to a microcomputer system that includes a central processing unit (CPU), monitor, keyboard, mouse, printer, and drives. If you are not sure what equipment you will be operating, check with your instructor. The computer system shown in Figure G.1 consists of six components. Each component is discussed separately in the material that follows.

**Figure G.1  Microcomputer System**

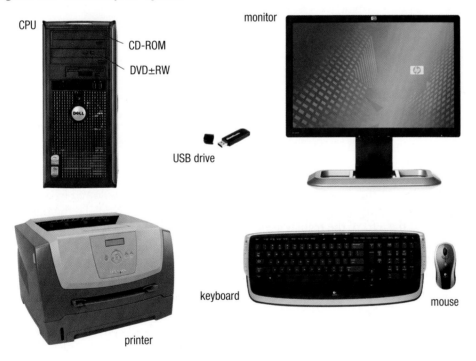

## CPU

The central processing unit (CPU) is the brain of the computer and is where all processing occurs. Silicon chips containing miniaturized circuitry, are placed on boards that are plugged into slots within the CPU. Whenever an instruction is given to the computer, it is processed through the circuitry in the CPU.

## Monitor

A computer monitor looks like a television screen. It displays both the information of the program being run by the computer and the text being input at the keyboard. The quality of a display for monitors varies depending on the type of monitor and the level of resolution. Monitors can also vary in size, generally ranging from 13 inches to 26 inches or larger.

## Keyboard

A keyboard is used to input information into the computer. The number and location of keys on a keyboard can vary. In addition to letters, numbers, and symbols, most computer keyboards contain function keys, arrow keys, and a numeric keypad. Figure G.2 shows a computer keyboard.

**Figure G.2 Microcomputer Keyboard**

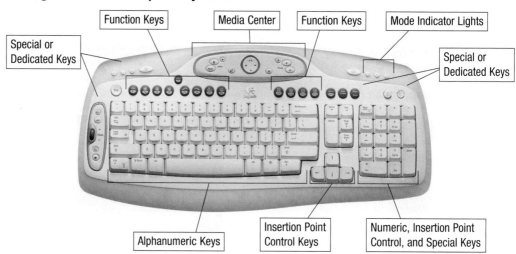

The 12 keys at the top of a keyboard, labeled with the letter F followed by a number, are called *function keys*. Use these keys to perform functions in Word. To the right (and sometimes to the left) of the regular keys is a group of *special* or *dedicated keys*. These keys are labeled with specific functions that will be performed when you press the key. Below the special keys are arrow keys. Use these keys to move the insertion point in the document screen.

Some keyboards include mode indicator lights. When you select certain modes, a light appears on the keyboard. For example, if you press the Caps Lock key, which disables the lowercase alphabet, a light appears next to Caps Lock. Similarly, pressing the Num Lock key will disable the special functions on the numeric keypad, which is located at the right side of the keyboard.

## Drives and Ports

Depending on the computer system you are using, Word 2013 is installed on a hard drive or as part of a network system. Whether you are using Word on a hard drive or network system, you will need to have available a CD or DVD drive to complete the projects and assessments in this book. If you plan to use a USB drive as your storage medium, you will also need a USB port. You will insert the CD that accompanies this textbook into the CD or DVD drive and then copy folders from the disc to your storage medium. You will also save documents you create to folders on your storage medium.

## Printer

A document you create in Word is considered ***soft copy***. If you want to create a ***hard copy*** of a document, you need to print it. To print documents, you will need to access a printer, which will probably be either a laser printer or an ink-jet printer. A laser printer uses a laser beam combined with heat and pressure to print documents, while an ink-jet printer prints a document by spraying a fine mist of ink on the page.

## Mouse or Touchpad

Many functions in Word are designed to be performed using a ***mouse*** or a similar pointing device. A mouse is an input device that sits on a flat surface next to the computer. You can operate a mouse with your left or right hand. When you move the mouse on the flat surface, a corresponding mouse pointer moves on the screen, and clicking the left or right mouse buttons allows you to select various objects and comments. Figure G.1 shows an illustration of a mouse.

If you are working on a laptop computer, you may use a ***touchpad*** instead of a mouse. A touchpad allows you to move the mouse pointer by moving your finger across a surface at the base of the keyboard. You click by using your thumb to press the button located at the bottom of the touchpad.

### Using the Mouse

The Word program can be operated with the keyboard and a mouse. The mouse generally has two buttons on top, which you press to execute specific functions and commands. A mouse may also contain a wheel, which can be used to scroll in a window or as a third button. To use the mouse, rest it on a flat surface or a mouse pad. Put your hand over it with your palm resting on top of the mouse, your wrist resting on the table surface, and your index finger resting on the left mouse button. As you move your hand, and thus the mouse, a corresponding pointer moves on the screen.

When using the mouse, you should understand four terms—point, click, double-click, and drag. When operating the mouse, you may need to *point* to a specific command, button, or icon. To ***point*** means to position the mouse pointer on the desired item. With the mouse pointer positioned on the desired item, you may need to click a button on the mouse to select the item. To ***click*** means to quickly tap a mouse button once. To complete two steps at one time, such as choosing and then executing a function, double-click the mouse button. To ***double-click*** means to tap the left mouse button twice in quick succession. To ***drag*** means to press and hold the left mouse button, move the mouse pointer to a specific location, and then release the button.

### Using the Mouse Pointer

The mouse pointer changes appearance depending on where you have positioned it and what function you are performing. The following are some of the ways the mouse pointer can appear when you are working in Word:

- The mouse pointer appears as an I-beam (called the ***I-beam pointer***) when you are inserting text in a document. The I-beam pointer can be used to move the insertion point or to select text.

- The mouse pointer appears as an arrow pointing up and to the left (called the ***arrow pointer***) when it is moved to the Title bar, Quick Access toolbar, ribbon, or an option in a dialog box, among other locations.

- The mouse pointer becomes a double-headed arrow (either pointing left and right, pointing up and down, or pointing diagonally) when you perform certain functions, such as changing the size of an object.

- In certain situations, such as when you move an object or image, the mouse pointer displays with a four-headed arrow attached. The four-headed arrow indicates that you can move the object left, right, up, or down.

- When a request is being processed or when a program is being loaded, the mouse pointer may appear as a moving circle. The moving circle means "please wait." When the process is completed, the circle is replaced with a normal arrow pointer.

- When the mouse pointer displays as a hand with a pointing index finger, it indicates that more information is available about an item. The mouse pointer also displays as a hand with a pointing index finger when you hover the mouse over a hyperlink.

## Choosing Commands

In Word, you can use several methods to choose commands. A ***command*** is an instruction that tells the program to do something. You can choose a command using the mouse or the keyboard. When Word is open, the ribbon contains buttons and options for completing tasks, as well as tabs you can click to display additional buttons and options. To choose a button on the Quick Access toolbar or on the ribbon, position the tip of the mouse arrow pointer on a button and then click the left mouse button.

Word provides ***accelerator keys*** you can press to use a command in a program. Press the Alt key on the keyboard to display KeyTips that identify the accelerator key you can press to execute a command. For example, press the Alt key in a document and KeyTips display, as shown in Figure G.3 on the next page. Continue pressing accelerator keys until you execute the desired command. For example, if you want to begin spell checking a document, you would press the Alt key, press the R key on the keyboard to display the REVIEW tab, and then press the S key on the keyboard.

**Figure G.3  Accelerator Keys KeyTips**

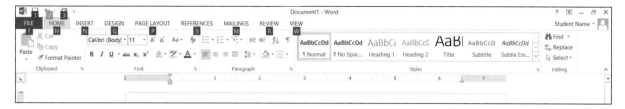

# Choosing Commands from Drop-down Lists

To choose a command from a drop-down list with the mouse, position the mouse pointer on the desired option and then click the left mouse button. To make a selection from a drop-down list with the keyboard, type the underlined letter in the desired option.

Some options at a drop-down list may appear in gray (dimmed), indicating that the option is currently unavailable. If an option at a drop-down list displays preceded by a check mark, the check mark indicates that the option is currently active. If an option at a drop-down list displays followed by an ellipsis (…), a dialog box will display when that option is chosen.

**Figure G.4  Font Dialog Box**

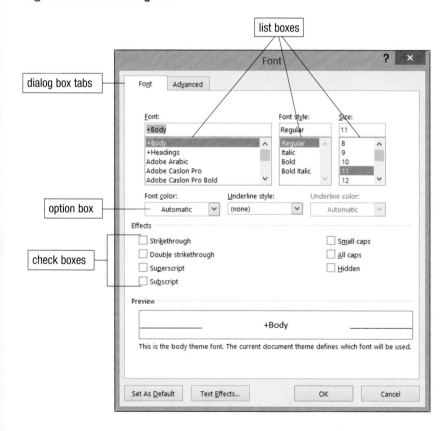

## Choosing Options from a Dialog Box

A ***dialog box*** contains options for applying formatting to a document or to data in a document. Some dialog boxes display with tabs along the top, which provide additional options. For example, the Font dialog box, as shown in Figure G.4 on the previous page, contains two tabs—the Font tab and the Advanced tab. The tab that displays in front is the active tab. To make a tab active using the mouse, position the arrow pointer on the desired tab and then click the left mouse button. If you are using the keyboard, press Ctrl + Tab or press Alt + the underlined letter on the desired tab.

To choose options from a dialog box with the mouse, position the arrow pointer on the desired option and then click the left mouse button. If you are using the keyboard, press the Tab key to move the insertion point forward from option to option. Press Shift + Tab to move the insertion point backward from option to option. You can also hold down the Alt key and then press the underlined letter of the desired option. When an option is selected, it displays with a blue background or surrounded by a dashed box called a ***marquee***. A dialog box contains one or more of the following elements: text boxes, list boxes, check boxes, option buttons, measurement boxes, and command buttons.

### Text Boxes

Text boxes are options in a dialog box that require you to enter text. For example, the boxes to the right of the *Find what* and *Replace with* options at the Find and Replace dialog box, as shown in Figure G.5, are text boxes. In a text box, you type text or edit existing text. You can edit text in a text box in the same manner you would edit text in a document. (You will learn to edit text in a document in Chapter 1.) Use the Left and Right Arrow keys on the keyboard to move the insertion point without deleting text and use the Delete key or Backspace key to delete text.

**Figure G.5  Find and Replace Dialog Box**

### List Boxes and Option Boxes

Some dialog boxes, such as the Font dialog box shown in Figure G.4 and the Building Blocks Organizer dialog box shown in Figure G.6, contain a ***list box***. To make a selection from a list box with the mouse, move the arrow pointer to the desired option and then click the left mouse button.

**Figure G.6  Building Blocks Organizer Dialog Box**

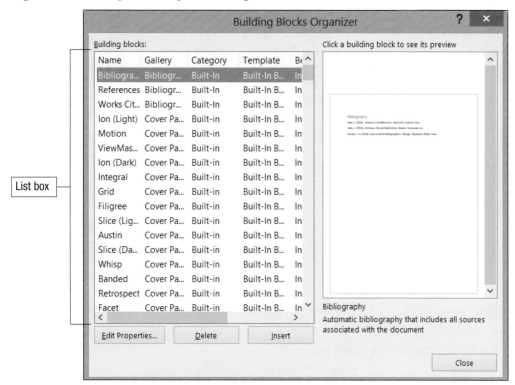

Some list boxes may contain a scroll bar. This scroll bar displays at the right side of the list box (a vertical scroll bar) or at the bottom of the list box (a horizontal scroll bar). Use a vertical scroll bar or a horizontal scroll bar to move through the list if the list is longer than the box. To move down through a list on a vertical scroll bar, position the arrow pointer on the down-pointing arrow and hold down the left mouse button. To scroll up through the list in a vertical scroll bar, position the arrow pointer on the up-pointing arrow and hold down the left mouse button. You can also move the arrow pointer above the scroll box and click the left mouse button to scroll up the list or move the arrow pointer below the scroll box and click the left mouse button to move down the list. To move through a list with a horizontal scroll bar, click the left-pointing arrow to scroll to the left of the list or click the right-pointing arrow to scroll to the right of the list.

To make a selection from a list using the keyboard, move the insertion point into the box by holding down the Alt key and pressing the underlined letter of the desired option. Press the Up and/or Down Arrow keys on the keyboard to move through the list, and press Enter once the desired option is selected.

In some dialog boxes, not enough room is available for a list box. In these dialog boxes, options are contained in a drop-down list box called an ***option box***. Option boxes display with a down-pointing arrow. For example, in Figure G.4, the font color options are contained in an option box. To display the different color options, click the down-pointing arrow at the right of the Font color option box. If you are using the keyboard, press Alt + C.

## Check Boxes

Some dialog boxes contain options preceded by a box. A check mark may or may not appear in the box. The Font dialog box, shown in Figure G.4, displays a variety of check boxes within the *Effects* section. If a check mark appears in the box, the option is active (turned on). If the check box does not contain a check mark, the option is inactive (turned off). Any number of check boxes can be active. For example, in the Font dialog box, you can insert a check mark in any or all of the boxes in the *Effects* section and these options will be active.

To make a check box active or inactive with the mouse, position the tip of the arrow pointer in the check box, and then click the left mouse button. If you are using the keyboard, press Alt + the underlined letter of the desired option.

## Option Buttons

The Insert Table dialog box shown in Figure G.7 contains options in the *AutoFit behavior* section preceded by ***option buttons***. Only one option button can be selected at any time. When an option button is selected, a blue or black circle displays in the button. To select an option button with the mouse, position the tip of the arrow pointer inside the option button, and then click the left mouse button. To make a selection with the keyboard, hold down the Alt key and then press the underlined letter of the desired option.

**Figure G.7  Insert Table Dialog Box**

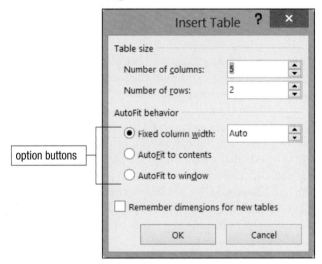

## Measurement Boxes

Some options in a dialog box contain measurements or amounts you can increase or decrease. These options are generally located in a ***measurement box***. For example, the Paragraph dialog box, as shown in Figure G.8 on the next page, contains the *Left, Right, Before,* and *After* measurement boxes. To increase a number in a measurement box, position the tip of the arrow pointer on the up-pointing arrow to the right of the desired option, and then click the left mouse button. To decrease the number, click the down-pointing arrow. If you are using the keyboard, press Alt + the underlined letter of the desired option, and then press the Up Arrow key to increase the number or the Down Arrow key to decrease the number.

**Figure G.8  Paragraph Dialog Box**

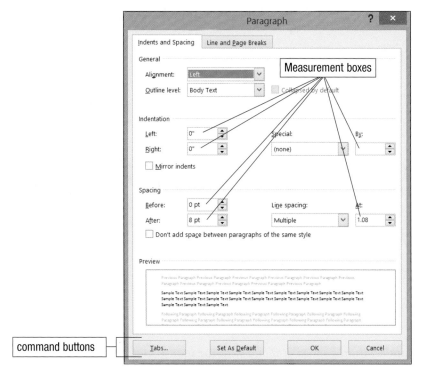

## Command Buttons

The buttons at the bottom of the Paragraph dialog box in Figure G.8 are called *command buttons*. Use a command button to execute or cancel a command. Some command buttons display with an ellipsis (…). A command button that displays with an ellipsis opens another dialog box when chosen. To choose a command button with the mouse, position the arrow pointer on the desired button and then click the left mouse button. To choose a command button with the keyboard, press the Tab key until the desired command button is surrounded by a marquee and then press the Enter key.

## Choosing Commands with Keyboard Shortcuts

Word offers a variety of keyboard shortcuts you can use to executive specific commands. Keyboard shortcuts generally require two or more keys. For example, the keyboard shortcut to display the Open dialog box is Ctrl + F12. To use this keyboard shortcut, hold down the Ctrl key, press the F12 key, and then release the Ctrl key. For a list of keyboard shortcuts, refer to the Help files.

## Choosing Commands with Shortcut Menus

Word includes shortcut menus that display commands and options related to the position of the mouse pointer or the insertion point. To display a shortcut menu, click the right mouse button or press Shift + F10. For example, if you position the mouse pointer in a paragraph of text in a document and then click the right mouse button, the shortcut menu shown in Figure G.9 on the next page displays in the document (along with the Mini toolbar).

**Figure G.9  Shortcut Menu**

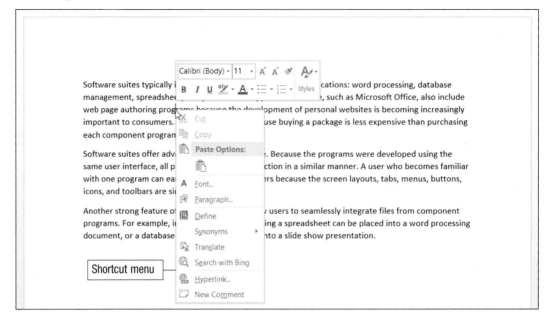

To select an option from a shortcut menu with the mouse, click the desired option. If you are using the keyboard, press the Up or Down Arrow key until the desired option is selected, and then press the Enter key. To close a shortcut menu without choosing an option, click anywhere outside the shortcut menu or press the Esc key.

## Customizing Settings

Before beginning computer exercises in this textbook, you may need to customize your monitor's settings and turn on the display of file extensions. Exercises in the chapters in this textbook assume that the monitor display is set at 1600 × 900 pixels and that the display of file extensions is turned on.

Before you begin learning Word 2013, take a moment to check the display settings on the computer you are using. Your monitor's display settings are important because the ribbon in Word adjusts to the screen resolution setting of your computer monitor. A computer monitor set at a high resolution will have the ability to show more buttons on the ribbon than will a monitor set to a low resolution. The illustrations in this textbook were created with a screen resolution display set at 1600 × 900 pixels. In Figure G.10 on the next page, the Word ribbon is shown three ways: at a lower screen resolution (1366 × 768 pixels), at the screen resolution featured throughout this textbook, and at a higher screen resolution (1920 × 1080 pixels). Note the variances in the ribbon in all three examples. If possible, set your display to 1600 × 900 pixels to match the illustrations you will see in this textbook.

## Figure G.10 Monitor Resolution

**1366 × 768 screen resolution**

**1600 × 900 screen resolution**

**1920 × 1080 screen resolution**

---

## Exercise G.1  Setting Monitor Display to 1600 × 900

1. At the Windows 8 desktop, right-click a blank area of the screen.
2. At the shortcut menu, click the *Screen resolution* option.
3. At the Screen Resolution window, click the *Resolution* option box. (This displays a slider bar. Your slider bar may display differently than what you see in the image at the right.)
4. Drag the button on the slider bar until *1600 × 900* displays to the right of the slider bar.
5. Click in the Screen Resolution window to remove the slider bar.
6. Click the Apply button.
7. Click the Keep Changes button.
8. Click the OK button.

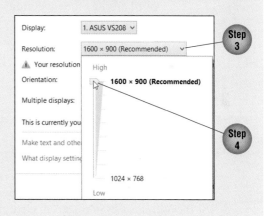

## Exercise G.2 Displaying File Extensions

1. At the Windows 8 desktop, position the mouse pointer in the lower left corner of the Taskbar until the Start screen thumbnail displays and then click the right mouse button.
2. At the pop-up list, click the *File Explorer* option.
3. At the Computer window, click the View tab on the ribbon and then click the *File name extensions* check box in the Show/hide group to insert a check mark.
4. Close the Computer window.

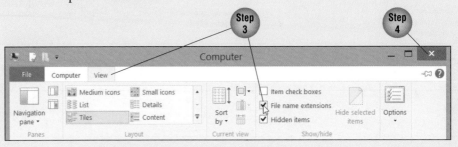

## Completing Computer Exercises

Some exercises in this textbook require that you open an existing file. Exercise files are saved on the Student Resources CD in individual chapter folders. Before beginning a chapter, copy the necessary folder from the CD to your storage medium (such as a USB flash drive or your SkyDrive) using the Computer window. To maximize storage capacity, delete previous chapter folders before copying a new chapter folder onto your storage medium.

## Exercise G.3 Copying a Folder from the Student Resources CD to a USB Flash Drive

1. Insert the CD that accompanies this textbook into your computer's CD/DVD drive.
2. Insert your USB flash drive into an available USB port.
3. At the Windows 8 Start screen, click the Desktop tile.
4. Open File Explorer by clicking the File Explorer button on the Taskbar.
5. Click *Computer* in the Navigation pane at the left side of the File Explorer window.
6. Double-click the CD/DVD drive that displays with the name *SW13StudentResources* preceded by the drive letter.
7. Double-click **StudentDataFiles** in the Content pane.
8. Click once on the desired chapter (or unit performance assessment) folder name to select it.
9. Click the Home tab and then click the Copy button in the Clipboard group.
10. Click your USB flash drive that displays in the Navigation pane at the left side of the window.
11. Click the Home tab and then click the Paste button in the Clipboard group.
12. Close the File Explorer window by clicking the Close button located in the upper right corner of the window.

## Exercise G.4  Copying a Folder from the Student Resources CD to your SkyDrive Account

*Note: SkyDrive is updated periodically, so the steps to create folders and upload files may vary from the steps below.*

1. Insert the CD that accompanies this textbook into your computer's CD/DVD drive.
2. At the Windows 8 Start screen, click the Desktop tile.
3. Open Internet Explorer by clicking the Internet Explorer button on the Taskbar.
4. At the Internet Explorer home page, click in the Address bar, type **www.skydrive.com**, and then press Enter.
5. At the Microsoft SkyDrive login page, type your Windows Live ID (such as your email address).
6. Press the Tab key, type your password, and then press Enter.
7. Click the Documents tile in your SkyDrive.
8. Click the Create option on the SkyDrive menu bar and then click *Folder* at the drop-down list.
9. Type the name of the folder that you want to copy from the Student Resources CD and then press the Enter key.
10. Click the folder tile you created in the previous step.
11. Click the Upload option on the menu bar.
12. Click the CD/DVD drive that displays in the Navigation pane at the left side of the Choose File to Upload dialog box.
13. Open the chapter folder on the CD that contains the required student data files.
14. Select all of the files in the folder by pressing Ctrl + A and then click the Open button.


## Exercise G.5  Deleting a Folder

*Note: Check with your instructor before deleting a folder.*

1. Insert your storage medium (such as a USB flash drive) into your computer's USB port.
2. At the Windows desktop, open File Explorer by right-clicking the Start screen thumbnail and then clicking *File Explorer* at the shortcut menu.
3. Double-click the drive letter for your storage medium (the drive containing your USB flash drive, such as *Removable Disk (F:)*).
4. Click the chapter folder in the Content pane.
5. Click the Home tab and then click the Delete button in the Organize group.
6. At the message asking if you want to delete the folder, click the Yes button.
7. Close the Computer window by clicking the Close button located in the upper right corner of the window.

# UNIT 1

## Preparing Documents

# Creating, Printing, and Editing Documents

## Performance Objectives

Upon successful completion of Chapter 1, you will be able to:

- Open Microsoft Word
- Create, save, name, print, and close a Word document
- Create a new document
- Open a saved document
- Save a document with *Save As*
- Close Word
- Edit a document
- Select text in a document
- Use the Undo and Redo buttons
- Use the Help feature

In this chapter, you will learn to create, save, name, print, open, close, and edit a Word document. Before continuing, make sure you read the *Getting Started* section presented at the beginning of this book. This section contains information about computer hardware and software, using the mouse, executing commands, and customizing settings.

*Note: Before beginning computer exercises for this chapter, copy to your storage medium the Chapter01 folder from the CD that accompanies this textbook. Steps on how to copy a folder are presented on the inside back cover of this textbook. Do this for each chapter before starting the chapter's exercises.*

In this chapter, students will produce the following documents:

Exercise 1.1. C01-E01-WebResumes.docx
Exercise 1.2. C01-E02-EmailResumes.docx
Exercise 1.4. C01-E04-LtrKCC.docx
Exercise 1.5. C01-E05-SoftwareSuites.docx

Model answers for these exercises are shown on the following pages.

Web page resumes fall into two categories: individuals who build a personal web page and bring it to the employer's attention; and companies that allow you to enter your details either into their standard resume form or by cutting and pasting your file on to their site. The resume is then indexed and stored on their site for future employers to search through. If you intend to set up your web page as a substitute resume, you must apply the same level of professionalism that you would to a conventional resume. The key difference with a web page resume is that you can include far more information, provided that it is appropriately indexed and the site is easily navigable. However, the initial key pages of the site should convey all the critical information of a conventional resume. Use the extra potential of a website for additional optional information in links that employers can choose to follow. Keep in mind that website resumes become public documents, which potentially can be accessed by anyone, including your current boss.

This document was written Wednesday, November 18, 2015.
Please insert this information as the 3$^{rd}$ paragraph in the 7$^{th}$ section.

**Exercise 1.1**

C01-E01-WebResumes.docx

Emailing Resumes

As an alternative to mailing your resume, some employers are now happy to receive them electronically via email. This can speed up the hiring process and can save money, too. If you are applying for a job that requires some IT knowledge, sending your resume by email will demonstrate that you are comfortable with this type of technology.

As with scanned resumes, you should keep to a maximum of 70 to 80 characters per line. Any more characters and you risk losing the formatting. You should send the resume as an attachment. Do not be tempted to copy and paste it into the body of the email—you will lose most of the formatting. Even though you may have a fancy email program that allows you to include formatting and graphics in the message body, the majority of email programs do not allow this, and all you will do is send an unintelligible mess to your prospective employer.

Another option to consider is to paste a text version of your resume into the body of the email. Some people advise you to do this because some recruiters may worry about opening attachments to emails for fear of any viruses they may contain. The pros of this are that you get your information to the recruiter. The downside is that we know that the visual appeal of the resume has a dramatic effect on the recruiter, and this type of resume is not visually appealing.

**Exercise 1.2**

C01-E02-EmailResumes.docx

Chapter One

**Exercise 1.4**

C01-E04-LtrKCC.docx

November 4, 2015

Dr. Avery Reynolds
Kodiak Community College
310 Northern Lights Boulevard
Anchorage, AK 99033

Dear Dr. Reynolds:

I enjoyed meeting you and discussing the implementation of a Pharmacy Tech program into the Business Information Technology curriculum. As I mentioned, we added a pharmacy tech program to our department at Cascade Community College last year.

We advertised it in our college schedule and sent brochures to all high school seniors in our district. Thirty people registered for the program, and student evaluations, which were completed last semester, were very favorable.

If you would like more information about the program, please call me at (712) 555-3400. I will be attending the National Computer Technology conference. I hope to see you there.

Sincerely,


Kerry Brown

XX
LtrKCC.docx

Software suites typically include the four most widely used applications: word processing, database management, spreadsheet, and presentation applications. Some, such as Microsoft Office, also include web page authoring programs because the development of personal websites is becoming increasingly important to consumers. Suites are popular because buying a package is less expensive than purchasing each component program separately.

Software suites offer advantages other than price. Because the programs were developed using the same user interface, all programs in the suite function in a similar manner. A user who becomes familiar with one program can easily learn to use the others because the screen layouts, tabs, menus, buttons, icons, and toolbars are similar.

Another strong feature of suites is that they allow users to seamlessly integrate files from component programs. For example, information produced using a spreadsheet can be placed into a word processing document, or a database table can be imported into a slide show presentation.

**Exercise 1.5**

C01-E05-SoftwareSuites.docx

**Open Word**
1. Click Word 2013 tile at Windows 8 Start screen.
2. Click *Blank document* template.

# Opening Microsoft Word

Microsoft Office 2013 contains a word processing program named Word that you can use to create, save, edit, and print documents. The steps to open Word may vary depending on your system setup. Generally, to open Word, click the Word 2013 tile at the Windows 8 Start screen. At the Word 2013 opening screen, click the *Blank document* template.

# Creating, Saving, Naming, Printing, and Closing a Document

When you click the *Blank document* template, a blank document displays on the screen, as shown in Figure 1.1. The features of the document screen are described in Table 1.1.

**Figure 1.1  Blank Document**

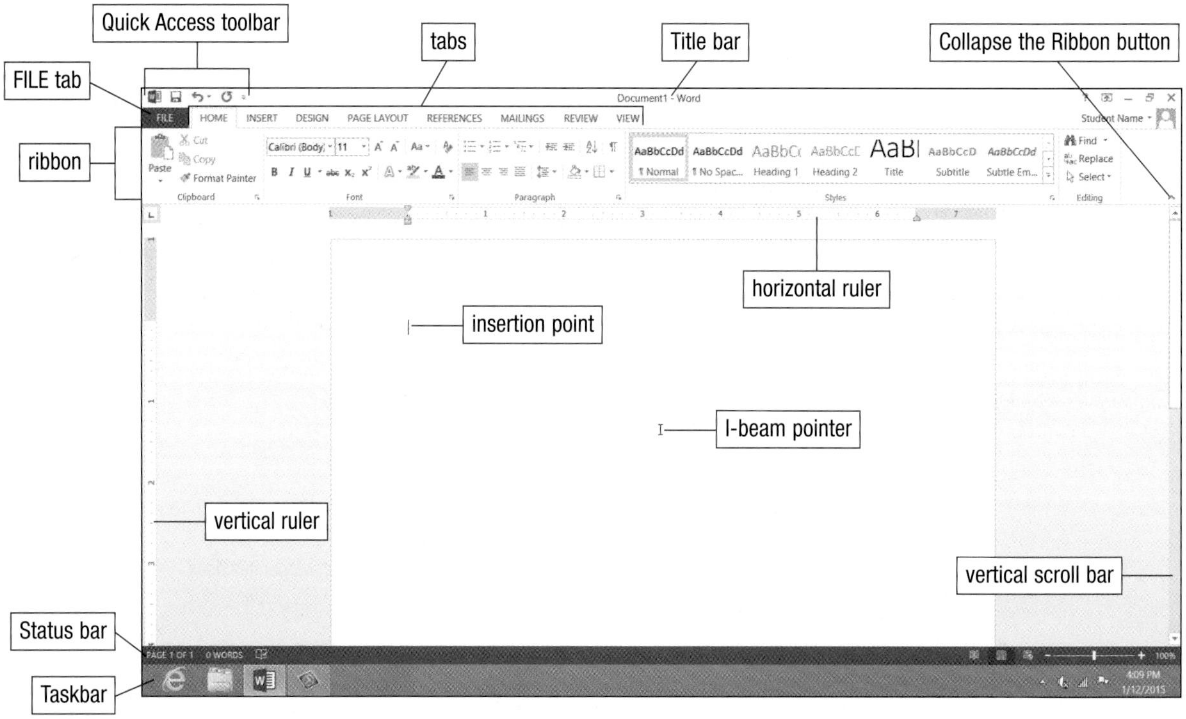

- Quick Access toolbar
- tabs
- Title bar
- Collapse the Ribbon button
- FILE tab
- ribbon
- horizontal ruler
- insertion point
- I-beam pointer
- vertical ruler
- vertical scroll bar
- Status bar
- Taskbar

**Table 1.1 Microsoft Word Screen Features**

| Feature | Description |
|---------|-------------|
| Quick Access toolbar | contains buttons for commonly used commands |
| FILE tab | when clicked, displays the backstage area that contains buttons and tabs for working with and managing documents |
| Title bar | displays the document name followed by the program name |
| tabs | contain commands and features organized into groups |
| ribbon | contains the tabs, with options and commands divided into groups |
| Collapse the Ribbon button | when clicked, removes the ribbon from the screen |
| horizontal ruler | used to set margins, indents, and tabs |
| vertical ruler | used to set top and bottom margins |
| I-beam pointer | used to move the insertion point or select text |
| insertion point | indicates the location of the next character entered at the keyboard |
| vertical scroll bar | used to view various parts of the document beyond the screen |
| Status bar | displays the number of pages and words, view buttons, and Zoom slider bar |

At a blank document, type information to create a document. A document can contain any information and have any format you choose—for instance, a letter, report, term paper, table, and so on. Some things to consider when typing text are:

- **Word wrap:** As you type to create a document, you do not need to press the Enter key at the end of each line because Word wraps text from one line to the next. A word is wrapped to the next line if it begins before the right margin and continues past the right margin. The only times you need to press Enter are to end a paragraph, create a blank line, and end a short line.

- **AutoCorrect:** Word contains a feature that automatically corrects certain words as you type them. For example, if you type *adn* instead of the word *and*, Word automatically corrects it when you press the spacebar after the word. AutoCorrect also superscripts the letters that follow an ordinal number (a number indicating a position in a series). For example, if you type *2nd* and then press the spacebar or Enter key, Word will convert this ordinal number to $2^{nd}$.

- **Automatic spelling checker:** By default, Word automatically inserts a red wavy line below any word that is not contained in its Spelling dictionary or automatically corrected by AutoCorrect. These words may include misspelled words, proper names, some terminology, and some foreign words. If the Spelling dictionary underlines a word that is spelled correctly, leave the word as written. However, if the word is spelled incorrectly, you have two choices: delete the word and then type it correctly or position the I-beam pointer on the word, click the *right* mouse button, and then click the correct spelling in the pop-up list that displays.

- **Automatic grammar checker:** Word includes an automatic grammar checker. If the grammar checker detects a sentence that contains a possible grammatical error, Word inserts a blue wavy line below the error in the sentence. You can leave the sentence as written or position the I-beam pointer on the sentence, click the *right* mouse button, and choose from the pop-up list of possible corrections.

- **Spacing punctuation:** Typically, Word uses Calibri, a proportional typeface, as the default typeface. (You will learn more about typefaces in Chapter 2.) When typing text in a proportional typeface, space once (rather than twice) after end-of-sentence punctuation such as a period, question mark, or exclamation point, and after a colon. The letters in a proportional typeface are set closer together, so it is unnecessary to add extra white space at the end of a sentence or after a colon.

- **Option buttons:** As you insert or edit text in a document, you may notice an option button popping up in your text. The name and appearance of this button vary depending on the action. If a word you type is corrected by AutoCorrect, if you create an automatic list, or if you apply autoformatting to text, the AutoCorrect Options button appears. Click this button to undo the specific automatic action. If you paste text in a document, the Paste Options button appears near the text. Click this button to display the Paste Options gallery with buttons for controlling how the pasted text is formatted.

- **AutoComplete:** Microsoft Word and other Office applications include an AutoComplete feature that inserts an entire item when you type a few identifying characters. For example, type the letters *Mond* and *Monday* displays in a ScreenTip above the letters. Press the Enter key or press the F3 key and Word inserts *Monday* in the document.

## Using the New Line Command

A Word document is based on a template that applies default formatting. Some basic formatting includes 1.08 line spacing and 8 points of spacing after a paragraph. Each time you press the Enter key, a new paragraph begins and 8 points of spacing is inserted after the paragraph. If you want to move the insertion point down to the next line without including the additional 8 points of spacing, use the New Line command, Shift + Enter.

| **Exercise 1.1A**   Creating a Document | Part 1 of 2 |
| --- | --- |

1. Open Word by clicking the Word 2013 tile at the Windows 8 Start screen. At the Word opening screen, click the *Blank document* template. (These steps may vary. Check with your instructor for specific instructions.)
2. At the blank document, type the information shown in Figure 1.2 on the next page with the following specifications:
   a. Correct any errors highlighted by the spelling checker or grammar checker as they occur.
   b. Press the spacebar once after end-of-sentence punctuation.
   c. To insert the word *Wednesday* near the end of the document, type **Wedn** and then press the F3 key. (This is an example of the AutoComplete feature.)
   d. To insert the word *November*, type **Nove** and then press the Enter key. (This is another example of the AutoComplete feature.)
   e. Press Shift + Enter after typing *November 18, 2015*. (This moves the insertion point to the next line without adding 8 points of additional spacing.)
   f. When typing the last line (the line containing the ordinal numbers), type the ordinal number text and AutoCorrect will automatically convert the letters in the ordinal numbers to superscripts.
3. When you are finished typing the text, press the Enter key once.

**Figure 1.2 Exercise 1.1A**

Web page resumes fall into two categories: individuals who build a personal web page and bring it to the employer's attention; and companies that allow you to enter your details either into their standard resume form or by cutting and pasting your file on to their site. The resume is then indexed and stored on their site for future employers to search through. If you intend to set up your web page as a substitute resume, you must apply the same level of professionalism that you would to a conventional resume. The key difference with a web page resume is that you can include far more information, provided that it is appropriately indexed and the site is easily navigable. However, the initial key pages of the site should convey all the critical information of a conventional resume. Use the extra potential of a website for additional optional information in links that employers can choose to follow. Keep in mind that website resumes become public documents, which potentially can be accessed by anyone, including your current boss.

This document was written Wednesday, November 18, 2015.
Please insert this information as the 3$^{rd}$ paragraph in the 7$^{th}$ section.

## Saving a Document

Save a document if you want to use it in the future. You can choose from a variety of methods to save a document, such as clicking the Save button on the Quick Access toolbar, clicking the FILE tab and then clicking the *Save* or *Save As* option, and using the keyboard shortcut Ctrl + S. When you choose one of these options, the Save As backstage area displays, as shown in Figure 1.3. At this backstage area, click the desired location for saving your document. For example, click the *SkyDrive* option preceded by your name if you are saving to your SkyDrive or click the *Computer* option if you are saving to your computer.

**QUICK STEPS**

**Save a Document**
1. Click Save button on Quick Access toolbar.
2. Click desired location.
3. Click Browse button.
4. Type document name in *File name* text box.
5. Press Enter or click Save button.

**Figure 1.3 Save As Backstage Area**

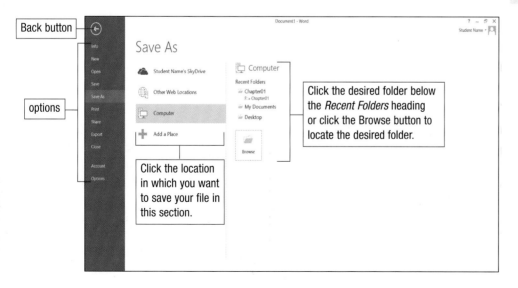

Save

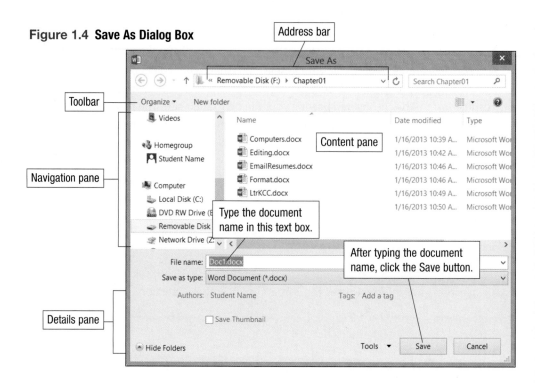

**Figure 1.4 Save As Dialog Box**

After specifying the place, click the Browse button and the Save As dialog box displays, as shown in Figure 1.4. If you are saving to your computer, double-click the *Computer* option to display the Save As dialog box. At this dialog box, type the name of the document in the *File name* text box and then press Enter or click the Save button. You can go directly to the Save As dialog box without displaying the Save As backstage area by pressing the F12 key.

## Naming a Document

Document names created in Word and other applications in the Office suite can be up to 255 characters in length, including the drive letter and any folder names, and may include spaces. File names cannot include any of the following characters:

| | |
|---|---|
| forward slash (/) | question mark (?) |
| backslash (\) | quotation mark (") |
| greater-than symbol (>) | colon (:) |
| less-than symbol (<) | semicolon (;) |
| asterisk (*) | pipe symbol (\|) |

## Printing a Document

**Print a Document**
Click Quick Print button on Quick Access toolbar.
OR
1. Click FILE tab.
2. Click *Print* option.
3. Click Print button.

Click the FILE tab and the backstage area displays. The buttons and options at the backstage area change depending on the option selected at the left side of the backstage area. If you want to remove the backstage area without completing an action, click the Back button located in the upper left corner of the backstage area or press the Esc key on your keyboard.

Many of the files you create will need to be printed. A printing of a document on paper is referred to as ***hard copy***, and a document displayed on the screen is referred to as ***soft copy***. Print a document with options at the Print backstage area, shown in Figure 1.5 on the next page. To display this backstage area, click the FILE tab and then

**Figure 1.5 Print Backstage Area**

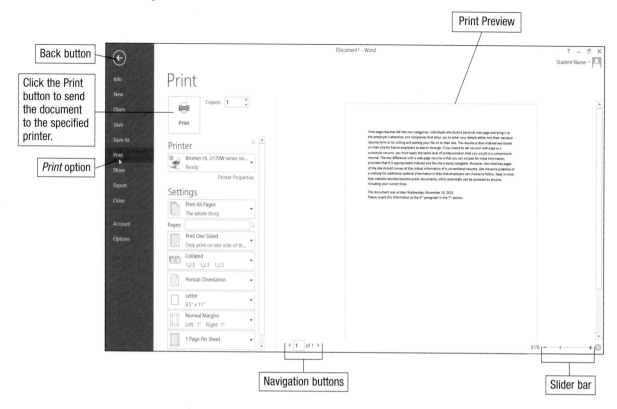

Print Preview

Back button

Click the Print button to send the document to the specified printer.

*Print* option

Navigation buttons

Slider bar

click the *Print* option. Another method for displaying the Print backstage area is to use the keyboard shortcut Ctrl + P.

Click the Print button, located near the upper left side of the backstage area, to send the document to the printer and specify the number of copies you want printed with the *Copies* option. Below the Print button are two categories: *Printer* and *Settings*. Use the gallery in the *Printer* category to specify the desired printer. The *Settings* category contains a number of galleries, each with options for specifying how you want your document printed, including whether you want the pages collated when printed; the orientation, page size, and margins of your document; and how many pages of your document you want to print on a sheet of paper.

Another method for printing a document is to insert the Quick Print button on the Quick Access toolbar and then click the button. This sends the document directly to the printer without displaying the Print backstage area. To insert the button on the Quick Access toolbar, click the Customize Quick Access Toolbar button that displays at the right side of the toolbar and then click *Quick Print* at the drop-down list. To remove the Quick Print button from the Quick Access toolbar, right-click the button and then click *Remove from Quick Access Toolbar* at the drop-down list.

Quick Print

Customize Quick Access Toolbar

## Closing a Document

When you save a document, it is saved on your SkyDrive or other storage medium and remains in the document screen. To remove the document from the screen, click the FILE tab and then click the *Close* option or use the keyboard shortcut Ctrl + F4. When you close a document, it is removed and a blank screen displays. At this screen, you can open a previously saved document, create a new document, or close Word.

**QUICK STEPS**

**Close a Document**
1. Click FILE tab.
2. Click *Close* option.
OR
Press Ctrl + F4.

1. Save the document you created in Exercise 1.1A and name it **C01-E01-WebResumes** (for Chapter 1, Exercise 1, web resumes document) by completing the following steps:
   a. Click the Save button on the Quick Access toolbar.
   b. At the Save As backstage area, click the SkyDrive option preceded by your name if you are saving to your SkyDrive or click the *Computer* option if you are saving to your computer or USB flash drive.
   c. Click the Browse button.
   d. At the Save As dialog box, if necessary, navigate to the Chapter01 folder.
   e. Click in the *File name* text box (this selects any text in the box), type **C01-E01-WebResumes**, and then press the Enter key.

2. Print the document by clicking the FILE tab, clicking the *Print* option, and then clicking the Print button at the Print backstage area.

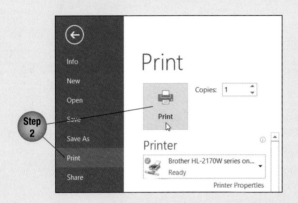

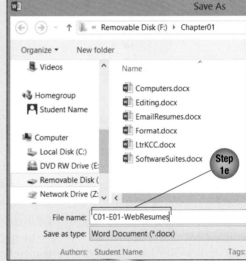

3. Close the document by clicking the FILE tab and then clicking the *Close* option.

## Creating a New Document

When you close a document, a blank screen displays. To create a new document, first display a blank document. To do this, click the FILE tab, click the *New* option, and then click the *Blank document* template. You can also open a new document using the keyboard shortcut Ctrl + N or by inserting a New button on the Quick Access toolbar. To insert the button, click the Customize Quick Access Toolbar button that displays at the right side of the toolbar and then click *New* at the drop-down list.

## Opening a Document

After you save and close a document, you can open it at the Open dialog box, shown in Figure 1.6 on the next page. To display this dialog box, click the FILE tab and then click the *Open* option. This displays the Open backstage area. You can also display the Open backstage area by using the keyboard shortcut Ctrl + O, inserting an Open button on the

**Figure 1.6 Open Dialog Box**

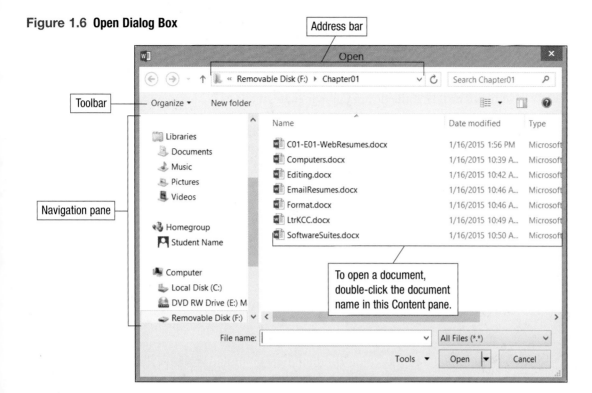

Quick Access toolbar, or clicking the <u>Open Other Documents</u> hyperlink that displays in the lower left corner of the Word 2013 opening screen.

At the Open backstage area, click the desired location (such as your SkyDrive or *Computer*) and then click the Browse button. (If you are opening a document from your computer or USB flash drive, double-click the *Computer* option.) When you click the Browse button (or double-click the *Computer* option), the Open dialog box displays. You can go directly to the Open dialog box without displaying the Open backstage area by pressing Ctrl + F12. At the Open dialog box, open a document by double-clicking the document name in the Content pane.

If a document is open, Word will display the folder name where the document is located below the *Current Folder* heading in the Open backstage area with your SkyDrive or the *Computer* option selected. Click this folder name to display the folder contents. In addition to the current folder, the Open backstage area also displays a list of the most recently accessed folders below the *Recent Folders* heading. Open a folder by clicking the folder name.

**QUICK STEPS**

**Open a Document**
1. Click FILE tab.
2. Click *Open* option.
3. Click desired location.
4. Click Browse button.
5. Double-click document name.

## Opening a Document from the Recent Documents List

At the Open backstage area with *Recent Documents* selected, the Recent Documents list displays the most recently opened documents. By default, Word displays the 25 most recently opened documents. To open a document from the Recent Documents list, scroll down the list and then click the desired document. The Word 2013 opening screen also displays a list of the most recently opened documents. Click a document name in the Recent list at the opening screen to open the document.

## Pinning a Document to the Recent Documents List

If you want a document to remain in the Recent Documents list at the Open backstage area, "pin" the document to the list. To pin a document, position the mouse pointer over the desired document name and then click the small, left-pointing stick pin that displays at the right side of the document name. This changes the left-pointing pin to a down-pointing stick pin. The next time you display the Open backstage area, the document you "pinned" displays at the top of the Recent Documents list.

You can also pin a document to the Recent list at the Word 2013 opening screen. When you pin a document, it displays at the top of the Recent list as well as the Recent Documents list at the Open backstage area. To "unpin" a document from the Recent or Recent Documents list, click the pin to change it from a down-pointing pin to a left-pointing pin. You can pin more than one document to a list. Another method for pinning and unpinning documents is to use the shortcut menu. Right-click a document name and then click *Pin to list* or *Unpin from list*.

In addition to pinning documents to a list, you can pin a folder to the Recent Folders list. Pin a folder in the same manner as you pin a document. If you access a particular folder on a regular basis, consider pinning it to the list.

---

## Exercise 1.2A   Opening and Pinning/Unpinning a Document          Part 1 of 2

1. Open the **EmailResumes.docx** document by completing the following steps:
   a. Click the FILE tab and then click the *Open* option.
   b. At the Open backstage area, click the desired location. (For example, click your SkyDrive if you are using your SkyDrive account or click the *Computer* option if you are opening a document from your computer's hard drive or a USB flash drive.)
   c. Click the *Chapter01* folder that displays below the *Recent Folders* heading. (If the folder name does not display, click the Browse button and then navigate to the Chapter01 folder.)
   d. At the Open dialog box, double-click **EmailResumes.docx** in the Content pane.
2. Close **EmailResumes.docx**.
3. Open **Computers.docx** by completing steps similar to those in Step 1.
4. Close **Computers.docx**.
5. Pin the **EmailResumes.docx** document to the Recent Documents list by completing the following steps:
   a. Click the FILE tab and then, if necessary, click the *Open* option.

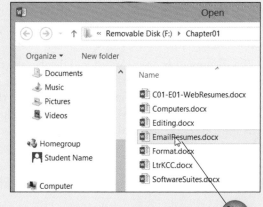

Step 1d

---

b. Hover the mouse pointer over **EmailResumes.docx** in the Recent Documents list and then click the left-pointing stick pin that displays at the right side of the document. (This moves the document to the top of the list and changes the left-pointing stick pin to a down-pointing stick pin.

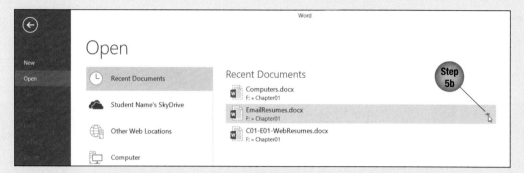

6. Click **EmailResumes.docx** at the top of the Recent Documents list to open the document.
7. With the insertion point positioned at the beginning of the document, type the text shown in Figure 1.7.
8. Unpin the **EmailResumes.docx** from the Recent Documents list by completing the following steps:
   a. Click the FILE tab and then click the *Open* option.
   b. Click the down-pointing stick pin that displays at the right of **EmailResumes.docx** in the Recent Documents list. (This changes the pin from a down-pointing stick pin to a left-pointing stick pin.)
9. Click the Back button to return to the document.

**Figure 1.7 Exercise 1.2A**

Emailing Resumes

As an alternative to mailing your resume, some employers are now happy to receive them electronically via email. This can speed up the hiring process and can save money, too. If you are applying for a job that requires some IT knowledge, sending your resume by email will demonstrate that you are comfortable with this type of technology.

# Saving a Document with *Save As*

If you open a previously saved document and want to give it a new name, use the *Save As* option at the backstage area rather than the *Save* option. Click the FILE tab and then click the *Save As* option. At the Save As backstage area, click the desired location and then click the Browse button or click the desired folder below the *Current Folder* or *Recent Folders* heading. At the Save As dialog box, type the new name for the document in the *File name* text box and then press Enter.

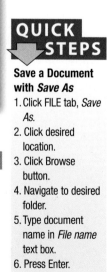

QUICK STEPS

Save a Document with *Save As*
1. Click FILE tab, *Save As*.
2. Click desired location.
3. Click Browse button.
4. Navigate to desired folder.
5. Type document name in *File name* text box.
6. Press Enter.

# Closing Word

When you are finished working with Word and have saved all necessary information, close Word by clicking the Close button located in the upper right corner of the screen. You can also close Word with the keyboard shortcut Alt + F4.

Close

---

## Exercise 1.2B    Saving a Document Using *Save As*    Part 2 of 2

1. With **EmailResumes.docx** open, save the document with a new name by completing the following steps:
    a. Click the FILE tab and then click the *Save As* option.
    b. At the Save As backstage area, click the *Chapter01* folder below the *Current Folder* heading or *Recent Folders* heading. (If the folder does not display, double-click your SkyDrive or the *Computer* option and then navigate to the Chapter01 folder.)
    c. At the Save As dialog box, press the Home key on your keyboard to move the insertion point to the beginning of the file name and then type **C01-E02-**. (Pressing the Home key saves you from having to type the entire document name.)
    d. Press the Enter key.
2. Print the document by clicking the FILE tab, clicking the *Print* option, and then clicking the Print button at the Print backstage area. (If your Quick Access toolbar contains the Quick Print button, click the button to send the document directly to the printer.)
3. Close the document by pressing Ctrl + F4.

---

## Editing a Document

When editing a document, you may decide to insert or delete text. To edit a document, use the mouse, the keyboard, or the mouse in combination with the keyboard to move the insertion point to specific locations in the document. To move the insertion point using the mouse, position the I-beam pointer where you want to place the insertion point and then click the left mouse button.

You can also scroll in a document, which changes the text display but does not move the insertion point. Use the mouse with the ***vertical scroll bar***, located at the right side of the screen, to scroll through text in a document. Click the up scroll arrow at the top of the vertical scroll bar to scroll up through the document; click the down scroll arrow to scroll down through the document.

A scroll box on the scroll bar indicates the location of the text on the document screen in relation to the remainder of the document. To scroll up one screen at a time, position the arrow pointer above the scroll box (but below the up scroll arrow) and then click the left mouse button. Position the arrow pointer below the scroll box and click the left button to scroll down a screen. If you hold down the left mouse button, the action becomes continuous. You can also position the arrow pointer on the scroll box, hold down the left mouse button, and then drag the scroll box along the scroll bar to reposition text on the document screen. As you drag the scroll box along the vertical scroll bar in a multiple-page document, page numbers display in a box at the right side of the document screen.

---

<table>
<tr><td>Exercise 1.3A</td><td>Scrolling in a Document</td><td>Part 1 of 2</td></tr>
</table>

1. Open **Computers.docx** from the Chapter01 folder on your storage medium.
2. Save the document with Save As and name it **C01-E03-Computers**.
3. Position the I-beam pointer at the beginning of the first paragraph and then click the left mouse button.
4. Click the down scroll arrow on the vertical scroll bar several times. (This scrolls down lines of text in the document.) With the mouse pointer on the down scroll arrow, hold down the left mouse button and keep it down until the end of the document displays.

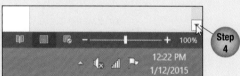

5. Position the mouse pointer on the up scroll arrow and hold down the left mouse button until the beginning of the document displays.
6. Position the mouse pointer below the scroll box and then click the left mouse button. Continue clicking the mouse button (with the mouse pointer positioned below the scroll box) until the end of the document displays.
7. Position the mouse pointer on the scroll box in the vertical scroll bar. Hold down the left mouse button, drag the scroll box to the top of the vertical scroll bar, and then release the mouse button. (The document page numbers displayed in a box at the right side of the document screen as you dragged the scroll box to the top of the vertical scroll bar.)
8. Click on the title at the beginning of the document. (This moves the insertion point to the location of the mouse pointer.)

---

## Moving the Insertion Point to a Specific Line or Page

Word includes a Go To feature that you can use to move the insertion point to a specific location in a document, such as a line or page. To use the feature, click the Find button arrow located in the Editing group on the HOME tab and then click *Go To* at the drop-down list. At the Find and Replace dialog box with the Go To tab selected, move the insertion point to a specific page by typing the page number in the *Enter page number* text box and then pressing Enter. Move to a specific line by clicking the *Line* option in the *Go to what* list box, typing the line number in the *Enter line number* text box, and then pressing Enter. Click the Close button to close the dialog box.

Find

## Moving the Insertion Point with the Keyboard

To move the insertion point with the keyboard, use the arrow keys located to the right of the regular keyboard or use the arrow keys on the numeric keypad. If you use these keys, make sure Num Lock is off. Use the arrow keys together with other keys to move the insertion point to various locations in the document, as shown in Table 1.2.

When moving the insertion point, Word considers a word to be any series of characters between spaces. A paragraph is any text that is followed by a stroke of the Enter key. A page is text that is set off by a soft or hard page break.

**Table 1.2 Insertion Point Movement Commands**

| To move insertion point | Press |
| --- | --- |
| one character left | Left Arrow |
| one character right | Right Arrow |
| one line up | Up Arrow |
| one line down | Down Arrow |
| one word left | Ctrl + Left Arrow |
| one word right | Ctrl + Right Arrow |
| to end of line | End |
| to beginning of line | Home |
| to beginning of current paragraph | Ctrl + Up Arrow |
| to beginning of next paragraph | Ctrl + Down Arrow |
| up one screen | Page Up |
| down one screen | Page Down |
| to top of previous page | Ctrl + Page Up |
| to top of next page | Ctrl + Page Down |
| to beginning of document | Ctrl + Home |
| to end of document | Ctrl + End |

## Resuming Reading or Editing in a Document

If you open a previously saved document, you can move the insertion point to where the insertion point was last located when the document was closed by pressing Shift + F5. When you work in a multiple-page document and then close the document, Word remembers the page where the insertion point was last positioned. When you reopen the document, Word displays a "Welcome back!" message at the right side of the screen near the vertical scroll bar. The message tells you that you can pick up where you left off and identifies the page where your insertion point was last located. Click the message and the insertion point is positioned at the top of that page.

1. With **C01-E03-Computers.docx** open, move the insertion point to page 3 by completing the following steps:

   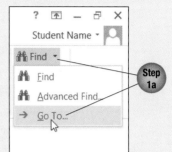

   a. Click the Find button arrow located in the Editing group on the HOME tab and then click *Go To* at the drop-down list.
   b. At the Find and Replace dialog box with the Go To tab selected, click *Line* in the *Go to what* list box.
   c. Click in the *Enter line number* text box, type **15**, and then press Enter.

   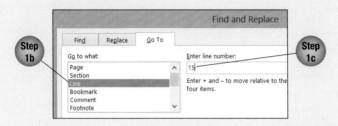

   d. Click *Page* in the *Go to what* box, click in the *Enter page number* text box, type **3**, and then press Enter.
   e. Click the Close button to close the Find and Replace dialog box.

   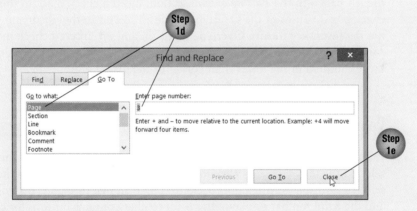

2. Close the document.
3. Open the document by clicking the FILE tab and then clicking the document name ***C01-E03-Computers.docx*** that displays at the top of the Recent Documents list.
4. Move the mouse pointer to the right side of the screen to display the "Welcome back!" message. Hover the mouse pointer over the message and then click the left mouse button. (This positions the insertion point at the top of the third page—the page where the insertion point was positioned when you closed the document.)

5. Press Ctrl + Home to move the insertion point to the beginning of the document.
6. Practice using the keyboard commands shown in Table 1.2 on the previous page to move the insertion point within the document.
7. Close **C01-E03-Computers.docx**.

## Inserting and Deleting Text

Editing a document may include inserting or deleting text. To insert text in a document, position the insertion point in the desired location and then type the text. Existing characters move to the right as you type the text. A number of options are available for deleting text. Some deletion commands are shown in Table 1.3.

**Table 1.3 Deletion Commands**

| *To delete* | *Press* |
|---|---|
| character right of insertion point | Delete key |
| character left of insertion point | Backspace key |
| text from insertion point to beginning of word | Ctrl + Backspace |
| text from insertion point to end of word | Ctrl + Delete |

If you want to type over existing text rather than have it move to the right as you insert new text, you will need to turn on the Overtype mode. With the Overtype mode on, anything you type will replace existing text. To turn on the Overtype mode, click the FILE tab and then click *Options*. At the Word Options dialog box, click *Advanced* in the left panel. In the *Editing options* section, insert a check mark in the *Use overtype mode* check box if you want the Overtype mode always on in the document. If you want to use the Insert key to turn Overtype mode on and off, insert a check mark in the *Use the Insert key to control overtype mode* check box. After making your selection, click the OK button located in the lower right corner of the dialog box.

# Selecting Text

Use the mouse or the keyboard to select a specific amount of text. Once you have selected the text, you can delete it or perform other Word functions on it. When text is selected, it displays with a gray background, as shown in Figure 1.8 on the next page, and the Mini toolbar displays. The Mini toolbar contains buttons for common tasks. (You will learn more about the Mini toolbar in Chapter 2.)

**Figure 1.8** Selected Text and Mini Toolbar

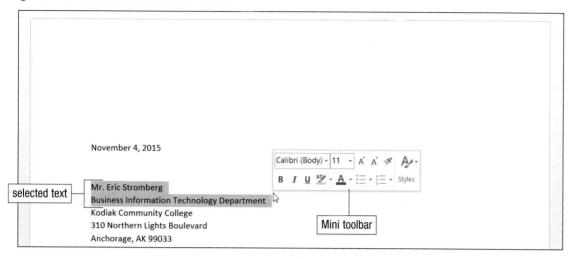

## Selecting Text with the Mouse

Use the mouse to select a word, line, sentence, paragraph, or entire document. Table 1.4 indicates the steps to follow to select various amounts of text. For example, to select a line, click in the selection bar. The selection bar is the space located toward the left side of the document screen between the left edge of the page and the text. When the mouse pointer is positioned in the selection bar, the pointer turns into an arrow pointing up and to the right.

**Table 1.4** Selecting Text with the Mouse

| To select | Complete these steps using the mouse |
|---|---|
| a word | Double-click the word. |
| a line of text | Click in the selection bar to the left of the line. |
| multiple lines of text | Drag in the selection bar to the left of the lines. |
| a sentence | Hold down the Ctrl key and then click anywhere in the sentence. |
| a paragraph | Double-click in the selection bar next to the paragraph or triple-click anywhere in the paragraph. |
| multiple paragraphs | Drag in the selection bar. |
| an entire document | Triple-click in the selection bar or click the Select button in the the Editing group on the HOME tab and then click *Select All*. |

To select sections of text other than a word, sentence, or paragraph, position the I-beam pointer on the first character of the text to be selected, hold down the left mouse button, drag the I-beam pointer to the last character of the text to be selected, and then release the mouse button. You can also select all of the text between the current insertion point and the I-beam pointer. To do this, position the insertion point where you want the selection to begin, hold down the Shift key, click the I-beam pointer at the end of the selection, and then release the Shift key. To cancel a selection using the mouse, click anywhere in the document screen outside the selected text.

Select text vertically in a document by holding down the Alt key while dragging with the mouse. This feature is especially useful when selecting a group of text, such as text set in columns.

## Selecting Text with the Keyboard

To select a specific amount of text using the keyboard, turn on the Selection mode by pressing the F8 key. With the Selection mode activated, use the arrow keys to select the desired text. If you want to cancel the selection, press the Esc key and then press any arrow key. You can also select text with the commands shown in Table 1.5.

You can customize the Status bar to display text indicating that the Selection mode is activated. To do this, right-click any blank location on the Status bar and then click *Selection Mode* at the pop-up list. When you press the F8 key to turn on the Selection mode, the words *EXTEND SELECTION* display on the Status bar.

**Table 1.5  Selecting Text with the Keyboard**

| To select | Press |
| --- | --- |
| one character to right | Shift + Right Arrow |
| one character to left | Shift + Left Arrow |
| to end of word | Ctrl + Shift + Right Arrow |
| to beginning of word | Ctrl + Shift + Left Arrow |
| to end of line | Shift + End |
| to beginning of line | Shift + Home |
| one line up | Shift + Up Arrow |
| one line down | Shift + Down Arrow |
| to beginning of paragraph | Ctrl + Shift + Up Arrow |
| to end of paragraph | Ctrl + Shift + Down Arrow |
| one screen up | Shift + Page Up |
| one screen down | Shift + Page Down |
| to end of document | Ctrl + Shift + End |
| to beginning of document | Ctrl + Shift + Home |
| entire document | Ctrl + A |

1. Open **LtrKCC.docx**. (This document is located in the Chapter01 folder you copied to your storage medium.)
2. Save the document with Save As and name it **C01-E04-LtrKCC**.
3. Delete the name, *Mr. Eric Stromberg*, and the department, *Business Information Technology Department*, using the mouse by completing the following steps:
   a. Position the I-beam pointer on the *M* in *Mr.* (in the address).
   b. Hold down the left mouse button and then drag the mouse down until *Mr. Eric Stromberg* and *Business Information Technology Department* are selected.

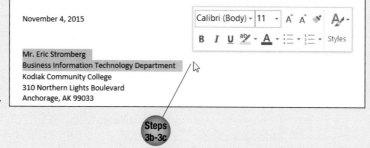

   c. Release the left mouse button.
   d. Press the Delete key.
4. Position the insertion point at the left margin of the line containing the text *Kodiak Community College*, type the name **Dr. Avery Reynolds**, and then press Shift + Enter.
5. Delete *Mr. Stromberg* in the salutation (after the word *Dear*) and then type **Dr. Reynolds**. (You choose the method for deleting.)

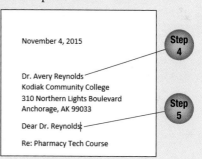

6. Delete the reference line, *Re: Pharmacy Tech Course*, using the Extend Selection key, F8, by completing the following steps:
   a. Position the insertion point on the *R* in *Re:*.
   b. Press the F8 key to turn on Selection mode.
   c. Press the Down Arrow key. (This selects the reference line and the spacing below it.)
   d. Press the Delete key.
7. Delete the first sentence in the first paragraph using the mouse by completing the following steps:
   a. Position the I-beam pointer anywhere in the sentence *The North Pacific Computer Technology conference that we attended last week was very educational.*
   b. Hold down the Ctrl key and then click the left mouse button.
   c. Press the Delete key.
8. Delete the first sentence in the second paragraph (the sentence that reads *Interest in the program has been phenomenal.*) using the keyboard by completing the following steps:
   a. Position the insertion point on the first letter of the sentence (the *I* in *Interest*).
   b. Hold down the Shift key and then press the Right Arrow key until the sentence is selected. Be sure to include the period at the end of the sentence and the space after the period.
   c. Press the Delete key.
9. Delete the third paragraph in the letter using the mouse by completing the following steps:
   a. Position the I-beam pointer anywhere in the third paragraph (the paragraph that begins *The instructor for the Medical Coding course*).
   b. Triple-click the left mouse button.
   c. Press the Delete key.
10. Save, print, and then close **C01-E04-LtrKCC.docx**.

# Using the Undo and Redo Buttons

If you make a mistake and delete text that you did not intend to delete or if you change your mind after deleting text and want to retrieve it, you can use the Undo or Redo button on the Quick Access toolbar. For example, if you type text and then click the Undo button, the text will be removed. You can undo text or commands. For example, if you add formatting such as bolding to text and then click the Undo button, the bolding is removed.

Undo

Redo

If you use the Undo button and then decide you do not want to reverse the original action, click the Redo button. For example, if you select and underline text and then decide to remove the underlining, click the Undo button. If you then decide you want the underlining back on, click the Redo button. Many Word actions can be undone or redone. Some actions, however, such as printing and saving, cannot be undone or redone.

Word maintains actions in temporary memory. If you want to undo an action that you performed earlier, click the Undo button arrow. This causes a drop-down list to display. To make a selection from this drop-down list, click the desired action and the action, along with any actions listed above it in the drop-down list, is undone.

---

## Exercise 1.5  Deleting and Restoring Text with the Undo and Redo Buttons  Part 1 of 1

1. Open **SoftwareSuites.docx**. (This document is located in the Chapter01 folder you copied to your storage medium.)
2. Save the document with Save As and name it **C01-E05-SoftwareSuites**.
3. Make the changes indicated by the proofreaders' marks in Figure 1.9 on the next page. (Proofreaders' marks are listed and described in Appendix A at the end of this textbook.)
4. Move the insertion point to the end of the document. Press the Backspace key until the last four words of the document *(or into a spreadsheet.)* are deleted. Be sure to delete the space before *or*.
5. Undo the deletion by clicking the Undo button on the Quick Access toolbar.
6. Redo the deletion by clicking the Redo button on the Quick Access toolbar.
7. Type a period after the word *presentation* to end the sentence.
8. Select the first sentence in the first paragraph and then delete it.
9. Select the second paragraph in the document and then delete it.
10. Undo the two deletions by completing the following steps:
    a. Click the down-pointing arrow to the right of the Undo button.
    b. Click the *second* Clear listed in the drop-down list. (This will redisplay the first sentence in the first paragraph and the second paragraph. The first sentence will be selected.)
11. With the first sentence of the paragraph selected, press the Delete key.
12. Save, print, and then close **C01-E05-SoftwareSuites.docx**.

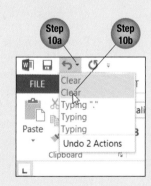

Step 10a    Step 10b

---

**Figure 1.9  Exercise 1.5**

Some commercial software vendors bundle and sell a group of software programs as a single package called a software suite, ~~also known as integrated software~~. Software suites typically include the four most widely used applications: word processing, database management, spreadsheet, and presentation ~~programs~~ *applications*. Some, such as Microsoft Office, also include Web page authoring programs because the development of personal Web sites is becoming increasingly important to consumers. Suites are popular because buying a package is ~~cheaper~~ *less expensive* than purchasing each component program separately.

Software suites offer advantages other than price. Because the programs were developed using the same user interface, all programs in the suite ~~work~~ *function* in a similar manner. A user who becomes familiar with one program can easily learn to use the others because the screen layouts, menus, *tabs,* buttons, icons, and toolbars are similar.

Another strong feature of suites is that they allow users to seamlessly integrate files from component programs. For example, information produced using a spreadsheet can be placed into a word processing document, or a database table can be imported into a slide show presentation or into a spreadsheet.

# Using Help

Word's Help feature is an on-screen reference manual containing information about Word features and commands. Word's Help feature is similar to the Help features in Excel, PowerPoint, and Access.

Get help by clicking the Microsoft Word Help button located in the upper right corner of the screen (a question mark) or by pressing the keyboard shortcut F1. This displays the Word Help window, as shown in Figure 1.10 on the next page. In this window, type a topic, feature, or question in the search text box and then press Enter. Topics related to the search text display in the Word Help window. Click a topic that interests you. If the topic window contains a Show All hyperlink in the upper right corner, click this hyperlink and the information expands to show all of the help information related to the topic. When you click the Show All hyperlink, it becomes the Hide All hyperlink.

The Word Help window contains five buttons that display to the left of the search text box. Use the Back and Forward buttons to navigate in the window. Click the Home button to return to the Word Help window opening screen. If you want to print information on a topic or feature, click the Print button and then click the Print button at the Print dialog box. Make the text in the Word Help window larger by clicking the Use Large Text button.

In addition to these five buttons, the Word Help window contains a Keep Help on Top button located near the upper right corner of the window. Click this button and the Word Help window remains on the screen even when you work in a document. Click the button again to remove the window from the screen.

**QUICK STEPS**

**Use the Help Feature**
1. Click Microsoft Word Help button.
2. Type topic or feature.
3. Press Enter.
4. Click desired topic.

Help

**Figure 1.10 Help Window**

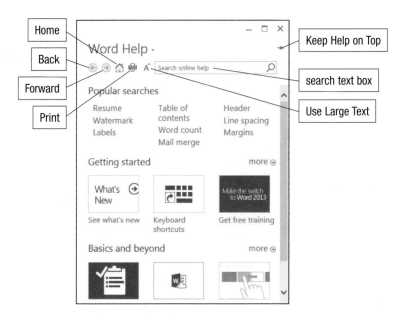

## Getting Help from a ScreenTip

If you hover your mouse pointer over certain buttons, the ScreenTip that displays may include a Help icon and the <u>Tell me more</u> hyperlink. Click <u>Tell me more</u> and the Word Help window opens with information about the button feature. You can also press the F1 key to display the Word Help window with information about the button feature.

---

## Exercise 1.6A  Using the Help Feature                                    Part 1 of 2

1. At a blank document, click the Microsoft Word Help button located in the upper right corner of the screen.
2. At the Word Help window, click in the search text box and then type **print**.
3. Press the Enter key.
4. When the list of topics displays, click the <u>Print and preview documents</u> hyperlinked topic.
5. Scroll down the Word Help window and read the information about printing and previewing documents.
6. Click the Print button in the Word Help window. This displays the Print dialog box. If you want to print the topic, click the Print button; otherwise, click the Cancel button to close the dialog box.

Step 1

Student Name

Find
Replace
Select
Editing

Step 2

Word Help -

print

**Print** labels
Article | How to print full pages of labels or a single label.

**Print** multiple copies of a document
Article | If you don't choose a certain number of copies to print, Word automatically prints one copy. But you can change that to almost any number you'd like.

Step 4

**Print** and preview documents
Article | You print and preview all your Word files

---

7. At the Word Help window, click the Use Large Text button to increase the size of the text in the window.
8. Click the Use Large Text button again to return the text to the normal size.

9. Click the Back button to return to the previous window.
10. Click the Forward button to redisplay the article on printing and previewing a document.
11. Click the Home button to return to the original Word Help screen.
12. Click the Close button to close the Word Help window.
13. Hover your mouse pointer over the Format Painter button in the Clipboard group on the HOME tab.
14. Click the Tell me more hyperlink that displays at the bottom of the ScreenTip.

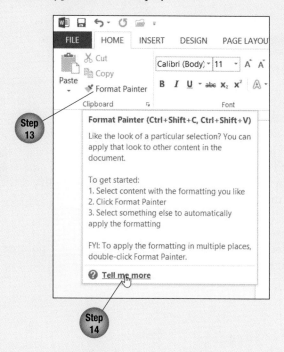

15. Read the information in the Word Help window about the Format Painter feature.
16. Click the Close button to close the Word Help window.

## Getting Help in a Dialog Box or Backstage Area

Some dialog boxes and backstage areas contain a Help button that you can click to display a Help window with specific information about the dialog box or backstage area. After reading and/or printing the information, close the dialog box by clicking the Close button located in the upper right corner of the dialog box or close the backstage area by clicking the Back button or pressing the Esc key.

---

**Exercise 1.6B**  Getting Help in a Dialog Box and Backstage Area  **Part 2 of 2**

1. At a blank document, click the Paragraph group dialog box launcher that displays in the lower right corner of the Paragraph group on the HOME tab. (The Paragraph group dialog box launcher is a small button containing a diagonally pointing arrow.)
2. Click the Help button that displays in the upper right corner of the dialog box.

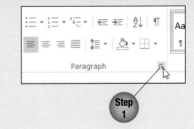

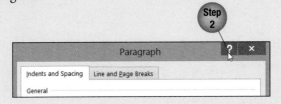

3. Read the information that displays in the Word Help window.
4. Close the Word Help window and then close the Paragraph dialog box by clicking the Cancel button located in the lower right corner of the dialog box.
5. Click the FILE tab and then click the *Save As* option.
6. At the Save As backstage area, click the Microsoft Word Help button that displays in the upper right corner of the backstage area.
7. Read the information that displays in the Word Help window.
8. Close the Word Help window.
9. Return to the blank document by clicking the Back button (left-pointing arrow inside a circle) that displays in the upper left corner of the backstage area.

---

# *Chapter Summary*

➤ Open Microsoft Word by clicking the Word 2013 tile at the Windows 8 Start screen. Refer to Figure 1.1 and Table 1.1 for an example and a list of key Word screen features, respectively.

➤ The Quick Access toolbar is located above the FILE tab and contains buttons for commonly used commands.

➤ Click the FILE tab and the backstage area displays containing options for working with and managing documents.

➤ The Title bar is located to the right of the Quick Access toolbar and displays the document name followed by the program name.

- The ribbon area contains tabs with commands and options divided into groups.
- The insertion point displays as a blinking vertical line and indicates the position of the next character to be entered in the document.
- The mouse pointer displays on the screen as an I-beam pointer or an up-pointing arrow.
- Use the vertical scroll bar to view various parts of the document.
- The Status bar displays the number of pages and words, view buttons, and Zoom slider bar.
- Word automatically wraps text to the next line as you type information. Press the Enter key only to end a paragraph, create a blank line, or end a short line.
- Word contains an AutoCorrect feature that automatically corrects certain words as they are typed.
- Word contains both an automatic spelling checker that inserts a red wavy line below words not contained in the Spelling dictionary and an automatic grammar checker that inserts a blue wavy line below text that may contain a grammatical error.
- The AutoComplete feature inserts an entire item when you type a few identifying characters and then press the Enter key or the F3 key.
- Document names can contain a maximum of 255 characters, including the drive letter and folder names, and may include spaces.
- You can move the insertion point by character, word, screen, or page and from the first to the last character in a document. Refer to Table 1.2 for keyboard insertion point movement commands.
- The scroll box on the vertical scroll bar indicates the location of the text in the document screen in relation to the remainder of the document.
- Delete text by character, word, line, several lines, or partial page using specific keys or by selecting text using the mouse or keyboard.
- A specific amount of text can be selected using the mouse or the keyboard. Refer to Table 1.4 for information on selecting text with the mouse and refer to Table 1.5 for information on selecting text with the keyboard.
- Use the Undo button on the Quick Access toolbar if you change your mind after typing, deleting, or formatting text and want to undo the action. Use the Redo button to reinstate something that has been undone with the Undo button.
- Word's Help feature is an on-screen reference manual that contains information about Word features and commands. Click the Microsoft Word Help button or press the F1 key to display the Word Help window.
- The Word Help window contains five buttons to the left of the search text box, including the Back, Forward, Home, Print, and Use Large Text buttons. Use the Keep Help on Top button in the Word Help window to keep the window on the screen even when working in a document.
- If you hover your mouse pointer over certain buttons, the ScreenTip that displays may include a Help icon and Tell me more hyperlink. Click this hyperlinked text to display the Word Help window with information about the button feature.
- Some dialog boxes and backstage areas contain a Help button that you can click to display information specific to the dialog box or backstage area.

# Commands Review

| FEATURE | RIBBON TAB, GROUP | BUTTON, OPTION | FILE TAB | KEYBOARD SHORTCUT |
|---|---|---|---|---|
| close document | | | *Close* | Ctrl + F4 |
| close Word | | ✕ | | Alt + F4 |
| Find and Replace dialog box with Go To tab selected | HOME, Editing | 🔍, *Go To* | | Ctrl + G |
| new blank document | | | *New, Blank document* | Ctrl + N |
| Open backstage area | | | *Open* | Ctrl + O |
| Open dialog box | | | | Ctrl + F12 |
| Save As backstage area | | 💾 | *Save* OR *Save As* | Ctrl + S |
| Save As dialog box | | | | F12 |
| Print backstage area | | | *Print* | Ctrl + P |
| Select document | HOME, Editing | ↖ | | Ctrl + A |
| redo action | | ↪ | | Ctrl + Y |
| undo action | | ↩ ▾ | | Ctrl + Z |
| Word Help window | | ? | | F1 |

# Key Points Review

**Completion:** In the space provided at the right, indicate the correct term, command, or number.

1. This is the area located near the top of the screen that contains tabs with commands and options divided into groups. _____

2. This bar, located near the bottom of the screen, displays the number of pages and words, view buttons, and Zoom slider bar. _____

3. This feature automatically corrects certain words as you type them. _____

4. This feature inserts an entire item when you type a few identifying characters and then press the Enter key or F3 key. _____

5. This toolbar contains the Save button. _____

6. Click this tab to display the backstage area. _____

7. Use this keyboard shortcut to display the Print backstage area. _____

8. Use this keyboard shortcut to close a document. _____

9. Use this keyboard shortcut to display a new blank document. _____

10. Use this keyboard command to move the insertion point to the beginning of the previous page. _____

11. Use this keyboard command to move the insertion point to the end of the document. _____

12. Press this key on the keyboard to delete the character left of the insertion point. _____

13. Using the mouse, do this to select one word. _____

14. To select various amounts of text using the mouse, click in this bar. _____

15. Use this keyboard shortcut to display the Word Help window. _____

# *Chapter Assessments*

## Applying Your Skills

Demonstrate your knowledge of features learned in this chapter by completing the following assessments.

### Assessment 1.1    Type a Document

1. At a blank document, type the text in Figure 1.11. (Correct any errors highlighted by the spelling checker as they occur and remember to space once after end-of-sentence punctuation.)
2. Save the document in the Chapter01 folder on your storage medium with the name **C01-A01-CoverLtrs**.
3. Print and then close **C01-A01-CoverLtrs.docx**.

**Figure 1.11  Assessment 1.1**

Cover letters are an essential component of your job search. During your search and transition, you will write many different letters or emails to "cover" your resume. In essence, cover letters tell your readers why you are contacting them. Often they are your very first opportunity to make an impression on a hiring decision-maker. They offer you the golden opportunity to link your unique set of skills, experiences, talents, and interests with a particular company or job opportunity. They are your formal introduction to people who can be extremely influential in your job search, and they prepare your reader for all of the details, experiences, and accomplishments you have highlighted in your resume.

### Assessment 1.2    Edit a Document Containing Proofreaders' Marks

1. Open **Editing.docx**.
2. Save the document with Save As and name it **C01-A02-Editing**.
3. Make the changes indicated by the proofreaders' marks in Figure 1.12 on the next page.
4. Save, print, and then close **C01-A02-Editing.docx**.

**Figure 1.12  Assessment 1.2**

*Editing is*
*lc*
The process of altering the contents of an existing document ~~is called editing~~. Editing
*when*
occurs ~~anytime~~ something is inserted, deleted, or modified within a document. Editing
features allow users to make changes until they are satisfied with the content. Perhaps the
most valued ~~word processing~~ editing feature is a spell checker, which matches each word in
*; and*
a document to a word list or dictionary. A spell checker is not context-sensitive ~~it~~ will not
flag words that have been spelled correctly but used incorrectly.

*No ¶* A grammar checker checks a document for common errors in grammar, usage, and
mechanics. Grammar checkers are no substitute for careful review by a knowledgeable
editor, but they can be useful for identifying such problems as run-on sentences, sentence
*double negatives,*
fragments, and misused apostrophes.

## Assessment 1.3    Edit a Document Containing Proofreaders' Marks

1.  Open **Format.docx**.
2.  Save the document with Save As and name it **C01-A03-Format**.
3.  Make the changes indicated by the proofreaders' marks in Figure 1.13.
4.  Save, print, and then close **C01-A03-Format.docx**.

**Figure 1.13  Assessment 1.3**

*which is*
Word processing programs allow many different types of formatting, ~~or~~ the manipulation
of text to change its appearance at the word, paragraph, or document level. Many word
*programs*
processing ~~applications~~ include text, paragraph, and document formatting.

*the*
Text formatting features include the ability to change font type, size, color, and style (such
*which is*
as bold, italic, or underlined). Users can also adjust the leading (the space between lines)
*which is*
and kerning (the amount of space that appears between letters).

*No ¶* Paragraph formatting changes the way a body of text flows on the page. Features related to
the appearance of a paragraph include placing the text in columns or tables; aligning the
*spacing*
text left, right, center, or justified within the margins; and double-, or single-spacing lines.

*No ¶* Document formatting lets users specify the form of a document as a whole, defining page
*Many word processing programs include a*
numbers, headers, footers, paper size, and margin width. A style ~~is a special shortcut~~
feature that formats text in a single step. Styles allow users to apply text and paragraph
*document        then*
formatting to a ~~page~~, and ~~the styles~~ automatically apply those same attributes to other
sections of text.

# Expanding Your Skills

Explore additional feature options or use Word Help to learn a new skill in creating these documents.

### Assessment 1.4   Compose a Document on Saving a Document

1. At a blank document, compose a paragraph explaining when you would use Save As when saving a document and what advantages this provides.
2. Save the document with the name **C01-A04-SaveAs**.
3. Print and then close **C01-A04-SaveAs.docx**.

### Assessment 1.5   Use Help to Learn about and Then Create a Document Describing Keyboard Shortcuts

1. Click the Microsoft Word Help button, click in the search text box, type **keyboard shortcuts,** and then press the Enter key.
2. At the Word Help window, click the Keyboard shortcuts for Microsoft Word hyperlink.
3. At the keyboard shortcut window, click the Show All hyperlink.
4. Read through the information in the Word Help window and then close the window.
5. Create a document describing four keyboard shortcuts.
6. Save the document with the name **C01-A05-KeyboardShortcuts**.
7. Print and then close **C01-A05-KeyboardShortcuts.docx**.

# Achieving Signature Status

Take your skills to the next level by completing this more challenging assessment.

### Assessment 1.6   Create a Cover Letter

1. At a blank document, click the No Spacing style thumbnail located in the Styles group on the HOME tab. (Clicking the No Spacing style changes the line spacing to single and removes the 8 points of spacing after each paragraph.)
2. Press the Enter key six times and then type the personal business letter shown in Figure 1.14 on the next page. Type the current date in place of the *Current Date* text and type your first and last names in place of the *Student Name* text. Refer to Appendix B at the end of this textbook for the formatting of a block style personal business letter.
3. Save the completed document with the name **C01-A06-CoverLtr**.
4. Print and then close the **C01-A06-CoverLtr.docx**.

**Figure 1.14  Assessment 1.6**

3120 Magnolia Drive
Columbia, SC 29167
Current Date


Mr. Nathaniel Jensen
Human Resources Director
Landmark Associates
4450 Seventh Avenue
Columbia, SC 29169

Dear Mr. Jensen:

In response to your advertisement on Monster.com, I would like to apply for the position of Sales Associate Trainee in the Sales and Marketing Department at your company. I have a strong interest in joining a dynamic organization such as Landmark Associates and feel I can make major contributions to the company in a short period of time.

I recently graduated from Columbia Technical College with a degree in Business Operations. For the past two years, I have been employed as an assistant in the Accounting Department at Atlantic Signs where I processed payroll and budget reports. My excellent communication skills and a strong work ethic make me a valuable asset to your training program.

I have enclosed my resume for your review. Please call me at (803) 555-3489 to schedule a meeting to discuss the Sales Associate Trainee position at Landmark Associates.

Sincerely,


Student Name

Enclosure

# Chapter 2

# Formatting Characters

## Performance Objectives

Upon successful completion of Chapter 2, you will be able to:

- Change fonts and font effects
- Apply styles from style sets
- Apply themes
- Customize style sets and themes

The term *format* refers to how a document looks on screen and when it is printed. As you learned in Chapter 1, Word uses a template to apply default formatting that affects the appearance of a document. Some default settings include 11-point Calibri font, line spacing of 1.08, 8 points of spacing after each paragraph, and left-aligned text. In this chapter, you will learn about character formatting, including how to change the typeface, type size, and typestyle, as well as how to apply font effects such as subscripting, superscripting, and highlighting.

*Note: Before beginning computer exercises for this chapter, copy to your storage medium the Chapter02 folder from the CD that accompanies this textbook and then make Chapter02 the active folder.*

In this chapter, students will produce the following documents:

Exercise 2.1. C02-E01-Terms.docx
Exercise 2.2. C02-E02-CompSecurity.docx

Model answers for these exercises are shown on the following page.

**GLOSSARY OF TERMS**

**A**

**Active desktop:** An on-screen desktop that can contain icons linked to the Web.

**Android:** A mobile *robot* designed to seem human.

**Applet:** A small computer application program, ~~generally created using the Java programming language,~~ that performs specific functions; applets are used to extend the capabilities of web pages.

**B**

**Beta version:** A prerelease version of a piece of software distributed so that users can test it to evaluate its features and identify any bugs.

**Bluetooth:** A technology that uses *infrared light signals* to send information.

**Buffer:** A temporary storage unit to which data can be written before being displayed, printed, or transmitted.

**C**

**Carpal tunnel syndrome:** A condition characterized by weakness, pain, or numbness of the hand(s), caused by compression of the median nerve as it passes through the wrist; the *syndrome* is associated with repetitive motion such as typing or using the computer mouse.

**Cell:** In a spreadsheet, the *intersection* of one row and one column into which text, numbers, formulas, links, or other elements may be entered.

**Chinese abacus:** Pebbles strung on a rod inside a frame. Pebbles in the upper part of an abacus correspond to $5 \times 10^0$, or 5, for the first column; $5 \times 10^1$, or 50, for the second column; $5 \times 10^2$, or 500, for the third column; and so on.

**Clip art:** Professionally designed graphic images sold for use in *word processing* and other types of documents; collections are sometimes included in a software program.

SUBMITTED BY MARCUS JACKSON

MONDAY, OCTOBER 12, 2015

**Exercise 2.1**　　　　　　　　　　　　　　C02-E01-Terms.docx

---

# COMPUTER VIRUSES

One of the most familiar forms of risk to computer security is the computer virus. A computer virus is a program written by a hacker or a cracker, designed to perform some kind of trick upon an unsuspecting victim's computer. In some cases, the trick performed is mild, such as drawing an offensive image on the victim's screen or changing all of the characters in a document to another language. Sometimes the trick is much more severe, such as reformatting the hard drive and erasing all the data or damaging the motherboard so that it cannot operate properly.

## Types of Viruses

Viruses can be categorized by their effects, which include being a nuisance, destroying data, facilitating espionage, and destroying hardware. A nuisance virus usually does no real damage but is an inconvenience. The most difficult part of a computer to replace is the data on the hard drive. The installed programs, documents, databases, and saved emails form the heart of a personal computer. A data-destructive virus is designed to destroy this data. Some viruses are designed to create a backdoor into a system to bypass security. Called espionage viruses, they do no damage but allow a hacker or cracker to enter the system later for the purpose of stealing data or spying on the work of the competitor. Very rarely, a virus is created to damage the hardware of the computer system itself. Called hardware-destructive viruses, these bits of programming can weaken or destroy chips, drives, and other components.

## Methods of Virus Operation

Viruses operate and are transmitted in a variety of ways. An email virus is normally transmitted as an attachment to a message sent over the Internet. Email viruses require the victim to click on the attachment, which causes the virus to execute. Another common mode of virus transmission is via a macro, a small subprogram that allows users to customize and automate certain functions. A macro virus is written for a specific program, which then becomes infected when it opens a file with the virus stored in its macros. The boot sector of a compact disc or hard drive contains a variety of information, including how the disk is organized and whether it is capable of loading an operating system. When a disc is left in a drive and the computer reboots, the operating system automatically reads the boot sector to learn about that disk and to attempt to start any operating system on it. A boot sector virus is designed to alter the boot sector of a disk so that whenever the operating system reads the boot sector, the computer will automatically become infected.

# SECURITY RISKS

Although hackers, crackers, and viruses garner the most attention as security risks, companies face a variety of other dangers to their hardware and software systems. Principally, these risks involve types of system failure, employee theft, and the cracking of software for copying.

## System Failure

A fundamental element in making sure that computer systems operate properly is protecting the electrical power that runs them. Power interruptions such as blackouts and brownouts have very adverse effects on computers. An inexpensive type of power strip called a surge protector can guard against power fluctuations and can also serve as an extension cord and splitter. A much more vigorous power protection system is an uninterruptible power supply (UPS), which provides a battery backup. Similar in nature to a power strip but much bulkier and a bit more expensive, a UPS provides steady, spike-free power and keeps a computer running during a blackout.

## Employee Theft

Although accurate estimates are difficult to pinpoint, businesses certainly lose millions of dollars a year in stolen computer hardware and software. In large organizations, such theft often goes unnoticed or unreported. Someone takes a hard drive or a scanner home for legitimate use, then leaves the job sometime later and keeps the machine. Sometimes, employees take components to add to their home PC systems, or thieves break into businesses and haul away computers. Such thefts cost far more than the price of the stolen computers because they also involve the cost of replacing the lost data, the cost of time lost while the machines are gone, and the cost of installing new machines and training people to use them.

## Cracking Software for Copying

A common goal of hackers is to crack a software protection scheme. A crack is a method of circumventing a security scheme that prevents a user from copying a program. A common protection scheme for software is to require the installation CD to be resident in the drive whenever the program runs. Making copies of the CD with a burner, however, easily fools this protection scheme. Some game companies are taking an extra step to make duplication difficult by scrambling some of the data on the original CDs, which CD burners will automatically correct when copying. When the copied and corrected CD is used, the software checks for the scrambled track information. If the error is not found, the software will not run.

**Exercise 2.2**　　　　　　　　　　C02-E02-CompSecurity.docx

# Changing Fonts

The Font group on the HOME tab, shown in Figure 2.1, contains a number of buttons for applying character formatting to text in a document. The top row contains buttons that change the font and font size, increase and decrease the font size, change the text case, and clear the formatting. To remove all character formatting (as well as paragraph formatting) that has been applied to text, click the Clear All Formatting button in the top row. To remove character formatting from selected text only, press the keyboard shortcut Ctrl + spacebar. The bottom row contains buttons for applying typestyles such as bold, italic, and underlining and applying text effects, highlighting, and color.

Clear All
Formatting

**Figure 2.1  Font Group Buttons**

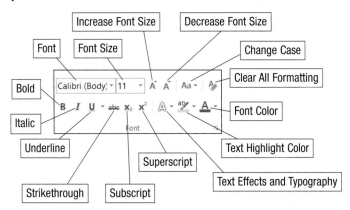

As noted earlier, 11-point Calibri is Word's default font. You may want to change this default to some other font for reasons such as creating a certain mood in the document, enhancing its appearance, or increasing its readability. A font consists of three elements: typeface, type size, and typestyle.

A typeface is a set of characters with a common design and shape. It can be decorative or plain, monospaced or proportional. Word refers to a typeface as a **font**. A monospaced typeface allots the same amount of horizontal space for each character, while a proportional typeface allots a varying amount of space for each character. Proportional typefaces are divided into two main categories: ***serif*** and ***sans serif***. A serif is a small line at the end of a character stroke. Because serifs help move the reader's eyes across the page, a serif font is a good choice for a text-intensive document. Sans serif typefaces are often used for headings, headlines, and advertisements. Some of the popular typefaces are shown in Table 2.1 on the next page.

**Table 2.1 Serif and Sans Serif Typefaces**

| Serif Typefaces | Sans Serif Typefaces | Monospaced Typefaces |
| --- | --- | --- |
| Cambria | Calibri | Consolas |
| Constantia | Candara | Courier |
| Times New Roman | Corbel | Letter Gothic |
| Bookman Old Style | Arial | |

**QUICK STEPS**

**Change the Font**
1. Click Font button arrow.
2. Click desired font at drop-down gallery.

**Change the Font Size**
1. Click Font Size button arrow.
2. Click desired font size at drop-down gallery.

Calibri (Body) ▾

Font

11 ▾

Font Size

Type is generally set in proportional size. The size of proportional type is measured vertically in units called **points**. A point is approximately ½ of an inch—the higher the point size, the larger the characters. Within a typeface, various typestyles may be available. Typestyles are divided into four main categories: regular, bold, italic, and bold italic.

Use the Font button in the Font group to change the font; use the Font Size button or the Decrease Font Size and Increase Font Size buttons to change the size. When you select text and then click the Font button arrow, a drop-down gallery displays font options. Hover your mouse pointer over a font option and the selected text in the document displays with the font applied. You can continue hovering your mouse pointer over different font options to see how the selected text displays in the specified font.

The Font button drop-down gallery is an example of the **live preview** feature in Word, which allows you to see how the font formatting affects your text without having to return to the document. The live preview feature is also available when you click the Font Size button arrow.

---

**Exercise 2.1A**  **Changing the Font**  **Part 1 of 4**

1. Open **Terms.docx**.
2. Save the document with Save As and name it **C02-E01-Terms**.
3. Change the typeface to Cambria by completing the following steps:
   a. Select the entire document by pressing Ctrl + A. (You can also select all of the text in the document by clicking the Select button in the Editing group on the HOME tab and then clicking *Select All* at the drop-down list.)

b.   Click the Font button arrow and then scroll down the Font drop-down gallery until *Cambria* displays. Hover the mouse pointer over *Cambria* to display a live preview of the document text set in Cambria.

c.   Click *Cambria*.

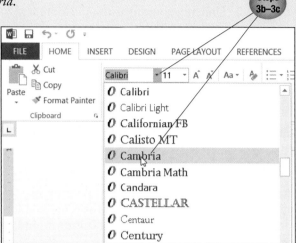

4.   Change the type size to 14 points by completing the following steps:

a.   With the text in the document still selected, click the Font Size button arrow.

b.   At the drop-down gallery that displays, hover the mouse pointer over *14* and look at the live preview of the text in 14-point size.

c.   Click *14*.

5.   Deselect the text by clicking anywhere in the document.

6.   Change the type size and typeface by completing the following steps:

a.   Press Ctrl + A to select the entire document.

b.   Click three times on the Decrease Font Size button in the Font group. (This decreases the size of the font to 10 points.)

c.   Click twice on the Increase Font Size button. (This increases the size of the font to 12 points.)

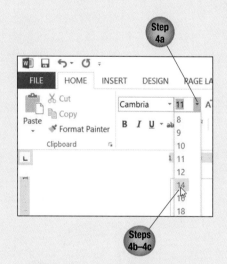

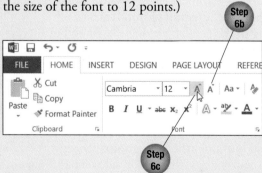

d.   With the text still selected, click the Font button arrow, scroll down the drop-down gallery, and then click *Constantia*. (The most recently used fonts display at the beginning of the gallery, followed by a list of all fonts.)

7.   Save **C02-E01-Terms.docx**.

## Choosing a Typestyle

**B** Bold    *I* Italic

**U** ▾ Underline

Apply a particular typestyle to text with the Bold, Italic, or Underline button in the bottom row in the Font group. You can apply more than one style to the same text. For example, you can bold and italicize the same text or apply all three styles to the same text. Click the Underline button arrow and a drop-down gallery displays with underlining options, such as a double line, dashed line, and thicker line. Click the *Underline Color* option at the Underline button drop-down gallery and a side menu displays with color options.

---

### Exercise 2.1B   Applying Character Formatting to Text as You Type   Part 2 of 4

1. With **C02-E01-Terms.docx** open, press Ctrl + Home to move the insertion point to the beginning of the document.
2. Type a heading for the document by completing the following steps:
   a. Click the Bold button in the Font group. (This turns on bold formatting.)
   b. Click the Underline button in the Font group. (This turns on underline formatting.)
   c. Type **Glossary of Terms**.

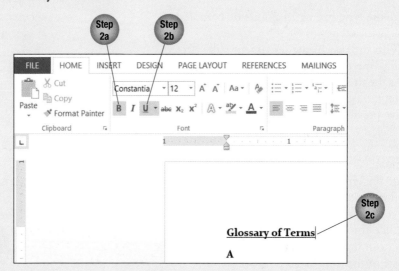

   d. Select *Glossary of Terms* and then click the Clear All Formatting button in the Font group. (This removes all formatting from the text.)
   e. Return formatting to the text by clicking the Undo button on the Quick Access toolbar.
3. Press Ctrl + End to move the insertion point to the end of the document.
4. Type the text shown in Figure 2.2 on the next page with the following specifications:
   a. While typing the text, make the appropriate text bold as shown in the figure by completing the following steps:
      1) Click the Bold button in the Font group. (This turns on bold formatting.)
      2) Type the text.
      3) Click the Bold button in the Font group. (This turns off bold formatting.)
   b. While typing the text, italicize the appropriate text as shown in the figure by completing the following steps:
      1) Click the Italic button in the Font group.
      2) Type the text.
      3) Click the Italic button in the Font group.

---

5. After typing the text, press the Enter key.
6. Change the underlining below the title *Glossary of Terms* by completing the following steps:
   a. Select the title *Glossary of Terms*.
   b. Click the Underline button arrow and then click the third underline option from the top of the drop-down gallery.
   c. Click the Underline button arrow, point to the *Underline Color* option, and then click the *Red* color (second color option in the *Standard Colors* section).
7. With the title *Glossary of Terms* still selected, change the font size to 14 points.
8. Save **C02-E01-Terms.docx**.

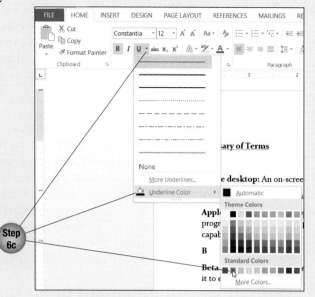

Step 6c

**Figure 2.2  Exercise 2.1B**

## C

**Carpal tunnel syndrome:** A condition characterized by weakness, pain, or numbness of the hand(s), caused by compression of the median nerve as it passes through the wrist; the *syndrome* is associated with repetitive motion such as typing or using the computer mouse.

**Cell:** In a spreadsheet, the *intersection* of one row and one column into which text, numbers, formulas, links, or other elements may be entered.

**Clip art:** Professionally designed graphic images sold for use in *word processing* and other types of documents; collections are sometimes included in a software program.

Change Case

Strikethrough

Subscript

Superscript

Text Effects and
Typography

Text Highlight Color

Font Color

## Choosing a Font Effect

Apply font effects with some of the buttons in the top and bottom rows in the Font group. Change the case of text with the Change Case button drop-down list. Click the Change Case button in the top row of the Font group and a drop-down list displays with the options *Sentence case, lowercase, UPPERCASE, Capitalize Each Word*, and *tOGGLEcASE*. You can also change the case of selected text with the keyboard shortcut Shift + F3. Each time you press Shift + F3, the selected text displays in the next case option in the list.

The bottom row in the Font group contains buttons for applying font effects. Use the Strikethrough button to draw a line through selected text. This has a practical application in some legal documents in which deleted text must be retained in the document. Use the Subscript button to create text that is lowered slightly below the line, as in the chemical formula $H_2O$. Use the Superscript button to create text that is raised slightly above the text line, as in the mathematical equation four to the third power (written as $4^3$). Click the Text Effects and Typography button in the bottom row and a drop-down gallery displays with effect options. Use the Text Highlight Color button to highlight specific text in a document and use the Font Color button to change the color of text.

## Using Keyboard Shortcuts

Keyboard shortcuts are available for several buttons in the Font group. For example, press Ctrl + B to turn on/off bold formatting and press Ctrl + I to turn on/off italic formatting. Position the mouse pointer on a button and an enhanced ScreenTip displays with the name of the button, the keyboard shortcut (if there is one), a description of the action performed by the button, and in some cases, access to the Word Help window. Table 2.2 identifies the keyboard shortcuts available for buttons in the Font group.

**Table 2.2 Font Button Keyboard Shortcuts**

| Font Group Button | Keyboard Shortcut |
|---|---|
| Font | Ctrl + Shift + F |
| Font Size | Ctrl + Shift + P |
| Increase Font Size | Ctrl + Shift + > |
| Decrease Font Size | Ctrl + Shift + < |
| Bold | Ctrl + B |
| Italic | Ctrl + I |
| Underline | Ctrl + U |
| Subscript | Ctrl + = |
| Superscript | Ctrl + Shift + + |
| Change Case | Shift + F3 |

## Formatting with the Mini Toolbar

When you select text, the Mini toolbar displays above the selected text. Click a button on the Mini toolbar to apply formatting to selected text. When you move the mouse pointer away from the Mini toolbar, it disappears.

If you do not want the Mini toolbar to display when you select text, you can turn it off. To do this, click the FILE tab and then click *Options*. At the Word Options dialog box with the *General* option selected in the left panel, click the *Show Mini Toolbar on selection* check box to remove the check mark.

## Exercise 2.1C  Applying Font Effects

Part 3 of 4

1. With **C02-E01-Terms.docx** open, move the insertion point to the beginning of the term *Clip art*, press the Enter key, and then press the Up Arrow key. Type the text shown in Figure 2.3. Create each superscript number by clicking the Superscript button, typing the number, and then clicking the Superscript button.

2. Change the case of text and remove underlining from the title by completing the following steps:
   a. Select the title *Glossary of Terms*.
   b. Remove all formatting from the title by clicking the Clear All Formatting button in the Font group.
   c. Click the Change Case button in the Font group and then click *UPPERCASE* at the drop-down list.
   d. Click the Text Effects and Typography button in the Font group and then click the *Gradient Fill - Blue, Accent 1, Reflection* option (second column, second row) at the drop-down gallery.

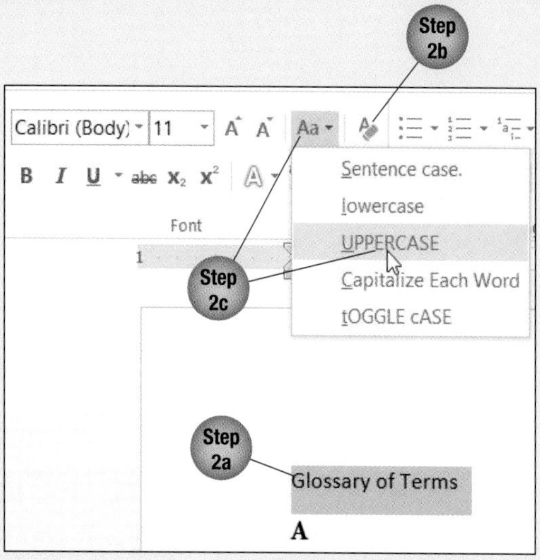

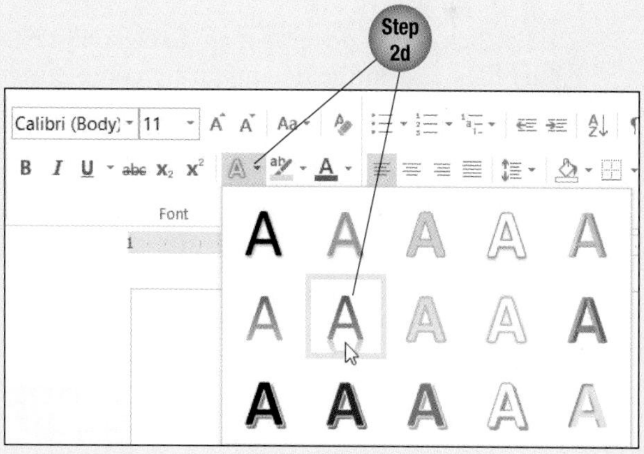

**Figure 2.3  Exercise 2.1C**

**Chinese abacus:** Pebbles strung on a rod inside a frame. Pebbles in the upper part of an abacus correspond to $5 \times 10^0$, or 5, for the first column; $5 \times 10^1$, or 50, for the second column; $5 \times 10^2$, or 500, for the third column; and so on.

3. Strike through text by completing the following steps:
   a. Select the commas and words , *generally created using the Java programming language,* located in the *Applet* definition.
   b. Click the Strikethrough button in the Font group.

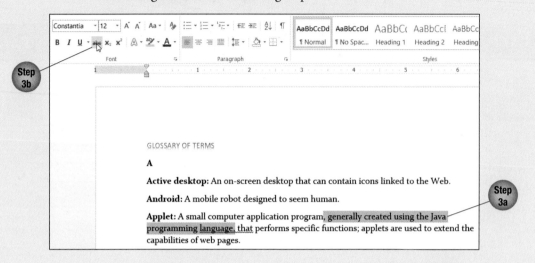

4. Change the font color by completing the following steps:
   a. Press Ctrl + A to select the entire document.
   b. Click the Font Color button arrow.
   c. Click the *Dark Red* color (first color option in the *Standard Colors* section) at the drop-down gallery.
   d. Click in the document to deselect all text.
5. Highlight text in the document by completing the following steps:
   a. Click the Text Highlight Color button arrow in the Font group and then click the *Yellow* color (first column, first row) at the drop-down palette. (This causes the mouse pointer to display as an I-beam pointer with a highlighter pen attached.)

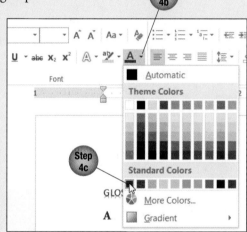

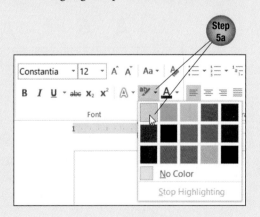

b. Select the term *Beta version* and the definition that follows.

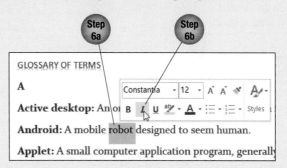

> **B**
>
> **Beta version:** A prerelease version of a piece of software distributed so that users can test it to evaluate its features and identify any bugs.
>
> **Bluetooth:** A technology that uses infrared light signals to send information.

Step 5b

c. Click the Text Highlight Color button arrow and then click the *Turquoise* color (third column, first row).
d. Select the term *Cell* and the definition that follows.
e. Click the Text Highlight Color button arrow and then click the *Yellow* color at the drop-down palette.
f. Click the Text Highlight Color button to turn off highlighting.

6. Apply italic formatting using the Mini toolbar by completing the following steps:

a. Select the word *robot* located in the *Android* definition. (When you select the word, the Mini toolbar displays.)
b. Click the Italic button on the Mini toolbar.
c. Select the words *infrared light signals* located in the *Bluetooth* definition and then click the Italic button on the Mini toolbar.

Step 6a    Step 6b

GLOSSARY OF TERMS

**A**

**Active desktop:** An o...

**Android:** A mobile robot designed to seem human.

**Applet:** A small computer application program, generally

7. Save **C02-E01-Terms.docx**.

## Changing Fonts at the Font Dialog Box

In addition to using the Font group buttons to apply font formatting, you can use options at the Font dialog box, shown in Figure 2.4 on the next page, to change the typeface, type size, and typestyle of text and to apply font effects. Display the Font dialog box by clicking the Font group dialog box launcher. The dialog box launcher is a small square containing a diagonal-pointing arrow that displays in the lower right corner of the Font group.

## Turning on the Display of Nonprinting Characters

The Font dialog box contains the *Hidden* option in the *Effects* section. With this option, you can select and then hide specific text. If you want to view the hidden text, turn on the display of nonprinting characters by clicking the Show/Hide ¶ button in the Paragraph group on the HOME tab or using the keyboard shortcut Ctrl + Shift + *. When the button is active, it displays with a light blue background. Hidden text displays with a dotted underline and other nonprinting characters display, as well, including paragraph symbols, tab symbols, and spacing characters. To redisplay hidden text, click the Show/Hide ¶ button to make it active, select the text, display the Font dialog box, and then remove the check mark from the *Hidden* option.

**QUICK STEPS**

**Change Fonts**
1. Click Font group dialog box launcher.
2. Choose desired options at dialog box.
3. Click OK.

**Display Nonprinting Characters**
Click Show/Hide ¶ button.
OR
Press Ctrl + Shift + *.

Show/Hide ¶

**Figure 2.4 Font Dialog Box**

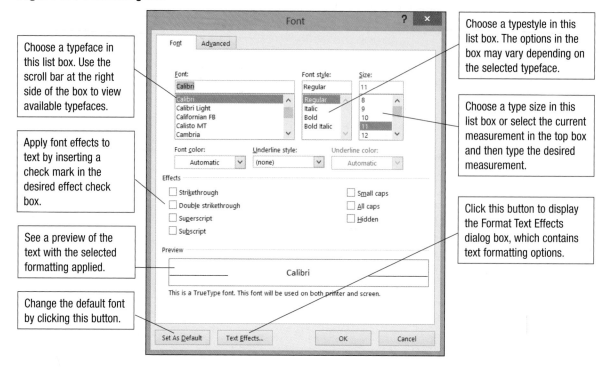

Choose a typeface in this list box. Use the scroll bar at the right side of the box to view available typefaces.

Choose a typestyle in this list box. The options in the box may vary depending on the selected typeface.

Apply font effects to text by inserting a check mark in the desired effect check box.

Choose a type size in this list box or select the current measurement in the top box and then type the desired measurement.

See a preview of the text with the selected formatting applied.

Click this button to display the Format Text Effects dialog box, which contains text formatting options.

Change the default font by clicking this button.

## Changing the Default Font

If you format most documents with a font other than the default of 11-point Calibri, change the default font with the Set as Default button at the Font dialog box. Make the desired change at the Font dialog box and then click the Set as Default button and a Microsoft Word message box displays asking if you want to change the default font and providing two options. The first option, *This document only,* is selected by default and indicates that the default font will change only for the current document. If you want the default font changed for all future documents, click the *All documents based on this Normal.dotm template* option.

**Exercise 2.1D**    Changing the Font at the Font Dialog Box      **Part 4 of 4**

1. With **C02-E01-Terms.docx** open, press Ctrl + End to move the insertion point to the end of the document. (Make sure the insertion point is positioned below the last line of text.)
2. Type **Submitted by Marcus Jackson** and then press the Enter key.
3. Type **Monday, October 12, 2015**.
4. Change the font to 13-point Calibri and the font color to Dark Blue for the entire document by completing the following steps:
   a. Press Ctrl + A to select the entire document.
   b. Click the Font group dialog box launcher.

Step 4b

c. At the Font dialog box, click the down-pointing arrow at the right side of the *Font* list box to scroll down the list box and then click *Calibri*.
d. Click in the *Size* text box and then type **13**.
e. Click the down-pointing arrow at the right side of the *Font color* option box and then click the *Dark Blue* color (ninth option in the *Standard Colors* section) at the drop-down color palette.
f. Click OK to close the dialog box.

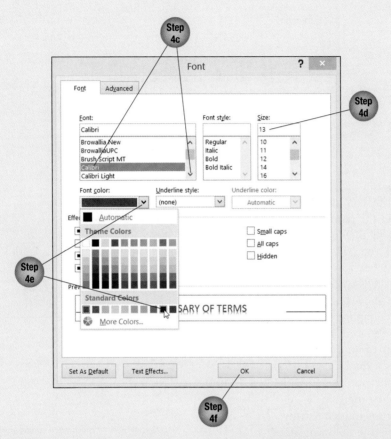

5. Double underline text by completing the following steps:
   a. Select *Monday, October 12, 2015*.
   b. Click the Font group dialog box launcher.
   c. At the Font dialog box, click the down-pointing arrow at the right side of the *Underline style* option box and then click the double-line option at the drop-down list.
   d. Click OK to close the dialog box.
6. Change text to small caps by completing the following steps:
   a. Select the text *Submitted by Marcus Jackson* and *Monday, October 12, 2015*.
   b. Display the Font dialog box.

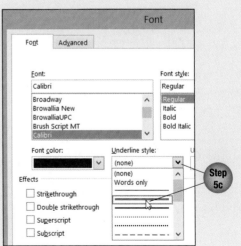

c.  Click the *Small caps* option in the *Effects* section. (This inserts a check mark in the check box.)

d.  Click OK to close the dialog box.

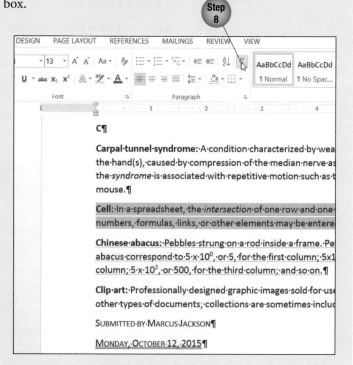

7.  Hide text by completing the following steps:
    a.  Select the term *Chinese abacus* and the definition that follows.
    b.  Display the Font dialog box.
    c.  Click the *Hidden* option in the *Effects* section. (This inserts a check mark in the check box.)
    d.  Click OK to close the dialog box.

8.  Click the Show/Hide ¶ button in the Paragraph group on the HOME tab to turn on the display of nonprinting characters. (The hidden text is now visible and displays with a dotted underline.)

9.  Redisplay the hidden text by completing the following steps:
    a.  Select the term *Chinese abacus* and the definition that follows.
    b.  Display the Font dialog box.
    c.  Click the *Hidden* option in the *Effects* section to remove the check mark.
    d.  Click OK to close the dialog box.

10. Click the Show/Hide ¶ button to turn off the display of nonprinting characters.

11. Save, print, and then close **C02-E01-Terms.docx**.

# Applying Styles from a Style Set

Word contains a number of predesigned formats grouped into style sets. Several thumbnails of the styles in the default style set display in the Styles group on the HOME tab. Display additional styles by clicking the More button that displays at the right side of the style thumbnails. This displays a drop-down gallery of style choices. To apply a style, select text or position the insertion point in the paragraph of text to which you want the style applied, click the More button at the right side of the style thumbnails in the Styles group, and then click the desired style at the drop-down gallery.

If you apply a heading style (such as Heading 1, Heading 2, and so on) to text, you can collapse and expand text below the heading(s). Hover your mouse pointer over text with a heading style applied and a collapse triangle (solid, right-and-down-pointing triangle) displays to the left of the heading. Click this collapse triangle and any text below the heading is collapsed (hidden). Redisplay the text below a heading by hovering the mouse pointer over the heading text until an expand triangle displays (hollow, right-pointing triangle) and then click the expand triangle. This expands (redisplays) the text below the heading.

As noted earlier, Word applies some default formatting to documents, including 8 points of spacing after paragraphs and line spacing of 1.08. You can remove this default formatting, as well as any character formatting applied to text in your document, by applying the No Spacing style to your text. This style is one of the styles that displays in the Styles group on the HOME tab.

Word contains a number of style sets you can use to apply formatting to a document. To change to a different style set, click the DESIGN tab and then click the desired style set thumbnail in the Document Formatting group.

**QUICK STEPS**

**Apply a Style**
1. Position insertion point in desired paragraph of text.
2. Click More button in Styles group.
3. Click desired style.

**Change the Style Set**
1. Click DESIGN tab.
2. Click desired style set thumbnail.

More

---

## Exercise 2.2A  Applying Styles and a Style Set                Part 1 of 3

1. Open **CompSecurity.docx**.
2. Save the document with Save As and name it **C02-E02-CompSecurity**.
3. Position the insertion point on any character in the title *COMPUTER VIRUSES* and then click the *Heading 1* style that displays in the Styles group.

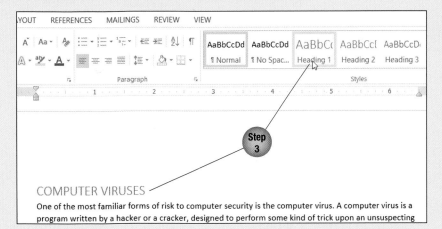

4. Position the insertion point on any character in the title *SECURITY RISKS* (located near the bottom of the first page) and then click the *Heading 1* style in the Styles group.

---

5. Position the insertion point on any character in the heading *Types of Viruses* and then click the *Heading 2* style that displays in the Styles group.

6. Position the insertion point on any character in the heading *Methods of Virus Operation* and then click the *Heading 2* style in the Styles group.

7. Apply the Heading 2 style to the remaining headings in the document: *System Failure*, *Employee Theft*, and *Cracking Software for Copying*.

8. Collapse and expand text below the titles with the Heading 1 style applied by completing the following steps:

   a. Hover the mouse pointer over the title *COMPUTER VIRUSES* until a collapse triangle displays at the left side of the title and then click the triangle. (This collapses all of the text below the first title.)

   b. Collapse the text below the second title, *SECURITY RISKS*, by hovering the mouse pointer at the left side of the title and then clicking the collapse triangle.

   c. Hover the mouse pointer over the title *SECURITY RISKS* until an expand triangle displays at the left side of the title and then click the triangle. (This redisplays the text below the second title.)

   d. Hover the mouse pointer over the left side of the title *COMPUTER VIRUSES* and then click the expand triangle.

9. Click the DESIGN tab.

10. Click the *Casual* style set thumbnail in the Document Formatting group. (Notice how the Heading 1 and Heading 2 formats change.)

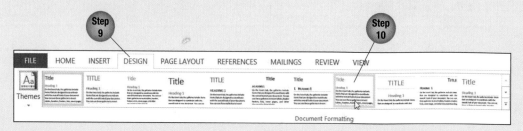

11. Save and then print **C02-E02-CompSecurity.docx**.

# Applying a Theme

Word provides a number of themes for formatting text in your document. A theme is a set of formatting choices that includes a color theme (a set of colors), font theme (a set of heading and body text fonts), and effects theme (a set of lines and fill effects). Applying a theme can give your documents a professional look.

To apply a theme, click the DESIGN tab and then click the Themes button in the Document Formatting group. At the drop-down gallery that displays, click the desired theme. Hover the mouse pointer over a theme and the live preview feature will display your document with the theme formatting applied. With the live preview feature, you can see how the theme formatting affects your document before you make your final choice.

**Apply a Theme**
1. Click DESIGN tab.
2. Click Themes button.
3. Click desired theme.

Themes

---

## Exercise 2.2B  Applying a Theme to a Document                    Part 2 of 3

1. With **C02-E02-CompSecurity.docx** open, if necessary, click the DESIGN tab and then click the Themes button in the Document Formatting group.
2. At the drop-down gallery, hover your mouse pointer over several themes and notice how the text formatting changes in your document.
3. Click the *Organic* theme.
4. Save and then print **C02-E02-CompSecurity.docx**.

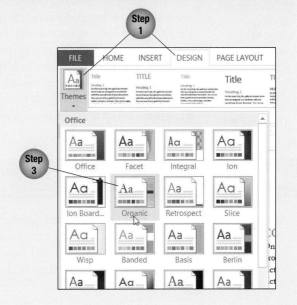

---

# Customizing Style Sets and Themes

Customize the color applied by a style or theme with the Colors button in the Document Formatting group. Click the Colors button and a drop-down gallery displays with named color schemes. Customize the fonts applied to text in a document with the Fonts button in the Document Formatting group. Click this button and a drop-down gallery displays with font choices. Each font group in the drop-down gallery contains two choices. The first choice in the group is the font that is applied to headings and the second choice is the font that is applied to body text in the document. If you are formatting a document containing graphics with lines and fills, you can apply a specific theme effect with options at the Effects button drop-down gallery.

The buttons in the Document Formatting group display a visual representation of the current theme. If you change the theme colors, the small color squares in the Themes button and Colors button reflect the change. Change the theme fonts and the letter *A*'s on the Themes button, as well as the uppercase letter *A* on the Fonts button, reflect the change. If you change the theme effects, the circle in the Effects button reflects the change.

The Paragraph Spacing button in the Document Formatting group on the DESIGN tab contains predesigned paragraph spacing options. To change paragraph spacing, click the Paragraph Spacing button and then click the desired option at the drop-down gallery. You can hover your mouse pointer over an option at the drop-down gallery and, after a moment, a ScreenTip displays with information about the formatting applied by the option. For example, if you hover the mouse pointer over the *Compact* option at the side menu, a ScreenTip displays telling you that the *Compact* option will change the spacing before paragraphs to 0 points, the spacing after paragraphs to 4 points, and the line spacing to 1.

Paragraph    Colors    Fonts
Spacing

---

## Exercise 2.2C    Customizing a Theme        Part 3 of 3

1. With **C02-E02-CompSecurity.docx** open, click the Colors button in the Document Formatting group on the DESIGN tab and then click *Red Orange* at the drop-down gallery. (Notice how the colors in the titles and headings change.)
2. Click the Fonts button arrow and then click the *Corbel* option. (Notice how the document text font changes.)

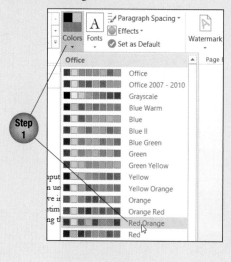 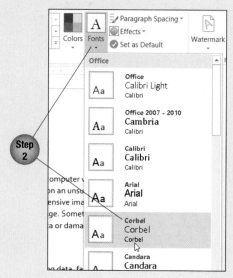

3. Apply the Centered style set by clicking the *Centered* thumbnail in the Document Formatting group.

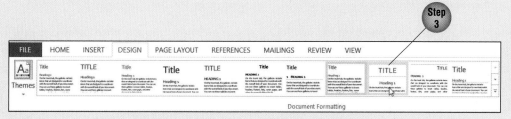

4. Click the Paragraph Spacing button and then, one at a time, hover the mouse pointer over each of the paragraph spacing options and read the ScreenTip that displays explaining the paragraph spacing applied by the option.
5. Click the *Double* option.

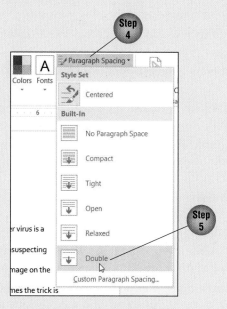

6. Scroll through the document and notice the paragraph spacing.
7. Change the paragraph spacing by clicking the Paragraph Spacing button and then clicking *Compact* at the drop-down gallery.
8. Save, print, and then close **C02-E02-CompSecurity.docx**.

# Chapter Summary

- The appearance of a document on the document screen and how it looks when printed is called the *format*.

- The top row in the Font group on the HOME tab contains buttons for changing the font and font size. The bottom row contains buttons for applying typestyles and effects.

- A font consists of three elements: typeface, type size, and typestyle.

- A typeface (font) is a set of characters with a common design and shape. Typefaces are either monospaced, allotting the same amount of horizontal space to each character, or proportional, allotting a varying amount of space for each character. Proportional typefaces are divided into two main categories: serif and sans serif.

- Type size is measured in point size—the higher the point size, the larger the characters.

- A typestyle is a variation of style within a certain typeface. Apply typestyle formatting with buttons in the Font group.

- With buttons in the Font group, you can apply font effects such as superscript, subscript, and strikethrough.

- Some buttons in the Font group have corresponding keyboard shortcuts. Refer to Table 2.2 on page 42 for a list of these shortcuts.

- The Mini toolbar automatically displays above selected text. Use buttons on this toolbar to apply formatting to selected text. Turn off the Mini toolbar by removing the check mark from the *Show Mini Toolbar on selection* option in the Word Options dialog box with the *General* option selected.

- With options at the Font dialog box, you can change the font, font size, and font style and apply specific effects. Display this dialog box by clicking the Font group dialog box launcher.

- Click the Show/Hide ¶ button in the Paragraph group on the HOME tab or press Ctrl + Shift + * to turn on/off the display of nonprinting characters. With the display of nonprinting characters turned on, hidden text will display with a dotted underline in the document.

- A Word document contains a number of predesigned formats grouped into style sets. Change to a different style set by clicking the DESIGN tab and then clicking the desired style set thumbnail in the Document Formatting group.

- Apply a theme and change theme colors, fonts, and effects with buttons in the Document Formatting group on the DESIGN tab.

- Click the Paragraph Spacing button in the Document Formatting group on the DESIGN tab to apply a predesigned paragraph spacing option to text in a document.

# *Commands* Review

| FEATURE | RIBBON TAB, GROUP | BUTTON | KEYBOARD SHORTCUT |
|---|---|---|---|
| bold text | HOME, Font | B | Ctrl + B |
| change case of text | HOME, Font | Aa ⌄ | Shift + F3 |
| clear all formatting | HOME, Font | | |
| clear character formatting | | | Ctrl + spacebar |
| decrease font size | HOME, Font | A⌄ | Ctrl + Shift + < |
| display nonprinting characters | HOME, Paragraph | ¶ | Ctrl + Shift + * |
| font | HOME, Font | Calibri (Body) ⌄ | |
| font color | HOME, Font | A ⌄ | |
| Font dialog box | HOME, Font | ⌟ | Ctrl + Shift + F |
| highlight text | HOME, Font | abⅽ ⌄ | |
| increase font size | HOME, Font | A⌃ | Ctrl + Shift + > |
| italicize text | HOME, Font | I | Ctrl + I |
| paragraph spacing | DESIGN, Document Formatting | | |
| strikethrough text | HOME, Font | abⅽ | |
| subscript text | HOME, Font | $x_2$ | Ctrl + = |
| superscript text | HOME, Font | $x^2$ | Ctrl + Shift + + |
| Text Effects and Typography | HOME, Font | A ⌄ | |
| theme colors | DESIGN, Document Formatting | | |
| theme fonts | DESIGN, Document Formatting | A | |
| themes | DESIGN, Document Formatting | Aa | |
| underline text | HOME, Font | U ⌄ | Ctrl + U |

# Key Points Review

**Completion:** In the space provided at the right, indicate the correct term, command, or number.

1. Click this button in the Font group to remove all formatting from selected text. _____

2. A font consists of a typeface, typestyle, and this. _____

3. Proportional typefaces are divided into two main categories: serif and this. _____

4. The Bold button is located in this group on the HOME tab. _____

5. Use this keyboard shortcut to apply italic formatting to selected text. _____

6. This term refers to text that is raised slightly above the regular text line. _____

7. This automatically displays above selected text. _____

8. Click this to display the Font dialog box. _____

9. Click this button in the Paragraph group on the HOME tab to turn on the display of nonprinting characters. _____

10. Apply a style set by clicking the style set thumbnail in this group on the DESIGN tab. _____

11. Apply a heading style to a title or heading in a document, hover your mouse pointer over the left side of the title or heading, and this displays. _____

12. Apply a theme and change theme colors, fonts, and effects with buttons in the Document Formatting group on this tab. _____

# Chapter Assessments

## Applying Your Skills

Demonstrate your knowledge of features learned in this chapter by completing the following assessments.

### Assessment 2.1   Create and Format a Utility Program Document

1. At a blank document, type the document shown in Figure 2.5 on the next page.
2. Apply bold, italic, and underline formatting to the text as shown.
3. Save the completed document with the name **C02-A01-UtilProgs**.
4. Print **C02-A01-UtilProgs.docx**.
5. Select the entire document and then change the font to 12-point Cambria.
6. Select *Utility Programs*, remove the underlining, and change the case style to uppercase letters.
7. For each of the following, remove the bold formatting from the text and apply underlining instead: *Antivirus software:*, *Backup utility:*, *File compression utility:*, *Device driver:*, and *Uninstaller utility:*. (Remove the bold formatting from the colon [:] after each utility, but do not underline the colon.)
8. Select and then hide the text *Backup utility:* and the sentence that follows it.
9. Select and then hide the last sentence in the last paragraph (the sentence that begins *Several companies produce software*).
10. Turn on the display of nonprinting characters and unhide the text *Backup utility:* and the sentence that follows it.
11. Turn off the display of nonprinting characters.
12. Save, print, and then close **C02-A01-UtilProgs.docx**.

**Figure 2.5 Assessment 2.1**

### Utility Programs

A *utility program* performs a single maintenance or repair task and is useful for correcting many of the problems that computer users are likely to encounter. Some of the most popular kinds of utility programs include the following:

**Antivirus software:** This type of software program protects the computer system from a virus attack.

**Backup utility:** This utility makes a backup copy of files on a separate disk.

**File compression utility:** Use this utility to reduce the size of files so they take up less disk space.

**Device driver:** This utility allows hardware devices, such as disk drives and printers, to work with the computer system.

**Uninstaller utility:** Remove programs and related system files with this utility.

An operating system typically includes several utility programs that are preinstalled at the factory. Users can also purchase and install additional utility programs of their choice. Several companies produce software suites containing a variety of utility programs.

## Assessment 2.2    Format a Memo

1. Open **BookMemo.docx**.
2. Save the memo with Save As and name it **C02-A02-BookMemo**.
3. Select the book title *Managing Network Security*, remove the underlining, and then apply italic formatting.
4. Select the book title *Network Management*, remove the underlining, and then apply italic formatting.
5. Select and apply bold formatting to the headings *TO:*, *FROM:*, *DATE:*, and *SUBJECT:*.
6. Insert your initials at the end of the document, replacing the *XX*. Change the document name below your initials from **BookMemo.docx** to **C02-A02-BookMemo.docx**.
7. Select the entire document and then change to the Cambria font.
8. Save, print, and then close **C02-A02-BookMemo.docx**.

## Assessment 2.3    Format a Training Announcement

1. Open **ManageData.docx**.
2. Save the document with Save As and name it **C02-A03-ManageData**.
3. Select the entire document.
4. Change the font to 16-point Candara bold and the font color to Red.
5. Select the title *MANAGING CRUCIAL DATA*, change the font size to 20 points, and apply the Fill - Black, Text 1, Outline - Background 1, Hard Shadow - Accent 1 text effect (second column, third row). ***Hint: Use the Text Effects and Typography button to apply the text effect.***
6. Save, print, and then close **C02-A03-ManageData.docx**.

## Assessment 2.4    Apply Styles, a Style Set, and a Theme to a Document

1. Open **WritingSteps.docx**.
2. Save the document with Save As and name it **C02-A04-WritingSteps**.
3. Apply the Heading 1 style to the title *Writing Steps*.
4. Apply the Heading 2 style to the five headings in the document: *Define Purpose*, *Identify Reader*, *Select and Organize Information*, *Write First Draft*, and *Edit and Proofread*.
5. Use the Paragraph Spacing button on the DESIGN tab to change the paragraph spacing to Compact.
6. Apply the Basic (Stylish) style set.
7. Apply the Integral theme.
8. Change the theme colors to Violet II.
9. Change the theme fonts to Candara.
10. Select the title *Writing Steps*, change the font color to Dark Blue, and then apply bold formatting.
11. Save, print, and then close **C02-A04-WritingSteps.docx**.

# Expanding Your Skills

Explore additional feature options or use Help to learn a new skill in creating these documents.

## Assessment 2.5    Create and Format a Memo

1. At a blank document, type the memo shown in Figure 2.6 in appropriate memo format. (Refer to Appendix C at the end of this textbook for information on typing a memo.) Apply italic, superscript, and subscript formatting to the text as shown in the memo.
2. After typing the memo, select the entire memo and then change the font to 12-point Constantia. (If necessary, realign the headings in the memo.)
3. Save the memo with the name **C02-A05-Memo**.
4. Print and then close **C02-A05-Memo.docx**.

**Figure 2.6  Assessment 2.5**

TO: Jolie Anderson; FROM: Ronald Chen; DATE: February 18, 2015; SUBJECT: Statistical Analysis

I have been running an analysis on the areas mentioned in your February 11 memo. Completing the computations has brought up the following questions:

With smaller sector ratios of $r^1$ and $r^2$ (.10 to .25)[1], what will be the yield increase?

What is the interaction effect on the scores of $X_1$, $X_2$, and $X_3$?

## Assessment 2.6    Research Text Effect Button

1. Research four options that display toward the bottom of the Text Effects and Typography button drop-down gallery—*Outline*, *Shadow*, *Reflection*, and *Glow*. Look at the four options to determine what effects are available and then write a memo to your instructor describing the options. Include in the memo at least three examples of the words *Text Effects and Typography Button Options* with various effects applied.
2. Save the completed memo and name it **C02-A06-TextEffects**.
3. Print and then close **C02-A06-TextEffects.docx**.

# Achieving Signature Status

Take your skills to the next level by completing these more challenging assessments.

## Assessment 2.7   Type and Format Text on Writing a Cover Letter

1. At a blank document, type the text in the document shown in Figure 2.7 and then apply the following formatting:
   - Select the entire document and then change the font to 11-point Constantia.
   - Change the font size for the title and subtitle to 14 points and the font size for the subheadings (*Assertive* and *Aggressive*) to 12 points.
   - Change the font color for the subtitle and subheadings to Blue.
   - Apply the Fill - Orange, Accent 2, Outline - Accent 2 text effect (third column, first row) to the title.
   - Apply any additional formatting so your document displays as shown in Figure 2.7.
2. Save the completed document and name it **C02-A07-WritingCoverLtr**.
3. Print and then close **C02-A07-WritingCoverLtr.docx**.

**Figure 2.7  Assessment 2.7**

WRITING A COVER LETTER

Assertive vs. Aggressive

We recommend an assertive closing when writing a cover letter, but do not become too aggressive. Keep the closing of your cover letter polite, positive, and pleasant. Try using language that "requests" rather than "demands." Consider the following examples of the difference between assertive and aggressive:

*Assertive:*

I will call within the next few days to see if we can schedule a time to meet. I would like to share my ideas for improving the productivity of your field technicians.

*Aggressive:*

I will call you at 10:00 a.m. on Tuesday. Please be available to discuss my ideas for improving the productivity of your field technicians.

*Assertive:*

I eagerly await your ideas and suggestions. I will call on Thursday in hopes of setting up a brief meeting at a time that is convenient for you.

*Aggressive:*

Your support is important for my job search, and I eagerly await all the leads you can give me. I will call on Thursday to see what names you have collected thus far.

## Assessment 2.8    Type a Business Letter

1. Open **NSSLtrhd.docx** and then save the document and name it **C02-A08-BCLtr**.
2. Click the *No Spacing* style thumbnail located in the Styles group on the HOME tab and then type the text in the document shown in Figure 2.8. Refer to Appendix D at the end of this textbook for the formatting of a block style business letter with the No Spacing style applied. (Replace the *XX* with your initials near the end of the letter.)
3. Save the completed document and name it **C02-A08-BCLtr**.
4. Print and then close **C02-A08-BCLtr.docx**.

### Figure 2.8  Assessment 2.8

February 17, 2015

Jessie Levigne, Manager
Technical Support Department
Baldwin Corporation
1590 28th Street
Springfield, IL 62126

Dear Mr. Levigne:

Based on our telephone conversation about your company data security training requirements, I suggest offering three workshops to employees at Baldwin Corporation. After attending the workshops, your employees will have the skills required to secure company data. The workshops I propose include:

**Rotating Backup Process:** In this workshop, participants will be briefed on the rotating backup process, which involves backing up data from specific departments on specific days of the week.

**Disaster Recovery:** The focus of this workshop is the development of a disaster recovery plan and will include data backup procedures, remote backup locations, and redundant systems.

**Data Security:** The third workshop I propose is data security and data encryption. In this workshop participants will learn about encryption schemes designed to scramble information before transferring it electronically.

I am confident that these three workshops will address your security issues. I have enclosed our standard contract for you to read. Please contact me to discuss the contract as well as the location, time, and equipment requirements for each workshop.

Sincerely,


Bryce Gyverson
Vice President

XX
C02-A08-BCLtr.docx

Enclosure

1-888-555-2200  ✦  www.emcp.net/nss

# Chapter 3

# Aligning and Indenting Paragraphs

## Performance Objectives

Upon successful completion of Chapter 3, you will be able to:

- Change the alignment of text in paragraphs
- Indent text in paragraphs
- Increase and decrease spacing before and after paragraphs
- Repeat the last action
- Automate formatting with Format Painter
- Change line spacing in a document
- Apply numbering and bullet formatting to text
- Reveal formatting
- Compare formatting

As you learned previously, a paragraph in Word is any amount of text followed by a paragraph mark, which is inserted by pressing the Enter key. Word provides a variety of options for formatting text in a paragraph. In this chapter, you will learn to change text alignment in a paragraph, indent text, change the line spacing, and format text using numbers and bullets. You will also learn how to apply formatting with Format Painter and how to reveal and compare paragraph formatting.

*Note: Before beginning computer exercises for this chapter, copy to your storage medium the Chapter03 folder from the CD that accompanies this textbook and then make Chapter03 the active folder.*

In this chapter, students will produce the following documents:

Exercise 3.1. C03-E01-CompIndustry.docx
Exercise 3.2. C03-E02-InternetSearch.docx
Exercise 3.3. C03-E03-CompIssues.docx

Model answers for these exercises are shown on the following pages.

**Page 1**

## COMPUTERS IN INDUSTRY

Computers were originally stand-alone devices, incapable of communicating with other computers. This changed in the 1970s and 1980s when the development of special telecommunications hardware and software led to the creation of the first private networks, allowing connected computers to exchange data. Exchanged data took the form of requests for information, replies to requests for information, and instructions on how to run programs stored on a network.

The linking of computers enables users to communicate and work together efficiently and effectively. Linked computers have become central to the communications and entertainment industries. They play a vital role in telecommunications, publishing, news services, and television and film.

### Telecommunications

The industry that provi[...]
telecommunications. The telec[...]
phone calls automatically over[...]
many other kinds of informatio[...]
Data can be sent from compute[...]
a modem. One kind of data free[...]
be sent from person to person [...]
innovation in telecommunicati[...]
locations to see and hear one a[...]

### Publishing

Just twenty-five years a[...]
typesetting machine and then [...]
to a computer and either a mo[...]
as electronic publishing. Write[...]
text. Artists and designers use [...]
graphics, or they use inexpens[...]
(turning them into computer-r[...]
combine text, illustrations, and[...]

**Exercise 3.1**

C03-E01-CompIndustry.docx

**Page 2**

files to printers for production of the film and plates from which books and magazines are printed.

### News Services

News providers rely on reporters located worldwide. Reporters use email to send, or upload, their stories to wire services. Increasingly, individuals get daily news reports from online services. News can also be accessed from specific providers, such as the *New York Times* or *USA Today*, via the Internet. One of the most popular Internet sites provides continuously updated weather reports.

### Television and Film

Many of the spectacular graphics and special effects seen on television and in movies today are created with computers. The original *Star Wars* films, for example, relied heavily on hand-constructed models and hand-drawn graphics. Twenty years after the first release of the films, they were re-released with many new special effects, including futuristic cityscape backgrou[...]
on computers and added to the [...]
on special effects, Jaclyn McFa[...]
computer simulation.

The film *Jurassic Park* b[...]
combining puppetry an[...]
dinosaurs. *Toy Story*, re[...]
animated commercial [...]

Software products are [...]
Industry analysts predict that [...]
enhance and improve the visu[...]

Fuller, F. & Larson, B. (2014) [...]
MN: Paradigm Publishi[...]

McFadden, J. M. (2015) *The ar*[...]
Dryers Publishing Hous[...]

**Page 3**

North, J. & Amundsen, R. (2014) *Computer gaming and system requirements*. Cleveland, OH: Blue Horizon Publishers.

Ziebel, K. M. & Weisenburg, H. L. (2015) *Computers and electronic publishing*. Seattle, WA: Greenlake Publishing House.

Prepared by Christian Samora
Edited by Martina Sanchez

**Internet Research**

Conduct Internet searches to find information to complete the activities described below. Write a brief report summarizing your research results. Be sure to document your sources, using the following format, which is recommended by the Modern Language Association (MLA):

- ➢ Author's name (if known)
- ➢ Title of document, in quotation marks
- ➢ Title of Internet page or online periodical, in italics (if not titled, put Home Page or give the name of the organization that created and maintains the page)
- ➢ Date of publication (for an article) or date site was last updated, if available
- ➢ Date you accessed the site
- ➢ URL, in angle brackets < >

**Activities**

1. Using online news sources, select a specific event that occurred in a country other than the United States within the past year. Find three separate news reports of the event and describe how each media source perceived the event.
2. Describe the kinds of information that are available on your government's website. Your summary should discuss the information available on a particular date.
3. Research the topic of high-tech stock investments as discussed in online news sources. What is the current trend as of the date of your research?
4. Robots with artificial intelligence are likely to play a large role in our future. Discuss possible applications for this new technology in the areas of manufacturing, health care, and home maintenance.

**Research and Writing**

1. Describe the components of a computer's central processing unit (CPU).
2. Identify at least four methods for inputting information into a computer.
3. Identify at least three methods for outputting information from a computer.
4. Explain the difference between read-only memory (ROM) and random-access memory (RAM).
5. Describe at least three types of network systems.

**Technology Objectives**

- ➢ Define the terms "input" and "processing."
- ➢ Categorize input devices for personal computers and explain their functions.
- ➢ Identify the main components of the system unit and explain their functions.
- ➢ Explain the four basic operations of a machine cycle.
- ➢ Describe the different types of computer memory and their functions.

**Exercise 3.2** C03-E02-InternetSearch.docx

**Solving Problems**

In groups or individually, brainstorm possible solutions to the issues presented.

- • Computers currently offer both *visual* and *audio* communications. Under development are devices and technologies that will allow users to smell various types of products while looking at them on the computer screen. What are some new applications of this technology for the food industry? Can you think of other industries that could use this capability?
- • Picture yourself working in the Information Technology department of a mid-sized company. Your responsibilities include evaluating employees' computer system needs and recommending equipment purchases. Recently, the company president hired a new employee and you must evaluate her computer system needs. Considering that you have a budget of $5,500 for equipping the new employee with the computer system (or systems) she needs, research possible configurations and prepare a report outlining your recommendations, including costs. Assume that for the office she needs a complete system, including a system unit, monitor, printer, speakers, keyboard, and mouse.

**Exercise 3.3** C03-E03-CompIssues.docx

Model Answers

# Changing Paragraph Alignment

The Paragraph group on the HOME tab contains a number of buttons for formatting paragraphs in a document. Four buttons in the bottom row of the Paragraph group change the alignment of text within a paragraph. In a Word document, paragraphs are aligned at the left margin and ragged at the right margin by default. You can change this alignment to center, right, or justified alignment with the alignment buttons in the Paragraph group, with keyboard shortcuts, or with the Alignment option at the Paragraph dialog box with the Indents and Spacing tab selected. The keyboard shortcuts and alignment buttons in the Paragraph group are shown in Table 3.1 on the next page.

You can change the text alignment before you type a paragraph or change the alignment of an existing paragraph. If you change the alignment before typing text, the alignment formatting is inserted in the paragraph mark. As you type text and press the Enter key, the paragraph formatting is continued. For example, if you click the Center button in the Paragraph group, type a paragraph of text, and then press the Enter key, the center alignment formatting is still active and the insertion point displays in the middle of the left and right margins.

To return to the default alignment (left-aligned), click the Align Left button in the Paragraph group. You can also return all paragraph formatting to the default settings with the keyboard shortcut Ctrl + Q. This keyboard shortcut removes paragraph formatting from selected text. If you want to remove all formatting—character and paragraph—from selected text, click the Clear All Formatting button in the Font group.

**QUICK STEPS**

**Change Paragraph Alignment**
Click desired alignment button in Paragraph group.
OR
Press desired keyboard shortcut.
OR
1. Click Paragraph group dialog box launcher.
2. Click *Alignment* option down-pointing arrow.
3. Click desired alignment.
4. Click OK.

Aligning and Indenting Paragraphs  **63**

**Table 3.1  Paragraph Alignment Buttons and Commands**

| To align text | Paragraph Group Button | Shortcut Command |
|---|:---:|:---:|
| at left margin | ☰ | Ctrl + L |
| between margins | ☰ | Ctrl + E |
| at right margin | ☰ | Ctrl + R |
| at left and right margins | ☰ | Ctrl + J |

To change the alignment of existing text in a paragraph, position the insertion point anywhere within the paragraph. You do not need to select the entire paragraph. To change the alignment of several adjacent paragraphs in a document, select a portion of the first paragraph through a portion of the last paragraph. You do not need to select all of the text in the paragraphs.

## Displaying Formatting Marks

Show/Hide ¶

As you learned in Chapter 2, you can turn on/off the display of nonprinting characters by clicking the Show/Hide ¶ button in the Paragraph group on the HOME tab. When you make a formatting change to a paragraph, the formatting is inserted in the paragraph mark, which is visible if the display of nonprinting characters is turned on.

By default, all nonprinting characters display on the screen when you click the Show/Hide ¶ button. You can turn on the display of specific characters only by using options at the Word Options dialog box with *Display* selected, as shown in Figure 3.1 on the next page. Display this dialog box by clicking the FILE tab, clicking *Options*, and then clicking *Display* in the left panel. Insert a check mark in the check boxes in the *Always show these formatting marks on the screen* section to select those nonprinting characters that you want to display.

**Figure 3.1  Word Options Dialog Box with Display Option Selected**

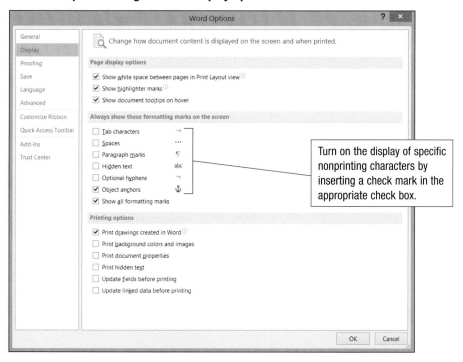

Turn on the display of specific nonprinting characters by inserting a check mark in the appropriate check box.

## Exercise 3.1A  Changing Paragraph Alignment

1. Open **CompIndustry.docx**.
2. Save the document with Save As and name it **C03-E01-CompIndustry**.
3. Click the Show/Hide ¶ button in the Paragraph group on the HOME tab to turn on the display of nonprinting characters.

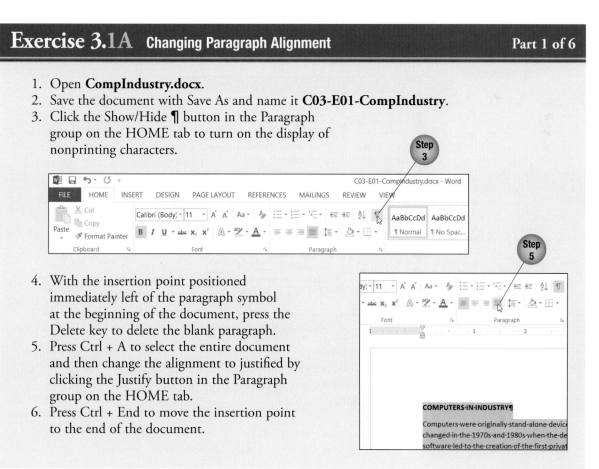

4. With the insertion point positioned immediately left of the paragraph symbol at the beginning of the document, press the Delete key to delete the blank paragraph.
5. Press Ctrl + A to select the entire document and then change the alignment to justified by clicking the Justify button in the Paragraph group on the HOME tab.
6. Press Ctrl + End to move the insertion point to the end of the document.

7. Press the Enter key once.
8. Press Ctrl + E to center the insertion point between the left and right margins.
9. Type **Prepared by Christian Samora**.
10. Press Shift + Enter and then type **Edited by Martina Sanchez**.

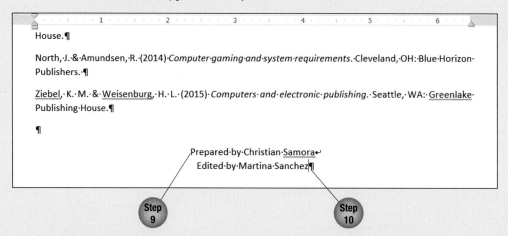

11. Click the Show/Hide ¶ button in the Paragraph group on the HOME tab to turn off the display of nonprinting characters.
12. Turn on the display of paragraph marks only by completing the following steps:
    a. Click the FILE tab and then click *Options*.
    b. At the Word Options dialog box, click the *Display* option in the left panel.
    c. Click the *Paragraph marks* check box in the *Always show these formatting marks on the screen* section to insert a check mark.

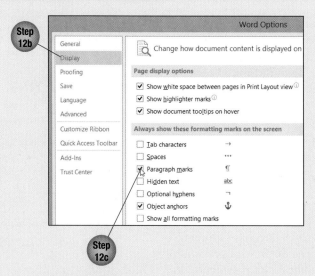

    d. Click OK to close the dialog box.
13. Scroll through the document and notice how the paragraph marks display.
14. Turn off the display of paragraph marks by completing steps similar to those in Step 12.
15. Save **C03-E01-CompIndustry.docx**.

## Changing Alignment at the Paragraph Dialog Box

In addition to using the alignment buttons in the Paragraph group or keyboard shortcuts to change paragraph alignment, you can also use the *Alignment* option at the Paragraph dialog box, as shown in Figure 3.2. Display this dialog box by clicking the Paragraph group dialog box launcher or by clicking the right mouse button and then clicking *Paragraph* at the shortcut menu that displays. At the Paragraph dialog box, click the down-pointing arrow at the right side of the *Alignment* drop-down list. At the drop-down list that displays, click the desired alignment option and then click OK to close the dialog box.

**Figure 3.2  Paragraph Dialog Box with Alignment Options Displayed**

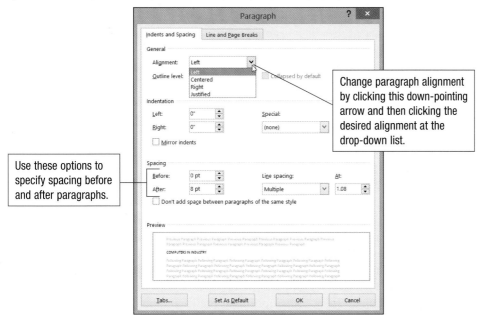

Change paragraph alignment by clicking this down-pointing arrow and then clicking the desired alignment at the drop-down list.

Use these options to specify spacing before and after paragraphs.

---

**Exercise 3.1B**  **Changing Paragraph Alignment at the Paragraph Dialog Box**    Part 2 of 6

1. With **C03-E01-CompIndustry.docx** open, change the paragraph alignment by completing the following steps:
    a. Select the entire document.
    b. Click the Paragraph group dialog box launcher.

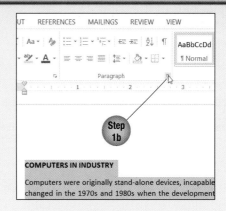

Step 1b

COMPUTERS IN INDUSTRY

Computers were originally stand-alone devices, incapable changed in the 1970s and 1980s when the development

c. At the Paragraph dialog box with the Indents and Spacing tab selected, click the down-pointing arrow at the right of the *Alignment* option box and then click *Left*.

d. Click OK to close the dialog box.

e. Deselect the text.

2. Change paragraph alignment by completing the following steps:

   a. Press Ctrl + End to move the insertion point to the end of the document.

   b. Position the insertion point on any character in the text *Prepared by Christian Samora*.

   c. Click the Paragraph group dialog box launcher.

   d. At the Paragraph dialog box with the Indents and Spacing tab selected, click the down-pointing arrow at the right of the *Alignment* option box and then click *Right*.

   e. Click OK. (The line of text containing the name *Christian Samora* and the line of text containing the name *Martina Sanchez* are both right-aligned because you used the New Line command, Shift + Enter, to separate the lines of text without creating a new paragraph.)

3. Save **C03-E01-CompIndustry.docx**.

# Indenting Text in Paragraphs

**QUICK STEPS**

**Indent Text in Paragraphs**
Drag indent marker(s) on horizontal ruler.
OR
Enter keyboard shortcut.
OR
1. Click Paragraph group dialog box launcher.
2. Insert measurement in *Left, Right,* and/or *By* text box.
3. Click OK.

By now you are familiar with the word wrap feature in Word, which ends a line and moves the insertion point to the beginning of the next line. You can indent the first line of text in a paragraph, indent all of the text in a paragraph, or indent the second and subsequent lines of a paragraph (called a *hanging indent*). You can indent text from the left margin, right margin, or both. Several methods are available for indenting text: using buttons in the Paragraph group on the HOME tab or PAGE LAYOUT tab, using markers on the horizontal ruler, using options at the Paragraph dialog box with the Indents and Spacing tab selected, and using keyboard shortcuts.

The various methods for indenting text are shown in Table 3.2 on the next page and indent examples are shown in Table 3.3 on page 70. The indent markers and Alignment button that display above the vertical ruler are shown in Figure 3.3. To display the horizontal ruler, as well as the vertical ruler, click the VIEW tab and then click the *Ruler* check box in the Show group to insert a check mark.

**Figure 3.3 Horizontal Ruler and Indent Markers**

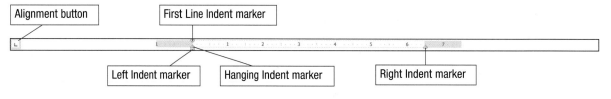

Alignment button

First Line Indent marker

Left Indent marker

Hanging Indent marker

Right Indent marker

**Table 3.2  Methods for Indenting Text**

| *Indent* | *Methods for Indenting* |
|---|---|
| first line of paragraph | • Press the Tab key. |
| | • Display the Paragraph dialog box, click the down-pointing arrow to the right of the *Special* list box, click *First line*, and then click OK. |
| | • Drag the First Line Indent marker on the horizontal ruler. |
| | • Click the Alignment button located above the vertical ruler until the First Line Indent button displays, and then click on the horizontal ruler at the desired location. |
| text from left margin | • Click the Increase Indent button in the Paragraph group on the HOME tab to increase the indent or click the Decrease Indent button to decrease the indent. |
| | • Display the Paragraph dialog box, type the desired indent measurement in the *Left* measurement box, and then click OK. |
| | • Drag the Left Indent marker on the horizontal ruler. |
| | • Press Ctrl + M to increase the indent or press Ctrl + Shift + M to decrease the indent. |
| | • Insert a measurement in the *Indent Left* measurement box in the Paragraph group on the PAGE LAYOUT tab. |
| text from right margin | • Display the Paragraph dialog box, type the desired indent measurement in the *Right* measurement box, and then click OK. |
| | • Drag the Right Indent marker on the horizontal ruler. |
| | • Insert a measurement in the *Indent Right* measurement box in the Paragraph group on the PAGE LAYOUT tab. |
| all lines of text except the first (called a hanging indent) | • Display the Paragraph dialog box, click the down-pointing arrow at the right side of the *Special* list box, click *Hanging*, and then click OK. |
| | • Press Ctrl + T. (Press Ctrl + Shift + T to remove a hanging indent.) |
| | • Click the Alignment button located above the vertical ruler until the Hanging Indent button displays and then click on the horizontal ruler at the desired location. |

**Table 3.3 Paragraph Indent Examples**

### First line indent example:

This is an example of text with the first line indented. Create the first line indent with the Tab key, options at the Paragraph dialog box, or the First Line indent marker on the horizontal ruler.

### Left indent example:

This is an example of text indented 0.5 inch from the left margin. Create left-indented text with the Increase Indent button in the Paragraph group on the HOME tab, options at the Paragraph dialog box, the *Indent Left* measurement box in the Paragraph group on the PAGE LAYOUT tab, the Left Indent marker on the horizontal ruler, or the keyboard shortcut Ctrl + M.

### Right indent example:

This is an example of text indented 0.5 inch from the right margin. Create right-indented text with options at the Paragraph dialog box, the Right Indent marker on the horizontal ruler, or the *Indent Right* measurement box in the Paragraph group on the PAGE LAYOUT tab.

### Hanging indent example:

This paragraph is an example of a hanging indent. This style of indenting is generally used in lists of sources on works cited and reference pages. Create a hanging indent with options at the Paragraph dialog box, the Hanging Indent button on the horizontal ruler, or the keyboard shortcut Ctrl + T.

This is another example of a paragraph formatted with a hanging indent. When creating a hanging indent, make sure you let the text wrap within the paragraph.

## Exercise 3.1C    Indenting Paragraphs                    Part 3 of 6

1. With **C03-E01-CompIndustry.docx** open, indent the first line of text in each paragraph by completing the following steps:

    a. Select the first two paragraphs of text in the document (the two paragraphs after the title *COMPUTERS IN INDUSTRY* and before the heading *Telecommunications*).

    b. Make sure the horizontal ruler displays. If it does not, click the VIEW tab and then click the *Ruler* check box in the Show group to insert a check mark.

    c. Position the mouse pointer on the First Line Indent marker on the horizontal ruler, hold down the left mouse button, drag the marker to the 0.5-inch mark, and then release the mouse button.

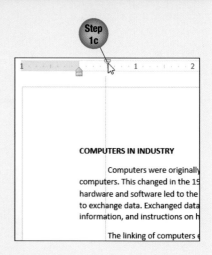

Step
1c

COMPUTERS IN INDUSTRY

Computers were originally
computers. This changed in the 19
hardware and software led to the
to exchange data. Exchanged data
information, and instructions on h

The linking of computers

d. Position the insertion point on any character in the paragraph below the *Telecommunications* heading and then drag the First Line Indent marker on the horizontal ruler to the 0.5-inch mark.

e. Indent to the 0.5-inch mark on the horizontal ruler the first line of the paragraph below the *Publishing* heading and the first line of the paragraph below the *News Services* heading.

f. Indent to the 0.5-inch mark the first line of the first paragraph and the first line of the third paragraph in the *Television and Film* heading.

2. Since the text in the second paragraph in the *Television and Film* section is a quotation, indent the text from the left and right margins by completing the following steps:

a. Position the insertion point anywhere within the second paragraph in the *Television and Film* section (the paragraph that begins *The film* Jurassic Park *brought*).

b. Click the Paragraph group dialog box launcher.

c. At the Paragraph dialog box, with the Indents and Spacing tab selected, select the current measurement in the *Left* measurement box and then type **0.5**.

d. Select the current measurement in the *Right* measurement box and then type **0.5**.

e. Click OK or press the Enter key.

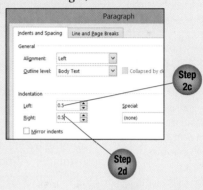

3. Create a hanging indent for the first paragraph in the *REFERENCES* section by positioning the insertion point anywhere in the first paragraph below *REFERENCES* and then pressing Ctrl + T.

4. Create a hanging indent for the second paragraph in the *REFERENCES* section by completing the following steps:

a. Position the insertion point anywhere in the second paragraph in the *REFERENCES* section.

b. Click the Alignment button located above the vertical ruler until the Hanging Indent button displays.

c. Click on the 0.5-inch mark on the horizontal ruler.

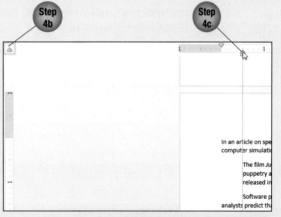

5. Create a hanging indent for the third and fourth paragraphs in the *REFERENCES* section by completing the following steps:

a. Select a portion of the third and fourth paragraphs.

b. Click the Paragraph group dialog box launcher.

c. At the Paragraph dialog box with the Indents and Spacing tab selected, click the down-pointing arrow at the right side of the *Special* list box and then click *Hanging* at the drop-down list.

d. Click OK or press the Enter key.

6. Save **C03-E01-CompIndustry.docx**.

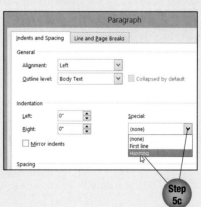

# Spacing Before and After Paragraphs

**QUICK STEPS**

**Change Paragraph Spacing**
1. Click PAGE LAYOUT tab.
2. Change spacing with *Spacing Before* and/or *Spacing After* measurement boxes.
OR
1. Click HOME tab or PAGE LAYOUT tab.
2. Click Paragraph group dialog box launcher.
3. Insert measurement in *Before* and/or *After* measurement boxes.
4. Click OK.

**Repeat the Last Action**
Press F4.
OR
Press Ctrl + Y.

As you learned earlier, inserting 8 points of spacing after each paragraph is one of the default settings in Word. You can remove this spacing, increase it, or decrease it. You can also insert spacing before a paragraph. To change spacing before or after a paragraph, use the *Spacing Before* and *Spacing After* measurement boxes located in the Paragraph group on the PAGE LAYOUT tab or the *Before* and/or *After* options at the Paragraph dialog box with the Indents and Spacing tab selected.

You can also add or remove paragraph spacing with the bottom two options from the Line and Paragraph Spacing button drop-down gallery. The two options will vary depending on the paragraph spacing in effect where the insertion point is positioned. For example, if you position the insertion point in a paragraph of text with the default spacing, the options display as *Add Space Before Paragraph* and *Remove Space After Paragraph*. Click the *Add Space Before Paragraph* option and Word adds 12 points of spacing before the paragraph or click the *Remove Space After Paragraph* option and Word removes the 8 points of spacing after the paragraph.

Spacing before or after a paragraph is part of that paragraph and it will be moved, copied, or deleted with the paragraph. If a paragraph, such as a heading, contains spacing before it and it falls at the top of a page, Word ignores the spacing.

Spacing before or after paragraphs is added in points. One vertical inch contains approximately 72 points. To add spacing before or after a paragraph, click the PAGE LAYOUT tab, select the current measurement in the *Spacing Before* or *Spacing After* measurement box, and then type the desired number of points. You can also click the up- and down-pointing arrows at the right sides of the *Spacing Before* and *Spacing After* measurement boxes to change the amount of spacing.

# Repeating the Last Action

If you apply formatting to a selection of text and then want to apply the same formatting to other text in the document, consider using the Repeat command. To use this command, apply the desired formatting, move the insertion point to the next location you want the formatting applied, and then press the F4 function key or the keyboard shortcut Ctrl + Y. The Repeat command will repeat only the last command you executed.

---

**Exercise 3.1D**  Spacing Before and After Paragraphs and Repeating Last Action    Part 4 of 6

1. With **C03-E01-CompIndustry.docx** open, change the spacing after paragraphs to 6 points by completing the following steps:
   a. Select the entire document.
   b. Click the PAGE LAYOUT tab.
   c. Click once on the down-pointing arrow at the right side of the *Spacing After* measurement box in the Paragraph group (which inserts *6 pt* in the box).

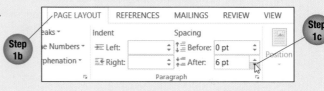

2. Add 18 points of spacing above and 12 points of spacing below the two titles by completing the following steps:
   a. Position the insertion point on any character in the title *COMPUTERS IN INDUSTRY*.
   b. Click three times on the up-pointing arrow at the right side of the *Spacing Before* measurement box (which changes the measurement to *18 pt*).
   c. Click once on the up-pointing arrow at the right side of the *Spacing After* measurement box (which changes the measurement to *12 pt*).

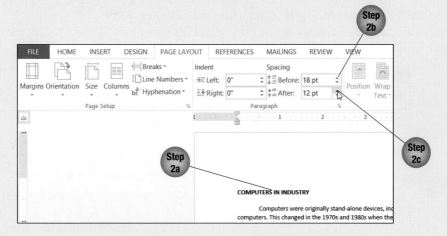

   d. Position the insertion point on any character in the title *REFERENCES* and then press F4 (the Repeat command).
3. Save **C03-E01-CompIndustry.docx**.

# Formatting with Format Painter

The Clipboard group on the HOME tab contains a button for copying formatting to different locations in the document. This button, labeled Format Painter, displays in the Clipboard group as a paintbrush.

To use the Format Painter button, position the insertion point on a character containing the desired formatting, click the Format Painter button, and then click or select the text to which you want the formatting applied. When you click the Format Painter button, the mouse I-beam pointer displays with a paintbrush attached. If you want to apply the formatting a single time, click the Format Painter button once. If you want to apply the formatting in more than one location in the document, double-click the Format Painter button, click or select the text at each location, and then click the Format Painter button or press the Esc key to turn the Format Painter off.

**Format with Format Painter**
1. Format text.
2. Double-click Format Painter button.
3. Click or select text.
4. Click Format Painter button.

Format Painter

1. With **C03-E01-CompIndustry.docx** open, click the HOME tab.
2. Select the entire document and then change the font to 12-point Cambria.
3. Select the title *COMPUTERS IN INDUSTRY*, click the Center button in the Paragraph group, and then change the font to 16-point Candara bold.
4. Use the Format Painter button and apply 16-point Candara bold and center formatting to the *REFERENCES* heading by completing the following steps:
   a. Click on any character in the title *COMPUTERS IN INDUSTRY*.
   b. Click once on the Format Painter button in the Clipboard group.

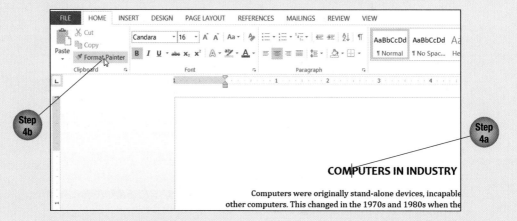

   c. Press Ctrl + End to move the insertion point to the end of the document and then click any character in the heading *REFERENCES*. (This applies the 16-point Candara bold formatting and centers the text.)
5. Select the heading *Telecommunications* and then change the font to 14-point Candara bold.
6. Use the Format Painter button and apply 14-point Candara bold formatting to the other headings by completing the following steps:
   a. Position the insertion point on any character in the heading *Telecommunications*.
   b. Double-click the Format Painter button in the Clipboard group.
   c. Using the mouse, click on any character in the heading *Publishing*.
   d. Using the mouse, select the heading *News Services*.
   e. Using the mouse, select the heading *Television and Film*.
   f. Click once on the Format Painter button in the Clipboard group. (This turns off the feature.)
   g. Deselect the heading.
7. Save **C03-E01-CompIndustry.docx**.

# Changing Line Spacing

The default line spacing in a Word document is 1.08. In certain situations, Word automatically adjusts the line spacing. For example, if you insert a large character or object, such as a graphic, Word increases the line spacing of that specific line. In some documents, you may want to change to a different line spacing, such as single spacing, 1.5 line spacing, or double spacing. Change line spacing using the Line and Paragraph Spacing button in the Paragraph group on the HOME tab, keyboard shortcuts, or options at the Paragraph dialog box. The keyboard shortcuts for changing line spacing are shown in Table 3.4.

**Table 3.4  Line Spacing Keyboard Shortcuts**

| Press | To change line spacing to |
|-------|---------------------------|
| Ctrl + 1 | single spacing |
| Ctrl + 2 | double spacing |
| Ctrl + 5 | 1.5 line spacing |

To change line spacing at the Paragraph dialog box, use the *Line spacing* option or *At* option. If you click the down-pointing arrow at the right side of the *Line spacing* option, a drop-down list displays with a variety of spacing options. To change the line spacing to double, click *Double* at the drop-down list. You can type a specific line spacing measurement in the *At* text box. For example, to change the line spacing to 1.75, type **1.75** in the *At* text box.

**QUICK STEPS**

**Change Line Spacing**
1. Click Line and Paragraph Spacing button in Paragraph group.
2. Click *Spacing* option at drop-down list.
OR
Press keyboard shortcut.
OR
1. Click Paragraph group dialog box launcher.
2. Click *Line Spacing* option down-pointing arrow.
3. Click desired line spacing option.
4. Click OK.
OR
1. Click Paragraph group dialog box launcher.
2. Type line measurement in *At* text box.
3. Click OK.

Line and Paragraph Spacing

---

**Exercise 3.1F**  Changing Line Spacing                                      Part 6 of 6

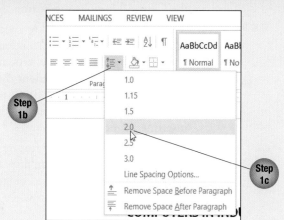

1. With **C03-E01-CompIndustry.docx** open, change the line spacing for all paragraphs to double spacing by completing the following steps:
   a. Select the entire document.
   b. Click the Line and Paragraph Spacing button in the Paragraph group on the HOME tab.
   c. Click *2.0* at the drop-down list.
2. With the entire document still selected, press Ctrl + 5. (This changes the line spacing to 1.5.)

3. Change the line spacing to 1.3 using the Paragraph dialog box by completing the following steps:

a. With the document still selected, click the Paragraph group dialog box launcher.

b. At the Paragraph dialog box with the Indents and Spacing tab selected, click in the *At* measurement box and then type **1.3**. (This measurement box is located to the right of the *Line spacing* list box.)

c. Click OK or press the Enter key.

d. Deselect the text.

4. Save, print, and then close **C03-E01-CompIndustry.docx**.

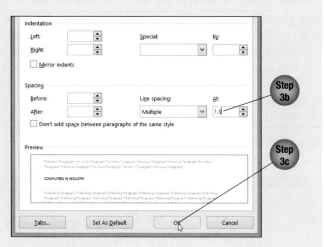

Step 3b

Step 3c

# Applying Numbering and Bullets

Automatically number paragraphs or insert bullets before paragraphs using buttons in the Paragraph group on the HOME tab. Use the Bullets button to insert bullets before specific paragraphs and use the Numbering button to insert numbers.

## Applying Numbering to Paragraphs

**Type Numbered Paragraphs**
1. Type **1**.
2. Press spacebar.
3. Type text.
4. Press Enter.

Numbering

If you type **1.** and then press the spacebar, Word indents the number approximately 0.25 inch from the left margin and then formats the text in the paragraph with a hanging indent that aligns approximately 0.5 inch from the left margin. Additionally, when you press Enter to end the first item, *2.* is inserted 0.25 inch from the left margin at the beginning of the next paragraph. Continue typing items and pressing Enter, and Word continues inserting the next number in the list.

To turn off numbering, press the Enter key twice or click the Numbering button in the Paragraph group. (You can also remove all paragraph formatting from a paragraph, including automatic numbering, with the keyboard shortcut Ctrl + Q. Remove all formatting, including character and paragraph formatting, from selected text by clicking the Clear All Formatting button in the Font group on the HOME tab.)

If you press the Enter key twice between numbered paragraphs, the automatic numbering turns off. To turn it back on, type the next number in the list (and the period) followed by a space, type the paragraph of text, and then press the Enter key. Word will automatically indent the number and format the text with a hanging indent. If you want to insert a line break without inserting a number, press Shift + Enter to insert the line break. This moves the insertion point down to the next line without inserting a number.

When the AutoFormat feature inserts numbering and indents the text, the AutoCorrect Options button displays. Click this button and a drop-down list displays with options for undoing and/or stopping the automatic numbering. An AutoCorrect Options button also displays when AutoFormat inserts automatic bulleting in a document.

1. Open **InternetSearch.docx**.
2. Save the document with Save As and name it **C03-E02-InternetSearch**.
3. Press Ctrl + End to move the insertion point to the end of the document and then type the text shown in Figure 3.5. When you type the numbered paragraphs, complete the following steps:
   a. Type **1.** and then press the spacebar. (This indents the number and period 0.25 inch from the left margin and moves the insertion point 0.5 inch from the left margin. Also, the AutoCorrect Options button displays. Use this button if you want to undo or stop automatic numbering.)
   b. Type the paragraph of text and then press the Enter key. (This moves the insertion point down to the next line, inserts *2.* indented 0.25 inch from the left margin, and indents the insertion point 0.5 inch from the left margin.)
   c. Continue typing the remaining text. (Remember, you do not need to type the paragraph number and period; both are automatically inserted.)
   d. After typing the last numbered item, press the Enter key twice. (This turns off paragraph numbering.)
4. Save **C03-E02-InternetSearch.docx**.

**Figure 3.5  Exercise 3.2A**

**Research and Writing**

1. Describe the components of a computer's central processing unit (CPU).
2. Identify at least four methods for inputting information into a computer.
3. Identify at least three methods for outputting information from a computer.
4. Explain the difference between read-only memory (ROM) and random-access memory (RAM).
5. Describe at least three types of network systems.

If you do not want automatic numbering in a document, turn off the feature at the AutoCorrect dialog box with the AutoFormat As You Type tab selected, as shown in Figure 3.6 on the next page. To display this dialog box, click the FILE tab and then click *Options*. At the Word Options dialog box, click *Proofing* in the left panel and then click the AutoCorrect Options button that displays in the *AutoCorrect options* section of the dialog box. At the AutoCorrect dialog box, click the AutoFormat As You Type tab and then click the *Automatic numbered lists* check box to remove the check mark. Click OK to close the AutoCorrect dialog box and then click OK to close the Word Options dialog box.

You can also automate the creation of numbered paragraphs with the Numbering button in the Paragraph group. To use this button, type the text (do not type the number) for each paragraph to be numbered, select the paragraphs to be numbered, and then click the Numbering button in the Paragraph group. You can insert or delete numbered paragraphs in a document.

**QUICK STEPS**

**Create Numbered Paragraphs**
1. Select text.
2. Click Numbering button in Paragraph group on HOME tab.

**Figure 3.6 AutoCorrect Dialog Box with the AutoFormat As You Type Tab Selected**

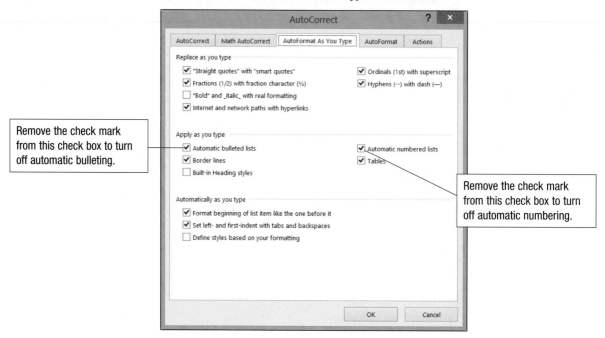

Remove the check mark from this check box to turn off automatic bulleting.

Remove the check mark from this check box to turn off automatic numbering.

---

## Exercise 3.2B  Inserting Paragraph Numbering

Part 2 of 4

1. With **C03-E02-InternetSearch.docx** open, apply numbering to paragraphs by completing the following steps:
   a. Select the three paragraphs of text in the *Activities* section.
   b. Click the Numbering button in the Paragraph group.

**Step 1b**

**Step 1a**

YOUT   REFERENCES   MAILINGS   REVIEW   V

Paragraph

**Activities**

Using online news sources, select a specific e States within the past year. Find three separ source perceived the event.

Describe the kinds of information that are av should discuss the information available on a

Robots with artificial intelligence are likely to for this new technology in the areas of manu

**Research and Writing**

2. Add the paragraph shown in Figure 3.7 between paragraphs 2 and 3 in the *Activities* section by completing the following steps:

    a. Position the insertion point immediately to the right of the period at the end of the second paragraph.

    b. Press the Enter key.

    c. Type the paragraph shown in Figure 3.7.

**Activities**

1. Using online news sources, select a specific event that occurred in a country other than the United States within the past year. Find three separate news reports of the event and describe how each media source perceived the event.
2. Describe the kinds of information that are available on your government's website. Your summary should discuss the information available on a particular date.
3. Research the topic of high-tech stock investments as discussed in online news sources. What is the current trend as of the date of your research?
4. Robots with artificial intelligence are likely to play a large role in our future. Discuss possible applications for this new technology in the areas of manufacturing, health care, and home maintenance.

Step 2c

3. Save **C03-E02-InternetSearch.docx**.

**Figure 3.7  Exercise 3.2B**

Research the topic of high-tech stock investments as discussed in online news sources. What is the current trend as of the date of your research?

## Applying Bullets to Paragraphs

In addition to automatically creating numbered paragraphs, the AutoFormat feature in Word creates bulleted paragraphs. Figure 3.8 on the next page shows an example of bulleted paragraphs. Word automatically creates bulleted lists with hanging indents when you begin a paragraph with one of the following symbols: *, >, or -. If you type one of the symbols and then press the spacebar, the AutoFormat feature inserts a bullet approximately 0.25 inch from the left margin and indents the text following the bullet another 0.25 inch.

    The type of bullet inserted depends on the type of character entered. For example, if you type an asterisk (*) symbol, a round bullet is inserted, and if you type a greater-than symbol (>), an arrow bullet is inserted. The automatic bulleting feature, like the automatic numbering feature, can be turned off at the AutoCorrect dialog box with the AutoFormat As You Type tab selected.

**QUICK STEPS**

**Type Bulleted Paragraphs**
1. Type *, >, or - symbol.
2. Press spacebar.
3. Type text.
4. Press Enter.

**Figure 3.8 Bulleted Paragraphs**

- This is a paragraph preceded by a bullet. A bullet indicates an item or a topic that is set off from the main text in a list format.
- This is another paragraph preceded by a bullet. You can easily create bulleted paragraphs by typing certain symbols before the text or with the Bullets button in the Paragraph group.

When typing bulleted text, pressing the Tab key will demote the bullet and text to the next tab and change the bullet to a hollow circle, creating an indented sublist. Pressing Shift + Tab when typing bulleted text will promote the text to the previous tab and change the bullet to the previous style, restoring the text to the main list.

## Exercise 3.2C   Typing Bulleted Paragraphs                                       Part 3 of 4

1. With **C03-E02-InternetSearch.docx** open, press Ctrl + End to move the insertion point to the end of the document and then press the Enter key once.
2. Type the heading *Technology Objectives* in bold, as shown in Figure 3.9, and then press the Enter key.
3. Type a greater-than symbol (>), press the spacebar, type the text of the first bulleted paragraph in Figure 3.9, and then press the Enter key.
4. Type the text of the second bulleted paragraph and then press the Enter key.
5. Press the Tab key (which demotes the bullet to a hollow circle) and then type the bulleted text.
6. Press the Enter key (which displays another hollow circle bullet), type the bulleted text, and then press the Enter key.
7. Press Shift + Tab (which promotes the bullet to an arrow), type the bulleted text, and then press the Enter key twice (which turns off the bulleting).
8. Promote bulleted text by positioning the insertion point at the beginning of the text *Identify the main components...* and then pressing Shift + Tab. Promote the other hollow circle bullet to an arrow. (Each of the five paragraphs of text should be preceded by an arrow bullet.)
9. Save **C03-E02-InternetSearch.docx**.

**Figure 3.9 Exercise 3.2C**

**Technology Objectives**

- ➢ Define the terms "input" and "processing."
- ➢ Categorize input devices for personal computers and explain their functions.
    - o Identify the main components of the system unit and explain their functions.
    - o Explain the four basic operations of a machine cycle.
- ➢ Describe the different types of computer memory and their functions.

Another way to create bulleted paragraphs is with the Bullets button in the Paragraph group. To create bulleted paragraphs using the Bullets button, type the text (do not type the bullet) of the paragraphs, select the paragraphs, and then click the Bullets button in the Paragraph group.

**QUICK STEPS**

**Create Bulleted Paragraphs**
1. Select text.
2. Click Bullets button in Paragraph group on HOME tab.

Bullets

---

**Exercise 3.2D** — **Inserting Bullets Using the Bullets Button** — Part 4 of 4

1. With **C03-E02-InternetSearch.docx** open, insert bullets before the six paragraphs of text below the first paragraph in the *Internet Research* section by completing the following steps:
   a. Select the paragraphs of text in the *Internet Research* section from *Author's name (if known)* through *URL, in angle brackets < >.*
   b. Click the Bullets button in the Paragraph group. (Because the last bullet you inserted was an arrow bullet, an arrow is inserted before each paragraph of the selected text.)
2. Save, print, and then close **C03-E02-InternetSearch.docx**.

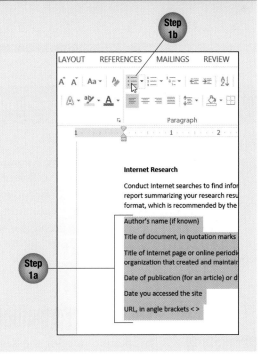

# Revealing Formatting

To identify formatting that has been applied to specific text in a document, access the Reveal Formatting task pane, shown in Figure 3.10 on the next page. The Reveal Formatting task pane displays font, paragraph, and section formatting applied to the text where the insertion point is positioned or to selected text. Display the Reveal Formatting task pane with the keyboard shortcut Shift + F1.

Generally, a collapse triangle (a solid right-and-down-pointing triangle) precedes *Font* and *Paragraph* in the *Formatting of selected text* list box in the Reveal Formatting task pane, and an expand triangle (a hollow right-pointing triangle) precedes *Section*. Click the collapse triangle to hide any items below a heading and click the expand triangle to reveal items. Some of the items below headings in the *Formatting of selected text* list box are hyperlinks. Click a hyperlink and a dialog box displays with the specific option.

**Figure 3.10 Reveal Formatting Task Pane**

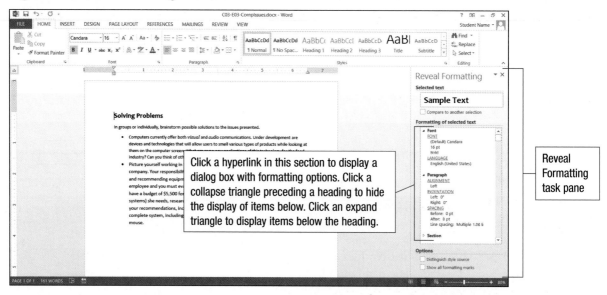

Click a hyperlink in this section to display a dialog box with formatting options. Click a collapse triangle preceding a heading to hide the display of items below. Click an expand triangle to display items below the heading.

Reveal Formatting task pane

---

**Exercise 3.3A**  **Revealing Formatting**                                          Part 1 of 2

1. Open **CompIssues.docx**.
2. Save the document with Save As and name it **C03-E03-CompIssues**.
3. Press Shift + F1 to display the Reveal Formatting task pane.
4. Click anywhere in the heading *Solving Problems* and then notice the formatting information that displays in the Reveal Formatting task pane.
5. Click in the bulleted paragraph and notice the formatting information that displays in the Reveal Formatting task pane.

---

## Comparing Formatting

**QUICK STEPS**

**Compare Formatting**
1. Press Shift + F1 to display Reveal Formatting task pane.
2. Click or select text.
3. Click *Compare to another selection* check box.
4. Click or select text.

In addition to using the Reveal Formatting task pane to identify formatting, you can use it to compare the formatting of two text selections to identify differences. To compare formatting, select the first text sample to be compared, click the *Compare to another selection* check box, and then select the second text sample. Any differences between the two selections display in the *Formatting differences* list box.

1. With **C03-E03-CompIssues.docx** open, make sure the Reveal Formatting task pane displays. If it does not, turn it on by pressing Shift + F1.
2. Select the first bulleted paragraph (which begins *Computers currently offer both*).
3. Click the *Compare to another selection* check box to insert a check mark.

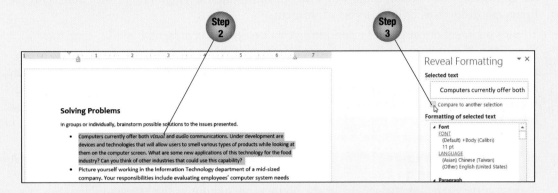

4. Select the second bulleted paragraph (which begins *Picture yourself working in the*).
5. Determine the formatting differences by reading the information in the *Formatting differences* list box. (The list box displays *11 pt -> 12 pt* below the FONT hyperlink, indicating that the difference is point size.)
6. Format the second bulleted paragraph so the text is set in 11-point size.
7. Click the *Compare to another selection* check box to remove the check mark.

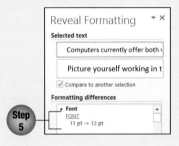

8. Select the word *visual* that displays in the first sentence in the first bulleted paragraph.
9. Click the *Compare to another selection* check box to insert a check mark.
10. Select the word *audio* that displays in the first sentence of the first bulleted paragraph.
11. Determine the formatting differences by reading the information in the *Formatting differences* list box.
12. Format the word *audio* so it matches the formatting of the word *visual*.

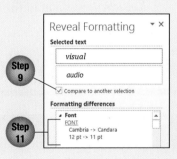

13. Click the *Compare to another selection* check box to remove the check mark.
14. Close the Reveal Formatting task pane by clicking the Close button (which contains an X) that displays in the upper right corner of the task pane.
15. Save, print, and then close **C03-E03-CompIssues.docx**.

# Chapter Summary

- In Word, a paragraph is any amount of text followed by a paragraph mark (a stroke of the Enter key). Paragraph formats are contained in the paragraph mark.

- By default, paragraphs in a Word document are aligned at the left margin and ragged at the right margin. Change this default alignment with buttons in the Paragraph group, with buttons at the Paragraph dialog box, or with keyboard shortcuts.

- To turn on or off the display of nonprinting characters such as paragraph marks, click the Show/Hide ¶ button in the Paragraph group on the HOME tab.

- Indent text in paragraphs with indent buttons in the Paragraph group on the HOME tab, indent buttons in the Paragraph group on the PAGE LAYOUT tab, keyboard shortcuts, options at the Paragraph dialog box, markers on the horizontal ruler, or the Alignment button on the horizontal ruler. Refer to Table 3.2 on page 69 for descriptions of the various methods for indenting text, and refer to Table 3.3 on page 70 for examples of various types of paragraph indents.

- Increase and decrease spacing before and after paragraphs using the *Spacing Before* and *Spacing After* measurement boxes in the Paragraph group on the PAGE LAYOUT tab, the *Before* and/or *After* options at the Paragraph dialog box, or the bottom two options at the Line and Paragraph Spacing button drop-down gallery.

- Repeat the last action by pressing the F4 key or Ctrl + Y.

- Use the Format Painter button in the Clipboard group on the HOME tab to copy character formatting that you have already applied to additional text at different locations in the document.

- Change line spacing with the Line and Paragraph Spacing button in the Paragraph group on the HOME tab, keyboard shortcuts, or options at the Paragraph dialog box.

- Number paragraphs with the Numbering button in the Paragraph group on the HOME tab and insert bullets before paragraphs with the Bullets button.

- Display the Reveal Formatting task pane to display formatting applied to text. Use the *Compare to another selection* option in the task pane to compare the formatting of two text selections.

# Commands Review

| FEATURE | RIBBON TAB, GROUP | BUTTON, OPTION | KEYBOARD SHORTCUT |
|---------|-------------------|----------------|-------------------|
| bullets | HOME, Paragraph | | |
| center text | HOME, Paragraph | | Ctrl + E |
| clear all formatting | HOME, Font | | |
| clear paragraph formatting | | | Ctrl + Q |
| Format Painter | HOME, Clipboard | | Ctrl + Shift + C |
| justify text | HOME, Paragraph | | Ctrl + J |

| FEATURE | RIBBON TAB, GROUP | BUTTON, OPTION | KEYBOARD SHORTCUT |
|---|---|---|---|
| left-align text | HOME, Paragraph | ☰ | Ctrl + L |
| line spacing | HOME, Paragraph | ⇕☰ ▾ | Ctrl + 1 (single)<br>Ctrl + 2 (double)<br>Ctrl + 5 (1.5) |
| numbering | HOME, Paragraph | ☷ ▾ | |
| Paragraph dialog box | HOME, Paragraph OR<br>PAGE LAYOUT, Paragraph | ⌹ | |
| repeat last action | | | F4 or Ctrl + Y |
| Reveal Formatting task pane | | | Shift + F1 |
| right-align text | HOME, Paragraph | ☰ | Ctrl + R |
| spacing after paragraph | PAGE LAYOUT, Paragraph | ⬇☰ After: 8 pt ⇕ | |
| spacing before paragraph | PAGE LAYOUT, Paragraph | ⬆☰ Before: 0 pt ⇕ | |

# *Key Points Review*

**Completion:** In the space provided at the right, indicate the correct term, command, or number.

1. This is the default paragraph alignment. _____

2. Return all paragraph formatting to the default settings with this keyboard shortcut. _____

3. Click this button in the Paragraph group on the HOME tab to align text at the right margin. _____

4. Click this button in the Paragraph group on the HOME tab to turn on the display of nonprinting characters. _____

5. In this type of paragraph, the first line of text aligns at the left margin and the remaining lines of text indent to the first tab. _____

6. Repeat the last action by pressing the F4 key or using this keyboard shortcut. _____

7. Use this button in the Clipboard group on the HOME tab to copy character formatting already applied to text to additional text at different locations in the document. _____

8. Change the line spacing to 1.5 with this keyboard shortcut. _____

9. The Numbering button is located in this group on the HOME tab. _____

10. This button displays when the AutoFormat feature inserts numbers. _____

11. A bulleted list with a hanging indent is automatically created when you begin a paragraph with an asterisk symbol (*), a hyphen (-), or this symbol. _____

12. Turn off automatic numbering and bulleting at the AutoCorrect dialog box with this tab selected. _____

13. Automate the creation of bulleted paragraphs with this button on the HOME tab. _____

14. Press these keys to display the Reveal Formatting task pane. _____

# Chapter Assessments

## Applying Your Skills

Demonstrate your knowledge of features learned in this chapter by completing the following assessments.

### Assessment 3.1    Apply Alignment and Spacing Formatting to a Document

1. At a blank document, click the *No Spacing* style in the Styles group on the HOME tab and then type the text shown in Figure 3.11 with the following specifications:
   a. Center and right-align text as indicated.
   b. After typing the text, select the centered text and change the font to 18-point Constantia bold.
   c. Select the right-aligned text and change the font to 10-point Constantia bold.
   d. Increase the paragraph spacing after each line of centered text by 12 points.
2. Save the document and name it **C03-A01-DataTraining**.
3. Print and then close **C03-A01-DataTraining.docx**.

**Figure 3.11  Assessment 3.1**

DATA SECURITY
Technical Support Training
Building C, Room 250
Thursday, April 9, 2015
3:00 to 5:30 p.m.

Technical Support Department
Support and Services Team

### Assessment 3.2    Apply Character and Paragraph Formatting to a Document

1. Open **Presentation.docx**.
2. Save the document with Save As and name it **C03-A02-Presentation**.
3. Select the entire document and then change the line spacing to 1.0.
4. Select the five lines of text below the first paragraph in the *Choose a Suitable Topic* section (*Getting a driver's license* through *Applying for financial aid*) and then apply the numbering format.

5. Select the second through fourth paragraphs of text in the *Develop Well-Organized Directions* section, apply bullet formatting, and then indent the right margin 0.5 inch.
6. Apply the Shaded style set.
7. Center the title.
8. Save and then print **C03-A02-Presentation.docx**.
9. Select the entire document and then change the line spacing to 1.15.
10. Select from the first paragraph of text below the title to the end of the document and then change the alignment to justified.
11. Delete the paragraph numbered as 4.
12. Select the four lines of numbered text and then apply bullet formatting.
13. Save the document with Save As and name it **C03-A02B-Presentation**.
14. Print and then close **C03-A02B-Presentation.docx**.

## Assessment 3.3    Create and Format a Bibliography

1. At a blank document, create the document shown in Figure 3.12 with the following specifications:
   a. Click the *No Spacing* style.
   b. Change the line spacing to double.
   c. Center the text and apply bold and italic formatting as indicated.
   d. Create hanging indents as indicated. (Make sure you let the text wrap within paragraphs to create the hanging indents correctly.)
   e. Change the alignment of paragraphs to justified.
2. Save the document and name it **C03-A03-Biblio**.
3. Print and then close **C03-A03-Biblio.docx**.

**Figure 3.12  Assessment 3.3**

**BIBLIOGRAPHY**

Albright, A. A. (2015). *Managing telecommunications* (2nd ed.) (pp. 24-33). Salt Lake City, UT: Blue Ridge

    Publishing Company.

Brown-Smythe, L. N. (2014). *Creating and maintaining local area networks* (pp. 19-22). Boston:

    Northhampton Publishers.

Lopez, V. C. (2015). *The future of nanotechnology* (pp. 43-51). Philadelphia: Graystone and Jefferson

    Publishing House.

Okada, D. G. (2015). *Electronic commerce* (2nd ed.) (pp. 38-42). New Orleans, LA: Pontchartrain

    Publishing, Inc.

## Assessment 3.4 Apply Character and Paragraph Formatting to a Travel Document

1. Open **TravelAdv.docx**.
2. Save the document with Save As and name it **C03-A04-TravelAdv**.
3. Move the insertion point to the end of the document and then type the text shown in Figure 3.13.
4. Select text from the first heading, *Rainy Day Activities*, to the end of the document and then add 6 points of spacing after each paragraph.
5. Select the title *HAWAIIAN ADVENTURES*, change the font to 16-point Constantia, and then apply the Gradient Fill - Blue, Accent 1, Reflection text effect (second column, second row).
6. Select the heading *Rainy Day Activities*, change the font to 12-point Constantia, and then apply the Gradient Fill - Blue, Accent 1, Reflection text effect. Use Format Painter to apply the same formatting to the other two headings in the document (*Kauai Sights* and *Photo Opportunities*).
7. Select the second through the fifth paragraphs of text in the *Rainy Day Activities* section and then apply bullet formatting.
8. Select the paragraphs of text in the *Kauai Sights* section and then apply bullet formatting.
9. Insert the following paragraph of text between paragraphs 2 and 3 in the *Kauai Sights* section: **Tree tunnel: Fragrant eucalyptus trees provide a canopy of green en route to Koloa and Poipu.**
10. Select the bulleted text below the *Photo Opportunities* heading and then increase the left paragraph indent to 2.1 inch.
11. Save, print, and then close **C03-A04-TravelAdv.docx**.

**Figure 3.13 Assessment 3.4**

Photo Opportunities
> Hanalei Pier and Bay
> Green Waioli Huiia Church
> Lumahai Beach
> Coconut Grove
> Fern Grotto
> Sleeping Giant

# Expanding Your Skills

Explore additional feature options or use Help to learn a new skill in creating this document.

## Assessment 3.5 Insert Symbol Bullets

1. At a blank document, click the Bullets button arrow, click the *Define New Bullet* option that displays at the bottom of the drop-down list, and then experiment with creating a symbol bullet.
2. Open **PlanResume.docx** and then save the document and name it **C03-A05-PlanResume**.
3. Select the paragraphs of text in the document (except the title) and then apply a new symbol bullet of your choosing.
4. After inserting the symbol bullets, move the insertion point to the end of the document. Type an explanation of the steps you followed to insert the new bullet and then number the steps.
5. Save, print, and then close the **C03-A05-PlanResume.docx**.

# Achieving Signature Status

Take your skills to the next level by completing these more challenging assessments.

## Assessment 3.6    Format a Document on Resume Strategies

1. Open **ResumeStrategies.docx** and then save the document and name it **C03-A06-ResumeStrategies**.
2. Apply character and paragraph formatting so your document appears as shown in Figure 3.14.
3. Save, print, and then close **C03-A06-ResumeStrategies.docx**.

**Figure 3.14  Assessment 3.6**

**NINE STRATEGIES FOR AN EFFECTIVE RESUME**

Following are the nine core strategies for writing an effective and successful resume:

1. Who are you and how do you want to be perceived?
2. Sell it to me … don't tell it to me.
3. Use keywords.
4. Use the "big" and save the "little."
5. Make your resume "interviewable."
6. Eliminate confusion with structure and content.
7. Use function to demonstrate achievement.
8. Remain in the realm of reality.
9. Be confident.

**Writing Style**

Always write in the first person, dropping the word "I" from the front of each sentence. This style gives your resume a more aggressive and more professional tone than the passive third person voice. Here are some examples:

***First Person***

> Manage 22-person team responsible for design and marketing of a new portfolio of PC-based applications for Landmark's consumer-sales division.

***Third Person***

> Ms. Sanderson manages a 22-person team responsible for design and marketing of a new portfolio of PC-based application for Landmark's consumer-sales division.

**REFERENCES**

Kurzweil, M. J. & Middleton, C. A. (2015). Designing a sure-fire resume (pp. 6-10). Indianapolis, IN: Rushton-Jansen Publishing House.

Perreault, R. M. and Engstrom, E. L. (2014). Writing resumes and cover pages (pp. 31-34). Los Angeles: Pacific Blue Printing.

## Assessment 3.7    Type a Business Letter

1. Open **BGLtrhd.docx** and then save the document and name it **C03-A07-PSPLetter**.
2. Type the text in the document shown in Figure 3.15 with the following specifications:
   - Click the *No Spacing* style before typing text. (Refer to Appendix D at the back of this book for information on formatting a business letter with the No Spacing style applied.)
   - Insert bullets as shown in the figure.
   - Indent the bulleted paragraphs of text 0.5 inch from the right margin.
   - Change the alignment to justified for the paragraphs of text in the body of the letter.
   - Replace the *XX* with your initials near the end of the letter.
3. Save, print, and then close **C03-A07-PSPLetter.docx**.

**Figure 3.15  Assessment 3.7**

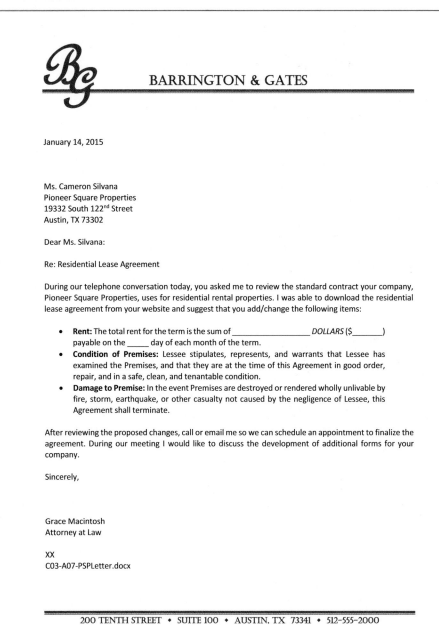

# Chapter 4

# Customizing Paragraphs

## Performance Objectives

Upon successful completion of Chapter 4, you will be able to:

- Insert paragraph borders and shading
- Sort paragraphs of text
- Set, delete, and move tabs on the horizontal ruler and at the Tabs dialog box
- Delete, cut, copy, and paste text within a document
- Copy and paste text between documents

In the last chapter, you learned some of the options Word provides for formatting text in a paragraph. In this chapter, you will learn additional options, including how to apply borders and shading, sort paragraphs, and manipulate tabs both on the horizontal ruler and at the Tabs dialog box. You will also learn to perform edits—such as selecting and then deleting, moving, or copying text—using buttons on the HOME tab or keyboard shortcuts.

*Note: Before beginning computer exercises for this chapter, copy to your storage medium the Chapter04 folder from the CD that accompanies this textbook and then make Chapter04 the active folder.*

In this chapter, students will produce the following documents:

Exercise 4.1. C04-E01-Quiz.docx
Exercise 4.2. C04-E02-IntlCorres.docx
Exercise 4.3. C04-E03-Tabs.docx
Exercise 4.4. C04-E04-LtrFormat.docx
Exercise 4.5. C04-E05-ManageData.docx
Exercise 4.6. C04-E06-FinalAgrmnt.docx

Model answers for these exercises are shown on the following pages.

**Exercise 4.1**

C04-E01-Quiz.docx

---

**CHAPTER 10 QUIZ**

**Directions:** For each item, circle the letter of the best answer from those provided.

1. Processed data that can be used immediately or stored in computer-usable form for later use is called
   a. Input
   b. Output
   c. Data retrieval
   d. Manipulated data

2. A tiny single point in anything being displayed on a screen is called a
   a. Dot
   b. Screen point
   c. Pixel
   d. Microsync

3. A term that describes the number of pixels in the display, or the quality of the text and graphics being displayed, is
   a. Resolution
   b. Density
   c. Coordination
   d. Element filtering

4. The component that converts digital signals into text so it can be displayed on a monitor is called a(n)
   a. Hypertext card
   b. RAM chip
   c. Graphics adapter
   d. Analog adapter

5. The most common type of device for producing hardcopy output is the
   a. Monitor
   b. Printer
   c. Plotter
   d. Speaker

---

**International Correspondence**

With the increased number of firms conducting business worldwide, international written communication has assumed new importance. Follow these guidelines when corresponding internationally, especially with people for whom English is not the primary language:

- Avoid slang, jargon, and idioms.
- Develop an awareness of cultural differences that may interfere with the communication process.
- Use a direct writing style and clear, precise words.

**International Addresses**

Use the company's letterhead or a business card as a guide for spelling and other information. Include the following when addressing international correspondences:

Line 1: Addressee's Name, Title
Line 2: Company Name
Line 3: Street Address
Line 4: City and Codes
Line 5: COUNTRY NAME (capitalized)

**Canadian Codes and Provinces**

AB – Alberta
BC – British Columbia
MB – Manitoba
NB – New Brunswick
NL – Newfoundland and Labrador
NS – Nova Scotia
ON – Ontario
PE – Prince Edward Island
QC – Quebec
SK – Saskatchewan

**Canadian Codes and Territories**

NT – Northwest Territories
NU – Nunavut
YT – Yukon

**Exercise 4.2**

C04-E02-IntlCorres.docx

---

**Exercise 4.3**
C04-E03-Tabs.docx

**TRAINING**

| Title | Date | Time |
|---|---|---|
| Producing Documents | March 4 | 10:00 a.m. to 3:30 p.m. |
| Preparing Spreadsheets | March 12 | 9:00 a.m. to Noon |
| Designing Newsletters | March 26 | 1:00 to 5:00 p.m. |
| Managing Databases | April 2 | 9:00 a.m. to 5:00 p.m. |
| Preparing Presentations | April 14 | 1:30 to 4:30 p.m. |
| Managing Client Records | April 21 | 2:00 to 5:00 p.m. |

**NEW EMPLOYEE TRAINING**

| | |
|---|---|
| January 6 | February 3 |
| January 15 | February 12 |
| January 20 | February 17 |
| January 22 | February 24 |

## CONTENTS

The Writing Process ............................................................... 1

Editing and Proofreading ..................................................... 3

Grammar .................................................................................. 5

Punctuation............................................................................ 12

Capitalization ........................................................................ 15

Abbreviations and Symbols ............................................... 19

Spelling and Word Division ................................................ 24

| Employee | Hire Date | Department |
|---|---|---|
| Marilyn Cameron | July 1, 2015 | Administration |
| Hayden St. Germaine | July 1, 2015 | Research & Development |
| Gerald Ahmad | July 1, 2015 | Maintenance Services |
| Charles Metzger | August 1, 2015 | Public Relations |
| Victoria Peterson | August 1, 2015 | Technical Services |

---

**Letter Formatting**

Achieving a balanced overall appearance to enhance readability is the primary goal of letter formatting. When you prepare business letters, consider the following formatting guidelines:

**Spacing:** Generally, single space lines in business letters but double space between paragraphs.

**Justification:** A ragged right edge aids readability because no unnecessary spacing appears within lines of text. Use left justification (ragged right edge) for business letters.

**Margins:** To achieve a balanced appearance, use equal margins on the left and right and approximately equal margins at the top and bottom, with the bottom margin two or three spaces greater than the top.

**Attention Line:** Use the attention line when you want a specific person to receive a letter containing a message intended for an entire company or group within a company. The attention line appears as the first line of the inside address and may include a person's name or simply a job title or department name.

**Date Line:** Include the month, day, and year with no abbreviations.

**Adjusting for Letter Length:** To achieve a balanced appearance, exceptionally long or short letters may require one or more of the following margin or spacing adjustments:

- Place the date higher or lower on the page.
- Delete space between the date and the inside address.
- Adjust side margins from three-quarters of an inch as a minimum and one and one-half inches as a maximum.
- Delete space between the complimentary close and the writer's signature line, leaving enough space for the signature.
- Allow long letters to go beyond a single page.

When a letter goes beyond a single page, use a header on all pages after the first to avoid confusion if the pages become separated. In addition, make sure isolated words or lines of text (often called *widows* and *orphans*) do not begin or end a page.

**Exercise 4.4**
C04-E04-LtrFormat.docx

**Exercise 4.5**

C04-E05-ManageData.docx

MANAGING CRUCIAL DATA
Technical Support Training
Building C, Room 250
Tuesday, April 15, 2015
9:00 a.m. to 11:30 a.m.

MANAGING CRUCIAL DATA
Technical Support Training
Building C, Room 250
Tuesday, April 15, 2015
9:00 a.m. to 11:30 a.m.

MANAGING CRUCIAL DATA
Technical Support Training
Building C, Room 250
Tuesday, April 15, 2015
9:00 a.m. to 11:30 a.m.

MANAGING CRUCIAL DATA
Technical Support Training
Building C, Room 250
Tuesday, April 15, 2015
9:00 a.m. to 11:30 a.m.

MANAGING CRUCIAL DATA
Technical Support Training
Building C, Room 250
Tuesday, April 15, 2015
9:00 a.m. to 11:30 a.m.

MANAGING CRUCIAL DATA
Technical Support Training
Building C, Room 250
Tuesday, April 15, 2015
9:00 a.m. to 11:30 a.m.

**CONTRACT NEGOTIATION ITEMS**

1. The Employer agrees that, during the term of this Agreement, it shall not cause or initiate any lockout of Employees.

2. During the term of this Agreement, the **TWU** agrees not to engage in, authorize, sanction, or support any strike, slowdown, or other acts of curtailment or work stoppage.

3. A differential of one dollar and seventy cents ($1.70) will be paid for work performed on Shift 3.

4. MBP agrees to negotiate with TWU for wage rates for jobs that may be established in the future and which are not included in said minimum wage schedule.

5. No MBP employee shall be compelled to work more than five (5) hours without being permitted to have a lunch period.

6. Payroll calculations are based on the week beginning 12:01 a.m. Sunday and ending noon Saturday. The payroll day runs from midnight to midnight.

**NEGOTIATING TEAM**

- Max Tillman, Chief Negotiator
- Jill Monahan
- William Nordyke
- Candace Rutledge
- Anthony Ceriotti
- Luanne Hayes

**Exercise 4.6**

C04-E06-FinalAgrmnt.docx

# Inserting Paragraph Borders and Shading

Every paragraph you create in Word is surrounded by an invisible frame, and a border can be applied to that frame. You can apply a border to a specific side of the paragraph or to all sides, customize the type of border line, and add shading to fill the area inside the border. Apply borders and shading to paragraphs using the Borders button and Shading button in the Paragraph group on the HOME tab or with options at the Borders and Shading dialog box.

Borders

Shading

## Inserting Paragraph Borders

When you add a border to a paragraph of text, the border expands and contracts as you insert or delete text from the paragraph. You can create a border around a single paragraph or around multiple paragraphs. One method for creating a border is to use options from the Borders button in the Paragraph group. Click the Borders button arrow and a drop-down list displays, as shown in Figure 4.1.

**QUICK STEPS**

**Insert a Paragraph Border**
1. Select text.
2. Click Borders button arrow.
3. Click desired border at drop-down list.

**Figure 4.1 Borders Button Drop-down List**

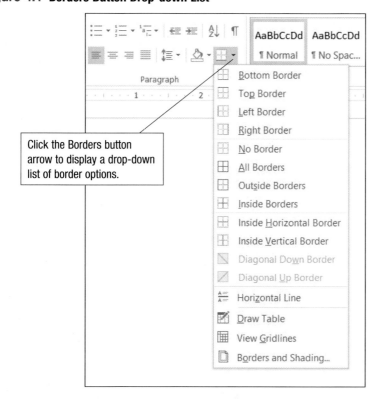

Click the Borders button arrow to display a drop-down list of border options.

At the drop-down list, click the option that will insert the desired border. Clicking an option adds the border to the paragraph where the insertion point is located. For example, to insert a border at the bottom of the paragraph, click the *Bottom Border* option. To add a border to more than one paragraph, select the paragraphs first and then click the desired border option.

1. Open **Quiz.docx** and save the document with the name **C04-E01-Quiz**.
2. Make the following changes to the document.
   a. Select the entire document, change the font to 12-point Cambria, and then deselect the text.
   b. Center the title *CHAPTER 10 QUIZ*.
3. Insert borders above and below the title by completing the following steps:
   a. Position the insertion point on any character in the title *CHAPTER 10 QUIZ*.
   b. Click the Borders button arrow and then click *Bottom Border* at the drop-down list.
   c. Click the Borders button arrow and then click *Top Border* at the drop-down list.

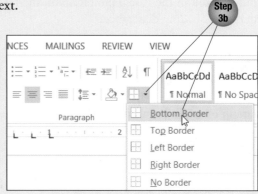

4. Insert an outside border to specific text by completing the following steps:
   a. Select the text for the first item (including the multiple-choice options).
   b. Click the Borders button arrow and then click *Outside Borders* at the drop-down list.

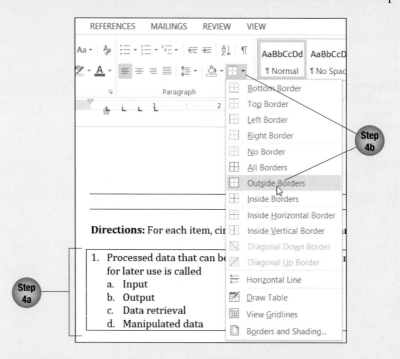

5. Select the text for the second item (including the multiple-choice options) and then press the Repeat command, key F4. (This command repeats the last function.)
6. Select individually each of the remaining items and multiple-choice options and press F4.
7. Save **C04-E01-Quiz.docx**.

# Adding Paragraph Shading

Use the Shading button in the Paragraph group to add shading behind a paragraph or selected text. If you want shading applied behind specific text, select the text, click the Shading button arrow, and then click the desired color at the drop-down gallery, as shown in Figure 4.2. If you want shading applied behind an entire paragraph, position the insertion point in the paragraph without selecting text, click the Shading button arrow, and then click the desired color at the drop-down gallery.

**Apply Paragraph Shading**
1. Select text or click in desired paragraph.
2. Click Shading button arrow.
3. Click desired shade in drop-down gallery.

**Figure 4.2  Shading Button Drop-down Gallery**

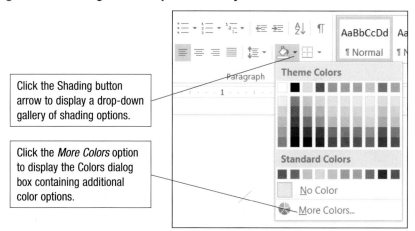

Click the Shading button arrow to display a drop-down gallery of shading options.

Click the *More Colors* option to display the Colors dialog box containing additional color options.

The shading colors are arranged in color themes. Choose one of the theme colors or one of the standard colors that display at the bottom of the gallery, or click the *More Colors* option to display the Colors dialog box. At this dialog box with the Standard tab selected, click the desired color or click the Custom tab and then specify a custom color.

## Exercise 4.1B  Applying Shading to Paragraphs                    Part 2 of 2

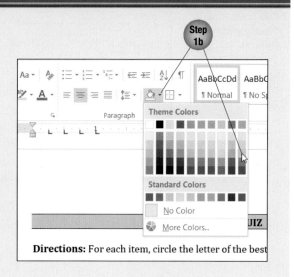

1. With **C04-E01-Quiz.docx** open, apply paragraph shading by completing the following steps:
   a. Position the insertion point on any character in the title *CHAPTER 10 QUIZ.*
   b. Click the Shading button arrow and then click the *Green, Accent 6, Lighter 40%* option (last column, fourth row in the *Theme Colors* section).
2. Apply shading to the number 1. item text by completing the following steps:
   a. Position the insertion point on any character in the number 1. text.

Step 1b

**Directions:** For each item, circle the letter of the best

b. Click the Shading button arrow and then click the *Green, Accent 6, Lighter 60%* option (last column, third row in the *Theme Colors* section). (Clicking this option applies shading to the number 1. text but not to the multiple-choice options.)

3. Use the Repeat command, key F4, to apply the same formatting to the remaining numbered items (but not the multiple-choice options).

4. Save, print, and then close **C04-E01-Quiz.docx**.

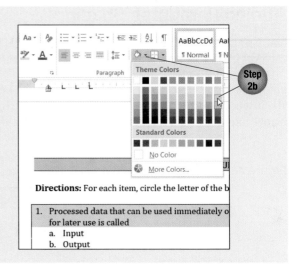

## Customizing Borders and Shading

**QUICK STEPS**

**Customize Borders**
1. Click Borders button arrow.
2. Click *Borders and Shading* at drop-down list.
3. Specify desired border, style, color, and width.
4. Click OK.

**Customize Shading**
1. Click Borders button arrow.
2. Click *Borders and Shading* at drop-down list.
3. Click Shading tab.
4. Specify desired shading.
5. Click OK.

If you want to further customize paragraph borders and shading, use options at the Borders and Shading dialog box. Display this dialog box by clicking the Borders button arrow and then clicking *Borders and Shading* at the drop-down list. With the Borders tab selected, as shown in Figure 4.3, the Borders and Shading dialog box contains options for specifying the border style, color, and width. Click the Shading tab and the dialog box displays with options for applying fill colors and patterns, as shown in Figure 4.4 on the next page.

**Figure 4.3 Borders and Shading Dialog Box with the Borders Tab Selected**

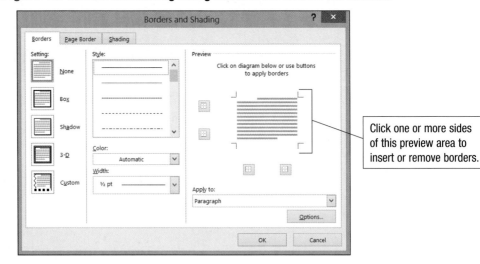

Click one or more sides of this preview area to insert or remove borders.

**Figure 4.4 Borders and Shading Dialog Box with the Shading Tab Selected**

Click this down-pointing arrow to display a drop-down list of shading options.

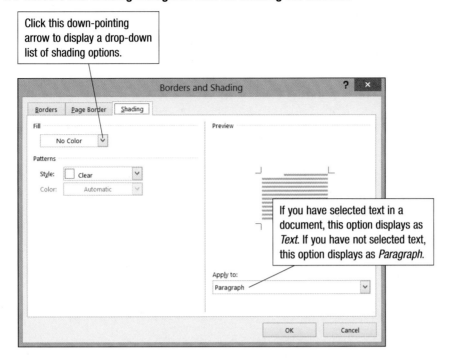

If you have selected text in a document, this option displays as *Text*. If you have not selected text, this option displays as *Paragraph*.

**Exercise 4.2A** Adding a Customized Border and Shading to a Document

Part 1 of 3

1. Open **IntlCorres.docx** and save the document with the name **C04-E02-IntlCorres**.
2. Insert a custom border and add shading to a heading by completing the following steps:
   a. Move the insertion point to any character in the heading *International Correspondence*.
   b. Click the Borders button arrow and then click *Borders and Shading* at the drop-down list.
   c. At the Borders and Shading dialog box with the Borders tab selected, click the down-pointing arrow at the right side of the *Color* option box and then click the *Dark Blue* color (ninth option in the *Standard Colors* section).

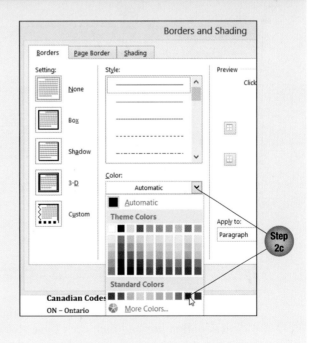

d.  Click the down-pointing arrow at the right of the *Width* option box and then click *1 pt* at the drop-down list.
e.  Click the top border of the box in the *Preview* section of the dialog box.

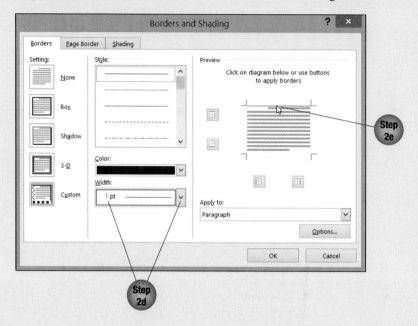

f.  Click the down scroll arrow in the *Style* list box and then click the first thick-thin line combination.
g.  Click the bottom border of the box in the *Preview* section of the dialog box.

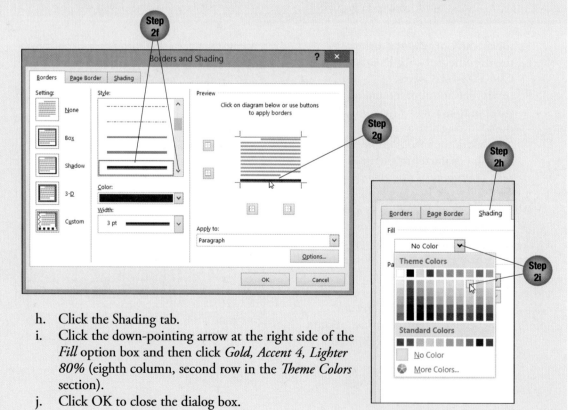

h.  Click the Shading tab.
i.  Click the down-pointing arrow at the right side of the *Fill* option box and then click *Gold, Accent 4, Lighter 80%* (eighth column, second row in the *Theme Colors* section).
j.  Click OK to close the dialog box.

3. Use Format Painter to apply the same border and shading formatting to the remaining headings by completing the following steps:
   a. Position the insertion point on any character in the heading *International Correspondence*.
   b. Double-click the Format Painter button in the Clipboard group on the HOME tab.
   c. Select the heading *International Addresses*.
   d. Select the heading *Canadian Codes and Provinces*.
   e. Select the heading *Canadian Codes and Territories*.
   f. Click the Format Painter button once.
4. Save **C04-E02-IntlCorres.docx**.

## Changing Borders and Shading Options

By default, a paragraph border displays and prints with 1 point of spacing from the text to the top and bottom borders and 4 points of spacing from the text to the left and right borders. These defaults can be changed with options at the Border and Shading Options dialog box, as shown in Figure 4.5. Display this dialog box by clicking the Options button at the Borders and Shading dialog box with the Borders tab selected. To increase the amount of spacing between the text and a paragraph border, increase the number in the appropriate measurement box in the dialog box.

**Figure 4.5  Border and Shading Options Dialog Box**

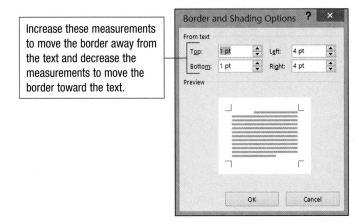

Increase these measurements to move the border away from the text and decrease the measurements to move the border toward the text.

If you apply shading to a paragraph of text but not a paragraph border, changing the measurements at the Border and Shading Options dialog box will not affect the shading. However, if the paragraph contains both borders and shading, changes to the measurements at the Border and Shading Options dialog box will affect the borders as well as the shading.

1. With **C04-E02-IntlCorres.docx** open, increase the spacing above and below the border and shading applied to the heading *International Correspondence* by completing the following steps:
   a. Position the insertion point on any character in the heading *International Correspondence*.
   b. Click the Borders button arrow and then click *Borders and Shading* at the drop-down list.
   c. At the Borders and Shading dialog box with the Borders tab selected, click the Options button that displays in the lower right corner.
   d. At the Border and Shading Options dialog box, click the up-pointing arrow at the right side of the *Top* measurement box until *6 pt* displays.
   e. Select the current measurement in the *Bottom* measurement box and then type **6**.
   f. Click OK to close the Border and Shading Options dialog box.

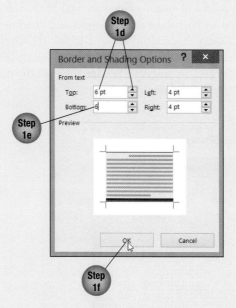

   g. Click OK to close the Borders and Shading dialog box.
2. Apply the same formatting to the other headings by completing the following steps:
   a. Position the insertion point on any character in the heading *International Addresses* and then press the F4 key (the Repeat command).
   b. Position the insertion point on any character in the heading *Canadian Codes and Provinces* and then press the F4 key.
   c. Position the insertion point on any character in the heading *Canadian Codes and Territories* and then press the F4 key.
3. Save **C04-E02-IntlCorres.docx**.

# Sorting Text in Paragraphs

You can sort text that is arranged in paragraphs alphabetically by the first character of each paragraph. That character can be a number, symbol (such as $ or #), or letter. Type the paragraphs you want to sort at the left margin or indent them to a tab. Unless you select specific paragraphs to be sorted, Word sorts the entire document.

To sort text in paragraphs, open the document. If you do not want to sort all of the paragraphs in the document, select the specific paragraphs of text you do want sorted. Click the Sort button in the Paragraph group and the Sort Text dialog box displays, as shown in Figure 4.6. At this dialog box, click OK. If you select text and then display the dialog box, the *Sort by* option is set at *Paragraphs*. If the text you select is numbers, then *Numbers* displays in the Sort Text dialog box.

**QUICK STEPS**

**Sort Text in Paragraphs**
1. Select desired paragraphs.
2. Click Sort button.
3. Make any needed changes at Sort Text dialog box.
4. Click OK.

**Figure 4.6  Sort Text Dialog Box**

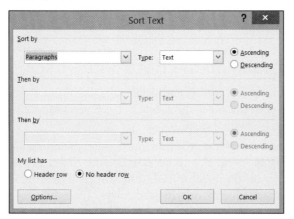

Sort

---

## Exercise 4.2C  Sorting Paragraphs                              Part 3 of 3

1. With **C04-E02-IntlCorres.docx** open, sort the bulleted paragraphs of text alphabetically by completing the following steps:
   a. Select the bulleted paragraphs in the *International Correspondence* section.
   b. Click the Sort button in the Paragraph group.
   c. At the Sort Text dialog box, make sure that *Paragraphs* displays in the *Sort by* option box and the *Ascending* option is selected.
   d. Click OK.

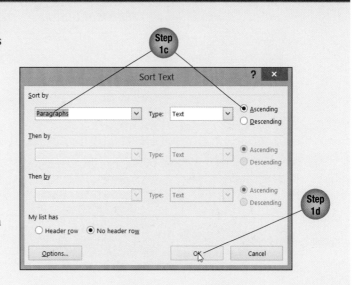

2. Sort the paragraphs that begin with *Line* followed by a number by completing the following steps:
   a. Select the paragraphs in the *International Addresses* section that begin with *Line*.
   b. Click the Sort button in the Paragraph group.
   c. Click OK at the Sort Text dialog box.
3. Follow the steps outlined in Step 2 to sort the names of the Canadian provinces alphabetically and then the names of the Canadian territories.
4. Save, print, and then close **C04-E02-IntlCorres.docx**.

# Manipulating Tabs

When you work with a document, Word provides a variety of default settings. One of these defaults is that left tabs are set every 0.5 inch. For some documents, these default tabs are appropriate; for others, you may want to create your own tabs. Tabs can be set on the horizontal ruler and at the Tabs dialog box.

## Manipulating Tabs on the Horizontal Ruler

Use the horizontal ruler to set, move, and delete tabs. If the ruler is not visible, click the VIEW tab and then click the *Ruler* check box in the Show group. By default, tabs are set every 0.5 inch on the horizontal ruler.

Five types of tabs can be set on the horizontal ruler, including a left tab (which is the default) and center, right, decimal, and bar tab. Use the Alignment button that displays above the vertical ruler to specify tabs. Each time you click the Alignment button, a different tab or paragraph alignment symbol displays. Table 4.1 shows the tab alignment buttons and which type of tab each button sets.

**Table 4.1 Tab Alignment Symbols**

| ***Alignment Button*** | ***Type of Tab*** |
|---|---|
|  | left tab |
|  | center tab |
|  | right tab |
|  | decimal tab |
|  | bar tab |

## Setting Tabs

To set a left tab on the horizontal ruler, make sure the left alignment symbol (see Table 4.1) displays in the Alignment button. Position the arrow pointer on the tick mark where you want the tab symbol to appear and then click the left mouse button. (Tick marks are the short vertical lines that indicate units on the ruler.) When you set a tab on the horizontal ruler, any default tabs to the left are automatically deleted by Word. Set a center, right, decimal, or bar tab on the horizontal ruler in a similar manner. When you set tabs on the horizontal ruler, a dotted guideline displays to help align the tabs.

Before setting a tab on the horizontal ruler, click the Alignment button that displays above the vertical ruler until the appropriate tab symbol displays. If you change the tab symbol in the Alignment button, that type of tab remains in effect until you change it again or close Word. If you close and then reopen Word, the Alignment button displays with the left tab symbol.

If you want to set a tab at a specific measurement on the horizontal ruler, hold down the Alt key, position the arrow pointer at the desired position, and then hold down the left mouse button. Two measurements are displayed on the horizontal ruler. The first measurement displays the location of the arrow pointer on the ruler in relation to the left margin. The second measurement is the distance from the location of the arrow pointer on the ruler to the right margin. With the left mouse button held down, position the tab symbol at the desired location and then release the mouse button and Alt key.

If you change tab settings and then type tabbed text using the New Line command, Shift + Enter, the tab formatting is stored in the paragraph mark at the end of the typed text. If you want to make changes to the tab settings for the text in the columns, position the insertion point anywhere within the columns (you do not have to select all of the text in the columns) and then make the changes. If you want to make changes to tab settings for the text in columns that you created by pressing the Enter key at the end of each line (rather than the New Line command, Shift + Enter), you need to select all of the lines of text in the columns and then make the changes.

**QUICK STEPS**

**Set Tabs on the Horizontal Ruler**
1. Click Alignment button above vertical ruler.
2. Click desired location on horizontal ruler.

---

**Exercise 4.3A**  **Setting Left, Center, and Right Tabs on the Horizontal Ruler**    **Part 1 of 5**

1. Press Ctrl + N to display a blank document.
2. Type **TRAINING**, center it, and apply bold formatting, as shown in Figure 4.7 on page 107.
3. Press the Enter key and then return the paragraph alignment back to left alignment and turn off bold formatting.
4. Set a left tab at the 0.5-inch mark on the horizontal ruler, a center tab at the 3.25-inch mark, and a right tab at the 6-inch mark by completing the following steps:
   a. Click the Show/Hide ¶ button in the Paragraph group on the HOME tab to turn on the display of nonprinting characters.
   b. Make sure the horizontal ruler is displayed. (If not, click the VIEW tab and then click the *Ruler* check box in the Show group.)

c. Make sure the left tab symbol displays in the Alignment button above the vertical ruler.
d. Position the arrow pointer on the 0.5-inch mark on the horizontal ruler and then click the left mouse button.

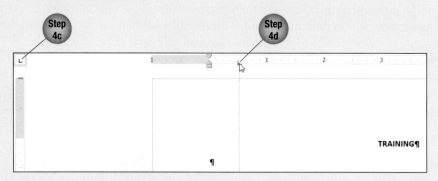

e. Position the arrow pointer on the Alignment button above the vertical ruler and then click the left mouse button to display the center tab symbol (see Table 4.1).
f. Position the arrow pointer below the 3.25-inch mark on the horizontal ruler. Hold down the Alt key and then the left mouse button. Make sure the first measurement on the horizontal ruler displays as *3.25"* and then release the mouse button and the Alt key.

g. Position the arrow pointer on the Alignment button above the vertical ruler and then click the left mouse button to display the right tab symbol (see Table 4.1).
h. Position the arrow pointer below the 6-inch mark on the horizontal ruler. Hold down the Alt key and then the left mouse button. Make sure the first measurement on the horizontal ruler displays as *6"* and then release the mouse button and the Alt key.

5. Type the text in columns, as shown in Figure 4.7 on the next page. (Make sure you bold the column headings.) Press the Tab key before typing each column entry and press Shift + Enter after typing each entry in the third column.
6. After typing the last column entry, press the Enter key twice.
7. Press Ctrl + Q to remove paragraph formatting (tab settings).
8. Click the Show/Hide ¶ button to turn off the display of nonprinting characters.
9. Save the document and name it **C04-E03-Tabs**.

**Figure 4.7  Exercise 4.3A**

|  | TRAINING |  |
|---|---|---|
| **Title** | **Date** | **Time** |
| Producing Documents | March 4 | 10:00 a.m. to 3:30 p.m. |
| Preparing Spreadsheets | March 12 | 9:00 a.m. to Noon |
| Designing Newsletters | March 26 | 1:00 to 5:00 p.m. |
| Managing Databases | April 2 | 9:00 a.m. to 5:00 p.m. |
| Preparing Presentations | April 14 | 1:30 to 4:30 p.m. |
| Managing Client Records | April 21 | 2:00 to 5:00 p.m. |

## Moving Tabs

After a tab has been set on the horizontal ruler, it can be moved to a new location. To move a tab, position the arrow pointer on the tab symbol on the ruler, hold down the left mouse button, drag the symbol to the new location on the ruler, and then release the mouse button.

## Deleting Tabs

To delete a tab from the horizontal ruler, position the arrow pointer on the tab symbol, hold down the left mouse button, drag the symbol down and away from the ruler, and then release the mouse button.

---

**Exercise 4.3B  Moving Tabs**                                        **Part 2 of 5**

1. With **C04-E03-Tabs.docx** open, position the insertion point on any character in the first entry in the tabbed text (*Title*).
2. Position the arrow pointer on the left tab symbol at the 0.5-inch mark, hold down the left mouse button, drag the left tab symbol to the 1-inch mark on the horizontal ruler, and then release the mouse button. ***Hint: Use the Alt key to help you position the tab symbol precisely.***
3. Position the arrow pointer on the right tab symbol at the 6-inch mark, hold down the left mouse button, drag the right tab symbol to the 5.5-inch mark on the horizontal ruler, and then release the mouse button. ***Hint: Use the Alt key to help you position the tab symbol precisely.***
4. Save **C04-E03-Tabs.docx**.

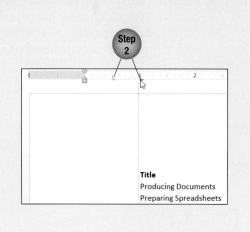

## Manipulating Tabs at the Tabs Dialog Box

**Set Tabs at the Tabs Dialog Box**
1. Click Paragraph group dialog box launcher.
2. Click Tabs button.
3. Specify tab positions, alignments, and leader options.
4. Click OK.

Use the Tabs dialog box, shown in Figure 4.8, to set tabs at specific measurements. You can also use the Tabs dialog box to set tabs with preceding leaders and to clear one tab or all tabs. To display the Tabs dialog box, click the Paragraph group dialog box launcher. At the Paragraph dialog box, click the Tabs button located in the bottom left corner of the dialog box.

**Figure 4.8 Tabs Dialog Box**

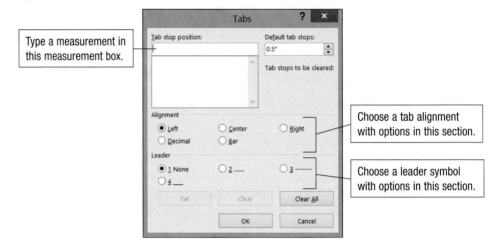

### Clearing Tabs

At the Tabs dialog box, you can clear an individual tab or all tabs. To clear all tabs, click the Clear All button. To clear an individual tab, specify the tab position and then click the Clear button.

### Setting Tabs

At the Tabs dialog box, you can set any type of tab: left, right, center, decimal, or bar. You can also set a left, right, center, or decimal tab with preceding leaders. To change the type of tab using the Tabs dialog box, display the dialog box and then click the desired tab in the *Alignment* section. Type the desired measurement for the tab in the *Tab stop position* measurement box.

1. With **C04-E03-Tabs.docx** open, press Ctrl + End to move the insertion point to the end of the document.
2. Type the title **NEW EMPLOYEE TRAINING**, center it, and apply bold formatting, as shown in Figure 4.9. Press the Enter key, change the paragraph alignment back to left, and then turn off bold formatting.
3. Display the Tabs dialog box and then set left tabs and a bar tab by completing the following steps:
    a. Click the Paragraph group dialog box launcher.
    b. At the Paragraph dialog box, click the Tabs button located in the lower left corner of the dialog box.
    c. Make sure *Left* is selected in the *Alignment* section of the dialog box.
    d. Type **1.75** in the *Tab stop position* measurement box and then click the Set button.
    e. Type **4** in the *Tab stop position* measurement box and then click the Set button.
    f. Type **3.25** in the *Tab stop position* measurement box, click *Bar* in the *Alignment* section, and then click the Set button.
    g. Click OK to close the Tabs dialog box.

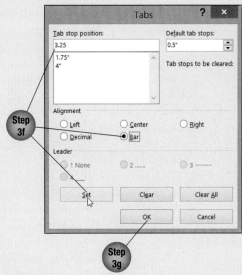

4. Type the text in columns as shown in Figure 4.9. Press the Tab key before typing each column entry and press Shift + Enter to end each line.
5. After typing *February 24*, complete the following steps:
    a. Press the Enter key.
    b. Clear all of the tabs by displaying the Tabs dialog box, clicking the Clear All button, and then clicking OK.
    c. Press the Enter key.
6. Remove the 8 points of spacing after the last entry in the text by completing the following steps:
    a. Position the insertion point on any character in the *January 22* entry.
    b. Click the Line and Paragraph Spacing button in the Paragraph group on the HOME tab.
    c. Click the *Remove Space After Paragraph* option at the drop-down gallery.
7. Save **C04-E03-Tabs.docx**.

**Figure 4.9  Exercise 4.3C**

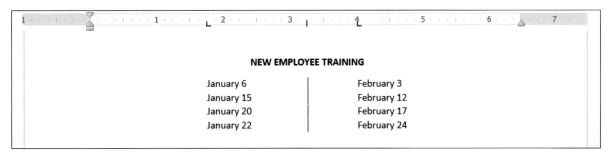

## Setting Leader Tabs

Left, right, decimal, and center tabs can be set with leaders at the Tabs dialog box (not on the horizontal ruler). Leaders are useful in a table of contents or other document in which you want to direct the reader's eyes across the page. Figure 4.10 shows an example of leaders. Leaders can be periods (.), hyphens (-), or underlines (_). To add leaders to a tab, click the type of leader desired in the *Leader* section of the Tabs dialog box.

---

## Exercise 4.3D  Setting a Left Tab and a Right Tab with Dot Leaders        Part 4 of 5

1. With **C04-E03-Tabs.docx** open, press Ctrl + End to move the insertion point to the end of the document.
2. Type the title **CONTENTS**, center it, and apply bold formatting, as shown in Figure 4.10 on the next page.
3. Press the Enter key and then return the paragraph alignment back to left and turn off bold formatting.
4. Set a left tab and then a right tab with period leaders by completing the following steps:

   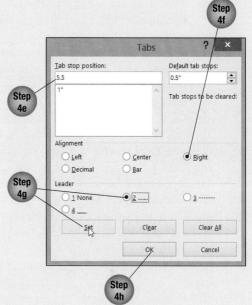

   a. Click the Paragraph group dialog box launcher.
   b. Click the Tabs button located in the lower left corner of the Paragraph dialog box.
   c. At the Tabs dialog box, make sure *Left* is selected in the *Alignment* section of the dialog box.
   d. With the insertion point positioned in the *Tab stop position* measurement box, type **1** and then click the Set button.
   e. Type **5.5** in the *Tab stop position* measurement box.
   f. Click *Right* in the *Alignment* section of the dialog box.
   g. Click *2 ......* in the *Leader* section of the dialog box and then click the Set button.
   h. Click OK to close the dialog box.
5. Type the text in columns as shown in Figure 4.10. Press the Tab key before typing each column entry and press the Enter key to end each line. (Do not use the New Line command, Shift + Enter.)
6. After typing the last column of text, press the Enter key twice and then press Ctrl + Q to remove the paragraph formatting.
7. Save **C04-E03-Tabs.docx**.

---

**Figure 4.10 Exercise 4.3D**

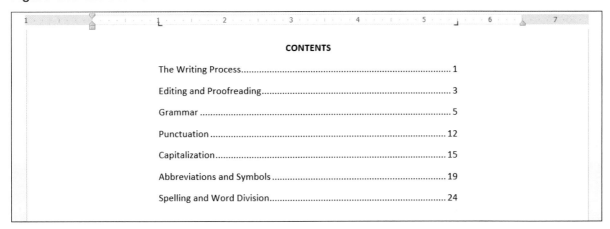

## Determining Tab Settings

When you are setting tabs for typing columns of text, try to balance the columns on the page. To do this, leave the same amount of space between columns and the same amount of space from the left margin to the first column and from the right margin to the end of text in the last column. For example, if the first column of text begins at the 1-inch mark on the horizontal ruler, you want the text in the last column to end at the 5.5-inch mark on the hotizontal ruler, which is 1 inch from the right margin. To do this, set tabs at approximate locations for each column and then type the text. After typing the text in columns, select the text and then move the tab markers on the horizontal ruler until the columns appear balanced.

In Figure 4.11, notice that the columns are set so the space from the left edge of the page to the first column of text is approximately the same as the space from the right edge of the page to the end of text in the third column. Also notice that the first and second columns of text are separated by approximately the same amount of space as the second and third columns.

---

### Exercise 4.3E  Determining Tab Settings                          Part 5 of 5

1. With **C04-E03-Tabs.docx** open, press Ctrl + End to move the insertion point to the end of the document.
2. Click the *No Spacing* style in the Styles group on the HOME tab. (This changes the line spacing to single and the spacing after paragraphs to 0 pt.)
3. Looking at the columns of text in Figure 4.11 on the next page, determine the approximate locations on the horizontal ruler to set a left tab (for the first column of text), a center tab (for the middle column of text), and a right tab (for the third column of text).
4. Type the text in columns as shown in Figure 4.11. Press the Enter key after typing each line of text. (Do not use the New Line command, Shift + Enter.)
5. Select the lines of text you just typed and then drag the tab markers on the horizontal ruler until the three columns are balanced on the page. Make sure that the first column begins at about the same distance from the left margin as the last column ends from the right margin.
6. Save, print, and then close **C04-E03-Tabs.docx**.

**Figure 4.11 Exercise 4.3E**

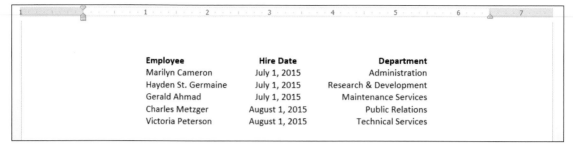

| Employee | Hire Date | Department |
|---|---|---|
| Marilyn Cameron | July 1, 2015 | Administration |
| Hayden St. Germaine | July 1, 2015 | Research & Development |
| Gerald Ahmad | July 1, 2015 | Maintenance Services |
| Charles Metzger | August 1, 2015 | Public Relations |
| Victoria Peterson | August 1, 2015 | Technical Services |

# Cutting, Copying, and Pasting Text

When editing a document, you may need to delete specific text, move it to a different location, or copy it to several locations in the document. You can complete these tasks using the Cut, Paste, and Copy buttons in the Clipboard group on the HOME tab.

## Deleting Selected Text

Cut

Word offers several methods for deleting text from a document. To delete a single character, use the Delete key or Backspace key. To delete more than a single character, select the text and then press the Delete key on the keyboard or click the Cut button in the Clipboard group. If you press the Delete key, the text is deleted permanently. (Deleted text can be restored with the Undo button on the Quick Access toolbar.) The Cut button in the Clipboard group removes the selected text from the document and inserts it in the ***Clipboard***. The Clipboard feature in Word is an area of temporary memory. The Clipboard holds text while it is being moved or copied to a new location in the document or to a different document or file.

## Cutting and Pasting Text

**Move Selected Text**
1. Select text.
2. Click Cut button.
3. Move to desired location.
4. Click Paste button.

To move text to a different location in the document, select the text, click the Cut button in the Clipboard group, position the insertion point at the location you want the text inserted, and then click the Paste button in the Clipboard group.

You can also move selected text with a shortcut menu. To do this, select the text and then position the I-beam pointer inside the selected text until it turns into an arrow pointer. Click the right mouse button (not the left button) and then click *Cut* at the shortcut menu. Position the insertion point where you want the text inserted, click the right mouse button (not the left), and then click *Paste* at the shortcut menu. Keyboard shortcuts are also available for cutting and pasting text. Use Ctrl + X to cut text and Ctrl + V to paste text.

Paste

When selected text is cut from a document and inserted in the Clipboard, it stays in the Clipboard until other text is inserted there. For this reason, you can paste text from the Clipboard more than once. For example, if you cut text and insert it in the Clipboard, you can paste this text in different locations within the document or other documents as many times as desired.

1. Open **LtrFormat.docx** and save the document with the name **C04-E04-LtrFormat**.
2. Move a paragraph by completing the following steps:
   a. Select the *Spacing* paragraph by positioning the mouse pointer in the paragraph and then triple-clicking the left mouse button.
   b. Click the Cut button in the Clipboard group on the HOME tab.

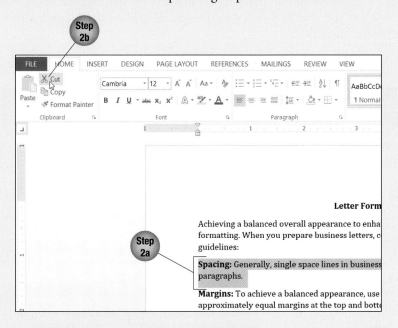

   c. Position the insertion point at the beginning of the *Justification* paragraph.
   d. Click the Paste button in the Clipboard group.

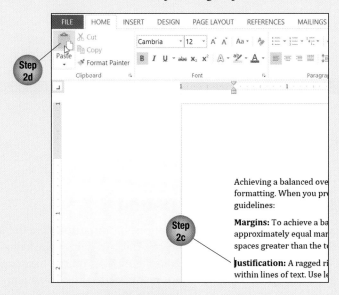

3. Complete steps similar to those in Step 2 to move the *Margins* paragraph before the *Date Line* paragraph.
4. Save **C04-E04-LtrFormat.docx**.

## Moving Text by Dragging with the Mouse

**Move Text with the Mouse**
1. Select text.
2. Position mouse pointer in selected text.
3. Hold down left mouse button and drag to desired location.

You can also use the mouse to move text. To do this, select the text to be moved and then position the I-beam pointer inside the selected text until it turns into an arrow pointer. Hold down the left mouse button and then drag in the document. The arrow pointer displays with a gray box attached and the insertion point displays as a black vertical bar. As you drag the arrow pointer, the insertion point (black vertical bar) moves in the document and the message *Move to where?* displays at the left side of the Status bar. When the insertion point is positioned in the desired location, release the mouse button. If you drag and then drop the selected text in the wrong location, immediatley click the Undo button.

---

**Exercise 4.4B**    **Moving Text by Dragging with the Mouse**      Part 2 of 3

1. With **C04-E04-LtrFormat.docx** open, use the mouse to select the *Date Line* paragraph.
2. Move the I-beam pointer inside the selected text until it becomes an arrow pointer.
3. Hold down the left mouse button, drag the arrow pointer (which displays with a small gray box attached) so that the insertion point (which displays as a black vertical bar) is positioned below the *Attention Line* paragraph, and then release the mouse button.

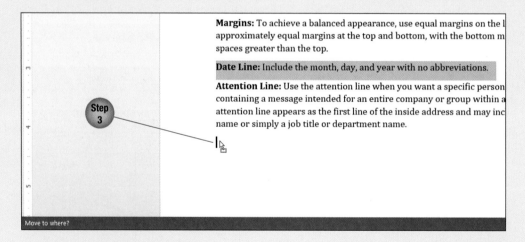

4. Deselect the text.
5. Save **C04-E04-LtrFormat.docx**.

---

## Using the Paste Options Button

Paste Options

When selected text is pasted, the Paste Options button displays in the lower right corner of the text. Click this button (or press the Ctrl key on the keyboard) and the Paste Options gallery displays, as shown in Figure 4.12 on the next page. Use buttons from this gallery to specify how you want text pasted in the document. Hover the mouse pointer over a button in the gallery and the live preview displays the text in the document as it will appear when pasted.

By default, pasted text retains the formatting of the selected text. You can choose to match the formatting of the pasted text with the formatting of the destination text or

---

**Figure 4.12 Paste Options Button Drop-Down List**

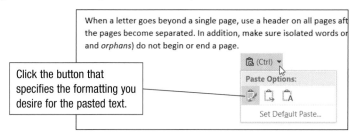

Click the button that specifies the formatting you desire for the pasted text.

to paste the text without retaining formatting. To determine the function of a button in the Paste Options gallery, hover the mouse pointer over a button and a ScreenTip displays with an explanation of the button's function along with its keyboard shortcut. For example, hover the mouse pointer over the first button in the Paste Options gallery and the ScreenTip displays with the information *Keep Source Formatting (K)*. If you click this button or press the letter *K* on the keyboard, the pasted text keeps its original formatting.

---

## Exercise 4.4C  Using the Paste Options Button                    Part 3 of 3

1. With **C04-E04-LtrFormat.docx** open, open **LtrLength.docx**.
2. Press Ctrl + A to select the entire **LtrLength** document and then click the Cut button in the Clipboard group.
3. Close **LtrLength.docx** without saving the changes.
4. Move the insertion point to the end of **C04-E04-LtrFormat.docx**.
5. Click the Paste button in the Clipboard group.
6. Click the Paste Options button that displays at the end of the paragraph and then click the second button in the Paste Options gallery (Merge Formatting [M] button). (This changes the font so it matches the font used in the paragraphs before the pasted paragraphs.)

> - Adjust side margins from three-quarters of an inch as a minimum and one and one-half inches as a maximum.
>
> - Delete space between the complimentary close and the writer's signature line, leaving enough space for the signature.
>
> - Allow long letters to go beyond a single page.
>
> When a letter goes beyond a single page, use a header on all pages after the first to avoid confusion if the pages become separated. In addition, make sure isolated words or lines of text (often called *widows* and *orphan* Paste Options: a page.
>
>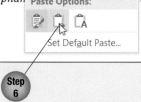

Step 6

7. Apply Green, Accent 6, Lighter 60% paragraph shading to the title of the document.
8. Save, print, and then close **C04-E04-LtrFormat.docx**.

---

## Copying and Pasting Text

**Copy Selected Text**
1. Select text.
2. Click Copy button.
3. Move to desired location.
4. Click Paste button.

Copying selected text can be useful in documents that contain repeated portions of text. Use the copy and paste features to insert duplicated text in a document instead of retyping it. After you have selected the text, copy it to a different location with the Copy and Paste buttons in the Clipboard group on the HOME tab or by using the mouse. You can also use the keyboard shortcut Ctrl + C to copy text.

Copy

---

## Exercise 4.5A  Copying Text                                   Part 1 of 2

1. Open **ManageData.docx** and save the document with the name **C04-E05-ManageData**.
2. Make the following changes to the document:
   a.  Press Ctrl + A to select the entire document.
   b.  Change the line spacing to single.
   c.  Change the spacing after paragraphs from 8 pt to 3 pt. (You will need to select *8 pt* in the measurement box and then type **3**.)
   d.  Change the font to 12-point Candara bold.
   e.  Press Ctrl + End to move the insertion point to the end of the document and then press the Enter key.
3. Copy the text in the document to the end of the document by completing the following steps:
   a.  Press Ctrl + A to select the entire document.
   b.  Click the Copy button in the Clipboard group.

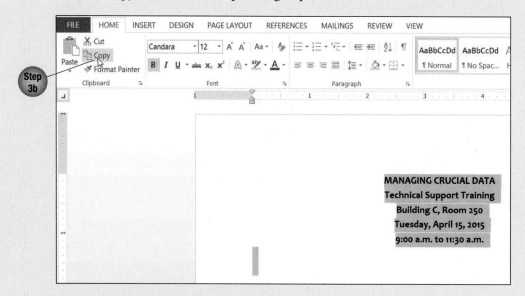

   c.  Move the insertion point to the end of the document.
   d.  Click the Paste button in the Clipboard group.

---

4. Copy the text again at the end of the document. To do this, position the insertion point at the end of the document and then click the Paste button in the Clipboard group. (This inserts a copy of the text from the Clipboard.)
5. Save **C04-E05-ManageData.docx**.

To use the mouse to copy text, select the text and then position the I-beam pointer inside the selected text until it becomes an arrow pointer. Hold down the left mouse button and hold down the Ctrl key. Drag the arrow pointer (which displays with both a small gray box and a box containing a plus [+] symbol) to the location you want to insert the copied text (making sure the insertion point, which displays as a black vertical bar, is positioned in the desired location), and then release the mouse button and then the Ctrl key.

1. With **C04-E05-ManageData.docx** open, select all of the text in the document using the mouse.
2. Move the I-beam pointer inside the selected text until it becomes an arrow pointer.
3. Hold down the Ctrl key and then the left mouse button. Drag the arrow pointer (which displays with a box with a plus [+] symbol inside) to the end of the document, release the mouse button, and then release the Ctrl key.

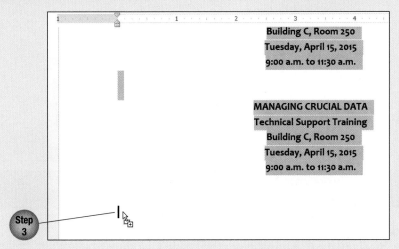

4. Deselect the text.
5. Delete some of the blank lines in the document to make all of the text fit on one page.
6. Save, print, and then close **C04-E05-ManageData.docx**.

# Using the Clipboard

**QUICK STEPS**

**Use the Clipboard**
1. Click Clipboard task pane launcher.
2. Select and copy desired text.
3. Move to desired location.
4. Click desired option in Clipboard task pane.

Use the Clipboard task pane to collect up to 24 different items and paste multiple items in various locations. To display the Clipboard task pane, click the Clipboard task pane launcher located in the lower right corner of the Clipboard group. The Clipboard task pane displays at the left side of the screen in a manner similar to that shown in Figure 4.13.

Select a section of text or an object you want to copy and then click the Copy button in the Clipboard group. Continue selecting items and clicking the Copy button. To insert an item, position the insertion point in the desired location and then click the button in the Clipboard task pane representing the item. If the copied item is text, the first 50 characters display in the Clipboard task pane list box. When all desired items are inserted, click the Clear All button to remove any remaining items. As noted previously, the Clipboard provides temporary storage. When you close Word, any items remaining in the Clipboard are deleted. To save Clipboard content permanently, save it as a separate document.

**Figure 4.13  Clipboard Task Pane**

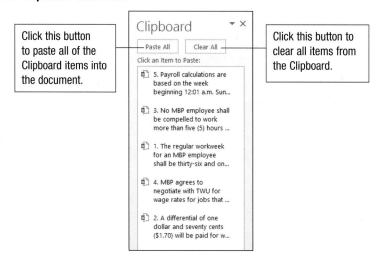

Click this button to paste all of the Clipboard items into the document.

Click this button to clear all items from the Clipboard.

---

## Exercise 4.6A  Collecting and Pasting Paragraphs of Text          Part 1 of 2

1. Open **ContItems.docx.**
2. Turn on the display of the Clipboard task pane by clicking the Clipboard task pane launcher located in the lower right corner of the Clipboard group. (If the Clipboard task pane list box contains any text, click the Clear All button located near the top of the task pane.)
3. Select paragraph 1 in the document (the *1.* is not selected) and then click the Copy button in the Clipboard group.
4. Select paragraph 3 in the document (the *3.* is not selected) and then click the Copy button in the Clipboard group.
5. Close **ContItems.docx.**

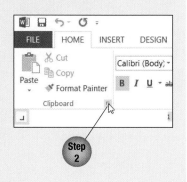

Step 2

6. Paste the paragraphs by completing the following steps:
   a. Press Ctrl + N to display a new blank document. (If the Clipboard task pane does not display, click the Clipboard task pane launcher.)
   b. Type **CONTRACT NEGOTIATION ITEMS** and center it and apply bold formatting.
   c. Press the Enter key, turn off bold formatting, and return the paragraph alignment to left.
   d. Click the Paste All button in the Clipboard task pane to paste both paragraphs in the document.
   e. Click the Clear All button in the Clipboard task pane.
7. Open **UnionAgrmnt.docx.**
8. Select and then copy each of the following paragraphs:
   a. Paragraph 2 in the *Wages* section.
   b. Paragraph 4 in the *Wages* section.
   c. Paragraph 1 in the *Workweek* section.
   d. Paragraph 3 in the *Workweek* section.
   e. Paragraph 5 in the *Workweek* section.
9. Close **UnionAgrmnt.docx.**
10. Make sure the insertion point is positioned at the end of the document and then paste the paragraphs by completing the following steps:
    a. Click the button in the Clipboard task pane representing paragraph 2. (When the paragraph is inserted in the document, the paragraph number changes to 3.)
    b. Click the button in the Clipboard task pane representing paragraph 4.
    c. Click the button in the Clipboard task pane representing paragraph 3.
    d. Click the button in the Clipboard task pane representing paragraph 5.
11. Click the Clear All button located near the top of the Clipboard task pane.
12. Close the Clipboard task pane.
13. Save the document and name it **C04-E06-FinalAgrmnt.**

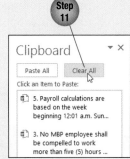

# Using Paste Special

Use options at the Paste Special dialog box, shown in Figure 4.14 on the next page, to specify the format for pasted text. Display this dialog box by clicking the Paste button arrow in the Clipboard group and then clicking *Paste Special* at the drop-down list. The options in the *As* list box vary depending on the cut or copied text or object and the source application. For example, in Exercise 4.6B, you will select and copy text from one document and paste it into another document without the formatting.

**Figure 4.14 Paste Special Dialog Box**

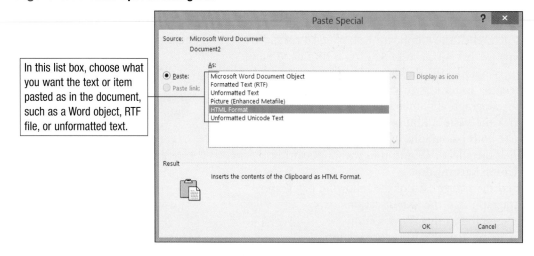

In this list box, choose what you want the text or item pasted as in the document, such as a Word object, RTF file, or unformatted text.

---

**Exercise 4.6B**  Copying Text Using the Paste Special Dialog Box          Part 2 of 2

1. With **C04-E06-FinalAgrmnt.docx** open, press Ctrl + End to move the insertion point to the end of the document and then press the Enter key once.
2. Open the document named **TeamMembers.docx**.
3. Press Ctrl + A to select the entire document and then click the Copy button.
4. Close **TeamMembers.docx**.
5. At the **C04-E06-FinalAgrmnt.docx** document, click the Paste button arrow and then click *Paste Special* at the drop-down list.
6. At the Paste Special dialog box, click *Unformatted Text* in the *As* list box.
7. Click OK to close the dialog box.

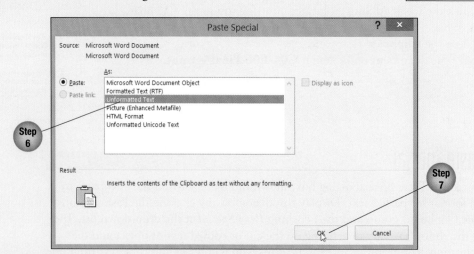

8. Select the title *Negotiating Team* and apply bold formatting to it.
9. Select the names below the title and format them as a bulleted list by clicking the Bullets button.
10. Save, print, and then close **C04-E06-FinalAgrmnt.docx**.

---

# Chapter Summary

➤ A paragraph created in Word contains an invisible frame and you can insert a border around this frame. Click the Borders button arrow to display a drop-down list of border choices.

➤ Apply shading to selected text by clicking the Shading button arrow and then clicking the desired color at the drop-down gallery.

➤ Use options at the Borders and Shading dialog box with the Borders tab selected to add a customized border to a paragraph or selected paragraphs. Use options with the Shading tab selected to add shading or a pattern to a paragraph or selected paragraphs.

➤ Use options at the Border and Shading Options dialog box to move a paragraph border closer to or farther away from the paragraph text.

➤ Use the Sort button in the Paragraph group on the HOME tab to sort text arranged in paragraphs alphabetically by the first character in each paragraph, which includes numbers, symbols, and letters.

➤ By default, tabs are set every 0.5 inch and these defaults can be changed using the horizontal ruler or with options at the Tabs dialog box.

➤ Use the Alignment button that displays above the vertical ruler to select any of the five types of tabs: left, right, center, decimal, or bar. When you set a tab on the horizontal ruler, any default tabs to the left are automatically deleted.

➤ A tab set on the horizontal ruler can be moved or deleted using the mouse.

➤ At the Tabs dialog box, you can set any of the five types of tabs at a specific measurement. You can also set left, right, center, and decimal tabs with preceding leaders and clear one tab or all tabs. Preceding leaders can be periods, hyphens, or underlines.

➤ Cut, copy, and paste text using buttons in the Clipboard group or with keyboard shortcuts.

➤ When selected text is pasted, the Paste Options button displays in the lower right corner of the text. Click the button and the Paste Options gallery displays with buttons for specifying how you want text pasted in the document.

➤ Use the Clipboard to collect up to 24 items and then paste them in various locations within one document or between several documents.

# Commands Review

| FEATURE | RIBBON TAB, GROUP | BUTTON, OPTION | KEYBOARD SHORTCUT |
|---|---|---|---|
| borders | HOME, Paragraph | ⊞ ▾ | |
| Border and Shading Options dialog box | HOME, Paragraph | ⊞ ▾ , *Borders and Shading, Options* | |
| Borders and Shading dialog box | HOME, Paragraph | ⊞ ▾ , *Borders and Shading* | |
| clear character and paragraph formatting | HOME, Font | 🄰̷ | |
| clear paragraph formatting | | | Ctrl + Q |

| FEATURE | RIBBON TAB, GROUP | BUTTON, OPTION | KEYBOARD SHORTCUT |
|---------|-------------------|----------------|-------------------|
| Clipboard task pane | HOME, Clipboard | ⬚ | |
| copy text | HOME, Clipboard | ⬚ | Ctrl + C |
| cut text | HOME, Clipboard | ✂ | Ctrl + X |
| New Line command | | | Shift + Enter |
| Paragraph dialog box | HOME, Paragraph OR PAGE LAYOUT, Paragraph | ⬚ | |
| paste text | HOME, Clipboard | 📋 | Ctrl + V |
| shading | HOME, Paragraph | 🪣 ▾ | |
| Sort Text dialog box | HOME, Paragraph | A↓Z↓ | |
| Tabs dialog box | HOME, Paragraph | ⬚ , *Tabs* | |

# *Key Points Review*

**Completion:** In the space provided at the right, indicate the correct term, symbol, or command.

1. The Borders button is located in this group on the HOME tab.

2. Use options at this dialog box with the Borders tab selected to add a customized border to a paragraph or selected paragraphs.

3. Sort text arranged in paragraphs alphabetically by the first character in each paragraph, which can be a number, symbol, or this.

4. By default, tabs are set apart from each other by this measurement.

5. This is the default tab type.

6. When setting tabs on the horizontal ruler, choose the tab type with this button.

7. Press this combination of keys to end a line with the New Line command.

8. Tabs can be set on the horizontal ruler or here.

9. This group on the HOME tab contains the Cut, Copy, and Paste buttons.

10. Use this keyboard shortcut to paste text.

11. To copy selected text with the mouse, hold down this key while dragging the selected text.

12. With this task pane, you can collect up to 24 items and then paste them in various locations in the document.

# Chapter *Assessments*

## Applying Your Skills

Demonstrate your knowledge of features learned in this chapter by completing the following assessments.

### Assessment 4.1    Format an Abbreviations Document

1. Open **Abbre.docx** and save the document with the name **C04-A01-Abbre**.
2. Type the text shown in Figure 4.15 immediately below the *R.N. Registered Nurse* text. Make sure you tab to the correct tab stop and press the Enter key to end each line.
3. Apply the Heading 1 style to the title *Abbreviations* and apply the Heading 2 style to the two headings *Personal Names* and *Academic, Professional, and Religious Designations*.
4. Apply the Lines (Simple) style set.
5. Apply the Frame theme.
6. Select the columns of text in the *Personal Names* section and then drag the left tab at the 1-inch mark on the horizontal ruler to the 0.5-inch mark. Also drag the left tab at the 3.5-inch mark on the horizontal ruler to the 1.5-inch mark.
7. Select the columns of text in the *Academic, Professional, and Religious Designations* section and then complete the following:
    a. Sort the text alphabetically.
    b. Drag the left tab at the 1-inch mark on the horizonal ruler to the 0.5-inch mark.
    c. Drag the left tab at the 3.5-inch mark on the horizontal ruler to the 1.5-inch mark.
8. Center the title *Abbreviations*.
9. Apply a top border to the title *Abbreviations* (in the same color as the bottom border) and apply Gold, Accent 2, Lighter 80% shading (sixth column, second row in the *Theme Colors* section).
10. Apply the same shading to the other two headings in the document.
11. Save, print, and then close **C04-A01-Abbre.docx**.

 **Grade It**

**Figure 4.15  Assessment 4.1**

| M.D. | Doctor of Medicine |
|------|--------------------|
| Ed.D. | Doctor of Education |
| D.D.S. | Doctor of Dental Science |
| D.D. | Doctor of Divinity |

### Assessment 4.2    Type and Format a Table of Contents

1. At a blank document, type the document shown in Figure 4.16 on the next page with the following specifications:
    a. Change the font to 11-point Cambria.
    b. Center the title and apply bold formatting as shown.
    c. Before typing the text in columns, display the Tabs dialog box and set these tabs: left tabs at the 1-inch mark and 1.5-inch mark and a right tab with period leaders at the 5.5-inch mark.
2. Save the document with the name **C04-A02-TofC**.
3. Print **C04-A02-TofC.docx**.

 **Grade It**

**START** From Scratch

4. Select the text in columns and then move the tab symbols on the horizontal ruler as follows:
   a. Delete the left tab symbol that displays at the 1.5-inch mark.
   b. Set a new left tab at the 0.5-inch mark.
   c. Move the right tab at the 5.5-inch mark to the 6-inch mark.
   d. Deselect the text.
5. Insert single-line top and bottom borders to the title *TABLE OF CONTENTS* and apply Blue, Accent 1, Lighter 60% shading (fifth column, third row in the *Theme Colors* section).
6. Save, print, and then close **C04-A02-TofC.docx**.

**Figure 4.16  Assessment 4.2**

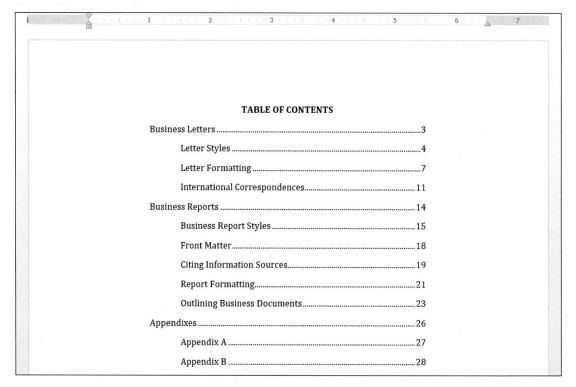

## Assessment 4.3    Type an Employee List

1. At a blank document, create the document shown in Figure 4.17 on the next page with the following specifications:
   a. Click the *No Spacing* style in the Styles group on the HOME tab.
   b. Change the font to 12-point Candara.
   c. Apply bold formatting to the text as shown in the figure.
   d. When typing the text in columns, set a left tab for the first column, a center tab for the second column, and a right tab for the third column.
   e. Apply Blue, Accent 1, Lighter 60% shading (fifth column, third row in the *Theme Colors* section) to the title *MOBILE BAY PRODUCTS* and the subtitle *New Employees*. Apply the same shading to the row containing the column headings.
   f. Apply Blue, Accent 1, Lighter 80% shading (fifth column, second row in the *Theme Colors* section) to the blank line between the subtitle and column headings and then apply the same shading to the text in the columns below the column headings.
2. Save the document and name it **C04-A03-NewEmp**.
3. Print and then close **C04-A03-NewEmp.docx**.

**Figure 4.17  Assessment 4.3**

| MOBILE BAY PRODUCTS New Employees | | |
|---|---|---|
| **Employee** | **Hire Date** | **Department** |
| Smith-Larsen, Beth | 07/06/2015 | Public Relations |
| Moranski, Adam | 06/22/2015 | Finance |
| Newton, Katherine | 07/06/2015 | Technical Support |
| Oh, Soo-Yean | 08/03/2015 | Finance |
| Crowley, Nicholas | 10/12/2015 | Technical Support |
| Espinoza, Enrique | 09/14/2015 | Training |

## Assessment 4.4  Format a Beta Testing Agreement

1. Open **BetaTestAgrmnt.docx** and save the document with the name **C04-A04-BetaTestAgrmnt**.
2. Select and then delete the paragraph that begins *Licensee agrees that Software includes*.
3. Move the paragraph that begins *This Agreement shall be governed, construed and* above the paragraph that begins *In consideration of the mutual covenants*.
4. Open **AgrmntItems.docx**.
5. Turn on the display of the Clipboard task pane. (If necessary, clear the contents.)
6. Select and then copy the first paragraph.
7. Select and then copy the second paragraph.
8. Select and then copy the third paragraph.
9. Select and then copy the fifth paragraph.
10. Close **AgrmntItems.docx**.
11. With **C04-A04-BetaTestAgrmnt.docx** open, make sure the Clipboard task pane displays.
12. Paste the paragraph that begins *Licensee shall comply with* above the paragraph that begins *In consideration of the mutual*.
13. Paste the paragraph that begins *This Agreement constitutes the entire* above the paragraph that begins *Stylus Enterprises:*.
14. Paste the paragraph that begins *IN WITNESS WHEREOF, parties hereto* above the paragraph that begins *Stylus Enterprises:*.
15. Clear all items from the Clipboard task pane and then close it.
16. Save, print, and then close **C04-A04-BetaTestAgrmnt.docx**.

# Expanding Your Skills

Explore additional feature options or use Help to learn a new skill in creating this document.

## Assessment 4.5  Write a Letter on Changing the Paste Options Default

**START** From Scratch

1. As you learned in this chapter, the Paste Options button displays when you paste text in a document. When you click the Paste Options button, the Paste Options gallery displays with three buttons. By default, the first button from the left (Keep Source Formatting) is active. You can change this default with options at the Word Options dialog box with *Advanced* selected in the left panel. Display this dialog box by pasting

text, clicking the Paste Options button, and then clicking the *Set Default Paste* option at the bottom of the Paste Options gallery. (You can also display this dialog box by clicking the FILE tab, clicking *Options*, and then clicking the *Advanced* option in the left panel.)

At a blank document, open the Word Options dialog box. Figure out how to change the default paste options when pasting text within and between documents from the default *Keep Source Formatting* to *Merge Formatting*. (Do not actually make the change.)

2. After learning how to change the paste options default, write a letter to your instructor using the personal business letter style (refer to Appendix B). Include in the letter information on the three buttons that display in the Paste Options button gallery. In addition, include steps on how to change the options for pasting within and between documents from the defaults to *Merge Formatting*.

3. Save the completed letter and name it **C04-A05-PasteOptions**.

4. Print and then close **C04-A05-PasteOptions.docx**.

## Achieving Signature Status

Take your skills to the next level by completing these more challenging assessments.

### Assessment 4.6    Create an Open House Notice

1. At a blank document, create the document shown in Figure 4.18 on the next page with the following specifications:
    - Change the font to Candara, the line spacing to single, and the spacing after paragraphs to 4 points.
    - Press the Enter key once and then type the text shown in the top box in Figure 4.18.
    - Apply character and paragraph formatting to the text and set tabs so the text in your document appears similar to that in Figure 4.18. Press the Enter key three times after typing the text *Refreshments available.*
    - Select the text in your document from the beginning of the document to the blank line below *Refreshments available.* (without including the last two blank lines in the document) and then apply the border shown in Figure 4.18 using the third line option from the bottom of the *Styles* list box, applying the Blue color in the *Standard Colors* section, and changing the width to 4 1/2 pt. Apply the Green, Accent 6, Lighter 80% paragraph shading to the text as shown in the figure.
    - After creating the first box, copy it and paste it two times in the document so your document contains a total of three boxes, as shown in Figure 4.18.
2. Save the document and name it **C04-A06-OpenHouse**.
3. Print and then close **C04-A06-Openhouse.docx**.

**Figure 4.18  Assessment 4.6**

**OPEN HOUSE**

Sponsored by the Marketing Department

Location.................................................................................. Room 100

Date ...........................................................................Friday, May 15

Time ........................................................................1:00 to 3:30 p.m.

*Refreshments available.*

---

**OPEN HOUSE**

Sponsored by the Marketing Department

Location.................................................................................. Room 100

Date ...........................................................................Friday, May 15

Time ........................................................................1:00 to 3:30 p.m.

*Refreshments available.*

---

**OPEN HOUSE**

Sponsored by the Marketing Department

Location.................................................................................. Room 100

Date ...........................................................................Friday, May 15

Time ........................................................................1:00 to 3:30 p.m.

*Refreshments available.*

## Assessment 4.7    Create and Format a Table of Contents

1. At a blank document, create the table of contents document in Figure 4.19 with the following specifications:
   - When creating the document, press the Enter key, change the spacing after paragraphs to 0 points, and then press the Enter key again.
   - Type the title and subtitle, press the Enter key three times, and then change the spacing after paragraphs back to 8 points.
   - Apply the borders and shading and set tabs as shown in the figure.
2. Save the completed document and name it **C04-A07-Ch01TofC**.
3. Print and then close **C04-A07-Ch01TofC.docx**.

**Figure 4.19  Assessment 4.7**

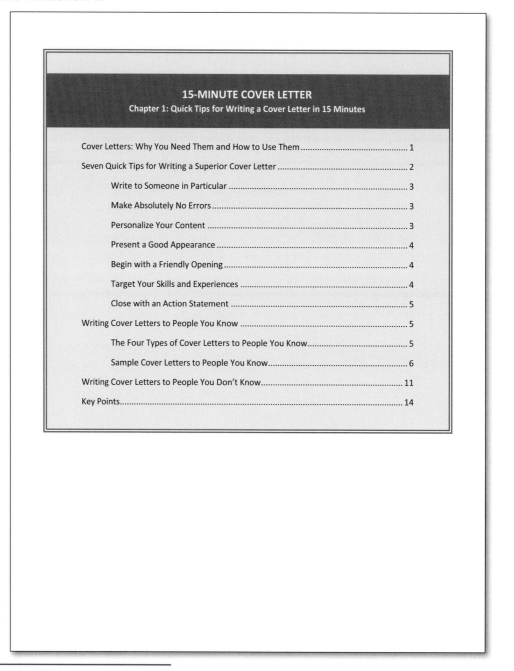

### 15-MINUTE COVER LETTER
#### Chapter 1: Quick Tips for Writing a Cover Letter in 15 Minutes

# Chapter 5

# Proofing Documents

## Performance Objectives

Upon successful completion of Chapter 5, you will be able to:

- Complete a spelling check and a grammar check on text in a document
- Create a custom dictionary and change the default dictionary
- Display document word, paragraph, and character counts
- Use the thesaurus to display synonyms and antonyms for specific words
- Use the dictionary to define specific words
- Use the translation feature to translate words from English to other languages

Microsoft Word includes proofing tools to help you create thoughtful and well-written documents. These tools include a spelling checker, grammar checker, thesaurus, and dictionary. Word also includes options for translating words from English to other languages, as well as a Mini Translator, which will translate specific words in a document. In this chapter, you will learn how to use these proofing tools and how to create a custom dictionary.

*Note: Before beginning computer exercises for this chapter, copy to your storage medium the Chapter05 folder from the CD that accompanies this textbook and then make Chapter05 the active folder.*

In this chapter, students will produce the following documents:

Exercise 5.1. C05-E01-VacAdventure.docx
Exercise 5.2. C05-E02-Interfaces.docx
Exercise 5.3. C05-E03-Photography.docx
Exercise 5.4. C05-E04-LetterFormat.docx
Exercise 5.4. C05-E04-TranslateTerms.docx

Model answers for these exercises are shown on the following pages.

**VACATION ADVENTURES – "FUN2016"**

**VACATION ADVENTURES – "FUN2016"**

Hurry and book now for one of our special FUN2016 vacation packages. Book within the next two weeks and you will be eligible for our special discount savings as well as earn a complimentary $100 gift card you can use at any of the resorts in our FUN2016 plan.

**FUN2016 Disneyland Adventure**

- Roundtrip air fare into Los Angeles, California
- Three-night hotel accommodations and hotel taxes
- Three-day Resort Ticket
- 24-hour traveler assistance

**FUN2016 Florida Adventure**

- Roundtrip airfare to Orlando, Florida
- Seven-night hotel accommodations and hotel taxes
- Four-day Resort Ticket
- Two-day Bonus Ticket
- Free transportation to some sites

**FUN2016 Cancun Adventure**

- Roundtrip airfare to Cancun, Mexico
- Five-night hotel accommodations and hotel taxes
- Free shuttle to and from the airport
- Two excursion tickets

Book a complete air/hotel FUN2016 vacation package and SAVE on fall travel! Bookings must be made by October 14, 2015, for travel January 1 through June 30, 2016 (blackout dates apply). Take advantage of these fantastic savings!

**Exercise 5.1**

C05-E01-VacAdventures.docx

**Sophisticated Natural Interfaces**

As computers continue to shrink in size and grow in power, it only makes sense that we will eventually be wearing our PCs. Wearing our computers, however, will require one critical difference in the type of interface used. Keyboards, mice, and monitors are far too cumbersome to hang from a person's body. This is where artificial intelligence (AI) comes in. Wearable computers will require a natural interface to operate. The most natural and easily foreseeable new interface would be speech-based.

Imagine a full PC system the size of a watch that weighs only a few ounces and could be strapped on a wrist. Any style and color would be available, of course. How could you control such a computer? Perhaps it would come with a tiny earpiece that users could use to hear whatever their PC had to say. Other systems might allow users to wear an acoustical system that rests on the person's inner ear. When the computer speaks, only the wearer could hear it.

**Exercise 5.2**

C05-E02-Interfaces.docx

*"Photography, as a powerful medium of expression and communication, offers an infinite variety of perception, interpretation, and execution." Ansel Adams*

## Photography

Photography is a process of picture making based on principles of light, optics, and chemistry. The word "photography" comes from the Greek words *photos* meaning "light" and *graphein* meaning "to draw." The scientist Sir John F. W. Herschel was the first to use the word in 1839. The first fixed image was taken by Joseph Nicephore Niepce in 1827. At about the same time, Louis Jacques Mande Daguerre was experimenting with methods for capturing an image. Approximately twelve years later, Daguerre was able to reduce the exposure time to less than 30 minutes, ushering in the age of modern photography. Daguerre partnered with Niepce to improve the process Niepce developed to take the first permanent photograph. Daguerre developed an effective method of photography that he named after himself—the daguerreotype. Daguerreotypes were metal sheets on which a positive silver image was affixed. He and Niepce's son sold the right for the daguerreotype to the French government.

William Henry Fox Talbot, a contemporary of Daguerre, was the inventor of the first process using a negative to make multiple prints. Another medium, tintypes, was patented by Hamilton Smith. The tintype method used a thin sheet of iron to provide a base for light-sensitive material, producing a positive image.

In 1889, George Eastman saw the potential for mass marketing and produced a newly invented film with a bendable and unbreakable base that could be rolled. Eastman sold simple cameras that contained factory-installed film. The photographer pushed a button to produce a negative and then, when the film was used up, mailed the camera back to the Kodak factory. At the factory, the film was removed from the camera and then processed and printed. The camera was reloaded with film and then returned to the owner.

Color film, introduced in 1935, was commercially available beginning in the early 1940s. Color film used the technology of dye-coupled colors in which a chemical process connected the three dye layers together to create a color image.

The Leitz Company in Germany introduced the Leica camera in 1925. It was one of the first cameras to use 35-millimeter film, which was small-sized film designed for motion pictures. The Leitz camera was light and compact and became popular with amateur and professional photographers.

## Camera Basics

Photographs are taken by letting light into a light-sensitive medium, which records the image. A camera consists of a light-tight box that stores a light-sensitive device and a lens that magnifies and focuses the image onto the light-sensitive device through a hole in the box called the aperture. A shutter opens and closes when the user presses the shutter release, exposing the film to the light. Cameras share some of the following common features:

- Light-sensitive medium to capture the image
- Lens aperture, which controls the amount of light reaching the medium
- Shutter, which opens and closes to allow light to act for a specified time
- Viewfinder or screen

Some additional camera features include a tripod screw of standard size to fit any tripod, a method for setting the distance, and a method for setting the film speed. Cameras vary in the amount of control a user has over the aperture, shutter, and distance settings, and whether these can be set automatically.

## Digital Cameras

A digital camera is a camera equipped with an electronic photosensitive sensor that stores photographs in a digital format directly in the camera's memory. The photographs can be downloaded to a computer. Some digital camera terminology includes white balance, pixel, ppi, and dpi.

### Pixels

The word *pixel* is a contraction of the term *picture element.* Digital images are made up of small squares. Each pixel in an image has a numerical value of 0 to 255 and is made up of three colors—red, green, and blue. Over 16 million combinations of colors are available with each one presenting a different color. A common method for categorizing digital cameras is in the number of pixel count. This represents the number of individual pixels that go into making each image. This number can range from approximately one million to 14 million or more. One million pixels equal one megapixel, which is written as MP. So, a 1MP digital camera has one million pixels and a 5MP camera has five million pixels.

### White Balance

White balance is the process of removing unrealistic color casts so that objects appearing white in person appear white in a photograph. Camera white balance takes into account the "color temperature" of a light source, which is the relative warmth or coolness of white light. Our eyes are good at judging what is white under different light sources; however, digital cameras often have difficulty with auto white balance. With a digital camera, the user can pick the *white balance* to suit the light source, so that white looks white, not yellow or blue. Normally, a camera automatically determines the white balance setting to use. Most digital cameras have settings for *sunlight, shade, electronic flash, fluorescent lighting,* and *tungsten lighting*. Some have a *manual* or *custom* setting where the user points the camera at a white card and lets the camera figure out what setting to use to make it white.

*"Photography can never grow up if it imitates some other medium. It has to walk alone; it has to be itself." Berenice Abbott*

**Exercise 5.4**

C05-E04-LetterFormat.docx

## Letter Formatting

Achieving a balanced overall appearance to enhance readability is the primary goal of letter formatting. When you prepare business letters, consider the following formatting guidelines:

Spacing

Generally, single space lines in business letters but double space between paragraphs

Margins

To achieve a balanced appearance, use equal margins on the left and right and approximately equal margins at the top and bottom, with the bottom margin two or three spaces greater than the top.

Justification

A ragged right edge aids readability because no unnecessary spacing appears within lines of text. Use left justification (ragged right edge) for business letters.

Date Line

Include the month, day, and year with no abbreviations.

Attention Line

Use the attention line when you want a specific person to receive a letter containing a message intended for an entire company or group within a company. The attention line appears as the first line of the inside address and may include a person's name or simply a job title or department name.

## Formato de carta

Lograr un aspecto general equilibrado para mejorar la legibilidad es el objetivo principal del formato de la carta. Cuando prepare cartas comerciales, tenga en cuenta las siguientes pautas de formato:

Espaciado

Generalmente, solo líneas de espacio en cartas comerciales pero doble espacio entre párrafos

Márgenes

Para lograr una apariencia equilibrada, utilice márgenes iguales a la izquierda y derecha y aproximadamente igual a los márgenes superior e inferior, con los espacios de margen dos o tres inferior mayores que la parte superior.

Justificación

Un borde derecho desigual ayuda legibilidad porque ningún espacio innecesario aparece dentro de las líneas de texto. Usar justificación izquierda (borde derecho desigual) para cartas comerciales.

Línea de fecha

Incluyen el mes, día y año con sin abreviaturas.

Línea de atención

Utilice la línea de atención cuando desee una persona para recibir una carta que contiene un mensaje destinado a una empresa o grupo dentro de una empresa. La línea de atención aparece como la primera línea del interior dirección y puede incluir el nombre de una persona o simplemente un título o departamento nombre de trabajo.

| TRANSLATION | | |
| --- | --- | --- |
| English to Spanish | | |
| English to French | | |
| **Term** | **Spanish** | **French** |
| Central | central | le centre |
| Data | datos | donnees |
| Directory | directorio | repertoire |
| External | externo | exterieur |

**Exercise 5.4**

C05-E04-TranslateTerms.docx

# Checking the Spelling and Grammar in a Document

As you learned in Chapter 1, Word automatically inserts a red wavy line below any word that is not contained in the spelling dictionary and inserts a blue wavy line below a possible grammar error in a sentence. Possible spelling and grammar errors can be corrected with Word's spelling checker and grammar checker tools. These and other tools are available in the Proofing group on the REVIEW tab.

The spelling checker in Word finds misspelled words and offers replacement words. It also finds duplicate words and irregular capitalizations. When you spell check a document, the spelling checker compares the words in your document to the words in its dictionary. If the spelling checker finds a match, it passes over the word. If it does not find a match, the spelling checker stops and selects the following:

- a misspelled word, when the misspelling does not match another word that exists in the dictionary
- typographical errors (such as transposed letters)
- double word occurrences (such as *and and*)
- irregular capitalizations
- some proper nouns, such as names
- jargon and some technical terms

The grammar checker searches a document for errors in grammar, punctuation, and word usage. Word's spelling checker and grammar checker can help you produce a well-written document but they do not replace the need for proofreading.

Before checking the spelling or grammar of a document, first save the document if you are working in it or open a saved document. Begin to check the spelling and grammar by clicking the REVIEW tab and then clicking the Spelling and Grammar button. (You can also use the keyboard shortcut by pressing key F7.) If Word detects a possible spelling error, the text containing the error is selected and the Spelling task pane displays, similar to the one shown in Figure 5.1 on the next page. Possible corrections for the word display in the Spelling task pane list box, along with buttons you can click to change or ignore the spelling error, as described in Table 5.1. The Spelling task pane also displays a definition of the selected word in the task pane list box.

**QUICK STEPS**

**Check Spelling and Grammar**
1. Click REVIEW tab.
2. Click Spelling & Grammar button.
3. Change or ignore error.
4. Click OK.

Spelling & Grammar

**Table 5.1 Spelling Task Pane and Grammar Task Pane Buttons**

| *Button* | *Function* |
|---|---|
| Ignore | During spell checking, skips that occurrence of the word; during grammar checking, leaves currently selected text as written. |
| Ignore All | During spell checking, skips that occurrence of the word and all other occurrences of the word in the document. |
| Add | Adds the selected word to the main spell check dictionary. |
| Delete | Deletes the currently selected word(s). |
| Change | Replaces the selected word with the selected word in the task pane list box. |
| Change All | Replaces the selected word and all other occurrences of it with a word in the task pane list box. |

**Figure 5.1 Spelling Task Pane with Error Selected**

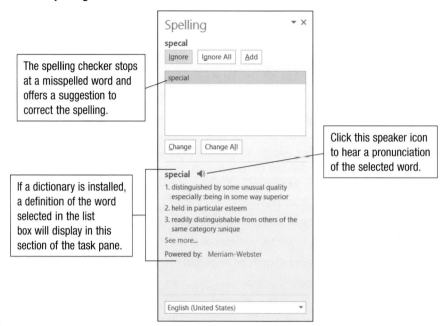

The spelling checker stops at a misspelled word and offers a suggestion to correct the spelling.

If a dictionary is installed, a definition of the word selected in the list box will display in this section of the task pane.

Click this speaker icon to hear a pronunciation of the selected word.

If Word detects a possible grammar error, the word(s) or sentence is selected and possible corrections display in the Grammar task pane. Depending on the error selected, some of the buttons described in Table 5.1 may display in the Grammar task pane. A description of the grammar rule with suggestions on how to correct the grammar error may display in the lower half of the Grammar task pane. Choose to ignore or change an error found by the grammar checker.

## Editing While Spelling and Grammar Checking

When checking the spelling or grammar in a document, you can temporarily leave the Spelling task pane or Grammar task pane, make corrections in the document, and then resume spelling or grammar checking. Click in the document outside the task pane, make the changes or edits, and then click the Resume button in the task pane by clicking the Change, Change All, Ignore, or Ignore All buttons.

## Using the Pronunciation Feature

The Spelling task pane and Grammar task pane include a pronunciation feature that will pronounce the word currently selected in the task pane list box. To hear the word pronounced, click the speaker icon located to the right of the word below the task pane list box. For this feature to work, you must have your computer's speakers turned on.

**Change Spelling Options**
1. Click FILE tab.
2. Click *Options.*
3. Click *Proofing.*
4. Specify options.
5. Click OK.

## Customizing Spell Checking

Customize the spell checker with options at the Word Options dialog box with the *Proofing* option selected, as shown in Figure 5.2 on the next page. Display this dialog box by clicking the FILE tab and then clicking *Options.* At the Word Options dialog box, click *Proofing* in the left panel. Use options at this dialog box to customize spell checking by identifying what you want the spelling checker to review or ignore. You can also create or edit a custom dictionary.

**Figure 5.2 Word Options Dialog Box with Proofing Selected**

Click *Proofing* to display options for checking spelling and grammar.

Insert or remove a check mark from the options in this section that you want active or inactive.

Click this button to create a custom dictionary.

You can change this option from *Grammar Only* to *Grammar & Style*.

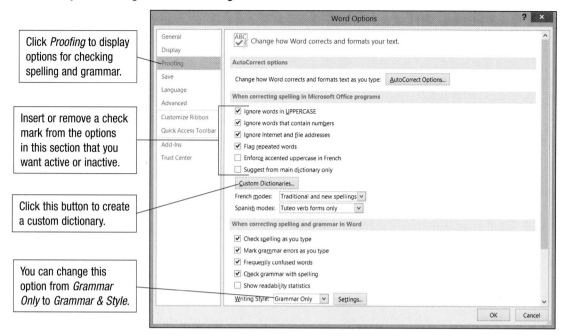

---

## Exercise 5.1   Spell Checking a Document with Words in Uppercase and with Numbers   Part 1 of 1

1. Open **VacAdventures.docx** and save the document with the name **C05-E01-VacAdventure**.
2. Check spell checking options by completing the following steps:
   a. Click the FILE tab.
   b. Click *Options*.
   c. At the Word Options dialog box, click *Proofing* in the left panel.
   d. Make sure the *Ignore words in UPPERCASE* check box and *Ignore words that contain numbers* check box each contains a check mark.
   e. Click OK to close the dialog box.

   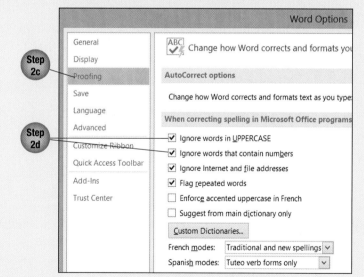

   Step 2c

   Step 2d

3. Complete a spelling check on the document by completing the following steps:
   a. Click the REVIEW tab.
   b. Click the Spelling & Grammar button in the Proofing group.

c. The spelling checker selects the word *specal* and displays the Spelling task pane. The proper spelling, *special*, is selected in the Spelling task pane list box and a definition of *special* displays below the list box. Click the Change button (or Change All button) to accept the proper spelling.

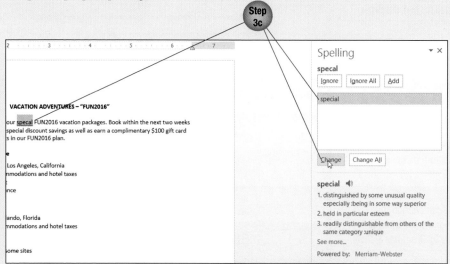

d. The spelling checker selects the word *elagible* and displays the proper spelling, *eligible*, in the task pane list box. Listen to the pronunciation of the word *eligible* by clicking the speaker icon that displays at the right of the word *eligible* located below the list box. (You must have your computer's speakers turned on to hear the pronunciation.)

e. With the proper spelling of *eligible* selected in the task pane list box, click the Change button.

f. The spelling checker selects the word *itnte*. The proper spelling of *into* is not selected in the task pane list box but it is one of the words suggested. Click *into* in the task pane list box and then click the Change button.

g. The spelling checker selects *Florada*. The proper spelling is selected in the task pane list box so click the Change button.

h. The spelling checker selects *accomodations*. The proper spelling is selected in the task pane list box so click the Change button.

i. When the message displays telling you that the spelling and grammar check is complete, click the OK button.

4. Save, print, and then close **C05-E01-VacAdventures.docx**.

# Checking the Grammar in a Document

When performing a spelling and grammar check, Word stops and highlights certain text that may contain a grammatical error and displays the Grammar task pane, similar to what is shown in Figure 5.3. Like the spelling checker, the grammar checker does not find every error in a document and may stop at correct sentences. Using the grammar checker can help you create well-written documents, but does not replace the need for proofreading.

If the grammar checker detects a possible grammatical error in the document, Word selects the sentence containing the possible error and inserts a possible correction in the Grammar task pane list box. The Grammar task pane may also display information on the grammar rule that may have been broken and offer possible methods for correcting the error. You can choose to ignore or change errors found by the grammar checker by clicking the Change, Change All, Ignore, or Ignore All buttons.

**Figure 5.3  Grammar Task Pane with Grammar Error Selected**

The grammar checker selects a sentence or word that contains a possible grammatical error and offers a suggestion to correct it.

This section of the Grammar task pane displays information about the grammar error.

---

**Exercise 5.2A**   Checking Grammar in a Document                     Part 1 of 3

1. Open **Interfaces.docx** and save the document with the name **C05-E02-Interfaces**.
2. Check the grammar in the document by completing the following steps:
   a. Click the REVIEW tab.
   b. Click the Spelling & Grammar button in the Proofing group.
   c. The grammar checker selects the sentence that begins *As computer's continue to shrink in size* and displays *computers* in the Grammar task pane list box. Read the information on plural and possessive forms that displays below the list box in the task pane.
   d. Click the Change button to replace *computer's* with *computers*.
   e. The grammar checker selects *to* in the document and displays *too* in the task pane. Read the definitions of *to* and *too* and then click the Change button.

f.  The grammar checker selects *there* in the document and displays *their* in the list box. Read the definitions of *there* and *their* in the task pane and then click the Change button.

g.  At the message telling you that the spelling and grammar check is complete, click OK.

3.  Save **C05-E02-Interfaces.docx**.

## Changing Grammar Checking Options

**Change Grammar Checking Options**
1. Click FILE tab.
2. Click *Options*.
3. Click *Proofing*.
4. Specify options.
5. Click OK.

Customize the type of grammar checking you perform on a document with options in the *When correcting spelling and grammar in Word* section of the Word Options dialog box with *Proofing* selected (see Figure 5.2 on page 135). Remove the check mark from those options that you do not want active in checking a document.

By default, the grammar checker checks only the grammar in a document. The *Writing Style* option at the Word Options dialog box with *Proofing* selected has a default setting of *Grammar Only*. You can change this default setting to *Grammar and Style*. To determine what style issues the grammar checker will select, click the Settings button to display the Grammar Settings dialog box with grammar and style options available. Insert check marks for those options you want active and remove the check marks from those options you want inactive during a grammar check.

1. With **C05-E02-Interfaces.docx** open, change the grammar settings by completing the following steps:
   a. Click the FILE tab.
   b. Click *Options*.
   c. At the Word Options dialog box, click *Proofing* in the left panel.
   d. Click the down-pointing arrow at the right side of the *Writing Style* option box and then click *Grammar & Style* at the drop-down list.
   e. Click the Recheck Document button.
   f. At the message that displays, click Yes.
   g. Click OK to close the Word Options dialog box.

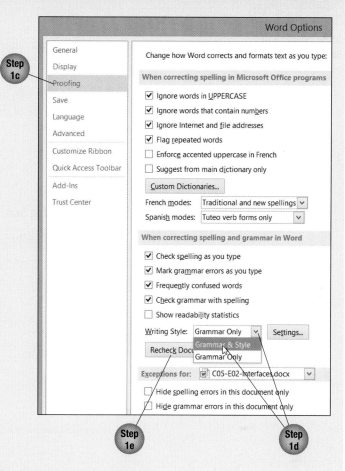

2. Complete a grammar and style check on the document by completing the following steps:
   a. Press Ctrl + Home to move the insertion point to the beginning of the document.
   b. Make sure the REVIEW tab is selected.
   c. Click the Spelling & Grammar button in the Proofing group.
   d. When the grammar checker selects the sentence that begins *Imagine a full PC system the size*, read the information on number agreement that displays below the task pane list box. Click *on a wrist* in the task pane list box and then click the Change button.

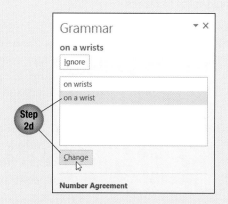

   e. When the grammar checker selects the same sentence again, read the information on verb use that displays below the task pane list box and then click the Ignore button.
   f. When the grammar checker selects the sentence that begins *When the computer speaks only*, read the information on comma use that displays below the task pane list box. Click the Change button to insert a comma after the word *speaks*.
   g. At the message telling you that the spelling and grammar check is complete, click OK.
3. Save and then print **C05-E02-Interfaces.docx**.

## Displaying Readability Statistics

**Show Readability Statistics**
1. Click FILE tab.
2. Click *Options*.
3. Click *Proofing*.
4. Click *Show readability statistics* check box.
5. Click OK.
6. Complete spelling and grammar check.

When completing a spelling and grammar check, you can display readability statistics about the document. Figure 5.4 shows the dialog box and readability statistics for **C05-E02-Interfaces.docx**.

Readability statistics include word, character, paragraph, and sentence count; average number of sentences per paragraph, words per sentence, and characters per word; and readability information such as the percentage of passive sentences in the document, the Flesch Reading Ease score, and the Flesch-Kincaid grade-level rating, which are described in Table 5.2. Control the display of readability statistics with the *Show readability statistics* check box in the Word Options dialog box with *Proofing* selected.

### Figure 5.4 Readability Statistics Dialog Box

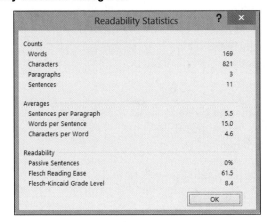

### Table 5.2 Readability Statistics

| | |
|---|---|
| **Flesch Reading Ease** | This score is based on the average number of syllables per word and average number of words per sentence. The higher the score, the greater the number of people who will be able to understand the text in the document. Standard writing generally scores in the 60–70 range. |
| **Flesch-Kincaid Grade Level** | This rating is based on the average number of syllables per word and average number of words per sentence. The score indicates a grade level. Standard writing is generally written at the seventh- or eighth-grade level. |

1. With **C05-E02-Interfaces.docx** open, display readability statistics for the document by completing the following steps:

   a. Click the FILE tab and then click *Options*.

   b. At the Word Options dialog box, click *Proofing* in the left panel.

   c. Click the *Show readability statistics* check box to insert a check mark.

   d. Click OK to close the Word Options dialog box.

   e. At the document, make sure the REVIEW tab is selected and then click the Spelling & Grammar button.

   f. Look at the readability statistics that display in the Readability Statistics dialog box and then click OK to close the dialog box.

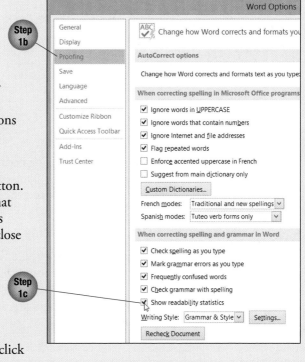

2. Change the grammar options back to the default settings by completing the following steps:

   a. Click the FILE tab and then click *Options*.

   b. At the Word Options dialog box, click *Proofing* in the left panel.

   c. Click the *Show readability statistics* check box to remove the check mark.

   d. Click the down-pointing arrow at the right side of the *Writing Style* option box and then click *Grammar Only* at the drop-down list.

   e. Click OK to close the Word Options dialog box.

3. Save and then close **C05-E02-Interfaces.docx**.

# Creating a Custom Dictionary

When completing a spelling check on a document, Word uses the RoamingCustom.dic custom dictionary by default. You can add or remove words from this default dictionary. In a multiple-user environment, you might also consider adding your own custom dictionary and then selecting it as the default. Using this feature, multiple users can create their own dictionaries to use when spell checking documents.

To create a custom dictionary, display the Word Options dialog box with *Proofing* selected and then click the Custom Dictionaries button. This displays the Custom Dictionaries dialog box, shown in Figure 5.5 on the next page. At this dialog box, click the New button to display the Create Custom Dictionary dialog box. Type a name for the dictionary in the *File name* text box and then press the Enter key. The new dictionary name will display in the *Dictionary List* box in the Custom Dictionaries dialog box. You can use more than one dictionary when spell checking a document. Insert a check mark in the check box next to the name of each dictionary you want to use.

**QUICK STEPS**

**Create a Custom Dictionary**
1. Click FILE tab.
2. Click *Options*.
3. Click *Proofing*.
4. Click Custom Dictionaries button.
5. Click New button.
6. Type name for dictionary; press Enter.

**Figure 5.5 Custom Dictionaries Dialog Box**

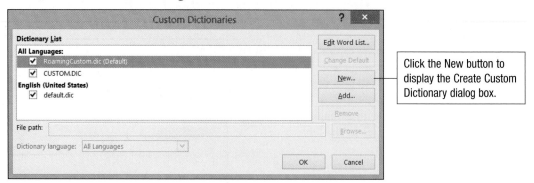

Click the New button to display the Create Custom Dictionary dialog box.

**QUICK STEPS**

**Remove a Custom Dictionary**
1. Click FILE tab.
2. Click *Options*.
3. Click *Proofing*.
4. Click Custom Dictionaries button.
5. Click custom dictionary name.
6. Click Remove.
7. Click OK.

## Changing the Default Dictionary

At the Custom Dictionaries dialog box, the name of the default dictionary displays in the *Dictionary List* box followed by *(Default)*. Change this default by clicking the desired dictionary name in the list box and then clicking the Change Default button.

## Removing a Dictionary

Remove a custom dictionary with the Remove button at the Custom Dictionaries dialog box. To do this, display the Custom Dictionaries dialog box, click the dictionary name in the *Dictionary List* box, and then click the Remove button. You are not prompted to confirm the removal of the dictionary, so make sure you select the correct name before clicking the Remove button.

---

**Exercise 5.3A**  Creating a Custom Dictionary and Changing the Default Dictionary       Part 1 of 4

1. Open **Photography.docx**, notice the red wavy lines indicating words that are not recognized by the spelling checker (that is, words not in the RoamingCustom.dic dictionary), and then close the document.
2. At a blank document, create a custom dictionary, add words to it, and then change the default dictionary by completing the following steps:
   a. Click the FILE tab and then click *Options*.
   b. At the Word Options dialog box, click *Proofing* in the left panel.
   c. Click the Custom Dictionaries button.
   d. At the Custom Dictionaries dialog box, click the New button.
   e. At the Create Custom Dictionary dialog box, type your first and last names (without a space between them) in the *File name* text box and then press the Enter key.

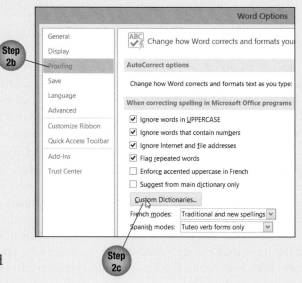

Step 2b

Step 2c

f. At the Custom Dictionaries dialog box, add a word to your dictionary by completing the following steps:
   1) Click your dictionary name in the *Dictionary List* box.
   2) Click the Edit Word List button.

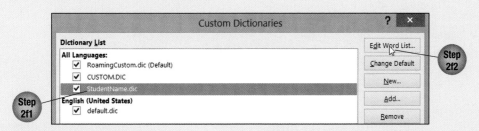

   3) At your custom dictionary dialog box, type **graphein** in the *Word(s)* text box.
   4) Click the Add button.
g. Complete the steps outlined in Steps 2f3 and 2f4 to add the following words:
   Nicephore
   Niepce
   Mande
   Leitz
   ppi
h. When all of the words have been added, click the OK button to close the dialog box.
i. At the Custom Dictionaries dialog box with your dictionary name selected in the *Dictionary List* box, click the Change Default button. (Notice that the word *(Default)* displays after the name of your custom dictionary.)

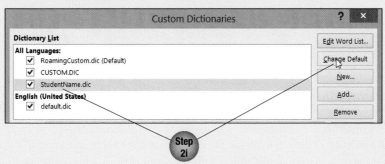

j. Click OK to close the Custom Dictionaries dialog box.
k. Click OK to close the Word Options dialog box.
3. Open **Photography.docx** and then save the document and name it **C05-E03-Photography**.
4. Complete a spelling and grammar check on your document. (The spelling checker will not stop at the words you added to your custom dictionary except for the word *Niepce's*.)
5. Save and then print **C05-E03-Photography.docx**.
6. Change the default dictionary and then remove your custom dictionary by completing the following steps:
   a. Click the FILE tab and then click *Options*.
   b. At the Word Options dialog box, click *Proofing* in the left panel.

c. Click the Custom Dictionaries button.
d. At the Custom Dictionaries dialog box, click *RoamingCustom.dic* in the *Dictionary List* box.
e. Click the Change Default button. (This changes the default back to the *Roaming Custom.dic* dictionary.)
f. Click your dictionary name in the *Dictionary List* box.
g. Click the Remove button.
h. Click OK to close the Custom Dictionaries dialog box.
i. Click OK to close the Word Options dialog box.

## Displaying Word Count

**QUICK STEPS**

**Display the Word Count Dialog Box**
Click word count section of Status bar.
OR
1. Click REVIEW tab.
2. Click Word Count button.

Word counts the words as you type them and displays the total number of words in your document in the Status bar. If you want to display more information—such as the number of pages, paragraphs, and lines—display the Word Count dialog box, as shown in Figure 5.6. Display this dialog box by clicking the word count section of the Status bar or by clicking the REVIEW tab and then clicking the Word Count button in the Proofing group. If you want to count the words in only a portion of the document, select the text first.

Word Count

**Figure 5.6 Word Count Dialog Box**

## Using the Thesaurus

**QUICK STEPS**

**Use the Thesaurus**
1. Click REVIEW tab.
2. Click Thesaurus button.
3. Type word in search text box.
4. Press Enter.

Word offers a Thesaurus feature for finding synonyms, antonyms, and related words for a particular word. Synonyms are words that have the same or nearly the same meaning and antonyms are words with opposite meanings. The thesaurus can help you to improve the clarity of business documents.

To use the thesaurus, click the REVIEW tab and then click the Thesaurus button in the Proofing group. (You can also use the keyboard shortcut Shift +F7.) This displays the Thesaurus task pane. Click in the search text box located near the top of the Thesaurus task pane, type the word for which you want to find synonyms and antonyms, and then press the Enter key or click the Start searching button (which is labeled with a magnifying glass). This causes a list of synonyms and antonyms to display in the task pane list box. Figure 5.7 on the next page shows the Thesaurus task pane with synonyms for the word *principle* displayed.

Thesaurus

**Figure 5.7  Thesaurus Task Pane**

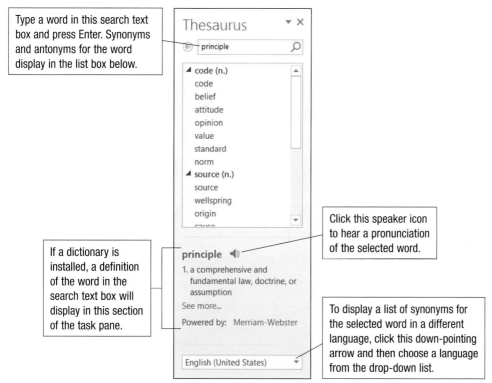

Type a word in this search text box and press Enter. Synonyms and antonyms for the word display in the list box below.

Thesaurus

principle

◢ code (n.)
  code
  belief
  attitude
  opinion
  value
  standard
  norm
◢ source (n.)
  source
  wellspring
  origin

Click this speaker icon to hear a pronunciation of the selected word.

If a dictionary is installed, a definition of the word in the search text box will display in this section of the task pane.

**principle** 🔊
1. a comprehensive and fundamental law, doctrine, or assumption
See more...
Powered by:  Merriam-Webster

To display a list of synonyms for the selected word in a different language, click this down-pointing arrow and then choose a language from the drop-down list.

English (United States)

Depending on the word you are looking up, the words in the Thesaurus task pane list box may be followed by *(n.)* for *noun*, *(adj.)* for *adjective*, or *(adv.)* for *adverb*. Antonyms may display for some words and appear at the end of the list of related synonyms; each antonym is followed by the word *(Antonym)*. If you have a dictionary installed on your computer, a definition of the selected word will display below the task pane list box.

The thesaurus provides synonyms for the selected word along with a list of related synonyms. For example, in the task pane list box shown in Figure 5.7, the main synonym *code* displays for *principle* and is preceded by a collapse triangle (right-and-down-pointing triangle). The collapse triangle indicates that the list of related synonyms is displayed. Click the collapse triangle and the list of related synonyms is removed from the task pane list box and the collapse triangle changes to an expand triangle (right-pointing triangle). Click a word in the Thesaurus task pane list box to see synonyms for that word.

As you look up synonyms and antonyms for various words, you can display the list for a previous word by clicking the Back button (left-pointing arrow) located to the left of the search text box. Click the down-pointing triangle located to the left of the Close button in the upper right corner of the task pane and a drop-down list displays with options for moving, sizing, and closing the task pane.

Replace the selected word in the document with a word in the Thesaurus task pane by hovering the mouse pointer over the word in the task pane until a down-pointing arrow displays. Click the down-pointing arrow and then click *Insert* at the drop-down list.

Like the Spelling task pane and Grammar task pane, the Thesaurus task pane includes a pronunciation feature that will pronounce the word currently selected. To hear the word pronounced, click the speaker icon located to the right of the word below the task pane list box. The Thesaurus task pane also includes a language option for displaying synonyms of the selected word in a different language. To use this feature, click the down-pointing arrow at the right side of the option box located at the bottom of the task pane and then click the desired language at the drop-down list.

## Exercise 5.3B  Displaying Word Count and Using the Thesaurus    Part 2 of 4

1. With **C05-E03-Photography.docx** open, click the word count section of the Status bar.
2. After reading the statistics in the Word Count dialog box, click the Close button.
3. Redisplay the Word Count dialog box by clicking the REVIEW tab and then clicking the Word Count button in the Proofing group.

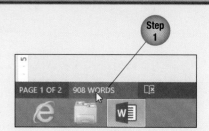

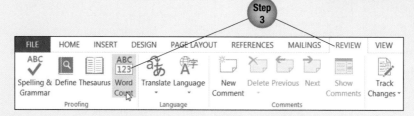

4. Click the Close button to close the Word Count dialog box.
5. Change the word *method* in the first paragraph to *process* using the thesaurus by completing the following steps:
   a. Click on any character in the word *method* located in the first sentence of the first paragraph.
   b. Click the REVIEW tab.
   c. Click the Thesaurus button in the Proofing group.
   d. At the Thesaurus task pane, hover the mouse pointer over the synonym *process*, click the down-pointing arrow that displays at the right of the word, and then click *Insert* at the drop-down list.

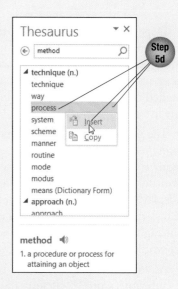

6. Find synonyms for the word *obtained* by completing the following steps:
   a. Click on any character in the word *obtained* located in the fourth sentence in the first paragraph.
   b. Click the Thesaurus button in the Proofing group.
   c. Hover the mouse pointer over the synonym *taken* in the Thesaurus task pane list box, click the down-pointing arrow at the right of the word, and then click *Insert* at the drop-down list.
7. Hear a pronunciation of the word *daguerreotype* by completing the following steps:
   a. Click on any character in the word *daguerreotype* located in the eighth sentence in the first paragraph.
   b. Click the Thesaurus button in the Proofing group.
   c. Click the speaker icon next to *daguerreotype* located below the task pane list box.
8. Close the Thesaurus task pane by clicking the Close button located in the upper right corner of the task pane.
9. Save **C05-E03-Photography.docx**.

Another method of displaying synonyms for a word is to use a shortcut menu. To do this, position the mouse pointer on the word and then click the right mouse button (not the left mouse button). At the shortcut menu that displays, point to *Synonyms* and then click the desired synonym at the side menu. Click the *Thesaurus* option located near the bottom of the side menu to display synonyms and antonyms for the word in the Thesaurus task pane.

## Exercise 5.3C  Replacing Synonyms Using a Shortcut Menu  Part 3 of 4

1. With **C05-E03-Photography.docx** open, position the mouse pointer on the word *flexible* located in the first sentence in the third paragraph of text.
2. Click the *right* mouse button.
3. At the shortcut menu that displays, point to *Synonyms* and then click *bendable* at the side menu.
4. Save **C05-E03-Photography.docx**.

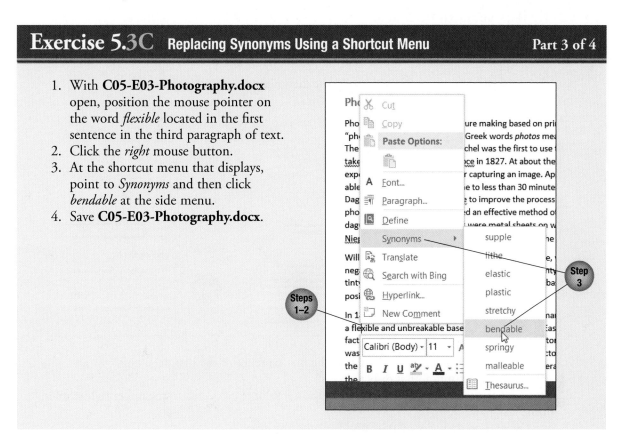

# Defining Words

If a dictionary is installed on your computer, the Thesaurus task pane displays a definition of the selected word. Another method for displaying the definition of a word is to click the Define button in the Proofing group on the REVIEW tab. A dictionary task pane opens at the right side of the screen with a definition of the word. If your computer does not have a dictionary installed, a list of dictionaries that you can download will display. Click the dictionary you want to use and then click *Download*.

Define

*Note: A dictionary must be installed on your computer to complete this project.*

1. With **C05-E03-Photography.docx** open, display definitions for words by completing the following steps:
   a. Click on any character in the word *Photography* at the beginning of the first paragraph of text.
   b. Make sure the REVIEW tab is active and then click the Define button in the Proofing group.
   c. Read the definition that displays in the dictionary task pane.

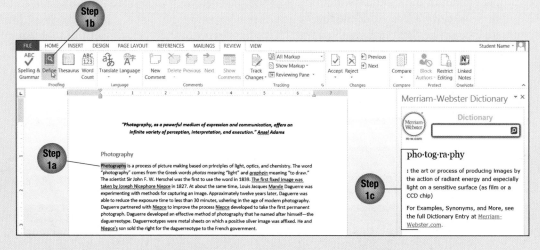

   d. Select the word *principles* located in the first sentence of the first paragraph.
   e. Read the definition that displays.
2. Close the dictionary task pane by clicking the Close button located in the upper right corner of the task pane.
3. Save, print, and then close **C05-E03-Photography.docx**.

# Translating Text to and from Different Languages

Word provides features for translating text from one language to another. The Thesaurus task pane provides one method for translating words. The Translate button in the Language group on the REVIEW tab provides additional translation methods. Click the Translate button and a drop-down list displays with options for translating the entire document or selected text and for turning on the Mini Translator.

Click the first option, *Translate Document*, and Word sends your document for translation by Microsoft Translator. When you click the option, a message displays telling you that Word is about to send your document for translation in unencrypted HTML (hypertext markup language) format and asking if you want to continue. To continue to the translator, click the Send button.

Click the second option, *Translate Selected Text*, and Microsoft Translator will translate the selected text in a document and insert the translation in the Research task pane. The Research task pane displays at the right side of the screen and includes options for translating text to and from different languages.

Click the third option, *Mini Translator*, to turn on this feature. With the Mini Translator turned on, point to a word or select a phrase in your document and the translation of the text displays in a box above the text. To turn off the Mini Translator, click the *Mini Translator* option at the Translate button drop-down list. When the Mini Translator is turned on, the icon positioned to the left of the Mini Translator option displays with a light blue background.

Use the fourth option from the Translate button, *Choose Translation Language*, to specify the language from which you want to translate and the language to which you want to translate. When you click the option, the Translation Language Options dialog box displays, as shown in Figure 5.8. At this dialog box, specify the translation language and whether you want to translate the entire document or turn on the Mini Translator. You may need to specify languages in the *Translate from* and *Translate to* option boxes before using the Mini Translator.

## Preparing Documents for Translation

The translation features in Word are considered machine translations because a machine rather than a person is translating text from one language to another. While machine translation is useful for basic information, important or sensitive information should be translated by a human to ensure that the translation reflects the full meaning of the information.

When using Word's translation features, consider the following content standards and guidelines when translating information to reduce confusion or errors and optimize the translation:

- Use standard, formal language
- Use proper punctuation and grammar
- Spell words correctly
- Avoid abbreviations and acronyms
- Avoid using slang, colloquialisms, and idioms
- Avoid ambiguities and vague references
- Write sentences that are direct and express only one idea
- Use articles (such as *the*) in sentences whenever possible
- Repeat the noun in a sentence instead of using a pronoun
- Apply predesigned heading styles to headings in a document

**Translate Selected Text**
1. Select text.
2. Click REVIEW tab.
3. Click Translate button.
4. Click *Translate Selected Text*.

**Turn on the Mini Translator**
1. Click REVIEW tab.
2. Click Translate button.
3. Click *Mini Translator*.

Translate

**Figure 5.8 Translation Language Options Dialog Box**

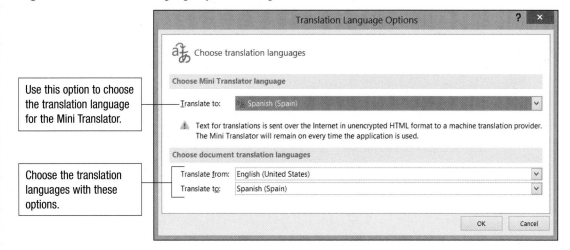

Use this option to choose the translation language for the Mini Translator.

Choose the translation languages with these options.

*Note: Check with your instructor before completing this exercise.*

1. Open **LetterFormat.docx** and save the document with the name **C05-E04-LetterFormat**.
2. Change the translation language to Spanish by completing the following steps:
   a. Click the REVIEW tab.
   b. Click the Translate button in the Language group and then click the *Choose Translation Language* option at the drop-down list.

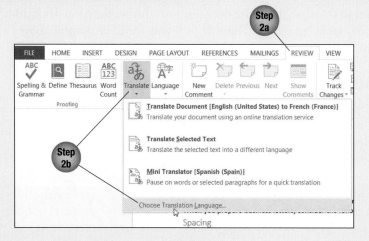

   c. At the Translation Language Options dialog box, make sure that *English (United States)* displays in the *Translate from* option box.
   d. Click the down-pointing arrow at the right of the *Translate to* option box in the *Choose document translation languages* section and then click *Spanish (Spain)* at the drop-down list. (Skip this step if *Spanish (Spain)* is already selected.)
   e. Click OK to close the dialog box.

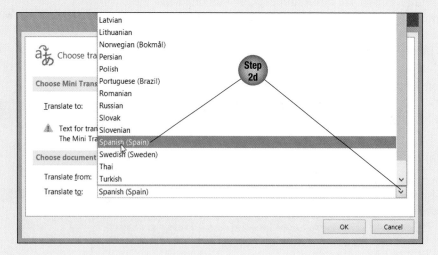

3. Translate the entire document to Spanish by completing the following steps:
   a. Click the Translate button and then click the *Translate Document [English (United States) to Spanish (Spain)]* option.

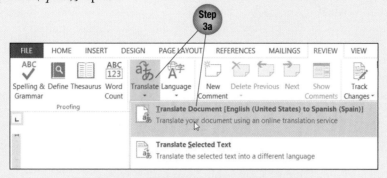

   b. At the message telling you that Word is about to send the document for translation over the Internet in unencrypted HTML format, click the Send button.
   c. In a few moments, the Microsoft Translator window will open. (If the window does not display, check the Status bar and click the button on the bar representing the translator.)
   d. Select the translated text.
   e. Press Ctrl + C to copy the text.
   f. Close the Microsoft Translator window.
   g. At the **C05-E04-LetterFormat.docx** document, press Ctrl + End to move the insertion point to the end of the document and then press Ctrl + V to insert the copied text. (The translated text may vary slightly from what displays in the model answer at the beginning of the chapter because the translation feature is continuously updated.)
4. Save, print, and then close **C05-E04-LetterFormat.docx**.
5. Open **TranslateTerms.docx** and save the document with the name **C05-E04-TranslateTerms**.
6. Translate the word *central* into Spanish by completing the following steps:
   a. Click the REVIEW tab.
   b. Click the Translate button and then click the *Choose Translation Language* option at the drop-down list.
   c. At the Translation Language Options dialog box, click the down-pointing arrow at the right of the *Translate to* option box in the *Choose Mini Translator language* section and then click *Spanish (Spain)* at the drop-down list. (Skip this step if *Spanish (Spain)* is already selected.)
   d. Click OK to close the dialog box.
   e. Click the Translate button and then click *Mini Translator [Spanish (Spain)]* at the drop-down list. (This turns on the Mini Translator.)

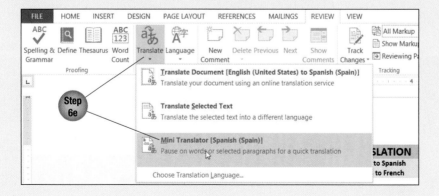

f. Hover the mouse pointer over the word *central* in the table. (The mini toolbar displays dimmed above the word.)

g. Move the mouse pointer to the Mini Translator and then choose one of the Spanish terms and type it in the *Spanish* column.

h. Complete steps similar to those in Steps 6f and 6g to display Spanish translations for the remaining terms. For each term, type the corresponding Spanish term in the appropriate location in the table. Type all of the terms without any accents or special symbols.

7. Use the Mini Translator to translate terms into French by completing the following steps:

a. Click the Translate button and then click the *Choose Translation Language* option at the drop-down list.

b. At the Translation Language Options dialog box, click the down-pointing arrow at the right of the *Translate to* option box in the *Choose Mini Translator language* section and then click *French (France)* at the drop-down list.

c. Click OK to close the dialog box.

d. With the Mini Translator turned on, hover the mouse pointer over the word *Central* in the table. (The Mini Translator displays dimmed above the word.)

e. Move the mouse pointer to the Mini Translator and then choose one of the French terms and type it in the *French* column.

f. Complete steps similar to those in Steps 7d and 7e to display French translations for the remaining terms. For each term, type the corresponding French term in the appropriate location in the table and omit any accents or special symbols.

8. Turn off the Mini Translator by clicking the Translate button and then clicking *Mini Translator [French (France)]* at the drop-down list.

9. Save, print, and then close **C05-E04-TranslateTerms.docx**.

# Chapter *Summary*

➤ The spelling checker matches the words in your document with the words in its dictionary. If a match is not found, the word is selected and possible corrections are suggested.

➤ When checking the spelling or grammar in a document, you can temporarily leave the Spelling task pane or Grammar task pane, make corrections in the document, and then resume checking.

➤ Customize spell checking options at the Word Options dialog box with *Proofing* selected in the left panel.

➤ With the grammar checker, you can search a document for correct grammar, style, punctuation, and word usage.

➤ Customize grammar checking with options in the *When correcting spelling and grammar in Word* section of the Word Options dialog box with *Proofing* selected.

➤ To display readability statistics for a document, insert a check mark in the *Show readability statistics* check box in the Word Options dialog box with *Proofing* selected and then complete a spelling and grammar check.

➤ Word uses the RoamingCustom.dic custom dictionary when spell checking a document. Add your own custom dictionary at the Custom Dictionaries dialog box. Display this dialog box by clicking the Custom Dictionaries button at the Word Options dialog box with *Proofing* selected.

➤ The Word Count dialog box displays the number of pages, words, characters, paragraphs, and lines in a document. Display this dialog box by clicking the word count section of the Status bar or clicking the Word Count button in the Proofing group on the REVIEW tab.

➤ Use the Thesaurus feature to find synonyms and antonyms for words in your document. Display synonyms and antonyms at the Thesaurus task pane or by right-clicking a word and then pointing to *Synonyms* at the shortcut menu.

➤ Use the Translate button in the Language group on the REVIEW tab to translate a document, selected text, or single word from one language to another.

# Commands *Review*

| FEATURE | RIBBON TAB, GROUP | BUTTON, OPTION | KEYBOARD SHORTCUT |
|---|---|---|---|
| Mini Translator | REVIEW, Language | [aあ] , *Mini Translator* | |
| spelling and grammar checking | REVIEW, Proofing | [ABC ✓] | F7 |
| Thesaurus task pane | REVIEW, Proofing | [📖] | Shift + F7 |
| translate selected text | REVIEW, Language | [aあ] , *Translate Selected Text* | |
| translate text | REVIEW, Language | [aあ] , *Translate Document* | |
| Translation Language Options dialog box | REVIEW, Language | [aあ] , *Choose Translation Language* | |
| Word Count dialog box | REVIEW, Proofing | [ABC 123] | |
| Word Options dialog box | FILE, Options | | |

# Key Points *Review*

**Completion:** In the space provided at the right, indicate the correct term, symbol, or command.

1. Click this tab to display the Proofing group.

2. Use this keyboard shortcut to begin checking the spelling and grammar in a document.

3. Click this button in the Spelling task pane to skip the occurrence of the word and all other occurrences of the word when checking the document.

4. Click this button in the Spelling task pane to replace the selected word in the document with the selected word in the list box.

5. This is the default setting for the *Writing Style* option at the Word Options dialog box with *Proofing* selected.

6. This readability score is based on the average number of syllables per word and average number of words per sentence.

7. When spell checking a document, Word uses this custom dictionary by default.

8. Use this keyboard shortcut to display the Thesaurus task pane.

9.  Click the Translate button and then click the *Translate Document* option and this online service translates the text in the document.                                    _____

10. Turn on this feature to point to a word or selected text and view a quick translation of it.                                    _____

# *Chapter Assessments*

## Applying Your Skills

Demonstrate your knowledge of features learned in this chapter by completing the following assessments.

### Assessment 5.1    Complete a Spelling and Grammar Check and Format a Style Document on Numbers

1.  Open **Numbers.docx** and save the document with the name **C05-A01-Numbers**.
2.  Complete a spelling and grammar check on the document.
3.  Display the Word Count dialog box for the document and then complete the following steps:
    a.  Make a note of the number of words, paragraphs, and lines in the document.
    b.  Move the insertion point to the end of the document, type **Words:**, press the spacebar, and then type the number of words identified in the Word Count dialog box.
    c.  Press the Enter key, type **Paragraphs:**, press the spacebar, and then type the number of paragraphs identified in the Word Count dialog box.
    d.  Press the Enter key, type **Lines:**, press the spacebar, and then type the number of lines identified in the Word Count dialog box.
4.  Make the following formatting changes to the document:
    a.  Apply the Heading 1 style to the title *NUMBERS* and apply the Heading 2 style to the two headings *Time Expressions* and *Dates*.
    b.  Apply the Basic (Elegant) style set.
    c.  Select the indented text in the *Time Expressions* section and then format the text as bulleted paragraphs.
    d.  Select the indented text in the *Dates* section and then format the text as bulleted paragraphs.
5.  Save, print, and then close **C05-A01-Numbers.docx**.

### Assessment 5.2    Complete a Spelling and Grammar Check and Proofread a Document

1.  Open **PrepareResume.docx** and save the document with the name **C05-A02-PrepareResume**.
2.  Complete a spelling and grammar check on the document.
3.  Proofread the document and make necessary changes. (The document contains mistakes that the spelling and grammar checker will not find.)
4.  Sort the numbered paragraphs in ascending order (lowest number to highest number) and then indent them 0.25 inch from the left margin.
5.  Use the thesaurus to replace the word *circumstances*, located in the last paragraph in the document, with the synonym *situations*.
6.  Use the thesaurus to replace the word *tasks*, located in the last paragraph in the document, with the synonym *responsibilities*.

7. Make the following changes to the document:
   a. Apply the Title style to the title and apply the Heading 1 style to the two headings in the document.
   b. Apply the Centered style set.
   c. Apply the Dividend theme and change the theme colors to Orange.
8. Save, print, and then close **C05-A02-PrepareResume.docx**.

### Assessment 5.3    Create and Format a Document Featuring Translated Terms

1. At a blank document, use the translation feature to find the Spanish and French translations for the following terms:
   memory
   logic
   navigate
   register
   system
   utility
   voice
2. Type the English words followed by the Spanish and French translations. Set the text in columns and then apply formatting to enhance the appearance of the document.
3. Save the document with the name **C05-A03-Translations**.
4. Print and then close **C05-A03-Translations.docx**.

## Expanding Your Skills

Explore additional feature options or use Help to learn a new skill in creating this document.

### Assessment 5.4    Write and Translate Steps for Customizing the Grammar Check

1. At a blank document, display the Word Options dialog box with *Proofing* selected in the left panel and then experiment with the options in each section.
2. Write a paragraph of text that briefly describes the options in the Word Options dialog box with *Proofing* selected.
3. Create an appropriate title for the document.
4. Translate the entire document into a language other than French or Spanish. ***Hint: Make sure you change the translation language at the Translation Language Options dialog box and then use the*** **Translate Document** ***option from the*** **Translate** ***button drop-down list.***
5. Copy the translated text from the website to your document.
6. Save the document and name it **C05-A04-OptionsTranslate**.
7. Print and then close **C05-A04-OptionsTranslate.docx**.

# Achieving Signature Status

Take your skills to the next level by completing these more challenging assessments.

## Assessment 5.5    Format a Document on Resume Writing

1. Open **WriteResume.docx** and save the document with the name **C05-A05-WriteResume**.
2. Complete a spelling and grammar check and apply character and paragraph formatting so your document appears as shown in Figure 5.9. (The font used is 12-point Cambria and the title is set in 14-point Cambria.)
3. Proofread the document and make any additional edits so that your document contains the same text as the document in Figure 5.9.
4. Save, print, and then close **C05-A05-WriteResume.docx**.

**Figure 5.9  Assessment 5.5**

---

### WRITING YOUR RESUME

**Contact Information**

Before getting into the major sections of the resume, let's briefly address the very top section: your name and contact information.

*Name*

You would think that writing your name would be the easiest part of writing your resume but you should consider the following factors:

- Although most people choose to use their full, formal name at the top of a resume, using the name by which you prefer to be called is becoming more acceptable.
- Keep in mind that it is to your advantage that readers feel comfortable when calling you for an interview. Their comfort level may decrease if your name is gender-neutral, difficult to pronounce, or very unusual; they don't know how to ask for you. You can make it easier for them by following these examples:

Lynn T. Cowles (Mr.)

(Ms.) Michael Murray

Tzirina (Irene) Kahn

Ndege "Nick" Vernon

*Address*

You should always include your home address on your resume. If you use a post office box for mail, include both your mailing address and your physical residence address. An exception to this is when you are posting your resume on the Internet. For security purposes, include just your phone and email contact as well as possibly your city and state with no street address.

*Telephone Number(s)*

Your home telephone number must be included so that people can pick up the phone and call you immediately. In addition, you can also include a cell phone number.

*Email Address*

Without question, if you have an email address, include it on your resume. Email is now often the preferred method of communication in job search, particularly in the early stages of each contact. If you do not have an email account, you can obtain a free, accessible-anywhere address from a provider such as www.yahoo.com, www.microsoft.com, or www.gmail.com.

## Assessment 5.6  Type a Business Letter

1. Open **NSSLtrhd.docx** and save the document with the name **C05-A06-MtgLtr**.
2. Type the text in the document shown in Figure 5.10 with the following specifications:
   - Insert bullets before the bulleted paragraphs of text as shown in the figure.
   - Change the alignment to justify the text in the body of the letter.
   - Replace the *XX* with your initials located near the end of the letter.
3. Check the spelling and grammar in the document.
4. Save, print, and then close **C05-A06-MtgLtr.docx**.

**Figure 5.10  Assessment 5.6**

Northland Security Systems
3200 North 22nd Street ✦ Springfield ✦ IL ✦ 62102

January 7, 2015

Dr. Gene Krezel
2310 North 122nd Street
Peoria, IL 61612

Dear Dr. Krezel:

RE: Shareholder's Annual General Meeting

You are cordially invited to attend the 2015 annual general meeting of shareholders of Northland Security Systems. The meeting will be held at the Evergreen Auditorium at the principal executive offices of Northland Security Systems. During the meeting, the Board will ask for your vote on the following issues:

- The election of four directors.
- The approval of an amendment to the company's long-term incentive plan to reduce the number of shares authorized for issuance under the plan.
- The ratification of the appointment by the audit committee of the company's independent auditor.
- The transaction of such other business as may be properly brought before the meeting or any adjournment or postponement of the meeting.

As an owner of shares, you can vote one of four ways. You can vote by attending the annual general meeting, by registering your vote at the company's website, by calling the company's toll-free telephone number and registering your vote, or by mailing your official ballot. If you need assistance or further information, please contact one of our support representatives available at our company website or by calling our support line.

Sincerely,

Faith Isenberg
Chief Executive Officer

XX
C05-A06-MtgLtr.docx

1-888-555-2200  ✦  www.emcp.net/nss

# Performance Assessments

**UNIT** *1*

## Preparing Documents

## ASSESSING PROFICIENCIES

In this unit, you have learned to create, edit, save, and print Word documents; use writing tools such as the spelling checker, grammar checker, and Thesaurus feature; and format characters and paragraphs.

*Note: Before beginning computer assessments, copy to your storage medium the Unit01PA folder from the CD that accompanies this textbook and then make Unit01PA the active folder.*

### Assessment U1.1    Format an Online Shopping Document

1. Open **ShopOnline.docx** and save the document with the name **U1-PA01-ShopOnline**.
2. Select the entire document and then change the font to 12-point Cambria.
3. Apply 14-point Calibri bold formatting to the two titles (*ONLINE SHOPPING* and *REFERENCES*) and three headings (*Advantages of Online Shopping, Online Shopping Venues,* and *Online Shopping Safety Tips*).
4. Center the titles *ONLINE SHOPPING* and *REFERENCES*.
5. Select the second through the fifth paragraphs in the *Advantages of Online Shopping* section and then apply bullet formatting.
6. Select the first sentence of each bulleted paragraph and apply bold formatting.
7. Select and then sort in ascending order the numbered paragraphs in the *Online Shopping Safety Tips* section.
8. Apply a hanging indent to the paragraphs of text below the *REFERENCES* title.
9. Apply Gold, Accent 4, Lighter 80% paragraph shading (eighth column, second row in the *Theme Colors* section) and a bottom border line to each of the two titles.
10. Move the insertion point to the *REFERENCES* title and then add 18 points of spacing before the title.
11. Save, print, and then close **U1-PA01-ShopOnline.docx**.

### Assessment U1.2    Format a Corporate Report

1. Open **ComReport.docx** and save the document with the name **U1-PA02-ComReport**.
2. Make the following changes to the document:
    a. Change the bullets in the *Compensation Philosophy* section to custom bullets of your choosing.
    b. Apply the Heading 1 style to the title *Compensation Committee Report*.
    c. Select the heading *Compensation Philosophy* and then apply the Emphasis style. Select the heading *Competitive Compensation* and then apply the Emphasis style.
    d. Apply the Shaded style set.
    e. Apply the Dividend theme.
    f. Apply the Blue theme colors.
    g. Center the title.
3. Save, print, and then close **U1-PA02-ComReport.docx**.

## Assessment U1.3    Create, Format, and Copy a Training Announcement

1. At a blank document, click the *No Spacing* style in the Styles group on the HOME tab, press the Enter key, and then type the text shown in Figure U1.1 with the following specifications:
   a. Center and right-align the text as indicated.
   b. After typing the text, press the Enter key four times.
   c. Set the centered text in 16-point Candara and change the font color to Dark Blue (ninth option in the *Standard Colors* section).
   d. Set the right-aligned text in 10-point Candara and change the font color to Dark Blue.
   e. Select from the blank line at the beginning of the document through one blank line below the right-aligned text, apply a thick-thin paragraph border and change the border color to Blue, Accent 1, Darker 25% (fifth column, fifth row in the *Theme Colors* section), and then apply the Green, Accent 6, Lighter 80% shading (last column, second row in the *Theme Colors* section).
   f. Copy the text (including the borders and shading) and paste it two times in the document. (The document should have a total of three announcements that fit on one page and are evenly distributed.)
2. Save the document and name it **U1-PA03-ManageData**.
3. Print and then close **U1-PA03-ManageData.docx**.

**Figure U1.1 Assessment U1.3**

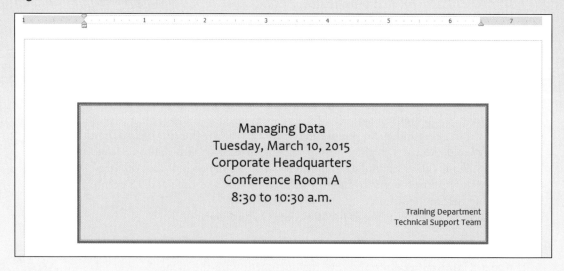

Managing Data
Tuesday, March 10, 2015
Corporate Headquarters
Conference Room A
8:30 to 10:30 a.m.

Training Department
Technical Support Team

## Assessment U1.4    Format a Software Document

1. Open **ProdSoftware.docx** and save the document with the name **U1-PA04-ProdSoftware**.
2. Select text from the beginning of the first paragraph of text below the title to the end of the document and then make the following changes:
   a. Change the spacing after paragraphs to 0 points.
   b. Change the line spacing to 1.5.
   c. Change the font to 12-point Constantia.
3. Indent the paragraphs that begin with bold text 0.5 inch from both the left and right margins.
4. Select the title and then change the font to 14-point Constantia bold.

5. Center the title and then apply Orange, Accent 2, Lighter 80% paragraph shading to the title (sixth column, second row in the *Theme Colors* section).
6. Insert a double-line border above the title and a single-line border below the title.
7. Save, print, and then close **U1-PA04-ProdSoftware.docx**.

## Assessment U1.5    Format a Travel Document

1. Open **CedarMeadows.docx** and save the document with the name **U1-PA05-CedarMeadows**.
2. Move the insertion point to the end of the document and then type the text shown in Figure U1.2.
3. Select the entire document and then add 6 points of spacing after paragraphs.
4. Apply the Heading 1 style to the title.
5. Apply the Heading 2 style to the two headings *Fast Facts* and *Special Highlights*.
6. Apply the Lines (Stylish) style set.
7. Apply the Wood Type theme.
8. Select the paragraphs of text in the *Fast Facts* section and then apply paragraph numbering.
9. Insert the following paragraph between paragraphs 3 and 4: **Ski School: The Cedar Meadows Ski School employs over 225 certified ski instructors and offers a variety of programs.**
10. Apply bold formatting to the words (and the colons) that begin the six numbered paragraphs.
11. Save, print, and then close **U1-PA05-CedarMeadows.docx**.

**Figure U1.2 Assessment U1.5**

Special Highlights
- ➤ 4,800 acres
- ➤ 79 trails
- ➤ 25 lifts
- ➤ Largest bi-state ski resort
- ➤ 3,500-foot vertical drop and 5.5-mile mountain descent
- ➤ 250 inches annual snowfall

## Assessment U1.6    Set Tabs and Create a Training Costs Document

1. At a blank document, create the document shown in Figure U1.3 on the next page. Set a left tab for the text in the first column and set right tabs for the text in the second and third columns.
2. After typing the text, make the following changes:
   a. Select the title and subtitle and change the font size to 14 points.
   b. Apply Dark Blue paragraph shading to the title (ninth option in the *Standard Colors* section). (Doing this will change the title text color to white.)
   c. Apply Gold, Accent 4, Lighter 80% paragraph shading to the subtitle (eighth column, second row in the *Theme Colors* section).
   d. Move the insertion point to the end of the document on the line below the text and then apply the Dark Blue paragraph shading.
3. Save the document with the name **U1-PA06-TrainCosts**.
4. Print and then close **U1-PA06-TrainCosts.docx**.

**Figure U1.3  Assessment U1.6**

| SMITH-ALLEN ENTERPRISES | | |
|---|---|---|
| **Training Costs** | | |
| **Department** | **Jan-June** | **July-Dec** |
| Human Resources | $20,250 | $23,500 |
| Production | 21,230 | 18,075 |
| Ancillary Services | 1,950 | 3,400 |
| Sales and Marketing | 10,375 | 9,500 |
| Finances | 15,300 | 17,200 |

## Assessment U1.7   Set Tabs and Create a Vacation Packages Document

1. At a blank document, create the document shown in Figure U1.4 on the next page. Set a left tab for the text in the first column and set a right tab with leaders for the text in the second column.
2. After typing the text, make the following changes:
   a. Apply the Heading 1 style to the title, *Rates and Packages*.
   b. Apply the Heading 2 style to the headings *Value Season*, *Peak Season*, and *Holiday Season*.
   c. Apply the Lines (Stylish) style set.
   d. Change the theme fonts to Arial. (Change the theme *fonts*, not the theme.)
   e. Center and bold the title, insert a top single-line border (in the same color as the bottom border), apply Blue-Gray, Text 2, Lighter 80% paragraph shading (fourth column, second row in the *Theme Colors* section), change the spacing from the title text to the top paragraph border to 3 points, and change the spacing from the title text to the bottom paragraph border to 4 points. ***Hint: Do this at the Border and Shading Options dialog box.***
   f. Change the paragraph spacing before the three headings to 12 points and the spacing after each of the three headings to 6 points.
3. Save the document with the name **U1-PA07-Rates**.
4. Print and then close **U1-PA07-Rates.docx**.

**Figure U1.4  Assessment U1.7**

**Rates and Packages**

Value Season

Hotel Room. . . . . . . . . . . . . . . . . . . . . . . . . . . . . . . $90 to $115

One-Bedroom Suite . . . . . . . . . . . . . . . . . . . . . . . . $115 to $140

Two-Bedroom Suite . . . . . . . . . . . . . . . . . . . . . . . . $145 to $170

Peak Season

Hotel Room. . . . . . . . . . . . . . . . . . . . . . . . . . . . . . $100 to $130

One-Bedroom Suite . . . . . . . . . . . . . . . . . . . . . . . . $130 to $160

Two-Bedroom Suite . . . . . . . . . . . . . . . . . . . . . . . . $165 to $195

Holiday Season

Hotel Room. . . . . . . . . . . . . . . . . . . . . . . . . . . . . . $140 to $150

One-Bedroom Suite . . . . . . . . . . . . . . . . . . . . . . . . $160 to $175

Two-Bedroom Suite . . . . . . . . . . . . . . . . . . . . . . . . $180 to $200

## Assessment U1.8    Customize Grammar Checking and Check Spelling and Grammar in a Document

1. Open **Activities.docx** and save the document with the name **U1-PA08-Activities**.
2. Display the Word Options dialog box with *Proofing* selected, change the *Writing Style* option to *Grammar & Style*, and then close the dialog box.
3. Complete a spelling and grammar check on the document.
4. Proofread the document and make any necessary changes.
5. Apply formatting to enhance the appearance of the document.
6. Display the Word Options dialog box with *Proofing* selected, change the *Writing Style* option to *Grammar Only*, and then close the dialog box.
7. Save, print, and then close **U1-PA08-Activities.docx**.

## Assessment U1.9    Format Resume Formats

1. At a blank document, create the document shown in Figure U1.5. Apply character and paragraph formatting so the document appears as shown in the figure.
2. Save the completed document and name it **U1-PA09-ResumeFormat**.
3. Print and then close **U1-PA09-ResumeFormat.docx**.

**Figure U1.5  Assessment U1.9**

**Executive Education Format**

| EDUCATION |
|---|
| Executive Leadership Program.............................................................................. STANFORD UNIVERSITY |
| Executive Development Program ...................................................... NORTHWESTERN UNIVERSITY |
| Master of Business Administration degree...............................................HARVARD UNIVERSITY |
| Bachelor of Science degree........................................................UNIVERSITY OF PENNSYLVANIA |

**Certification Format**

| TECHNICAL CERTIFICATIONS & DEGREES |
|---|
| Registered Nurse, University of Maryland, 2014 |
| Certified Nursing Assistant, University of Maryland, 2012 |
| Certified Nursing Aide, State of Maryland, 2009 |
| Bachelor of Science in Nursing, University of Maryland, 2014 |

## Assessment U1.10     Format a Job Announcement

1. Open **JobAnnounce.docx** and save the document with the name **U1-PA10-JobAnnounce**. (The medical center letterhead appears in the document header.)
2. Apply formatting so the document appears as shown in Figure U1.6. *Hint: Change the spacing from the text in the title* **JOB ANNOUNCEMENT** *to the top and bottom paragraph borders to 4 points with measurements at the Border and Shading Options dialog box.*
3. Save, print, and then close **U1-PA10-JobAnnounce.docx**.

**Figure U1.6  Assessment U1.10**

**Green Lake Medical Center**
100 Ninth Avenue Southeast
Newark, NJ 07102
(201) 555-1000

### JOB ANNOUNCEMENT

JOB TITLE...................................................................................................... Medical Office Assistant
STATUS........................................................................................................... Full-time employment
SALARY .......................................................................................................... Depending on experience
CLOSING......................................................................................................... February 1, 2015

**JOB SUMMARY**

- Register new patients; assist with form completion
- Retrieve charts
- Enter patient data into computer database
- Maintain and file medical records
- Schedule patients
- Call patients with appointment reminders
- Answer telephones and route messages
- Call and/or fax pharmacy for prescription order refills
- Mail lab test results to patients
- Perform other clerical duties as required

**REQUIRED SKILLS**

- Keyboarding (35+ wpm)
- Knowledge of Microsoft Word, Excel, and PowerPoint
- Thorough understanding of medical terms
- Excellent grammar and spelling skills
- Excellent customer service skills

**EDUCATION**

- High school diploma
- Post-secondary training as a medical office assistant, CMA or RMA preferred
- CPR certification

*For further information, contact Olivia Summers (201) 555-1057.*

# CREATING ORIGINAL DOCUMENTS

The activities in Assessments U1.11, U1.12, and U1.13 give you the opportunity to practice your writing skills as well as demonstrate your mastery of the important Word features presented in this unit. Use correct grammar, precise word choices, and clear sentence construction. Follow the steps below to improve your writing skills.

# THE WRITING PROCESS

**Plan:** Gather ideas, select the information to include, and choose the order in which to present it.

**Checkpoints**
- What is the purpose of your document?
- What information do readers need to reach your intended conclusion?

**Write:** Keeping readers in mind and following the information plan, draft the document using clear, direct sentences that say what you mean.

**Checkpoints**
- What are the subpoints that support each main point?
- How can you connect paragraphs so readers move smoothly from one idea to the next?

**Revise:** Improve what you have written by changing, deleting, rearranging, or adding words, sentences, and paragraphs.

**Checkpoints**
- Is the meaning clear?
- Do the ideas follow a logical order?
- Have you included any unnecessary information?
- Have you built your sentences around strong verbs and nouns?

**Edit:** Check spelling, sentence construction, word use, punctuation, and capitalization.

**Checkpoints**
- Can you spot any redundancies or clichés?
- Can you reduce any phrases to effective words (for example, change *the fact that* to *because*)?
- Have you used commas only where there is a strong reason for doing so?
- Did you proofread the document for errors that your spelling checker cannot identify?

**Publish:** Prepare a final copy that can be reproduced and shared with others.

**Checkpoints**
- Which design elements (for example, bolding and different fonts) will help highlight important ideas and sections?
- Will charts or other graphics help clarify meaning?

## Assessment U1.11    Create and Format an Announcement

**Situation:** You work in the public relations department at Coleman Development Corporation, and your supervisor has asked you to prepare an announcement about the appointment of the new corporate president using the following information:

- The board of trustees has appointed Stephanie Branson as president of Coleman Development Corporation.

- She has 25 years of experience in the land management field and has spent the past 11 years as president of Lancaster, Inc.

- The selection process began over six months ago and included several interviews with board members and visitations by board members to Lancaster. An open house is planned for Friday, August 14, 2015, from 1:30 to 5:00 p.m., in the corporation's conference room.

Provide a title for the announcement. Save the announcement and name it **U1-PA11-Announce**. Print and then close **U1-PA11-Announce.docx**.

## Assessment U1.12    Create and Format a Word Commands Document

**Situation:** You work in the training department at Crossroads Industries, and your supervisor has asked you to prepare a brief summary of some Word commands for use in Microsoft Word training classes. She has asked you to include the following information:

- A brief explanation of how to move the insertion point to a specific page
- Keyboard commands to move the insertion point to the beginning and end of a line and to the beginning and end of a document
- Commands to delete text from the insertion point to the beginning of a word and from the insertion point to the end of a word
- Steps to select a word, sentence, paragraph, and entire document using the mouse
- Keyboard command to select the entire document

Save the document with the name **U1-PA12-WordCommands**. Print and then close **U1-PA12-WordCommands.docx**.

## Assessment U1.13    Prepare a Memo Illustrating Font Use

**Situation:** You work as the assistant to the public relations manager at your local chamber of commerce. The manager, Makenzie Keenan, wants to maintain a consistent style for articles published in the chamber's monthly newsletter. She wants you to explore the use of various handwriting, decorative, and plain fonts. She would like you to choose two handwriting fonts, two decorative fonts, and two plain fonts and then prepare a memo to her that illustrates the use of each font. (Refer to Appendix C for information on formatting a memo.) When typing information about a font, set the text in the font you are describing. Save the completed memo and name it **U1-PA13-Fonts**. Print and then close **U1-PA13-Fonts.docx**.

# UNIT 2

## Formatting and Managing Documents

# Chapter 6

# Formatting Pages

## Performance Objectives

Upon successful completion of Chapter 6, you will be able to:

- Change the document view
- Change the page setup, including the margins, page orientation, and paper size in a document
- Insert section breaks in a document
- Create and format text in columns
- Hyphenate words automatically and manually
- Insert line numbers in a document
- Format the page background using a watermark, page color, and page border

A Word document, by default, displays in Print Layout view, with portrait orientation, and one-inch top, bottom, left, and right margins. In this chapter you will learn how to change the default view, orientation, and page margins. You will also learn how to insert section breaks and then apply formatting to specific sections in a document, format text in columns, hyphenate words, and insert line numbering. Additionally, you will learn how to insert document elements such as a watermark, page background color, and page borders.

*Note: Before beginning computer exercises for this chapter, copy to your storage medium the Chapter06 folder from the CD that accompanies this textbook and then make Chapter06 the active folder.*

In this chapter, students will produce the following documents:

Exercise 6.1. C06-E01-WebReport.docx
Exercise 6.2. C06-E02-BestFitResume.docx
Exercise 6.3. C06-E03-CompCommunications.docx
Exercise 6.4. C06-E04-CompAccess.docx

Model answers for these exercises are shown on the following pages.

## Page 1

### NAVIGATING THE WEB

Since so many people create web pages, the Web should be chaotic. However, underlying systems are in place specifying how pages are organized on the Web and how they are delivered to your computer. This system involves unique addresses used to access each web page, a unique address for each computer, and browser features for locating and retrieving online content.

#### IPS AND URLS

An *Internet Protocol (IP) address* is a series of numbers that uniquely identifies a location on the Internet. An IP address consists of four groups of numbers separated by periods. For example: 225.73.110.102. A nonprofit organization called ICANN keeps track of IP numbers around the world.

Because numbers would be difficult to remember for retrieving pages, we use a text-based address referred to as a *uniform resource locator (URL)* to go to a website. A URL, also called a *web address*, has several parts separated by a colon (:), slashes (/), and dots (.). The first part of a URL is called a *protocol* and identifies a certain way for interpreting computer information in the transmission process. *Http*, which stands for *hypertext transfer protocol*, and *ftp*, for *file transfer protocol*, are examples of protocols. Some sites use a secondary identifier for the type of site being contacted, such as *www* for *World Wide Web* site, but this is often optional.

The next part of the URL is the *domain name*, which identifies the group of servers (the domain) to which the site belongs and the particular com... the domain. For example, the *.com* ... exists such as *.com*, *.net*, *.org*, *.edu*,...

Table A: Common Top-Level Domain Suffi...

| Suffix | Type of Organization |
|---|---|
| .biz | business site |
| .com | company or commercial institution |
| .edu | educational institution |
| .gov | government site |
| .int | international organizati... endorsed by treaty |
| .mil | military site |
| .net | administrative site for I... |
| .org | nonprofit or private org... |

#### BROWSING WEB PAGES

You may already be quite comfortal... browsers move around the Web an... be linked to another page using a h... be inserted in text or a graphical ob...

## Page 2

A website is a series of related web pages that are linked together. You get to a website by entering the URL, such as www.amazon.com, in your browser. Every website has a starting page, called the *home page*, which is displayed when you enter the site URL. You can also enter a URL to jump to a specific page on a site, such as the Video-On-Demand page at Amazon's site, www.amazon.com/Video-On-Demand.

### SEARCHING THE WEB

A search engine, such as Google.com, Ask.com, and Yahoo.com, catalogs and indexes web pages for you. A type of search engine, called a search directory, can also catalog pages into topics such as *finance*, *health*, *news*, *shopping*, and so on. Search engines may seem to be free services, but in reality they are typically financed by selling advertising. Some also make money by selling information about your online activities and interests to advertisers.

#### SEARCH ENGINES

The newest wave of search engines, including Microsoft Bing and Google Squared, not only search for content but also make choices among... example, to ask for a list of fe... for you. Table B shows some o... ability to catalog pages in dire...

Table B: Common Search Tools

| Search Tool | URL |
|---|---|
| Ask | www.ask.c... |
| Bing | www.bing.... |
| Dogpile | www.dogp... |
| Google | www.goog... |
| MSN | www.msn.... |
| Yahoo! | www.yaho... |

#### HOW SEARCH ENGINES...

So how do search engines wo... typing your search text, which... information about the interna... box and press the Enter key. Y... types of results such as image...

You can get more targeted sea... you gain through practice. For... more than eighty million resu... keyword phrase like "space st... include or exclude certain res...

## Page 3

and .net) to limit your search results to educational and government sites. Table C offers some ways you can narrow your search by entering your keywords in various ways.

Table C: Advanced Search Parameters

| Item | What It Does | Example |
|---|---|---|
| Quotes ("") | Instruction to use exact word or words in the exact order given | "Pearl Harbor" |
| Minus symbol (-) | Excludes words preceded by the minus symbol from the search | jaguar –car |
| Wildcard (*) | Treat the asterisk as a placeholder for any possible word | *bird for bluebird, redbird, etc. |
| Or | Allow either one word or the other | Economy 2010 or Economy 2011 |

#### METASEARCH ENGINES

A metasearch engine, such as dogpile.com, searches keywords across several websites at the same time. For example, imagine you need to fly from Atlanta to Seattle. Instead of checking available flights on three different airline websites, you can use a metasearch engine to check all of the airline sites at once.

3

Exercise 6.1

C06-E01-WebReport.docx

**BEST FIT RESUME**

**The Right Fit**

Recruitment consultants often talk about the job "fit." The way they see recruitment and the way many firms think about it is in terms of getting a good fit between the employer and the employee. Merely putting your life history on a resume is highly unlikely to demonstrate the best fit. This is why tailoring your resume to the particular position is so important.

Fit is all about matching a candidate to a particular job. The best candidate for the job will be the one that best matches all of the requirements of the job. Employers tend to think about fit in terms of four different qualities:

- **Knowledge:** The experience and qualifications you possess and the ability to demonstrate knowledge.
- **Skills:** The skills you have demonstrated (perhaps evidenced by your qualifications).
- **Abilities:** Potential to carry out a range of different tasks beyond your immediate skills or knowledge.
- **Attitudes:** The degree to which you are enthusiastic, flexible, and positive in approach.

**Preparing the "Best Fit" Resume**

To produce the best fitting resume, you need to know about yourself and about the job to which you are applying. Before you do anything else, ask yourself why you are preparing a resume. The answer to this question is going to vary from one person to the next. Here are nine reasons for writing a resume:

1. You have seen a job advertised in the paper that appeals to you.
2. You have seen a job on an Internet job site that appeals to you.
3. Your friends or family told you of a job opening at a local company.
4. You want to work for the local company and thought that sending a resume to the company might get the company's attention.
5. You have seen a job advertised internally at work.
6. You are going for a promotion.
7. You want to market yourself to win a contract or a proposal or be elected to a committee or organization.
8. You are about to be downsized and want to update your resume to be ready for any good opportunities.
9. You are feeling fed up and writing down all your achievements will cheer you up and might motivate you to look for a better job.

All of these certainly are good reasons to write a resume, but the resume serves many different purposes. One way of seeing the differences is to identify who is going to read the resume.

**The Right Mix**

In some situations you will have a good idea of what the employer is looking for because you have a job advertisement in front of you and can tailor you resume accordingly. For others, you have no idea what the employer might want to see. Updating your resume from time to time is a good idea so you do not forget important details. Note that the result of such a process will not be a winning resume but a useful list of tasks and achievements.

**Exercise 6.2**  C06-E02-BestFitResume.docx

Model Answers

---

**COMPUTERS IN COMMUNICATIONS**

Computers were originally stand-alone devices, incapable of communicating with other computers. This changed in the 1970s and 1980s when the development of special telecommunications hardware and software led to the creation of the first private networks, allowing connected computers to exchange data. Exchanged data took the form of requests for information, replies to requests for information, or instructions on how to run programs stored on the network.

The ability to link computers enables users to communicate and work together efficiently and effectively. Linked computers have become central to the communications industry. They play a vital role in telecommunications, publishing, and news services.

**Telecommunications**

The industry that provides for communication across distances is called telecommunications. The telephone industry uses computers to switch and route phone calls automatically over telephone lines. In addition to the spoken word, many other kinds of information move over such lines, including faxes and computer data. Data can be sent from computer to computer over telephone lines using a device known as a modem. One kind of data frequently sent by modem is electronic mail, or email, which can be sent from person to person via the Internet or an online service. A more recent innovation in telecommunications is teleconferencing, which allows people in various locations to see and hear one another and thus hold virtual meetings.

**Publishing**

Just twenty-five years ago, book manuscripts were typeset mechanically on a typesetting machine and then reproduced on a printing press. Now anyone who has access to a computer and either a modem or a printer can undertake what has come to be known as electronic publishing. Writers and editors use word processing applications to produce text. Artists and designers use drawing and painting applications to create original graphics, or they use inexpensive scanners to digitize illustrations and photographs (turn them into computer-readable files). Typesetters use personal computers to combine text, illustrations, and photographs. Publishers typically send computer-generated files to printers for production of the film and plates from which books and magazines are printed.

**News Services**

News providers rely on reporters located worldwide. Reporters use email to send, or upload, their stories to wire services. Increasingly, individuals get daily news reports from online services. News can also be accessed from specific providers, such as the *New York Times* or *USA Today*, via the Internet. One of the most popular Internet sites provides continuously updated weather reports.

**Exercise 6.3**  C06-E03-CompCommunications.docx

**Exercise 6.4**

C06-E04-CompAccess.docx

## UNAUTHORIZED ACCESS

Like uncharted wilderness, the Internet lacks borders. This inherent openness is what makes the Internet so valuable and yet so vulnerable. Over its short life, the Internet has grown so quickly that the legal system has not been able to keep pace. The security risks posed by networks and the Internet can be grouped into three categories: unauthorized access, information theft, and denial of service.

Hackers, individuals who gain access to computers and networks illegally, are responsible for most cases of unauthorized access. Hackers tend to exploit sites and programs that have poor security measures in place. However, they also gain access to more challenging sites by using sophisticated programs and strategies. Many hackers claim they hack merely because they like the challenge of trying to defeat security measures. They rarely have a more malicious motive, and they generally do not aim to destroy or damage the sites that they invade. In fact, hackers dislike being identified with those who seek to cause damage. They refer to hackers with malicious or criminal intent as *crackers*.

### User IDs and Passwords

To gain entry over the Internet to a secure computer system, most hackers focus on finding a working user ID and password combination. User IDs are easy to come by and are generally not secure information. Sending an email, for example, displays the sender's user ID in the return address, making it very public. The only missing element is the password. Hackers know from experience which passwords are common; they have programs that generate thousands of likely passwords and they try them systematically over a period of hours or days.

### System Backdoors

Programmers can sometimes inadvertently aid hackers by providing unintentional entrance to networks and information systems. One such unintentional entrance is a system "backdoor," which is a user ID and password that provides the highest level of authorization. Programmers innocently create a "backdoor" in the early days of system development to allow other programmers and team members to access the system to fix problems. Through negligence or by design, the user ID and password are sometimes left behind in the final version of the system. People who know about them can then enter the system, bypassing the security perhaps years later, when the backdoor has been forgotten.

### Spoofing

A sophisticated way to break into a network via the Internet involves spoofing, which is the process of fooling another computer by pretending to send information from a legitimate source. It works by altering the address that the system automatically puts on every message sent. The address is changed to one that the receiving computer is programmed to accept as a trusted source of information.

### Spyware

t allows an intruder to spy upon someone else's computer. This age of loopholes in the computer's security systems and allows a other person's every mouse click or keystroke on the monitor as it es and gain access to passwords and credit card information. Spyware all it on the machine that is being spied upon, so it is highly unlikely

that random strangers on the Internet could simply begin watching your computer. In the workplace, however, someone might be able to install the software without the victim's knowledge. Disguised as an email greeting, for example, the program can operate like a virus that gets the unwary user to install the spyware unknowingly.

## INFORMATION THEFT

Information can be a company's most valuable possession. Stealing corporate information, a crime included in the category of industrial espionage, is unfortunately both easy to do and difficult to detect. This is due in part to the invisible nature of software and data. If a cracker breaks into a company network and manages to download the company database from the network onto a disk, there is no visible sign to the company that anything is amiss. The original database is still in place, working the same way it always has.

### Wireless Device Security

The growing number of wireless devices has created a new opportunity for data theft. Wireless devices such as cameras, Web phones, networked computers, PDAs, and input and output peripherals are inherently less secure than wired devices. Security is quite lax, and in some cases nonexistent, in new wireless technologies for handheld computers and cell phone systems. In a rush to match competition, manufacturers have tended to sacrifice security to move a product to the marketplace faster. Already, viruses are appearing in emails for cell phones and PDAs. With little protection available for these new systems, hackers and spies are enjoying a free hand with the new technology. One of the few available security protocols for wireless networks is Wired Equivalent Privacy (WEP), developed in conjunction with the standard for wireless local area networks. Newer versions of WEP with enhanced security features make it more difficult for hackers to intercept and modify data transmissions sent by radio waves or infrared signals.

### Data Browsing

Data browsing is a less damaging form of information theft that involves an invasion of privacy. Workers in many organizations have access to networked databases that contain private information about people. Accessing this information without an official reason is against the law. The IRS had a particularly large problem with data browsing in the late 1990s. Some employees were fired and the rest were given specialized training in appropriate conduct.

# Changing the View

By default, a Word document displays in Print Layout view. In this view, the document displays on the screen as it will appear when printed. Other views are also available, such as Draft, Web Layout, and Read Mode. Change views with buttons in the view area on the Status bar or options on the VIEW tab. Figure 6.1 identifies the buttons in the view area on the Status bar. Along with the View buttons, the Status bar also contains a Zoom slider bar. Drag the button on the Zoom slider bar to increase or decrease the display size, or click the Zoom Out button to decrease the display size and click the Zoom In to increase the display size.

Zoom Out

Zoom In

Figure 6.1 **Viewing Buttons and Zoom Slider Bar**

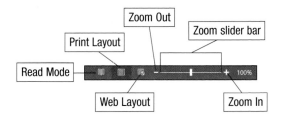

## Displaying a Document in Draft View

Change to Draft view and the document displays in a format for efficient editing and formatting. In this view, margins and features such as headers and footers do not display on the screen. Change to Draft view by clicking the VIEW tab and then clicking the Draft button in the Views group.

Draft    Web Layout

## Displaying a Document in Web Layout View

Use Web Layout view to see how the document displays as a web page. In Web Layout view, text is wrapped to fit the window, backgrounds are visible, and graphics appear as they display in a browser. Display a document in Web Layout view by clicking the VIEW tab and then clicking the Web Layout button in the Views group or by clicking the Web Layout button in the view area on the Status bar.

Web Layout
(Status bar)

## Displaying a Document in Read Mode View

The Read Mode view displays a document in a format for easy viewing and reading by automatically fitting the page layout to the screen and displaying text in columns and in a larger point size. Change to Read Mode view by clicking the Read Mode button in the view area on the Status bar or by clicking the VIEW tab and then clicking the Read Mode button in the Views group.

You can navigate in Read Mode view using the keys on the keyboard, as shown in Table 6.1 on the next page. You can also navigate with the mouse by clicking at the right side of the screen or clicking the Next button (right-pointing triangle in a circle) to display the next page or by clicking at the left side of the screen or clicking the Previous button (left-pointing triangle in a circle) to display the previous page.

The FILE, TOOLS, and VIEW tabs display in the upper left corner of the screen in Read Mode view. Click the FILE tab to display the backstage area. Click the TOOLS tab and a drop-down list displays options for finding specific text in the document and searching for information on the Internet using the Bing search engine. Click the VIEW tab and options display for customizing what you see in Read Mode view. You

**QUICK STEPS**

**Display a Document in Read Mode**
Click Read Mode button in view area on Status bar.
OR
1. Click VIEW tab.
2. Click Read Mode button.

Read Mode
(Status bar)

Read Mode

**Table 6.1 Keyboard Commands in Read Mode View**

| Press this key . . . | to complete this action |
|---|---|
| Page Down key, Right Arrow key, or spacebar | display next two pages |
| Page Up key, Left Arrow key, or Backspace key | display previous two pages |
| Home | display first page in document |
| End | display last page in document |
| Esc | return to previous view |

can display the Navigation pane to navigate to specific locations in the document, show comments inserted in the document, change the widths of the columns or change to a different page layout, and change the page colors in Read Mode view.

If your document contains an object such as a table, SmartArt graphic, image, or shape, you can zoom in on the object in Read Mode view. To do this, double-click the object. When you double-click an object, a button containing a magnifying glass with a plus symbol inside displays just outside the upper right corner of the object. Click this button to zoom in even more on the object. Click the button again and the object returns to the original zoom size. Click once outside the object to return it to its original size.

To close Read Mode view and return to the previous view, press the Esc key on your keyboard, click the VIEW tab, and then click *Edit Document* at the drop-down list or click the Print Layout button on the Status bar.

## Changing Ribbon Display Options

Ribbon Display Options

If you want to view more of your document, use the Ribbon Display Options button that displays in the upper right corner of the screen to the right of the Microsoft Word Help button. Click the Ribbon Display Options button and a drop-down list displays three options: *Auto-hide Ribbon*, *Show Tabs*, and *Show Tabs and Commands*.

Collapse the Ribbon

The default is *Show Tabs and Commands*, which displays the Quick Access toolbar, ribbon, and Status bar on the screen. Click the first option, *Auto-hide Ribbon*, and the Quick Access toolbar, ribbon, and Status bar are hidden, allowing you to see more of your document. To temporarily redisplay these features, click at the top of the screen. Turn these features back on by clicking the Ribbon Display Options button and then clicking the *Show Tabs and Commands* option. Click the *Show Tabs* option at the drop-down list and only the tabs display on the ribbons—not the buttons and commands.

You can also turn off the display of the ribbon by clicking the Collapse the Ribbon button located above the vertical scroll bar or with the keyboard shortcut Ctrl + F1. Redisplay the ribbon by double-clicking any tab or pressing Ctrl + F1.

---

**Exercise 6.1A** Changing Views **Part 1 of 4**

1. Open **WebReport.docx** and save the document with the name **C06-E01-WebReport**.
2. Click the VIEW tab and then click the Draft button in the Views group.

3. Using the mouse, drag the Zoom slider bar button located in the view area on the Status bar to the left to decrease the size of the document display to approximately 60%. (The percentage displays at the right side of the Zoom In button.)

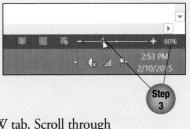

Step 3

4. Drag the Zoom slider bar button back to the middle until *100%* displays at the right side of the Zoom In button.
5. Click the Web Layout button in the Views group on the VIEW tab. Scroll through the document and notice that it has wider margins and does not contain any page breaks.
6. Click the Print Layout button in the view area on the Status bar. Press Ctrl + Home to move the insertion point to the beginning of the document.
7. Click the Read Mode button located in the view area on the Status bar.
8. Click the Next button (right-pointing triangle in a circle) to display the next two pages in the viewing window.

Step 8

9. Click the left side of the screen above the Previous button (left-pointing triangle in a circle) to display the previous two pages.
10. Increase the display of the table located at the right side of the screen by double-clicking the table. (If the table is not visible, click the Next button located at the right side of the screen to view the next page.)
11. Click the button (contains a magnifying glass with a plus [+] symbol) that displays outside the upper right corner of the table. (This increases the zoom.)
12. Click outside the table to return the table to the original size.
13. Change the width of columns by clicking the VIEW tab, pointing to *Column Width*, and then clicking *Narrow* at the side menu.

Step 13

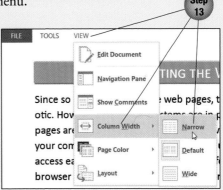

14. Return the column width back to the default by clicking the VIEW tab, pointing to *Column Width*, and then clicking *Default* at the side menu.
15. Change the page color by clicking the VIEW tab, pointing to *Page Color*, and then clicking *Sepia* at the side menu.
16. Remove page color by clicking the VIEW tab, pointing to *Page Color*, and then clicking *None* at the side menu.
17. Change the layout by clicking the VIEW tab, pointing to *Layout*, and then clicking *Paper Layout* at the side menu.
18. Return to the Column Layout by clicking the VIEW tab, pointing to *Layout*, and then clicking *Column Layout* at the side menu.
19. Practice navigating in Read Mode view using the actions shown in Table 6.1 on the previous page.
20. Press the Esc key to return to Print Layout view.
21. Click the Ribbon Display Options button that displays in the upper right corner of the screen to the right of the Microsoft Word Help button and then click *Auto-hide Ribbon* at the drop-down list.

Step 21

22. Press Ctrl + End to display the last page in the document and then press the Page Up key until the beginning of the document displays.
23. Click at the top of the screen to temporarily redisplay the Quick Access toolbar, ribbon, and Status bar.
24. Click the Ribbon Display Options button and then click *Show Tabs and Commands* at the drop-down list.

# Changing Page Setup

**Change the Margins**
1. Click PAGE LAYOUT tab.
2. Click Margins button.
3. Click desired margin option.

Margins

The Page Setup group on the PAGE LAYOUT tab contains a number of options for changing the setup of pages in a document. Use options in the Page Setup group to perform actions such as changing the margins, page orientation, and page size and inserting page breaks.

## Changing Margins

As noted earlier, the default measurements for the top, bottom, left, and right margins are 1 inch. You can change these page margins with options at the Margins drop-down list, shown in Figure 6.2. To display this drop-down list, click the PAGE LAYOUT tab and then click the Margins button in the Page Setup group. Change the margins by clicking one of the preset options that displays at the drop-down list.

**Figure 6.2  Margins Drop-down List**

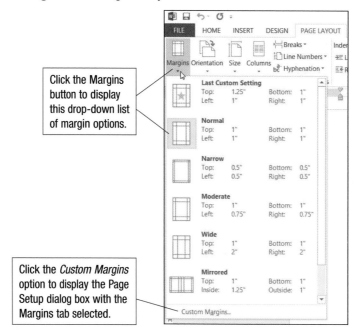

Click the Margins button to display this drop-down list of margin options.

Click the *Custom Margins* option to display the Page Setup dialog box with the Margins tab selected.

## Changing Page Orientation

**Change the Page Orientation**
1. Click PAGE LAYOUT tab.
2. Click Orientation button.
3. Click desired orientation.

Orientation

Click the Orientation button in the Page Setup group on the PAGE LAYOUT tab and two options for orienting pages in a document display: *Portrait* and *Landscape*. In Portrait orientation, which is the default, the page is 11 inches tall and 8.5 inches wide. In Landscape orientation, the page is 8.5 inches tall and 11 inches wide. When you change the page orientation, the page margins change automatically.

Can you imagine some instances in which you might use a landscape orientation? Suppose you are preparing a company's annual report and need to include a couple of tables that have several columns of text. If you use the default portrait orientation, the columns will need to be quite narrow, possibly so narrow that reading them becomes difficult. Changing the orientation to landscape provides 2.5 more inches of usable space. Also, you can use both portrait and landscape in the same document. To do this, select the text, display the Page Setup dialog box, click the desired orientation, and change the *Apply to* option to *Selected text*.

1. With **C06-E01-WebReport.docx** open, click the PAGE LAYOUT tab.
2. Click the Margins button in the Page Setup group and then click the *Narrow* option.
3. Return the margins back to the default settings by clicking the Margins button and then clicking the *Normal* option.
4. Click the Orientation button in the Page Setup group.
5. Click *Landscape* at the drop-down list.
6. Scroll through the document and notice how the text displays on the page in landscape orientation.
7. Click the Orientation button in the Page Setup group and then click *Portrait* at the drop-down list. (This changes the orientation back to the default.)
8. Save **C06-E01-WebReport.docx**.

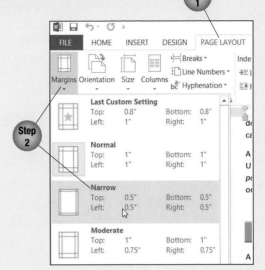

## Changing Page Size

The template Word uses to apply default formatting is based on a page size of 8.5 inches wide and 11 inches tall. Change this default setting with options at the *Size* drop-down list, as shown in Figure 6.3. Display this drop-down list by clicking the Size button in the Page Setup group on the PAGE LAYOUT tab.

**QUICK STEPS**

**Change the Page Size**
1. Click PAGE LAYOUT tab.
2. Click Size button.
3. Click desired size option.

Size

**Figure 6.3  Size Button Drop-down List**

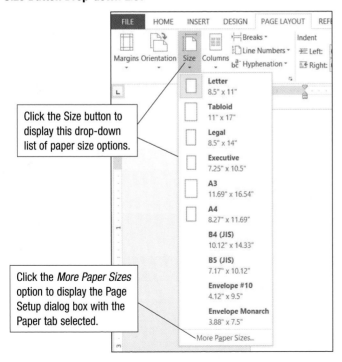

Click the Size button to display this drop-down list of paper size options.

Click the *More Paper Sizes* option to display the Page Setup dialog box with the Paper tab selected.

1. With **C06-E01-WebReport.docx** open, make sure the PAGE LAYOUT tab is selected.
2. Click the Size button in the Page Setup group.
3. Click the *Executive* option (displays with *7.25" × 10.5"* below *Executive*). If this option is not available, choose an option with a similar size.
4. Scroll through the document and notice how the text displays on the page.
5. Click the Size button and then click *Legal* (displays with *8.5" × 14"* below *Legal*).
6. Scroll through the document and notice how the text displays on the page.
7. Click the Size button and then click *Letter* (displays with *8.5" × 11"* below *Letter*). (This returns the size back to the default.)
8. Save **C06-E01-WebReport.docx**.

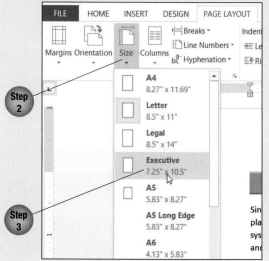

## Changing Margins at the Page Setup Dialog Box

The Margins button drop-down list provides a number of preset margins. If these margins do not fit your needs, you can set specific margins at the Page Setup dialog box with the Margins tab selected, as shown in Figure 6.4 on the next page. Display this dialog box by clicking the Page Setup group dialog box launcher or by clicking the Margins button and then clicking *Custom Margins* at the bottom of the drop-down list.

To change one of the margins, select the current measurement in the *Top*, *Bottom*, *Left*, or *Right* measurement box and then type the new measurement. You can also increase a measurement by clicking the up-pointing arrow at the right of the measurement box. Decrease a measurement by clicking the down-pointing arrow. As you change the margin measurements at the Page Setup dialog box, the sample page in the *Preview* section illustrates the effects of the changes.

**Figure 6.4 Page Setup Dialog Box with Margins Tab Selected**

Notice the default settings for the top, bottom, left, and right margins.

The changes you make to the margins are reflected in this preview page.

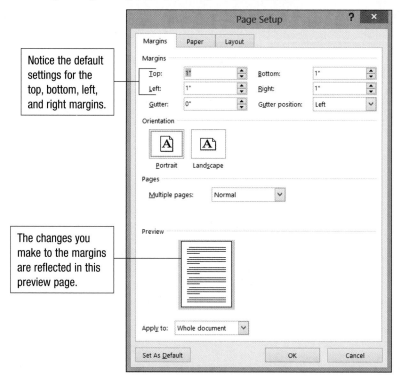

## Changing Paper Size at the Page Setup Dialog Box

The Size button drop-down list contains a number of preset page sizes. If these sizes do not fit your needs, specify a page size at the Page Setup dialog box with the Paper tab selected. Display this dialog box by clicking the Size button in the Page Setup group and then clicking *More Paper Sizes,* which displays at the bottom of the drop-down list.

**QUICK STEPS**

**Change Page Size at the Page Setup Dialog Box**
1. Click PAGE LAYOUT tab.
2. Click Size button.
3. Click *More Paper Sizes* at drop-down list.
4. Specify desired size.
5. Click OK.

1. With **C06-E01-WebReport.docx** open, make sure the PAGE LAYOUT tab is selected.
2. Click the Page Setup group dialog box launcher.
3. At the Page Setup dialog box with the Margins tab selected, click the down-pointing arrow at the right side of the *Top* measurement box until *0.5"* displays.
4. Click the down-pointing arrow at the right side of the *Bottom* measurement box until *0.5"* displays.
5. Select the current measurement in the *Left* measurement box and then type **0.75**.
6. Select the current measurement in the *Right* measurement box and then type **0.75**.

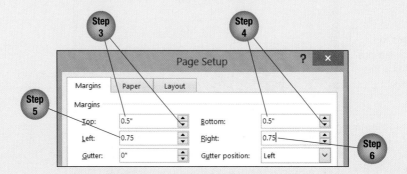

7. Click OK to close the dialog box.
8. Click the Size button in the Page Setup group and then click *More Paper Sizes* at the drop-down list.
9. At the Page Setup dialog box with the Paper tab selected, click the down-pointing arrow at the right side of the *Paper size* option and then click *A4* at the drop-down list.
10. Click OK to close the dialog box.
11. Scroll through the document and notice how the text displays on the page.
12. Click the Size button in the Page Setup group and then click *Letter* at the drop-down list.
13. Click the Margins button and then click *Custom Margins* at the drop-down list. At the Page Setup dialog box, type **1.2** in the *Top* measurement box and then press Enter.
14. Save, print, and then close **C06-E01-WebReport.docx**.

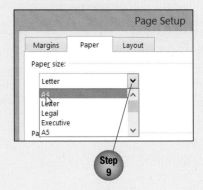

# Inserting a Section Break

Change the layout and formatting of specific parts of a document by inserting section breaks. For example, you can change the margins for a portion of text by inserting section breaks before and after the text. Similarly, you can format specific text in a document into columns after inserting section breaks before and after the text.

Insert a section break in a document by clicking the PAGE LAYOUT tab, clicking the Breaks button in the Page Setup group, and then clicking the desired option in the *Section Breaks* section of the drop-down list, as shown in Figure 6.5. The first option, *Next Page*, inserts a section break and continues the text on the next page. The second option inserts a continuous section break, which separates the document into parts but does not begin a new page. The *Even Break* option inserts a section break and begins the new section on the next even-numbered page and the *Odd Page* option begins the new section on the next odd-numbered page.

A section break inserted in a document is not visible in Print Layout view. If you change to Draft view or click the Show/Hide ¶ button on the HOME tab to turn on the display of nonprinting characters, a section break displays as a double row of dots with the words *Section Break* in the middle. Depending on the type of section break you insert, text follows the words *Section Break*. For example, if you insert a continuous section break, the words *Section Break (Continuous)* display in the middle of the row of dots.

To delete a section break, change to Draft view, click on the words *Section Break*, and then press the Delete key. Another option is to click the Show/Hide ¶ button to turn on the display of nonprinting characters, position the insertion point at the beginning of the section break, and then press the Delete key. If you delete a section break, the text that follows the section break takes on the formatting of the text preceding the break.

**QUICK STEPS**

**Insert a Section Break**
1. Click PAGE LAYOUT tab.
2. Click Breaks button.
3. Click section break type at drop-down list.

Breaks

**QUICK STEPS**

**Delete a Section Break**
1. Click VIEW tab.
2. Click Draft button.
3. Click on section break.
4. Press Delete key.

**Figure 6.5  Breaks Button Drop-down List**

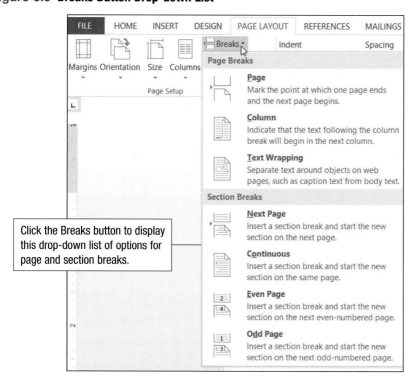

Click the Breaks button to display this drop-down list of options for page and section breaks.

1. Open **BestFitResume.docx** and save the document with the name **C06-E02-BestFitResume**.
2. Select the entire document and then change the font size to 12 points.
3. Insert a section break in the document that continues the text on an odd page by completing the following steps:

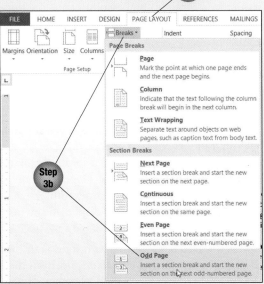

   a. Press Ctrl + Home to position the insertion point at the beginning of the document (at the beginning of the title) and click the PAGE LAYOUT tab.
   b. Click the Breaks button in the Page Setup group and then click *Odd Page* at the drop-down list.
4. Move the insertion point to the beginning of the heading *The Right Mix* (located on the last page) and then insert a section break that continues the text on an even page by clicking the Breaks button in the Page Setup group and then clicking *Even Page* at the drop-down list.
5. Move the insertion point to the beginning of the document and notice that the blank page at the beginning of the document is identified at the left side of the Status bar as *Page 1 of 6*. Scroll through the other pages and notice that the last page of the document is identified as *Page 6 of 6*.
6. Move the insertion point to the beginning of the document and then delete the section breaks by completing the following steps:
   a. Click the VIEW tab and then click the Draft button in the Views group.
   b. Position the insertion point on the section break above the title (displays as a double row of dots across the screen with the words *Section Break (Odd Page)* centered in the middle) and then press the Delete key.

   c. Position the insertion point on the section break above the heading *The Right Mix* and then delete the even-page section break.
7. Select the entire document and then change the font size to 11 points.
8. Click the Print Layout button in the view area on the Status bar.
9. Move the insertion point to the beginning of the heading *Preparing the "Best Fit" Resume* and then insert a continuous section break by clicking the PAGE LAYOUT tab, clicking the Breaks button, and then clicking *Continuous* at the drop-down list.
10. Move the insertion point to the beginning of the heading *The Right Mix* and then insert a continuous section break.
11. Click in the first paragraph of text below the heading *Preparing the "Best Fit" Resume* and then change the left and right margins to 1.25 inches.
12. Scroll through the document and notice that the margin changes affect only the text between the two continuous section breaks.
13. Save and then print **C06-E02-BestFitResume.docx**.

# Creating Columns

When you prepare any document that contains text, the readability of the document is one of your most important considerations. As you learned in the last chapter, the term *readability* refers to the ease with which a person can read and understand text. Line length in a document is one of the factors that can affect the readability of the text. If the length is too long, the reader may lose his or her place on the line and have a difficult time moving to the next line below.

To improve the readability of documents such as newsletters and reports, you may want to set the text in columns. One commonly used type of column is the newspaper column, which is typically used for text in newspapers, newsletters, and magazines. To read this kind of text, the reader scans down to the bottom of one column and then to the top of the next column, continuing across the page.

Set text in columns with the Columns button in the Page Setup group on the PAGE LAYOUT tab or with options at the Columns dialog box. Use the Columns button to create columns of equal width and use the Columns dialog box to create columns of varying widths. A document can include as many columns as space permits on the page. Word determines how many columns can be included based on the page width, margin width, and size and spacing of the columns. Columns must be at least 0.5 inch in width. Making changes in columns affects the entire document or section of the document in which the insertion point is positioned.

**Create Columns**
1. Click PAGE LAYOUT tab.
2. Click Columns button.
3. Click desired number of columns.

Columns

---

## Exercise 6.2B  Formatting Text into Columns                    Part 2 of 3

1. With **C06-E02-BestFitResume.docx** open, delete the section breaks by completing the following steps:
   a. Click the HOME tab and then click the Show/Hide ¶ button to turn on the display of nonprinting characters.
   b. Position the insertion point at the beginning of the section break above the heading *Preparing the "Best Fit" Resume*.

   > • → **Abilities:** Potential to carry out a range of different tasks beyond your immediate skills or knowledge.¶
   > • → **Attitudes:** The degree to which you are enthusiastic, flexible, and positive in approach.¶
   > ¶———————————————————Section Break (Continuous)———————————————————
   > **Preparing the "Best Fit" Resume¶**
   > ¶
   > To produce the best fitting resume, you need to know about yourself and about the job to which you are applying. Before you do anything else, ask yourself why you are preparing a

   Step 1b

   c. Press the Delete key.
   d. Position the insertion point on the section break above the heading *The Right Mix* and then press the Delete key.
   e. Click the Show/Hide ¶ button to turn off the display of nonprinting characters.
2. Move the insertion point to the beginning of the heading *The Right Fit* (located immediately below the title of the document) and then insert a continuous section break.
3. Format the text (except the title) into two columns by completing the following steps:
   a. Make sure the insertion point is positioned below the section break.
   b. If necessary, click the PAGE LAYOUT tab.

---

c. Click the Columns button in the Page Setup group and then click *Two* at the drop-down list.
4. Scroll through the document and notice that the text after the section break is set in two columns.
5. Save **C06-E02-BestFitResume.docx**.

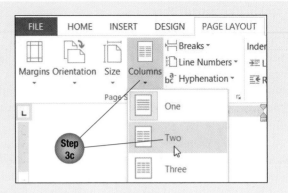

By inserting section breaks in a document, you can format specific text in a document into columns. In Exercise 6.2B, you inserted a section break and then formatted the text into two columns from the section break to the end of the document. You can also create columns within text by inserting two continuous section breaks: one at the beginning of the text you want to format into columns and one at the location you want the columns of text to end.

## Exercise 6.2C  Formatting Text into Columns within a Document        Part 3 of 3

1. With **C06-E02-BestFitResume.docx** open, delete the continuous section break and return the text to one column by completing the following steps:
   a. Click the VIEW tab and then click the Draft button in the Views group.
   b. Position the insertion point on the continuous section break above the heading *The Right Fit* and then press the Delete key.
   c. Click the PAGE LAYOUT tab, click the Columns button, and then click *One* at the drop-down list. (This returns the document text to one column and also changes the document view to Print Layout view.)
2. Format the bulleted paragraphs of text into two columns by completing the following steps:
   a. Position the insertion point at the beginning of the word *Knowledge* that displays after the first bullet in the bulleted paragraphs and then insert a continuous section break.
   b. Insert a continuous section break at the blank line after the last bulleted paragraph of text.
   c. Move the insertion point to any character in the bulleted text.
   d. With the PAGE LAYOUT tab active, click the Columns buttons and then click *Two* at the drop-down list.
3. Completing steps similar to those in Step 2, format the numbered paragraphs of text into two columns. ***Hint: Insert a continuous section break at the beginning of the first numbered paragraph and insert a continuous section break at the blank line after the last numbered paragraph.***
4. Select the entire document and then change the font to Cambria.
5. Move the insertion point to the title *BEST FIT RESUME* and then change the bottom margin to 0.8 inch. ***Hint: Do this at the Page Setup dialog box with the Margins tab selected.***
6. Save, print, and then close **C06-E02-BestFitResume.docx**.

# Creating Columns with the Columns Dialog Box

Use the Columns dialog box to create newspaper columns that are equal or unequal in width. To display the Columns dialog box, shown in Figure 6.6, click the Columns button in the Page Setup group on the PAGE LAYOUT tab and then click *More Columns* at the drop-down list.

## Figure 6.6 Columns Dialog Box

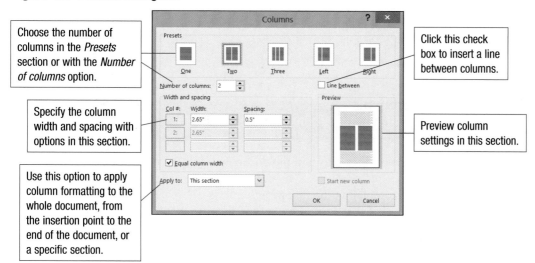

Choose the number of columns in the *Presets* section or with the *Number of columns* option.

Specify the column width and spacing with options in this section.

Use this option to apply column formatting to the whole document, from the insertion point to the end of the document, or a specific section.

Click this check box to insert a line between columns.

Preview column settings in this section.

Use options at the Columns dialog box to specify the style and number of columns, enter your own column measurements, create unequal columns, and insert a line between columns. By default, column formatting is applied to the whole document. With the *Apply to* option at the bottom of the Columns dialog box, you can change this from *Whole document* to *This point forward*. When you select the *This point forward* option, a section break is inserted and the column formatting is applied to text from the location of the insertion point to the end of the document or until other column formatting is encountered. The *Preview* section of the dialog box displays an example of how the columns will appear in the document.

## Removing Column Formatting

To remove column formatting using the Columns button, position the insertion point in the section containing columns, click the PAGE LAYOUT tab, click the Columns button, and then click *One* at the drop-down list. You can also remove column formatting at the Columns dialog box by selecting the *One* option in the *Presets* section.

**Create Columns at the Columns Dialog Box**
1. Click PAGE LAYOUT tab.
2. Click Columns button.
3. Click *More Columns* at drop-down list.
4. Specify column options.
5. Click OK.

## Inserting a Column Break

**Insert a Column Break**

1. Position insertion point at desired location.
2. Click PAGE LAYOUT tab.
3. Click Breaks button.
4. Click *Column* at drop-down list.

When Word formats text into columns, it automatically breaks the columns to fit the page. At times, column breaks may appear in undesirable locations. You can insert a column break by positioning the insertion point where you want the column to end and the new column to begin, clicking the PAGE LAYOUT tab, clicking the Breaks button, and then clicking *Column* at the drop-down list. You can also insert a column break with the keyboard shortcut Ctrl + Shift + Enter.

---

## Exercise 6.3A  Formatting Columns at the Columns Dialog Box     Part 1 of 4

1. Open **CompCommunications.docx** and save the document with the name **C06-E03-CompCommunications**.
2. Format text in columns by completing the following steps:
   a. Position the insertion point at the beginning of the first paragraph of text in the document.
   b. Click the PAGE LAYOUT tab.
   c. Click the Columns button in the Page Setup group and then click *More Columns* at the drop-down list.
   d. At the Columns dialog box, click *Two* in the *Presets* section.
   e. Click the up-pointing arrow at the right of the *Spacing* option box to display *0.6".*
   f. Click the *Line between* check box to insert a check mark.
   g. Click the down-pointing arrow at the right side of the *Apply to* option box and then click *This point forward* at the drop-down list.
   h. Click OK to close the dialog box.

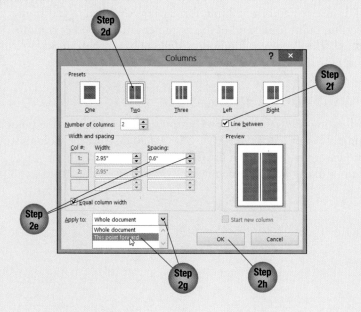

---

3. Insert a column break by completing the following steps:
   a. Position the insertion point at the beginning of the *News Services* heading.
   b. Click the Breaks button in the Page Setup group and then click *Column* at the drop-down list.
4. Save and then print **C06-E03-CompCommunications.docx**.

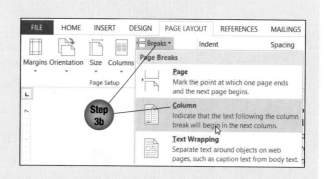

## Balancing Columns on a Page

In documents that contain text formatted into columns, Word automatically lines up (balances) the last line of text at the bottom of each column, except on the last page. Text in the first column of the last page may flow to the end of the page, while the text in the second column may end far short of the end of the page. You can balance columns by inserting a continuous section break at the end of the text.

---

**Exercise 6.3B**  Formatting and Balancing Columns of Text                Part 2 of 4

---

1. With **C06-E03-CompCommunications.docx** open, delete the column break by completing the following steps:
   a. Position the insertion point at the beginning of the *News Services* heading.
   b. Click the VIEW tab and then click the Draft button in the Views group.
   c. Position the insertion point on the column break.

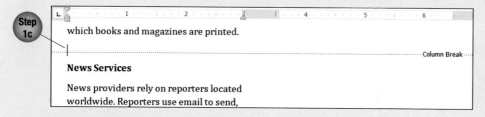

   d. Press the Delete key.
   e. Click the Print Layout button in the view area on the Status bar.
2. Select the entire document and then change the font to Constantia.
3. Move the insertion point to the end of the document and then balance the columns by clicking the PAGE LAYOUT tab, clicking the Breaks button, and then clicking *Continuous* at the drop-down list.
4. Apply the Blue, Accent 1, Lighter 60% paragraph shading (fifth column, third row in the *Theme Colors* section) to the title *COMPUTERS IN COMMUNICATIONS*.
5. Apply the Blue, Accent 1, Lighter 80% paragraph shading (fifth column, second row in the *Theme Colors* section) to each of the headings in the document.
6. Save **C06-E03-CompCommunications.docx**.

# Hyphenating Words

**QUICK STEPS**

**Use Automatic Hyphenation**
1. Click PAGE LAYOUT tab.
2. Click Hyphenation button.
3. Click *Automatic* at drop-down list.

**Use Manual Hyphenation**
1. Click PAGE LAYOUT tab.
2. Click Hyphenation button.
3. Click *Manual* at drop-down list.
4. Click Yes or No to hyphenate or not hyphenate selected words.
5. When complete, click OK.

Hyphenation

In some Word documents, especially documents that have left and right margins wider than 1 inch or text set in columns, the right margin may appear quite ragged. To improve the display of the text, consider hyphenating long words that fall at the ends of the lines. With the hyphenation feature in Word, you can hyphenate words in a document automatically or manually.

## Automatically Hyphenating Words

To hyphenate words automatically, click the PAGE LAYOUT tab, click the Hyphenation button in the Page Setup group, and then click *Automatic* at the drop-down list. Scroll through the document and check to see if hyphens display in appropriate locations within the words. If after hyphenating words in a document you want to remove all of the hyphens, immediately click the Undo button on the Quick Access toolbar.

## Manually Hyphenating Words

If you want to control where a hyphen appears in a word, choose manual hyphenation. To do this, click the PAGE LAYOUT tab, click the Hyphenation button in the Page Setup group, and then click *Manual* at the drop-down list. This displays the Manual Hyphenation dialog box, as shown in Figure 6.7. (The word in the *Hyphenate at* text box will vary.) At this dialog box, click Yes to hyphenate the word as indicated in the *Hyphenate at* text box, click No if you do not want the word hyphenated, or click Cancel to cancel hyphenation. If you continue hyphenating text in the document, keep clicking Yes or No at the Manual Hyphenation dialog box. At the message indicating that hyphenation is complete, click OK.

At the Manual Hyphenation dialog box, you can reposition the hyphen in the word in the *Hyphenate at* text box. Word displays the word with syllable breaks indicated by hyphens. The position at which the word will be hyphenated displays as a blinking bar. If you want to hyphenate the word at a different location, position the blinking bar where you want the hyphen and then click Yes.

Be careful with words ending in *-ed*. Several two-syllable words can be divided before that final syllable—for example, *noted*. However, one-syllable words ending in *-ed* should not be divided. An example is *served*. Watch for this type of occurrence and click No to cancel the hyphenation. At the hyphenation complete message, click OK.

**Figure 6.7  Manual Hyphenation Dialog Box**

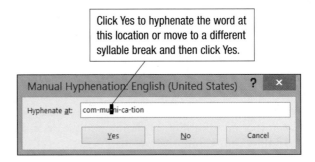

1. With **C06-E03-CompCommunications.docx** open, press Ctrl + Home and then hyphenate words automatically by completing the following steps:
   a. Click the PAGE LAYOUT tab.
   b. Click the Hyphenation button in the Page Setup group and then click *Automatic* at the drop-down list.

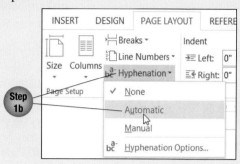

2. Scroll through the document and notice the automatic hyphenation.
3. Click the Undo button to remove the hyphens.
4. Manually hyphenate words by completing the following steps:
   a. Click the Hyphenation button in the Page Setup group and then click *Manual* at the drop-down list.
   b. At the Manual Hyphenation dialog box, make one of the following choices:
      - Click Yes to hyphenate the word as indicated in the *Hyphenate at* text box.
      - Move the hyphen in the word to a more desirable location and then click Yes.
      - Click No if you do not want the word hyphenated.

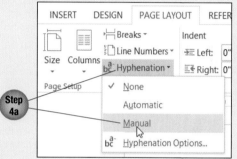

   c. Continue clicking Yes or No at the Manual Hyphenation dialog box as you work through the document.
   d. At the hyphenation complete message, click OK.
5. Save **C06-E03-CompCommunications.docx**.

# Inserting Line Numbers

Use the Line Numbers button in the Page Setup group on the PAGE LAYOUT tab to insert line numbers in a document. Numbering lines has practical applications for certain legal papers and reference purposes. To number lines in a document, click the PAGE LAYOUT tab, click the Line Numbers button in the Page Setup group, and then click the desired line number option at the drop-down list.

If you want more control over inserting line numbers in a document, click the Line Numbers button and then click *Line Numbering Options* at the drop-down list. At the Page Setup dialog box with the Layout tab selected, click the Line Numbers button that displays at the bottom of the dialog box. This displays the Line Numbers dialog box, as shown in Figure 6.8. Use options at this dialog box to insert line numbering and to specify the starting number, the location line numbers are printed, the interval between printed line numbers, and whether line numbers are consecutive or start over at the beginning of each page.

**Insert Line Numbers**
1. Click PAGE LAYOUT tab.
2. Click Line Numbers button.
3. Click desired line number option.

**OR**
1. Click PAGE LAYOUT tab.
2. Click Line Numbers button.
3. Click *Line Numbering Options* at drop-down list.
4. Click Line Numbers button.
5. Specify line numbering options at dialog box.
6. Click OK.
7. Click OK.

**Figure 6.8  Line Numbers Dialog Box**

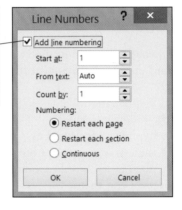

Click this check box to turn on line numbering and make the remaining options active. Use options at this dialog box to customize how line numbers appear in the document.

Line Numbers

---

## Exercise 6.3D    Inserting Line Numbers                          Part 4 of 4

1. With **C06-E03-CompCommunications.docx** open, insert line numbers by completing the following steps:
   a. Position the insertion point at the beginning of the first paragraph below the title *COMPUTERS IN COMMUNICATIONS*.
   b. If necessary, click the PAGE LAYOUT tab.
   c. Click the Line Numbers button in the Page Setup group.
   d. Click *Continuous* at the drop-down list.
   e. Scroll through the document and notice how the line numbers appear.
   f. Turn off line numbering by clicking the Line Numbers button and then clicking *None*.

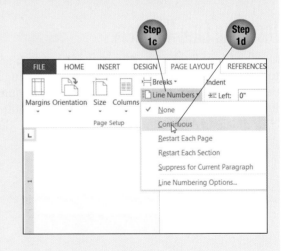

2. Insert line numbers at the Line Numbers dialog box by completing the following steps:

   a. With the insertion point positioned at the beginning of the first paragraph below the title *COMPUTERS IN COMMUNICATIONS*, click the Line Numbers button and then click *Line Numbering Options* at the drop-down list.

   b. At the Page Setup dialog box with the Layout tab selected, click the Line Numbers button that displays at the bottom of the dialog box.

   c. At the Line Numbers dialog box, click the *Add line numbering* check box to insert a check mark.

   d. Click the up-pointing arrow at the right side of the *Count by* option to display *2* in the text box.

   e. Click OK to close the Line Numbers dialog box.

   f. Click OK to close the Page Setup dialog box.

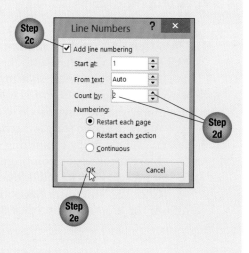

3. Scroll through the document and notice the appearance of the line numbers.
4. Remove line numbering by clicking the Line Numbers button and then clicking *None*.
5. If the heading *News Services* displays at the bottom of the first page, insert a page break at the beginning of the heading.
6. Save, print, and then close **C06-E03-CompCommunications.docx**.

# Formatting the Page Background

The Page Background group on the DESIGN tab contains three buttons for customizing a page background. Click the Watermark button and choose a predesigned watermark from a drop-down list. If a document is going to be viewed on screen or on the Web, consider adding a page color. In Chapter 4, you learned how to apply borders and shading to text at the Borders and Shading dialog box. This dialog box also contains options for inserting a page border.

## Inserting a Watermark

A **watermark** is a lightened image that displays behind the text in a document. Use a watermark to add visual appeal to a document or identify a document as a draft, sample, or confidential document. Word provides a number of predesigned watermarks you can insert in a document. Display them by clicking the Watermark button in the Page Background group on the DESIGN tab. Scroll through the list of watermarks and then click the desired option.

## Changing Page Color

Use the Page Color button in the Page Background group to apply background color to a document. This background color is intended for viewing a document on screen or on the Web. The color is visible on the screen but does not print. Insert a page color by clicking the Page Color button and then clicking the desired color at the color palette.

**Insert a Watermark**
1. Click DESIGN tab.
2. Click Watermark button.
3. Click desired option at drop-down list.

**Change the Page Color**
1. Click DESIGN tab.
2. Click Page Color button.
3. Click desired option at color palette.

Watermark

Page Color

1. Open **CompAccess.docx** and save the document with the name **C06-E04-CompAccess**.
2. Make the following changes to the document:
   a. Apply the Heading 1 style to the two titles in the document: *UNAUTHORIZED ACCESS* and *INFORMATION THEFT*.
   b. Apply the Heading 2 style to all of the headings in the document.
   c. Apply the Basic (Elegant) style set.
3. Insert a watermark by completing the following steps:
   a. Move the insertion point to the beginning of the document.
   b. If necessary, click the DESIGN tab.
   c. Click the Watermark button in the Page Background group.
   d. At the drop-down list, click the *CONFIDENTIAL 1* option.

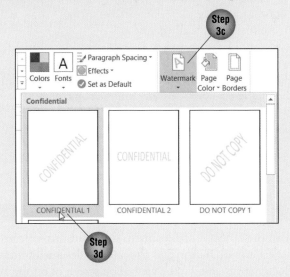

4. Scroll through the document and notice how the watermark displays behind the text.
5. Remove the watermark and insert a different one by completing the following steps:
   a. Click the Watermark button in the Page Background group and then click *Remove Watermark* at the drop-down list.
   b. Click the Watermark button and then click the *DO NOT COPY 1* option at the drop-down list.
6. Scroll through the document and notice how the watermark displays.
7. Move the insertion point to the beginning of the document.

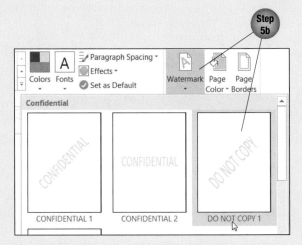

8. Click the Page Color button in the Page Background group and then click *Gold, Accent 4, Lighter 80%* at the color palette (eighth column, second row in the *Theme Colors* section).
9. Save **C06-E04-CompAccess.docx**.

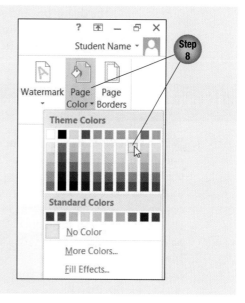

## Inserting a Page Border

To improve the visual interest of a document, consider adding a page border. When you insert a page border in a multiple-page document, the border prints on each page. To insert a page border, click the Page Borders button in the Page Background group on the DESIGN tab. This displays the Borders and Shading dialog box with the Page Border tab selected, as shown in Figure 6.9. At this dialog box, specify the border style, color, and width.

**Insert a Page Border**
1. Click DESIGN tab.
2. Click Page Borders button.
3. Specify desired options at dialog box.

Page Borders

**Figure 6.9  Borders and Shading Dialog Box with Page Border Tab Selected**

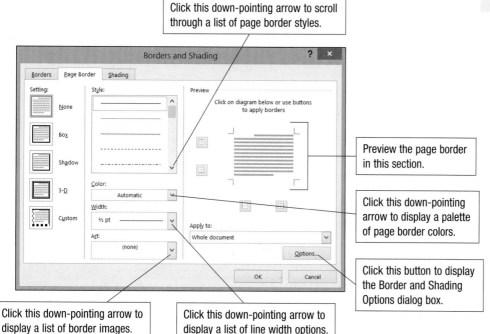

The dialog box includes an option for inserting a page border that contains an image. To display the images available, click the down-pointing arrow at the right of the *Art* option box. Scroll down the drop-down list and then click the desired image.

## Exercise 6.4B    Inserting a Page Border

1. With **C06-E04-CompAccess.docx** open, remove the page color by clicking the Page Color button in the Page Background group on the DESIGN tab and then clicking *No Color* at the color palette.
2. Insert a page border by completing the following steps:
   a. Click the Page Borders button in the Page Background group on the DESIGN tab.
   b. Click the *Box* option in the *Setting* section.
   c. Scroll down the list of line styles in the *Style* list box until the end of the list displays and then click the third line from the end.
   d. Click the down-pointing arrow at the right of the *Color* list box and then click *Dark Blue* at the color palette (ninth option in the *Standard Colors* section).
   e. Click OK to close the dialog box.
3. Save and then print **C06-E04-CompAccess.docx**.
4. Insert an image page border by completing the following steps:
   a. Click the Page Borders button in the Page Background group.
   b. Click the down-pointing arrow at the right side of the *Art* option box and then click the border image shown at the right (located approximately one-third of the way down the drop-down list).
   c. Click OK to close the dialog box.
5. Save **C06-E04-CompAccess.docx**.

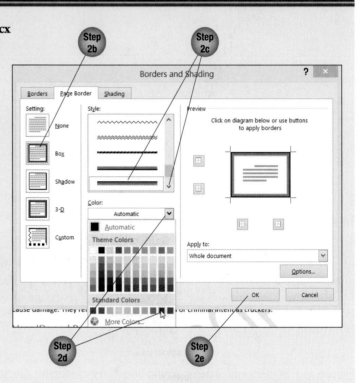

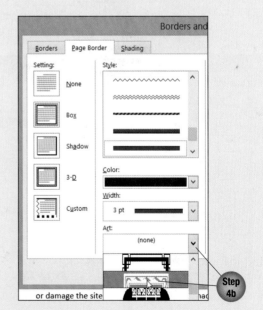

By default, a page border displays and prints 24 points from the top, left, right, and bottom edges of the page. Some printers, particularly inkjet printers, have a nonprinting area around the outside edges of the page that can interfere with the printing of a border. Before printing a document with a page border, click the FILE tab and then click the *Print* option. Look at the preview of the page at the right side of the Print backstage area and determine whether the entire border is visible. If part of the border is not visible in the preview page (generally at the bottom and right side of the page), consider changing measurements at the Border and Shading Options dialog box, as shown in Figure 6.10. You can also change measurements at the Border and Shading Options dialog box to control the location of the page border on the page.

**Figure 6.10  Border and Shading Options Dialog Box**

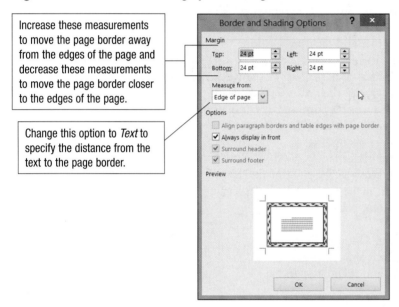

Increase these measurements to move the page border away from the edges of the page and decrease these measurements to move the page border closer to the edges of the page.

Change this option to *Text* to specify the distance from the text to the page border.

Display the Border and Shading Options dialog box by clicking the DESIGN tab and then clicking the Page Borders button. At the Borders and Shading dialog box with the Page Border tab selected, click the Options button that displays in the lower right corner of the dialog box. The options at the Border and Shading Options dialog box change depending on whether you click the Options button at the Borders and Shading dialog box with the Borders tab selected or the Page Border tab selected. In Chapter 4, you learned about changing measurements for paragraph borders at the Border and Shading Options dialog box. At the Border and Shading Options dialog box for page borders, you can increase and/or decrease the spacing between the page border and edges of the page with the Top and Bottom measurement boxes in the *Margin* section.

The *Measure from* option box at the Border and Shading Options dialog box has the default setting *Edge of page*. You can change this option to *Text*, which changes the top and bottom measurements to 1 point and the left and right measurements to 4 points and moves the page border into the page. Use the measurement boxes to specify the distance you want the page border displayed and printed from the text in the document.

1. With **C06-E04-CompAccess.docx** open, increase the spacing from the page border to the edges of the page by completing the following steps:
   a. Click the DESIGN tab and then click the Page Borders button.
   b. At the Borders and Shading dialog box with the Page Border tab selected, click the Options button located in the lower right corner.
   c. At the Border and Shading Options dialog box, click the up-pointing arrow at the right side of the *Top* measurement box until *31 pt* displays. (This is the maximum measurement allowed.)
   d. Increase the measurements for the *Left, Bottom,* and *Right* measurement boxes to 31 points.
   e. Click OK to close the Border and Shading Options dialog box.
   f. Click OK to close the Borders and Shading dialog box.
2. Save **C06-04-CompAccess.docx** and then print only page 1.
3. Change the page border and page border options by completing the following steps:
   a. With the DESIGN tab active, click the Page Borders button.
   b. At the Borders and Shading dialog box, scroll down the *Style* list box and then click the third line option from the bottom.
   c. Click the down-pointing arrow at the right of the *Color* option box and then make sure the *Dark Blue* option is selected at the color palette.
   d. Click the Options button.
   e. At the Border and Shading Options dialog box, click the down-pointing arrow at the right of the *Measure from* option box and then click *Text* at the drop-down list.
   f. Click the up-pointing arrow at the right of the *Top* measurement box until *10 pt* displays.
   g. Increase the measurement for the *Bottom* measurement box to 10 points and the measurements in the *Left* and *Right* measurement boxes to 14 points.
   h. Click the *Surround header* check box to remove the check mark.
   i. Click the *Surround footer* check box to remove the check mark.
   j. Click OK to close the Border and Shading Options dialog box.
   k. Click OK to close the Borders and Shading dialog box.
4. Save, print, and then close **C06-04-CompAccess.docx**.

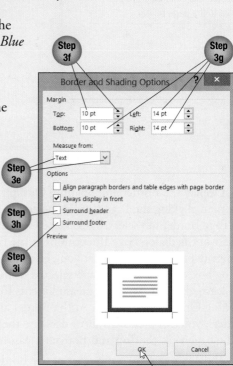

# Chapter Summary

- Change the document view with buttons in the view area on the Status bar or with options on the VIEW tab.

- Use the Zoom slider bar, located on the Status bar, to change the percentage of the display.

- Print Layout is the default view and it can be changed to other views, such as Draft view, Web Layout view, and Read Mode view.

- Draft view displays the document in a format for efficient editing and formatting.

- Read Mode view displays a document in a format for easy viewing and reading.

- Navigate in Read Mode view using keys on the keyboard, with the Next and Previous buttons, or by clicking at the left and right sides of the screen.

- Use options at the Ribbon Display Options button drop-down list to specify whether you want the Quick Access toolbar, ribbon, and Status bar visible or hidden.

- By default, a Word document contains 1-inch top, bottom, left, and right margins. Change margins with preset margin settings at the Margins button drop-down list or with options at the Page Setup dialog box with the Margins tab selected.

- The default page orientation is portrait and it can be changed to landscape with the Orientation button in the Page Setup group on the PAGE LAYOUT tab.

- The default page size is 8.5 by 11 inches and it can be changed with options at the Size button drop-down list or options at the Page Setup dialog box with the Paper tab selected.

- Insert a section break in a document to apply formatting to a portion of a document. Insert a continuous section break or a section break that begins a new page. View and/or delete a section break in Draft view or by clicking the Show/Hide ¶ button to turn on the display of nonprinting characters.

- Set text in columns to improve the readability of documents such as newsletters and reports. Format text in columns using the Columns button in the Page Setup group on the PAGE LAYOUT tab or with options at the Columns dialog box.

- Remove column formatting with the Columns button on the PAGE LAYOUT tab or at the Columns dialog box.

- Balance column text on the last page of a document by inserting a continuous section break at the end of the text.

- Improve the display of text by hyphenating long words that fall at the ends of lines. You can automatically or manually hyphenate words in a document.

- Number lines in a document with options at the Line Numbers button drop-down list or the Line Numbers dialog box.

- A watermark is a lightened image that displays behind the text in a document. Use the Watermark button in the Page Background group on the DESIGN tab to insert a watermark.

- Insert page color in a document with the Page Color button in the Page Background group on the DESIGN tab. Page color is designed for viewing a document on screen and does not print.

- Click the Page Borders button in the Page Background group on the DESIGN tab and the Borders and Shading dialog box displays with the Page Border tab selected. Use options at this dialog box to insert a page border in a document.

- By default, a page border displays and prints 24 points from the top, left, right, and bottom edges of the page. Change this default spacing at the Border and Shading Options dialog box.

- At the Border and Shading Options dialog box, select *Text* at the *Measure from* option box to specify the distance from text in a document to the page border.

# Commands *Review*

| FEATURE | RIBBON TAB, GROUP | BUTTON, OPTION |
|---------|-------------------|----------------|
| Border and Shading Options dialog box | DESIGN, Page Background | , *Options* |
| Borders and Shading dialog box with Page Border tab selected | DESIGN, Page Background | |
| collapse the ribbon | | |
| columns | PAGE LAYOUT, Page Setup | |
| Columns dialog box | PAGE LAYOUT, Page Setup | , *More Columns* |
| continuous section break | PAGE LAYOUT, Page Setup | , *Continuous* |
| Draft view | VIEW, Views | |
| hyphenate words automatically | PAGE LAYOUT, Page Setup | , *Automatic* |
| hyphenate words manually | PAGE LAYOUT, Page Setup | , *Manual* |
| line numbers | PAGE LAYOUT, Page Setup | |
| margins | PAGE LAYOUT, Page Setup | |
| page color | DESIGN, Page Background | |
| page orientation | PAGE LAYOUT, Page Setup | |
| Page Setup dialog box with Margins tab selected | PAGE LAYOUT, Page Setup | , *Custom Margins*; OR |
| Page Setup dialog box with Paper tab selected | PAGE LAYOUT, Page Setup | , *More Paper Sizes* |
| page size | PAGE LAYOUT, Page Setup | |
| Print Layout view | VIEW, Views | |
| Read Mode view | VIEW, Views | OR |
| ribbon display options | | |
| section break | PAGE LAYOUT, Page Setup | |
| watermark | DESIGN, Page Background | |
| Web Layout view | VIEW, Views | OR |

# Key Points *Review*

**Completion:** In the space provided at the right, indicate the correct term, symbol, or command.

1. This view displays a document in a format for efficient editing and formatting.  _____

2. This view displays a document in a format for easy viewing and reading.  _____

3. This is the default measurement for the top, bottom, left, and right margins.  _____

4. This is the default page orientation.  _____

5. Set specific margins at this dialog box with the Margins tab selected.  _____

6. Balance column text on the last page of a document by inserting this type of break at the end of the text.  _____

7. Use this view to display a section break.  _____

8. Format text into columns with the Columns button located in this group on the PAGE LAYOUT tab.  _____

9. If you hyphenate words in a document and then decide to remove the hyphens, click this button immediately.  _____

10. A lightened image that displays behind the text in a document is called this.  _____

11. The Page Borders button displays in this group on the DESIGN tab.  _____

12. Change the position of the page border from the edges of the page with options at this dialog box.  _____

# Chapter *Assessments*

## Applying Your Skills

Demonstrate your knowledge of features learned in this chapter by completing the following assessments.

### Assessment 6.1    Apply Formatting to a Computers in Industry Report

1. Open **CompIndustry.docx** and save the document with the name **C06-A01-CompIndustry**.
2. Apply the Heading 1 style to the titles *COMPUTERS IN INDUSTRY* and *REFERENCES*.
3. Apply the Heading 2 style to the headings in the report.
4. Apply the Centered style set.
5. Format the paragraphs of text below the *REFERENCES* title using a hanging indent.
6. Change the top, left, and right margins to 1.25 inches.
7. Manually hyphenate the text in the document. (Do not hyphenate proper nouns, such as names.)

8. Insert the SAMPLE 1 watermark in the document. (You will need to scroll down the list box to display this watermark.)
9. Insert a double-line page border in Blue color with a weight of 1½ points. (Choose the first double-line border in the *Style* list box at the Borders and Shading dialog box and apply the Blue color in the *Standard Colors* section.)
10. Display the Border and Shading Options dialog box and then change the top, left, bottom, and right measurements to 31 points. ***Hint: Display the Border and Shading Options dialog box by clicking the Options button at the Borders and Shading dialog box with the Page Border tab selected.***
11. Save, print, and then close **C06-A01-CompIndustry.docx**.

### Assessment 6.2    Apply Formatting to a Data Security Training Notice

1. Open **DataTraining.docx** and save the document with the name **C06-A02-DataTraining**.
2. Change the font for the entire document to 12-point Candara.
3. Set the title in 14-point Candara bold and center it.
4. Change the page orientation to landscape.
5. Change the top margin to 2.5 inches and the left and right margins to 1.8 inches.
6. Insert the ASAP 1 watermark in the document.
7. Insert a page border using the third option from the end of the list in the *Style* list box and change the color of the border to Dark Red (in the *Standard Colors* section). (Display the document in the Print backstage area and determine whether the entire page border will print. If the entire page border is not visible, display the Border and Shading Options dialog box and change the top, left, bottom, and right measurements to 31 points.)
8. Save, print, and then close **C06-A02-DataTraining.docx**.

### Assessment 6.3    Apply Formatting to an Interface Applications Report

1. Open **InterfaceApps.docx** and save the document with the name **C06-A03-InterfaceApps**.
2. Change the top margin to 1.5 inches.
3. Format the text from the first paragraph to the end of the document into two columns with 0.6-inch spacing and a line between columns.
4. Balance the columns on the second page.
5. Manually hyphenate the text in the document.
6. Insert an art page border using the first star images option that displays in the *Art* drop-down list and change the line width of the border to 10 points.
7. Save, print, and then close **C06-A03-InterfaceApps.docx**.

## Expanding Your Skills

Explore additional feature options or use Help to learn a new skill in creating this document.

### Assessment 6.4    Apply a Picture Watermark

1. Open **BGClientLtr.docx** and save the document with the name **C06-A04-BGClientLtr**.
2. Click the DESIGN tab, click the Watermark button, and then click *Custom Watermark* at the drop-down list.
3. At the Printed Watermark dialog box, determine how to insert a picture as a watermark into a document.
4. Insert the picture named **BG.jpg** (located in the Chapter06 folder) as a watermark.
5. Insert your initials in place of the *XX* that displays above the document name located at the end of the letter.
6. Save, print, and then close **C06-A04-BGClientLtr.docx**.

# Achieving Signature Status

Take your skills to the next level by completing these more challenging assessments.

## Assessment 6.5    Create and Format an Announcement

1. At a blank document, create the announcement shown in Figure 6.11. Set the text in Constantia, change the orientation to landscape, change the left and right margins to 2 inches, and set appropriate tabs for the tabbed text. Insert the watermark and page border as shown. (The page border is an art border located approximately two-thirds of the way down the list in the *Art* option box.) Change the color of the page border to Dark Red and the text color to Dark Blue.
2. Display the document in the Print backstage area and determine whether the entire page border will print. If the entire page border is not visible, display the Border and Shading Options dialog box and change the top, left, bottom, and right measurements to 31 points.
3. Save the completed document and name it **C06-A05-Announce**.
4. Print and then close **C06-A05-Announce.docx**.

**Figure 6.11  Assessment 6.5**

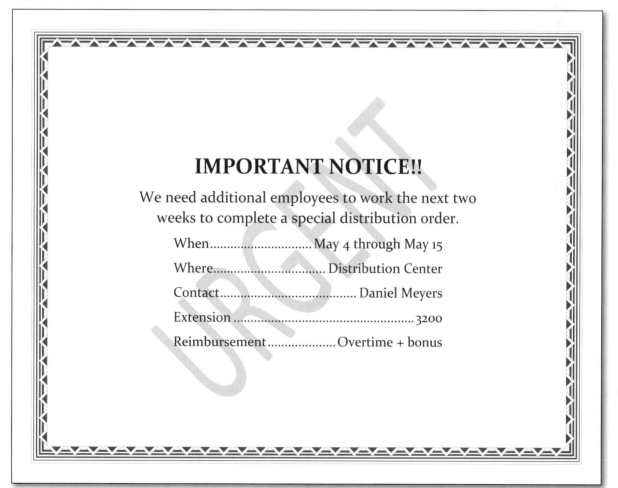

## Assessment 6.6 Format a Report on Delivering a Presentation

1. Open **DeliverPres.docx** and save the document with the name **C06-A06-DeliverPres**.
2. Change the top margin to 1.25 inches.
3. Apply bold and italic formatting to text and create bulleted paragraphs as shown in Figure 6.12.
4. Set the text from the beginning of the first paragraph to the end of the document in two columns with a line between them.
5. Apply the paragraph shading and border to the title as shown in the figure. (Apply the Blue, Accent 5, Lighter 60% paragraph shading.)
6. Apply the page border and change the page border color to Blue, Accent 5, Darker 50%. (The page border is an art border located approximately three-quarters of the way down the list in the *Art* option box—approximately the twentieth border option from the bottom of the list.)
7. Display the document in the Print backstage area and determine whether the entire page border will print. If the entire page border is not visible, display the Border and Shading Options dialog box and change the top, left, bottom, and right measurements to 31 points.
8. Save, print, and then close **C06-A06-DeliverPres.docx**.

**Figure 6.12 Assessment 6.6**

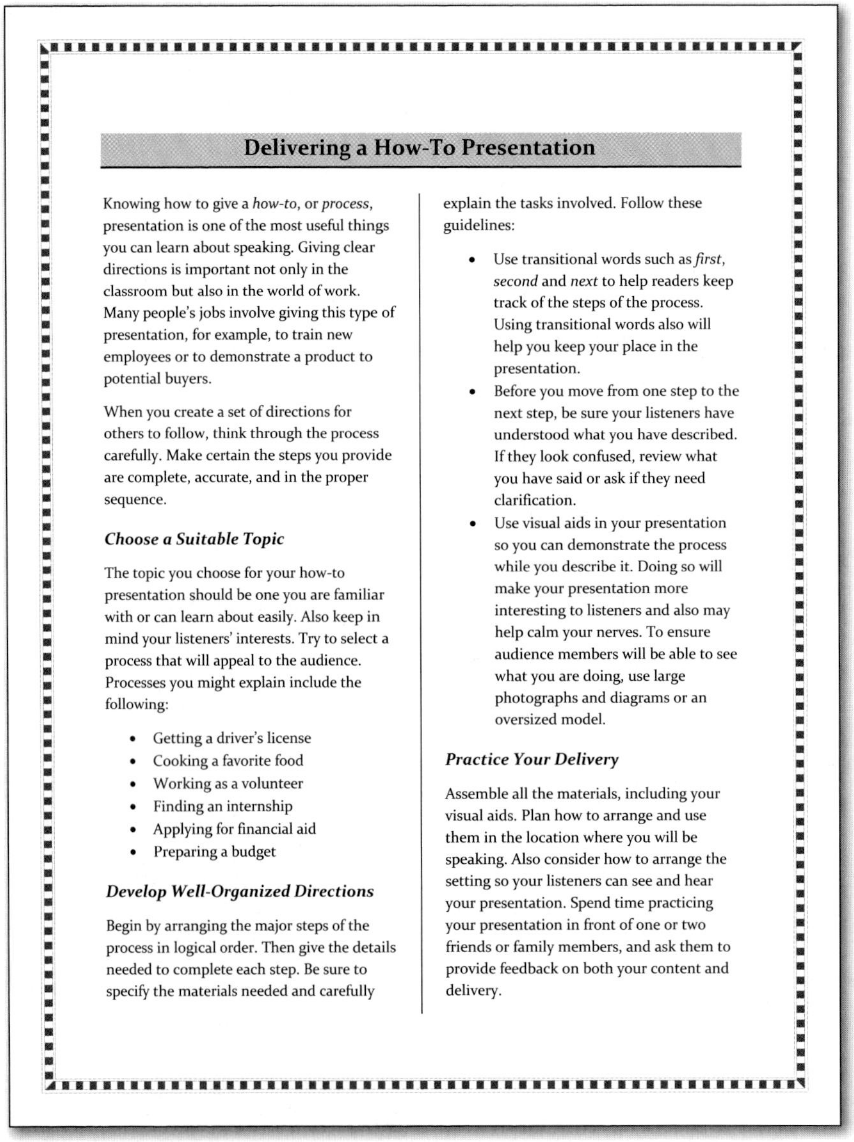

### Delivering a How-To Presentation

Knowing how to give a *how-to*, or *process*, presentation is one of the most useful things you can learn about speaking. Giving clear directions is important not only in the classroom but also in the world of work. Many people's jobs involve giving this type of presentation, for example, to train new employees or to demonstrate a product to potential buyers.

When you create a set of directions for others to follow, think through the process carefully. Make certain the steps you provide are complete, accurate, and in the proper sequence.

#### Choose a Suitable Topic

The topic you choose for your how-to presentation should be one you are familiar with or can learn about easily. Also keep in mind your listeners' interests. Try to select a process that will appeal to the audience. Processes you might explain include the following:

- Getting a driver's license
- Cooking a favorite food
- Working as a volunteer
- Finding an internship
- Applying for financial aid
- Preparing a budget

#### Develop Well-Organized Directions

Begin by arranging the major steps of the process in logical order. Then give the details needed to complete each step. Be sure to specify the materials needed and carefully explain the tasks involved. Follow these guidelines:

- Use transitional words such as *first*, *second* and *next* to help readers keep track of the steps of the process. Using transitional words also will help you keep your place in the presentation.
- Before you move from one step to the next step, be sure your listeners have understood what you have described. If they look confused, review what you have said or ask if they need clarification.
- Use visual aids in your presentation so you can demonstrate the process while you describe it. Doing so will make your presentation more interesting to listeners and also may help calm your nerves. To ensure audience members will be able to see what you are doing, use large photographs and diagrams or an oversized model.

#### Practice Your Delivery

Assemble all the materials, including your visual aids. Plan how to arrange and use them in the location where you will be speaking. Also consider how to arrange the setting so your listeners can see and hear your presentation. Spend time practicing your presentation in front of one or two friends or family members, and ask them to provide feedback on both your content and delivery.

# Chapter 7

# Customizing Page Formatting

## Performance Objectives

Upon successful completion of Chapter 7, you will be able to:

- Insert a page break, blank page, and cover page
- Insert page numbering
- Insert and edit headers and footers
- Find and replace text
- Use the Click and Type feature to position the insertion point within the document
- Align text vertically

**Tutorial 7.1**
Inserting a Blank Page and a Cover Page
**Tutorial 7.2**
Inserting Page Numbers and Page Breaks
**Tutorial 7.3**
Creating Headers and Footers
**Tutorial 7.4**
Finding and Replacing Text
**Tutorial 7.5**
Using Click and Type
**Tutorial 7.6**
Using Vertical Alignment

In Chapter 6, you learned how to format pages in a Word document by changing the margins, page orientation, and paper size; inserting section breaks and setting text in columns; hyphenating words; and inserting line numbers, watermarks, page colors, and page borders. In this chapter, you will learn how to insert other elements into a document, such as cover pages, blank pages, page breaks, page numbers, and headers and footers. You will also learn how to align text vertically; how to use the Click and Type feature, which allows you to insert text in specific locations in a document; and how to use the Find and Replace feature, which allows you to search for specific text and replace it with other text.

*Note: Before beginning computer exercises for this chapter, copy to your storage medium the Chapter07 folder from the CD that accompanies this textbook and then make Chapter07 the active folder.*

In this chapter, students will produce the following documents:

Exercise 7.1. C07-E01-CompAccess.docx
Exercise 7.2. C07-E02-LtrWriting.docx
Exercise 7.3. C07-E03-Lease.docx
Exercise 7.4. C07-E04-WordTrain.docx

Model answers for these exercises are shown on the following pages.

**Exercise 7.1**
C07-E01-CompAccess.docx

2015

# Computer Security

Student Name
Northland Security
2/11/2015

## UNAUTHORIZED ACCESS

Like uncharted wilderness, the Internet lacks borders. This inherent openness is what makes the Internet so valuable and yet so vulnerable. Over its short life, the Internet has grown so quickly that the legal system has not been able to keep pace. The security risks posed by networks and the Internet can be grouped into three categories: unauthorized access, information theft, and denial of service.

Hackers, individuals who gain access to computers and networks illegally, are responsible for most cases of unauthorized access. Hackers tend to exploit sites and programs that have poor security measures in place. However, they also gain access to more challenging sites by using sophisticated programs and strategies. Many hackers claim they hack merely because they like the challenge of trying to defeat security measures. They rarely have a more malicious motive, and they generally do not aim to destroy or damage the sites that they invade. In fact, hackers dislike being identified with those who seek to cause damage. They refer to hackers with malicious or criminal intent as *crackers*.

### User IDs and Passwords

To gain entry over the Internet to a secure computer system, most hackers focus on finding a working user ID and password combination. User IDs are easy to come by and are generally not secure information. Sending an email, for example, displays the sender's user ID in the return address, making it very public. The only missing element is the password. Hackers know from experience which passwords are common; they have programs that generate thousands of likely passwords and they try them systematically over a period of hours or days.

### System Backdoors

Programmers can sometimes inadvertently aid hackers by providing unintentional entrance to networks and information systems. One such unintentional entrance is a system "backdoor," which is a user ID and password that provides the highest level of authorization. Programmers innocently create a "backdoor" in the early days of system development to allow other programmers and team members to access the system to fix problems. Through negligence or by design, the user ID and password are sometimes left behind in the final version of the system. People who know about them can then enter the system, bypassing the security perhaps years later, when the backdoor has been forgotten.

### Spoofing

A sophisticated way to break into a network via the Internet involves spoofing, which is the process of fooling another computer by pretending to send information from a legitimate source. It works by altering the address that the system automatically puts on every message sent. The address is changed to one that the receiving computer is programmed to accept as a trusted source of information.

1

## Spyware

Spyware is a type of software that allows an intruder to spy upon someone else's computer. This alarming technology takes advantage of loopholes in the computer's security systems and allows a stranger to witness and record another person's every mouse click or keystroke on the monitor as it occurs. The spy can record activities and gain access to passwords and credit card information. Spyware generally requires the user to install it on the machine that is being spied upon, so it is highly unlikely that random strangers on the Internet could simply begin watching your computer. In the workplace, however, someone might be able to install the software without the victim's knowledge. Disguised as an email greeting, for example, the program can operate like a virus that gets the unwary user to install the spyware unknowingly.

2

Page 3

## INFORMATION THEFT

Information can be a company's most valuable possession. Stealing corporate information, a crime included in the category of industrial espionage, is unfortunately both easy to do and difficult to detect. This is due in part to the invisible nature of software and data. If a cracker breaks into a company network and manages to download the company database from the network onto a disk, there is no visible sign to the company that anything is amiss. The original database is still in place, working the same way it always has.

### Wireless Device Security

The growing number of wireless devices has created a new opportunity for data theft. Wireless devices such as cameras, Web phones, networked computers, PDAs, and input and output peripherals are inherently less secure than wired devices. Security is quite lax, and in some cases nonexistent, in new wireless technologies for handheld computers and cell phone systems. In a rush to match competition, manufacturers have tended to sacrifice security to move a product to the marketplace faster. Already, viruses are appearing in emails for cell phones and PDAs. With little protection available for these new systems, hackers and spies are enjoying a free hand with the new technology. One of the few available security protocols for wireless networks is Wired Equivalent Privacy (WEP), developed in conjunction with the standard for wireless local area networks. Newer versions of WEP with enhanced security features make it more difficult for hackers to intercept and modify data transmissions sent by radio waves or infrared signals.

### Data Browsing

Data browsing is a less damaging form of information theft that involves an invasion of privacy. Workers in many organizations have access to networked databases that contain private information about people. Accessing this information without an official reason is against the law. The IRS had a particularly large problem with data browsing in the late 1990s. Some employees were fired and the rest were given specialized training in appropriate conduct.

3

Page 4

**Exercise 7.2**
C07-E02-LtrWriting.docx

## LETTER FORMATTING

Achieving a balanced overall appearance to enhance readability is the primary goal of letter formatting. When you prepare business letters, consider the following formatting guidelines:

- **Spacing:** Generally, single space lines in business letters but double space between paragraphs.
- **Margins:** To achieve a balanced appearance, use equal margins on the left and right and approximately equal margins at the top and bottom, with the bottom margin two or three spaces greater than the top.
- **Justification:** A ragged right edge aids readability because no extra spacing appears within lines of text. Use left justification (ragged right edge) for business letters.
- **Date Line:** Include the month, day, and year with no abbreviations.
- **Attention Line:** Use the attention line when you want a specific person to receive a letter containing a message intended for an entire company or group within a company. The attention line appears as the first line of the inside address and may include a person's name or simply a job title or department name.
- **Adjusting for Letter Length:** To achieve a balanced appearance, exceptionally long or short letters may require one or more of the following margin or spacing adjustments:
  - Place the date higher or lower on the page.
  - Delete space between the date and the inside address.
  - Adjust side margins from three-quarters of an inch as a minimum and one and a half inches as a maximum.
  - Delete space between the complimentary close and the writer's signature line, leaving enough space for the signature.
  - Allow long letters to go beyond a single page.

When a letter goes beyond a single page, use a header on all pages after the first to avoid confusion if the pages become separated. In addition, make sure isolated words or lines of text (widows and orphans) do not begin or end a page.

Page 1

## LETTER STYLES

Business letters are formatted in one of three styles: block, modified block, or simplified:

- **Block Style:** The block style is recommended for its efficiency and streamlined appearance. The block-style letter begins each letter part and paragraph at the left margin.
- **Modified Block Style:** The indented date, complimentary close, and signature block of this style allows some formatting flexibility, especially to balance letterhead that may be flush with the left margin.
- **Simplified Style:** By using a subject line to replace the salutation, this letter style provides a comfortable option when writing to groups or to people whose names you do not know. This style does not use a complimentary close.

Page 2

## INTERNATIONAL CORRESPONDENCE

With the increased number of firms conducting business worldwide, international written communication has assumed new importance. Follow these guidelines when corresponding internationally, especially with people for whom English is not the primary language:

- Use a direct writing style and clear, precise words.
- Avoid slang, jargon, and idioms.
- Develop an awareness of cultural differences that may interfere with the communication process.

## INTERNATIONAL ADDRESSES

Use the company's letterhead or a business card as a guide for spelling and other information. Include the following when addressing international correspondences:

Line 1: Addressee's Name, Title
Line 2: Company Name
Line 3: Street Address
Line 4: City and Codes
Line 5: COUNTRY NAME (capitalized)

### Canadian Codes and Provinces

ON – Ontario
QC – Quebec
NS – Nova Scotia
NB – New Brunswick
MB – Manitoba
BC – British Columbia
PE – Prince Edward Island
SK – Saskatchewan
AB – Alberta
NL – Newfoundland and Labrador

### Canadian Codes and Territories

NT – Northwest Territories
YT – Yukon
NU – Nunavut

**Letter Formatting**

Page 3

Model Answers

**Exercise 7.3**

C07-E03-Lease.docx

---

**RENT AGREEMENT**

**THIS RENT AGREEMENT** (hereinafter referred to as the "Agreement") made and entered into this DAY of MONTH, YEAR, by and between Maggie Branson and Lee Gardella.

**WITNESSETH:**

**WHEREAS,** Maggie Branson is the owner of real property and is desirous of renting the Premises to Lee Gardella upon the terms and conditions as contained herein.

**NOW, THEREFORE,** for and in consideration of the covenants and obligations contained herein and other good and valuable consideration, the receipt and sufficiency of which is hereby acknowledged, the parties hereto agree as follows:

1. **TERM.** Maggie Branson rents to Lee Gardella and Lee Gardella rents from Maggie Branson the Premises.
2. **RENT.** The total rent for the premise is RENT due on the first day of each month minus any set off for approved repairs.
3. **DAMAGE DEPOSIT.** Upon the due execution of this Agreement, Lee Gardella shall deposit with Maggie Branson the sum of DEPOSIT receipt of which is hereby acknowledged by Maggie Branson, as security for any damage caused to the Premises during the term hereof. Such deposit shall be returned to Lee Gardella, without interest, and minus any set off for damages to the Premises upon the termination of this Agreement.
4. **USE OF PREMISES.** The Premises shall be used and occupied by Lee Gardella and Lee Gardella's immediate family, exclusively, as a private single family dwelling, and no part of the Premises shall be used at any time during the term of this Agreement by Lee Gardella for the purpose of carrying on any business, profession, or trade of any kind, or for any purpose other than as a private single family dwelling. Lee Gardella shall not allow any other person, other than Lee Gardella's immediate family, to occupy the Premises.
5. **CONDITION OF PREMISES.** Lee Gardella stipulates, represents, and warrants that Lee Gardella has examined the Premises, and that they are in good order, repair, and in a safe, clean and tenantable condition.
6. **ALTERATIONS AND IMPROVEMENTS.** Lee Gardella shall make no alterations or improvements on the Premises or construct any building or make any other improvements on the Premises without the prior written consent of Maggie Branson.
7. **NON-DELIVERY OF POSSESSION.** In the event Maggie Branson cannot deliver possession of the Premises to Lee Gardella upon the commencement of the term, through no fault of Maggie Branson or its agents, then Maggie Branson or its agents shall have no liability, but the rental herein provided shall abate until possession is given. Maggie Branson or its agents shall have thirty (30) days in which to give possession, and if possession is tendered within such time, Lee Gardella agrees to accept the demised

---

Premises and pay the rental herein provided from that date. In the event possession cannot be delivered within such time, through no fault of Maggie Branson or its agents, then this Agreement and all rights hereunder shall terminate.

8. **UTILITIES.** Lee Gardella shall be responsible for arranging for and paying for all utility services required on the Premises.

**IN WITNESS WHEREOF** the parties have reviewed the information above and certify, to the best of their knowledge, that the information provided by the signatory is true and accurate.

_____
Maggie Branson

_____
Lee Gardella

**Exercise 7.4**

C07-E04-WordTrain.docx

MICROSOFT WORD TRAINING

Formatting Company Documents

Wednesday, May 20, 2015

Technology Department Training Center

8:30 a.m. to 11:30 a.m.

Sponsored by
Culver Training Services

# Inserting Page Elements

The Pages group on the INSERT tab contains three buttons for inserting and then formatting or modifying elements in a document. With these buttons, you can insert a page break, blank page, and predesigned cover page.

## Inserting a Page Break

Word assumes that you are using standard-sized paper, which is 8.5 inches wide and 11 inches long. With default top and bottom margins of 1 inch, a Word document contains approximately 9 inches of text on a page. At approximately the 10-inch mark, Word automatically inserts a page break. You can insert your own page break in a document with the keyboard shortcut Ctrl + Enter or with the Page Break button in the Pages group on the INSERT tab.

A page break that is automatically inserted by Word is considered a *soft* page break and a page break that you insert is considered a *hard* page break. A soft page break adjusts automatically when you add or delete text from a document. A hard page break does not adjust and is therefore less flexible than a soft page break.

If you add or delete text from a document with hard page breaks, check the breaks to determine whether they are still in desirable locations. Display hard page breaks along with other nonprinting characters by clicking the Show/Hide ¶ button in the Paragraph

**Insert a Page Break**
1. Click INSERT tab.
2. Click Page Break button.
OR
Press Ctrl + Enter.

Page Break

group on the HOME tab. A hard page break displays as a row of dots with the words *Page Break* in the center.

To delete a hard page break, position the insertion point at the beginning of the page break and then press the Delete key. If the display of nonprinting characters is turned off, delete a hard page break by positioning the insertion point immediately above the page break and then pressing the Backspace key.

---

## Exercise 7.1A  Inserting Page Breaks
Part 1 of 3

1. Open **CompAccess.docx** and save the document with the name **C07-E01-CompAccess**.
2. Make the following formatting changes:
   a. Apply the Heading 1 style to the two titles: *UNAUTHORIZED ACCESS* and *INFORMATION THEFT*.
   b. Apply the Heading 2 style to the six headings: *User IDs and Passwords, System Backdoors, Spoofing, Spyware, Wireless Device Security,* and *Data Browsing*.
   c. Apply the Centered style set.
   d. Change the theme fonts to Century Gothic-Palatino Linotype.

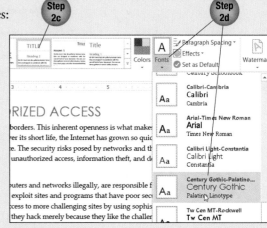

3. Insert a page break by completing the following steps:
   a. Position the insertion point at the beginning of the title *INFORMATION THEFT* (located on page 2).
   b. Click the INSERT tab and then click the Page Break button in the Pages group.

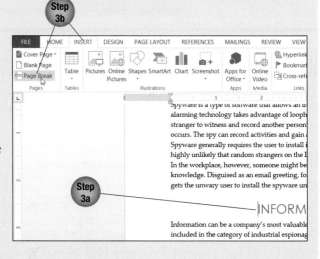

4. Move the insertion point to the beginning of the heading *Spoofing* and then press Ctrl + Enter to insert a page break.
5. Scroll through the document and notice the page breaks.
6. Delete a page break by completing the following steps:
   a. Position the insertion point at the end of the paragraph in the *System Backdoors* section.
   b. Click the HOME tab.
   c. Click the Show/Hide ¶ button in the Paragraph group.
   d. Position the insertion point at the beginning of the page break (displays with the words *Page Break*) and then press the Delete key.
   e. Press the Delete key again to remove the blank line.
   f. Click the Show/Hide ¶ button to turn off the display of nonprinting characters.
7. Save **C07-E01-CompAccess.docx**.

# Inserting a Blank Page

Click the Blank Page button in the Pages group on the INSERT tab to insert a blank page at the position of the insertion point. Inserting a blank page can be useful as a spaceholder in a document when you want to insert an illustration, graphic, or figure.

# Inserting a Cover Page

If you are preparing a document for distribution to others or if you simply want to improve the appearance of a document, consider inserting a cover page. With the Cover Page button in the Pages group on the INSERT tab, you can insert a predesigned and formatted cover page and then type text in specific locations on the page to personalize it. Click the Cover Page button and a drop-down list displays similar to the one shown in Figure 7.1. The drop-down list provides a visual representation of each cover page option. Scroll through the list and then click the cover page you want to use.

These predesigned cover pages contain location placeholders for entering specific information. For example, a cover page might contain the placeholder *[Document title]*. Click anywhere in the placeholder and then type the desired text. The first time you click placeholder text, all of the text is selected. If you have typed text in a placeholder, clicking in the text will position the insertion point at that location. If you want to delete the entire placeholder, click the placeholder tab and then press the Delete key. To delete the text but not the placeholder, select only the text in the placeholder and then press the Delete key.

**QUICK STEPS**

**Insert a Blank Page**
1. Click INSERT tab.
2. Click Blank Page button.

**Insert a Cover Page**
1. Click INSERT tab.
2. Click Cover Page button.
3. Click desired cover page at drop-down list.

Blank Page

Cover Page

**Figure 7.1 Cover Page Drop-down List**

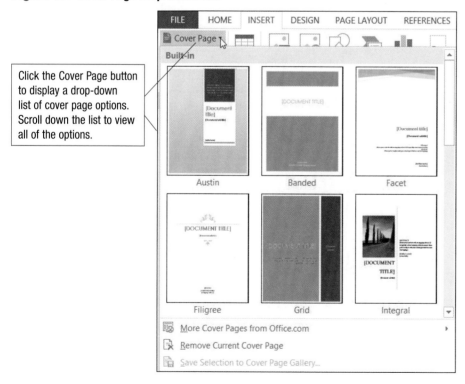

Click the Cover Page button to display a drop-down list of cover page options. Scroll down the list to view all of the options.

1. With **C07-E01-CompAccess.docx** open, create a blank page by completing the following steps:

   a. Move the insertion point to the beginning of the heading *Spoofing* (located on the first page).

   b. Click the INSERT tab.

   c. Click the Blank Page button in the Pages group.

2. Insert a cover page by completing the following steps:

   a. Press Ctrl + Home to move the insertion point to the beginning of the document.

   b. Click the Cover Page button in the Pages group on the INSERT tab.

   c. At the drop-down list, scroll down and then click the *Motion* cover page.

   d. Click in the placeholder text *[Year]*, click the down-pointing arrow that displays at the right of the placeholder, and then click the Today button that displays at the bottom of the drop-down calendar.

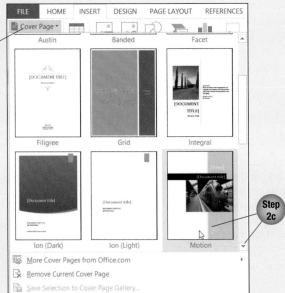

e.   Click in the placeholder text *[Document title]* and then type **Computer Security**.

f.   Click in the placeholder text *[Company name]* and then type **Northland Security**.

g.   Select the name that displays above the company name and then type your first and last names. If instead of a name, the *[Author name]* placeholder displays above the company name, click in the placeholder and then type your first and last names.

3.   Remove the blank page you created in Step 1 by completing the following steps:

a.   Move the insertion point to the end of the paragraph in the *System Backdoors* section.

b.   Press the Delete key until the *Spoofing* heading displays below the paragraph.

> password are sometimes left behind in the final version of the system. People who know about them can then enter the system, bypassing the security perhaps years later, when the backdoor has been forgotten.
>
> Spoofing
>
> A sophisticated way to break into a network via the Internet involves spoofing, which is the process of fooling another computer by pretending to send information from a legitimate source. It works by

4.   Save **C07-E01-CompAccess.docx**.

# Inserting Predesigned Page Numbering

**Insert Page Numbering**
1. Click INSERT tab.
2. Click Page Number button.
3. Click desired option at drop-down list.

Page Number

By default, Word does not print page numbers on document pages. If you want to insert page numbers in a document, use the Page Number button in the Header & Footer group on the INSERT tab. When you click the Page Number button, a drop-down list displays with options for specifying where on the page you want the page number inserted. Point to an option at this list and a drop-down list displays with predesigned page formats. Scroll through the options in the drop-down list and then click the desired option. If you want to change the format, you can remove page numbering from a document by clicking the Page Number button and then clicking *Remove Page Numbers* at the drop-down list.

## Exercise 7.1C  Inserting Predesigned Page Numbering                    Part 3 of 3

1. With **C07-E01-CompAccess.docx** open, insert page numbering by completing the following steps:
   a. Move the insertion point to the beginning of the title *UNAUTHORIZED ACCESS*.
   b. Click the INSERT tab.
   c. Click the Page Number button in the Header & Footer group and then point to *Top of Page*.
   d. Scroll down the drop-down list and then click the *Brackets 2* option.

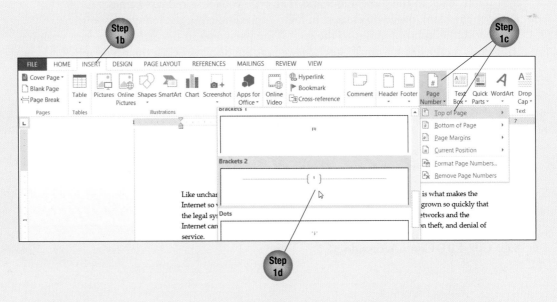

2. Double-click in the document to make it active and then scroll through the document to view the page numbering that displays at the top of each page except the cover page.
3. Remove the page numbering by clicking the INSERT tab, clicking the Page Number button, and then clicking *Remove Page Numbers* at the drop-down list.

4. Click the Page Number button, point to *Bottom of Page*, scroll down the drop-down list, and then click the *Thin Line* option.

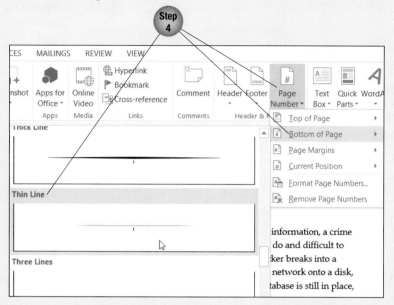

5. Click the Close Header and Footer button that displays at the right side of the HEADER & FOOTER TOOLS DESIGN tab to make the document active and then scroll through the document and view the page numbering.
6. Save, print, and then close **C07-E01-CompAccess.docx**.

# Inserting Predesigned Headers and Footers

Text that appears at the top of every page of a multipage document is called a ***header*** and text that appears at the bottom of every page is called a ***footer***. The use of headers and footers is common in manuscripts, textbooks, reports, and other publications.

Insert a predesigned header in a document by clicking the INSERT tab and then clicking the Header button in the Header & Footer group. This displays the drop-down list shown in Figure 7.2 on the next page. At this list, click the predesigned header you want to use and the header is inserted in the document. The header is visible in Print Layout view but not in Draft view.

A predesigned header or footer, like a predesigned cover page, may contain location placeholders where you can enter specific information. For example, a header might contain the placeholder *[Document title]*. Click in the placeholder and then type the desired text. The first time you click placeholder text, all of the text is selected. If you have typed text in a placeholder, clicking in the text will position the insertion point at that location. If you want to delete the entire placeholder, click the placeholder tab and then press the Delete key. To delete the text but not the placeholder, select only the text in the placeholder and then press the Delete key.

To return to your document after inserting a header or footer, double-click in the document. You can also return to the document by clicking the Close Header and Footer button in the Close group on the HEADER & FOOTER TOOLS DESIGN tab.

**Insert a Predesigned Header**
1. Click INSERT tab.
2. Click Header button.
3. Click desired option at drop-down list.
4. Type text in specific placeholders in header.

Header

Figure 7.2 **Header Button Drop-down List**

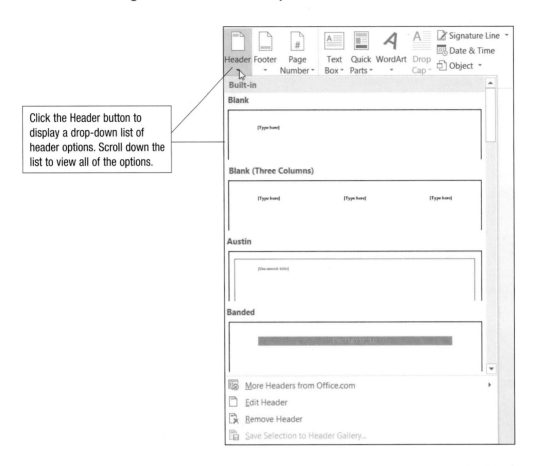

Click the Header button to display a drop-down list of header options. Scroll down the list to view all of the options.

---

## Exercise 7.2A  Inserting a Predesigned Header in a Document     Part 1 of 3

1. Open **LtrWriting.docx** and save the document with the name **C07-E02-LtrWriting**.
2. Apply the Minimalist style set.
3. Move the insertion point to the beginning of the heading *INTERNATIONAL CORRESPONDENCE* (located on page 2) and then insert a page break by clicking the INSERT tab and then clicking the Page Break button in the Pages group.
4. Press Ctrl + Home to move the insertion point to the beginning of the document and then insert a header by completing the following steps:

Step 2

a. Click the Header button in the Header & Footer group on the INSERT tab.
b. Scroll down the drop-down list and then click the *Integral* header.

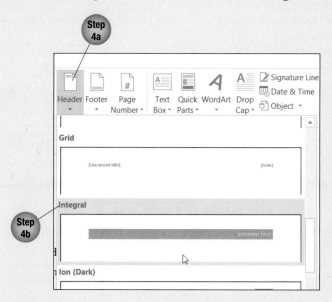

c. Click anywhere in the placeholder text *[DOCUMENT TITLE]* and then type **letter formatting**. (The header placeholder will change the text you type to uppercase letters.)

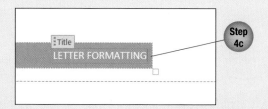

d. Close the header and return to the document by clicking the Close Header and Footer button that displays at the right side of the HEADER & FOOTER TOOLS DESIGN tab.
5. Scroll through the document to see how the header will print.
6. Save and then print **C07-E02-LtrWriting.docx**.

Insert a predesigned footer in the same manner you inserted a predesigned header. Click the Footer button in the Header & Footer group on the INSERT tab and a drop-down list displays similar to the Header button drop-down list shown in Figure 7.2 on the previous page. Click the desired footer and the predesigned footer is inserted in the document. Like a header, a footer displays in Print Layout view but not in Draft view.

## Removing a Header or Footer

Remove a header from a document by clicking the INSERT tab and then clicking the Header button in the Header & Footer group. At the drop-down list that displays, click the *Remove Header* option. Complete similar steps to remove a footer.

**Insert a Predesigned Footer**
1. Click INSERT tab.
2. Click Footer button.
3. Click desired option at drop-down list.
4. Type text in specific placeholders in footer.

Footer

1. With **C07-E02-LtrWriting.docx** open, press Ctrl + Home to move the insertion point to the beginning of the document.
2. Remove the header by clicking the INSERT tab, clicking the Header button in the Header & Footer group, and then clicking the *Remove Header* option at the drop-down list.
3. Insert a footer in the document by completing the following steps:
   a. Click the Footer button in the Header & Footer group.
   b. Scroll down the drop-down list and then click the *Integral* footer.

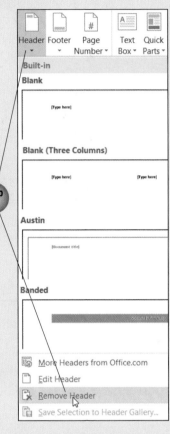

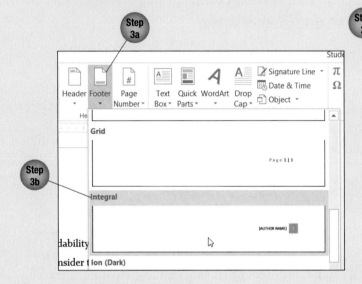

   c. Select the name that displays in the *[Author]* placeholder and then type your first and last names. (If a name does not display in the placeholder, click in the placeholder and then type your first and last names.)

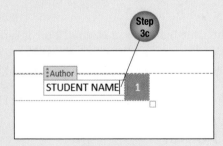

   d. Double-click in the document text. (This makes the document text active and dims the footer.)
4. Scroll through the document to see how the footer will print.
5. Save and then print **C07-E02-LtrWriting.docx**.

## Editing a Predesigned Header or Footer

Predesigned headers and footers contain elements such as page numbers, the document title, and the author name. You can change the formatting of an element by clicking it and then applying the desired formatting. You can also select and then delete an element. In Print Layout view, you can display the header or footer pane for editing by double-clicking a header or footer, respectively. You can also display the header pane for editing by clicking the INSERT tab, clicking the Header button, and then clicking the *Edit Header* option. To edit a footer, click the Footer button on the INSERT tab and then click *Edit Footer* at the drop-down list.

---

**Exercise 7.2C**   Formatting and Deleting Header and Footer Elements        **Part 3 of 3**

1. With **C07-E02-LtrWriting.docx** open, remove the footer by clicking the INSERT tab, clicking the Footer button, and then clicking *Remove Footer* at the drop-down list.
2. Insert and then format a header by completing the following steps:
   a. Click the Header button in the Header & Footer group on the INSERT tab, scroll down the drop-down list, and then click *Motion (Odd Page)*. (This header inserts the document title as well as the page number.)

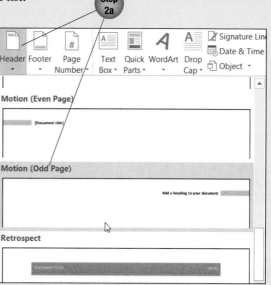

   b. Delete the document title from the header by clicking anywhere in the text *Letter Formatting*, selecting the text, and then pressing the Delete key.
   c. Double-click in the document text.
3. Insert and then format a footer by completing the following steps:
   a. Click the INSERT tab.
   b. Click the Footer button, scroll down the drop-down list, and then click *Motion (Odd Page)*.
   c. Click in the *[Date]* placeholder and then type **Letter Formatting**. (If the date displays in the placeholder, select the date and then type **Letter Formatting**.)
   d. Select the text you just typed (*Letter Formatting*) and then click the HOME tab.
   e. Apply bold formatting and change the font size to 12 points.
   f. Double-click in the document text.
4. Scroll through the document to see how the header and footer will print.
5. Save, print, and then close **C07-E02-LtrWriting.docx**.

# Finding and Replacing Text

Find

Replace

Use the Find feature in Word to search in a document for specific characters or types of formatting. Use the Find and Replace feature to search for specific characters or types of formatting and replace them with other characters or formatting. The Find button and Replace button are located in the Editing group on the HOME tab.

## Finding Text

**QUICK STEPS**

**Find Text**
1. Click HOME tab.
2. Click Find button.
3. Type search text.
4. Click Find Next button.

Click the Find button in the Editing group on the HOME tab (or press the keyboard shortcut Ctrl + F) and the Navigation pane displays at the left side of the screen with the RESULTS tab selected. With this tab selected, type the text to be searched for in the search text box and each occurrence of the text in the document is highlighted. A fragment of the text surrounding the search text also displays in a thumbnail in the Navigation pane. For example, search for *Lessee* in the **Lease.docx** document and the screen displays, as shown in Figure 7.3. Notice that each occurrence of *Lessee* displays highlighted in yellow in the document and the Navigation pane displays thumbnails of the text surrounding the occurrences of *Lessee*.

**Figure 7.3 Navigation Pane Showing Search Results**

Click a text thumbnail in the Navigation pane and the occurrence of the search text is selected in the document. If you hover your mouse over a text thumbnail in the Navigation pane, the page number location displays in a small box near the mouse pointer. You can also move to the next occurrence of the search text by clicking the Next button (which contains a down-pointing triangle) that displays below and to the right of the search text box. Click the Previous button (which contains an up-pointing triangle) to move to the previous occurrence of the search text.

Click the down-pointing arrow at the right of the search text box and a drop-down list displays. It shows options for displaying dialog boxes, such as the Find Options dialog box and Find and Replace dialog box, and also options for specifying what you want to find in the document, such as figures, tables, and equations.

You can also highlight search text in a document with options at the Find and Replace dialog box with the Find tab selected. Display this dialog box by clicking the Find button arrow in the Editing group on the HOME tab and then clicking the *Advanced Find* option at the drop-down list. You can also display the Find and Replace dialog box with the Find tab selected by clicking the down-pointing arrow at the right of the search text box in the Navigation pane and then clicking the *Advanced Find* option at the drop-down list. To highlight search text, type the search text in the *Find what* text box, click the Reading Highlight button, and then click *Highlight All* at the drop-down list. All occurrences of the text in the document are highlighted. To remove highlighting, click the Reading Highlight button and then click *Clear Highlighting* at the drop-down list.

## Exercise 7.3A   Finding and Highlighting Text                          Part 1 of 3

1. Open **Lease.docx** and save the document with the name **C07-E03-Lease**.
2. Find all occurrences of *lease* by completing the following steps:
   a. Click the Find button in the Editing group on the HOME tab.
   b. Click the RESULTS tab in the Navigation pane.
   c. Type **lease** in the search text box in the Navigation pane.
   d. After a moment, all occurrences of *lease* in the document are highlighted and text thumbnails display in the Navigation pane. Click a couple of the text thumbnails in the Navigation pane to select the text in the document.
   e. Click the Previous button (which contains an up-pointing triangle) to select the previous occurrence of *lease* in the document.

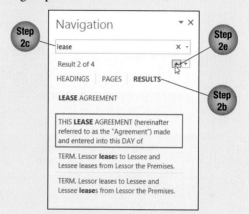

3. Use the Find and Replace dialog box with the Find tab selected to highlight all occurrences of *Premises* in the document by completing the following steps:
   a. Press Ctrl + Home to move the insertion point to the beginning of the document.
   b. Click the down-pointing arrow at the right of the search text box in the Navigation pane and then click *Advanced Find* at the drop-down list.

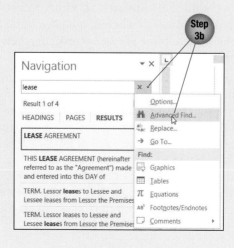

c.  At the Find and Replace dialog box with the Find tab selected (and *lease* selected in the *Find what* text box), type **Premises**.

d.  Click the Reading Highlight button and then click *Highlight All* at the drop-down list.

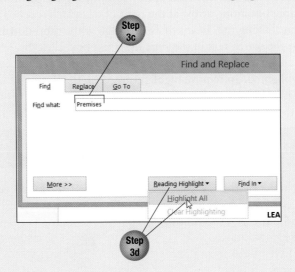

e.  Click in the document to make it active and then scroll through the document and notice the occurrences of highlighted text.

f.  Click in the dialog box to make it active.

g.  Click the Reading Highlight button and then click *Clear Highlighting* at the drop-down list.

h.  Click the Close button to close the Find and Replace dialog box.

4.  Close the Navigation pane by clicking the Close button that displays in the upper right corner of the pane.

5.  Save **C07-E03-Lease.docx**.

## Finding and Replacing Text

**Find and Replace Text**

1. Click HOME tab.
2. Click Replace button.
3. Type search text.
4. Press Tab key.
5. Type replacement text.
6. Click Replace or Replace All button.

To find and replace text, click the Replace button in the Editing group on the HOME tab or use the keyboard shortcut Ctrl + H. Either action displays the Find and Replace dialog box with the Replace tab selected, as shown in Figure 7.4 on the next page. Type the text you want to find in the *Find what* text box, press the Tab key, and then type the replacement text in the *Replace with* text box.

The Find and Replace dialog box contains several command buttons. Click the Find Next button to tell Word to find the next occurrence of the text. Click the Replace button to replace the text and find the next occurrence. If you know that you want all occurrences of the text in the *Find what* text box replaced with the characters in the *Replace with* text box, click the Replace All button. This replaces every occurrence from the location of the insertion point to the beginning or end of the document (depending on the search direction). Click the Cancel button to close the Find and Replace dialog box. If you make a mistake when replacing text, close the Find and Replace dialog box and then click the Undo button on the Quick Access toolbar.

**Figure 7.4 Find and Replace Dialog Box with the Replace Tab Selected**

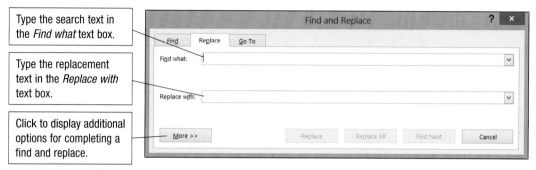

Type the search text in the *Find what* text box.

Type the replacement text in the *Replace with* text box.

Click to display additional options for completing a find and replace.

---

## Exercise 7.3B  Finding and Replacing Text

Part 2 of 3

1. With **C07-E03-Lease.docx** open, make sure the insertion point is positioned at the beginning of the document.
2. Find all occurrences of *Lessor* and replace them with *Maggie Branson* by completing the following steps:
   a. Click the Replace button in the Editing group on the HOME tab.
   b. At the Find and Replace dialog box with the Replace tab selected, type **Lessor** in the *Find what* text box.
   c. Press the Tab key to move the insertion point to the *Replace with* text box.
   d. Type **Maggie Branson**.
   e. Click the Replace All button.
   f. At the message telling you that 13 replacements were made, click OK. (Do not close the Find and Replace dialog box.)

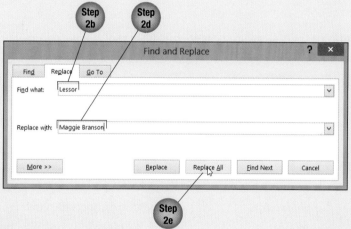

3. With the Find and Replace dialog box still open, complete steps similar to those in Step 2 to find all occurrences of *Lessee* and replace them with *Lee Gardella.* (Word should make 18 replacements.)
4. Close the Find and Replace dialog box.
5. Save **C07-E03-Lease.docx**.

---

## Choosing Check Box Options

The Find and Replace dialog box contains a variety of search option check boxes for completing a search. To display these options, click the More button located at the bottom of the dialog box. This causes the Find and Replace dialog box to expand, as shown in Figure 7.5. Each option and what will occur if it is selected is described in Table 7.1 on the next page. To remove the display of options, click the Less button, which was previously the More button. (Using wildcards with the Find or Find and Replace feature and finding and replacing formatting is covered in Chapter 18.)

**Figure 7.5 Expanded Find and Replace Dialog Box**

Click to remove the display of search options.

Specify search options by clicking the desired check boxes in this section.

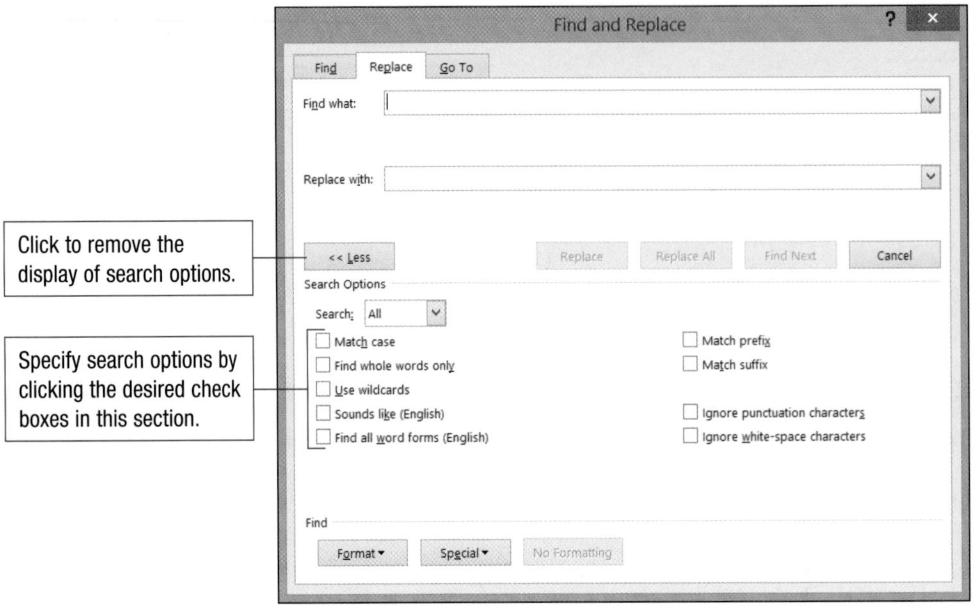

**Table 7.1 Options Available at the Expanded Find and Replace Dialog Box**

| Choose this option | To |
|---|---|
| *Match case* | Exactly match the case of the search text. For example, if you search for *Book* and select the *Match case* option, Word will stop at *Book* but not *book* or *BOOK*. |
| *Find whole words only* | Find a whole word, not a part of a word. For example, if you search for *her* and do not select *Find whole words only*, Word will stop at there, here, hers, etc. |
| *Use wildcards* | Use wildcards, special characters, or special search operators. |
| *Sounds like* | Match words that sound alike but are spelled differently, such as *know* and *no*. |
| *Find all word forms* | Find all forms of the word entered in the *Find what* text box. For example, if you enter *hold*, Word will stop at *held* and *holding*. |
| *Match prefix* | Find only those words that begin with the letters in the *Find what* text box. For example, if you enter *per*, Word will stop at words such as *perform* and *perfect* but skip words such as *super* and *hyperlink*. |
| *Match suffix* | Find only those words that end with the letters in the *Find what* text box. For example, if you enter *ly*, Word will stop at words such as *accurately* and *quietly* but skip over words such *catalyst* and *lyre*. |
| *Ignore punctuation characters* | Ignore punctuation within characters. For example, if you enter *US* in the *Find what* text box, Word will stop at *U.S.* |
| *Ignore white-space characters* | Ignore spaces between letters. For example, if you enter *F B I* in the *Find what* text box, Word will stop at *FBI*. |

1. With **C07-E03-Lease.docx** open, make sure the insertion point is positioned at the beginning of the document.
2. Find all word forms of the word *lease* and replace them with *rent* by completing the following steps:

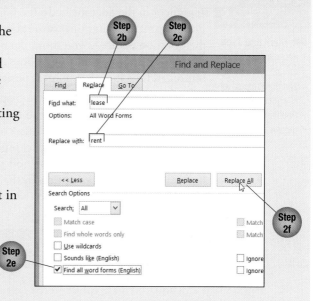

   a. Click the Replace button in the Editing group on the HOME tab.
   b. At the Find and Replace dialog box with the Replace tab selected, type **lease** in the *Find what* text box.
   c. Press the Tab key and then type **rent** in the *Replace with* text box.
   d. Click the More button.
   e. Click the *Find all word forms* option. (This inserts a check mark in the check box.)
   f. Click the Replace All button.
   g. At the message telling you that *Replace All* is not recommended with *Find all word forms*, click OK.
   h. At the message telling you that five replacements were made, click OK.
   i. Click the *Find all word forms* option to remove the check mark.
3. Find the word *less* and replace each occurrence with the word *minus* and specify that you want Word to find only those words that end in *less* by completing the following steps:

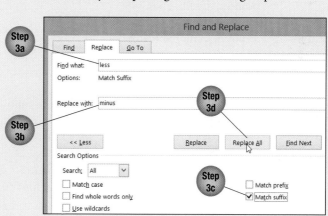

   a. At the expanded Find and Replace dialog box, select the text in the *Find what* text box and then type **less**.
   b. Select the text in the *Replace with* text box and then type **minus**.
   c. Click the *Match suffix* check box to insert a check mark and tell Word to find only words that end in *less*.
   d. Click the Replace All button.
   e. At the message telling you that two replacements were made, click OK.
   f. Click the *Match suffix* check box to remove the check mark.
   g. Click the Less button.
   h. Close the Find and Replace dialog box.
4. Save, print, and then close **C07-E03-Lease.docx**.

# Using the Click and Type Feature

**QUICK STEPS**

**Use Click and Type**
1. Hover mouse at left margin, between left and right margin, or at right margin.
2. Double-click left mouse button.

Use Word's Click and Type feature to position the insertion point at a specific location and alignment in the document. To use Click and Type, make sure the document displays in Print Layout view and then hover the mouse pointer at the location you want to position the insertion point. As you move the mouse pointer, you will notice that the pointer displays with varying horizontal lines representing the alignment. Double-click the mouse button and the insertion point is positioned at the location of the mouse pointer.

If the horizontal lines do not display next to the mouse pointer when you double-click the mouse button, a left tab is set at the position of the insertion point. If you want to change the alignment and not set a tab, make sure the horizontal lines display near the mouse pointer before double-clicking the mouse. You can turn off the Click and Type feature by clicking the FILE tab and then clicking *Options*. At the Word Options dialog box, click the *Advanced* option in the left panel, click the *Enable click and type* check box to remove the check mark, and then click OK.

## Exercise 7.4A  Using Click and Type                          Part 1 of 2

1. At a blank document, create the centered text shown in Figure 7.6 on the next page by completing the following steps:
   a. Position the I-beam pointer between the left and right margins at about the 3.25-inch mark on the horizontal ruler and at the top of the vertical ruler.
   b. When the center alignment lines display below the I-beam pointer, double-click the left mouse button.

Step 1b

   c. Type the centered text shown in Figure 7.6. Press Shift + Enter to end each text line.
2. Change to right alignment by completing the following steps:
   a. Position the I-beam pointer near the right margin at approximately the 1.5-inch mark on the vertical ruler until the right-alignment lines display at the left side of the I-beam pointer.
   b. Double-click the left mouse button.
   c. Type the right-aligned text shown in Figure 7.6. Press Shift + Enter to end the text line.
3. Select the centered text and then change the font to 14-point Constantia bold and the line spacing to double.
4. Select the right-aligned text, change the font to 10-point Constantia bold, and then deselect the text.
5. Save the document and name it **C07-E04-WordTrain.**

**Figure 7.6 Exercise 7.4A**

MICROSOFT WORD TRAINING
Formatting Company Documents
Wednesday, May 20, 2015
Technology Department Training Center
8:30 a.m. to 11:30 a.m.

Sponsored by
Culver Training Services

# Vertically Aligning Text

Text in a Word document is aligned at the top of the page by default. You can change this alignment with the *Vertical alignment* option at the Page Setup dialog box with the Layout tab selected, as shown in Figure 7.7. Display this dialog box by clicking the PAGE LAYOUT tab, clicking the Page Setup group dialog box launcher, and then clicking the Layout tab at the Page Setup dialog box.

The *Vertical alignment* option box in the Page Setup dialog box contains four choices: *Top*, *Center*, *Justified*, and *Bottom*. The default setting is *Top*, which aligns text at the top of the page. Choose *Center* if you want text centered in the middle of the page vertically. The *Justified* option adds space between paragraphs of text (not within) to fill the page from the top to bottom margins. If you center or justify text, it does not display as centered or justified in Draft view, but it does display centered or justified in Print Layout view. Choose the *Bottom* option to align text in the document vertically along the bottom of the page.

**QUICK STEPS**

**Vertically Align Text**
1. Click PAGE LAYOUT tab.
2. Click Page Setup group dialog box launcher.
3. Click Layout tab.
4. Click down-pointing arrow at right of *Vertical alignment* option.
5. Click desired alignment.
6. Click OK.

**Figure 7.7 Page Setup Dialog Box with Layout Tab Selected**

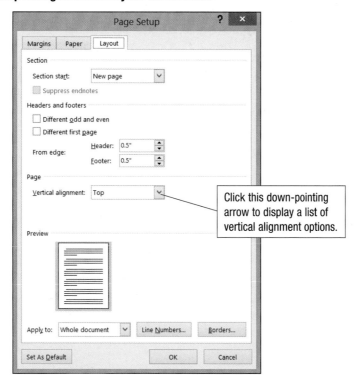

Click this down-pointing arrow to display a list of vertical alignment options.

1. With **C07-E04-WordTrain.docx** open, click the PAGE LAYOUT tab and then click the Page Setup group dialog box launcher.
2. At the Page Setup dialog box, click the Layout tab.
3. Click the down-pointing arrow at the right of the *Vertical alignment* option box and then click *Center* at the drop-down list.
4. Click OK to close the dialog box.
5. Save, print, and then close **C07-E04-WordTrain.docx**.

# Chapter Summary

➤ The page break that Word inserts automatically is a soft page break. A page break that you insert is a hard page break. Insert a hard page break by clicking the Page Break button in the Pages group on the INSERT tab or by pressing Ctrl + Enter.

➤ Insert a blank page in a document by clicking the Blank Page button in the Pages group on the INSERT tab.

➤ Insert a predesigned and formatted cover page by clicking the Cover Page button in the Pages group on the INSERT tab and then clicking the desired option at the drop-down list.

➤ Insert predesigned and formatted page numbering by clicking the Page Number button in the Header & Footer group on the INSERT tab, specifying the desired location of the page numbers, and then clicking the desired page numbering option.

➤ Text that appears at the top of every page is called a header; text that appears at the bottom of every page is called a footer.

➤ Insert predesigned headers and footers in a document with the Header button and Footer button in the Header & Footer group on the INSERT tab.

➤ A header or footer displays in Print Layout view but not in Draft view.

➤ You can remove or edit predesigned headers and footers.

➤ Use the Navigation pane to search for specific text in a document. Display the Navigation pane by clicking the Find button in the Editing group on the HOME tab or by pressing Ctrl + F.

➤ If you type search text in the search text box in the Navigation pane, any occurrence of the text is highlighted in the document and thumbnails of the search text display in the Navigation pane.

➤ Use the Find and Replace feature to search for specific characters and types of formatting and replace them with other characters and formatting.

- At the Find and Replace dialog box, click the Find Next button to find the next occurrence of specific text, click the Replace button to replace the text and find the next occurrence, and click the Replace All button to replace all occurrences of the text.
- Click the More button at the Find and Replace dialog box to display additional options for completing a search.
- Use the Click and Type feature to center, right-align, and left-align text.
- Vertically align text in a document with the *Vertical alignment* option at the Page Setup dialog box with the Layout tab selected.

# Commands *Review*

| FEATURE | RIBBON TAB, GROUP | BUTTON, OPTION | KEYBOARD SHORTCUT |
|---|---|---|---|
| blank page | INSERT, Pages | ▯ | |
| cover page | INSERT, Pages | ▦ | |
| Find and Replace dialog box with Find tab selected | HOME, Editing | 🔍 , *Advanced Find* | |
| Find and Replace dialog box with Replace tab selected | HOME, Editing | ab↔ac | Ctrl + H |
| footer | INSERT, Header & Footer | ▯ | |
| header | INSERT, Header & Footer | ▯ | |
| Navigation pane | VIEW, Show | | Ctrl + F |
| page break | INSERT, Pages | ⊢⊣ | Ctrl + Enter |
| page numbering | INSERT, Header & Footer | # | |
| Page Setup dialog box | PAGE LAYOUT, Page Setup | ⌐ | |

# Key Points *Review*

**Completion:** In the space provided at the right, indicate the correct term, symbol, or command.

1. Press this combination of keys on the keyboard to insert a page break.                                  _____

2. The Cover Page button is located in the Pages group on this tab.                                  _____

3. A predesigned cover page generally contains these, which are locations where you can enter specific information.                                  _____

4. The Page Number button is located in this group on the INSERT tab.

5. Text that appears at the top of every page is called this.

6. A footer displays in Print Layout view but not this view.

7. Click this button in the Editing group on the HOME tab to display the Navigation pane.

8. Use this keyboard shortcut to display the Find and Replace dialog box with the Replace tab selected.

9. If you want to replace every occurrence of what you are searching for in a document, click this button at the Find and Replace dialog box.

10. Click this option at the Find and Replace dialog box if you are searching for a word and all of its forms.

11. Use this feature to position the insertion point at a specific location and alignment in a document.

12. Vertically align text with the *Vertical alignment* option at the Page Setup dialog box with this tab selected.

# *Chapter Assessments*

## Applying Your Skills

Demonstrate your knowledge of features learned in this chapter by completing the following assessments.

### Assessment 7.1    Format and Insert a Cover Page in a Document

1. Open **Strategies.docx** and save the document with the name **C07-A01-Strategies**.
2. Apply the Heading 1 style to the title of the document and apply the Heading 2 style to the headings in the document.
3. Apply the Casual style set.
4. Apply the Basis theme.
5. Change the theme colors to Blue Warm.
6. Center the title.
7. Insert a page break at the beginning of the heading *Using Visual Aids*.
8. Move the insertion point to the beginning of the document and then insert the Slice (Light) cover page. Insert the following text in the specified placeholders:
   a. Type **computer manuals** in the *[DOCUMENT TITLE]* placeholder.
   b. Type **Strategies for Reading Computer Manuals** in the *[Document subtitle]* placeholder.
   c. Delete the *[School]* placeholder. **Hint: To delete a placeholder, click in the placeholder text, click the placeholder tab, and then press the Delete key.**
   d. Type your first and last names in the *[Course title]* placeholder.
9. Move the insertion point to any character in the title *Strategies for Reading Computer Manuals* in the main document (not in the cover page) and then insert the Thin Line page numbering at the bottoms of the pages. (The page numbering will not appear on the cover page.)
10. Save, print, and then close **C07-A01-Strategies.docx**.

## Assessment 7.2 Format and Insert a Header and Footer in a Report

1. Open **QuoteMarks.docx** and save the document with the name **C07-A02-QuoteMarks**.
2. Change the top margin to 1.25 inches.
3. Apply the Banded theme.

4. Insert a page break at the beginning of the heading *Indicate Titles*.
5. Move the insertion point to the beginning of the document, insert the Retrospect header, and then make the following changes:
   a. Type **quotation marks** in the *[DOCUMENT TITLE]* placeholder.
   b. Click in the *[DATE]* placeholder, click the down-pointing arrow that displays, and then click the Today button at the drop-down calendar.
6. Insert the Retrospect footer, select the name that displays at the left side of the footer, and then type your first and last names. If an *[AUTHOR]* placeholder displays, click in the placeholder and then type your first and last names.
7. Save and then print **C07-A02-QuoteMarks.docx**.
8. Remove the header and footer.
9. Insert the Facet (Odd Page) header.
10. Insert the Ion (Dark) footer and then make the following changes:
    a. Make sure the title *QUOTATION MARKS* displays at the left side of the footer. If the title does not display, click the *[DOCUMENT TITLE]* placeholder and then type **quotation marks**.
    b. Select the name that displays at the right side of the footer and then type your first and last names.
    c. Select all of the text in the footer, apply bold formatting, and then change the font size to 10 points.
11. Insert the DRAFT 1 watermark in the document.
12. Save, print, and then close **C07-A02-QuoteMarks.docx**.

## Assessment 7.3 Find and Replace Text in a Real Estate Agreement

1. Open **REAgrmnt.docx** and save the document with the name **C07-A03-REAgrmnt**.
2. Find all occurrences of *BUYER* (matching the case) and replace with *Craig Metzner*.
3. Find all occurrences of *SELLER* (matching the case) and replace with *Carol Winters*.
4. Find all forms of the word *buy* and replace them with *purchase*.
5. Insert a page break at the beginning of the paragraph that begins *Default and attorney's fees:*.
6. Insert the Bold Numbers 2 page numbers at the bottoms of the pages.
7. Save, print, and then close **C07-A03-REAgrmnt.docx**.

## Assessment 7.4 Create a Notice Using Click and Type

1. At a blank document, use the Click and Type feature to create the document shown in Figure 7.8.
2. Select the centered text and then change the font to 16-point Candara bold in Dark Blue.
3. Select the right-aligned text and then change the font to 12-point Candara bold in Dark Blue.
4. Change the vertical alignment of the text to center alignment.
5. Save the document and name it **C07-A04-CoData**.
6. Print and then close **C07-A04-CoData.docx**.

**Figure 7.8 Assessment 7.4**

Securing Company Data

Systems for Backing up Crucial Data

Thursday, March 19, 2015

Corporate Training Center

1:30 to 4:00 p.m.

Sponsored by
Madison Security Systems

# Expanding Your Skills

Explore additional feature options or use Help to learn a new skill in creating these documents.

## Assessment 7.5 Insert a Header, Footer, and Cover Page from Office.com

1. Open **Presentation.docx** and save the document with the name **C07-A05-Presentation**.
2. Make the following changes to the document:
   a. Change the top margin to 1.25 inches.
   b. Apply the Title style to the title in the document, the Heading 1 style to the subtitle, and the Heading 2 style to the three headings in the document.
   c. Apply the Centered style set.
   d. Change the theme colors to Orange.
3. Additional headers, footers, and cover pages are available from Office.com. Click the INSERT tab, click the Header button, click the *More Headers from Office.com* option, and then choose a header from the side menu.
4. Choose a footer from Office.com.
5. Choose a cover page from Office.com and insert the appropriate text in the cover page placeholders. (Consider deleting placeholders if they are not pertinent to the document.)
6. Save, print, and then close **C07-A05-Presentation.docx**.

# Achieving Signature Status

Take your skills to the next level by completing this more challenging assessment.

## Assessment 7.6    Format a Resume

1. Open **ResumeInfo.docx** and save the document with the name **C07-A06-ResumeInfo**.
2. Format the document so it appears as shown in Figure 7.9 with the following specifications:
   a. Apply the Heading 1 style to the title and the Heading 2 style to the headings. Also, apply the Lines (Stylish) style set and change the theme colors to Blue Green.
   b. Insert the Banded cover page and insert text in the placeholders and delete placeholders so your cover page looks like the cover page in Figure 7.9.
   c. Insert the Ion (Dark) header.
   d. Insert the Ion (Dark) footer.
   e. Apply any other formatting necessary so your document appears as shown in Figure 7.9.
3. Save, print, and then close **C07-A06-ResumeInfo.docx**.

**Figure 7.9  Assessment 7.6**

**Figure 7.9 Assessment 7.6 (continued)**

## Becoming a Job Detective

Imagine the scene: an office in the city, but there is someone missing from one desk. Witnesses say the missing person is dynamic, well qualified, and pays exceptional attention to detail. Every employer has a "prime suspect" in mind when they advertise a position, and they tend to leave clues to that person's identity in their job description. In this chapter, we teach you to become a job detective, so that you can pick up all the clues and solve the mystery—what would the ideal candidate for this job look like?

To produce the best "fitting" resume, you need to know about yourself and the job you are applying for. Before you do anything else, ask yourself why you are preparing a resume. The answer to this question is going to vary from one person to the next, and here are our top ten reasons for writing a resume:

1. You have seen a job that appeals to you advertised in the newspaper.
2. You want to market yourself to win a contract or a proposal or be elected to a committee or organization.
3. You have seen a job that appeals to you on an Internet job site.
4. Your friends or family told you of a job opening at a local company.
5. You want to work for the local company and thought that sending a resume to the company might get the company's attention.
6. You have seen a job advertised internally at work.
7. You are going for a promotion.
8. You are about to be downsized and want to update your resume to be ready for any good opportunities.
9. You are feeling fed up, and writing down all your achievements will cheer you up and might motivate you to look for a better job.
10. You are thinking "Oh, so that's a resume! I've never done one. I suppose I ought to try to remember what I've been doing with my life."

All of these certainly are good reasons to write a resume, but the resume serves many different purposes. One way of understanding the differences is to ask yourself who is going to read the resume in each case.

Resumes 1 through 5 will be read by potential employers who probably do n[...]
likely to be read by your boss or other people who know you. Resumes 8 thr[...]
benefit and should not be considered as suitable for sending out to employe[...]

### The Right Mix

Think about the list of reasons again. How else can you divide up these reaso[...]
is that, in some cases, you will have a good idea of what the employer is look[...]
advertisement in front of you and can tailor your resume accordingly. For oth[...]
reader might want to see. Updating your resume from time to time is a good [...]

RESUME WRITING

Page 1

---

important details, but remember that the result of such a process will not be a winning resume. It will be a useful list of tasks and achievements.

Writing a resume is like baking a cake. You need all the right ingredients: flour, butter, eggs, and so on. It is what you do with the ingredients that makes the difference between a great resume (or cake) and failure. Keeping your resume up-to-date is like keeping a stock of ingredients in the pantry—it's potentially very useful, but do not imagine that is the end of it!

### Information about the Job

You should tailor the information in your resume to the main points in the job advertisement. That sounds fine, but how do you do it? Get as much information about the job and the company as you can. The main sources of information about a job are normally the following:

- A job advertisement
- A job description
- A friend in the company
- The media
- Gossip and rumor
- Someone already doing the job or something similar

There is no substitute for experience. Talking to someone who does a job similar to the one you wish to apply for in the same company may well provide you with a good picture of what the job is really like. Bear in mind, of course, that this source of information is not always reliable. You may react differently than the way that person does, and therefore his or her experience with a company may be very different than yours. However, someone with reliable information can provide a golden opportunity. Make sure you do not waste the chance to get some information.

### Information about the Company

The main sources of information about an employer are normally the following:

- The media
- Annual reports/company brochures
- Industry/trade magazines or journals
- The Internet—on the company's own site or at general sites
- Industry directories
- Gossip and Rumor

Other sources of information about companies are available; if you are serious about wanting to know more about a potential employer (and you should be), it is worth a visit to your local library. Ask a reference librarian to help you with your search. It will help if you explain to the librarian that you are looking for information on a specific company to help with your job search.

RESUME WRITING                                                                 STUDENT NAME

Page 2

# Inserting Elements and Navigating in a Document

## Performance Objectives

Upon successful completion of Chapter 8, you will be able to:

- Insert symbols and special characters
- Insert a drop cap
- Insert the date and time
- Insert a file into an open document
- Navigate in a document using the Navigation pane and bookmarks
- Insert hyperlinks to a location in the same document, a different document, and a file in another program
- Create a cross-reference

You can insert a variety of elements into a Word document to serve a variety of purposes. In this chapter, you will learn how to insert symbols, special characters, and drop capital letters to add visual interest. You will also learn how to insert the date and/or time in a number of formats, making it possible to identify when a document was created and automatically update the information to reflect when a document was revised. You will learn how to insert one file into another to efficiently combine the content of two documents, and you will learn how to insert hyperlinks, bookmarks, and cross-references to provide additional information for readers and allow for more efficient navigation within a document.

*Note: Before beginning computer exercises for this chapter, copy to your storage medium the Chapter08 folder from the CD that accompanies this textbook and then make Chapter08 the active folder.*

In this chapter, students will produce the following documents:

Exercise 8.1. C08-E01-ProdSoftware.docx
Exercise 8.2. C08-E02-VirusesSecurity.docx

Model answers for these exercises are shown on the following pages.

**Exercise 8.1**

C08-E01-ProdSoftware.docx

Productivity Software

Productivity software is designed to improve efficiency and performance on the job and at home. It is the largest category of application software for individual use. Employment notices appearing in newspapers and magazines often list required computer skills, such as word processing or spreadsheet expertise. Some employment notices even specify that an applicant must be certified in a particular application.

In-depth knowledge of productivity software applications and skill in using them can make a potential employee more valuable to a business, organization, or agency. Productivity software includes the following categories:

**Word processing:** Used to write, format, and print letters, memos, reports, and other documents.

**Desktop publishing:** Used to produce newsletters, advertisements, and other high-quality documents.

**Spreadsheet:** Used to produce spreadsheets and manipulate financial and other numerical data.

**Project management:** Used to schedule and manage projects.

**Presentation graphics:** Used to create and display slide shows.

**Computer-aided design:** Used to create and edit detailed designs of products.

Personal-use Software

Shoppers browsing in computer stores are likely to see numerous software applications designed for home and personal use. Among the many products available are applications for writing letters, making out wills, designing a new home, landscaping a lawn, preparing and filing tax returns, and managing finances. Software suites are also available for home and personal use, although sometimes the suites available for home use do not contain all the features found in business versions.

More than one-half of U.S. homes now include a personal computer on which a variety of software applications has been installed. Most application software programs are relatively inexpensive. Some vendors advertise popular word processing programs for as little as $99.

e includes the following categories:

**are:** Assists users with paying bills, balancing checkbooks, he and expenses, and maintaining investment records.

1

- **Tax preparation software:** Designed to aid in analyzing federal and state tax status, as well as to prepare and transmit tax returns.
- **Legal documents software:** Designed to help analyze, plan, and prepare a variety of legal documents, including wills and trusts.
- **Games and entertainment software:** Designed to provide fun as well as challenges to users and includes interactive games, videos, and music.

Created by: Rueben Cedeño

Northland Security Systems®

February 11, 2015

2:19:27 PM

2

Cover Page

**Exercise 8.2**

C08-E02-VirusesSecurity.docx

---

1

## CHAPTER 1: UNAUTHORIZED ACCESS

Like uncharted wilderness, the Internet lacks borders. This inherent openness is what makes the Internet so valuable and yet so vulnerable. Over its short life, the Internet has grown so quickly that the legal system has not been able to keep pace. The security risks posed by networks and the Internet can be grouped into three categories: unauthorized access, information theft, and denial of service.

Hackers, individuals who gain access to computers and networks illegally, are responsible for most cases of unauthorized access. Hackers tend to exploit sites and programs that have poor security measures in place. However, they also gain access to more challenging sites by using sophisticated programs and strategies. Many hackers claim they hack merely because they like the challenge of trying to defeat security measures. They rarely have a more malicious motive, and they generally do not aim to destroy or damage the sites that they invade. In fact, hackers dislike being identified with those who seek to cause damage. They refer to hackers with malicious or criminal intent as crackers. Types of Viruses

### User IDs and Passwords

To gain entry over the Internet to
user ID and password combinatio
information. Sending an email, fo
very public. The only missing ele
are common; they have program
systematically over a period of h

Programmers can sometimes ina
and information systems. One su
password that provides the highe
the early days of system develop
system to fix problems. Through
behind in the final version of the
bypassing the security, perhaps y

A sophisticated way to break into
fooling another computer by pre
altering the address that the syst
one that the receiving computer

COMPUTER SECURITY

Page 1

---

2

### Spyware

Spyware is a type of software that allows an intruder to spy upon someone else's computer. This alarming technology takes advantage of loopholes in the computer's security systems and allows a stranger to witness and record another person's every mouse click or keystroke on the monitor as it occurs. The spy can record activities and gain access to passwords and credit card information. Spyware generally requires the user to install it on the machine that is being spied upon, so it is highly unlikely that random strangers on the Internet could simply begin watching your computer. In the workplace, however, someone might be able to install the software without the victim's knowledge. Disguised as an email greeting, for example, the program can operate like a virus that gets the unwary user to install the spyware unknowingly.

## CHAPTER 2: INFORMATION THEFT

Information can be a company's most valuable possession. Stealing corporate information, a crime included in the category of industrial espionage, is unfortunately both easy to do and difficult to detect. This is due in part to the invisible nature of software and data. If a cracker breaks into a company network and manages to download the company database from the network onto a disk, there is no visible sign to the company that anything is amiss. The original database is still in place, working the same way it always has.

### Wireless Device Security

The growing number of wireless devices has created a new opportunity for data theft. Wireless devices such as cameras, Web phones, networked computers, PDAs, and input and output peripherals are inherently less secure than wired devices. Security is quite lax, and in some cases nonexistent, in new wireless technologies for handheld computers and cell phone systems. In a rush to match competition, manufacturers have tended to sacrifice security to move a product to the marketplace faster. Already, viruses are appearing in emails for cell phones and PDAs. With little protection available for these new systems, hackers and spies are enjoying a free hand with the new technology. One of the few available security protocols for wireless networks is Wired Equivalent Privacy (WEP), developed in conjunction with the standard for wireless local area networks. Newer versions of WEP with enhanced security features make it more difficult for hackers to intercept and modify data transmissions sent by radio waves or infrared signals.

### Data Browsing

Data browsing is a less damaging form of information theft that involves an invasion of privacy. Workers in many organizations have access to networked databases that contain private information about people. Accessing this information without an official reason is against the law. The IRS had a particularly

COMPUTER SECURITY                                                                    STUDENT NAME

Page 2

Model Answers

**Page 3**

3

large problem with data browsing in the late 1990s. Some employees were fired and the rest were given specialized training in appropriate conduct.

### CHAPTER 3: COMPUTER VIRUSES

One of the most familiar forms of risk to computer security is the computer virus. A computer virus is a program written by a hacker or cracker designed to perform some kind of trick upon an unsuspecting victim. The trick performed in some cases is mild, such as drawing an offensive image on the screen, or changing all of the characters in a document to another language. Sometimes the trick is much more severe, such as reformatting the hard drive and erasing all the data, or damaging the motherboard so that it cannot operate properly. Computer Virus Protection

#### Types of Viruses

Viruses can be categorized by their effect, which include nuisance, data-destructive, espionage, and hardware-destructive. A nuisance virus usually does no real damage, but is rather just an inconvenience. The most difficult part of a comp... documents, databases, and saved... is designed to destroy this data. S... security. Called espionage viruses... system later for the purpose of st... is created that attempts to damag... destructive viruses, these bits of g... components. (For more informati...

Viruses can create effects that ra... and transmitted by a variety of m... message sent over the Internet. E... execute. Another common form o... to customize and automate certa... then becomes infected when it op... disk or hard disk contains a variet... capable of loading an operating sy... operating system automatically re... operating system on that disk. A b... whenever the operating system r...

Other methods of virus infection... program or data file, and the stea...

COMPUTER SECURITY

**Page 4**

4

Polymorphic viruses alter themselves to prevent antivirus software from detecting them by examining familiar patterns. Polymorphic viruses alter themselves randomly as they move from computer to computer, making detection more difficult. Multipartite viruses alter their form of attack. Their name derives from their ability to attack in several different ways. They may first infect the boot sector and then later move on to become a Trojan horse type by infecting a disk file. These viruses are more sophisticated, and therefore more difficult to guard against. Another type of virus is the logic bomb, which generally sits quietly dormant waiting for a specific event or set of conditions to occur. A famous logic bomb was the widely publicized Michelangelo virus, which infected personal computers and caused them to display a message on the artist's birthday.

### CHAPTER 4: SECURITY RISKS

Although hackers, crackers, and viruses garner the most attention as security risks, a company faces a variety of other dangers to its hardware and software systems. Principally, these risks involve types of system failure, employee theft, and the cracking of software for copying. Click to view types of unauthorized access

A fundamental element in makin... electrical power that runs them... effects on computers. An inexper... power fluctuations and can also s... protection system is an uninterru... nature to a power strip, but muc... spike-free power, but also keeps...

Although accurate estimates are... stolen computer hardware and s... unreported. Someone takes a ha... sometime later, and keeps the m... PC systems or a thief breaks into... the price of the stolen computers... the time lost while the machines... use them.

COMPUTER SECURITY

**Page 5**

5

#### Cracking Software for Copying

A common goal of hackers is to crack a software protection scheme. A crack is a method of circumventing a security scheme that prevents a user from copying a program. A common protection scheme for software is to require that the installation CD be resident in the drive whenever the program runs. Making copies of the CD with a burner, however, easily fools this protection scheme. Some game companies are taking the extra step of making duplication difficult by scrambling some of the data on the original CDs, which CD burners will automatically correct when copying. When the copied and corrected CD is used, the software checks for the scrambled track information. If the error is not found, the software will not run.

*Hold down the Ctrl key and then click the logo shown below to display a list of training courses offered by Northland Security Systems.*

Click to send an email

COMPUTER SECURITY                                                                STUDENT NAME

# Inserting Symbols and Special Characters

Use the Symbol button in the Symbols group on the INSERT tab to insert special symbols in a document. Click the button to display a drop-down list with the most recently inserted symbols and the *More Symbols* option. Click one of the symbols that displays in the list to insert it in the document or click the *More Symbols* option to display the Symbol dialog box, as shown in Figure 8.1. At the Symbol dialog box, double-click the symbol you want to insert and then click Close, or click the symbol you want to insert, click the Insert button, and then click Close.

**QUICK STEPS**

**Insert a Symbol**
1. Click INSERT tab.
2. Click Symbol button.
3. Click desired symbol at drop-down list.
OR
1. Click INSERT tab.
2. Click Symbol button.
3. Click *More Symbols*.
4. Select desired font.
5. Double-click desired symbol.
6. Click Close.

Symbol

**Figure 8.1 Symbol Dialog Box with Symbols Tab Selected**

Use the *Font* option to select the desired set of characters.

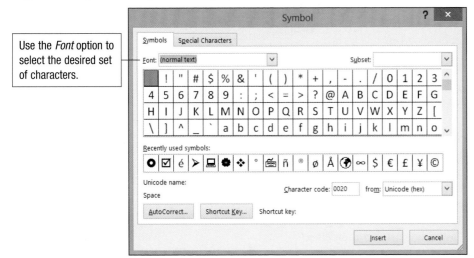

The Symbol dialog box contains a number of fonts and each font provides different symbols. To change to a different font, click the down-pointing arrow at the right side of the *Font* option box and then click the desired font at the drop-down list. Click the Special Characters tab and a list of special characters displays along with the keyboard shortcuts to create them.

---

## Exercise 8.1A  Inserting Symbols and Special Characters                    Part 1 of 4

1. Open **ProdSoftware.docx** and save the document with the name **C08-E01-ProdSoftware**.
2. Press Ctrl + End to move the insertion point to the end of the document.
3. Type **Created by:** and then press the spacebar once.
4. Type the first name **Rueben** and then press the spacebar.
5. Insert the last name *Cedeño* by completing the following steps:
   a. Type **Cede**.
   b. Click the INSERT tab.
   c. Click the Symbol button in the Symbols group.
   d. Click *More Symbols* at the drop-down list.

e.  At the Symbol dialog box, make sure the *Font* option displays as *(normal text)* and then double-click the ñ symbol (located in approximately the tenth through twelfth rows).

f.  Click the Close button.

g.  Type **o**.

6.  Press Shift + Enter.

7.  Insert the computer laptop symbol (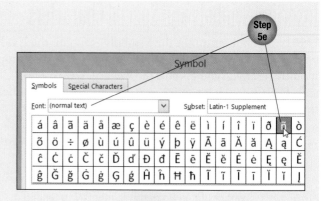) by completing the following steps:

a.  Click the Symbol button and then click *More Symbols*.

b.  At the Symbol dialog box, click the down-pointing arrow at the right of the *Font* option and then click *Wingdings* at the drop-down list. (You will need to scroll down the list to display this option.)

c.  Double-click 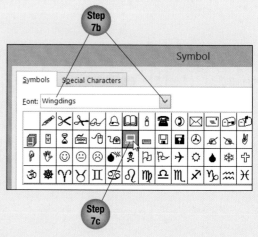 (located in approximately the second row).

d.  Click the Close button.

8.  Type **Northland Security Systems**.

9.  Insert the registered trademark symbol (®) by completing the following steps:

a.  Click the Symbol button and then click *More Symbols*.

b.  At the Symbol dialog box, click the Special Characters tab.

c.  Double-click the ® symbol (tenth option from the top).

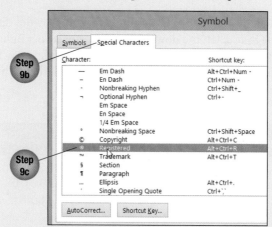

d.  Click the Close button.

e.  Press Shift + Enter.

10.  Select the computer laptop symbol (□) and then change the font size to 18 points.

11.  Save **C08-E01-ProdSoftware.docx**.

# Creating a Drop Cap

A ***drop cap*** is a design element in which the first letter of the first word of a paragraph is enlarged and set into the paragraph to extend (drop) more than one line space. Drop caps identify the beginning of major sections or parts of a document and are often used to enhance the appearance of the text. They generally look best when they are used in paragraphs that contain text set in a proportional font.

Create a drop cap with the Drop Cap button in the Text group on the INSERT tab. You can choose to set the drop cap in the paragraph or margin. At the Drop Cap dialog box, specify the font, number of lines you want the letter to drop, and distance you want the letter positioned from the text of the paragraph. To make the first letter in a paragraph a drop cap, position the insertion point in the word and then click the Drop Cap button.

**QUICK STEPS**

**Create a Drop Cap**
1. Click INSERT tab.
2. Click Drop Cap button.
3. Click desired type at drop-down list.

Drop Cap

---

## Exercise 8.1B  Inserting a Drop Cap                              Part 2 of 4

1. With **C08-E01-ProdSoftware.docx** open, create a drop cap by completing the following steps:
   a. Position the insertion point in the first word of the first paragraph of text below the title (*Productivity*).
   b. Click the INSERT tab.
   c. Click the Drop Cap button in the Text group.
   d. Click *In margin* at the drop-down gallery.
2. To see how the size and location of a drop cap affect the appearance of the document, make the drop smaller and change the location of the letter by completing the following steps:
   a. With the *P* selected in the word *Productivity*, click the Drop Cap button in the Text group and then click *None* at the drop-down gallery.
   b. Click the Drop Cap button and then click *Drop Cap Options* at the drop-down gallery.
   c. At the Drop Cap dialog box, click *Dropped* in the *Position* section.
   d. Click the down-pointing arrow at the right side of the *Font* option box, scroll down the drop-down list, and then click *Cambria*.
   e. Click the down arrow at the right side of the *Lines to drop* measurement box to change the number to 2.
   f. Click OK to close the dialog box.
   g. Click outside the drop cap to deselect it.
3. Save **C08-E01-ProdSoftware.docx**.

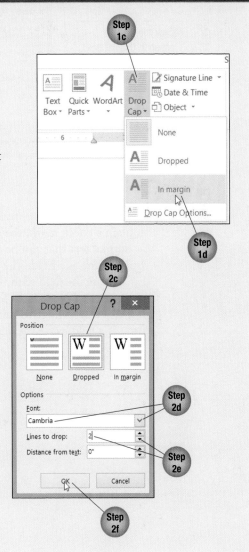

# Inserting the Date and Time

**Insert the Date and Time**
1. Click INSERT tab.
2. Click Date and Time button.
3. Click desired option in list box.
4. Click OK.

Use the Date & Time button in the Text group on the INSERT tab to insert the current date and time into a document. Click this button and the Date and Time dialog box displays, as shown in Figure 8.2. (Your date will vary from what you see in the figure.) At the Date and Time dialog box, click the desired date and/or time format in the *Available formats* list box.

**Figure 8.2  Date and Time Dialog Box**

Date & Time

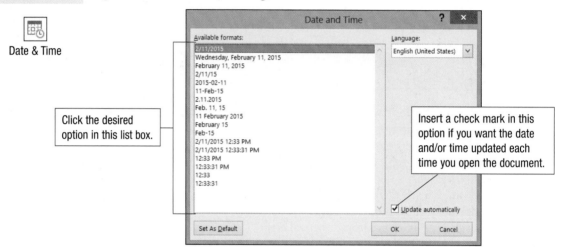

Click the desired option in this list box.

Insert a check mark in this option if you want the date and/or time updated each time you open the document.

If the *Update automatically* check box at the bottom of the dialog box does not contain a check mark, the date and/or time that you click are inserted in the document as normal text that can be edited in the usual manner. You can also insert the date and/or time as a field. The advantage to inserting the date or time as a field is that you can update the field with the Update Field keyboard shortcut, key F9. Insert a check mark in the *Update automatically* check box to insert the date and/or time as a field. You can also insert the date as a field using the keyboard shortcut Alt + Shift + D and the time as a field using the keyboard shortcut Alt + Shift + T.

1. With **C08-E01-ProdSoftware.docx** open, press Ctrl + End and make sure the insertion point is positioned below the company name.
2. Insert the current date by completing the following steps:
   a. Click the Date & Time button in the Text group on the INSERT tab.
   b. At the Date and Time dialog box, click the third option from the top in the *Available formats* list box. (Your date and time will vary from what you see in the image at the right.)
   c. If necessary, click in the *Update automatically* check box to insert a check mark.
   d. Click OK to close the dialog box.

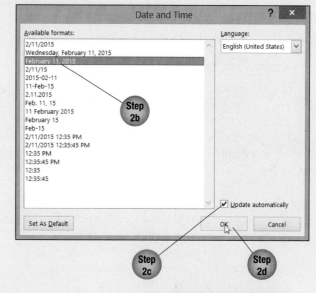

Step 2b

Step 2c

Step 2d

3. Press Shift + Enter.
4. Insert the current time by completing the following steps:
   a. Click the Date & Time button.
   b. At the Date and Time dialog box, click the third option from the *bottom* in the *Available formats* list box.
   c. Click OK to close the dialog box.

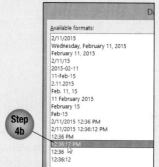

Step 4b

5. Save **C08-E01-ProdSoftware.docx**.
6. Update the time by clicking the time and then pressing key F9.
7. Save and then print **C08-E01-ProdSoftware.docx**.

# Inserting a File

If you want to insert the contents of one document into another, use the Object button in the Text group on the INSERT tab. Open the document into which you want to insert the contents of another file, click the Object button arrow, and then click *Text from File*. This displays the Insert File dialog box, which is similar to the Open dialog box. Navigate to the desired folder and then double-click the document you want to insert in the open document.

**QUICK STEPS**

**Insert a File**
1. Open document.
2. Click INSERT tab.
3. Click Object button arrow.
4. Click *Text from File*.
5. Navigate to desired folder.
6. Double-click document name.

Object

1. With **C08-E01-ProdSoftware.docx** open, insert a file into the open document by completing the following steps:
   a. Move the insertion point to the blank line above the text *Created by: Rueben Cedeño*.
   b. Click the INSERT tab.
   c. Click the Object button arrow in the Text group.
   d. Click *Text from File* at the drop-down list.
   e. At the Insert File dialog box, navigate to the Chapter08 folder and then double-click **PersSoftware.docx**.

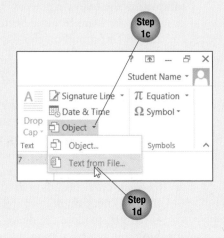

2. Make the following changes to the document:
   a. Apply the Heading 2 style to the two headings in the document.
   b. Select the four paragraphs of text in the *Personal-use Software* section that begin with bolded text and then click the Bullets button in the Paragraph group.
   c. Change the top margin to 1.5 inches.
   d. Apply the Basic (Stylish) style set.
   e. Apply the Wisp theme.
   f. Insert page numbers centered at the bottom of each page.
3. Save, print, and then close **C08-E01-ProdSoftware.docx**.

# Navigating in a Document

**QUICK STEPS**

**Display the Navigation Pane**
1. Click VIEW tab.
2. Click *Navigation Pane* check box.

Word includes a number of features for navigating in a document. Along with the navigating features you have already learned, you can also navigate using the Navigation pane and by inserting bookmarks.

## Navigating Using the Navigation Pane

To navigate using the Navigation pane, as shown in Figure 8.3 on the next page, click the VIEW tab and then click the *Navigation Pane* check box in the Show group. The Navigation pane displays at the left side of the screen and includes a search text box and pane with three tabs. Click the HEADINGS tab and titles and headings with styles applied display in the Navigation pane. Click a title or heading in the pane and the insertion point moves to that title or heading. Click the PAGES tab to display thumbnails of each page in the pane. Click a thumbnail to move the insertion point to that specific page. Click the RESULTS tab to browse the current search results in the document. Close the Navigation pane by clicking the *Navigation Pane* check box in the Show group on the VIEW tab or by clicking the Close button located in the upper right corner of the pane.

**Figure 8.3 Navigation Pane**

Click the PAGES tab to display a thumbnail of each page in the Navigation pane.

Click the RESULTS tab to browse the current search results in the document.

Click the HEADINGS tab and titles and headings with styles applied display in the Navigation pane.

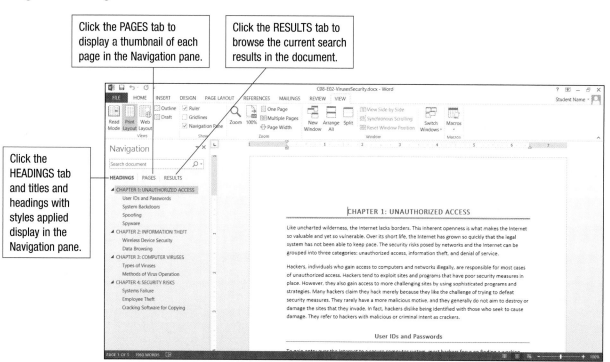

---

# Exercise 8.2A   Navigating Using the Navigation Pane

Part 1 of 5

1. Open **VirusesSecurity.docx** and save the document with the name **C08-E02-VirusesSecurity**.
2. Since this document has heading styles applied, you can easily navigate in it with the Navigation pane by completing the following steps:
   a. Click the VIEW tab.
   b. Click the *Navigation Pane* check box in the Show group to insert a check mark. (This displays the Navigation pane at the left side of the screen.)
   c. Click the *CHAPTER 2: INFORMATION THEFT* heading in the Navigation pane.
   d. Click the *CHAPTER 4: SECURITY RISKS* heading in the Navigation pane.
   e. Click *Spoofing* in the Navigation pane.

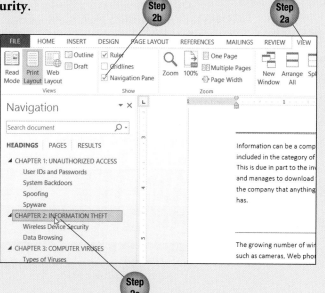

Step 2b

Step 2a

Step 2c

3. Navigate in the document using thumbnails by completing the following steps:
   a. Click the PAGES tab in the Navigation pane. (This displays page thumbnails in the pane.)
   b. Click the page 2 thumbnail in the Navigation pane.
   c. Scroll down the Navigation pane and then click the page 3 thumbnail.
4. Close the Navigation pane by clicking the Close button located in the upper right corner of the Navigation pane.
5. Save **C08-E02-VirusesSecurity.docx**.

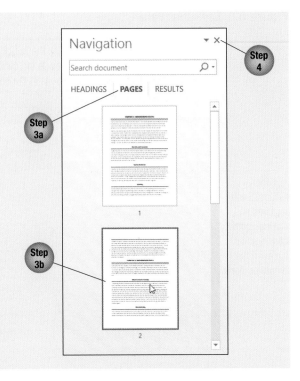

## Navigating with Bookmarks

**Create a Bookmark**
1. Position insertion point at desired location.
2. Click INSERT tab.
3. Click Bookmark button.
4. Type name for bookmark.
5. Click Add button.

In a long document, you may find it useful to mark a location with a bookmark so you can quickly move the insertion point to that location. Create bookmarks for locations in a document at the Bookmark dialog box.

To create a bookmark, position the insertion point at the desired location, click the INSERT tab, and then click the Bookmark button in the Links group. This displays the Bookmark dialog box, as shown in Figure 8.4. Type a name for the bookmark in the *Bookmark name* text box and then click the Add button. Repeat these steps as many times as needed to insert the desired bookmarks. Give each bookmark a unique and meaningful name. A bookmark name must begin with a letter; it can contain numbers but not spaces. Use the underscore character if you want to separate the words in a bookmark name.

**Figure 8.4 Bookmark Dialog Box**

Bookmark

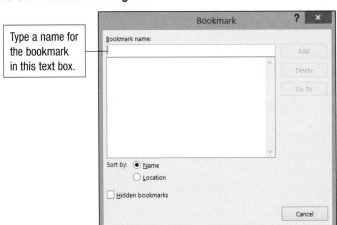

Type a name for the bookmark in this text box.

By default, bookmarks are not visible in the document. Turn on the display of bookmarks at the Word Options dialog box with *Advanced* selected. Display this dialog box by clicking the FILE tab and then clicking *Options*. At the Word Options dialog box, click the *Advanced* option in the left panel. Click the *Show bookmarks* check box in the *Show document content* section to insert a check mark. Complete similar steps to turn off the display of bookmarks. A bookmark displays in the document as an I-beam marker.

You can also create a bookmark for selected text. To do this, first select the text and then complete the steps to create a bookmark. When you create a bookmark for selected text, a left bracket ([) indicates the beginning of the selected text and a right bracket (]) indicates the end of the selected text. The bookmark brackets do not print.

After you have inserted bookmarks in a document, you can move the insertion point to a specific bookmark. To do this, display the Bookmark dialog box and then double-click the bookmark name or click the bookmark name and then click the Go To button. When Word stops at the location of the bookmark, click the Close button to close the dialog box. If you move the insertion point to a bookmark created with selected text, Word moves the insertion point to the bookmark and selects the text. Delete bookmarks in the Bookmark dialog box by clicking the bookmark name in the list box and then clicking the Delete button.

**QUICK STEPS**

**Navigate with Bookmarks**
1. Click INSERT tab.
2. Click Bookmark button.
3. Double-click desired bookmark name.
OR
1. Click INSERT tab.
2. Click Bookmark button.
3. Click bookmark name.
4. Click Go To button.

---

## Exercise 8.2B  Inserting, Navigating with, and Deleting Bookmarks  Part 2 of 5

1. With **C08-E02-VirusesSecurity.docx** open, turn on the display of bookmarks by completing the following steps:
   a. Click the FILE tab and then click *Options*.
   b. At the Word Options dialog box, click *Advanced* in the left panel.
   c. Scroll down the dialog box and then click the *Show bookmarks* check box in the *Show document content* section to insert a check mark.
   d. Click OK to close the dialog box.
2. Insert a bookmark by completing the following steps:
   a. Move the insertion point to the beginning of the first paragraph in the document (below the heading *CHAPTER 1: UNAUTHORIZED ACCESS*).
   b. Click the INSERT tab.
   c. Click the Bookmark button in the Links group.
   d. At the Bookmark dialog box, type **Access** in the *Bookmark name* text box.
   e. Click the Add button.

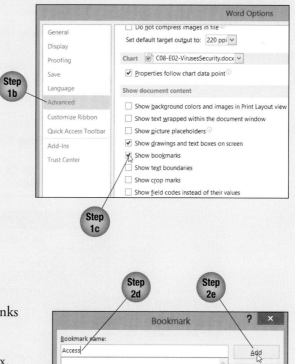

3. Using steps similar to those in Steps 2a through 2e, insert a bookmark named *Viruses* at the beginning of the paragraph in the *Types of Viruses* section (located on page 3).
4. Using steps similar to those in Steps 2a through 2e, insert a bookmark named *Electrical* at the beginning of the first paragraph in the *Systems Failure* section (located on page 4).
5. Navigate to the Viruses bookmark by completing the following steps:
   a. If necessary, click the INSERT tab.
   b. Click the Bookmark button in the Links group.
   c. At the Bookmark dialog box, click *Viruses* in the list box.
   d. Click the Go To button.
6. With the Bookmark dialog box open, navigate to the Access bookmark by double-clicking *Access* in the list box.
7. With the Bookmark dialog box open, delete the *Electrical* bookmark by clicking *Electrical* in the list box and then clicking the Delete button.
8. Click the Close button to close the Bookmark dialog box.
9. Save **C08-E02-VirusesSecurity.docx**.

## Inserting Hyperlinks

**QUICK STEPS**

**Insert a Hyperlink**
1. Click INSERT tab.
2. Click Hyperlink button.
3. Make desired changes at Insert Hyperlink dialog box.
4. Click OK.

A hyperlink in a document can serve a number of purposes: Click it to navigate to a specific location in the document, to display a different document, to open a file in a different program, to create a new document, or to link to an email address.

Insert a hyperlink by clicking the Hyperlink button located in the Links group on the INSERT tab. This displays the Insert Hyperlink dialog box, as shown in Figure 8.5. You can also display the Insert Hyperlink dialog box by pressing Ctrl + K. At this dialog box, identify what you want to link to and the location of the link. Click the ScreenTip button to customize the hyperlink ScreenTip.

Hyperlink

**Figure 8.5 Insert Hyperlink Dialog Box**

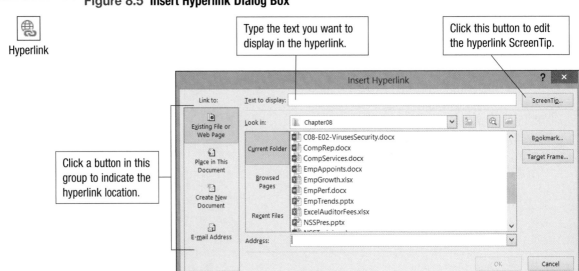

Type the text you want to display in the hyperlink.

Click this button to edit the hyperlink ScreenTip.

Click a button in this group to indicate the hyperlink location.

## Linking to a Place in the Document

To create a hyperlink to another location in the document, you need to mark the location by applying heading styles to text or inserting bookmarks. To hyperlink to a heading or bookmark in a document, display the Insert Hyperlink dialog box and then click the Place in This Document button in the *Link to* section. This displays text with heading styles applied and bookmarks in the *Select a place in this document* list box. Click the desired heading style or bookmark name and the heading or bookmark name displays in the *Text to display* text box. Leave the text as displayed or select the text and then type the text you want to appear in the document.

## Navigating Using Hyperlinks

Navigate to a hyperlink by hovering the mouse over the hyperlink text, holding down the Ctrl key, and then clicking the left mouse button. When you hover the mouse over hyperlink text, a ScreenTip displays with the name of the heading or bookmark. If you want specific information to display in the ScreenTip, click the ScreenTip button in the Insert Hyperlink dialog box, type the desired text in the Set Hyperlink ScreenTip dialog box, and then click OK.

---

**Exercise 8.2C**  **Inserting a Hyperlink to a Location in the Document**  **Part 3 of 5**

1. With **C08-E02-VirusesSecurity.docx** open, insert a hyperlink to a bookmark in the document by completing the following steps:
   a. Position the insertion point at the immediate right of the period that ends the first paragraph of text in the *CHAPTER 4: SECURITY RISKS* section (located on page 4).
   b. Press the spacebar once.
   c. If necessary, click the INSERT tab.
   d. Click the Hyperlink button in the Links group.
   e. At the Insert Hyperlink dialog box, click the Place in This Document button in the *Link to* section.
   f. Scroll down the *Select a place in this document* list box and then click *Access,* which displays below *Bookmarks* in the list box.
   g. Select the text that displays in the *Text to display* text box and then type **Click to view types of unauthorized access**.
   h. Click the ScreenTip button located in the upper right corner of the dialog box. At the Set Hyperlink ScreenTip dialog box, type **View types of unauthorized access to computers** and then click OK.
   i. Click OK to close the Insert Hyperlink dialog box.

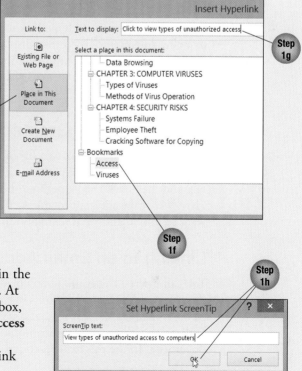

---

2. Navigate to the hyperlinked location by hovering the mouse over the <u>Click to view types of unauthorized access</u> hyperlink, holding down the Ctrl key, and then clicking the left mouse button.
3. Insert a hyperlink to a heading in the document by completing the following steps:
   a. Press Ctrl + Home to move the insertion point to the beginning of the document.
   b. Move the insertion point to the immediate right of the period that ends the second paragraph in the document and then press the spacebar.
   c. Click the Hyperlink button on the INSERT tab.
   d. At the Insert Hyperlink dialog box with the Place in This Document button selected in the *Link to* section, click the *Types of Viruses* heading in the *Select a place in this document* list box.
   e. Click OK to close the Insert Hyperlink dialog box.
4. Navigate to the hyperlinked heading by hovering the mouse over the <u>Types of Viruses</u> hyperlink, holding down the Ctrl key, and then clicking the left mouse button.
5. Save **C08-E02-VirusesSecurity.docx**.

## Linking to a File in Another Program

In some situations, you may want to provide information to your readers in a variety of formats. You may want to provide information in a Word document, Excel workbook, and/or PowerPoint presentation. To link a Word document to a file in another application, display the Insert Hyperlink dialog box and then click the Existing File or Web Page button in the *Link to* section. Use the *Look in* option to navigate to the folder containing the desired file and then click the file. Make other changes in the Insert Hyperlink dialog box as needed and then click OK.

## Linking to a New Document

In addition to creating a hyperlink to an existing document, you can create a hyperlink to a new document. To do this, display the Insert Hyperlink dialog box and then click the Create New Document button in the *Link to* section. Type a name for the new document in the *Name of new document* text box and then specify if you want to edit the document now or later.

## Linking Using a Graphic

You can create a hyperlink to a file or website using a graphic, such as a clip art image, picture, or text box. To hyperlink with a graphic, select the graphic, click the INSERT tab, and then click the Hyperlink button or right-click the graphic and then click *Hyperlink* at the shortcut menu. At the Insert Hyperlink dialog box, specify where you want to link to and what text you want to display in the hyperlink.

## Linking to an Email Address

You can insert a hyperlink to an email address at the Insert Hyperlink dialog box. To do this, click the E-mail Address button in the *Link to* section, type the desired address in the *E-mail address* text box, and type a subject for the email in the *Subject* text box. Click in the *Text to display* text box and then type the text you want to display in the document. To use this feature, the email address you use must be set up in Outlook.

1. The Word document **C08-E02-VirusesSecurity.docx** contains information used by Northland Security Systems. The company also has a PowerPoint presentation that contains similar information. Link the document with the presentation by completing the following steps:
   a. Move the insertion point to the immediate right of the period that ends the paragraph in the *CHAPTER 3: COMPUTER VIRUSES* section and then press the spacebar.
   b. If necessary, click the INSERT tab.
   c. Click the Hyperlink button in the Links group.
   d. At the Insert Hyperlink dialog box, click the Existing File or Web Page button in the *Link to* section.
   e. Click the down-pointing arrow at the right side of the *Look in* list box and then navigate to the Chapter08 folder on your storage medium.
   f. Click the presentation named **NSSPres.pptx** in the list box.
   g. Select the text in the *Text to display* text box in the dialog box and then type **Computer Virus Presentation**.

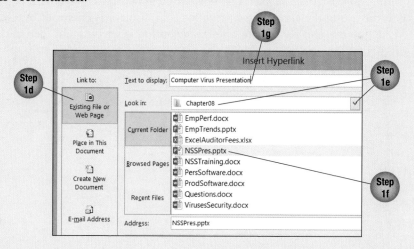

   h. Click OK to close the Insert Hyperlink dialog box.
2. View the PowerPoint presentation by completing the following steps:
   a. Position the mouse pointer over the Computer Virus Presentation hyperlink, hold down the Ctrl key, and then click the left mouse button.
   b. At the PowerPoint presentation, click the Slide Show button in the view area on the Status bar.
   c. Click the left mouse button to advance each slide.
   d. Click the left mouse button at the black screen that displays the message *End of slide show, click to exit*.
   e. Close the presentation and PowerPoint by clicking the Close button (contains an X) that displays in the upper right corner of the screen.

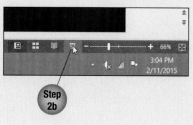

3. Insert a hyperlink with a graphic by completing the following steps:
   a. Press Ctrl + End to move the insertion point to the end of the document.
   b. Click the compass image to select it.
   c. Click the Hyperlink button on the INSERT tab.
   d. At the Insert Hyperlink dialog box, make sure the Existing File or Web Page button is selected in the *Link to* section.
   e. Navigate to the Chapter08 folder on your storage medium and then double-click the document named ***NSSTraining.docx***. (This selects the document name and closes the dialog box.)
4. Navigate to the **NSSTraining.docx** document by hovering the mouse pointer over the compass image, holding down the Ctrl key, and then clicking the left mouse button.
5. Close the document by clicking the FILE tab and then clicking the *Close* option.
6. Insert a hyperlink to a new document by completing the following steps:
   a. Move the insertion point to the immediate right of the period that ends the paragraph in the *User IDs and Passwords* section and then press the spacebar.
   b. Click the Hyperlink button on the INSERT tab.
   c. Click the Create New Document button in the *Link to* section.
   d. In the *Name of new document* text box, type **PasswordSuggestions**.
   e. Edit the text in the *Text to display* text box so it displays as **Password Suggestions**.
   f. Make sure the *Edit the new document now* option is selected and then click OK.

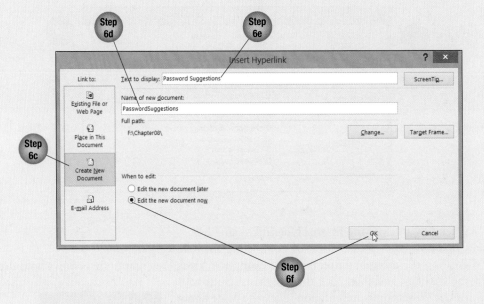

   g. At the blank document, turn on bold formatting, type **Please type any suggestions you have for creating secure passwords:**, turn off bold formatting, and then press the Enter key.
   h. Save and then close the document.
7. Press Ctrl + End to move the insertion point to the end of the document and then press the Enter key four times.

8. Insert a hyperlink to your email address or your instructor's email address by completing the following steps:

    a. Click the Hyperlink button.

    b. At the Insert Hyperlink dialog box, click the E-mail Address button in the *Link to* section.

    c. Type your email address or your instructor's email address in the *E-mail address* text box.

    d. Select the current text in the *Text to display* text box and then type **Click to send an email**.

    e. Click OK to close the dialog box.

    ***Optional: If you have Outlook set up, click the Click to send an email hyperlink and then send a message indicating that you have completed inserting hyperlinks in C08-E02-VirusesSecurity.docx.***

9. Save **C08-E02-VirusesSecurity.docx**.

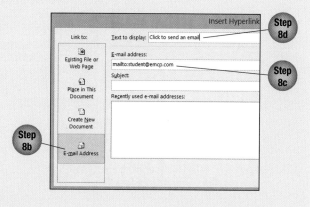

# Creating a Cross-reference

A ***cross-reference*** in a Word document refers the reader to another location within the document. Cross-referencing is useful in a long document or a document that contains related information in another location. Insert a reference to an item such as a heading, figure, or table. For example, you can insert a cross-reference that refers readers to another location with more information about the topic or to a specific table or page. By default, cross-references are inserted in a document as hyperlinks.

To insert a cross-reference, type introductory text, click the INSERT tab, and then click the Cross-reference button in the Links group. Clicking the Cross-reference button displays the Cross-reference dialog box, similar to the one shown in Figure 8.6 on the next page. At the Cross-reference dialog box, identify the reference type (what you are referencing), where the reader should refer, and the specific text.

The reference identified in the Cross-reference dialog box displays immediately after the introductory text. To move to the specified reference, hold down the Ctrl key, position the mouse pointer over the introductory text (the pointer turns into a hand), and then click the left mouse button.

**Insert a Cross-reference**

1. Type introductory text.
2. Click INSERT tab.
3. Click Cross-reference button.
4. Identify reference type, where to refer, and specific text.
5. Click Insert.
6. Click Close.

Cross-reference

**Figure 8.6 Cross-reference Dialog Box**

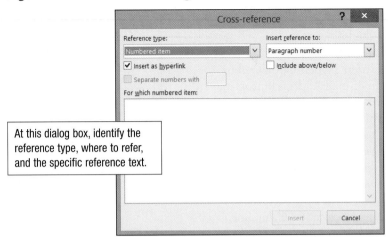

At this dialog box, identify the reference type, where to refer, and the specific reference text.

## Exercise 8.2E  Inserting and Navigating with Cross-references

1. With **C08-E02-VirusesSecurity.docx** open, insert a cross-reference in the document by completing the following steps:
   a. Move the insertion point so it is positioned at the immediate right of the period that ends the paragraph in the *Types of Viruses* section (located on page 3).
   b. Press the spacebar once and then type (**For more information, refer to**.
   c. Press the spacebar once.
   d. If necessary, click the INSERT tab.
   e. Click the Cross-reference button in the Links group.
   f. At the Cross-reference dialog box, click the down-pointing arrow at the right side of the *Reference type* list box and then click *Heading* at the drop-down list.
   g. Click *Spyware* in the *For which heading* list box.
   h. Click the Insert button.
   i. Click the Close button to close the dialog box.
   j. At the document, type a period followed by the right parenthesis.

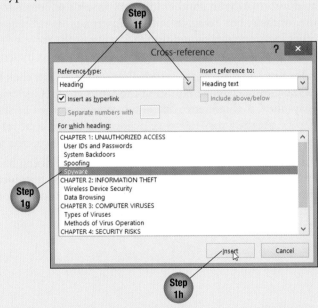

2. Move to the reference text by holding down the Ctrl key, positioning the mouse pointer over *Spyware* until the pointer turns into a hand, and then clicking the left mouse button.
3. Save **C08-E02-VirusesSecurity.docx**.

4. Apply the following formatting to the document:
   a. Insert page numbers that print at the top of each page at the right margin using the *Plain Number 3* option.
   b. Insert the Ion (Light) footer. Click the *[DOCUMENT TITLE]* placeholder and then type **Northland Security Systems**. Select the name that displays at the right side of the footer and then type your first and last names.
   c. Insert the Austin cover page and then make the following changes:
      • Delete the [abstract] placeholder.
      • Click the *[Document title]* placeholder (may display with the text *Northland Security Systems*) and then type **Computer Security**.
      • Delete the *[Document subtitle]* placeholder.
      • Type your name in place of the name that displays on the cover page.
5. Check the page breaks in the document. If a heading displays at the bottom of a page and the paragraph of text that follows displays on the next page, then insert a page break at the beginning of the heading.
6. Save and then print **C08-E02-VirusesSecurity.docx**.
7. Turn off the display of bookmarks by completing the following steps:
   a. Click the FILE tab and then click *Options*.
   b. At the Word Options dialog box, click *Advanced* in the left panel.
   c. Click the *Show bookmarks* check box in the *Show document content* section to remove the check mark.
   d. Click OK to close the dialog box.
8. Close **C08-E02-VirusesSecurity.docx**.

# Chapter Summary

➤ Insert symbols with options at the Symbol dialog box with the Symbols tab selected. Insert special characters with options at the Symbol dialog box with the Special Characters tab selected.

➤ Use drop caps to identify the beginnings of major sections or parts of a document and to enhance the appearance of the text. Create drop caps with the Drop Cap button in the Text group on the INSERT tab.

➤ Click the Date & Time button in the Text group on the INSERT tab to display the Date and Time dialog box. Insert the date and/or time with options at this dialog box or with keyboard shortcuts. If the date or time is inserted as a field, update the field with the Update Field key, F9.

➤ Insert a document into an open document by clicking the INSERT tab, clicking the Object button arrow, and then clicking *Text from File* at the drop-down list. At the Insert File dialog box, double-click the desired document.

➤ Navigate in a document with the Navigation pane or by inserting bookmarks.

➤ Insert bookmarks with options at the Bookmark dialog box.

➤ Insert hyperlinks in a document with options at the Insert Hyperlink dialog box. You can insert a hyperlink to an existing file or web page, a location in the current document, a new document, or an email. You can also use a graphic to link to a file or website.

➤ Create cross-references with options at the Cross-reference dialog box.

# Commands *Review*

| FEATURE | RIBBON TAB, GROUP | BUTTON, OPTION | KEYBOARD SHORTCUT |
|---|---|---|---|
| Bookmark dialog box | INSERT, Links | ⚑ | |
| Cross-reference dialog box | INSERT, Links | ⊟ | |
| Date and Time dialog box | INSERT, Text | 🗓 | |
| drop cap | INSERT, Text | A | |
| insert date | | | Alt + Shift + D |
| insert file | INSERT, Text | 📑 | |
| Insert Hyperlink dialog box | INSERT, Links | 🌐 | Ctrl + K |
| insert time | | | Alt + Shift + T |
| Navigation pane | VIEW, Show | *Navigation Pane* | |
| Symbol dialog box | INSERT, Symbols | Ω | |
| update field | | | F9 |

# Key Points *Review*

**Completion:** In the space provided at the right, indicate the correct term, symbol, or command.

1. The Symbol button is located on this tab. _____
2. Click this option at the Symbol button drop-down list to display the Symbol dialog box. _____
3. The first letter of the first word of a paragraph that is set into a paragraph is called this. _____
4. The Date & Time button is located in this group on the INSERT tab. _____
5. This is the Update Field keyboard shortcut. _____
6. Use this keyboard shortcut to insert the current date. _____
7. Use this keyboard shortcut to insert the current time. _____
8. Display the Insert File dialog box by clicking the Object button arrow on the INSERT tab and then clicking this option. _____
9. The *Navigation Pane* check box is located in the Show group on this tab. _____

10. Turn on the display of bookmarks in a document with the *Show bookmarks* check box in this dialog box with *Advanced* selected. _____

11. The Bookmark button is located in this group on the INSERT tab. _____

12. Navigate to a hyperlink by hovering the mouse over the hyperlink text, holding down this key, and then clicking the left mouse button. _____

13. To link a Word document to a file in another application, click this button in the *Link to* section in the Insert Hyperlink dialog box. _____

14. By default, cross-references are inserted in a document as this. _____

# *Chapter* Assessments

## Applying Your Skills

Demonstrate your knowledge of features learned in this chapter by completing the following assessments.

### Assessment 8.1  Apply Headers and Footers to Employee Orientation Documents

 **Grade It**

1. Open **EmpAppoints.docx** and save the document with the name **C08-A01-EmpAppoints**.
2. Press Ctrl + End to move the insertion point to the end of the document and then insert the file named **EmpPerf.docx**.
3. Press Ctrl + End to move the insertion point to the end of the document and then type **Séverin Technologies®**.
4. Press Shift + Enter and then insert the current date using the third option in the *Available formats* list box at the Date and Time dialog box.
5. Press Shift + Enter and then insert the current time with the keyboard shortcut Alt + Shift + T.
6. Create a drop cap with the first letter of the first paragraph of text (the word *Acceptance*) and specify that the drop cap drops two lines.
7. Make the following changes to the document:
   a. Apply the Heading 1 style to the two titles in the document: *EMPLOYMENT APPOINTMENTS* and *EMPLOYEE PERFORMANCE*.
   b. Apply the Heading 2 style to the four headings: *Types of Appointments*, *Work Performance Standards*, *Performance Evaluation*, and *Employment Records*.
   c. Apply the Black & White (Capitalized) style set.
   d. Apply the Frame theme.
   e. Change the theme colors to Blue Green.
   f. Center the two titles.
   g. Insert the Integral header and type **employee handbook** in the [DOCUMENT TITLE] placeholder.
   h. Insert the Integral footer and type your first and last names in the [author] placeholder.
   i. Insert a page break at the beginning of the title *EMPLOYEE PERFORMANCE* located on the second page.
8. Save, print, and then close **C08-A01-EmpAppoints.docx**.

## Assessment 8.2    Format and Navigate in Corporate Report Documents

1. Open **AuditRep.docx** and save the document with the name **C08-A02-AuditRep**.
2. Move the insertion point to the end of the document and then insert the document named **CompRep.docx**.
3. Apply the following formatting:
   a. Insert a page break at the beginning of the heading *Compensation Committee Report*.
   b. Apply the Minimalist style set.
   c. Insert the Austin footer.
4. Turn on the display of bookmarks.
5. Move the insertion point to the end of the third paragraph in the document (the paragraph that begins *The audit committee selects*) and then insert a bookmark named *Audit*.
6. Move the insertion point to the end of the first paragraph in the *Fees to Independent Auditor* section, following the *(Excel Worksheet)* text, and then insert a bookmark named *Audit_Fees*.
7. Move the insertion point to the end of the last paragraph of text in the document and then insert a bookmark named *Compensation*.
8. Navigate in the document using the bookmarks.
9. Move the insertion point to the end of the first paragraph in the *Committee Responsibilities* section and then insert a hyperlink to the *Audit_Fees* bookmark.
10. Select the text *(Excel Worksheet)* that displays at the end of the first paragraph in the *Fees to Independent Auditor* section and then insert a hyperlink to the Excel file named **ExcelAuditorFees.xlsx** that is located in the Chapter08 folder on your storage medium.
11. Hold down the Ctrl key and then click the <u>(Excel Worksheet)</u> hyperlink. Print the Excel worksheet that displays by clicking the FILE tab, clicking the *Print* option, and then clicking the Print button at the Print backstage area.
12. Close the Excel program without saving the workbook.
13. Save, print, and then close **C08-A02-AuditRep.docx**.

# Expanding Your Skills

Explore additional feature options or use Help to learn a new skill in creating these documents.

## Assessment 8.3    Customize Drop Cap Options

1. Open **CompServices.docx** and save the document with the name **C08-A03-CompServices**.
2. Display the Drop Cap dialog box and then determine how to change the drop cap font and distance from the text.
3. Create a drop cap for the first letter below the title and each heading in the document with the following specifications:
   - Position the drop cap within the text.
   - Change the drop cap font to Castellar.
   - Drop the cap two lines.
   - Change the *Distance from text* option to 0.1″.
   - With the drop cap selected, change the font color to Orange, Accent 6, Darker 50%.
4. Save, print, and then close **C08-A03-CompServices.docx**.
5. At a blank document, write a memo to your instructor describing the steps you took to create the drop caps in **C08-A03-CompServices.docx**. (Refer to Appendix C for information about the proper formatting of a memo.)
6. Save the completed memo and name it **C08-A03-DropCapMemo**.
7. Print and then close **C08-A03-DropCapMemo.docx**.

## Assessment 8.4 Determine Symbol Keyboard Shortcuts and Write a Letter

1. You work for a computer services and training company, and your supervisor has asked you to send a letter to a client regarding symbols and keyboard shortcuts. To begin, open **BMCLtrhd. docx** and save the document with the name **C08-A04-BMCClientLtr**.

2. You can insert some symbols in a document using keyboard shortcuts. If a symbol has a keyboard shortcut, it will display in the Symbol dialog box when the symbol is selected. Display the Symbol dialog box with the *(normal text)* font selected and then click the cent symbol (¢) (located in approximately the sixth row). Notice that the *Shortcut key:* option located toward the bottom of the dialog box is followed by *Ctrl + /,C*. This keyboard shortcut indicates that to insert a cent symbol in a document, you hold down the Ctrl key, press the / key on the keyboard, release the Ctrl key, and then type the letter **c**. If you click the Japanese Yen symbol (¥), *Shortcut key: Alt + 0165* displays toward the bottom of the Symbol dialog box. To insert the Yen symbol using the keyboard, press the Num Lock key on the numeric keypad if it is not active, hold down the Alt key, type **0165**, and then release the Alt key. At the Symbol dialog box, identify and write down the keyboard shortcuts for the following symbols:

   - Cent symbol (¢)
   - Yen symbol (¥)
   - British pound symbol (£)
   - Copyright symbol (©)
   - Registered symbol (®)
   - Paragraph symbol (¶)

3. Your supervisor has asked you to type a letter to a client that describes the steps to follow to insert a symbol from the Symbol dialog box and includes information on how to insert the symbols listed in item 2 using keyboard shortcuts. Address the letter to the following name and address using the block-style business letter style (refer to Appendix D):

   Patrick Shaughnessy, President
   A-line Manufacturing
   4512 Northeast 18th Avenue
   Casper, WY 82605

4. After typing the letter, save, print, and then close **C08-A04-BMCClientLtr.docx**.

# Achieving Signature Status

Take your skills to the next level by completing this more challenging assessment.

**Assessment 8.5**   **Create and Format a Document on Resumes for Career Changers**

1. At a blank document, create the document shown in Figure 8.7 on the next pages with the following specifications:
   a. The bulleted paragraphs of text are saved in a file named **Questions.docx**. Insert that file into your document instead of typing the bulleted text.
   b. Apply the Heading 1 style to the title and the Heading 3 style to the headings.
   c. Apply the Shaded style set.
   d. Apply the Wisp theme and change the theme colors to Violet II.
   e. Insert the Retrospect footer.
   f. Apply character formatting and insert a page break as indicated in Figure 8.7. (Center the title and apply bold formatting to the three headings.)
   g. Select the text *(Top-ten Growth Industries)* and then create a hyperlink that links to the Excel workbook named **EmpGrowth.xlsx**.
   h. Select the text *(Employment Trends)* and then create a hyperlink that links to the PowerPoint presentation named **EmpTrends.pptx**.
   i. Apply any other formatting required to ensure that your document appears the same as the document in Figure 8.7.
2. Hold down the Ctrl key and then click the hyperlink to display the **EmpGrowth.xlsx** Excel workbook. After viewing the workbook, close Excel without saving the workbook.
3. Hold down the Ctrl key and then click the hyperlink to display the **EmpTrends.pptx** PowerPoint presentation. Run the presentation by clicking the Slide Show button that displays in the view area on the Status bar. Click the left mouse button to advance each slide. After viewing the presentation, close PowerPoint.
4. Save the document and name it **C08-A05-CareerChangers**.
5. Print and then close **C08-A05-CareerChangers.docx**.

**Figure 8.7  Assessment 8.5**

RÉSUMÉS FOR CAREER CHANGERS

The fact that you are seeking to change careers will dictate almost everything that you write in your résumé, how you write it, and where it is positioned. Your goal is to paint a picture of the "new" you and not simply reiterate what you have done in the past, expecting a prospective employer to figure out that you can do the "new" thing just as well. If you fall into the career-changer category, the critical questions you must ask yourself about your résumé and your job search are the following:

- *How are you going to paint a picture of the "new" you?* What are you going to highlight about your past experience that ties directly to your current objectives? What accomplishments, skills, and qualifications are you going to "sell" in your résumé to support your "new" career objective?
- *What résumé format are you going to use?* Is a chronological, functional, or hybrid résumé format going to work best for you? Which format will give you the greatest flexibility to highlight the skills you want to bring to the forefront in support of your career change?
- *Where are you going to look for a job?* Assuming you know the type of position and industry you want to enter at this point in your career, how are you going to identify and approach those companies?

When you can answer the how, what, and where, you will be prepared to write your résumé and launch your search campaign. Your résumé should focus on your skills, achievements, and qualifications, demonstrating the value and benefit you bring to a prospective employer as they relate to your current career goals. The focus is on the "new" you and not necessarily what you have done professionally in the past.

CAREER OBJECTIVES

Before you begin writing your résumé, you will need to begin by defining your career or job objectives such as the types of positions, companies, and industries in which you are interested. This is critical because a haphazard, unfocused job search will lead you nowhere.

EMPLOYMENT TRENDS

One of the best ways to begin identifying your career objectives is to look at what opportunities are available today, in the immediate future, and in the longer-term future. A useful tool is the U.S. Department of Labor's Bureau of Labor Statistics. (Top-ten Growth Industries)

Numerous employment opportunities across diverse sectors within our economy, from advanced technology positions to hourly wage jobs in construction and home health care are available. Some of the most interesting findings that you will discover when investigating potential industry and job targets are listed in a PowerPoint presentation. (Employment Trends)

STUDENT NAME                                                                 1

**Figure 8.7  Assessment 8.5 (continued)**

## JOB SEARCH AND YOUR CAREER

To take advantage of these opportunities, you must be an educated job seeker. This means you must know what you want in your career, where the hiring action is, what qualifications and credentials you need to attain your desired career goals, and how best to market your qualifications.

The employment market has changed dramatically from only a few years ago. According to the U.S. Department of Labor, you should expect to hold between 10 and 20 different jobs during your career. No longer is stability the status quo. Today, the norm is movement, onward and upward, in a fast-paced and intense employment market where many opportunities are available for career changers. To take advantage of all of the opportunities, every job seeker must proactively control and manage his/her career.

STUDENT NAME

2

# Chapter 9

## Maintaining Documents

### Performance Objectives

Upon successful completion of Chapter 9, you will be able to:

- Manage files by copying, moving, printing, and renaming documents; opening multiple documents; and creating new folders and renaming existing folders
- Customize the display of folders and documents
- Share documents by exporting and saving them in different formats
- Create a document using a Word template

**Tutorial 9.1**
Managing Folders on Your Computer
**Tutorial 9.2**
Managing Documents
**Tutorial 9.3**
Changing Dialog Box Views
**Tutorial 9.4**
Saving a Document in a Different Format
**Tutorial 9.5**
Creating Documents Using a Word Template

Nearly every company that conducts business maintains a filing system. The system may consist of paper documents, folders, and file cabinets, or it may consist of electronic files and folders stored on a computer hard drive or other storage medium. Whatever type of system a company uses, the daily maintenance of files is important to its operations. In this chapter, you will learn to maintain files (documents) in Word, including how to create folders and copy, move, and rename documents. You will also learn how to create a document using a Word template.

*Note: Before beginning computer exercises for this chapter, copy to your storage medium the Chapter09 folder from the CD that accompanies this textbook and then make Chapter09 the active folder.*

In this chapter, students will produce the following documents:

Exercise 9.2. C09-E02-IntlCorres.docx
Exercise 9.2. C09-E02-IntlCorres-Word97-2003.doc
Exercise 9.2. C09-E02-IntlCorres-PlainTxt.txt
Exercise 9.2. C09-E02-IntlCorres-RichTxt.rtf
Exercise 9.2. C09-E02-NSS.docx
Exercise 9.3. C09-E03-LtrLuncheon.docx

Model answers for these exercises are shown on the following pages.

## INTERNATIONAL CORRESPONDENCE

With the increased number of firms conducting business worldwide, international written communication has assumed new importance. Follow these guidelines when corresponding internationally, especially with people for whom English is not the primary language:

- Use a direct writing style and clear, precise words.
- Avoid slang, jargon, and idioms.
- Develop an awareness of cultural differences that may interfere with the communication process.

## INTERNATIONAL ADDRESSES

Use the company's letterhead or a business card as a guide for spelling and other information. Include the following when addressing international correspondences:

Line 1: Addressee's Name, Title

Line 2: Company Name

Line 3: Street Address

Line 4: City and Codes

Line 5: COUNTRY NAME (capitalized)

## CANADIAN CODES AND PROVINCES

ON – Ontario

QC – Quebec

NS – Nova Scotia

NB – New Brunswick

MB – Manitoba

BC – British Columbia

PE – Prince Edward Island

SK – Saskatchewan

AB – Alberta

NL – Newfoundland and Labrador

## CANADIAN CODES AND TERRITORIES

NT – Northwest Territories

YT – Yukon

NU – Nunavut

**Exercise 9.2**

C09-E02-IntlCorres.docx

C09-E02-IntlCorres-Word97-2003.doc

C09-E02-IntlCorres-RichTxt.rtf

```
INTERNATIONAL CORRESPONDENCE
With the increased number of firms conducting business worldwide,
international written communication has assumed new importance. Follow
these guidelines when corresponding internationally, especially with
people for whom English is not the primary language:
* Use a direct writing style and clear, precise words.
* Avoid slang, jargon, and idioms.
* Develop an awareness of cultural differences that may interfere with
the communication process.

INTERNATIONAL ADDRESSES
Use the company's letterhead or a business card as a guide for spelling
and other information. Include the following when addressing
international correspondences:
Line 1: Addressee's Name, Title
Line 2: Company Name
Line 3: Street Address
Line 4: City and Codes
Line 5: COUNTRY NAME (capitalized)

CANADIAN CODES AND PROVINCES
ON - Ontario
QC - Quebec
NS - Nova Scotia
NB - New Brunswick
MB - Manitoba
BC - British Columbia
PE - Prince Edward Island
SK - Saskatchewan
AB - Alberta
NL - Newfoundland and Labrador

CANADIAN CODES AND TERRITORIES
NT - Northwest Territories
YT - Yukon
NU - Nunavut
```

**Exercise 9.2**

C09-E02-IntlCorres-PlainTxt.txt

## NORTHLAND SECURITY SYSTEMS MISSION

Northland Security Systems is a full-service computer information security management and consulting firm offering a comprehensive range of services to help businesses protect electronic data.

## SECURITY SERVICES

Northland Security Systems is dedicated to helping business, private and public, protect vital company data through on-site consultation, product installation and training, and 24-hour telephone support services. We show you how computer systems can be compromised and steps you can take to protect your company's computer system.

## SECURITY SOFTWARE

We offer a range of security management software to protect your business against viruses, spyware, adware, intrusion, spam, and policy abuse.

**Exercise 9.2**

C09-E02-NSS.docx

---

2/12/2015

Student Name
Franklin Securities
210 Benton Boulevard
Kansas City, MO 64111

Ms. Rebecca Brunson
21220 N.E. 100ᵗʰ St.
Kansas City, MO 64112

Dear Ms. Brunson:

I am pleased you can join me for lunch Wednesday, October 14, from 11:30 a.m. to 1:00 p.m. This event will be held at the company corporate headquarters. The attached map shows the location of the corporate headquarters building.

Franklin Securities is continually involved in a strategic planning process that attempts to respond to the needs of the community we serve. We are hosting a series of luncheons to tell community leaders about our work and to discuss how we can work together to strengthen our community.

I look forward to seeing you Wednesday and hearing your views on future community planning. If you have any questions, please call me at 816-555-8550.

Sincerely,


Student Name
Vice President
Franklin Securities

**Exercise 9.3**

C09-E03-LtrLuncheon.docx

# Maintaining Documents

Many file (document) management tasks in Word can be completed at either the Open or Save As dialog box. These tasks include copying, moving, printing, and renaming documents; opening multiple documents; and creating new folders and renaming existing folders.

Directions and projects in this chapter are based on the assumption that you are managing documents and folders on a USB flash drive or computer hard drive. If you are using SkyDrive, some of the document and folder management tasks may vary.

## Using Print Screen

A computer keyboard has a Print Screen button that will capture the contents of the screen as a file. That file can then be inserted into a Word document. Press the Print Screen key to capture the entire screen as an image or press Alt + Print Screen to capture only a dialog box or window that is open on the screen. The Print Screen feature is useful for file management in that capturing and then printing folder content can help you keep track of documents.

To use the Print Screen key, display the desired information on the screen and then press the Print Screen key on your keyboard (generally located in the top row) or press Alt + Print Screen to capture a dialog box or window on the screen. When you press the Print Screen key or Alt + Print Screen, nothing seems to happen, but in fact the screen image, dialog box, or window is captured in a file that is inserted in the Clipboard. To insert this file in a document, click the Paste button in the Clipboard group on the HOME tab. You can also paste the file by right-clicking in a blank location in a document and then clicking the *Paste* option at the shortcut menu or by pressing the keyboard shortcut Ctrl + V.

## Creating a Folder

**QUICK STEPS**

**Create a Folder**
1. Display Open dialog box.
2. Click New folder button.
3. Type folder name.
4. Press Enter.

Word documents, like paper documents, should be grouped logically and placed in *folders*. The main folder on a storage medium is called the ***root folder*** and additional folders can be created within the root folder. At both the Open and Save As dialog boxes, documents display in the Content pane preceded by the document icon (⊞) and folders display preceded by the folder icon (▯).

Create a new folder by clicking the New folder button located on either dialog box toolbar. This inserts a folder in the Content pane that contains the text *New folder*. Type a name for the folder (the name you type replaces *New folder*) and then press the Enter key. A folder name can contain a maximum of 255 characters. Numbers, spaces, and symbols can be used in the folder name, except those symbols listed in the *Naming a Document* section of Chapter 1.

To make the new folder active, double-click the folder name in the Open dialog box Content pane. The current folder path displays in the Address bar in the Open dialog box, as shown in Figure 9.1 on the next page. The path includes the current folder and any previous folders. If the folder is located on an external storage device, the drive letter and name may display in the path. For example, if you create a folder named *Contracts* in the Chapter09 folder on your storage medium, the Address bar displays *Chapter09* followed by a right-pointing triangle and then *Contracts*. Two left-pointing arrows display before *Chapter09*. These arrows indicate that Chapter09 is a subfolder within a folder or in a drive. Click the two left-pointing arrows and a drop-down list displays with the folder name or drive letter that is up one level from Chapter09. The drop-down list also includes other common folders and locations.

**Figure 9.1  Open Dialog Box**

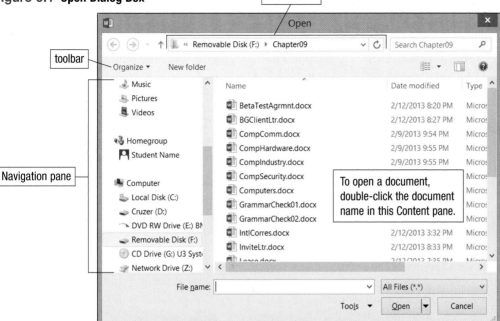

To open a document, double-click the document name in this Content pane.

## Exercise 9.1A  Creating a Folder                                          Part 1 of 7

1. Press Ctrl + N to open a blank document and then press Ctrl + F12 to display the Open dialog box.
2. In the *Computer* list in the Navigation pane, click the drive containing your storage medium. (You may need to scroll down the list to display the drive.)
3. Double-click the *Chapter09* folder in the Content pane.
4. Click the New folder button on the dialog box toolbar.
5. Type **Documents** and then press the Enter key.
6. Capture the Open dialog box as an image file and insert the image in a document by completing the following steps:
   a. With the Open dialog box displayed, hold down the Alt key and then press the Print Screen key on your keyboard (which is generally located in the top row of your keyboard).
   b. Close the Open dialog box.
   c. At the blank document, click the Paste button in the Clipboard group on the HOME tab.
   d. With the print screen file inserted in the document, print the document by clicking the FILE tab, clicking the *Print* option, and then clicking the Print button at the Print backstage area.
7. Close the document without saving it.

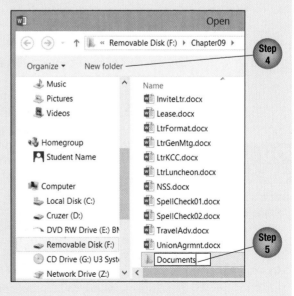

## Renaming a Folder

**Rename a Folder**
1. Display Open dialog box.
2. Right-click folder.
3. Click *Rename*.
4. Type new name.
5. Press Enter.

Organize ▾

As you organize your files and folders, you may decide to rename a folder. You can rename a folder using the Organize button in the Open or Save As dialog box or by using a shortcut menu. To rename a folder using the Organize button, display the Open or the Save As dialog box, click the folder you want to rename, click the Organize button located on the dialog box toolbar, and then click *Rename* at the drop-down list. Clicking *Rename* selects the folder name and inserts a border around it. Type the new name for the folder and then press the Enter key. To rename a folder using a shortcut menu, display the Open or Save As dialog box, right-click the folder you want to rename, and then click *Rename* at the shortcut menu. Type the new name for the folder and then press the Enter key.

---

### Exercise 9.1B    Renaming a Folder                          Part 2 of 7

1. Press Ctrl + F12 to display the Open dialog box and then right-click the *Documents* folder name in the Content pane.
2. Click *Rename* at the shortcut menu.
3. Type **Letters** and then press the Enter key.

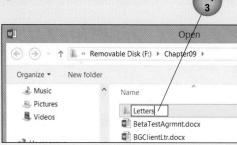

## Selecting Documents

You can complete document management tasks on one or more selected documents. To select one document, display the Open dialog box and then click the desired document. To select several adjacent documents (documents that display next to each other), click the first document, hold down the Shift key, and then click the last document. To select documents that are not adjacent, click the first document, hold down the Ctrl key, click any other desired documents, and then release the Ctrl key.

## Deleting Documents

**Delete a Document**
1. Display Open dialog box.
2. Click document name.
3. Click Organize button.
4. Click *Delete* at drop-down list.
5. Click Yes.

At some point, you may want to delete certain documents from your storage medium or any other drive or folder in which you may be working. To delete a document, display the Open or Save As dialog box, click the document, click the Organize button on the toolbar, and then click *Delete* at the drop-down list. If you are deleting a document from an external drive, such as a USB flash drive, click the Yes button at the message that displays asking you to confirm the deletion. This message does not display if you are deleting a document from the computer's hard drive. To delete a document using a shortcut menu, right-click the document name in the Content pane and then click *Delete* at the shortcut menu. If a confirmation message displays, click the Yes button.

## Deleting to the Recycle Bin

When you delete a document from your storage medium, it is deleted permanently. (Recovery programs are available, however, that will help you recover deleted text. If you accidentally delete a document or documents from a storage medium such as a USB flash drive, do not do anything more with the drive until you run a recovery program.) In contrast, when you delete a document from your hard drive, it is automatically sent to the Windows Recycle Bin. If you accidentally delete a document from the hard drive, sending it to the Recycle Bin, you can easily restore it. To free space on the drive, empty the Recycle Bin periodically.

Restoring a document from or emptying the contents of the Recycle Bin is completed at the Windows desktop (not in Word). To empty the Recycle Bin, complete the following steps:

1. Display the Windows desktop. If you are currently working in Word, click the Minimize button at the right side of the Title bar. The Minimize button is marked with a single underline symbol ( _ ).
2. At the Windows desktop, double-click the *Recycle Bin* icon (usually located at the left side of the desktop).
3. At the Recycle Bin window, click the Recycle Bin Tools Manage tab.
4. Click the Empty Recycle Bin button.
5. At the question asking if you are sure you want to empty the Recycle Bin, click Yes.

If you want to remove only specific documents from the Recycle Bin, hold down the Ctrl key while clicking the documents to be removed. Position the mouse pointer on one of the selected documents, click the right mouse button, and then click *Delete* at the shortcut menu. At the question asking if you want to delete the selected documents, click Yes.

A document or selected documents can also be restored from the Recycle Bin and returned to its original location. To do this, complete the following steps:

1. At the Windows desktop, double-click the *Recycle Bin* icon.
2. At the Recycle Bin window, click the document to be restored. (If you are restoring more than one document, hold down the Ctrl key while clicking the desired documents.)
3. Click the Recycle Bin Tools Manage tab.
4. Click the Restore the selected items button.

At the Recycle Bin window, you can also restore a document by positioning the mouse pointer on the document to be restored, clicking the right mouse button, and then clicking *Restore* at the shortcut menu.

If you minimized the Word program by clicking the Minimize button, maximize (display the Word screen) the Word program on the desktop by clicking the Word button located on the Taskbar (at the bottom of the screen).

1. Open **Computers.docx** and save the document with the name **C09-E01-Computers**.
2. Close **C09-E01-Computers.docx**.
3. Delete **C09-E01-Computers.docx** by completing the following steps:
   a. Display the Open dialog box with Chapter09 the active folder.
   b. Click *C09-E01-Computers.docx* to select it.
   c. Click the Organize button on the toolbar and then click *Delete* at the drop-down list.
   d. At the question asking if you want to delete **C09-E01-Computers.docx**, click Yes.
4. Delete selected documents by completing the following steps:
   a. At the Open dialog box, click *CompComm.docx*.
   b. Hold down the Shift key and then click *CompSecurity.docx*.
   c. Position the mouse pointer on a selected document and then click the right mouse button.
   d. At the shortcut menu that displays, click *Delete*.
   e. At the question asking if you want to delete the items, click Yes.
5. Open **LtrKCC.docx** and save the document with the name **C09-E01-LtrKCC**.
6. Save a copy of **C09-E01-LtrKCC.docx** in the Letters folder by completing the following steps:
   a. With **C09-E01-LtrKCC.docx** open, press the F12 function key to display the Save As dialog box.
   b. At the Save As dialog box, double-click the *Letters* folder located at the beginning of the Chapter09 Content pane. (Folders are listed before documents.)
   c. Click the Save button located in the lower right corner of the dialog box.
7. Close **C09-E01-LtrKCC.docx**.
8. Press Ctrl + F12 to display the Open dialog box and then click *Chapter09* in the Address bar.

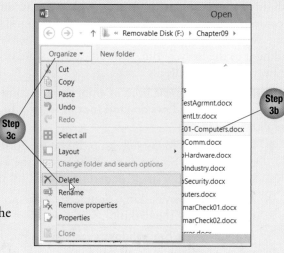

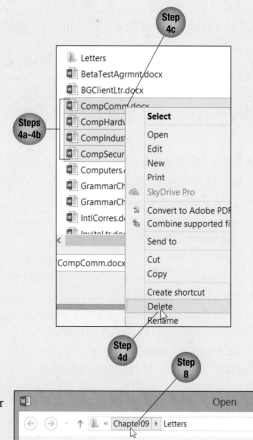

## Copying and Moving Documents

You can copy a document to another folder without opening the document first. To do this, use the *Copy* and *Paste* options from the Organize button drop-down list or the shortcut menu at the Open or Save As dialog box. You can copy a document or selected documents into the same folder. When you do this, Word adds a hyphen and the word *Copy* to the document name.

Remove a document from one folder and insert it into another folder using the *Cut* and *Paste* options from the Organize button drop-down list or the shortcut menu at the Open dialog box. To do this with the Organize button, display the Open dialog box, select the desired document, click the Organize button, and then click *Cut* at the drop-down list. Navigate to the desired folder, click the Organize button, and then click *Paste* at the drop-down list. To do this with the shortcut menu, display the Open dialog box, position the arrow pointer on the document to be removed (cut), click the right mouse button, and then click *Cut* at the shortcut menu. Navigate to the desired folder, position the arrow pointer in a white area in the Content pane, click the right mouse button, and then click *Paste* at the shortcut menu.

To move or copy files or folders on your SkyDrive, go to skydrive.com, make sure you are logged in to your account, and then use the SkyDrive.com toolbar to move a document or folder to another location or copy and then move a document or folder to another location.

**QUICK STEPS**

**Copy or Move a Document**
1. Display Open dialog box.
2. Right-click document name.
3. Click *Copy* or *Cut*.
4. Navigate to desired folder.
5. Right-click in white area.
6. Click *Paste*.

## Exercise 9.1D  Copying Documents                    Part 4 of 7

1. At the Open dialog box with Chapter09 the active folder, copy a document to another folder by completing the following steps:
   a. Click **LtrGenMtg.docx** in the Content pane, click the Organize button, and then click *Copy* at the drop-down list.
   b. Navigate to the Letters folder by double-clicking *Letters* at the beginning of the Content pane.
   c. Click the Organize button and then click *Paste* at the drop-down list.
2. Go back to the Chapter09 folder by clicking *Chapter09* in the Address bar.
3. Copy several documents to the Letters folder by completing the following steps:
   a. Click once on **LtrFormat.docx**. (This selects the document.)
   b. Hold down the Ctrl key, click **LtrKCC.docx**, click **LtrLuncheon.docx**, and then release the Ctrl key.
   c. Position the arrow pointer on one of the selected documents, click the right mouse button, and then click *Copy* at the shortcut menu.
   d. Double-click the *Letters* folder.
   e. Position the arrow pointer in a white area in the Content pane, click the right mouse button, and then click *Paste* at the shortcut menu.
4. Click *Chapter09* in the Address bar.

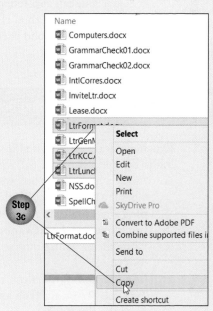

Step 3c

5. Move **TravelAdv.docx** to the Letters folder by completing the following steps:
   a. Position the arrow pointer on **TravelAdv.docx**, click the right mouse button, and then click *Cut* at the shortcut menu.
   b. Double-click *Letters* to make it the active folder.
   c. Position the arrow pointer in a white area in the Content pane, click the right mouse button, and then click *Paste* at the shortcut menu.
6. Capture the Open dialog box as an image and insert the image in a document by completing the following steps:
   a. With the Open dialog box displayed, hold down the Alt key and then press the Print Screen key on your keyboard.
   b. Close the Open dialog box.
   c. At a blank document, click the Paste button in the Clipboard group on the HOME tab. (If a blank document does not display on your screen, press Ctrl + N to open a blank document.)
   d. With the dialog box image inserted in the document, print the document by clicking the FILE tab, clicking the *Print* option, and then clicking the Print button at the Print backstage area.
7. Close the document without saving it.
8. Display the Open dialog box and make Chapter09 the active folder.

**QUICK STEPS**

## Renaming Documents

**Rename a Document**
1. Display Open dialog box.
2. Click document name.
3. Click Organize button and then *Rename*.
4. Type new name.
5. Press Enter.

At the Open dialog box, use the *Rename* option from the Organize button drop-down list to give a document a different name. The *Rename* option changes the name of the document but keeps it in the same folder. To use *Rename*, display the Open dialog box, click once on the document to be renamed, click the Organize button, and then click *Rename* at the drop-down list. When you click *Rename*, a black border surrounds the document name and the name is selected. Type the new name and then press the Enter key. You can also rename a document by right-clicking the document name at the Open dialog box and then clicking *Rename* at the shortcut menu. Type the desired name for the document and then press the Enter key.

### Exercise 9.1E  Renaming Documents                          Part 5 of 7

1. Rename a document located in the Letters folder by completing the following steps:
   a. At the Open dialog box with the Chapter09 folder active, double-click the *Letters* folder to make it active.
   b. Click once on **LtrKCC.docx** to select it.
   c. Click the Organize button on the toolbar.
   d. Click *Rename* at the drop-down list.
   e. Type **LtrPharmacyTech** and then press the Enter key.

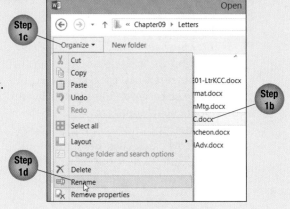

2. Capture the Open dialog box as an image and insert the image in a document by completing the following steps:
   a. Hold down the Alt key and then press the Print Screen key on your keyboard.
   b. Close the Open dialog box.
   c. At a blank document, click the Paste button in the Clipboard group on the HOME tab. (If a blank document does not display on your screen, press Ctrl + N to open a blank document.)
   d. With the dialog box image inserted in the document, print the document.
3. Close the document without saving it.
4. Display the Open dialog box and make Chapter09 the active folder.

## Deleting a Folder

As you learned earlier in this chapter, you can delete a selected document or several selected documents. Delete a folder and all of its contents in the same way you would delete a document.

## Using Open Button Options

Click the Open button arrow in the Open dialog box and a drop-down list displays with options for how to open the document. Click the *Open Read-Only* option to open a document that cannot be edited and then saved with the same name. This option is useful in a situation in which you do not want the original document modified. With some of the other options at the drop-down list, you can open a document as a copy, open the document in a web browser, and open and repair the document.

## Opening Multiple Documents

To open more than one document, select the documents in the Open dialog box and then click the Open button. You can also open multiple documents by positioning the arrow pointer on one of the selected documents, clicking the right mouse button, and then clicking *Open* at the shortcut menu.

**QUICK STEPS**

**Delete a Folder**
1. Display Open dialog box.
2. Click folder name.
3. Click Organize button and then *Delete*.
4. Click Yes.

**Open Multiple Documents**
1. Display Open dialog box.
2. Select desired documents.
3. Click Open button.

---

**Exercise 9.1F**  Deleting a Folder and Opening Multiple Documents          Part 6 of 7

1. At the Open dialog box, click the *Letters* folder to select it.
2. Click the Organize button and then click *Delete* at the drop-down list. (If a message displays asking if you want to delete the folder and its contents, click Yes.)
3. Open a document as read-only by completing the following steps:
   a. At the Open dialog box, click **LtrFormat.docx** in the Content pane to select it.

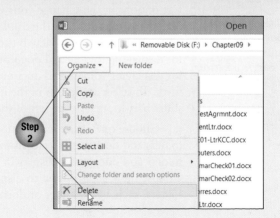

Step 2

---

b. Click the Open button arrow (located near the lower right corner of the dialog box) and then click *Open Read-Only* at the drop-down list. (This opens the document in Read Mode.)

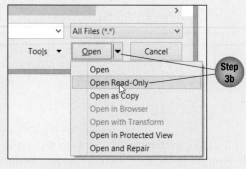

Step 3b

c. Display the document in Print Layout view by clicking the Print Layout button in the view area on the Status bar.

d. Notice that the Title bar displays the name *LtrFormat.docx [Read-Only]*.

e. Click the Save button on the Quick Access toolbar and notice that the Save As dialog box displays. (This is because you cannot save a read-only document with the original name.)

f. Click the Cancel button to close the Save As dialog box.

g. Close **LtrFormat.docx [Read-Only]**.

4. Open a document as a copy by completing the following steps:

a. Display the Open dialog box with Chapter09 the active folder and then click **LtrGenMtg.docx** in the Content pane to select it.

b. Click the Open button arrow and then click *Open as Copy* at the drop-down list.

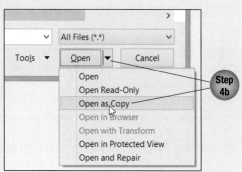

Step 4b

c. Notice that the Title bar displays the name *Copy (1)LtrGenMtg.docx*.

d. Close **Copy (1)LtrGenMtg.docx**.

5. Open multiple documents by completing the following steps:

a. Display the Open dialog box with Chapter09 the active folder and then select **LtrFormat.docx**, **LtrGenMtg.docx**, and **LtrKCC.docx**.

b. Click the Open button located near the lower right corner of the dialog box.

6. Close the open documents.

## Changing Dialog Box Views

Use options in the Change your view button drop-down list at the Open or Save As dialog box to customize the display of folders and documents in the Content pane. Click the Change your view button arrow and a drop-down list displays with options for displaying folders and documents as extra large, large, medium, or small icons and for displaying folders and documents in a list, with specific details, as tiles, or in content form. To select an option in the drop-down list, click the desired option or drag the slider bar (located at the left of the list) to the desired option.

Choose one of the icon options (extra large, large, medium, or small) to display folders and documents as icons in the Content pane. With the *List* option selected, folders and documents display in the Content pane in alphabetical order by name. Choose the *Details* option to display additional information about documents and folders, such as the folder or document type and modification date, as well as document size. With the *Tiles* option selected, folders and documents display as icons along with information about the folder or document type and size. Choose the *Content* option and document names display along with the author's name, date the document was modified, and document size.

You can cycle through the various views by clicking the Change your view button. Each time you click the button, the next view displays. Continue clicking the Change your view button until the desired view is selected.

## Displaying Document Properties

If you want to learn more about a specific document—such as the document location, size, creation date, modification dates, and date last accessed—display the document properties. You can do this with the *Properties* option at the Organize button drop-down list in the Open dialog box or Save As dialog box. Figure 9.2 displays the properties dialog box for the document **UnionAgrmnt.docx**. (The dates and times in the dialog box will vary.)

**Display Document Properties**
1. Display Open dialog box.
2. Click desired document.
3. Click Organize button.
4. Click *Properties*.

**Figure 9.2  Properties Dialog Box**

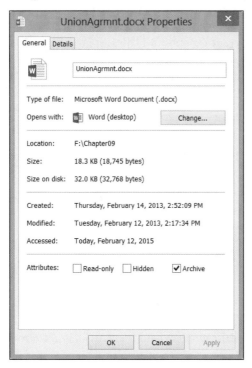

The properties dialog box generally displays with at least two tabs—General and Details. Other tabs that may display in the dialog box include Previous Versions, Sharing, and Customize. Each tab displays additional information about the document.

QUICK
STEPS

**Change the Dialog Box Layout**
1. Display Open dialog box.
2. Click Organize button.
3. Point to *Layout*.
4. Click desired option.

# Changing Dialog Box Layout

Generally, the Open dialog box displays with the Navigation pane at the left and Content pane at the right. You can customize this layout with options at the Organize button *Layout* side menu. Click the Organize button in the Open dialog box, point to *Layout*, and a side menu displays with options for turning on or off the display of the Details pane, Preview pane, and Navigation pane. Click the Organize button in the Save As dialog box, point to *Layout*, and the side menu displays with an option for turning on or off the display of the Navigation pane. A check mark displays before each option that is turned on.

**Exercise 9.1G** Changing Views, Displaying Properties, and Changing Layout                    Part 7 of 7

1. Display the Open dialog box with Chapter09 the active folder.
2. Change the views at the Open dialog box by completing the following steps:
   a. Click the Change your view button arrow on the toolbar.
   b. At the drop-down list that displays, drag the button on the slider bar that displays at the left of the list to the *Extra large icons* option. (This displays the folders and documents in the Content pane as large icons.)

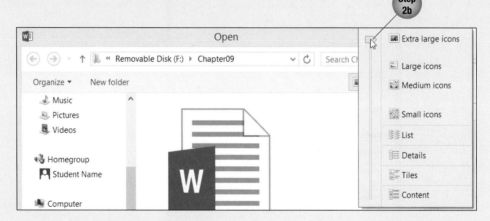

   c. Scroll through the Content pane and notice that the folders and documents are displayed as extra large icons.
   d. Click the Change your view button arrow and then click *Medium icons* at the drop-down list.

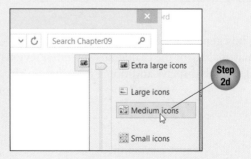

e. Scroll through the Content pane and notice that the folders and documents are displayed as medium-sized icons.

f. Click the Change your view button arrow and then drag the button on the slider bar to the *Details* option.

g. Scroll through the list of documents in the Content pane and notice that information is displayed on the documents' last modification dates, types, and sizes.

h. Click the Change your view button until the documents in the Content pane display as a list.

3. Display document properties for specific documents by completing the following steps:

a. At the Open dialog box, click **UnionAgrmnt.docx**.

b. Click the Organize button and then click *Properties* at the drop-down list.

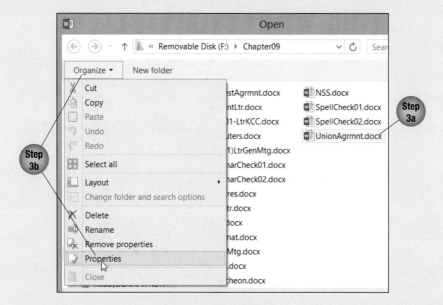

c. At the UnionAgrmnt.docx Properties dialog box, notice the properties information that displays in the dialog box with the General tab selected.

d. Click the Details tab and read the information that displays in the dialog box.

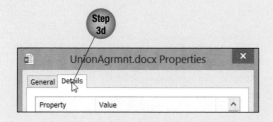

e. Click the Cancel button to close the UnionAgrmnt.docx Properties dialog box.

f. At the Open dialog box, click **IntlCorres.docx**, click the Organize button, and then click *Properties* at the drop-down list.

g. Notice the properties information that displays for the document and then close the properties dialog box.

4. Customize the layout of the Open dialog box by completing the following steps:
   a. At the Open dialog box, click the Organize button, point to *Layout* at the drop-down list, and then click *Navigation pane* at the side menu. (Doing this should remove the Navigation pane from the dialog box.)

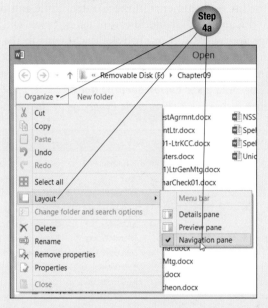

   b. Click the Organize button, point to *Layout*, and then click *Details pane*. (Doing this should display the Details pane along the bottom of the Open dialog box.)
   c. Click the Organize button, point to *Layout*, and then click *Preview pane*. (Doing this should display the Preview pane at the right side of the dialog box.)
5. Capture an image of the Open dailog box and insert the image in a document by completing the following steps:
   a. With the Open dialog box displayed, press Alt + Print Screen.
   b. Close the Open dialog box.
   c. At a blank document, click the Paste button.
   d. Print the document.
   e. Close the document without saving it.
6. Return the display of the Open dialog box back to the default settings by completing the following steps:
   a. Display the Open dialog box, click the Organize button, point to *Layout* at the drop-down list, and then click *Navigation pane* at the side menu. (Doing this should display the Navigation pane at the left side of the dialog box.)
   b. Click the Organize button, point to *Layout,* and then click *Details pane*. (Doing this should remove the display of the Details pane.)
   c. Click the Organize button, point to *Layout,* and then click *Preview pane*. (Doing this should remove the Preview pane from the right side of the dialog box.)
7. Close the Open dialog box.

# Saving a Document in a Different Format

When you save a document, the document is automatically saved as a Word document with the *.docx* file extension. If you need to share a document with someone who is using a different word processing program or different version of Word, you may want to save the document in another format. At the Export backstage area, click the *Change File Type* option and the backstage area displays, as shown in Figure 9.3. Display the Export backstage area by clicking the FILE tab and then clicking the *Export* option.

**QUICK STEPS**

**Save a Document in a Different Format**
1. Click FILE tab.
2. Click *Export* option.
3. Click *Change File Type* option.
4. Click desired format in *Document File Types* or *Other File Types* section.
5. Click Save As button.

**Figure 9.3** **Export Backstage Area with *Change File Type* Option Selected**

Click the *Change File Type* option to display options for saving a file in a different format.

With options in the *Document File Types* section below the *Change File Type* heading, you can choose to save a Word document with the default file format, in a previous version of Word, in OpenDocument Text format, or as a template. The OpenDocument Text format is a file format based on extensible markup language (XML). This format is used for displaying, storing, and editing files such as word processing, spreadsheet, and presentation files. OpenDocument Text format is free from any licensing, royalty payments, and other restrictions. Saving a document in OpenDocument Text format also ensures that the information in the file can be accessed, retrieved, and used now and in the future. This is a valuable feature considering how rapidly technology changes.

Additional file types are available in the *Other File Types* section. If you need to send your document to another user who does not have access to Microsoft Word, consider saving the document in plain text or rich text file format. Use the *Plain Text (*.txt)* option to save the document with all of the formatting removed; this is a good format for universal file exchange. Use the *Rich Text Format (*.rtf)* option to save the document with most of the character formatting applied to the text in the document—such as bold, italic, underline, bullets, and fonts—as well as some paragraph formatting. Before the widespread use of Adobe's portable document format (PDF), rich text format was the most portable file format used to exchange files. With the *Single File Web Page (*.mht, *.mhtml)* option, you can save your document as a single-page web document.

Click the *Save as Another File Type* option and the Save As dialog box displays. Click the *Save as type* option box and a drop-down list displays with a variety of available file type options.

<br>

**Exercise 9.2A**  **Saving a Document in Different File Formats**  **Part 1 of 3**

1. Open **IntlCorres.docx** and save the document with the name **C09-E02-IntlCorres**.
2. Save the document in Word 97-2003 format by completing the following steps:
   a. Click the FILE tab and then click the *Export* option.
   b. At the Export backstage area, click the *Change File Type* option.
   c. Click the *Word 97-2003 Document (*.doc)* option in the *Document File Types* section and then click the Save As button.

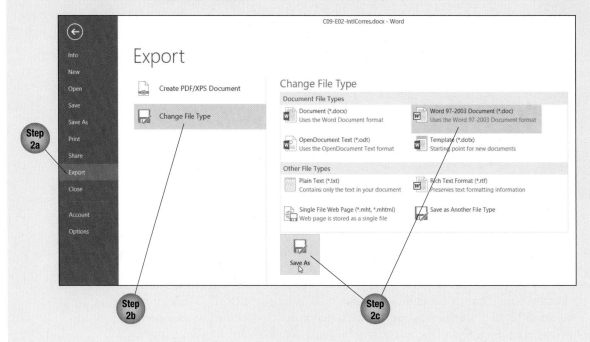

d. At the Save As dialog box with the *Save as type* option changed to *Word 97-2003 Document (*.doc)*, type **C09-E02-IntlCorres-Word97-2003** and then press the Enter key.

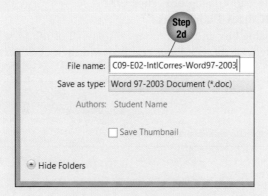

Step
2d

File name:  C09-E02-IntlCorres-Word97-2003

Save as type:  Word 97-2003 Document (*.doc)

Authors:  Student Name

☐ Save Thumbnail

⊙ Hide Folders

3. At the document, notice that the Title bar displays the words *[Compatibility Mode]* after the document name.
4. Click the DESIGN tab and notice that the Themes, Colors, and Fonts buttons are dimmed. (This is because the themes features were not available in Word 97 through 2003.)
5. Close **C09-E02-IntlCorres-Word97-2003.docx**.
6. Open **C09-E02-IntlCorres.docx**.
7. Save the document in plain text format by completing the following steps:
   a. Click the FILE tab and then click the *Export* option.
   b. At the Export backstage area, click the *Change File Type* option.
   c. Click the *Plain Text (*.txt)* option in the *Other File Types* section and then click the Save As button.

C09-E02-IntlCorres.docx - Word

Export

Create PDF/XPS Document

Change File Type

Change File Type

Document File Types

Document (*.docx)
Uses the Word Document format

Word 97
Uses the

OpenDocument Text (*.odt)
Uses the OpenDocument Text format

Template
Starting

Other File Types

Plain Text (*.txt)
Contains only the text in your document

Rich Text
Preserves

Single File Web Page (*.mht, *.mhtml)
Web page is stored as a single file

Save as A

Save As

Step
7a

Info
New
Open
Save
Save As
Print
Share
Export
Close
Account
Options

Step
7b

Step
7c

    d.  At the Save As dialog box, type **C09-E02-IntlCorres-PlainTxt** and then press the
        Enter key.
    e.  At the File Conversion dialog box, click OK.
8.  Close **C09-E02-IntlCorres-PlainTxt.txt**.
9.  Display the Open dialog box and if necessary display all of the files. To do this, click the file
    type button at the right of the *File name* text box and then click *All Files (\*.\*)* at the drop-
    down list.

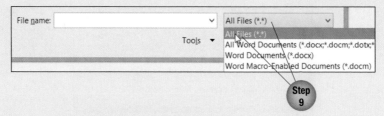

10. Double-click ***C09-E02-IntlCorres-PlainTxt.txt***. (If a File Conversion dialog box displays,
    click OK.) Notice that the character formatting and paragraph formatting have been
    removed from the document.
11. Close **C09-E02-IntlCorres-PlainTxt.txt**.

In addition to saving a document using options in the Export backstage area with
the *Change File Type* option selected, you can save a document in a different format using
the *Save as type* option box at the Save As dialog box. Click the *Save as type* option box
and a drop-down list displays, as shown in Figure 9.4. The drop-down list contains all of
the available file formats for saving a document. Click the desired format and then click
the Save button.

**Figure 9.4  Save As Dialog Box with *Save as type* Option Box Drop-down List**

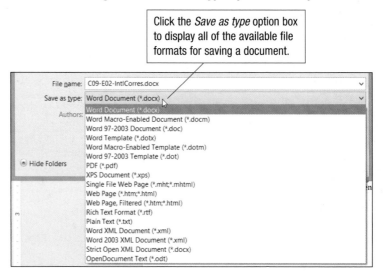

Click the *Save as type* option box
to display all of the available file
formats for saving a document.

1. Open **C09-E02-IntlCorres.docx**.
2. Save the document in rich text format by completing the following steps:
   a. Press the F12 function key to display the Save As dialog box.
   b. At the Save As dialog box, type **C09-E02-IntlCorres-RichTxt** in the *File name* text box.
   c. Click the *Save as type* option box.
   d. Scroll down the drop-down list and then click *Rich Text Format (*.rtf)*.

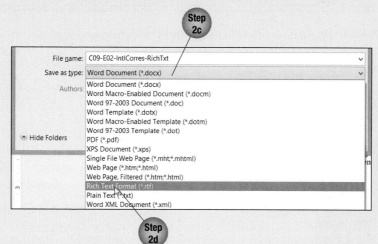

Step 2c

Step 2d

   e. Click the Save button.
3. Close the document.
4. Display the Open dialog box and, if necessary, display all of the files.
5. Double-click **C09-E02-IntlCorres-RichText.rtf**. Notice that the formatting is retained in the document.
6. Close the document.

## Saving in PDF or XPS Format

A Word document can be saved in PDF or XPS file format. The abbreviation *PDF* stands for *portable document format*, which is a file format that preserves fonts, formatting, and images in a printer-friendly version that looks the same on most computers. Someone who receives a Word file saved in PDF format does not need to have the Word application on his or her computer to open, read, and print the file. Exchanging PDF files is a popular method for collaborating with others. Because this file type has cross-platform compatibility, users can open PDF files on Windows-based personal computers, Macintosh computers, tablets, and smartphones.

The abbreviation *XPS* stands for *XML paper specification*. XPS is a fixed-layout format with all formatting preserved (similar to PDF). The XPS format was developed by Microsoft.

To save a document in PDF or XPS format, click the FILE tab, click the *Export* option, and then click the Create PDF/XPS button. This displays the Publish as PDF or XPS dialog box with the *PDF (*.pdf)* option selected in the *Save as type* option box. If you want to save the document in XPS format, click the *Save as type* option box and then click *XPS Document (*.xps)* at the drop-down list. At the Save As dialog box, type a name in the *File name* text box and then click the Publish button.

**QUICK STEPS**

**Save a Document in PDF or XPS Format**
1. Open document.
2. Click FILE tab.
3. Click *Export* option.
4. Click Create PDF/XPS button.
5. At Publish as PDF or XPS dialog box, specify PDF or XPS format.
6. Click Publish button.

A PDF file will open in Adobe Reader, Internet Explorer, Microsoft Word, and Windows Read. An XPS file will open in Internet Explorer, Windows Reader, and XPS Viewer. One method for opening a PDF or XPS file is to open File Explorer, navigate to the folder containing the file, right-click the file, and then point to *Open with*. This displays a side menu with the programs you can choose from to open the file. You can also open a PDF file in Word and make edits to the file, but you cannot open an XPS file in Word.

## Exercise 9.2C  Saving a Document in PDF Format and Editing a PDF File in Word                 Part 3 of 3

1. Open **NSS.docx** and then save the document in PDF format by completing the following steps:
   a. Click the FILE tab and then click the *Export* option.
   b. At the Export backstage area, click the Create PDF/XPS button.

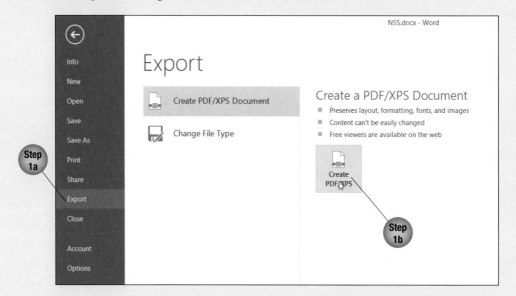

   c. At the Publish as PDF or XPS dialog box, make sure that *PDF (\*.pdf)* is selected in the *Save as type* option box and that the *Open file after publishing* check box contains a check mark and then click the Publish button. (When you click the Publish button, the document will automatically open in Adobe Reader if the program is installed on your computer. If Adobe Reader is not installed on your computer, the file will open in Windows Reader.)
2. Scroll through the document in Adobe Reader and then close Adobe Reader by clicking the Close button, located in the upper right corner of the window. (If the file opened in Windows Reader, close the window by positioning the mouse pointer at the top of the window [the mouse turns into a hand], holding down the left mouse button, dragging down to the bottom of the screen, and then releasing the mouse button. At the Windows 8 Start screen, click the Desktop icon.)
3. Close **NSS.docx**.
4. Open **NSS.pdf** in Windows Reader by completing the following steps:
   a. Click the File Explorer button on the Taskbar.
   b. At the Libraries dialog box, navigate to the Chapter09 folder on your storage medium.
   c. Right-click the **NSS.pdf** file in the Content pane, point to *Open with* at the shortcut menu, and then click *Reader* at the side menu.

d. After scrolling through the file in Windows Reader, close the window by positioning the mouse pointer at the top of the window (the mouse turns into a hand), holding down the left mouse button, dragging down to the bottom of the screen, and then releasing the mouse button.

e. At the Windows 8 Start screen, click the Desktop icon. (This step may vary.)

f. Close the Chapter09 window.

5. In Word, open the **NSS.pdf** file you saved to your Chapter09 folder. At the message that displays telling you that Word will convert the file to an editable Word document, click the OK button.

6. Notice that in Word, the text formatting is slightly different than the original PDF formatting and that the graphic is moved to the second page. Edit the file by completing the following steps:

a. Click the DESIGN tab and then click the *Lines (Distinctive)* style set.

b. Delete the text *We are* in the text below the first heading and replace it with *Northland Security Systems is.*

7. Save the file with Save As and name it **C09-E02-NSS**. (The file will save in the .docx file format.)

8. Close **C09-E02-NSS.docx**.

9. Capture the dialog box as an image by completing the following steps:

a. Press Ctrl + N to open a blank document.

b. Display the Open dialog box with the Chapter09 folder active.

c. Make sure that all files with any file extension display in the Content pane. To do this, check the option that displays at the right side of the *File name* text box. If *All Files (*.*)* does not display in the option box, click the option box and then click the *All Files (*.*)* option at the drop-down list.

d. Check to make sure that the documents display in List view. If they do not, click the Change your view button arrow and then click *List* at the drop-down list.

e. Hold down the Alt key and then press the Print Screen key.

f. Close the Open dialog box.

g. At the blank document, click the Paste button.

h. Print the document and then close the document without saving it.

# Creating a Document Using a Template

Word includes a number of template documents that are formatted for specific uses. Each Word document is based on a template document with the Normal template the default. With Word templates, you can easily create a variety of documents with special formatting, such as letters, calendars, and awards. Display the available templates by clicking the FILE tab and then clicking the *New* option. This displays the New backstage area, as shown in Figure 9.5 on the next page.

In addition to the templates that display at the New backstage area, you can download templates from the Office.com website. To do this, click in the search text box, type the search text or category, and then press Enter. Templates that match the search text or category display in the New backstage area. Click the desired template once and then click the Create button or double-click the desired template. Doing this downloads the template from the Office.com website and opens a document based on the template. Locations for personalized text may display in placeholders in the document. Click in the placeholder or select placeholder text and then type the personalized text.

**QUICK STEPS**

**Create a Document Using a Template**
1. Click FILE tab.
2. Click *New* option.
3. Double-click desired template.
OR
1. Click FILE tab.
2. Click *New* option.
3. Type search text or category in search text box.
4. Press Enter.
5. Double-click desired template.

If you use a template on a regular basis, consider "pinning" the template to the New backstage area. To do this, search for the desired template, hover your mouse over the template, and then click the gray left-pointing stick pin (*Pin to list*) that displays to the right of the template name. To unpin a template, click the down-pointing stick pin (*Unpin from list*).

**Figure 9.5  New Backstage Area**

Exercise 9.3  Creating a Letter Using a Template                        Part 1 of 1

## Exercise 9.3  Creating a Letter Using a Template                        Part 1 of 1

1. Click the FILE tab and then click the *New* option.
2. At the New backstage area, click in the search text box, type **letter**, and then press Enter.
3. When templates display that match *letter*, notice the *Category* list box that displays at the right side of the New backstage area.
4. Click the *Business* option in the *Category* list box. (Doing this displays only business letter templates.)

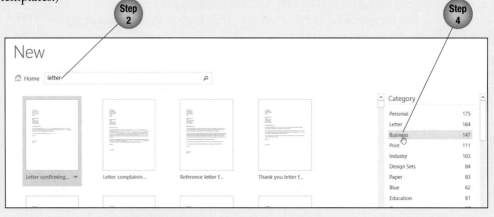

5. Scroll down the template list and then double-click the *Letter (Equity theme)* template.

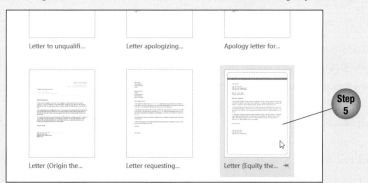

6. When the letter document displays on the screen, click the placeholder text *[Pick the date]*, click the down-pointing arrow at the right of the placeholder, and then click the Today button located below the calendar.

7. Click in the name that displays below the date, select the name, and then type your first and last names.

8. Click the placeholder text *[Type the sender company name]* and then type **Franklin Securities**.

9. Click the placeholder text *[Type the sender company address]*, type **210 Benton Boulevard**, press the Enter key, and then type **Kansas City, MO 64111**.

10. Click the placeholder text *[Type the recipient name]* and then type **Ms. Rebecca Brunson**.

11. Click the placeholder text *[Type the recipient address]*, type **21220 N.E. 100th St.**, press the Enter key, and then type **Kansas City, MO 64112**.

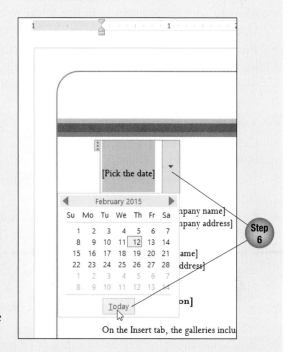

12. Click the placeholder text *[Type the salutation]* and then type **Dear Ms. Brunson:**. Select the text you just typed and then remove the bold formatting.

13. Insert a file in the document by completing the following steps:
    a. Click anywhere in the three paragraphs of text in the body of the letter and then click the Delete key.
    b. Click the INSERT tab.
    c. Click the Object button arrow in the Text group and then click *Text from File* at the drop-down list.
    d. At the Insert File dialog box, navigate to the Chapter09 folder on your storage medium and then double-click **LtrLuncheon.docx**.
    e. Press the Delete key once to remove the blank space above the complimentary close.

14. Click the placeholder text *[Type the closing]* and then type **Sincerely,**.

15. Click the placeholder text *[Type the sender title]* and then type **Vice President**.

16. Save the document with the name **C09-E03-LtrLuncheon**. (If a message displays telling you that your document will be upgraded to the newest file format, click OK.)

17. Print and then close **C09-E03-LtrLuncheon.docx**.

# Chapter Summary

➤ Group Word documents logically into folders. Create a new folder with the New folder button at the Open or Save As dialog box.

➤ Select one or several documents at the Open dialog box and then copy, move, rename, delete, print, or open the document or selected documents.

➤ Delete documents and/or folders with the *Delete* option at the Organize button drop-down list at the Open or Save As dialog box or with the *Delete* option from the shortcut menu.

➤ Documents deleted from the hard drive are sent to the Windows Recycle Bin. You can empty or recover documents from the Recycle Bin.

➤ Move or copy a document from one folder to another using the *Cut*, *Copy*, and *Paste* options from the Organize button drop-down list or the Open or Save As dialog box shortcut menu.

➤ Rename documents with the *Rename* option from the Open dialog box Organize button drop-down list or shortcut menu.

➤ Use options from the Open button arrow in the Open dialog box to open a document in a different format, such as read-only or a copy.

➤ You can open multiple documents from the Open dialog box.

➤ Change views in the Open dialog box or Save As dialog box with options from the Change your view button arrow drop-down list.

➤ Use the *Properties* option at the Organize button drop-down list to display information about the currently selected document in the Content pane.

➤ Customize the layout of the Open or Save As dialog box with layout options from the Organize button *Layout* side menu.

➤ Click the *Change File Type* option at the Export backstage area to display options for saving a document in a different file format, such as OpenDocument Text, plain text, rich text format, single-file web page, a previous version of Word, or a template.

➤ You can also save documents in a different file format with the *Save as type* option box at the Save As dialog box.

➤ Save a document in PDF or XPS format with the *Create PDF/XPS Document* option at the Export backstage area.

➤ Available templates display in the New backstage area. Double-click a template to open a document based on that template. Search for templates online by typing the search text or category in the search text box and then pressing Enter.

# Commands *Review*

| FEATURE | RIBBON TAB, GROUP | BUTTON, OPTION | KEYBOARD SHORTCUT |
|---|---|---|---|
| Export backstage area | FILE | *Export* | |
| New backstage area | FILE | *New* | |
| Open dialog box | FILE | *Open*, double-click *Computer* | Ctrl + F12 |
| Recycle Bin | |  | |
| Save As dialog box | FILE | *Save As*, double-click *Computer* | F12 |

# Key Points *Review*

SNAP

**Completion:** In the space provided at the right, indicate the correct term, command, or number.

1. Create a new folder with this button in the Open or Save As dialog box.

2. To make the previous folder active, click the folder name in this bar in the Open or Save As dialog box.

3. Using the mouse, select adjacent documents at the Open dialog box by holding down this key while clicking the desired documents.

4. Using the mouse, select nonadjacent documents at the Open dialog box by holding down this key while clicking the desired documents.

5. Documents deleted from the hard drive are automatically sent to this bin.

6. Copy a document to another folder without opening the document using the *Copy* option and this option from the Open dialog box shortcut menu.

7. Use this option from the Open dialog box Organize button drop-down list to give a document a different name.

8. Choose this option at the Open dialog box Change your view button drop-down list to display folders and documents alphabetized by name.

9. Choose this option at the Open dialog box Change your view button arrow drop-down list to display information about folders and documents such as modification date, type, and size.

10. Saving a document in this file format removes all of the formatting.

11. You can save a document in a different file format with this option box at the Save As dialog box.

12. The abbreviation PDF stands for this. _____

13. Click this button at the Export backstage area to display the
    Publish as PDF or XPS dialog box. _____

14. In addition to the templates that display at the New backstage
    area, templates can be downloaded from this website. _____

# Chapter *Assessments*

## Applying Your Skills

Demonstrate your knowledge of features learned in this chapter by completing the following assessments.

### Assessment 9.1    Create a Folder and Copy and Rename Documents

1. Display the Open dialog box with Chapter09 as the active folder and then create a new folder named *CheckingTools*.
2. Copy (be sure to copy and not cut) into the CheckingTools folder all of the documents that have names beginning with *SpellCheck* and *GrammarCheck*.
3. With the CheckingTools folder active, rename **SpellCheck01.docx** as **VacationAdventures.docx**.
4. Rename **GrammarCheck01.docx** as **NaturalInterfaces.docx**.
5. Press Alt + Print Screen key to capture an image of the Open dialog box, close the Open dialog box, insert the file in a blank document, print the document, and then close the document without saving it.
6. Display the Open dialog box and make Chapter09 the active folder.
7. Delete the CheckingTools folder and all of the documents within it.

### Assessment 9.2    Save a Document in Different Formats

1. Open **Lease.docx** and save the document with the name **C09-A02-Lease**.
2. Make the following changes to the document:
   a. Apply the Heading 1 style to the title *LEASE AGREEMENT*.
   b. Apply the Centered style set.
   c. Apply the Wisp theme.
3. Save and then print **C09-A02-Lease.docx**.
4. With **C09-A02-Lease.docx** open, save the document in Word 97-2003 format with the name **C09-A02-Lease-W97-2003**.
5. Close **C09-A02-Lease-W97-2003.doc**.
6. Open **C09-A02-Lease.docx** and then save the document in plain text format with the name **C09-A02-Lease-PlainTxt**.
7. Close **C09-A02-Lease-PlainTxt.txt**.
8. Open **C09-A02-Lease.docx** and then save the document in PDF format with the name **C09-A02-Lease-PDF**. After viewing the document in Adobe Reader, click the Close button located in the upper right corner of the screen. (If the file opened in Windows Reader, position the mouse pointer at the top of the window, hold down the left mouse button, drag down to the bottom of the screen, and then release the mouse button.)
9. Open the **C09-A02-Lease-PDF.pdf** file in Word and click OK at the message telling you that Word will convert the PDF to an editable Word document.

10. Select the entire document and then change the font to Candara (if necessary, delete the blank page at the end of the document).
11. Save the document with the default name (**C09-A02-Lease-PDF.docx**) and then print and close the document.
12. Close **C09-A02-Lease.docx** without saving changes.

### Assessment 9.3    Use a Template to Create a Fax Document

1. Search for and download the Fax (Equity theme) template and then type the following information in the specified fields:

> *To:* **Charlene Renquist**
> *From:* (your first and last names)
> *Fax:* **(816) 555-9010**
> *Pages:* **3**
> *Phone:* **(816) 555-9005**
> *Date:* (insert current date)
> *Re:* **Financial Contract**
> *CC:* **Eric Young**
> *For Review check box:* (insert an X)
> *Comments:* **Please review the Financial Contract and advise me of any legal issues.**

2. Save the fax document with the name **C09-A03-Fax**.
3. Print and then close **C09-A03-Fax.docx**.

## Expanding Your Skills

Explore additional feature options or use Help to learn a new skill in creating this document.

### Assessment 9.4    Create a Calendar and Write a Memo

1. Search for and download a calendar template of your choosing from Office.com. Insert text in the calendar as needed.
2. When you have completed the calendar, print the first page.
3. Save the document and name it **C09-A04-Calendar**.
4. Close **C09-A04-Calendar.docx**.
5. At a blank document, write a memo to your instructor describing the steps you followed to download and create the calendar in **C09-A04-Calendar.docx**.
6. Save the completed memo and name it **C09-A04-Memo**.
7. Print and then close **C09-A04-Memo.docx**.

## Achieving Signature Status

Take your skills to the next level by completing these more challenging assessments.

### Assessment 9.5    Create a Folder and Save Documents in Different Formats

1. Look at the Open dialog box shown in Figure 9.6 on the next page. Create a new folder named *FileFormats* as shown in the figure. Open the documents from the Chapter09 folder on your storage medium and then save them in the FileFormats folder in the four file formats shown in the Content pane in the figure. ***Hint: Look at the file extension of each document and the information in the* Type *column to determine the four formats in which you need to save the document.***

2.  When you have completed saving the documents in the appropriate file formats, display the Open dialog box with the FileFormats folder active, change the view to Details, and then press Alt + Print Screen to capture an image of the Open dialog box. Paste the image into a blank document, print the document, and then close the document without saving it.

**Figure 9.6  Assessment 9.5**

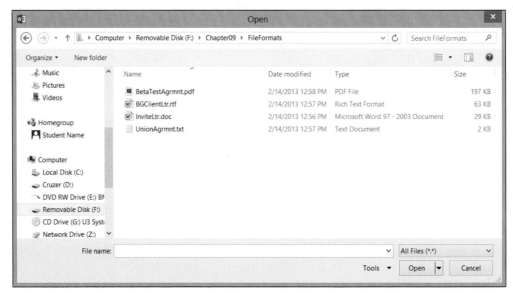

## Assessment 9.6  Create an Invitation

1.  Create the company annual picnic invitation shown in Figure 9.7 on the next page with the following specifications:
    a.  Search for and download the company picnic invitation flyer shown in the figure.
    b.  Edit the information so it displays as shown in the figure. (Type your first and last names in place of *Student Name* located near the bottom of the invitation.)
    c.  Insert the page border with the following specifications:
        •  Use the border style third from the bottom in the *Style* list box.
        •  Change the line width to 4½ points.
        •  Change the color to Blue, Accent 1 (fifth column, first row in the *Theme Colors* section).
2.  Save the completed invitation and name it **C09-A06-Invitation**.
3.  Print and then close **C09-A06-Invitation.docx**.

**Figure 9.7** **Assessment 9.6**

# Chapter 10

# Managing and Printing Documents

## Performance Objectives

Upon successful completion of Chapter 10, you will be able to:

- Open, close, arrange, split, maximize, minimize, and restore documents
- Manage the list of most recently opened documents
- Preview and print pages or sections of a document
- Create and print envelopes
- Create and print labels

When you work in Word, you can view a single document or multiple documents on the screen. You can also open and close windows; arrange windows; and maximize, minimize, and restore documents. In this chapter, you will learn how to complete these tasks and how to customize printing and create and print envelopes and labels.

*Note: Before beginning computer exercises for this chapter, copy to your storage medium the Chapter10 folder from the CD that accompanies this textbook and then make Chapter10 the active folder.*

In this chapter, students will produce the following documents:

Exercise 10.1. C10-E01-CompSoftware.docx
Exercise 10.2. C10-E02-Env.docx
Exercise 10.3. C10-E03-GSHLtr.docx
Exercise 10.4. C10-E04-Labels.docx
Exercise 10.5. C10-E05-BGCLabels.docx

Model answers for these exercises are shown on the following pages.

## SECTION 1: GRAPHICS AND MULTIMEDIA SOFTWARE

Graphics and multimedia software allows both professional and home users to work with graphics, video, and audio. A variety of application software is focused in this area including painting and drawing software, image-editing software, video and audio editing software, and computer-aided design (CAD) software.

### Painting and Drawing Software

Painting and drawing programs are available for both professional and home users. The more expensive professional versions typically include more features and greater capabilities than do the less expensive personal versions. Both painting programs and drawing programs provide an intuitive interface through which users can draw pictures, make sketches, create various shapes, and edit images. Programs typically include a variety of templates that simplify painting or drawing procedures.

### Image-Editing Software

The market demand for image-editing programs has increased concurrently w[...]
An image-editing program allows a user to touch up, modify, and enhance ima[...]
stored in a variety of forms and inserted into other files, such as letters, adver[...]

### Video and Audio Editing Software

As digital video cameras and other portable technologies have become more c[...]
ability to create and modify recorded video and audio clips using video and au[...]
video or audio files, home users can often use basic video and audio editing so[...]
computer's operating system. Some users prefer the additional features of an [...]

### Computer-aided Design Software

Computer-aided design software is a sophisticated kind of drawing software, [...]
professionals to create architectural, engineering, product, and scientific desig[...]
design buildings or bridges, and scientists can create graphical designs of plan[...]
Some software programs display designs in three-dimensional form so they ca[...]
Once a design has been created, changes can be easily made until it is finalized[...]

## SECTION 2: PERSONAL-USE SOF[...]

When browsing computer stores, shoppers are likely to see numerous softwa[...]
household. Among the many products available are applications for writing le[...]
new home, landscaping a lawn, preparing and filing tax returns, and managing[...]
available for home and personal use, although sometimes the suites available [...]
features in business versions.

**Page 1**

### Personal Finance

Personal finance software assists users with paying bills, balancing checkbooks, keeping track of income and expenses, maintaining investments records, and other financial activities. The software also enables users to readily view how their money is being spent. Some personal finance software provides online services available on the Internet and Web. These services allow users to go online to learn the status of their investments and insurance coverage. They can also conduct normal banking transactions, including accessing and printing bank statements showing monthly transaction summaries.

### Tax Preparation

Tax preparation software is designed to aid in analyzing federal and state tax status, as well as to prepare and transmit tax returns. Most of the programs provide tips for preparing tax documents that can help identify deductions, possibly resulting in great savings. Some programs include actual state and federal tax forms for entering tax data. Programs that do not include forms provide instructions for downloading them from the software publisher's website. Finished tax returns can be printed for mailing or filing electronically. Because federal and state tax laws change frequently, as do tax forms, users will probably need to obtain the software version for the appropriate taxable years or period.

### Legal Documents

Legal software is designed to help analyze, plan, and prepare a variety of legal documents, including wills and trusts. It can also be used to prepare other legal documents, such as the forms required for real estate purchases or sales, rental contracts, and estate planning. Included in most packages are standard templates for various legal documents, along with suggestions for preparing them.

### Educational and Reference Software

The widespread use of home computers has brought about an increase in the availability of educational and reference software, making computers popular learning and reference tools. Examples of educational and reference software include encyclopedias, dictionaries, and tutorials.

**Page 2**

**Exercise 10.1**

C10-E01-CompSoftware.docx

---

JOSEPH DEROUSSE
1005 E 102 AVE
KANSAS CITY MO 64110-2089

CRYSTAL BERGMAN
8975 N 32 ST
KANSAS CITY MO 64119-4201

**Exercise 10.2**

C10-E02-Env.docx

Mr. Victor Durham
Good Samaritan Hospital
1201 James Street
St. Louis, MO 62033

Mr. Victor Durham
Good Samaritan Hospital
1201 James Street
St. Louis, MO 62033

Mr. Victor Durham
Good Samaritan Hospital
1201 James Street
St. Louis, MO 62033

Mr. Victor Durham
Good Samaritan Hospital
1201 James Street
St. Louis, MO 62033

Mr. Victor Durham
Good Samaritan Hospital
1201 James Street
St. Louis, MO 62033

Mr. Victor Durham
Good Samaritan Hospital
1201 James Street
St. Louis, MO 62033

Mr. Victor Durham
Good Samaritan Hospital
1201 James Street
St. Louis, MO 62033

Mr. Victor Durham
Good Samaritan Hospital
1201 James Street
St. Louis, MO 62033

Mr. Victor Durham
Good Samaritan Hospital
1201 James Street
St. Louis, MO 62033

Mr. Victor Durham
Good Samaritan Hospital
1201 James Street
St. Louis, MO 62033

Mr. Victor Durham
Good Samaritan Hospital
1201 James Street
St. Louis, MO 62033

Mr. Victor Durham
Good Samaritan Hospital
1201 James Street
St. Louis, MO 62033

Mr. Victor Durham
Good Samaritan Hospital
1201 James Street
St. Louis, MO 62033

Mr. Victor Durham
Good Samaritan Hospital
1201 James Street
St. Louis, MO 62033

Mr. Victor Durham
Good Samaritan Hospital
1201 James Street
St. Louis, MO 62033

**Exercise 10.3**

C10-E03-GSHLtr.docx

DEBRA FOSTER
9054 N 23 ST
BOISE ID 83709

CHARLES MOZONNE
12003 203 ST SE
BOISE ID 83799

CASSANDRA REID
9045 VISTA AVE
BOISE ID 83719

BEN AND JILL NYE
6013 FAIRVIEW AVE
BOISE ID 83720

MARK CHAVEZ
805 ORCHARD ST
BOISE ID 83720

KARL KNOWLES
23102 HARRISON BLVD
BOISE ID 83722

**Exercise 10.4**

C10-E04-Labels.docx

Model Answers

**Exercise 10.5**

C10-E05-BGCLabels.docx

# Working with Windows

In Word, you can open multiple documents and move the insertion point among them. This feature allows you to move and copy information or compare content between documents. The maximum number of documents you can have open at one time depends on the memory capacity of your computer and the amount of data in each document. When you open a new window, it displays on top of any previously opened window(s) that you have not closed or minimized. When you have multiple windows open, you can resize them to see all of one document or a portion of each document on the screen.

When a document is open, a Word button displays on the Taskbar. Hover the mouse over this button and a thumbnail of the document displays. If you have more than one document open, the Word button on the Taskbar displays another layer in a cascaded manner. The layer behind the Word button displays only a portion of the edge at the right of the button. If you have multiple documents open, hovering the mouse over the Word button on the Taskbar will cause thumbnails of all of the documents to display above the button. To change to the desired document, click the thumbnail that represents that document.

Switch Windows

Another method for determining which documents are open is to click the VIEW tab and then click the Switch Windows button in the Window group. The document name that displays in the list with a check mark in front of it is the ***active document***. The active document contains the insertion point. To make one of the other documents active, click the document name. If you are using a keyboard, type the number shown in front of the desired document.

**QUICK STEPS**

**Arrange Windows**
1. Open documents.
2. Click VIEW tab.
3. Click Arrange All.

## Arranging Windows

If you have more than one document open, you can arrange them on the screen so that a portion of each is visible. To do this, click the VIEW tab and then click the Arrange All button in the Window group. Figure 10.1 on the next page shows a document screen with four open documents that have been arranged to make a portion of each visible.

Arrange All

## Maximizing, Restoring, and Minimizing Documents

Use the Maximize and Minimize buttons, located in the upper right corner of the active document, to change the size of the window. These two buttons are located to the left of the Close button. (The Close button is marked with an X.) The Minimize button is located immediately to the left of the Maximize button.

Maximize

Minimize

If you arrange all of the open documents and then click the Maximize button in the active document, the active document expands to fill the document screen. In addition, the Maximize button becomes the Restore Down button. To return the active document to its former size, click the Restore Down button. If you click the Minimize button in the active document, the document is reduced and displays as a layer behind the Word button on the Taskbar. To maximize a document that has been minimized, click the Word button on the Taskbar and then click the thumbnail representing the document.

Restore Down

**Figure 10.1 Arranged Documents**

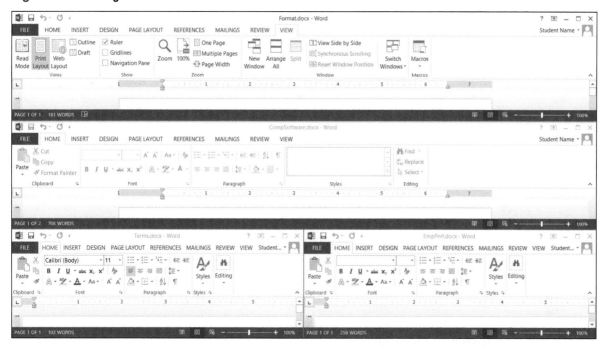

# Exercise 10.1A  Arranging, Maximizing, Restoring, and Minimizing Windows

Part 1 of 8

*Note: If you are using Word on a network that contains a virus checker, you may not be able to open multiple documents at once. Continue by opening each document individually.*

1. Open the following documents: **CompSoftware.docx**, **EmpPerf.docx**, **Format.docx**, and **Terms.docx**.
2. Arrange the windows by clicking the VIEW tab and then clicking the Arrange All button in the Window group.
3. Make sure that **Format.docx** is the active document by clicking the Switch Windows button and then clicking *Format.docx* at the drop-down list.
4. Close **Format.docx** by clicking the Close button located in the upper right corner of the **Format.docx** document.
5. Make **EmpPerf.docx** active and then close it.
6. Make **CompSoftware.docx** active and then minimize it by clicking the Minimize button in the upper right corner of the window.
7. Maximize **Terms.docx** by clicking the Maximize button at the right side of the Title bar. (The Maximize button is the button at the right of the Title bar, immediately left of the Close button.)
8. Close **Terms.docx**.

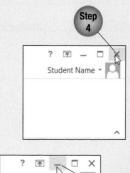

Step 4

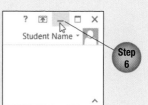

Step 6

9. Restore **CompSoftware.docx** by clicking the Word button on the Taskbar.
10. Maximize **CompSoftware.docx**.

Step 9

## Splitting a Window

**Split a Window**
1. Open document.
2. Click VIEW tab.
3. Click Split button.

Split

Remove Split

You can divide a window into two *panes*, which is helpful if you want to view different parts of a document at one time. For example, you may want to display an outline for a report in one pane and the portion of the report you are editing in the other. The original window is split into two panes that extend horizontally across the screen.

To split a window, click the VIEW tab and then click the Split button in the Window group. This splits the window in two with a split bar and another horizontal ruler. You can change the location of the split bar by positioning the mouse pointer on the bar until the pointer displays as an up-and-down-pointing arrow with two small lines in the middle, holding down the left mouse button, dragging to the desired position, and then releasing the mouse button.

When a window is split, the insertion point is positioned in the bottom pane. To move the insertion point to the other pane with the mouse, position the I-beam pointer in the other pane and then click the left mouse button. To remove the split bar from the document, click the VIEW tab and then click the Remove Split button in the Window group. You can also double-click the split bar or drag the split bar to the top or bottom of the screen.

## Exercise 10.1B  Moving Selected Text between Split Windows        Part 2 of 8

1. With **CompSoftware.docx** open, save the document with the name **C10-E01-CompSoftware**.
2. Click the VIEW tab and then click the Split button in the Window group.
3. Move the first section of the document below the second section by completing the following steps:

Step 2

REVIEW   VIEW

New Window | Arrange All | Split | View Side by Side | Synchronous Scrolling | Reset Window Position | Switch Windows
Window

   a. Click in the top pane and then click the HOME tab.
   b. Select the *SECTION 1: PERSONAL-USE SOFTWARE* section from the title to immediately above *SECTION 2: GRAPHICS AND MULTIMEDIA SOFTWARE*.
   c. Click the Cut button in the Clipboard group on the HOME tab.
   d. Click in the bottom pane and then move the insertion point to the end of the document.
   e. Click the Paste button in the Clipboard group on the HOME tab.
   f. Change the numbers in the two titles to *SECTION 1: GRAPHICS AND MULTIMEDIA SOFTWARE* and *SECTION 2: PERSONAL-USE SOFTWARE*.
4. Remove the split from the window by clicking the VIEW tab and then clicking the Remove Split button in the Window group.
5. Save **C10-E01-CompSoftware.docx**.

# Viewing Documents Side by Side

If you want to compare the contents of two documents, open both, click the VIEW tab, and then click the View Side by Side button in the Window group. Both documents display on the screen arranged side by side, as shown in Figure 10.2.

By default, synchronous scrolling is active. With this feature active, scrolling in one document results in the same scrolling in the other document. This feature is useful when you want to compare text, formatting, or other features between documents. If you want to scroll in one document but not the other, click the Synchronous Scrolling button in the Window group on the VIEW tab to turn off synchronous scrolling.

When you have arranged documents on the screen or are viewing documents side by side, you can drag the document window borders to increase or decrease the size of a document. To change the size of a document window, position the mouse pointer on a window border until the pointer displays as a two-headed arrow, hold down the left mouse button, and then drag the border to the desired location. If you change the size of documents you are viewing side by side, click the Reset Window Position button in the Window group on the VIEW tab to reset the document windows so that both display equally on the divided screen.

**QUICK STEPS**

**View Documents Side by Side**
1. Open two documents.
2. Click VIEW tab.
3. Click View Side by Side button.

View Side by Side

Synchronous Scrolling

Reset Window Position

**Figure 10.2 Viewing Documents Side by Side**

> Click the View Side by Side button to compare the formatting of two different documents.

SECTION 1: PERSONAL-USE SOFTWARE

When browsing computer stores, shoppers are likely to see numerous software applications designed for use in the household. Among the many products available are applications for writing letters, making out wills, designing a new home, landscaping a lawn, preparing and filing tax returns, and managing finances. Software suites are also available for home and personal use although sometimes the suites available for home use do not contain all the features in business versions.

**Personal Finance**

Personal finance software assists users with paying bills, balancing checkbooks, keeping track of income and expenses, maintaining investments records, and other financial activities. The software also enables users to readily view how their money is being spent. Some personal finance software provides online services available on the Internet and Web. These services allow users to go online to learn the status of their investments and insurance coverage. They can also conduct normal banking transactions, including accessing and printing bank statements showing monthly transaction summaries.

**Tax Preparation**

SECTION 1: GRAPHICS AND MULTIMEDIA SOFTWARE

Graphics and multimedia software allows both professional and home users to work with graphics, video, and audio. A variety of application software is focused in this area including painting and drawing software, image-editing software, video and audio editing software, and computer-aided design (CAD) software.

**Painting and Drawing Software**

Painting and drawing programs are available for both professional and home users. The more expensive professional versions typically include more features and greater capabilities than less expensive personal versions. Both painting programs and drawing programs provide an intuitive interface through which users can draw pictures, make sketches, create various shapes and edit images. Programs typically include a variety of templates that simplify painting or drawing procedures.

**Video and Audio Editing Software**

As digital video cameras and other portable technologies have become more common, users desired the ability to create and modify recorded video and audio clips using video and audio editing software. To create digital video or audio files, home users can often use basic video

1. With **C10-E01-CompSoftware.docx** open, open **Software.docx**.
2. Click the VIEW tab and then click the View Side by Side button in the Window group.

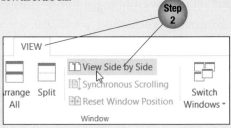

3. Scroll through both documents simultaneously and notice the differences between the two documents. Change the formatting of the titles and headings in **C10-E01-CompSoftware.docx** so the font and font color match the titles and headings in **Software.docx**. *Hint: Use the Format Painter to copy the formats.*

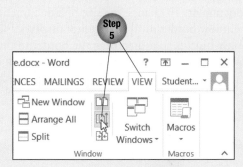

4. With **C10-E01-CompSoftware.docx** active, click the Save button on the Quick Access toolbar.
5. Turn off synchronous scrolling by clicking the VIEW tab and then clicking the Synchronous Scrolling button in the Window group.
6. Scroll through the document and notice that the other document does not scroll.
7. Decrease the size of the **Software.docx** document by completing the following steps:
    a. Make **Software.docx** active and then position the mouse pointer on the right edge of the document until the mouse pointer turns into a double-headed arrow.
    b. Hold down the left mouse button, drag left approximately one inch, and then release the mouse button.

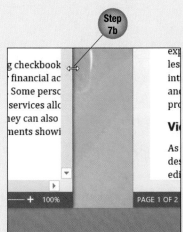

8. Increase the size of the **C10-E01-CompSoftware.docx** document by completing the following steps:
    a. Position the mouse pointer on the left edge of the **C10-E01-CompSoftware.docx** document until the pointer turns into a double-headed arrow.
    b. Hold down the left mouse button and drag to the left until the left edge of the **C10-E01-CompSoftware.docx** document border lines up with the right border of the **Software.docx** document.
9. Reset the windows by clicking the VIEW tab and then clicking the Reset Window Position button in the Window group.
10. Make **Software.docx** the active document and then close it.

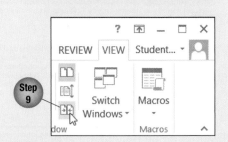

## Opening a New Window

In addition to splitting a document to view two locations of the same document, you can open a new window containing the same document. When you open a new window, the document name in the Title bar displays followed by *:2*. Any change you make to the document in one window is reflected in the document in the other window. If you want to view both documents on the screen, click the Arrange All button to arrange them horizontally or click the View Side by Side button to arrange them vertically.

New Window

---

**Exercise 10.1D**   Opening a New Window                          **Part 4 of 8**

1. With **C10-E01-CompSoftware.docx** open, open a new window by clicking the New Window button in the Window group on the VIEW tab. (Notice that the document name in the Title bar displays followed by *:2*.)
2. Click the VIEW tab and then click the View Side by Side button in the Window group.
3. Click the Synchronous Scrolling button to turn off synchronous scrolling.
4. With **C10-E01-CompSoftware.docx:2** the active document, look at the first paragraph of text and notice the order in which the types of software are listed in the last sentence (*painting and drawing software, image-editing software, video and audio editing software, and computer-aided design (CAD) software*).
5. Click in the **C10-E01-CompSoftware.docx:1** window and then copy and paste the headings and text so the types of software display in the order listed in the paragraph.
6. Click the Save button on the Quick Access toolbar.
7. Close the second version of the document by hovering the mouse pointer over the Word button on the Taskbar and then clicking the Close button in the upper right corner of the **C10-E01-CompSoftware.docx:2** thumbnail (the thumbnail that displays above the Word button on the Taskbar).

---

## Changing Document Zoom

In Chapter 6, you learned to increase and decrease the display of a document on the screen with buttons on the Zoom slider bar. You can also increase and decrease the display of a document with buttons in the Zoom group on the VIEW tab.

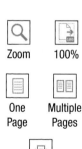

Zoom  100%

One Page  Multiple Pages

Page Width

Click the Zoom button and the Zoom dialog box displays. This is the same dialog box that displays when you click the percentage number next to the Zoom slider bar on the Status bar. Use options at the Zoom dialog box to change the percentage of display. If you change the document display, you can return it to the normal display (100%) by clicking the 100% button in the Zoom group. Click the One Page button in the Zoom group to display the entire page on the screen and click the Multiple Pages button to display multiple pages on the screen. Click the Page Width button and the document expands across the screen.

## Hiding/Showing White Space in Print Layout View

In Print Layout view, a page displays as it will appear when printed, including the white spaces at the top and bottom of the page that represent the page margins. To save space on the screen in Print Layout view, you can remove the white space. To do this, position the mouse pointer at the top edge or bottom edge of a page or between pages until the pointer displays as the Hide White Space icon and then double-click the left mouse button. To redisplay the white space, position the mouse pointer on the thin gray line separating the pages until the pointer turns into the Show White Space icon and then double-click the left mouse button.

The display of white space can also be turned on or off at the Word Options dialog box. To do this, click the FILE tab and then click *Options*. At the Word Options dialog box, click the *Display* option in the left panel. Click the *Show white space between pages in Print Layout view* check box to remove the check mark and then click OK to close the dialog box. Redisplay the white space between pages by displaying the Word Options dialog box with the *Display* option selected, inserting a check mark in the *Show white space between pages in Print Layout view* check box, and then clicking OK.

---

## Exercise 10.1E   Zooming in a Document and Hiding/Showing White Space                     Part 5 of 8

1. With **C10-E01-CompSoftware.docx** open, press Ctrl + Home.
2. Click the VIEW tab.
3. Click the Zoom button in the Zoom group.
4. At the Zoom dialog box, click the *Text width* option.
5. Click OK to close the dialog box.
6. After viewing the document at text width, click the 100% button in the Zoom group.
7. Click the Zoom button, click *200%* in the *Zoom to* section in the Zoom dialog box, and then click OK to close the dialog box.
8. After viewing the document at 200%, click the 100% button in the Zoom group.
9. Click the Multiple Pages button in the Zoom group.
10. Click the Page Width button.
11. Click the 100% button.
12. Hide the white spaces at the top and bottom of the document pages by positioning the mouse pointer at the top edge of a page until the pointer turns into the Hide White Space icon and then double-clicking the left mouse button.
13. Scroll through the document and notice how the pages display.
14. Redisplay the white spaces at the tops and bottoms of pages by positioning the mouse pointer on any thin gray line separating pages until the pointer turns into the Show White Space icon and then double-clicking the left mouse button.
15. Save and then close **C10-E01-CompSoftware.docx**.

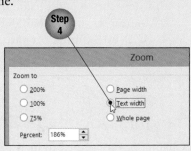

Step 4

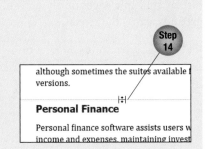

Step 12

Step 14

although sometimes the suites available versions.

**Personal Finance**

Personal finance software assists users w income and expenses, maintaining invest

---

# Managing the Recent List

As you learned in Chapter 1, Word keeps a list of the most recently opened documents in the Recent Documents list at the Open backstage area and the Recent list at the Word opening screen. Generally, the names of the 25 most recently opened documents display at the Open backstage area with *Recent Documents* selected or at the Word opening screen. You can also display a list of the most recently opened documents in the left panel of the backstage area. Do this with options in the *Display* section of the Word Options dialog box with *Advanced* selected in the left panel, as shown in Figure 10.3.

Display the Word Options dialog box by clicking the FILE tab and then clicking *Options*. At the Word Options dialog box, click *Advanced* in the left panel and then scroll down the dialog box to the *Display* section. To display the most recently opened document names in the backstage area, click the *Quickly access this number of Recent Documents* check box to insert a check mark. Use the measurement box that displays to the right of the option to specify the number of documents you want displayed. The maximum number is 25.

Use the *Show this number of Recent Documents* measurement box to increase or decrease the number of document names that display in the Recent Documents list at the Open backstage area or the Recent list at the Word opening screen. Use the *Show this number of unpinned Recent Folders* measurement box to increase or decrease the number of unpinned folder names that display in the *Recent Folders* section of the Open backstage area or Save As backstage area with your SkyDrive or the *Computer* option selected.

If you close a document without saving it, you can recover it with the Recover Unsaved Documents button located below the Recent Documents list at the Open backstage area with *Recent Documents* selected. Click the Recover Unsaved Documents button and the Open dialog box displays with the UnsavedFiles folder active. (This folder contains the documents that Word has automatically saved.) At this dialog box, double-click the desired document name to open the document.

**Figure 10.3 Word Options Dialog Box with *Advanced* Selected**

Insert a check mark in this check box and the four most recently opened document names display below *Options* in the left panel of the backstage area.

Word Options

General

Display

Proofing          Display

Save              Show this number of Recent Documents:          25

Language          ☐ Quickly access this number of Recent Documents:     4

Advanced          Show this number of unpinned Recent Folders:     5

Customize Ribbon  Show measurements in units of:          Inches

Quick Access Toolbar  Style area pane width in Draft and Outline views:   0"

Add-Ins           ☐ Show pixels for HTML features

Trust Center      ☑ Show shortcut keys in ScreenTips
                  ☑ Show horizontal scroll bar
                  ☑ Show vertical scroll bar
                  ☑ Show vertical ruler in Print Layout view
                  ☐ Optimize character positioning for layout rather than readability
                  ☐ Disable hardware graphics acceleration
                  ☑ Update document content while dragging
                  ☑ Use subpixel positioning to smooth fonts on screen

Use this option to increase/decrease the number of recently opened document names that display in the Recent Documents list.

Use this option to increase/decrease the number of recently opened document names that display below *Options* in the left panel of the backstage area.

Clear the contents (except the pinned documents) of the Recent or Recent Documents list by right-clicking a document name in the list and then clicking *Clear unpinned Documents* at the shortcut menu. At the message asking if you are sure you want to remove the items, click the Yes button.

1. Display the names of the six most recently opened documents in the left panel of the backstage area and change the number of unpinned folder names that display in the Recent Folders list by completing the following steps:
   a. Click the FILE tab and then click *Options*.
   b. At the Word Options dialog box, click *Advanced* in the left panel.
   c. Scroll down the dialog box to the *Display* section.
   d. Click the *Quickly access this number of Recent Documents* check box to insert a check mark and then click the up arrow in the measurement box until *6* displays.
   e. Select the current number in the *Show this number of unpinned Recent Folders* measurement box and then type **2**.
   f. Click OK to close the dialog box.

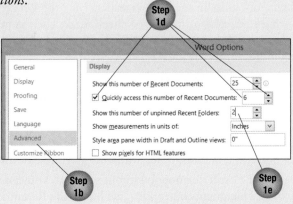

2. Click the FILE tab and then notice the document names that display near the bottom of the left panel. Click ***C10-E01-CompSoftware.docx*** in the left panel to open the document.
3. Click the FILE tab and then click the *Open* option.
4. Click the *Computer* option and then notice the folders below the *Recent Folders* heading.
5. Click the *Recent Documents* option, scroll to the bottom of the Recent Documents list, and then click the Recover Unsaved Documents button.
6. At the Open dialog box that displays, look at any unsaved document names that display in the content pane and then click the Cancel button.
7. Return options to the default settings at the Word Options dialog box by completing the following steps:
   a. Click the FILE tab and then click *Options*.
   b. At the Word Options dialog box, click *Advanced* in the left panel.
   c. Scroll down the dialog box to the *Display* section.
   d. Click the *Quickly access this number of Recent Documents* check box to remove the check mark.
   e. Select the current number in the *Show this number of unpinned Recent Folders* measurement box and then type **5**.
   f. Click OK to close the dialog box.

## Previewing and Printing a Document

Use options at the Print backstage area, shown in Figure 10.4 on the next page, to specify the pages that you want to print and to preview the pages before printing. To display the Print backstage area, click the FILE tab and then click the *Print* option.

**Figure 10.4** **Print Backstage Area**

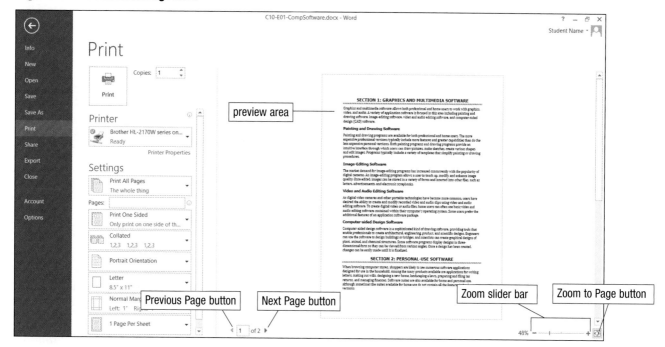

## Previewing Pages in a Document

When you display the Print backstage area, a preview of the page on which the insertion point is positioned displays at the right side (see Figure 10.4). Click the Next Page button (right-pointing triangle), located below and at the left of the page, to view the next page in the document and click the Previous Page button (left-pointing triangle) to view the previous page in the document. Use the Zoom slider bar to increase or decrease the size of the page and click the Zoom to Page button to fit the page in the preview area in the Print backstage area.

**QUICK STEPS**

**Preview a Document**
1. Click FILE tab.
2. Click *Print* option.

---

## Exercise 10.1G  Previewing the Document                    Part 7 of 8

1. With **C10-E01-CompSoftware.docx** open, press Ctrl + Home to move the insertion point to the beginning of the document.
2. Preview the document by clicking the FILE tab and then clicking the *Print* option.
3. At the Print backstage area, click the Next Page button located below and at the left of the preview page. (This displays page 2 in the preview area.)
4. Click twice on the Zoom In button (plus [+] symbol) that displays at the right of the Zoom slider bar. (This increases the size of the preview page.)
5. Click twice on the Zoom Out button (minus [–] symbol) that displays at the left of the Zoom slider bar.

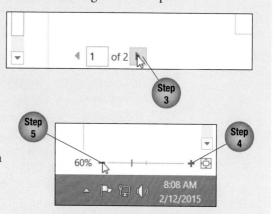

6. Change the zoom at the Zoom dialog box by completing the following steps:
   a. Click the percentage number that displays at the left side of the Zoom slider bar.
   b. At the Zoom dialog box, click the *Many pages* option in the *Zoom to* section.
   c. Click OK to close the dialog box. (Notice that the two pages in the document display as thumbnails in the preview area.)
7. Click the Zoom to Page button that displays at the right side of the Zoom slider bar. (This returns the page to the default size.)
8. Click the Back button to return to the document.

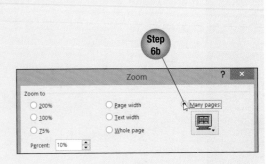

## Printing Pages in a Document

Specify what pages you want to print using options at the Print backstage area. Click the first gallery in the *Settings* category and a drop-down list displays with options for printing all of the pages in the document, selected text, the current page, or a custom range of pages.

If you want to select and then print a portion of the document, choose the *Print Selection* option. With this option, only the text that you have selected in the current document prints. (This option is dimmed unless text is selected in the document.) Click the *Print Current Page* option to print only the page on which the insertion point is located. With the *Custom Print* option, you can identify a specific page, multiple pages, or a range of pages to print. To print specific pages, type the page numbers in the *Pages* text box. Separate the numbers using a comma (,) to indicate *and* and a hyphen (-) to indicate *through*. For example, to print pages 2 and 5, type **2,5** in the *Pages* text box. To print pages 6 through 10, type **6-10**.

With the other galleries available in the *Settings* category of the Print backstage area, you can specify whether to print on one or both sides of the page, change the page orientation (portrait or landscape), identify how you want the pages collated, choose the page size, and set the margins of the document. The last gallery contains options for printing 1, 2, 4, 6, 8, or 16 pages of a multiple-page document on a single sheet of paper. This gallery also contains the *Scale to Paper Size* option. Click this option and then use the side menu to choose the paper size to which to scale the document.

If you want to print more than one copy of a document, specify the number of copies using the *Copies* text box located to the right of the Print button. If you print several copies of a document that has multiple pages, Word collates the pages as they print. For example, if you print two copies of a three-page document, pages 1, 2, and 3 print and then the same pages print a second time. Printing collated pages is helpful for assembly but takes more printing time. To reduce printing time, tell Word *not* to print collated pages. To do this, click the *Collated* gallery in the *Settings* category and then click *Uncollated*.

If you want to send a document directly to the printer without displaying the Print backstage area, consider adding the Quick Print button to the Quick Access toolbar. To do this, click the Customize Quick Access Toolbar button located at the right of the toolbar and then click *Quick Print* at the drop-down gallery. When you click the Quick Print button, all of the pages of the active document print.

1. With **C10-E01-CompSoftware.docx** open, print selected text by completing the following steps:

   a. Select the heading *Painting and Drawing Software* and the paragraph of text that follows it.

   b. Click the FILE tab and then click the *Print* option.

   c. At the Print backstage area, click the first gallery in the *Settings* category and then click *Print Selection* at the drop-down list.

   d. Click the Print button.

2. Change the margins and page orientation and then print only the first page by completing the following steps:

   a. Press Ctrl + Home to move the insertion point to the beginning of the document.

   b. Click the FILE tab and then click the *Print* option.

   c. At the Print backstage area, click the fourth gallery (displays with *Portrait Orientation*) in the *Settings* category and then click *Landscape Orientation* at the drop-down list.

   d. Click the sixth gallery (displays with *Normal Margins*) in the *Settings* category and then click *Narrow* at the drop-down list.

   e. Click the first gallery (displays with *Print All Pages*) in the *Settings* category and then click *Print Current Page* at the drop-down list.

   f. Click the Print button. (The first page of the document prints in landscape orientation with 0.5-inch margins.)

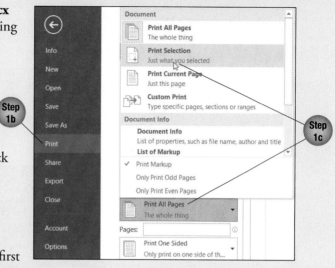

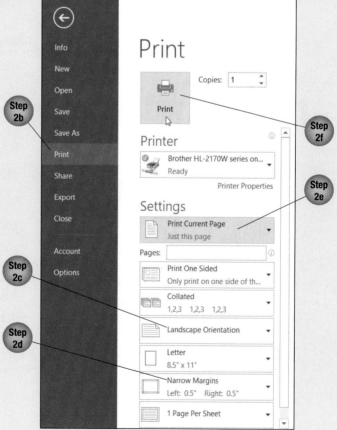

3. Print all of the pages as thumbnails on one sheet of paper by completing the following steps:
   a. Click the FILE tab and then click the *Print* option.
   b. At the Print backstage area, click the bottom gallery (displays with *1 Page Per Sheet*) in the *Settings* category and then click *4 Pages Per Sheet* at the drop-down list.
   c. Click the first gallery (displays with *Print Current Page*) in the *Settings* category and then click *Print All Pages* at the drop-down list.
   d. Click the Print button.
4. Select the entire document, change the line spacing to 1.5, and then deselect the text.
5. Print two copies of specific pages by completing the following steps:
   a. Click the FILE tab and then click the *Print* option.
   b. Click the fourth gallery (displays with *Landscape Orientation*) and then click *Portrait Orientation* at the drop-down list.
   c. Click in the *Pages* text box (located below the first gallery in the *Settings* category) and then type **1,3**.
   d. Click the up-pointing arrow at the right side of the *Copies* text box (located to the right of the Print button) to display *2*.
   e. Click the third gallery (displays with *Collated*) in the *Settings* category and then click *Uncollated* at the drop-down list.
   f. Click the sixth gallery (displays with *Narrow Margins*) in the *Settings* category and then click *Wide* at the drop-down list.
   g. Click the bottom gallery (displays with *4 Pages Per Sheet*) in the *Settings* category and then click *1 Page Per Sheet* at the drop-down list.
   h. Click the bottom gallery, point to *Scale to Paper Size*, and then click the A5 paper size at the side menu. (If the A5 paper size is not available, choose another style.)
   i. Click the Print button. (The first page of the document will print twice and then the third page will print twice.)
6. Save and then close **C10-E01-CompSoftware.docx**.

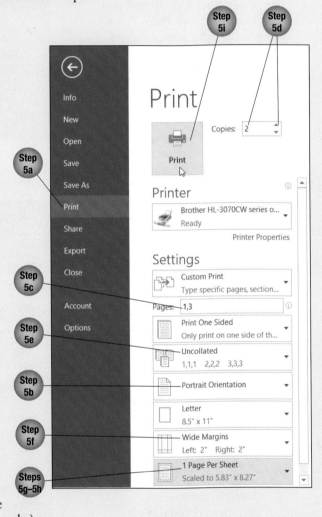

# Creating and Printing Envelopes

Word automates the creation of envelopes with options at the Envelopes and Labels dialog box with the Envelopes tab selected, as shown in Figure 10.5. Display this dialog box by clicking the MAILINGS tab and then clicking the Envelopes button in the Create group. At the dialog box, type the delivery address in the *Delivery address* text box and type the return address in the *Return address* text box. Send the envelope directly to the printer by clicking the Print button or insert the envelope in an open document by clicking the Add to Document button.

**QUICK STEPS**

**Create an Envelope**
1. Click MAILINGS tab.
2. Click Envelopes button.
3. Type delivery address.
4. Click in *Return address* text box.
5. Type return address.
6. Click Add to Document button or Print button.

**Figure 10.5 Envelopes and Labels Dialog Box with Envelopes Tab Selected**

Type the delivery name and address in this text box.

Type the return name and address in this text box.

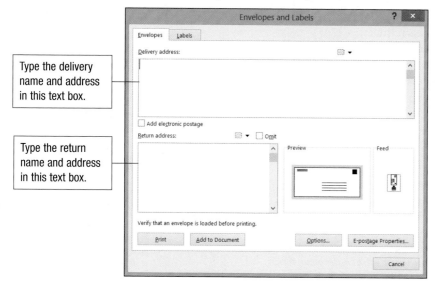

Envelopes

If you enter a return address before printing the envelope, Word displays the question *Do you want to save the new return address as the default return address?* At this question, click Yes if you want the current return address available for future envelopes and click No if you do not want the current return address used as the default. If a default return address displays in the *Return address* section of the dialog box, tell Word to omit the return address when printing the envelope by clicking the *Omit* check box to insert a check mark.

The Envelopes and Labels dialog box contains a *Preview* sample box and *Feed* sample box. The *Preview* sample box shows how the envelope will appear when printed and the *Feed* sample box shows how the envelope should be inserted into the printer.

When addressing envelopes, consider following the general guidelines issued by the United States Postal Service (USPS). For instance, USPS guidelines suggest using all capital letters, with no commas or periods, for return and delivery addresses. USPS guidelines also suggest using abbreviations for street designations (such as *ST* for *Street* and *AVE* for *Avenue*). Figure 10.6 on the next page shows delivery and return addresses that follow the USPS guidelines. For a complete list of address abbreviations, visit www.emcp.net/usps and search for *Official USPS Abbreviations*.

If you want the same return address printed on most or all envelopes, consider inserting the return address in the Word Options dialog box with *Advanced* selected. At the dialog box with *Advanced* selected, scroll down to the end of the list box and then type the desired name and address in the *Mailing address* text box in the *General* section.

1. At a blank document, create an envelope that prints the delivery address and return address shown in Figure 10.6. Begin by clicking the MAILINGS tab.
2. Click the Envelopes button in the Create group.
3. At the Envelopes and Labels dialog box with the Envelopes tab selected, type the delivery address shown in Figure 10.6 (the one containing the name *CRYSTAL BERGMAN*). Press the Enter key to end each line in the name and address.

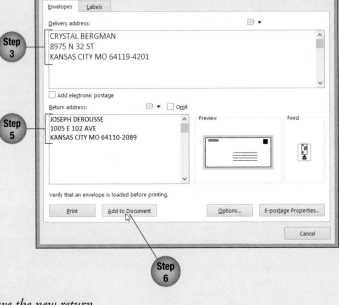

4. Click in the *Return address* text box. (If any text displays in the *Return address* text box, select and then delete it.)
5. Type the return address shown in Figure 10.6 (the one containing the name *JOSEPH DEROUSSE*). Press the Enter key to end each line in the name and address.
6. Click the Add to Document button.
7. At the message *Do you want to save the new return address as the default return address?*, click No.
8. Save the document with the name **C10-E02-Env**.
9. Print and then close **C10-E02-Env.docx**. *Note: Manual feed of the envelope may be required. Please check with your instructor.*

**Figure 10.6 Exercise 10.2**

JOSEPH DEROUSSE
1005 E 102 AVE
KANSAS CITY MO 64110-2089

CRYSTAL BERGMAN
8975 N 32 ST
KANSAS CITY MO 64119-4201

If you open the Envelopes and Labels dialog box in a document that contains a name and address with each line ending with a press of the Enter key (not Shift + Enter), Word automatically inserts the name and address in the *Delivery address* text box of the dialog box. To automatically insert a delivery address, open a document containing a name and address and then display the Envelopes and Labels dialog box. The name and address are inserted in the *Delivery address* text box as they appear in the letter and may not conform to USPS guidelines. The USPS guidelines for addressing envelopes are only suggestions, however, not requirements.

---

**Exercise 10.3A**  **Creating an Envelope in an Existing Document**  **Part 1 of 2**

1. Open **GSHLtr.docx**.
2. Click the MAILINGS tab.
3. Click the Envelopes button in the Create group.
4. At the Envelopes and Labels dialog box with the Envelopes tab selected, make sure the delivery address contained in **GSHLtr.docx** displays properly in the *Delivery address* text box.
5. If any text displays in the *Return address* text box, insert a check mark in the *Omit* check box (located at the right of the *Return address* option). This tells Word not to print the return address on the envelope.
6. Click the Print button. (Manual feed of the envelope into the printer may be necessary.)

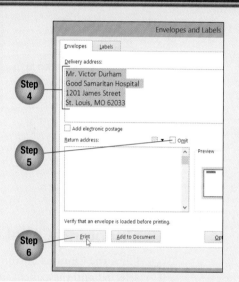

Step 4

Step 5

Step 6

---

# Creating and Printing Labels

Use the labels feature in Word to print text on mailing labels, file labels, disc labels, or other types of labels. This feature includes a variety of predefined formats for labels that can be purchased at an office supply store.

Using the labels feature, you can create a sheet of mailing labels with the same name and address or image or enter a different name and address on each label. To create a sheet of mailing labels with the same name and address using the default settings, click the Labels button in the Create group on the MAILINGS tab. At the Envelopes and Labels dialog box with the Labels tab selected, as shown in Figure 10.7 on the next page, type the desired address in the *Address* text box. Click the New Document button to insert the mailing label in the new document or click the Print button to send the mailing label directly to the printer.

If you open the Envelopes and Labels dialog box with the Labels tab selected in a document that contains a name and address with each line ending with a press of the Enter key (not Shift + Enter), Word automatically inserts the name and address in the dialog box *Address* text box.

**QUICK STEPS**

**Create Labels**
1. Click MAILINGS tab.
2. Click Labels button.
3. Type desired address(es).
4. Click New Document button or Print button.

Labels

**Figure 10.7 Envelopes and Labels Dialog Box with Labels Tab Selected**

Figure 10.7 Envelopes and Labels Dialog Box with Labels Tab Selected

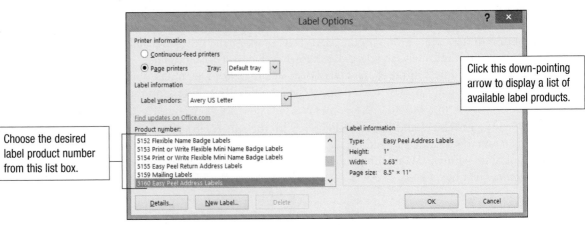

Type the label address in this text box.

Click the Print button to send the label directly to the printer.

Click the New Document button to insert the mailing label in a new document.

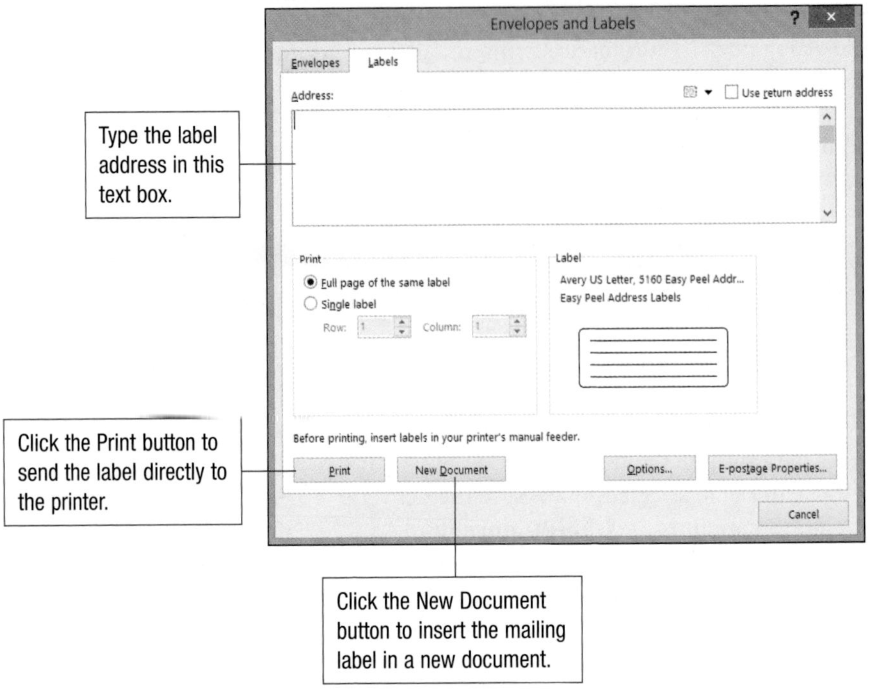

## Changing Label Options

Click the Options button at the Envelopes and Labels dialog box with the Labels tab selected and the Label Options dialog box displays, as shown in Figure 10.8. At the Label Options dialog box, choose the type of printer, desired label product, and product number. This dialog box also displays information about the selected label, such as type, height, width, and paper size. When you select a label, Word automatically determines the label margins. If you want to customize these default settings, click the Details button at the Label Options dialog box.

**Figure 10.8 Label Options Dialog Box**

Click this down-pointing arrow to display a list of available label products.

Choose the desired label product number from this list box.

1. With **GSHLtr.docx** open, create mailing labels with the delivery address. Begin by clicking the MAILINGS tab.
2. Click the Labels button in the Create group.
3. At the Envelopes and Labels dialog box with the Labels tab selected, click the Options button.
4. At the Label Options dialog box, click the down-pointing arrow at the right of the *Label vendors* option and then click *Avery US Letter* at the drop-down list.
5. Scroll down the *Product number* list box and then click *5160 Easy Peel Address Labels*.

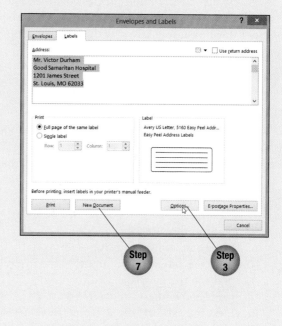

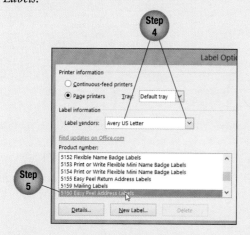

6. Click OK or press the Enter key.
7. At the Envelopes and Labels dialog box, click the New Document button.
8. Save the mailing label document with the name **C10-E03-GSHLtr**.
9. Print and then close **C10-E03-GSHLtr.docx**.
10. Close **GSHLtr.docx**.

To create a sheet of mailing labels with a different name and address in each label, start with a blank document, display the Envelopes and Labels dialog box with the Labels tab selected, and then click the New Document button. The Envelopes and Labels dialog box is removed from the screen and the document displays with label forms. The insertion point is positioned in the first label form. Type the name and address in this label and then press the Tab key to move the insertion point to the next label. Press Shift + Tab to move the insertion point back to the preceding label.

1. Press Ctrl + N to display a blank document and then click the MAILINGS tab.
2. Click the Labels button in the Create group.
3. At the Envelopes and Labels dialog box with the Labels tab selected, click the Options button.
4. At the Label Options dialog box, make sure *Avery US Letter* is selected. If not, click the down-pointing arrow at the right of the *Label vendors* option and then click *Avery US Letter* at the drop-down list.
5. Scroll down the *Product number* list box and then click *5810 Address Labels*.
6. Click OK or press the Enter key.
7. At the Envelopes and Labels dialog box, click the New Document button.
8. At the document, type in the first label the first name and address shown in Figure 10.9 (the name and address for DEBRA FOSTER).
9. Press the Tab key twice to move the insertion point to the next label and then type the second name and address shown in Figure 10.9.
10. Press the Tab key twice to move the insertion point to the next label and then type the third name and address shown in Figure 10.9.
11. Press the Tab key once. (Doing this moves the insertion point to the second row of labels.)
12. Type the fourth name and address shown in Figure 10.9. Continue in this manner until you have typed all of the names and addresses.
13. Save the document and name it **C10-E04-Labels**.
14. Print and then close **C10-E04-Labels.docx**.
15. At the blank document, close the document without saving changes.

**Figure 10.9 Exercise 10.4**

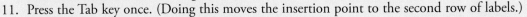

| DEBRA FOSTER | CHARLES MOZONNE | CASSANDRA REID |
|---|---|---|
| 9054 N 23 ST | 12003 203 ST SE | 9045 VISTA AVE |
| BOISE ID 83709 | BOISE ID 83799 | BOISE ID 83719 |
| | | |
| BEN AND JILL NYE | MARK CHAVEZ | KARL KNOWLES |
| 6013 FAIRVIEW AVE | 805 ORCHARD ST | 23102 HARRISON BLVD |
| BOISE ID 83720 | BOISE ID 83720 | BOISE ID 83722 |

## Creating Mailing Labels with an Image

You can create labels that include a graphic image. For example, you may want to provide a company's logo or slogan with its name and address on the mailing labels. Create labels with a graphic image by inserting the image in a blank document, clicking the MAILINGS tab, and then clicking the Labels button. At the Envelopes and Labels dialog box, make sure the desired label vendor and product number are selected and then click the New Document button.

---

**Exercise 10.5**    Creating Mailing Labels with an Image      **Part 1 of 1**

1. At a blank document, insert a graphic image by completing the following steps:
   a. Click the INSERT tab and then click the Pictures button in the Illustrations group.
   b. At the Insert Picture dialog box, make sure the Chapter10 folder on your storage medium is active and then double-click *BGCLabels.png*.
2. With the image selected in the document, click the MAILINGS tab and then click the Labels button.
3. At the Envelopes and Labels dialog box, click the Options button.
4. At the Label Options dialog box, make sure that *Avery US Letter* is selected in the *Label vendors* option box.
5. Scroll up (or down) the *Product number* list box and then click *5160 Easy Peel Address Labels* at the drop-down list.
6. Click OK to close the Label Options dialog box.
7. At the Envelopes and Labels dialog box, click the New Document button.
8. Save the document and name it **C10-E05-BGCLabels**.
9. Print and then close **C10-E05-BGCLabels.docx**.
10. Close the document containing the image without saving changes.

# Chapter Summary

➤ Move among open documents on your screen by clicking the Word button on the Taskbar and then clicking the thumbnail representing the desired document or by clicking the VIEW tab, clicking the Switch Windows button in the Window group, and then clicking the desired document name.

➤ View portions of all open documents by clicking the VIEW tab and then clicking the Arrange All button in the Window group.

➤ Use the Minimize, Maximize, and Restore Down buttons, located in the upper right corner of the window, to reduce or increase the size of the active window.

➤ Divide a window into two panes by clicking the VIEW tab and then clicking the Split button in the Window group. Doing this enables you to view different parts of the same document at one time.

➤ View the contents of two open documents side by side by clicking the VIEW tab and then clicking the View Side by Side button in the Window group.

➤ By default, synchronous scrolling is turned on when you view documents side by side. To scroll through each document individually, turn off the feature by clicking the Synchronous Scrolling button.

➤ If you have changed the size of side-by-side document windows, click the Reset Window Position button to reset the windows and display the documents equally on the divided screen.

➤ Use buttons in the Zoom group on the VIEW tab to increase or decrease the visual display of a document.

➤ In Print Layout view, you can remove the white spaces at the tops and bottoms of pages.

➤ Use options in the *Display* section of the Word Options dialog box with *Advanced* selected in the left panel to display a list of the most recently opened documents in the left panel of the backstage area, specify the number of files you want displayed in the panel, specify the number of recent document names you want displayed in the Recent list at the Open backstage area or the Recent list at the Word opening screen, and specify the number of folders that display in the *Recent Folders* section of the Open or Save As backstage area.

➤ Click the Recover Unsaved Documents button, located below the Recent Documents list at the Open backstage area with *Recent Documents* selected, to display the Open dialog box with the UnsavedFiles folder active. Open an unsaved document by double-clicking the document name in the Content pane.

➤ Preview a document at the Print backstage area. Scroll through the pages in the document with the Next Page and Previous Page buttons that display below the preview page. Use the Zoom slider bar to increase or decrease the display size of the preview page.

➤ Use options at the Print backstage area to change the page orientation, size, and margins; specify how many pages to print on one sheet of paper; specify the number of copies and whether to collate the pages; and specify the printer.

➤ Use options at the Envelopes and Labels dialog box with the Envelope tab selected to create and print an envelope.

➤ If you open the Envelopes and Labels dialog box in a document that contains a name and address with each line ending with a press of the Enter key (not Shift + Enter), that information is automatically inserted in the *Delivery address* text box in the dialog box.

➤ Use the labels feature to print text on mailing labels, file labels, disk labels, and other types of labels.

# Commands *Review*

| FEATURE | RIBBON TAB, GROUP | BUTTON, OPTION | KEYBOARD SHORTCUT |
|---------|-------------------|----------------|-------------------|
| arrange documents | VIEW, Window | | |
| Envelopes and Labels dialog box with Envelopes tab selected | MAILINGS, Create | | |
| Envelopes and Labels dialog box with Labels tab selected | MAILINGS, Create | | |
| maximize document | | | |
| minimize document | | | |
| new window | VIEW, Window | | |
| Print backstage area | FILE | *Print* | Ctrl + P |
| reset window position | VIEW, Window | | |
| restore down | | | |
| split window | VIEW, Window | | |
| synchronous scrolling | VIEW, Window | | |
| view document at 100% | VIEW, Zoom | | |
| view document at page width | VIEW, Zoom | | |
| view documents side by side | VIEW, Window | | |
| view multiple pages | VIEW, Zoom | | |
| view one page | VIEW, Zoom | | |
| Zoom dialog box | VIEW, Zoom | | |

# Key Points *Review*

**Completion:** In the space provided at the right, indicate the correct term, command, or number.

1. To determine which documents are open, click the VIEW tab and then click this button in the Window group. _____

2. Click this button in the Window group on the VIEW tab to arrange all open documents so a portion of each document displays. _____

3. Click this button and the active document fills the editing window. _____

4. Click this button and the active document is reduced to the Word button on the Taskbar. _____

5. To display documents side by side, click this button in the Window group on the VIEW tab. _____

6. If you are viewing documents side by side and decide you want to scroll in one document but not the other, click this button in the Window group on the VIEW tab. _____

7. When viewing documents side by side, click this button in the Window group on the VIEW tab to reset the document windows so they display equally on the divided screen. _____

8. To remove white spaces from the tops and bottoms of pages, double-click this icon. _____

9. Click this button, located below the Recent Documents list at the Open backstage area with *Recent Documents* selected, to display the Open dialog box with the UnsavedFiles folder active. _____

10. Type this in the *Pages* text box in the *Settings* category at the Print backstage area to print pages 3 through 6 of the open document. _____

11. Type this in the *Pages* text box in the *Settings* category at the Print backstage area to print pages 4 and 9 of the open document. _____

12. The Envelopes button is located in the Create group on this tab. _____

13. If you open the Envelopes and Labels dialog box in a document containing a name and address, the name and address are automatically inserted in this text box of the dialog box. _____

# *Chapter* Assessments

## Applying Your Skills

Demonstrate your knowledge of features learned in this chapter by completing the following assessments.

### Assessment 10.1    Arrange Documents

1. Open **BetaTestAgrmnt.docx**, **CompHardware.docx**, and **CompSecurity.docx**.
2. Make **CompHardware.docx** the active document.
3. Make **BetaTestAgrmnt.docx** the active document.
4. Arrange all of the windows.
5. Make **CompSecurity.docx** the active document and then minimize it.
6. Minimize the remaining documents.
7. Restore **BetaTestAgrmnt.docx**.
8. Restore **CompHardware.docx**.
9. Restore **CompSecurity.docx**.

10. Maximize and close **BetaTestAgrmnt.docx** and then maximize and close **CompSecurity.docx**.
11. Maximize **CompHardware.docx** and then save the document and name it
    **C10-A01-CompHardware**.
12. Open **Hardware.docx**.
13. View **C10-A01-CompHardware.docx** and **Hardware.docx** side by side.
14. Scroll through both documents simultaneously. Notice the formatting differences between the two documents. Change the font size and paragraph shading in **C10-A01-CompHardware. docx** so they match the formatting in **Hardware.docx**.
15. Make **Hardware.docx** active and then close it.
16. Save, print, and then close **C10-A01-CompHardware.docx**.

## Assessment 10.2    Create an Envelope

1. At a blank document, create an envelope with the text shown in Figure 10.10.
2. Save the envelope document with the name **C10-A02-Envelope**.
3. Print and then close **C10-A02-Envelope.docx**.

**Figure 10.10  Assessment 10.2**

SHAWN FINNEGAN
3078 SIXTH AVE
SALT LAKE CITY UT 84119




                              DR DAVID TOMOLLA
                              12039 CHAMBER ST
                              SALT LAKE CITY UT 84110

## Assessment 10.3    Create Mailing Labels

1. Create mailing labels with the names and addresses shown in Figure 10.11 on the next page. Use a label option of your choosing. (You may need to check with your instructor before choosing an option.)
2. Save the document with the name **C10-A03-Labels**.
3. Print and then close **C10-A03-Labels.docx**.
4. At the blank document, close the document without saving changes.

**Figure 10.11 Assessment 10.3**

| | | |
|---|---|---|
| LINDA GOULD<br>3210 CRANSTON ST<br>PROVIDENCE RI 02903 | ROBERT ALBRIGHT<br>10228 123 ST NE<br>PROVIDENCE RI 02908 | TRAVIS KANE<br>5532 S BROAD ST<br>PROVIDENCE RI 02905 |
| CHARLES WHITE<br>887 N 42 ST<br>PROVIDENCE RI 02903 | RAY PETROVICH<br>12309 45 AVE N<br>PROVIDENCE RI 02904 | BLAINE ISHAM<br>12110 141 ST SE<br>PROVIDENCE RI 02907 |

## Expanding Your Skills

Explore additional feature options or use Help to learn a new skill in creating these documents.

### Assessment 10.4    Create and Format Labels

1. At a blank document, display the Envelopes and Labels dialog box with the Labels tab selected.
2. Type the following name and address in the *Address* text box:
   Barrington & Gates
   200 Tenth Street, Suite 100
   Austin, TX 73341
3. Click the New Document button.
4. In a previous chapter, you learned how to indent paragraphs of text using the Left Indent marker on the horizontal ruler. You can also use this marker to increase the indent of text within labels. Increase the indent of the labels text by completing the following steps:
   a. Press Ctrl + A to select all of the labels.
   b. Drag the Left Indent marker on the horizontal ruler to the 0.5-inch marker.
   c. Click in any label to deselect the text.
5. With the insertion point positioned in a label, the TABLE TOOLS tabs display on the ribbon. With options on the TABLE TOOLS LAYOUT tab, you can adjust the vertical alignment of text within labels. You decide that the label text will look better if it is centered vertically in each label. To do this, complete the following steps:
   a. Click the TABLE TOOLS LAYOUT tab.
   b. Click the Select button at the left side of the TABLE TOOLS LAYOUT tab and then click *Select Table* at the drop-down list.
   c. With the text in all of the labels selected, click the Align Center Left button located in the Alignment group on the TABLE TOOLS LAYOUT tab.
   d. Click in any label to deselect the text.
6. Save the label document and name it **C10-A04-BGLabels**.
7. Print and then close **C10-A04-BGLabels.docx**.

## Achieving Signature Status

Take your skills to the next level by completing these more challenging assessments.

### Assessment 10.5    Create Custom Labels

1. You can create a sheet of labels with the same information in each label either by typing the information in the *Address* text box at the Envelopes and Labels dialog box or by typing the desired information, selecting it, and then creating the label.

Using the second technique, create the sheet of labels shown in Figure 10.12 with the following specifications:

- At a blank document, type the company name and address (shown in the first label in Figure 10.12).
- Set the text in 14-point Harlow Solid Italic and set the *S* in *Southland* and the *A* in *Aviation* in 20-point size. Change the font color to Blue.
- Select the company name and address and then create the labels by displaying the Envelopes and Labels dialog box with the Labels tab selected and then clicking the New Document button. Use the Avery US Letter label, product number 5160 when creating the labels.
- At the labels document, select the entire document and then click the Center button. (Doing this centers all of the names and addresses in each label.)

2. Save the completed labels document and name it **C10-A05-SALabels**.
3. Print and then close the document.

**Figure 10.12 Assessment 10.5**

## Assessment 10.6  Create Personal Labels

1. At a blank document, type your name and address and then apply formatting to enhance the appearance of the text. (You determine the font, font size, and font color.)
2. Create labels with your name and address. (You determine the label vendor and product number.)
3. Save the label document and name it **C10-A06-PersonalLabels**.
4. Print and then close the document.

# *Performance* Assessments

**UNIT 2**

## Formatting and Managing Documents

## ASSESSING PROFICIENCIES

In this unit, you have learned to format the pages of a document by changing page margins, orientation, and size. You have learned to improve the appearance of a document by inserting a cover page, page color, page border, drop cap, and watermark, as well as other elements such as special symbols and characters, page numbers, headers and footers, and the date and time. You have also learned how to hyphenate words, navigate within a document, insert hyperlinks, and maintain and print documents.

*Note: Before beginning computer assessments, copy to your storage medium the Unit02PA folder from the CD that accompanies this textbook and then make Unit02PA the active folder.*

### Assessment U2.1    Format a Corporate Report

 **Grade It**

1. Open **Terra.docx** and save the document with the name **U2-PA01-Terra**.
2. Move the insertion point to the beginning of the heading *Manufacturing* and then insert the file named **R&D.docx**.
3. Apply the Heading 1 style to the title and the Heading 2 style to the headings in the document.
4. Apply the Basic (Stylish) style set and then center the title *TERRA ENERGY COMPANY REPORT*.
5. Apply the Frame theme and then change the theme colors to Blue II.
6. Insert a continuous section break at the beginning of the first paragraph (the paragraph that begins *Terra Energy Corporation is a*).
7. Format the text below the section break into two columns.
8. Balance the columns on the second page.
9. Create a drop cap with the first letter of the first word *Terra* (which begins the first paragraph of text) and make the drop cap two lines in height.
10. Manually hyphenate the text in the document.
11. Insert page numbering that prints at the bottom center of each page.
12. Insert the Motion cover page and type the appropriate text in the placeholders.
13. Save, print, and then close **U2-PA01-Terra.docx**.

### Assessment U2.2    Create and Format an Announcement

 **Grade It**

**START From Scratch**

1. At a blank document, use the Click and Type feature to create the document shown in Figure U2.1 on the next page.
2. Select the centered text and then change the font to 20-point Cambria and the font color to Orange, Accent 2, Darker 50%.
3. Select the right-aligned text and then change the font to 14-point Cambria and the font color to Orange, Accent 2, Darker 50%.
4. Change the vertical alignment of the text to Center.
5. Insert a page border using the first double-line option in the *Style* list box. Change the width to 2¼ points and the font color to Dark Blue.
6. Save the document with the name **U2-PA02-InvestDisc**.

7. Print **U2-PA02-InvestDisc.docx**.
8. Change the page orientation to landscape.
9. Save, print, and then close **U2-PA02-InvestDisc.docx**.

**Figure U2.1  Assessment U2.2**

**INVESTMENT SERVICES PANEL DISCUSSIONS**

Fiduciary Responsibility in Retirement Plans

Best Practices in Technology

Redefining Investment Advice

Small Business Succession Planning

Sponsored by
Qualité Group®

### Assessment U2.3    Format a Computer Security Report

1. Open **ComputerViruses.docx** and save the document with the name **U2-PA03-ComputerViruses**.
2. Apply the following formatting:
   a.  Apply the Centered style set.
   b.  Apply the Dividend theme.
   c.  Insert the Retrospect footer and type your first and last names at the left side of the footer.
3. Move to the end of the paragraph in the *Types of Viruses* section, press the spacebar, and then type **(Pie Chart)**.
4. If necessary, turn on the display of bookmarks. (Do this at the Word Options dialog box with *Advanced* selected in the left panel.)
5. Move the insertion point to the end of the paragraph in the *Types of Viruses* section (following the *(Pie Chart)* text), press the spacebar, and then insert a bookmark named *Types*.
6. Move the insertion point to the end of the first paragraph in the *Methods of Virus Operation* section and then insert a bookmark named *Effects*.
7. Move the insertion point to the end of the second paragraph in the *Methods of Virus Operation* section and then insert a bookmark named *Infection*.
8. Navigate in the document using the bookmarks.
9. Move the insertion point to the end of the first paragraph in the *HARDWARE AND SOFTWARE SECURITY RISKS* section, press the spacebar once, and then insert a hyperlink to the *Effects* bookmark with the display text *Click to display virus effects*.
10. Select the text *(Pie Chart)* that you inserted at the end of the paragraph in the *Types of Viruses* section and then insert a hyperlink to the Excel file named **Viruses.xlsx,** located in the Unit02PA folder on your storage medium.

11. Hold down the Ctrl key, click the (Pie Chart) hyperlink and then print the Excel worksheet that displays by clicking the FILE tab, clicking the *Print* option, and then clicking the Print button. Close the Excel program.
12. Insert the DRAFT1 watermark in the document.
13. Save, print, and then close **U2-PA03-ComputerViruses.docx**.

## Assessment U2.4  Create a Business Letter Using a Template

1. Search for and then download the Letter (Equity theme) template at the New backstage area. (If more than one Letter (Equity theme) template displays, use the one without the orange circle in the lower left corner of the page.) Type the following information in the specified fields:

> *[Pick the date]:* (Insert today's date)
> *Name:* (Click in the name that displays below the date, select the name, and then type your first and last names.)
> *Sender company name:* **Mobile Bay Products**
> *Sender company address:* **700 Michigan Avenue**
> **Mobile, AL 36606**
> *Recipient name:* **Dr. Erin Sutton**
> *Recipient address:* **5110 Third Avenue**
> **Prichard, AL 36610**
> *Salutation:* **Dear Dr. Sutton:**

2. Select the salutation text and remove the bold formatting.
3. Delete the three paragraphs of text in the body of the letter and then insert **AnnualMtg.docx.** (Press the Delete key once to remove the blank space above the complimentary close.)
4. Type the following information in the specified fields:

> *Closing:* **Sincerely,**
> *Sender title:* **President**

5. Save the document with the name **U2-PA04-AnnualMtg**.
6. Print and then close **U2-PA04-AnnualMtg.docx**.

## Assessment U2.5  Format an Employment Appointments Document

1. Open **EmpAppoints.docx** and save the document with the name **U2-PA05-EmpAppoints**.
2. Change the top, left, and right margins to 1.25 inches.
3. Apply the Heading 1 style to the title *EMPLOYMENT APPOINTMENTS* and the Heading 2 style to the heading *Types of Appointments*.
4. Apply the Minimalist style set.
5. Apply the Slice theme.
6. Insert a page break at the beginning of the text *Reappointment*.
7. Move the insertion point to the end of the document and then insert the current date and time.
8. Insert the Austin header and type **Employee Handbook** for the document title.
9. Insert the Austin footer.
10. Save, print, and then close **U2-PA05-EmpAppoints.docx**.

## Assessment U2.6    Create an Envelope

START From Scratch

1. At a blank document, create an envelope with the text shown in Figure U2.2.
2. Save the envelope document with the name **U2-PA06-Env**.
3. Print and then close **U2-PA06-Env.docx**.

**Figure U2.2  Assessment U2.6**

DR ERIN SUTTON
5110 THIRD AVE
PRICHARD AL 36610

MRS VIOLET KOHLBERG
12032 145TH ST E
MOBILE AL 36607

## Assessment U2.7    Create Mailing Labels

START From Scratch

1. Create mailing labels with the name and address for Dr. Erin Sutton shown in Figure U2.2. Use the label vendor and product of your choosing.
2. Save the document with the name **U2-PA07-Labels**.
3. Print and then close **U2-PA07-Labels.docx**.

## Assessment U2.8    Format a Report

1. Open **VisualAids.docx** and save the document with the name **U2-PA08-VisualAids**.
2. Format the report so it appears as shown in Figure U2.3 on the next page with the following specifications:
   - Change the top margin to 1.5 inches.
   - Set the text in 12-point Cambria and set the title in 16-point Cambria.
   - Set the text in columns as shown in the figure.
   - Apply bullets to the text as shown in the figure and then decrease the indent so the bullets align at the left margin.
   - Apply the Blue II theme colors.
   - Insert the Ion (Dark) header and footer.
   - Apply other character and paragraph formatting so the report displays as shown in the figure.
   - Use the hyphenation feature and manually hyphenate the text in the report. (Figure U2.3 does not show manual hyphenation.)
3. Save, print, and then close **U2-PA08-VisualAids.docx**.

**Figure U2.3  Assessment U2.8**

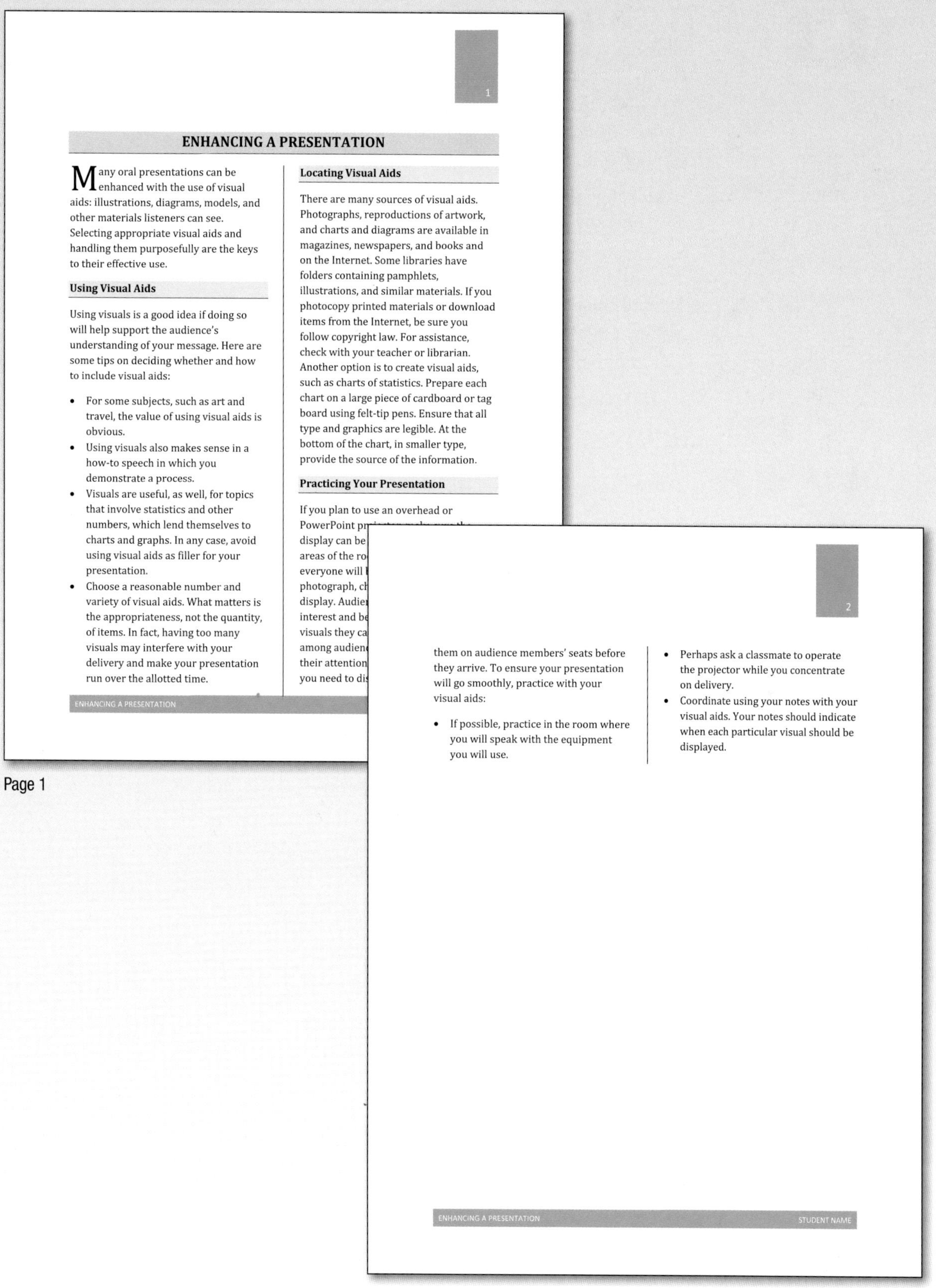

---

**1**

## ENHANCING A PRESENTATION

**M**any oral presentations can be enhanced with the use of visual aids: illustrations, diagrams, models, and other materials listeners can see. Selecting appropriate visual aids and handling them purposefully are the keys to their effective use.

### Using Visual Aids

Using visuals is a good idea if doing so will help support the audience's understanding of your message. Here are some tips on deciding whether and how to include visual aids:

- For some subjects, such as art and travel, the value of using visual aids is obvious.
- Using visuals also makes sense in a how-to speech in which you demonstrate a process.
- Visuals are useful, as well, for topics that involve statistics and other numbers, which lend themselves to charts and graphs. In any case, avoid using visual aids as filler for your presentation.
- Choose a reasonable number and variety of visual aids. What matters is the appropriateness, not the quantity, of items. In fact, having too many visuals may interfere with your delivery and make your presentation run over the allotted time.

### Locating Visual Aids

There are many sources of visual aids. Photographs, reproductions of artwork, and charts and diagrams are available in magazines, newspapers, and books and on the Internet. Some libraries have folders containing pamphlets, illustrations, and similar materials. If you photocopy printed materials or download items from the Internet, be sure you follow copyright law. For assistance, check with your teacher or librarian. Another option is to create visual aids, such as charts of statistics. Prepare each chart on a large piece of cardboard or tag board using felt-tip pens. Ensure that all type and graphics are legible. At the bottom of the chart, in smaller type, provide the source of the information.

### Practicing Your Presentation

If you plan to use an overhead or PowerPoint projector, make sure the display can be [seen in all] areas of the ro[om so that] everyone will [see each] photograph, ch[art, or other] display. Audie[nce members'] interest and be[havior depend on] visuals they ca[n see. To direct] among audien[ce members and] their attention [to the visuals] you need to dis[play...]

---

**2**

them on audience members' seats before they arrive. To ensure your presentation will go smoothly, practice with your visual aids:

- If possible, practice in the room where you will speak with the equipment you will use.

- Perhaps ask a classmate to operate the projector while you concentrate on delivery.
- Coordinate using your notes with your visual aids. Your notes should indicate when each particular visual should be displayed.

Page 1

Page 2

### Assessment U2.9    Prepare a Gift Certificate

1. Create the gift certificates shown in Figure U2.4 on the next page with the following specifications:
    - At the New backstage area, search for and then download the gift certificate from Office.com. Use the search words *summer santa design* to find the certificate.
    - Insert the appropriate information in the certificates, as shown in the figure.
    - Change the font size to 28 points and the color to Dark Blue for the company name *World Wide Travel* in all three certificates.
    - Delete the text *Cut along dotted line* that displays above each certificate. (To do this, click in the text, click the dashed border surrounding the text, and then press the Delete key.)
2. Save the gift certificate document and name it **U2-PA09-GiftCert**.
3. Print and then close **U2-PA09-GiftCert.docx**.

**Figure U2.4  Assessment U2.9**

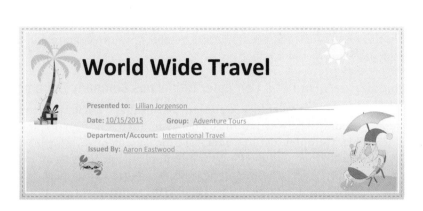

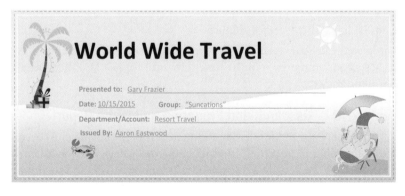

# CREATING ORIGINAL DOCUMENTS

The activities in Assessments 10, 11, and 12 give you the opportunity to practice your writing skills while demonstrating your mastery of some of the important Word features presented in this unit. When composing the documents, use correct grammar, precise word choices, and clear sentence structure.

### Assessment U2.10    Format a Computer Guidelines Company Document

**Situation:** You work in the technology support department at Mobile Bay Products and your supervisor has asked you to format a document that outlines computer use guidelines. Open **CompGuidelines.docx**, save the document with the name **U2-PA10-CompGuidelines**, and then format it by applying or inserting at least the following elements: a style set; a heading style; a header, footer, and/or page numbers; and a cover page. Save, print, and then close **U2-PA10-CompGuidelines.docx**. Use one of the Word letter templates and write a letter to your instructor describing how you formatted **U2-PA10-CompGuidelines.docx**, including the reasons you chose specific formats. Save the completed letter with the name **U2-PA10-Ltr**. Print and then close **U2-PA10-Ltr.docx**.

### Assessment U2.11    Create a Calendar Using a Calendar Template

**Situation:** You are responsible for monitoring employee vacation days and decide to use a Word calendar template to record the information. Download a calendar that allows you to enter information for the current year. In the appropriate calendar months (use months for the current year), enter the following data on employee vacation days:

- Mariah Brown, first two weeks of June
- Jaden Holland, second week of July
- Maddie O'Hara, last two weeks of July
- Evan Noland, first week of August

Save the completed calendar document with the name **U2-PA11-Calendar**. Print only those pages containing the months June, July, and August and then close **U2-PA11-Calendar.docx**.

### Assessment U2.12    Research and Prepare a Netiquette Report

**Situation:** Your supervisor at Mobile Bay Products wants to provide employees with a document that describes netiquette ("Internet etiquette" rules). She has asked you to research the topic and then create a document that will be distributed to employees. Use the Internet (or other resources available to you) and search for information on "rules of netiquette." Locate at least two sources that provide information on netiquette. Using this information, create a document that describes netiquette rules and apply formatting to enhance the appearance of the document. Be sure to use your own words when describing netiquette rules; cutting and pasting text from Internet sources is plagiarism. At the end of the document, type the web addresses for the sites you used as references. Save the document with the name **U2-PA12-Netiquette**. Print and then close **U2-PA12-Netiquette.docx**.

# UNIT 3

## Enhancing Documents

# Chapter 11

# Inserting Images

## Performance Objectives

Upon successful completion of Chapter 11, you will be able to:

- Insert, format, size, and move pictures and clip art images
- Customize pictures and clip art images
- Create and format SmartArt graphics and organizational charts

**Tutorial 11.1**
Inserting and Formatting a
Picture Image
**Tutorial 11.2**
Inserting, Sizing, and Moving
Images
**Tutorial 11.3**
Customizing and Formatting an
Image
**Tutorial 11.4**
Applying Advanced Formatting to
Images
**Tutorial 11.5**
Creating SmartArt
**Tutorial 11.6**
Arranging and Moving SmartArt
**Tutorial 11.7**
Creating an Organizational Chart
with SmartArt

Inserting images into your documents can further increase their visual appeal and attract readers' attention. In this chapter, you will learn to insert images such as pictures and clip art and display data in more interesting ways by creating SmartArt graphics. The SmartArt feature provides a number of predesigned graphics, such as diagrams and organizational charts.

*Note: Before beginning computer exercises for this chapter, copy to your storage medium the Chapter11 folder from the CD that accompanies this textbook and then make Chapter11 the active folder.*

In this chapter, students will produce the following documents:

Exercise 11.1. C11-E01-EditedPictures.docx
Exercise 11.2. C11-E02-SummerRates.docx
Exercise 11.3. C11-E03-Presentation.docx
Exercise 11.4. C11-E04-TTSMaui.docx
Exercise 11.5. C11-E05-WritingSteps.docx
Exercise 11.6. C11-E06-Graphics.docx
Exercise 11.7. C11-E07-OrgChart.docx

Model answers for these exercises are shown on the following pages.

**Exercise 11.1**

C11-E01-EditedPictures.docx

**Exercise 11.2**

C11-E02-SummerRates.docx

## DELIVERING A HOW-TO PRESENTATION

Knowing how to give a *how-to*, or *process*, presentation is one of the most useful things you can learn about speaking. Giving clear directions is important not only in the classroom but also in the world of work. Many people's jobs involve giving this type of presentation, for example, to train new employees or to demonstrate a product to potential buyers. When you create a set of directions for others to follow, think through the process carefully. Make certain the steps you provide are complete, accurate, and in the proper sequence.

### Choose a Suitable Topic

The topic you choose for your how-to presentation should be one you are familiar with or can learn about easily. Also keep in mind your listeners' interests. Try to select a process that will appeal to the audience. Processes you might explain include the following:

- Getting a driver's license
- Cooking a favorite food
- Working as a volunteer
- Finding an internship
- Applying for financial aid

### Develop Well-Organized Directions

Begin by arranging the major steps of the process in logical order. Then give the details needed to complete each step. Be sure to specify the materials needed and carefully explain the tasks involved. Follow these guidelines:

- Use transitional words such as *first*, *second*, and *next* to help readers keep track of the steps of the process. Using transitional words also will help you keep your place in the presentation.
- Before you move from one step to the next step, be sure your listeners have understood what you have described. If they look confused, review what you have said or ask if they need clarification.
- Use visual aids in your presentation so you can demonstrate the process while you describe it. Doing so will make your presentation more interesting to listeners and also may help calm your nerves. To ensure audience members will be able to see what you are doing, use large photographs and diagrams or an oversized model.

### Practice Your Delivery

Assemble all the materials, including your visual aids. Plan how to arrange and use them in the location where you will be speaking. Also consider how to arrange the setting so yo[...] presentation. Spend time practicing your presentation in front of one or tw[...] ask them to provide feedback on both your content and delivery. In particu[...] the steps you present in explaining your process.

**Exercise 11.3**

C11-E03-Presentation.docx

**Exercise 11.4**

C11-E04-TTSMaui.docx

**Terra Travel Services**

#### MAUI SITES

- Haleakala
- Hana
- Makena Beach
- Iao Valley
- Kapalua Beach
- Molokini
- Lahaina
- Maui Ocean Center
- Pools of Oheo
- Kaanapali Beach

#### MAUI ACTIVITIES

Whether you are vacationing in Kihei or relaxing in Lahaina, Maui offers a wide range of activities. Choose one of the activities listed below or create your own Maui adventure.

- Parasailing fun: Enjoy an hour of parasailing over the beautiful and exotic coastline of West Maui.
- Jet skiing experience: Sign up for an afternoon of jet skiing and feel the thrill of zooming across the spectacular waters of West Maui.
- Zip line adventure: Enjoy an unforgettable four-hour zip line adventure in the Maui rainforest.
- Helicopter tour: Soar over the magnificent West Maui Mountains, get a spectacular view of the island rainforest, and experience the beauty of the Maui coastline in a 45-minute helicopter flight.
- Surfing lesson: Sign up for an individual one-hour surfing lesson and learn how to "surf Maui."

1050 Marietta Street ❖ Atlanta, GA 30315 ❖ 1-888-555-2288 ❖ www.emcp.net/terratravel

## Writing Steps

A document that communicates clearly is the result of good writing and good rewriting; you can usually improve anything you have written. The writing process includes the following steps:

### Define Purpose

Knowing your purpose for writing is the foundation for any written project. Before you begin writing your memo, letter, or other document, ask yourself the following questions:

- What am I trying to accomplish?
- What is my purpose for writing?
- To request information or products?
- To respond to a question or request?
- To persuade someone?
- To direct someone?

### Identify Reader

As you define your purpose, you will need to develop a good picture of the person who will be reading your document. Ask yourself:

- Who is my reader?
- What do I know about my reader that will help determine the best approach?
- Is the audience one person or a group?
- Is my reader a coworker, a subordinate, a superior, or a customer?
- How is the reader likely to feel about my message?

### Select and Organize Information

Once you have defined your purpose and identified your reader, decide what information you will include. Ask yourself questions such as:

- What does my reader want or need to know?
- What information must I include?
- What information will help my reader respond positively?
- What information should I not include?

### Write First Draft

A first effort is rarely a final draft, even for the best writers; therefore, write something to get started. Let your purpose, reader, and organizational plan guide you, but do not let them stifle you. Keep going even if you occasionally lose your focus. Once you have a full draft, you can add or delete information, reorganize, and edit sentences.

### Edit and Proofread

Editing and proofreading are essential to good writing. Planning and drafting allow you to get your information on paper; editing and proofreading help you communicate your ideas as clearly as possible to the reader.

**Exercise 11.5** C11-E05-WritingSteps.docx

**Exercise 11.6** C11-E06-Graphics.docx      Page 1

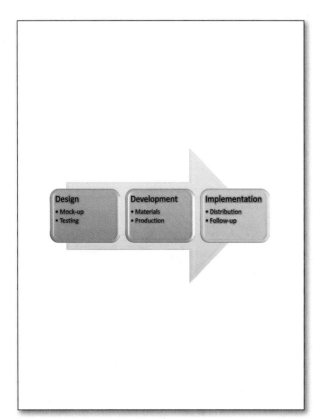

**Exercise 11.6** C11-E06-Graphics.docx      Page 2

**Exercise 11.7** C11-E07-OrgChart.docx

# Inserting an Image

Use buttons in the Illustrations group on the INSERT tab to insert a picture or clip art image into a document. Click the Pictures button to display the Insert Picture dialog box, where you can specify the desired picture file you want to insert, or click the Online Pictures button and search online for images such as pictures and clip art.

## Customizing and Formatting an Image

When you insert an image in a document, the image is selected and the PICTURE TOOLS FORMAT tab, shown in Figure 11.1, becomes active. Use buttons on this tab to format the image.

With buttons in the Adjust group, you can remove unwanted portions of the image, correct the brightness and contrast, change the image color, apply artistic effects, compress the size of the image file, change to a different image, and reset the image back to the original formatting. Use buttons in the Picture Styles group to apply a predesigned style to the image, change the image border, and apply other effects to the image. Use the Remove Background button to remove unwanted portions of the picture. With options in the Arrange group, you can position the image on the page, specify how text will wrap around the image, align the image with other elements in the document, and rotate the image. Use the Crop button in the Size group to remove any unnecessary parts of the image, and specify the image size with the *Shape Height* and *Shape Width* measurement boxes.

In addition to using options on the PICTURE TOOLS FORMAT tab, you can format an image using options at the shortcut menu. Display this menu by right-clicking the image. Use options at the shortcut menu to change the picture, insert a caption, choose text wrapping, size and position the image, and display the Format Picture task pane.

**QUICK STEPS**

**Insert a Picture**
1. Click INSERT tab.
2. Click Pictures button.
3. Navigate to desired folder.
4. Double-click desired picture in Insert Picture dialog box.

Pictures

**Figure 11.1 PICTURE TOOLS FORMAT Tab**

---

## Exercise 11.1  Inserting a Picture                                  Part 1 of 1

1. Press Ctrl + N to display a blank document.
2. Click the INSERT tab and then click the Pictures button in the Illustrations group.
3. At the Insert Picture dialog box, navigate to your Chapter11 folder and then double-click *Olympics.jpg*.

4. Click the Artistic Effects button in the Adjust group and then click the *Cutout* option at the drop-down gallery (first column, fifth row).
5. Click the Corrections button in the Adjust group and then click the *Brightness: +20% Contrast: +20%* option at the drop-down gallery (fourth column, fourth row in the *Brightness/Contrast* section).

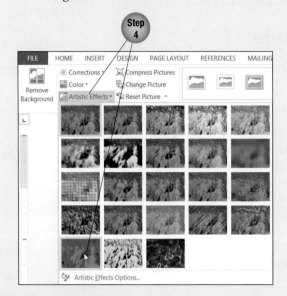

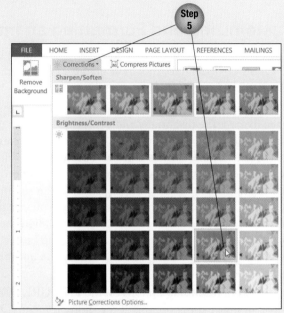

6. Reset the picture by clicking the Reset Picture button in the Adjust group. After looking at the picture, you decide to reapply the formatting. To do this, click the Undo button on the Quick Access toolbar.
7. Click the Corrections button in the Adjust group and then click the *Sharpen: 50%* option at the drop-down gallery (last option in the *Sharpen/Soften* section).
8. Click the More button at the right of the picture style thumbnails in the Picture Styles group and then click the *Perspective Shadow, White* option at the drop-down gallery (fourth column, third row).

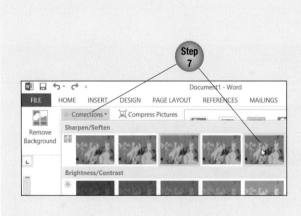

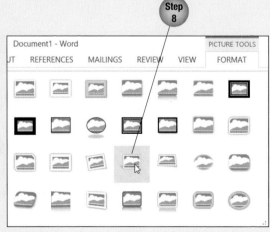

9. Click the Picture Border button arrow in the Picture Styles group and then click the *Blue, Accent 1, Lighter 40%* option (fifth column, fourth row in the *Theme Colors* section).

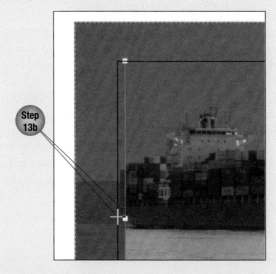

10. Press Ctrl + End and then press the Enter key twice.
11. Click the INSERT tab and then click the Pictures button.
12. At the Insert Picture dialog box, make sure your Chapter11 folder is active and then double-click *Ship.jpg*.
13. With the ship picture selected, remove some of the background by completing the following steps:
    a. Click the Remove Background button in the Adjust group on the PICTURE TOOLS FORMAT tab.
    b. Using the left middle sizing handle, drag the border to the left to include the back of the ship (see image below).

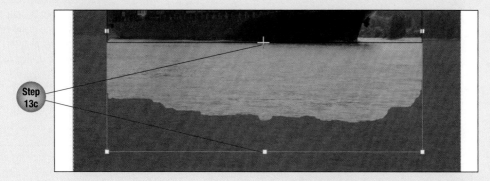

    c. Using the bottom middle sizing handle, drag the border up to the bottom edge of the ship (see image below).

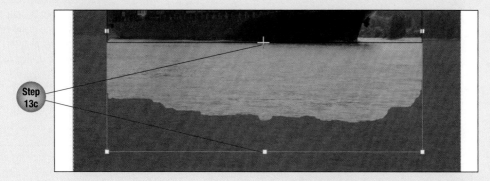

    d. Using the right middle sizing handle, drag the border to the left so the border is near the front of the ship.

e. Click the Keep Changes button in the Close group on the BACKGROUND REMOVAL tab.

14. Click the Corrections button in the Adjust group and then click the *Brightness: +40% Contrast: +20%* option at the drop-down gallery (last column, fourth row in the *Brightness/Contrast* section).

15. Click the Corrections button in the Adjust group and then click the *Sharpen: 50%* option at the drop-down gallery (last option in the *Sharpen/Soften* section).

16. Click outside the picture to deselect it.

17. Save the document and name it **C11-E01-EditedPictures**.

18. Print and then close **C11-E01-EditedPictures.docx**.

## Changing an Image Layout

When you insert a picture or image into a document, the default text wrapping style is *Top and Bottom*. With this wrapping style, text wraps above and below the image. Change the wrapping style with the Position button and Wrap Text button on the PICTURE TOOLS FORMAT tab and with options from the Layout Options button side menu, as shown in Figure 11.2. The Layout Options button displays just outside the upper right corner of a selected image. Click this button to display a side menu with wrapping options and click the <u>See more</u> hyperlink that displays at the bottom of the side menu to display the Layout dialog box, which contains additional options for positioning the image on the page. Close the Layout Options button side menu by clicking the button or clicking the Close button located in the upper right corner of the side menu.

Figure 11.2 **Layout Options Button Side Menu**

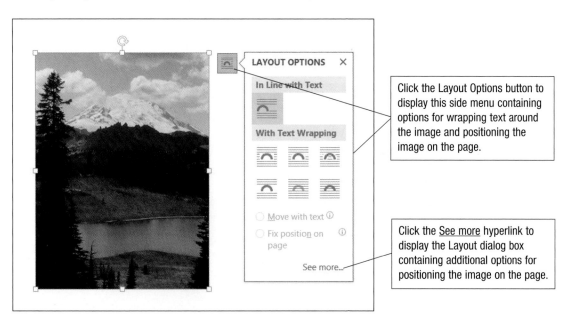

Click the Layout Options button to display this side menu containing options for wrapping text around the image and positioning the image on the page.

Click the <u>See more</u> hyperlink to display the Layout dialog box containing additional options for positioning the image on the page.

## Sizing an Image

Change the size of an image with the *Shape Height* and *Shape Width* measurement boxes in the Size group on the PICTURE TOOLS FORMAT tab or with the sizing handles that display around a selected image, as shown in Figure 11.3. To increase or decrease the image size with a sizing handle, position the mouse pointer on a handle until the pointer turns into a double-headed arrow and then hold down the left mouse button. Drag the sizing handle in to decrease or out to increase the size of the image and then release the mouse button. Use the middle sizing handles at the left and right sides of the image to make the image wider or thinner. Use the middle sizing handles at the top and bottom of the image to make the image taller or shorter. Use the sizing handles at the corners of the image to change both the width and height at the same time.

**Figure 11.3 Selected Image**

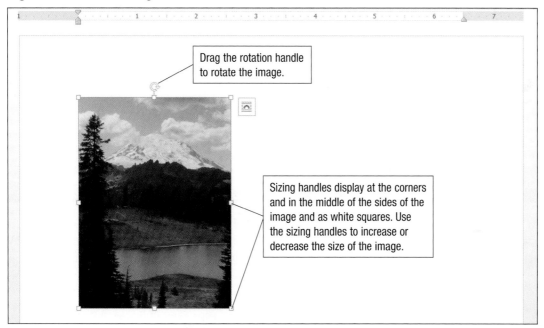

Drag the rotation handle to rotate the image.

Sizing handles display at the corners and in the middle of the sides of the image and as white squares. Use the sizing handles to increase or decrease the size of the image.

## Moving an Image

Move an image to a specific location on the page with options from the Position button drop-down gallery. The Position button is located in the Arrange group on the PICTURE TOOLS FORMAT tab. When you choose an option at the Position button drop-down gallery, the image is moved to the specified location on the page and the text wraps around the image.

Position

You can also move an image by dragging it to the desired location. Before dragging an image, however, you must first choose how the text will wrap around it by clicking the Wrap Text button in the Arrange group and then clicking the desired wrapping style at the drop-down list. After choosing a wrapping style, move the image by positioning the mouse pointer on the image until the arrow pointer displays with a four-headed arrow attached. Hold down the left mouse button, drag the image to the desired position, and then release the mouse button. A third way to move a selected image is by pressing an arrow key on the keyboard.

Wrap Text

As you move an image to the top, left, right, or bottom margin or to the center of the document, green alignment guides display. Use these alignment guides to help you position the image on the page. You can also turn on gridlines to help you position an image precisely. Do this by clicking the Align button in the Arrange group and then clicking *View Gridlines*.

To rotate an image, use the rotation handle (see Figure 11.3 on the previous page) or the Rotate Objects button in the Arrange group. To use the rotation handle, position the mouse pointer on the round rotation handle (circular arrow) that displays above the image until the pointer displays with a black circular arrow attached. Hold down the left mouse button, drag in the desired direction, and then release the mouse button.

**Figure 11.4 Exercise 11.2**

BLUE MOUNTAIN SPA AND RESORT

Special Summer Rates

Complimentary Breakfast Buffet

June 1 through August 31

## Exercise 11.2   Inserting and Customizing a Picture                    Part 1 of 1

1. At a blank document, press the Enter key two times and then type the text and center it, as shown in Figure 11.4.
2. Select the text and then change the font to 18-point Franklin Gothic Heavy and the text color to Dark Blue.
3. Press Ctrl + Home to move the insertion point to the beginning of the document.
4. Insert a picture by completing the following steps:
   a. Click the INSERT tab.
   b. Click the Pictures button in the Illustrations group.
   c. At the Insert Picture dialog box, navigate to your Chapter11 folder.
   d. Double-click *Mountain.jpg* in the list box.
5. Save the document and name it **C11-E02-SummerRates**.
6. Close **C11-E02-SummerRates.docx**.
7. Display the Open dialog box, right-click the **C11-E02-SummerRates.docx** document, and then click *Properties* at the shortcut menu.
8. At the Properties dialog box with the General tab selected, notice the size information that displays after *Size* and *Size on disk* and then close the Properties dialog box.
9. Open **C11-E02-SummerRates.docx**.

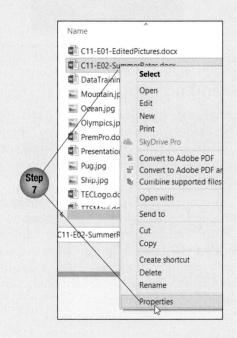

10. Compress the picture by completing the following steps:
    a. Click the picture to select it. (Make sure sizing handles display around the image.)
    b. Click the PICTURE TOOLS FORMAT tab.
    c. Click the Compress Pictures button in the Adjust group.

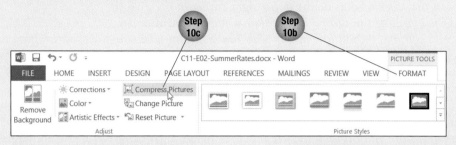

    d. At the Compress Pictures dialog box, make sure the *Apply only to this picture* check box and *Delete cropped areas of pictures* check box both contain check marks.
    e. Click the *E-mail (96 ppi): minimize document size for sharing* option in the *Target output* section.
    f. Click OK to close the dialog box.
11. Click outside the picture to deselect it.
12. Save and then close **C11-E02-SummerRates.docx**.
13. Display the Open dialog box, right-click the **C11-E02-SummerRates.docx** document, and then click *Properties* at the shortcut menu.
14. At the Properties dialog box with the General tab selected, notice the size information that displays after *Size* and *Size on disk*. (The numbers are less than the original numbers.)
15. Close the Properties dialog box.
16. At the Open dialog box, double-click **C11-E02-SummerRates.docx**.
17. Click the picture to select it and then crop the picture by completing the following steps:
    a. Click the PICTURE TOOLS FORMAT tab and then click the Crop button in the Size group.
    b. Position the mouse pointer on the bottom middle crop handle (which displays as a short black line) until the pointer turns into the crop tool (which displays as a small black T).
    c. Hold down the left mouse button, drag up to just below the mountain (as shown at the right), and then release the mouse button.
    d. Click the Crop button in the Size group to turn off the feature.

18. Increase the size of the picture by selecting the current measurement in the *Shape Width* measurement box, typing **6**, and then pressing the Enter key.

19. Move the picture behind the text by clicking the Layout Options button that displays outside the upper right corner of the picture and then clicking the *Behind Text* option at the side menu (second column, second row in the *With Text Wrapping* section). Close the side menu by clicking the Close button located in the upper right corner of the side menu.

20. Position the mouse pointer on the border of the selected picture until the pointer turns into a four-headed arrow and then drag the picture to the right so it is positioned as shown below. Use the green alignment guide to position the image aligned at the top margin and between the left and right margins. (If the green alignment guides do not display, click the Align button in the Arrange group on the PICTURE TOOLS FORMAT tab, and then click *Use Alignment Guides* at the drop-down list.)

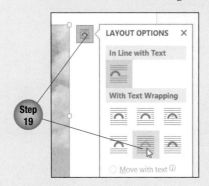

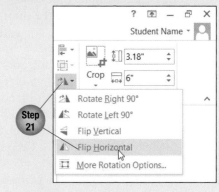

21. Rotate the image by clicking the Rotate Objects button in the Arrange group and then clicking *Flip Horizontal* at the drop-down list.

22. Click the Corrections button in the Adjust group and then click the *Brightness: 0% (Normal) Contrast: +40%* option at the drop-down gallery (third column, bottom row in the *Brightness/Contrast* section).

23. Click the Color button in the Adjust group and then click the *Temperature: 4700 K* option (first option in the *Color Tone* section).

24. Click the More button at the right of the picture style thumbnails in the Picture Styles group and then click the *Drop Shadow Rectangle* option at the drop-down gallery (fourth option in top row).

25. Save, print, and then close **C11-E02-SummerRates.docx**.

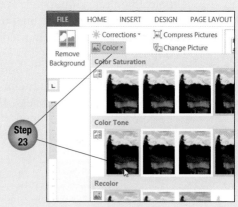

## Inserting an Image from Office.com

Microsoft Office provides a gallery of media images you can insert into a document, including both clip art and photographs. To insert an image from the Office.com website into a Word document, click the INSERT tab and then click the Online Pictures button in the Illustrations group. This displays the Insert Pictures window, as shown in Figure 11.5.

At the Insert Pictures window, click in the search text box to the right of *Office.com Clip Art*, type the search term or topic, and then press Enter. Images that match your search term or topic display in the window. To insert an image, click the desired image and then click the Insert button or double-click the image. This downloads the image from the Office.com website to your document.

When you insert an image in the document, the image is selected and the PICTURE TOOLS FORMAT tab is active. Use buttons on this tab to customize an image, just as you learned to customize a picture image.

**QUICK STEPS**

**Insert a Clip Art Image**
1. Click INSERT tab.
2. Click Online Pictures button.
3. Type search word or topic.
4. Press Enter.
5. Double-click desired image.

Online Pictures

**Figure 11.5  Insert Pictures Window**

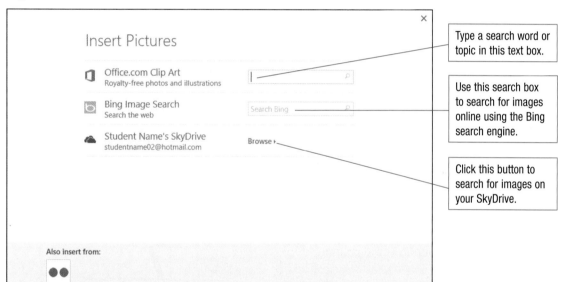

---

### Exercise 11.3  Inserting a Clip Art Image                    Part 1 of 1

1. Open **Presentation.docx** and save the document with the name **C11-E03-Presentation**.
2. Insert a clip art image by completing the following steps:
   a. Click the INSERT tab.
   b. Click the Online Pictures button in the Illustrations group.
   c. At the Insert Pictures window, click in the Office.com Clip Art text box.

d. Type **communications female presentation** and then press Enter.

e. Double-click the clip art image in the list box, as shown below.

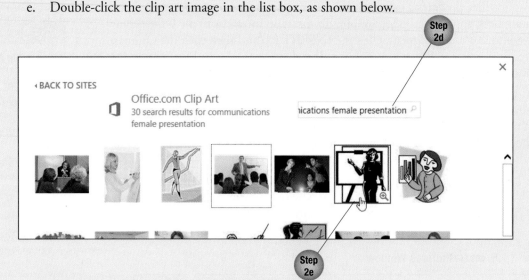

3. Decrease the size of the clip art by clicking in the *Shape Height* measurement box, typing **1.8**, and then pressing the Enter key.

4. Change the position of the image by clicking the Position button in the Arrange group and then clicking *Position in Top Right with Square Text Wrapping* (last column, first row in the *With Text Wrapping* section).

5. Rotate the image by clicking the Rotate Objects button in the Arrange group and then clicking *Flip Horizontal* at the drop-down list.

6. Change the color of the image by clicking the Color button and then clicking the *Turquoise, Accent color 2 Light* option (third column, third row).

7. Click the Picture Effects button in the Picture Styles group, point to *Shadow*, and then click the *Offset Diagonal Top Right* option (first column, third row in the *Outer* section).

8. Click outside the clip art image to deselect it.

9. Save, print, and then close **C11-E03-Presentation.docx**.

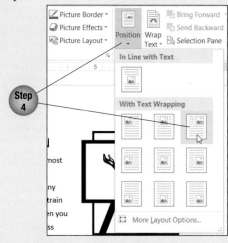

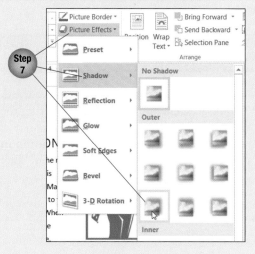

# Customizing Images

Word provides a number of methods for formatting and customizing pictures and clip art images. Format pictures and clip art images with buttons on the PICTURE TOOLS FORMAT tab and further customize images with options at the Layout dialog box and the Format Picture task pane.

## Customizing Layout

Customize the layout of images with options at the Layout dialog box. Display the Layout dialog box by clicking the Size group dialog box launcher on the PICTURE TOOLS FORMAT tab. The Layout dialog box contains three tabs. Click the Position tab and the dialog box displays, as shown in Figure 11.6.

**Figure 11.6 Layout Dialog Box with Position Tab Selected**

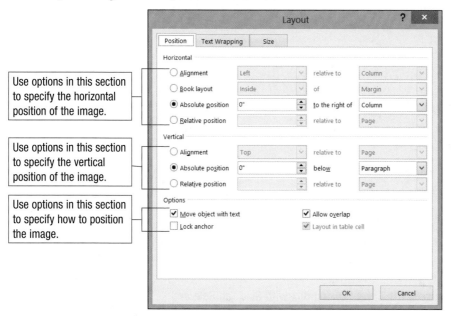

Use options in this section to specify the horizontal position of the image.

Use options in this section to specify the vertical position of the image.

Use options in this section to specify how to position the image.

Use options at the Layout dialog box with the Position tab selected to specify horizontal and vertical layout options. In the *Horizontal* section, choose the *Alignment* option to specify how to position the image horizontally left-, center-, or right-aligned relative to the margin, page, column, or character. Choose the *Book layout* option to align the image with the inside or outside margin on the page. Use the *Absolute position* option to align the image horizontally with the specified amount of space between the left edge of the image and left edge of the page, column, left margin, or character.

In the *Vertical* section of the dialog box, use the *Alignment* option to align the image at the top, bottom, center, inside, or outside relative to the page, margin, or line. In the *Options* section, you can attach (anchor) the image to a paragraph so that the image and paragraph move together. Choose the *Move object with text* option if you want the image to move up or down on the page with the paragraph to which it is anchored. Keep the image anchored in the same place on the page by choosing the *Lock anchor* option. Choose the *Allow overlap* option if you want images with the same wrapping style to overlap.

Use options at the Layout dialog box with the Text Wrapping tab selected, as shown in Figure 11.7, to specify the wrapping style for the image. You can also specify which sides you want the text to wrap around and the amount of space you want between the text and top, bottom, left, and right edges of the image.

**Figure 11.7  Layout Dialog Box with Text Wrapping Tab Selected**

Choose options in this dialog box to specify text wrapping around the image and the distance from the image to text.

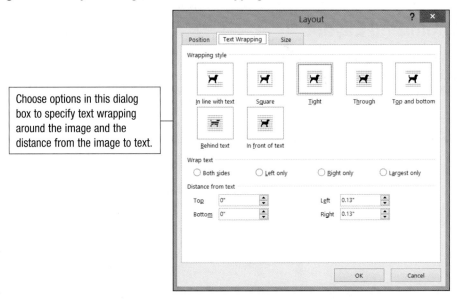

Click the Size tab at the Layout dialog box and the dialog box displays, as shown in Figure 11.8. The dialog box contains options for specifying the height and width measurements of the image relative to the margin, page, top margin, bottom margin, inside margin, or outside margin. Use the *Rotation* option to rotate the image by degrees and use options in the *Scale* section to change the percentage of the height and width scale. Reset the image size by clicking the Reset button located in the lower right corner of the dialog box.

**Figure 11.8  Layout Dialog Box with Size Tab Selected**

Use options in this dialog box to specify the image height, width, rotation, and scale and to reset the size of the image.

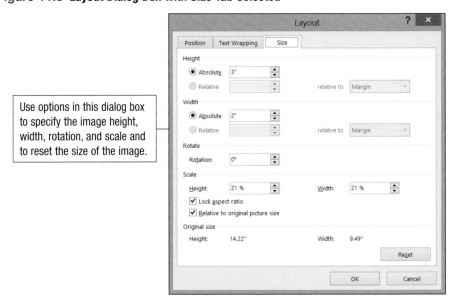

1. Open **TTSMaui.docx** and save the document with the name **C11-E04-TTSMaui**.
2. Insert a clip art image by completing the following steps:
   a. Click the INSERT tab and then click the Online Pictures button in the Illustrations group.
   b. At the Insert Pictures window, click in the *Office.com Clip Art* text box, type **banners, Hawaii**, and then press the Enter key.
   c. Double-click the clip art image in the list box, as shown below.

3. Click the Wrap Text button in the Arrange group on the PICTURE TOOLS FORMAT tab and then click *In Front of Text* at the drop-down list.
4. Change the size of the image and position the image precisely on the page by completing the following steps:

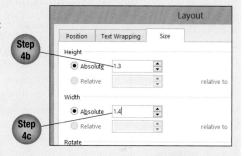

   a. Click the Size group dialog box launcher. (This displays the Layout dialog box with the Size tab selected.)
   b. Select the current measurement in the *Absolute* measurement box in the *Height* section and then type **1.3**.
   c. Select the current measurement in the *Absolute* measurement box in the *Width* section and then type **1.4**.
   d. Click the Position tab.
   e. Make sure the *Absolute position* option is selected in the *Horizontal* section.
   f. Select the current measurement in the box to the right of the *Absolute position* option and then type **6.2**.
   g. Click the down-pointing arrow at the right of the *to the right of* option box and then click *Page* at the drop-down list.
   h. Click the *Absolute position* option in the *Vertical* section.

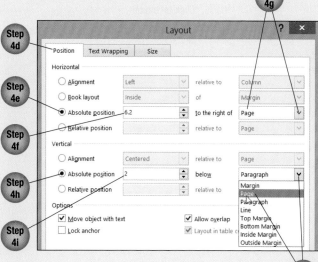

   i. Select the current measurement in the box to the right of the *Absolute position* option and then type **2**.
   j. Click the down-pointing arrow at the right of the *below* option box and then click *Page* at the drop-down list.
   k. Click OK to close the Layout dialog box.

5. Click the *Drop Shadow Rectangle* style thumbnail in the Picture Styles group (fourth thumbnail from left).
6. Click the Color button in the Adjust group and then click the *Blue, Accent color 1 Light* option (second column, third row).
7. Click outside the clip art image to deselect it.
8. Save **C11-E04-TSSMaui.docx**.

## Applying Formatting at the Format Picture Task Pane

Options for formatting an image are available at the Format Picture task pane, as shown in Figure 11.9. Display this task pane box by clicking the Picture Styles group task pane launcher on the PICTURE TOOLS FORMAT tab. The options in the task pane vary depending on the icon selected. You may need to display (expand) the formatting options within the icons. For example, click *SHADOW* in the task pane with the Effects icon selected to display options for applying shadow effects to an image.

Many of the options available at the Format Picture task pane are also available on the PICTURE TOOLS FORMAT tab. The task pane is a central location for formatting options and also includes some additional advanced formatting options.

**Figure 11.9 Format Picture Task Pane**

Click an icon to display the options available for formatting an image.

Format Picture

▷ SHADOW
▷ REFLECTION
▷ GLOW
▷ SOFT EDGES
▷ 3-D FORMAT
▷ 3-D ROTATION
▷ ARTISTIC EFFECTS

Click an option to expand the list of available formatting options.

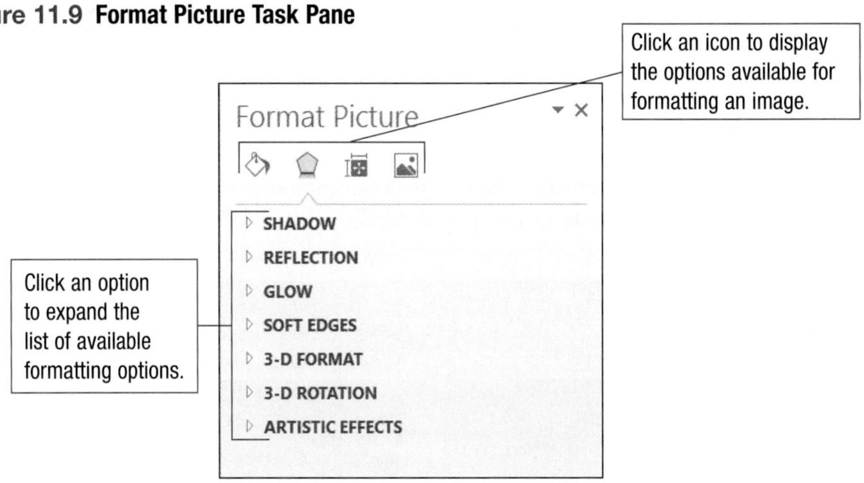

1. With **C11-E04-TTSMaui.docx** open, press Ctrl + End to move the insertion point to the end of the document and then insert a photograph by completing the following steps:
   a. Click the INSERT tab and then click the Online Pictures button in the Illustrations group.
   b. Type **surfer riding wave** in the *Office.com Clip Art* text box and then press the Enter key.
   c. Double-click the image in the list box, as shown below.

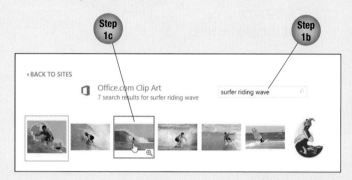

2. With the surfing photograph selected, click the Picture Effects button in the Picture Styles group, point to *Bevel*, and then click the first option in the *Bevel* section (*Circle*).
3. Click the Artistic Effects button in the Adjust group and then click the *Cutout* option (first column, bottom row).
4. After looking at the formatting, remove the formatting by clicking the Reset Picture button in the Adjust group.
5. Select the current measurement in the *Shape Height* measurement box, type **1.4**, and then press Enter.

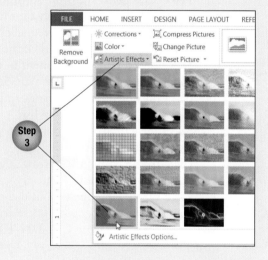

6. Format the photograph by completing the following steps:
   a. Click the Picture Styles group task pane launcher.
   b. At the Format Picture task pane, click *REFLECTION* to expand the reflection options in the task pane.
   c. Click the Presets button and then click the *Tight Reflection, touching* option (first option in the *Reflection Variations* section).
   d. Click *ARTISTIC EFFECTS* in the task pane to expand the artistic effect options.
   e. Click the Artistic Effect button and then click the *Paint Brush* option (third column, second row).
   f. Close the task pane by clicking the Close button located in the upper right corner of the task pane.

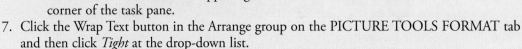

7. Click the Wrap Text button in the Arrange group on the PICTURE TOOLS FORMAT tab and then click *Tight* at the drop-down list.
8. Position the photograph precisely on the page by completing the following steps:
   a. With the photograph selected, click the Size group dialog box launcher.
   b. At the Layout dialog box, click the Position tab.
   c. Select the current measurement in the *Absolute position* measurement box in the *Horizontal* section and then type **5.3**.
   d. Click the down-pointing arrow to the right of the *to the right of* option box and then click *Page* at the drop-down list.
   e. Select the current measurement in the *Absolute position* measurement box in the *Vertical* section and then type **6.6**.
   f. Click the down-pointing arrow at the right of the *below* option box and then click *Page* at the drop-down list.
   g. Click OK to close the Layout dialog box.
9. Click outside the photograph to deselect it.
10. Save, print, and then close **C11-E04-TTSMaui.docx**.

## Ungrouping Images

If you want to edit the individual components of a clip art image, you must first ungroup the image. To do this, click the clip art image to make it active, click the Group Objects button in the Arrange group on the PICTURE TOOLS FORMAT tab, and then click *Ungroup* at the drop-down list. A message will display telling you that the image is an imported picture and not a group and asking if you want to convert the image to a Microsoft Office drawing object. At this message, click the Yes button. With the image ungrouped, click the specific component that you want to format and the DRAWING TOOLS FORMAT tab becomes actives. Use options and buttons on the tab to format individual components of the image.

1. Open **WritingSteps.docx** and then save the document with the name **C11-E05-WritingSteps**.

2. Insert a clip art image by completing the following steps:

   a. Click the INSERT tab and then click the Online Pictures button in the Illustrations group.
   b. At the Insert Pictures window, click in the *Office.com Clip Art* text box, type **academics, offices, pens, writing**, and then press Enter.
   c. Double-click the clip art image in the list box, as shown at the right.

3. Ungroup the clip art image by completing the following steps:

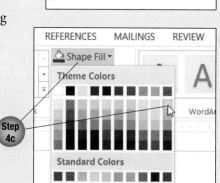

   a. Click the Group Objects button in the Arrange group on the PICTURE TOOLS FORMAT tab and then click *Ungroup* at the drop-down list.
   b. At the message telling you the image is an imported picture and not a group and asking if you want to convert it to a Microsoft Office drawing object, click the Yes button.

4. Format specific components of the image by completing the following steps:
   a. Click the blue color inside the image.
   b. Click the DRAWING TOOLS FORMAT tab to make it active.
   c. Click the Shape Fill button arrow in the Shape Styles group and then click the *Blue-Gray, Accent 6, Lighter 80%* option (last column, second row in the *Theme Colors* section).
   d. Click the curved black line.
   e. Click the Shape Fill button arrow in the Shape Styles group and then click the *Red* color (second option in the *Standard Colors* section).

5. Position the image and change its size by completing the following steps:
   a. Click on the border of the image. (This selects the entire image, not just a component of the image.)
   b. Click the Position button in the Arrange group and then click the *Position in Bottom Right with Square Text Wrapping* option (last option in the *With Text Wrapping* section).
   c. Click in the *Shape Height* measurement box, type **1.2**, and then press the Enter key.

6. Save, print, and then close **C11-E05-WritingSteps.docx**.

# Creating SmartArt

Use the SmartArt feature in Word to insert graphics such as diagrams and organizational charts into a document. A variety of predesigned graphics is available at the Choose a SmartArt Graphic dialog box, as shown in Figure 11.10. At this dialog box, *All* is selected in the left panel by default and all of the predesigned SmartArt graphics display in the middle panel.

**Figure 11.10 Choose a SmartArt Graphic Dialog Box**

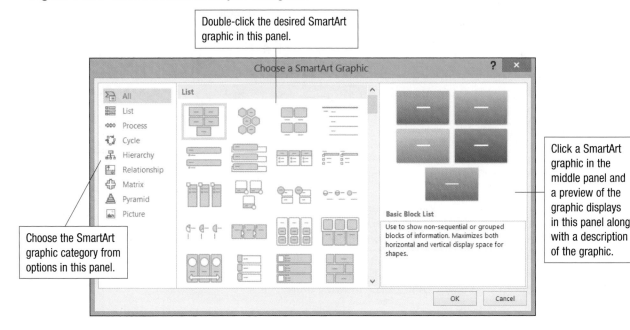

Double-click the desired SmartArt graphic in this panel.

Choose the SmartArt graphic category from options in this panel.

Click a SmartArt graphic in the middle panel and a preview of the graphic displays in this panel along with a description of the graphic.

## Inserting and Formatting a SmartArt Graphic

**Insert a SmartArt Graphic**
1. Click INSERT tab.
2. Click SmartArt button.
3. Double-click desired graphic.

SmartArt

Predesigned graphics display in the middle panel of the Choose a SmartArt Graphic dialog box. Use the scroll bar at the right of the middle panel to scroll down the list of graphic choices. Click a graphic in the middle panel and the name and a preview of the graphic display in the right panel along with a description of the graphic type. SmartArt includes graphics for presenting lists of data; showing data processes, cycles, and relationships; and presenting data in matrixes and pyramids. Double-click a graphic in the middle panel of the dialog box and the graphic is inserted in the document.

When the graphic is inserted in the document, a text pane may display at the left of the graphic. You can insert text in the graphic by typing in the text pane or typing directly in the graphic. Apply design formatting to a graphic with options on the SMARTART TOOLS DESIGN tab, as shown in Figure 11.11. This tab is active when the graphic is inserted in the document. With options and buttons on this tab, you can add objects, change the graphic layout, apply a style to the graphic, and reset the graphic back to the original formatting.

**Figure 11.11 SMARTART TOOLS DESIGN Tab**

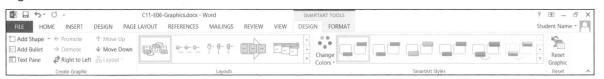

1. At a blank document, insert the graphic shown in Figure 11.12 on the next page by completing the following steps:

   a. Click the INSERT tab.

   b. Click the SmartArt button in the Illustrations group.

   c. At the Choose a SmartArt Graphic dialog box, click *Process* in the left panel and then double-click the *Alternating Flow* graphic (see image at right).

   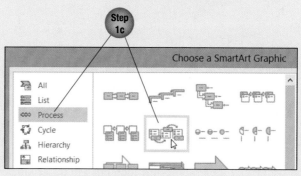

   d. If a *Type your text here* text pane does not display at the left side of the graphic, click the Text Pane button in the Create Graphic group to display the pane.

   e. With the insertion point positioned after the top bullet in the *Type your text here* text pane, type **Design**.

   f. Click *[Text]* that displays below *Design* and then type **Mock-up**.

   g. Continue clicking occurrences of *[Text]* and typing text so the text pane displays as shown at the right.

   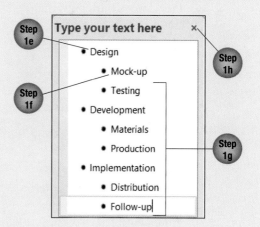

   h. Close the text pane by clicking the Close button (marked with an X) that displays in the upper right corner of the pane. (You can also click the Text Pane button in the Create Graphic group.)

   i. Click inside the graphic border but outside any shape. (This deselects the shape but keeps the graphic selected.)

2. Change the graphic colors by clicking the Change Colors button in the SmartArt Styles group on the SMARTART TOOLS DESIGN tab and then clicking the *Colorful - Accent Colors* option (first option in the *Colorful* section).

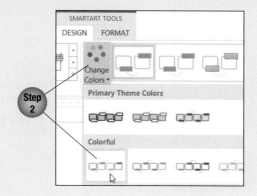

3. Apply a style by clicking the More button that displays at the right of the thumbnails in the SmartArt Styles group and then clicking the *Inset* option (second column, first row in the *3-D* section).

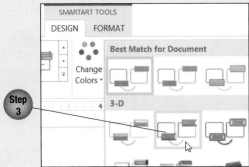

4. Copy the graphic and then change the layout by completing the following steps:
   a. Click the HOME tab.
   b. Click the Copy button in the Clipboard group.
   c. Press Ctrl + End, press the Enter key once, and then press Ctrl + Enter to insert a page break.
   d. Click the Paste button in the Clipboard group.
   e. Click the bottom graphic in the document.
   f. Click the SMARTART TOOLS DESIGN tab.
   g. Click the More button that displays at the right of the thumbnails in the Layouts group and then click the *Continuous Block Process* layout.
   h. Click outside the graphic to deselect it.
5. Save the document and name it **C11-E06-Graphics**.

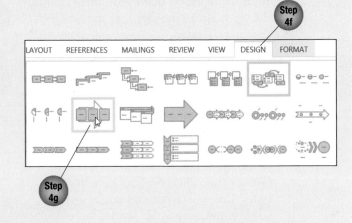

Figure 11.12 Exercise 11.6A

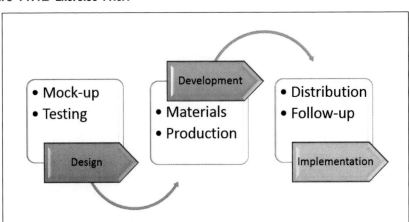

Apply formatting to a graphic with options on the SMARTART TOOLS FORMAT tab, as shown in Figure 11.13. Use options and buttons on this tab to change the sizes and shapes of objects in the graphic; apply shape styles and WordArt styles; change the shape fill, outline, and effects; and arrange and size the graphic.

**Figure 11.13 SMARTART TOOLS FORMAT Tab**

## Arranging and Moving a SmartArt Graphic

Position a SmartArt graphic by clicking the Arrange button on the SMARTART TOOLS FORMAT tab, clicking the Position button, and then clicking the desired position option at the drop-down gallery. Along with positioning the SmartArt graphic, the options at the Position button drop-down gallery apply the Square text wrapping. You can also apply text wrapping by clicking the Arrange button, clicking the Wrap Text button, and then clicking the desired wrapping style at the drop-down gallery or by using options from the Layout Options button that displays outside the upper right corner of the selected SmartArt graphic.

Move a SmartArt graphic by positioning the arrow pointer on the graphic border until the pointer displays with a four-headed arrow attached, holding down the left mouse button, and then dragging the graphic to the desired location. Nudge the SmartArt graphic or a shape or selected shapes in the graphic using the up, down, left, or right arrow keys on the keyboard.

## Exercise 11.6B  Formatting SmartArt Graphics                    Part 2 of 2

1. With **C11-E06-Graphics.docx** open, format shapes by completing the following steps:
   a. Click the SmartArt graphic on the first page to select it. (A border surrounds the graphic.)
   b. Click the SMARTART TOOLS FORMAT tab.
   c. In the SmartArt graphic, click the rectangle shape containing the word *Design*.
   d. Hold down the Shift key and then click the shape containing the word *Development*.
   e. With the Shift key still down, click the shape containing the word *Implementation*. (All three shapes should now be selected.)
   f. Click the Change Shape button in the Shapes group.
   g. Click the *Pentagon* shape (seventh column, second row in the *Block Arrows* section).
   h. With the shapes still selected, click the Larger button in the Shapes group.

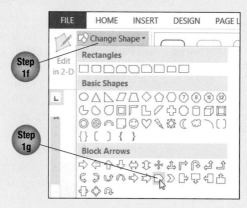

i. With the shapes still selected, click the Shape Outline button arrow in the Shape Styles group and then click the *Dark Blue* color (ninth option in the *Standard Colors* section).

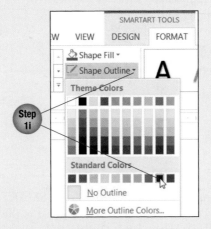

j. Click the Text Fill button arrow in the WordArt Styles group and then click *Black, Text 1* at the drop-down list (second column, first row in the *Theme Colors* section).
k. Click inside the graphic border but outside any shape. (This deselects the shapes but keeps the graphic selected.)

2. Change the size of the graphic by completing the following steps:

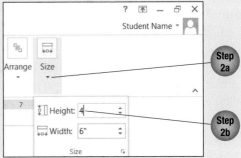

   a. Click the Size button located at the right side of the tab.
   b. Select the current measurement in the *Shape Height* measurement box, type 4, and then press the Enter key.

3. Position the graphic by completing the following steps:

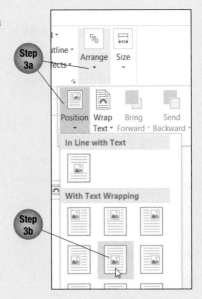

   a. Click the Arrange button on the SMARTART TOOLS FORMAT tab and then click the Position button at the drop-down list.
   b. Click the *Position in Middle Center with Square Text Wrapping* option (second column, second row in the *With Text Wrapping* section).
   c. Click outside the graphic to deselect it.

4. Format the bottom SmartArt graphic by completing the following steps:
   a. Press Ctrl + End to move to the end of the document and then click in the bottom SmartArt graphic to select it.
   b. Hold down the Shift key and then click each of the three rectangle shapes.
   c. Click the More button at the right of the style thumbnails in the WordArt Styles group.

d.  Click the *Fill - Black, Text 1, Shadow* option (first column, first row).
e.  Click the Text Outline button arrow in the WordArt Styles group and then click the *Dark Blue* color (ninth color in the *Standard Colors* section).
f.  Click the Text Effects button in the WordArt Styles group, point to *Glow* at the drop-down list, and then click the *Blue, 8 pt glow, Accent color 1* option (first column, second row in the *Glow Variations* section).

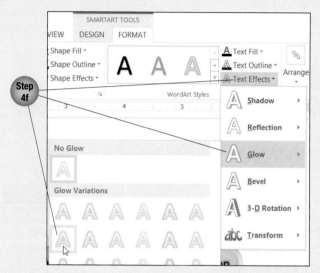

g.  Click inside the SmartArt graphic border but outside any shape.
5.  Arrange the SmartArt graphic by clicking the Arrange button, clicking the Position button, and then clicking the *Position in Middle Center with Square Text Wrapping* option (second column, second row in the *With Text Wrapping* section).
6.  Save, print, and then close **C11-E06-Graphics.docx**.

## Creating an Organizational Chart with SmartArt

If you want to represent hierarchical data visually, consider creating an organizational chart using a SmartArt option. To display SmartArt options for organizational charts, click the INSERT tab and then click the SmartArt button in the Illustrations group. At the Choose a SmartArt Graphic dialog box, click *Hierarchy* in the left panel.

Organizational chart options display in the middle panel of the dialog box. Double-click the desired organizational chart and the chart is inserted into the document. Type text in a chart by selecting the shape and then typing text in the shape, or type text in the *Type your text here* window that displays at the left of the graphic. Format a SmartArt organizational chart with options and buttons on the SMARTART TOOLS DESIGN tab, similar to the one shown in Figure 11.11 on page 358; the SMARTART TOOLS FORMAT tab, similar to the one shown in Figure 11.13 on page 361; and the Layout Options button.

**Insert an Organizational Chart**
1. Click INSERT tab.
2. Click SmartArt button.
3. Click *Hierarchy*.
4. Double-click desired organizational chart.

1. At a blank document, create the organizational chart shown in Figure 11.14. Begin by clicking the INSERT tab.
2. Click the SmartArt button in the Illustrations group.
3. At the Choose a SmartArt Graphic dialog box, click *Hierarchy* in the left panel of the dialog box and then double-click the *Organization Chart* option (first option in middle panel).

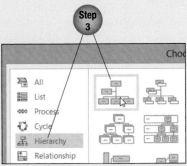

4. If a *Type your text here* pane displays at the left side of the organizational chart, close the pane by clicking the Text Pane button in the Create Graphic group.
5. Delete one of the boxes in the organizational chart by clicking the border of the box in the lower right corner to select it and then pressing the Delete key. (Make sure that the selection border that surrounds the box is a solid line and not a dashed line. If a dashed line displays, click the box border again. This should change it to a solid line.)
6. With the bottom right box selected, click the Add Shape button arrow and then click the *Add Shape Below* option.

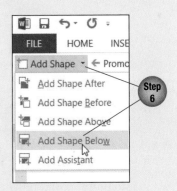

7. Click *[Text]* in the top box, type **Susan Garner**, press Shift + Enter, and then type **President**. Click in each of the remaining boxes and type the text as shown in Figure 11.14 on the next page. (Press Shift + Enter after typing each name.)
8. Click the More button located at the right of the style thumbnails in the SmartArt Styles group and then click the *Inset* style (second column, first row in the *3-D* section).
9. Click the Change Colors button in the SmartArt Styles group and then click the *Colorful Range - Accent Colors 4 to 5* option (fourth option in the *Colorful* section).

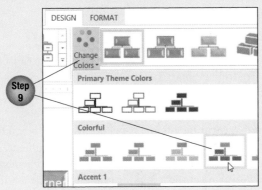

10. Click the SMARTART TOOLS FORMAT tab.
11. Click the text pane control (displays with a left-pointing arrow) that displays at the left side of the graphic border. (This displays the *Type your text here* window.)
12. Using the mouse, select all of the text that displays in the *Type your text here* window.
13. Click the Change Shape button in the Shapes group and then click the *Round Same Side Corner Rectangle* option (eighth option in the *Rectangles* section).
14. Click the Shape Outline button in the Shape Styles group and then click the *Dark Blue* color (ninth option in the *Standard Colors* section).
15. Close the *Type your text here* window by clicking the Close button (marked with an *X*) located in the upper right corner of the window.
16. Click inside the organizational chart border but outside any shape.
17. Click the Size button, click in the *Shape Height* measurement box, and then type **4**.
18. Click in the *Shape Width* measurement box, type **6.5**, and then press the Enter key.
19. Click outside the organizational chart to deselect it.
20. Save the document with the name **C11-E07-OrgChart**.
21. Print and then close the **C11-E07-OrgChart.docx**.

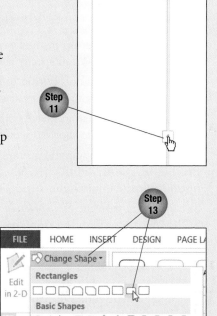

**Figure 11.14 Exercise 11.7**

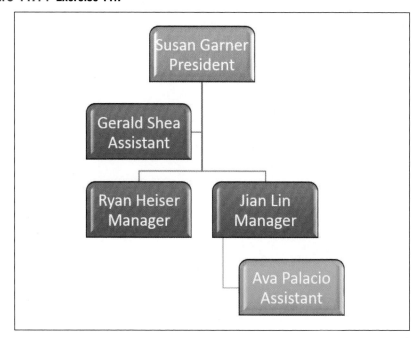

# Chapter Summary

- ➤ Click the Pictures button in the Illustrations group on the INSERT tab to display the Insert Picture dialog box, where you can specify the desired picture file to insert in the document.

- ➤ Click the Online Pictures button in the Illustrations group on the INSERT tab to display the Online Pictures window, where you can search for and download images at Office.com.

- ➤ Customize and format an image with options and buttons on the PICTURE TOOLS FORMAT tab or with options at the shortcut menu. Display the shortcut menu by right-clicking the image.

- ➤ Change the text wrapping of an image with the Position button or Wrap Text button on the PICTURE TOOLS FORMAT tab and with options from the Layout Options button that displays just outside the upper right corner of a selected image.

- ➤ Size an image with the *Shape Height* and *Shape Width* measurement boxes on the PICTURE TOOLS FORMAT tab or with the sizing handles that display around a selected image.

- ➤ Move an image by using options from the Position button drop-down gallery located on the PICTURE TOOLS FORMAT tab, dragging the image with the mouse, or using arrow keys on the keyboard.

- ➤ Green alignment guides display in a document when an image is moved to the top, left, right, or bottom margin or to the center of the document.

- ➤ Customize the layout of an image with options at the Layout dialog box. Display this dialog box by clicking the Size group dialog box launcher on the PICTURE TOOLS FORMAT tab.

- ➤ The Layout dialog box contains three tabs. Click the Position tab to specify the position of the image in the document, click the Text Wrapping tab to specify a wrapping style for the image, and click the Size tab to specify the height and width of the image.

- ➤ Format an image with options in the Format Picture task pane. Display this task pane by clicking the Picture Styles group task pane launcher.

- ➤ To edit individual components of a clip art image, first ungroup the image with the Group button in the Arrange group on the PICTURE TOOLS FORMAT tab.

- ➤ Use the SmartArt feature to insert predesigned graphics, such as diagrams and organizational charts, in a document.

- ➤ Choose a SmartArt graphic at the Choose a SmartArt Graphic dialog box. Display this dialog box by clicking the INSERT tab and then clicking the SmartArt button in the Illustrations group.

- ➤ Format a SmartArt graphic with options and buttons on the SMARTART TOOLS DESIGN tab and SMARTART TOOLS FORMAT tab.

- ➤ To move a SmartArt graphic, first choose a text wrapping style with the Position button or Wrap Text button on the SMARTART TOOLS FORMAT tab. After applying a wrapping style, move the graphic by positioning the arrow pointer on the graphic border until the pointer displays with a four-headed arrow attached, holding down the left mouse button, and then dragging the graphic to the desired location.

# Commands *Review*

| FEATURE | RIBBON TAB, GROUP | BUTTON |
|---|---|---|
| Choose a SmartArt Graphic dialog box | INSERT, Illustrations | |
| Format Picture task pane | PICTURE TOOLS FORMAT, Picture Styles | |
| Insert Picture dialog box | INSERT, Illustrations | |
| Insert Pictures window | INSERT, Illustrations | |
| Layout dialog box | PICTURE TOOLS FORMAT, Size | |

# Key Points *Review*

**Completion:** In the space provided at the right, indicate the correct term, symbol, or command.

1. Insert an image in a document with buttons in this group on the INSERT tab. _____

2. Click the Pictures button on the INSERT tab and this dialog box displays. _____

3. Customize and format an image with options and buttons on this tab. _____

4. Size an image with the sizing handles that display around the selected image or with these measurement boxes on the PICTURE TOOLS FORMAT tab. _____

5. Change text wrapping with the options from the Position button, the Wrap Text button, or this button, which displays just outside the upper right corner of a selected image. _____

6. Click the Online Pictures button on the INSERT tab and this window displays. _____

7. With options in the Layout dialog box with this tab selected, you can specify horizontal and vertical layout options. _____

8. The Layout dialog box contains three tabs: Position, Size, and this. _____

9. Click this group task pane launcher on the PICTURE TOOLS FORMAT tab to display the Format Picture task pane. _____

10. If you want to edit individual components of a clip art image, you must first do this to the image. _____

11. Insert a SmartArt graphic in a document and this tab is active. _____

12. To represent hierarchical data visually, consider creating this with the SmartArt feature. _____

13. The SmartArt button is located on this tab. _____

14. Click the SmartArt button and this dialog box displays. _____

# Chapter *Assessments*

## Applying Your Skills

Demonstrate your knowledge of features learned in this chapter by completing the following assessments.

### Assessment 11.1    Create a Flyer with a Picture and Text

1. At a blank document, press the Enter key three times, type **Ocean View Condominiums**, press the Enter key, and then type **1-888-555-6570**.
2. Press Ctrl + Home and then insert the picture **Ocean.jpg** with the following specifications:
   a. Change the position to Position in Top Center with Square Text Wrapping.
   b. Change the text wrapping to Behind Text.
   c. Change the width to 4.5 inches.
   d. Change the brightness and contrast to Brightness: -20% Contrast: +20%.
3. Select the text, change the font to 26-point Script MT Bold and the text color to White, and then center the text.
4. Save the document with the name **C11-A01-OVC**.
5. Print and then close **C11-A01-OVC.docx**.

### Assessment 11.2    Insert and Format a Clip Art Image

1. Open **PremPro.docx** and save the document with the name **C11-A02-PremPro**.
2. Insert a clip art image from Office.com with the following specifications:
   a. At the Insert Picture window, use the word *cornucopia* to search for and then download the image shown in Figure 11.16 on the next page.
   b. Change the height of the clip art image to 1.4 inches.
   c. Change the brightness and contrast to Brightness: 0% (Normal) Contrast: +20%.
   d. Change the position to Position in Middle Right with Square Text Wrapping.
   e. Apply the Offset Diagonal Bottom Left picture effect shadow. ***Hint: Use the Picture Effects button in the Pictures Styles group and then point to* Shadow.**
3. Save, print, and then close **C11-A02-PremPro.docx**.

**Figure 11.16** Assessment 11.2

## PREMIUM PRODUCE

3500 Fairview Drive ❧ Lincoln, NE 74932 ❧ (402) 555-8900 ❧ www.emcp.net/prempro

**Farm-fresh and Organic Produce**

Premium Produce is your source for local, farm-fresh produce. All of our produce is organically grown without pesticides, herbicides or other sprays. We ship our produce daily to a seven-state region in the Midwest.

**Featured Product of the Month**

Many fruits and vegetables are being harvested now while they are at the peak of their flavor. Featured produce this month include:

- ❧ Squash
- ❧ Potatoes
- ❧ Apples

**Ordering from Premium Produce**

Before ordering from Premium Produce, check our sale prices for the current month. After viewing the sale prices, call our toll-free number at 1-800-555-8900.

---

**Assessment 11.3** **Insert and Format a Clip Art Image in a Data Security Training Notice**

 Grade It

1. Open **DataTraining.docx** and save the document with the name **C11-A03-DataTraining**.
2. Insert the clip art image shown in Figure 11.17 on the next page using the search words *computer* and *padlock icon* at the Insert Pictures window.
3. Rotate the image by flipping it horizontally.
4. Click the Picture Styles group task pane launcher to display the Format Picture task pane and then make the following changes:
   a. Click the Fill & Line icon located toward the top of the task pane.
   b. Click *FILL* to expand the options, click the *Gradient fill* option, click the Preset gradients button, and then click the *Light Gradient - Accent 6* option (last column, first row).
   c. Click the *Effects* icon.
   d. Click *SHADOW* to expand the options, click the Presets button, and then click the *Offset Diagonal Bottom Right* option (first option in the *Outer* section).
   e. Click *REFLECTION* to expand the options, click the Presets button, and then click the *Tight Reflection, touching* option (first option in the *Reflection Variations* section).
5. Change the text wrapping to Square.
6. Change the shape height measurement to 1.3 inches.
7. Display the Layout dialog box with the Position tab selected and then change the horizontal absolute position to 6.2 inches to the right of the left margin and the vertical absolute position to 2.2 inches below the page. ***Hint: Display the Layout dialog box by clicking the Size group dialog box launcher on the PICTURE TOOLS FORMAT tab.***
8. Save, print, and then close **C11-A03-DataTraining.docx**.

**Figure 11.17 Assessment 11.3**

### DATA SECURITY TRAINING

The technical support team is preparing three workshops focusing on protecting and securing company data. The workshops are open to all employees; however, participants must obtain approval from their immediate supervisor.

The first workshop, scheduled for Tuesday, April 7, from 9:00 to 11:30 a.m., will cover backing up crucial data. Participants will be briefed on the company's new rotating backup process, which involves backing up data from specific departments on specific days of the week.

The second workshop, scheduled for Wednesday, April 15, from 1:30 to 3:00 p.m., will focus on disaster recovery plan formulation and will include data backup procedures, remote backup locations, and redundant systems.

The third and final workshop, scheduled for Thursday, April 23, from 3:00 to 5:30 p.m., will focus on data security and will cover data encryption. Participants will learn about encryption schemes designed to scramble information before transferring it electronically.

---

## Assessment 11.4    Insert, Ungroup, and Recolor a Clip Art Image in a Vacation Document

1. Open **VacAdventure.docx** and save the document with the name **C11-A04-VacAdventure**.
2. Insert the clip art image shown in Figure 11.18 on the next page with the following specifications:
   a. Use the words *illustrations of sunglasses, mountains and the sun* to search for the clip art image.
   b. Change the text wrapping of the clip art image to Square.
   c. Change the shape height measurement to 2.3 inches.
   d. Ungroup the clip art image.
   e. Recolor individual components in the clip art so it appears as shown in Figure 11.18. (Apply the Orange shape fill color to the sun, the Green shape fill color to the mountains, and the Blue shape fill color to the water shapes.)
   f. Change the position of the image to Position in Middle Right with Square Text Wrapping.
3. Save, print, and then close **C11-A04-VacAdventure.docx**.

## Assessment 11.5    Create and Format a Cycle SmartArt Graphic

1. At a blank document, create the SmartArt cycle graphic shown in Figure 11.19 on the next page with the following specifications:
   a. Use the Basic Radial cycle graphic.
   b. Add a shape.
   c. Apply the Polished SmartArt style.
   d. Change the colors to Colorful Range - Accent Colors 3 to 4.
   e. Change the height of the SmartArt graphic to 5.5 inches and the width to 6.5 inches.
   f. Type the text in the shapes as shown in Figure 11.19.
2. Save the completed document and name it **C11-A05-TECGraphic**.
3. Print and then close **C11-A05-TECGraphic.docx**.

**Figure 11.18  Assessment 11.4**

## "FUN2016" VACATION ADVENTURES

Hurry and book now for one of our special FUN2016 vacation packages. Book within the next two weeks and you will be eligible for our special discount savings as well as earn a complimentary $100 gift card you can use at any of the resorts in our FUN2016 plan.

**FUN2016 Disneyland Adventure**

Roundtrip air fare to Los Angeles, California
Three-night hotel accommodations
Three-day Resort Ticket
24-hour traveler assistance

**FUN2016 Florida Adventure**

Roundtrip airfare to Orlando, Florida
Seven-night hotel accommodations
Four-day Resort Ticket
Two-day Bonus Ticket
Free transportation to some sites

**FUN2016 Cancun Adventure**

Roundtrip airfare to Cancun, Mexico
Five-night hotel accommodations and hotel taxes
Free shuttle to and from the airport
Two excursion tickets

Book a complete air/hotel FUN2016 vacation package and SAVE on fall travel! Bookings must be made by October 1, 2016, for travel October 30 through December 19, 2016 (blackout dates apply). Take advantage of these fantastic savings!

**Figure 11.19  Assessment 11.5**

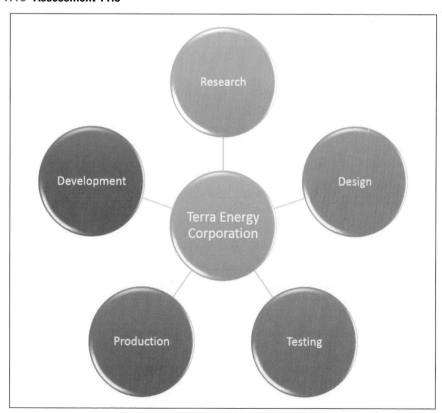

## Assessment 11.6    Create and Format a SmartArt Organizational Chart

1. At a blank document, create the organizational chart shown in Figure 11.20 with the following specifications:
   a. Use the Hierarchy organizational chart in the *Hierarchy* section.
   b. Select the top text box and insert a shape above it.
   c. Select the text box at the right in the third row and then add a shape below it.
   d. Apply the *Colorful Range - Accent Colors 3 to 4* option.
   e. Increase the height to 4.5 inches and the width to 6.5 inches.
   f. Type the text in each text box as shown in Figure 11.20.
   g. Position the organizational chart in the middle of the page.
2. Save the document with the name **C11-A06-OrgChart**.
3. Print and then close **C11-A06-OrgChart.docx**.

**Figure 11.20  Assessment 11.6**

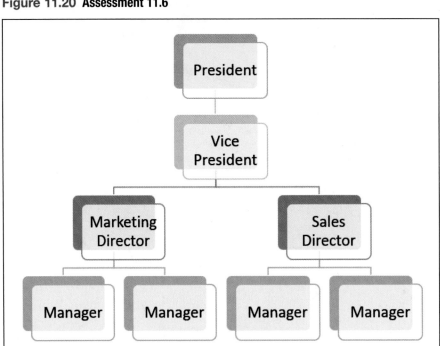

# Expanding Your Skills

Explore additional feature options or use Help to learn a new skill in creating this document.

## Assessment 11.7    Create a Flyer

1. Create the flyer shown in Figure 11.21 on the next page with the following specifications:
   - Set the text in Comic Sans MS. (You determine the point size.)
   - Insert and format the paragraph borders and page border as shown in the figure. (Create the border below the title as a bottom border of the title *Pugs on Parade!* At the Borders and Shading dialog box, choose the first double-line style in the *Style* list box, change the color to Dark Red, and change the width similar to what is shown in Figure 11.21. Create the page border using the first thick-thin line style in the *Style* list box, change the color to Dark Red, and change the width similar to what is shown in the figure.)

- Insert the **Pug.jpg** picture from your Chapter11 folder. (Use the Pictures button on the INSERT tab.)
- Click the Remove Background button on the PICTURE TOOLS FORMAT tab and then experiment with the options for marking areas to keep and marking areas to remove. Learn how to use the Delete Mark, Discard All Changes, and Keep Changes buttons. Remove and/or keep backgrounds so your picture displays as shown in Figure 11.21. (It may take some practice to remove and/or keep the necessary backgrounds for the picture.)
- Change the text wrapping for the picture to Behind Text and then size and position the picture as shown in the figure.
- Make any other changes needed so your document appears the same as Figure 11.21.

2. Check to make sure the entire page border will print. If it will not, increase the measurements at the Border and Shading Options dialog box.
3. Save the completed document and name it **C11-A07-PugFlyer**.
4. Print and then close **C11-A07-PugFlyer.docx**.

**Figure 11.21  Assessment 11.7**

# Achieving Signature Status

Take your skills to the next level by completing these more challenging assessments.

## Assessment 11.8    Ungroup and Recolor a Clip Art Image

1. At a blank document, create the document shown in Figure 11.22 with the following specifications:
   a. Insert the clip art image by opening the document named **TECLogo.docx** and then copying the clip art image from **TECLogo.docx** and pasting it into the blank document. (Do not use the Online Pictures button to do this.)
   b. Flip the clip art image, ungroup the image, and recolor the components so your clip art image displays the same as the image in Figure 11.22.
   c. Type the text in the document as shown in Figure 11.22.
   d. Set the title in 20-point Copperplate Gothic bold. Make any other formatting changes needed so your document is formatted the same as the document in Figure 11.22.
2. Save the completed document and name it **C11-A08-TECRevs**.
3. Print and then close **C11-A08-TECRevs.docx**.
4. Close **TECLogo.docx** without saving changes.

**Figure 11.22  Assessment 11.8**

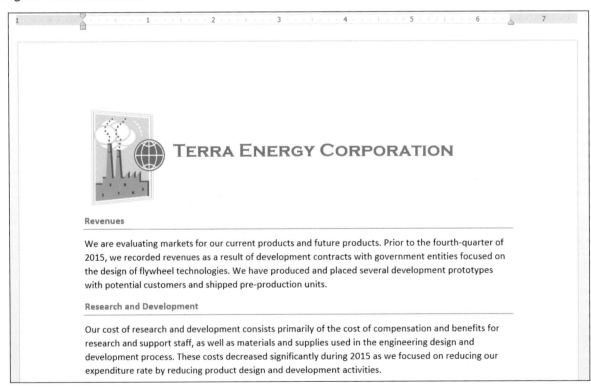

**TERRA ENERGY CORPORATION**

**Revenues**

We are evaluating markets for our current products and future products. Prior to the fourth-quarter of 2015, we recorded revenues as a result of development contracts with government entities focused on the design of flywheel technologies. We have produced and placed several development prototypes with potential customers and shipped pre-production units.

**Research and Development**

Our cost of research and development consists primarily of the cost of compensation and benefits for research and support staff, as well as materials and supplies used in the engineering design and development process. These costs decreased significantly during 2015 as we focused on reducing our expenditure rate by reducing product design and development activities.

## Assessment 11.9    Create and Format a SmartArt Graphic

1. At a blank document, create the SmartArt graphic shown in Figure 11.23 with the
   following specifications:
   a. Use the Pyramid List graphic.
   b. Apply the Inset SmartArt style.
   c. Change the colors to Colorful Range - Accent Colors 5 to 6.
   d. Apply Light Green shape fill color to the bottom shape, Light Blue fill color to the middle
      shape, and Red fill color to the top shape.
   e. Type the text in each shape as shown in Figure 11.23.
2. Save the document with the name **C11-A09-Levels**.
3. Print and then close **C11-A09-Levels.docx**.

**Figure 11.23  Assessment 11.9**

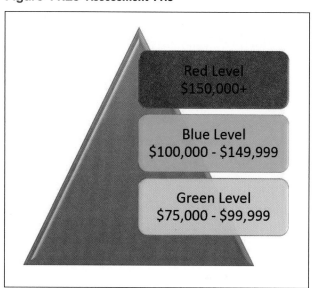

# Chapter 12

## Using Shapes, WordArt, and Advanced Character Formatting

### Performance Objectives

Upon successful completion of Chapter 12, you will be able to:

- Insert and format screenshot images
- Draw and format shapes
- Select and align objects
- Insert and format text boxes
- Link and unlink text boxes
- Insert and format WordArt
- Apply character formatting, such as spacing, OpenType features, and text effects

In the previous chapter, you learned to use the Pictures, Online Pictures, and SmartArt buttons in the Illustrations group on the INSERT tab. The Illustrations group also contains a Screenshot button that you can use to capture all or part of the contents of a screen as an image. In this chapter, you will learn how to create and insert screenshot images into a document. You will also learn how to insert other elements (such as shapes, text boxes, and WordArt) to enhance the appearance of your documents, and how to apply formatting to text in a document using options at the Font dialog box with the Advanced tab selected.

*Note: Before beginning computer exercises for this chapter, copy to your storage medium the Chapter12 folder from the CD that accompanies this textbook and then make Chapter12 the active folder.*

In this chapter, students will produce the following documents:

Exercise 12.1. C12-E01-BackstageAreas.docx
Exercise 12.1. C12-E01-SFHCoverPages.docx
Exercise 12.2. C12-E02-LelandFS.docx
Exercise 12.3. C12-E03-Hawaii.docx
Exercise 12.4. C12-E04-PRDonorApp.docx

Model answers for these exercises are shown on the following pages.

Print Backstage Area

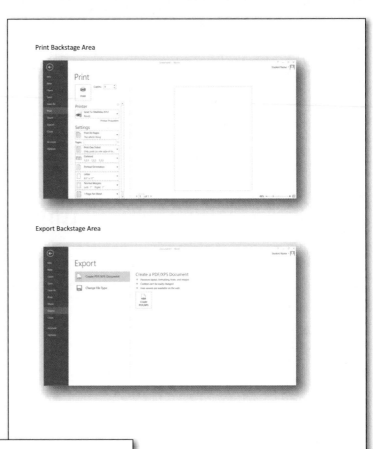

Export Backstage Area

**Exercise 12.1A**

C12-E01-BackstageAreas.docx

## ST. FRANCIS HOSPITAL

### SAMPLE COVER PAGES

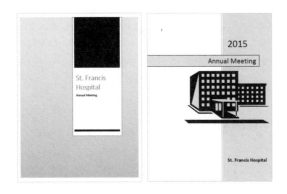

**Exercise 12.1B**

C12-E01-SFHCoverPages.docx

3500 MEEKER BOULEVARD ∝ REDFIELD, NE 68304 ∝ 308-555-5000

## LELAND FINANCIAL SERVICES

Our customers have high expectations for their financial security, and our company offers superior services in personal interactions with clients and investment advice and recommendations from our highly trained investment specialists. Leland Financial Services helps customers establish financial goals, and we provide structure, advice, and investments opportunities to meet the goals. With fewer companies offering full pension plans, personal retirement planning is crucial. Retirement savings need to be a priority rather than an afterthought. Our investment specialists focus on the customer's goals and priorities to prepare a personalized investment portfolio. Ongoing monitoring of financial investments is part of our commitment to help our customers reach their financial objectives. In the midst of today's ever-shifting financial and economic markets, financial planning is more important than ever to ensure retirement security.

"Ongoing monitoring of financial investments is part of our commitment to our customers..."

Let Leland Financial Services help you plan for retirement and provide

you with information to determine your financial direction.

Page 1

**Exercise 12.2**

C12-E02-LelandFS.docx

Page 2

Free seminar!

1-888-555-4588

Page 3

Model Answers

**Exercise 12.3**

C12-E03-Hawaii.docx

### RAINY DAY ACTIVITIES

Expect to have a rainy day or two during your vacation, especially in the winter months between November and March. With a little planning, you can have just as much fun indoors as outdoors. To make the most of a rainy day, enjoy one of the activities listed below.

- Movies: Take advantage of matinee prices. The Sunshine Marketplace Theaters offer discount tickets and current feature films.
- Shopping: Most of the area shopping centers are "open-air" complexes with some roof covering, ideal havens from the rain. Visit the Coconut Grove Shopping Center or the Kukui Shopping Village.
- Museums: Learn about the history of Hawaii through murals, artifacts, and artwork by visiting one of several museums located throughout the islands. Most museums offer special family activities the first Saturday of each month.
- Theater: Several local community performing arts centers offer annual productions for children and adults. Admission prices are very affordable, and most theaters have special matinee prices.

### KAUAI SIGHTS

- Na Pali Coast: Unless you are a rugged hiker, you can see this fifteen-mile, spectacular landmark only by air or boat.
- North Shore: Find shadowy mountains, lush valleys, and spectacular coastlines along a string of one-lane bridges.
- Hanalei Valley Lookout: Pull over to see wetland taro fields with a backdrop of purple mountains.
- Kilauea Point: This National Wildlife Refuge is home to nesting seabirds and an original lighthouse.
- Sleeping Giant: Nounou Mountain provides the "man in repose" profile best seen from Kuhio Highway 56 in Kapaa.
- Coconut Coast: You will know when you are here because palm trees line Kuhio Highway 56 on the island's east side.

# Phoenix Rising

## Donor Appreciation

Enjoy the "flavor of Tanzania"
and an evening of cultural entertainment...

We want to show our appreciation to all of our donors by offering an evening of fine foods, cultural entertainment, and a presentation by our international advocate. Your evening begins at 6:00 p.m. and includes:

- Social hour from 6:00 to 7:00 p.m.
- Opening remarks by the president of Phoenix Rising
- Five-course meal of traditional Tanzanian dishes
- Tanzanian music and entertainment
- Presentation by Renate Santorini, the international advocate for Phoenix Rising

Donation Goal for 2016 – 2017
$3,500,000

Please call the Phoenix Rising office to let us know if you will be joining us.

1500 Frontier Avenue • Eugene, OR 97440 • 541-555-4110

**Exercise 12.4**

C12-E04-PRDonorApp.docx

# Creating Screenshots

The Illustrations group on the INSERT tab contains a Screenshot button that you can use to capture the contents of a screen as an image or to capture a specific part of the screen as an image. If you want to capture the entire screen as an image, open a new document, click the INSERT tab, click the Screenshot button, and then click the desired screen thumbnail at the drop-down list. The currently active document does not display as a thumbnail at the drop-down list; only the other documents and programs you have open display. When you click the desired thumbnail, the screenshot is inserted as an image into the open document, the image is selected, and the PICTURE TOOLS FORMAT tab is active. Use buttons on this tab to customize the screenshot image.

**Insert a Screenshot**
1. Open blank document.
2. Open another document and display desired information.
3. Make blank document active.
4. Click INSERT tab.
5. Click Screenshot button.
6. Click desired window at drop-down list.

Screenshot

---

## Exercise 12.1A  Inserting and Formatting a Screenshot     Part 1 of 2

1. Press Ctrl + N to open a blank document.
2. Press Ctrl + N to open a second blank document.
3. Type **Print Backstage Area** at the left margin and then press the Enter key.
4. Save the document and name it **C12-E01-BackstageAreas**.
5. Point to the Word button on the Taskbar and then click the thumbnail representing the blank document.

6. Display the Print backstage area by clicking the FILE tab and then clicking the *Print* option.
7. Point to the Word button on the Taskbar and then click the **C12-E01-BackstageAreas.docx** thumbnail.

8. Insert and format a screenshot of the Print backstage area by completing the following steps:
   a. Click the INSERT tab.
   b. Click the Screenshot button in the Illustrations group and then click the thumbnail that displays in the drop-down list. (This inserts a screenshot of the Print backstage area in the document.)

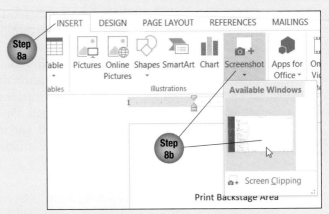

   c. With the screenshot image selected, click the *Drop Shadow Rectangle* picture style (fourth option in Picture Styles group).
   d. Click in the *Shape Width* measurement box, type **5.5**, and then press the Enter key.
9. Press Ctrl + End and then press the Enter key. (This moves the insertion point below the screenshot image.)
10. Type **Export Backstage Area** at the left margin and then press the Enter key.
11. Point to the Word button on the Taskbar and then click the thumbnail representing the blank document.
12. At the backstage area, click the *Export* option. (This displays the Export backstage area.)
13. Click the Word button on the Taskbar and then click the **C12-E01-BackstageAreas.docx** thumbnail.
14. Insert and format a screenshot of the Export backstage area by completing steps similar to those in Step 8.
15. Press Ctrl + Home to move the insertion point to the beginning of the document.
16. Save, print, and then close **C12-E01-BackstageAreas.docx**.
17. At the Export backstage area, press the Esc key to redisplay the blank document and then close the document without saving it.

**QUICK STEPS**

**Insert a Screen Clipping**
1. Open blank document.
2. Open another document.
3. Display desired information in document.
4. Make blank document active.
5. Click INSERT tab.
6. Click Screenshot button.
7. Click *Screen Clipping*.
8. Drag to specify area in document to capture.

In addition to making a screenshot of an entire screen, you can make a screenshot of a specific portion of the screen by clicking the *Screen Clipping* option at the Screenshot button drop-down list. When you click this option, the other open document, file, or Windows desktop displays in a dimmed manner and the mouse pointer displays as crosshairs (+). Using the mouse, draw a border around the specific area of the screen you want to capture. The specific area you identified is inserted in the other document as an image, the image is selected, and the PICTURE TOOLS FORMAT tab is active. If you have only one document or file open when you click the Screenshot button, clicking the *Screen Clipping* option will cause the Windows Start screen or desktop to display.

1. Open **SFHLtrhd.docx** and then save the document and name it **C12-E01-SFHCoverPages**.
2. Type the text **Sample Cover Pages** and then press the Enter key twice.
3. Select the text you just typed, change the font to 18-point Copperplate Gothic Bold, and then center the text.
4. Press Ctrl + End to move the insertion point below the text.
5. Open the document **SFHCoverPg01.docx** and then change the zoom to 40% by clicking six times on the Zoom Out button located at the left side of the Zoom slider bar on the Status bar.
6. Point to the Word button on the Taskbar and then click the **C12-E01-SFHCoverPages.docx** thumbnail.
7. Create and format a screen clipping by completing the following steps:
   a. Click the INSERT tab.
   b. Click the Screenshot button in the Illustrations group and then click *Screen Clipping*.

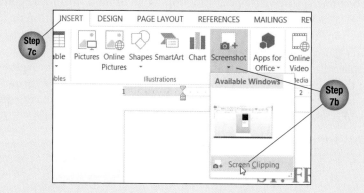

   c. When **SFHCoverPg01.docx** displays in a dimmed manner, position the mouse crosshairs in the upper left corner of the cover page, hold down the left mouse button, drag down to the lower right corner of the cover page, and then release the mouse button. (See the image at the right.)
   d. With the cover page screenshot image inserted in **C12-E01-SFHCoverPages.docx**, make sure the image is selected (sizing handles display around the cover page image).
   e. Click in the *Shape Width* measurement box, type **3**, and then press the Enter key.
   f. Click the Wrap Text button in the Arrange group on the PICTURE TOOLS FORMAT tab and then click *Square* at the drop-down gallery.
8. Point to the Word button on the Taskbar and then click the **SFHCoverPg01.docx** thumbnail.

9. Close **SFHCoverPg01.docx**.
10. Open **SFHCoverPg02.docx** and, if necessary, change the zoom to 40%.
11. Point to the Word button on the Taskbar and then click the **C12-E01-SFHCoverPages.docx** thumbnail.
12. Create and format a screenshot by completing steps similar to those in Step 7.
13. Position the two cover page screenshot images side by side in the document.
14. Save, print, and then close **C12-E01-SFHCoverPages.docx**.
15. Close **SFHCoverPg02.docx**.

# Drawing Shapes

**Draw a Shape**
1. Click INSERT tab.
2. Click Shapes button.
3. Click desired shape in drop-down list.
4. Click or drag in document to create shape.

Shapes

Use the Shapes button on the INSERT tab to draw a variety of objects in a document, such as lines, basic geometric shapes, block arrows, flow chart shapes, callouts, stars, and banners. Click a shape at the drop-down list and the mouse pointer displays as crosshairs. Click in the document to insert the shape or position the crosshairs where you want the shape to begin, hold down the left mouse button, drag to create the shape, and then release the mouse button. This inserts the shape in the document and also displays the DRAWING TOOLS FORMAT tab, as shown in Figure 12.1. Use buttons on this tab to replace the shape with another shape, apply a style to the shape, position or arrange the shape, or change the size of the shape. This tab contains many of the same options and buttons as the PICTURE TOOLS FORMAT tab.

**Figure 12.1 DRAWING TOOLS FORMAT Tab**

## Drawing Lines

The Shapes button drop-down list includes lines and enclosed shapes. To draw a line, click an option in the *Lines* group. When the mouse pointer changes to crosshairs, position the crosshairs in the document and then drag to draw the line. If you want to draw a straight horizontal or vertical line, hold down the Shift key while dragging with the mouse.

1. Open **LelandFS.docx** and then save the document and name it **C12-E02-LelandFS**. If necessary, change the zoom to 100%.
2. Insert and format the line below the text as shown in Figure 12.2 on the next page by completing the following steps:
   a. Click the INSERT tab.
   b. Click the Shapes button and then click the *Double Arrow* option (third option in the *Lines* section).
   c. Hold down the Shift key and then drag to create a horizontal line below the title that is approximately 6 inches in length (see Figure 12.2).
   d. With the line selected, click the More button at the right of the thumbnails in the Shape Styles group and then click the *Intense Line - Accent 6* option (last option in the last row).

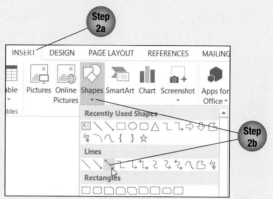

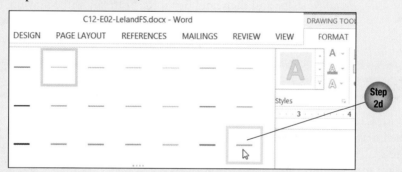

   e. Click the Shape Outline button arrow in the Shape Styles group and then click the *Green, Accent 6, Darker 25%* option (last column, fifth row in the *Theme Colors* section).
   f. Click the Shape Effects button in the Shape Styles group, point to *Shadow*, and then click the *Offset Bottom* option (second column, first row in the *Outer* section).

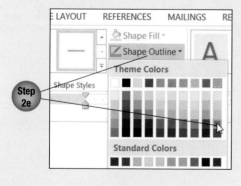

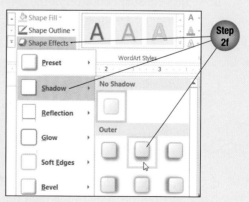

3. Click outside the line to deselect it.
4. Save **C12-E02-LelandFS.docx**.

**Figure 12.2 Exercise 12.2A**

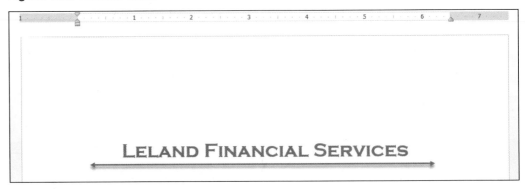

LELAND FINANCIAL SERVICES

## Drawing Enclosed Shapes

If you choose a shape in the *Lines* section of the Shapes button drop-down list, the shape you draw is considered a **line drawing**. If you choose an option in one of the other sections of the drop-down list, the shape you draw is considered an **enclosed shape**. When you draw an enclosed shape, you can maintain its proportions by holding down the Shift key while dragging to create the shape. For example, to draw a square, choose the *Rectangle* shape and then hold down the Shift key while drawing the shape. To draw a circle, choose the *Oval* shape and then hold down the Shift key while drawing the shape.

---

**Exercise 12.2B** **Drawing and Formatting an Arrow Shape**                    Part 2 of 10

1. With **C12-E02-LelandFS.docx** open, press Ctrl + End to move the insertion point to the end of the document.
2. Press Ctrl + Enter to insert a page break.
3. Make sure the horizontal and vertical rulers are visible. If not, click the VIEW tab and then click the *Ruler* check box.

4. Draw and format the arrow shape shown in Figure 12.3 on the next page by completing the following steps:
   a. Click the INSERT tab.
   b. Click the Shapes button in the Illustrations group and then click the *Striped Right Arrow* shape (fifth column, second row in the *Block Arrows* section).
   c. Position the mouse pointer (which displays as crosshairs) in the document at approximately the 1-inch mark on the horizontal ruler and the 0.5-inch mark on the vertical ruler.
   d. Hold down the Shift key and the left mouse button, drag to the right until the tip of the arrow is positioned at approximately the 5.5-inch mark on the horizontal ruler, and then release the mouse button and Shift key.

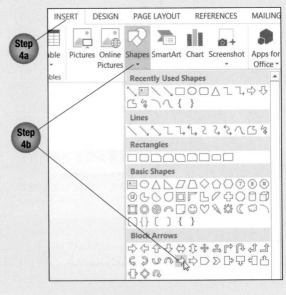

5. Format the arrow by completing the following steps:
   a. Click in the *Shape Height* measurement box in the Size group and then type **2.4**.
   b. Click in the *Shape Width* measurement box in the Size group, type **4.5**, and then press the Enter key.
   c. Click the More button at the right of the thumbnails in the Shape Styles group and then click the *Subtle Effect - Green, Accent 6* option (last column, fourth row).
   d. Click the Shape Effects button, point to *Bevel*, and then click the *Angle* option (first column, second row in the *Bevel* section).
   e. Click the Shape Outline button arrow and then click *Dark Blue* (ninth option in the *Standard Colors* section).

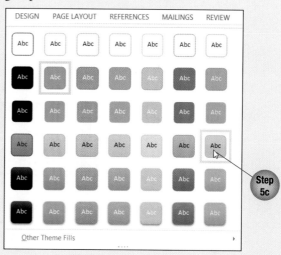

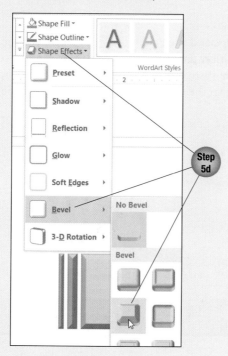

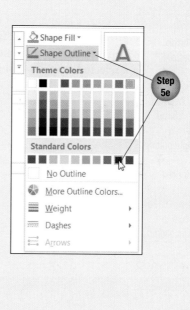

6. Save **C12-E02-LelandFS.docx**.

**Figure 12.3  Exercise 12.2B**

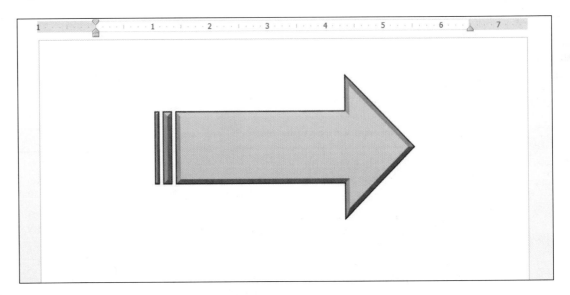

## Copying Shapes

To copy a shape, select the shape and then click the Copy button in the Clipboard group on the HOME tab. Position the insertion point at the location you want the copied shape and then click the Paste button in the Clipboard group. You can also copy a selected shape by holding down the Ctrl key while dragging the shape to the desired location.

**Copy a Shape**
1. Select desired shape.
2. Click Copy button.
3. Position insertion point at desired location.
4. Click Paste button.
**OR**
1. Select desired shape.
2. Hold down Ctrl key.
3. Drag shape to desired location.

---

**Exercise 12.2C**   Copying a Shape                    Part 3 of 10

---

1. With **C12-E02-LelandFS.docx** open, copy the arrow by completing the following steps:
   a. With the arrow selected, position the mouse pointer on the arrow border until the mouse pointer displays with a four-headed arrow attached and then hold down the Ctrl key.
   b. Drag down until the copied arrow displays just below the top (original) arrow, release the mouse button, and then release the Ctrl key.

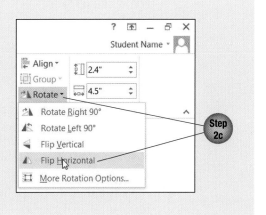

   c. Copy the arrow again by holding down the
      Ctrl key and then dragging the copied arrow
      just below the second arrow.
2. Flip the middle arrow by completing the
   following steps:
   a. Click the middle arrow to select it.
   b. If necessary, click the DRAWING TOOLS
      FORMAT tab.
   c. Click the Rotate button in the Arrange group
      and then click *Flip Horizontal* at the drop-
      down gallery.
3. Save **C12-E02-LelandFS.docx**.

## Selecting and Aligning Shapes

If you are working with multiple shapes, select the shapes and then apply formatting
to all of them. To select multiple shapes, hold down the Shift key, click each shape you
want to select, and then release the Shift key. You can also hold down the Ctrl key and
then click the desired shapes.

The Align button in the Arrange group on the DRAWING TOOLS FORMAT tab
contains options for aligning multiple shapes in a document. To align shapes, click the
desired shapes, click the Align button in the Arrange group, and then click the desired
alignment option at the drop-down list. For example, if you want to align all of the
shapes at the left side of the page, click the *Align Left* option at the Align button drop-
down list. If you want to distribute the selected shapes horizontally on the page, click
the *Distribute Horizontally* option at the Align button drop-down list or click *Distribute
Vertically* if you want to distribute the shapes vertically on the page.

---

**Exercise 12.2D**     Selecting and Aligning Arrow Shapes          Part 4 of 10

1. With **C12-E02-LelandFS.docx** open, display the arrows on the second page.
2. Select and align the arrows by completing the following steps:
   a. Click the top arrow to select it.
   b. Hold down the Shift key.
   c. Click the middle arrow and then click the
      bottom arrow.
   d. Release the Shift key.
   e. With the three arrows selected, click the
      Align button in the Arrange group on the
      DRAWING TOOLS FORMAT tab and then
      click *Align Left* at the drop-down list.
3. Distribute the arrows vertically by clicking the Align
   button and then clicking *Distribute Vertically* at the
   drop-down list.
4. Save **C12-E02-LelandFS.docx**.

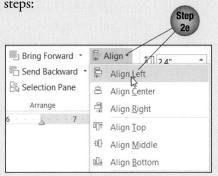

## Inserting Text in a Shape

When you draw a shape in a document, you can type text directly in the shape. Select the text and then use options in the WordArt Styles group on the DRAWING TOOLS FORMAT tab to format text. You can also apply formatting to text in a shape with options available at other tabs, such as the HOME tab.

## Editing a Shape and Points in a Shape

**Edit Shape**

The DRAWING TOOLS FORMAT tab contains an Edit Shape button in the Insert Shapes group. Click this button and a drop-down list displays with options to change the shape and customize the shape with edit points.

Click the Edit Shape button and then point to the *Change Shape* option and a side menu displays with shape options. Click the desired shape option and the shape in the document conforms to the chosen shape.

Click the *Edit Points* option at the Edit Shape button drop-down list and the selected shape displays with edit points around the shape. The edit points display as small black squares at the intersecting points in the shape. To use an edit point, position the mouse pointer on the desired point until the mouse pointer displays as a small square surrounded by an up-pointing, right-pointing, down-pointing, and left-pointing triangle. Hold down the left mouse button, drag to the desired position, and then release the mouse button.

---

## Exercise 12.2E    Inserting Text in a Shape and Editing Points    Part 5 of 10

1. With **C12-E02-LelandFS.docx** open, press Ctrl + End to move the insertion point to the end of the document. (The insertion point will display above the shapes.) Insert a page break by pressing Ctrl + Enter. (The shapes will remain on the previous page.)
2. Insert a shape by completing the following steps:
   a. Click the INSERT tab.
   b. Click the Shapes button in the Illustrations group and then click the *5-Point Star* shape (fourth column, first row in the *Stars and Banners* section).
   c. Hold down the Shift key, drag in the document to create a star shape that is approximately 4 inches in height and width, and then release the mouse button and then the Shift key.
   d. With the DRAWING TOOLS FORMAT tab active, click in the *Shape Height* measurement box and then type **4**.
   e. Click in the *Shape Width* measurement box, type **4**, and then press the Enter key.

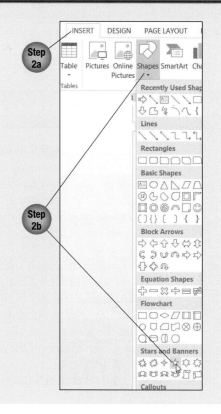

Step 2a

Step 2b

---

3. Change the shape by clicking the Edit Shape button in the Insert Shapes group on the DRAWING TOOLS FORMAT tab, pointing to *Change Shape*, and then clicking the *7-Point Star* shape in the shapes side menu (sixth column, first row in the *Stars and Banners* section).

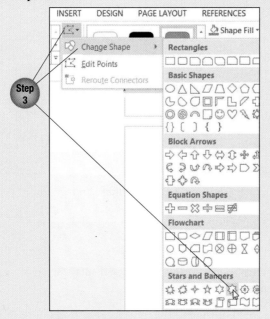

4. Format the shape by completing the following steps:
   a. Click the More button at the right of the thumbnails in the Shape Styles group and then click the *Subtle Effect – Green, Accent 6* option (last column, fourth row).

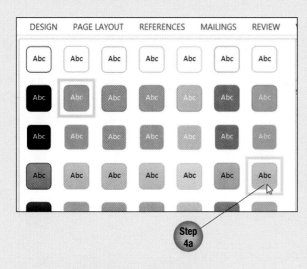

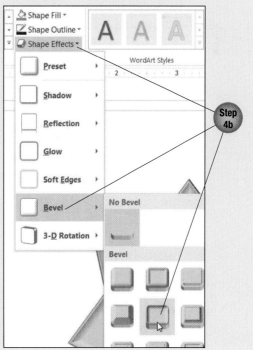

   b. Click the Shape Effects button in the Shape Styles group, point to *Bevel*, and then click the *Soft Round* option (second column, second row in the *Bevel* section).

5. Edit points in the shape by completing the following steps:
   a. Click the Edit Shape button and then click *Edit Points* at the drop-down list.
   b. Position the mouse pointer on the edit point at the outside of the top left point, drag up and out as shown in the image at the right, and then release the mouse button.

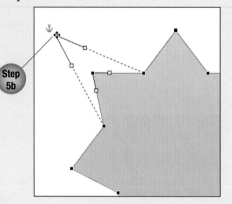

Step 5b

   c. Position the mouse pointer on the edit point at the outside of the top right point, drag out as shown in the image below, and then release the mouse button.

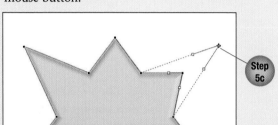

Step 5c

   d. Continue dragging edit points until your image displays similarly to the image shown in Figure 12.4 on the next page.
   e. Click outside the shape to remove the edit points.
6. Insert and format text in the shape by completing the following steps:
   a. Click in the shape to select it.
   b. Make sure the DRAWING TOOLS FORMAT tab is active.
   c. Type **Free seminar!**, press the Enter key, and then type **1-888-555-4588**. (This text will appear in the middle of the shape.)
   d. Select the text you just typed.
   e. Click the Text Fill button arrow in the WordArt Styles group on the DRAWING TOOLS FORMAT tab and then click the *Green, Accent 6, Darker 50%* option at the drop-down palette (last column, bottom row in the *Theme Colors* section).

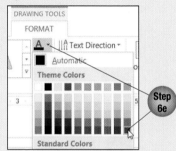

Step 6e

   f. Click the Text Effects button in the WordArt Styles group, point to *Glow*, and then click the *Blue, 8 pt glow, Accent color 1* option (first column, second row in the *Glow Variations* section).

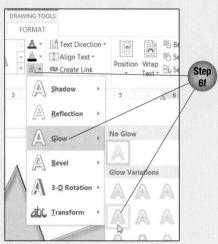

Step 6f

   g. Click the HOME tab.
   h. Click the Font Size button arrow and then click *18* at the drop-down gallery.
   i. Horizontally align the star on the page by clicking the border of the shape to select the entire shape, clicking the Align button in the Arrange group, and then clicking *Distribute Horizontally* at the drop-down list. Vertically align the star on the page by clicking the Align button and then clicking *Distribute Vertically* at the drop-down list.
   j. Click outside the shape. (Your text and shape should appear similar to what you see in Figure 12.4.)
7. Save **C12-E02-LelandFS.docx**.

**Figure 12.4 Exercise 12.2E**

# Inserting and Formatting Text Boxes

Use the Text Box button in the Text group on the INSERT tab to insert a predesigned text box or draw a text box and then apply formatting with options and buttons on the DRAWING TOOLS FORMAT tab (see Figure 12.1 on page 384). Click the Text Box button and a drop-down list displays with a variety of predesigned text boxes. Click one of the text boxes to insert it in the document or click the *Draw Text Box* option and then click in the document or drag in the document to create a text box.

Text Box

## Inserting a Predesigned Text Box

You can insert a predesigned text box in a document to create a pull quote, which is a quote that is "pulled" from an article and is enlarged and displayed in a strategic or attractive location on the page. Use pull quotes in an article to attract readers' attention. Some advantages of using pull quotes are that they reinforce important concepts, summarize the message, and break up blocks of text to make the article easier to read.

Insert a pull quote in a document by clicking the INSERT tab, clicking the Text Box button, and then clicking the desired predesigned text box at the drop-down list. Type the quote you have selected inside the text box and then format the text and/or customize the text box with buttons on the DRAWING TOOLS FORMAT tab.

**QUICK STEPS**

**Insert a Predesigned Text Box**
1. Click INSERT tab.
2. Click Text Box button in Text group.
3. Click predesigned text box at drop-down list.

1. With **C12-E02-LelandFS.docx** open, press Ctrl + Home to move the insertion point to the beginning of the document.
2. Insert and format the pull quote text box shown in Figure 12.5 on the next page by completing the following steps:

    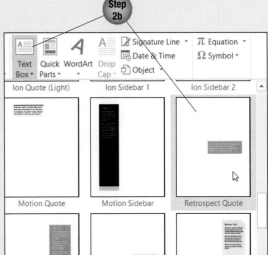

    a. Click the INSERT tab.
    b. Click the Text Box button in the Text group, scroll down the drop-down list, and then click the *Retrospect Quote* pull quote text box.
    c. With the insertion point positioned in the text box, type "**Ongoing monitoring of financial investments is part of our commitment to our customers...**".
    d. Click the Shape Fill button arrow in the Shapes Styles group and then click the *Green, Accent 6, Darker 25%* option (last column, fifth row in the *Theme Colors* section).

    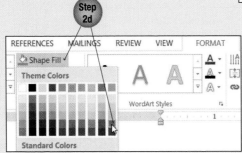

    e. Click in the *Shape Width* measurement box, type **2.8**, and then press Enter.
3. Drag the text box up so that three lines of paragraph text display above the box and three and one half lines display below the box.
4. Align the text box at the right margin by clicking the Align button in the Arrange group on the DRAWING TOOLS FORMAT tab and then clicking *Align Right* at the drop-down list.
5. Save **C12-E02-LelandFS.docx**.

**Figure 12.5 Exercise 12.2F**

## LELAND FINANCIAL SERVICES

Our customers have high expectations for their financial security, and our company offers superior services in personal interactions with clients and investment advice and recommendations from our highly trained investment specialists. Leland Financial Services helps customers establish financial goals, and we provide structure, advice, and investments opportunities to meet the goals. With fewer companies offering full pension plans, personal retirement planning is crucial. Retirement savings need to be a priority rather than an afterthought. Our investment specialists focus on the customer's goals and priorities to prepare a personalized investment portfolio. Ongoing monitoring of financial investments is part of our commitment to help our customers reach their financial objectives. In the midst of today's ever-shifting financial and economic markets, financial planning is more important than ever to ensure retirement security.

"Ongoing monitoring of financial investments is part of our commitment to our customers..."

## Drawing and Formatting a Text Box

Along with inserting predesigned pull quote text boxes, you can draw text boxes in a document using the Text Box button. To draw a text box, click the INSERT tab, click the Text box button, and then click *Draw Text Box* at the drop-down list. Position the mouse pointer, which displays as crosshairs, in the document and then drag to create the text box. You can also just click in the document, which inserts a small text box in the document with the insertion point inside it.

**QUICK STEPS**

**Draw a Text Box**
1. Click INSERT tab.
2. Click Text Box button in Text group.
3. Click *Draw Text Box*.
4. Click or drag in document to create box.

## Exercise 12.2G  Inserting and Formatting Text Boxes        Part 7 of 10

1. With **C12-E02-LelandFS.docx** open, press Ctrl + Home.
2. Create and format the text box shown in Figure 12.6 on page 397. Begin by clicking the INSERT tab.
3. Click the Text Box button in the Text group and then click the *Draw Text Box* option at the drop-down list.
4. Click in the document to the immediate right of the insertion point that displays at the beginning of the document at the left margin. (This inserts a text box in the document.)
5. Type "**Retirement savings need to be a priority rather than an afterthought.**".

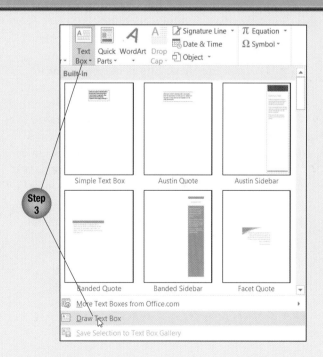

6. Customize the text box and text by completing the following steps:

a. With the DRAWING TOOLS FORMAT tab active, click in the *Shape Height* measurement box and then type **0.6**.

b. Click in the *Shape Width* measurement box, type **2.7**, and then press the Enter key.

c. Click the More button at the right of the style thumbnails in the Shape Styles group and then click the *Colored Fill - Green, Accent 6* option at the drop-down gallery (last column, second row).

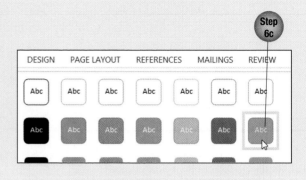

Step 6c

d. Click the Shape Effects button, point to *Shadow*, and then click the *Offset Diagonal Bottom Right* option at the side menu (first option in the *Outer* section).

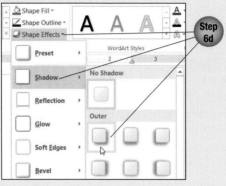

Step 6d

e. Click the Shape Effects button, point to *3-D Rotation*, and then click the *Perspective Below* option at the side menu (last column, first row in the *Perspective* section).

f. Click the Shape Effects button, point to *Bevel*, and then click the *Cool Slant* option (last column, first row in the *Bevel* section).

g. Click the Position button in the Arrange group and then click the *Position in Top Center with Square Text Wrapping* option at the drop-down gallery (second column, first row in the *With Text Wrapping* section).

h. Press Ctrl + E to center the text in the text box.

i. Press Ctrl + B to apply bold formatting to the text in the text box.

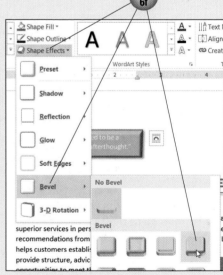

Step 6f

7. Save **C12-E02-LelandFS.docx**.

**Figure 12.6 Exercise 12.2G**

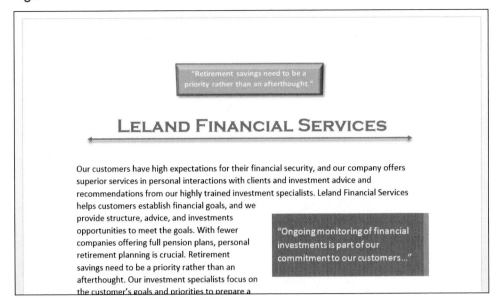

## Inserting a Text Box in a Shape

In addition to typing text directly in a shape, you can draw a text box in a shape, type text in the text box, and then customize the text box and the text with options and buttons on the DRAWING TOOLS FORMAT tab. When you draw a text box in a shape, the text box is actually added as a layer on top of the shape. If you want to move the shape and the text box, select both objects. To select a shape and a text box inside a shape, click the text box, hold down the Shift key, and then click the shape.

**Exercise 12.2H** Inserting and Copying Text Boxes Part 8 of 10

1. With **C12-E02-LelandFS.docx** open, display page 2 (the page containing the three arrows).
2. Insert text boxes in the tips of the arrows as shown in Figure 12.7 on the next page. To begin, insert a text box in the top arrow by completing the following steps:

   a. Click the INSERT tab, click the Text Box button in the Text group, and then click *Draw Text Box* at the drop-down list.
   b. Click in the top arrow. (This inserts a small text box on top of the shape.)
   c. Press Ctrl + E to change the alignment to center and then type **Reliable**.
   d. Click the Text Direction button and then click *Rotate all text 90°* at the drop-down list.
   e. Click in the *Shape Height* measurement box and then type **1.4**.

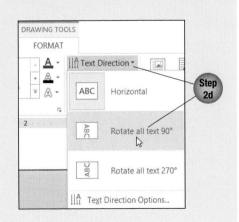

f. Click in the *Shape Width* measurement box, type **0.5**, and then press the Enter key.

g. Click the Shape Fill button arrow in the Shape Styles group and then click *No Fill* at the drop-down gallery.

h. Click the Shape Outline button arrow in the Shape Styles group and then click *No Outline* at the drop-down gallery.

i. Click the border to make it a solid line.

j. Drag the text box so it is positioned in the tip of the arrow. (Refer to Figure 12.7.)

k. Click on any character in the word *Reliable*.

l. Select *Reliable*.

m. Click the HOME tab.

n. Change the font size to 16 points, apply bold formatting, and then change the font color to Green, Accent 6, Darker 50% (last column, last row in the *Theme Colors* section).

o. Click outside the text box.

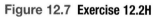

3. Complete steps similar to those in Step 2 to insert the word *Responsible* in the middle arrow *except* click *Rotate all text 270°* in Step 2d.

4. Complete steps similar to those in Step 2 to insert the word *Committed* in the bottom arrow.

5. Save **C12-E02-LelandFS.docx**.

Figure 12.7  Exercise 12.2H

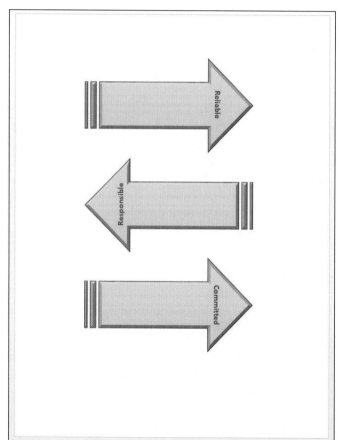

# Linking and Unlinking Text Boxes

You can create several text boxes and then have text flow from one to another by linking the boxes. To do this, draw the desired text boxes and then select the first text box that you want in the link. Click the Create Link button in the Text group on the DRAWING TOOLS FORMAT tab and the mouse pointer displays with a link image attached. Click an empty text box to link it with the selected text box. To break a link between two boxes, select the first text box in the link and then click the Break Link button in the Text group. When you break a link, all of the text is placed in the selected text box.

**QUICK STEPS**

**Link Text Boxes**
1. Select first text box.
2. Click Create Link button.
3. Click empty text box.

Create Link    Break Link

---

1. With **C12-E02-LelandFS.docx** open, press Ctrl + Home to move the insertion point to the beginning of the document.
2. Create the arrows and text boxes as shown in Figure 12.8 on page 402. Begin by drawing and formatting an arrow below the paragraph of text on page 1 by completing the following steps:
   a. Click the INSERT tab.
   b. Click the Shapes button in the Illustrations group and then click the *Notched Right Arrow* option (sixth column, second row in the *Block Arrows* section).
   c. Drag in the document below the paragraph of text to create an arrow that is approximately 4 inches wide and 2 inches tall.
   d. Click the More button at the right of the thumbnails in the Shape Styles group and then click the *Subtle Effect - Green, Accent 6* option (last column, fourth row).

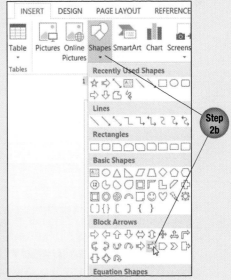

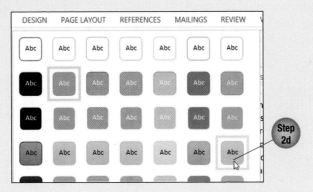

e. Click the Shape Effects button, point to *Bevel*, and then click the *Circle* option (first column, first row in the *Bevel* section).

f. Click in the *Shape Height* measurement box in the Size group and then type **2**.

g. Click in the *Shape Width* measurement box in the Size group, type **4**, and then press the Enter key.

h. Click the Align button in the Arrange group and then click *Distribute Horizontally* at the drop-down list.

3. With the arrow selected, copy it by holding down the Ctrl key, dragging the arrow below the original arrow, and releasing the mouse button and then the Ctrl key.

4. With the bottom arrow selected, click the Rotate button in the Arrange group and then click *Flip Horizontal* at the drop-down list.

5. Make sure both arrows fit on page 1. If not, move the arrows so they are positioned on page 1.

6. Insert a text box inside the top arrow and format the text box by completing the following steps:

a. Click in the top arrow to select it.

b. Click the INSERT tab.

c. Click the Text Box button in the Text group and then click *Draw Text Box* at the drop-down list.

d. Draw a text box on top of the arrow as shown at the right.

7. Format the text box by completing the following steps:

a. Change the height measurement to 0.8 inch and the width measurement to 2 inches.

b. Click the Shape Fill button arrow and then click *No Fill*.

c. Make sure the text box is visually centered in the arrow. (If you need to move the text box, click the text box border so it turns into a solid line and then use the mouse to drag the text box to the desired position.)

8. With the text box selected, copy it to the bottom arrow by holding down the Ctrl key, dragging the text box on top of the bottom arrow, releasing the mouse button, and then releasing the Ctrl key.

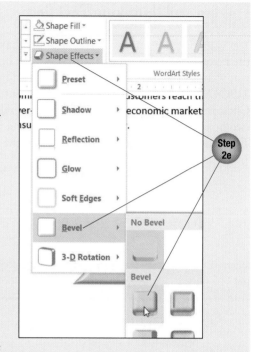

9. Link the text boxes by completing the following steps:
   a. Click in the text box in the top arrow to select it.
   b. Click the Create Link button in the Text group.
   c. Click the text box in the second arrow.

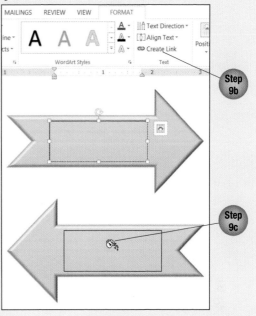

Step 9b

Step 9c

10. With the top text box selected, make the following changes:
    a. Click the HOME tab.
    b. Change the font size to 12 points, change the font color to Green, Accent 6, Darker 50% (last column, bottom row in the *Theme Colors* section), and apply bold formatting.
    c. Click the Center button in the Paragraph group.
    d. Type **Let Leland Financial Services help you plan for retirement and provide you with information to determine your financial direction.**. (The text will flow to the text box in the bottom arrow.)

11. Remove the border around the text boxes by completing the following steps:
    a. Click in the text box in the top arrow.
    b. With the top text box selected, click the DRAWING TOOLS FORMAT tab.
    c. Click the Shape Outline button arrow and then click *No Outline*.
    d. Click the bottom text box.
    e. Click the Shape Outline button arrow and then click *No Outline*.

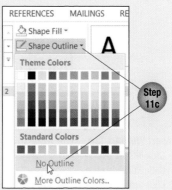

Step 11c

12. Align the shapes and text boxes by completing the following steps:
    a. Click the top arrow to select it.
    b. Hold down the Shift key and click the text box in the top arrow, click the bottom arrow, and then click the text box in the bottom arrow.
    c. Release the mouse button and then the Shift key.
    d. Make sure the DRAWING TOOLS FORMAT tab is active, click the Align button in the Arrange group, and then click the *Align Center* option at the drop-down list.
    e. Click outside the shapes and text boxes to deselect them. (Your arrows and text boxes should appear as shown in Figure 12.8 on the next page.)

13. Save **C12-E02-LelandFS.docx**.

14. Break the link between the text boxes by completing the following steps:
    a. Click in the text in the top arrow. (This inserts a dashed border around the text box.)
    b. Click the DRAWING TOOLS FORMAT tab.
    c. Click the Break Link button in the Text group. (Notice that the text in the bottom arrow disappears. The text is actually part of the text box in the first arrow.)

15. Link the text boxes again by clicking the Create Link button in the Text group, hovering the mouse over the bottom arrow until the pointer displays as a tipping pitcher, and then clicking the left mouse button. (If the mouse pointer is not positioned over the text box in the bottom arrow, the pointer displays as an upright pitcher.)

16. Click in a white portion of the document to deselect the text box and then save **C12-E02-LelandFS.docx**.

**Figure 12.8 Exercise 12.2I**

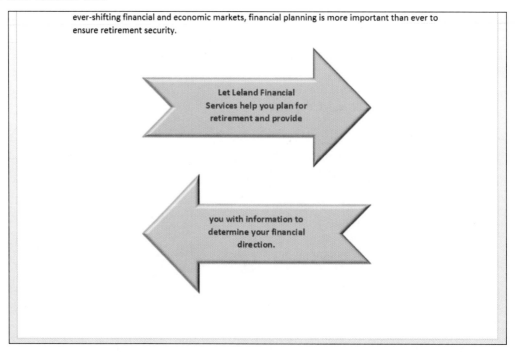

ever-shifting financial and economic markets, financial planning is more important than ever to ensure retirement security.

Let Leland Financial Services help you plan for retirement and provide

you with information to determine your financial direction.

# Inserting WordArt

**Insert WordArt Text**
1. Click INSERT tab.
2. Click WordArt button.
3. Click desired WordArt option at drop-down list.
4. Type desired WordArt text.

WordArt

Use the WordArt feature to distort or modify text to conform to a variety of shapes. This is useful for creating company logos, letterhead, flyer titles, and headings. To insert WordArt in a document, click the INSERT tab and then click the WordArt button in the Text group. This displays the WordArt drop-down list, as shown in Figure 12.9. Select the desired option at the drop-down list and a WordArt text box is inserted in the document containing the words *Your text here* and the DRAWING TOOLS FORMAT

**Figure 12.9 WordArt Drop-down List**

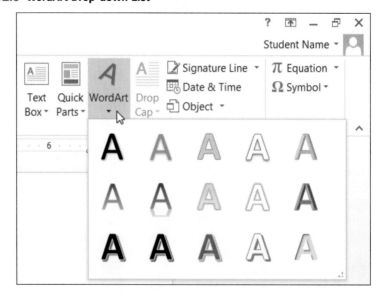

tab is active. Type the desired WordArt text and then format the WordArt with options on the DRAWING TOOLS FORMAT tab. WordArt can also be created by selecting text in a document, clicking the INSERT tab, and then clicking the WordArt button.

## Formatting WordArt Text

Use options in the WordArt Styles group on the DRAWING TOOLS FORMAT tab to apply formatting to the WordArt text. You can apply a predesigned WordArt style, change the WordArt text color or text outline color, and apply a text effect such as Shadow, Reflection, Glow, Bevel, 3-D Rotation, or Transform. Use the *Transform* option to conform the WordArt text to a specific shape. To do this, click the Text Effects button, point to *Transform*, and then click the desired shape at the side menu. Use options in the Arrange group to specify the position, alignment, and rotation of the WordArt text, and specify the size of the WordArt with options in the Size group.

---

**Exercise 12.2**    Inserting and Formatting WordArt      Part 10 of 10

1. With **C12-E02-LelandFS.docx** open, press Ctrl + End to move the insertion point to the end of the document. (The insertion point should be positioned above the shape on page 3.)
2. Type **Leland Financial Services**.
3. Create WordArt with selected text by completing the following steps:
   a. Select *Leland Financial Services*.
   b. Click the INSERT tab.
   c. Click the WordArt button in the Text group and then click the *Fill - Orange, Accent 2, Outline - Accent 2* option (third column, first row).

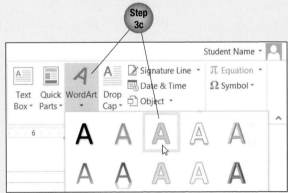

4. Format the WordArt text by completing the following steps:
   a. Click the Text Fill button arrow in the WordArt Styles group on the DRAWING TOOLS FORMAT tab and then click the *Green, Accent 6, Darker 25%* option (last column, fifth row in the *Theme Colors* section).
   b. Click the Text Outline button arrow in the WordArt Styles group and then click the *Green, Accent 6, Lighter 40%* option (last column, fourth row in the *Theme Colors* section).
   c. Click the Text Effects button, point to *Glow*, and then click the *Blue, 5 pt glow, Accent color 1* option (first option in the *Glow Variations* section).

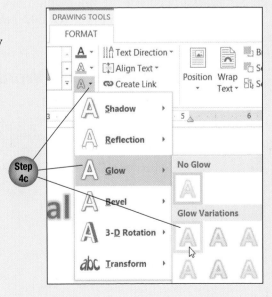

---

d.  Click the Text Effects button, point to *3-D Rotation*, and then click the *Perspective Above* option (first column, second row in the *Perspective* section).

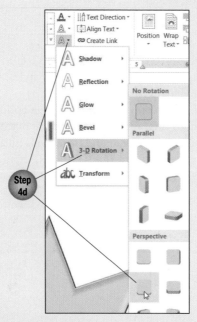

e.  Click in the *Shape Height* measurement box and then type **1**.
f.  Click in the *Shape Width* measurement box, type **6.5**, and then press the Enter key.
g.  Click the Text Effects button, point to *Transform*, scroll down the side menu, and then click the *Deflate* option (second column, sixth row in the *Warp* section).
h.  Make sure the WordArt text box is positioned at the beginning of page 3 between the left and right margins.
i.  Click outside the WordArt text box to deselect it.

5.  Save, print, and then close **C12-E02-LelandFS.docx**.

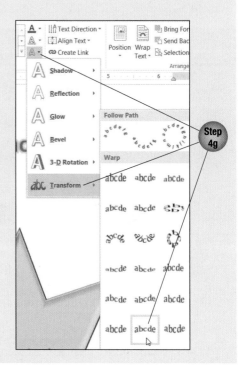

## Formatting the WordArt Text Box

WordArt text is inserted in a text box and the text box can be customized with options in the Shape Styles group on the DRAWING TOOLS FORMAT tab. Use options in this group to apply a predesigned style to the WordArt text box, change the text box fill color and outline color, and apply an effect to the WordArt text box, such as Shadow, Reflection, Glow, Soft Edges, Bevel, and 3-D Rotation.

1. Open **Hawaii.docx** and then save the document and name it **C12-E03-Hawaii**.
2. Create and customize the WordArt text shown in Figure 12.10 on the next page. Begin by clicking the INSERT tab.
3. Click the WordArt button in the Text group and then click the *Fill - Blue, Accent 1, Outline - Background 1, Hard Shadow - Accent 1* option (third column, bottom row).

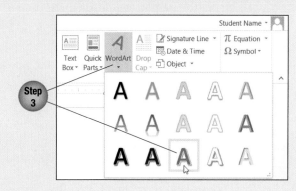

4. Type **HAWAII**.
5. Click the outside border of the WordArt text box so the border displays as a solid line.
6. Click the More button at the right of the thumbnails in the Shape Styles group and then click the *Subtle Effect - Blue, Accent 1* option (second column, fourth row).
7. Click the Text Fill button arrow and then click the Blue option (eighth color in the *Standard Colors* section).

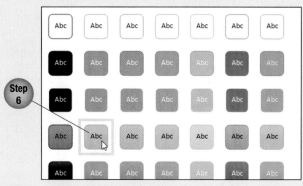

8. Click the Text Outline button arrow and then click the Dark Blue option (ninth color in the *Standard Colors* section).
9. Click the Shape Effects button, point to *Glow*, and then click the *Blue, 8 pt glow, Accent color 1* option (first column, second row in the *Glow Variations* section).
10. Click the Shape Effects button, point to *Bevel*, and then click the *Riblet* option (second column, third row in the *Bevel* section).

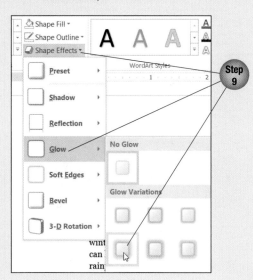

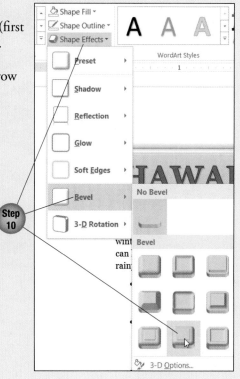

11. Click the Wrap Text button and then click *Tight* at the drop-down list.
12. Click the Rotate button and then click *Rotate Left 90°* at the drop-down list.
13. Click in the *Shape Height* measurement box and then type **1.3**.
14. Click in the *Shape Width* measurement box, type **7**, and then press Enter.
15. Click the Text Effects button, point to *Transform*, and then click the *Square* option (first option in the *Warp* section).
16. Using the mouse, drag the WordArt so it is positioned as shown in Figure 12.10.
17. Save, print, and then close **C12-E03-Hawaii.docx**.

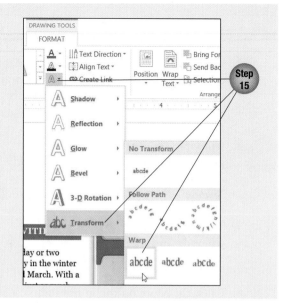

**Figure 12.10  Exercise 12.3**

**RAINY DAY ACTIVITIES**

Expect to have a rainy day or two during your vacation, especially in the winter months between November and March. With a little planning, you can have just as much fun indoors as outdoors. To make the most of a rainy day, enjoy one of the activities listed below.

- Movies: Take advantage of matinee prices. The Sunshine Marketplace Theaters offer discount tickets and current feature films.
- Shopping: Most of the area shopping centers are "open-air" complexes with some roof covering, ideal havens from the rain. Visit the Coconut Grove Shopping Center or the Kukui Shopping Village.
- Museums: Learn about the history of Hawaii through murals, artifacts, and artwork by visiting one of several museums located throughout the islands. Most museums offer special family activities the first Saturday of each month.
- Theater: Several local community performing arts centers offer annual productions for children and adults. Admission prices are very affordable, and most theaters have special matinee prices.

**KAUAI SIGHTS**

- Na Pali Coast: Unless you are a rugged hiker, you can see this fifteen-mile, spectacular landmark only by air or boat.
- North Shore: Find shadowy mountains, lush valleys, and spectacular coastlines along a string of one-lane bridges.
- Hanalei Valley Lookout: Pull over to see wetland taro fields with a backdrop of purple mountains.
- Kilauea Point: This National Wildlife Refuge is home to nesting seabirds and an original lighthouse.
- Sleeping Giant: Nounou Mountain provides the "man in repose" profile best seen from Kuhio Highway 56 in Kapaa.
- Coconut Coast: You will know when you are here because palm trees line Kuhio Highway 56 on the island's east side.

# Applying Character Formatting

With the WordArt feature, you format text to improve its appearance. You can also format text to improve its appearance by applying a specific font and choosing font options at the Font dialog box with the Advanced tab selected. At this dialog box, specify character spacing for text, apply OpenType features, and apply text effects to selected text.

## Adjusting Character Spacing

Each typeface is designed with a specific amount of space between characters. This character spacing can be changed with options in the *Character Spacing* section of the Font dialog box with the Advanced tab selected, as shown in Figure 12.11. Display this dialog box by clicking the Font group dialog box launcher on the HOME tab and then clicking the Advanced tab at the dialog box.

**Figure 12.11 Font Dialog Box with Advanced Tab Selected**

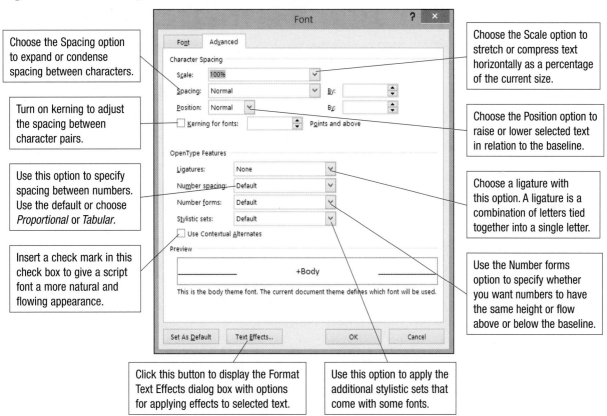

Choose the Spacing option to expand or condense spacing between characters.

Turn on kerning to adjust the spacing between character pairs.

Use this option to specify spacing between numbers. Use the default or choose *Proportional* or *Tabular*.

Insert a check mark in this check box to give a script font a more natural and flowing appearance.

Choose the Scale option to stretch or compress text horizontally as a percentage of the current size.

Choose the Position option to raise or lower selected text in relation to the baseline.

Choose a ligature with this option. A ligature is a combination of letters tied together into a single letter.

Use the Number forms option to specify whether you want numbers to have the same height or flow above or below the baseline.

Click this button to display the Format Text Effects dialog box with options for applying effects to selected text.

Use this option to apply the additional stylistic sets that come with some fonts.

Choose the *Scale* option to stretch or compress text horizontally as a percentage of the current size. You can choose a percentage from 1 to 600. Expand or condense the spacing between characters with the *Spacing* option. Choose the *Expanded* or *Condensed* option and then enter the desired point size in the *By* text box. Raise or lower selected text in relation to the baseline with the *Position* option. Choose the *Raised* or *Lowered* option and then enter the point size in the *By* text box.

Insert a check mark in the *Kerning* check box to apply kerning to selected text in a document. **Kerning** refers to the adjustment of spacing between certain character combinations by positioning two characters closer together than normal and uses the shapes and slopes of the characters to improve their appearance. Kerning allows more text to be fit in a specific amount of space and also looks more natural and helps the eye move along the text. Consider kerning text set in larger font sizes, such as 14 points and higher, and text set in italics. Figure 12.12 displays text with and without kerning applied. Notice how the letters *Te* and *Va* are closer together in the kerned text compared to the text that is not kerned.

Turn on automatic kerning by displaying the font dialog box with the Advanced tab selected and then inserting a check mark in the *Kerning for fonts* check box. Specify the beginning point size that you want kerned in the *Points and above* measurement box.

**Figure 12.12  Text with and without Kerning Applied**

# Tennison Valley (not kerned)
# Tennison Valley (kerned)

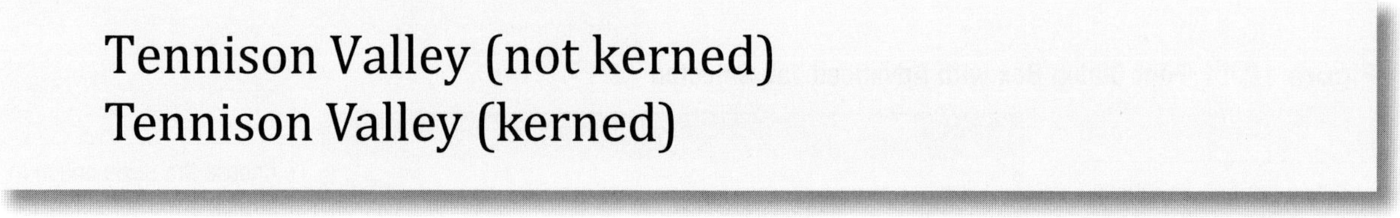

**Exercise 12.4A    Adjusting Character Spacing and Kerning Text**                    Part 1 of 4

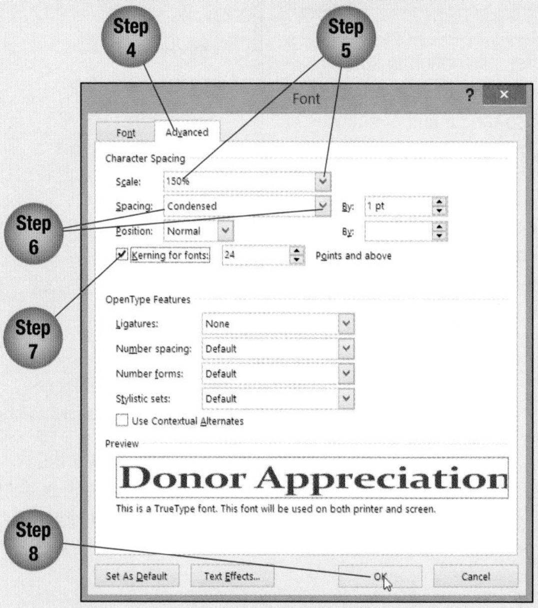

1. Open **PRDonorApp.docx** and then save the document with Save As and name it **C12-E04-PRDonorApp**.
2. Select the title *Donor Appreciation*.
3. With the HOME tab active, click the Font group dialog box launcher.
4. At the Font dialog box, click the Advanced tab.
5. Click the down-pointing arrow at the right of the *Scale* option box and then click *150%* at the drop-down list.
6. Click the down-pointing arrow at the right of the *Spacing* option box and then click *Condensed* at the drop-down list.
7. Click the *Kerning for fonts* check box to insert a check mark.
8. Click OK to close the dialog box.
9. Select the text *Enjoy the "flavor of Tanzania" and an evening of cultural entertainment...*
10. Click the Font group dialog box launcher to display the Font dialog box with the Advanced tab selected.
11. Click the *Kerning for fonts* check box to insert a check mark and then click OK to close the dialog box.
12. Save **C12-E04-PRDonorApp.docx**.

Step 4
Step 5
Step 6
Step 7
Step 8

Font

Font    Advanced

Character Spacing

Scale:       150%
Spacing:   Condensed        By:  1 pt
Position:   Normal           By:
☑ Kerning for fonts:  24    Points and above

OpenType Features

Ligatures:        None
Number spacing:  Default
Number forms:    Default
Stylistic sets:    Default
☐ Use Contextual Alternates

Preview

**Donor Appreciation**

This is a TrueType font. This font will be used on both printer and screen.

Set As Default    Text Effects...    OK    Cancel

## Using OpenType Features

The OpenType font file format was developed by Adobe and Microsoft to work on both Macintosh and Windows computers. The benefits of the OpenType format are cross-platform compatibility, which means you can move font files between Macintosh and Windows computers; the ability to support expanded character sets and layout figures; and the capability for Web page designers to create high-quality on-screen fonts for online documents.

Microsoft Word offers some advanced OpenType features in the Font dialog box with the Advanced tab selected (see Figure 12.11 on page 407) that desktop publishers and web and graphic designers can use to enhance the appearance of text. At the Font dialog box with the Advanced tab selected, *Ligatures* is the first option in the *OpenType Features* section. A **ligature** is a combination of characters joined into a single letter. The OpenType standard specifies four categories of ligatures: *Standard Only, Standard and Contextual, Historical and Discretionary*, and *All*. The font designer decides which category to support and in which group to put combinations of characters.

With the *Standard Only* option selected, the standard set of ligatures that most typographers and font designers determine are appropriate for the font are applied to text. Common ligatures include letter combinations with the letter *f*, as shown in Figure 12.13. Notice how the *fi* and *fl* letter combinations are combined when ligatures are applied.

**Figure 12.13  Ligature Combination Examples**

final flavor (not using ligatures)
final flavor (using ligatures)

With the other ligature options, you can specify *Contextual* ligatures, which are ligatures that the font designer believes are appropriate for use with the font but are not standard. Choose the option *Historical and Discretionary* to apply ligatures that were once standard but are no longer commonly used; you can use them to create a historical or "period" effect. You can also choose the *All* ligatures option, which applies all of the ligature combinations to selected text. Another method for applying ligatures is to click the Text Effects and Typography button in the Font group, point to *Ligatures* at the drop-down gallery, and then click an option at the side menu.

Text Effects
and Typography

The *Number spacing* option in the *OpenType Features* section is set at *Default*, which means the spacing between numbers is determined by the font designer. You can choose *Proportional*, which adjusts the spacing for numbers with varying widths. Three Microsoft fonts—Candara, Constantial, and Corbel—use proportional number spacing by default. Use the *Tabular* option if you want to specify that each number is the same width. This is useful in a situation in which the numbers are set in columns and you want all of the numbers to align vertically. The Cambria, Calibri, and Consolas fonts use tabular spacing by default.

Like the *Number spacing* option, the *Number forms* option is set at *Default*, which means the font designer determines the number form. Change this option to *Lining* if you want all of the numbers to be the same height and not extend below the baseline of the text. Generally, lining numbers are used in tables and forms because they are easier to read. The Cambria, Calibri, and Consolas fonts use lining number forms by default. With the

*Old-style* option, the lines of the numbers can flow above or below the baseline of the text. For some fonts, changing the *Number forms* option to *Old-style* results in numbers such as *3* and *5* extending below the baseline or being centered higher on the line. Three fonts that use *Old-style* number forms include Candara, Constantia, and Corbel. The *Number Styles* option at the Text Effects and Typography button drop-down gallery combines number spacing and number forms options and displays the combined options in a side menu. Display the side menu by hovering the mouse pointer over the *Number Styles* option.

## Exercise 12.4B  Applying a Ligature and Number Form    Part 2 of 4

1. With **C12-E04-PRDonorApp.docx** open, select the text *Enjoy the "flavor of Tanzania" and an evening of cultural entertainment....*
2. Click the Font group dialog box launcher. (If necessary, click the Advanced tab.)
3. At the Font dialog box with the Advanced tab selected, click the down-pointing arrow at the right of the *Ligatures* option box and then click *Standard and Contextual* at the drop-down list.
4. Click OK to close the dialog box.
5. Select the text *2016 – 2017* and *$3,500,000*.
6. Click the Text Effects and Typography button in the Font group, point to *Number Styles* at the drop-down gallery, and then click *Tabular Old-style* at the side menu.
7. Save **C12-E04-PRDonorApp.docx**.

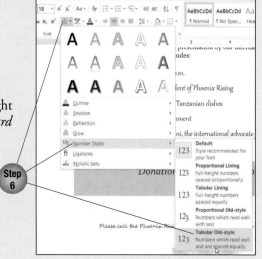

A font designer may include a number of stylistic sets for a specific font. A different stylistic set may apply additional formatting to the characters in a font. For example, the sentences in Figure 12.14 are set in 16-point Gabriola. Notice the slight variations in characters in some of the stylistic sets. Choose a stylistic set and see a visual representation of the characters with the stylistic set applied in the *Preview* section of the dialog box. You can also choose a stylistic set by clicking the Text Effects and Typography button in the Font group, pointing to *Stylistic Sets* at the drop-down gallery, and then clicking the desired stylistic set at the side menu.

**Figure 12.14  Examples of Gabriola Font Stylistic Sets**

Typography refers to the appearance of printed characters on the page. (Default set)

Typography refers to the appearance of printed characters on the page. (Stylistic set 4)

Typography refers to the appearance of printed characters on the page. (Stylistic set 5)

Typography refers to the appearance of printed characters on the page. (Stylistic set 6)

Insert a check mark in the *Use Contextual Alternates* option in the Font dialog box with the Advanced tab selected to fine-tune letter combinations based on the surrounding characters. Use this feature to give script fonts a more natural and flowing appearance. Figure 12.15 shows text set in 12-point Segoe Script. The first line of text is set with the default setting and the second line of text is set with the *Use Contextual Alternates* option selected. Notice the slight differences in letters such as *t*, *n*, *s*, and *h*.

**Figure 12.15 Examples of Segoe Script Font with and without *Use Contextual Alternates* Selected**

A font designer determines the appearance of each character in a font.

A font designer determines the appearance of each character in a font.

Not all fonts contain ligature combinations, number spacing and forms, stylistic sets, or contextual alternates. Experiment with fonts using the options in the Font dialog box with the Advanced tab selected to select the font and font options for your document.

## Exercise 12.4C  Applying a Stylistic Set and Using Contextual Alternates  Part 3 of 4

1. With **C12-E04-PRDonorApp.docx** open, select the bulleted text.
2. Display the Font dialog box with the Advanced tab selected.
3. Click the down-pointing arrow at the right of the *Stylistic sets* option box and then click *4* at the drop-down list.
4. Click OK to close the dialog box.
5. Select the text *Please call the Phoenix Rising office to let us know if you will be joining us.*
6. Display the Font dialog box with the Advanced tab selected.
7. Click the *Use Contextual Alternates* check box to insert a check mark.
8. Click OK to close the Font dialog box.
9. Save **C12-E04-PRDonorApp.docx**.

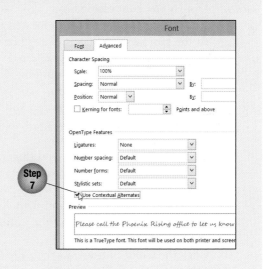

## Applying Text Effects

When you click the Text Effects button that displays at the bottom of the Font dialog box with the Advanced tab selected, the Format Text Effects dialog box displays with the Text Fill & Outline icon selected, as shown in Figure 12.16 on the next page. Click *TEXT FILL* or *TEXT OUTLINE* to display the text formatting options. Click the Text Effects icon to display additional effects formatting options. Many of the options available at the dialog box also are available by clicking the Text Effects and Typography button in the Font group on the HOME tab.

**Figure 12.16 Format Text Effects Dialog Box**

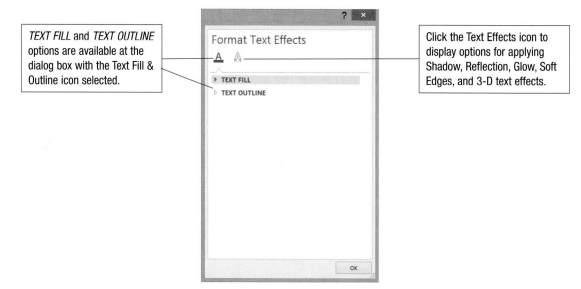

TEXT FILL and TEXT OUTLINE options are available at the dialog box with the Text Fill & Outline icon selected.

Click the Text Effects icon to display options for applying Shadow, Reflection, Glow, Soft Edges, and 3-D text effects.

## Exercise 12.4D  Applying Text Effects

Part 4 of 4

1. With **C12-E04-PRDonorApp.docx** open, select the title *Donor Appreciation*.
2. Display the Font dialog box.
3. Click the Text Effects button located near the bottom of the dialog box.
4. At the Format Text Effects dialog box with the Text Fill & Outline icon selected, click *TEXT FILL* to expand the options.
5. Click the *Gradient fill* option.
6. Click the Preset gradients button and then click the *Medium Gradient - Accent 6* option (last column, third row).
7. Click the Direction button and then click the *Linear Down* option (second column, first row).
8. Scroll down the task pane and then click *TEXT OUTLINE* to expand the options.
9. Click the *Solid line* option.
10. Click the Color button and then click the *Orange, Accent 6, Darker 50%* option (last option in the *Theme Colors* section).
11. Click the Text Effects icon.
12. Click *SHADOW* to expand the options.
13. Click the Presets button and then click the *Offset Left* option (last column, second row in the *Outer* section).
14. Click *GLOW* to expand the options.
15. Click the Presets button in the *GLOW* section and then click the *Orange, 5 pt glow, Accent color 6* option (last column, first row in the *Glow Variations* section).
16. Click OK to close the Format Text Effects dialog box.
17. Click OK to close the Font dialog box and then deselect the title.
18. Save, print, and then close **C12-E04-PRDonorApp.docx**.

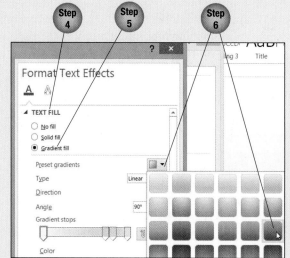

# Chapter *Summary*

- ➤ Use the Screenshot button in the Illustrations group on the INSERT tab to capture all or part of the contents of a screen.
- ➤ Use buttons on the PICTURE TOOLS FORMAT tab to customize a screenshot image.
- ➤ Draw shapes in a document by clicking the Shapes button in the Illustrations group on the INSERT tab, clicking the desired shape at the drop-down list, and then clicking or dragging in the document to draw the shape.
- ➤ Draw lines or enclosed shapes with options at the Shapes button drop-down list.
- ➤ When drawing a line, hold down the Shift key to draw a straight horizontal or vertical line. When drawing an enclosed shape, maintain the proportions of the shape by holding down the Shift key while dragging in the document to create the shape.
- ➤ Copy a shape by holding down the Ctrl key while dragging the selected shape.
- ➤ Customize a shape with options on the DRAWING TOOLS FORMAT tab.
- ➤ Select multiple shapes by holding down the Shift key or Ctrl key while clicking each desired shape.
- ➤ Use the Align button in the Arrange group on the DRAWING TOOLS FORMAT tab to align multiple shapes in a document.
- ➤ Insert text in a shape by clicking in the shape and then typing the desired text.
- ➤ Change the shape of a selected shape by clicking the Edit Shape button on the DRAWING TOOLS FORMAT tab, pointing to the *Change Shape* option, and then clicking the desired shape at the side menu.
- ➤ Modify a shape by dragging the edit points. Display the edit points by clicking the Edit Shape button on the DRAWING TOOLS FORMAT tab and then clicking *Edit Points* at the drop-down list.
- ➤ Insert a pull quote in a document with a predesigned text box by clicking the INSERT tab, clicking the Text Box button, and then clicking the desired text box at the drop-down list.
- ➤ Format a pull quote text box with options on the DRAWING TOOLS FORMAT tab.
- ➤ Draw a text box by clicking the Text Box button in the Text group on the INSERT tab, clicking *Draw Text Box* at the drop-down list, and then clicking or dragging in the document.
- ➤ Format and customize a text box with buttons on the DRAWING TOOLS FORMAT tab.
- ➤ Link text boxes you have drawn with the Create Link button in the Text group on the DRAWING TOOLS FORMAT tab. Break a link with the Break Link button in the Text group.
- ➤ Use WordArt to distort or modify text to conform to a variety of shapes.
- ➤ Insert WordArt text by clicking the INSERT tab, clicking the WordArt button in the Text group, and then clicking the desired WordArt option at the drop-down list.
- ➤ Customize WordArt with options on the DRAWING TOOLS FORMAT tab.
- ➤ Use options in the *Character Spacing* section of the Font dialog box with the Advanced tab selected to adjust character spacing and turn on kerning.
- ➤ The *OpenType Features* section of the Font dialog box with the Advanced tab selected includes options for choosing a ligature style, specifying number spacing and form, and applying stylistic sets.
- ➤ The Text Effects and Typography button in the Font group on the HOME tab contains options for applying number styles, ligatures, and stylistic sets.
- ➤ Click the Text Effects button at the Font dialog box to display the Format Text Effects dialog box. Use options at this dialog box to apply text effects to selected text.

# Commands *Review*

| FEATURE | RIBBON TAB, GROUP | BUTTON, OPTION |
|---------|-------------------|----------------|
| break text box link | DRAWING TOOLS FORMAT, Text | |
| create text box link | DRAWING TOOLS FORMAT, Text | |
| draw text box | INSERT, Text | , *Draw Text Box* |
| edit shape | DRAWING TOOLS FORMAT, Insert Shapes | |
| Font dialog box | HOME, Font | |
| predesigned text box | INSERT, Text | |
| screenshot | INSERT, Illustrations | |
| shapes | INSERT, Illustrations | |
| Text Effects and Typography button | HOME, Font | |
| WordArt | INSERT, Text | |

# Key Points *Review*

**Completion:** In the space provided at the right, indicate the correct term, symbol, or command.

1. To capture a portion of a screen, click the Screenshot button in the Illustrations group on the INSERT tab and then click this option at the drop-down list. _____

2. The Shapes button is located on this tab. _____

3. To draw a straight horizontal or vertical line, hold down this key while dragging in the document. _____

4. To copy a selected shape, hold down this key while dragging the shape. _____

5. Select multiple shapes by holding down the Ctrl key or this key while clicking the shapes. _____

6. The Align button is located in this group on the DRAWING TOOLS FORMAT tab. _____

7. Change the shape of a selected shape by clicking this button on the DRAWING TOOLS FORMAT tab, pointing to *Change Shape*, and then clicking the desired shape at the side menu. _____

8. Modify a shape by dragging these points. _____

9. Display available predesigned pull quote text boxes by clicking the INSERT tab and then clicking this button in the Text group. _____

10. Format a pull quote text box with options on this tab. _____

11. Link text boxes with this button in the Text group on the DRAWING TOOLS FORMAT tab. _____

12. The WordArt button is located in this group on the INSERT tab. _____

13. Turn on kerning with the *Kerning for fonts* check box located in this section of the Font dialog box with the Advanced tab selected. _____

14. This term refers to a combination of characters joined into a single letter. _____

15. Use this option at the Font dialog box with the Advanced tab selected to specify if numbers should be the same height or extend above or below the baseline. _____

16. Click this button at the Font dialog box to display the Format Text Effects dialog box. _____

# Chapter *Assessments*

## Applying Your Skills

Demonstrate your knowledge of features learned in this chapter by completing the following assessments.

### Assessment 12.1    Create a Screenshot

1. Open **CruiseShip01.docx** and then open **ImagesMemo.docx**.
2. Type your instructor's name after the *TO:* heading, type your name after the *FROM:* heading, and type the current date after the *DATE:* heading.
3. With **ImagesMemo.docx** the active document, move the insertion point to the end of the document and then create and insert a screenshot screen clipping of the cruise ship image in **CruiseShip01.docx**.
4. Change the text wrapping of the screenshot screen clipping image to Tight, change the height of the image to 2.3 inches, and then deselect the image.
5. Make **CruiseShip01.docx** the active document and then close the document.
6. Open **CruiseShip02.docx** and then make **ImagesMemo.docx** the active document.
7. Create and then insert a screenshot screen clipping of the cruise ship image in **CruiseShip02.docx**.
8. Change the text wrapping of the screenshot screen clipping image to Tight, change the height of the image to 2.3 inches, and then deselect the image. (Move the two images so they display side by side in the memo.)
9. Press the Enter key approximately eight times to move the insertion point below the screenshot image, **type your two initials**, press Shift + Enter, and then type **C12-A01-ImagesMemo.docx**.
10. Save the document with Save As and name it **C12-A01-ImagesMemo**.
11. Print and then close **C12-A01-ImagesMemo.docx**.
12. Close **CruiseShip02.docx**.

### Assessment 12.2    Create a Letterhead with Text and a Drawn Line

1. At a blank document, type the text **Blue Water Charters**, as shown in Figure 12.17 on the next page, with the following specifications:
   a. Change the font to 56-point Freestyle Script bold and the font color to Blue. (To change the font size to 56 points, you will need to select the current point size in the Font Size text box and then type **56**.)
   b. Center the text.

START From Scratch

2. Select the text *Blue Water Charters*, display the Format Text Effects dialog box (by clicking the Text Effects button at the Font dialog box), and then apply the following effects:
   a. Click *TEXT FILL* to expand the options, click the *Gradient fill* option, click the Preset gradients button, and then click the *Medium Gradient - Accent 1* option (first column, third row).
   b. Scroll down the dialog box and then click *TEXT OUTLINE* to expand the options.
   c. Click the *Solid line* option, click the Color button, and then click the *Dark Blue* option (ninth option in the *Standard Colors* section).
   d. Click the Text Effects icon.
   e. Click *SHADOW* to expand the options, click the Presets button, and then click the *Offset Diagonal Bottom Right* option (first option in the *Outer* section).
   f. Click *3-D FORMAT* to expand the options, click the Top bevel button, and then click the *Circle* option (first option in the *Bevel* section).
   g. Close both dialog boxes.
3. Draw the line below the text with the *Line* option at the *Shapes* drop-down list and then apply the following formatting:
   a. Apply the Intense Line - Accent 1 shape style.
   b. Change the shape outline color to Blue.
   c. Apply the Offset Bottom shadow effect.
4. Save the document with the name **C12-A02-BWC**.
5. Print and then close **C12-A02-BWC.docx**.

**Figure 12.17  Assessment 12.2**

## Assessment 12.3    Create an Announcement with a Shape and Text Box

1. At a blank document, create the shape shown in Figure 12.18 on the next page with the following specifications:
   a. Use the Bevel shape (located in the *Basic Shapes* section of the drop-down list).
   b. Change the height to 3.3 inches and the width to 5.7 inches.
   c. Apply the Subtle Effect - Gold, Accent 4 shape style.
   d. Apply the Offset Diagonal Top Right shadow effect.
   e. Apply the Orange, 8 pt glow, Accent color 2 glow effect.
   f. Change the position of the text box to Position in Top Center with Square Text Wrapping. ***Hint: Use the Position button in the Arrange group.***
2. Type the text inside the shape as shown in Figure 12.18. After typing the text, select it and then change the font to 36-point Monotype Corsiva bold and the color to Orange, Accent 2, Darker 50%.
3. Save the document and name it **C12-A03-EmpofMonth**.
4. Print and then close **C12-A03-EmpofMonth.docx**.

**Figure 12.18  Assessment 12.3**

## Assessment 12.4    Insert a Pull Quote Text Box and WordArt in a Document

1. Open **SoftwareCycle.docx** and save the document with the name **C12-A04-SoftwareCycle**.
2. Position the insertion point at the beginning of the first paragraph of text, insert the Sideline Quote predesigned text box in the document, and then type the following text in the text box: **"The commercial software life cycle is repeated every time a new version of a program is needed."**
3. With the DRAWING TOOLS FORMAT tab active, change the shape width to 2.6 inches.
4. Change the position of the text box to Position in Middle Left with Square Text Wrapping.
5. Select the title *COMMERCIAL LIFE CYCLE* and then create WordArt with the text with the following specifications (see Figure 12.19):
   a. Use the Fill - Black, Text 1, Outline - Background 1, Hard Shadow - Accent 1 WordArt style (second column, last row).
   b. Apply the Blue text fill color (eighth color option in the *Standard Colors* section).
   c. Use the Text Effects button in the WordArt Styles group to apply the Green, 5 pt glow, Accent color 6 glow text effect (last column, first row in the *Glow Variations* section).
   d. Use the Text Effects button in the WordArt Styles group to apply the Perspective Below 3-D rotation text effect (last column, first row in the *Perspective* section).
   e. Change the height to 1 inch and the width to 6.5 inches.
   f. Apply the Inflate Top transform text effect (first column, seventh row in the *Warp* section).
6. Save, print, and then close **C12-A04-SoftwareCycle.docx**.

**Figure 12.19  Assessment 12.6**

## Assessment 12.5    Create a Flyer with Shapes and a Text Box

1. At a blank document, create the left circular arrow shown in Figure 12.20 with the following specifications:
   a. Draw the shape using the Curved Right Arrow shape (located in the *Block Arrows* section of the drop-down list).
   b. Change the height of the arrow to 4.8 inches and the width to 3 inches.
   c. Apply the Moderate Effect - Orange, Accent 2 shape style.
   d. Change the shape outline color to Dark Blue.
2. Copy the arrow shape to the right and then flip the arrow horizontally and vertically.
3. Change the alignment of the left arrow to Align Left and change the alignment of the right arrow to Align Right. ***Hint: Use options at the Align button drop-down list.***
4. Select only the right arrow and then move it up slightly so it is positioned as shown in Figure 12.20.
5. Draw a text box between the arrows that is 1.3 inches tall and 4 inches wide and then change the shape outline to No Outline.
6. Type the text inside the text box with the following specifications:
   a. Change the paragraph alignment to Center.
   b. Change the font to 28-point Franklin Gothic Heavy and the font color to Dark Blue.
7. Drag the text box so the text is positioned between the arrows, as shown in Figure 12.20.
8. Save the document and name it **C12-A05-TeamBuildFlyer**.
9. Print and then close **C12-A05-TeamBuildFlyer.docx**.

**Figure 12.20  Assessment 12.5**

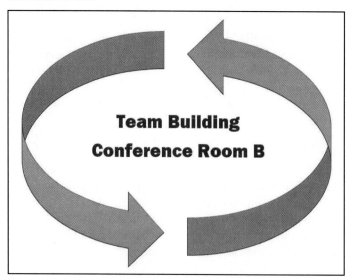

## Assessment 12.6    Apply Character Spacing and OpenType Features

1. Open **PRDonations.docx** and then save the document and name it **C12-A06-PRDonations**.
2. Select the quote text *"In every community there is work to be done. In every nation there are wounds to heal. In every heart there is the power to do it."* and then change the stylistic set to 4. (Do this at the Font dialog box with the Advanced tab selected.)
3. Select the heading *Domestic Donations*, change the scale to 90%, and change the spacing to Expanded. (Do this at the Font dialog box with the Advanced tab selected.)
4. Apply the same formatting in Step 3 to the heading *International Donations*.

5. Select the numbers in the *Domestic Donations* section. **Hint: To select only the numbers, position the mouse pointer at the beginning of $450,000, hold down the Alt key, and then use the mouse to drag and select the four numbers in the second column.** With the numbers selected, change the number spacing to Tabular. (Do this at the Font dialog box with the Advanced tab selected.)
6. Select the numbers in the *International Donations* section and then change the number spacing to Tabular.
7. Select the text *We are dedicated to working toward a more just and peaceful world.* and then insert a check mark in the *Use Contextual Alternates* check box at the Font dialog box with the Advanced tab selected.
8. Save, print, and then close **C12-A06-PRDonations.docx**.

# Expanding Your Skills

Explore additional feature options or use Help to learn a new skill in creating these documents.

## Assessment 12.7    Edit a Drawn Line

1. Open **C12-A02-BWC.docx** and save the document with the name **C12-A07-BWC**.
2. Click the horizontal line to select it, click the DRAWING TOOLS FORMAT tab, and then click the Shape Styles group task pane launcher. This displays the Format Shape task pane with additional options for customizing the shape.
3. Look at the options in the Format Shape task pane with the Fill & Line icon selected. If necessary, click *LINE* to expand the options. Use options in the Format Shape task pane to change the line color to Blue, Accent 1, Lighter 40% (fifth column, fourth row in the *Theme Colors* section), change the line width to 4 points, and change the beginning arrow type and ending arrow type to Diamond Arrow. **Hint: Do this with the Begin Arrow type and End Arrow type buttons in the task pane.**
4. Click the Effects icon and then click *GLOW* to expand the options. Click the Color button and then click the *Dark Blue* color in the *Standard Colors* section. Change the size to 3 point and then close the task pane.
5. Save, print, and then close **C12-A07-BWC.docx**.

## Assessment 12.8    Format and Insert WordArt Text in a Travel Document

1. Open **CedarMeadows.docx** and then save the document with the name **C12-A08-CedarMeadows**.
2. Select the paragraphs of text below the *Fast Facts* heading and then apply bulleted list formatting.
3. Change the left and right margins to 1.5 inches.
4. Insert the WordArt text, as shown in Figure 12.21 on the next page, using the Gradient Fill - Blue, Accent 1, Reflection WordArt style.
5. Click the WordArt text box border to make it a solid line and then click the WordArt Styles group task pane launcher. Explore the options available at the task pane with each icon selected. After exploring the options in the task pane, make the following changes:
   a. Click the Text Fill & Outline icon, click *TEXT FILL* to expand the options, and then change the gradient fill direction to Linear Up. **Hint: Use the Direction button.**
   b. Click the Text Effects icon, click *SHADOW* to expand the options, and then apply the Offset Diagonal Top Left shadow effect. **Hint: Use the Presets button.** Change the shadow color to Blue (in the *Standard Colors* section).
   c. Click *REFLECTION* to expand the options and then apply the *Tight Reflection, touching* reflection. **Hint: Use the Presets button.**
   d. Click *3-D FORMAT* to expand the options and then apply the Slope bevel format. **Hint: Use the Top bevel button.**
   e. Close the task pane.

6. With the WordArt text box selected (solid line), make the following changes:
   a. Change the height to 1 inch and the width to 5.5 inches.
   b. Change the position to Position in Top Center with Square Text Wrapping.
   c. Apply the Square transform text effect.
7. Save, print, and then close **C12-A08-CedarMeadows.docx**.

**Figure 12.21  Assessment 12.8**

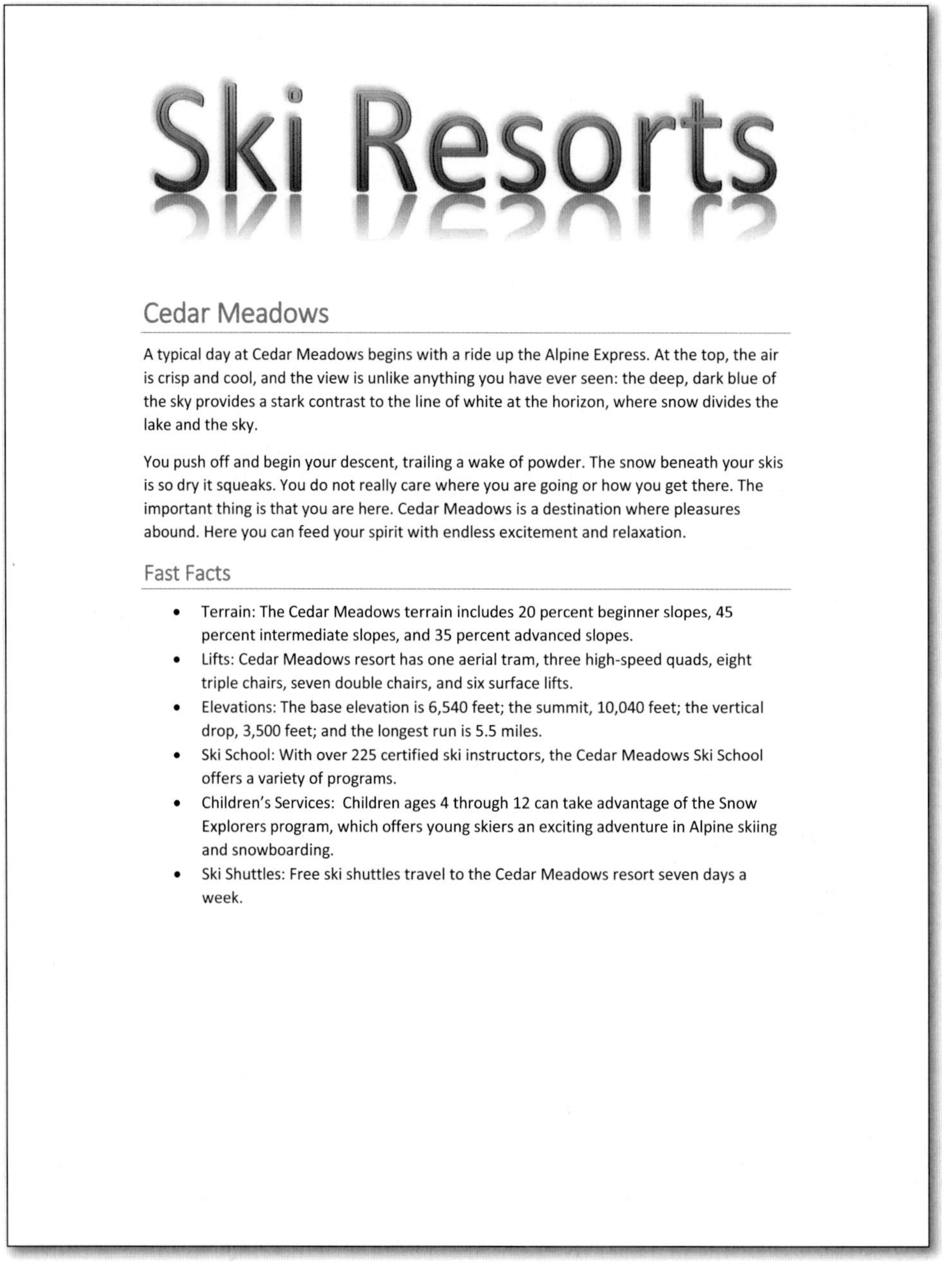

## Ski Resorts

### Cedar Meadows

A typical day at Cedar Meadows begins with a ride up the Alpine Express. At the top, the air is crisp and cool, and the view is unlike anything you have ever seen: the deep, dark blue of the sky provides a stark contrast to the line of white at the horizon, where snow divides the lake and the sky.

You push off and begin your descent, trailing a wake of powder. The snow beneath your skis is so dry it squeaks. You do not really care where you are going or how you get there. The important thing is that you are here. Cedar Meadows is a destination where pleasures abound. Here you can feed your spirit with endless excitement and relaxation.

### Fast Facts

- Terrain: The Cedar Meadows terrain includes 20 percent beginner slopes, 45 percent intermediate slopes, and 35 percent advanced slopes.
- Lifts: Cedar Meadows resort has one aerial tram, three high-speed quads, eight triple chairs, seven double chairs, and six surface lifts.
- Elevations: The base elevation is 6,540 feet; the summit, 10,040 feet; the vertical drop, 3,500 feet; and the longest run is 5.5 miles.
- Ski School: With over 225 certified ski instructors, the Cedar Meadows Ski School offers a variety of programs.
- Children's Services:  Children ages 4 through 12 can take advantage of the Snow Explorers program, which offers young skiers an exciting adventure in Alpine skiing and snowboarding.
- Ski Shuttles: Free ski shuttles travel to the Cedar Meadows resort seven days a week.

# Achieving Signature Status

Take your skills to the next level by completing these more challenging assessments.

## Assessment 12.9    Create an Announcement

1. At a blank document, create the announcement shown in Figure 12.22 on the next page. Insert the WordArt text with the following specifications:
   a. Use the Fill - Blue, Accent 1, Outline - Background 1, Hard Shadow - Accent 1 WordArt style.
   b. Select the WordArt text box and then apply the Dark Blue text fill.
   c. Apply the Blue text outline.
   d. Apply the Inside Diagonal Top Left shadow text effect. ***Hint: Use the Text Effects button.***
   e. Apply the Subtle Effect - Blue, Accent 1 shape style.
   f. Apply the Offset Top shadow shape effect. ***Hint: Use the Shape Effects button.***
   g. Apply the Square transform text effect. ***Hint: Use the Text Effects button.***
2. Insert the caduceus clip art image, as shown in Figure 12.22, with the following specifications:
   a. Use the word *caduceus* at the Insert Pictures window to search online for the clip art image.
   b. Change the text wrapping to Tight.
   c. Change the clip art image color to Blue, Accent color 1 Light.
   d. Change the brightness and contrast to Brightness: -20% Contrast: +40%.
   e. Size and move the clip art image as shown in the figure.
3. Apply character, paragraph, and page formatting so your document appears similar to the document in Figure 12.22. (Set the text in the Candara font.)
4. Check to make sure the entire page border will print. If it will not, increase the measurements in the Border and Shading Options dialog box.
5. Save the completed announcement and name it **C12-A09-FirstAidCourse**.
6. Print and then close **C12-A09-FirstAidCourse.docx**.

**Figure 12.22  Assessment 12.9**

# First Aid at Work

The Safety Committee is offering a two-day first aid course for employees. The objective of the course is to equip employees with the essential knowledge and practical experience to enable them to carry out first aid in the workplace. Course content includes health and safety administration, handling an incident and developing an action plan, recognizing and treating injuries and illnesses, and cardiopulmonary resuscitation (CPR).

Dates ...................................................... March 9 and 10

Times ........................................... 9:00 a.m. to 4:30 p.m.

Location .................................... Administration Building

Room............................................ Conference Room 200

Registration is available from February 15 until the course begins on March 9. Before registering, please check with your immediate supervisor to ensure that you can be excused from your normal duties for the two days.

**For more information, contact Caleb Sullivan at extension 3505.**

## Assessment 12.10    Insert Screenshots in a Memo

1. Open **FirstAidMemo.docx** and then save it and name it **C12-A10-FirstAidMemo**.
2. Insert screenshots so your document appears as shown in Figure 12.23. Use **FirstAidAnnounce .docx** to create the first screenshot and use **C12-A09-FirstAidCourse.docx** (the document you created in Assessment 12.9) for the second screenshot. Before making either screenshot, make sure the entire announcement page displays on the screen. If you cannot see the entire page, adjust the zoom.
3. Save, print, and then close **C12-A10-FirstAidMemo.docx**.

**Figure 12.23  Assessment 12.10**

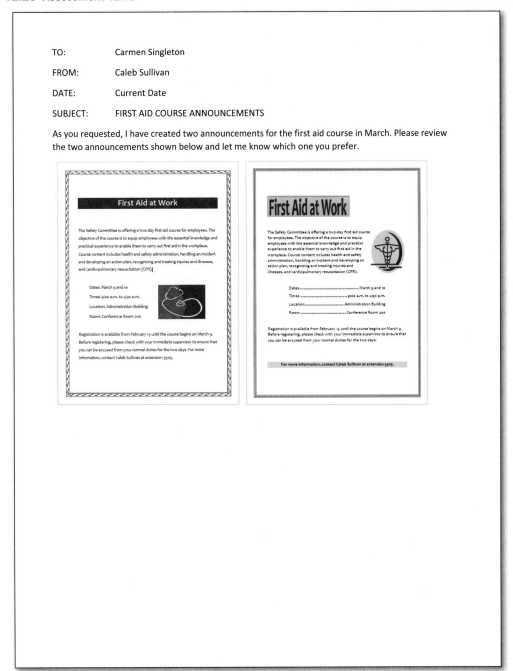

# Chapter 13

# Creating Tables

## Performance Objectives

Upon successful completion of Chapter 13, you will be able to:

- Create and format a table
- Format a table by selecting specific cells
- Change the table design
- Draw a table
- Insert an Excel spreadsheet into a Word document
- Insert a predesigned table into a document

The use of tables provides a systematic way to organize and display data within a document. With the Tables feature in Word, data such as text, numbers, and formulas can be organized into columns and rows to create a variety of tables. In this chapter, you will learn to create tables using several different methods, including inserting a predesigned table called a Quick Table. You will also learn how to format data in a table and apply table styles.

*Note: Before beginning computer exercises for this chapter, copy to your storage medium the Chapter13 folder from the CD that accompanies this textbook and then make Chapter13 the active folder.*

In this chapter, students will produce the following documents:

Exercise 13.1. C13-E01-Tables.docx
Exercise 13.2. C13-E02-YrlySales.docx
Exercise 13.3. C13-E03-WMExecs.docx
Exercise 13.4. C13-E04-Worksheet.docx
Exercise 13.5. C13-E05-Calendar.docx

Model answers for these exercises are shown on the following pages.

## TECHNICAL SUPPORT PERSONNEL

| Name | Title | Telephone Number |
|------|-------|------------------|
| Alan Hubbard | Manager | 555-3203 Ext. 5401 |
| Debbie Morrissey | Assistant Manager | 555-3312 Ext. 5320 |
| Christopher Sorenson | Technician | 555-3938 Ext. 5327 |
| Donna Grabowski | Technician | 555-3894 Ext. 5411 |
| William Koehler | Technician | 555-3809 Ext. 5388 |

## HUMAN RESOURCES PERSONNEL

| Name | Title | Telephone Number |
|------|-------|------------------|
| Melissa Clemensen | Manager | 555-7463 Ext. 2100 |
| Joseph Reeves | Assistant | 555-7601 Ext. 3211 |
| Stephanie Tomasi | Assistant | 555-7548 Ext. 2408 |
| Myong Han | Assistant Manager | 555-7487 Ext. 2105 |
| David Hoover | Assistant | 555-7444 Ext. 2238 |

**Exercise 13.1**

C13-E01-Tables.docx

**WOODRIDGE MANUFACTURING**

**YEARLY SALES**

| State | First Quarter | Second Quarter | Third Quarter | Fourth Quarter |
|-------|---------------|----------------|---------------|----------------|
| Maine | $100,340 | $105,249 | $110,985 | $123,679 |
| New Hampshire | $105,674 | $101,563 | $100,257 | $110,947 |
| Massachusetts | $152,491 | $162,490 | $153,276 | $160,054 |
| Connecticut | $104,239 | $97,639 | $100,574 | $106,379 |

**Exercise 13.2**

C13-E02-YrlySales.docx

**Exercise 13.3**

C13-E03-WMExecs.docx

| WOODRIDGE MANUFACTURING | |
|---|---|
| Ethan Sanchez | President |
| Shawna Richards | Vice President |
| Jennifer Powell | Director |
| Chase Selden | Director |
| Lee Kazlowski | Director |

**Exercise 13.4**

C13-E04-Worksheet.docx

| NATIONAL SALES | | |
|---|---|---|
| Division | Amount | 2% Inc. |
| North | $1,683,000 | $171,666,000 |
| South | $1,552,000 | $158,304,000 |
| Central | $1,024,000 | $104,448,000 |
| East | $1,778,000 | $181,356,000 |
| West | $1,299,000 | $132,498,000 |

## January

| Sun | Mon | Tue | Wed | Thu | Fri | Sat |
|---|---|---|---|---|---|---|
| | | | | 1 | 2 | 3 |
| 4 | 5 | 6 | 7 | 8 | 9 | 10 |
| 11 | 12 | 13 | 14 | 15 | 16 | 17 |
| 18 | 19 | 20 | 21 | 22 | 23 | 24 |
| 25 | 26 | 27 | 28 | 29 | 30 | 31 |
| | | | | | | |

**Exercise 13.5**

C13-E05-Calendar.docx

# Creating a Table

**Create a Table**
1. Click INSERT tab.
2. Click Table button.
3. Drag to create desired number of columns and rows.
4. Click mouse button.
OR
1. Click INSERT tab.
2. Click Table button.
3. Click *Insert Table*.
4. Specify number of columns and rows.
5. Click OK.

Table

A table is made up of information boxes called *cells*. A cell is the intersection between a column and a row. Cells can contain text, numbers, characters, graphics, and formulas. You can use the Tables feature to create cells and organize data in columns and rows. To create a table, click the INSERT tab, click the Table button in the Tables group, drag down and to the right until the correct numbers of columns and rows display in the grid, and then click the mouse button.

Figure 13.1 shows a sample table with four columns and three rows. Various features of a Word table are identified in the figure, such as gridlines, end-of-cell markers, end-of-row markers, move table column markers, the table move handle, and the resize handle. In a Word table, nonprinting characters identify the end of a cell and the end of a row. The end-of-cell marker displays inside each cell and the end-of-row marker displays at the end of each row of cells. To view these characters, click the Show/Hide ¶ button in the Paragraph group on the HOME tab.

**Figure 13.1 Sample Table**

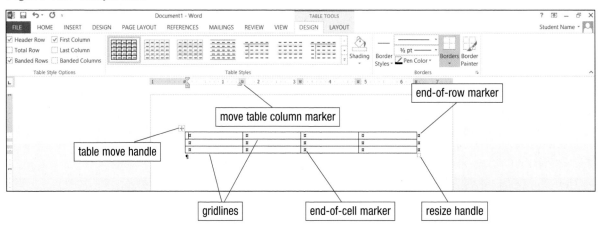

Each cell in a table has a cell designation. The columns in a table are lettered from left to right, beginning with *A*; the rows in a table are numbered from top to bottom, beginning with *1*. The cell in the upper left corner of the table is cell A1. The cell to the right of A1 is B1, the cell to the right of B1 is C1, and so on. When you create a table, the insertion point displays in cell A1 (in the upper left corner of the table).

When the insertion point is positioned in a cell in the table, the move table column markers display on the horizontal ruler (see Figure 13.1). If the horizontal ruler is not displayed, you can display it—and the markers—by clicking the VIEW tab and then clicking the *Ruler* check box in the Show group. The move table column markers represent the ends of the columns and are useful when changing column widths.

## Entering Text in Cells

With the insertion point positioned in a cell, type or edit the cell contents. If the text you type does not fit on one line, it wraps to the next line within the same cell. If you press the Enter key within a cell, the insertion point moves to the next line within that cell. The cell lengthens vertically to accommodate the text and all of the cells in that row also lengthen.

## Moving the Insertion Point within a Table

To move the insertion point to a different cell within a table using the mouse, click in the desired cell. To move the insertion point to a different cell using the keyboard, use the keyboard commands shown in Table 13.1.

If you want to move the insertion point to a tab stop within a cell, press Ctrl + Tab. If the insertion point is located in the last cell of the table and you press the Tab key, Word adds another row to the table. You can insert a page break within a table by pressing Ctrl + Enter. The page break is inserted between rows, not within a row.

**Table 13.1 Insertion Point Movement within a Table Using the Keyboard**

| To move the insertion point | Press these keys |
| --- | --- |
| to next cell | Tab |
| to preceding cell | Shift + Tab |
| forward one character | Right Arrow key |
| backward one character | Left Arrow key |
| to previous row | Up Arrow key |
| to next row | Down Arrow key |
| to first cell in row | Alt + Home |
| to last cell in row | Alt + End |
| to top cell in column | Alt + Page Up |
| to bottom cell in column | Alt + Page Down |

---

**Exercise 13.1A   Creating a Table**                                          Part 1 of 3

1. At a blank document, turn on bold formatting and then type the title **TECHNICAL SUPPORT PERSONNEL**, as shown in Figure 13.2 on the next page.
2. Turn off bold formatting and then press the Enter key.

3. Create the table shown in Figure 13.2 by completing the following steps:
   a. Click the INSERT tab.
   b. Click the Table button in the Tables group.
   c. Move the mouse pointer down and to the right until the number above the grid displays as *3x6* and then click the mouse button.
4. Type the text in the cells as indicated in Figure 13.2. Press the Tab key to move to the next cell or press Shift + Tab to move to the preceding cell. To indent the text in the cells in the middle column, press Ctrl + Tab to move the insertion point to a tab within the cells and then type the text. (If you accidentally press the Enter key within a cell, immediately press the Backspace key. Do not press the Tab key after typing the text in the last cell. If you do, another row is inserted in the table. If this happens, immediately click the Undo button on the Quick Access toolbar.)
5. Save the table in the Chapter13 folder on your storage medium with the name **C13-E01-Tables**.

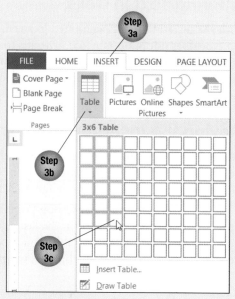

**Figure 13.2 Exercise 13.1A**

**TECHNICAL SUPPORT PERSONNEL**

| Name | Title | Telephone Number |
|---|---|---|
| Alan Hubbard | Manager | 555-3203 Ext. 5401 |
| Debbie Morrissey | Assistant Manager | 555-3312 Ext. 5320 |
| Christopher Sorenson | Technician | 555-3938 Ext. 5327 |
| Donna Grabowski | Technician | 555-3894 Ext. 5411 |
| William Koehler | Technician | 555-3809 Ext. 5388 |

You can also create a table with options at the Insert Table dialog box, as shown in Figure 13.3 on the next page. To display this dialog box, click the INSERT tab, click the Table button in the Tables group, and then click *Insert Table* at the drop-down list. At the Insert Table dialog box, enter the desired number of columns and rows and then click OK.

Use options in the *AutoFit behavior* section of the Insert Table dialog box to specify column widths in the table. The first option, *Fixed column width*, has a default setting of *Auto*. At this setting, Word automatically determines the width of the columns. Click the up or down arrow in the *Fixed column width* measurement box to set a specific width for columns. Choose the *AutoFit to contents* option and a table is created with very narrow columns. As you type text in the cells in the columns, the columns automatically adjust to fit the text. Use the *AutoFit to window* option and the table is automatically fit between the left and right margins of the document with evenly spaced columns. This option creates the same width of columns as the *Fixed Column width* option with *Auto* selected. Insert a check mark in the *Remember dimensions for new tables* if you want to create new tables with the same numbers of rows and columns and column widths.

**Figure 13.3 Insert Table Dialog Box**

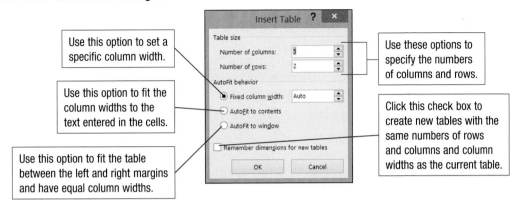

Use this option to set a specific column width.

Use this option to fit the column widths to the text entered in the cells.

Use this option to fit the table between the left and right margins and have equal column widths.

Use these options to specify the numbers of columns and rows.

Click this check box to create new tables with the same numbers of rows and columns and column widths as the current table.

---

**Exercise 13.1B**  **Creating a Table with the Insert Table Dialog Box**  Part 2 of 3

1. With **C13-E01-Tables.docx** open, press Ctrl + End to move the insertion point below the table and then press the Enter key twice.
2. Turn on bold formatting and then type the title **HUMAN RESOURCES PERSONNEL**, as shown in Figure 13.4.
3. Turn off bold formatting and then press the Enter key.
4. Insert the table by completing the following steps:
   a. Click the INSERT tab.
   b. Click the Table button in the Tables group and then click *Insert Table* at the drop-down list.
   c. At the Insert Table dialog box, type **3** in the *Number of columns* text box. (The insertion point is automatically positioned in this text box.)
   d. Press the Tab key. (This moves the insertion point to the *Number of rows* option.)
   e. Type **6**.
   f. Click the *Autofit to contents* option.
   g. Click OK.
5. Type the text in the cells as indicated in Figure 13.4. Press the Tab key to move to the next cell or press Shift + Tab to move to the preceding cell.
6. Save **C13-E01-Tables.docx**.

*Step 4c*
*Step 4e*
*Step 4f*
*Step 4g*

---

**Figure 13.4 Exercise 13.1B**

**HUMAN RESOURCES PERSONNEL**

| Name | Title | Telephone Number |
|------|-------|------------------|
| Melissa Clemensen | Manager | 555-7463 Ext. 2100 |
| Myong Han | Assistant Manager | 555-7487 Ext. 2105 |
| David Hoover | Assistant | 555-7444 Ext. 2238 |
| Joseph Reeves | Assistant | 555-7601 Ext. 3211 |
| Stephanie Tomasi | Assistant | 555-7548 Ext. 2408 |

# Selecting Cells

Text in a table can be formatted in several ways. For example, the alignment of text within cells and rows can be changed; rows or columns can be selected and then moved; and character formatting, such as bold, italic, and underline formatting, can be applied to text. To format specific cells, rows, or columns, you must first select them.

## Selecting in a Table with the Mouse

Use the mouse pointer to select a cell, column, row, or entire table. Table 13.2 provides instructions for selecting specific portions of a table or an entire table with the mouse. The left edge of each cell—between the left column border and the end-of-cell marker or first character in the cell—is called the *cell selection bar*. When you position the mouse pointer in the cell selection bar, the pointer turns into a black arrow pointing up and to the right (instead of the left). Each row in a table contains a *row selection bar*, which is the space just to the left of the left edge of the table. When you position the mouse pointer in the row selection bar, the pointer turns into an arrow pointing up and to the right.

**Table 13.2  Selecting in a Table with the Mouse**

| To select this | Do this |
|---|---|
| cell | Position the mouse pointer in the cell selection bar at the left edge of the cell until it turns into a black arrow pointing up and to the right and then click the left mouse button. |
| row | Position the mouse pointer in the row selection bar at the left edge of the table until it turns into an arrow pointing up and to the right and then click the left mouse button. To select nonadjacent rows, hold down the Ctrl key while selecting the desired rows. |
| column | Position the mouse pointer on the uppermost horizontal gridline of the table in the appropriate column until it turns into a short down-pointing arrow and then click the left mouse button. To select nonadjacent columns, hold down the Ctrl key while selecting columns. |
| adjacent cells | Position the mouse pointer in the first cell to be selected, hold down the left mouse button, drag the mouse pointer to the last cell to be selected, and then release the mouse button. |
| all cells in a table | Click the table move handle or position the mouse pointer in the row selection bar for the first row at the left edge of the table until it turns into an arrow pointing up and to the right, hold down the left mouse button, drag down to select all of the rows in the table, and then release the left mouse button. |
| text within a cell | Position the mouse pointer at the beginning of the text and then hold down the left mouse button as you drag the mouse across the text. (When a cell is selected, the cell background color changes to gray. When text within a cell is selected, only those lines containing text are selected.) |

## Selecting in a Table with the Keyboard

Another way to select specific cells within a table is to use the keyboard. Table 13.3 presents the commands for using the keyboard to select specific portions of a table.

If you want to select only the text within a cell rather than the entire cell, press the F8 key to turn on the Extend mode and then move the insertion point with an arrow key. When a cell is selected, the cell background color changes to gray. When text within a cell is selected, only those lines containing text are selected. You can move text to a different cell by selecting the text and then dragging it to a different cell.

**Table 13.3 Selecting in a Table with the Keyboard**

| *To select* | *Press* |
|---|---|
| next cell | Tab |
| preceding cell | Shift + Tab |
| entire table | Alt + 5 (on numeric keypad with Num Lock off) |
| adjacent cells | Hold down the Shift key and then press an arrow key repeatedly. |
| column | Position the insertion point in the top cell of the column, hold down the Shift key, and then press the down-pointing arrow key until the column is selected. |

**Exercise 13.1C**    **Selecting Cells, Applying Formatting, and Moving Rows**        Part 3 of 3

1. With **C13-E01-Tables.docx** open, select the heading *TECHNICAL SUPPORT PERSONNEL*, change the font to 14-point Candara, and then center the text.
2. Select the heading *HUMAN RESOURCES PERSONNEL* and then change the font to 14-point Candara.
3. Change the formatting for the entire top table by completing the following steps:
   a. Hover the mouse pointer over any cell in the top table until the table move handle displays in the upper left corner of the table.
   b. Position the mouse pointer over the table move handle until the pointer displays with a four-headed arrow attached and then click the left mouse button. (This selects the entire table.)
   c. Make sure the HOME tab is active.
   d. Click the Font button arrow and then click *Candara* at the drop-down gallery.
   e. Deselect the table by clicking in any cell.

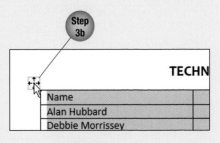

Step 3b

4. Center the text in the cells in the third column of the top table by completing the following steps:
   a. Position the mouse pointer in the cell below the heading *Telephone Number* (the cell containing *555-3203 Ext. 5401*).
   b. Hold down the left mouse button and drag down to the bottom cell in the table (the cell containing *555-3809 Ext. 5388*).
   c. Click the Center button in the Paragraph group on the HOME tab.

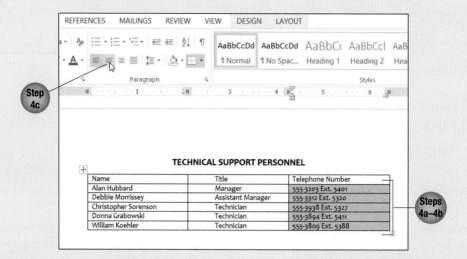

5. Apply formatting to the first row in the top table by completing the following steps:
   a. Position the mouse pointer in the row selection bar at the left side of the first row until the pointer turns into an arrow pointing up and to the right and then click the left mouse button. (This selects the entire first row of the top table.)
   b. Click the Bold button in the Font group on the HOME tab.
   c. Click the Center button in the Paragraph group.
   d. Click the Shading button arrow and then click the *Dark Blue* color (ninth option in the *Standard Colors* section). (This automatically changes the font color to white.)

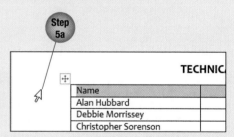

6. Apply paragraph shading to the rows in the top table by completing the following steps:
   a. Click immediately right of the name *Alan Hubbard*.
   b. Hold down the Shift key and then press the Right Arrow key on the keyboard until the entire row is selected.
   c. Click the Shading button arrow and then click the *Gold, Accent 4, Lighter 80%* option (eighth column, second row in the *Theme Colors* section).

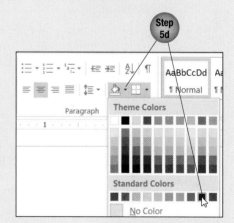

d. Select the fourth row in the table (begins with the name *Christopher Sorenson*) by positioning the mouse pointer in the row selection bar at the left edge of the fourth row until the pointer turns into an arrow pointing up and to the right and then click the left mouse button.

e. Press the F4 key. (This is the Repeat command, which repeats the last action.)

f. Select the sixth row (begins with the name *William Koehler*) and then press the F4 key.

7. Apply bold formatting and center the text in the first row in the bottom table.

8. Move two rows in the bottom table by completing the following steps:

a. Position the mouse pointer in the row selection bar at the left side of the row containing the name *Joseph Reeves*, hold down the left mouse button, and drag down to select two rows (the *Joseph Reeves* row and the *Stephanie Tomasi* row).

b. Click the HOME tab and then click the Cut button in the Clipboard group.

c. Move the insertion point so it is positioned at the beginning of the name *Myong Han* and then click the Paste button in the Clipboard group.

9. Save, print, and then close **C13-E01-Tables.docx**.

# Changing the Table Design

When you insert a table into a document, the TABLE TOOLS DESIGN tab, as shown in Figure 13.5, becomes active. This tab contains options for applying, customizing, and changing table styles. The tab also contains buttons for formatting cell borders.

**Figure 13.5 TABLE TOOLS DESIGN Tab**

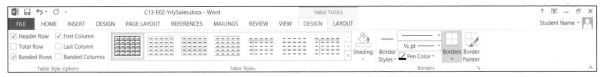

## Applying Table Styles

Word provides a number of predesigned styles for formatting a table. The Table Styles group on the TABLE TOOLS DESIGN tab displays several styles. Display a drop-down gallery of additional styles by clicking the More button that displays at the right of the styles. Hover the mouse pointer over a formatting option and the table in the document displays with that formatting applied.

You can further customize predesigned style formatting with options in the Table Style Options group. For example, if your table contains a *Total* row, you can insert a check mark in the *Total Row* option. If your table contains data in the first column that you would like to set off from the other columns of data, insert a check mark in the *First Column* check box.

1. At a blank document, create the table shown in Figure 13.6 on the next page by completing the following steps:
   a. Type the heading **WOODRIDGE MANUFACTURING** centered and with bold formatting applied.
   b. Type the subheading **YEARLY SALES** centered and with bold formatting applied.
   c. Press the Enter key once after typing the subheading, change the paragraph alignment back to Left, turn off bold formatting, and then click the INSERT tab.
   d. Click the Table button in the Tables group.
   e. Move the mouse pointer down and to the right until 5×5 displays above the grid and then click the left mouse button.
   f. Type the text in the cells as shown in Figure 13.6.
2. Center the text in all of the columns except the first column by completing the following steps:
   a. Position the mouse pointer at the top of the second column until the pointer displays as a down-pointing black arrow, hold down the left mouse button, drag to the fifth column, and then release the mouse button.
   b. Press Ctrl + E.
3. Apply a table style by completing the following steps:
   a. Make sure the insertion point is positioned in a cell in the table and that the TABLE TOOLS DESIGN tab is active.
   b. Click the More button that displays at the right side of the table styles in the Table Styles group.
   c. Click the *Grid Table 4 - Accent 6* style (last column, fourth row in the *Grid Tables* section).
   d. Click the *First Column* check box in the Table Style Options group to remove the check mark.
4. Save the document with the name **C13-E02-YrlySales**.
5. Print **C13-E02-YrlySales.docx**.
6. With the document open, make the following changes:
   a. Make sure the TABLE TOOLS DESIGN tab is active.
   b. Remove the check mark from the *Banded Rows* check box in the Table Style Options group.
   c. Insert check marks in the *First Column* check box and *Banded Columns* check box.
   d. Make sure the *Header Row* check box contains a check mark.
7. Save **C13-E02-YrlySales.docx**.

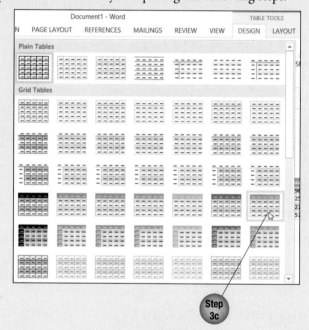

Step 3c

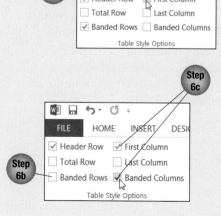

Step 3d

Step 6c

Step 6b

**Figure 13.6  Exercise 13.2A**

**WOODRIDGE MANUFACTURING**

**YEARLY SALES**

| State | First Quarter | Second Quarter | Third Quarter | Fourth Quarter |
|-------|---------------|----------------|---------------|----------------|
| Maine | $100,340 | $105,249 | $110,985 | $123,679 |
| New Hampshire | $105,674 | $101,563 | $100,257 | $110,947 |
| Massachusetts | $152,491 | $162,490 | $153,276 | $160,054 |
| Connecticut | $104,239 | $97,639 | $100,574 | $106,379 |

## Applying Shading and Borders

Apply shading to a table by clicking the Shading button arrow in the Table Styles group and then clicking the desired shading color at the drop-down gallery. Apply predesigned border styles by clicking the Border Styles button arrow in the Borders group and then clicking the desired border style at the drop-down list.

Choosing a border style changes the mouse pointer to a pen and also makes the Border Painter button active. Using the mouse, click or drag along a border to apply the border style. Turn off border formatting by clicking the Border Painter button. Use the Line Style button in the Borders group to choose a border line style and use the Line Weight button to choose a line weight. Change the border color by clicking the Pen Color button arrow and then clicking the desired color at the drop-down palette.

Another method for applying a border is to click the Borders button arrow in the Borders group and then click the desired border at the drop-down list. If you want more control over shading and borders, click the *Borders and Shading* option at the Borders button drop-down list. This displays the Borders and Shading dialog box with the Borders tab selected, as shown in Figure 13.7.

**Figure 13.7  Borders and Shading Dialog Box with Borders Tab Selected**

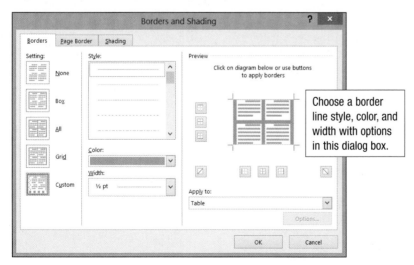

**QUICK STEPS**

**Apply Shading to a Table**
1. Click TABLE TOOLS DESIGN tab.
2. Click Shading button arrow.
3. Click desired shading color.

**Apply a Border Style**
1. Click TABLE TOOLS DESIGN tab.
2. Click Border Styles button arrow.
3. Click or drag along table gridlines and/or borders.

**Apply Borders to a Table**
1. Click TABLE TOOLS DESIGN tab.
2. Click Borders button arrow.
3. Click desired border option at drop-down list.

Shading   Border Styles

Pen Color   Borders

Border Painter

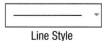

Line Style

½ pt ———

Line Weight

1. With **C13-E02-YrlySales.docx** open, change cell shading by completing the following steps:

   a. Make sure the TABLE TOOLS DESIGN tab is active.

   b. Select all of the cells in the second column *except* the first cell.

   c. Click the Shading button arrow in the Table Styles group.

   d. Click the *Blue, Accent 1, Lighter 80%* color (fifth column, second row in the *Theme Colors* section).

   e. Select all of the cells in the fourth column *except* the first cell and then press the F4 key.

   f. Select all of the cells in the third column *except* the first cell.

   g. Click the Shading button arrow in the Table Styles group.

   h. Click the *Green, Accent 6, Lighter 80%* option at the drop-down gallery (last column, second row in the *Theme Colors* section.

   i. Select all of the cells in the fifth column *except* the first cell and then press the F4 key.

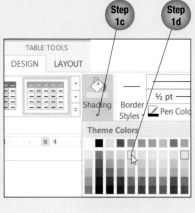

2. Change cell borders by completing the following steps:

   a. Select the first column in the table.

   b. Click the Border Styles button arrow and then click the *Single solid line, 1 1/2 pt, Acccent 6* option (last column, second row).

   c. Click the Borders button arrow in the Borders group and then click the *Left Border* option at the drop-down list.

   d. Select the fifth column in the table.

   e. Click the Borders button arrow in the Borders group and then click the *Right Border* option at the drop-down list.

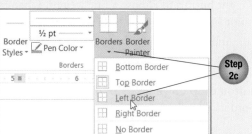

3. Customize cell borders by completing the following steps:

   a. Select the entire table by hovering the mouse pointer over the table and then clicking the table move handle.

   b. Click the Borders button arrow in the Borders group and then click the *Borders and Shading* option located at the bottom of the drop-down list.

   c. At the Borders and Shading dialog box with the Borders tab selected, click the down-pointing arrow at the right of the *Color* option.

   d. Click the *Dark Blue* color (ninth option in the *Standard Colors* section).

   e. Click the *Box* option in the *Setting* section.

   f. Click OK to close the dialog box. (The borders you inserted in Step 2 are removed.)

   g. Click anywhere in the table to deselect the text.

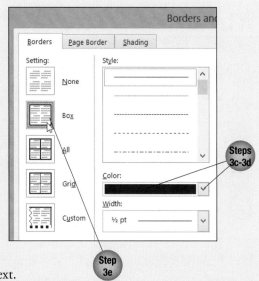

4. Draw a double-line border by completing the following steps:
   a. Click the Line Style button arrow in the Borders group and then click the first double-line option at the drop-down list. (This turns on the Border Painter button and changes the mouse pointer to a pen.)
   b. Click the Line Weight button arrow and then click ¾ pt at the drop-down list.

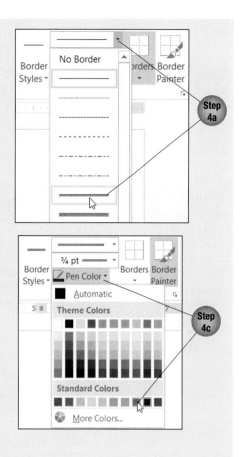

Step 4a

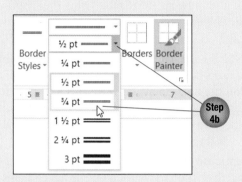

Step 4b

Step 4c

   c. Click the Pen Color button arrow and then click the *Blue* color (eighth option in the *Standard Colors* section).
   d. Drag with the pen pointer along the bottom border of the first row from the first cell to the last cell in the row.

**WOODRIDGE MANUFACTURING**

**YEARLY SALES**

Step 4d

| State | First Quarter | Second Quarter | Third Quarter | Fourth Quarter |
|---|---|---|---|---|
| Maine | $100,340 | $105,249 | $110,985 | $123,679 |
| New Hampshire | $105,674 | $101,563 | $100,257 | $110,947 |
| Massachusetts | $152,491 | $162,490 | $153,276 | $160,054 |
| Connecticut | $104,239 | $97,639 | $100,574 | $106,379 |

5. Draw single-line borders between the columns by completing the following steps:
   a. Click the Line Style button arrow and then click the single-line option that displays near the top of the drop-down list.
   b. Click the Line Weight button arrow and then click ¼ pt at the drop-down list.
   c. Leave the pen color as Blue.
   d. Draw along the right side of the cells in the first column from the bottom of the first row to the last row.
   e. Draw along the right side of the cells in the second column from the bottom of the first row to the last row.
   f. Draw along the right side of the cells in the third column from the bottom of the first row to the last row.
   g. Draw along the right side of the cells in the fourth column from the bottom of the first row to the last row.
   h. Click the Border Painter button to deactivate it.

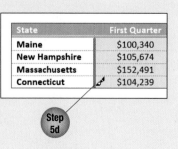

| State | First Quarter |
|---|---|
| Maine | $100,340 |
| New Hampshire | $105,674 |
| Massachusetts | $152,491 |
| Connecticut | $104,239 |

Step 5d

6. Select the heading and subheading in the document (*WOODRIDGE MANUFACTURING* and *YEARLY SALES*) and then change the font color to Dark Blue (ninth option in the *Standard Colors* section). (Do this with the Font Color button on the HOME tab.)

7. Save, print, and then close **C13-E02-YrlySales.docx**.

# Drawing a Table

**QUICK STEPS**

**Draw a Table**
1. Click INSERT tab.
2. Click Table button.
3. Click *Draw Table* at drop-down list.
4. Drag pen pointer in document to create table.

Eraser

In Exercise 13.2B, you used options in the Borders group to draw borders within and around an existing table. You can also draw an entire table using these options together with the *Draw Table* option at the Table button drop-down list or the Draw Table button in the Draw group on the TABLE TOOLS LAYOUT tab.

To draw a table, click the INSERT tab, click the Table button in the Tables group, and then click *Draw Table* at the drop-down list. This turns the mouse pointer into a pencil and displays guidelines on the horizontal and vertical rulers that identify the location of the pencil in the document. Drag the pencil pointer in the document to create the table using the guidelines as a reference. In addition to horizontal and vertical lines, you can draw diagonal lines in a table.

The first time you release the mouse button when drawing a table, the TABLE TOOLS LAYOUT tab becomes active. The Draw group on the tab contains the Draw Table button and Eraser button. The Draw Table button displays with a blue background, indicating that it is active. If you make a mistake while drawing a table, click the Eraser button in the Draw group (which changes the mouse pointer to an eraser) and then drag over any border lines you want to erase.

## Exercise 13.3  Drawing a Table                    Part 1 of 1

1. At a blank document, draw the table shown in Figure 13.8 on page 442 by completing the following steps:
   a. Click the INSERT tab.
   b. Click the Table button in the Tables group and then click *Draw Table* at the drop-down list.
   c. Move the pencil pointer to approximately the 2-inch marker on the horizontal ruler and the 1-inch marker on the vertical ruler. (Use the guidelines to position the pencil.)
   d. Hold down the left mouse button, drag down and to the right until the guideline displays at approximately the 4.5-inch marker on the horizontal ruler and the 3-inch marker on the vertical ruler, and then release the mouse button.

Step 1d

e. Click the TABLE TOOLS DESIGN tab.

f. Click the Line Style button arrow and then click the first thick/thin line option at the drop-down list.

g. Click the Pen Color button in the Borders group and then click *Black, Text 1* at the drop-down list (second column, first row in the *Theme Colors* section).

h. Click each border of the table to change it to a thick/thin line.

i. Click the TABLE TOOLS DESIGN tab.

j. Click the Line Style button arrow and then click the first double-line option at the drop-down list.

k. Drag to create the first row with the double-line border.

l. Click the TABLE TOOLS DESIGN tab.

m. Click the Line Style button arrow and then click the single-line option.

n. Drag in the table to create the remaining rows and columns, as shown in Figure 13.8. If you are not satisfied with a table border, click the Eraser button in the Draw group on the TABLE TOOLS LAYOUT tab and then drag across the border line you want to remove.

o. Click the Draw Table button on the TABLE TOOLS LAYOUT tab to deactivate it.

2. Type the text in the table, as shown in Figure 13.8 on the next page.

3. Click on any character in the title in the first row.

4. Click the TABLE TOOLS DESIGN tab, click the Shading button arrow, and then click the *Dark Blue* color (ninth color in the *Standard Colors* section).

5. Center the title in row 1.

6. Draw diagonal lines in the cell containing the name *Chase Selden* by completing the following steps:

a. Click the TABLE TOOLS LAYOUT tab.

b. Click the Draw Table button to make it active.

c. Using the mouse, drag from the upper left corner of the cell containing the name *Chase Selden* to the lower right corner of the cell.

d. Using the mouse, drag from the upper right corner of the cell containing the name *Chase Selden* to the lower left corner of the cell.

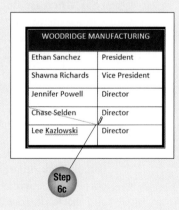

e. Click the Draw Table button to deactivate it.

7. Save the document with the name **C13-E03-WMExecs**.

8. Print and then close **C13-E03-WMExecs.docx**.

**Figure 13.8 Exercise 13.3**

| WOODRIDGE MANUFACTURING | |
|---|---|
| Ethan Sanchez | President |
| Shawna Richards | Vice President |
| Jennifer Powell | Director |
| Chase Selden | Director |
| Lee Kazlowski | Director |

# Inserting an Excel Spreadsheet

You can insert an Excel spreadsheet into a Word document, which provides you with some Excel functions. To insert an Excel spreadsheet, click the INSERT tab, click the Table button in the Tables group, and then click the *Excel Spreadsheet* option at the drop-down list. This inserts a small worksheet in the document with two columns and two rows visible. Increase or decrease the number of visible cells by dragging the sizing handles that display around the worksheet. Use buttons on the Excel ribbon tabs to format the worksheet. Click outside the worksheet and the Excel ribbon tabs are removed. Double-click the table to display the Excel ribbon tabs.

## Exercise 13.4  Inserting and Formatting an Excel Spreadsheet          Part 1 of 1

1. Open **SalesIncrease.docx** in the Chapter13 folder on your storage medium.
2. Press Ctrl + N to open a blank document.
3. Insert an Excel spreadsheet into the blank document by clicking the INSERT tab, clicking the Table button in the Tables group, and then clicking *Excel Spreadsheet* at the drop-down list.
4. Decrease the size of the worksheet by completing the following steps:
   a. Position the mouse pointer on the sizing handle (small black square) located in the lower right corner of the worksheet until the pointer displays as a black, diagonal, two-headed arrow.
   b. Hold down the left mouse button, drag up and to the left, and release the mouse button. Continue dragging the sizing handles until columns A, B, and C and rows 1 through 7 are visible.

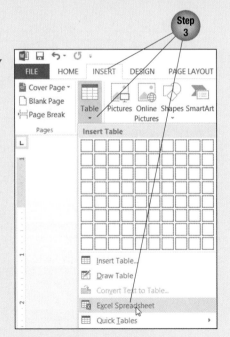

5. Copy a table into the Excel worksheet by completing the following steps:
   a. Hover the mouse pointer over the Word button on the Taskbar and then click the thumbnail representing **SalesIncrease.docx**.
   b. Hover your mouse pointer over the table and then click the table move handle (small square containing a four-headed arrow) that displays in the upper left corner of the table. (This selects all of the cells in the table.)
   c. Click the Copy button in the Clipboard group on the HOME tab.
   d. Close **SalesIncrease.docx**.
   e. With the first cell in the worksheet active, click the Paste button in the Clipboard group.
6. Format the worksheet and insert a formula by completing the following steps:
   a. Increase the width of the second column by positioning the mouse pointer on the column boundary between columns B and C and double-clicking the left mouse button.
   b. Click in cell C3, type the formula =**B3\*102**, and then press Enter.

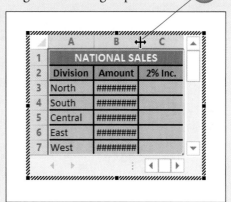

7. Copy the formula in cell C3 to cells C4 through C7 by completing the following steps:
   a. Position the mouse pointer (white plus [+] symbol) in cell C3, hold down the left mouse button, drag down to cell C7, and then release the mouse button.
   b. Click the Fill button in the Editing group on the HOME tab and then click *Down* at the drop-down list.
8. Click outside the worksheet to remove the Excel ribbon tabs.
9. Position the table by completing the following steps:
   a. Click in the table.
   b. Click the PAGE LAYOUT tab.
   c. Click the Position button in the Arrange group and then click *Position in Top Center with Square Text Wrapping* at the drop-down gallery (second column, first row in the *With Text Wrapping* section).

10. Save the document and name it **C13-E04-Worksheet**.
11. Print and then close **C13-E04-Worksheet.docx**.

# Inserting a Quick Table

**Insert a Quick Table**
1. Click INSERT tab.
2. Click Table button.
3. Point to *Quick Tables* in drop-down list.
4. Click desired table at side menu.

Word includes a Quick Tables feature that you can use to insert predesigned tables into a document. To insert a predesigned table, click the INSERT tab, click the Table button, point to *Quick Tables,* and then click the desired table at the side menu. When the table is inserted in the document, the TABLE TOOLS DESIGN tab becomes active. Use options on this tab to customize the table.

## Exercise 13.5   Inserting a Quick Table                    Part 1 of 1

1. At a blank document, click the INSERT tab.
2. Click the Table button, point to *Quick Tables*, and then click *Calendar 3* at the side menu.

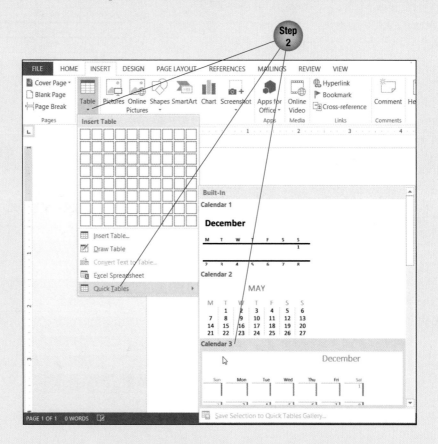

3. Edit the text in each cell so the month and day reflect the current date.
4. Save the completed monthly calendar with the name **C13-E05-Calendar**.
5. Print and then close **C13-E05-Calendar.docx**.

# Chapter Summary

- Use the Tables feature to arrange information in columns and rows. A cell is the intersection between a column and a row.

- A table can contain text, characters, numbers, data, graphics, and formulas.

- Create a table by clicking the INSERT tab, clicking the Table button in the Tables group, dragging the mouse pointer down and to the right until the desired number of columns and rows display in the grid, and then clicking the left mouse button. You can also create a table with options at the Insert Table dialog box.

- Columns in a table are lettered from left to right, beginning with A. Rows are numbered from top to bottom, beginning with 1.

- The lines that form the cells of the table are called gridlines.

- To move the insertion point to a different cell within the table using the mouse, click in the desired cell.

- To move the insertion point to a different cell within the table using the keyboard, refer to Table 13.1 on page 429.

- Position the mouse pointer on the cell selection bar, row selection bar, or the uppermost horizontal gridline of a column to select a cell, row, or column, respectively. Click the table move handle to select the entire table.

- Refer to Table 13.3 on page 433 for a list of keyboard commands for selecting specific cells within a table.

- When you insert a table in a document, the TABLE TOOLS DESIGN tab is active.

- Apply formatting to a table with the table styles available in the Table Styles group on the TABLE TOOLS DESIGN tab.

- Fine-tune predesigned style formatting applied to columns and rows with options in the Table Style Options group on the TABLE TOOLS DESIGN tab.

- Use the Shading button in the Table Styles group on the TABLE TOOLS DESIGN tab to apply shading to a cell or selected cells.

- Use the Borders button in the Borders group on the TABLE TOOLS DESIGN tab to apply borders to a table or selected cells.

- Customize shading and borders with options at the Borders and Shading dialog box. Display this dialog box by clicking the Borders button arrow and then clicking *Borders and Shading*.

- Use options in the Borders group on the TABLE TOOLS DESIGN tab to change the border style, line style, and line weight and to choose a pen color.

- Draw a table in a document by clicking the INSERT tab, clicking the Table button, and then clicking *Draw Table*. Using the mouse, drag in the document to create the table.

- Use the Draw Table button in the Draw group on the TABLE TOOLS LAYOUT tab to draw a table and use the Eraser button in the Draw group to erase specific borders in a table.

- Insert an Excel spreadsheet into a Word document to provide Excel functions by clicking the INSERT tab, clicking the Table button in the Tables group, and then clicking *Excel Spreadsheet* at the drop-down list.

- Quick Tables are predesigned tables you can insert into a document. To do so, click the INSERT tab, click the Table button, point to *Quick Tables*, and then click the desired option at the side menu.

# Commands *Review*

| FEATURE | RIBBON TAB, GROUP | BUTTON, OPTION | KEYBOARD SHORTCUT |
|---|---|---|---|
| create table | INSERT, Tables | ▦ , drag in grid | |
| draw table | INSERT, Tables | ▦ , *Draw Table* | |
| insert Excel spreadsheet | INSERT, Tables | ▦ , *Excel Spreadsheet* | |
| insert page break within table | | | Ctrl + Enter |
| insert Quick Table | INSERT, Tables | ▦ , *Quick Tables* | |
| Insert Table dialog box | INSERT, Tables | ▦ , *Insert Table* | |
| move insertion point to next cell | | | Tab |
| move insertion point to previous cell | | | Shift + Tab |
| move insertion point to tab stop within cell | | | Ctrl + Tab |

# Key Points *Review*

**Completion:** In the space provided at the right, indicate the correct term, symbol, or command.

1. This term refers to the intersection between a row and a column. _____

2. The Table button is located on this tab. _____

3. When you hover the mouse pointer over a table, this displays in the upper left corner of the table. _____

4. Press this key to move the insertion point to the next cell. _____

5. Press this combination of keys to move the insertion point to the previous cell. _____

6. The space just to the left of the left edge of the table is referred to as this. _____

7. When you insert a table in a document, this tab is active. _____

8. The Line Style and Line Weight buttons are located in this group on the TABLE TOOLS DESIGN tab. _____

9. When you click the Borders button arrow and then click *Borders and Shading,* the Borders and Shading dialog box displays with this tab active. _____

10. To remove a border line, click this button in the Draw group on the TABLE TOOLS LAYOUT tab and then drag across the border. _____

11. Use this feature to insert a predesigned table in a document. _____

# Chapter *Assessments*

## Applying Your Skills

Demonstrate your knowledge of features learned in this chapter by completing the following assessments.

### Assessment 13.1    Create and Format a Table in a Letter

1. Open **LtrCofC.docx** and save the document with the name **C13-A01-LtrCofC**.
2. Move the insertion point to the blank line between the two paragraphs of text in the body of the letter and then create the table shown in Figure 13.9 with the following specifications:
   a. Create a table with three columns and eight rows.
   b. Apply bold and italic formatting and center the text in the first row.
   c. Apply bold formatting to the text in the cells below the *Name* heading.
   d. Apply Blue, Accent 5, Darker 50% shading (ninth column, bottom row in the *Theme Colors* section) to the first row.
   e. Apply Green, Accent 6, Lighter 80% shading (last column, second row in the *Theme Colors* section) to the second, fourth, sixth, and eighth rows.
   f. Apply Blue, Accent 1, Lighter 80% shading (fifth column, second row in the *Theme Colors* section) to the third, fifth, and seventh rows.
3. Save, print, and then close **C13-A01-LtrCofC.docx**.

**Figure 13.9** **Assessment 13.1**

| Name | Title | Department |
|---|---|---|
| Shawn Kilpatrick | Chief Executive Officer | Administration |
| Gerald Palmer | President | Administration |
| Emily Higgins | Vice President | Administration |
| Ryan Keaton | Finances Manager | Finance |
| Jim Everson | Resources Coordinator | Purchasing |
| Isabelle Brown | Training Coordinator | Support and Training Services |
| Sandy Romano-Ellison | Public Relations Manager | Public Relations |

### Assessment 13.2    Create and Format a Tour Package Table

1. At a blank document, create the text and table shown in Figure 13.10 on the next page with the following specifications:
   a. Set the title *BAYSIDE TRAVEL TOUR PACKAGES* in 16-point bold.
   b. Use the Insert Table dialog box to create a table with three columns and five rows and choose the *Autofit to contents* option at the dialog box.
   c. Type the text in the cells as shown in Figure 13.10.
   d. Apply the Grid Table 4 - Accent 1 table style (second column, fourth row in the *Grid Tables* section).
   e. Remove the check mark from the *First Column* check box.
2. Save the document with the name **C13-A02-TourPkgs**.
3. Print and then close **C13-A02-TourPkgs.docx**.

**Figure 13.10  Assessment 13.2**

## BAYSIDE TRAVEL TOUR PACKAGES

| Name | Duration | Costs |
|---|---|---|
| Hawaiian Fun in the Sun | 5 days and 4 nights | From $709 to $1049 |
| Hawaiian Nights | 8 days and 7 nights | From $1079 to $1729 |
| Hawaiian Fun Tours | 10 days and 9 nights | From $1999 to $2229 |
| Hawaiian Island Tours | 14 days and 13 nights | From $2499 to $3099 |

### Assessment 13.3    Format a Contacts List Table

1. Open **Contacts.docx** and save the document with the name **C13-A03-Contacts**.
2. Select the entire table and then change the font to Candara.
3. Apply the Grid Table 2 - Accent 4 table style (fifth column, second row in the *Grid Table* section) and then remove the check mark from the *First Column* check box.
4. Display the Borders and Shading dialog box with the Borders tab selected, choose the first thick-thin line style, change the color to Dark Blue, click the *Box* option, and then close the dialog box.
5. Click the Border Styles button arrow, click the *Double solid lines, 1/2 pt* option (first column, bottom row in the *Theme Borders* section), and then drag along the bottom of the first row.
6. Save, print, and then close **C13-A03-Contacts.docx**.

## Expanding Your Skills

Explore additional feature options or use Help to learn a new skill in creating these documents.

### Assessment 13.4    Draw and Format an Employment Information Table

1. At a blank document, type the title **JOBS IN DEMAND**, press the Enter key, draw a table, and then in the table type the following text:

| Position | Weekly Income | Yearly Openings |
|---|---|---|
| Accountants/Auditors | $975 | 852 |
| Financial Managers | $895 | 343 |
| Loan Officers | $875 | 301 |
| Registered Nurses | $852 | 1,550 |
| Teachers, Elementary | $780 | 1,112 |
| Teachers, Secondary | $750 | 1,258 |

2. Apply formatting to enhance the appearance of the table.
3. Save the document with the name **C13-A04-Jobs**.
4. Print and then close **C13-A04-Jobs.docx**.

### Assessment 13.5    Create a Monthly Calendar with a Quick Table

1. Use the Quick Tables feature to create a monthly calendar for next month.
2. Apply any additional formatting to enhance the appearance of the calendar.
3. Save the document with the name **C13-A05-MoCalendar**.
4. Print and then close **C13-A05-MoCalendar.docx**.

# Achieving Signature Status

Take your skills to the next level by completing this more challenging assessment.

## Assessment 13.6    Create and Format Tables

<image name="START from Scratch" />

1. At a blank document, create the document shown in Figure 13.11 with the following specifications:
   - Use the Insert Table dialog box to create the table and choose the *AutoFit to contents* option.
   - Apply to both tables the Grid Table 3 - Accent 5 table style and remove the check marks from the *Header Row* and *First Column* check boxes.
   - Vertically center the text on the page.
2. Save the completed document and name it **C13-A06-ResumeWords**.
3. Print and then close the document.

**Figure 13.11  Assessment 13.6**

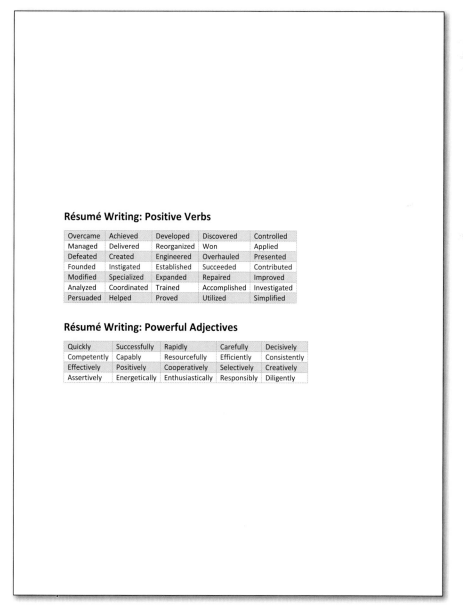

**Résumé Writing: Positive Verbs**

| | | | | |
|---|---|---|---|---|
| Overcame | Achieved | Developed | Discovered | Controlled |
| Managed | Delivered | Reorganized | Won | Applied |
| Defeated | Created | Engineered | Overhauled | Presented |
| Founded | Instigated | Established | Succeeded | Contributed |
| Modified | Specialized | Expanded | Repaired | Improved |
| Analyzed | Coordinated | Trained | Accomplished | Investigated |
| Persuaded | Helped | Proved | Utilized | Simplified |

**Résumé Writing: Powerful Adjectives**

| | | | | |
|---|---|---|---|---|
| Quickly | Successfully | Rapidly | Carefully | Decisively |
| Competently | Capably | Resourcefully | Efficiently | Consistently |
| Effectively | Positively | Cooperatively | Selectively | Creatively |
| Assertively | Energetically | Enthusiastically | Responsibly | Diligently |

# Chapter 14

## Enhancing Tables

### Performance Objectives

Upon successful completion of Chapter 14, you will be able to:

- Change the table design and layout
- Change between table and text formats and sort text in a table
- Perform calculations on data in a table

In Chapter 13, you learned to create tables and format them by applying table styles, borders, and shading. In this chapter, you will learn how to enhance the appearance of tables by changing the layout; inserting and deleting columns and rows; merging and splitting cells; and changing cell size, alignment, and margins. You will also learn to change between text and table formats, sort text in a table, and perform calculations on data in a table.

*Note: Before beginning computer exercises for this chapter, copy to your storage medium the Chapter14 folder from the CD that accompanies this textbook and then make Chapter14 the active folder.*

In this chapter, students will produce the following documents:

Exercise 14.1. C14-E01-LoanTables.docx
Exercise 14.2. C14-E02-EmpTable.docx
Exercise 14.3. C14-E03-SalesDivTable.docx
Exercise 14.4. C14-E04-Sales&Support.docx

Model answers for these exercises are shown on the following pages.

**MORTGAGE BANKERS**

| Mortgage Banker | Mortgage Loans | Home Equity Loans |
|---|---|---|
| Brittany Stevens | $2,490,520 | $1,101,340 |
| Vernon Rosenfeld | $1,905,348 | $1,003,265 |
| Janelle Fisher | $2,005,476 | $1,057,422 |
| Joseph Lundeen | $2,315,380 | $1,320,341 |
| Marilyn Luo | $1,058,394 | $1,429,554 |
| William Morrisette | $2,409,822 | $1,539,588 |

**CONTACT INFORMATION, NORTH**

| Name | Title | Company | Telephone | |
|---|---|---|---|---|
| Kimberly Gibson | Vice President | First Financial Trust | (412) 555-3948 | Ext. 231 |
| Neville Lewis | Loan Officer | Prime One Savings | (503) 555-9986 | |
| Chandra Hall | Manager | Horizon Mutual | (712) 555-0331 | |

**CONTACT INFORMATION, SOUTH**

| Name | Title | Company | Telephone | |
|---|---|---|---|---|
| Harrison Brooks | Vice President | Mainland Bank | (313) 555-8555 | |
| Richard Osaka | President | Meridian Savings | (603) 555-9002 | Ext. 782 |
| Julio Rivas | Loan Officer | Mountain Bank | (206) 555-1048 | |

| Waiting Period | Plan 2016 Employees | Basic Plan Employees |
|---|---|---|
| 30 days | 0.85% | 0.81% |
| 60 days | 0.79% | 0.67% |
| 90 days | 0.59% | 0.49% |
| 120 days | 0.35% | 0.30% |
| 180 days | 0.26% | 0.23% |

**CONTACT INFORMATION, NORTH**

| Name | Title | Company | Telephone |
|---|---|---|---|
| Donna Gould | President | Freestone Bank | (206) 555-9002 |
| John DePaolo | Vice President | North Sound Bank | (253) 555-5300 |
| Dean Zuniga | President | Cornerstone Savings | (425) 555-1048 |
| Joaquin Morgan | Loan Officer | Miles Bank | (206) 555-2102 |
| Maureen Grand | Vice President | National Savings | (253) 555-4215 |
| Noel Nielson | Loan Officer | Hill Savings and Loan | (253) 555-0033 |
| Dennis Keenan | President | Central Bank | (425) 555-1050 |
| Dara Vaughn | Vice President | Touchstone Savings | (206) 555-3285 |

**CONTACT INFORMATION, NORTH**

| Name | Title | Company | Telephone |
|---|---|---|---|
| Aaron Wilson | Loan Officer | Timberline Bank | (425) 555-4892 |
| Rose Simpson | President | Fir Crest Mortgage | (206) 555-2348 |
| Megan Henning | Vice President | Valley Bank | (425) 555-3444 |

**Exercise 14.1** C14-E01-LoanTables.docx    Page 1    Page 2

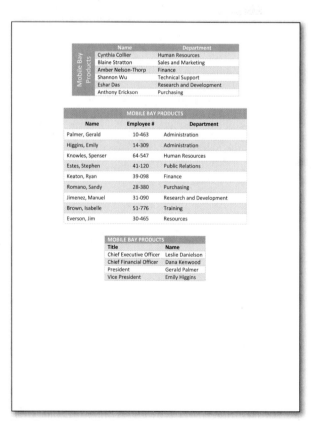

| | Name | Department |
|---|---|---|
| Mobile Bay Products | Cynthia Collier | Human Resources |
| | Blaine Stratton | Sales and Marketing |
| | Amber Nelson-Thorp | Finance |
| | Shannon Wu | Technical Support |
| | Eshar Das | Research and Development |
| | Anthony Erickson | Purchasing |

**MOBILE BAY PRODUCTS**

| Name | Employee # | Department |
|---|---|---|
| Palmer, Gerald | 10-463 | Administration |
| Higgins, Emily | 14-309 | Administration |
| Knowles, Spenser | 64-547 | Human Resources |
| Estes, Stephen | 41-120 | Public Relations |
| Keaton, Ryan | 39-098 | Finance |
| Romano, Sandy | 28-380 | Purchasing |
| Jimenez, Manuel | 31-090 | Research and Development |
| Brown, Isabelle | 51-776 | Training |
| Everson, Jim | 30-465 | Resources |

**MOBILE BAY PRODUCTS**

| Title | Name |
|---|---|
| Chief Executive Officer | Leslie Danielson |
| Chief Financial Officer | Dana Kenwood |
| President | Gerald Palmer |
| Vice President | Emily Higgins |

**Exercise 14.2** C14-E02-EmpTable.docx

**Exercise 14.3**

C14-E03-SalesDivTable.docx

| MOBILE BAY PRODUCTS |||
| Sales Division |||

| Salesperson | Sales, 2014 | Sales, 2015 |
|---|---|---|
| Hubbard, Christopher | $320,348 | $400,570 |
| Washington, Isaac | $395,675 | $402,530 |
| Barclay, Kurt | $400,394 | $425,304 |
| Tanaka, Diana | $428,528 | $399,511 |
| Coulter, Jolene | $600,340 | $597,288 |
| Kohler, Roger | $610,476 | $700,387 |
| Owens, Kendra | $700,328 | $675,329 |
| Total | $3,456,089 | $3,600,919 |
| Average | $493,727 | $514,417 |
| Top Sales | $700,328 | $700,387 |

| Region | First Qtr. | Second Qtr. | Third Qtr. | Fourth Qtr. | Total |
|---|---|---|---|---|---|
| Northwest | $225,420 | $157,090 | $239,239 | $220,340 | $842,089 |
| Southwest | $133,450 | $143,103 | $153,780 | $142,498 | $572,831 |
| Northeast | $275,340 | $299,342 | $278,098 | $266,593 | $1,119,373 |
| Southeast | $211,349 | $222,330 | $201,849 | $239,432 | $874,960 |
| Total | $845,559 | $821,865 | $872,966 | $868,863 | $3,409,253 |
| Average | $211,390 | $205,466 | $218,242 | $217,216 | $852,313 |

Model Answers

| FIRST QUARTER DIVISION SALES ||||
|---|---|---|---|
| Customer | Actual | Planned | Difference |
| JR Systems | $20,450.75 | $20,000.00 | $450.75 |
| Linden Production | $94,375.50 | $70,000.00 | $24,375.50 |
| Danner Designs | $14,540.00 | $12,000.00 | $2,540.00 |
| Valley Supplies | $68,947.00 | $70,000.00 | ($1,053.00) |
| Sunset Enterprises | $58,390.00 | $65,000.00 | ($6,610.00) |

| TECHNICAL SUPPORT - EMPLOYEE HOURS ||||
|---|---|---|---|
| Name | Hours | Rate | Salary |
| Jessie Levigne | 40 | $45.00 | $1800.00 |
| Eduardo Quintana | 30 | $40.00 | $1200.00 |
| Carol Runyon | 40 | $39.50 | $1580.00 |
| Chad Mahoney | 40 | $35.00 | $1400.00 |
| Kyung Shin | 25 | $35.00 | $875.00 |

**Exercise 14.4**

C14-E04-Sales&Support.docx

Enhancing Tables

453

# Changing Table Layout

When you insert a table into a document, the TABLE TOOLS DESIGN tab becomes active. In Chapter 13, you learned how to use options on this tab to format tables. You can also format a table with options on the TABLE TOOLS LAYOUT tab, as shown in Figure 14.1. Use options and buttons on the tab to select specific cells within the table, delete and insert rows and columns, merge and split cells, specify the heights and widths of cells, sort data in cells, and insert formulas. Some of these table layout options are also available at a shortcut menu that can be viewed by right-clicking on a table.

**Figure 14.1  TABLE TOOLS LAYOUT Tab**

## Selecting in a Table with the Select Button

Select

As you learned in Chapter 13, you can select a specific cell, column, or row in a table using either the mouse or the keyboard. You can also select cells, columns, or rows in a table with the Select button, located in the Table group on the TABLE TOOLS LAYOUT tab. To select with this button, position the insertion point in the desired cell, column, or row and then click the Select button. At the drop-down list that displays, specify what you want to select: the entire table or a column, row, or cell.

## Inserting and Deleting Rows and Columns

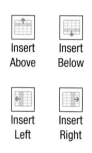

Insert Above

Insert Below

Insert Left

Insert Right

Delete

With buttons in the Rows & Columns group on the TABLE TOOLS LAYOUT tab, you can insert rows or columns and delete rows or columns. Click the button in the group that inserts the row or column in the desired location, such as above, below, to the left, or to the right of the row or column you have selected. To delete a row or column or the entire table, click the Delete button and then click the option specifying what you want to delete.

You can also insert a row or column with insert icons. Display the insert row icon (a plus [+] symbol in a circle and a border line) by positioning the mouse pointer just outside the left border of the table at the left of the desired row border. When the insert row icon displays, click the icon and a row is inserted below the icon border line. To insert a column, position the mouse pointer above the column border line until the insert column icon displays and then click the icon. This inserts a new column immediately left of the insert column icon border line. Like the insert row icon, the insert column icon displays as a plus symbol in a circle and a border line.

## Exercise 14.1A  Inserting and Deleting Columns, Rows, and Tables                Part 1 of 4

1. Open **LoanTables.docx** and save the document with the name **C14-E01-LoanTables**.
2. Insert a new row in the top table and type text in the new cells by completing the following steps:
   a. Click in the cell containing the name *Joseph Lundeen*.

b. Click the TABLE TOOLS LAYOUT tab.

c. Click the Insert Above button in the Rows & Columns group.

d. Type **Janelle Fisher** in the first cell of the new row, press the Tab key, and then type **$2,005,476** in the middle cell of the new row. Press the Tab key again and then type **$1,057,422** in the third cell of the new row.

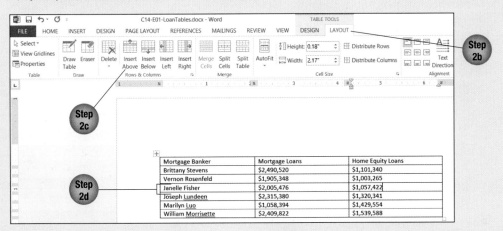

3. Insert a new row in the middle table by clicking in any cell in the middle table, positioning the mouse pointer at the left side of the middle table next to the border line below the row containing *Neville Lewis* until the insert row icon displays, and then clicking the icon. (See image at right.)

4. Type **Chandra Hall** in the first cell in the new row, **Horizon Mutual** in the second cell, and **(712) 555-0331** in the third cell.

5. Insert two new rows in the middle table and type text in the new cells by completing the following steps:

a. Select the two rows of cells that begin with the names *Chandra Hall* and *Ivy Talmadge*.

b. Click the Insert Below button in the Rows & Columns group.

c. Type the following text in the new cells:

| | | |
|---|---|---|
| **Harrison Brooks** | **Mainland Bank** | **(313) 555-8555** |
| **Richard Osaka** | **Meridian Savings** | **(603) 555-9002** |

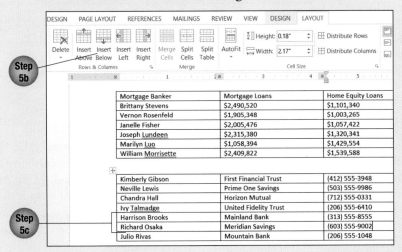

6. Delete a row in the middle table by completing the following steps:
   a. Click in the cell containing the name *Ivy Talmadge*.
   b. Click the Delete button in the Rows & Columns group and then click *Delete Rows* at the drop-down list.
7. Insert a new column in the middle table and type text in the new cells by completing the following steps:
   a. Position the mouse pointer immediately above the border line between the first and second columns in the middle table until the insert column icon displays. (See image at right.)
   b. Click the insert column icon.
   c. Type the following text in the new cells:

   > B1: **Vice President**
   > B2: **Loan Officer**
   > B3: **Manager**
   > B4: **Vice President**
   > B5: **President**
   > B6: **Loan Officer**

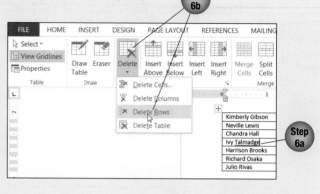

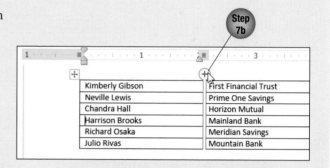

8. Delete the bottom table by completing the following steps:
   a. Click in any cell in the bottom table.
   b. Make sure the TABLE TOOLS LAYOUT tab is active.
   c. Click the Delete button in the Rows & Columns group and then click *Delete Table* at the drop-down list.
9. After deleting the table, you decide you want the table back in the document. To do this, click the Undo button on the Quick Access toolbar.
10. Save **C14-E01-LoanTables.docx**.

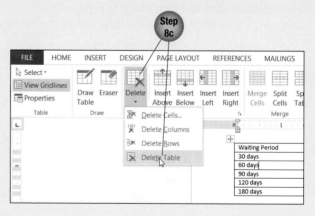

## Merging and Splitting Cells and Tables

Click the Merge Cells button in the Merge group on the TABLE TOOLS LAYOUT tab to merge selected cells and click the Split Cells button to split the currently active cell. When you click the Split Cells button, the Split Cells dialog box displays. At this dialog box, specify the number of columns or rows into which you want to split the active cell. If you want to split one table into two tables, position the insertion point in a cell in the row that you want to be the first row in the new table and then click the Split Table button.

Merge Cells

Split Cells

Split Table

1. With **C14-E01-LoanTables.docx** open, insert a new row in the top table and merge cells in the row by completing the following steps:

   a. Click in the cell containing the text *Mortgage Banker*.
   b. Click the Insert Above button in the Rows & Columns group on the TABLE TOOLS LAYOUT tab.
   c. With all of the cells in the new row selected, click the Merge Cells button in the Merge group.
   d. Type **MORTGAGE BANKERS** and then press Ctrl + E to center the text in the cell.

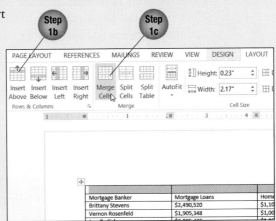

2. Insert rows and text in the middle table and merge cells by completing the following steps:

   a. Click in the cell containing the name *Kimberly Gibson*.
   b. Make sure the TABLE TOOLS LAYOUT tab is active.
   c. Click the Insert Above button twice. (This inserts two rows at the top of the table.)
   d. With the cells in the top row selected, click the Merge Cells button in the Merge group.
   e. Type **CONTACT INFORMATION, NORTH** and then press Ctrl + E to center the text in the cell.
   f. Type the following text in the four cells in the new second row: **Name**, **Title**, **Company**, and **Telephone**, respectively.

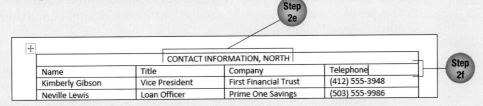

3. Split a cell by completing the following steps:

   a. Click in the cell containing the telephone number *(412) 555-3948*.
   b. Make sure the TABLE TOOLS LAYOUT tab is active.
   c. Click the Split Cells button in the Merge group.
   d. At the Split Cells dialog box, click OK. (The telephone number will wrap to a new line. You will change this in the next exercise.)
   e. Click in the new cell.
   f. Type **Ext. 231** in the new cell.

4. Split the cell containing the telephone number *(603) 555-9002* and then type **Ext. 782** in the new cell.

5. Split the middle table into two tables by completing the following steps:
   a. Click in the cell containing the name *Harrison Brooks*.
   b. Click the Split Table button in the Merge group.
   c. Click in the cell containing the name *Harrison Brooks* (in the first row of the new table) and then, if necessary, click the TABLE TOOLS LAYOUT tab.
   d. Click the Insert Above button.
   e. With the new row selected, click the Merge Cells button.
   f. Type **CONTACT INFORMATION, SOUTH** in the new row and then press Ctrl + E to center the text in the cell.
6. Insert a new row in the third table and type text in the new cells by completing the following steps:
   a. Click in the cell containing the name *Harrison Brooks*.
   b. Make sure the TABLE TOOLS LAYOUT tab is active.
   c. Click the Insert Above button in the Rows & Columns group.
   d. Type **Name** in the first cell, **Title** in the second cell, **Company** in the third cell, and **Telephone** in the fourth cell.
7. Save **C14-E01-LoanTables.docx**.

## Changing Column Widths and Heights

Distribute Rows

Distribute Columns

When you create a table, the column widths and row heights are equal. Customize the widths of columns and heights of rows with buttons in the Cell Size group on the TABLE TOOLS LAYOUT tab. Use the *Table Row Height* measurement box to increase or decrease the heights of rows and use the *Table Column Width* measurement box to increase or decrease the widths of columns. The Distribute Rows button distributes the heights of selected rows equally and the Distribute Columns button distributes the widths of selected columns equally.

You can also change column widths using the move table column markers on the horizontal ruler or by using the table gridlines. To change the width of a column using the move table column markers, position the mouse pointer on a marker until it turns into a left-and-right-pointing arrow and then drag the marker to the desired position. Hold down the Shift key and then drag a table column marker, and the horizontal ruler remains stationary while the table column marker moves. Hold down the Alt key and then drag a table column marker, and measurements display on the horizontal ruler. To change the width of a column using gridlines, position the arrow pointer on the gridline separating two columns until the pointer turns into a left-and-right-pointing arrow crossed by a double vertical line and then drag the gridline to the desired position. If you want to see the column measurements on the horizontal ruler as you drag the gridline, hold down the Alt key.

Adjust row heights in a manner similar to that used to adjust column widths. You can drag the adjust table row marker on the vertical ruler or drag the gridline separating two rows. Hold down the Alt key while dragging the adjust table row marker or row gridline and measurements display on the vertical ruler.

AutoFit

Use the AutoFit button in the Cell Size group to make the column widths in a table automatically fit the contents. To do this, position the insertion point in any cell in the table, click the AutoFit button in the Cell Size group, and then click *AutoFit Contents* at the drop-down list.

In addition to changing column widths and row heights with measurement boxes in the Cell Size group on the TABLE TOOLS LAYOUT tab, you can use options at the Properties dialog box to change these measurements. To change the width of a column, click in a cell in the column and then click the Properties button in the Table group on the TABLE TOOLS LAYOUT tab. At the Table Properties dialog box, click the Column tab, insert the desired measurement in the *Preferred width* measurement box, and then click OK to close the dialog box. To change the height of a row, click in a cell in the row and then click the Properties button. At the Table Properties dialog box, click the Row tab, insert the desired measurement in the *Specify height* measurement box, and then click OK to close the dialog box.

Properties

---

## Exercise 14.1C   Changing Column Widths and Row Heights          Part 3 of 4

1. With **C14-E01-LoanTables.docx** open, change the width of the first column in the second table by completing the following steps:
   a. Click in the cell containing the name *Kimberly Gibson*.
   b. Position the mouse pointer on the move table column marker that displays just right of the 1.5-inch mark on the horizontal ruler until the pointer turns into a left-and-right-pointing arrow.
   c. Hold down the Shift key and then the left mouse button.
   d. Drag the marker to the 1.25-inch mark, release the Shift key, and then release the mouse button.

2. Complete steps similar to those in Step 1 to drag the move table column marker that displays just right of the 3-inch mark on the horizontal ruler to the 2.5-inch mark. (Make sure you hold down the Shift key and then drag the marker.)

3. Change the width of the third column in the second table by completing the following steps:
   a. Position the mouse pointer on the gridline separating the third and fourth columns until the pointer turns into a left-and-right-pointing arrow crossed by a double vertical line.
   b. Hold down the Alt key and then the left mouse button, drag the gridline to the left until the measurement for the third column on the horizontal ruler displays approximately as *1.3"*, release the Alt key, and then release the mouse button.

4. Position the mouse pointer on the gridline that separates the telephone number *(412) 555-3948* from the extension *Ext. 231* and then drag the gridline to the 5.25-inch mark on the horizontal ruler.

5. Click in the cell containing the text *Ext. 231* and then drag the right border of the second table to the 6-inch mark on the horizontal ruler.

6. Click in any cell in the third table and then drag the column boundaries so they match the boundaries in the second table. ***Hint: Use the guidelines that display when dragging boundaries to help you position the column boundaries.***

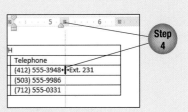

7. AutoFit the columns in the top table by completing the following steps:
   a. Click in any cell in the top table and, if necessary, click the TABLE TOOLS LAYOUT tab.
   b. Click the AutoFit button in the Cell Size group and then click *AutoFit Contents* at the drop-down list.

8. Increase the height of the first row in the top table by completing the following steps:
   a. Make sure the insertion point is located in one of the cells in the top table.
   b. Position the mouse pointer on the top adjust table row marker on the vertical ruler.
   c. Hold down the left mouse button and hold down the Alt key.
   d. Drag the adjust table row marker down until the first row measurement on the vertical ruler displays as *0.4"*, release the mouse button, and then release the Alt key.

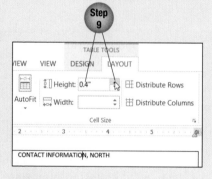

9. In the second table, click in the cell containing the text *CONTACT INFORMATION, NORTH* and then click the up-pointing arrow at the right of the *Height* measurement box in the Cell Size group on the TABLE TOOLS LAYOUT tab until *0.4"* displays in the box.

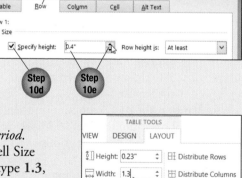

10. Change the height of the top row in the third table by completing the following steps:
   a. Click in the cell containing the text *CONTACT INFORMATION, SOUTH*.
   b. Click the Properties button in the Table group on the TABLE TOOLS LAYOUT tab.
   c. At the Table Properties dialog box, click the Row tab.
   d. Click the *Specify height* check box to insert a check mark.
   e. Click the up-pointing arrow at the right of the *Specify height* measurement box until *0.4"* displays.
   f. Click OK to close the dialog box.

11. Change the width of the first and second columns in the bottom table by completing the following steps:
   a. Click in the cell containing the text *Waiting Period*.
   b. Click in the *Width* measurement box in the Cell Size group on the TABLE TOOLS LAYOUT tab, type **1.3**, and then press the Enter key.
   c. Click in the cell containing the text *Plan 2016 Employees* and then click the down-pointing arrow at the right of the *Width* measurement box until *1.6"* displays in the box.

12. Change the width of the third column in the bottom table by completing the following steps:
   a. Click in the cell containing the text *Basic Plan Employees*.

b. Click the Properties button in the Table group on the TABLE TOOLS LAYOUT tab.
c. At the Table Properties dialog box, click the Column tab.
d. Click the down-pointing arrow at the right of the *Preferred width* measurement box until *1.8"* displays in the box.
e. Click OK to close the dialog box.

13. Save **C14-E01-LoanTables.docx**.

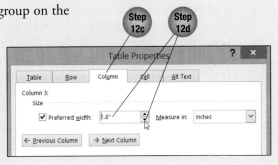

## Changing Cell Alignment

The Alignment group on the TABLE TOOLS LAYOUT tab includes a number of buttons for specifying the horizontal and vertical alignment of text in cells. Each button contains a visual representation of the alignment, and hovering the mouse pointer over a button will also show the alignment.

In addition, the alignment of text in a cell can be changed with options at the Table Properties dialog box with the Cell tab selected. Display this dialog box by clicking the Properties button in the Table group on the TABLE TOOLS LAYOUT tab. Click the Cell tab and the *Vertical alignment* section of the dialog box displays options to align text at the top, center, or bottom of the cells.

## Viewing Gridlines

When you create a table, cell borders are identified by horizontal and vertical gridlines, which are thin black lines. You can remove a cell border gridline but maintain the cell border. If you remove the cell border gridlines or apply a table style that removes the gridlines, the gridlines display as dashed lines. Turn on or off the display of dashed gridlines with the View Gridlines button in the Table group on the TABLE TOOLS LAYOUT tab.

## Repeating a Header Row

If a table is split across pages, consider repeating the header row that appears at the beginning of the table at the top of the next page. Repeating this row helps the reader understand the data that displays in each column. To repeat a header row, click in the header row and then click the Repeat Header Rows button in the Data group on the TABLE TOOLS LAYOUT tab. If you want to repeat more than one header row, select the rows and then click the Repeat Header Rows button.

## Exercise 14.1D   Aligning Text in Cells                              Part 4 of 4

1. With **C14-E01-LoanTables.docx** open, vertically align and apply bold formatting to text in the first two rows in the top table by completing the following steps:
   a. Select the first and second rows of the top table.
   b. Click the Align Center button in the Alignment group on the TABLE TOOLS LAYOUT tab.
   c. Press Ctrl + B.

2. Select the first and second rows of the second table, click the Align Center button in the Alignment group, and then press Ctrl + B.
3. Select the first and second rows of the third table, click the Align Center button in the Alignment group, and then press Ctrl + B.
4. Apply a table style to the fourth (bottom) table by completing the following steps:
   a. Click in any cell in the table.
   b. Click the TABLE TOOLS DESIGN tab.
   c. Click the More button that displays at the right of the table style thumbnails in the Table Style group.
   d. Click the *List Table 3 - Accent 2* table style (third column, third row in the *List Tables* section).
   e. Click the *First Column* check box in the Table Style Options group to remove the check mark.

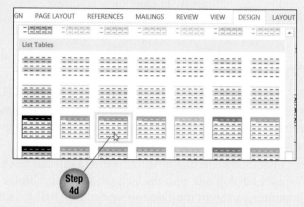

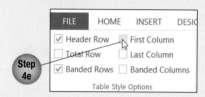

Step 4e

Step 4d

   f. Select the second and third columns of the bottom table and then press Ctrl + E.
5. The table style that you applied to the bottom table removed some of the border gridlines. If you do not see dashed gridlines in the table, turn on the display of these gridlines by positioning your insertion point in any cell in the table and then clicking the View Gridlines button in the Table group on the TABLE TOOLS LAYOUT tab.
6. Press Ctrl + End to move the insertion point to the end of the document, press the Enter key, and then insert a table into the current document by completing the following steps:
   a. Click the INSERT tab.
   b. Click the Object button arrow in the Text group and then click *Text from File* at the drop-down list.
   c. At the Insert File dialog box, navigate to the Chapter14 folder on your storage medium and then double-click ***ContactsNorth.docx***.

Step 7c

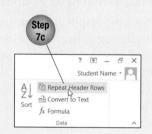

7. Repeat the header row by completing the following steps:
   a. Select the first two rows in the table you just inserted.
   b. Click the TABLE TOOLS LAYOUT tab.
   c. Click the Repeat Header Rows button in the Data group.
8. Save, print, and then close ***C14-E01-LoanTables.docx***.

## Changing Cell Margin Measurements

Cell Margins

Cells in a Word table have specific default margin settings. The top and bottom margins in a cell have default measurements of 0 inches and the left and right margins have default measurements of 0.08 inch.

These default settings can be changed with options at the Table Options dialog box, as shown in Figure 14.2 on the next page. Display this dialog box by clicking the Cell Margins button in the Alignment group on the TABLE TOOLS LAYOUT tab. Use the options in the *Default cell margins* section to change the top, bottom, left, and right cell margin measurements. If you want to insert space between cells, click the *Allow spacing between cells* check box to insert a check mark and then use the measurement box at the right to specify how much space to add. Word will automatically adjust the size of a column to fit the content. If you want the column width to remain constant, click the *Automatically resize to fit contents* check box to remove the check mark.

Changing the cell margins affects all of the cells in a table. If you want to change the cell margin measurements for only one cell or selected cells, position the insertion point in the cell or select the desired cells and then click the Properties button in the Table group on the TABLE TOOLS LAYOUT tab. (You can also click the Cell Size group dialog box launcher.) At the Table Properties dialog box, click the Cell tab and then click the Options button that displays in the lower right corner of the dialog box. This displays the Cell Options dialog box, as shown in Figure 14.3.

Before you can set new cell margin measurements, you must remove the check mark from the *Same as the whole table* option. When the check mark is removed from this option, the cell margin options become available. Specify the new cell margin measurements and then click OK to close the dialog box. If you want the text in the cell to fit within the cell, insert a check mark in the *Fit text* check box.

**Figure 14.2 Table Options Dialog Box**

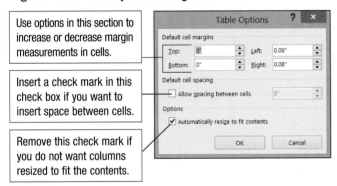

**Figure 14.3 Cell Options Dialog Box**

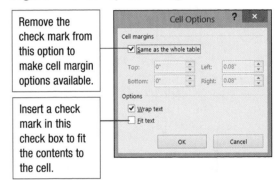

**Exercise 14.2A**   **Changing Cell Margin Measurements**                                Part 1 of 4

1. Open **EmpTable.docx** and save the document with the name **C14-E02-EmpTable**.
2. Change the top and bottom margins for all of the cells in the table by completing the following steps:
    a. Position the insertion point in any cell in the table and then click the TABLE TOOLS LAYOUT tab.
    b. Click the Cell Margins button in the Alignment group.
    c. At the Table Options dialog box, change the cell margins in the *Top* and *Bottom* measurement boxes to 0.05 inch.
    d. Click the *Allow spacing between cells* check box to insert a check mark and then click twice on the up-pointing arrow in the measurement box.
    e. Click OK to close the Table Options dialog box.

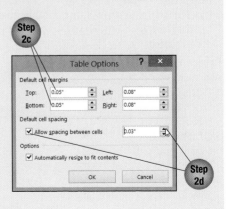

3. Change the top and bottom cell margin measurements for the first row of cells by completing the following steps:
   a. Select the first row of cells (the cells containing *Name* and *Department*).
   b. Click the Properties button in the Table group.
   c. At the Table Properties dialog box, click the Cell tab.
   d. Click the Options button.
   e. At the Cell Options dialog box, remove the check mark from the *Same as the whole table* option.
   f. Change the *Top* and *Bottom* measurement boxes to *0.1"*.
   g. Click OK to close the Cell Options dialog box.
   h. Click OK to close the Table Properties dialog box.

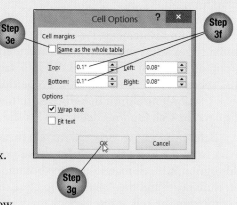

4. Change the left cell margin measurement for specific cells by completing the following steps:
   a. Select all of the rows in the table *except* the top row.
   b. Click the Cell Size group dialog box launcher.
   c. At the Table Properties dialog box, click the Cell tab.
   d. Click the Options button.
   e. At the Cell Options dialog box, remove the check mark from the *Same as the whole table* option.
   f. Change the cell margin in the *Left* measurement box to *0.3"*.
   g. Click OK to close the Cell Options dialog box.
   h. Click OK to close the Table Properties dialog box.

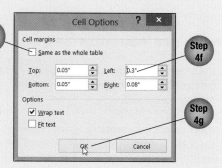

5. Save **C14-E02-EmpTable.docx**.

**QUICK STEPS**

**Change Cell Direction**
1. Click in desired cell.
2. Click TABLE TOOLS LAYOUT tab.
3. Click Text Direction button until text is in desired position.

**Change Table Alignment**
1. Click in table.
2. Click TABLE TOOLS LAYOUT tab.
3. Click Properties button.
4. Click Table tab.
5. Click desired alignment option.

## Changing Cell Direction

Change the direction of text in a cell with the Text Direction button in the Alignment group on the TABLE TOOLS LAYOUT tab. Each time you click the Text Direction button, the text in the cell rotates 90 degrees.

## Changing Table Alignment and Dimensions

By default, a table aligns at the left margin of a document. Change this alignment with options at the Table Properties dialog box with the Table tab selected, as shown in Figure 14.4 on the next page. To change the alignment, click the desired alignment option in the *Alignment* section of the dialog box. Change table dimensions by clicking the *Preferred width* check box to insert a check mark. This makes active both the width measurement box and *Measure in* option box. Type a width in the *Preferred width* measurement box and specify whether the measurement type is inches or a percentage with the *Measure in* option box.

Text Direction

**Figure 14.4** Table Properties Dialog Box with Table Tab Selected

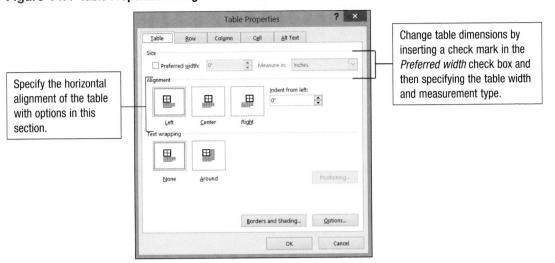

Specify the horizontal alignment of the table with options in this section.

Change table dimensions by inserting a check mark in the *Preferred width* check box and then specifying the table width and measurement type.

---

Exercise 14.2B    **Changing Table Alignment and Dimensions**    Part 2 of 4

1. With **C14-E02-EmpTable.docx** open, insert a new column and change the text direction by completing the following steps:
   a. Click in any cell in the first column and then click the TABLE TOOLS LAYOUT tab.
   b. Click the Properties button in the Table group.
   c. At the Table Properties dialog box, click the Table tab and then click the Options button.
   d. Click the *Allow spacing between cells* check box to remove the check mark.
   e. Click OK to close the Table Options dialog box and then click OK to close the Table Properties dialog box.
   f. With the insertion point positioned in any cell in the first column, click the Insert Left button in the Rows & Columns group.
   g. With the cells in the new column selected, click the Merge Cells button in the Merge group.
   h. Type **Mobile Bay Products**.
   i. Click the Align Center button in the Alignment group.
   j. Click twice on the Text Direction button in the Alignment group.
   k. With *Mobile Bay Products* selected, click the HOME tab, increase the font size to 14 points, and if necessary, apply bold formatting.

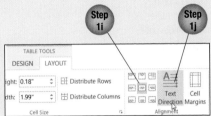

2. AutoFit the contents by completing the following steps:
   a. Click in any cell in the table.
   b. Click the TABLE TOOLS LAYOUT tab.
   c. Click the AutoFit button in the Cell Size group and then click *AutoFit Contents* at the drop-down list.

3. Change the table dimension and alignment by completing the following steps:
   a. Click the Properties button in the Table group on the TABLE TOOLS LAYOUT tab.
   b. At the Table Properties dialog box, click the Table tab.
   c. Click the *Preferred width* check box.
   d. Select the measurement value in the measurement box and then type **4.5**.
   e. Click the *Center* option in the *Alignment* section.
   f. Click OK.
4. Select the two cells containing the text *Name* and *Department* and then click the Align Center button in the Alignment group.
5. Save **C14-E02-EmpTable.docx**.

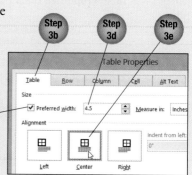

## Changing Table Size with the Resize Handle

**QUICK STEPS**

**Change Table Size with the Resize Handle**
1. Hover mouse pointer over table.
2. Position mouse pointer on resize handle in lower right corner of table.
3. Drag resize handle to increase or decrease size and proportion of table.

**Move a Table**
1. Position mouse pointer on table move handle until pointer displays with four-headed arrow.
2. Drag table to desired position.
3. Release mouse button.

When you hover the mouse pointer over a table, a resize handle displays as a small white square in the lower right corner of the table. Drag this resize handle to increase or decrease the size and proportion of the table.

## Moving a Table

Position the mouse pointer in a table and a table move handle displays in the upper left corner. Use this handle to move the table in the document. To move a table, position the mouse pointer on the table move handle until the pointer displays with a four-headed arrow attached, hold down the left mouse button, drag the table to the desired position, and then release the mouse button.

---

**Exercise 14.2C** Resizing and Moving Tables                    Part 3 of 4

---

1. With **C14-E02-EmpTable.docx** open, insert a table into the current document by completing the following steps:
   a. Press Ctrl + End to move the insertion point to the end of the document and then press the Enter key.
   b. Click the INSERT tab.

c. Click the Object button arrow in the Text group and then click *Text from File* at the drop-down list.

d. At the Insert File dialog box, navigate to your Chapter14 folder and then double-click ***EmpDept.docx***.

2. AutoFit the bottom table by completing the following steps:
   a. Click in any cell in the table.
   b. Click the TABLE TOOLS LAYOUT tab.
   c. Click the AutoFit button in the Cell Size group and then click *AutoFit Contents* at the drop-down list.

3. Format the bottom table by completing the following steps:
   a. Click the TABLE TOOLS DESIGN tab.
   b. Click the More button that displays at the right side of the style thumbnails in the Table Styles group and then click the *List Table 4 - Accent 6* table style (last column, fourth row in the *List Tables* section).

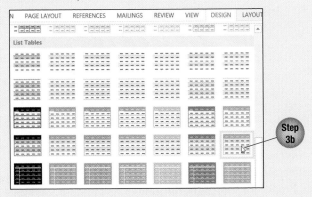

Step 3b

c. Click the *First Column* check box in the Table Style Options group to remove the check mark.

d. Select the first and second rows, click the TABLE TOOLS LAYOUT tab, and then click the Align Center button in the Alignment group.

e. Select the second row and then press Ctrl + B to apply bold formatting.

4. Resize the bottom table by completing the following steps:
   a. Position the mouse pointer on the resize handle located in the lower right corner of the table.
   b. Hold down the left mouse button, drag down and to the right until the width and height of the table increase approximately 1 inch, and then release the mouse button.

| MOBILE BAY PRODUCTS | | |
|---|---|---|
| Name | Employee # | Department |
| Palmer, Gerald | 10-463 | Administration |
| Higgins, Emily | 14-309 | Administration |
| Knowles, Spenser | 64-547 | Human Resources |
| Estes, Stephen | 41-120 | Public Relations |
| Keaton, Ryan | 39-098 | Finance |
| Romano, Sandy | 28-380 | Purchasing |
| Jimenez, Manuel | 31-090 | Research and Development |
| Brown, Isabelle | 51-776 | Training |
| Everson, Jim | 30-465 | Resources |

Steps 4a-4b

5. Move the bottom table by completing the following steps:
   a. Hover the mouse pointer over the table.
   b. Position the mouse pointer on the table move handle until the pointer displays with a four-headed arrow attached.
   c. Hold down the left mouse button, drag the table so it is positioned equally between the left and right margins, and then release the mouse button.

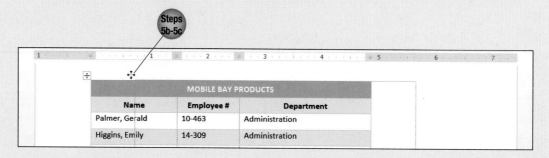

6. Select the cells in the column below the heading *Employee #* and then click the Align Top Center button in the Alignment group.
7. Center-align the text vertically in the cells by completing the following steps:
   a. Select all of the cells in the three columns below the headings *Name*, *Employee #*, and *Department*. (Begin with the cell containing *Palmer, Gerald* and select through the cell containing *Resources*.)
   b. Click the Properties button in the Table group.
   c. At the Table Properties dialog box, click the Cell tab.
   d. Click the *Center* option in the *Vertical alignment* section.
   e. Click OK to close the dialog box.
8. Save **C14-E02-EmpTable.docx**.

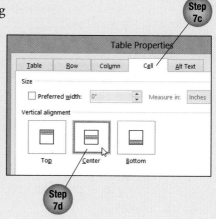

**Convert Text to a Table**
1. Select text.
2. Click INSERT tab.
3. Click Table button.
4. Click *Convert Text to Table*.
5. Make any necessary changes at the Convert Text to Table dialog box.
6. Click OK.

# Converting Text

For some text in documents, you may want to format the text in a table to make the text easier to read and understand. Or, in some documents, you may want to remove table formatting from text. Convert text to a table with the *Convert Text to Table* option at the Table button drop-down list and remove table formatting from text in a document with the Convert to Text button in the Data group on the TABLE TOOLS LAYOUT tab.

## Converting Text to a Table

To convert text to a table, first type the text. Use a separator character, such as a comma or tab, to identify where you want the text to be divided into columns. To create the table, select the text, click the INSERT tab, click the Table button in the Tables group, and then click *Convert Text to Table* at the drop-down list. At the Convert Text to Table dialog box, make any necessary changes and then click OK.

# Converting a Table to Text

Convert a table to text by positioning the insertion point in any cell of the table, clicking the TABLE TOOLS LAYOUT tab, and then clicking the Convert to Text button in the Data group. At the Convert Table to Text dialog box, specify the desired separator and then click OK.

---

## Exercise 14.2D  Converting Text to a Table and a Table to Text  Part 4 of 4

1. With **C14-E02-EmpTable.docx** open, press Ctrl + End to move the insertion point to the end of the document. (Make sure the insertion point is positioned approximately a double space below the bottom table.)
2. Insert **MBExecs.docx** into the current document.
3. Convert the text to a table by completing the following steps:
   a.   Select the text you just inserted.
   b.   Click the INSERT tab.
   c.   Click the Table button in the Tables group and then click *Convert Text to Table* at the drop-down list.
   d.   At the Convert Text to Table dialog box, type **2** in the *Number of columns* text box.
   e.   Click the *AutoFit to contents* option in the *AutoFit behavior* section.
   f.   Click the *Commas* option in the *Separate text at* section.
   g.   Click OK.

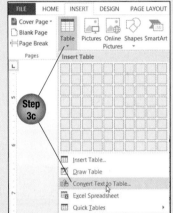

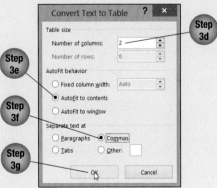

4. Select and merge the cells in the top row (containing the title *MOBILE BAY PRODUCTS)* and then change the alignment to Center.
5. Apply the List Table 4 - Accent 6 table style (last column, fourth row in the *List Tables* section) and remove the check mark from the *First Column* check box in the Table Style Options group on the TABLE TOOLS DESIGN tab.
6. Drag the table so it is centered below the table above.
7. Apply the List Table 4 - Accent 6 table style to the top table. (Increase the width of the columns so the text *MOBILE BAY PRODUCTS* is visible.)
8. Drag the table so it is centered above the middle table. Make sure the three tables fit on one page.
9. Save and then print **C14-E02-EmpTable.docx**.

10. Convert a table to text by completing the following steps:
    a. Select the middle table.
    b. Click the Copy button in the Clipboard group on the HOME tab.
    c. Press Ctrl + N (which displays a blank document).
    d. Click the Paste button in the Clipboard group.
    e. Select the table and then click the TABLE TOOLS LAYOUT tab.
    f. Click the Convert to Text button in the Data group.
    g. At the Convert Table to Text dialog box, click the *Tabs* option in the *Separate text with* section and then click OK.
    h. Select and then apply bold formatting to the title *MOBILE BAY PRODUCTS*.
    i. Print the document.
    j. Close the document without saving it.
11. Save and then close **C14-E02-EmpTable.docx**.

Step 10g

## Sorting Text in a Table

Use the Sort button in the Data group on the TABLE TOOLS LAYOUT tab to sort text in selected cells in a table in ascending or descending alphabetic or numeric order or by date. To sort text, select the desired rows in the table and then click the Sort button in the Data group. At the Sort dialog box, specify the column containing the text on which you want to sort and then click OK.

---

**Exercise 14.3A**  Sorting Text in a Table                    Part 1 of 2

1. Open **SalesDivTable.docx** and save the document with the name **C14-E03-SalesDivTable**.
2. Sort text in the top table by completing the following steps:

   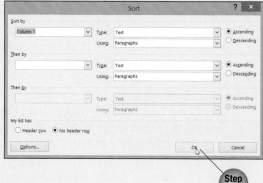

   a. Select all of the rows containing names (from *Kohler, Roger* through *Washington, Isaac*).
   b. Click the TABLE TOOLS LAYOUT tab.
   c. Click the Sort button in the Data group.
   d. At the Sort dialog box, click OK. (This sorts the last names in the first column in alphabetical order.)

Step 2d

3. Re-sort the table by 2014 sales by completing the following steps:
    a. With the rows still selected, click the Sort button in the Data group.
    b. At the Sort dialog box, click the down-pointing arrow at the right side of the *Sort by* option box and then click *Column 2* at the drop-down list.
    c. Click OK.
    d. Deselect the rows.
4. Save **C14-E03-SalesDivTable.docx**.

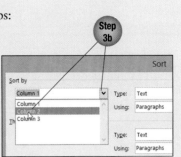

# Performing Calculations in a Table

Use the Formula button in the Data group on the TABLE TOOLS LAYOUT tab to insert formulas that perform calculations on the data in a table. You can add, subtract, multiply, and divide the numbers in cells in a table. In addition, you can perform other calculations, such as determine averages, count items, and identify minimum and maximum values. Although you can calculate data in a Word table, an Excel worksheet is more suitable for complex calculations.

Formula

To perform a calculation on data in a table, position the insertion point in the cell in which you want the result inserted and then click the Formula button in the Data group on the TABLE TOOLS LAYOUT tab. This displays the Formula dialog box, as shown in Figure 14.5. At this dialog box, accept the default formula that displays in the *Formula* text box or type the desired calculation and then click OK.

In the default formula, the SUM part of the formula is called a ***function***. Word provides other functions you can use to write a formula. These functions are available at the *Paste function* drop-down list in the Formula dialog box. For example, you can use the AVERAGE function to determine the average of numbers in cells. Specify the numbering format at the *Number format* drop-down list in the Formula dialog box. For example, if you are calculating money amounts, you can specify that the calculated numbers display with no numbers or with two numbers following the decimal point.

**Figure 14.5 Formula Dialog Box**

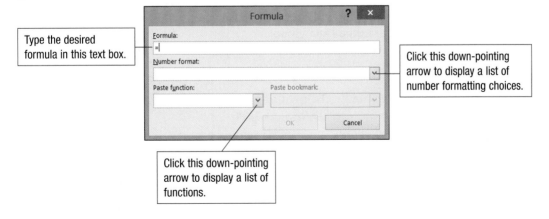

1. With **C14-E03-SalesDivTable.docx** open, insert a formula by completing the following steps:
   a. In the top table, click in cell B9 (the empty cell immediately below the cell containing the amount *$700,328*).
   b. Click the TABLE TOOLS LAYOUT tab.
   c. Click the Formula button in the Data group.
   d. At the Formula dialog box, make sure that *=SUM(ABOVE)* displays in the *Formula* option box.
   e. Click the down-pointing arrow at the right side of the *Number format* option box and then click *#,##0* at the drop-down list (top option).
   f. Click OK to close the Formula dialog box.

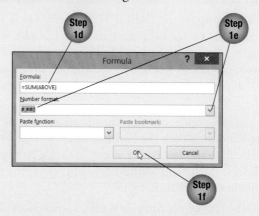

Step 1d

Step 1e

Step 1f

   g. In the table, type a dollar sign ($) before the number just inserted in cell B9.
2. Complete steps similar to those in Steps 1c through 1g to insert the SUM formula in cell C9 (the empty cell immediately below the cell containing the amount *$675,329*).
3. In the bottom table, complete steps similar to those in Steps 1c through 1g to insert SUM formulas that calculate totals in the cells in the *Total* row.
4. In the bottom table, complete steps similar to those in Steps 1c through 1g to insert in cell F2 (the cell below the *Total* heading) a SUM formula that calculates the total of cells in the row. (The Formula dialog box should display *=SUM(LEFT)* instead of *=SUM(ABOVE)*.)
5. Insert a formula in the second cell below the *Total* heading (cell F3) by completing the following steps:
   a. Click in cell F3.
   b. Click the Formula button in the Data group.
   c. At the Formula dialog box, press the Backspace key to delete *ABOVE)*.
   d. Type **LEFT)**.
   e. Click the down-pointing arrow at the right side of the *Number format* option box and then click *#,##0* at the drop-down list (top option).
   f. Click OK to close the Formula dialog box.
   g. In the table, type a dollar sign before the number just inserted in cell F3.

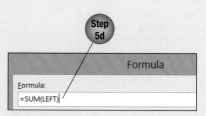

Step 5d

Formula

Formula:

=SUM(LEFT)

6. In the bottom table, complete steps similar to those in Steps 5b through 5g to insert SUM formulas that calculate the totals of cells in the rows in the *Total* column.

7. Insert a formula that calculates the average of amounts by completing the following steps:
   a. Click in cell B10 in the top table (the empty cell immediately right of the cell containing the word *Average*).
   b. Click the Formula button in the Data group.
   c. At the Formula dialog box, delete the formula in the *Formula* text box but *not* the equals sign (=).
   d. With the insertion point positioned immediately right of the equals sign, click the down-pointing arrow at the right side of the *Paste function* option box and then click *AVERAGE* at the drop-down list.
   e. With the insertion point positioned between the left and right parentheses, type **B2:B8**.

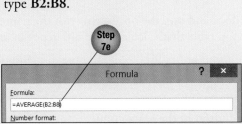

   f. Click the down-pointing arrow at the right side of the *Number format* option box and then click *#,##0* at the drop-down list (top option).
   g. Click OK to close the Formula dialog box.
   h. Type a dollar sign before the number just inserted in cell B10.
8. Complete steps similar to those in Steps 7b through 7h to insert in the top and bottom tables formulas that calculate averages. Insert formulas in the *Average* rows of both tables. (When inserting an AVERAGE formula in a cell in the bottom table, identify only those amounts in rows 2 through 5.)
9. Insert a formula that calculates the maximum number by completing the following steps:
   a. Click in cell B11 in the top table (the empty cell immediately right of the cell containing the words *Top Sales*).
   b. Click the Formula button in the Data group.
   c. At the Formula dialog box, delete the formula in the *Formula* text box but *not* the equals sign.
   d. With the insertion point positioned immediately right of the equals sign, click the down-pointing arrow at the right side of the *Paste function* option box and then click *MAX* at the drop-down list. (You will need to scroll down the list to display the *MAX* option.)
   e. With the insertion point positioned between the left and right parentheses, type **B2:B8**.
   f. Click the down-pointing arrow at the right side of the *Number format* option box and then click *#,##0* at the drop-down list (top option).
   g. Click OK to close the Formula dialog box.
   h. Type a dollar sign before the number just inserted in cell B10.
10. Complete steps similar to those in Steps 9b through 9h to insert the maximum number in cell C11.
11. Save, print, and then close **C14-E03-SalesDivTable.docx**.

## Writing Formulas

In addition to using the functions provided in the Formula dialog box, you can write your own formulas. Use the four basic operators when you write a formula, including the plus sign (+) for addition, the minus sign (–) for subtraction, the asterisk (*) for multiplication, and the forward slash (/) for division. If a calculation contains two or more operators, Word calculates from left to right. If you want to change the order of the calculations, put parentheses around the part of the calculation to be performed first.

---

**Exercise 14.4A**  Writing Formulas in Tables                                                                 Part 1 of 2

1. Open **Sales&Support.docx** and save the document with the name **C14-E04-Sales&Support**.
2. Write a formula in the top table that calculates the difference in amounts by completing the following steps:
   a. Click in cell D3 (the empty cell immediately below the cell containing the heading *Difference*).
   b. Click the TABLE TOOLS LAYOUT tab.
   c. Click the Formula button in the Data group.
   d. At the Formula dialog box, press the Backspace key to delete *SUM(LEFT)* that displays in the *Formula* option box. (Do not delete the equals sign.)
   e. Type **B3-C3**.
   f. Click OK to close the Formula dialog box.

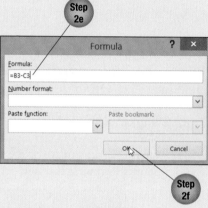

3. Click in cell D4 and then complete steps similar to those in Steps 2c through 2f, except type **B4-C4** in the *Formula* text box in the Formula dialog box. (Amounts enclosed in parentheses are negative amounts.)
4. Insert the correct formula in each remaining cell in column D. (Make sure you change the cell designation for each formula. For example, type **B5-C5** when inserting the formula in cell D5.)
5. Write a formula in the bottom table that calculates salary amounts by completing the following steps:
   a. Click in cell D3 (the empty cell immediately below the cell containing the heading *Salary*).
   b. If necessary, click the TABLE TOOLS LAYOUT tab.
   c. Click the Formula button in the Data group.
   d. At the Formula dialog box, press the Backspace key to delete *SUM(LEFT)* that displays in the *Formula* option box. (Do not delete the equals sign.)
   e. Type **C3*B3**.
   f. Click OK to close the Formula dialog box.

6. Click in cell D4 and then complete steps similar to those in Steps 5c through 5f, except type **C4*B4** in the *Formula* text box in the Formula dialog box.

7. Insert the correct formula in each remaining cell in column D. (Make sure you change the cell designation for each formula. For example, type **C5*B5** when inserting the formula in cell D5.)
8. Make the following changes to the top table:
   a. AutoFit the contents of the table.
   b. Apply the Grid Table 2 - Accent 6 table style.
   c. Remove the check mark from the *First Column* check box in the Table Style Options group on the TABLE TOOLS DESIGN tab.
   d. Select all of the cells containing amounts, click the TABLE TOOLS LAYOUT tab, and then click the Align Top Right button in the Alignment group.
9. Make the following changes to the bottom table:
   a. AutoFit the contents of the table.
   b. Apply the Grid Table 2 - Accent 6 table style.
   c. Remove the check mark from the *First Column* check box in the Table Style Options group on the TABLE TOOLS DESIGN tab.
   d. Select the cells containing amounts in the *Rate* and *Salary* columns, click the TABLE TOOLS LAYOUT tab, and then click the Align Top Right button in the Alignment group.
   e. Select the hour numbers below the *Hours* heading and then click the Align Top Center button in the Alignment group.
10. Center each table between the left and right margins of the document.
11. Save and then print **C14-E04-Sales&Support.docx**.

## Recalculating a Formula

If you change the numbers in cells that are part of a formula, you must recalculate the formula. To do this, select the result of the formula and then press the F9 key. This recalculates the formula and inserts the new result in the cell. You can recalculate adjacent cells by selecting the cells and then pressing F9. You can also recalculate by selecting the result of the formula, clicking the Formula button on the TABLE TOOLS LAYOUT tab, and then clicking OK at the Formula dialog box.

| Exercise 14.4B | Recalculating Formulas | Part 2 of 2 |
| --- | --- | --- |

1. With **C14-E04-Sales&Support.docx** open, make the following changes to amounts in the top table:
   a. Change the amount in cell B4 from *$65,375.50* to *$94,375.50*.
   b. Change the amount in cell B6 from *$75,328.20* to *$68,947.00*.
2. Recalculate the amounts in cells D4 and D6 in the top table by completing the following steps:
   a. Click the number in cell D4 and then press the F9 key.
   b. Click the number in cell D6 and then press the F9 key.
3. Make the following changes to numbers in the bottom table:
   a. Change the number in cell B4 from *40* to *30*.
   b. Change the amount in cell C5 from *$38.00* to *$39.50*.
4. Recalculate the amounts in cells D4 and D5 in the bottom table by selecting cells D4 and D5 and then pressing the F9 key.
5. Save, print, and then close **C14-E04-Sales&Support.docx**.

# Chapter *Summary*

➤ Change the layout of a table with options and buttons on the TABLE TOOLS LAYOUT tab.

➤ You can select a cell, row, column, or table using the Select button in the Table group on the TABLE TOOLS LAYOUT tab.

➤ Insert and delete columns and rows with buttons in the Rows & Columns group on the TABLE TOOLS LAYOUT tab.

➤ Merge selected cells with the Merge Cells button and split cells with the Split Cells button. Both buttons are located in the Merge group on the TABLE TOOLS LAYOUT tab.

➤ Three options are available for changing column widths and row heights: by using the height and width measurement boxes in the Cell Size group on the TABLE TOOLS LAYOUT tab; by dragging the move table column markers on the horizontal ruler, the adjust table row markers on the vertical ruler, or the gridlines in the table; or by using the AutoFit button in the Cell Size group.

➤ Change the alignment of data in cells with buttons in the Alignment group on the TABLE TOOLS LAYOUT tab.

➤ If a table splits across two pages, you can repeat the header row above the rows that extend to the next page. To do this, click in the header row or select the desired header rows at the beginning of the table and then click the Repeat Header Rows button in the Data group on the TABLE TOOLS LAYOUT tab.

➤ Change cell margins with options at the Table Options dialog box.

➤ Change text direction in a cell with the Text Direction button in the Alignment group.

➤ Change table alignment at the Table Properties dialog box with the Table tab selected.

➤ Use the resize handle to change the size of the table and use the table move handle to move the table.

➤ Convert text to a table with the *Convert Text to Table* option at the Table button drop-down list. Convert a table to text with the Convert to Text button in the Data group on the TABLE TOOLS LAYOUT tab.

➤ Sort selected rows in a table with the Sort button in the Data group.

➤ Perform calculations on data in a table by clicking the Formula button in the Data group on the TABLE TOOLS LAYOUT tab and then specifying the formula and number format at the Formula dialog box.

➤ Write a formula with basic operators, including the plus sign for addition, the minus sign for subtraction, the asterisk for multiplication, and the forward slash for division.

➤ Recalculate a formula by clicking in the cell containing the result of the formula and then pressing the F9 key or by clicking the Formula button on the TABLE TOOLS LAYOUT tab and then clicking OK at the Formula dialog box.

# Commands *Review*

| FEATURE | RIBBON TAB, GROUP | BUTTON, OPTION |
|---------|-------------------|----------------|
| AutoFit table contents | TABLE TOOLS LAYOUT, Cell Size | |
| change cell alignment | TABLE TOOLS LAYOUT, Alignment | |
| change cell direction | TABLE TOOLS LAYOUT, Alignment | |
| convert table to text | TABLE TOOLS LAYOUT, Data | |

| FEATURE | RIBBON TAB, GROUP | BUTTON, OPTION |
|---------|-------------------|----------------|
| convert text to table | INSERT, Tables | ⊞, Convert Text to Table |
| delete column | TABLE TOOLS LAYOUT, Rows & Columns | ✕, Delete Columns |
| delete row | TABLE TOOLS LAYOUT, Rows & Columns | ✕, Delete Rows |
| delete table | TABLE TOOLS LAYOUT, Rows & Columns | ✕, Delete Table |
| distribute columns | TABLE TOOLS LAYOUT, Cell Size | ⊞ |
| distribute rows | TABLE TOOLS LAYOUT, Cell Size | ⊞ |
| Formula dialog box | TABLE TOOLS LAYOUT, Data | $f_x$ |
| insert column at left | TABLE TOOLS LAYOUT, Rows & Columns | ⊞ |
| insert column at right | TABLE TOOLS LAYOUT, Rows & Columns | ⊞ |
| insert row above | TABLE TOOLS LAYOUT, Rows & Columns | ⊞ |
| insert row below | TABLE TOOLS LAYOUT, Rows & Columns | ⊞ |
| merge cells | TABLE TOOLS LAYOUT, Merge | ⊞ |
| repeat header row | TABLE TOOLS LAYOUT, Data | ▦ |
| select table | TABLE TOOLS LAYOUT, Table | ⬉ |
| sort text in table | TABLE TOOLS LAYOUT, Data | A Z↓ |
| Split Cells dialog box | TABLE TOOLS LAYOUT, Merge | ⊞ |
| split table | TABLE TOOLS LAYOUT, Merge | ⊞ |
| Table Options dialog box | TABLE TOOLS LAYOUT, Alignment | ▯ |
| Table Properties dialog box | TABLE TOOLS LAYOUT, Table | ▤ |
| view gridlines | TABLE TOOLS LAYOUT, Table | ▦ |

# *Key Points Review*

**Completion:** In the space provided at the right, indicate the correct term, command, or number.

1. Insert and delete columns and rows with buttons in this group on the TABLE TOOLS LAYOUT tab. _____

2. Click this button on the TABLE TOOLS LAYOUT tab to insert a column at the left of the column containing the insertion point. _____

3. Click this button on the TABLE TOOLS LAYOUT tab to merge selected cells. _____

4. One method of changing the column width is dragging this on the horizontal ruler. _____

5. Use this measurement box on the TABLE TOOLS LAYOUT tab to increase or decrease the height of a row. _____

6. When you hold down this key while dragging a table column marker, measurements display on the horizontal ruler. _____

7. Use this button in the Cell Size group on the TABLE TOOLS LAYOUT tab to make the column widths automatically fit the contents. _____

8. The left and right margins in a cell both have this default setting. _____

9. Change the table alignment at this dialog box with the Table tab selected. _____

10. Hover the mouse pointer over a table and this displays in the lower right corner of the table. _____

11. Position the mouse pointer within a table and this displays in the upper left corner. _____

12. Click this button to display the *Convert Text to Table* option. _____

13. The Sort button is located in this group on the TABLE TOOLS LAYOUT tab. _____

14. When writing a formula, use this symbol to indicate multiplication. _____

15. When writing a formula, use this symbol to indicate division. _____

# *Chapter* Assessments

## Applying Your Skills

Demonstrate your knowledge of features learned in this chapter by completing the following assessments.

### Assessment 14.1    Create and Format a Supply Request Form Table

1. At a blank document, create the table shown in Figure 14.6 on the next page with the following specifications:

   a. Create a table with five columns and eight rows.
   b. Insert three additional rows in the table.
   c. Merge the cells in the first row.
   d. Type the text in the cells as shown in Figure 14.6.
   e. Change the row height of the first row to 0.58 inch.
   f. Select the text in the first row and then change the font size to 22 points.
   g. Select rows 2 through 11 and then change the row height for the selected cells to 0.3 inch.
   h. Apply the Grid Table 4 - Accent 5 table style (sixth column, fourth row in the *Grid Tables* section).
   i. Remove the check mark from the *First Column* option in the Table Style Options group.
   j. Change the alignment of the text in the first row to centered.
   k. Change the alignment of the text in the second row to centered and apply bold formatting.

2. Save the document with the name **C14-A01-SupplyForm**.

3. Print and then close **C14-A01-SupplyForm.docx**.

**Figure 14.6  Assessment 14.1**

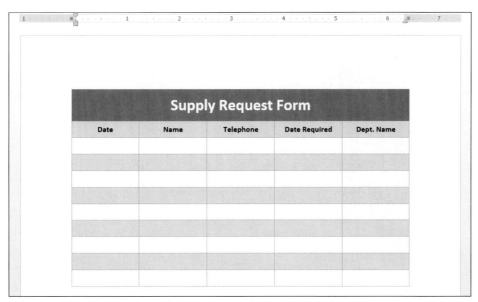

| Supply Request Form | | | | |
|---|---|---|---|---|
| Date | Name | Telephone | Date Required | Dept. Name |
| | | | | |
| | | | | |
| | | | | |
| | | | | |
| | | | | |
| | | | | |
| | | | | |
| | | | | |

## Assessment 14.2    Format a Transportation Services Table

1. Open **Services.docx** and save the document with the name **C14-A02-Services**.
2. Format the table so it appears as shown in Figure 14.7 on the next page with the following specifications:
   a. Delete the row that begins with *City Travel 24-hour customer service.*
   b. Click in the cell containing the text *Edgewood City Transit*, insert four new rows above it, and then type the following text in the new rows:
      Valley Rail Road
      Railway information     (208) 555-8775
      Status hotline          (208) 555-8740
      Travel information      (208) 555-8442
   c. Select the cells containing the text *Railway information*, *Status hotline*, and *Travel information* that you just typed and then change the left cell margin measurement to 0.3 inch. ***Hint: Refer to Exercise 14.2A, Step 4.***
   d. Select the two cells below *City Travel Card* (the cells containing indented text) and then change the left cell margin measurement to 0.3 inch.
   e. Select the three cells below *Edgewood City Transit* (the cells containing indented text) and then change the left cell margin measurement to 0.3 inch.
   f. Select the three cells below *Mainline Bus* (the cells containing indented text) and then change the left cell margin measurement to 0.3 inch.
   g. Insert a column at the left of the first column and then merge the cells in the new column. Type the text **Edgewood Area Transportation Services**, change the text direction so it displays as shown in Figure 14.7 on the next page, and then change the alignment to centered. With the text selected, change the font size to 18 points.
   h. Change the width of the first column to 1 inch, the width of the second column to 2.2 inches, and the width of the third column to 1.1 inches.
   i. Apply bold and italic formatting to the text as shown in Figure 14.7.
   j. Apply shading to the cells as shown in Figure 14.7. (Use Dark Blue for the first column and first row and Gold, Accent 4, Lighter 80% and Blue, Accent 5, Lighter 80% for the other cells.)
3. Center the table between the left and right margins of the document.
4. Save, print, and then close **C14-A02-Services.docx**.

**Figure 14.7  Assessment 14.2**

| | Service | Telephone |
|---|---|---|
| **Edgewood Area Transportation Services** | **City Travel Card** | |
| | City Travel office | (208) 555-6500 |
| | Card inquiries | (208) 555-9005 |
| | **Valley Rail Road** | |
| | Railway information | (208) 555-8775 |
| | Status hotline | (208) 555-8740 |
| | Travel information | (208) 555-8442 |
| | **Edgewood City Transit** | |
| | Subway and bus information | (208) 555-5475 |
| | Service status hotline | (208) 555-1194 |
| | Travel information | (208) 555-9043 |
| | **Mainline Bus** | |
| | Bus routes | (208) 555-4355 |
| | Emergency hotline | (208) 555-5121 |
| | Travel information | (208) 555-4550 |

## Assessment 14.3    Create and Format a Training Costs Table

1. At a blank document, create the table shown in Figure 14.8 with the following specifications:
   a. Create a table with two columns and seven rows.
   b. Merge the cells in the top row and then change the alignment to centered.
   c. Type the text in the cells as shown in Figure 14.8.
   d. Change the alignment to top right for the cells containing the money amounts and the blank line below the last amount (cells B2 through B7).
   e. AutoFit the contents of the cells.
   f. Apply the Grid Table 5 Dark - Accent 6 table style (last column, fifth row in the *Grid Tables* section).
   g. Change the font size to 14 points for the text in cell A1.
   h. Click the Cell Margins button on the TABLE TOOLS LAYOUT tab to display the Table Options dialog box and then specify that you want to allow 0.02-inch spacing between cells.
2. Insert a formula in cell B7 that sums the amounts in cells B2 through B6. (Type a dollar sign before the number inserted by the formula.)
3. Save the document with the name **C14-A03-TrainCosts**.
4. Print and then close **C14-A03-TrainCosts.docx**.

**Figure 14.8  Assessment 14.3**

| TRAINING COSTS | |
|---|---|
| Human Resources | $23,150.50 |
| Research and Development | $78,455.00 |
| Public Relations | $10,348.20 |
| Purchasing | $22,349.55 |
| Administration | $64,352.00 |
| Total | |

## Assessment 14.4     Insert Formulas and Format a Training Department Table

1. Open **TrainDept.docx** and save the document with the name **C14-A04-TrainDept**.
2. Insert formulas in the cells below the *Average* heading that calculate the averages of the numbers in the modules columns. Change the number format to 0 at the Formula dialog box.
3. Change the number in cell B6 from *78* to *90* and change the number in cell B7 from *76* to *90*. Recalculate the averages in cells E6 and E7.
4. Apply the Grid Table 2 - Accent 4 table style (fifth column, second row in the *Grid Tables* section). Remove the check mark from the *First Column* check box in the Table Style Options group.
5. Save, print, and then close **C14-A04-TrainDept.docx**.

## Assessment 14.5     Insert Formulas and Format a Financial Analysis Table

1. Open **FinAnalysis.docx** and save the document with the name **C14-A05-FinAnalysis**.
2. Insert a formula in cell B13 that sums the amounts in cells B6 through B12.
3. Insert a formula in cell C13 that sums the amounts in cells C6 through C12.
4. Insert a formula in cell B14 that subtracts the amount in cell B13 from the amount in cell B4. ***Hint: The formula should look like this: =B4-B13***.
5. Insert a formula in cell C14 that subtracts the amount in cell C13 from the amount in cell C4. ***Hint: The formula should look like this: =C4-C13***. (Make sure you insert dollar signs before the numbers inserted by the formulas.)
6. Apply the Grid Table 4 - Accent 2 table style (third column, fourth row in the *Grid Tables* section). Remove the check mark from the *First Column* check box in the Table Style Options group.
7. Select the top two rows in the table and then change the alignment to centered.
8. Save, print, and then close **C14-A05-FinAnalysis.docx**.

# Expanding Your Skills

Explore additional feature options or use Help to learn a new skill in creating these documents.

## Assessment 14.6     Insert an Average Formula

1. Open **NSSQuizAverages.docx** and save the document with the name **C14-A06-NSSQuizAverages**.
2. Position the insertion point in the last cell in the *Average* column containing data (the cell containing *67%*). Display the Formula dialog box, determine how the formula was written to calculate the quiz averages, determine the number format, and then close the dialog box.
3. Move the insertion point to the empty cell below *67%* and then insert a formula to calculate the averages. Click in the next empty cell in the *Average* column and then press the F4 key to repeat the last function (which was inserting the formula). Continue moving the insertion point to the next empty cell in the *Average* column and pressing the F4 key.
4. Display the Table Options dialog box (click the Cell Margins button) and then specify that you want to allow 0.01-inch spacing between cells.
5. Save and then close **C14-A06-NSSQuizAverages.docx**.

## Assessment 14.7     Insert a Table in a Document and Repeat a Header Row

1. Open **NSSQuizAveLtr.docx** and save the document with the name **C14-A07-NSSQuizAveLtr**.
2. Move the insertion point to the beginning of the second paragraph in the letter and then insert **C14-A06-NSSQuizAverages.docx** into the letter. ***Hint: Do this with the Object button arrow in the Text group on the INSERT tab.***
3. Specify that you want the first row in the table to display as a header row at the top of the table on the second page.
4. Insert your initials at the end of the letter in place of the *XX*.
5. Save, print, and then close **C14-A07-NSSQuizAveLtr.docx**.

# Achieving Signature Status

Take your skills to the next level by completing this more challenging assessment.

## Assessment 14.8 Create a Cover Letter Containing a Table

1. At a blank document, create the document shown in Figure 14.9. Create and format the table as shown in the figure.
2. Save the completed document and name it **C14-A08-CoverLtr**.
3. Print and then close **C14-A08-CoverLtr.docx**.

**Figure 14.9 Assessment 14.8**

4523 Parkland Road
Indianapolis, IN 46211
March 3, 2015

Mr. Alan Lundgren
Orion News Tribune
211 South 42nd Street
Indianapolis, IN 46204

Dear Mr. Lundgren:

Your advertised opening for a corporate communications staff writer describes interesting challenges. As you can see from the table below, my skills are excellent matches for the position.

| QUALIFICATIONS AND SKILLS | |
|---|---|
| **Your Requirements** | **My Experience, Skills, and Value Offered** |
| Two years of business writing experience | Four years of experience creating diverse business messages, from corporate communications to feature articles and radio broadcast material. |
| Ability to complete projects on deadline | Proven project coordination skills and tight deadline focus. My current role as producer of a daily, three-hour talk-radio program requires planning, coordination, and execution of many detailed tasks, always in the face of inflexible deadlines. |
| Oral presentation skills | Unusually broad experience, including high-profile roles as an on-air radio presence and "the voice" for an on-hold telephone message company. |
| Relevant education (BA or BS) | BA in Mass Communications, one year post-graduate study in Multimedia Communications. |

As you will note from the enclosed resume, my experience encompasses corporate, print media, and multimedia environments. I offer a diverse and proven skill set that can help your company create and deliver its message to various audiences to build image, market presence, and revenue. I look forward to meeting with you to discuss the value I can offer your company.

Sincerely,

Justine Brock

Enclosure: Resume

# Chapter 15

# Creating Charts

## Performance Objectives

Upon successful completion of Chapter 15, you will be able to:

- Create charts
- Format charts using the chart buttons
- Change the chart design
- Format charts and chart elements

In Chapters 13 and 14, you learned to create tables to organize data. Although a table provides an adequate way to present and display data, a chart can provide a more visual representation. Sometimes referred to as a *graph,* a chart is a picture of numeric data. You can choose from 10 different chart types to represent data in a Word document.

*Note: Before beginning computer exercises for this chapter, copy to your storage medium the Chapter15 folder from the CD that accompanies this textbook and then make Chapter15 the active folder.*

In this chapter, students will produce the following documents:

Exercise 15.1. C15-E01-TECSales.docx
Exercise 15.2. C15-E02-Singapore.docx
Exercise 15.3. C15-E03-CIRevs.docx

Model answers for these exercises are shown on the following pages.

**Exercise 15.1**

C15-E01-TECSales.docx

**TANDEM ENERGY CORPORATION**

**Sales and Marketing**

Our products are marketed directly to customers to build market interest through power-quality manufacturers' representatives and through lead generation via advertising, trade press articles, participation in industry conferences, technical presentations to potential customers, and limited direct mail to specific power-quality customers. This strategy has seen an increase in sales in most regions of the country as shown in the sales chart.

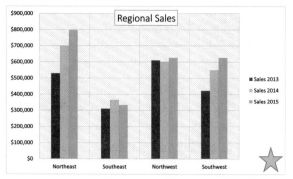

Our marketing strategy has been to identify key prospects and to work with those companies to formulate our product plan, pricing, initial installation, and service strategies. We will continue to perform market analysis to identify opportunities for installations that fit the unique characteristics of those products and to emphasize the value proposition of our high-energy products. Potential customers for these products include businesses with heightened needs for 100 percent reliability, such as hospitals, data centers, call centers, and other critical-use facilities. We believe that our high-energy products will also be attractive to customers with power sources that are very expensive to replace or maintain due to their location or other factors, or power sources located where high or low prevailing temperatures or dramatic changes in temperatures exist.

## Singapore

Steeped in tradition, yet contemporary in outlook, Singapore is the ideal destination for travelers in pursuit of that elusive and eclectic cultural mix. Before you experience Singapore's unique lifestyle options, take a look at some of the basic facts about this fascinating country.

### Language

Of the four official languages (Malay, Mandarin, Tamil, and English), Malay is the national language, although English is the one most widely spoken and understood. Most Singaporeans are bilingual; they speak their mother tongue as well as English.

### Population

Over the past 50 years, the population of Singapore has changed 214 percent. The population reached a record low of 1.7 million in December of 1960 with an all-time high of 5.2 million in December of 2011. The following chart shows the population change from 1980 to 2010.

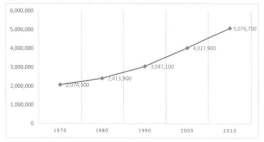

**Exercise 15.2**

C15-E02-Singapore.docx

### Climate

Singapore's climate is warm and humid, ideal for sunbathing, swimming, sailing, surfing, and other water sports. But there is respite for those who need a break from the tropical climate: almost all shops, hotels, office buildings, and restaurants in Singapore are air-conditioned.

Although the monsoon extends from November to January, Singaporeans are accustomed to sudden, refreshing showers all year round.

### Currency

Other than the Singapore dollar, the U.S. and Australian dollars, the Yen, and the British pound are accepted in most major shopping centers and department stores.

Page 1

## Religion

Singapore is an eclectic mix of people and religions. Buddhism, Christianity, Islam, Hinduism, Sikhism, Judaism, and Zoroastrianism coexist harmoniously. Towering cathedrals, exquisite mosque minarets, intricate Chinese temple architecture, and minutely wrought figurines in Hindu temples are all embedded in Singapore's rich heritage.

## Entertainment

When in Singapore, the party never stops! The nightlife in Singapore is designed to keep you dancing 'til dawn. Whether you're into jazz or house music, tribal or techno, Singapore offers a wide variety of dance clubs that cater to every mood and occasion.

For those in a mellower mood, you can relax and have a drink in a number of pubs and jazz lounges. And, if you're looking for fun, what better than an all-night bowling session?

All this activity is bound to stir your appetite. You can head for one of the 24-hour coffee houses in the city or take a look at the scrumptious fare offered at the superb food stalls scattered throughout the island.

## Museums

Singapore has a number of superbly maintained museums that offer a glimpse into Asia's cultural variety. Exhibitions, workshops, and other activities organized by the museums enliven history and artistic tradition. The artifacts and paintings on display are sure to hold your attention for hours.

# Caswell Industries

### Revenues

We are evaluating markets for our current and future products. Prior to the fourth quarter of 2015, we increased the percentage of our revenues from contracts with government entities. While we saw an increase in our revenue percentage from government contracts, we maintained and, in some quarters, exceeded our projects on revenue percentages from domestic and foreign sales.

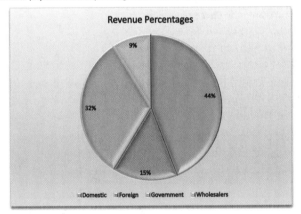

### Research and Development

Our cost of research and development consists primarily of the cost of compensation and benefits for research and support staff, as well as materials and supplies used in the engineering design and development process. These costs decreased significantly during 2015 as we focused on reducing our expenditure rate by reducing product design and development activities.

### Preferred Stock Dividends

Prior to our initial public offering of our common stock, we had various classes of preferred stock outstanding, each of which was entitled to receive dividends. We accrued dividend expenses monthly according to the requirements of each class of preferred stock.

**Exercise 15.3**

C15-E03-CIRevs.docx

# Creating a Chart

**Insert a Chart**
1. Click INSERT tab.
2. Click Chart button.
3. Click desired chart type and style.
4. Click OK.
5. Enter data in Excel spreadsheet.
6. Close Excel.

Chart

In Word, you can create a variety of charts, including bar and column charts, pie charts, area charts, and many other types. Table 15.1 describes the 10 basic chart types you can create in Word.

To create a chart, click the INSERT tab and then click the Chart button in the Illustrations group. This displays the Insert Chart dialog box, as shown in Figure 15.1 on the next page. At this dialog box, choose the type of chart you want to create from the list at the left side of the dialog box, click the chart style, and then click OK.

When you click OK, a sample chart is inserted into your Word document and Excel opens with sample data, as shown in Figure 15.2 on the next page. Type the desired data in the Excel worksheet cells over the existing data. To type data in the Excel worksheet, click in the desired cell, type the data, and then press the Tab key to make the next cell active. Press Shift + Tab to make the previous cell active or press the Enter key to make the cell below active. As you type data in the Excel worksheet, the entries are reflected in the chart in the Word document.

The sample worksheet contains a data range of four columns and five rows and the cells in the data range display with a light fill color. Excel uses the data in the range to create the chart in the slide. You are not limited to creating charts with only four columns and five rows, however. Simply type data in cells outside the data range and Excel will expand the data range and incorporate the new data in the chart. This happens because the table AutoExpansion feature is on by default. If you type data in a cell outside the data range, an AutoCorrect Options button displays in the lower right corner of the cell when you move away from the cell. Use this button if you want to turn off AutoExpansion.

**Table 15.1  Types of Charts**

| Chart | Description |
|---|---|
| area | Emphasizes the magnitude of change over time, rather than the rate of change. Also shows the relationship of the parts to the whole by displaying the sum of the plotted values. |
| bar | Shows individual figures at a specific time or shows variations between components but not in relationship to the whole. |
| column | Compares separate (noncontinuous) items as they vary over time. |
| combo | Combines two or more chart types to make data easy to understand. |
| line | Shows trends and overall change across time at even intervals. Emphasizes the rate of change over time, rather than the magnitude of change. |
| pie | Shows proportions and relationships of the parts to the whole. |
| radar | Emphasizes differences and amounts of change over time and variations and trends. Each category has its own value axis radiating from the center point. Lines connect all values in the same series. |
| stock | Shows five values for a stock: open, high, low, volume, and close. |
| surface | Shows trends in values across two dimensions in a continuous curve. |
| XY (scatter) | Shows the relationships among numeric values in several data series or plots the interception points between *x* and *y* values. Shows uneven intervals of data and is commonly used in scientific data. |

**Figure 15.1  Insert Chart Dialog Box**

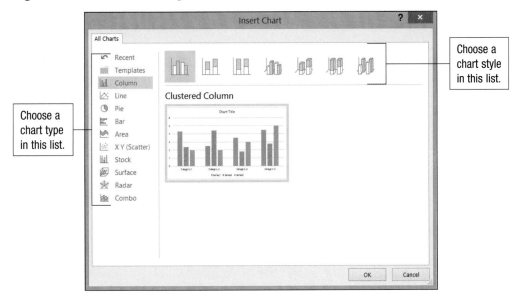

Choose a chart type in this list.

Choose a chart style in this list.

**Figure 15.2  Sample Chart**

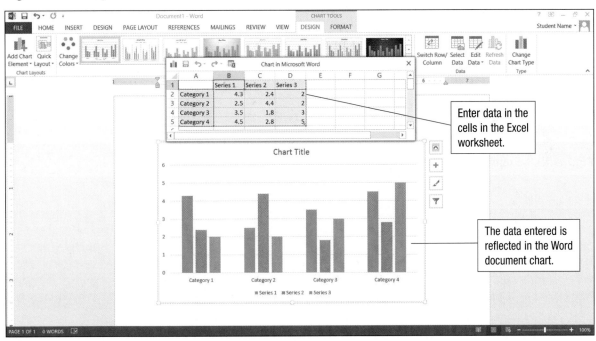

Enter data in the cells in the Excel worksheet.

The data entered is reflected in the Word document chart.

If you do not insert data into all four columns and five rows, then decrease the size of the data range. To do this, position the mouse pointer on the small, square, blue icon that displays in the lower right corner of cell E5 until the pointer displays as a diagonally pointing, two-headed arrow. Drag the arrow up to decrease the number of rows in the range and/or drag the arrow to the left to decrease the number of columns.

When you have entered all of the data in the worksheet, click the Close button that displays in the upper right corner of the Excel window. This closes the Excel window, expands the Word document window, and displays the chart in the document.

Close

1. Open **TECSales.docx** and save the document with the name **C15-E01-TECSales**.
2. Move the insertion point to the blank line between the two paragraphs of text in the document and then insert a chart by completing the following steps:
   a. Click the INSERT tab.
   b. Click the Chart button in the Illustrations group.
   c. At the Insert Chart dialog box, click OK.
3. Type **Sales 2013** in cell B1 in the Excel worksheet.

4. Press the Tab key and then type **Sales 2014** in cell C1.
5. Press the Tab key and then type **Sales 2015** in cell D1.
6. Press the Tab key. (This makes cell A2 active.)
7. Continue typing the remaining data in the cells as shown in Figure 15.3. After typing the last entry, click in cell A1.
8. When all of the data is entered, click the Close button that displays in the upper right corner of the Excel window.
9. Save **C15-E01-TECSales.docx**.

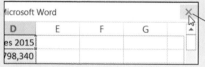

**Figure 15.3  Exercise 15.1A**

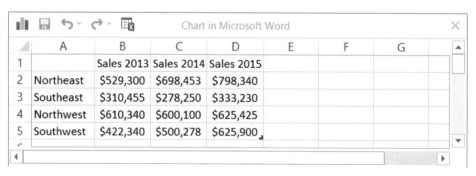

| | A | B | C | D | E | F | G |
|---|---|---|---|---|---|---|---|
| 1 | | Sales 2013 | Sales 2014 | Sales 2015 | | | |
| 2 | Northeast | $529,300 | $698,453 | $798,340 | | | |
| 3 | Southeast | $310,455 | $278,250 | $333,230 | | | |
| 4 | Northwest | $610,340 | $600,100 | $625,425 | | | |
| 5 | Southwest | $422,340 | $500,278 | $625,900 | | | |

# Formatting with Chart Buttons

When you insert a chart in a document, four buttons display at the right side of the chart border, as shown in Figure 15.4. These buttons provide options for applying formatting to the entire chart.

## Applying Text Wrapping with the Layout Options Button

Click the top button, Layout Options, that displays at the right side of the chart border and a side menu displays with text wrapping options. The default setting is *In Line with Text*. Use options in the *With Text Wrapping* section of the side menu to apply a text wrapping option to the chart.

When you apply text wrapping, the *Move with text* and *Fix position on page* options become available. The *Move with text* option is active by default. With this option selected, the chart moves on the page as text is added or removed from the document. With the *Fix position on page* option selected, the chart is anchored to a specific location on the page. Click the <u>See more</u> hyperlink that displays at the bottom of the Layout Options side menu and the Layout dialog box displays.

## Adding and Removing Elements with the Chart Elements Button

Click the second button, Chart Elements, and a side menu displays with chart elements such as axis title, chart title, data labels, data table, gridlines, and legend. Elements containing check marks in the check boxes are included in the chart. Add other elements by inserting check marks in the check boxes for those elements.

Hover the mouse pointer over an option in the Chart Elements side menu and a right-pointing triangle displays. Click this right-pointing triangle and another side menu displays with additional options. For example, position the mouse pointer over the *Chart Title* option, click the right-pointing triangle, and a side menu displays with options for centering or overlaying the chart title or displaying the Format Chart Title task pane. Click *More Options* at the side menu to display the task pane.

**QUICK STEPS**

**Apply Text Wrapping with Layout Options Button**
1. Click Layout Options button at right side of chart.
2. Click text wrapping option at side menu

**Add/Remove Chart Elements with Chart Elements Button**
1. Click Chart Elements button at right side of the chart.
2. Add or remove check marks from elements at side menu.

**Figure 15.4  Chart Buttons**

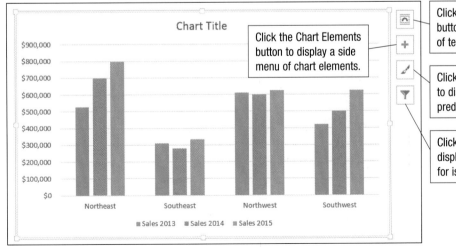

Click the Layout Options button to display a side menu of text wrapping options.

Click the Chart Elements button to display a side menu of chart elements.

Click the Chart Styles button to display a side menu of predesigned style options.

Click the Chart Filters button to display a side menu with options for isolating specific data.

1. With **C15-E01-TECSales.docx** open, make sure the chart is selected.
2. Click the Layout Options button that displays outside the upper right border of the chart and then click the *Top and Bottom* option in the side menu (first column, second row in the *With Text Wrapping* section).
3. Click the *Fix position on page* option to anchor the chart to the current location on the page.
4. Click the Chart Elements button that displays below the Layout Options button outside the upper right border of the chart.
5. At the Chart Elements side menu, remove the chart title by clicking the *Chart Title* check box to remove the check mark.

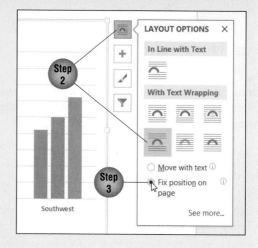

6. Add data labels above the columns in the chart by completing the following steps:
   a. Click the *Data Labels* check box in the side menu to insert a check mark.
   b. Click the right-pointing triangle that displays to the right of the *Data Labels* option.
   c. Click the *Center* option at the side menu.
7. Add a data table at the bottom of the chart by completing the following steps:
   a. Click the *Data Table* check box to insert a check mark.
   b. Click the right-pointing triangle that displays to the right of the *Data Table* option.
   c. Click the *No Legend Keys* option at the side menu.

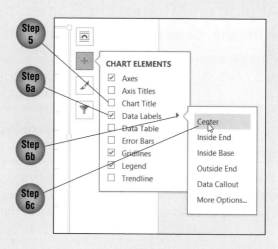

8. Remove the data labels centered on the columns by clicking the *Data Labels* check box to remove the check mark.
9. Add additional gridlines to the chart by completing the following steps:
   a. Hover the mouse pointer over the *Gridlines* option in the Chart Elements button side menu and then click the right-pointing triangle that displays.
   b. Click the *Primary Major Vertical* check box to insert a check mark.
   c. Click the *Primary Minor Horizontal* check box to insert a check mark.
10. Click the Chart Elements button to remove the side menus.
11. Save **C15-E01-TECSales.docx**.

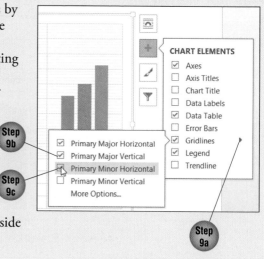

## Applying Chart Styles with the Chart Styles Button

Click the Chart Styles button that displays at the right side of the selected chart and a side menu gallery of styles displays. Scroll down the gallery, hover your mouse over an option, and the style formatting is applied to your chart. Using this feature, you can scroll down the gallery and preview a style before applying it to your chart.

In addition to applying a chart style, you can change the chart colors by using the Chart Styles button side menu gallery. Click the Chart Styles button, click the COLOR tab that displays to the right of the STYLE tab, and then click the desired color option at the palette that displays. Hover your mouse pointer over a color option to view how the color change affects the elements in your chart. Hover your mouse pointer over the text *How do I change these colors?* that displays at the bottom of the side menu and a box displays with a message telling you how to change colors. To do this, go to the DESIGN tab, click the Theme Colors button in the Document Formatting group, and then select a theme color from the drop-down gallery.

## Filtering Chart Data with the Chart Filters Button

Use the Chart Filters button that displays at the right side of the selected chart to isolate specific data in your chart. When you click the button, a side menu displays with check boxes before series and categories. Isolate specific data by removing the check marks from the specific series or categories that you do not want to display in the chart. After removing the desired check marks, click the Apply button that displays toward the bottom of the side menu. Click the NAMES tab at the Chart Filters button side menu and options display for turning on and off the display of column and row names.

**QUICK STEPS**

**Apply Chart Style with Chart Styles Button**
1. Click Chart Styles button at right side of chart.
2. Click chart style at side menu gallery.

**Change Chart Colors with Chart Styles Button**
1. Click Chart Styles button at right side of chart.
2. Click COLOR tab.
3. Click color option at palette.

**Filter Data with the Chart Filters Button**
1. Click Chart Filters button at right side of chart.
2. Add or remove check marks from series or categories.
3. Click Apply button.

---

**Exercise 15.1C**   Applying a Style, Changing Colors, and Filtering Data in a Chart                     Part 3 of 6

---

1. With **C15-E01-TECSales.docx** open, apply a different chart style by completing the following steps:
   a. Click the Chart Styles button that displays below the Chart Elements button.
   b. At the side menu gallery, click the *Style 3* option (third option in the gallery).
   c. Click the COLOR tab at the top of the side menu.
   d. Click the *Color 4* option at the drop-down gallery (fourth row of color options in the *Colorful* section).

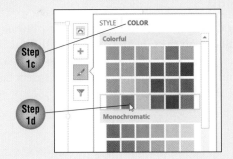

   e. Click the Chart Styles button to close the side menu.

2. Display only the *Northeast* and *Southeast* categories of sales and remove the category names by completing the following steps:
   a. Click the Chart Filters button that displays below the Chart Styles button.
   b. Click the *Northwest* check box in the CATEGORIES section to remove the check mark.
   c. Click the *Southwest* check box in the CATEGORIES section to remove the check mark.
   d. Click the NAMES tab.
   e. Click the *(None)* option in the CATEGORIES section.
   f. Click the Apply button that displays near the bottom of the side menu.

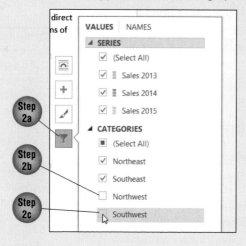
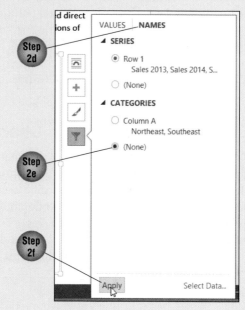

3. Redisplay the category names by completing the following steps:
   a. Click the *Column A* option in the CATEGORIES section of the NAMES tab of the Chart Filters button side menu.
   b. Click the Apply button that displays near the bottom of the side menu.
4. Click the Chart Filters button to close the side menu.
5. After viewing only the *Northeast* and *Southeast* sales categories, redisplay the other regions by clicking the Chart Filters button, clicking the *Northwest* and *Southwest* check boxes, and then clicking the Apply button.
6. Click the Chart Filters button to close the side menu.
7. Save **C15-E01-TECSales.docx**.

# Changing the Chart Design

In addition to the buttons that display outside the chart border, buttons and options for customizing a chart are available on the CHART TOOLS DESIGN tab. Use the buttons and options on this tab, as shown in Figure 15.5 on the next page, to add a chart element, change the chart layout and colors, apply a chart style, select data and switch rows and columns, and change the chart type.

**Figure 15.5 CHART TOOLS DESIGN Tab**

## Adding Chart Elements

Click the Add Chart Element button on the CHART TOOLS DESIGN tab and a drop-down list displays with a variety of chart elements that can be added to a chart. Hover the mouse pointer over one of these options at the drop-down list, and a side menu displays with additional options. The options at this drop-down list and side menus are similar to the options available at the Chart Elements button that displays at the right side of a selected chart.

## Changing the Chart Layout, Colors, and Style

Word provides a number of preformatted layouts that can be applied to a chart. To apply a preformatted layout, click the Quick Layout button on the CHART TOOLS DESIGN tab and then click the desired layout at the drop-down gallery. Hover the mouse over a layout and the formatting is applied to the chart in the document.

The Chart Styles group on the CHART TOOLS DESIGN tab contains the Change Colors button and predesigned chart styles. Change chart colors by clicking the Change Colors button and then clicking the desired color option at the drop-down gallery. Apply a predesigned chart style by clicking a chart style thumbnail in the Chart Styles group. Additional chart styles are available by clicking the More button at the right side of the chart style thumbnails.

**QUICK STEPS**

**Add/Remove Chart Elements with Button on Ribbon**
1. Click Add Chart Element button on CHART TOOLS DESIGN tab.
2. Hover mouse over option at drop-down list.
3. Click option at side menu.

**Apply Chart Layout**
1. Click Quick Layout button on CHART TOOLS DESIGN tab.
2. Click layout at drop-down gallery.

**Apply Chart Style with Button on Ribbon**
1. Click chart style thumbnail in Chart Styles group.
OR
1. Click More button.
2. Click chart style at drop-down gallery.

---

**Exercise 15.1D**  **Adding Chart Elements and Applying a Chart Style**  **Part 4 of 6**

1. With **C15-E01-TECSales.docx** open, make sure that the chart is selected and the CHART TOOLS DESIGN tab is active.
2. Change to a different layout by clicking the Quick Layout button in the Chart Layouts group and then clicking the *Layout 3* option (third option in the drop-down gallery).
3. Click the *Style 7* thumbnail that displays in the Chart Styles group (seventh thumbnail option).
4. Change the chart colors by clicking the Change Colors button and then clicking the *Color 3* option (third row in the *Colorful* section).

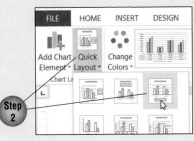

5. Click the Add Chart Element button in the Chart Layouts group, point to *Chart Title* at the drop-down list, and then click *Centered Overlay* at the side menu.
6. Type **Regional Sales** as the chart title.
7. Click the chart border to deselect the chart title.
8. Move the legend to the right side of the chart by clicking the Add Chart Element button, pointing to *Legend*, and then clicking *Right* at the side menu.
9. Save **C15-E01-TECSales.docx**

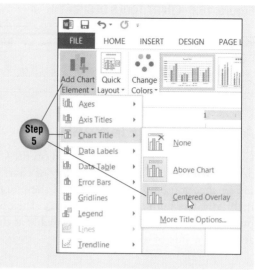

## Managing Data

**Edit Data in Chart**
1. Click Edit Data button.
2. Make changes in Excel worksheet.
3. Click Close button.

**Change Chart Type**
1. Click Change Chart Type button.
2. Click chart and chart type at Insert Chart dialog box.
3. Click OK.

Use options in the Data group on the CHART TOOLS DESIGN tab to change the order of data in the chart, select specific data, edit data, and refresh data. When you create a chart, the cells in the Excel worksheet are linked to the chart in the Word document. If you need to edit data in the chart, click the Edit Data button and the Excel worksheet opens. Make the desired changes to the cells in the Excel worksheet and then click the Close button.

Click the Select Data button in the Data group and the Select Data Source dialog box displays. Use options in this dialog box to switch the rows and columns of data; add, edit, and remove chart entries; and filter and isolate specific data in the chart.

## Changing the Chart Type

Click the Change Chart Type button on the CHART TOOLS DESIGN tab and the Change Chart Type dialog box displays. This dialog box contains the same options as the Insert Chart dialog box. Use options at this dialog box to change the selected chart to a different type.

---

**Exercise 15.1E**    **Managing Data and Changing the Chart Type**      Part 5 of 6

1. With **C15-E01-TECSales.docx** open and the chart selected, edit the data by completing the following steps:
   a. Click the Edit Data button in the Data group.
   b. Click in cell C3.
   c. Type **375,250**. (The text you type replaces the original amount of $278,250.)
   d. Click in cell C5, type **550,300**, and then press the Tab key.
   e. Click the Close button that displays in the upper right corner of the Excel window.

2. Reverse the columns and rows and isolate specific data by completing the following steps:
   a. Click the Select Data button in the Data group.
   b. At the Select Data Source dialog box, click the Switch Row/Column button.
   c. Click the *Northeast* check box in the *Legend Entries (Series)* list box to remove the check mark.
   d. Click the *Southeast* check box to remove the check mark.
   e. Click OK to close the dialog box.

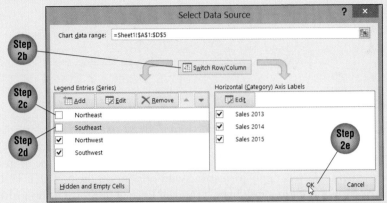

3. With the Excel worksheet open in the document, click in the chart outside the Excel worksheet and then click the Switch Row/Column button in the Data group on the CHART TOOLS DESIGN tab. (This reverses the columns and rows again.)

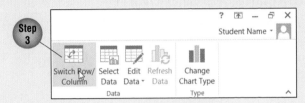

4. Close the Excel worksheet.
5. Change the chart type by completing the following steps:
   a. Click the Change Chart Type button in the Type group on the CHART TOOLS DESIGN tab.
   b. At the Change Chart Type dialog box, click *Bar* in the list at the left.
   c. Click the *3-D Clustered Bar* option that displays near the top of the dialog box (fourth option from the left).
   d. Click OK to close the dialog box.
6. Save and then print **C15-E01-TECSales.docx**.
7. Remove the filter from the chart by completing the following steps:
   a. Make sure the chart is selected.
   b. Click the Chart Filters button that displays at the right side of the chart.
   c. Click the *Northeast* check box in the CATEGORIES section to insert a check mark.
   d. Click the *Southeast* check box in the CATEGORIES section to insert a check mark.
   e. Click the Apply button located near the bottom of the side menu.
   f. Click the Chart Filters button to remove the side menu.
8. Change the chart type by clicking the Change Chart Type button, clicking *Column* in the list at the left side of the Choose a Chart Type dialog box, and then clicking OK.
9. Save **C15-E01-TECSales.docx**.

# Formatting the Chart

Use buttons on the CHART TOOLS FORMAT tab, as shown in Figure 15.6, to format a chart and the chart elements. With options on the tab, select chart elements, insert a shape, apply a shape style and WordArt style, and arrange and size the chart or chart element.

**Figure 15.6  CHART TOOLS FORMAT Tab**

## Selecting Elements

**Select Chart Element**
1. Click element in chart.
OR
1. Click Chart Elements button.
2. Click element at drop-down list.

**Insert Shape in Chart**
1. Click shape in shape gallery.
2. Click or drag in chart.
OR
1. Click More button.
2. Click shape at drop-down list.
3. Click or drag in chart.

To format or modify a specific element in a chart, first select the element. To do this, click the element or click the Chart Elements button in the Current Selection group on the CHART TOOLS FORMAT tab and then click the element at the drop-down list. With the element selected, apply formatting with options on the CHART TOOLS FORMAT tab or with options at a task pane. (You will learn about formatting with a task pane later in this chapter.) If you make changes to the chart and then want to return to the original formatting, click the Reset to Match Style button in the Current Selection group.

## Inserting Shapes in a Chart

The Insert Shapes group on the CHART TOOLS FORMAT tab contains options for inserting a shape in a chart. Click the desired shape in the shape gallery or click the More button and then click the desired shape at the drop-down list. With the shape selected, click or draw in the chart to insert the shape.

## Applying Shape and WordArt Styles

Options in the Shape Styles group on the CHART TOOLS FORMAT tab apply formatting to an element in a chart. The Shape Styles group contains predesigned shape styles that can be applied to an element in a chart, buttons to change the fill color and outline color of an element, and a button to apply effects to a chart element.

Use options in the WordArt Styles group on the CHART TOOLS FORMAT tab to apply formatting to the text in a chart. The WordArt Styles group contains predesigned WordArt formatting, buttons for changing the fill color and outline color of text, and a button for applying effects to text.

1. With **C15-E01-TECSales.docx** open, apply a
   shape style to the chart title by completing the
   followings steps:
   a. With the chart selected, click the CHART
      TOOLS FORMAT tab.
   b. Click the Chart Elements button arrow in the
      Current Selection group.
   c. Click *Chart Title* at the drop-down list.
   d. Click the *Colored Outline - Blue, Accent 1* option
      (second thumbnail in the Shape Styles gallery).

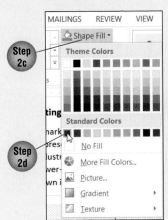

2. Change the color of the *Sales 2013* series by completing
   the followings steps:
   a. Click the Chart Elements button arrow in the Current Selection group.
   b. Click *Series "Sales 2013"* at the drop-down list.
   c. Click the Shape Fill button arrow in the Shapes Styles group.
   d. Click the *Dark Red* option (first color option in the *Standard Colors* section).

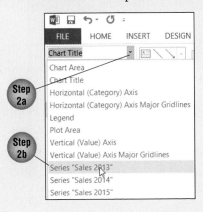

3. Apply a WordArt style to all of the text in the chart by completing the following steps:
   a. Click the Chart Elements button arrow.
   b. Click *Chart Area* at the drop-down list.
   c. Click the *Fill - Black, Text 1, Shadow* option in the WordArt Styles group (first
      thumbnail in the WordArt Styles gallery).
4. Draw a shape in the lower right corner of the chart by completing the following steps:
   a. Click the More button that displays at the right side of the shape gallery in the Insert
      Shapes group.
   b. Click the *5-Point Star* shape at the drop-down list (fourth column, first row in the *Stars
      and Banners* section).
   c. Click in the lower right corner of the chart. (This inserts the star shape in the chart and
      also makes the DRAWING TOOLS FORMAT tab active.)
   d. Click in the *Shape Height* measurement box and then type **0.5**.
   e. Click in the *Shape Width* measurement box, type **0.5**, and then press Enter.
   f. Click the Shape Fill button arrow and then click the *Orange* color (third option in the
      *Standard Colors* section).
   g. Drag the star shape to the lower right corner of the chart.
5. Save, print, and then close **C15-E01-TECSales.docx**.

## Arranging and Sizing a Chart

The Arrange and Size groups on the CHART TOOLS FORMAT tab contain buttons and options for changing the location of a chart, changing the chart's position relative to other elements, and changing the height and width of a chart. The options in the two groups are the same as the options in the Arrange and Size groups on the DRAWING TOOLS FORMAT tab.

---

**Exercise 15.2   Creating and Formatting a Line Chart**                                   Part 1 of 1

1. Open **Singapore.docx** and save the document with the name **C15-E02-Singapore**.
2. Create a line chart by completing the following steps:
   a.   Click the INSERT tab.
   b.   Click the Chart button in the Illustrations group.
   c.   At the Insert Chart dialog box, click the *Line* option in list at the the left.
   d.   Click the *Line with Markers* chart style that displays near the top of the dialog box (fourth option).

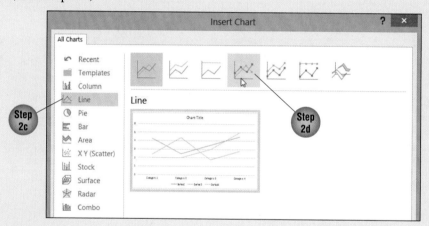

   e.   Click OK.
3. Decrease the size of the data range in the Excel worksheet by completing the following steps:
   a.   Position the mouse pointer on the small blue icon that displays in the lower right corner of cell E5 until the pointer displays as a diagonally pointing two-headed arrow.
   b.   Drag to the left to decrease the number of columns so only columns A and B are in the data range.
4. Type the text in the cells as shown in Figure 15.7 on the next page. After typing the last entry, click in cell A2.
5. Click the Close button that displays in the upper right corner of the Excel window.
6. Click the Quick Layout button on the CHART TOOLS DESIGN tab and then click the *Layout 9* option at the drop-down gallery (third column, third row).
7. Click the More button at the right side of the chart style thumbnails in the Chart Styles group and then click *Style 11* at the drop-down gallery (third column, bottom row).

8. Remove the legend from the chart by clicking the Add Chart Element button, pointing to *Legend*, and then clicking *None* at the side menu.
9. Remove the chart title by clicking the Add Chart Element button, pointing to *Chart Title*, and then clicking *None* at the side menu.
10. Change the size of the chart by completing the following steps:
    a. Click the CHART TOOLS FORMAT tab.
    b. Click in the *Shape Height* measurement box and then type **2.8**.
    c. Click in the *Shape Width* measurement box, type **4**, and then press Enter.
11. Change the position of the chart by clicking the Position button in the Arrange group on the CHART TOOLS FORMAT tab and then clicking the *Position in Middle Left with Square Text Wrapping* option at the drop-down gallery (first column, second row in the *With Text Wrapping* section).

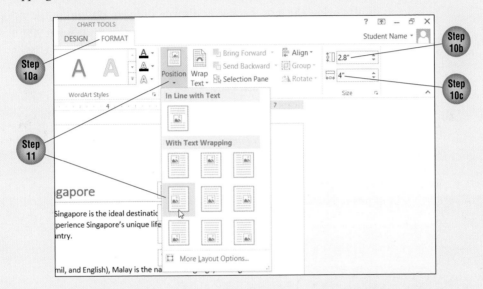

12. Change the text wrapping by clicking the Wrap Text button and then clicking *Top and Bottom* at the drop-down gallery.
13. Click in the *Shape Width* measurement box, type **5.5**, and then press Enter.
14. Change the alignment of the chart by clicking the Align button in the Arrange group and then clicking *Align Center* at the drop-down list.
15. Save, print, and then close **C15-E02-Singapore.docx**.

**Figure 15.7 Exercise 15.2**

| | A | B | C | D | E | F | G |
|---|---|---|---|---|---|---|---|
| 1 | | Population | Series 2 | Series 3 | | | |
| 2 | 1970 | 2,074,500 | 2.4 | 2 | | | |
| 3 | 1980 | 2,413,900 | 4.4 | 2 | | | |
| 4 | 1990 | 3,047,100 | 1.8 | 3 | | | |
| 5 | 2000 | 4,027,900 | 2.8 | 5 | | | |
| 6 | 2010 | 5,076,700 | | | | | |
| 7 | | | | | | | |

## Formatting with Task Pane Options

Additional formatting options are available at various task panes. To display a task pane, click the Format Selection button or click a group task pane launcher. The Shape Styles and WordArt Styles groups on the CHART TOOLS FORMAT tab both contain task pane launchers. The task pane that opens at the right side of the screen depends on the chart or chart element selected. For example, select a chart, click the Shape Styles group task pane launcher, and the Format Chart Area task pane displays, as shown in Figure 15.8.

The Format Chart Area task pane contains two tabs located near the top of the task pane with the CHART OPTIONS tab active. With this tab active, options display in the task pane for formatting the chart. Click the TEXT OPTIONS tab and options display for formatting the text in a chart.

Icons display below the tabs. Each icon displays different options in the task pane and the options may or may not be expanded. To expand an option, click the option or the expand triangle that displays to the left of the option.

**Figure 15.8 Format Chart Area Task Pane**

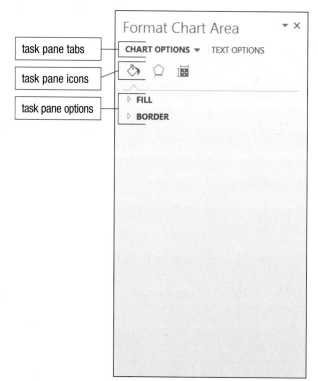

## Formatting with Layout Dialog Box Options

In Chapter 11, you learned about the Layout dialog box, which contains options for formatting the position, text wrapping, and size of an image. The same dialog box is available for formatting a chart. Display the Layout dialog box by clicking the Size group dialog box launcher on the CHART TOOLS FORMAT tab. You can also display the dialog box by clicking the Layout Options button that displays at the right side of a selected chart and then clicking the *See more* option that displays at the bottom of the side menu.

1. Open **CIRevs.docx** and save the document with the name **C15-E03-CIRevs**.
2. Create a pie chart by completing the following steps:
   a. Click the INSERT tab and then click the Chart button in the Illustrations group.
   b. At the Insert Chart dialog box, click *Pie* in the list at the left.
   c. Click OK.
3. Type the data in the Excel worksheet cells as shown in Figure 15.9 on page 503. After typing the last entry, click in cell A1 and then click the Close button located in the upper right corner of the Excel window.
4. Click on the title *Percentage* and then type **Revenue Percentages**.
5. Add data labels to the pie chart by completing the following steps:
   a. Click the Add Chart Element button in the Chart Layouts group on the CHART TOOLS DESIGN tab.
   b. Point to *Data Labels* at the drop-down list and then click *Inside End* at the side menu.

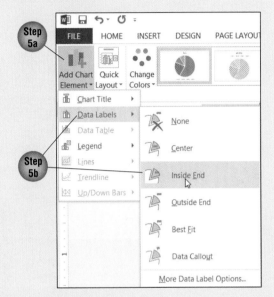

6. Click on the chart border to select the chart and not a chart element.
7. Click the CHART TOOLS FORMAT tab.
8. Apply formatting to the chart with options at the Format Chart Area task pane by completing the following steps:
   a. With the chart selected, click the Shape Styles group task pane launcher.
   b. At the Format Chart Area task pane with the Fill & Line icon selected, click *FILL*. (This expands the options below FILL.)
   c. Click the *Gradient fill* option.
   d. Click the Effects icon located near the top of the task pane.
   e. Click *SHADOW* to expand the shadow options.
   f. Click the Presets button.
   g. Click the *Offset Bottom* option (second column, first row in the *Outer* section).

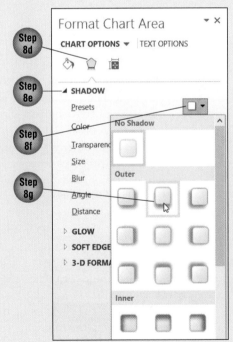

h.  Click the TEXT OPTIONS tab that displays near the top of the task pane to the right of the CHART OPTIONS tab.
i.  Click *TEXT OUTLINE* to expand the options.
j.  Click the *Solid line* option.
k.  Click the Color button and then click the *Dark Blue* option (ninth color in the *Standard Colors* section).

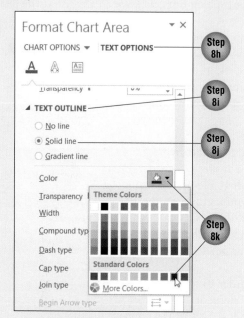

9.  Format the pie chart by completing the following steps:
a.  Click in any "piece" of the pie. (This selects all of the pieces of the pie.) Notice that the task pane name changes to *Format Data Series*.
b.  Click the Effects icon that displays near the top of the task pane.
c.  Click *3-D FORMAT* to expand the options.
d.  Click the Top bevel button.
e.  Click the *Soft Round* option at the drop-down list (second column, second row in the *Bevel* section).
f.  Close the task pane by clicking the Close button that displays in the upper right corner of the task pane.

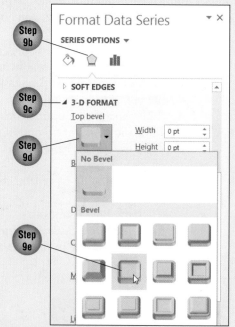

10. Click the chart border to select the chart and not a chart element.
11. Size and position the chart using the Layout dialog box by completing the following steps:
a.  With the CHART TOOL FORMAT tab active, click the Size group dialog box launcher.
b.  At the Layout dialog box with the Size tab selected, select the current measurement in the *Absolute* measurement box in the *Height* section and then type **3.75**.
c.  Select the current measurement in the *Absolute* measurement box in the *Width* section and then type **5.5**.

d. Click the Text Wrapping tab.
e. Click the *Top and bottom* option.
f. Click once on the up arrow at the right side of the *Top* measurement box in the *Distance from text* section. (This displays *0.1"* in the measurement box.)
g. Click twice on the up arrow at the right side of the *Bottom* measurement box in the *Distance from text* section. (This displays *0.2"* in the measurement box.)
h. Click the Position tab.
i. Click the *Alignment* option in the *Horizontal* section.
j. Click the down-pointing arrow at the right side of the *Alignment* option box and then click *Centered* at the drop-down list.
k. With the *Absolute position* option selected in the *Vertical* section, select the current measurement in the *Absolute position* measurement box in the *Vertical* section and then type **3.2**.
l. Click the down-pointing arrow at the right side of the option box to the right of *below* in the *Vertical* section and then click *Top Margin* at the drop-down list.
m. Click OK to close the Layout dialog box.

12. Save, print, and then close **C15-E03-CIRevs.docx**.

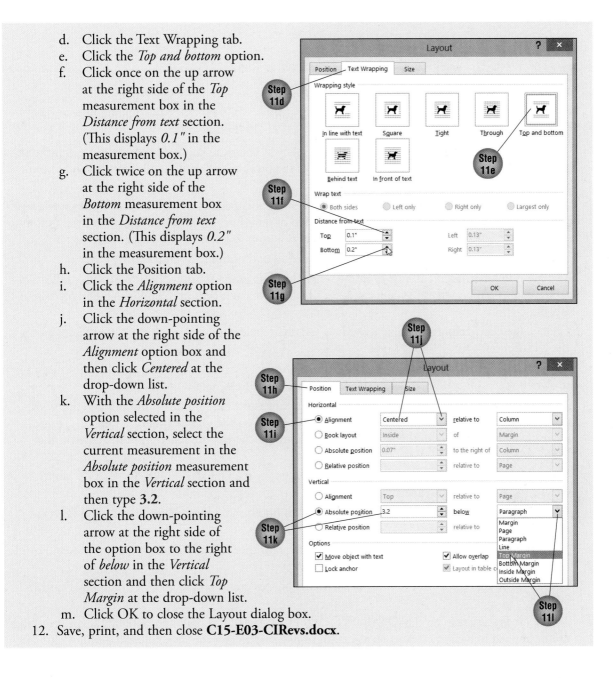

**Figure 15.9 Exercise 15.3**

| | A | B | C | D | E | F | G | H |
|---|---|---|---|---|---|---|---|---|
| 1 | | Percentage | | | | | | |
| 2 | Domestic | 44% | | | | | | |
| 3 | Foreign | 15% | | | | | | |
| 4 | Government | 32% | | | | | | |
| 5 | Wholesalers | 9% | | | | | | |

# Chapter Summary

- To present data visually, create a chart with the Chart button on the INSERT tab.

- At the Insert Chart dialog box, choose one of 10 available chart types: column, line, pie, bar, area, X Y scatter, stock, surface, radar, or combo.

- Enter the data for a chart in an Excel worksheet. As you enter the data, press the Tab key to make the next cell active, press the Shift + Tab keys to make the previous cell active, and press the Enter key to make the cell below active.

- Four buttons display at the right side of a selected chart. Use the Layout Options button to apply a text wrapping option, the Chart Elements button to add or remove chart elements, the Chart Syles button to apply a predesigned chart style, and the Chart Filters button to isolate specific data in the chart.

- The CHART TOOLS DESIGN tab contains buttons and options for customizing a chart.

- Use the Add Chart Element button in the Chart Layouts group on the CHART TOOLS DESIGN tab to add or remove chart elements and use the Quick Layout button to apply a predesigned chart layout.

- Change the chart colors and apply a predesigned chart style with options in the Chart Styles group on the CHART TOOLS DESIGN tab.

- Use options in the Data group on the CHART TOOLS DESIGN tab to manage data (for instance, to switch rows and columns), select data, edit data, and refresh data.

- The cells in the Excel worksheet that are used to create a chart are linked to the chart in the Word document. Click the Edit Data button in the Data group on the CHART TOOLS DESIGN tab, make changes to the text in the Excel worksheet, and the changes are reflected in the chart in the Word document.

- Use the Change Chart Type button in the Type group on the CHART TOOLS DESIGN tab to change the type of the existing chart.

- Apply formatting to a chart and chart elements with options and buttons on the CHART TOOLS FORMAT tab.

- Select chart elements with the Chart Elements button in the Current Selection group on the CHART TOOLS FORMAT tab.

- Insert a shape in a chart with options in the Insert Shapes group on the CHART TOOLS FORMAT tab.

- The Shape Styles group on the CHART TOOLS FORMAT tab contains predesigned shape styles that can be applied to a chart or chart elements, buttons for changing the shape fill and outline color and applying shape effects, and buttons for applying WordArt styles, text fills and outline colors, and text effects.

- Use options in the Arrange group on the CHART TOOLS FORMAT tab to position and arrange a chart in a document.

- Change the height and width of a chart with measurement boxes in the Size group on the CHART TOOLS FORMAT tab.

- Additional formatting options are available in task panes. Display a task pane by clicking the Format Selection button or a group task pane launcher. The task pane that displays depends on what is selected in the chart.

- The Layout dialog box contains options for formatting the position, text wrapping, and size of a chart. Display this dialog box by clicking the Size group dialog box launcher or the *See more* option at the Layout Options button side menu.

# *Commands* Review

| FEATURE | RIBBON TAB, GROUP | BUTTON, OPTION | KEYBOARD SHORTCUT |
|---------|-------------------|----------------|-------------------|
| Change Chart Type dialog box | CHART TOOLS DESIGN, Type | ▮▮ | |
| edit chart data | CHART TOOLS DESIGN, Data | ▦ | |
| format selection | CHART TOOLS FORMAT, Current Selection | ⬚ | |
| Insert Chart dialog box | INSERT, Illustrations | ▮▮ | |
| Layout dialog box | CHART TOOLS FORMAT, Size | ⬛ | |
| make cell below active | | | Enter |
| make next cell active | | | Tab |
| make previous cell active | | | Shift + Tab |
| select chart elements | CHART TOOLS FORMAT, Current Selection | Chart Area ▾ | |
| task pane | CHART TOOLS FORMAT, Shape Styles | ⬛ | |

# *Key Points* Review

**Completion:** In the space provided at the right, indicate the correct term, symbol, or command.

1. This is the number of chart types available at the Insert Chart dialog box. _____

2. Use this type of chart to show trends and overall change over time. _____

3. Use this type of chart to show proportions and relationships of the parts to the whole. _____

4. When creating a chart, enter the data in this. _____

5. Use this button, which displays at the right side of the selected chart, to apply a text wrapping option. _____

6. Use this button, which displays at the right side of the selected chart, to isolate specific data. _____

7. The Quick Layout button is located on this tab. _____

8. Click this button to open the Excel worksheet containing the chart data. _____

9. The Chart Elements button is located in this group on the CHART TOOLS FORMAT tab. _____

10. Control the position of a chart in a document with options and buttons in this group on the CHART TOOLS FORMAT tab. _____

11. One method for displaying a task pane is to click the task pane launcher in this group on the CHART TOOLS FORMAT tab. _____

12. Display the Layout dialog box by clicking the dialog box launcher in this group on the CHART TOOLS FORMAT tab. _____

# Chapter Assessments

## Applying Your Skills

Demonstrate your knowledge of features learned in this chapter by completing the following assessments.

### Assessment 15.1    Create and Format a Column Chart

1. At a blank document, use the data in Figure 15.10 to create a 3-D clustered column chart with the following specifications:
   a. Use the Chart Elements button that displays at the right side of the selected chart to insert a data table with legend keys.
   b. Remove the legend.
   c. Change the chart title to **Sales by State**.
   d. Use the Chart Styles button that displays at the right side of the selected chart to apply the Style 11 chart style and the Color 4 color option.
   e. Add Primary Major Vertical gridlines to the chart.
   f. Filter the data in the chart so only the sales for Florida and Georgia display.
2. Save the document with the name **C15-A01-StSalesChart**.
3. Print **C15-A01-StSalesChart.docx**.
4. Remove the filters so the data for all four states displays.
5. Change the chart type to a clustered bar chart. *Hint: Do this with the Change Chart Type button in the Type group on the CHART TOOLS DESIGN tab.*
6. Click the Select Data button on the CHART TOOLS DESIGN tab, click the Switch Row/Column button at the dialog box, and then click OK.
7. Use the Chart Elements button that displays at the right side of the selected chart to remove the axes from the chart.
8. Save, print, and then close **C15-A01-StSalesChart.docx**.

Figure 15.10  Assessment 15.1

|  | Sales 2013 | Sales 2014 | Sales 2015 |
|---|---|---|---|
| Florida | $356,750 | $400,790 | $325,490 |
| Georgia | $475,230 | $385,675 | $425,450 |
| Alabama | $225,545 | $300,245 | $312,680 |
| Mississippi | $178,878 | $210,907 | $200,578 |

## Assessment 15.2    Create and Format a Pie Chart

1. At a blank document, use the data in Figure 15.11 to create a pie chart with the following specifications:
   a. Apply the Layout 4 quick layout.
   b. Apply the Style 9 chart style.
   c. Add the chart title *DEPARTMENT EXPENSES* above the chart and apply the Subtle Effect - Blue, Accent 1 shape style to the title.
   d. Click a "piece" of the pie to select all of the pie pieces and then click the Shape Styles group task pane launcher. At the Format Data Series task pane, click the *Effects* icon, click *3-D FORMAT* to expand the options, and then apply the Circle top bevel.
   e. Change the position of the pie chart to Position in Middle Center with Square Text Wrapping.
2. Save the document and name it **C15-A02-ExpChart**.
3. Print **C15-A02-ExpChart.docx**.
4. With the chart selected, display the Excel worksheet and edit the data in the worksheet by changing the following:
   a. Change the *Salaries* percentage from *67%* to *62%*.
   b. Change the *Travel* percentage from *15%* to *17%*.
   c. Change the *Equipment* percentage from *11%* to *14%*.
5. Save, print, and then close **C15-A02-ExpChart.docx**.

**Figure 15.11  Assessment 15.2**

| Category | Percentage |
|----------|-----------|
| Salaries | 67% |
| Travel | 15% |
| Equipment | 11% |
| Supplies | 7% |

## Assessment 15.3    Create and Format a Bar Chart

1. At a blank document, use the data in Figure 15.12 on the next page to create a 3-D clustered bar chart with the following specifications:
   a. Use the Chart Elements button that displays at the right side of the selected chart to remove the legend and add Primary Minor Vertical gridlines to the chart.
   b. Use the Chart Elements button on the CHART TOOLS FORMAT tab to select *Series "Sales in Millions"*, apply the Dark Red shape fill color (first option in the *Standard Colors* section), and then apply the Light Blue shape outline color (seventh color option in the *Standard Colors* section).
   c. Select the chart area and then apply the Dark Blue text fill color (ninth option in the *Standard Colors* section).
   d. Change the height of the chart to 4.5 inches and the width to 6.5 inches.
2. Save the document with the name **C15-A03-CoSalesChart**.
3. Print and then close **C15-A03-CoSalesChart.docx**.

**Figure 15.12** Assessment 15.3

|  | Sales in Millions |
| --- | --- |
| Africa | 2.8 |
| Asia | 7.5 |
| Europe | 10.3 |
| North America | 12.2 |
| South America | 4.8 |

## Assessment 15.4 Create and Format a Line Chart

1. Open **Middleton.docx** and save the document with the name **C15-A04-Middleton**.
2. Use the data in Figure 15.13 to create a line chart with the following specifications:
   a. Choose the Line with Markers line chart type.
   b. Switch the rows and columns.
   c. Apply the Style 11 chart style.
   d. Remove the chart title.
   e. Select the chart area, display the Format Chart Area task pane, and then apply gradient fill.
   f. With the chart area still selected, apply the Fill - Black, Text 1, Shadow WordArt style (first WordArt style).
3. Display the Layout dialog box and then make the following changes:
   a. With the Size tab selected, change the absolute height measurement to 2.5 inches and the absolute width measurement to 5 inches.
   b. With the Text Wrapping tab selected, change the wrapping style to Top and bottom and change the distance from text bottom measurement to 0.2 inches.
   c. With the Position tab selected, change the horizontal alignment to centered and change the vertical absolute position to 4.8 inches below the top margin.
4. Save, print, and then close **C15-A04-Middleton.docx**.

**Figure 15.13** Assessment 15.4

|  | 1970 | 1980 | 1990 | 2000 | 2010 |
| --- | --- | --- | --- | --- | --- |
| Lanville | 58,980 | 61,248 | 65,320 | 53,120 | 78,340 |
| Mill Creek | 68,458 | 70,538 | 55,309 | 64,328 | 70,537 |

# Expanding Your Skills

Explore additional feature options or use Help to learn a new skill in creating these documents.

## Assessment 15.5 Create and Format a Chart

1. At a blank document, create a chart and chart type of your choosing with the data shown in Figure 15.14 on the next page. You determine the design and format of the chart and chart elements. Insert a chart title with the text *Taxes*.
2. Save the document with the name **C15-A05-TaxesChart**.
3. Print and then close **C15-A05-TaxesChart.docx**.

**Figure 15.14  Assessment 15.5**

|        | Budgeted | Actual   |
|--------|----------|----------|
| City   | $15,000  | $17,350  |
| County | $22,000  | $24,100  |
| Federal| $53,500  | $48,750  |

## Assessment 15.6    Type a Business Letter Containing a Column Chart

1. Open **BMCLtrhd.docx** and save the document with the name **C15-A06-LtrtoCP**.
2. Type the letter and insert and format the chart as shown in Figure 15.15. Apply the Style 5 chart style, change the color to Color 2, and change the font size of the title to 12 points. Size and position the chart as shown in the figure. Insert your initials in place of the *XX* that display near the bottom of the letter.
3. Save, print, and then close **C15-A06-LtrtoCP.docx**.

**Figure 15.15  Assessment 15.6**

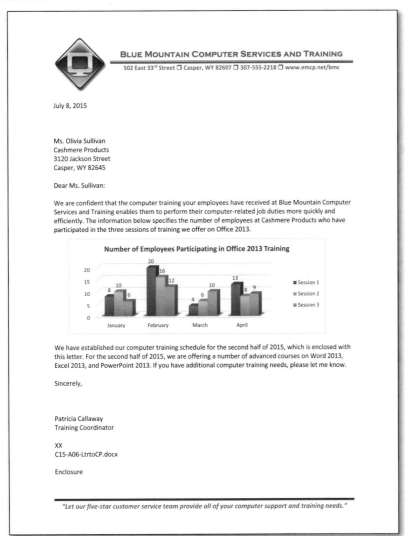

# Achieving Signature Status

Take your skills to the next level by completing this more challenging assessment.

## Assessment 15.7    Create and Format a Pie Chart

1. Open **NSSLtrhd.docx** and save the document with the name **C15-A07-NSSExpChart**.
2. Create and format the pie chart shown in Figure 15.16 with the following specifications:
   - Use the *3-D Pie* chart option.
   - Enter the data in the Excel worksheet in this order: Salaries, Benefits, Production, Development, Material, and Administration.
   - Remove the legend, insert the Data Callout data labels, change the text fill color to black, apply bold formatting to the text, and change the font size of the title to 28 points.
   - Remove the shape outline from the chart.
   - Increase the size of the chart and then position the chart in the middle of the page.
3. Save, print, and then close **C15-A07-NSSExpChart.docx**.

**Figure 15.16  Assessment 15.7**

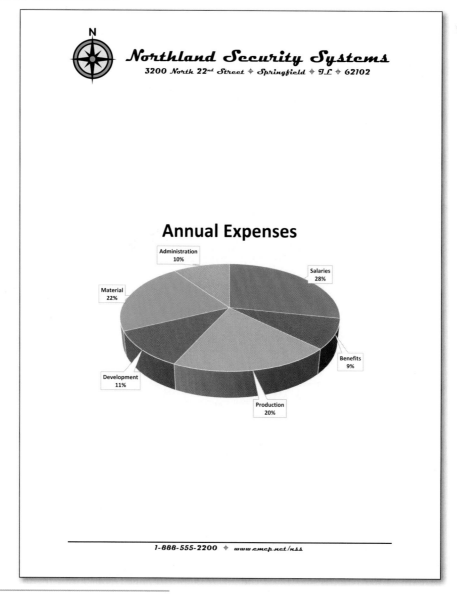

# *Performance Assessments*

UNIT 3

## Enhancing Documents

## ASSESSING PROFICIENCIES

In this unit, you learned to improve the appearance of documents by inserting, customizing, and formatting pictures, clip art images, screen images, shapes, text boxes, and WordArt. You also learned how to present data visually in tables, SmartArt graphics, and charts.

*Note: Before beginning computer assessments, copy to your storage medium the Unit03PA folder from the CD that accompanies this textbook and then make Unit03PA the active folder.*

**Assessment U3.1      Create a Flyer with WordArt and a Clip Art Image**

1. Create the flyer shown in Figure U3.1 with the following specifications:
   a. Create the WordArt with the following specifications:
      - Use the Fill - White, Outline - Accent 1, Shadow option (first row, fourth column) at the WordArt button drop-down gallery.
      - Increase the width to 6.5 inches and the height to 1 inch.
      - Apply the Deflate text effect transform shape (second column, sixth row in the *Warp* section).
      - Change the text fill color to Green, Accent 6, Lighter 40%.
   b. Type the text shown in the figure set in 22-point Calibri and then apply bold formatting and center the text.
   c. Insert the clip art image shown in the figure (use the keywords *Eiffel Tower Paris* to find the clip art) and then change the wrapping style to Square. Change the height and width of the clip art image to 2.2 inches and position the image as shown in the figure.
2. Save the document and name it **U3-PA01-TravelFlyer**.
3. Print and then close **U3-PA01-TravelFlyer.docx**.

 **Grade It**

START

**Figure U3.1  Assessment U3.1**

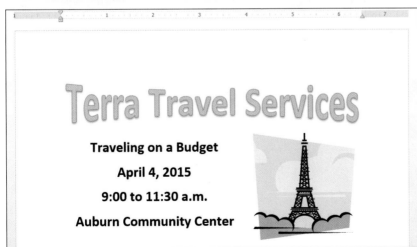

**Create and Format an Organizational Chart**

1. Use the Hierarchy SmartArt graphic to create an organizational chart for the text below (in the arrangement shown). Change the color to Colorful Range - Accent Colors 4 to 5 and apply the Metallic Scene SmartArt style.

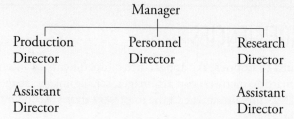

2. Save the completed document with the name **U3-PA02-OrgChart**.
3. Print and then close **U3-PA02-OrgChart.docx**.

**Create and Format a SmartArt Cycle Graphic**

1. At a blank document, create the SmartArt graphic shown in Figure U3.2 with the following specifications:
   a. Create the cycle graphic using the Basic Radial SmartArt graphic, insert two additional shapes, and then type the text (applying bold formatting) in the shapes as shown in the figure.
   b. Change the color to Colorful Range - Accent Colors 4 to 5.
   c. Apply the Cartoon SmartArt style.
   d. Increase the height to 4.5 inches and the width to 6.5 inches.
   e. Change the position of the graphic to Position in Middle Center with Square Text Wrapping.
   f. Change the text fill color to Black, Text 1.
2. Save the document with the name **U3-PA03-ServerGraphic**.
3. Print and then close **U3-PA03-ServerGraphic.docx**.

Figure U3.2 **Assessment U3.3**

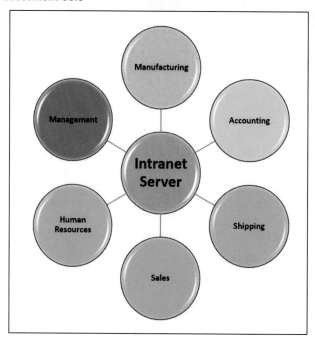

## Assessment U3.4    Create and Format a Training Announcement

1. Create the announcement shown in Figure U3.3 with the following specifications:
   a. Use the Bevel shape in the *Basic Shapes* section of the Shapes drop-down list to create the shape.
   b. Apply the Moderate Effect - Green, Accent 6 style to the shape.
   c. Change the shape outline color to Dark Blue.
   d. Apply the Offset Diagonal Top Left shadow to the shape.
   e. Change the shape height to 2.8 inches and the shape width to 6 inches.
   f. Change the position of the shape to Position in Middle Center with Square Text Wrapping.
   g. Type the text inside the bevel shape as shown in the figure. Set the text in 20-point Candara with bold formatting applied and then change the font color to Dark Blue.
2. Save the completed document with the name **U3-PA04-NetworkTrain**.
3. Print and then close **U3-PA04-NetworkTrain.docx**.

**Figure U3.3 Assessment U3.4**

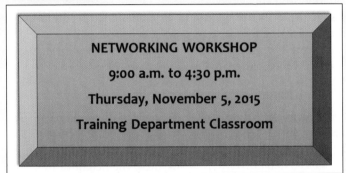

## Assessment U3.5    Create an Announcement with a Picture and Text

1. At a blank document, insert the picture **River.jpg** located in the Unit03PA folder on your storage medium. (Insert the picture using the Pictures button.)
2. Crop out some of the trees at the left and right and part of the hill at the top.
3. Change the brightness and contrast to Brightness: 0% (Normal) Contrast: +20%.
4. Change the width of the picture to 5 inches.
5. Change the position of the picture to Position in Top Center with Square Text Wrapping.
6. Specify that the picture should wrap behind the text.
7. Change the font to 22-point Constantia and apply bold formatting; change the font color to White, Background 1; and then change the alignment to Center. Press the Enter key two times and then type **Riverside Apartments**. Press the Enter key and then type **1-888-555-8800**.
8. Save the document with the name **U3-PA05-RAAnnounce**.
9. Print and then close **U3-PA05-RAAnnounce.docx**.

**Format a Photography Report**

**Grade It**

1. Open **Photography.docx** and save the document with the name **U3-PA06-Photography**.
2. Select the text *Photography* that displays at the beginning of the document and then create WordArt with the following specifications:
   a. Use the *Fill - Black, Text 1,* Shadow WordArt option.
   b. Change the height to 0.7 inches and the width to 4 inches.
   c. Change the position to Position in Top Center with Square Text Wrapping.
   d. Change the text wrapping to Top and Bottom.
   e. Apply the Square transform text effect (first option in the *Warp* section).
3. Insert the Motion Quote text box and then change the position of the text box to Position in Middle Center with Square Text Wrapping. Type **"Photography, as a powerful medium of expression and communication, offers an infinite variety of perception, interpretation, and execution." Ansel Adams** in the text box. Select the text in the text box, change the font size to 11 points, apply bold formatting, and then change the width of the text box to 3.1 inches.
4. Select the quote (including the author's name) that displays at the bottom of the document, display the Font dialog box with the Advanced tab selected, and then make the following changes:
   a. Change the character spacing to Expanded by 0.3 points.
   b. Turn on kerning for fonts 16 points and above.
   c. Change the *Stylistic sets* option to 4 and then close the dialog box.
5. Save, print, and then close **U3-PA06-Photography.docx**.

Assessment U3.7 **Create and Format a Table**

**Grade It**

START From Scratch

1. At a blank document, create the table shown in Figure U3.4 with the following specifications:
   a. Merge and center the cells and type the text as shown in the figure below.
   b. Change the height of row 1 to 0.7 inch, the height of row 2 to 0.4 inch, and the heights of the remaining rows to 0.3 inch.
   c. Change the font size to 16 points for the text in the first row.
   d. Center and apply bold formatting to the text in the first three rows.
   e. Apply shading as shown. (Use Green, Accent 6, Lighter 40% for the first and third rows and use Gold, Accent 4, Lighter 80% for the second row.)

Figure U3.4 **Assessment U3.7**

| COLEMAN DEVELOPMENT CORPORATION | | |
|---|---|---|
| Community Development Committee Members | | |
| Name | Company | Address |
| | | |
| | | |
| | | |
| | | |
| | | |
| | | |

2. Save the document with the name **U3-PA07-ComMembers**.
3. Print and then close **U3-PA07-ComMembers.docx**.

## Assessment U3.8    Format a Travel Table

1. Open **TravelPkgs.docx** and save the document with the name **U3-PA08-TravelPkgs**.
2. Format the table so it displays as shown in Figure U3.5 with the following specifications:
   a.  Select the entire table and then change the font to 12-point Candara.
   b.  Change the column widths so the columns display as shown in the figure.
   c.  Apply the Grid Table 4 - Accent 4 table style. Remove the check mark from the *First Column* option in the Table Style Options group.
   d.  Center the text in the first three rows.
   e.  Increase the font size of the text in row 1 to 18 points.
   f.  Apply bold formatting to the text in rows 2 and 3.
   g.  Slightly increase the heights of rows 1 and 2 as shown in Figure U3.5.
   h.  Center the text in the columns below the headings *Length* and *Estimated Cost*.
3. Save and then print **U3-PA08-TravelPkgs**.
4. With **U3-PA08-TravelPkgs.docx** open, open the document named **TTSLtrtoMA.docx** and then save the document with the name **U3-PA08-TTSLtrtoMA**.
5. Make **U3-PA08-TravelPkgs.docx** active, select the table, and then click the Copy button on the HOME tab. Make **U3-PA08-TTSLtrtoMA.docx** active, position the insertion point on the blank line immediately above the second paragraph of text in the letter, and then click the Paste button on the HOME tab.
6. Select and then delete the first row of the table.
7. Change the alignment of the table to Center. (Do this at the Table Properties dialog box with the Table tab selected.)
8. Replace the initials *XX* that display near the end of the letter with your initials.
9. Save, print, and then close **U3-PA08-TTSLtrtoMA.docx**.
10. Close **U3-PA08-TravelPkgs.docx**.

**Figure U3.5** **Assessment U3.8**

| TERRA TRAVEL SERVICES | | |
|---|---|---|
| Family Fun Ski and Snowboard Vacations | | |
| Package | Length | Estimated Cost |
| Lake Tahoe, Nevada | 3 days, 2 nights | $229 to $259 |
| Lake Tahoe, Nevada | 7 days, 6 nights | $459 to $599 |
| Sun Valley, Idaho | 3 days, 2 nights | $249 to $279 |
| Sun Valley, Idaho | 7 days, 6 nights | $499 to $629 |
| Jackson Hole, Wyoming | 3 days, 2 nights | $239 to $269 |
| Jackson Hole, Wyoming | 7 days, 6 nights | $469 to $629 |

## Assessment U3.9  Calculate Averages in a Table

1. Open **EmpOrient.docx** and save the document with the name **U3-PA09-EmpOrient**.
2. Insert formulas in the appropriate cells that calculate the averages of the quizzes. (Change the *Number Format* option at the Formula dialog box to 0.)
3. Use the AutoFit feature to format the contents of the table.
4. Apply a table style of your choosing to the table.
5. Apply any other formatting to improve the appearance of the table.
6. Save, print, and then close **U3-PA09-EmpOrient.docx**.

## Assessment U3.10  Calculate Quantities and Totals in a Table

1. Open **PurOrder.docx** and save the document with the name **U3-PA10-PurOrder**.
2. In the appropriate cells, insert formulas that multiply the quantity by the unit price. In the bottom cell in the fourth column, insert a formula that totals the amounts in the cells above.
3. Save, print, and then close **U3-PA10-PurOrder.docx**.

## Assessment U3.11  Create and Format a Column Chart

1. At a blank document, use the data in Figure U3.6 to create a column chart with the following specifications:
   a. Choose the 3-D Clustered Column chart type.
   b. Apply the Layout 3 chart layout.
   c. Apply the Style 5 chart style.
   d. Change the chart title to *2015 Sales*.
   e. Insert a data table with legend keys.
   f. Select the chart area, apply the Subtle Effect - Green, Accent 6 shape style (last column, fourth row), and apply the Offset Bottom shadow shape effect.
   g. Select the *Second Half* series and then change the shape fill to Dark Red.
   h. Change the chart height to 4 inches and the chart width to 6.25 inches.
   i. Use the Position button in the Arrange group to position the chart in the middle of the page with square text wrapping.
2. Save the document with the name **U3-PA11-SalesChart**.
3. Print **U3-PA11-SalesChart.docx**.
4. With the chart selected, display the Excel worksheet and edit the data in the worksheet by changing the following:
   a. Change the amount in cell C2 from *$285,450* to *$302,500*.
   b. Change the amount in cell C4 from *$180,210* to *$190,150*.
5. Save, print, and then close **U3-PA11-SalesChart.docx**.

Figure U3.6  **Assessment U3.11**

| Salesperson | First Half | Second Half |
|---|---|---|
| Bratton | $235,500 | $285,450 |
| Daniels | $300,570 | $250,700 |
| Hughes | $170,200 | $180,210 |
| Marez | $358,520 | $376,400 |

## Assessment U3.12　Create and Format a Pie Chart

1. At a blank document, use the data in Figure U3.7 to create a pie chart with the following specifications:
   a. Apply the Layout 6 chart layout.
   b. Apply the Style 3 chart style.
   c. Change the chart title to *District Expenditures*.
   d. Move the legend to the left side of the chart.
   e. Select the chart area, apply Gold, Accent 4, Lighter 80% shape fill (eighth column, second row in the *Theme Colors* section), and apply the Gray-50%, 11 pt glow, Accent color 3 glow shape effect (third column, third row in the *Glow Variations* section).
   f. Select the legend and apply the Blue shape outline color (eighth option in the *Standard Colors* section).
   g. Apply the WordArt style Fill - Blue, Accent 1, Outline - Background 1, Hard Shadow - Accent 1 (third column, third row) to the chart title text.
   h. Move the data labels to the inside ends of the pie "pieces."
   i. Select the legend and then move it so it is centered between the left edge of the chart border and the pie.
   j. Use the Position button in the Arrange group to center the chart at the top of the page with square text wrapping.
2. Save the document with the name **U3-PA12-ExpendChart**.
3. Print and then close **U3-PA12-ExpendChart.docx**.

**Figure U3.7  Assessment U3.12**

|  | Percentage |
|---|---|
| Basic Education | 42% |
| Special Needs | 20% |
| Support Services | 19% |
| Vocational | 11% |
| Compensatory | 8% |

# CREATING ORIGINAL DOCUMENTS

The activities in Assessments U3.13 through U3.16 give you the opportunity to practice your writing skills as well as demonstrate your mastery of the important Word features presented in this unit. When you compose the documents, use correct grammar, precise word choices, and clear sentence construction.

## Assessment U3.13　Write Steps Describing How to Use SmartArt

**Situation:** You work in the training department of Coleman Development Corporation and are responsible for preparing a training document on how to use Word 2013. Create a document that describes the SmartArt feature and the types of graphics a user can create with it. Provide specific steps describing how to create an organizational chart using the Organizational Chart graphic and how to create a radial cycle graphic using the Radial Cycle graphic. Save the completed document with the name **U3-PA13-SmartArt**. Print and then close **U3-PA13-SmartArt.docx**.

**Create an Expenditures Table**

**Situation:** You are the vice president of Coleman Development Corporation and need to prepare a table showing the equipment expenditures for each department, as shown below:

### COLEMAN DEVELOPMENT CORPORATION
**Equipment Expenditures**

| Department | Amount |
|---|---|
| Personnel | $20,400 |
| Research | $58,300 |
| Finance | $14,900 |
| Production | $90,100 |
| Sales | $51,000 |
| Marketing | $52,600 |

Create a table with the data and apply appropriate formatting to it. Save the document with the name **U3-PA14-EquipExpend**. Print and then close **U3-PA14-EquipExpend.docx**.

**Create a Column Chart**

**Situation:** You decide that the data in the table you created in Assessment U3.14 will be easier to visualize if it is inserted in a chart. Using the information from the table, create a column chart and apply formatting to enhance the appearance of the chart. Save the completed document with the name **U3-PA15-EquipExpChart**. Print and then close **U3-PA15-EquipExpChart.docx**.

**Create a Store Letterhead**

**Situation:** You work for Evergreen Sports, a sports equipment store that specializes in hiking gear. You have been asked to design a letterhead for the store. When designing the letterhead, include an appropriate clip art image along with the following information:

Evergreen Sports
4500 Lowell Avenue
Portland, OR 99821
(503) 555-8220

Save the completed letterhead document with the name **U3-PA16-ESLtrhd**. Print and then close **U3-PA16-ESLtrhd.docx**.

# UNIT 4

## Managing Data

# Chapter 16

# Merging Documents

## Performance Objectives

Upon successful completion of Chapter 16, you will be able to:

- Create and merge a main document and a data source file
- Merge files to create envelopes, labels, and directories
- Edit main documents and data source files
- Insert additional fields
- Merge a main document with other data sources
- Use the Mail Merge wizard to merge documents

Word includes a Mail Merge feature that you can use to create customized letters, envelopes, labels, directories, email messages, and faxes. The Mail Merge feature is useful when you need to send the same letter to a number of people but want to personalize it and create an envelope or mailing label for each person. Use Mail Merge to create a main document that contains a letter, envelope, or other data and then merge the main document with a data source. In this chapter, you will use Mail Merge to create customized letters, envelopes, labels, and directories.

*Note: Before beginning computer exercises for this chapter, copy to your storage medium the Chapter16 folder from the CD that accompanies this textbook and then make Chapter16 the active folder.*

In this chapter, students will produce the following documents:

Exercise 16.1. C16-E01-CofELtrs.docx
Exercise 16.2. C16-E02-CofEEnvs.docx
Exercise 16.3. C16-E03-CofELabels.docx
Exercise 16.4. C16-E04-CofEDirectory.docx
Exercise 16.5. C16-E05-Labels.docx
Exercise 16.6. C16-E06-Directory.docx
Exercise 16.7. C16-E07-CofELetters.docx
Exercise 16.8. C16-E08-BTTourLtrs.docx
Exercise 16.9. C16-E09-BTTourLtrs.docx
Exercise 16.10. C16-E10-BTTourLtrs.docx
Exercise 16.12. C16-E12-PRLtrs.docx

Model answers for these exercises are shown on the following pages.

**Exercise 16.1** C16-E01-CofELtrs.docx

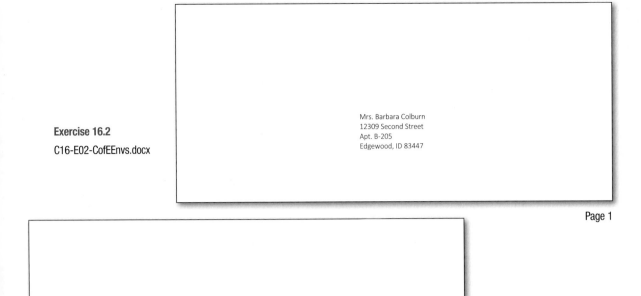

**Exercise 16.2**

C16-E02-CofEEnvs.docx

Mrs. Barbara Colburn
12309 Second Street
Apt. B-205
Edgewood, ID 83447

Mr. Brian Kosel
345 Rosewood Avenue
Edgewood, ID 83445

Mrs. Barbara Colburn
12309 Second Street
Apt. B-205
Edgewood, ID 83447

Mr. Brian Kosel
345 Rosewood Avenue
Edgewood, ID 83445

Mr. Gordon Costanzo
13115 132nd Street
Apt. 5
Edgewood, ID 83445

Dr. Tracy Malone
7485 North Collins
Edgewood, ID 83447

**Exercise 16.3**

C16-E03-CofELabels.docx

| Last Name | First Name | Membership |
|-----------|-----------|-----------|
| Colburn | Barbara | Gold |
| Kosel | Brian | Platinum |
| Costanzo | Gordon | Premium |
| Malone | Tracy | Platinum |

**Exercise 16.4**

C16-E04-CofEDirectory.docx

Mrs. Claudia Levinson
1521 North 32nd Street
Lexington, KY 40511

Ms. Laurel Kittner
12303 North 141st
Apt. 3-B
Lexington, KY 40507

Dr. Miguel Trivelas
5840 North 132nd
P.O. Box 9045
Lexington, KY 40517

Mr. Ryan Wright
10291 South 41st
Lexington, KY 40511

Mr. Arthur Washbaugh
1203 24th Street
Lexington, KY 40511

Mrs. Kayla Stuben
450 Madison Street
P.O. Box 3643
Lexington, KY 40526

**Exercise 16.5**

C16-E05-Labels.docx

| Name | Home Phone | Cell Phone |
|------|-----------|-----------|
| Levinson, Claudia | (859) 555-5579 | (859) 555-5879 |
| Diaz, Jeffrey | (859) 555-2386 | (859) 555-9902 |
| Kittner, Laurel | (859) 555-5889 | (859) 555-8349 |
| Hershey, Karl | (859) 555-1214 | (859) 555-5611 |
| Pirone, Mary | (859) 555-5540 | (859) 555-1200 |
| Trivelas, Miguel | (859) 555-4585 | (859) 555-7522 |
| Wright, Ryan | (859) 555-0899 | (859) 555-1233 |
| Carmichael, Dale | (859) 555-7900 | (859) 555-5628 |
| Novak, Marianne | (859) 555-3499 | (859) 555-5890 |
| Washbaugh, Arthur | (859) 555-4523 | (859) 555-2903 |
| Stuben, Kayla | (859) 555-8891 | (859) 555-9703 |
| Montague, Amanda | (859) 555-2047 | (859) 555-5563 |

**Exercise 16.6**

C16-E06-Directory.docx

# CITY OF EDGEWOOD

September 22, 2015

Mrs. Barbara Colburn
12309 Second Street
Apt. B-205
Edgewood, ID 83447

Dear Mrs. Colburn:

The next meeting of the Edgewood Volunteers Group will be Monday, October 5, 2015, at 7:00 p.m. The meeting was previously scheduled for the meeting hall in the community center but has been changed to the conference room at the library.

As we prepare our budget for the next year, we need to confirm our members' pledges. According to our records, you have pledged $2,500 for 2016. Please contact us if you want to change this pledge.

In January, we will be printing our membership directory. Currently, Mrs. Colburn, we have you listed as a Gold member. Please let us know if your membership or any of your personal information has changed. Also, we are interested in recruiting additional members so please call or email us if you have a referral.

Sincerely,

Stacey Levine

XX
C16-E01-CofELetterMD-1.docx

*"The City of Possibilities"*
1900 Center Street, Edgewood, ID 83440, 208-555-1900

**Exercise 16.7** C16-E07-CofELetters.docx          Page 1

---

# CITY OF EDGEWOOD

September 22, 2015

Mr. Brian Kosel
345 Rosewood Avenue
Edgewood, ID 83445

Dear Mr. Kosel:

The next meeting of the Edgewood Volunteers Group will be Monday, October 5, 2015, at 7:00 p.m. The meeting was previously scheduled for the meeting hall in the community center but has been changed to the conference room at the library.

As we prepare our budget for the next year, we need to confirm our members' pledges. According to our records, you have pledged $10,000 for 2016. Please contact us if you want to change this pledge. We hope you will continue your Platinum membership and enjoy the benefits of supporting your local community.

In January, we will be printing our membership directory. Currently, Mr. Kosel, we have you listed as a Platinum member. Please let us know if your membership or any of your personal information has changed. Also, we are interested in recruiting additional members so please call or email us if you have a referral.

Sincerely,

Stacey Levine

XX
C16-E01-CofELetterMD-2.docx

*"The City of Possibilities"*
1900 Center Street, Edgewood, ID 83440, 208-555-1900

Page 2

---

# CITY OF EDGEWOOD

September 22, 2015

Mr. Gordon Costanzo
13115 132nd Street
Apt. 5
Edgewood, ID 83445

Dear Mr. Costanzo:

The next meeting of the Edgewood Volunteers Group will be Monday, October 5, 2015, at 7:00 p.m. The meeting was previously scheduled for the meeting hall in the community center but has been changed to the conference room at the library.

As we prepare our budget for the next year, we need to confirm our members' pledges. According to our records, you have pledged $5,000 for 2016. Please contact us if you want to change this pledge.

In January, we will be printing our membership directory. Currently, Mr. Costanzo, we have you listed as a Premium member. Please let us know if your membership or any of your personal information has changed. Also, we are interested in recruiting additional members so please call or email us if you have a referral.

Sincerely,

Stacey Levine

XX
C16-E01-CofELetterMD-3.docx

*"The City of Possibilities"*
1900 Center Street, Edgewood, ID 83440, 208-555-1900

Page 3

---

# CITY OF EDGEWOOD

September 22, 2015

Dr. Tracy Malone
7485 North Collins
Edgewood, ID 83447

Dear Dr. Malone:

The next meeting of the Edgewood Volunteers Group will be Monday, October 5, 2015, at 7:00 p.m. The meeting was previously scheduled for the meeting hall in the community center but has been changed to the conference room at the library.

As we prepare our budget for the next year, we need to confirm our members' pledges. According to our records, you have pledged $10,000 for 2016. Please contact us if you want to change this pledge. We hope you will continue your Platinum membership and enjoy the benefits of supporting your local community.

In January, we will be printing our membership directory. Currently, Dr. Malone, we have you listed as a Platinum member. Please let us know if your membership or any of your personal information has changed. Also, we are interested in recruiting additional members so please call or email us if you have a referral.

Sincerely,

Stacey Levine

XX
C16-E01-CofELetterMD-4.docx

*"The City of Possibilities"*
1900 Center Street, Edgewood, ID 83440, 208-555-1900

Page 4

**Bayside Travel**

April 8, 2015

Mr. Jeremiah Roberts
5532 Logan Street
San Francisco, CA 94122

Dear Mr. Roberts:

At Bayside Travel, we strive to provide our clients with fun- and adventure-filled travel vacations. We have created an exciting new vacation tour that you do not want to miss! Our tour explores the beauty, culture, and history of Slovenia, Croatia, Albania, and Greece—all countries located in the Balkans region along the Adriatic Sea.

Bayside Travel is offering a 13-night, 14-day travel tour that combines all types of transportation—from airplanes to all-terrain vehicles. The tour begins in Slovenia, ends in Greece, and includes the following countries and activities:

- Days 1 through 3: Travel to Slovenia and tour the country by boat and bus.
- Days 4 through 6: Travel to Croatia and tour the country by boat, bus, and all-terrain vehicle.
- Days 7 through 9: Travel to Montenegro and tour the country by all-terrain vehicle.
- Days 10 through 11: Travel to Albania and tour the country by bus.
- Days 12 through 14: Travel to Greece and tour the country by ferry, bus, and all-terrain vehicle.

We are offering this exciting adventure only one time this year, so don't miss this opportunity to visit these beautiful countries along the Adriatic Sea. Visit our website or call one of our travel consultants for more information on this tour.

Sincerely,

Mandy Takada
Travel Consultant

XX
BTTourLtr.docx

5530 Bayside Drive ❖ San Francisco CA 94320 ❖ 1-888-555-8890 ❖ www.emcp.net/bayside

**Exercise 16.8** C16-E08-BTTourLtrs.docx          Page 1

---

**Bayside Travel**

April 8, 2015

Mrs. Carrie Chen
10233 North 52nd Avenue
Daly City, CA 94015

Dear Mrs. Chen:

At Bayside Travel, we strive to provide our clients with fun- and adventure-filled travel vacations. We have created an exciting new vacation tour that you do not want to miss! Our tour explores the beauty, culture, and history of Slovenia, Croatia, Albania, and Greece—all countries located in the Balkans region along the Adriatic Sea.

Bayside Travel is offering a 13-night, 14-day travel tour that combines all types of transportation—from airplanes to all-terrain vehicles. The tour begins in Slovenia, ends in Greece, and includes the following countries and activities:

- Days 1 through 3: Travel to Slovenia and tour the country by boat and bus.
- Days 4 through 6: Travel to Croatia and tour the country by boat, bus, and all-terrain vehicle.
- Days 7 through 9: Travel to Montenegro and tour the country by all-terrain vehicle.
- Days 10 through 11: Travel to Albania and tour the country by bus.
- Days 12 through 14: Travel to Greece and tour the country by ferry, bus, and all-terrain vehicle.

We are offering this exciting adventure only one time this year, so don't miss this opportunity to visit these beautiful countries along the Adriatic Sea. Visit our website or call one of our travel consultants for more information on this tour.

Sincerely,

Mandy Takada
Travel Consultant

XX
BTTourLtr.docx

5530 Bayside Drive ❖ San Francisco CA 94320 ❖ 1-888-555-8890 ❖ www.emcp.net/bayside

Page 2

---

**Bayside Travel**

April 8, 2015

Mrs. Leanne Blaylock
18872 West 78th
San Francisco, CA 94127

Dear Mrs. Blaylock:

At Bayside Travel, we strive to provide our clients with fun- and adventure-filled travel vacations. We have created an exciting new vacation tour that you do not want to miss! Our tour explores the beauty, culture, and history of Slovenia, Croatia, Albania, and Greece—all countries located in the Balkans region along the Adriatic Sea.

Bayside Travel is offering a 13-night, 14-day travel tour that combines all types of transportation—from airplanes to all-terrain vehicles. The tour begins in Slovenia, ends in Greece, and includes the following countries and activities:

- Days 1 through 3: Travel to Slovenia and tour the country by boat and bus.
- Days 4 through 6: Travel to Croatia and tour the country by boat, bus, and all-terrain vehicle.
- Days 7 through 9: Travel to Montenegro and tour the country by all-terrain vehicle.
- Days 10 through 11: Travel to Albania and tour the country by bus.
- Days 12 through 14: Travel to Greece and tour the country by ferry, bus, and all-terrain vehicle.

We are offering this exciting adventure only one time this year, so don't miss this opportunity to visit these beautiful countries along the Adriatic Sea. Visit our website or call one of our travel consultants for more information on this tour.

Sincerely,

Mandy Takada
Travel Consultant

XX
BTTourLtr.docx

5530 Bayside Drive ❖ San Francisco CA 94320 ❖ 1-888-555-8890 ❖ www.emcp.net/bayside

**Exercise 16.9** C16-E09-BTTourLtrs.docx          Page 1

---

**Bayside Travel**

April 8, 2015

Mr. Issac Cousineau
4500 Williams Road
Daly City, CA 94015

Dear Mr. Cousineau:

At Bayside Travel, we strive to provide our clients with fun- and adventure-filled travel vacations. We have created an exciting new vacation tour that you do not want to miss! Our tour explores the beauty, culture, and history of Slovenia, Croatia, Albania, and Greece—all countries located in the Balkans region along the Adriatic Sea.

Bayside Travel is offering a 13-night, 14-day travel tour that combines all types of transportation—from airplanes to all-terrain vehicles. The tour begins in Slovenia, ends in Greece, and includes the following countries and activities:

- Days 1 through 3: Travel to Slovenia and tour the country by boat and bus.
- Days 4 through 6: Travel to Croatia and tour the country by boat, bus, and all-terrain vehicle.
- Days 7 through 9: Travel to Montenegro and tour the country by all-terrain vehicle.
- Days 10 through 11: Travel to Albania and tour the country by bus.
- Days 12 through 14: Travel to Greece and tour the country by ferry, bus, and all-terrain vehicle.

We are offering this exciting adventure only one time this year, so don't miss this opportunity to visit these beautiful countries along the Adriatic Sea. Visit our website or call one of our travel consultants for more information on this tour.

Sincerely,

Mandy Takada
Travel Consultant

XX
BTTourLtr.docx

5530 Bayside Drive ❖ San Francisco CA 94320 ❖ 1-888-555-8890 ❖ www.emcp.net/bayside

Page 2

## Bayside Travel

April 8, 2015

Donald Rutledge
3730 Rodesco Drive
Oakland, CA 94604

Dear Donald Rutledge:

At Bayside Travel, we strive to provide our clients with fun- and adventure-filled travel vacations. We have created an exciting new vacation tour that you do not want to miss! Our tour explores the beauty, culture, and history of Slovenia, Croatia, Albania, and Greece—all countries located in the Balkans region along the Adriatic Sea.

Bayside Travel is offering a 13-night, 14-day travel tour that combines all types of transportation—from airplanes to all-terrain vehicles. The tour begins in Slovenia, ends in Greece, and includes the following countries and activities:

- Days 1 through 3: Travel to Slovenia and tour the country by boat and bus.
- Days 4 through 6: Travel to Croatia and tour the country by boat, bus, and all-terrain vehicle.
- Days 7 through 9: Travel to Montenegro and tour the country by all-terrain vehicle.
- Days 10 through 11: Travel to Albania and tour the country by bus.
- Days 12 through 14: Travel to Greece and tour the country by ferry, bus, and all-terrain vehicle.

We are offering this exciting adventure only one time this year, so don't miss this opportunity to visit these beautiful countries along the Adriatic Sea. Visit our website or call one of our travel consultants for more information on this tour.

Sincerely,


Mandy Takada
Travel Consultant

XX
BTTourLtr.docx

5530 Bayside Drive ❖ San Francisco CA 94320 ❖ 1-888-555-8890 ❖ www.emcp.net/bayside

**Exercise 16.10**  C16-E10-BTTourLtrs.docx

---

## Bayside Travel

April 8, 2015

Patricia Kaelin
4818 Cedar Boulevard
Oakland, CA 94618

Dear Patricia Kaelin:

At Bayside Travel, we strive to provide our clients with fun- and adventure-filled travel vacations. We have created an exciting new vacation tour that you do not want to miss! Our tour explores the beauty, culture, and history of Slovenia, Croatia, Albania, and Greece—all countries located in the Balkans region along the Adriatic Sea.

Bayside Travel is offering a 13-night, 14-day travel tour that combines all types of transportation—from airplanes to all-terrain vehicles. The tour begins in Slovenia, ends in Greece, and includes the following countries and activities:

- Days 1 through 3: Travel to Slovenia and tour the country by boat and bus.
- Days 4 through 6: Travel to Croatia and tour the country by boat, bus, and all-terrain vehicle.
- Days 7 through 9: Travel to Montenegro and tour the country by all-terrain vehicle.
- Days 10 through 11: Travel to Albania and tour the country by bus.
- Days 12 through 14: Travel to Greece and tour the country by ferry, bus, and all-terrain vehicle.

We are offering this exciting adventure only one time this year, so don't miss this opportunity to visit these beautiful countries along the Adriatic Sea. Visit our website or call one of our travel consultants for more information on this tour.

Sincerely,


Mandy Takada
Travel Consultant

XX
BTTourLtr.docx

5530 Bayside Drive ❖ San Francisco CA 94320 ❖ 1-888-555-8890 ❖ www.emcp.net/bayside

---

December 2, 2015

Mr. Donald Reyes
14332 150th Street East
Eugene, OR 97408

Dear Mr. Reyes:

Phoenix Rising is a global community supporting individuals in more than twenty countries who are survivors of war and violence and who are rebuilding their lives. Our organization includes dedicated staff, dedicated volunteers, and generous donors like you. For more than three decades, Phoenix Rising has provided direct financial and emotional support to individuals living on the edge of hope.

Your generosity makes economic independence possible for people while we provide vocational skills training, small business development, and income-generation support. All of these things are needed for long-term peace, stability, and security.

As we look to the new year, we ask you to continue to support those individuals we serve by making a monetary contribution. With your ongoing support, Phoenix Rising can continue to address their immediate and long-term needs, work to improve their status and opportunities, and work toward a more just and peaceful world.

Sincerely,


Neela Shamae
Executive Director

XX
C16-E08-PRLtrs.docx

1500 Frontier Avenue • Eugene, OR 97440 • 541-555-4110

**Exercise 16.12**  C16-E12-PRLtrs.docx

---

December 2, 2015

Ms. Hannah Devereaux
9005 Fifth Street
Springfield, OR 97478

Dear Ms. Devereaux:

Phoenix Rising is a global community supporting individuals in more than twenty countries who are survivors of war and violence and who are rebuilding their lives. Our organization includes dedicated staff, dedicated volunteers, and generous donors like you. For more than three decades, Phoenix Rising has provided direct financial and emotional support to individuals living on the edge of hope.

Your generosity makes economic independence possible for people while we provide vocational skills training, small business development, and income-generation support. All of these things are needed for long-term peace, stability, and security.

As we look to the new year, we ask you to continue to support those individuals we serve by making a monetary contribution. With your ongoing support, Phoenix Rising can continue to address their immediate and long-term needs, work to improve their status and opportunities, and work toward a more just and peaceful world.

Sincerely,


Neela Shamae
Executive Director

XX
C16-E08-PRLtrs.docx

1500 Frontier Avenue • Eugene, OR 97440 • 541-555-4110

Merging Documents          527

# Completing a Merge

A merge generally requires two files: a ***main document*** and a ***data source file***. The main document contains the standard text and/or fields that identify where variable information will be inserted during the merge. The data source file contains the variable information that will be inserted into the main document.

Use the Start Mail Merge button on the MAILINGS tab, as shown in Figure 16.1, to specify the type of main document you want to create. Use the Select Recipients button to create a data source file or to choose an existing data source file.

## Figure 16.1 MAILINGS Tab

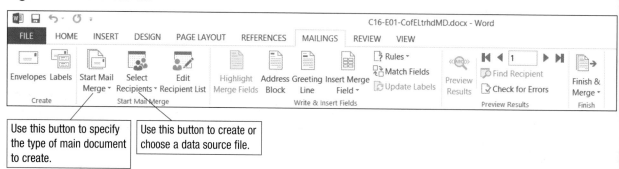

Use this button to specify the type of main document to create.

Use this button to create or choose a data source file.

## Creating a Data Source File

You begin a mail merge by clicking the MAILINGS tab, clicking the Start Mail Merge button, and selecting the type of main document that you want to create from the drop-down list. Before you create the main document, determine what type of correspondence you will be creating and the type of information you will need to insert in it. Word provides predetermined field names in a data source for this purpose. Use these field names if they represent the data you are creating.

Variable information in a data source file is saved as a ***record.*** A record is a series of fields and each record contains all of the information for one unit (for example, a person, family, customer, client, or business). A data source file is a series of records.

Create a data source file by clicking the Select Recipients button in the Start Mail Merge group on the MAILINGS tab and then clicking *Type a New List* at the drop-down list. At the New Address List dialog box, shown in Figure 16.2 on the next page, use the predesigned fields offered by Word and type the required data, or edit the fields by deleting and/or inserting custom fields and then typing the data. When you have entered all of the records, click OK.

At the Save Address List dialog box, navigate to the desired folder, type a name for the data source file, and then click OK. Word saves a data source file as an Access database. You do not need Access on your computer to complete a merge with a data source file.

Start Mail Merge

Select Recipients

**Figure 16.2 New Address List Dialog Box**

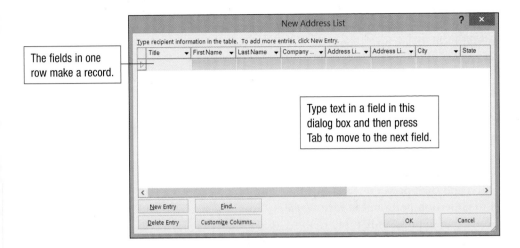

The fields in one row make a record.

Type text in a field in this dialog box and then press Tab to move to the next field.

## Exercise 16.1A  Creating a Data Source File                    Part 1 of 3

1. Open **CofELtrhd.docx** from the Chapter16 folder on your storage medium and then save the document with the name **C16-E01-CofELetterMD.docx**.
2. Click the MAILINGS tab.
3. Click the Start Mail Merge button in the Start Mail Merge group and then click *Letters* at the drop-down list.
4. Click the Select Recipients button in the Start Mail Merge group and then click *Type a New List* at the drop-down list.
5. At the New Address List dialog box, predesigned fields display in the list box. Delete the fields you do not need by completing the following steps:
    a. Click the Customize Columns button.
    b. At the Customize Address List dialog box, click *Company Name* to select it and then click the Delete button.
    c. At the message asking if you are sure that you want to delete the field, click Yes.
    d. Complete steps similar to those in Steps 5b and 5c to delete the following fields:
        *Country or Region*
        *Home Phone*
        *Work Phone*
        *E-mail Address*

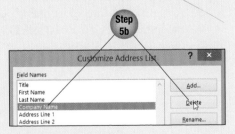

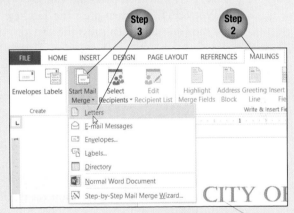

6. Insert a custom field by completing the following steps:
   a. At the Customize Address List dialog box, click the Add button.
   b. At the Add Field dialog box, type **Membership** and then click OK.
   c. Click the OK button to close the Customize Address List dialog box.

7. At the New Address List dialog box, enter the following information for the first client by completing the following steps:
   a. Make sure the insertion point is positioned in the *Title* text box.
   b. Type **Mrs.** and then press the Tab key. (This moves the insertion point to the *First Name* field. You can also press Shift + Tab to move to the previous field.)
   c. Type **Barbara** and then press the Tab key.
   d. Type **Colburn** and then press the Tab key.
   e. Type **12309 Second Street** and then press the Tab key.
   f. Type **Apt. B-205** and then press the Tab key.
   g. Type **Edgewood** and then press the Tab key.
   h. Type **ID** and then press the Tab key.
   i. Type **83447** and then press the Tab key.
   j. Type **Gold** and then press the Tab key.

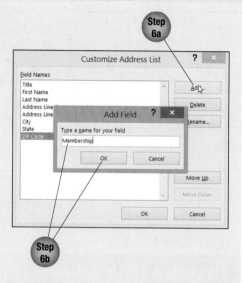

Step 6a

Step 6b

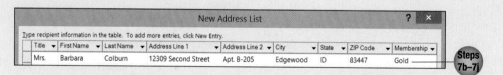

Steps 7b–7j

   k. With the insertion point positioned in the *Title* field, complete steps similar to those in Steps 7b through 7j to enter the information for the three clients shown in Figure 16.3 on the next page.

8. After entering all of the information for the last client in Figure 16.3 (Dr. Tracy Malone), click the OK button located in the bottom right corner of the New Address List dialog box.

9. At the Save Address List dialog box, navigate to the Chapter16 folder on your storage medium, type **C16-E01-CofEDS** in the *File name* text box, and then click the Save button.

**Figure 16.3 Exercise 16.1A**

Title: **Mr.**
First Name: **Brian**
Last Name: **Kosel**
Address Line 1: **345 Rosewood Avenue**
Address Line 2: (leave this blank)
City: **Edgewood**
State: **ID**
ZIP Code: **83445**
Membership: **Platinum**

Title: **Dr.**
First Name: **Tracy**
Last Name: **Malone**
Address Line 1: **7485 North Collins**
Address Line 2: (leave this blank)
City: **Edgewood**
State: **ID**
ZIP Code: **83447**
Membership: **Platinum**

Title: **Mr.**
First Name: **Gordon**
Last Name: **Costanzo**
Address Line 1: **13115 132nd Street**
Address Line 2: **Apt. 5**
City: **Edgewood**
State: **ID**
ZIP Code: **83445**
Membership: **Premium**

## Creating a Main Document

After creating and typing records in the data source file, type the main document. As you type, insert fields identifying where you want variable information to appear when the document is merged with the data source file. Use buttons in the Write & Insert Fields group to insert fields and field blocks in the main document.

Insert all of the fields required for the inside address of a letter with the Address Block button in the Write & Insert Fields group. Click this button and the Insert Address Block dialog box displays with a preview of how the fields will be inserted in the document to create the inside address. The Insert Address dialog box also contains buttons and options for customizing the fields. Click OK and «*AddressBlock*» is inserted into the document. The «*AddressBlock*» field is an example of a composite field that groups a number of fields.

Click the Greeting Line button and the Insert Greeting Line dialog box displays with options for customizing how the fields are inserted in the document to create the greeting line. When you click OK at the dialog box, the «*GreetingLine*» composite field is inserted into the document.

If you want to insert an individual field from the data source file, click the Insert Merge Field button arrow and then click the desired field at the drop-down list containing the fields in the data source file. You can also click the Insert Merge Field button and then click the desired field at the Insert Merge Field dialog box.

**QUICK STEPS**

**Create a Main Document**
1. Click MAILINGS tab.
2. Click Start Mail Merge button.
3. Click desired document type at drop-down list.
4. Type main document text and insert fields as needed.

Address Block

Greeting Line

Insert Merge Field

*Note: If a message displays while you are completing exercises that indicates opening a document will run the SQL command, click Yes.*

1. With **C16-E01-CofELetterMD** open, type the date **September 22, 2015**, as shown in Figure 16.4 on the next page, and then press the Enter key four times.

2. Insert address fields by completing the following steps:

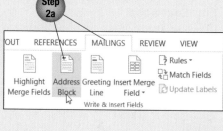

Step 2a

   a. If necessary, click the MAILINGS tab and then click the Address Block button in the Write & Insert Fields group.
   b. At the Insert Address Block dialog box, click the OK button.
   c. Press the Enter key twice.

3. Insert greeting line fields by completing the following steps:
   a. Click the Greeting Line button in the Write & Insert Fields group.

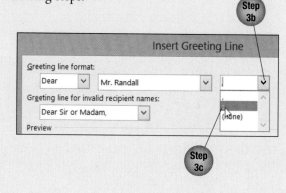

Step 3b

Step 3c

   b. At the Insert Greeting Line dialog box, click the down-pointing arrow at the right of the option box containing the comma (the box to the right of the box containing *Mr. Randall*).
   c. At the drop-down list that displays, click the colon (:).
   d. Click OK to close the Insert Greeting Line dialog box.
   e. Press the Enter key twice.

4. Type the letter text shown in Figure 16.4. When you reach the «*Title*» field, insert the field by clicking the Insert Merge Field button arrow and then clicking *Title* at the drop-down list.

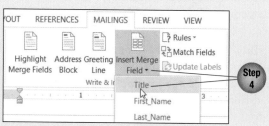

Step 4

5. Press the spacebar and then insert the «*Last_Name*» field by clicking the Insert Merge Field button arrow and then clicking *Last_Name* at the drop-down list.

6. When you reach the «*Membership*» field, insert the field by clicking the Insert Merge Field button arrow and then clicking *Membership* at the drop-down list.

7. Type the remainder of the letter text as shown in Figure 16.4. (Replace the *XX* at the end of the letter with your initials.)

8. Save **C16-E01-CofELetterMD.docx**.

**Figure 16.4 Exercise 16.1B**

September 22, 2015


«AddressBlock»

«GreetingLine»

The next meeting of the Edgewood Volunteers Group will be Monday, October 5, 2015, at 7:00 p.m. The meeting was previously scheduled for the meeting hall in the community center but has been changed to the conference room at the library.

We will be discussing the annual holiday food drive. The director of the food bank will give a short presentation on the agency and how it serves the community. In addition to discussing the food drive, we will decide on other community service activities.

In January, we will be printing our membership directory. Currently, «Title» «Last_Name», we have you listed as a «Membership» member. Please let us know if your membership or any of your personal information has changed. Also, we are interested in recruiting additional members so please call or email us if you have a referral.

Sincerely,


Stacey Levine

XX
C16-E01-CofELetterMD.docx


## Previewing a Merge

To view the main document as it will appear when merged with the first record in the data source file, click the Preview Results button on the MAILINGS tab. To view the main document merged with other records, use the navigation buttons in the Preview Results group, which include the First Record, Previous Record, Next Record, and Last Record buttons, and the *Go to Record* text box. Click the button that will display the main document merged with the record you want to view. To use the *Go to Record* text box, click in the text box, type the number of the desired record, and then press the Enter key. Turn off the preview feature by clicking the Preview Results button.

The Preview Results group on the MAILINGS tab also includes a Find Recipient button. If you want to search for and preview merged documents with specific entries, click the Preview Results button and then click the Find Recipient button. This displays the Find Entry dialog box, as shown in Figure 16.5 on the next page. At this dialog box,

Preview Results

First Record    Previous Record

Next Record    Last Record

Find Recipient

type the specific field entry for which you are searching in the *Find* text box and then click the Find Next button. Continue clicking the Find Next button until Word displays a message telling you that there are no more entries that contain the text you typed. At this message, click OK.

**Figure 16.5 Find Entry Dialog Box**

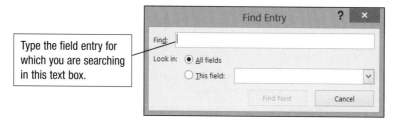

Type the field entry for which you are searching in this text box.

## Checking for Errors

Check for Errors

Before merging documents, you can check for errors using the Check for Errors button in the Preview Results group on the MAILINGS tab. Click this button and the Checking and Reporting Errors dialog box, as shown in Figure 16.6, displays containing three options. Click the first option, *Simulate the merge and report errors in a new document*, to have Word test the merge, not make any changes, and report the errors in a new document. Choose the second option, *Complete the merge, pausing to report each error as it occurs*, to have Word merge the documents and display errors as they occur during the merge. Choose the third option, *Complete the merge without pausing. Report errors in a new document*, to have Word complete the merge without pausing and report any errors in a new document.

**Figure 16.6 Checking and Reporting Errors Dialog Box**

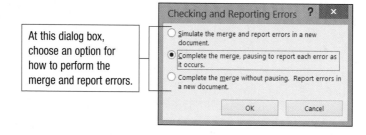

At this dialog box, choose an option for how to perform the merge and report errors.

**QUICK STEPS**

**Merge Documents**
1. Click Finish & Merge button.
2. Click *Edit Individual Documents* at drop-down list.
3. Make sure *All* is selected in Merge to New Document dialog box.
4. Click OK.

Finish & Merge

## Merging Documents

To complete the merge, click the Finish & Merge button in the Finish group on the MAILINGS tab. At the drop-down list that displays, you can choose to merge the records and create a new document, send the merged documents directly to the printer, or send the merged documents by email.

To merge the documents and create a new document with the merged records, click the Finish & Merge button and then click *Edit Individual Documents* at the drop-down list. At the Merge to New Document dialog box, make sure *All* is selected in the *Merge records* section and then click OK. This merges the records in the data source file with the main document and inserts the merged documents in a new document.

Identify specific records you want merged with options at the Merge to New Document dialog box, as shown in Figure 16.7 on the next page. Display this dialog box by clicking the Finish & Merge button in the Mailings tab and then clicking the *Edit Individual Documents* option at the drop-down list. Click the *All* option to merge all of the records in the data source. Click the *Current record* option if you want to merge only the current record. If you have not previewed the merge and changed record numbers, the *Current record* option will merge only the first record in the data source. If you want to merge a different record, click the Preview Results to turn it on and then click the Next Record button until the desired merged record displays. Click the Finish & Merge button, click the *Edit Individual Documents* option, click *Current record* at the Merge to New Document dialog box, and then click OK. Use the *From* and *To* text boxes to specify a range of records. For example, if you want to merge only records 1 through 3, you would type **1** in the *From* text box and **3** in the *To* text box and then click OK.

**Figure 16.7 Merge to New Document Dialog Box**

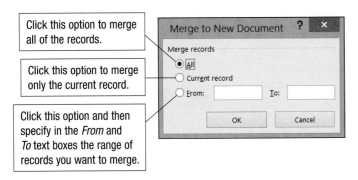

**Exercise 16.1C   Merging the Main Document with the Data Source File**                                          **Part 3 of 3**

1. With **C16-E01-CofELetterMD.docx** open, preview the main document merged with the first record in the data source file by clicking the Preview Results button on the MAILINGS tab.
2. Click the Next Record button to view the main document merged with the second record in the data source file.
3. Click the Last Record button to view the main document merged with the last record in the data source file.
4. Click the First Record button to view the first record merged.

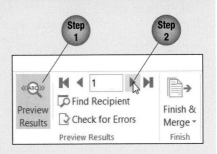

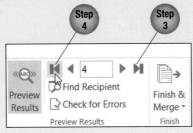

5. Find records with the zip code *83445* by completing the following steps:
   a. Click the Find Recipient button in the Preview Results group.
   b. At the Find Entry dialog box, type **83445** in the *Find* text box and then click the Find Next button.

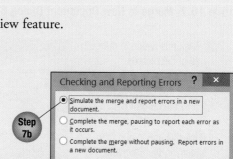

   c. Continue clicking the Find Next button (noticing the merged letters that display) until a message displays telling you that there are no more entries that contain the text you typed. At this message, click OK.
   d. Click the Cancel button to close the Find Entry dialog box.
6. Click the Preview Results button to turn off the preview feature.
7. Check for errors by completing the following steps:
   a. Click the Check for Errors button in the Preview Results group on the MAILINGS tab.
   b. At the Checking and Reporting Errors dialog box, click the first option, *Simulate the merge and report errors in a new document.*
   c. Click OK.
   d. If a new document displays with any errors, print the document and then close it without saving it. If a message displays telling you that no errors were found, click OK.
8. Click the Finish & Merge button in the Finish group and then click *Edit Individual Documents* at the drop-down list.

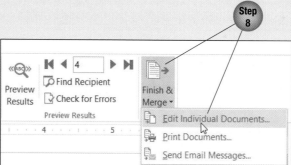

9. At the Merge to New Document dialog box, make sure *All* is selected and then click OK.
10. Save the merged letters document with the name **C16-E01-CofELtrs**.
11. Print **C16-E01-CofELtrs.docx**. (This document will print four letters.)
12. Close **C16-E01-CofELtrs.docx**.
13. Save and then close **C16-E01-CofELettersMD.docx**.

# Merging Envelopes

If you create a letter as your main document and then merge it with a data source file, you will likely need properly addressed envelopes to send copies of the letter. To create customized envelopes, prepare an envelope main document to be merged with the data source file. To do this, click the MAILINGS tab, click the Start Mail Merge button and then click *Envelopes* at the drop-down list. This displays the Envelope Options dialog box, as shown in Figure 16.8. At this dialog box, specify the desired envelope size, make any other changes, and then click OK.

**Figure 16.8 Envelope Options Dialog Box**

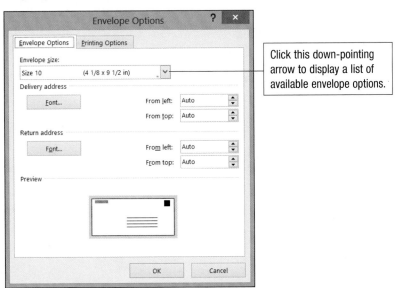

Click this down-pointing arrow to display a list of available envelope options.

After selecting an envelope as the main document type, the next step in the envelope merge process is to create a data source file to merge with the envelope document or identify an existing file to use. To identify an existing data source file, click the Select Recipients button in the Start Mail Merge group and then click *Use an Existing List* at the drop-down list. At the Select Data Source dialog box, navigate to the folder that contains the data source file you want to use and then double-click the file.

With the data source file attached to the envelope main document, insert the appropriate fields. Click in the approximate location where the recipient's address will appear and a box with a dashed gray border displays. Click the Address Block button in the Write & Insert Fields group and then click OK at the Insert Address Block dialog box.

1. At a blank document, click the MAILINGS tab.
2. Click the Start Mail Merge button in the Start Mail Merge group and then click *Envelopes* at the drop-down list.

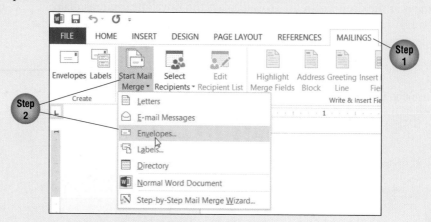

3. At the Envelope Options dialog box, make sure the envelope size is 10 and then click OK.
4. Click the Select Recipients button in the Start Mail Merge group and then click *Use an Existing List* at the drop-down list.
5. At the Select Data Source dialog box, navigate to the Chapter16 folder on your storage medium and then double-click the data source file named **C16-E01-CofEDS.mdb**.

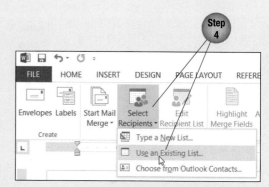

6. In the envelope document, click in the approximate location where the recipient's address will appear. (This causes a box with a dashed gray border to display. If you do not see this box, try clicking in a different location in the envelope.)

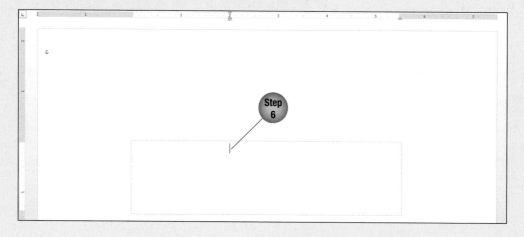

7. Click the Address Block button in the Write & Insert Fields group.
8. At the Insert Address Block dialog box, click the OK button.
9. Click the Preview Results button to view the envelope merged with the first record in the data source file.
10. Click the Preview Results button to turn off the preview feature.
11. Click the Finish & Merge button in the Finish group and then click *Edit Individual Documents* at the drop-down list.
12. At the Merge to New Document dialog box, specify that you want only the first two records to merge by completing the following steps:

    a. Click in the *From* text box and then type **1**.
    b. Click in the *To* text box and then type **2**.
    c. Click OK. (This merges only the first two records and opens a document with two merged envelopes.)

13. Save the merged envelopes document with the name **C16-E02-CofEEnvs**.
14. Print **C16-E02-CofEEnvs.docx**. (This document will print two envelopes. Manual feed of the envelopes may be required. Please check with your instructor.)
15. Close **C16-E02-CofEEnvs.docx**.
16. Save the envelope main document with the name **C16-E02-EnvMD**.
17. Close **C16-E02-EnvMD.docx**.

## Merging Labels

You can create mailing labels for records in a data source file in much the same way that you create envelopes. Click the Start Mail Merge button and then click *Labels* at the drop-down list. This displays the Label Options dialog box, as shown in Figure 16.9. Make sure that the label product number you want to use is selected and then click OK to close the dialog box. For the address information, you can create the data source file or identify an existing data source file to use. With the data source file attached to the label main document, insert the appropriate fields and then complete the merge.

**Figure 16.9 Label Options Dialog Box**

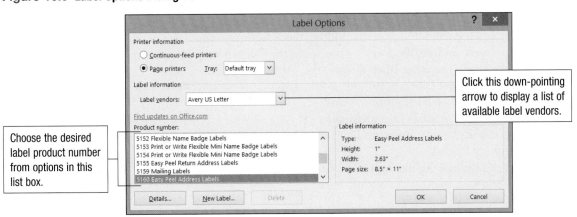

1. At a blank document, click the MAILINGS tab. (If you just completed Exercise 16.2, change the document zoom back to 100%.)
2. Click the Start Mail Merge button in the Start Mail Merge group and then click *Labels* at the drop-down list.
3. At the Label Options dialog box, complete the following steps:
   a. If necessary, click the down-pointing arrow at the right of the *Label vendors* option and then click *Avery US Letter* at the drop-down list. (If this option is not available, choose a vendor that offers labels that print on a full page.)
   b. Scroll in the *Product number* list box and then click *5160 Easy Peel Address Labels*. (If this option is not available, choose a label number that prints labels in two or three columns on a full page.)
   c. Click OK to close the dialog box.

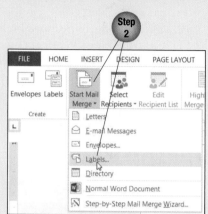

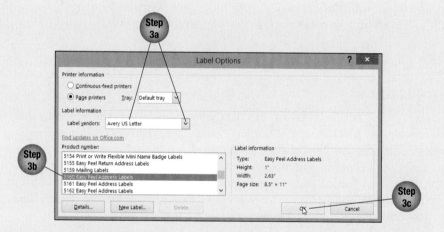

4. Click the Select Recipients button in the Start Mail Merge group and then click *Use an Existing List* at the drop-down list.
5. At the Select Data Source dialog box, navigate to the Chapter16 folder on your storage medium and then double-click the data source file named **C16-E01-CofEDS.mdb**.
6. At the labels document, click the Address Block button in the Write & Insert Fields group.
7. At the Insert Address Block dialog box, click the OK button. (This inserts «*AddressBlock*» in the first label. The other labels contain the «*Next Record*» field.)
8. Click the Update Labels button in the Write & Insert Fields group. (This adds the «*AddressBlock*» field after each «*Next Record*» field in the second and subsequent labels.)
9. Click the Preview Results button to view the labels merged with the records in the data source file.

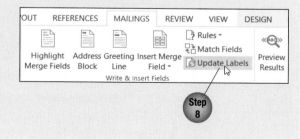

10. Click the Preview Results button to turn off the preview feature.
11. Click the Finish & Merge button in the Finish group and then click *Edit Individual Documents* at the drop-down list.
12. At the Merge to New Document dialog box, make sure *All* is selected and then click OK.
13. Format the labels by completing the following steps:
    a. Click the TABLE TOOLS LAYOUT tab.
    b. Click the Select button in the Table group and then click *Select Table*.
    c. Click the Align Center Left button in the Alignment group.
    d. Click the HOME tab and then click the Paragraph group dialog box launcher.
    e. At the Paragraph dialog box, click the up-pointing arrow at the right of the *Before* measurement box to change the measurement to 0 points.
    f. Click the up-pointing arrow at the right of the *After* measurement box to change the measurement to 0 points.
    g. Click the up-pointing arrow at the right of the *Inside* measurement box until *0.3* displays in the measurement box.
    h. Click OK.

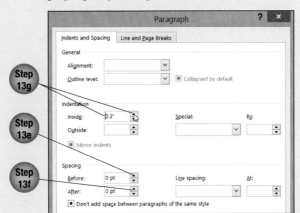

14. Save the merged labels document with the name **C16-E03-CofELabels**.
15. Print and then close **C16-E03-CofELabels.docx**.
16. Save the label main document with the name **C16-E03-CofELabelsMD**.
17. Close **C16-E03-CofELabelsMD.docx**.

## Merging a Directory

When merging letters, envelopes, or mailing labels, a new form is created for each record. For example, if the data source file merged with a letter contains eight records, eight letters are created. If the data source file merged with a mailing label contains 20 records, 20 labels are created. In some situations, you may want merged information to remain on the same page. This is useful when you want to create a list such as a directory or address list.

To create a merged directory, click the Start Mail Merge button and then click *Directory*. Create or identify an existing data source file and then insert the desired fields in the directory document. Set tabs if you want to insert the text in columns.

---

**Exercise 16.4**  Merging a Directory                                    Part 1 of 1

---

1. At a blank document, click the MAILINGS tab.
2. Click the Start Mail Merge button in the Start Mail Merge group and then click *Directory* at the drop-down list.
3. Click the Select Recipients button in the Start Mail Merge group and then click *Use an Existing List* at the drop-down list.

4. At the Select Data Source dialog box, navigate to the Chapter16 folder on your storage medium and then double-click the data source file named **C16-E01-CofEDS.mdb**.
5. At the document, set left tabs on the horizontal ruler at the 1-inch mark, the 2.5-inch mark, and the 4-inch mark.
6. Press the Tab key. (This moves the insertion point to the tab set at the 1-inch mark.)
7. Click the Insert Merge Field button arrow and then click *Last_Name* at the drop-down list.
8. Press the Tab key to move the insertion point to the 2.5-inch mark.
9. Click the Insert Merge Field button arrow and then click *First_Name* at the drop-down list.
10. Press the Tab key to move the insertion point to the 4-inch mark.
11. Click the Insert Merge Field button arrow and then click *Membership* at the drop-down list.
12. Press the Enter key once.
13. Click the Finish & Merge button in the Finish group and then click *Edit Individual Documents* at the drop-down list.
14. At the Merge to New Document dialog box, make sure *All* is selected and then click OK. (This merges the fields in the document.)
15. Press Ctrl + Home, press the Enter key once, and then press the Up Arrow key once.
16. Press the Tab key, apply bold formatting, and then type **Last Name**.
17. Press the Tab key and then type **First Name**.
18. Press the Tab key and then type **Membership**.

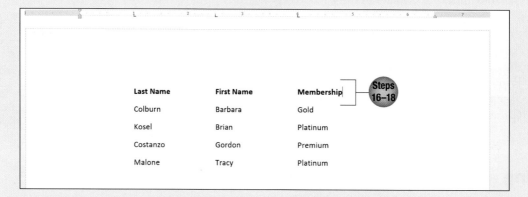

19. Save the directory document with the name **C16-E04-CofEDirectory**.
20. Print and then close **C16-E04-CofEDirectory.docx**.
21. Close the directory main document without saving it.

# Editing a Data Source File

Edit a main document in the normal manner. Open the document, make the required changes, and then save the document. Since a data source file is actually an Access database file, you cannot open it in the usual manner. Open a data source file for editing using the Edit Recipient List button in the Start Mail Merge group on the MAILINGS tab. When you click the Edit Recipient List button, the Mail Merge Recipients dialog box displays, as shown in Figure 16.10 on the next page. Select or edit records at this dialog box.

Edit Recipient List

**Figure 16.10 Mail Merge Recipients Dialog Box**

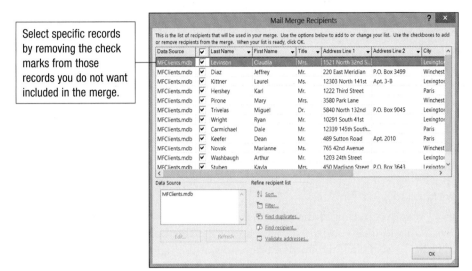

Select specific records by removing the check marks from those records you do not want included in the merge.

## Selecting Specific Records

Each record in the Mail Merge Recipients dialog box contains a check mark before the first field. To select specific records, remove the check marks from those records you do not want included in the merge. This feature allows you to select and then merge only certain records in the data source file with the main document.

---

### Exercise 16.5 Selecting Records and Merging Mailing Labels    Part 1 of 1

1. At a blank document, create mailing labels for clients living in Lexington. Begin by clicking the MAILINGS tab.
2. Click the Start Mail Merge button in the Start Mail Merge group and then click *Labels* at the drop-down list.
3. At the Label Options dialog box, make sure that *Avery US Letter* displays in the *Label products* option box and that *5160 Easy Peel Address Labels* displays in the *Product number* list box, and then click OK.
4. Click the Select Recipients button in the Start Mail Merge group and then click *Use an Existing List* at the drop-down list.
5. At the Select Data Source dialog box, navigate to the Chapter16 folder on your storage medium and then double-click the data source file named **MFClients.mdb**.
6. Click the Edit Recipient List button in the Start Mail Merge group.
7. At the Mail Merge Recipients dialog box, complete the following steps:
   a. Click the check box located immediately left of the *Last Name* field to remove the check mark. (This removes all of the check marks from the check boxes.)

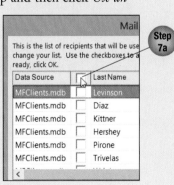

---

b. Click the check box immediately left of each of the following last names: *Levinson, Kittner, Trivelas, Wright, Washbaugh,* and *Stuben*. (These are the clients who live in Lexington.)

c. Click OK to close the dialog box.

8. At the labels document, click the Address Block button in the Write & Insert Fields group.

9. At the Insert Address Block dialog box, click the OK button.

10. Click the Update Labels button in the Write & Insert Fields group.

11. Click the Finish & Merge button in the Finish group and then click *Edit Individual Documents* at the drop-down list.

12. At the Merge to New Document dialog box, make sure *All* is selected and then click OK.

13. Format the labels by completing the following steps:

a. Click the TABLE TOOLS LAYOUT tab.

b. Click the Select button in the Table group and then click *Select Table*.

c. Click the Align Center Left button in the Alignment group.

d. Click the HOME tab and then click the Paragraph group dialog box launcher.

e. At the Paragraph dialog box, click the up-pointing arrow at the right of the *Before* measurement box to change the measurement to 0 points.

f. Click the up-pointing arrow at the right of the *After* measurement box to change the measurement to 0 points.

g. Click the up-pointing arrow at the right of the *Inside* measurement box until *0.3* displays in the box.

h. Click OK.

14. Save the merged labels document with the name **C16-E05-Labels**.

15. Print and then close **C16-E05-Labels.docx**.

16. Close the main labels document without saving it.

## Editing Records

A data source file may need periodic editing to add and delete customer names, update fields, insert new fields, and delete existing fields. To edit a data source file, click the Edit Recipient List button in the Start Mail Merge group. At the Mail Merge Recipients dialog box, click the data source file name in the *Data Source* list box and then click the Edit button that displays below the list box. This displays the Edit Data Source dialog box, as shown in Figure 16.11. At this dialog box, you can add a new entry, delete an existing entry, find a particular entry, and customize columns.

**Figure 16.11  Edit Data Source Dialog Box**

Edit the fields in the records in the data source file at this dialog box.

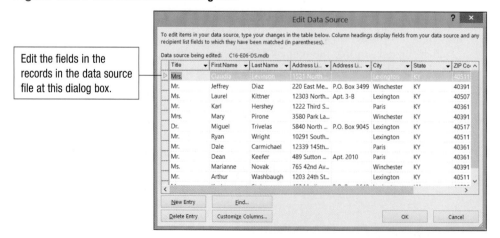

1. Make a copy of the **MFClients.mdb** file by completing the following steps:
    a. Display the Open dialog box and make Chapter16 on your storage medium the active folder.
    b. If necessary, change the file type button to *All Files (\*.\*)*.
    c. Right-click ***MFClients.mdb*** and then click *Copy* at the shortcut menu.
    d. Position the mouse pointer in an empty area in the Content pane of the Open dialog box (outside any file name), click the *right* mouse button, and then click *Paste* at the shortcut menu. (This inserts a copy of the file in the dialog box Content pane and names the file **MFClients - Copy.mdb**.)
    e. Right-click ***MFClients - Copy.mdb*** and then click *Rename* at the shortcut menu.
    f. Type **C16-E06-DS** and then press the Enter key.
    g. Close the Open dialog box.
2. At a blank document, click the MAILINGS tab.
3. Click the Select Recipients button and then click *Use an Existing List* from the drop-down list.
4. At the Select Data Source dialog box, navigate to the Chapter16 folder on your storage medium and then double-click the data source file named **C16-E06-DS.mdb**.
5. Click the Edit Recipient List button in the Start Mail Merge group.
6. At the Mail Merge Recipients dialog box, click **C16-E06-DS.mdb** that displays in the *Data Source* list box (located in the lower left of the dialog box) and then click the Edit button.

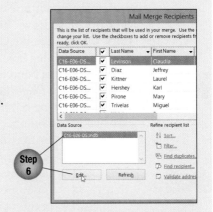

**Step 6**

7. Delete the record for *Dean Keefer* by completing the following steps:
    a. Click the square that displays at the beginning of the row for *Mr. Dean Keefer*.
    b. Click the Delete Entry button.
    c. At the message asking if you want to delete the entry, click the Yes button.
8. Insert a new record by completing the following steps:
    a. Click the New Entry button in the dialog box.
    b. Type the following text in the new record in the specified fields:

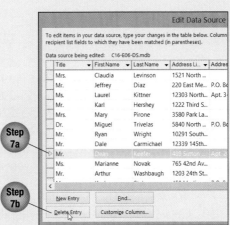

**Step 7a**

**Step 7b**

         Title = **Mrs.**
         First Name = **Amanda**
         Last Name = **Montague**
         Address Line 1 = **632 Tenth Street**
         Address Line 2 = (none)
         City = **Lexington**
         State = **KY**
         ZIP Code = **40506**
         Home Phone = **(859) 555-2047**

9. Insert a new field and type text in it by completing the following steps:
   a. At the Edit Data Source dialog box, click the Customize Columns button.
   b. At the message asking if you want to save the changes made to the data source file, click Yes.
   c. At the Customize Address List dialog box, click *ZIP Code* in the *Field Names* list box.
   d. Click the Add button.
   e. At the Add Field dialog box, type **Cell Phone** and then click OK.
   f. Change the order of the fields so the *Cell Phone* field displays after the *Home Phone* field. To move the *Cell Phone* field, make sure it is selected and then click the Move Down button.
   g. Click OK to close the Customize Address List dialog box.
   h. At the Edit Data Source dialog box, scroll to the right to display the *Cell Phone* field (last field in the file) and then type the following cell phone numbers. (After typing each cell phone number except the last number, press the Down Arrow key to make the next cell below active.)

   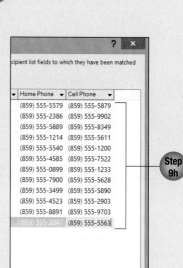

   Record 1: **(859) 555-5879**
   Record 2: **(859) 555-9902**
   Record 3: **(859) 555-8349**
   Record 4: **(859) 555-5611**
   Record 5: **(859) 555-1200**
   Record 6: **(859) 555-7522**
   Record 7: **(859) 555-1233**
   Record 8: **(859) 555-5628**
   Record 9: **(859) 555-5890**
   Record 10: **(859) 555-2903**
   Record 11: **(859) 555-9703**
   Record 12: **(859) 555-5563**

   i. Click OK to close the Edit Data Source dialog box.
   j. At the message asking if you want to update the recipient list and save the changes, click Yes.
   k. At the Mail Merge Recipients dialog box, click OK.
10. Create a directory by completing the following steps:
    a. Click the Start Mail Merge button and then click *Directory* at the drop-down list.
    b. At the blank document, set left tabs on the horizontal ruler at the 1-inch mark, 3-inch mark, and 4.5-inch mark.
    c. Press the Tab key. (This moves the insertion point to the first tab, set at the 1-inch mark.)
    d. Click the Insert Merge Field button arrow and then click *Last_Name* at the drop-down list.
    e. Type a comma and then press the spacebar.
    f. Click the Insert Merge Field button arrow and then click *First_Name* at the drop-down list.

    g.   Press the Tab key, click the Insert Merge Field button arrow, and then click *Home_Phone* at the drop-down list.

    h.   Press the Tab key, click the Insert Merge Field button arrow, and then click *Cell_Phone* at the drop-down list.

    i.   Press the Enter key once.

    j.   Click the Finish & Merge button in the Finish group and then click *Edit Individual Documents* at the drop-down list.

    k.   At the Merge to New Document dialog box, make sure *All* is selected and then click OK. (This merges the fields in the document. If the merge is missing a field of information, close the merged document without saving changes and complete the merge again.)

11. Press Ctrl + Home, press the Enter key once, and then press the Up Arrow key once.

12. Press the Tab key, apply bold formatting, and then type **Name**.

13. Press the Tab key and then type **Home Phone**.

14. Press the Tab key and then type **Cell Phone**.

15. Save the directory document with the name **C16-E06-Directory**.

16. Print and then close **C16-E06-Directory.docx**.

17. Close the directory main document without saving it.

| Name | Home Phone | Cell Phone | |
|---|---|---|---|
| Levinson, Claudia | (859) 555-5579 | (859) 555-5879 | Steps 12–14 |
| Diaz, Jeffrey | (859) 555-2386 | (859) 555-9902 | |
| Kittner, Laurel | (859) 555-5889 | (859) 555-8349 | |

# Inserting Additional Fields

The Mail Merge feature provides a number of methods for inserting fields into a main document. In addition to the methods you have used so far, you can also insert fields with the Rules button in the Write & Insert Fields group on the MAILINGS tab. Click the Rules button to display a drop-down list of additional fields.

Rules

## Inputting Text during a Merge

Word's Merge feature contains a large number of fields that you can insert into a main document. One such field, the Fill-in field, is used to input information with the keyboard during a merge.

In some situations, you may not need to keep all of the variable information in a data source file. For example, variable information that changes on a regular basis might include a customer's monthly balance, a product price, and so on. Insert a Fill-in field in a main document to input variable information into a document during the merge using the keyboard.

To insert a Fill-in field in a main document, click the Rules button in the Write & Insert Fields group on the MAILINGS tab and then click *Fill-in* at the drop-down list. This displays the Insert Word Field: Fill-in dialog box, as shown in Figure 16.12 on the next page. At this dialog box, type a short message indicating what should be entered with the keyboard and then click OK. At the Microsoft Word dialog box, the message you entered displays in the upper left corner. Type the text you want to display in the document and then click OK.

**Insert a Fill-in Field in the Main Document**
1. Click Rules button.
2. Click *Fill-in* at drop-down list.
3. Type prompt text.
4. Click OK.
5. Type text to be displayed in document.
6. Click OK.

**Figure 16.12  Insert Word Field: Fill-in Dialog Box**

In this text box, type a short message indicating what should be entered at the keyboard.

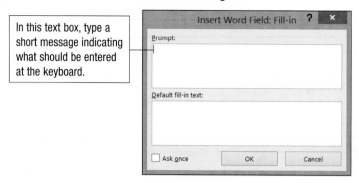

When you have added a Fill-in field or fields, save the main document in the normal manner. A document can contain any number of Fill-in fields.

When you merge the main document with the data source file, the first record is merged and the Microsoft Word dialog box displays with the message you entered displayed in the upper left corner. Type the required information for the first record in the data source file and then click OK. Word displays the dialog box again. Type the required information for the second record in the data source file and then click OK. Continue in this manner until you have entered the required information for each record in the data source file. Word then completes the merge.

## Inserting a Record Number

If you are merging a small number of records, you can look at each merged document to determine if all of the records merged and printed. If you have a large number of records in a data source and want to ensure that each document merges and prints, consider inserting a Merge Record # field in the document. This field will insert a record number in each merged document. For example, if you are merging letters, the code will insert number 1 in the first merged letter, number 2 in the second, and so on. With the merge record number in each letter, you can ensure that all of the letters print.

To insert a Merge Record # field, click the Rules button in the Write & Insert Fields group on the MAILINGS tab and then click *Merge Record #* at the drop-down list. This inserts the field «*Merge Record #*» in the document.

## Inserting an If...Then...Else... Field

Use an If...Then...Else... field to tell Word to compare two values and then, depending on what is determined, enter one set of text or the other. When you click *If...Then...Else...* at the Rules button drop-down list, the Insert Word Field: IF dialog box displays, as shown in Figure 16.13 on the next page.

**Figure 16.13 Insert Word Field: IF Dialog Box**

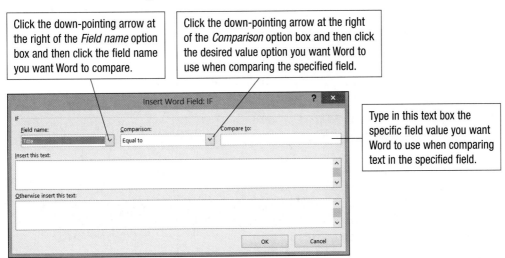

Click the down-pointing arrow at the right of the *Field name* option box and then click the field name you want Word to compare.

Click the down-pointing arrow at the right of the *Comparison* option box and then click the desired value option you want Word to use when comparing the specified field.

Type in this text box the specific field value you want Word to use when comparing text in the specified field.

Specify the field you want Word to compare with the *Field name* option. Click the down-pointing arrow at the right of the *Field name* option box and then click the desired field at the drop-down list. The drop-down list displays all of the fields you specified when creating the data source. Use the *Comparison* option to identify how you want Word to compare values. By default, *Equal to* displays in the *Comparison* option box. Click the down-pointing arrow at the right of the option box and a drop-down list displays with a variety of value options, such as *Not equal to, Less than, Greater than*, and so on. In the *Compare to* text box, type the specific field value you want Word to use. For example, if you want to include a statement in a letter for all customers with the zip code 98405, click the down-pointing arrow at the right of the *Field name* option box and then click *ZIP_Code* at the drop-down list. Then click in the *Compare to* text box and type **98405**.

Once you have established the field name and specific field entry, type in the *Insert this text* text box the text you want inserted if the field entry is matched, and type in the *Otherwise insert this text* text box the text you want inserted if the field entry is not matched. You can also leave the *Otherwise insert this text* text box empty. This tells Word not to insert any text if the specific entry value is not matched.

By default, an If…Then…Else… field does not display in the document. If you want to make the field visible, press the keys Alt + F9. To turn off the display, press the keys Alt + F9 again. Turning on the display of field codes also expands other merge codes.

**Figure 16.14 Exercise 16.7**

As we prepare our budget for the next year, we need to confirm our members' pledges. According to our records, you have pledged (pledge) for 2016. Please contact us if you want to change this pledge.

## Exercise 16.7  Adding Fields to a Main Document with the Rules Button    Part 1 of 1

1. Open the document named **C16-E01-CofELetterMD.docx** and save it with the name **C16-E07-CofELetterMD**. (At the message indicating that opening the document will run the SQL command, click Yes.)
2. Change the second paragraph in the body of the letter to the paragraph shown in Figure 16.14. When you reach the text *(pledge)*, insert the Fill-in field *(pledge)* by completing the following steps:
   a. Click the MAILINGS tab.
   b. Click the Rules button in the Write & Insert Fields group and then click *Fill-in* at the drop-down list.
   c. At the Insert Word Field: Fill-in dialog box, type **Insert pledge amount** in the *Prompt* text box and then click OK.
   d. At the Microsoft Word dialog box with *Insert pledge amount* displayed in the upper left corner, type **(pledge)** and then click OK.

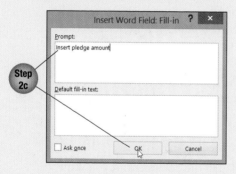

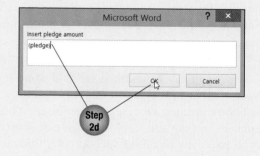

   e. Continue typing the remaining text shown in Figure 16.14.
3. Insert an If…Then…Else… field that tells Word to add text if the membership code is equal to *Platinum* by completing the following steps:
   a. Position the insertion point to the right of the period that ends the new second paragraph you just typed and press the spacebar.
   b. Click the Rules button in the Write & Insert Fields group and then click *If…Then…Else…* at the drop-down list.

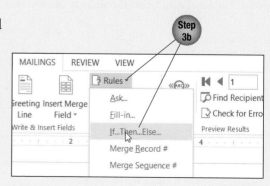

    c.    At the Insert Word Field: IF dialog box, click the down-pointing arrow at the right of the *Field name* option box and then click *Membership* at the drop-down list. (Scroll down the list box to display this field.)

    d.    Click in the *Compare to* text box and then type **Platinum**.

    e.    Click in the *Insert this text* text box and then type **We hope you will continue your Platinum membership and enjoy the benefits of supporting your local community.**

    f.    Click OK to close the dialog box.

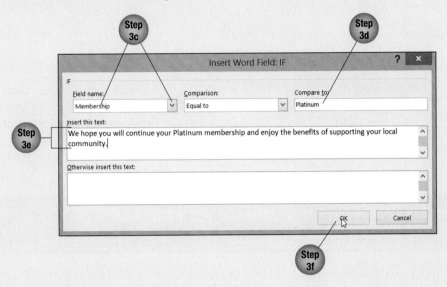

    g.    View the If…Then…Else… field code (and expand the other merge codes) by pressing keys Alt + F9.

    h.    After viewing the expanded fields, press keys Alt + F9 again to turn off the display.

4.  Change the file name after your initials toward the bottom of the letter to **C16-E07-CofELetterMD**.

5.  Insert a Merge Record # field by completing the following steps:

    a.    Position the insertion point immediately right of the letters *MD* in the document name **C16-E07-CofELetterMD.docx**.

    b.    Type a hyphen.

    c.    Click the Rules button in the Write & Insert Fields group and then click *Merge Record #* at the drop-down list.

6.  Save **C16-E07-CofELetterMD.docx**.

7.  Merge the main document with the data source file by completing the following steps:

    a.    Click the Finish & Merge button and then click *Edit Individual Documents* at the drop-down list.

    b.    At the Merge to New Document dialog box, make sure *All* is selected and then click OK.

    c.    When Word merges the main document with the first record, a dialog box displays with the message *Insert pledge amount* and the text *(pledge)* selected. At this dialog box, type **$2,500** and then click OK.

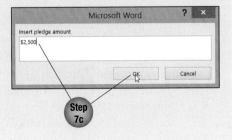

    d.    At the dialog box with the message *Insert pledge amount*, type **$10,000** (over *$2,500*) and then click OK.

e.  At the dialog box with the message *Insert pledge amount*, type **$5,000** (over *$10,000*) and then click OK.

f.  At the dialog box with the message *Insert pledge amount*, type **$10,000** (over *$5,000*) and then click OK and close the dialog box.

8.  Save the merged document with the name **C16-E07-CofELetters**.

9.  Print and then close **C16-E07-CofELetters.docx**.

10. Save and then close **C16-E07-CofELetterMD.docx**.

# Merging with Other Data Sources

In this chapter, you have merged a main document with a data source. Word saves a data source as an Access database with the *.mdb* file extension. (In Access 2013, a database file is saved with the *.accdb* file extension.) You can also merge a main document with other data sources, such as a Word document containing data in a table, an Excel worksheet, an Access database table, and an Outlook contacts list.

---

**Exercise 16.8**  **Merging a Main Document with a Word Table Data Source**    **Part 1 of 1**

1.  Open **BTTourLtr.docx** located in the Chapter16 folder on your storage medium.

2.  Save the document with Save As and name it **C16-E08-BTTourLtrMD**.

3.  Identify a Word table as the data source by completing the following steps:
    a.  Click the MAILINGS tab.
    b.  Click the Select Recipients button in the Start Mail Merge group and then click *Use an Existing List* at the drop-down list.
    c.  At the Select Data Source dialog box, navigate to the Chapter16 folder on your storage medium and then double-click **BTClientTable.docx**.

4.  Press the Down Arrow key four times and then click the Address Block button in the Write & Insert Fields group.

5.  At the Insert Address Block dialog box, click OK.

6.  Press the Enter key twice.

7.  Insert the greeting line fields by completing the following steps:
    a.  Click the Greeting Line button in the Write & Insert Fields group.
    b.  At the Insert Greeting Line dialog box, click the down-pointing arrow at the right of the option box containing the comma (the box to the right of the box containing *Mr. Randall*).
    c.  At the drop-down list that displays, click the colon.
    d.  Click OK to close the Insert Greeting Line dialog box.

8.  Scroll to the end of the letter. Replace the *XX* with your initials.

9.  Merge the document by clicking the Finish & Merge button in the Finish group and then clicking *Edit Individual Documents* at the drop-down list. At the Merge to New Document dialog box, click OK.

10. Save the merged letters with the name **C16-E08-BTTourLtrs**.

11. Print the first two pages (letters) of the document and then close it.

12. Save and then close **C16-E08-BTTourLtrMD.docx**.

If the fields in a data source do not match the fields in the address block, use options at the Match Fields dialog box to match the field names. Display the Match Fields dialog box by clicking the Match Fields button in the Write & Insert group or by clicking the Match Fields button in the Insert Address Block dialog box or the Greeting Line dialog box. To match the fields, click the down-pointing arrow at the right side of the field you want to match and then click the desired field at the drop-down list of fields in the data source. For example, in Exercise 16.9, you will use an Excel worksheet as a data source. One of the fields, *MailingAddress*, does not have a match in the address block, so you will use the Match Fields button to match the *Address 1* field in the address block to the *MailingAddress* field in the Excel worksheet.

## Exercise 16.9  Merging a Main Document with an Excel Worksheet Data Source    Part 1 of 1

1. Open **BTTourLtr.docx** and then save the document with Save As and name it **C16-E09-BTTourLtrMD**.
2. Identify an Excel worksheet as the data source by completing the following steps:
   a. Click the MAILINGS tab.
   b. Click the Select Recipients button in the Start Mail Merge group and then click *Use an Existing List* at the drop-down list.
   c. At the Select Data Source dialog box, navigate to the Chapter16 folder on your storage medium and then double-click **BTClientsExcel.xlsx**.
   d. At the Select Table dialog box, click OK.

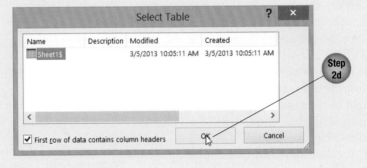

3. Press the Down Arrow key four times and then insert the address block by completing the following steps:
   a.  Click the Address Block button in the Write & Insert Fields group.
   b.  At the Insert Address Block dialog box, click the Match Fields button.

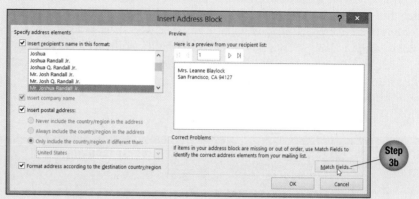

   c.  At the Match Fields dialog box, click the down-pointing arrow at the right side of the *Address 1* field and then click *MailingAddress* at the drop-down list.
   d.  Click OK to close the Match Fields dialog box.
   e.  Click OK to close the Insert Address Block dialog box.
4. Press the Enter key twice.
5. Insert the greeting line fields by completing the following steps:
   a.  Click the Greeting Line button in the Write & Insert Fields group.
   b.  At the Insert Greeting Line dialog box, click the down-pointing arrow at the right of the option box containing the comma (the box to the right of the box containing *Mr. Randall*).
   c.  At the drop-down list that displays, click the colon.
   d.  Click OK to close the Insert Greeting Line dialog box.

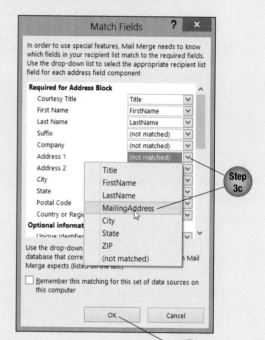

6. Scroll to the end of the letter and then replace the *XX* with your initials.
7. Merge the document by clicking the Finish & Merge button in the Finish group and then clicking *Edit Individual Documents* at the drop-down list. At the Merge to New Document dialog box, click OK.
8. Save the merged letters with the name **C16-E09-BTTourLtrs**.
9. Print the first two pages (letters) of the document and then close it.
10. Save and then close **C16-E09-BTTourLtrMD.docx**.

In addition to using a Word table or Excel worksheet as a data source, you can use an Access database table. To choose an Access database table, display the Select Data Source dialog box, navigate to the desired folder, and then double-click the desired database. At the Select Table dialog box, select the desired table and then click OK.

---

**Exercise 16.10**  Merging a Main Document with an Access Database Table Data Source      Part 1 of 1

1. Open **BTTourLtr.docx** and then save the document with Save As and name it **C16-E10-BTTourLtrMD**.
2. Identify an Access table as the data source by completing the following steps:
   a. Click the MAILINGS tab.
   b. Click the Select Recipients button in the Start Mail Merge group and then click *Use an Existing List* at the drop-down list.
   c. At the Select Data Source dialog box, navigate to the Chapter16 folder on your storage medium and then double-click *BaysideTravel.accdb*.
   d. At the Select Table dialog box, click the *Clients* table and then click OK.

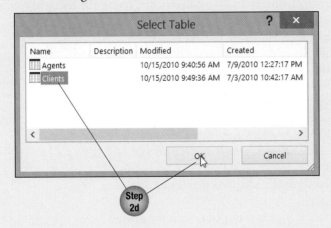
Step 2d

3. Press the Down Arrow key four times.
4. Click the Address Block button in the Write & Insert Fields group and then click OK at the Insert Address Block dialog box.
5. Press the Enter key twice.
6. Insert the greeting line fields by completing the following steps:
   a. Click the Greeting Line button in the Write & Insert Fields group.
   b. At the Insert Greeting Line dialog box, click the down-pointing arrow at the right of the option box containing the comma (the box to the right of the box containing *Mr. Randall*).
   c. At the drop-down list that displays, click the colon.
   d. Click OK to close the Insert Greeting Line dialog box.
7. Scroll to the end of the letter and then replace the *XX* with your initials.
8. Merge the document by clicking the Finish & Merge button in the Finish group and then clicking *Edit Individual Documents* at the drop-down list. At the Merge to New Document dialog box, click OK.
9. Save the merged letters with the name **C16-E10-BTTourLtrs**.
10. Print the first two pages (letters) of the document and then close it.
11. Save and then close **C16-E10-BTTourLtrMD.docx**.

If you use Outlook to send emails, you can use an Outlook contact list as a data source. Create the email message in a Word document, identify it as an email message, and then send it to contacts in the contact list. To do this, open the document containing the email message or type the email message in a blank document. Click the MAILINGS tab, click the Start Mail Merge button in the Start Mail Merge group, and then click *E-mail Messages* at the drop-down list. This changes the display of the document on the screen. Click the Select Recipients button in the Start Mail Merge group and then click *Select from Outlook Contacts* at the drop-down list. Complete the steps to identify the specific Outlook contact list and then merge the email message with the names in the list.

## Exercise 16.11   Merging a Main Document with an Outlook Contact List Data Source   Part 1 of 1

***Note: You must have Outlook set up to send emails to complete this exercise.***

1. Open **BTTourLtr.docx** and then save the document with Save As and name it **C16-E11-BTTourLtrMD**.
2. Identify the main document as an email by completing the following steps:
   a. Click the MAILINGS tab.
   b. Click the Start Mail Merge button in the Start Mail Merge group and then click *E-mail Messages* at the drop-down list.
3. Identify an Outlook Contacts list as the data source by completing the following steps:
   a. Click the Select Recipients button in the Start Mail Merge group and then click *Choose from Outlook Contacts* at the drop-down list.

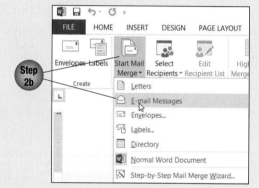

   b. If a Choose Profile dialog box displays, click OK.
   c. At the Select Contacts dialog box, click the desired contact list name in the list box and then click OK.
   d. At the Mail Merge Recipients dialog box, make sure the desired contact names are selected and then click OK.

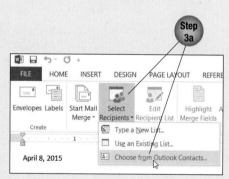

4. Press the Down Arrow key four times.
5. Insert the greeting line fields by completing the following steps:
   a. Click the Greeting Line button in the Write & Insert Fields group.
   b. At the Insert Greeting Line dialog box, click the down-pointing arrow at the right of the option box containing the comma (the box to the right of the box containing *Mr. Randall*).
   c. At the drop-down list that displays, click the colon.
   d. Click OK to close the Insert Greeting Line dialog box.
6. Scroll to the end of the email and then replace the *XX* with your initials.

7. Merge the emails by completing the following steps:
   a. Click the Finish & Merge button in the Finish group.
   b. Click *Send E-mail Messages* at the drop-down list.
   c. At the Merge to E-mail dialog box, click in the *Subject line* text box and then type **Adriatic Tour**.
   d. Click OK.
8. Save and then close **C16-E11-BTTourLtrMD.docx**.

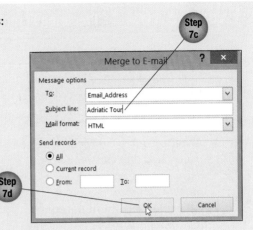

# Using the Mail Merge Wizard

The Mail Merge feature includes a Mail Merge wizard that guides you through the merge process. To access the wizard, click the MAILINGS tab, click the Start Mail Merge button, and then click the *Step-by-Step Mail Merge Wizard* at the drop-down list. The first of six Mail Merge task panes displays at the right side of the screen. Completing the tasks at one task pane displays the next task pane. The options in each task pane may vary depending on the type of merge you are performing. Generally, you complete one of the following steps at each successive task pane:

Step 1: Select the type of document you want to create (letter, email message, envelope, label, or directory).

Step 2: Specify if you want to use the current document window to create the main document, to start from a template, or to start from an existing document.

Step 3: Specify if you are typing a new list (for the variable information), using an existing list, or selecting from an Outlook contacts list. Depending on the choice you make, you may need to select a specific data source file or create a new data source file.

Step 4: Use the items in this task pane to help you prepare the main document. For example, if you are creating a letter, click the Address Block button in the Write & Insert Fields group on the MAILINGS tab and the wizard inserts the required codes in the main document for merging names and addresses. Click the Greeting Line button in the Write & Insert Fields group and the wizard inserts codes for a greeting. You can also click the More Fields button to display a list of fields that can be inserted in the document.

Step 5: Preview the merged documents.

Step 6: Complete the merge. At this step, send the merged document to the printer and/or edit the merged document.

1. At a blank document, click the MAILINGS tab, click the Start Mail Merge button in the Start Mail Merge group, and then click *Step-by-Step Mail Merge Wizard* at the drop-down list.
2. At the first Mail Merge task pane, make sure *Letters* is selected in the *Select document type* section and then click the <u>Next: Starting document</u> hyperlink located near the bottom of the task pane.
3. At the second Mail Merge task pane, click the *Start from existing document* option in the *Select starting document* section.
4. Click the Open button in the *Start from existing* section of the task pane.
5. At the Open dialog box, navigate to the Chapter16 folder on your storage medium and then double-click ***PRLtrMD.docx***.
6. Click the <u>Next: Select recipients</u> hyperlink located near the bottom of the task pane.
7. At the third Mail Merge task pane, click the <u>Browse</u> hyperlink that displays in the *Use an existing list* section of the task pane.
8. At the Select Data Source dialog box, navigate to the Chapter16 folder on your storage medium and then double-click ***PRClients.mdb***.

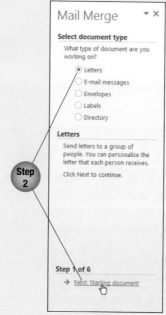

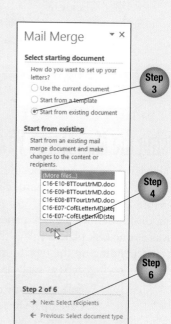

9. At the Mail Merge Recipients dialog box, click OK.
10. Click the <u>Next: Write your letter</u> hyperlink that displays near the bottom of the task pane.
11. At the fourth Mail Merge task pane, enter fields in the form letter by completing the following steps:
    a. Position the insertion point a double-space above the first paragraph of text in the letter.
    b. Click the <u>Address block</u> hyperlink located in the *Write your letter* section of the task pane.

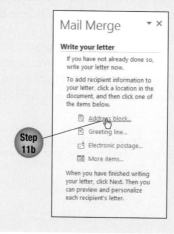

   c.   At the Insert Address Block dialog box, click the OK button.

   d.   Press the Enter key twice and then click the <u>Greeting line</u> hyperlink located in the *Write your letter* section of the task pane.

   e.   At the Insert Greeting Line dialog box, click the down-pointing arrow at the right of the option box containing the comma (the box to the right of the box containing *Mr. Randall*).

   f.   At the drop-down list that displays, click the colon.

   g.   Click OK to close the Insert Greeting Line dialog box.

12.  Click the <u>Next: Preview your letters</u> hyperlink located near the bottom of the task pane.

13.  At the fifth Mail Merge task pane, look over the letter that displays in the document window and make sure the information merged properly. If you want to see the letters for the other recipients, click the button in the Mail Merge task pane containing the right-pointing arrow.

14.  Click the Preview Results button in the Preview Results group to turn off the preview feature.

15.  Click the <u>Next: Complete the merge</u> hyperlink that displays near the bottom of the task pane.

16.  At the sixth Mail Merge task pane, click the <u>Edit individual letters</u> hyperlink that displays in the *Merge* section of the task pane.

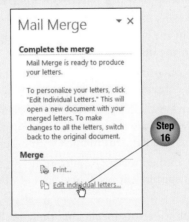

17.  At the Merge to New Document dialog box, make sure *All* is selected and then click the OK button.

18.  Save the merged letters document with the name **C16-E12-PRLtrs**.

19.  Print only the first two pages of **C16-E12-PRLtrs.docx**. (This document contains seven pages.)

20.  Close **C16-E12-PRLtrs.docx**.

21.  At the sixth Mail Merge task pane, close the letter main document without saving it.

# Chapter Summary

➤ Use the Mail Merge feature to create letters, envelopes, labels, and directories for multiple recipients, all with personalized information.

➤ A merge generally takes two documents: the data source file, which contains information that varies for each recipient, and the main document, which contains standard text (text intended for all recipients) along with fields identifying where the variable information will be inserted during the merge process.

➤ Variable information in a data source file is saved as a record. A record contains all of the information for one unit. A series of fields makes one record and a series of records makes a data source file.

➤ A data source file is saved as an Access database but you do not need Access on your computer to complete a merge with a data source file.

➤ Use predesigned fields when creating a data source file or create your own custom fields at the Customize Address List dialog box.

➤ Use the Address Block button in the Write & Insert Fields group on the MAILINGS tab to insert all of the fields required for the inside address of a letter. This inserts the «AddressBlock» field, which is considered a composite field because it groups a number of fields.

➤ Click the Greeting Line button in the Write & Insert Fields group on the MAILINGS tab to insert the «GreetingLine» composite field in the document.

➤ Click the Insert Merge Field button arrow in the Write & Insert Fields group on the MAILINGS tab to display a drop-down list of fields contained in the data source file.

➤ Click the Preview Results button on the MAILINGS tab to view the main document merged with the first record in the data source. Use the navigation buttons in the Preview Results group on the MAILINGS tab to display the main document merged with other records.

➤ Click the Find Recipient button in the Preview Results group on the MAILINGS tab to search for and preview merged documents with specific entries. Click the Find Recipient button and the Find Entry dialog box displays.

➤ Before merging documents, check for errors by clicking the Check for Errors button in the Preview Results group on the MAILINGS tab. This displays the Checking and Reporting Errors dialog box with three options for checking and reporting errors.

➤ Click the Finish & Merge button on the MAILINGS tab to complete the merge.

➤ Select specific records for merging by inserting or removing the check marks preceding the desired records at the Mail Merge Recipients dialog box. Display this dialog box by clicking the Edit Recipient List button on the MAILINGS tab.

➤ Edit specific records in a data source file at the Edit Data Source dialog box. Display this dialog box by clicking the Edit Recipient List button on the MAILINGS tab, clicking the desired data source file name in the *Data Source* list box, and then clicking the Edit button.

➤ Use a Fill-in field in a main document to insert variable information with the keyboard during a merge.

➤ Insert the Merge Record # field in a main document to insert a record number in each merged document. To insert this field, click the Rules button in the Write & Insert Fields group on the MAILINGS tab and then click *Merge Record #* at the drop-down list.

➤ Use an If...Then...Else... field to compare two values and then, depending on what is determined, enter one set of text or another. To insert this field, click the Rules button in the Write & Insert Fields group on the MAILINGS tab and then click *If...Then...Else...* at the drop-down list. At the Insert Word Field: IF dialog box that displays, make the desired changes and then click OK.

- You can merge a main document with a Word table, Excel worksheet, Access table, or Outlook contact list data source.
- If fields in a data source do not match the fields used in the address block, use options at the Match Fields dialog box to match the fields.
- Word includes a Mail Merge wizard to guide you through the process of creating letters, envelopes, labels, directories, and email messages with personalized information.

# Commands *Review*

| FEATURE | RIBBON TAB, GROUP | BUTTON, OPTION |
|---|---|---|
| address block fields | MAILINGS, Write & Insert Fields | |
| Checking and Reporting Errors dialog box | MAILINGS, Preview Results | |
| directory main document | MAILINGS, Start Mail Merge | , *Directory* |
| envelope main document | MAILINGS, Start Mail Merge | , *Envelopes* |
| Fill-in merge field | MAILINGS, Write & Insert Fields | , *Fill-in* |
| Find Entry dialog box | MAILINGS, Preview Results | |
| greeting line fields | MAILINGS, Write & Insert Fields | |
| insert merge fields | MAILINGS, Write & Insert Fields | |
| Insert Word Field: IF dialog box | MAILINGS, Write & Insert Fields | , *If…Then…Else* |
| label main document | MAILINGS, Start Mail Merge | , *Labels* |
| letter main document | MAILINGS, Start Mail Merge | , *Letters* |
| Mail Merge Recipients dialog box | MAILINGS, Start Mail Merge | |
| Mail Merge wizard | MAILINGS, Start Mail Merge | , *Step-by-Step Mail Merge Wizard* |
| Match Fields dialog box | MAILINGS, Start Mail Merge | |
| Merge Record # field | MAILINGS, Write & Insert Fields | , *Merge Record #* |
| New Address List dialog box | MAILINGS, Start Mail Merge | , *Type a New List* |
| preview merge results | MAILINGS, Preview Results | |

# Key Points Review

**Completion:** In the space provided at the right, indicate the correct term, command, or number.

1. A merge generally takes two files: a data source file and this.

2. This term refers to all of the information for one unit in a data source file.

3. Create a data source file by clicking this button on the MAILINGS tab and then clicking *Type a New List* at the drop-down list.

4. Create your own custom fields in a data source file with options at this dialog box.

5. A data source file is saved as this type of file.

6. Use this button on the MAILINGS tab to insert all of the required fields for the inside address in a letter.

7. The «*GreetingLine*» field is considered this type of field because it includes all of the fields required for the greeting line.

8. Click this button on the MAILINGS tab to display the first record merged with the main document.

9. Click this button in the Preview Results group on the MAILINGS tab to display the Find Entry dialog box.

10. Before merging a document, check for errors using this button in the Preview Results group on the MAILINGS tab.

11. To complete a merge, click this button in the Finish group on the MAILINGS tab.

12. Select specific records in a data source file by inserting or removing check marks from the records in this dialog box.

13. Use this field to insert variable information with the keyboard during a merge.

14. Insert this field in a main document to insert a record number in each merged document.

15. Insert this field in a main document to tell Word to compare two values and then enter one set of text or the other.

16. Click this option at the Start Mail Merge button drop-down list to begin the Mail Merge wizard.

# Chapter *Assessments*

## Applying Your Skills

Demonstrate your knowledge of features learned in this chapter by completing the following assessments.

### Assessment 16.1    Create a Data Source File

1. At a blank document, display the New Address List dialog box and then display the Customize Address List dialog box.
2. At the Customize Address List dialog box, delete the following fields—*Company Name*, *Country or Region*, *Work Phone*, and *E-mail Address*—and then add a custom field named *Cell Phone*.
3. Close the Customize Address List dialog box and then type the following information in the New Address List dialog box as the first record:
   *Title:* **Mrs.**
   *First Name:* **Tina**
   *Last Name:* **Cardoza**
   *Address Line 1:* **2314 Magnolia Drive**
   *Address Line 2:* **P.O. Box 231**
   *City:* **San Francisco**
   *State:* **CA**
   *ZIP Code:* **94120**
   *Home Phone:* **(415) 555-2265**
   *Cell Phone:* **(415) 555-7523**
4. Type the following information as the second record:
   *Title:* **Mr.**
   *First Name:* **Lucas**
   *Last Name:* **Yarborough**
   *Address Line 1:* **12110 South 142nd Street**
   *Address Line 2:* (leave blank)
   *City:* **Daly City**
   *State:* **CA**
   *ZIP Code:* **94015**
   *Home Phone:* **(415) 555-4883**
   *Cell Phone:* **(415) 555-0221**
5. Type the following information as the third record:
   *Title:* **Mrs.**
   *First Name:* **Lucille**
   *Last Name:* **Alvarez**
   *Address Line 1:* **2542 Ranchero Drive**
   *Address Line 2:* **Apt. 115**
   *City:* **Daly City**
   *State:* **CA**
   *ZIP Code:* **94017**
   *Home Phone:* **(415) 555-8372**

SNAP Grade It

*Cell Phone:* **(415) 555-4411**

6. Type the following information as the fourth record:
   *Title:* **Mr.**
   *First Name:* **Daryl**
   *Last Name:* **Gillette**
   *Address Line 1:* **13181 North 42nd Street**
   *Address Line 2:* (leave blank)
   *City:* **San Francisco**
   *State:* **CA**
   *ZIP Code:* **94128**
   *Home Phone:* **(415) 555-8302**
   *Cell Phone:* **(415) 555-6455**
7. Save the data source file and name it **C16-A01-BTDS**.
8. Close the blank document without saving the changes.

## Assessment 16.2  Create a Main Document and Merge with a Data Source File

1. Open **BTVacPkgs.docx** and then save the document with Save As and name it **C16-A02-BTVacPkgsMD**.
2. Select **C16-A01-BTDS.mdb**, which you created in Assessment 1, as the data source file.
3. Move the insertion point to the beginning of the first paragraph of text in the body of the letter, insert the *«AddressBlock»* field, and then press Enter twice.
4. Insert the *«GreetingLine»* field specifying a colon rather than a comma as the greeting line format and then press Enter twice.
5. Move the insertion point one space to the right of the period that ends the third paragraph of text in the body of the letter and then type the following text inserting the *«Title»*, *«Last_Name»*, *«Home_Phone»*, *«Cell_Phone»* fields where indicated:
   **Currently, *«Title» «Last_Name»*, our records indicate your home telephone number is *«Home_Phone»* and your cell phone number is *«Cell_Phone»*. If this information is not accurate, please contact our office with the correct numbers and let us know a good time to reach you.**
6. Merge the main document with all of the records in the data source file.
7. Save the merged letters document as **C16-A02-BTVacPkgsLetters**.
8. Print and then close **C16-A02-BTVacPkgsLetters.docx**.
9. Save and then close **C16-A02-BTVacPkgsMD.docx**.

## Assessment 16.3  Create an Envelope Main Document and Merge with a Data Source File

1. Create an envelope main document using the standard size 10 envelope.
2. Select **C16-A01-BTDS.mdb** as the data source file.
3. Insert the *«AddressBlock»* field in the appropriate location in the envelope document.
4. Merge the envelope main document with all of the records in the data source file.
5. Save the merged envelopes document and name it **C16-A03-BTEnvs**.
6. Print and then close the envelope document. (Check with your instructor before printing the envelopes.)
7. Close the envelope main document without saving it.

## Assessment 16.4 Create a Label Main Document and Merge with a Data Source File

1. Create a label main document using the *Avery US Letter 5160 Easy Peel Address Labels* option.
2. Select **C16-A01-BTDS.mdb** as the data source file.
3. Insert the «*AddressBlock*» field.
4. Update the labels.
5. Merge the label main document with all of the records in the data source file.
6. Select the entire document and then apply the No Spacing style.
7. Save the merged label document and name it **C16-A04-BTLabels**.
8. Print and then close the label document.
9. Close the label main document without saving it.

## Assessment 16.5 Edit a Data Source File

1. Open **C16-A02-BTVacPkgsMD.docx** (at the message asking if you want to continue, click Yes) and then save the main document with Save As and name it **C16-A05-BTVacPkgsMD**.
2. Edit the **C16-A01-BTDS.mdb** data source file by making the following changes:
   a. Display the record for Mrs. Tina Cardoza and then change the last name from *Cardoza* to *Cordova*.
   b. Display the record for Mr. Daryl Gillette, change the street address from *13181 North 42nd Street* to *9843 22nd Street South*, and change the zip code from *94128* to *94102*.
   c. Delete the record for Mr. Lucas Yarborough.
   d. Insert two new records with the following information:

   Mr. Curtis Jackson                Ms. Tanya Forrester
   13201 North Fourth Street          575 Taylor Street
   (leave blank)                      Apt. 120
   Daly City, CA 94017                San Francisco, CA 94127
   Home Phone: (415) 555-9743         Home Phone: (415) 555-2211
   Cell Phone: (415) 555-1027         Cell Phone: (415) 555-7913

3. At the main document, add the following sentence at the beginning of the third paragraph in the letter. (Insert a Fill-in field for *(vacation)* shown in the sentence below; you determine the prompt.) **Last summer we booked a fabulous (vacation) for you and your entire family.**
4. Move the insertion point immediately below the file name, type **Letter**, press the spacebar once, and then insert a Merge Record # field.
5. Move the insertion point immediately after the job title in the closing of the letter. Press the Enter key twice and then insert an If...Then...Else... field with the following specifications:
   a. At the Insert Word Field: IF dialog box, specify the *City* field in the *Field name* option box.
   b. Type **Daly City** in the *Compare to* text box.
   c. In the *Insert this text* text box, type the text shown below and then close the dialog box:

      **P.S. A representative from Wildlife Eco-Tours will present information on upcoming tours at our Daly City branch office the first Saturday of next month. Come by and hear about exciting and adventurous eco-tours.**

6. Change the file name below your reference initials to **C16-A05-BTVacPkgs-MD.docx**.
7. Merge the main document with the data source file and type the following text for each of the records:
   Record 1: **Ocean Vista Mexican cruise**
   Record 2: **Disneyland California vacation**
   Record 3: **Ocean Vista Caribbean cruise**
   Record 4: **River Rafting Adventure vacation**
   Record 5: **Disney World Florida vacation**

8. Save the merged document with the name **C16-A05-BTVacPkgsLetters**.
9. Print and then close **C16-A05-BTVacPkgsLetters.docx**.
10. Save and then close **C16-A05-BTVacPkgsMD.docx**.

### Assessment 16.6    Use the Mail Merge Wizard to Create Envelopes

1. At a blank document, use the Mail Merge wizard to merge the records in the **PRClients.mdb** data source with an envelope main document. (Use the standard size 10 envelope.)
2. Save the merged envelope document with the name **C16-A06-PREnvs**.
3. Print only the first two envelopes in the document and then close **C16-A06-PREnvs.docx**.
4. Close the envelope main document without saving it.

## Expanding Your Skills

Explore additional feature options or use Help to learn a new skill in creating these documents.

### Assessment 16.7    Create a Client Directory

1. Make a copy of the **PRClients.mdb** file located in your Chapter16 folder and insert the copy into the same folder. Rename the copied file **C16-A07-PRClients.mdb**.
2. At a blank document, create a directory main document and specify **C16-A07-PRClients.mdb** as the data source file.
3. Add a new field named *Telephone* to the **C16-A07-PRClients.mdb** data source file. ***Hint: To do this, click the Edit Recipient List button, click the* C16-A07-PRClients.mdb *file name in the* Data Source *list box, and then click the Edit button. At the Edit Data Source dialog box, click the Customize Columns button. Add the new* Telephone *field and then move it so it displays after the* ZIP Code *field.***
4. Type the following telephone numbers in the specified fields:

   Reyes: **(541) 555-3904**
   Devereaux: **(541) 555-6675**
   Heaton: **(541) 555-4982**
   LeBlanc: **(541) 555-0012**
   Seydell: **(541) 555-6599**
   Pena: **(541) 555-2189**
   Morrisey: **(541) 555-9922**

5. Add the following records to the data source file (in the appropriate fields):

   Mr. Greg Parker
   3411 45th Street
   Eugene, OR 97405
   (541) 555-4188

   Dr. Jane Takahara
   10293 Mountain Drive
   Springfield, OR 97477
   (541) 555-9441

   Mrs. Karen Jennings
   1302 Washington Avenue
   Eugene, OR 97402
   (541) 555-6817

   Mr. Chris Martinez
   109 Voss Drive
   Springfield, OR 97478
   (541) 555-4045

6. At the blank directory document, set left tabs at the 1-inch mark and 4-inch mark.
7. Insert the «*Last_Name*» field at the 1-inch tab, type a comma, press the spacebar, and then insert the «*First_Name*» field. Press the tab key, insert the «*Telephone*» field, and then press the Enter key.
8. Merge the directory main document with the data source file.
9. Insert the heading *Name* with bold formatting applied above the column containing the last and first names. Insert the heading *Telephone* with bold formatting applied above the column containing the telephone numbers.

10. Save the directory and name it **C16-A07-PRDirectory**. (If the merge is missing a field of information, close the merged document without saving changes and then complete the merge again.)
11. Print **C16-A07-PRDirectory.docx**.
12. Select the text in the document and then convert it to a table. *Hint: Use the Table button in the Tables group on the INSERT tab*.
13. With the text converted to a table, delete the first column (which is empty), format the contents of the table using the AutoFit feature, and then apply a table style of your choosing. Make other formatting changes to enhance the display of the table.
14. Save, print, and then close **C16-A07-PRDirectory.docx**.
15. Close the directory main document without saving it.

## Assessment 16.8    Merge Specific Records

1. Open **PRLtrMD.docx** and save it with the name **C16-A08-PRLtrMD**.
2. Identify **C16-A07-PRClients.mdb** as the data source file.
3. Insert the appropriate fields in the letter main document.
4. Change the file name below the reference initials at the bottom of the letter to **C16-A08-PRLtrMD.docx**.
5. Merge only records 8 through 11. *Hint: Do this at the Merge to New Document dialog box*.
6. Save the merged letter document and name it **C16-A08-PRLtrs8-11**.
7. Print and then close the **C16-A08-PRLtrs8-11.docx** document.
8. Save and then close the **C16-A08-PRLtrMD.docx** document.

## Assessment 16.9    Merge Labels with an Excel Worksheet

1. Use the Mail Merge feature to prepare name badges with the following specifications:
   a. Click the Start Mail Merge button on the MAILINGS tab and then click *Labels* at the drop-down list. At the Label Options dialog box, change the *Label vendors* option to *Avery US Letter* and then click the *42395 EcoFriendly Name Badges* option in the *Product number* list box. Click OK to close the dialog box.
   b. Specify the **BTClientsExcel.xlsx** workbook as the data source. Click OK at the Select table dialog box.
   c. Use the Insert Merge Field button on the MAILINGS tab to insert the *FirstName* field. Press the spacebar and then insert the *LastName* field. Press the Enter key, insert the *City* field, type a comma, press the spacebar, and then insert the *State* field.
   d. Update the labels and then merge the labels.
2. At the label document, click the table move handle (displays in the upper left corner of the table) to select the entire table. If necessary, click the HOME tab and then change the font size to 20 points. Click the TABLE TOOLS LAYOUT tab and then click the Align Center button in the Alignment group.
3. Save the name badge document and name it **C16-A09-BTNameBadges**.
4. Print and then close **C16-A09-BTNameBadges.docx**.
5. Close the label main document without saving it.

# Achieving Signature Status

Take your skills to the next level by completing this more challenging assessment.

## Assessment 16.10 Create and Merge a Data Source and Main Document

1. Open **NSSLtrhd.docx** and then save the document with the name **C16-A10-NSSLtrMD**.
2. Look at the information shown in Figure 16.15 and Figure 16.16 on the next page, respectively. Use the Mail Merge feature to prepare six letters using the information shown in the figures. Name the data source file **C16-A10-NSS-DS.mdb**. (When creating the records in the data source file, make sure to add a *Department* field.)
3. Prepare the main document with the following specifications:
   a. Insert the current date at the beginning of the letter.
   b. Since the «*AddressBlock*» composite field will not insert the *Department* field, you need to insert each individual field required for the inside address. To do this, use the Insert Merge Field button to insert the fields so they appear as follows (inserting spaces where necessary):
      «*Title*» «*First_Name*» «*Last_Name*»
      «*Department*»
      «*Company_Name*»
      «*Address_Line_1*»
      «*City*», «*State*» «*ZIP_Code*»
   c. Insert the appropriate greeting line field.
   d. Type the appropriate complimentary close and type your first and last names in the complimentary close.
   e. Type the document name in the appropriate location in the letter.
   f. After typing the letter, insert the Merge Record # field near the bottom of the letter. (You determine the location.)
   g. Insert an If...Then...Else field at the beginning of the last paragraph of text in the letter (the paragraph that begins *As a valued client...*). Specify the *City* field in the *Field name* option box, type **Peoria** in the *Compare to* text box, and then type the following information in the *Insert this text* text box. (Make sure you press the spacebar once after typing the text.) **At our Peoria NSS Training Academy, we are offering two additional courses including *Network Security* and *Web Applications Security*. Please call for more information about these courses.**
4. Before merging the letters, check for errors.
5. Complete the merge and then save the merged letters document and name it **C16-A10-NSSCoursesLtrs**.
6. Print and then close **C16-A10-NSSCoursesLtrs.docx**.
7. Save and then close **C16-A10-NSSLtrMD.docx**.

**Figure 16.15** Assessment 16.10

Mrs. Sylvia Patterson
Human Resources Department
Rolling Hills Manufacturing
31203 33rd Street South
Springfield, IL 62133
(217) 555-3310

Mr. Dale Marshall
Training Department
Providence Care
2712 Martin Luther King, Jr. Way
Peoria, IL 61639
(309) 555-0775

Mr. Russell Navarro
Technology Department
Woodmark Products
8844 South 24th Street
Peoria, IL 61623
(309) 555-1800

Ms. Amanda Sperring
Human Resources Department
Frontier Steel
310 Riddell Avenue
Decatur, IL 62524
(217) 555-9742

Mr. Wade Townsend
IT Department
Keystone Technologies
145 South 95th Street
Springfield, IL 62129
(217) 555-7770

Mrs. Emma Battner
Training Department
Franklin Services
2010 Patterson Court East
Peoria, IL 61618
(309) 555-3153

**Figure 16.16** Assessment 16.10

We have scheduled the Springfield NSS Training Academy course offerings for next month. If you have additional data security training needs, please give us a call and we can customize a training course for your company. Courses next month at the Springfield NSS Training Academy include:

| Course Title | Total Hours | Cost |
|---|---|---|
| Securing Windows | 8 hours | $375 |
| Intrusion Detection | 3 hours | $250 |
| Basic Security Essentials | 6 hours | $350 |
| Advanced Security Essentials | 4 hours | $295 |
| Perimeter Protection | 3 hours | $195 |

As a valued client of Northland Security Systems, we are offering your company a 10 percent discount on all courses offered next month. To qualify for the discount, participants must be signed up before the first of the month. You can register employees at our website or by calling us at 1-888-555-2200.

# Chapter 17

**Managing Lists**

## Performance Objectives

Upon successful completion of Chapter 17, you will be able to:

- Insert custom numbers and bullets
- Insert multilevel list numbering
- Insert special characters, such as symbols, hyphens, and nonbreaking spaces

Inserting a bullet before each item in a list draws a reader's attention to the content. Similarly, inserting numbers before items listed in sequence emphasizes their order. You can insert numbers and bullets and create multiple-level bulleted and numbered paragraphs with buttons in the Paragraph group on the HOME tab. Use options from the drop-down lists at these buttons to customize bullets and numbers and create customized multilevel numbering. In this chapter, you will learn how to create and insert customized bullets and numbers and how to insert special characters, such as intellectual property protection symbols, hyphens, and nonbreaking spaces.

*Note: Before beginning computer exercises for this chapter, copy to your storage medium the Chapter17 folder from the CD that accompanies this textbook and then make Chapter17 the active folder.*

In this chapter, students will produce the following documents:

Exercise 17.1. C17-E01-TDAgenda.docx
Exercise 17.2. C17-E02-TravelAdv.docx
Exercise 17.3. C17-E03-CSList.docx
Exercise 17.4. C17-E04-SpecialCharacters.docx

Model answers for these exercises are shown on the following pages.

**Exercise 17.1**

C17-E01-TDAgenda.docx

## TRAINING DEPARTMENT

I) Approval of Minutes
II) Introductions
III) Organizational Overview
IV) Review of Goals
V) Expenses
VI) Technology
VII) Resources
VIII) Future Goals
IX) Proposals
X) Adjournment

## RESEARCH DEPARTMENT AGENDA

I) Approval of Minutes
II) Introductions
III) Review of Goals
IV) Current Projects
V) Materials
VI) Staffing
VII) Future Projects
VIII) Adjournment

## Hawaiian Adventures

### Rainy Day Activities

Expect to have a rainy day or two during your vacation, especially in the winter months between November and March. With a little planning, you can have just as much fun indoors as outdoors. To make the most of a rainy day, enjoy one of the activities listed below.

- Movies: Take advantage of matinee prices. The Sunshine Marketplace Theaters offer discount tickets and current feature films.
- Shopping: Most of the area shopping centers are "open-air" complexes with some roof covering, ideal havens from the rain. Visit the Coconut Grove Shopping Center or the Kukui Shopping Village.
- Museums: Learn about the history of Hawaii through murals, artifacts, and artwork by visiting one of several museums located throughout the island. Most museums offer special family activities the first Saturday of each month.
- Theater: Several local community performing arts centers offer annual productions for children and adults. Admission prices are very affordable, and most theaters have special matinee prices.

### Kauai Sights

- Na Pali Coast: Unless you are a rugged hiker, you can see this fifteen-mile, spectacular landmark only by air or boat.
- North Shore: Find shadowy mountains, lush valleys, and spectacular coastlines along a string of one-lane bridges.
- Hanalei Valley Lookout: Pull over to see wetland taro fields with a backdrop of purple mountains.
- Kilauea Point: This national wildlife refuge is home to nesting seabirds and an original lighthouse.
- Sleeping Giant: Nounou Mountain provides the "man in repose" profile best seen from Kuhio Highway 56 in Kapaa.
- Coconut Coast: You will know when you are here because palm trees line Kuhio Highway 56 on the island's east side.

**Exercise 17.2**

C17-E02-TravelAdv.docx

## COMPUTER SECURITY

A. Security Issues
    1. Network Security Risks
        a) Unauthorized Access
        b) Information Theft
        c) Denial of Service Attacks
    2. Computer Viruses
        a) Virus Types
        b) Virus Methods
        c) Virus Symptoms
B. Security Strategies
    1. Computer Protection
        a) Anti-virus Software
        b) Firewalls
    2. Security Strategies
        a) Data Backup
        b) Data Encryption
        c) Passwords
        d) User ID

**Exercise 17.3**

C17-E03-CSList.docx

## NETWORKS

A. Networking over the Web
    1. Data Transmission
        a) Bandwidth
        b) Analog and Digital Transmission
        c) Parallel and Serial Transmission
    2. Communications Media
        a) Wired Communications Media
        b) Wireless Communications Media
B. Network Design
    1. Network Topologies
        a) Bus Topologies
        b) Star Topologies
        c) Ring Topologies
        d) Hybrid Topologies
    2. Network Hardware
        a) Hubs
        b) Repeaters
        c) Routers
        d) Gateways
        e) Bridges

### INTELLECTUAL PROPERTY PROTECTION

A copyright protects original works in areas such as publishing, music, literature, and drama. Use the © symbol to identify copyrighted intellectual property. Create this symbol by typing (c), using the keyboard shortcut Alt + Ctrl + C, or by clicking the symbol in the Symbol dialog box with the Special Characters tab selected.

A trademark identifies a word, symbol, device, or name such as a brand name. Use the ™ symbol to identify a trademarked name or product. Create this symbol (tm), using the keyboard shortcut Alt + Ctrl + T, or by clicking the symbol in the Symbol dialog box with the Special Characters tab.

A registered trademark is a trademark that has been registered with the U.S. Patent & Trademark Office. Use the ® symbol to identify a registered trademark. Create this symbol by typing (r), using the keyboard shortcut Alt + Ctrl + R, or by clicking the symbol in the Symbol dialog box with the Special Character tab selected.

### SOFTWARE TRAINING

The Microsoft® Office Word training is scheduled for Thursday, March 5, 2015, from 9:00–10:30 a.m. Additional training for other applications in the Office suite—Excel, PowerPoint, and Access—will be available during the month of April. Contact the Training Department for additional information. All Tri-State employees are eligible for the training.

### KEYBOARD SHORTCUTS

Microsoft Word includes a number of keyboard shortcuts you can use to access features and commands. The ScreenTip for some buttons displays the keyboard shortcut you can use to execute the command. For example, hovering the mouse over the Font button causes the ScreenTip to display Ctrl + Shift + F as the keyboard shortcut. Additional HOME tab Font group keyboard shortcuts include Ctrl + B to bold text, Ctrl + I to italicize text, and Ctrl + U to underline text. You can also press Ctrl + Shift + + to turn on superscript and press Ctrl + = to turn on subscript.

**Exercise 17.4**

C17-E04-SpecialCharacters.docx

# Inserting Custom Numbers and Bullets

Numbering

Bullets

In Chapter 3, you learned to number paragraphs and insert bullets automatically using the Numbering button and Bullets button in the Paragraph group on the HOME tab. After you insert numbers or bullets, you can customize them by clicking the Numbering button arrow or Bullets button arrow and then choosing an option from the drop-down gallery.

## Inserting Custom Numbers

As you learned earlier, you can insert numbers as you type text or you can type text, select it, and then apply numbering formatting. Whether you insert numbers as you type text or click the Numbering button in the Paragraph group to apply number formatting after you type text, Word inserts arabic numbers (1., 2., 3., and so on) in the document by default. You can change this default numbering by clicking the Numbering button arrow and then clicking the option you desire at the Numbering drop-down gallery, as shown in Figure 17.1.

To change list levels, click the Numbering button arrow, point to the *Change List Level* option located near the bottom of the drop-down gallery, and then click the desired list level at the side menu. Set the numbering value with options at the Set Numbering Value dialog box. Display this dialog box by clicking the Numbering button arrow and then clicking the *Set Numbering Value* option located at the bottom of the drop-down gallery.

**Figure 17.1** **Numbering Drop-down Gallery**

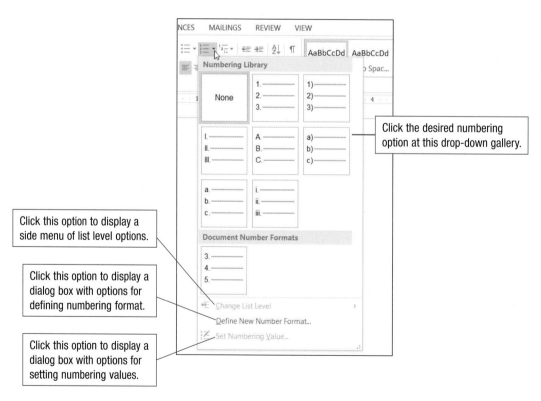

Click the desired numbering option at this drop-down gallery.

Click this option to display a side menu of list level options.

Click this option to display a dialog box with options for defining numbering format.

Click this option to display a dialog box with options for setting numbering values.

1. Open **TDAgenda.docx** and save the document with the name **C17-E01-TDAgenda**.
2. Restart the numbering of list items at 1 by completing the following steps:
   a. Select the numbered paragraphs.
   b. Click the Numbering button arrow and then click *Set Numbering Value* at the drop-down gallery.
   c. At the Set Numbering Value dialog box, select the number in the *Set value to* option box, type **1**, and then press the Enter key.

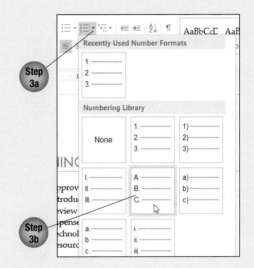

3. Change the numbering of the paragraphs to letters by completing the following steps:
   a. With the numbered paragraphs selected, click the Numbering button arrow.
   b. At the Numbering drop-down gallery, click the option that uses capital letters, as shown at the right. (The location of the option may vary.)
4. Add text to the agenda by positioning the insertion point immediately to the right of the text *Introductions*, pressing the Enter key, and then typing **Organizational Overview**.
5. Demote the lettered list by completing the following steps:
   a. Select the lettered paragraphs.
   b. Click the Numbering button arrow, point to the *Change List Level* option, and then click the *a.* option (*Level 2*) at the side menu.
6. With the paragraphs still selected, promote the list by clicking the Decrease Indent button in the Paragraph group on the HOME tab. (This changes back to capital letters.)

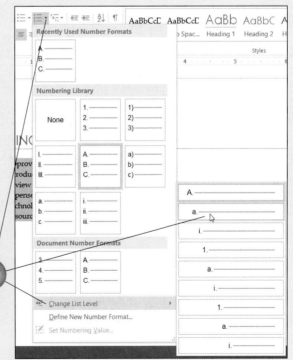

7. Move the insertion point to the end of the document and then type **The meeting will stop for lunch, which is catered and will be held in the main conference center from 12:15 to 1:30.**

8. Press the Enter key twice and then click the Numbering button.

9. Click the AutoCorrect Options button that displays next to the *A.* inserted in the document and then click the *Continue Numbering* option at the drop-down list. (This change the letter from *A.* to *H.*)

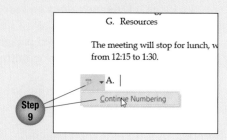

10. Type **Future Goals**, press the Enter key, type **Proposals**, press the Enter key, and then type **Adjournment**.

11. Press the Enter key and the letter *K.* is inserted in the document. Turn off the list format by clicking the Numbering button arrow and then clicking the *None* option at the drop-down gallery.

12. Save and then print **C17-E01-TDAgenda.docx**.

13. Select and then delete the paragraph of text in the middle of the list, including the blank lines above and below the text. (All of the lettered items should be listed consecutively and have the same spacing between them.)

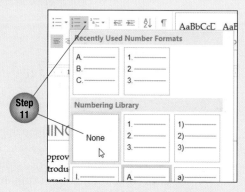

14. Select the lettered paragraphs, click the Numbering button arrow, and then click the option that uses a number followed by a right parenthesis (*1*), *2*), *3*), and so on).

15. Save **C17-E01-TDAgenda.docx**.

**QUICK STEPS**

**Define a Numbering Formatting**
1. Click Numbering button arrow.
2. Click *Define New Number Format* at drop-down gallery.
3. Choose desired number formatting option.
4. Click OK.

## Defining a Numbering Format

In addition to using the default numbering format or a custom numbering format in the *Numbering Library* section in the Numbering button drop-down gallery, you can define your own numbering format with options at the Define New Number Format dialog box, as shown in Figure 17.2 on the next page. Display this dialog box by clicking the Numbering button arrow and then clicking *Define New Number Format* at the drop-down gallery. Use options at the dialog box to specify the number style, font, and alignment and preview the formatting in the *Preview* section.

When a numbering format is defined at the Define New Number Format dialog box, it is automatically included in the *Numbering Library* section in the Numbering button drop-down gallery. Remove a numbering format from the drop-down gallery by right-clicking it and then clicking *Remove* at the shortcut menu.

**Figure 17.2** Define New Number Format Dialog Box

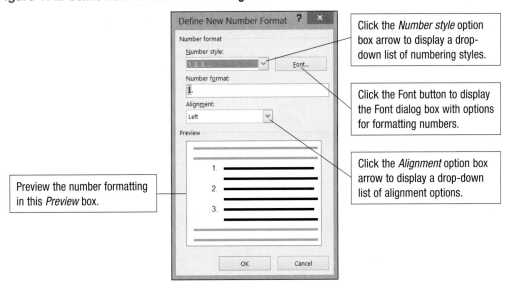

Click the *Number style* option box arrow to display a drop-down list of numbering styles.

Click the Font button to display the Font dialog box with options for formatting numbers.

Click the *Alignment* option box arrow to display a drop-down list of alignment options.

Preview the number formatting in this *Preview* box.

---

## Exercise 17.1B  Defining a Numbering Format

Part 2 of 2

1. With **C17-E01-TDAgenda.docx** open, define a new number format by completing the following steps:
   a. Position the insertion point on any character in the numbered text.
   b. Click the Numbering button arrow.
   c. Click *Define New Number Format* at the drop-down gallery.
   d. At the Define New Number Format dialog box, click the down-pointing arrow at the right of the *Number style* option and then click the *1st, 2nd, 3rd …* option.
   e. Click the Font button that displays at the right of the *Number style* option box.

Step 1b

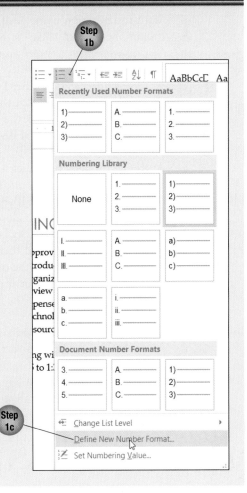

Step 1d

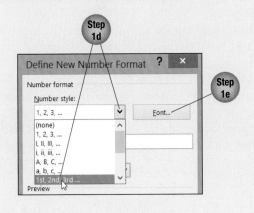

Step 1e

Step 1c

f.  At the Font dialog box, scroll down the *Font* list box and then click *Candara*.
g.  Click *Bold* in the *Font style* list box.
h.  Click OK to close the Font dialog box.
i.  Click the down-pointing arrow at the right of the *Alignment* option box and then click *Right* at the drop-down list.

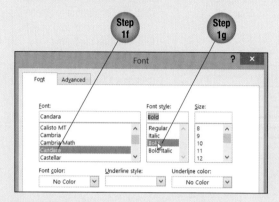

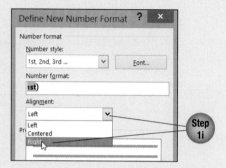

j.  Click OK to close the Define New Number Format dialog box. (This applies the new formatting to the numbered paragraphs in the document.)
2.  After looking at the numbering with the new formatting applied, define another number format by completing the following steps:
    a.  With the insertion point positioned on any character in the numbered text, click the Numbering button arrow.
    b.  Click *Define New Number Format* at the drop-down gallery.
    c.  At the Define New Number Format dialog box, click the down-pointing arrow at the right of the *Number style* option box and then click the *I, II, III, ...* option.

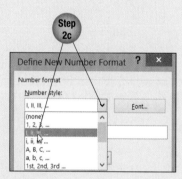

    d.  Click the Font button that displays at the right of the *Number style* option box.
    e.  At the Font dialog box, click *Cambria* in the *Font* list box.
    f.  Check to make sure *Bold* is selected in the *Font style* list box and then click OK to close the Font dialog box.
    g.  At the Define New Number Format dialog box, make sure *Right* is selected in the *Alignment* option box and then click OK. (This applies the new formatting to the numbered paragraphs in the document.)
3.  Insert a file into the current document by completing the following steps:
    a.  Press Ctrl + End to move the insertion point to the end of the document.
    b.  Click the INSERT tab.
    c.  Click the Object button arrow and then click *Text from File* at the drop-down list.
    d.  At the Insert File dialog box, navigate to your Chapter17 folder and then double-click **RDAgenda.docx**.
4.  Position the insertion point on any character in the title *RESEARCH DEPARTMENT AGENDA*, click the HOME tab, and then click the *Heading 1* style in the Styles group.

5. Select the text below the title *RESEARCH DEPARTMENT AGENDA*, click the Numbering button arrow, and then click the roman numeral style that you defined.
6. Click in the title *RESEARCH DEPARTMENT AGENDA* and then change the spacing after paragraphs to 12.
7. Save, print, and then close **C17-E01-TDAgenda.docx**.

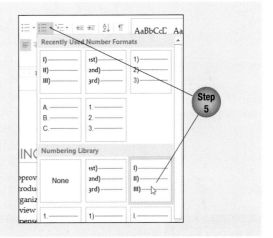

## Defining and Inserting Custom Bullets

When you click the Bullets button in the Paragraph group, round bullets are inserted before selected paragraphs in the document. You can insert custom bullets by clicking the Bullets button arrow and then clicking the desired bullet type at the drop-down gallery. This drop-down gallery displays the most recently used bullets along with an option for defining new bullets.

Click the *Define New Bullet* option and the Define New Bullet dialog box displays, as shown in Figure 17.3. With options at this dialog box, you can choose a symbol or picture bullet, change the font size of the bullet, and specify the alignment of the bullet. When you choose a custom bullet, consider matching the theme or mood of the document to maintain a consistent look or consider creating a picture bullet to add visual interest.

**QUICK STEPS**

**Define a Custom Bullet**
1. Click Bullets button arrow.
2. Click *Define New Bullet* at drop-down gallery.
3. Click Symbol button or Picture button.
4. Click desired symbol or picture.
5. Click OK.
6. Click OK.

**Figure 17.3 Define New Bullet Dialog Box**

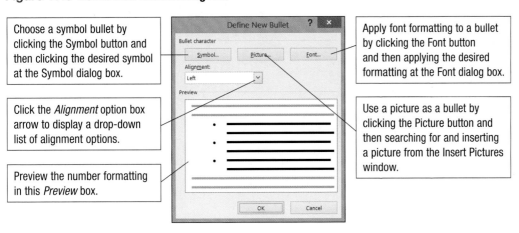

Choose a symbol bullet by clicking the Symbol button and then clicking the desired symbol at the Symbol dialog box.

Apply font formatting to a bullet by clicking the Font button and then applying the desired formatting at the Font dialog box.

Click the *Alignment* option box arrow to display a drop-down list of alignment options.

Use a picture as a bullet by clicking the Picture button and then searching for and inserting a picture from the Insert Pictures window.

Preview the number formatting in this *Preview* box.

When you define a new bullet at the Define New Bullet dialog box, that bullet is automatically included within the *Bullet Library* section in the Bullets button drop-down gallery. Remove a bullet from the drop-down gallery by right-clicking the bullet and then clicking *Remove* at the shortcut menu.

As you can with a numbered list, you can change the level of a bulleted list. Click the item or select the items you want to change, click the Bullets button arrow, and then point to *Change List Level*. At the side menu of bullet options that display, click the desired bullet. With the *Change List Level* option, you can change a single-level list into a multilevel list. To insert a line break in the list while the automatic bulleting feature is on without inserting a bullet, press Shift + Enter. (You can also insert a line break in a numbered list without inserting a number by pressing Shift + Enter.)

## Exercise 17.2 Defining and Inserting Custom Bullets
Part 1 of 1

1. Open **TravelAdv.docx** and save the document with the name **C17-E02-TravelAdv**.
2. Make the following changes to the document:
   a. Select the entire document and then change the line spacing to 1.15.
   b. Apply the Heading 1 style to the title *Hawaiian Adventures*.
   c. Apply the Heading 2 style to the two headings *Rainy Day Activities* and *Kauai Sights*.
   d. Change the style set to Lines (Stylish).
   e. Change the theme colors to Blue.
3. Define and insert a picture bullet by completing the following steps:
   a. Select text in the *Rainy Day Activities* section from the paragraph that begins with *Movies* through the paragraph that begins with *Theater*.
   b. Click the HOME tab.
   c. Click the Bullets button arrow and then click *Define New Bullet* at the drop-down gallery.
   d. At the Define New Bullet dialog box, click the Picture button.
   e. At the Insert Pictures window, click in the *Office.com Clip Art* search text box, type **bullets, icons** and then press Enter.
   f. When the search results display, double-click the round blue bullet shown to the right.
   g. Click OK to close the Define New Bullet dialog box. (This applies the new bullet to the selected paragraphs.)

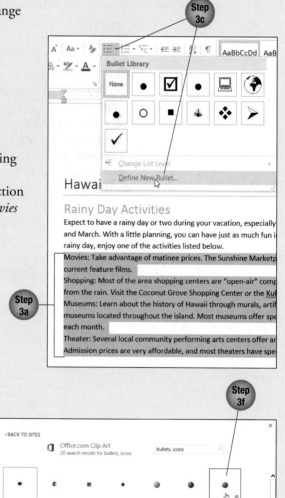

4. Define and insert a symbol bullet by completing the following steps:
   a. Select the paragraphs of text below the heading *Kauai Sights*.
   b. Click the Bullets button arrow and then click *Define New Bullet* at the drop-down gallery.
   c. At the Define New Bullet dialog box, click the Symbol button.
   d. At the Symbol dialog box, click the down-pointing arrow at the right of the *Font* option, scroll down the drop-down list, and then click *Wingdings*.
   e. Click the flower symbol shown below.

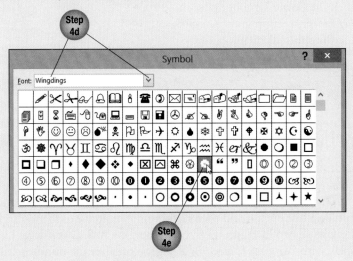

   f. Click OK to close the Symbol dialog box.
   g. At the Define New Bullet dialog box, click the Font button.
   h. At the Font dialog box, click *14* in the *Size* list box.
   i. Click the down-pointing arrow at the right of the *Font color* option and then click the color *Dark Blue, Text 2, Lighter 40%* (fourth column, fourth row in the *Theme Colors* section).

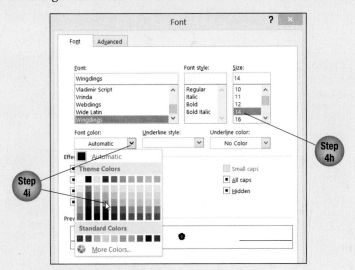

   j. Click OK to close the Font dialog box.
   k. At the Define New Bullet dialog box, click OK.

5. Remove from the Bullet Library the two bullets you have just defined by completing the following steps:
   a. Click the Bullets button arrow.
   b. Right-click the round blue picture bullet in the *Bullet Library* section and then click *Remove* at the shortcut menu.
   c. Click the Bullets button arrow.
   d. Right-click the flower symbol bullet in the *Bullet Library* section and then click *Remove* at the shortcut menu.
6. Save, print, and then close **C17-E02-TravelAdv.docx**.

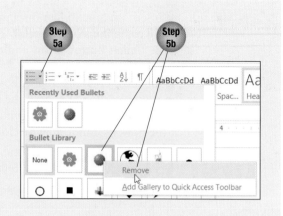

# Inserting Multilevel List Numbering

**QUICK STEPS**

**Insert Multilevel List Numbering**
1. Click Multilevel List button.
2. Click desired style at drop-down gallery.

Use the Multilevel List button in the Paragraph group on the HOME tab to specify the type of numbering for paragraphs of text at the left margin, first tab, second tab, and so on. Apply predesigned multilevel numbering to text in a document by clicking the Multilevel List button and then clicking the desired numbering style at the drop-down gallery, as shown in Figure 17.4. Some options at the Multilevel List drop-down gallery display with *Heading 1*, *Heading 2*, and so on after the number. Click one of these options and Word inserts the numbering and applies the heading style to the text.

Multilevel List

**Figure 17.4  Multilevel List Drop-down Gallery**

Click the Multilevel List button to display this drop-down gallery of multilevel list options.

Click the *Define New Multilevel List* option to display the Define new Multilevel list dialog box with options for creating a custom multilevel list.

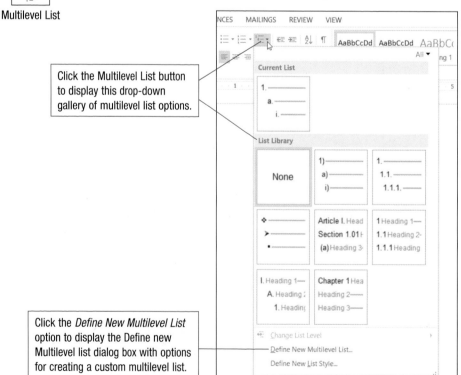

1. Open **CSList.docx** and save the document with the name **C17-E03-CSList**.
2. Change the tab settings by completing the following steps:
   a. Select the paragraphs of text below the title.
   b. Click the Paragraph group dialog box launcher.
   c. At the Paragraph dialog box, click the Tabs button located in the lower left corner of the dialog box.
   d. At the Tabs dialog box, select *0.5″* in the *Default tab stops* measurement box and then type **0.25**.

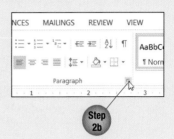

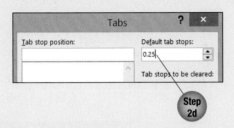

Step 2d

Step 3a     Step 3b

   e. Click OK to close the Tabs dialog box.
3. With the text still selected, apply multilevel list numbering by completing the following steps:
   a. Click the Multilevel List button in the Paragraph group on the HOME tab.
   b. At the drop-down gallery, click the middle option in the top row of the *List Library* section.
   c. Deselect the text.
4. Save and then print **C17-E03-CSList.docx**.

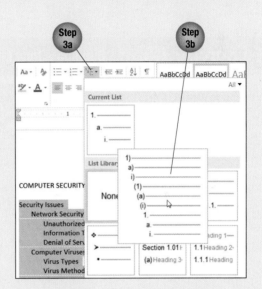

## Defining a Multilevel List

The Multilevel List button drop-down gallery contains options for predesigned multiple-level numbering. If the gallery does not contain the type of numbering you want to use, you can define your own. To do this, click the Multilevel List button and then click *Define New Multilevel List*. This displays the Define new Multilevel list dialog box, as shown in Figure 17.5 on the next page. At this dialog box, click a level in the *Click level to modify* option box and then specify the number format, style, position, and alignment. When you define a multilevel list style, you can mix numbers and bullets in the same list.

**QUICK STEPS**

**Define a Multilevel List**
1. Click Multilevel List button.
2. Click *Define New Multilevel List* at drop-down gallery.
3. Click desired level, number format, and/or position.
4. Click OK.

**Figure 17.5  Define New Multilevel List Dialog Box**

Click a level in this option box and then specify the number format, style, position, and alignment.

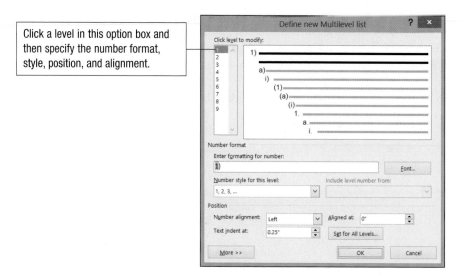

## Exercise 17.3B  Defining a New Multilevel List

Part 2 of 3

1. With **C17-E03-CSList.docx** open, define a multilevel list by completing the following steps:
   a. Select the paragraphs of text below the title.
   b. Click the Multilevel List button in the Paragraph group on the HOME tab.
   c. Click the *Define New Multilevel List* option at the drop-down gallery.
   d. At the Define new Multilevel list dialog box, make sure *1* is selected in the *Click level to modify* list box.
   e. Click the down-pointing arrow at the right of the *Number style for this level* option and then click *A, B, C, ...* at the drop-down list.
   f. Click in the *Enter formatting for number* text box, delete any text that displays after *A*, and then type a period (.). (The entry in the text box should now display as *A*.)
   g. Click the up-pointing arrow at the right of the *Aligned at* measurement box until *0.3"* displays.
   h. Click the up-pointing arrow at the right of the *Text indent at* measurement box until *0.6"* displays.

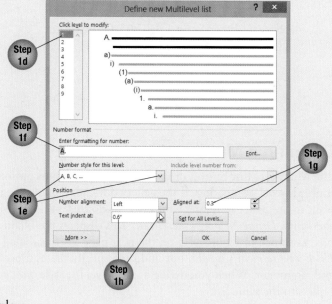

Step 1d

Step 1f

Step 1e

Step 1g

Step 1h

i. Click *2* in the *Click level to modify* list box.
j. Click the down-pointing arrow at the right of the *Number style for this level* option and then click *1, 2, 3, ...* at the drop-down list.
k. Click in the *Enter formatting for number* text box, delete any text that displays after the *1*, and then type a period (.).
l. Click the up-pointing arrow at the right of the *Aligned at* measurement box until *0.6"* displays.
m. Click the up-pointing arrow at the right of the *Text indent at* measurement box until *0.9"* displays.
n. Click *3* in the *Click level to modify* list box.
o. Click the down-pointing arrow at the right of the *Number style for this level* option and then click *a, b, c, ...* at the drop-down list.
p. Make sure *a)* displays in the *Enter formatting for number* text box. (If not, delete any text that displays after the *a* and then type a right parenthesis.)
q. Click the up-pointing arrow at the right of the *Aligned at* measurement box until *0.9"* displays.
r. Click the up-pointing arrow at the right of the *Text indent at* measurement box until *1.2"* displays.
s. Click OK to close the dialog box. (This applies the new multilevel list numbering to the selected text.)

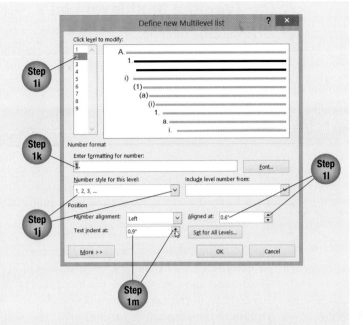

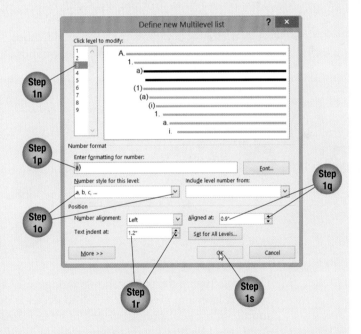

2. Make the following formatting changes to the document:
   a. Apply the Heading 1 style to the title *COMPUTER SECURITY*.
   b. Change the style set to Lines (Stylish).
3. With the document still open, make the following changes:
   a. Select and then delete *Network Sniffers* in the *Computer Protection* section.
   b. Move the insertion point immediately right of the text *Data Encryption*, press the Enter key, and then type **Passwords**.
4. Save **C17-E03-CSList.docx**.

## Typing a Multilevel List

You can select text and apply a multilevel list to it or you can apply the list and then type the text. As you type text, press the Tab key to move to the next level and press Shift + Tab to move to the previous level.

---

1. With **C17-E03-CSList.docx** open, type the text shown in Figure 17.6 on the next page in a multilevel list by completing the following steps:

   a. Press Ctrl + End to move the insertion point to the end of the document and then press the Enter key.

   b. Type **NETWORKS** and then press the Enter key twice.

   c. Apply the multilevel list format you defined in Exercise 17.3B by clicking the Multilevel List button and then clicking the list. (The list displays in the *Lists in Current Documents* section of the drop-down gallery.)

   d. Type **Networking over the Web** as shown below and in Figure 17.6.

   e. Press the Enter key, press the Tab key, and then type **Data Transmission** as shown below and in Figure 17.6.

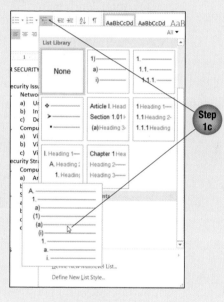

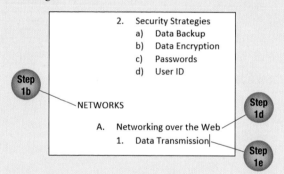

   f. Continue typing the text as shown in Figure 17.6. Press the Tab key to indent text to the next level and press Shift + Tab to decrease the indent to the previous level. (The multilevel list will apply letter and number formatting.)

   g. Apply the Heading 1 style to the title *NETWORKS*.

2. Save, print, and then close **C17-E03-CSList.docx**.

---

**Figure 17.6** **Exercise 17.3C**

NETWORKS

Networking over the Web
      Data Transmission
           Bandwidth
           Analog and Digital Transmission
           Parallel and Serial Transmission
      Communications Media
           Wired Communications Media
           Wireless Communications Media
Network Design
      Network Topologies
           Bus Topologies
           Star Topologies
           Ring Topologies
           Hybrid Topologies
      Network Hardware
           Hubs
           Repeaters
           Routers
           Gateways
           Bridges

# Inserting Special Characters

In Chapter 8, you learned how to insert symbols and special characters with options at the Symbol dialog box with the Symbols tab or Special Characters tab selected. You can also insert special symbols and characters by typing a sequence of characters or by using keyboard shortcuts. Word creates some special characters automatically as you type text.

## Inserting Intellectual Property Symbols

Among the symbols you can insert in Word are three intellectual property protection symbols: ©, ™, and ®. Insert the © symbol to identify copyrighted intellectual property, use the ™ symbol to identify a trademark, and use the ® symbol to identify a registered trademark.

You can insert these symbols with options at the Symbol dialog box with the Special Characters tab selected, by typing a sequence of characters, or by using a keyboard shortcut. Insert a © symbol by typing (c) or pressing Alt + Ctrl + C, insert a ™ symbol by typing (tm) or pressing Alt + Ctrl + T, and insert a ® symbol by typing (r) or pressing Alt + Ctrl + R.

## Exercise 17.4A Inserting Intellectual Property Symbols Part 1 of 3

1. At a blank document, type the text shown in Figure 17.7. Insert each intellectual property symbol using the appropriate sequence of characters or keyboard shortcut. To insert (c), (tm), and (r) in the document rather than the corresponding symbol, type the sequence of characters and then immediately click the Undo button. This changes the symbol back to the sequence of characters.
2. Save the document with the name **C17-E04-SpecialCharacters.**

**Figure 17.7** Exercise 17.4A

**INTELLECTUAL PROPERTY PROTECTION**

A copyright protects original works in areas such as publishing, music, literature, and drama. Use the © symbol to identify copyrighted intellectual property. Create this symbol by typing (c), using the keyboard shortcut Alt + Ctrl + C, or by clicking the symbol in the Symbol dialog box with the Special Characters tab selected.

A trademark identifies a word, symbol, device, or name such as a brand name. Use the ™ symbol to identify a trademarked name or product. Create this symbol by typing (tm), using the keyboard shortcut Alt + Ctrl + T, or by clicking the symbol in the Symbol dialog box with the Special Characters tab selected.

A registered trademark is a trademark that has been registered with the U.S. Patent & Trademark Office. Use the ® symbol to identify a registered trademark. Create this symbol by typing (r), using the keyboard shortcut Alt + Ctrl + R, or by clicking the symbol in the Symbol dialog box with the Special Characters tab selected.

## Inserting Hyphens

In Chapter 6, you learned how to use the Hyphenation button in the Page Setup group on the PAGE LAYOUT tab to hyphenate words automatically or manually. In addition to inserting a regular hyphen in a document, you can insert an optional hyphen and nonbreaking hyphen, as well as an en dash and em dash.

One method for inserting a regular hyphen is to press the hyphen key on the keyboard and use it to create a compound word, such as *fresh-looking* or *sister-in-law*. An optional hyphen is one inserted by Word when you automatically hyphenate a document. An optional hyphen will display only if the word falls at the end of the line and the word is divided across two lines. Word does not display the optional hyphen if the word is not divided across lines. Optional hyphens display as hyphens if you turn on the display of nonprinting characters.

You may not want some hyphenated text divided across lines. For example, you may not want a company name such as *Knowles-Myers Corporation* divided between *Knowles* and *Myers* and set on two lines. To avoid a break like this, insert a nonbreaking hyphen by clicking the *Nonbreaking Hyphen* option at the Symbol dialog box with the Special Characters tab selected or with the keyboard shortcut Ctrl + Shift + -.

Em dashes (—) are used to indicate a break in thought or to highlight a term or phrase by separating it from the rest of the sentence. Em dashes are particularly useful in long sentences and sentences with multiple phrases and commas. For example, the sentence "The main focus of this document is on general-purpose, single-user computers—personal computers—that enable users to complete a variety of computing tasks." contains two em dashes before and after the term *personal computers*.

To create an em dash in a Word document, type the word, type two hyphens, type the next word, and then press the spacebar. When you press the spacebar, Word automatically converts the two hyphens to an em dash. If automatic formatting of em dashes is turned off, you can insert an em dash with the *Em Dash* option at the Symbol dialog box with the Special Characters tab selected or with the keyboard shortcut Alt + Ctrl + - (on the numeric keypad). (You must use the hyphen key on the numeric keypad rather than the hyphen key, which is located between the 0 key and = key.)

En dashes (–) are used between inclusive dates, times, and numbers to mean "through." For example, in the text *9:30–11:00 a.m.*, the numbers should be separated by an en dash rather than a regular hyphen. Word does not automatically convert hyphens to en dashes, as it does with em dashes. To create an en dash, click the *En Dash* option at the Symbol dialog box with the Special Characters tab selected or with the keyboard shortcut Ctrl + - (on the numeric keypad).

---

**Exercise 17.4B**  **Inserting Hyphens**                                  **Part 2 of 3**

1. With **C17-E04-SpecialCharacters.docx** open, press Ctrl + End, press the Enter key, and then type the text shown in Figure 17.8 with the following specifications:
   a. Type an en dash between the times *9:00* and *10:30 a.m.* by pressing Ctrl + - (on the numeric keypad).
   b. Create the em dashes before and after the phrase *Excel, PowerPoint, and Access* by typing hyphens (two hyphens for each em dash).
   c. Insert a nonbreaking hyphen within *Tri-State* by pressing Ctrl + Shift + -.
2. Save **C17-E04-SpecialCharacters.docx**.

---

**Figure 17.8 Exercise 17.4B**

**SOFTWARE TRAINING**

The Microsoft® Office Word training is scheduled for Thursday, March 5, 2015, from 9:00–10:30 a.m. Additional training for other applications in the Office suite—Excel, PowerPoint, and Access—will be available during the month of April. Contact the Training Department for additional information. All Tri-State employees are eligible for the training.

## QUICK STEPS

**Insert Nonbreaking Spaces**

1. Click INSERT tab.
2. Click Symbol button.
3. Click *More Symbols.*
4. Click Special Characters tab.
5. Double-click *Nonbreaking Space* option.
6. Click Close.

OR

Press Ctrl + Shift + spacebar.

# Inserting Nonbreaking Spaces

As you type text in a document, Word makes decisions about where to end lines and automatically wraps text to the beginnings of new lines. In some situations, a line may break between two words or phrases that should remain together. To control where text breaks across lines, consider inserting nonbreaking spaces between words you want to stay together.

Insert a nonbreaking space with the *Nonbreaking Space* option at the Symbol dialog box with the Special Characters tab selected or with the keyboard shortcut Ctrl + Shift + spacebar. If nonprinting characters are turned on, a normal space displays as a dot and a nonbreaking space displays as a degree symbol.

## Exercise 17.4C Inserting Nonbreaking Spaces    Part 3 of 3

1. With **C17-E04-SpecialCharacters.docx** open, click the Show/Hide ¶ button in the Paragraph group on the HOME tab.
2. Press Ctrl + End, press the Enter key, and then type the text in Figure 17.9. Insert nonbreaking spaces in the keyboard shortcuts by pressing Ctrl + Shift + spacebar before and after each plus (+) symbol.
3. Turn off the display of nonprinting characters.
4. Save, print, and then close **C17-E04-SpecialCharacters.docx**.

**Figure 17.9 Exercise 17.4C**

### KEYBOARD SHORTCUTS

Microsoft Word includes a number of keyboard shortcuts you can use to access features and commands. The ScreenTip for some buttons displays the keyboard shortcut you can use to execute the command. For example, hovering the mouse over the Font button causes the ScreenTip to display Ctrl + Shift + F as the keyboard shortcut. Additional HOME tab Font group keyboard shortcuts include Ctrl + B to bold text, Ctrl + I to italicize text, and Ctrl + U to underline text. You can also press Ctrl + Shift ++ to turn on superscript and press Ctrl + = to turn on subscript.

# Chapter Summary

➤ Use the Bullets button to insert bullets before specific paragraphs of text and use the Numbering button to insert numbers.

➤ Insert custom numbers or letters by clicking the Numbering button arrow and then clicking the desired option at the drop-down gallery.

➤ Set the numbering value with options at the Set Numbering Value dialog box. Display this dialog box by clicking the Numbering button arrow and then clicking *Set Numbering Value* at the drop-down gallery.

➤ Define your own numbering format with options at the Define New Number Format dialog box. Display this dialog box by clicking the Numbering button arrow and then clicking *Define New Number Format* at the drop-down gallery.

➤ Insert custom bullets by clicking the Bullets button arrow and then clicking the desired option at the drop-down gallery.

➤ Define your own custom bullet with options at the Define New Bullet dialog box. Display this dialog box by clicking the Bullets button arrow and then clicking *Define New Bullet* at the drop-down gallery.

➤ Apply multilevel numbering to paragraphs of text by clicking the Multilevel List button in the Paragraph group on the HOME tab.

➤ Define your own multilevel list numbering format with options at the Define new Multilevel list dialog box. Display this dialog box by clicking the Multilevel List button and then clicking *Define New Multilevel List* at the drop-down gallery.

➤ When you type a multilevel list, press the Tab key to move to the next level and press Shift + Tab to move to the previous level.

➤ Insert special characters and symbols with options at the Symbol dialog box with the Special Characters tab selected, by typing a sequence of characters, or with keyboard shortcuts.

➤ Use the © symbol to identify copyrighted intellectual property, use the ™ symbol to identify a trademark, and use the ® symbol to identify a registered trademark.

➤ Insert regular, optional, and nonbreaking hyphens, as well as en dashes and em dashes, for specific purposes.

➤ Insert a nonbreaking hyphen by clicking the *Nonbreaking Hyphen* option at the Symbol dialog box with the Special Characters tab selected or by using the keyboard shortcut Ctrl + Shift + -.

➤ Use em dashes to indicate a break in a thought or to highlight a term or phrase by separating it from the rest of the sentence. To insert an em dash, type a word, type two hyphens, type the next word, and press the spacebar. You can also insert an em dash with the keyboard shortcut Alt + Ctrl + - (on the numeric keypad) or at the Symbol dialog box with the Special Characters tab selected.

➤ Use en dashes to indicate inclusive dates, times, and numbers. To insert an en dash, click the *En Dash* option at the Symbol dialog box with the Special Characters tab selected or use the keyboard shortcut Ctrl + - (on the numeric keypad).

➤ Insert nonbreaking spaces between words that you do not want to separate across a line break. Insert a nonbreaking space by clicking the *Nonbreaking Space* option at the Symbol dialog box with the Special Characters tab selected or with the keyboard shortcut Ctrl + Shift + spacebar.

# Commands *Review*

| FEATURE | RIBBON TAB, GROUP | BUTTON, OPTION | KEYBOARD SHORTCUT |
|---------|-------------------|----------------|-------------------|
| bulleted list | HOME, Paragraph | [button] | |
| copyright symbol © | | | Alt + Ctrl + C |
| Define New Bullet dialog box | HOME, Paragraph | [button], *Define New Bullet* | |
| Define new Multilevel list dialog box | HOME, Paragraph | [button], *Define New Multilevel List* | |
| Define New Number Format dialog box | HOME, Paragraph | [button], *Define New Number Format* | |
| em dash | | | Alt + Ctrl + - (on numeric keypad) |
| en dash | | | Ctrl + - (on numeric keypad) |
| multilevel list | HOME, Paragraph | [button] | |
| nonbreaking hyphen | | | Ctrl + Shift + - |
| nonbreaking space | | | Ctrl + Shift + spacebar |
| numbered list | HOME, Paragraph | [button] | |
| registered trademark symbol ® | | | Alt + Ctrl + R |
| Symbol dialog box | INSERT, Symbols | Ω, *More Symbols* | |
| trademark symbol ™ | | | Alt + Ctrl + T |

# Key Points *Review*

**Completion:** In the space provided at the right, indicate the correct term, symbol, or command.

1. The Numbering button is located in this group on the HOME tab.   _____

2. Define your own numbering format with options at this dialog box.   _____

3. When you define a bullet at the Define New Bullet dialog box, it is automatically included in this section in the Bullets button drop-down gallery.   _____

4. Click this button to number paragraphs of text at the left margin, first tab, second tab, and so on. _____

5. As you type a multilevel list, press this combination of keys to move to the previous level. _____

6. Type this sequence of characters on the keyboard to insert a copyright symbol. _____

7. This is the keyboard shortcut to insert the ® symbol. _____

8. Use this type of dash in a sentence to indicate a break in thought or to highlight a term or phrase. _____

9. Use this type of dash to indicate inclusive dates, times, and numbers. _____

10. Use this keyboard shortcut to insert a nonbreaking space. _____

# Chapter *Assessments*

## Applying Your Skills

Demonstrate your knowledge of features learned in this chapter by completing the following assessments.

**Assessment 17.1**     **Insert Custom Bullets and Numbering in a Technology Document**

1. Open **ElecTech.docx** and save the document with the name **C17-A01-ElecTech**.
2. Apply the following formatting to the document:
   a. Apply the Lines (Simple) style set.
   b. Apply the Frame theme.
3. Select the questions below the heading *Technology Information Questions* and then insert check mark (✔) bullets.
4. Create a computer disc symbol bullet in 14-point font size and then apply the symbol bullet to the eight paragraphs of text below the heading *Technology Timeline: Storage Devices and Media.* ***Hint: You can find the disc symbol in the Wingdings font (located in approximately the second row).***
5. Select the paragraphs of text below the heading *Information Systems and Commerce*, click the Multilevel List button, and then click the middle option in the top row of the *List Library* section.
6. Select the paragraphs of text below the heading *Internet* and then apply the same multilevel list numbering.
7. Save and then print **C17-A01-ElecTech.docx**.
8. Select the paragraphs of text below the heading *Information Systems and Commerce* and then define a new multilevel list with the following specifications:
   a. Level 1 that inserts arabic numbers (1, 2, 3) followed by periods and aligned at 0 inch and indented at 0.25 inch.
   b. Level 2 that inserts capital letters (A, B, C) followed by periods and aligned at 0.25 inch and indented at 0.5 inch.
   c. Level 3 that inserts arabic numbers (1, 2, 3) followed by right parentheses and aligned at 0.5 inch and indented at 0.75 inch.
   d. Make sure the new multilevel list numbering is applied to the selected paragraphs.
9. Select the paragraphs of text below the heading *Internet* and then apply the new multilevel list numbering.
10. Save, print, and then close **C17-A01-ElecTech.docx**.

## Assessment 17.2 Type a Corporate Report Document That Contains Special Characters

1. At a blank document, type the text shown in Figure 17.10. with the following specifications:
   a. Insert nonbreaking hyphens in the corporate name (Perez-Lin-Hyatt).
   b. Insert en dashes in the money amount ($20–25 million) and the meeting times (in the Department Meetings section).
   c. Insert em dashes around the text *an important indicator of current demand*.
   d. Insert the ™ and © symbols correctly.
   e. Insert nonbreaking spaces within keyboard shortcuts.
2. Save the document with the name **C17-A02-CorpReport**.
3. Print and then close **C17-A02-CorpReport.docx**.

**Figure 17.10 Assessment 17.2**

---

**Corporate Report**

During 2015, Perez-Lin-Hyatt Industrial invested $28 million on capital expenditures and an additional $20–25 million on research and engineering. All major projects undergo a rigorous financial analysis to ensure they meet all investment return objectives. Employees completed two major projects at PerezLinHyatt including expansion of Asian and northern European markets. Major effect at PerezLinHyatt centered on development of product line extensions of our Tubular™ and ReedBit™ drill technology. The outlook for 2016 is encouraging. The backlog for our products—an important indicator of current demand—grew to a record $265 million at year-end 2015.

PerezLinHyatt Industrial Corporate Report©

**Department Meetings**

Finance: Tuesday, 9:30–11:00 a.m.

Purchasing: Wednesday, 3:00–4:30 p.m.

Training: Thursday, 8:30–9:30 a.m.

**Keyboard Shortcuts**

Word includes keyboard shortcuts you can use for creating, viewing, and saving documents. Press Ctrl + N to display a new blank document, or press Ctrl + O to open a document. Use the shortcut Ctrl + W to close the currently open document. Additional keyboard shortcuts include pressing Alt + Ctrl + S to split the document window and pressing Alt + Shift + C to remove the document window split.

---

# Expanding Your Skills

Explore additional feature options or use Help to learn a new skill in creating this document.

## Assessment 17.3  Create and Insert a Picture Bullet in a Document

1. Create the document shown in Figure 17.11 with the following specifications:
   a. Change the left and right margins to 1.5 inches.
   b. Set the text in 36-point Angsana New. (If this typeface is not available, choose a similar typeface.)
   c. In addition to symbols and pictures provided by Microsoft, you can create bullets with your own pictures. Use the Picture button in the Define New Bullet dialog box to insert the **WhiteHorse.jpg** image located in your Chapter17 folder as the picture bullets. After inserting the picture bullets, click the first bullet (which selects all of the bullets) and then change the font size to 36 points.
   d. As shown in the figure, apply Green, Accent 6, Darker 25% shading to the title, change the title text font color to White, Background 1, and apply bold formatting.

**Figure 17.11  Assessment 17.3**

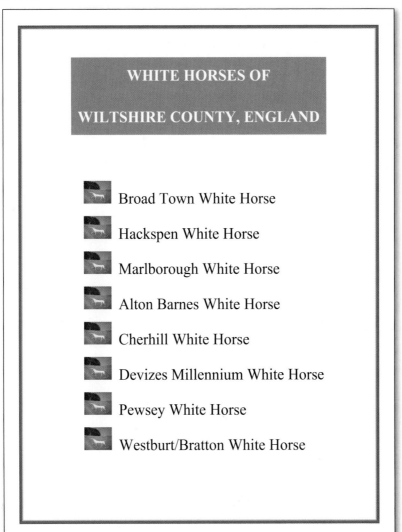

e. Insert the page border as shown in the figure. *Hint: Use the third option from the bottom in the* **Style** *list box at the Borders and Shading dialog box with the Page Border tab selected and change the color to Green, Accent 6, Darker 25%.*

f. Make any other formatting changes so your document appears as shown in Figure 17.11.

2. Save the document and name it **C17-A03-WhiteHorses**.

3. Print and then close the document.

## Achieving Signature Status

Take your skills to the next level by completing this more challenging assessment.

### Assessment 17.4    Type a Business Letter

1. Open **NSSLtrhd.docx** and save the document with the name **C17-A04-TrainingLtr**.

2. Type the letter shown in Figure 17.12 on the next page with the following specifications:

   a. Insert the current date in place of *Current date* in the letter.

   b. Insert the symbols as shown in the figure.

   c. Insert a nonbreaking space between the words *Mont* and *Tremblant* in the company name.

   d. Insert en dashes between the times in the third column in the table.

   e. Format the table as shown. *Hint: Apply the Grid Table 2 - Accent 3 table style, center the table, and make any other changes so your table appears as shown in Figure 17.12.*

   f. Type your first and last names in place of *Student Name* in the letter.

3. Save, print, and then close **C17-A04-TrainingLtr.docx**.

**Figure 17.12  Assessment 17.4**

# Northland Security Systems
### 3200 North 22nd Street ❖ Springfield ❖ IL ❖ 62102

Current Date

Ms. Chloë St. Jérôme
Mont Tremblant-Broughton
4500-320 St. Laurent
Montréal, QC H3Y 1C4
CANADA

Dear Ms. St. Jérôme:

Thank you for contracting with Northland Security Systems to provide training to employees at
Mont Tremblant-Broughton. As our agreement states, we will be providing the following on-site
software training for employees at your company:

| Software | Date | Times |
|---|---|---|
| Adobe® InDesign | Tuesday, March 10 | 9:00–11:30 a.m. and 1:00–5:00 p.m. |
| | Thursday, March 12 | 9:00–11:30 a.m. and 1:00–3:00 p.m. |
| Microsoft® Word 2013 | Wednesday, March 11 | 8:00–11:30 a.m. and 1:00–5:00 p.m. |
| Microsoft® Excel 2013 | Tuesday, March 17 | 8:00–11:30 a.m. and 1:00–3:00 p.m. |
| | Thursday, March 19 | 9:00–11:30 a.m. and 1:00–3:00 p.m. |
| Intuit® QuickBooks | Wednesday, March 18 | 8:00–11:30 a.m. and 1:00–5:00 p.m. |

Our training coordinator, Barbara Goodwin, will contact you this week to confirm the number of
employees that will be attending each training session, the training location, and equipment needs. She
may also contact you for a referral on lodging near your company headquarters.

We look forward to conducting the training sessions and are confident that employees of
Mont Tremblant-Broughton will acquire the skills they needs to manage the software applications they
use on the job. If you need to contact me or Ms. Goodwin, please give us a call at 1-888-555-2200.

Sincerely,

Student Name

C17-A04-TrainingLtr.docx

*1-888-555-2200 ❖ www.emcp.net/nss*

# Chapter 18

# Sorting and Selecting; Finding and Replacing Data

## Performance Objectives

Upon successful completion of Chapter 18, you will be able to:

- Sort text in paragraphs, columns, and tables
- Sort records in a data source file
- Select specific records in a data source file for merging
- Find specific records in a data source file
- Find and replace formatting and special characters and use wildcard characters

Word is primarily a word processing program but it also includes some basic database functions. For example, you can sort text that is set in paragraphs, columns, or tables; sort records in a data source file; and select specific records from a data source file to merge with a main document. In addition to finding or finding and replacing text, you can find or find and replace formatting and special characters and use wildcard characters. In this chapter, you will learn how to sort text in paragraphs, column, tables, and records in a data source file; specify records in a data source file for merging; find and replace formatting and special characters; and use wildcard characters to find and replace data.

*Note: Before beginning computer exercises for this chapter, copy to your storage medium the Chapter18 folder from the CD that accompanies this textbook and then make Chapter18 the active folder.*

In this chapter, students will produce the following documents:

Exercise 18.1. C18-E01-MBSortDoc.docx
Exercise 18.2B. C18-E02-MFLabels-01.docx
Exercise 18.2C. C18-E02-MFLabels-02.docx
Exercise 18.2D. C18-E02-MFLabels-03.docx
Exercise 18.2E. C18-E02-MFLabels-04.docx
Exercise 18.3. C18-E03-LeaseAgrmnt.docx
Exercise 18.4. C18-E04-CompanyInfo.docx
Exercise 18.5. C18-E05-ComLease.docx

Model answers for these exercises are shown on the following pages.

**MOBILE BAY PRODUCTS**
**Sales Division**

**ADMINISTRATION**
Danielson, Leslie, Chief Executive Officer
Higgins, Emily, Vice President
Kenwood, Dana, Chief Financial Officer
Palmer, Gerald, President

**TECHNICAL SUPPORT TEAM**
Jonathon Bear, Hardware Team Member
Jessie Levigne, Team Leader
Chad Mahoney, Software Team Member
Eduardo Quintana, Supervisor
Carol Runyon, Software Specialist
Kyung Shin, Software Team Member
Mel Sogura, Hardware Team Member
Terry Ulrich, Hardware Specialist

**NEW EMPLOYEES**

| Employee | Department | Hire Date |
|---|---|---|
| Moranski, Adam | Finances | 09/10/2014 |
| Oh, Soo-Yean | Finances | 08/06/2015 |
| Hartford, Gina | Public Relations | 08/06/2012 |
| Smith-Larsen, Beth | Public Relations | 07/02/2013 |
| Crowley, Nicholas | Technical Support | 10/01/2014 |
| Newton, Katherine | Technical Support | 07/02/2012 |
| Espinoza, Enrique | Training | 09/10/2013 |

| Salesperson | Sales, 2014 | Sales, 2015 |
|---|---|---|
| Owens, Kendra | $700,328 | $675,329 |
| Kohler, Roger | $610,476 | $700,387 |
| Coulter, Jolene | $600,340 | $597,288 |
| Tanaka, Diana | $428,528 | $399,511 |
| Barclay, Kurt | $400,394 | $425,304 |
| Washington, Aaron | $395,675 | $402,530 |
| Hubbard, Christopher | $320,348 | $400,570 |

**Exercise 18.1** C18-E01-MBSortDoc.docx

---

Mr. Dale Carmichael
12339 145th Southeast
Paris, KY 40361

Mr. Karl Hershey
1222 Third Street
Paris, KY 40361

Mr. Dean Keefer
489 Sutton Road
Apt. 2010
Paris, KY 40361

Mr. Jeffrey Diaz
220 East Meridian
P.O. Box 3499
Winchester, KY 40391

Ms. Marianne Novak
765 42nd Avenue
Winchester, KY 40391

Mrs. Mary Pirone
3580 Park Lane
Winchester, KY 40391

Ms. Laurel Kittner
12303 North 141st
Apt. 3-B
Lexington, KY 40507

Mrs. Claudia Levinson
1521 North 32nd Street
Lexington, KY 40511

Mr. Arthur Washbaugh
1203 24th Street
Lexington, KY 40511

Mr. Ryan Wright
10291 South 41st
Lexington, KY 40511

Dr. Miguel Trivelas
5840 North 132nd
P.O. Box 9045
Lexington, KY 40517

Mrs. Kayla Stuben
450 Madison Street
P.O. Box 3643
Lexington, KY 40526

**Exercise 18.2B** C18-E02-MFLabels-01.docx

---

Ms. Laurel Kittner
12303 North 141st
Apt. 3-B
Lexington, KY 40507

Mrs. Claudia Levinson
1521 North 32nd Street
Lexington, KY 40511

Mr. Arthur Washbaugh
1203 24th Street
Lexington, KY 40511

Mr. Ryan Wright
10291 South 41st
Lexington, KY 40511

Dr. Miguel Trivelas
5840 North 132nd
P.O. Box 9045
Lexington, KY 40517

Mrs. Kayla Stuben
450 Madison Street
P.O. Box 3643
Lexington, KY 40526

**Exercise 18.2C** C18-E02-MFLabels-02.docx

Mr. Dale Carmichael
12339 145th Southeast
Paris, KY 40361

Mr. Karl Hershey
1222 Third Street
Paris, KY 40361

Mr. Dean Keefer
489 Sutton Road
Apt. 2010
Paris, KY 40361

Mr. Jeffrey Diaz
220 East Meridian
P.O. Box 3499
Winchester, KY 40391

Ms. Marianne Novak
765 42nd Avenue
Winchester, KY 40391

Mrs. Mary Pirone
3580 Park Lane
Winchester, KY 40391

Mrs. Claudia Levinson
1521 North 32nd Street
Lexington, KY 40511

Mr. Arthur Washbaugh
1203 24th Street
Lexington, KY 40511

Mr. Ryan Wright
10291 South 41st
Lexington, KY 40511

**Exercise 18.2D**  C18-E02-MFLabels-03.docx

**Exercise 18.2E**  C18-E02-MFLabels-04.docx

---

**LEASE AGREEMENT**

**THIS LEASE AGREEMENT** (hereinafter referred to as the "Agreement") made and entered into this DAY of MONTH, YEAR, by and between Lessor and Lessee.

**WITNESSETH:**

**WHEREAS,** Lessor is the owner of real property and is desirous of leasing the Premises to Lessee upon the terms and conditions as contained herein.

**NOW, THEREFORE,** for and in consideration of the covenants and obligations contained herein and other good and valuable consideration, the receipt and sufficiency of which is hereby acknowledged, the parties hereto agree as follows:

1. **TERM.** Lessor leases to Lessee and Lessee leases from Lessor the Premises.
2. **RENT.** The total rent for the premise is RENT due on the first day of each month less any set off for approved repairs.
3. **DAMAGE DEPOSIT.** Upon the due execution of this Agreement, Lessee shall deposit with Lessor the sum of DEPOSIT receipt of which is hereby acknowledged by Lessor, as security for any damage caused to the Premises during the term hereof. Such deposit shall be returned to Lessee, without interest, and less any set off for damages to the Premises upon the termination of this Agreement.
4. **USE OF PREMISES.** The Premises shall be used and occupied by Lessee and Lessee's immediate family, exclusively, as a private single family dwelling, and no part of the Premises shall be used at any time during the term of this Agreement by Lessee for the purpose of carrying on any business, profession, or trade of any kind, or for any purpose other than as a private single family dwelling. Lessee shall not allow any other person, other than Lessee's immediate family, to occupy the Premises.
5. **CONDITION OF PREMISES.** Lessee stipulates, represents, and warrants that Lessee has examined the Premises, and that they are in good order, repair, and in a safe, clean and tenantable condition.
6. **ALTERATIONS AND IMPROVEMENTS.** Lessee shall make no alterations or improvements on the Premises or construct any building or make any other improvements on the Premises without the prior written consent of Lessor.
7. **NON-DELIVERY OF POSSESSION.** In the event Lessor cannot deliver possession of the Premises to Lessee upon the commencement of the term, through no fault of Lessor or its agents, then Lessor or its agents shall have no liability, but the rental herein provided shall abate until possession is given. Lessor or its agents shall have thirty (30) days in which to give possession, and if possession is tendered within such time, Lessee agrees to accept the demised Premises and pay the rental herein provided from that date. In the event possession cannot be delivered within such time, through no fault of Lessor or its agents, then this Agreement and all rights hereunder shall terminate.

8. **UTILITIES.** Lessee shall be responsible for arranging for and paying for all utility services required on the Premises.

**IN WITNESS WHEREOF** the parties have reviewed the information above and certify, to the best of their knowledge, that the information provided by the signatory is true and accurate.

_____
Lessor

_____
Lessee

**Exercise 18.3**  C18-E03-LeaseAgrmnt.docx

Page 1

Page 2

## EMPLOYEE APPOINTMENTS

Acceptance by an applicant of an offer of employment by an appointing authority and their mutual agreement to the date of hire is known as an appointment.

### TYPES OF APPOINTMENTS

**New Hire:** When you initially accept an appointment, you are considered a new hire. As a new hire, you will be required to serve a probationary period—six months or one year.

**Reemployment:** Reemployment is a type of appointment that does not result in a break in service. The following are types of reemployment:

1. Military reemployment: Any remaining portion of a probationary period must be completed upon return to the company.

2. Reemployment of a permanent employee who has been laid off: Completion of a new probationary period department.

3. Reemployment due

4. Reemployment of s

5. Reemployment due

Further information on this or a representative in the h

**Reinstatement:** If you hav standing, you may be reinst termination.

The probationary period fo compete in promotional ex You cannot be reinstated to higher grade level than the

**Reappointment:** You may class if you meet the curren approval. If you are a proba cannot be reappointed to a level than the position you

**Demotion:** An employee n grade level if the employee approves. You may not dem higher if the position is allo

Page 1

---

**Promotion:** Promotion is advancement to a vacant position in a class that has a higher grade than the class previously held. As an employee of the company, you may compete in recruitments for promotional openings when you have served six months (full-time equivalent) of consecutive service. When you accept a promotion, you will be required to serve a trial period of either six months or one year. If you fail to attain permanent status in a vacant position to which you were promoted, you shall be restored to your former position.

## EMPLOYEE PERFORMANCE

### WORK PERFORMANCE STANDARDS

Work performance standards are written statements of the results and/or behavior expected of an employee when his or her job elements are satisfactorily performed under existing working conditions. Each employee in a permanent position must be provided with a current set of work performance standards for his or her position.

### PERFORMANCE EVALUATION

If you are serving a six-mont evaluate your performance a year (full-time equivalent) p the third, seventh, and eleve Once you have attained perr the month prior to your pay

Each evaluation will include goals and methods to achiev progress in the job. Evaluatic standards.

Your official personnel file is resources department maint department. Your file includi performance evaluations, an of commendation, training c supervisor has requested to l

E

The compensation schedule grade are ten steps. As an em

Page 2

---

the grade for the class to which you are appointed. Your pay is further determined by the compensation schedule applicable to your participation in the company's retirement system.

### DIRECT DEPOSIT OPTION

You have the option to forward your paycheck directly to a checking or savings account in a bank of your choice. The company payroll center representative can provide you with a direct deposit authorization card.

### PAY PROGRESSION

You will receive a merit salary increase annually on your pay progression date if your last performance evaluation was standard or better, and you have not reached the top step in your grade. The maximum merit salary increase is an adjustment of one step annually.

If your date of promotion coincides with your pay progression date, the merit salary increase will be computed first and the promotional increase applied to your new pay rate. If you continue to do satisfactory work, you will remain eligible for annual merit salary increases until you have reached the maximum step within your grade. In addition to merit salary increases, your salary may be adjusted by general salary increases granted by the company.

### OVERTIME

Under state law, overtime is any time worked in excess of eight hours a day, eight hours in a 16-hour period, or 40 hours in a week. Employees who choose and are approved for variable/innovative workday schedules earn overtime after 40 hours in a week.

Cash payment is the principal method of compensation for overtime. Payments are computed based on the employee/employer-paid salary schedule. Agreements may be reached with your employer to provide for compensatory time off in lieu of cash payments. Compensatory time must be taken within a reasonable time after accrual at the direction of the appointing authority. If you request compensatory time off and give at least two weeks' notice, it cannot be unreasonably denied.

### SHIFT DIFFERENTIAL

Shift differential is an adjustment in pay equivalent to an additional 5 percent of an employee's normal rate of pay. To qualify, a nonexempt employee must work in a unit requiring multiple shifts in a 24-hour period and be assigned to a period of work of at least 8 hours of which at least four hours fall between 6:00 p.m. and 7:00 a.m. Employees working a qualifying shift that is reduced due to daylight savings time will still receive shift differential pay for that shift.

Page 3

**COMMERCIAL LEASE AGREEMENT**

This Commercial Lease Agreement ("Lease") is made and effective February 1, 2015, by and between Evergreen Management and Arigalason Investments. Evergreen Management is the owner of land and improvements commonly known as the Tenth Street Building. Evergreen Management makes available for lease a portion of the Tenth Street Building designated as Suite 242 (the "Leased Premises").

Evergreen Management desires to lease the Leased Premises to Arigalason Investments, and Arigalason Investments desires to lease the Leased Premises from Evergreen Management for the term, at the rental and upon the covenants, conditions and provisions herein set forth.

THEREFORE, in consideration of the mutual promises herein, contained and other good and valuable consideration, it is agreed:

**Term**

Evergreen Management leases the Leased Premises to Arigalason Investments, and Arigalason Investments hereby leases the same from Evergreen Management, for an "Initial Term" beginning February 1, 2015, and ending January 31, 2016. Evergreen Management shall use its best efforts to give Arigalason Investments possession as nearly as possible at the beginning of the Lease term. If Evergreen Management is unable to provide the Leased Premises in a timely manner, rent shall abate for the period of delay. Arigalason Investments shall make no other claim against Evergreen Management for any such delay.

Arigalason Investments may renew the Lease for one extended term of one year. Arigalason Investments shall exercise such renewal option, if at all, by giving written notice to Evergreen Management not less than ninety (90) days prior to the expiration of the Initial Term. The renewal term shall be at the rental set forth below and otherwise upon the same covenants, conditions and provisions as provided in this Lease.

**Rental**

Arigalason Investments shall pay to Evergreen Management during the Initial Term rental of $36,000 per year, payable in installments of $3,000 per month. Each installment payment shall be due in advance on the first day of each calendar month during the lease term to Evergreen Management. The rental payment amount for any partial calendar months included in the lease term shall be prorated on a daily basis. Arigalason Investments shall also pay to Evergreen Management a "Security Deposit" in the amount of $5,000.

**Use**

Notwithstanding the forgoing, Arigalason Investments shall not use the Leased Premises for the purposes of storing, manufacturing or selling any explosives, flammables or other inherently dangerous substance, chemical, thing or device.

**Sublease and Assignment**

Arigalason Investments shall have the right without Evergreen Management's consent, to assign this Lease to a corporation with which Arigalason Investments may merge or consolidate, to any subsidiary of Arigalason Investments, to any corporation under common control with Arigalason Investments, or to

a purchaser of substantially all of Arigalason Investments' assets. Except as set forth above, Arigalason Investments shall not sublease all or any part of the Leased Premises, or assign this Lease in whole or in part without Evergreen Management's consent, such consent not to be unreasonably withheld or delayed.

**Repairs**

During the Lease term, Arigalason Investments shall make, at Arigalason Investments' expense, all necessary repairs to the Leased Premises. Repairs shall include such items as routine repairs of floors, walls, ceilings, and other parts of the Leased Premises damaged or worn through normal occupancy, except for major mechanical systems or the roof, subject to the obligations of the parties otherwise set forth in this Lease.

**Property Taxes**

Evergreen Management shall pay, prior to delinquency, all general real estate taxes and installments of special assessments coming due during the Lease term on the Leased Premises, and all personal property taxes with respect to Evergreen Management's personal property, if any, on the Leased Premises. Arigalason Investments shall be responsible for paying all personal property taxes with respect to Arigalason Investments' personal property at the Leased Premises.

_____

Evergreen Management Representative

_____

Arigalason Investments Representative

**Exercise 18.5** C18-E05-ComLease.docx    Page 1    Page 2

# Sorting Text

In Word, you can sort text in paragraphs, text in columns within a table, and records in a data source file. As shown in Table 18.1 on the next page, Word can perform three types of sorts: text, number, and date.

## Sorting Text in Paragraphs

As you learned in Chapter 4, text arranged in paragraphs can be sorted by the first character of each paragraph. That character can be a number or symbol (such as $ or #). In an alphanumeric sort, Word sorts paragraphs beginning with a punctuation mark or special symbol first, followed by paragraphs beginning with a number and then paragraphs beginning with a letter.

Remember, in Word, a paragraph can be a single word or line followed by a press of the Enter key. Also, if you sort paragraphs alphanumerically or numerically, Word treats dates as regular text. Unless you select specific paragraphs to be sorted, Word sorts the entire document.

To sort text arranged in paragraphs, select the text and then click the Sort button in the Paragraph group on the HOME tab. This displays the Sort Text dialog box, as shown in Figure 18.1 on the next page, which contains sorting options. The default setting for the *Sort by* option is *Paragraphs*. This default setting changes depending on the text in the document. For example, if you are sorting text in a table, the *Sort by* option has a default setting of *Column 1*.

**QUICK STEPS**

**Sort Text in Paragraphs**
1. Select text.
2. Click Sort button.
3. Make any needed changes at Sort Text dialog box.
4. Click OK.

Sort

**Figure 18.1  Sort Text Dialog Box**

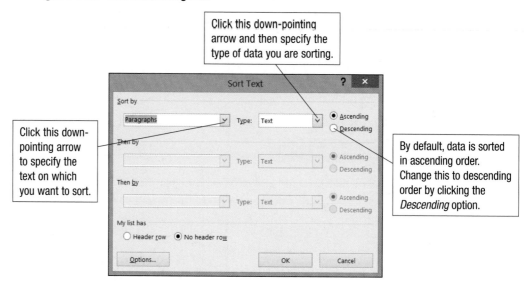

Click this down-pointing arrow and then specify the type of data you are sorting.

Click this down-pointing arrow to specify the text on which you want to sort.

By default, data is sorted in ascending order. Change this to descending order by clicking the *Descending* option.

The *Type* option at the Sort Text dialog box has a default setting of *Text*. This can be changed to *Number* or *Date*. Table 18.1 describes how Word sorts numbers and dates. When Word sorts paragraphs that are separated by more than a single space, the extra hard returns (strokes of the Enter key) are removed and inserted before the paragraphs selected for the sort.

**Table 18.1  Types of Sorts**

| | |
|---|---|
| **Text** | In a text sort, Word arranges text in the following order: first, text beginning with special symbols, such as $ and #; second, text preceded by numbers; and third, alphabetically by letter. Word can also sort letters by case—text beginning with uppercase letters first, followed by text beginning with lowercase letters. |
| **Number** | In a number sort, Word arranges text in numeric order and ignores any alphabetic text. Only the numbers 0 through 9 and symbols pertaining to numbers are recognized. These symbols include $, %, ( ), a decimal point, a comma, and the symbols for the four basic operations: + (addition), - (subtraction), * (multiplication), and / (division). Word can sort numbers in ascending or descending order. |
| **Date** | In a date sort, Word chronologically sorts dates that are expressed in a common date format, such as 06-01-2015; 06/01/2015; June 1, 2015; or 1 June 2015. Word does not sort dates that include abbreviated month names without periods. Word does not sort dates that are expressed as a month, day, or year only. Like a numeric sort, a date sort can be in ascending or descending order. |

1. Open **MBSortDoc.docx** and save the document with the name **C18-E01-MBSortDoc**.
2. Sort the names under the *ADMINISTRATION* heading alphabetically by last name by completing the following steps:
   a. Select the four lines of text below the *ADMINISTRATION* heading.
   b. Click the Sort button in the Paragraph group on the HOME tab.
   c. At the Sort Text dialog box, click OK.
3. Save **C18-E01-MBSortDoc.docx**.

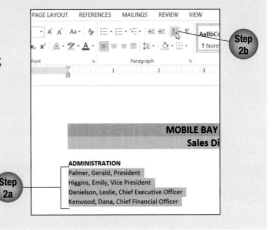

## Changing Sort Options

The *Sort by* options at the Sort Text dialog box vary depending on the options selected in the Sort Options dialog box, as shown in Figure 18.2. To display this dialog box, click the Options button at the Sort Text dialog box.

**QUICK STEPS**

**Display the Sort Options Dialog Box**
1. Click Sort button.
2. Click Options button at Sort Text dialog box.

**Figure 18.2  Sort Options Dialog Box**

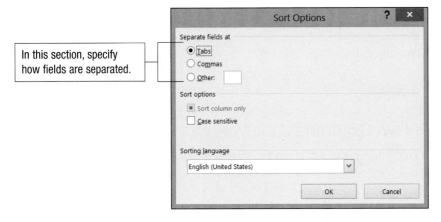

In this section, specify how fields are separated.

The *Separate fields at* section of the dialog box contains three options. The first option, *Tabs*, is the default setting. At this setting, Word assumes that the text to be sorted is divided by tabs. This setting can be changed to *Commas* or *Other*. With the *Other* setting, specify the text-dividing character by which to sort. For example, suppose a document contains paragraphs of first and last names separated by spaces and you want to sort by last name. To do this, you would click *Other* at the Sort Options dialog box and then press the spacebar. This inserts a space, which is not visible, in the *Other* text box. If the names are separated by a comma, click the *Commas* option.

The Sort Options dialog box contains two choices in the *Sort options* section. The first choice, *Sort column only*, sorts only the selected column. This choice is dimmed unless a column of text is selected. If a check mark appears in the *Case sensitive* check box, Word will sort text so that a word that begins with a capital letter is sorted before any word that begins with the same letter but lowercase. This option is available only if *Text* is selected in the *Type* option box at the Sort Text dialog box.

When you make changes at the Sort Options dialog box, those changes are reflected in the choices available with the *Sort by* option at the Sort Text dialog box. For example, if you click *Other* at the Sort Options dialog box and then press the spacebar, the choices for *Sort by* at the Sort Text dialog box will include *Word 1*, *Word 2*, *Word 3*, and so on.

## Exercise 18.1B  Sorting Text Separated by Spaces                Part 2 of 6

1. With **C18-E01-MBSortDoc.docx** open, sort the names of the technical support team alphabetically by last name by completing the following steps:
   a. Select the eight lines of text below the *TECHNICAL SUPPORT TEAM* heading.
   b. Click the Sort button.
   c. At the Sort Text dialog box, click the Options button.
   d. At the Sort Options dialog box, click *Other* and then press the spacebar. (This indicates the first and last names are separated by spaces.)
   e. Click OK.
   f. At the Sort Text dialog box, click the down-pointing arrow at the right of the *Sort by* option and then click *Word 2* at the drop-down list.
   g. Click OK.
2. Save **C18-E01-MBSortDoc.docx**.

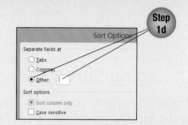

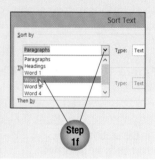

**QUICK STEPS**

**Sort Text in Columns**
1. Select specific text.
2. Click Sort button.
3. Click Options button.
4. Specify *Tabs* as separator.
5. Click OK.
6. Make any needed changes at Sort Text dialog box.
7. Click OK.

## Sorting Text in Columns

To sort text set in columns, the text must be separated by tabs. When Word sorts text in columns, it sorts by field. Word considers text typed at the left margin to be *Field 1*, text typed at the first tab stop to be *Field 2*, text typed at the second tab stop to be *Field 3*, and so on.

To sort text arranged in columns, display the Sort Text dialog box and then click the Options button. At the Sort Options dialog box, make sure that *Tabs* is selected in the *Separate fields at* section and then click OK. At the Sort Text dialog box, display the appropriate field number in the *Sort by* option box and then click OK.

When you sort text in columns, make sure the columns are separated by only one tab. If you press the Tab key more than once between columns, Word recognizes each tab as a separate column. In this case, the field number you specify may correspond to an empty column rather than the desired column.

1. With **C18-E01-MBSortDoc.docx** open, sort text in columns by completing the
following steps:
   a. Select the seven lines of text set in columns that display below the headings *Employee*,
   *Department*, and *Hire Date*.
   b. Click the Sort button.
   c. Click the Options button.
   d. At the Sort Options dialog box, make sure the *Separate fields at* option is set at *Tabs* and
   then click OK to close the dialog box.

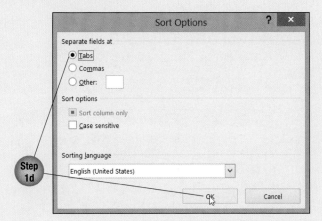

   e. At the Sort Text dialog box, make sure *Field 2* displays in the *Sort by* option box. (If not,
   click the down-pointing arrow at the right of the *Sort by* option and then click *Field 2* at
   the drop-down list.)
   f. Click OK.
2. With the columns of text still selected, sort by the third column of text by date by completing
the following steps:
   a. Click the Sort button.
   b. Click the down-pointing arrow at the right of the *Sort by* option and then click *Field 4*
   at the drop-down list.
   c. Click OK.
3. Save **C18-E01-MBSortDoc.docx**.

## Specifying a Header Row

In Exercise 18.1C, you identified columns by field numbers. You can also identify
columns by headings. If the columns of text you are sorting have column headings, you
can specify this at the Sort Text dialog box by clicking the *Header row* option in the
*My list has* section. Clicking the *Header row* option changes the sort options from field
numbers to column heading names.

For example, in Exercise 18.1D, you will sort column text by department. To do
this, you will select the columns of text (including the header row), display the Sort
Text dialog box, and then click the *Header row* option in the *My list has* section. When
you click the down-pointing arrow at the right of the *Sort by* option, the drop-down list
displays the options *Employee*, *Department*, and *Hire Date* instead of field numbers. (The
drop-down list will also contain the option *(Field 1)*, which identifies the left margin.)

1. With **C18-E01-MBSortDoc.docx** open, sort text in columns by department by completing the following steps:
   a. Select all eight lines of text set in columns beginning with the row containing the column headings *Employee*, *Department*, and *Hire Date*.
   b. Click the Sort button.
   c. At the Sort Text dialog box, click the *Header row* option in the *My list has* section.
   d. Click the Options button.
   e. At the Sort Options dialog box, make sure the *Separate fields at* option is set at *Tabs* and then click OK to close the dialog box.
   f. At the Sort Text dialog box, click the down-pointing arrow at the right of the *Sort by* option and then click *Department* at the drop-down list.
   g. Click OK.

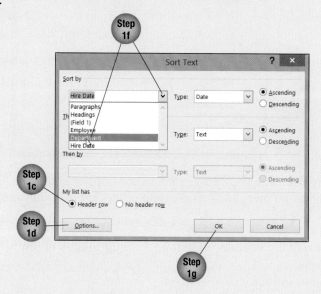

2. With the columns of text still selected, sort by the first column alphabetically by completing the following steps:
   a. Click the Sort button.
   b. At the Sort Text dialog box, click the *Header row* option in the *My list has* section.
   c. Click the down-pointing arrow at the right side of the *Sort by* option and then click *Employee* at the drop-down list.
   d. Click OK.
3. Save **C18-E01-MBSortDoc.docx**.

## Sorting on More Than One Field

Text can be sorted on more than one field. For example, in Exercise 18.1E, you will sort the department entries alphabetically and then sort the employee names alphabetically within the departments. To do this, you will specify the department column in the *Sort by* option and then specify the employee column in the *Then by* option.

1. With **C18-E01-MBSortDoc.docx** open, sort two columns by completing the following steps:

   a. Make sure the eight lines of text set in columns are still selected (including the header row).
   b. Click the Sort button.
   c. At the Sort Text dialog box, click the *Header row* option in the *My list has* section of the dialog box.
   d. Click the down-pointing arrow at the right of the *Sort by* option and then click *Department*.
   e. Click the down-pointing arrow at the right of the *Then by* option and then click *Employee* at the drop-down list.
   f. Click OK.

2. Save **C18-E01-MBSortDoc.docx**.

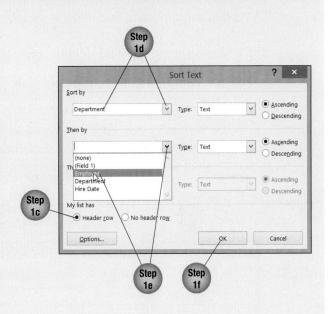

# Sorting Text in Tables

You can sort text in columns within a table in much the same way that you can sort columns of text separated by tabs. If a table contains a header, click the *Header row* option at the Sort dialog box. The Sort Text dialog box becomes the Sort dialog box when you are sorting in a table. If you want to sort only specific cells in a table, select the cells and then complete the sort.

**Sort Text in a Table**
1. Position insertion point in table.
2. Click Sort button.
3. Make any needed changes at Sort dialog box.
4. Click OK.

1. With **C18-E01-MBSortDoc.docx** open, sort text in the first column of the table that displays near the bottom of the page by completing the following steps:
   a. Position the insertion point in any cell in the table.
   b. Click the Sort button.

c. At the Sort dialog box, make sure the *Header row* option is selected in the *My list has* section.

d. Click the down-pointing arrow at the right of the *Sort by* option and then click *Salesperson* at the drop-down list.

e. Click OK.

2. Sort the numbers in the second column in descending order by completing the following steps:

a. Select all of the cells in the table except the cells in the first row.

b. Click the Sort button.

c. At the Sort dialog box, click the down-pointing arrow at the right of the *Sort by* option and then click *Column 2* at the drop-down list.

d. Click *Descending*.

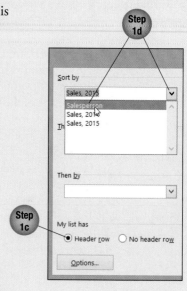

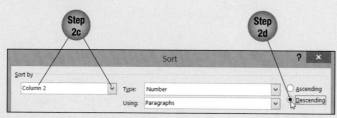

e. Click OK.

3. Save, print, and then close **C18-E01-MBSortDoc.docx**.

## QUICK STEPS

**Sort Records in a Data Source**
1. Click MAILINGS tab.
2. Click Select Recipients button.
3. Click *Use an Existing List* at drop-down list.
4. Double-click desired file.
5. Click Edit Recipient List button.
6. At Mail Merge Recipients dialog box, sort by specific field by clicking field column heading.
7. Click OK.

Select Recipients

Edit Recipient List

# Sorting Records in a Data Source

To sort records in a data source file, click the MAILINGS tab, click the Select Recipients button, and then click *Use an Existing List*. At the Select Data Source dialog box, navigate to the folder that contains the data source file you want to use and then double-click the file. Click the Edit Recipient List button in the Start Mail Merge group on the MAILINGS tab to display the Mail Merge Recipients dialog box, which is shown in Figure 18.3 on the next page with the data for Exercise 18.2A.

Click the field column heading to sort data in ascending order in a specific field. To perform additional sorts, click the down-pointing arrow at the right of the field column heading and then click the desired sort order.

**Figure 18.3 Mail Merge Recipients Dialog Box**

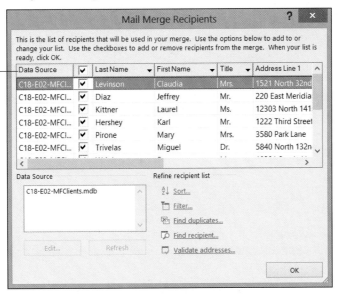

To sort on a specific field, click the appropriate column heading.

---

## Exercise 18.2A  Sorting Data in a Data Source                          Part 1 of 5

1. Make a copy of the **MFClients.mdb** file by completing the following steps:
   a. Press Ctrl + F12 to display the Open dialog box
   b. Make Chapter18 the active folder.
   c. If necessary, change the file type button to *All Files (*.*)*.
   d. Right-click on the *MFClients.mdb* file and then click *Copy* at the shortcut menu.
   e. Position the mouse pointer in a white portion of the Open dialog box Content pane (outside any file name), click the *right* mouse button, and then click *Paste* at the shortcut menu. (This inserts a copy of the file in the dialog box Content pane and names the file **MFClients - Copy.mdb**.)
   f. Right-click on the file name *MFClients - Copy.mdb* and then click *Rename* at the shortcut menu.
   g. Type **C18-E02-MFClients** and then press the Enter key.
   h. Close the Open dialog box.
2. At a blank document, click the MAILINGS tab, click the Start Mail Merge button in the Start Mail Merge group, and then click *Labels* at the drop-down list.

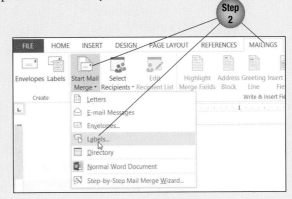

---

3. At the Label Options dialog box, click the down-pointing arrow at the right of the *Label vendors* option and then click *Avery US Letter* at the drop-down list.
4. Scroll down the *Product number* list box, click *5360 Mailing Labels*, and then click OK.

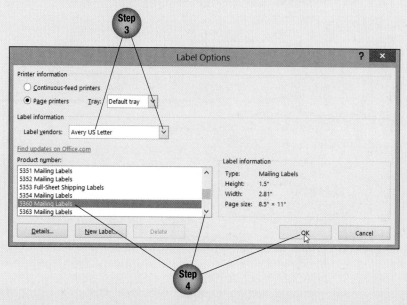

5. Click the Select Recipients button in the Start Mail Merge group and then click *Use an Existing List* at the drop-down list.
6. At the Select Data Source dialog box, navigate to your Chapter18 folder and then double-click the data source file named *C18-E02-MFClients.mdb*.
7. Click the Edit Recipient List button.
8. At the Mail Merge Recipients dialog box, click the *Last Name* column heading. (This sorts the last names in ascending alphabetical order.)
9. Scroll to the right to display the *City* field and then click the *City* column heading.
10. Click OK to close the Mail Merge Recipients dialog box.
11. Save the labels main document and name it *C18-E02-MFLabelsMD*.

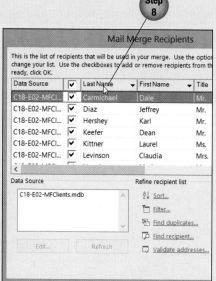

If you want more control over the sort or if you want to sort on more than one field, click the Sort hyperlink located in the *Refine recipient list* section of the Mail Merge Recipients dialog box. Clicking this hyperlink displays the Filter and Sort dialog box with the Sort Records tab selected, as shown in Figure 18.4 on the next page. The options at this dialog box are similar to the options available at the Sort Text (and Sort) dialog box.

**Figure 18.4  Filter and Sort Dialog Box with Sort Records Tab Selected**

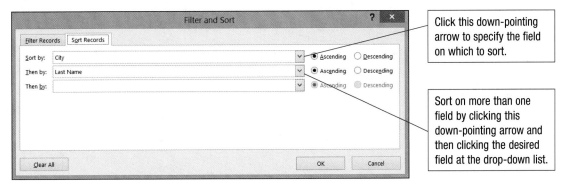

Click this down-pointing arrow to specify the field on which to sort.

Sort on more than one field by clicking this down-pointing arrow and then clicking the desired field at the drop-down list.

## Exercise 18.2B   Refining a Sort

Part 2 of 5

1. With **C18-E02-MFLabelsMD.docx** open, sort records by zip code and then by last name by completing the following steps:
   a. Click the Edit Recipient List button.
   b. At the Mail Merge Recipients dialog box, click the Sort hyperlink located in the *Refine recipient list* section.
   c. At the Filter and Sort dialog box with the Sort Records tab selected, click the down-pointing arrow at the right of the *Sort by* option box and then click *ZIP Code* at the drop-down list. (You will need to scroll down the list to display the *ZIP Code* field.)
   d. Make sure that *Last Name* displays in the *Then by* option box.
   e. Click OK to close the Filter and Sort dialog box.

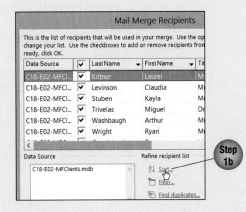

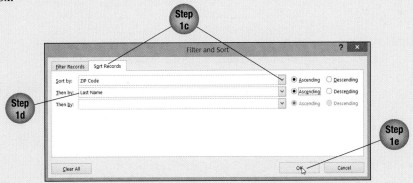

   f. Click OK to close the Mail Merge Recipients dialog box.
2. At the label document, click the Address Block button in the Write & Insert Fields group.
3. At the Insert Address Block dialog box, click OK.
4. Click the Update Labels button in the Write & Insert Fields group.

5. Click the Finish & Merge button in the Finish group and then click *Edit Individual Documents* at the drop-down list.
6. At the Merge to New Document dialog box, make sure that *All* is selected and then click OK.
7. Save the merged labels and name the document **C18-E02-MFLabels-01**.
8. Print and then close **C18-E02-MFLabels-01.docx**.
9. Save **C18-E02-MFLabelsMD.docx**.

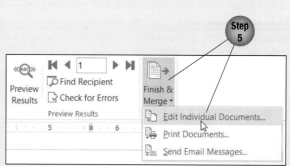

# Selecting Records

If a data source file contains numerous records, you may at some point want to merge only some of those records with the main document. For example, you may want to send a letter to customers who have a specific zip code or live in a particular city.

As you learned in Chapter 16, one method for selecting specific records is to display the Mail Merge Recipients dialog box and then insert or remove check marks from specific records. Using check boxes to select specific records is useful when a data source contains a limited number of records but this selection method may not be practical when a data source contains many records.

For a large data source file, use options at the Filter and Sort dialog box with the Filter Records tab selected, as shown in Figure 18.5. To display this dialog box, click the <u>Filter</u> hyperlink that displays in the *Refine recipient list* section of the Mail Merge Recipients dialog box.

Figure 18.5  **Filter and Sort Dialog Box with Filter Records Tab Selected**

Click this down-pointing arrow to specify the field on which to select.

Use the *Comparison* and *Compare to* options to specify records matching certain criteria.

| Filter and Sort | ? | × |
|---|---|---|

| Filter Records | Sort Records |
|---|---|

| Field: | Comparison: | Compare to: |
|---|---|---|

Clear All    OK    Cancel

When you select a field from the *Field* drop-down list, Word automatically inserts *Equal to* in the *Comparison* option box. To make other comparisons, click the down-pointing arrow to the right of the *Comparison* option box. A drop-down list displays with these additional options: *Not equal to, Less than, Greater than, Less than or equal, Greater than or equal, Is blank,* and *Is not blank.* Use one of these options to create a select equation.

## Exercise 18.2C  Selecting Records
Part 3 of 5

1. With **C18-E02-MFLabelsMD.docx** open, find records with a zip code greater than *40400* by completing the following steps:
   a. Click the Edit Recipient List button.
   b. At the Mail Merge Recipients dialog box, click the <u>Filter</u> hyperlink in the *Refine recipient list* section.
   c. At the Filter and Sort dialog box, click the down-pointing arrow at the right of the *Field* option and then click *ZIP Code* at the drop-down list. (You will need to scroll down the list to display *ZIP Code.*) Notice that when *ZIP Code* is inserted in the *Field* option box, *Equal to* is inserted in the *Comparison* option box and the insertion point is positioned in the *Compare to* text box.
   d. Click the down-pointing arrow at the right of the *Comparison* option box and then click *Greater than* at the drop-down list.
   e. Type **40400** in the *Compare to* text box.
   f. Click OK to close the Filter and Sort dialog box.

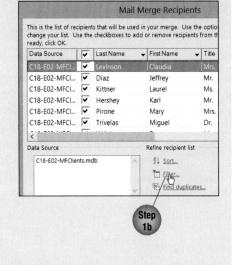

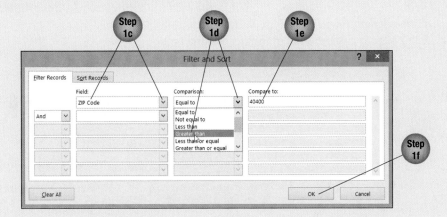

   g. Click OK to close the Mail Merge Recipients dialog box.
2. At the label document, click the Finish & Merge button in the Finish group and then click *Edit Individual Documents* at the drop-down list.
3. At the Merge to New Document dialog box, make sure that *All* is selected and then click OK.
4. Save the merged labels and name the document **C18-E02-MFLabels-02**.
5. Print and then close **C18-E02-MFLabels-02.docx**.
6. Save **C18-E02-MFLabelsMD.docx**.

When you select a field from the *Field* option box, Word automatically inserts *And* in the first box at the left side of the dialog box. You can change this to *Or* if needed. With the *And* and *Or* options, you can specify more than one condition for selecting records. For example, in Exercise 18.2D, you will select all of the records for clients living in the city of Paris or Winchester. If the data source file contained another field, such as a specific financial plan for each customer, you could select all customers in a specific city who subscribe to a specific financial plan. For this situation, you would use the *And* option.

If you want to clear the current options at the Filter and Sort dialog box, with the Filter Records tab selected, click the Clear All button. This clears all of the text from text boxes and leaves the dialog box on the screen. Click the Cancel button if you want to close the Filter and Sort dialog box without specifying any records.

---

## Exercise 18.2D  Selecting Records with Specific Cities                    Part 4 of 5

1. With **C18-E02-MFLabelsMD.docx** open, find all of the records for recipients who live in the city of Paris or Winchester by completing the following steps:
   a. Click the Edit Recipient List button.
   b. At the Mail Merge Recipients dialog box, click the <u>Filter</u> hyperlink in the *Refine recipient list* section of the dialog box.
   c. At the Filter and Sort dialog box, click the Clear All button that displays in the lower left corner.
   d. Click the down-pointing arrow at the right of the *Field* option and then click *City* at the drop-down list. (You will need to scroll down the list to display this field.)
   e. Type **Paris** in the *Compare to* text box.
   f. Click the down-pointing arrow to the right of the first option box containing the word *And* (at the left side of the dialog box) and then click *Or* at the drop-down list.
   g. Click the down-pointing arrow at the right of the second *Field* option box and then click *City* at the drop-down list. (You will need to scroll down the list to display this field.)
   h. With the insertion point positioned in the second *Compare to* text box (the one below the box containing *Paris*), type **Winchester**.
   i. Click OK to close the Filter and Sort dialog box.

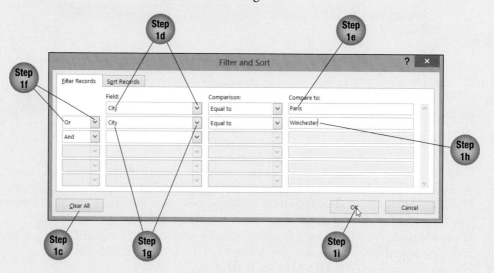

   j. Click OK to close the Mail Merge Recipients dialog box.

2. At the label document, click the Finish & Merge button in the Finish group and then click *Edit Individual Documents* at the drop-down list.
3. At the Merge to New Document dialog box, make sure that *All* is selected and then click OK.
4. Save the merged labels and name the document **C18-E02-MFLabels-03**.
5. Print and then close **C18-E02-MFLabels-03.docx**.
6. Save **C18-E02-MFLabelsMD.docx**.

# Finding Records

The <u>Find duplicates</u> and <u>Find recipient</u> hyperlinks in the *Refine recipient list* section of the Mail Merge Recipients dialog box can be useful for finding records in an extensive data source file. Use the <u>Find duplicates</u> hyperlink to locate duplicate records that appear in the data source file. Use the <u>Find recipient</u> hyperlink to find a record or records that meet a specific criterion. The <u>Validate addresses</u> hyperlink in the *Refine recipient list* section is available only if you have installed address validation software. (Visit the Microsoft Office website to find more information about address validation software.)

When you click the <u>Find duplicates</u> hyperlink, any duplicate records display in the Find Duplicates dialog box. At this dialog box, remove the check mark from the duplicate record that you do not want to include in the merge. To find a specific record in a data source file, click the <u>Find recipient</u> hyperlink. At the Find Entry dialog box, type the text that you want to find and then click the Find Next button. Continue clicking the Find Next button until a message displays telling you that there are no more entries that contain the text you typed. By default, Word searches for the specified text in all of the fields of all of the records in the data source file. You can limit the search by clicking the down-pointing arrow at the right of the *This field* option box and then clicking the specific field. Type the text to find in the *Find* text box and then click OK.

**Exercise 18.2E**   **Finding Records**                                    **Part 5 of 5**

1. With **C18-E02-MFLabelsMD.docx** open, remove the filter by completing the following steps:
   a. Click the Edit Recipient List button.
   b. At the Mail Merge Recipients dialog box, click the <u>Filter</u> hyperlink in the *Refine recipient list* section.
   c. At the Filter and Sort dialog box, click the Clear All button that displays in the lower left corner.
   d. Click OK to close the Filter and Sort dialog box.
   e. At the Mail Merge Recipients dialog box, click the <u>Find duplicates</u> hyperlink in the *Refine recipient list* section.
   f. At the Find Duplicates dialog box, which indicates that there are no duplicate items, click OK.

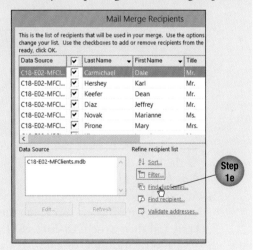

2. Find all records containing the zip code *40511* by completing the following steps:

   a. At the Mail Merge Recipients dialog box, click the <u>Find recipient</u> hyperlink in the *Refine recipient list* section.

   b. At the Find Entry dialog box, click the down-pointing arrow at the right of the *This field* option box and then click *ZIP Code* at the drop-down list. (You will need to scroll down the list to display this option.)

   c. Click in the *Find* text box and then type **40511**.

   d. Click the Find Next button.

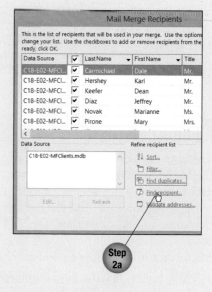

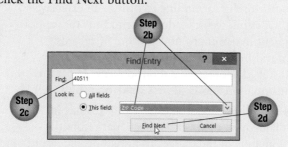

   e. When the first record is selected containing the zip code *40511*, click the Find Next button.

   f. Continue clicking the Find Next button until a message displays telling you that there are no more entries that contain the text you typed. At this message, click OK.

   g. Click the Cancel button to close the Find Entry dialog box.

3. Select and then merge records of those clients with a zip code of *40511* by completing the following steps:

   a. At the Mail Merge Recipients dialog box, click the <u>Filter</u> hyperlink in the *Refine recipient list* section of the dialog box.

   b. At the Filter and Sort dialog box, click the down-pointing arrow at the right of the *Field* option and then click *ZIP Code* at the drop-down list. (You will need to scroll down the list to display this field.)

   c. Type **40511** in the *Compare to* text box.

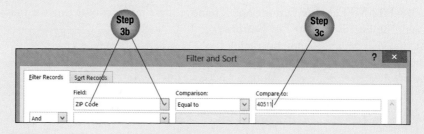

   d. Click OK to close the Filter and Sort dialog box.

   e. Click OK to close the Mail Merge Recipients dialog box.

4. At the label document, click the Finish & Merge button in the Finish group and then click *Edit Individual Documents* at the drop-down list.

5. At the Merge to New Document dialog box, make sure that *All* is selected and then click OK.

6. Save the merged labels and name the document **C18-E02-MFLabels-04**.

7. Print and then close **C18-E02-MFLabels-04.docx**.

8. Save and then close **C18-E02-MFLabelsMD.docx**.

# Finding and Replacing Formatting and Special Characters and Using Wildcard Characters

In Chapter 7, you used the Navigation pane and the Find and Replace dialog box with the Find tab selected to find specific text in a document. You also used the Find and Replace dialog box with the Replace tab selected to find specific text and replace it with other text. In addition to finding and replacing text, you can find and replace specific formatting and special characters and find or find and replace text using wildcard characters.

## Finding and Replacing Formatting

To find formatting in a document, display the Find and Replace dialog box with the Find tab selected, click the More button to expand the dialog box, and then click the Format button that displays near the bottom of the dialog box. At the drop-down list that displays, identify the type of formatting you want to find. The formatting that you specify displays below the *Find what* text box.

Complete similar steps to find formatting in a document and replace it with other formatting. Display the Find and Replace dialog box with the Replace tab selected and then click the More button to expand the dialog box. With the insertion point positioned in the *Find what* text box, click the Format button and then specify the formatting that you want to find. Click in the *Replace with* text box, click the Format button, and then specify the replacement formatting.

---

## Exercise 18.3   Finding and Replacing Formatting                        Part 1 of 1

1. Open **LeaseAgrmnt.docx** and save the document with the name **C18-E03-LeaseAgrmnt.docx**.
2. Find text set in 11-point Calibri with bold formatting and the Dark Red color applied and replace it with text set in 12-point Cambria with bold formatting and the Dark Blue color applied by completing the following steps:
   a. Click the Replace button in the Editing group on the HOME tab.
   b. At the Find and Replace dialog box, make sure the *Find what* and *Replace with* text boxes are empty.
   c. Click the More button. (If a check mark displays in any of the check boxes, click the option to remove the check mark.)
   d. With the insertion point positioned in the *Find what* text box, click the Format button located near the bottom of the dialog box and then click *Font* at the drop-down list.
   e. At the Find Font dialog box, click *Calibri* in the *Font* list box, *Bold* in the *Font style* list box, and *11* in the *Size* list box and then change the font color to Dark Red (first color option in *Standard Colors* section).

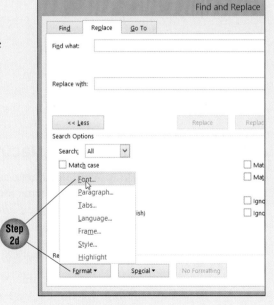

Step 2d

---

f.  Click OK to close the Find Font dialog box.
g.  At the Find and Replace dialog box, click in the *Replace with* text box.
h.  Click the Format button located near the bottom of the dialog box and then click *Font* at the drop-down list.
i.  At the Replace Font dialog box, click *Cambria* in the *Font* list box, *Bold* in the *Font style* list box, and *12* in the *Size* list box and then change the font color to Dark Blue (ninth color option in the *Standard Colors* section).
j.  Click OK to close the Replace Font dialog box.

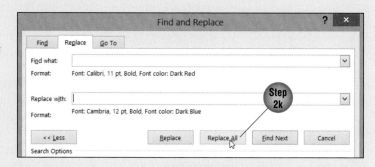

k.  At the Find and Replace dialog box, click the Replace All button.
l.  At the message telling you that the search of the document is complete and 13 replacements were made, click OK.

3.  Clear formatting from the Find and Replace dialog box by completing the following steps:

a.  Click in the *Find what* text box and then click the No Formatting button.
b.  Click in the *Replace with* text box and then click the No Formatting button.
c.  Click the Less button and then close the Find and Replace dialog box.

4.  Save, print, and then close **C18-E03-LeaseAgrmnt. docx**.

## Finding and Replacing Body and Heading Fonts

By default, a Word document has the Office theme applied, which applies theme colors, fonts, and effects. The theme fonts include a body font and heading font. The default settings for theme fonts are *Calibri (Body)* and *Calibri Light (Headings)*. These fonts display at the beginning of the Font button drop-down gallery. If you have applied a different theme, the body and heading fonts will be different and can be viewed at the Font button drop-down gallery.

You can search a document for a body or heading font and then replace it with a different font. To do this, display the Find and Replace dialog box with the Replace tab selected. Expand the dialog box, click the Format button, and then click *Font* at the

drop-down list. At the Find Font dialog box, scroll up the *Font* list box and then click
*+Body* if you are searching for the body font or click *+Headings* if you are searching
for the heading font. Click in the *Replace with* text box and then complete the steps to
insert the replacement font.

## Exercise 18.4A  Finding and Replacing Body and Heading Fonts     Part 1 of 2

1. Open **CompanyInfo.docx** and save the document with the name **C18-E04-CompanyInfo**.
2. This document contains text formatted with the default font *Calibri (Body)* and text
   formatted with the default font *Calibri Light (Headings)* (text with Heading 1 and Heading 2
   styles applied). Search for the *+Body* font and replace it with Constantia by completing the
   following steps:
   a.  Click the Replace button in the Editing group on the HOME tab.
   b.  At the Find and Replace dialog box, click the More button. (If a check mark displays in
       any of the check boxes, click the option to remove the check mark.)
   c.  Clear text and formatting from the *Find what* and *Replace with* text box. (See Exercise
       18.3, Steps 3a and 3b.)
   d.  With the insertion point positioned in the *Find what* text box, click the Format button
       located near the bottom of the dialog box and then click *Font* at the drop-down list.
   e.  At the Find Font dialog box, scroll up the *Font* list box and then click *+Body*.

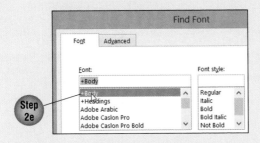

   f.  Click OK to close the Find Font dialog box.
   g.  At the Find and Replace dialog box, click in the *Replace with* text box.
   h.  Click the Format button located near the bottom of the dialog box and then click *Font*
       at the drop-down list.
   i.  At the Replace Font dialog box, scroll down the *Font* list box and then click *Constantia*.
   j.  Click OK to close the Replace Font dialog box.
   k.  At the Find and Replace dialog box, click the Replace All button.
   l.  At the message telling you that the search of the document is complete and 10
       replacements were made, click OK.
3. With the Find and Replace dialog box open, search for the *+Headings* font and replace it with
   Corbel and then change the paragraph alignment to center by completing the following steps:
   a.  With the insertion point positioned in the *Find what* text box, click the No Formatting
       button that displays near the bottom of the dialog box.
   b.  Click the Format button located near the bottom of the dialog box and then click *Font*
       at the drop-down list.
   c.  At the Find Font dialog box, click *+Headings* in the *Font* list box.
   d.  Click OK to close the Find Font dialog box.
   e.  At the Find and Replace dialog box, click in the *Replace with* text box.
   f.  Click the No Formatting button that displays near the bottom of the dialog box.

g. Click the Format button located near the bottom of the dialog box and then click *Font* at the drop-down list.
h. At the Replace Font dialog box, scroll down the *Font* list box and then click *Corbel*.
i. Click OK to close the Replace Font dialog box.
j. At the Find and Replace dialog box, click the Format button and then click *Paragraph* at the drop-down list.

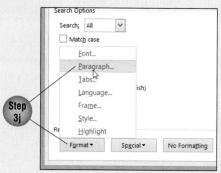

k. At the Replace Paragraph dialog box, click the down-pointing arrow at the right side of the *Alignment* option box and then click *Centered* at the drop-down list.

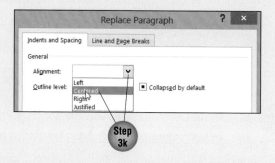

l. Click OK to close the Replace Paragraph dialog box.
m. Click the Replace All button.
n. At the message telling you that the search of the document is complete and 10 replacements were made, click OK.
4. Click the Less button and then close the Find and Replace dialog box.
5. Scroll through the document and notice that the text with the Heading 1 style and Heading 2 style applied are now set in Corbel and centered.
6. Save **C18-E04-CompanyInfo.docx**.

# Finding and Replacing Special Characters

You can find or find and replace special characters in a document. To see a list of the special characters you can search for in a document, display the Find and Replace dialog box with the Find or Replace tab selected, expand the dialog box, and then click the Special button. This displays a pop-up list similar to the one shown in Figure 18.6.

**Figure 18.6** **Special Button Pop-up List**

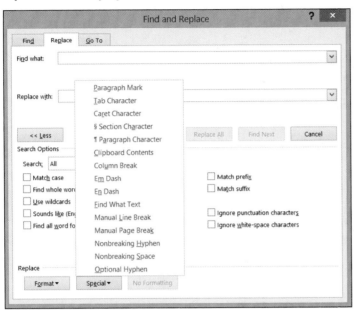

Click a special character in the pop-up list and a code representing the character is inserted into the text box where the insertion point is positioned. For example, with the insertion point positioned in the *Find what* text box, clicking *Paragraph Mark* at the Special button pop-up list inserts the code ^p in the text box. If you know the specific code for a character, you can type the code directly in the *Find what* or *Replace with* text box.

---

**Exercise 18.4B**   Finding and Replacing Special Characters          Part 2 of 2

1. With **C18-E04-CompanyInfo.docx** open, search for and delete all of the section breaks by completing the following steps:
   a. Click the Replace button in the Editing group on the HOME tab.
   b. At the Find and Replace dialog box, click the More button.
   c. With the insertion point positioned in the *Find what* text box, delete any text in the text box and then click the No Formatting button to remove any formatting.
   d. Click the Special button that displays near the bottom of the dialog box.

e. At the pop-up list, click *Section Break*. (This inserts ^b in the *Find what* text box.)

f. Click in the *Replace with* text box, delete any text in the text box, and then click the No Formatting button to remove any formatting. (The text box must be empty because you want to replace the section breaks with nothing.)

g. Click the Replace All button.

h. At the message telling you that 2 replacements were made, click OK.

2. With the expanded Find and Replace dialog box open, find all occurrences of two hyphens and replace them with an em dash by completing the following steps:

a. With ^b selected in the *Find what* text box, type -- (two hyphens).

b. Press the Tab key to move the insertion point to the *Replace with* text box.

c. Click the Special button located near the bottom of the dialog box and then click *Em Dash* at the pop-up list.

d. Click the Replace All button.

e. At the message telling you that the search of the document is complete and 3 replacements were made, click OK.

3. Search for en dashes and replace them with regular hyphens by completing the following steps:

a. With -- selected in the *Find what* text box, click the Special button and then click *En Dash* at the pop-up list.

b. Press the Tab key and then type - (a hyphen) in the *Replace with* text box.

c. Click the Replace All button.

d. At the message telling you that 11 replacements were made, click OK.

e. Click the Less button.

f. Close the Find and Replace dialog box.

4. Save, print, and then close **C18-E04-CompanyInfo.docx**.

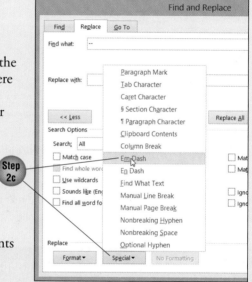

### Using Wildcards

The expanded Find and Replace dialog box contains a *Use wildcards* check box. Insert a check mark in this check box if you want to use wildcard characters in a search to find or find and replace data. For example, if you want to find the company name *Hansen Products* and think it may also appear in the document as *Hanson Products*, you can find both spellings by typing *Hans?n* in the *Find what* text box. Word will find *Hansen* and *Hanson* if the *Use wildcards* check box contains a check mark. If the *Use wildcards* check box does not contain a check mark, Word will try to find the exact spelling *Hans?n* and not find either spelling in the document.

Table 18.2 on the next page identifies some common wildcard characters along with the functions they perform. For additional wildcard characters, refer to Word help.

**Table 18.2 Wildcard Characters**

| Wildcard character | Function |
|---|---|
| * | Indicates any characters. For example, type **le\*s** and Word finds *less, leases,* and *letters.* |
| ? | Indicates one character. For example, type **gr?y** and Word finds *gray* and *grey.* |
| @ | Indicates any occurrence of the previous character. For example, type **cho@se** and Word finds *chose* and *choose.* |
| < | Indicates the beginning of a word. For example, type **<(med)** and Word finds *medical, medicine,* and *media.* |
| > | Indicates the ending of a word. For example, type **(tion)>** and Word finds *election, deduction,* and *education.* |

## Exercise 18.5   Finding and Finding and Replacing Using a Wildcard Character   Part 1 of 1

1. Open **ComLease.docx** and save the document with the name **C18-E05-ComLease**.
2. Use a wildcard character to search for words beginning with *leas* by completing the following steps:
   a. Click the Find button arrow in the Editing group on the HOME tab and then click *Advanced Find* at the drop-down list.
   b. At the Find and Replace dialog box, make sure that the *Find what* text box is empty and no formatting displays below the text box.
   c. Click the More button.
   d. Click the *Use wildcards* check box to insert a check mark.
   e. With the insertion point positioned in the *Find what* text box, type **<(leas)**.

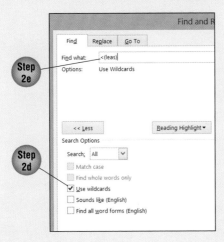

   f. Click the Find Next button to find the first occurrence of a word that begins with *leas.*
   g. Click the Find Next button four more times.
   h. Press the Esc key to end the find and remove the Find and Replace dialog box from the screen.

3. The name *Arigalason* is spelled a variety of ways in the document. Use a wildcard character to search for all of the versions of the name and replace them with the correct spelling by completing the following steps:

   a. Press Ctrl + Home to move the insertion point to the beginning of the document.

   b. Click the Replace button in the Editing group on the HOME tab.

   c. At the Find and Replace dialog box, delete the text in the *Find what* text box and then type **Ar?galas?n**.

   d. Make sure that the dialog box is expanded and the *Use wildcards* check box contains a check mark.

   e. Press the Tab key.

   f. Type **Arigalason** (the correct spelling) in the *Replace with* text box.

   g. Click the Replace All button.

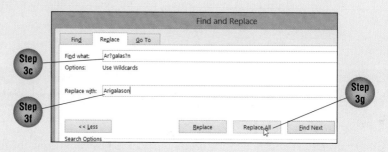

   h. At the message telling you that 23 replacements were made, click OK.

4. Close the Find and Replace dialog box.

5. Save, print, and then close **C18-E05-ComLease.docx**.

# Chapter *Summary*

➤ Word is a word processing program that includes some basic database functions for alphabetizing information, arranging numbers numerically, and selecting specific records from a data source.

➤ You can sort text in paragraphs, columns, and tables. You can also sort records in a data source file and select specific records for merging with a main document.

➤ Word can perform three types of sorts: text, number, and date.

➤ Unless specific text is selected, Word sorts text in the entire document.

➤ Use the Sort button in the Paragraph group on the HOME tab to sort text in paragraphs, columns, and tables.

➤ The *Sort by* option at the Sort Text dialog box has a default setting of *Paragraphs*. This default setting changes depending on the text in the document.

➤ Click the Options button in the Sort Text dialog box to display the Sort Options dialog box. Use the *Separate fields at* section to specify the character that divides the text to be sorted.

➤ To sort text in columns, the text must be separated with tabs. When Word sorts text set in columns, it considers the left margin to be *Field 1*, the first column to be *Field 2*, and so on.

➤ Use the *Header row* option in the *My list has* option in the Sort Text dialog box to sort all of the text in columns except the first row.

➤ You can sort on more than one field with the *Sort by* and *Then by* options at the Sort dialog box.

➤ You can sort text in the columns of a table much the same way that you sort columns of text. The Sort Text dialog box becomes the Sort dialog box when you sort in a table.

➤ Sort the records in a data source file at the Mail Merge Recipients dialog box by clicking the column heading. You can also sort by clicking the <u>Sort</u> hyperlink in the *Refine recipient list* section of the Mail Merge Recipients dialog box. This displays the Filter and Sort dialog box with the Sort Records tab selected.

➤ Select specific records in a data source file by inserting or removing check marks from the check boxes preceding those records or with options at the Filter and Sort dialog box with the Filter Records tab selected. Display this dialog box by clicking the <u>Filter</u> hyperlink that displays in the *Refine recipient list* section.

➤ Use the *Comparison* option box in the Filter and Sort dialog box to refine your search to records that meet specific criteria.

➤ Use the <u>Find duplicates</u> hyperlink in the *Refine recipient list* section of the Mail Merge Recipients dialog box to find duplicate records in a data source file, and use the <u>Find recipient</u> hyperlink to search for records that match a specific criterion.

➤ Use the Format button at the expanded Find and Replace dialog box to specify formatting that you want to find or formatting that you want to find and replace with other formatting.

➤ By default, Word applies the Office theme fonts to a document, which includes a body font and heading font. To find a body or heading font, display the expanded Find and Replace dialog box, click the Format button, and then click *Font* at the drop-down-list. At the Find Font dialog box, scroll up the *Font* list box and then click *+Body* if you are searching for the body font or click *+Headings* if you are searching for the heading font.

➤ You can find or find and replace special characters in a document. Display special characters by clicking the Special button at the expanded Find and Replace dialog box.

➤ Wildcard characters can be used to find text in a document. To use wildcard characters in a find or find and replace, display the expanded Find and Replace dialog box and then click the *Use wildcards* check box to insert a check mark.

# Commands *Review*

| FEATURE | RIBBON TAB, GROUP | BUTTON, OPTION |
|---|---|---|
| Filter and Sort dialog box with Select Records tab selected | MAILINGS, Start Mail Merge | , *Filter* |
| Filter and Sort dialog box with Sort Records tab selected | MAILINGS, Start Mail Merge | , *Sort* |
| Find and Replace dialog box Find tab selected | HOME, Editing | , *Advanced Find* |
| Find and Replace dialog box with Replace tab selected | HOME, Editing | ab↨ac |
| Sort Options dialog box | HOME, Paragraph | A↓Z , *Options* |
| Sort Text dialog box | HOME, Paragraph | A↓Z |

# Key Points *Review*

**Completion:** In the space provided at the right, indicate the correct term, symbol, or command.

1. You can sort text in paragraphs, columns, or these. _____

2. The three types of sorts you can perform in a document include text, number, and this. _____

3. The Sort button is located in this group on the HOME tab. _____

4. Click the Sort button with paragraphs of text selected and this dialog box displays. _____

5. This is the default setting for the *Separate fields at* option at the Sort Options dialog box. _____

6. When you sort text in columns, Word considers the left margin to be this field number. _____

7. If you select column text, including the column headings, click this option in the *My list has* section of the Sort Text dialog box. _____

8. With the insertion point positioned in a table, clicking the Sort button displays this dialog box. _____

9. Click this at the Mail Merge Recipients dialog box to sort data in a specific column. _____

10. Click this hyperlink at the Mail Merge Recipients dialog box and the Filter and Sort dialog box displays with the Sort Records tab selected. _____

11. Click this button at the Filter and Sort dialog box with the Filter Records tab selected to clear any text from text boxes. _____

12. Click this hyperlink in the Mail Merge Recipients dialog box to search for records that match a specific criterion. _____

13. Display the Find Font dialog box by clicking this button at the expanded Find and Replace dialog box and then clicking *Font* at the drop-down list.

_____

14. To find the body font in a document, click this option in the *Font* list box at the Find Font dialog box.

_____

15. Display a list of characters you can search for in a document by clicking this button at the Find and Replace dialog box.

_____

16. Use this wildcard character to indicate a single character in a search to find or find and replace data.

_____

# Chapter Assessments

## Applying Your Skills

Demonstrate your knowledge of features learned in this chapter by completing the following assessments.

### Assessment 18.1    Sort Text in a Company Document

1. Open **SFSortDoc.docx** and save the document with the name **C18-A01-SFSortDoc**.
2. Sort the nine lines of text below the heading *Executive Team* in ascending alphabetical order by last name.
3. Select the columns of text below the heading *New Employees* and then sort the columns alphabetically by last name in the first column.
4. Sort by the *Salesperson* column in the table located near the bottom of the document in ascending order.
5. Save, print, and then close **C18-A01-SFSortDoc.docx**.

### Assessment 18.2    Sort Text in a Health Services Document

1. Open **RHSSortDoc.docx** and save the document with the name **C18-A02-RHSSortDoc**.
2. Sort the five lines of text below the title *RHODES HEALTH SERVICES* by clinic name in ascending order.
3. Sort the columns of text below the heading *EXECUTIVE TEAM* by last name in ascending order.
4. Sort by the column *Second Half Expenses* in the table located near the bottom of the document in descending order.
5. Save, print, and then close **C18-A02-RHSSortDoc.docx**.

### Assessment 18.3    Create Labels for Key Life Customers

1. Make a copy of the **KLCustomers.mdb** file by completing the following steps:
   a. Display the Open dialog box and make Chapter18 the active folder.
   b. If necessary, change the file type button to *All Files (\*.\*)*.
   c. Right-click on the **KLCustomers.mdb** file and then click *Copy* at the shortcut menu.
   d. Position the mouse pointer in a white portion of the Open dialog box Content pane (outside any file name), click the *right* mouse button, and then click *Paste* at the shortcut menu. (This inserts a copy of the file in the dialog box Content pane and names the file **KLCustomers - Copy.mdb**.)

e. Right-click on the file name *KLCustomers - Copy.mdb* and rename it **C18-A03-KLCustomersDS** and then press the Enter key.

f. Close the Open dialog box.

2. At a blank document, use the Mail Merge feature to create mailing labels with the Avery US Letter 5360 label product using the existing data source **C18-A03-KLCustomersDS.mdb**.

3. Display the Mail Merge Recipients dialog box and sort the records first by zip code in ascending order and then by last name in ascending order.

4. Complete the merge and then save the label document with the name **C18-A03-KLLabels**.

5. Print and then close **C18-A03-KLLabels.docx**.

6. Close the label main document without saving it.

### Assessment 18.4    Create Labels for Key Life Boston Customers

1. At a blank document, use the Mail Merge feature to create mailing labels with the Avery US Letter 5360 label product. Use the existing data source **C18-A03-KLCustomersDS.mdb** for the labels.

2. Display the Mail Merge Recipients dialog box, display the Filter and Sort dialog box with the Filter Records tab selected, and then select those customers living in Boston.

3. Complete the merge and then save the labels document with the name **C18-A04-KLLabelsBoston**.

4. Print and then close **C18-A04-KLLabelsBoston.docx**.

5. Close the label main document without saving it.

### Assessment 18.5    Finding and Replacing Formatting and Special Characters and Using Wildcard Characters

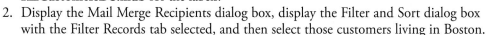

1. Open **EmpGuide.docx** and save the document with the name **C18-A05-EmpGuide**.

2. Find text set in the *+Body* font and replace with Constantia.

3. Find text set in Candara with bold formatting applied and replace it with Corbel with bold formatting applied.

4. Find all of the section breaks in the document and replace them with nothing.

5. Find all of the em dashes and replace each dash with a colon (:) followed by a space (a press of the spacebar).

6. Using a wildcard character, find all of the occurrences of *Ne?land?Davis* and replace them with *Newland-Davis*.

7. Save, print, and then close **C18-A05-EmpGuide.docx**.

# Expanding Your Skills

Explore additional feature options or use Help to learn a new skill in creating this document.

### Assessment 18.6    Create Name Tag Labels for Contacts in New York

1. At a blank document, click the MAILINGS tab, click the Start Mail Merge button, and then click *Labels* at the drop-down list.

2. At the Label Options dialog box, make sure the *Label vendors* option displays with *Avery US Letter*, click *45395 EcoFriendly Name Badges* in the list box (scroll up or down the list box to find this label), and then click OK.

3. Click the Select Recipients button, and then click *Type a New List* at the drop-down list.

4. Create and customize a data source file so it appears as shown in Figure 18.7 on the next page. Type the information in the appropriate fields for the 14 records shown in the figure.

5. Name the data source file **ContactsDS**.

6. At the main document, insert the fields in the first label as shown below:

    «First_Name» «Last_Name»
    «Company_Name»
    «State»
    «Work_Phone»

7. Update the labels.
8. Edit **ContactsDS.mdb** and then sort by company name in ascending order and filter by the state of New York.
9. Merge the name tag labels.
10. With the name tag labels displayed, complete the following steps:
    a. Click in any label in the document and then click the TABLE TOOLS LAYOUT tab.
    b. Select the entire table. ***Hint: Use the Select button on the TABLE TOOLS LAYOUT tab.***
    c. Click the TABLE TOOLS DESIGN tab and then apply the Grid Table 3 - Accent 3 table style.
    d. Click the TABLE TOOLS LAYOUT tab and then change the alignment to center aligned.
    e. With the table selected, change the font to 16-point Lucida Calligraphy with bold formatting applied.
11. Save the name tag label document and name it **C18-A06-NYNameTags**.
12. Print and then close **C18-A06-NYNameTags.docx**.
13. Close the name tag label main document without saving it.

**Figure 18.7  Assessment 18.6**

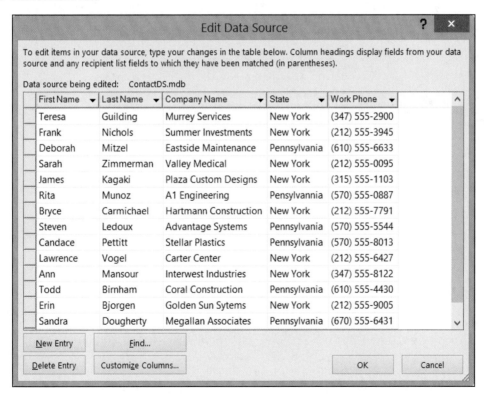

# Achieving Signature Status

Take your skills to the next level by completing this more challenging assessment.

## Assessment 18.7    Create a Contacts Table

1. Open **Contacts.docx** and save the document with the name **C18-A07-Contacts**.
2. Sort the text in ascending order by state and then by company name.
3. After sorting the text, select it and then convert it to a table. Split the table as shown in Figure 18.8.
4. Apply formatting so your document and tables display as shown in Figure 18.8.
5. Save, print, and then close **C18-A07-Contacts.docx**.

**Figure 18.8   Assessment 18.7**

### CORPORATE CONTACTS

| Company | Contact | State | Telephone |
|---|---|---|---|
| Carter Center | Lawrence Vogel | New York | (212) 555-6427 |
| Golden Sun Systems | Erin Bjorgen | New York | (212) 555-9005 |
| Hartmann Construction | Bryce Carmichael | New York | (212) 555-7791 |
| Interwest Industries | Ann Mansour | New York | (347) 555-8122 |
| Murrey Services | Teresa Guilding | New York | (347) 555-2900 |
| Plaza Custom Designs | James Kagaki | New York | (315) 555-1103 |
| Summer Investments | Frank Nichols | New York | (212) 555-3945 |
| Valley Medical | Sarah Zimmerman | New York | (212) 555-0095 |

| Company | Contact | State | Telephone |
|---|---|---|---|
| A1 Engineering | Rita Munez | Pennsylvania | (570) 555-0887 |
| Adventage Systems | Steven Ledoux | Pennsylvania | (570) 555-5544 |
| Coral Construction | Todd Birnham | Pennsylvania | (610) 555-4430 |
| Eastside Maintenance | Deborah Mitzel | Pennsylvania | (610) 555-6633 |
| Stellar Plastics | Candace Petit | Pennsylvania | (570) 555-8013 |

Tutorial 19.1
Customizing Page Numbers
Tutorial 19.2
Customizing Headers and Footers
Tutorial 19.3
Printing Sections of a Document
Tutorial 19.4
Keeping Text Together

# Chapter 19

# Managing Page Numbers, Headers, and Footers

## Performance Objectives

Upon successful completion of Chapter 19, you will be able to:

- Insert, format, and remove customized page numbers
- Insert, format, edit, and remove customized headers and footers
- Print specific pages or sections of a document
- Control page breaks to keep related text together

As you learned in Chapter 7, Word provides predesigned page numbers, headers, and footers that you can insert into a document. You can customize page numbers with options at the Page Number Format dialog box, and create and edit your own headers and footers with options on the HEADER & FOOTER TOOLS DESIGN tab. In this chapter, you will learn how to customize page numbers, create and customize headers and footers, print specific pages or sections of a document, and control page breaks to improve readability and appearance.

*Note: Before beginning computer exercises for this chapter, copy to your storage medium the Chapter19 folder from the CD that accompanies this textbook and then make Chapter19 the active folder.*

In this chapter, students will produce the following documents:

Exercise 19.1. C19-E01-CompAccess.docx
Exercise 19.2. C19-E02-ResumeReport.docx
Exercise 19.3. C19-E03-EmpHandbook.docx
Exercise 19.4. C19-E04-EmpHandbook.docx
Exercise 19.5. C19-E05-EmpHandbook.docx
Exercise 19.6. C19-E06-EmpHandbook.docx
Exercise 19.7. C19-E07-OnlineShop.docx

Model answers for these exercises are shown on the following pages.

**Exercise 19.1**

C19-E01-CompAccess.docx

## TABLE OF CONTENTS

i

## UNAUTHORIZED ACCESS

Like uncharted wilderness, the Internet lacks borders. This inherent openness is what makes the Internet so valuable and yet so vulnerable. Over its short life, the Internet has grown so quickly that the legal system has not been able to keep pace. The security risks posed by networks and the Internet can be grouped into three categories: unauthorized access, information theft, and denial of service.

Hackers, individuals who gain access to computers and networks illegally, are responsible for most cases of unauthorized access. Hackers tend to exploit sites and programs that have poor security measures in place. However, they also gain access to more challenging sites by using sophisticated programs and strategies. Many hackers claim they hack merely because they like the challenge of trying to defeat security measures. They rarely have a more malicious motive, and they generally do not aim to destroy or damage the sites that they invade. In fact, hackers dislike being identified with those who seek to cause damage. They refer to hackers with malicious or criminal intent as *crackers*.

### User IDs and Passwords

To gain entry over the Internet to a secure computer system, most hackers focus on finding a working user ID and password combination. User IDs are easy to come by and are generally not secure information. Sending an email, for example, displays the sender's user ID in the return address, making it very public. The only missing element is the password. Hackers know from experience which passwords are common; they have programs that generate thousands of likely passwords and they try them systematically over a period of hours or days.

### System Backdoors

Programmers can sometimes inadvertently aid hackers by providing unintentional entrance to networks and information systems. One such unintentional entrance is a system "backdoor," which is a user ID and password that provides the highest level of authorization. Programmers innocently create a "backdoor" in the early days of system development to allow other programmers and team members to access the system to fix problems. Through negligence or by design, the user ID and password are sometimes left behind in the final version of the system. People who know about them can then enter the system, bypassing the security perhaps years later, when the backdoor has been forgotten.

1

## Spoofing

A sophisticated way to break into a network via the Internet involves spoofing, which is the process of fooling another computer by pretending to send information from a legitimate source. It works by altering the address that the system automatically puts on every message sent. The address is changed to one that the receiving computer is programmed to accept as a trusted source of information.

## Spyware

Spyware is a type of software that allows an intruder to spy upon someone else's computer. This alarming technology takes advantage of loopholes in the computer's security systems and allows a stranger to witness and record another person's every mouse click or keystroke on the monitor as it occurs. The spy can record activities and gain access to passwords and credit card information. Spyware generally requires the user to install it on the machine that is being spied upon, so it is highly unlikely that random strangers on the Internet could simply begin watching your computer. In the workplace, however, someone might be able to install the software without the victim's knowledge. Disguised as an email greeting, for example, the program can operate like a virus that gets the unwary user to install the spyware unknowingly.

2

Page 3

## INFORMATION THEFT

Information can be a company's most valuable possession. Stealing corporate information, a crime included in the category of industrial espionage, is unfortunately both easy to do and difficult to detect. This is due in part to the invisible nature of software and data. If a cracker breaks into a company network and manages to download the company database from the network onto a disk, there is no visible sign to the company that anything is amiss. The original database is still in place, working the same way it always has.

## Wireless Device Security

The growing number of wireless devices has created a new opportunity for data theft. Wireless devices such as cameras, Web phones, networked computers, PDAs, and input and output peripherals are inherently less secure than wired devices. Security is quite lax, and in some cases nonexistent, in new wireless technologies for handheld computers and cell phone systems. In a rush to match competition, manufacturers have tended to sacrifice security to move a product to the marketplace faster. Already, viruses are appearing in emails for cell phones and PDAs. With little protection available for these new systems, hackers and spies are enjoying a free hand with the new technology. One of the few available security protocols for wireless networks is Wired Equivalent Privacy (WEP), developed in conjunction with the standard for wireless local area networks. Newer versions of WEP with enhanced security features make it more difficult for hackers to intercept and modify data transmissions sent by radio waves or infrared signals.

## Data Browsing

Data browsing is a less damaging form of information theft that involves an invasion of privacy. Workers in many organizations have access to networked databases that contain private information about people. Accessing this information without an official reason is against the law. The IRS had a particularly large problem with data browsing in the late 1990s. Some employees were fired and the rest were given specialized training in appropriate conduct.

3

Page 4

## Chapter 1 Resume Styles

You can write a resume several different ways. The three most popular resume styles include: chronological resumes, functional resumes, and hybrid resumes. To these three we will add the structured interview resume. Although not used often, this resume format enables people to set out the benefits that they offer an employer in a conversational style. It is inviting to read and enables you to convey a lot of targeted information. It is particularly useful if you are able to anticipate the types of questions that will be asked at an interview. By presenting your resume in this way, you provide the employer with an expectation of how you might perform in an interview, giving the employer a reason to consider your application further.

### The Chronological Resume

This resume style is the one many people use without thinking. It lists your training and jobs by the date you started each of them. Typically, people list their most recent training or jobs first and proceed backward to the first things they did in the past. This is called "reverse chronological" order. The components of this resume include:

- Personal contact information
- Employment history, including employers, dates of employment, positions held, and achievements
- Education qualifications
- Professional development

### The Functional Resume

This is the style that emphasizes the skills of the individual and his or her achievements. It is often used when the applicant lacks formal education, or his or her educational qualifications are judged obsolete or irrelevant. If you have had many different jobs with no clear pattern or progression, or your work history has several gaps, some people recommend this approach.

### The Hybrid Resume

This is an increasingly popular approach that combines the best of both the chronological resume and the functional resume. A hybrid resume retains much of the fixed order of the chronological resume, but includes more emphasis on skills and achievements—sometimes in a separate section. The hybrid approach is the one that we recommend to most people, in that it produces an excellent

1-1

**Exercise 19.2** C19-E02-ResumeReport.docx

---

clear structure but requires the candidate to carefully consider his or her achievements and what he or she has to offer. Obviously, there is a limit to how long your resume should be. If you decide to use a hybrid style, you may wish to just emphasize the skills, knowledge, and abilities you have.

1-2

---

## Chapter 2 Writing Your Resume

### Contact Information

Before getting into the major sections of the resume, let's briefly address the very top section: your name and contact information.

### Name

You would think that writing your name would be the easiest part of writing your resume but you should consider certain factors. Although most peoples choose to use their full, formal name at the top of a resume, using the name by which you prefer to be called is becoming more acceptable.

Keep in mind that it is to your advantage when readers feel comfortable when calling you for an interview. Their comfort level may decrease if your name is gender-neutral, difficult to pronounce, or very unusual; they don't know how to ask for you. You can make it easier for them by following these examples:

- Lynn T. Cowles (Mr.)
- (Ms.) Michael Murray
- Tzirina (Irene) Kahn
- Ndege "Nick" Vernon

### Address

You should always include your home address on your resume. If you use a post office box for mail, include both your mailing address and your physical residence address. An exception to this is when you are posting your resume on the Internet. For security purposes, include just your phone and email contact as well as possibly your city and state with no street address.

### Telephone Number(s)

Your home telephone number must be included so that people can pick up the phone and call you immediately. In addition, you can also include a cell phone number.

### Email Address

Without question, if you have an email address, include it on your resume. Email is now often the preferred method of communication in job search, particularly in the early stages of each contact. If

2-3

---

you do not have an email account, you can obtain a free, accessible-anywhere address from a provider such as www.yahoo.com, www.microsoft.com, or www.gmail.com.

2-4

---

# PROBATIONARY PERIODS

Acceptance by an applicant of an offer of employment by an appointing authority and their mutual agreement to the date of hire is known as an appointment.

## Types of Appointments

**New Hire:** When you initially accept an appointment, you are considered a new hire. As a new hire, you will be required to serve a probationary period of either six months or one year.

**Reemployment:** Reemployment is a type of appointment that does not result in a break in service. The following are types of reemployment:

1. Military reemployment: Any remaining portion of a probationary period must be completed upon return to the company.

2. Reemployment of a permanent employee who has been laid off: Completion of a new probationary period is required if you are reemployed in a different class or in a different department.

3. Reemployment due to reclassification of a position to a lower class.

4. Reemployment of seasonal employees.

5. Reemployment due to a permanent disability arising from an injury sustained at work.

Further information on this subject can be obtained by contacting your personnel representative or a representative in the human resources department.

**Reinstatement:** If you have resigned from company service as a permanent employee in good standing, you may be reinstated to the same or a similar class within a two-year period following termination.

The probationary period following reinstatement may be waived, but you will not be eligible to compete in promotional examinations until you have completed six months of permanent service. You cannot be reinstated to a position that is at grade 20 or above if the position is allocated at a higher grade level than the position you held at the time of termination.

**Reappointment:** You may be reappointed to a class that you formerly held or to a comparable class if you meet the current minimum qualifications and receive the appointing authority's approval. If you are a probationary employee, you must complete a new probationary period. You cannot be reappointed to a position at grade 20 or above if the position is allocated at a higher level than the position you formerly held.

Student Name_____1_____C19-E03-EmpHandbook.docx

---

**Demotion:** An employee may request or accept a demotion to a position in a class with a lower grade level if the employee meets the minimum qualifications and if the appointing authority approves. You may not demote through non-competitive means to a position at grade 20 or higher if the position is allocated to a higher grade level than the position you currently hold.

**Promotion:** Promotion is advancement to a vacant position in a class that has a higher grade than the class previously held. As an employee of the company, you may compete in recruitments for promotional openings when you have served six months (full-time equivalent) of consecutive service. When you accept a promotion, you will be required to serve a trial period of either six months or one year. If you fail to attain permanent status in a vacant position to which you were promoted, you shall be restored to your former position.

## EMPLOYEE PERFORMANCE

## Work Performance Standards

Work performance standards are written statements of the results and/or behavior expected of an employee when his or her job elements are satisfactorily performed under existing working conditions. Each employee in a permanent position must be provided with a current set of work performance standards for his or her position.

## Performance Evaluation

If you are serving a six-month (full-time equivalent) probationary period, your supervisor will evaluate your performance at the end of the second and fifth months. If you are completing a one-year (full-time equivalent) probationary period, your evaluations will be conducted at the end of the third, seventh, and eleventh months. You will receive a copy of each performance report. Once you have attained permanent status, your performance will be evaluated annually during the month prior to your pay progression date.

Each evaluation will include a discussion between you and your supervisor to review and clarify goals and methods to achieve them. The evaluation will also include a written report of your progress in the job. Evaluations will be made with reference to established work performance standards.

## Employment Records

Your official personnel file is maintained in the human resources department. The human resources department maintains a working file with copies of the documentation in your specific department. Your file includes personnel action documents, mandatory employment forms, your performance evaluations, and documentation of disciplinary action. Your file may include letters of commendation, training certificates, or other work-related documents that you or your supervisor has requested to be included in your file.

Student Name_____2_____C19-E03-EmpHandbook.docx

---

# COMPENSATION

## Rate of Pay

The compensation schedule for employees consists of pay ranges for each grade. Within each grade are ten steps. As an employee of the company, your pay will be set at one of the steps within the grade for the class to which you are appointed. Your pay is further determined by the compensation schedule applicable to your participation in the company's retirement system.

## Direct Deposit Option

You have the option to forward your paycheck directly to a checking or savings account in a bank of your choice. The company payroll center representative can provide you with a direct deposit authorization card.

## Pay Progression

You will receive a merit salary increase annually on your pay progression date if your last performance evaluation was standard or better, and you have not reached the top step in your grade. The maximum merit salary increase is an adjustment of one step annually.

If your date of promotion coincides with your pay progression date, the merit salary increase will be computed first and the promotional increase applied to your new pay rate. If you continue to do satisfactory work, you will remain eligible for annual merit salary increases until you have reached the maximum step within your grade. In addition to merit salary increases, your salary may be adjusted by general salary increases granted by the company.

## Overtime

Under state law, overtime is any time worked in excess of eight hours a day, eight hours in a 16-hour period, or 40 hours in a week. Employees who choose and are approved for variable/innovative workday schedules earn overtime after 40 hours in a week.

Cash payment is the principal method of compensation for overtime. Payments are computed based on the employee/employer-paid salary schedule. Agreements may be reached with your employer to provide for compensatory time off in lieu of cash payments. Compensatory time must be taken within a reasonable time after accrual at the direction of the appointing authority. If you request compensatory time off and give at least two weeks' notice, it cannot be unreasonably denied.

Student Name_____3_____C19-E03-EmpHandbook.docx

---

## Longevity Pay

When you have completed eight years of continuous service and have standard or better performance, you will be entitled to longevity pay based on a longevity chart. (Click to display Longevity Schedule.)

Eligible full-time or part-time employees who work less than full-time for a portion of the 6-month qualifying period are entitled to a prorated amount based on the semi-annual payment. Longevity payments are issued in July and December.

## Payment for Holidays

Nonexempt employees are entitled to receive payment for eleven holidays per year when they are in "paid status" during any portion of the shift immediately preceding the holiday. In addition, a nonexempt employee who works on a holiday is entitled to earn time and one-half cash payment or time and one-half compensatory time for the hours worked on the holiday. Exempt employees who work on a holiday do not receive additional compensation, but may have their schedule adjusted during the week in which the holiday occurs or in a subsequent week to recognize the holiday or additional time worked.

## Shift Differential

Shift differential is an adjustment in pay equivalent to an additional 5 percent of an employee's normal rate of pay. To qualify, a nonexempt employee must work in a unit requiring multiple shifts in a 24-hour period and be assigned to a period of work of at least 8 hours of which at least four hours fall between 6:00 p.m. and 7:00 a.m. Employees working a qualifying shift that is reduced due to daylight savings time will still receive shift differential pay for that shift.

Student Name_____4_____C19-E03-EmpHandbook.docx

## PROBATIONARY PERIODS

Acceptance by an applicant of an offer of employment by an appointing authority and their mutual agreement to the date of hire is known as an appointment.

### Types of Appointments

**New Hire:** When you initially accept an appointment, you are considered a new hire. As a new hire, you will be required to serve a probationary period of either six months or one year.

**Reemployment:** Reemployment is a type of appointment that does not result in a break in service. The following are types of reemployment:

1. Military reemployment: Any remaining portion of a probationary period must be completed upon return to the company.

2. Reemployment of a permanent employee who has been laid off: Completion of a new probationary period is required if you are reemployed in a different class or in a different department.

3. Reemployment due to reclassification of a position to a lower class.

4. Reemployment of seasonal employees.

5. Reemployment due to a permanent disability arising from an injury sustained at work.

Further information on this subject can be obtained by contacting your personnel representative or a representative in the human resources department.

**Reinstatement:** If you have resigned from company service as a permanent employee in good standing, you may be reinstated to the same or a similar class within a two-year period following termination.

The probationary period following reinstatement may be waived, but you will not be eligible to compete in promotional examinations until you have completed six months of permanent service. You cannot be reinstated to a position that is at grade 20 or above if the position is allocated at a higher grade level than the position you held at the time of termination.

**Reappointment:** You may be reappointed to a class that you formerly held or to a comparable class if you meet the current minimum qualifications and receive the appointing authority's approval. If you are a probationary employee, you must complete a new probationary period. You cannot be reappointed to a position at grade 20 or above if the position is allocated at a higher level than the position you formerly held.

**Exercise 19.4  C19-E04-EmpHandbook.docx**

Page 1

---

**Demotion:** An employee may request or accept a demotion to a position in a class with a lower grade level if the employee meets the minimum qualifications and if the appointing authority approves. You may not demote through non-competitive means to a position at grade 20 or higher if the position is allocated to a higher grade level than the position you currently hold.

**Promotion:** Promotion is advancement to a vacant position in a class that has a higher grade than the class previously held. As an employee of the company, you may compete in recruitments for promotional openings when you have served six months (full-time equivalent) of consecutive service. When you accept a promotion, you will be required to serve a trial period of either six months or one year. If you fail to attain permanent status in a vacant position to which you were promoted, you shall be restored to your former position.

## EMPLOYEE PERFORMANCE

### Work Performance Standards

Work performance standards are written statements of the results and/or behavior expected of an employee when his or her job elements are satisfactorily performed under existing working conditions. Each employee in a permanent position must be provided with a current set of work performance standards for his or her position.

### Performance Evaluation

If you are serving a six-month (full-time equivalent) probationary period, your supervisor will evaluate your performance at the end of the second and fifth months. If you are completing a one-year (full-time equivalent) probationary period, your evaluations will be conducted at the end of the third, seventh, and eleventh months. You will receive a copy of each performance report. Once you have attained permanent status, your performance will be evaluated annually during the month prior to your pay progression date.

Each evaluation will include a discussion between you and your supervisor to review and clarify goals and methods to achieve them. The evaluation will also include a written report of your progress in the job. Evaluations will be made with reference to established work performance standards.

### Employment Records

Your official personnel file is maintained in the human resources department. The human resources department maintains a working file with copies of the documentation in your specific department. Your file includes personnel action documents, mandatory employment forms, your performance evaluations, and documentation of disciplinary action. Your file may include letters of commendation, training certificates, or other work-related documents that you or your supervisor has requested to be included in your file.

Page 2

---

## COMPENSATION

### Rate of Pay

The compensation schedule for employees consists of pay ranges for each grade. Within each grade are ten steps. As an employee of the company, your pay will be set at one of the steps within the grade for the class to which you are appointed. Your pay is further determined by the compensation schedule applicable to your participation in the company's retirement system.

### Direct Deposit Option

You have the option to forward your paycheck directly to a checking or savings account in a bank of your choice. The company payroll center representative can provide you with a direct deposit authorization card.

### Pay Progression

You will receive a merit salary increase annually on your pay progression date if your last performance evaluation was standard or better, and you have not reached the top step in your grade. The maximum merit salary increase is an adjustment of one step annually.

If your date of promotion coincides with your pay progression date, the merit salary increase will be computed first and the promotional increase applied to your new pay rate. If you continue to do satisfactory work, you will remain eligible for annual merit salary increases until you have reached the maximum step within your grade. In addition to merit salary increases, your salary may be adjusted by general salary increases granted by the company.

### Overtime

Under state law, overtime is any time worked in excess of eight hours a day, eight hours in a 16-hour period, or 40 hours in a week. Employees who choose and are approved for variable/innovative workday schedules earn overtime after 40 hours in a week.

Cash payment is the principal method of compensation for overtime. Payments are computed based on the employee/employer-paid salary schedule. Agreements may be reached with your employer to provide for compensatory time off in lieu of cash payments. Compensatory time must be taken within a reasonable time after accrual at the direction of the appointing authority. If you request compensatory time off and give at least two weeks' notice, it cannot be unreasonably denied.

Page 3

---

### Longevity Pay

When you have completed eight years of continuous service and have standard or better performance, you will be entitled to longevity pay based on a longevity chart. (Click to display Longevity Schedule.)

Eligible full-time or part-time employees who work less than full-time for a portion of the 6-month qualifying period are entitled to a prorated amount based on the semi-annual payment. Longevity payments are issued in July and December.

### Payment for Holidays

Nonexempt employees are entitled to receive payment for eleven holidays per year when they are in "paid status" during any portion of the shift immediately preceding the holiday. In addition, a nonexempt employee who works on a holiday is entitled to earn time and one-half cash payment or time and one-half compensatory time for the hours worked on the holiday. Exempt employees who work on a holiday do not receive additional compensation, but may have their schedule adjusted during the week in which the holiday occurs or in a subsequent week to recognize the holiday or additional time worked.

### Shift Differential

Shift differential is an adjustment in pay equivalent to an additional 5 percent of an employee's normal rate of pay. To qualify, a nonexempt employee must work in a unit requiring multiple shifts in a 24-hour period and be assigned to a period of work of at least 8 hours of which at least four hours fall between 6:00 p.m. and 7:00 a.m. Employees working a qualifying shift that is reduced due to daylight savings time will still receive shift differential pay for that shift.

Page 4

---

## PROBATIONARY PERIODS

Acceptance by an applicant of an offer of employment by an appointing authority and their mutual agreement to the date of hire is known as an appointment.

### Types of Appointments

**New Hire:** When you initially accept an appointment, you are considered a new hire. As a new hire, you will be required to serve a probationary period of either six months or one year.

**Reemployment:** Reemployment is a type of appointment that does not result in a break in service. The following are types of reemployment:

1. Military reemployment: Any remaining portion of a probationary period must be completed upon return to the company.

2. Reemployment of a permanent employee who has been laid off: Completion of a new probationary period is required if you are reemployed in a different class or in a different department.

3. Reemployment due to reclassification of a position to a lower class.

4. Reemployment of seasonal employees.

5. Reemployment due to a permanent disability arising from an injury sustained at work.

Further information on this subject can be obtained by contacting your personnel representative or a representative in the human resources department.

**Reinstatement:** If you have resigned from company service as a permanent employee in good standing, you may be reinstated to the same or a similar class within a two-year period following termination.

The probationary period following reinstatement may be waived, but you will not be eligible to compete in promotional examinations until you have completed six months of permanent service. You cannot be reinstated to a position that is at grade 20 or above if the position is allocated at a higher grade level than the position you held at the time of termination.

**Reappointment:** You may be reappointed to a class that you formerly held or to a comparable class if you meet the current minimum qualifications and receive the appointing authority's approval. If you are a probationary employee, you must complete a new probationary period. You cannot be reappointed to a position at grade 20 or above if the position is allocated at a higher level than the position you formerly held.

1

Exercise 19.5 C19-E05-EmpHandbook.docx

---

**Demotion:** An employee may request or accept a demotion to a position in a class with a lower grade level if the employee meets the minimum qualifications and if the appointing authority approves. You may not demote through non-competitive means to a position at grade 20 or higher if the position is allocated to a higher grade level than the position you currently hold.

**Promotion:** Promotion is advancement to a vacant position in a class that has a higher grade than the class previously held. As an employee of the company, you may compete in recruitments for promotional openings when you have served six months (full-time equivalent) of consecutive service. When you accept a promotion, you will be required to serve a trial period of either six months or one year. If you fail to attain permanent status in a vacant position to which you were promoted, you shall be restored to your former position.

## EMPLOYEE PERFORMANCE

### Work Performance Standards

Work performance standards are written statements of the results and/or behavior expected of an employee when his or her job elements are satisfactorily performed under existing working conditions. Each employee in a permanent position must be provided with a current set of work performance standards for his or her position.

### Performance Evaluation

If you are serving a six-month (full-time equivalent) probationary period, your supervisor will evaluate your performance at the end of the second and fifth months. If you are completing a one-year (full-time equivalent) probationary period, your evaluations will be conducted at the end of the third, seventh, and eleventh months. You will receive a copy of each performance report. Once you have attained permanent status, your performance will be evaluated annually during the month prior to your pay progression date.

Each evaluation will include a discussion between you and your supervisor to review and clarify goals and methods to achieve them. The evaluation will also include a written report of your progress in the job. Evaluations will be made with reference to established work performance standards.

### Employment Records

Your official personnel file is maintained in the human resources department. The human resources department maintains a working file with copies of the documentation in your specific department. Your file includes personnel action documents, mandatory employment forms, your performance evaluations, and documentation of disciplinary action. Your file may include letters of commendation, training certificates, or other work-related documents that you or your supervisor has requested to be included in your file.

2

---

## COMPENSATION

### Rate of Pay

The compensation schedule for employees consists of pay ranges for each grade. Within each grade are ten steps. As an employee of the company, your pay will be set at one of the steps within the grade to which you are appointed. Your pay is further determined by the compensation schedule applicable to your participation in the company's retirement system.

### Direct Deposit Option

You have the option to forward your paycheck directly to a checking or savings account in a bank of your choice. The company payroll center representative can provide you with a direct deposit authorization card.

### Pay Progression

You will receive a merit salary increase annually on your pay progression date if your last performance evaluation was standard or better, and you have not reached the top step in your grade. The maximum merit salary increase is an adjustment of one step annually.

If your date of promotion coincides with your pay progression date, the merit salary increase will be computed first and the promotional increase applied to your new pay rate. If you continue to do satisfactory work, you will remain eligible for annual merit salary increases until you have reached the maximum step within your grade. In addition to merit salary increases, your salary may be adjusted by general salary increases granted by the company.

### Overtime

Under state law, overtime is any time worked in excess of eight hours a day, eight hours in a 16-hour period, or 40 hours in a week. Employees who choose and are approved for variable/innovative workday schedules earn overtime after 40 hours in a week.

Cash payment is the principal method of compensation for overtime. Payments are computed based on the employee/employer-paid salary schedule. Agreements may be reached with your employer to provide for compensatory time off in lieu of cash payments. Compensatory time must be taken within a reasonable time after accrual at the direction of the appointing authority. If you request compensatory time off and give at least two weeks' notice, it cannot be unreasonably denied.

3

---

### Longevity Pay

When you have completed eight years of continuous service and have standard or better performance, you will be entitled to longevity pay based on a longevity chart. (Click to display Longevity Schedule.)

Eligible full-time or part-time employees who work less than full-time for a portion of the 6-month qualifying period are entitled to a prorated amount based on the semi-annual payment. Longevity payments are issued in July and December.

### Payment for Holidays

Nonexempt employees are entitled to receive payment for eleven holidays per year when they are in "paid status" during any portion of the shift immediately preceding the holiday. In addition, a nonexempt employee who works on a holiday is entitled to earn time and one-half cash payment or time and one-half compensatory time for the hours worked on the holiday. Exempt employees who work on a holiday do not receive additional compensation, but may have their schedule adjusted during the week in which the holiday occurs or in a subsequent week to recognize the holiday or additional time worked.

### Shift Differential

Shift differential is an adjustment in pay equivalent to an additional 5 percent of an employee's normal rate of pay. To qualify, a nonexempt employee must work in a unit requiring multiple shifts in a 24-hour period and be assigned to a period of work of at least 8 hours of which at least four hours fall between 6:00 p.m. and 7:00 a.m. Employees working a qualifying shift that is reduced due to daylight savings time will still receive shift differential pay for that shift.

4

## PROBATIONARY PERIODS

Exercise 19.6

C19-E06-EmpHandbook.docx

Acceptance by an applicant of an offer of employment by an appointing authority and their mutual agreement to the date of hire is known as an appointment.

### Types of Appointments

**New Hire:** When you initially accept an appointment, you are considered a new hire. As a new hire, you will be required to serve a probationary period of either six months or one year.

**Reemployment:** Reemployment is a type of appointment that does not result in a break in service. The following are types of reemployment:

1. Military reemployment: Any remaining portion of a probationary period must be completed upon return to the company.

2. Reemployment new probationa different departm

3. Reemployment

4. Reemployment

5. Reemployment work.

Further information on representative or a repr

**Reinstatement:** If you h good standing, you may following termination.

The probationary period to compete in promotio service. You cannot be r allocated at a higher gra

**Reappointment:** You m comparable class if you authority's approval. If y probationary period. Yo position is allocated at a

Section 1 Probationary P

**Page 1, Section 1**

## EMPLOYEE PERFORMANCE

### Work Performance Standards

Work performance standards are written statements of the results and/or behavior expected of an employee when his or her job elements are satisfactorily performed under existing working conditions. Each employee in a permanent position must be provided with a current set of work performance standards for his or her position.

### Performance Evaluation

If you are serving a six-month (full-time equivalent) probationary period, your supervisor will evaluate your performance at the end of the second and fifth months. If you are completing a one-year (full-time equivalent) probationary period, your evaluations will be conducted at the end of the third, seventh, and eleventh months. You will receive a copy of each performance report. Once you have attained permanent status, your performance will be evaluated annually d

Each evaluation will inclu clarify goals and methods of your progress in the jo performance standards.

### Employment F

Your official personnel fil resources department ma specific department. Your forms, your performance may include letters of co that you or your supervis

Section 2 Employee Perfor

**Page 1, Section 2**

## COMPENSATION

### Rate of Pay

The compensation schedule for employees consists of pay ranges for each grade. Within each grade are ten steps. As an employee of the company, your pay will be set at one of the steps within the grade for the class to which you are appointed. Your pay is further determined by the compensation schedule applicable to your participation in the company's retirement system.

### Direct Deposit Option

You have the option to forward your paycheck directly to a checking or savings account in a bank of your choice. The company payroll center representative can provide you with a direct deposit authorization card.

### Pay Progression

You will receive a merit salary increase annually on your pay progression date if your last performance evaluation was standard or better, and you have not reached the top step in your grade. The maximum merit salary increase is an adjustment of one step annually.

If your date of promotion coincides with your pay progression date, the merit salary increase will be computed first and the promotional increase applied to your new pay rate. If you continue to do satisfactory work, you will remain eligible for annual merit salary increases until you have reached the maximum step within your grade. In addition to merit salary increases, your salary may be adjusted by general salary increases granted by the company.

### Overtime

Under state law, overtime is any time worked in excess of eight hours a day, eight hours in a 16-hour period, or 40 hours in a week. Employees who choose and are approved for variable/innovative workday schedules earn overtime after 40 hours in a week.

Cash payment is the principal method of compensation for overtime. Payments are computed based on the employee/employer-paid salary schedule. Agreements may be reached with your employer to

Section 3 Compensation                                    Page 1

**Page 1, Section 3**

**ONLINE SHOPPING**

Online shopping, also called electronic shopping or e-shopping, is shopping that involves the use of a computer, modem, browser, and the Internet to locate, examine, select, and pay for products.

Many businesses encourage consumers to shop online because it saves employee time, thus reducing staffing needs and saving money for the company. For example, some major airlines offer special discounts to travelers who purchase their tickets over the Internet, and most are eliminating paper tickets altogether.

**Advantages of Online Shopping**

For the consumer, online shopping offers several distinct advantages over traditional shopping methods. These advantages include the following:

- More product information. At many online stores, you can find detailed information about a wide variety of p
- Ease of comparison shop
  similar stores and locate
- Convenience. With e-sho
  whenever you want fron
- Greater selection. Becau
  can offer you an almost

**Online Shopping Venues**

Just as consumers can visit a var
shopping malls, Internet shoppe
including online stores, supersto

*Online Stores*

An online store, also called a vir
purchase a merchant's products
services in categories that link to
desired category to view picture

**Exercise 19.7**

C19-E07-OnlineShop.docx

*Online Superstores*

Like brick-and-mortar superstores, online superstores offer an extensive array of products, from candy bars to household appliances. Some popular superstores also have online superstores. E-tailer superstores have proved especially popular with shoppers.

*Online Shopping Malls*

When shopping malls were introduced in the 1950s, consumers were delighted by the convenience of being able to shop in a wide variety of stores physically connected under one roof. Similar in concept, an online shopping mall connects its stores by hyperlinks on the mall's home page. Some businesses, in fact, do not have individual online stores but instead offer their products and services only at an online shopping mall.

**Online Shopping Safety Tips**

The number one concern consumers have about shopping online is security. The truth, however, is that shopping online is safe and secure if you know what to look for. Following these guidelines can help you avoid trouble.

- Never provide your social security number.
- Find out the privacy policy of shopping sites before you buy.
- Keep current on the latest Internet scams.
- Look for sites that follow privacy rules from a privacy watchdog such as TRUSTe.
- Answer only the minimum questions when filling out forms.
- Only buy at secure sites.

# Customizing Page Numbers

In Chapter 7, you learned to use the Page Number button in the Header & Footer group on the INSERT tab to insert page numbers in a document.
You inserted a page number by clicking the Page Number button, pointing to the desired position for the number at the drop-down list, and then clicking a predesigned page numbering option. You removed page numbers from a document by clicking the Page Number button and then clicking the *Remove Page Numbers* option at the drop-down list.

By default, Word inserts arabic numbers (1, 2, 3, and so on) and numbers pages sequentially beginning with 1. You can customize these default settings with options at the Page Number Format dialog box, as shown in Figure 19.1. To display this dialog box, click the INSERT tab, click the Page Number button in the Header & Footer group, and then click *Format Page Numbers* at the drop-down list.

**QUICK STEPS**

**Insert Page Numbers**
1. Click INSERT tab.
2. Click Page Number button.
3. Point to desired position.
4. Click desired predesigned page number option.

**Remove Page Numbers**
1. Click INSERT tab.
2. Click Page Number button.
3. Click *Remove Page Numbers* at drop-down list.

Page Number

**Figure 19.1  Page Number Format Dialog Box**

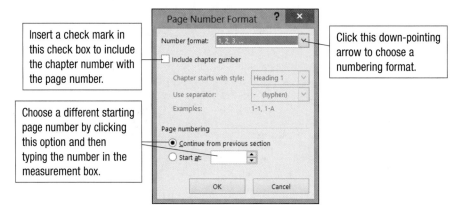

Insert a check mark in this check box to include the chapter number with the page number.

Click this down-pointing arrow to choose a numbering format.

Choose a different starting page number by clicking this option and then typing the number in the measurement box.

Click the *Number format* option in the Page Number Format dialog box to change from arabic numbers to one of the following options: arabic numbers preceded and followed by hyphens (- 1 -, - 2 -, - 3 -, and so on), lowercase letters (a, b, c, and so on), uppercase letters (A, B, C, and so on), lowercase roman numerals (i, ii, iii, and so on), or uppercase roman numerals (I, II, III, and so on).

By default, page numbering begins with 1 and continues sequentially from 1 through all of the pages and sections in a document. You can change the beginning page number with the *Start at* option at the Page Number Format dialog box. To do this, click the *Start at* option and then type the desired beginning page number in the measurement box. You can also click the up or down arrow in the measurement box to increase or decrease the number.

1. Open **CompAccess.docx** and save the document with the name **C19-E01-CompAccess**.
2. Insert section breaks that begin new pages by completing the following steps:
   a. With the insertion point positioned at the beginning of the title *UNAUTHORIZED ACCESS*, click the PAGE LAYOUT tab.
   b. Click the Breaks button in the Page Setup group and then click *Next Page* in the *Section Breaks* section of the drop-down list.
   c. Move the insertion point to the beginning of the title *INFORMATION THEFT*.
   d. Click the Breaks button in the Page Setup group and then click *Next Page* in the *Section Breaks* section of the drop-down list.

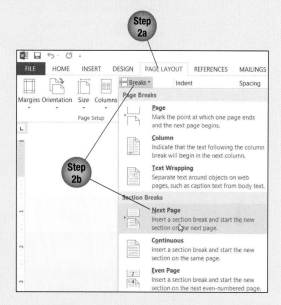

3. Insert a file by completing the following steps:
   a. Press Ctrl + Home to move the insertion point to the beginning of the document.
   b. Click the INSERT tab.
   c. Click the Object button arrow and then click *Text from File* at the drop-down list.
   d. At the Insert File dialog box, navigate to your Chapter19 folder and then double-click *TableofContents.docx*.
4. Apply the Heading 1 style to the title *TABLE OF CONTENTS*.
5. Apply the Minimalist style set.
6. Insert lowercase roman numeral page numbers for the table of contents page by completing the following steps:
   a. Press Ctrl + Home.
   b. Click the INSERT tab.
   c. Click the Page Number button in the Header & Footer group.
   d. Click *Format Page Numbers* at the drop-down list.
   e. At the Page Number Format dialog box, click the down-pointing arrow at the right of the *Number format* option and then click *i, ii, iii, …* at the drop-down list.
   f. Click OK to close the dialog box.

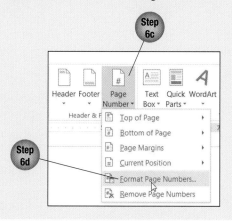

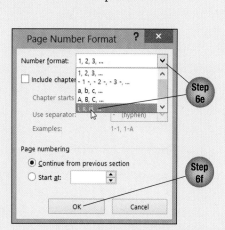

g. Click the Page Number button in the Header & Footer group, point to *Bottom of Page*, and then click the *Plain Number 2* option at the side menu.

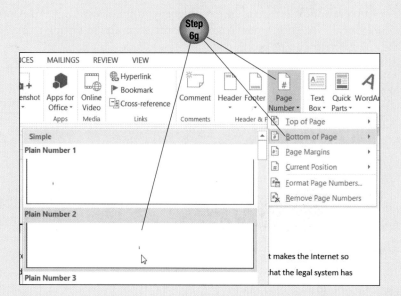

7. Begin the page numbering with 1 by completing the following steps:

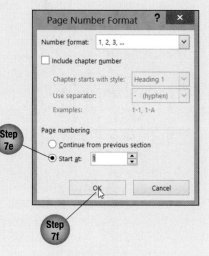

a. Click the Close Header and Footer button to return to the document.
b. Position the insertion point on any character in the title *UNAUTHORIZED ACCESS* (located on page 2).
c. Click the INSERT tab.
d. Click the Page Number button in the Header & Footer group and then click *Format Page Numbers* at the drop-down list.
e. At the Page Number Format dialog box, click the *Start at* option in the *Page numbering* section. (This inserts the number *1* in the *Start at* measurement box.)
f. Click OK to close the dialog box.
8. Save, print, and then close **C19-E01-CompAccess.docx**.

You can number the chapters in a document with an option at the Multilevel List button drop-down list on the HOME tab and then include chapter numbers in the page numbers in the document. To do this, click the *Include chapter number* check box at the Page Number Format dialog box and then specify with what page number the chapter starts and what separator to use between the chapter number and page number.

## Exercise 19.2    Inserting Page Numbers That Include Chapter Numbers     Part 1 of 1

1. Open **ResumeReport.docx** and save the document with the name **C19-E02-ResumeReport**.
2. Change the case style of the first title by completing the following steps:
   a. Select the title *RESUME STYLES*.
   b. Click the Change Case button in the Font group on the HOME tab.
   c. Click the *Capitalize Each Word* option.
3. Complete steps similar to those in Step 2 to change the case style of the other title in the document: *WRITING YOUR RESUME*.
4. Move the insertion point to the beginning of the title *Writing Your Resume* and then insert a section break that begins a new page.
5. Apply the Heading 1 style to the two titles in the document: *Resume Styles* and *Writing Your Resume*.
6. Apply the Centered style set.
7. Change the theme colors to Orange Red.
8. Apply chapter multilevel list numbering by completing the following steps:
   a. Press Ctrl + Home to move the insertion point to the beginning of the document.
   b. If necessary, click the HOME tab.
   c. Click the Multilevel List button in the Paragraph group.
   d. Click the last option in the *List Library* section of the drop-down gallery. (This inserts *Chapter 1* before the first title and *Chapter 2* before the second title.)
9. Include chapter numbers with the page numbers in the document by completing the following steps:
   a. With the insertion point positioned at the beginning of the document, click the INSERT tab.

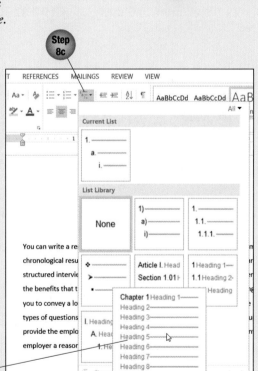

b. Click the Page Number button in the Header & Footer group and then click *Format Page Numbers* at the drop-down list.
c. At the Page Number Format dialog box, click the *Include chapter number* check box to insert a check mark.
d. Click OK.
e. Click the Page Number button in the Header & Footer group, point to *Bottom of Page*, and then click the *Plain Number 2* option.
f. Double-click in the document.
g. Move the insertion point so it is positioned on any character in the second title, *Chapter 2 Writing Your Resume*.
h. Click the INSERT tab.
i. Click the Page Number button in the Header & Footer group and then click *Format Page Numbers*.
j. At the Page Number Format dialog box, click the *Include chapter number* check box to insert a check mark.
k. Click OK to close the dialog box.
10. Scroll through the document and notice that the chapter number appears with each page number. (The page number for the first page displays as *1-1*, indicating page 1 of chapter 1. The number that precedes the page number changes to *2* for the pages in chapter 2.)
11. Save, print, and then close **C19-E02-ResumeReport.docx**.

# Inserting Headers and Footers

In Chapter 7, you learned to insert predesigned headers with the Header button on the INSERT tab and predesigned footers with the Footer button. If the predesigned headers and footers provided by Word do not meet your needs, you can create your own.

To create a header, click the INSERT tab, click the Header button in the Header & Footer group, and then click *Edit Header* at the drop-down list. This displays a header pane in the document along with the HEADER & FOOTER TOOLS DESIGN tab, as shown in Figure 19.2. With options on this tab, you can insert elements such as pictures, images, and shapes; navigate to other headers or footers in the document; and position headers and footers on different pages in a document.

Header    Footer

**Figure 19.2 HEADER & FOOTER TOOLS DESIGN Tab**

# Inserting Elements in Headers and Footers

Use buttons in the Insert group on the HEADER & FOOTER TOOLS DESIGN tab to insert elements in the header or footer such as the date and time, Quick Parts, and pictures and images.

Click the Date & Time button in the Insert group and the Date and Time dialog box displays. This is the same dialog box that displays when you click the Date & Time button in the Text group on the INSERT tab. Choose a date and time option in the *Available formats* list box and then click OK. Click the Document Info button to display a drop-down list of document information fields you can insert into the document. Hover the mouse pointer over the *Document Property* option to display a side menu of document properties such as *Author*, *Comments*, and *Company*. The Quick Parts button in the Insert group on the HEADER & FOOTER TOOLS DESIGN tab displays the same options at the drop-down list as the Quick Parts button on the INSERT tab. Click the Online Pictures button and the Insert Pictures window displays, where you can search for and then insert an image into the header or footer.

## QUICK STEPS

**Insert an Element in a Header**
1. Click INSERT tab.
2. Click Header button.
3. Click *Edit Header* at drop-down list.
4. Click desired element.

**Insert an Element in a Footer**
1. Click INSERT tab.
2. Click Footer button.
3. Click *Edit Footer* at drop-down list.
4. Click desired element.

Date & Time    Document Info

Pictures    Online Pictures

---

## Exercise 19.3A    Inserting Elements in a Header and Footer    Part 1 of 2

1. Open **EmpHandbook.docx** and save the document with the name **C19-E03-EmpHandbook**.
2. Change the theme colors to Blue.
3. Change the theme fonts to Century Gothic-Palatino Linotype.
4. Move the insertion point to the beginning of the document and then insert a header by completing the following steps:
   a. Click the INSERT tab.
   b. Click the Header button in the Header & Footer group.
   c. Click *Edit Header* at the drop-down list.
   d. With the insertion point positioned in the Header pane, click the Pictures button in the Insert group on the HEADER & FOOTER TOOLS DESIGN tab.

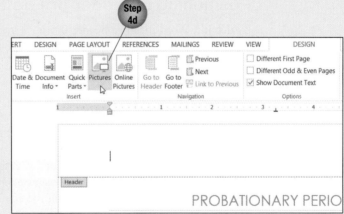

---

e.  At the Insert Picture dialog box, navigate to your Chapter19 folder and then double-click **WELogo.jpg**.

f.  With the image selected, click in the *Shape Height* measurement box, type **0.6**, and then press the Enter key.

g.  Click the Wrap Text button and then click *Behind Text* at the drop-down list.

h.  Drag the image up approximately one-third of an inch.

i.  Click to the right of the image to deselect it.

j.  Press the Tab key. (This moves the insertion point to approximately the middle of the page.)

k.  Click the HEADER & FOOTER TOOLS DESIGN tab.

l.  Click the Date & Time button in the Insert group.

m.  At the Date and Time dialog box, click the twelfth option from the top (the option that displays the date in numbers and the time in hours and minutes) and then click OK to close the dialog box.

n.  Select the date and time text, click the HOME tab, and then change the font to 10-point Palatino Linotype and apply bold formatting.

o.  Double-click in the document to make it active and dim the header.

5. Save **C19-E03-EmpHandbook.docx**.

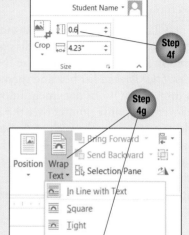

## Navigating in Headers and Footers

Go to Footer

Previous    Next

If a document contains a header and footer or is divided into sections, use the buttons in the Navigation group on the HEADER & FOOTER TOOLS DESIGN tab to navigate to various headers and footers. If a header pane is open, clicking the Go to Footer button will make active the footer on the same page. If a document is divided into sections, click the Previous or Next button to navigate between headers and footers.

## Positioning a Header or Footer

By default, Word inserts a header 0.5 inch from the top of the page and a footer 0.5 inch from the bottom of the page. You can change these default positions with buttons in the Position group on the HEADER & FOOTER TOOLS DESIGN tab. Use the *Header from Top* or *Footer from Bottom* measurement box to adjust the position of the header or footer, respectively, on the page.

By default, headers and footers contain two tab settings. A center tab is set at 3.25 inches on the horizontal ruler and a right tab is set at 6.5 inches. If the document contains default left and right margin settings of 1 inch, then the center tab set at 3.25 inches is the center of the document and the right tab set at 6.5 inches is at the right margin. If you make changes to the default margins, you may need to move the default tabs before inserting header or footer text at the center or right tabs.

You can also set and position tabs with the Insert Alignment Tab button in the Position group. Click this button and the Alignment Tab dialog box displays. Use options at this dialog box to change the tab alignment and set tabs with leaders. Tabs set at the Alignment Tab dialog box do not display on the horizontal ruler.

1. With **C19-E03-EmpHandbook.docx** open, create a footer by completing the following steps:

   a. Click the INSERT tab.

   b. Click the Footer button in the Header & Footer group and then click *Edit Footer* at the drop-down list.

   c. With the insertion point positioned in the footer pane, type your first and last names at the left margin.

   d. Click the Insert Alignment Tab button in the Position group on the HEADER & FOOTER TOOLS DESIGN tab.

   e. At the Alignment Tab dialog box, make sure that *Center* is selected in the *Alignment* section and *Margin* displays in the *Align relative to* option box, and then click *4 ___* in the *Leader* section. Close the dialog box by clicking OK.

   f. With the insertion point positioned at the center tab position, click the Page Number button in the Header & Footer group, point to *Current Position*, and then click *Plain Number 1* at the side menu.

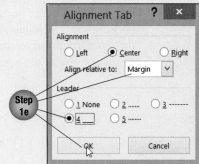

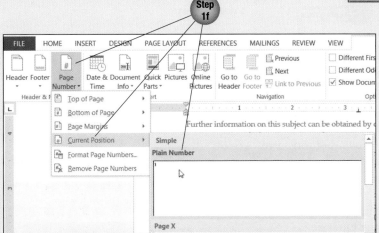

   g. Click the Insert Alignment Tab button.

   h. At the Alignment Tab dialog box, click *Right* in the *Alignment* section, click *4 ___* in the *Leader* section, and then click OK.

   i. With the insertion point positioned at the right tab position, type **C19-E03-EmpHandbook.docx**.

   j. Select all of the footer text and then change the font to 10-point Palatino Linotype and apply bold formatting.

   k. Click the Close Header and Footer button.

2. Change the left and right margins to 1.25 inches. Scroll down the document and notice that the tabs in the footer you inserted in Step 1 automatically adjusted to the new margins. (The tabs do not display on the horizontal ruler.)
3. Edit the header by completing the following steps:
   a. Click the INSERT tab, click the Header button in the Header & Footer group, and then click *Edit Header* at the drop-down list.
   b. Notice that the center tab and right tab are slightly out of position because the left and right margins in the document are set at 1.25 inches instead of 1 inch. The tabs did not automatically adjust when you changed the margins because the tabs were not set at the Tab Alignment dialog box. To align the centered text correctly, drag the Center tab marker to the 3-inch mark on the horizontal ruler. Even though the right-aligned text is aligned at the right margin instead of at the right tab, drag the Right tab marker to the 6-inch mark on the horizonal ruler. (If the horizonal ruler is not visible, display it by clicking the VIEW tab and then clicking the *Ruler* check box in the Show group.) Move the insertion point to the beginning of the date and then press the Tab key. (This right-aligns the text at the right margin.)

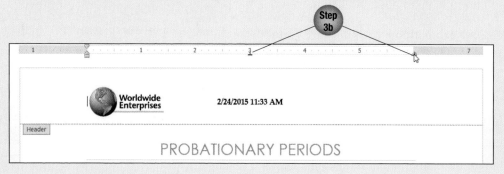

4. Change the positions of the header and footer by completing the following steps:
   a. With the HEADER & FOOTER TOOLS DESIGN tab active, click once on the down-pointing arrow at the right of the *Header from Top* measurement box to display *0.4"*.
   b. Click in the *Footer from Bottom* measurement box, type **0.8**, and then press the Enter key.
   c. Click the Close Header and Footer button.

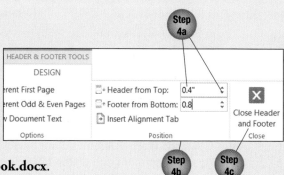

5. Save and then print **C19-E03-EmpHandbook.docx**.

## Creating a Different First Page Header or Footer

By default, Word inserts a header and footer on every page in the document. However, you can create different headers and footers within one document. For example, you can create a unique header and/or footer for the first page and then insert different headers and/or footers on subsequent pages.

To create a different first page header, click the INSERT tab, click the Header button, and then click *Edit Header* at the drop-down list. Click the *Different First Page* check box to insert a check mark and the First Page Header pane displays with the insertion point inside. Insert elements or type text to create the first page header and then click the Next button in the Navigation group. This displays the Header pane with the insertion point positioned inside it. Insert elements and/or type text to create the header. Complete similar steps to create a different first page footer.

In some situations, you may want the first page header or footer to be blank. For instance, if a document contains a title page, you may not want the header or footer to print at the top or bottom of that page.

**QUICK STEPS**

**Create a Different First Page Header or Footer**
1. Click INSERT tab.
2. Click Header or Footer button.
3. Click *Edit Header* or *Edit Footer* at drop-down list.
4. Click *Different First Page* check box.
5. Insert desired elements and/or text for first page.
6. Click Next button.
7. Insert desired elements and/or text for remaining pages.

---

## Exercise 19.4  Creating a Header That Prints on All Pages Except the First Page  Part 1 of 1

1. With **C19-E03-EmpHandbook.docx** open, save the document with Save As and name it **C19-E04-EmpHandbook**.
2. Remove the header and footer by completing the following steps:
   a. Click the INSERT tab.
   b. Click the Header button in the Header & Footer group and then click *Remove Header* at the drop-down list.
   c. Click the Footer button in the Header & Footer group and then click *Remove Footer* at the drop-down list.
3. Press Ctrl + Home and then create a header that prints on all pages except the first page by completing the following steps:
   a. With the INSERT tab active, click the Header button in the Header & Footer group.
   b. Click *Edit Header* at the drop-down list.
   c. Click the *Different First Page* check box located in the Options group.
   d. With the insertion point positioned in the First Page Header pane, click the Next button in the Navigation group. (This tells Word that the first page header is blank.)

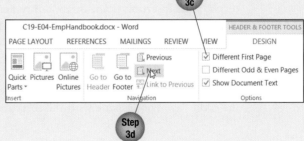

Step 3c

Step 3d

    e.  With the insertion point positioned in the header pane, click the Page Number button, point to *Top of Page*, and then click *Accent Bar 2* at the side menu.

    f.  Click the Close Header & Footer button.

4.  Scroll through the document and observe that the header appears on pages 2 through 4.

5.  Save and then print **C19-E04-EmpHandbook.docx**.

## Creating Odd and Even Page Headers or Footers

**QUICK STEPS**

**Create Odd and Even Page Headers or Footers**

1. Click INSERT tab.
2. Click Header or Footer button.
3. Click *Edit Header* or *Edit Footer* at drop-down list.
4. Click *Different Odd & Even Pages* check box.
5. Insert desired elements and/or text.

If your document will be read in book format with facing pages, consider inserting odd and even page headers and/or footers. When a document in book format has facing pages, the outside margin is the left side of the left page and the right side of the right page. In addition, the page at the right side is generally numbered with an odd page number and the page at the left side is generally numbered with an even page number.

You can create odd and even headers and/or footers to provide this type of page numbering. Use the *Different Odd & Even Pages* check box in the Options group on the HEADER & FOOTER TOOLS DESIGN tab to create odd and even headers and/or footers.

---

**Exercise 19.5**   Creating Even Page and Odd Page Footers        **Part 1 of 1**

1. With **C19-E04-EmpHandbook.docx** open, save the document with Save As and name it **C19-E05-EmpHandbook**.

2. Remove the headers from the document by completing the following steps:
   a.  Click the INSERT tab.
   b.  Click the Header button in the Header & Footer group and then click *Edit Header* at the drop-down list.
   c.  Click the *Different First Page* check box in the Options group to remove the check mark.
   d.  Click the Header button in the Header & Footer group on the HEADER & FOOTER TOOLS DESIGN tab and then click *Remove Header* at the drop-down list. (This displays the insertion point in an empty header pane.)

3. Create one footer that prints on odd-numbered pages and another that prints on even-numbered pages by completing the following steps:
   a.  Click the Go to Footer button in the Navigation group on the HEADER & FOOTER TOOLS DESIGN tab.
   b.  Click the *Different Odd & Even Pages* check box in the Options group. (This displays the Odd Page Footer pane with the insertion point inside.)

c. Click the Page Number button in the Header & Footer group, point to *Bottom of Page*, and then click *Plain Number 3* at the side menu.

d. Click the Next button in the Navigation group. (This displays the Even Page Footer pane with the insertion point inside it.)

e. Click the Page Number button in the Header & Footer group, point to *Current Position*, and then click *Plain Number 1* at the side menu.

f. Click in the *Footer from Bottom* measurement box, type **0.4**, and then press the Enter key.

g. Click the Close Header and Footer button.

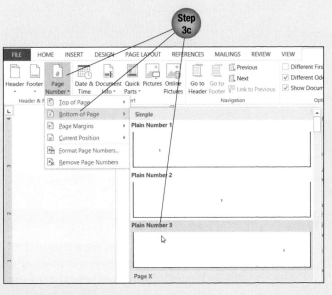

4. Scroll through the document and notice the page number at the right side of the odd page footer and the page number at the left side of the even page footer.

5. Save and then print **C19-E05-EmpHandbook.docx**.

## Creating Headers and Footers for Different Sections

You can divide a document into sections and then apply different formatting in each section. You can insert a section break that begins a new page, insert a continuous section break that starts a new section on the same page, and insert a section break that starts a new section on the next even-numbered or odd-numbered page.

If you want the pages in a document to have different headers and/or footers, divide the document into sections. For example, if a document contains several chapters, you can make each chapter a section and then create a different header and/or footer for each one. When you create sections for each chapter in a document, insert a section break for each chapter that begins a new page.

## Breaking a Section Link

When a header or footer is created for a specific section in a document, the header or footer can be applied to all of the previous and subsequent sections or only the subsequent sections. By default, each section in a document is linked to the other sections.

If you want a header or footer to print on only specific pages in a section and not pages in the previous or following sections, you must deactivate the Link to Previous button. This tells Word not to print the header or footer in previous sections. Word will, however, print the header or footer on pages in the following sections. If you do not want the header or footer to print in following sections, create a blank header or footer in the next section. When you create a header and/or footer for a specific section in a document, preview the document to determine if the headers and/or footers appear on the correct pages.

**QUICK STEPS**

**Create Headers/ Footers for Different Sections**
1. Insert section break in desired location.
2. Click INSERT tab.
3. Click Header or Footer button.
4. Click *Edit Header* or *Edit Footer* at drop-down list.
5. Click Link to Previous button to deactivate.
6. Insert desired elements and/or text.
7. Click Next button.
8. Insert desired elements and/or text.

Link to Previous

Some of the page formatting that is applied to the header or footer text will also apply to the text in the document. For example, if you change the margins in the header or footer, the margins also change within the document. If you create headers and footers for specific sections in a document and the section links have been deactivated, the page formatting changes you make in the header or footer in a section are applied to the document text only in that specific section.

**Exercise 19.6A**    **Creating Footers for Different Sections**      **Part 1 of 2**

1. With **C19-E05-EmpHandbook.docx** open, save the document with Save As and name it **C19-E06-EmpHandbook**.
2. Remove the odd and even page footers by completing the following steps:
    a. Click the INSERT tab.
    b. Click the Footer button and then click *Edit Footer* at the drop-down list.
    c. Click the *Different Odd & Even Pages* check box to remove the check mark.
    d. Click the Footer button and then click *Remove Footer* at the drop-down list.
    e. Click the Close Header and Footer button.
3. Insert a section break that begins a new page by completing the following steps:
    a. Move the insertion point to the beginning of the title *EMPLOYEE PERFORMANCE*.
    b. Click the PAGE LAYOUT tab.
    c. Click the Breaks button in the Page Setup group and then click *Next Page* in the *Section Breaks* section of the drop-down list.
4. Move the insertion point to the beginning of the title *COMPENSATION* and then insert an even page section break by clicking the Breaks button and then clicking *Odd Page* at the drop-down list.

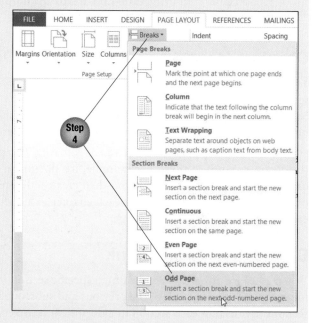

5. Create section titles and page numbering footers for the three sections in the document by completing the following steps:
    a. Position the insertion point at the beginning of the document.
    b. Click the INSERT tab.
    c. Click the Footer button in the Header & Footer group and then click *Edit Footer* at the drop-down list.
    d. At the Footer -Section 1- pane, change the font to 10-point Palatino Linotype and apply bold formatting, type **Section 1 Probationary Periods**, and then press the Tab key twice. (This moves the insertion point to the right margin.)
    e. Type **Page** and then press the spacebar.
    f. Click the HEADER & FOOTER TOOLS DESIGN tab.
    g. Click the Page Number button in the Header & Footer group, point to *Current Position*, and then click *Plain Number* at the side menu.

h. Click the Next button in the Navigation group.
i. Click the Link to Previous button to deactivate it. (This removes the message *Same as Previous* from the top right side of the footer pane.)
j. In the footer, change the text *Section 1 Probationary Periods* to *Section 2 Employee Performance.*

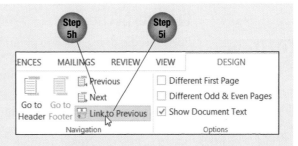

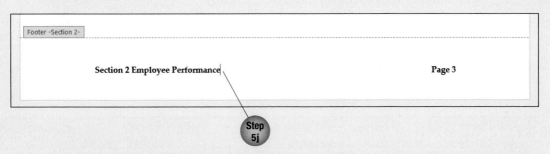

k. Click the Next button in the Navigation group.
l. Click the Link to Previous button to deactivate it. (This removes the message *Same as Previous* from the top right side of the footer pane.)
m. In the footer, change the text *Section 2 Employee Performance* to *Section 3 Compensation.*

6. Change the margins in the section 3 footer and section 3 of the document text by clicking the PAGE LAYOUT tab, clicking the Margins button, and then clicking *Wide* at the drop-down list.

7. Click the HEADER & FOOTER TOOLS DESIGN tab and then click the Close Header and Footer button. Scroll through the document and notice that changing the margins in the section 3 footer changed the margins in section 3 of the document text.

8. Begin the page numbering with 1 at the beginning of section 2 by completing the following steps:
   a. Position the insertion point on any character in the title *EMPLOYEE PERFORMANCE.*
   b. Click the INSERT tab.
   c. Click the Page Number button in the Header & Footer group and then click *Format Page Numbers.*
   d. At the Page Number Format dialog box, click the *Start at* option. (This inserts *1* in the *Start at* measurement box.)
   e. Click OK.

9. Begin the page numbering with 1 at the beginning of the *COMPENSATION* title by completing steps similar to those in Step 8.

10. Save **C19-E06-EmpHandbook.docx**.

# Printing Sections

**QUICK STEPS**

**Print a Section**
1. Click FILE tab.
2. Click *Print* option.
3. Click in *Pages* text box.
4. Type **s** followed by section number.
5. Click Print button.

Print specific pages in a document by entering the desired page numbers in the *Pages* text box at the Print backstage area. When entering page numbers, use a hyphen to indicate a range of consecutive pages for printing and a comma to specify nonconsecutive pages.

If a document contains sections, use the *Pages* text box at the Print backstage area to specify the section and pages within the section that you want to print. For example, if a document is divided into three sections and you want to print only section 2, type **s2** in the *Pages* text box. If a document contains six sections and you want to print sections 3 through 5, type **s3-s5** in the *Pages* text box.

You can also identify specific pages within or between sections for printing. For example, to print pages 2 through 5 of section 4, type **p2s4-p5s4**; to print from page 3 of section 1 through page 5 of section 4, type **p3s1-p5s4**; and to print page 1 of section 3, page 4 of section 5, and page 6 of section 8, type **p1s3,p4s5,p6s8**.

---

## Exercise 19.6B  Printing Sections                                    Part 2 of 2

1. With **C19-E06-EmpHandbook.docx** open, click the FILE tab and then click the *Print* option.
2. At the Print backstage area, specify that you want to print page 1 of section 1, page 1 of section 2, and page 1 of section 3 by clicking in the *Pages* text box and then typing **p1s1,p1s2,p1s3**.
3. Click the Print button.

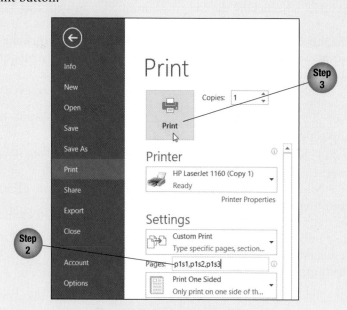

4. Save and then close **C19-E06-EmpHandbook.docx**.

# Keeping Text Together

In a multiple-page document, the soft page breaks automatically inserted by Word sometimes occur in undesirable locations. For example, a soft page break may cause a heading to display at the bottom of a page while the text connected to the heading displays at the top of the next page. A soft page break can also create a *widow* or *orphan*. A widow occurs when the short last line of text in a paragraph appears at the top of a page, and an orphan occurs when the first line of text in a paragraph appears at the bottom of a page.

Use options at the Paragraph dialog box with the Line and Page Breaks tab selected, as shown in Figure 19.3, to control widows and orphans and to keep a paragraph, group of paragraphs, or group of lines together. Display this dialog box by clicking the Paragraph group dialog box launcher on the HOME tab and then clicking the Line and Page Breaks tab at the dialog box.

By default, the *Widow/Orphan control* option is active and Word tries to avoid creating widows and orphans when inserting soft page breaks. The other three options in the *Pagination* section of the dialog box are not active by default. Use the *Keep with next* option to keep one line of text together with the next line. This is useful for keeping a heading together with the first line below it. To keep a group of selected lines together, use the *Keep lines together* option. Use the *Page break before* option to insert a page break before selected text.

**QUICK STEPS**

**Keep Text Together**
1. Click Paragraph group dialog box launcher.
2. Click Line and Page Breaks tab.
3. Click *Keep with next*, *Keep lines together*, and/or *Page break before*.
4. Click OK.

**Figure 19.3 Paragraph Dialog Box with Line and Page Breaks Tab Selected**

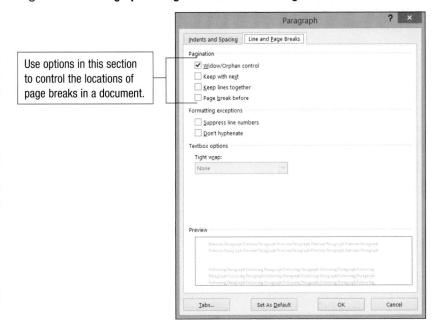

Use options in this section to control the locations of page breaks in a document.

1. Open **OnlineShop.docx** and save the document with the name **C19-E07-OnlineShop**.
2. Keep a heading together with the paragraph of text that follows it by completing the following steps:
   a. Move the insertion point to the beginning of the heading *Online Superstores* that displays at the bottom of the first page.
   b. Click the Paragraph group dialog box launcher.
   c. At the Paragraph dialog box, click the Line and Page Breaks tab.
   d. Click the *Keep with next* check box to insert a check mark.
   e. Click OK to close the dialog box.

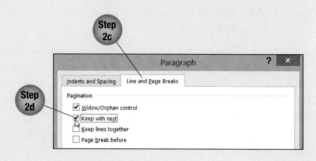

3. Insert a soft page break before text by completing the following steps:
   a. Move the insertion point to the end of the second page.
   b. Move the insertion point to the beginning of the heading *Online Shopping Safety Tips*.
   c. Click the Paragraph group dialog box launcher.
   d. At the Paragraph dialog box with the Line and Page Breaks tab selected, click the *Page break before* check box to insert a check mark.
   e. Click OK to close the dialog box.

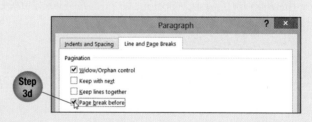

4. Insert a predesigned footer in the document by completing the following steps:
   a. Move the insertion point to the beginning of the document.
   b. Click the INSERT tab.
   c. Click the Footer button in the Header & Footer group.
   d. Scroll down the drop-down list and the click the *Filigree* option.
   e. Double-click in the document to close the footer pane.
5. Save, print, and then close **C19-E07-OnlineShop.docx**.

# Chapter Summary

➤ By default, Word inserts arabic numbers (1, 2, 3, and so on) as page numbers and numbers the pages in a document sequentially beginning with 1. You can change these default settings with options at the Page Number Format dialog box.

➤ Number the chapters in a document using an option at the Multilevel List button drop-down gallery and then include the chapter numbers with the page numbers using the *Include chapter number* option at the Page Number Format dialog box.

➤ You can insert predesigned headers and/or footers in a document or create your own.

➤ To create a header, click the INSERT tab, click the Header button, and then click *Edit Header*. At the header pane, insert the desired elements or text. Complete similar steps to create a footer.

➤ Use buttons in the Insert group on the HEADER & FOOTER TOOLS DESIGN tab to insert elements such as the date and time, Quick Parts, and pictures and images into a header or footer.

➤ Navigate to headers and footers with buttons in the Navigation group on the HEADER & FOOTER TOOLS DESIGN tab.

➤ By default, Word inserts headers and footers 0.5 inch from the edge of the page. You can reposition headers and footers with buttons in the Position group on the HEADER & FOOTER TOOLS DESIGN tab.

➤ You can create a unique header and/or footer on the first page; omit a header and/or footer on the first page; create different headers and/or footers for odd and even pages; and create different headers and/or footers for sections in a document. Use options in the Options group on the HEADER & FOOTER TOOLS DESIGN tab to specify the type of header and/or footer you want to create.

➤ To print sections or specific pages within a section, use the *Pages* text box at the Print backstage area. When specifying sections and pages, use the letter *s* before the section number and the letter *p* before the page number.

➤ Word attempts to avoid creating widows and orphans when inserting soft page breaks. Turn the widow/orphan control feature on or off at the Paragraph dialog box with the Line and Page Breaks tab selected. This dialog box also contains options for keeping a paragraph, group of paragraphs, or group of lines together and for inserting soft page breaks.

# Commands Review

| FEATURE | RIBBON TAB, GROUP | BUTTON, OPTION |
|---|---|---|
| edit footer | INSERT, Header & Footer | , *Edit Footer* |
| edit header | INSERT, Header & Footer | , *Edit Header* |
| insert footer | INSERT, Header & Footer | |
| insert header | INSERT, Header & Footer | |
| insert page number | INSERT, Header & Footer | |
| Page Number Format dialog box | INSERT, Header & Footer | , *Format Page Numbers* |
| Paragraph dialog box | HOME, Paragraph | |

# Key Points Review

**Completion:** In the space provided at the right, indicate the correct term, symbol, or command.

1. If you insert page numbers in a document, Word uses this type of number by default.

   _____

2. Customize page numbering with options at this dialog box.

   _____

3. To create your own header, click the INSERT tab, click the Header button in the Header & Footer group, and then click this option at the drop-down list.

   _____

4. This group on the HEADER & FOOTER TOOLS DESIGN tab contains the Date & Time and Pictures buttons.

   _____

5. By default, a header is positioned this distance from the top of the page.

   _____

6. By default, headers and footers contain two tab settings: a center tab and this type of tab.

   _____

7. When you create a header, clicking the *Different First Page* check box causes this pane to display.

   _____

8. Type this in the *Pages* text box at the Print backstage area to print section 5.

   _____

9. Type this in the *Pages* text box at the Print backstage area to print page 2 of section 4 and page 5 of section 8.

   _____

10. The *Keep lines together* option is available at the Paragraph dialog box with this tab selected.

   _____

# Chapter Assessments

## Applying Your Skills

Demonstrate your knowledge of features learned in this chapter by completing the following assessments.

### Assessment 19.1    Insert and Customize Page Numbers in a Computer Report

1. Open **CompSecurity.docx** and save the document with the name **C19-A01-CompSecurity**.
2. Make the following changes to the document:
   a. Apply the Heading 1 style to the two titles, *Computer Viruses* and *Security Risks*, and apply the Heading 2 style to the five headings.
   b. Insert at the beginning of the title *Security Risks* a section break that begins a new page.
   c. Apply the Centered style set.
   d. Apply chapter multilevel list numbering.
   e. Insert page numbers that include chapter numbers on all of the pages in the document. Position the page number at the bottom center of each page. *Hint: Refer to Exercise 19.2, Step 9.*
3. Save, print, and then close **C19-A01-CompSecurity.docx**.

## Assessment 19.2     Create Odd and Even Page Footers in a Robot Report

1. Open **Robots.docx** and save the document with the name **C19-A02-Robots**.
2. Make the following changes to the document:
   a. Apply the Heading 2 style to the title *ROBOTS AS ANDROIDS*.
   b. Apply the Heading 3 style to the headings *Visual Perception, Audio Perception, Tactile Perception, Locomotion*, and *Navigation*.
   c. Apply the Lines (Distinctive) style set.
   d. Change the paragraph spacing to Relaxed. (Use the Paragraph Spacing button in the Document Formatting group on the DESIGN tab.)
   e. Center the title *ROBOTS AS ANDROIDS*.
   f. Keep the heading *Navigation* together with the paragraph of text that follows it.
3. Create an odd page footer that includes the following:
   a. Insert the current date at the left margin. (Choose the date option that displays the month spelled out, such as *January 1, 2015*.)
   b. Insert a clip art image related to robots in the middle of the footer. Change the height of the robot image to approximately 0.6 inch and the text wrapping to *Behind Text*. Drag the robot image down so it is positioned below the footer pane border.
   c. At the right margin, type **Page**, press the spacebar, and then insert a page number at the current position.
4. Create an even page footer that includes the following:
   a. At the left margin, type **Page**, press the spacebar, and then insert a page number at the current position.
   b. Insert in the middle of the footer the same clip art image you inserted in the odd page footer.
   c. Insert the current date at the right margin in the same format you chose for the odd page footer.
5. Save, print, and then close **C19-A02-Robots.docx**.

## Assessment 19.3     Create and Edit Footers in a Software Report

1. Open **SoftwareChapters.docx** and save the document with the name **C19-A03-SoftwareChapters**.
2. Insert at the beginning of the title *CHAPTER 2: GRAPHICS AND MULTIMEDIA SOFTWARE* a section break that begins a new page.
3. Create a footer for the first section in the document that displays *Chapter 1* at the left margin, the page number in the middle, and your first and last names at the right margin.
4. Edit the footer for the second section so it displays as *Chapter 2* instead of *Chapter 1*. **Hint: Make sure you break the link.**
5. Begin page numbering with 1 at the beginning of the section 2.
6. Print page 1 of section 1 and page 1 of section 2.
7. Save and then close **C19-A03-SoftwareChapters.docx**.

# Expanding Your Skills

Explore additional feature options or use Help to learn a new skill in creating this document.

**Assessment 19.4    Insert a Horizontal Line in a Footer in an Online Shopping Report**

1. Open **OnlineShop.docx** and save the document with the name **C19-A04-OnlineShop**.
2. Keep the heading *Online Superstores* together with the paragraph following it.
3. Open the footer pane. Office.com provides a number of horizontal line images that you can insert in a document or in the header and/or footer in a document. Display horizontal line images by clicking the Online Pictures button in the Insert group to open the Insert Pictures window, typing **horizontal line** in the search text box, and then pressing the Enter key. Insert a horizontal line of your choosing in the footer pane. (To get a better view of the horizontal line options at the Insert Pictures window, hover your mouse over an option and then click the magnifying glass image that displays in the lower right corner of the option.) With the horizontal line selected, press Ctrl + E to center the line in the footer pane. Use the Color button on the PICTURE TOOLS FORMAT tab to apply a color that matches the colors in the document.
4. After inserting the horizontal line, press the Enter key and then insert the current date. Select the date, apply bold formatting, and change the font color to Dark Blue.
5. The HEADER & FOOTER TOOLS DESIGN tab contains a number of buttons for inserting data in a header or footer. With the Quick Parts button in the Insert group, you can insert pieces of content such as fields and document properties. To determine what options are available, click the Quick Parts button and then hover your mouse over or click the options at the drop-down list.
6. Close the footer pane.
7. Create a header that inserts an author document property. To do this, display the header pane, click the Quick Parts button, point to *Document Property*, and then click *Author* at the side menu. This inserts the *Author* placeholder, which contains a name. If the name is not your name, click the *Author* placeholder tab (which selects the text in the placeholder) and then type your first and last names.
8. Press the Right Arrow key to move the insertion point to the right of the *Author* placeholder and then press the Tab key twice.
9. Insert the file name as a field. To do this, click the Quick Parts button and then click *Field* at the drop-down list. At the Field dialog box, click *FileName* in the *Field names* list box and then click OK. (You will need to scroll down the list box to find the *FileName* option.) Select your name and the file name, apply bold formatting, and change the font color to Dark Blue.
10. Make the document active.
11. Save, print, and then close **C19-A04-OnlineShop.docx**.

# Achieving Signature Status

Take your skills to the next level by completing this more challenging assessment.

## Assessment 19.5    Format a Document with Headers, Footers, and Page Numbers

1. Open **InternetChapters.docx** and save the document with the name **C19-A05-InternetChapters**.
2. Make the following changes to the document:
   a. Insert a section break that begins a new page at the beginning of the title *Online Content* and at the beginning of the title *E-Commerce*.
   b. Apply chapter multilevel list numbering. (This will insert the word *Chapter* followed by the chapter number before each of the three titles with the Heading 1 style applied.)
   c. Move the insertion point to the beginning of the document and then create an odd page header that prints your name at the left margin and the current date at the right margin. Insert a border line below the text. (The border line will span from the left to the right margin.) Create an even page header that prints the current date at the left margin and your name at the right margin. Insert a border line below the text.
   d. Create an odd page footer that inserts a page number at the bottom right margin of each page that includes the chapter number. Insert a border line above the page number. Create an even page footer that inserts a page number at the bottom left margin of each page that includes the chapter number. Insert a border line above the page number.
   e. Move the insertion point to the chapter 1 title and then change the page numbering so it includes the chapter number.
   f. Move the insertion point to the chapter 2 title and then change the page numbering so it starts with 1 and includes the chapter number.
   g. Move the insertion point to the chapter 3 title and then change the page numbering so it starts with 1 and includes the chapter number.
3. Scroll through the document. Each odd page should have your name displayed at the top of the page at the left margin and the current date at the right margin with a border line below it, along with the page number (including the chapter number) at the bottom of the page at the right margin with a border line above it. Each even page should have the current date displayed at the top of the page at the left margin and your name at the right margin with a border line below it, along with the page number (including the chapter number) at the bottom of the page at the left margin with a border line above it. The page numbers for the first two pages should display as *1-1* and *1-2*. The third and fourth pages should display as *2-1* and *2-2*. (The pages are numbered like this because you specified to include chapter numbers with the page numbers and to start numbering each chapter with page 1.) The fifth page should display *3-1*.
4. Save **C19-A05-InternetChapters.docx**.
5. Print only the first pages of sections 1, 2, and 3.
6. Close **C19-A05-InternetChapters.docx**.
7. If a message displays asking if you want to save your building blocks, click the Don't Save button.

# Chapter 20

# Managing Shared Documents

## Performance Objectives

Upon successful completion of Chapter 20, you will be able to:

- Insert, edit, delete, display, print, and reply to comments
- Track the changes made to a document and customize tracking
- Compare documents and customize compare options
- Combine documents and manage style conflicts
- Embed and link data between Excel and Word

In a company environment, you may work with other employees and need to share and distribute documents to members of the company. You may be part of a workgroup in a company, which is a network of computers that share files, printers, and other resources. As a member of a workgroup, you can collaborate with other members and distribute documents for review and/or revision. In this chapter, you will perform workgroup activities such as inserting comments into a document, tracking changes in a document from multiple users, comparing documents, and combining documents from multiple users. You will also embed and link data between Excel and Word.

If a Word document (in the *.docx* format) is located on a server running Microsoft SharePoint Server, multiple users can edit the document concurrently. Concurrent editing allows a group of users to work on a document at the same time or a single user to work on the same document from different computers. If a document is not located on a server running SharePoint Server, Word supports only single-user editing. Exercises and assessments in this chapter assume that the files you are editing are not located on a server running SharePoint Server.

*Note: Before beginning computer exercises for this chapter, copy to your storage medium the Chapter20 folder from the CD that accompanies this textbook and then make Chapter20 the active folder.*

In this chapter, students will produce the following documents:

Exercise 20.1. C20-E01-NDMNewEmps.docx
Exercise 20.2. C20-E02-BldgAgrmnt.docx
Exercise 20.3. C20-E03-ComAgrmnt.docx
Exercise 20.4. C20-E04-CombinedLease.docx
Exercise 20.5. C20-E05-DIRevs.docx
Exercise 20.5. C20-E05-NSSCosts.docx

Model answers for these exercises are shown on the following pages.

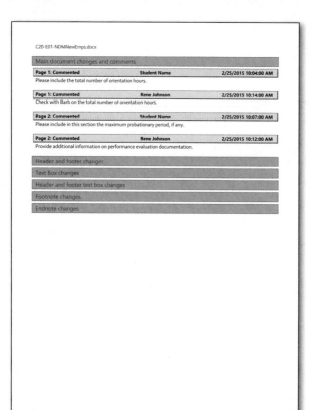

C20-E01-NDMNewEmps.docx

**Main document changes and comments**

| Page 1: Commented | Student Name | 2/25/2015 10:04:00 AM |

Please include the total number of orientation hours.

| Page 1: Commented | Rene Johnson | 2/25/2015 10:14:00 AM |

Check with Barb on the total number of orientation hours.

| Page 2: Commented | Student Name | 2/25/2015 10:07:00 AM |

Please include in this section the maximum probationary period, if any.

| Page 2: Commented | Rene Johnson | 2/25/2015 10:12:00 AM |

Provide additional information on performance evaluation documentation.

**Header and footer changes**

**Text Box changes**

**Header and footer text box changes**

**Footnote changes**

**Endnote changes**

**Exercise 20.1** C20-E01-NDMNewEmps.docx

---

**BUILDING CONSTRUCTION AGREEMENT**

**THIS AGREEMENT** made this _____ day of _____, 2015, by and between _____, hereinafter referred to as "builder," and _____, hereinafter referred to as "owner," the builder and the owner, for the considerations hereinafter named, agree as follows:

**Construction Loan and Financing Arrangements:** The owner either has or will obtain a construction loan to finance the work to be performed under this Agreement. If adequate financing has not been arranged within sixty (60) days of the date of this Agreement, or the owner cannot provide evidence to the builder of other financial ability to pay the full amount of the contract, then the builder at his option may treat this Agreement as null and void, and retain the down payment made on the execution of this Agreement.

**Supervision of Work:** Owner agrees that the direction and supervision of the working force including subcontractor, rests exclusively with the builder or his/her duly designated agent, and owner agrees not to issue any instructions to, or otherwise interfere with, same.

**Start of Construction:** The builder shall commence construction of the residence as soon as practical after signing of this Agreement and adequate financial arrangements satisfactory to the builder have been made.

**Changes and Alterations:** All changes in or departures from the plans and/or specifications shall be in writing. Where changes in or departures from plans and specifications requested in writing by owner will result in furnishing of additional labor and materials, the owner shall pay the builder for such extras at a price agreed upon in writing before commencement of said change. Where such change results in the omitting of any labor or materials, the builder shall allow the owner a credit therefore at a price agreed to in writing before commencement of said changes.

**Possession of Residence:** On final payment by owner and upon owner's request, builder will provide owner with affidavit stating that all labor, materials, and equipment used in the construction have been paid for or will be paid for in full by the builder unless otherwise noted. Builder shall not be required to give possession of the residence to the owner before final payment by owner. Final payment constitutes acceptance of the residence as being satisfactorily completed unless a separate escrow agreement is executed between the parties stipulating the unfinished items.

**Exclusions:** The owner is solely responsible for the purchase and installation of any septic tank or other individual subsurface sewage disposal system that may be required on the property.

**Builder's Right to Terminate the Contract:** Should the work be stopped by any public authority for a period of sixty (60) days or more, through no fault of the builder, or should the work be stopped through act or neglect of the owner for a period of seven days, or should the owner fail to pay the builder any payment within seven days after it is due, then the builder upon seven days written notice to the owner,

**Exercise 20.2** C20-E02-BldgAgrmnt.docx

Page 1

---

may stop work or terminate the contract and recover from the owner payment for all work executed and any loss sustained and reasonable profit and damages.

The owner acknowledges that she/he has read and fully understands the provisions of this Agreement.

**IN WITNESS WHEREOF,** the builder and owner have hereunto set their hands this _____ day of _____, 20____.

_____          _____
BUILDER                                                     OWNER

Page 2

---

Model Answers

**Exercise 20.3**

C20-E03-ComAgrmnt.docx

## COMMERCIAL LEASE AGREEMENT

**This Commercial Lease Agreement** ("Lease") is made by and between _____ ("Landlord") and _____ ("Tenant"). Landlord is the owner of land and improvements commonly known and numbered as _____ and legally described as follows (the "Building"): _____
_____. Landlord makes available for lease a portion of the Building designated as _____ (the "Leased Premises").

Landlord desires to lease the Leased Premises to Tenant, and Tenant desires to lease the Leased Premises from Landlord for the term at the rental, and upon the covenants, conditions, and provisions herein set forth.

**THEREFORE**, in consideration of the mutual promises herein contained, and other good and valuable consideration, it is agreed:

**Term**

A. Landlord hereby leases the Leased Premises to Tenant, and Tenant hereby leases the same from Landlord, for an "Initial Term" beginning _____ and ending _____. Landlord shall use his/her best efforts to give Tenant possession as nearly as possible at the beginning of the Lease term. If Landlord is unable to timely provide the Leased Premises, rent shall abate for the period of delay. Tenant shall make no other claim against Landlord for any such delay.

B. Tenant may renew the Lease for one extended term of _____. Tenant shall exercise such renewal option by giving written notice to Landlord not less than ninety (90) days prior to the expiration of the Initial Term. The renewal term shall be at the rental set forth below and otherwise upon the same covenants, conditions, and provisions as provided in this Lease.

**Rental**

A. Tenant shall pay to Landlord during the Initial Term rental of _____ per year, payable in installments of _____ per month. Each installment payment shall be due in advance on the first day of each calendar month during the lease term to Landlord at _____ or at such other place designated by written notice from Landlord or Tenant. The rental payment amount for any partial calendar months included in the lease term shall be prorated on a daily basis. Tenant shall also pay to Landlord a "Security Deposit" in the amount of _____.

B. The rental for any renewal lease term, if created as permitted under this Lease, shall be _____ per year payable in installments of _____ per month.

Page 1

**Use**

Notwithstanding the forgoing, Tenant shall not use the Leased Premises for manufacturing, or selling any explosives, flammables, or other inherently da chemical, item, or device.

**Repairs**

During the Lease term, Tenant shall make, at Tenant's expense, all necessary repairs to the Leased Premises. Repairs shall include such items as routine repairs of floors, walls, ceilings, and other parts of the Leased Premises damaged or worn through normal occupancy, except for major mechanical systems or the roof, subject to the obligations of the parties otherwise set forth in this Lease.

**Sublease and Assignment**

Tenant shall have the right, without Landlord's consent, to assign this Lease to a corporation with which Tenant may merge or consolidate, to any subsidiary of Tenant, to any corporation under common control with Tenant, or to a purchaser of substantially all of Tenant's assets. Except as set forth above, Tenant shall not sublease all or any part of the Leased Premises, or assign this Lease in whole or in part without Landlord's consent, such consent not to be unreasonably withheld or delayed.

**Property Taxes**

Landlord shall pay all general real estate taxes and installments of special assessments coming due during the Lease term on the Leased Premises, and all personal property taxes with respect to Landlord's personal property, if any, on the Leased Premises. Tenant shall be responsible for paying all personal property taxes with respect to Tenant's personal property at the Leased Premises.

_____

**Landlord**

_____

**Tenant**

Page 2

LEASE AGREEMENT

THIS LEASE AGREEMENT (hereinafter referred to as the "Agreement") is made and entered into this _____ day of _____, 2015, by and between Lessor and Lessee.

### Term

Lessor leases to Lessee and Lessee leases from Lessor the described Premises together with any and all appurtenances thereto, for a term of _____ year(s), such term beginning on _____, and ending at midnight on _____.

### Damage Deposit

Upon the due execution of this Agreement, Lessee shall deposit with Lessor the sum of _____ DOLLARS ($_____) receipt of which is hereby acknowledged by Lessor, as security for any damage caused to the Premises during the leasing term hereof. Such deposit shall be returned to Lessee, without interest, upon the termination of this leasing Agreement.

### Use of Premises

The Premises shall be used and occupied by Lessee and Lessee's immediate family, exclusively, as a private, single-family residence, and no part of the Premises shall be used at any time during the term of this Agreement by Lessee for the purpose of carrying on any business, profession, or trade of any kind, or for any purpose other than as a private single-family dwelling. Lessee shall not allow any other person, other than Lessee's immediate family or relatives and friends who are guests of Lessee, to use or occupy the Premises without first obtaining Lessor's written consent to such use.

### Rent

The total rent for the term hereof is the sum of _____ DOLLARS ($_____) less any reimbursements and payable on the _____ day of each month of the term. All such payments shall be made to Lessor at Lessor's address on or before the due date and without demand.

### Condition of Premises

Lessee stipulates, represents, and warrants that Lessee has examined the Premises, and that they are at the time of this Agreement in good order, repair, and in a safe, clean, and tenantable condition.

### Alterations and Improvements

Lessee shall make no improvements on the Premises without the prior written consent of Lessor. Any and all alterations, changes, and/or improvements built, constructed, or placed on the Premises by Lessee shall be and become the property of the Lessor and remain on the Premises at the expiration or earlier termination of this Agreement.

### Damage to Premises

In the event Premises are destroyed or rendered wholly unlivable by fire, storm, earthquake, or other casualty not caused by the negligence of Lessee, this Agreement shall terminate from such time except for the purpose of enforcing all rights that may have then accrued hereunder.

**Exercise 20.4**  C20-E04-CombinedLease.docx          Page 1

Page 2

# Dearborn Industries

## Revenues

Company revenues increased in 2015 as a result of development contracts with government entities focused on the design of flywheel technologies. Several development prototypes were produced and placed with potential customers and shipped and preproduction units have shipped. The increase in revenues is reflected in the following table:

| Customer | 1st Qtr | 2nd Qtr | 3rd Qtr | 4th Qtr | Total |
|---|---|---|---|---|---|
| Lakeside Trucking | $ 69,450 | $ 75,340 | $ 88,224 | $ 95,000 | $ 328,014 |
| Gresham Machines | 25,210 | 28,340 | 33,400 | 43,199 | 130,149 |
| Manchester County | 30,219 | 28,590 | 34,264 | 40,891 | 133,964 |
| Genesis Productions | 35,290 | 51,390 | 59,334 | 72,190 | 218,204 |
| Landower Company | 12,168 | 19,355 | 25,209 | 262,188 | 318,920 |
| Jewell Enterprises | 24,329 | 21,809 | 33,490 | 49,764 | 129,392 |
| Total | $ 196,666 | $ 224,824 | $ 273,921 | $ 563,232 | $ 1,258,643 |

**Exercise 20.4**  C20-E05-DIRevs.docx

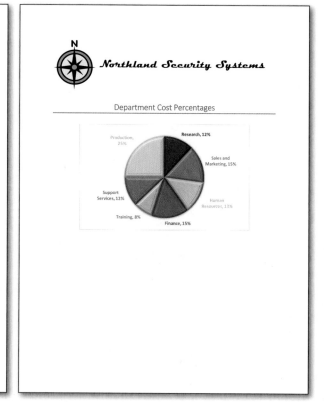

**Exercise 20.4**  C20-E05-NSSCosts.docx

# Inserting Comments

You can provide feedback and suggest changes to a document that someone else has written by inserting comments into it. Similarly, you can obtain feedback on a document that you have written by distributing it electronically to others and having them insert comments into it.

To insert a comment in a document, select the text or item you would like to comment on or position the insertion point at the end of that text, click the REVIEW tab, and then click the New Comment button in the Comments group. Generally, clicking the New Comment button displays a comment icon and comment balloon at the right margin, as shown in Figure 20.1. With the insertion point positioned in the comment balloon, type the comment text.

**Insert a Comment in a Balloon**
1. Select text.
2. Click REVIEW tab.
3. Click New Comment button.
4. Type comment.

New Comment

## Figure 20.1 Comment Balloon

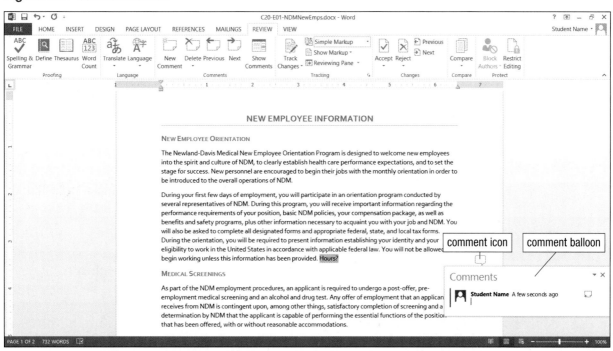

Depending on what previous settings have been applied, clicking the New Comment button may cause the Reviewing pane to display at the left side of the document rather than a comment icon and balloon at the right margin. If this happens, click the Show Markup button in the Tracking group on the REVIEW tab, point to *Balloons*, and then click *Show Only Comments and Formatting in Balloons* at the side menu. Also check to make sure the Display for Review button in the Tracking group is set to *Simple Markup*. If it is set to something else, click the Display for Review button and then click *Simple Markup* at the drop-down list.

Show Markup

Display for Review

1. Open **NDMNewEmps.docx** and save the document with the name **C20-E01-NDMNewEmps**.
2. Insert a comment by completing the following steps:
   a. Position the insertion point at the end of the second paragraph in the *NEW EMPLOYEE ORIENTATION* section.
   b. Press the spacebar once and then type **Hours?**.
   c. Select *Hours?*.
   d. Click the REVIEW tab.
   e. If the Show Comments button in the Comments group is active (displays with a light blue background), click the button to deactivate it.
   f. Click the New Comment button in the Comments group. (If the insertion point does not display in a comment balloon, click the Show Markup button in the Tracking group, point to *Balloons*, and then click *Show Only Comments and Formatting in Balloons* at the side menu. If the Reviewing pane displays, turn it off by clicking the Reviewing Pane button in the Tracking group.)
   g. Type **Please include the total number of orientation hours.** in the comment balloon.

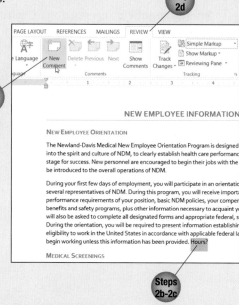

3. Insert another comment by completing the following steps:
   a. Move the insertion point to the end of the third (last) paragraph in the *MEDICAL SCREENINGS* section.
   b. Click the New Comment button in the Comments group on the REVIEW tab.
   c. Type **Specify the locations where drug tests are administered.** in the comment balloon. (Since you did not have text selected when you clicked the New Comment button, Word selected the word immediately left of the insertion point.)

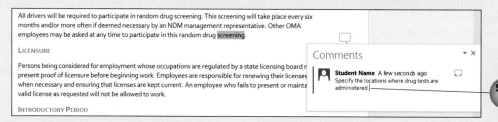

   d. Click in the document to close the comment balloons.
4. Save **C20-E01-NDMNewEmps.docx**.

# Inserting Comments in the Reviewing Pane

You may prefer to insert comments with the Reviewing pane displayed on the screen. The Reviewing pane displays inserted comments and changes made with the Track Changes feature. (You will learn about tracking changes later in this chapter.)

To display the Reviewing pane, click the Reviewing Pane button in the Tracking group. The Reviewing pane displays at the left side of the screen, as shown in Figure 20.2. Click the New Comment button in the Comments group and a comment icon and comment balloon display in the right margin, and the reviewer's name followed by "Commented" displays in the Reviewing pane. Type your comment and the text displays in the comment balloon as well as the Reviewing pane.

The Reviewing pane might display along the bottom of the screen rather than at the left side. To specify where you want the pane to display, click the Reviewing Pane button arrow in the Tracking group on the REVIEW tab and then click *Reviewing Pane Vertical* or *Reviewing Pane Horizontal*.

**Insert a Comment in the Reviewing Pane**
1. Click REVIEW tab.
2. Click Reviewing Pane button.
3. Click New Comment button.
4. Type comment.

Reviewing Pane

## Figure 20.2 Vertical Reviewing Pane

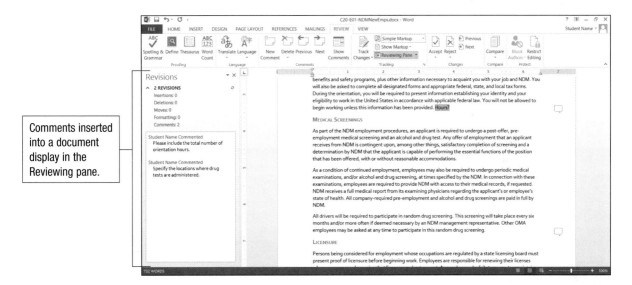

Comments inserted into a document display in the Reviewing pane.

The summary section at the top of the Reviewing pane provides counts of the number of comments inserted and types of changes made to the document. After typing your comment in the Reviewing pane, close the pane by clicking the Reviewing Pane button in the Tracking group or clicking the Close button (the button marked with an *X*) located in the upper right corner of the pane.

1. With **C20-E01-NDMNewEmps.docx** open, show the comments in the Reviewing pane by completing the following steps:

    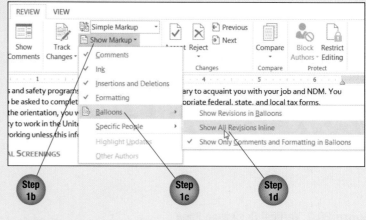

    a. Click the Reviewing Pane button in the Tracking group on the REVIEW tab.
    b. Click the Show Markup button in the Tracking group.
    c. Point to *Balloons* at the drop-down list.
    d. Click *Show All Revisions Inline* at the side menu.

2. Insert a comment by completing the following steps:

    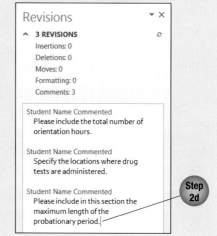

    a. Move the insertion point to the end of the paragraph of text in the *INTRODUCTORY PERIOD* section.
    b. Press the spacebar once, type **Maximum?**, and then select *Maximum?*.
    c. Click the New Comment button in the Comments group on the REVIEW tab.
    d. With the insertion point positioned in the Reviewing pane, type **Please include in this section the maximum length of the probationary period.**
3. Click the Reviewing Pane button in the Tracking group to turn off the display of the Reviewing pane.
4. Save **C20-E01-NDMNewEmps.docx**.

**QUICK STEPS**

**Edit a Comment**
1. Click REVIEW tab.
2. Click Reviewing Pane button.
3. Click in desired comment in pane.
4. Make desired changes.
OR
1. Click REVIEW tab.
2. Turn on display of comment balloons.
3. Click in comment balloon.
4. Make desired changes.

## Navigating between Comments

When working in a long document that has many inserted comments, you may find it helpful to use the Previous and Next buttons in the Comments group on the REVIEW tab. Click the Next button to move the insertion point to the next comment or click the Previous button to move the insertion point to the preceding comment.

## Editing Comments

You can edit a comment in the Reviewing pane or in a comment balloon. To edit a comment in the Reviewing pane, click the Reviewing Pane button to turn on the pane and then click in the comment that you want to edit. Make the desired changes to the comment and then close the Reviewing pane. To edit a comment in a comment balloon, turn on the display of comment balloons, click in the comment balloon, and then make the desired changes.

Previous    Next

## Showing Comments

The Comments group on the REVIEW tab contains a Show Comments button. Click this button and comments display at the right side of the document. The Show Comments button is available only when the Display for Review button in the Tracking group is set to *Simple Markup*.

Show Comments

---

## Exercise 20.1C   Editing Comments                                    Part 3 of 4

1. With **C20-E01-NDMNewEmps.docx** open, navigate from one comment to another by completing the following steps:
   a. Press Ctrl + Home to move the insertion point to the beginning of the document.
   b. Make sure the REVIEW tab is active and then click the Next button in the Comments group. (This moves the insertion point to the first comment, opens the Reviewing pane, and moves the insertion point to the pane.)
   c. Click the Next button to display the second comment.
   d. Click the Next button to display the third comment.
   e. Click the Previous button to display the second comment.
2. With the insertion point positioned in the Reviewing pane, edit the second comment to read **Specify the locations within NDM where drug tests are administered as well as any off-site locations.**
3. Click the Reviewing Pane button to close the pane.
4. Edit a comment in a comment balloon by completing the following steps:
   a. Click the Show Markup button in the Tracking group, point to *Balloons*, and then click *Show Only Comments and Formatting in Balloons* at the side menu.
   b. Click the Show Comments button in the Comments group to display the balloons on the right side of the document.
   c. Display the paragraph of text in the *INTRODUCTORY PERIOD* section and then click in the comment balloon that displays at the right.
   d. Edit the comment so it displays as **Please include in this section the maximum probationary period, if any.**

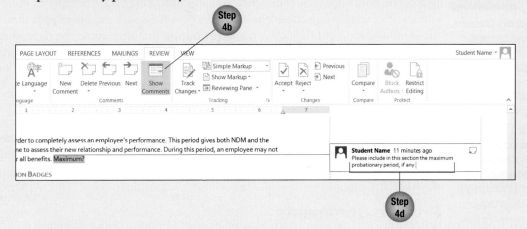

   e. Click in the document and click the Show Comments button to turn off the display of comments at the right side of the document.
   f. Click the Show Markup button, point to *Balloons*, and then click *Show All Revisions Inline*.
5. Save **C20-E01-NDMNewEmps.docx**.

---

## Distinguishing Comments from Other Users

**QUICK STEPS**

**Change the User Name and Initials**
1. Click FILE tab.
2. Click *Options*.
3. Type desired name in *User name* text box.
4. Type desired initials in *Initials* text box.
5. Click OK.

More than one user can make comments within a document. Word uses colors to distinguish comments made by different users, generally displaying the first user's comments in red and the second user's comments in blue. (These colors may vary.)

You can change the user name and initials at the Word Options dialog box with *General* selected, as shown in Figure 20.3. To change the user name, select the name that displays in the *User name* text box and then type the desired name. Complete similar steps to change the user initials in the *Initials* text box. You may also need to insert a check mark in the *Always use these values regardless of sign in to Office.* check box.

**Figure 20.3 Word Options Dialog Box with *General* Selected**

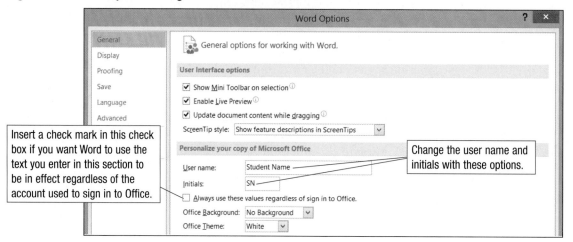

Insert a check mark in this check box if you want Word to use the text you enter in this section to be in effect regardless of the account used to sign in to Office.

Change the user name and initials with these options.

## Replying to Comments

**QUICK STEPS**

**Reply to a Comment**
1. Open comment balloon.
2. Hover mouse over comment text.
3. Click Reply button.
4. Type reply.

**Print a Document with Comments**
1. Click FILE tab.
2. Click *Print* option.
3. Click first gallery in *Settings* category.
4. If necessary, click *Print Markup* to insert check mark.
5. Click Print button.

In a document containing comments, you and others may want to reply to the comments. To reply to a comment, open the comment balloon, hover your mouse over the comment text, and then click the Reply button that displays to the right of the reviewer's name. Type the reply in the reply window that opens below the comment. You can also click in a comment and then click the New Comment button in the Comments group on the REVIEW tab or right-click in a comment and then click *Reply To Comment* at the shortcut menu.

Reply to a comment in the Reviewing pane by right-clicking the comment in the pane and then clicking *Reply To Comment* at the shortcut menu. This creates a new comment in the Reviewing pane. Another option is to click in the comment in the Reviewing pane and then click the New Comment button in the Comments group on the REVIEW tab.

## Printing Comments

To print a document with the comments included, display the Print backstage area and then click the first gallery in the *Settings* category. (This is the gallery containing the text *Print All Pages*.) At the drop-down list that displays, insert a check mark before the *Print Markup* option if you want to print the document with the comments. If you want to print the document without the comments, remove the check mark before the *Print Markup* option. If you want to print only the comments and not the document, click *List of Markup* at the drop-down list. This prints the contents of the Reviewing pane, which may include comments, tracked changes, and changes to headers, footers, text boxes, footnotes, and endnotes.

## Deleting Comments

Delete a comment by clicking the Next button in the Comments group on the REVIEW tab until the desired comment is selected and then clicking the Delete button in the Comments group. If you want to delete all of the comments in a document, click the Delete button arrow and then click *Delete All Comments in Document* at the drop-down list. You can also right-click a comment in the Reviewing pane and click *Delete Comment* from the shortcut menu.

A comment can also be dimmed in a document without deleting it. To dim a comment, right-click the comment and then click *Mark Comment Done* at the shortcut menu. Dimming a comment is useful when you are finished with a comment but are not ready to delete it.

**QUICK STEPS**

**Print Only the Comments**
1. Click FILE tab.
2. Click *Print* option.
3. Click first gallery in *Settings* category.
4. Click *List of Markup* in drop-down list.
5. Click Print button.

**Delete a Comment**
1. Click REVIEW tab.
2. Click Next button until desired comment is selected.
3. Click Delete button.

Delete

---

**Exercise 20.1D**  **Changing User Information and Inserting and Deleting Comments**  **Part 4 of 4**

1. With **C20-E01-NDMNewEmps.docx** open, change the user information by completing the following steps:
   a. Click the FILE tab.
   b. Click *Options*.
   c. At the Word Options dialog box, make sure *General* is selected in the left panel.
   d. Make a note of the current name and initials in the *Personalize your copy of Microsoft Office* section.
   e. Select the name displayed in the *User name* text box and then type **Rene Johnson**.
   f. Select the initials displayed in the *Initials* text box and then type **RJ**.
   g. Click in the *Always use these values regardless of sign in to Office.* check box to insert a check mark.
   h. Click OK to close the Word Options dialog box.

2. Insert a comment by completing the following steps:
   a. Move the insertion point to the end of the first paragraph of text in the *PERFORMANCE REVIEW* section.
   b. Click the New Comment button in the Comments group on the REVIEW tab.
   c. Type **Provide additional information on performance evaluation documentation.** in the Reviewing pane.
   d. Click the Reviewing Pane button to close the pane.
3. Respond to a comment by completing the following steps:
   a. Press Ctrl + Home to move the insertion point to the beginning of the document.
   b. Click the Show Markup button, point to *Balloons*, and then click *Show Only Comments and Formatting in Balloons* at the drop-down list.
   c. Click the Next button in the Comments group. (This opens the comment balloon for the first comment.)
   d. Click the Reply button that displays to the right of the reviewer's name in the comment balloon.

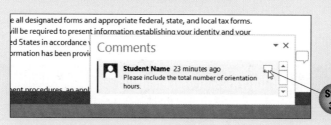

Step 3d

e. Type **Check with Barb on the total number of orientation hours.**

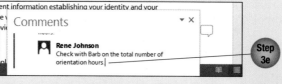

Step 3e

f. Click in the document. (This removes the comment balloon.)
4. Print only the information in the Reviewing pane by completing the following steps:
   a. Click the FILE tab and then click the *Print* option. (You can also display the Print backstage area by pressing Ctrl + P.)
   b. At the Print backstage area, click the first gallery in the *Settings* category and then click *List of Markup* in the drop-down list.
   c. Click the Print button.

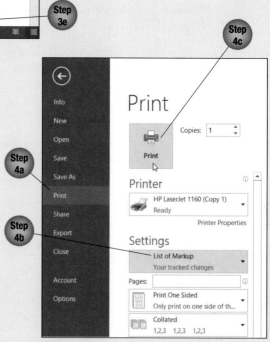

Step 4a

Step 4b

Step 4c

Step 2c

5.  Delete a comment by completing the following steps:
    a.  Press Ctrl + Home.
    b.  Click the Next button in the Comments group.
    c.  Click the Next button again.
    d.  Click the Next button again.
    e.  Click the Delete button in the Comments group to delete the comment.
6.  Print only the information in the Reviewing pane by repeating Step 4.
7.  Change the user information back to the default settings by completing the following steps:
    a.  Click the FILE tab and then click *Options*.
    b.  At the Word Options dialog box with *General* selected, select *Rene Johnson* in the *User name* text box and then type the original name.
    c.  Select the initials *RJ* in the *Initials* text box and then type the original initials.
    d.  Click the *Always use these values regardless of sign in to Office.* check box to remove the check mark.
    e.  Click OK to close the dialog box.
8.  Save and then close **C20-E01-NDMNewEmps.docx**.

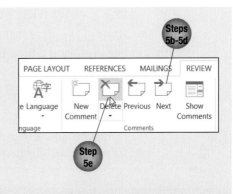

# Tracking Changes to a Document

If more than one person in a workgroup needs to review and edit a document, consider using the Track Changes feature in Word. When Track Changes is turned on, Word tracks each deletion, insertion, and formatting change made to a document. Word uses a different color (up to eight) for each person who makes changes to the document. This allows anyone looking at the document to identify which users made which changes.

## Displaying Changes for Review

The Display for Review button in the Tracking group on the REVIEW tab has a default setting of *Simple Markup*. At this setting, any changes you make to the document display in the document and Word inserts a line near the left margin where the change was made.

If you want to see the changes, click the Display for Review button and then click the *All Markup* option. With this option selected, each change displays in the document. For example, if you delete text, it stays in the document but displays in a different color with a line through it. You can also turn on the display of all markup by clicking a vertical change line that displays at the left margin where a change was made or by clicking a comment balloon.

If you have used Track Changes to revise a document, you can see what the final document will look like with the changes made by clicking the Display for Review button and then clicking *No Markup* at the drop-down list. This displays the document with the changes but does not make the changes to the document. If you want to see the original document without the changes, click the Display for Review button and then click *Original* at the drop-down list.

**Turn on Track Changes**
1. Click REVIEW tab.
2. Click Track Changes button.
OR
Press Ctrl + Shift + E.

Track Changes

## Showing Markup

With the display of all markup turned on, specify what tracking information displays in a document with options at the Balloons side menu. To show all of the revisions in balloons at the right margin, click the Show Markup button, point to *Balloons*, and then click *Show Revisions in Balloons* at the side menu. To display all of the changes in the document with vertical change lines at the left margin where the changes were made, click *Show All Revisions Inline*. To display insertions and deletions in the text and comments and formatting changes in balloons at the right margin, click the *Show Only Comments and Formatting in Balloons* option at the side menu.

---

## Exercise 20.2A  Tracking Changes in a Document                    Part 1 of 4

1. Open **BldgAgrmnt.docx** and save the document with the name **C20-E02-BldgAgrmnt**.

2. Turn on the Track Changes by clicking the REVIEW tab and then clicking the Track Changes button in the Tracking group.

3. Type the word **BUILDING** between the words *THIS* and *AGREEMENT* in the first paragraph of text. (Notice the vertical change line that displays at the left margin.)

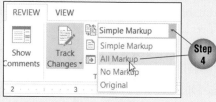

4. Show all markup by clicking the Display for Review button in the Tracking group on the REVIEW tab and then clicking *All Markup* at the drop-down list. (Notice that the text *BUILDING* you inserted is underlined and displays in red in the document.)

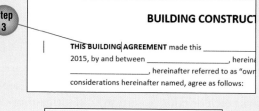

5. Select and then delete *thirty (30)* in the second paragraph. (The deleted text displays in the document as strikethrough text.)

6. Type **sixty (60)**.

7. Move a paragraph of text by completing the following steps:

    a. Select the paragraph of text that begins with *Supervision of Work:*, including the blank line below the paragraph.

    b. Press Ctrl + X to cut the text. (The paragraph stays in the document and displays in red as strikethrough text.)

    c. Position the insertion point at the beginning of the word *Start* (in the paragraph that begins *Start of Construction and Completion:*).

    d. Press Ctrl + V to insert the cut text. (The inserted text displays in green with double underlining in the new location and the text in the original location also displays in green with double-strikethrough characters.)

8. Turn off Track Changes by clicking the Track Changes button in the Tracking group.

9. Display the revisions in balloons by clicking the Show Markup button, pointing to *Balloons*, and then clicking *Show Revisions in Balloons* at the side menu.

10. After looking at the revisions in balloons, click the Show Markup button, point to *Balloons*, and then click *Show All Revisions Inline* at the side menu.

11. Save **C20-E02-BldgAgrmnt.docx**.

# Displaying Track Changes Information

Display information about a revision that was made by positioning the mouse pointer on a change. After approximately one second, a box displays above the change noting the author of the change, the date and time the change was made, and the type of change (for example, a deletion or insertion). You can also review information about tracked changes by displaying the Reviewing pane. Each change is listed separately in the pane. Use the up and down scroll arrows at the right of the Reviewing pane to scroll through and view all of the changes.

# Changing User Information

Word uses a different color (up to eight) for each person who makes changes to a document. That way, anyone looking at the document can identify which users made which changes. In the "Distinguishing Comments from Different Users" section earlier in this chapter, you learned how to change the user's name and initials.

# Locking Track Changes and Blocking Authors

If you want to ensure that no one can make changes to a document without tracking the changes, lock the Track Changes feature. To do this, click the Track Changes button arrow and then click *Lock Tracking* at the drop-down list. At the Lock Tracking dialog box, type a password, press the Tab key, type the password again, and then click OK. This locks Track Changes on so any changes made will be tracked. Unlock Track Changes by clicking the Track Changes button arrow and then clicking *Lock Tracking*. At the Unlock Tracking dialog box, type the password and then click OK.

If your document is saved to Microsoft SharePoint or to your Windows Live SkyDrive, the Block Authors button on the REVIEW tab is available. Use the Block Authors button to restrict authors from changing specific sections of a document by selecting the section and then clicking the Block Authors button. To remove a block, click in the blocked section, and then click the Block Authors button.

# Customizing the Markup Display

Customize which changes display in a document with options at the Show Markup button drop-down list. If you want to show only one type of change, remove the check marks before all of the options except the desired one. For example, to view only formatting changes and not other types of changes, such as insertions and deletions, remove the check mark before each option except *Formatting*.

**Lock Track Changes**
1. Click REVIEW tab.
2. Click Track Changes button arrow.
3. Click *Lock Tracking*.
4. Type password.
5. Press Tab.
6. Type password.
7. Click OK.

Block Authors

**Customize the Markup Display**
1. Click REVIEW tab.
2. Click Show Markup button.
3. Insert or remove check marks from options.
OR
1. Click REVIEW tab.
2. Click Tracking group dialog box launcher.
3. Insert or remove check marks from options.
4. Click OK.

**Figure 20.4 Track Changes Options Dialog Box**

Insert or remove check marks from the check boxes in this section to control which changes show in the document.

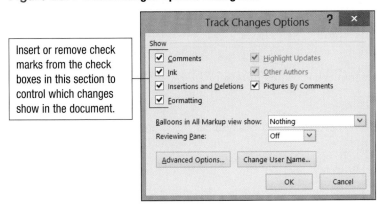

In addition to using the Show Markup button drop-down list, you can customize which changes display with options at the Track Changes Options dialog box, as shown in Figure 20.4 on the previous page. Display this dialog box by clicking the Tracking group dialog box launcher.

If the changes of more than one reviewer have been tracked in a document, you can choose to view only the changes of a particular reviewer. To do this, click the Show Markup button, point to *Specific People* at the drop-down list, and then click the *All Reviewers* check box to remove the check mark. Click the Show Markup button, point to *Reviewers*, and then click the check box of the desired reviewer.

---

### Exercise 20.2B   Changing User Information and Tracking Changes        Part 2 of 4

1.  With **C20-E02-BldgAgrmnt.docx** open, change the user information by completing the following steps:
    a.  Click the FILE tab and then click *Options*.
    b.  At the Word Options dialog box with *General* selected, select the name in the *User name* text box and then type **Lorrie Carter**.
    c.  Select the initials in the *Initials* text box and then type **LC**.
    d.  Click in the *Always use these values regardless of sign in to Office.* check box to insert a check mark.
    e.  Click OK to close the dialog box.
2.  Make additional changes to the contract and track the changes by completing the following steps:
    a.  Click the Track Changes button on the REVIEW tab.
    b.  Select the title *BUILDING CONSTRUCTION AGREEMENT* and then change the font size to 14 points.
    c.  Delete the text *at his option* located in the second sentence in the second paragraph. (Your tracking color may be different from what you see below.)
    d.  Delete the text *and Completion* (including the space before *and*) that displays at the beginning of the fourth paragraph.

> **Construction Loan and Financing Arrangements:** The owner either has or will obtain a construction loan to finance the work to be performed under this Agreement. If adequate financing has not been arranged within ~~thirty (30)~~ sixty (60) days of the date of this Agreement, or the owner cannot provide evidence to the builder of other financial ability to pay the full amount of the contract, then the builder ~~at his option~~ may treat this Agreement as null and void, and retain the down payment made on the execution of this Agreement.
>
> **Supervision of Work:** Owner agrees that the direction and supervision of the working force including subcontractor, rests exclusively with the builder or his/her duly designated agent, and owner agrees not to issue any instructions to, or otherwise interfere with, same.
>
> **Start of Construction** ~~and Completion~~**:** The builder shall commence construction of the residence as soon as practical after signing of this Agreement and adequate financial arrangements satisfactory to the builder have been made.

    e.  Delete *thirty (30)* in the paragraph that begins *Builder's Right to Terminate the Contract:* (located on the second page).
    f.  Type **sixty (60)**.
    g.  Select the text *IN WITNESS WHEREOF* that displays near the bottom of the document and then apply bold formatting.

3. Click the REVIEW tab and then click the Track Changes button to turn off the tracking feature.

4. Click the Reviewing Pane button to turn on the display of the pane, hover the mouse pointer in the pane, and then use the up- and down-pointing arrows at the right side of the Reviewing pane to review the changes.

5. View the changes in balloons by clicking the Show Markup button, pointing to *Balloons*, and then clicking *Show Revisions in Balloons*.

6. Click the Reviewing Pane button to turn off the display of the pane. Scroll through the document and view the changes in the balloons.

7. Click the Show Markup button, point to *Balloons*, and then click *Show All Revisions Inline* at the side menu.

8. Change the user information back to the information that displayed before you typed *Lorrie Carter* and the initials *LC* by completing the following steps:
   a. Click the FILE tab and then click *Options*.
   b. At the Word Options dialog box with *General* selected in the left panel, select *Lorrie Carter* in the *User name* text box and then type the original name.
   c. Select the initials *LC* in the *Initials* text box and then type the original initials.
   d. Click in the *Always use these values regardless of sign in to Office.* check box to remove the check mark.
   e. Click OK to close the dialog box.

9. Display only those changes made by Lorrie Carter by completing the following steps:
   a. Click the Show Markup button in the Tracking group, point to *Specific People*, and then click *All Reviewers* at the side menu. (This also removes the drop-down list.)
   b. Click the Show Markup button, point to *Specific People*, and then click *Lorrie Carter*.

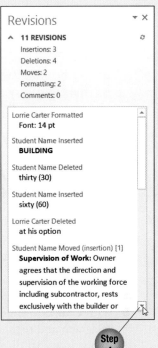

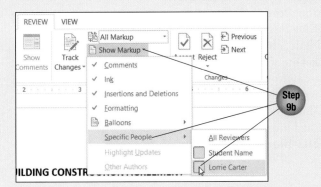

   c. Scroll through the document and notice that only changes made by Lorrie Carter display.
   d. Return the display to all reviewers by clicking the Show Markup button, pointing to *Specific People*, and then clicking *All Reviewers*.

10. Print the document with the markup by completing the following steps:
    a. Click the FILE tab and then click the *Print* option.
    b. At the Print backstage area, click the first gallery in the *Settings* category and then make sure a check mark displays before the *Print Markup* option that displays below the drop-down list. (If the *Print Markup* option is not preceded by a check mark, click the option.)
    c. Click the Print button.

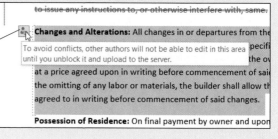

11. Save **C20-E02-BldgAgrmnt.docx**.

**Optional steps:**

12. Save **C20-E02-BldgAgrmnt.docx** to your SkyDrive and name it **C20-E02-BlockAuthors**.
13. With **C20-E02-BlockAuthors.docx** open in SkyDrive, select the *Changes and Alterations* paragraph and then click the Block Authors button on the REVIEW tab. (Notice the block author icon that displays to the left of the paragraph along with a dashed bracket, indicating the section that cannot be edited.)
14. Hover your mouse over the block author icon that displays to the left of the paragraph and read the information telling you that other authors will not be able to edit the area until you unblock and upload the text to the server.

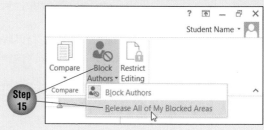

15. Remove the block by clicking the Block Authors button arrow and then clicking *Release All of My Blocked Areas* at the drop-down list. (Notice that the block author and dashed bracket are still displayed.)
16. Click the Save button on the Quick Access toolbar to save the document to your SkyDrive. (This removes the block author icon and dashed bracket.)
17. Close **C20-E02-BlockAuthors.docx**.

## Customizing Track Changes Options

Show Markup

Default settings determine how tracked changes display within a document. For example, with all markup showing, inserted text displays in red and is underlined and deleted text displays in red with strikethrough characters. Moved text displays in the original location in green with double-strikethrough characters and the text in the new location displays in green with a double-underline below it.

You can customize these options, along with others, at the Advanced Track Changes Options dialog box, as shown in Figure 20.5. Use options at this dialog box to customize the display of markup text, moved text, table cell highlighting, formatting, and balloons. Display this dialog box by clicking the Tracking group dialog box launcher. At the Track Changes Options dialog box, click the Advanced Options button.

**QUICK STEPS**

**Customize Track Changes Options**
1. Click REVIEW tab.
2. Click Tracking group dialog box launcher.
3. Click Advanced Options button.
4. Make desired changes at Advanced Track Changes Options dialog box.
5. Click OK.

**Figure 20.5  Advanced Track Changes Options Dialog Box**

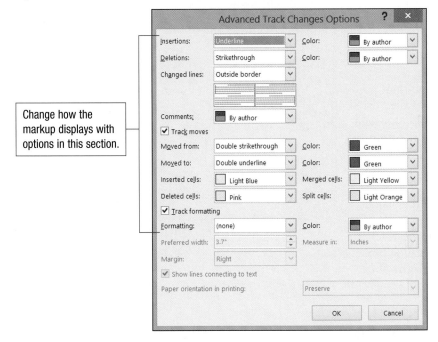

Change how the markup displays with options in this section.

---

**Exercise 20.2C**  Customizing Track Changes Options          Part 3 of 4

1. Open **C20-E02-BldgAgrmnt.docx** and then customize Track Changes options by completing the following steps:
   a. Click the REVIEW tab.
   b. Click the Tracking group dialog box launcher.
   c. Click the Advanced Options button at the Track Changes Options dialog box.
   d. At the Advanced Track Changes Options dialog box, click the down-pointing arrow at the right of the *Insertions* option and then click *Double underline* at the drop-down list.

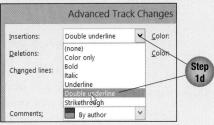

e. Click the down-pointing arrow at the right of the *Insertions* color option box and then click *Green* at the drop-down list. (You will need to scroll down the list to display this color.)

f. Click the down-pointing arrow at the right of the *Moved from* color option box and then click *Dark Blue* at the drop-down list.

g. Click the down-pointing arrow at the right of the *Moved to* color option box and then click *Violet* at the drop-down list. (You will need to scroll down the list to display this color.)

h. Click OK to close the dialog box.

i. Click OK to close the Track Changes Options dialog box.

2. Save **C20-E02-BldgAgrmnt.docx**.

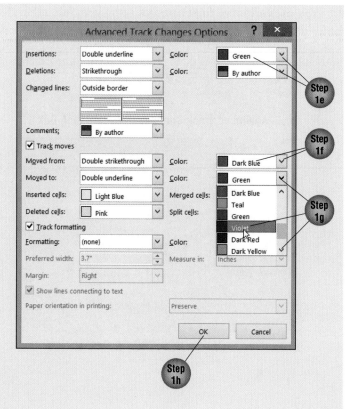

## Navigating to Revisions

Next    Previous

When reviewing a document, use the Next and Previous buttons in the Changes group on the REVIEW tab to navigate among revisions. Click the Next button to review the next revision in the document and click the Previous button to review the previous revision. If you turn on Track Changes, move text, and then turn on the display of revision balloons, a small Go button (a blue right-pointing arrow) displays in the lower right corner of any balloon identifying moved text. Click the Go button in one of the balloons to move the insertion point to the other balloon.

## Accepting and Rejecting Revisions

Accept    Reject

Tracked changes can be removed from a document only by accepting or rejecting them. Click the Accept button in the Changes group on the REVIEW tab to accept the change and move to the next change or click the Reject button to reject the change and move to the next change. Click the Accept button arrow and a drop-down list displays with options to accept the change and move to the next change, accept the change, accept all of the changes shown, and accept all of the changes and stop tracking. Similar options are available at the Reject button arrow drop-down list.

1. With **C20-E02-BldgAgrmnt.docx** open, display all of the changes *except* formatting changes by completing the following steps:

    a. Click the Show Markup button and then click *Formatting* at the drop-down list. (This removes the check mark before the option.)

    b. Scroll through the document and notice that the vertical change lines at the left sides of the formatting locations have been removed.

    c. Click the Show Markup button and then click *Formatting* at the drop-down list. (This inserts a check mark before the option.)

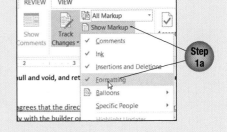

2. Navigate between the tracked changes by completing the following steps:

    a. Press Ctrl + Home to move the insertion point to the beginning of the document.

    b. Click the Next button in the Changes group to select the first change.

    c. Click the Next button again to select the second change.

    d. Click the Previous button to select the first change.

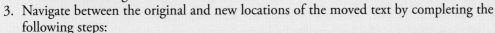

3. Navigate between the original and new locations of the moved text by completing the following steps:

    a. Press Ctrl + Home to move the insertion point to the beginning of the document.

    b. Click the Show Markup button, point to *Balloons*, and then click *Show Revisions in Balloons*.

    c. Click the Go button (small, blue, right-pointing arrow) that displays in the lower right corner of the *Moved* balloon. (This selects the text in the *Moved up* balloon.)

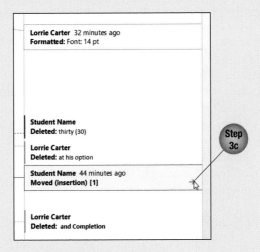

    d. Click the Go button in the lower right corner of the *Moved up* balloon. (This selects the text in the *Moved* balloon.)

    e. Click the Show Markup button, point to *Balloons*, and then click *Show All Revisions Inline*.

4. Press Ctrl + Home to move the insertion point to the beginning of the document.

5. Display and then accept only the formatting changes by completing the following steps:
   a. Click the Tracking group dialog box launcher.
   b. At the Track Changes Options dialog box, click in the *Comments* check box to remove the check mark.
   c. Click the *Ink* check box to remove the check mark.
   d. Click the *Insertions and Deletions* check box to remove the check mark.
   e. Click OK to close the Track Changes Options dialog box.
   f. Click the Accept button arrow and then click *Accept All Changes Shown* at the drop-down list. (This accepts only the formatting changes in the document because they are the only changes showing.)

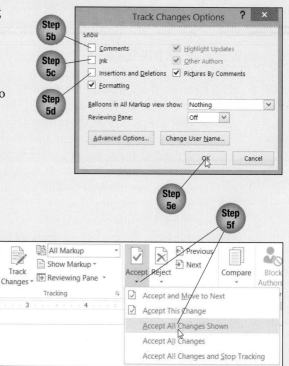

6. Redisplay all of the changes by completing the following steps:
   a. Click the Tracking group dialog box launcher.
   b. Click in the *Comments* check box to insert a check mark.
   c. Click in the *Ink* check box to insert a check mark.
   d. Click in the *Insertions and Deletions* check box to insert a check mark.
   e. Click OK to close the Track Changes Options dialog box.
7. Press Ctrl + Home to move the insertion point to the beginning of the document.
8. Reject the change inserting the word *BUILDING* by clicking the Next button in the Changes group and then clicking the Reject button. (This rejects the change and moves to the next revision in the document.)
9. Click the Accept button to accept the change deleting *thirty (30)*.
10. Click the Accept button to accept the change inserting *sixty (60)*.
11. Click the Reject button to reject the change deleting the words *at his option*.
12. Accept all of the remaining changes by clicking the Accept button arrow and then clicking *Accept All Changes* at the drop-down list.
13. Return the Track Changes options to the default settings by completing the following steps:
    a. Click the Tracking group dialog box launcher.
    b. At the Track Changes Options dialog box, click the Advanced Options button.
    c. At the Advanced Track Changes Options dialog box, click the down-pointing arrow at the right side of the *Insertions* option and then click *Underline* at the drop-down list.
    d. Click the down-pointing arrow at the right of the *Insertions Color* option box and then click *By author* at the drop-down list. (You will need to scroll up the list to display this color.)
    e. Click the down-pointing arrow at the right of the *Moved from Color* option box and then click *Green* at the drop-down list.
    f. Click the down-pointing arrow at the right of the *Moved to Color* option box and then click *Green* at the drop-down list.
    g. Click OK to close the dialog box.
    h. Click OK to close the Track Changes Options dialog box.

14. Check to make sure that all tracked changes are accepted or rejected by completing the following steps:
    a. Click the Reviewing Pane button in the Tracking group.
    b. Check the summary information that displays at the top of the Reviewing pane and make sure that a zero follows each option.
    c. Close the Reviewing pane.
15. Save, print, and then close **C20-E02-BldgAgrmnt.docx**.

# Comparing Documents

Word contains a Compare feature that compares two documents and displays the differences as tracked changes in a third document. To use this option, click the REVIEW tab, click the Compare button in the Compare group, and then click *Compare* at the drop-down list. This displays the Compare Documents dialog box, as shown in Figure 20.6.

At this dialog box, click the Browse for Original button. At the Open dialog box, navigate to the folder that contains the first of the two documents you want to compare (usually, the original) and then double-click the document. Click the Browse for Revised button in the Compare Documents dialog box, navigate to the folder containing the second of the two documents you want to compare (usually, a revision of the original), and then double-click the document. Click OK to close the dialog box and the compared document displays with track changes. You can also click the down-pointing arrow at the right of the *Original document* option box or the *Revised document* option box to display a drop-down list of the most recently opened documents.

**Compare Documents**
1. Click REVIEW tab.
2. Click Compare button.
3. Click *Compare* at drop-down list.
4. Click Browse for Original button.
5. Double-click desired document.
6. Click Browse for Revised button.
7. Double-click desired document.
8. Click OK.

Compare

**Figure 20.6 Compare Documents Dialog Box**

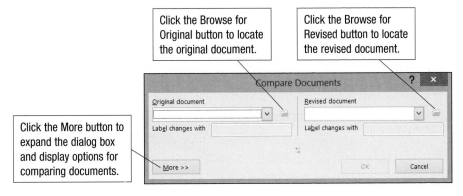

## Viewing Compared Documents

When you click OK at the Compare Documents dialog box, the compared document displays with the changes tracked. Other windows may also display, depending on the option selected at the Show Source Documents side menu. Display this side menu by clicking the Compare button and then pointing to *Show Source Documents*. You may see only the compared document or you may see the compared document plus the Reviewing pane, original document, and/or revised document.

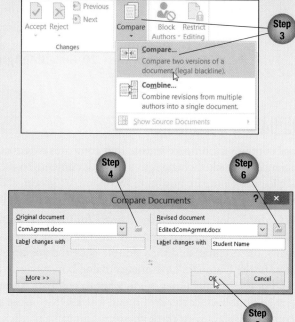

1. Close any open documents.
2. Click the REVIEW tab.
3. Click the Compare button and then click *Compare* at the drop-down list.
4. At the Compare Documents dialog box, click the Browse for Original button.
5. At the Open dialog box, navigate to your Chapter20 folder and then double-click *ComAgrmnt.docx*.
6. At the Compare Documents dialog box, click the Browse for Revised button.
7. At the Open dialog box, double-click *EditedComAgrmnt.docx*.
8. Click the OK button.
9. If the original and revised documents display along with the compared document, click the Compare button, point to *Show Source Documents* at the drop-down list, and then click *Hide Source Documents* at the side menu.
10. With the compared document active, print the document with the markup.
11. Click the FILE tab and then click the *Close* option. At the message asking if you want to save changes, click the Don't Save button.

## Customizing Compare Options

By default, Word compares the original document with the revised document and displays the differences as tracked changes in a third document. You can change this default setting along with others by expanding the Compare Documents dialog box. Expand the dialog box by clicking the More button. Additional options display as shown in Figure 20.7.

**Figure 20.7  Expanded Compare Documents Dialog Box**

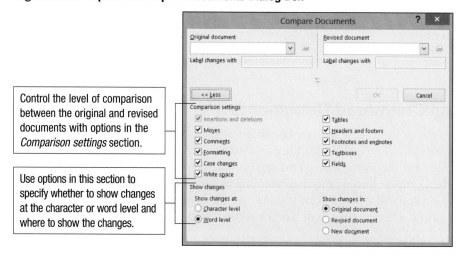

Control the level of comparison between the original and revised documents with options in the *Comparison settings* section.

Use options in this section to specify whether to show changes at the character or word level and where to show the changes.

Control the level of comparison that Word makes between the original and revised documents with options in the *Comparison settings* section of the dialog box. The *Show changes at* option in the *Show changes* section of the dialog box has a default setting of *Word level*. At this setting, Word shows changes to whole words rather than individual characters within a word. For example, if you delete the letters *ed* from the end of a word, Word displays the entire word as a change, not just the *ed*. If you want to show changes by character, click the *Character level* option.

By default, Word displays differences between compared documents in a new document. With options in the *Show changes in* section, you can change this to *Original document* or *Revised document*. If you change options in the expanded Compare Documents dialog box, the selected options will be the defaults the next time you open the dialog box.

## Exercise 20.3B Customizing Compare Options and Comparing Documents
Part 2 of 2

1. Close any open documents.
2. Click the REVIEW tab.
3. Click the Compare button and then click *Compare* at the drop-down list.
4. At the Compare Documents dialog box, click the Browse for Original button.
5. At the Open dialog box, navigate to your Chapter20 folder and then double-click **ComAgrmnt.docx**.
6. At the Compare Documents dialog box, click the Browse for Revised button.
7. At the Open dialog box, double-click **EditedComAgrmnt.docx**.
8. At the Compare Documents dialog box, click the More button. (Skip this step if the dialog box displays expanded and a Less button displays above the *Comparison settings* section.)
9. Click the *Moves* check box and then the *Formatting* check box to remove the check marks.
10. Click the OK button.
11. Print the document with the markup.
12. Close the document without saving it.
13. Return the options to the default settings by completing the following steps:
    a. Close any open documents.
    b. Click the REVIEW tab.
    c. Click the Compare button and then click *Compare* at the drop-down list.
    d. At the Compare Documents dialog box, click the Browse for Original button.
    e. At the Open dialog box, double-click **ComAgrmnt.docx**.
    f. At the Compare Documents dialog box, click the Browse for Revised button.
    g. At the Open dialog box, double-click **EditedComAgrmnt.docx**.
    h. At the Compare Documents dialog box, click the More button and then click the *Moves* check box and the *Formatting* check box to insert check marks.
    i. Click the Less button.
    j. Click the OK button.
14. At the new document, accept all of the changes.
15. Save the document and name it **C20-E03-ComAgrmnt**.
16. Print and then close the document.

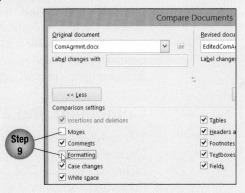

Step 9

# Combining Documents

If several people have made changes to a document, you can combine their changed versions with the original document. Combine the changed documents with the original document one at a time until you have incorporated all of the changes into the original document. To do this, click the Compare button on the REVIEW tab and then click *Combine* at the drop-down list. This displays the Combine Documents dialog box, as shown in Figure 20.8. The Combine Documents dialog box contains many of the same options as the Compare Documents dialog box.

**Figure 20.8 Combine Documents Dialog Box**

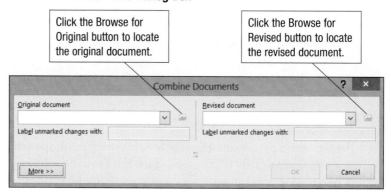

To combine documents at the Combine Documents dialog box, click the Browse for Original button, navigate to the desired folder, and then double-click the original document. To select the revised document, click the Browse for Revised button, navigate to the desired folder, and then double-click one of the documents containing revisions. You can also click the down-pointing arrow at the right of the *Original document* option box or the *Revised document* option box to display a drop-down list of the most recently opened documents.

## Combining and Merging Documents

You can control how changes are combined with options in the expanded Combine Documents dialog box. This dialog box contains many of the same options as the expanded Compare Documents dialog box. By default, Word merges the changes in the revised document into the original document. Change this default setting with options in the *Show changes in* section. You can choose to merge changes into the revised document or to merge changes into a new document.

## Managing Style Conflicts

If text in the original document has styles applied that are different than the styles applied to text in the revised document, Word determines that a style conflict exists when you try to combine the documents and displays a message similar to the one shown in Figure 20.9 on the next page. The message indicates that Word can store only one set of formatting changes in the final merged document.

You have the option of keeping the style formatting from the original document or applying the style formatting from the revised document. After specifying which document style to use, click the Continue with Merge button and Word combines the documents.

**Figure 20.9 Microsoft Word Message Box**

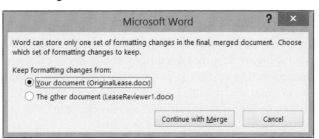

1. Close all open documents.
2. Click the REVIEW tab.
3. Click the Compare button in the Compare group and then click *Combine* at the drop-down list.
4. At the Combine Documents dialog box, click the More button to expand the Combine Documents dialog box.
5. Click the *Original document* option in the *Show changes in* section.

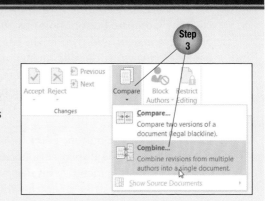

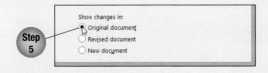

6. Click the Browse for Original button.
7. At the Open dialog box, navigate to your Chapter20 folder and then double-click **OriginalLease.docx**.
8. At the Combine Documents dialog box, click the Browse for Revised button.
9. At the Open dialog box, double-click **LeaseReviewer1.docx**.
10. Click the OK button.
11. At the Microsoft Word message box that displays, click the *The other document (LeaseReviewer1.docx)* option.
12. Click the Continue with Merge button.
13. Save the combined document with Save As and name it **C20-E04-CombinedLease**.

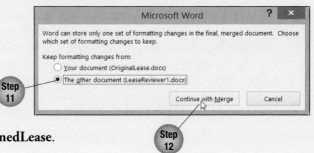

## Showing Source Documents

Use options in the Show Source Documents side menu to specify which source documents to display. Display this side menu by clicking the Compare button and then pointing to *Show Source Documents*. Four options display at the side menu: *Hide Source Documents, Show Original, Show Revised,* and *Show Both*.

With the *Hide Source Documents* option selected, the original and revised documents do not display on the screen; only the combined document displays. If you choose the *Show Original* option, the original document displays in a side pane at the right side of the document. Synchronous scrolling is selected, so scrolling in the combined document results in scrolling in the other document. If you choose the *Show Revised* option, the revised document displays in the panel at the right. Choose the *Show Both* option to display the original document in a panel at the right side of the screen and the revised document in a panel below the original document panel.

## Exercise 20.4B  Combining and Showing Documents  Part 2 of 2

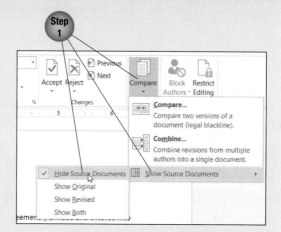

1. With **C20-E04-CombinedLease.docx** open, click the Compare button, point to *Show Source Documents*, and then, make sure *Hide Source Documents* at the side menu contains a check mark. If not, click the option to insert a check mark. (This displays the original document with the changes shown as tracked changes.)
2. Click the Compare button, point to *Show Source Documents*, and then click *Show Original* at the side menu. (This displays the original document at the right, the original document with tracked changes in the middle, and the Reviewing pane at the left side of the screen.)
3. Click the Compare button, point to *Show Source Documents*, and then click *Show Revised*.
4. Click the Compare button, point to *Show Source Documents*, and then click *Show Both*. Scroll in the combined document and notice that the original document and revised document also scroll simultaneously.
5. Click the Compare button, point to *Show Source Documents*, and then click *Hide Source Documents*.
6. Close the Reviewing pane.
7. Click the Compare button and then click *Combine* at the drop-down list.
8. At the Combine Documents dialog box, click the Browse for Original button.
9. At the Open dialog box, double-click **C20-E04-CombinedLease.docx**.
10. At the Combine Documents dialog box, click the Browse for Revised button.
11. At the Open dialog box, double-click **LeaseReviewer2.docx**.
12. At the Combine Documents dialog box, click the OK button.
13. At the Microsoft Word message box that displays, click the Continue with Merge button. (You want the combined document to retain the style formatting from the original lease document.)
14. Save **C20-E04-CombinedLease.docx**.
15. Print the document with the markup.
16. Accept all of the changes to the document.
17. Save, print, and then close **C20-E04-CombinedLease.docx**.

# Embedding and Linking Objects

Microsoft Word is part of the Microsoft Office suite and one reason the suite is used extensively in business is because it allows data from one program to be seamlessly integrated into another program. For example, a chart depicting sales projections created in Excel can easily be added to a corporate report prepared in Word.

*Integration* is the process of adding content from other sources to a file. Integrating content is different than simply copying and pasting it. While it makes sense to copy and paste objects from one application to another when the content is not likely to change, if the content is dynamic, the copy and paste method becomes problematic and inefficient. To illustrate this point, assume one of the outcomes from the presentation to the board of directors is a revision to the sales projections, which means that the chart originally created in Excel has to be updated to reflect the new projections. If the first version of the chart was copied and pasted into Word, it would need to be deleted and then the revised chart in Excel would need to be copied and pasted into the Word document again. Both Excel and Word would need to be opened and edited to reflect this change in projection. In this case, copying and pasting the chart would not be efficient.

To eliminate the inefficiency of the copy and paste method, you can integrate objects between programs. An *object* can be text in a document, data in a table, a chart, or picture, or any combination of data that you would like to share between programs. The program that was used to create the object is called the *source* and the program the object is linked or embedded to is called the *destination*.

Embedding and linking are two methods you can use to integrate data. *Embedding* an object means that the object is stored independently in both the source and the destination programs. When you edit an embedded object in the destination program, the source program opens to help you make the changes, but the changes will not be reflected in the version of the object stored in the source program. If the object is changed in the source program, the changes will not be reflected in the version of the object stored in the destination program.

*Linking* inserts a code into the destination file that connects the destination to the name and location of the source object. The object itself is not stored within the destination file. When an object is linked, changes made to the content in the source program are automatically reflected in the destination program. Your decision to integrate data by embedding or linking will depend on whether the data is dynamic or static. If the data is dynamic, then linking the object is the most efficient method of integration.

## Embedding Objects

An object that is embedded is stored in both the source and the destination programs. The content of the object can be edited in *either* the source or the destination; however, a change made in one will not be reflected in the other. The difference between copying and pasting and copying and embedding is that embedded objects can be edited with the source program's tabs and options.

Since embedded objects are edited within the source program, the source program must reside on the computer when the file is opened for editing. If you are preparing a

Word document that will be edited on another computer, you may want to check before embedding any objects to verify that the other computer has the same programs.

To embed an object, open both programs and both files. In the source program, click the desired object and then click the Copy button in the Clipboard group on the HOME tab. Click the button on the Taskbar representing the destination program file and then position the insertion point at the location where you want the object embedded. Click the Paste button arrow in the Clipboard group and then click *Paste Special* at the drop-down list. At the Paste Special dialog box, click the source of the object in the *As* list box and then click OK.

Edit an embedded object by double-clicking the object. This displays the object with the source program tabs and options. Make any desired changes and then click outside the object to close the source program tabs and options.

---

**Exercise 20.5A**  Embedding Excel Data in a Document                                 **Part 1 of 3**

---

1.  Open **DIRevs.docx** and save the document with the name **C20-E05-DIRevs**.
2.  Start Excel and then open **DISales.xlsx**, located in your
    Chapter20 folder.
3.  Select cells A2 through F9.
4.  Click the Copy button in the Clipboard group on the
    HOME tab.
5.  Click the Word button on the Taskbar.
6.  Press Ctrl + End to move the insertion point to the end
    of the document.
7.  Click the Paste button arrow and then click
    *Paste Special* at the drop-down list.
8.  At the Paste Special dialog box, click *Microsoft Excel
    Worksheet Object* in the *As* list box and
    then click OK.
9.  Save **C20-E05-DIRevs.docx**.
10. Click the Excel button on the Taskbar,
    close the workbook, and then close Excel.
11. With **C20-E05-DIRevs.docx** open,
    double-click in any cell in the Excel data.
    (This displays the Excel tabs and options
    for editing the data.)
12. Click in cell E3 (contains the amount
    *$89,231*), type **95000**, and then press Enter.
13. Click in cell F9 and then double-click the AutoSum button in the Editing
    group on the HOME tab. (This inserts the total *$1,258,643* in the cell.)
14. Click outside the Excel data to remove the Excel tabs and options.
15. Save, print, and then close **C20-E05-DIRevs.docx**.

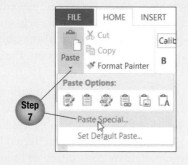

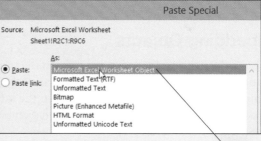

## Linking Objects

If the content of the object that you will integrate between programs is likely to change, you can link the object from the source program to the destination program. Linking the object establishes a direct connection between the source and destination programs. The object is stored in the source program only, and the destination program contains a code that indicates the name and location of the source of the object. Whenever the document containing the link is opened, a message displays indicating that the document contains links and asking if you want to update them.

To link an object, open both programs and program files. In the source program file, click the desired object and then click the Copy button in the Clipboard group on the HOME tab. Click the button on the Taskbar representing the destination program file and then position the insertion point in the desired location. Click the Paste button arrow in the Clipboard group on the HOME tab and then click *Paste Special* at the drop-down list. At the Paste Special dialog box, click the *Paste link* option located at the left side of the *As* list box, click the source program for the object in the *As* list box, and then click OK.

## Exercise 20.5B  Linking an Excel Chart to a Document  Part 2 of 3

1. Open **NSSCosts.docx** and save the document with the name **C20-E05-NSSCosts**.
2. Open Excel and then open **NSSDept%.xlsx** located in your Chapter20 folder.
3. Save the workbook and name it **C20-E05-NSSDept%**.
4. Copy and link the chart to the Word document by completing the following steps:
   a. Click the chart to select it.
   b. Click the Copy button in the Clipboard group on the HOME tab.
   c. Click the Word button on the Taskbar.
   d. Press Ctrl + End to move the insertion point to the end of the document.
   e. Click the Paste button arrow and then click *Paste Special* at the drop-down list.
   f. At the Paste Special dialog box, click the *Paste link* option.
   g. Click *Microsoft Excel Chart Object* in the *As* list box.

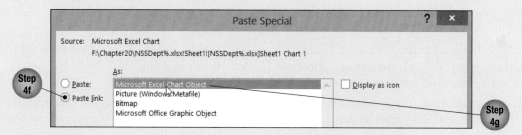

   h. Click OK.
5. Click the Excel button on the Taskbar, close **C20-E05-NSSDept%.xlsx**, and then close Excel.
6. With **C20-E05-NSSCosts.docx** open on the screen, save, print, and then close the document.

## Editing a Linked Object

Edit linked objects in the source program in which they were created. Open the file containing the object, make the changes as required, and then save and close the file. If both the source and destination programs are open at the same time, the changed content is reflected immediately in both programs.

---

**Exercise 20.5C**  Linking an Excel Chart to a Document                                    Part 3 of 3

1. Open Excel and then open **C20-E05-NSSDept%.xlsx**.
2. Make the following changes to the data:
   a. In cell B4, change *18%* to *12%*.
   b. In cell B6, change *10%* to *13%*.
   c. In cell B8, change *5%* to *8%*.
3. Click the Save button on the Quick Access toolbar to save the edited workbook.
4. Close **C20-E05-NSSDept%.xlsx** and then close Excel.
5. In Word, open **C20-E05-NSSCosts.docx**.
6. At the message telling you that the document contains links, click the Yes button. (Notice the changes to the chart data.)
7. Save, print, and then close **C20-E05-NSSCosts.docx**.

---

# *Chapter Summary*

➤ Insert a comment in a document by clicking the New Comment button in the Comments group on the REVIEW tab. When you click the New Comment button, a comment icon and comment balloon display at the right margin. If any previous settings have been applied, the Reviewing pane, rather than a comment balloon, may display.

➤ Turn the display of the Reviewing pane on and off with the Reviewing Pane button in the Tracking group on the REVIEW tab.

➤ You can insert comments in a document with the Reviewing pane displayed. The summary section of the Reviewing pane provides counts of the number of comments inserted and the number of changes made to the document.

➤ Navigate through the comments in a document using the Previous and Next buttons in the Comments group on the REVIEW tab.

➤ Edit a comment in the Reviewing pane by displaying the pane and then making the desired changes to the comment. Edit a comment in a comment balloon by turning on the display of balloons, clicking in the desired comment balloon, and then making the desired changes.

➤ If changes are made to a document by someone with different user information, the changes display in a different color. Change the user name and initials at the Word Options dialog box with *General* selected.

➤ Reply to a comment by clicking the Reply button that displays to the right of the reviewer's name in the comment balloon and then typing the reply.

➤ You can print a document along with the inserted comments or print only the comments and not the document.

➤ Delete a comment by clicking the Next button in the Comments group on the REVIEW tab until the desired comment is selected and then clicking the Delete button in the Comments group.

➤ Use Track Changes when more than one person is reviewing a document and making changes to it. Turn on Track Changes by clicking the Track Changes button in the Tracking group on the REVIEW tab.

➤ Control how editing marks display in a document with the Display for Review button in the Tracking group on the Review tab. Control the markup of changes that Word displays in a document with options at the Show Markup button drop-down list.

➤ Display information about tracked changes by positioning the mouse pointer on a change, and after approximately one second, a box displays above the change with information such as the author, date, time, and type of change.

➤ Lock the tracking feature on so any changes made to a document are tracked. Lock the feature by clicking the Track Changes button arrow in the Tracking group on the REVIEW tab and then clicking *Lock Tracking* at the drop-down list. At the Lock Tracking dialog box, type a password.

➤ Customize which type of tracked changes display in a document with options at the Show Markup button drop-down list or with options at the Track Changes Options dialog box. Display this dialog box by clicking the Tracking group dialog box launcher.

➤ Change Track Changes default settings with options at the Advanced Track Changes Options dialog box. Display this dialog box by clicking the Tracking group dialog box launcher and then clicking the Advanced Options button at the Track Changes Options dialog box.

➤ Move to the next change in a document by clicking the Next button in the Changes group on the REVIEW tab or move to the previous change by clicking the Previous button.

➤ Use the Accept and Reject buttons in the Changes group on the REVIEW tab to accept and reject changes made in a document.

➤ Use the Compare button in the Compare group on the REVIEW tab to compare two documents and display the differences between the documents as tracked changes.

➤ Customize options for comparing documents at the expanded Compare Documents dialog box. Click the More button to expand this dialog box.

➤ If you send a document to several people for review, you can combine their changes with the original document. Combine the revised documents with the original one at a time until all of the changes are incorporated. Combine documents with options at the Combine Documents dialog box.

➤ Customize options for combining documents at the expanded Combine Documents dialog box. Click the More button to expand this dialog box.

➤ Specify which source documents to display by clicking the Compare button in the Compare group on the REVIEW tab, pointing to *Show Source Documents*, and then clicking the desired option at the side menu.

➤ An object created in one program in the Microsoft Office suite can be copied, linked, or embedded into another program in the suite. The program containing the original object is called the source program and the program in which it is inserted is called the destination program.

➤ An embedded object is stored in both the source and the destination programs. A linked object is stored in the source program only. Link an object if you want the contents in the destination program to reflect any changes made to the object stored in the source program.

# Commands Review

| FEATURE | RIBBON TAB, GROUP | BUTTON, OPTION | KEYBOARD SHORTCUT |
|---|---|---|---|
| accept changes | REVIEW, Changes | | |
| Advanced Track Changes Options dialog box | REVIEW, Tracking | , Advanced Options | |
| balloons | REVIEW, Tracking | , Balloons | |
| Combine Documents dialog box | REVIEW, Compare | , Combine | |
| Compare Documents dialog box | REVIEW, Compare | , Compare | |
| delete comment | REVIEW, Comments | | |
| display for review | REVIEW, Tracking | Simple Markup | |
| new comment | REVIEW, Comments | | |
| next comment | REVIEW, Comments | | |
| next revision | REVIEW, Changes | | |
| Paste Special dialog box | HOME, Clipboard | , Paste Special | |
| previous comment | REVIEW, Comments | | |
| previous revision | REVIEW, Changes | | |
| reject changes | REVIEW, Changes | | |
| Reviewing pane | REVIEW, Tracking | | |
| show comments | REVIEW, Comments | | |
| show markup | REVIEW, Tracking | | |
| show source documents | REVIEW, Compare | , Show Source Documents | |
| Track Changes | REVIEW, Tracking | | Ctrl + Shift + E |
| Track Changes Options dialog box | REVIEW, Tracking | | |

# Key Points *Review*

**Completion:** In the space provided at the right, indicate the correct term, command, or number.

1. Insert a comment into a document by clicking this button in the Comments group on the REVIEW tab.

2. Navigate between comments by using these two buttons in the Comments group on the REVIEW tab.

3. Change user information with options at this dialog box.

4. If a document contains comments, you can print only the comments by displaying the Print backstage area, clicking the first gallery in the *Settings* category, clicking this option, and then clicking the Print button.

5. Turn on the Track Changes feature by clicking the Track Changes button on this tab.

6. Use this keyboard shortcut to turn on Track Changes.

7. Show all markup in a document by clicking this button arrow in the Tracking group on the REVIEW tab and then clicking *All Markup* at the drop-down list.

8. Display information about tracked changes in this pane.

9. When Track Changes is turned on, moved text displays in this color by default.

10. You can customize options for tracking changes at the Track Changes Options dialog box and this dialog box.

11. Click the *Combine* option at the Compare button drop-down list and this dialog box displays.

12. Specify which source documents to display by clicking the Compare button, pointing to this option, and then clicking the desired option or options at the side menu.

13. Do this to an object if you want the contents in the destination program to reflect any changes made to the object stored in the source program.

# Chapter *Assessments*

## Applying Your Skills

Demonstrate your knowledge of features learned in this chapter by completing the following assessments.

### Assessment 20.1    Insert Comments in a Web Report

1. Open **NavigateWeb.docx** and then save the document with the name **C20-A01-NavigateWeb**.
2. Delete the only comment in the document.
3. Position the insertion point at the end of the first paragraph in the section *IPs and URLs* and then insert a comment with the following text: **Please identify what the letters ICANN stand for.**

4. Position the insertion point at the end of the third paragraph in the section *IPs and URLs* and then insert a comment with the following text: **Insert a caption for the following table and the two other tables in the document.**
5. Position the insertion point at the end of the last paragraph in the document (above the table) and insert a comment with the following text: **Include in the following table additional examples of methods for narrowing a search.**
6. Save the document and print only the comments.
7. Close **C20-A01-NavigateWeb.docx**.

## Assessment 20.2    Track Changes in a Viruses Report

SNAP Grade It

1. Open **CompChapters.docx** and then save the document with the name **C20-A02-CompChapters**.
2. Turn on Track Changes and then make the following changes:
   a. Edit the first sentence in the document so it reads **The computer virus is one of the most familiar forms of risk to computer security.**
   b. Type the word **computer's** between *the* and *motherboard* in the last sentence in the first paragraph of the document.
   c. Delete the word *real* in the second sentence of the section *TYPES OF VIRUSES* and then type **significant**.
   d. Select and then delete the last sentence in the section *Methods of Virus Operation* (the sentence that begins *A well-known example of a logic bomb was the*).
   e. Turn off Track Changes.
3. Display the Word Options dialog box with *General* selected and then type **Stacey Phillips** in the *User Name* text box and **SP** in the *Initials* text box.
4. Turn on Track Changes and then make the following changes:
   a. Delete the words *or cracker* located in the seventh sentence in the section *Types of Viruses*.
   b. Delete the word *garner* in the first sentence in the section *CHAPTER 2: SECURITY RISKS* and then type **generate**.
   c. Select and then move the section *Employee Theft* below the section *Cracking Software for Copying*.
   d. Turn off Track Changes.
5. Display the Word Options dialog box with *General* selected and then change the user name and initials back to the original versions.
6. Print the document with all markup.
7. Accept all of the changes in the document *except* reject the change moving the section *EMPLOYEE THEFT* below the section *CRACKING SOFTWARE FOR COPYING*.
8. Save, print, and then close **C20-A02-CompChapters.docx**.

## Assessment 20.3    Compare Documents

1. Compare **Security.docx** with **EditedSecurity.docx** and insert the changes into a new document. *Hint: Choose* **New document** *at the expanded Compare Documents dialog box.*
2. Save the compared document and name it **C20-A03-Security.docx**.
3. Print only the list of markup (not the document).
4. Reject the changes made to all bulleted text and the last paragraph in the section *Disaster Recovery Plan* and accept all of the other changes.
5. Number the pages at the bottom center of each page.
6. Save the document, print only the document, and then close **C20-A03-Security.docx**.

## Assessment 20.4    Combine Documents

1. Open **LegalSummons.docx** and save the document with the name **C20-A04-LegalSummons**.
2. Close **C20-A04-LegalSummons.docx**.

3. At a blank screen, combine **C20-A04-LegalSummons** (the original document) with **Review1-LegalSummons.docx** (the revised document) into the original document. *Hint: Choose* Original document *at the Combine Documents expanded dialog box.*
4. Accept all of the changes to the document.
5. Save and then close **C20-A04-LegalSummons.docx**.
6. At a blank screen, combine **C20-A04-LegalSummons.docx** (the original document) with **Review2-LegalSummons.docx** (the revised document) into the original document.
7. Print only the list of markup.
8. Accept all of the changes to the document.
9. Save, print only the document, and then close **C20-A04-LegalSummons.docx**.

## Assessment 20.5    Link an Excel Chart with a Word Document

1. Open **WESales.docx** and save the document with the name **C20-A05-WESales**.
2. Open Excel and then open the workbook named **WESalesChart.xlsx**.
3. Save the Excel workbook with the name **C20-A05-WESalesChart**.
4. Link the Excel chart to the end of **C20-A05-WESales.docx**. (Make sure you use the Paste Special dialog box.)
5. Save, print, and then close **C20-A05-WESales.docx**.
6. With Excel the active program, make the following changes to the data in the specified cells:
   a.  Change the amount in cell F3 from *$500,750* to *$480,200*.
   b.  Change the amount in cell E4 from *$410,479* to *$475,500*.
7. Save and close **C20-A05-WESalesChart.xlsx** and then close Excel.
8. Open **C20-A05-WESales.docx** and click Yes at the message asking if you want to update the document.
9. Save, print, and then close **C20-A05-WESales.docx**.

# Expanding Your Skills

Explore additional feature options or use Help to learn a new skill in creating these documents.

## Assessment 20.6    Track Changes to a Table

1. Open **MBPSales.docx** and save the document with the name **C20-A06-MBPSales**.
2. You can track changes made to a table and customize the Track Changes options for the table. Display the Advanced Track Changes Options dialog box and then make the following changes:
   a.  Change the color for inserted cells to Light Purple.
   b.  Change the color for deleted cells to Light Green.
3. Turn on Track Changes and then make the following changes:
   a.  Insert a new row at the beginning of the table.
   b.  Merge the cells in the new row. (At the message telling you the action will not be marked as a change, click OK.)
   c.  Type **Mobile Bay Products** in the merged cell.
   d.  Delete the row *Barclay, Kurt*.
   e.  Insert a new row below *Tanaka, Diana* and then type **Caswell, Martin** in the first cell, **$495,678** in the second cell, and **$475,850** in the third cell.
   f.  Turn off Track Changes.
4. Save and then print the document with all markup.
5. Accept all of the changes.
6. Display the Advanced Track Changes Options dialog box and then return the inserted cells color back to Light Blue and the deleted cells color back to Pink.
7. Save, print, and then close **C20-A06-MBPSales.docx**.

# Achieving Signature Status

Take your skills to the next level by completing this more challenging assessment.

## Assessment 20.7    Track Changes in an Employee Performance Document

1. Open **NSSEmpPerf.docx** and then save the document and name it **C20-A07-NSSEmpPerf**.
2. Turn on Track Changes and then make the changes shown in Figure 20.10. (Make the editing changes before you move the *Employment Records* information below the *Performance Evaluation* information.)
3. Turn off Track Changes and then print only the list of markup.
4. Accept all of the changes to the document.
5. Save, print, and then close **C20-A07-NSSEmpPerf.docx**.
6. At a blank screen, combine **C20-A07-NSSEmpPerf.docx** (the original document) with **EditedNSSEmpPerf.docx** (the revised document) into the original document.
7. Accept all of the changes to the document.
8. Save, print, and then close **C20-A07-NSSEmpPerf.docx**.

**Figure 20.10  Assessment 20.7**

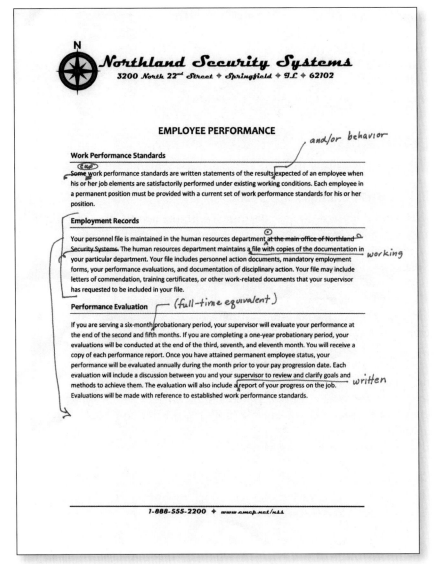

# *Performance Assessments*

UNIT 4

## Managing Data

## ASSESSING PROFICIENCIES

In this unit, you have learned to prepare customized letters, envelopes, labels, and directories and to sort text in paragraphs, columns, tables, and data source files. You learned how to select specific records from a data source file and merge the specific records with a main document. You also learned how to customize bullets, numbers, and lists; insert and customize headers and footers; insert comments; and track changes.

*Note: Before beginning computer assessments, copy to your storage medium the Unit04PA folder from the CD that accompanies this textbook and then make Unit04PA the active folder.*

### Assessment U4.1  Use Mail Merge to Create Letters to Customers

1. Open **MALtrhd.docx** and save the document with the name **U4-PA01-MA-MD**.
2. Look at the information shown in Figure U4.1 below and Figure U4.2 on the next page.
3. Use the Mail Merge feature to prepare six letters using the information shown in the figures.
4. Save the data source file and name it **U4-PA01-MA-DS**. Save the merged document and name it **U4-PA01-MALtrs**.
5. Print and then close **U4-PA01-MALtrs.docx**.
6. Save and then close **U4-PA01-MA-MD.docx**.

### Figure U4.1  Assessment U4.1

| | |
|---|---|
| Mr. Roy Heitzman<br>5043 Pleasant Street<br>Grand Rapids, MI 49518 | Mr. and Mrs. Lawrence Nesbitt<br>11023 South 32nd Street<br>Kentwood, MI 49506 |
| Ms. Julia Quintero<br>905 Randall Road<br>Kentwood, MI 49509 | Mr. Darren Butler<br>23103 East Avenue<br>Grand Rapids, MI 49523 |
| Ms. Lola Rose-Simmons<br>3312 South Meridian<br>Grand Rapids, MI 49510 | Mr. Samuel McClelland<br>660 Grove Street<br>Grand Rapids, MI 49507 |

**Figure U4.2  Assessment U4.1**

September 20, 2015


«AddressBlock»

«GreetingLine»

Because you are a valued customer of Motorway Autos, we are offering you a free oil change with your next 15,000-mile, 36,000-mile, or 60,000-mile car service appointment. Mention the free offer the next time you schedule a service appointment and the oil change is on us!

For the entire month of October, we are offering fantastic deals on new 2015 models. If you buy a new car from us, we will offer you top trade-in dollars for your used car. Along with our low, low prices, we are also offering low-interest and, in some cases, no-interest loans. Come in and talk with one of our sales representatives to see if you qualify for these special loans.

Please come down to visit our showroom and check out the best-priced automobiles in the region. We are open for your convenience Monday through Friday from 8:00 a.m. to 8:00 p.m., Saturday from 9:00 a.m. to 6:00 p.m., and Sunday from 9:00 a.m. to 5:00 p.m.

Sincerely,



Dusty Powell
Director of Sales


XX
U4-PA01-MA-MD.docx

### Assessment U4.2     Use Mail Merge to Create Envelopes

1. Use the Mail Merge feature to prepare envelopes for the letters you created in Assessment U4.1.
2. Specify **U4-PA01-MA-DS.mdb** as the data source document.
3. Save the merged envelope document with the name **U4-PA02-MAEnvs**.
4. Print and then close **U4-PA02-MAEnvs.docx**. (Check with your instructor before printing.)
5. Close the envelope main document without saving it.

## Assessment U4.3    Edit the Data Source and Main Document and Merge Letters

1.  Open **U4-PA01-MA-MD.docx** (at the SQL message, click Yes) and save the main document with the name **U4-PA03-MA-MD**.
2.  Edit the **U4-PA01-MA-DS.mdb** data source file by making the following changes:
    a.  Display the record for Mr. Darren Butler and then change the street address from *23103 East Avenue* to *715 South Fifth Street*.
    b.  Add *and Mrs.* in the title for Mr. Samuel McClelland. (The *Title* field should display as *Mr. and Mrs.*)
    c.  Delete the record for Ms. Lola Rose-Simmons.
    d.  Insert a new record with the following information:

    > Ms. Glenda Jefferson
    > 5048 Burton Street
    > Grand Rapids, MI 49503

3.  At the main document, add the sentence shown in Figure U4.3 to the end of the third paragraph in the body of the letter and include fill-in fields as shown in parentheses in the figure.
4.  Save **U4-PA03-MA-MD.docx**.
5.  Merge the records to a new document. At the dialog boxes asking for the number of automobiles and percentages, type the following:

    | | | |
    |---|---|---|
    | Record 1: | Number: **two automobiles** | Percent: **2%** |
    | Record 2: | Number: **one automobile** | Percent: **1%** |
    | Record 3: | Number: **one automobile** | Percent: **1%** |
    | Record 4: | Number: **three automobiles** | Percent: **3%** |
    | Record 5: | Number: **two automobiles** | Percent: **2%** |
    | Record 6: | Number: **one automobile** | Percent: **1%** |

6.  Save the merged document with the name **U4-PA03-MALtrs**.
7.  Print and then close **U4-PA03-MALtrs.docx**.
8.  Save and then close **U4-PA03-MA-MD.mdb**.

### Figure U4.3  Assessment U4.3

According to our records, you have purchased (Number) from us. This qualifies you for a special bonus of up to (Percent) off the purchase of a new automobile.

## Assessment U4.4    Use Mail Merge to Create Labels

1.  Use the Mail Merge feature to create mailing labels with the label product Avery US Letter 5360 Mailing Labels. Use the existing data source **U4-PA01-MA-DS.mdb** for the labels.
2.  Display the Mail Merge Recipients dialog box, display the Filter and Sort dialog box with the Filter Records tab selected, and then select only those customers living in Grand Rapids.
3.  Complete the merge and then save the label document with the name **U4-PA04-MALbls**.
4.  Print and then close **U4-PA04-MALbls.docx**.
5.  Close the label main document without saving it.

### Assessment U4.5    Use Mail Merge to Create a Directory

1. Use the Mail Merge feature to create a directory that uses the records in the **U4-PA01-MA-DS.mdb** data source file to print the customer title and first and last names at the left margin, the street address at a tab stop, and the city, state, and zip code at another tab stop.
2. After merging the records in the directory, create a heading for each column.
3. Select the merged information (including the headings) and then convert the text to a table. Apply formatting to enhance the appearance of the table.
4. Save the document and name it **U4-PA05-MADirectory**.
5. Print and then close **U4-PA05-MADirectory.docx**.
6. Close the directory main document without saving it.

### Assessment U4.6    Sort Data in Columns and a Table

1. Open **Sort.docx** and save the document with the name **U4-PA06-Sort**.
2. Sort the columns of text below the *CONTACTS* title in ascending order by last name.
3. Sort the amounts in the *Home Equity Loans* column in the table in descending order.
4. Save, print, and then close **U4-PA06-Sort.docx**.

### Assessment U4.7    Create and Apply Custom Bullets and a Multilevel List

1. Open **MBPStocks.docx** and save the document with the name **U4-PA07-MBPStocks**.
2. Apply the Title style to the title *Mobile Bay Products*.
3. Apply the Heading 1 style to the headings *Stock Awards* and *Employee Stock Plan*.
4. Apply the Centered style set.
5. Select the bulleted paragraphs of text and then define a new picture bullet. At the Insert Pictures window, search for *blue globe with grid lines* and download the image of a globe with blue grid lines and a black background.
6. Select the lines of text below the heading *Employee Stock Plan* and then apply a multilevel list (the middle option in the top row of the *List Library* section of the Multilevel List button drop-down gallery).
7. With the text still selected, define a new multilevel list that inserts capital letters followed by periods (A., B., C.) for level 2 and arabic numbers followed by periods (1., 2., 3.) for level 3. (Make sure the new multilevel list applies to the selected text.)
8. Save, print, and then close **U4-PA07-MBPStocks.docx**.

### Assessment U4.8    Keep Text Together and Insert Footers in a Report

1. Open **FutureEthics.docx** and save the document with the name **U4-PA08-FutureEthics**.
2. Keep the heading *Self-Replicating Robots* (located at the bottom of the first page) together with the paragraph of text that follows it.
3. Keep the title *REFERENCES* (located at the bottom of the second page) together with the paragraph of text that follows it.
4. Create an odd page footer that prints the document title *Future of Computer Ethics* at the left margin and the page number at the right margin.
5. Create an even page footer that prints the page number at the left margin and the document title at the right margin.
6. Save, print, and then close **U4-PA08-FutureEthics.docx**.

## Assessment U4.9    Insert Headers and Footers in Different Sections of a Document

1. Open **CompSoftware.docx** and then save the document with the name **U4-PA09-CompSoftware**.
2. Insert a section break that begins a new page at the title *SOFTWARE PRICING* (located on page 2).
3. Apply the Title style to the two titles in the document (*SOFTWARE DELIVERY* and *SOFTWARE PRICING*) and apply the Heading 1 style to the six headings in the document.
4. Apply the Centered style set.
5. Apply the Depth theme and change the theme colors to Blue II.
6. Create a header that prints the current date at the right margin in both sections in the document.
7. Create a footer for the first section in the document that prints *Software Delivery* at the left margin, the page number in the middle, and your first and last names at the right margin.
8. Edit the footer for the second section so it prints *Software Pricing* instead of *Software Delivery*. **Hint: Make sure that you click the Link to Previous button on the HEADER & FOOTER TOOLS DESIGN tab to turn off linking.**
9. Save, print, and then close **U4-PA09-CompSoftware.docx**.

## Assessment U4.10    Insert Comments and Track Changes in a Document

1. Open **OnlineShop.docx** and save the document with the name **U4-PA10-OnlineShop**.
2. Move the insertion point to the end of the first paragraph in the report and then insert the comment **Include the source where you found this definition.**
3. Move the insertion point to the end of the paragraph in the *Online Shopping Venues* section and then insert the comment **Include at least two of the most popular online shopping stores.**
4. Click the Display for Review button arrow and then click *All Markup* at the drop-down list.
5. Turn on Track Changes and then make the following changes:
   a. Delete the comma and the words *and most are eliminating paper tickets altogether* that display at the end of the last sentence in the second paragraph.
   b. Edit the heading *Advantages of Online Shopping* so it displays as *Online Shopping Advantages*.
   c. Apply bold formatting to the first sentence of each bulleted paragraph on the first page.
   d. Turn off Track Changes.
6. Display the Word Options dialog box with *General* selected and then type **Colleen Burton** as the user name and **CB** as the user initials. (Make sure that you insert a check mark in the *Always use these values regardless of sign in to Office.* check box.)
7. Turn on Track Changes and then make the following changes:
   a. Delete the words *the following* in the first paragraph in the *Online Shopping Advantages* section.
   b. Type the following bulleted text between the third and fourth bulleted paragraphs on the second page: **Keep thorough records of all transactions.**
   c. Turn off Track Changes.
8. Print the document with all of the markups.

9. Display the Word Options dialog box with *General* selected and then change the user name back to the original name and the initials back to the original initials. (Remove the check mark from the *Always use these values regardless of sign in to Office.* check box.)

10. Accept all of the changes in the document except reject the change deleting the words *and most are eliminating paper tickets altogether.* (Leave the comments in the document.)

11. Save, print, and then close **U4-PA10-OnlineShop.docx**.

### Assessment U4.11     Combine Documents

1. Open **Software.docx** and save the document with the name **U4-PA11-Software**.
2. Close **U4-PA11-Software.docx**.
3. At a blank document, combine **U4-PA11-Software.docx** (the original document) with **Software-AL.docx** (the revised document).
4. Save **U4-PA11-Software.docx**.
5. Print the document with all of the markup.
6. Accept all of the changes to the document.
7. Make the following changes to the document:
    a. Apply the Basic (Stylish) style set.
    b. Apply the Wisp theme.
    c. Apply the Red theme colors.
    d. Insert the Austin footer.
8. Save, print, and then close **U4-PA11-Software.docx**.

# CREATING ORIGINAL DOCUMENTS

The activity in Assessment U4.12 gives you the opportunity to practice your writing skills as well as demonstrate your mastery of some of the important Word features presented in this unit. When you compose the document, use correct grammar, precise word choices, and clear sentence construction.

### Assessment U4.12     Use Mail Merge to Create Letters to Volunteers

**Situation:** You are a volunteer coordinator for the Kentwood School District, and you have been asked to write a letter to the new reading volunteers listed on the next page, thanking them for their interest in volunteering for the reading literacy program and inviting them to an orientation meeting on Tuesday, September 22, 2015, from 7:00 to 8:30 p.m. In the letter, explain that during this orientation, volunteers will learn more about the reading program, including the program goals, the students served by the program, the reading levels included in the program, the time commitment required of volunteers, and the materials needed for the program. Use the Mail Merge feature to compose the main document letter and create a data source file with the names and addresses provided for the volunteers. Save the data source file with the name **U4-PA12-KSD-DS.mdb** and the letter main document with the name **U4-PA12-KSD-MD.docx**. Merge the main document with the records in the data source file and name the merged document **U4-PA12-VolLtrs**. Print and then close **U4-PA12-VolLtrs.docx** and then save and close **U4-PA12-KSD-MD.docx**.

Ms. Karen Lyons
9023 South 42nd Street
Kentwood, MI 48933

Mr. Bryan Hamilton
11023 12th Northeast
Kentwood, MI 48920

Mr. Richard Ulrich
453 Silverdale Road
Kentwood, MI 48930

Mrs. Lindsay Childers
8931 133rd Place Northwest
Kentwood, MI 48933

Mr. Juan Nunez
8329 Branchwood Drive
Kentwood, MI 48933

Ms. Lisa Taua
1129 Military Road South
Kentwood, MI 48930

# UNIT 5

## Customizing Documents and Features

# Inserting and Customizing Quick Parts

## Performance Objectives

Upon successful completion of Chapter 21, you will be able to:

- Sort and insert building blocks
- Create, edit, modify, and delete building blocks
- Insert document properties
- Insert, update, and customize fields

Word offers a number of features to help you streamline the formatting of documents. In this chapter, you will learn how to use predesigned building blocks to build a document. You will also learn how to create, save, and edit your own building blocks and how to insert fields in a document and then update them.

*Note: Before beginning computer exercises for this chapter, copy to your storage medium the Chapter21 folder from the CD that accompanies this textbook and then make Chapter21 the active folder.*

In this chapter, students will produce the following documents:

Exercise 21.1. C21-E01-CompViruses.docx
Exercise 21.2. C21-E02-PSLtr.docx
Exercise 21.3A. C21-E03-PSLtr.docx
Exercise 21.3B. C21-E03-PacificSkyAnnounce.docx
Exercise 21.4. C21-E04-SEBetaAgrmnt.docx

Model answers for these exercises are shown on the following pages.

**Exercise 21.1**

C21-E01-CompViruses.docx

FEBRUARY 26, 2015

# NORTHLAND SECURITY SYSTEMS

COMPUTER VIRUSES AND SECURITY RISKS

STUDENT NAME

Page 1

CONTENTS

Page 2

## CHAPTER 1: COMPUTER VIRUSES

One of the most familiar forms of risk to computer security is the computer virus. A computer virus is a program written by a hacker or cracker designed to perform some kind of trick upon an unsuspecting victim. The trick performed in some cases is mild, such as drawing an offensive image on the screen, or changing all of the characters in a document to another language. Sometimes the trick is much more severe, such as reformatting the hard drive and erasing all the data, or damaging the motherboard so that it cannot operate properly.

and are operated and transmitted by a variety of methods. An email virus is normally transmitted as an attachment to a message sent over the Internet. Email viruses require the victim to click on the attachment and cause it to execute. Another common form of virus transmission is by a macro, a small subprogram that allows users to customize and automate certain functions. A macro virus is written specifically for one program, which then becomes infected when it opens a file with the virus stored in its macros. The boot sector of a compact disc or hard drive contains a variety of information, including how the disc is organized and whether it is

### TYPES OF VIRUS

Viruses can be categorized by th
which include nuisance, data-de
espionage, and hardware-destru
nuisance virus usually does no
but is rather just an inconvenier
difficult part of a computer to re
data on the hard drive. The insta
programs, the documents, datab
saved emails form the heart of a
computer. A data-destructive vi
designed to destroy this data. S
are designed to create a backdo
system to bypass security. Calle
viruses, they do no damage, but
hacker or cracker to enter the sy
the purpose of stealing data or s
work of the competitor. Very ra
created that attempts to damage
hardware of the computer syste
Called hardware-destructive vir
bits of programming can weake
chips, drives, and other compon

### METHODS OF VIRUS OF

Viruses can create effects that r
minor and annoying to highly d

dormant waiting for a specific event or set of conditions to occur. A famous logic bomb was the widely publicized Michelangelo virus,

which infected personal computers and caused them to display a message on the artist's birthday.

## CHAPTER 2: SECURITY RISKS

Although hackers, crackers, and viruses garner the most attention as security risks, companies face a variety of other dangers to their hardware and software systems. Principally, these risks involve types of system failure, employee theft, and the cracking of software for copying.

### SYSTEMS FAILURE

A fundamental element in making sure that computer systems operate properly is protecting the electrical power that runs them. Power interruptions such as blackouts and brownouts have very adverse effects on computers. An inexpensive type of power strip called a surge protector can guard against power fluctuations and can also serve as an extension cord and splitter. A much more vigorous power protection system is an uninterruptible power supply (UPS), which provides a battery backup. Similar in nature to a power strip but much more bulky and a bit more expensive, a UPS provides not only steady spike-free power, but also keeps computers running during a blackout.

### EMPLOYEE THEFT

Although accurate estimates are difficult to pinpoint, businesses certainly lose millions of dollars a year in stolen computer hardware and software. Often, in large organizations,

such theft goes unnoticed or unreported. Someone takes a hard drive or a scanner home for legitimate use, then leaves the job some time later, and keeps the machine. Sometimes, employees take components to add to their home PC systems or a thief breaks into a business and hauls away computers. Such thefts cost far more than the price of the stolen computers because they also involve the cost of replacing the lost data, the cost of the time lost while the machines are gone, and the cost of installing new machines and training people to use them.

### CRACKING SOFTWARE FOR COPYING

A common goal of hackers is to crack a software protection scheme. A crack is a method of circumventing a security scheme that prevents a user from copying a program. A common protection scheme for software is to require that the installation CD be resident in the drive whenever the program runs. Making copies of the CD with a burner, however, easily fools this protection scheme. Some game companies are taking the extra step of making duplication difficult by scrambling some of the data on the original CDs, which CD burners will automatically correct when copying. When the copied and corrected CD is used, the software checks for the scrambled track information. If the error is not found, the software will not run.

**Exercise 21.2**

C21-E02-PSLtr.docx

# WORLD WIDE TRAVEL
### 2400 International Drive ⑤ Las Vegas, NV ⑤ 77534 1-800-555-3445
### www.emcp.net/worldwide

February 26, 2015

Mrs. Jody Lancaster
Pacific Sky Cruise Lines
120 Montgomery Boulevard
Los Angeles, CA 97032

Dear Jody:

Your colorful brochures have made quite an impression on our clients, and consequently, we have given away our entire stock. Please send us an additional box of brochures as well as information and fact sheets about the various specialized cruises coming up.

Are you planning to offer the "Northern Lights" cruise next year? The cruise has been very popular with our clients, and I have had three inquiries in the past three weeks regarding the cruise. As soon as you know the dates of the cruise and stateroom prices, please let me know.

Sincerely,


Student Name
Travel Consultant

C21-E02-PSLtr.docx


> **Visit our website at www.emcp.net/worldwide to learn about our weekly vacation specials!**

*"Making your travel dreams a reality"*

---

# WORLD WIDE TRAVEL
### 2400 International Drive ⑤ Las Vegas, NV ⑤ 77534 1-800-555-3445
### www.emcp.net/worldwide

February 26, 2015


Mrs. Jody Lancaster
Pacific Sky Cruise Lines
120 Montgomery Boulevard
Los Angeles, CA 97032

Dear Jody:

I imagine you are extremely busy finalizing the preparations for the Pacific Sky Cruise Line's inaugural trip to the Alaska Inside Passage. The promotional literature you provided our company has been very effective in enticing our clients to sign up. This letter is a confirmation of the thirty staterooms that we have reserved for our clients for the inaugural cruise. We have reserved ten each of the following staterooms:

- Category H: Inside stateroom with two lower beds
- Category D: Deluxe ocean-view stateroom with window, sitting area, and two lower beds
- Category B: Superior deluxe ocean-view stateroom with window, sitting area, and two lower beds
- Category S: Superior deluxe suite with ocean view, private balcony, sitting area, and two lower beds

With only a few weeks to go before the cruise, I want to make sure our clients' bookings are finalized so they can enjoy the eight-day, seven-night cruise to the Alaska Inside Passage. Please confirm the stateroom reservations, and send me a fax or email with the confirmation numbers.

Sincerely,


Student Name
Senior Travel Consultant

C21-E03-PSLtr.docx


*"Making your travel dreams a reality"*

**Exercise 21.3A**

C21-E03-PSLtr.docx

**Exercise 21.3B**

C21-E03-PacificSkyAnnounce.docx

# WORLD WIDE TRAVEL

2400 International Drive ⑤ Las Vegas, NV ⑤ 77534 1-800-555-3445
www.emcp.net/worldwide

**Pacific Sky Cruise Line**

**Alaska Inside Passage - Inaugural Cruise**

**Available Staterooms**

- **Category H:** Inside stateroom with two lower beds
- **Category D:** Deluxe ocean-view stateroom with window, sitting area, and two lower beds
- **Category B:** Superior deluxe ocean-view stateroom with window, sitting area, and two lower beds
- **Category S:** Superior deluxe suite with ocean view, private balcony, sitting area, and two lower beds

Visit our website at www.emcp.net/worldwide to learn about our weekly vacation specials!

February 2015

*"Making your travel dreams a reality"*

## BETA TESTING AGREEMENT

THIS AGREEMENT is made by and between Stylus Software Enterprises, and _____ ("Licensee") having a principal place of business located at _____.

In consideration of the mutual covenants and premises herein contained, the parties hereto agree as follows:

Stylus Software Enterprises grants to Licensee a non-exclusive, non-transferable license to use the Software on a single computer at Licensee's business location solely for beta testing and internal use until _____, 20__ at which time the Software and all copies shall be returned to Stylus Software Enterprises.

In consideration for receiving a copy of the Software for testing, Licensee agrees to serve as a beta testing site for the Software and will notify Stylus Software Enterprises of all problems and ideas for enhancements which come to Licensee's attention during the period of this Agreement, and hereby assigns to Stylus Software Enterprises all right, title and interest to such enhancements and all property rights therein including without limitation all patent, copyright, trade secret, mask work, trademark, moral right or other intellectual property rights.

This Agreement shall be governed, construed, and enforced in accordance with the laws of the United States of America and of the State of California. Any notice required by this Agreement shall be given by prepaid, first class, certified mail, return receipt requested.

Stylus Software Enterprises:                    Licensee:


_____          _____
Name                                              Name



First Draft
Current date and time: 2/26/2015 4:27 PM
File name and path: F:\CHAPTER21\C21-E04-SEBETAAGRMNT.DOCX

**Exercise 21.4**

C21-E04-SEBetaAgrmnt.docx

# Inserting Quick Parts

Quick Parts

Word provides a variety of tools for inserting data such as text, fields, objects, and other items to help build a document. To view some of the tools available, click the Quick Parts button in the Text group on the INSERT tab. Doing this displays a drop-down list of options for inserting document properties, fields, and predesigned building blocks, as well as options for saving selected data to the *AutoText* or *Quick Part* gallery.

## Inserting Building Blocks

**Insert a Building Block**
1. Click INSERT tab.
2. Click Quick Parts button.
3. Click *Building Blocks Organizer*.
4. Click desired building block.
5. Click Insert button.

Building blocks are tools used for developing, or "building," a document. Word provides a number of these reusable pieces of content that you can insert into a document. You can also create your own and save them for future use.

To insert one of the predesigned building blocks into a Word document, click the INSERT tab, click the Quick Parts button in the Text group, and then click *Building Blocks Organizer* at the drop-down list. This displays the Building Blocks Organizer dialog box, as shown in Figure 21.1. On the left, the dialog box displays six columns of information about the building blocks: its name, the gallery to which its belongs, its category, the template in which it is stored, its behavior, and its description. When you click the name of a building block, the dialog box also displays a preview of the building block, its name, and a brief description of it.

**Figure 21.1 Building Blocks Organizer Dialog Box**

Click the desired building block in the list box and then preview it in this preview area.

Click a column heading to sort column entries alphabetically.

Building Blocks Organizer

Building blocks:

| Name | Gallery | Category | Template | Be |
|------|---------|----------|----------|-----|
| Bibliogra... | Bibliogr... | Built-In | Built-In B... | In |
| Works Cit... | Bibliogr... | Built-In | Built-In B... | In |
| References | Bibliogr... | Built-In | Built-In B... | In |
| Semapho... | Cover Pa... | Built-in | Built-In B... | In |
| Slice (Da... | Cover Pa... | Built-in | Built-In B... | In |
| Banded | Cover Pa... | Built-in | Built-In B... | In |
| Retrospect | Cover Pa... | Built-in | Built-In B... | In |
| Whisp | Cover Pa... | Built-in | Built-In B... | In |
| Integral | Cover Pa... | Built-in | Built-In B... | In |
| Grid | Cover Pa... | Built-in | Built-In B... | In |
| Austin | Cover Pa... | Built-in | Built-In B... | In |
| Motion | Cover Pa... | Built-in | Built-In B... | In |
| Filigree | Cover Pa... | Built-in | Built-In B... | In |
| Slice (Lig... | Cover Pa... | Built-in | Built-In B... | In |
| Facet | Cover Pa... | Built-in | Built-In B... | In |
| ViewMas... | Cover Pa... | Built-in | Built-In B... | In |
| Sideline | Cover Pa... | Built-in | Built-In B... | In |

Click a building block to see its preview

Bibliography

Chen, J. (2003). *Citations and References.* New York: Citation Press.

Haas, J. (2005). *Creating a Formal Publication.* Boston: Proseware, Inc.

Kramer, J. D. (2006). *How to Write Bibliographies.* Chicago: Adventure Works Press.

Bibliography
Automatic bibliography that includes all sources associated with the document

Edit Properties...    Delete    Insert

Close

The Building Blocks Organizer dialog box is a central location for viewing all of the predesigned building blocks available in Word. You used building blocks in previous chapters when you inserted elements such as predesigned cover pages, headers, footers, page numbers, and watermarks into a document. You used various buttons on the INSERT tab to insert these elements. Other galleries of predesigned building blocks include bibliographies, equations, tables of contents, tables, and text boxes. The Building Blocks Organizer dialog box provides a convenient location for viewing and inserting building blocks.

## Sorting Building Blocks

When you open the Building Blocks Organizer dialog box, the building blocks display in a list box sorted by the *Gallery* column. Sort the building blocks by another column by clicking the column heading. For example, to sort the building blocks alphabetically by name, click the *Name* column heading.

QUICK STEPS

**Sort Building Blocks**
1. Click INSERT tab.
2. Click Quick Parts button.
3. Click *Building Blocks Organizer*.
4. Click desired column heading.

---

**Exercise 21.1**    **Inserting Predesigned Building Blocks**        Part 1 of 1

1. Open **CompViruses.docx** and save the document with the name **C21-E01-CompViruses**.
2. Make the following changes to the document:
   a. Insert a continuous section break at the beginning of the first paragraph below the title *CHAPTER 1: COMPUTER VIRUSES.*
   b. Insert a section break that begins a new page at the beginning of the title *CHAPTER 2: SECURITY RISKS* located in the middle of the second page.
   c. Insert a continuous section break at the beginning of the first paragraph below the title *CHAPTER 2: SECURITY RISKS.*
   d. Change the line spacing to 1.0 for the entire document.
   e. Format the paragraphs in the section below the title *CHAPTER 1: COMPUTER VIRUSES* into two columns of equal width.
   f. Balance the columns of text on the second page. **Hint: Balance columns by inserting a continuous section break.**
   g. Format the paragraphs in the section below the title *CHAPTER 2: SECURITY RISKS* into two columns of equal width.
   h. Balance the columns of text on the third page.
3. Sort the building blocks and then insert a table of contents building block by completing the following steps:
   a. Press Ctrl + Home, press Ctrl + Enter to insert a page break, and then press Ctrl + Home again to move the insertion point back to the beginning of the document.
   b. Click the INSERT tab.
   c. Click the Quick Parts button in the Text group and then click *Building Blocks Organizer* at the drop-down list.

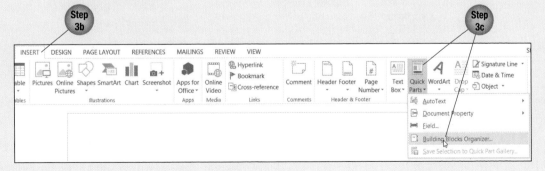

---

d.  At the Building Blocks Organizer dialog box, notice the arrangement of the building blocks in the list box. (The building blocks are most likely organized alphabetically by the *Gallery* column.)

e.  Click the *Name* column heading. (This sorts the building blocks alphabetically by name; however, some blank building blocks may display at the beginning of the list box.)

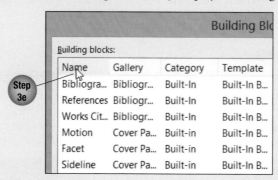

f.  Scroll down the list box and then click *Automatic Table 1*. (You may see only a portion of the name. Click the name and the full name as well as a description of the building block display in the dialog box below the preview.)

g.  Click the Insert button that displays near the bottom of the dialog box. (This inserts a contents page at the beginning of the document and uses the heading styles applied to the titles and headings in the document to create the table of contents.)

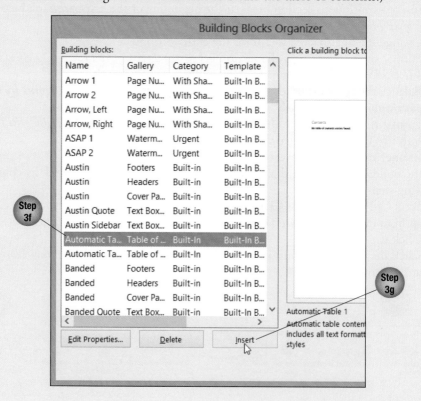

4. Insert a footer building block by completing the following steps:
   a. Click the Quick Parts button on the INSERT tab and then click *Building Blocks Organizer*.
   b. Scroll down the Building Blocks Organizer list box, click the *Semaphore* footer, and then click the Insert button.

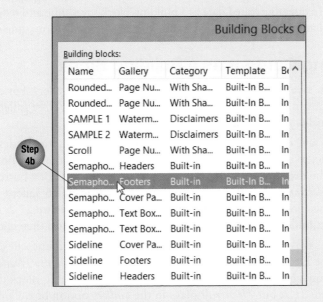

   c. Decrease the *Footer from Bottom* measurement to 0.3 inch (located in the Position group on the HEADER & FOOTER TOOLS DESIGN tab).
   d. Click the DESIGN tab, click the Theme Colors button, and then click *Red* at the drop-down list. (This changes the color of the footer text to red.)
   e. Double-click in the document.
5. Insert a cover page building block by completing the following steps:
   a. Press Ctrl + Home to move the insertion point to the beginning of the document.
   b. Click the INSERT tab, click the Quick Parts button, and then click *Building Blocks Organizer*.
   c. Scroll down the Building Blocks Organizer list box, click the *Semaphore* cover page, and then click the Insert button.
   d. Click the *[DATE]* placeholder and then type today's date.
   e. Click the *[DOCUMENT TITLE]* placeholder and then type **Northland Security Systems**. (The text you type will be converted to all uppercase letters.)
   f. Click the *[DOCUMENT SUBTITLE]* placeholder and then type **Computer Viruses and Security Risks**.
   g. Select the name that displays above the *[COMPANY NAME]* placeholder and then type your first and last names.
   h. Select and then delete the *[COMPANY NAME]* placeholder.
   i. Select and then delete the *[Company address]* placeholder.
6. Scroll through the document and look at each page. The Semaphore footer and cover page building blocks you inserted have similar formatting and are part of the Semaphore group. Using building blocks from the same group provides consistency in a document and gives it a polished and professional appearance.
7. Save, print, and then close **C21-E01-CompViruses.docx**.

# Saving Building Block Content

The Building Blocks Organizer dialog box contains reusable pieces of content organized by galleries such as *AutoText*, *Cover Page*, *Header*, *Footer*, and *Quick Part*. If you find yourself typing and formatting the same data regularly, consider saving the data as a building block. Saving frequently created data as a building block saves time and reduces the potential for errors that might occur each time you type data or apply formatting to it.

**QUICK STEPS**

**Save Content to the *Text Box* Gallery**
1. Select text box.
2. Click INSERT tab.
3. Click Text Box button.
4. Click *Save Selection to Text Box Gallery*.

**Save Content to the *Header* Gallery**
1. Select content.
2. Click INSERT tab.
3. Click Header button.
4. Click *Save Selection to Header Gallery*.

**Save Content to the *Footer* Gallery**
1. Select content.
2. Click INSERT tab.
3. Click Footer button.
4. Click *Save Selection to Footer Gallery*.

## Saving Content as a Building Block

You can save content as a building block in a specific gallery. For example, you can save a text box in the *Text Box* gallery, save content in the *Header* gallery, save content in the *Footer* gallery, and so on.

To save content in a specific gallery, use the button for the desired gallery. For example, to save a text box in the *Text Box* gallery, use the Text Box button. To do this, select the text box, click the INSERT tab, click the Text Box button, and then click the *Save Selection to Text Box Gallery* option at the drop-down gallery. At the Create New Building Block dialog box that displays, as shown in Figure 21.2, type a name for the text box building block, type a description if desired, and then click OK.

To save content in the *Header* gallery, select the content, click the INSERT tab, click the Header button, and then click the *Save Selection to Header Gallery* option at the drop-down gallery. This displays the Create New Building Block dialog box, as shown in Figure 21.2, but *Header* displays in the *Gallery* option box. Complete similar steps to save content to the *Footer* gallery or *Cover Page* gallery.

## Saving Building Blocks in a Specific Template

By default, the content you save as a building block is saved in the Building Block.dotx template or the Normal.dotm template, depending on the gallery you choose at the Create New Building Block dialog box. A building block saved in either of these templates is available each time you open a document in Word. In a public environment, such as a school, you may not be able to save data to one of these templates.

In Exercise 21.2A, you will create your own template and then save building blocks in it. To create a template, display the Save As dialog box and then change the *Save as type* option to *Word Template (*.dotx)*. When you choose this option, the Custom Office Templates folder is automatically selected. Type a name for the template, click the Save button, and the template is saved in the Custom Office Templates folder.

**Figure 21.2  Create New Building Block Dialog Box**

Type the building block name in this text box.

Use this option to specify the gallery in which you want the building block saved.

Type a description of the building block in this text box.

Click this down-pointing arrow and then click the template in which you want the building block saved.

To open a document based on your template, click the FILE tab and then click the *New* option. At the New backstage area, click the *PERSONAL* option that displays below the search text box. This displays thumbnails of the templates saved in the Custom Office Templates folder. Click the thumbnail of your template and a blank document opens based on the template.

To specify the template in which you want a building block saved, click the down-pointing arrow at the right side of the *Save in* option in the Create New Building Block dialog box and then click the desired template. You must open a document based on a template for the template name to display in the drop-down list.

## Saving Content to the *AutoText* Gallery

You can save content as a building block in the *AutoText* gallery. The building block can easily be inserted into a document by clicking the INSERT tab, clicking the Quick Parts button, pointing to *AutoText*, and then clicking the desired AutoText building block at the side menu. To save content in the *AutoText* gallery, type and format the desired content and then select the content. Click the INSERT tab, click the Quick Parts button, point to *AutoText*, and then click the *Save Selection to AutoText Gallery* option at the side menu. You can also press Alt + F3 to display the dialog box. At the Create New Building Block dialog box, type a name for the building block, type a description if desired, and then click OK.

## Saving Content to the *Quick Part* Gallery

In addition to saving content in the *AutoText* gallery, you can save selected content in the *Quick Part* gallery. To do this, select the desired content, click the INSERT tab, click the Quick Parts button, and then click the *Save Selection to Quick Part Gallery* option at the drop-down gallery. This displays the Create New Building Block dialog box with *Quick Parts* specified in the *Gallery* option box and *Building Blocks.dotx* specified in the *Save in* option box. Type a name for the building block, type a description if desired, and then click OK.

**QUICK STEPS**

**Save Content to the *AutoText* Gallery**
1. Select content.
2. Click INSERT tab.
3. Click Quick Parts button.
4. Point to *AutoText*.
5. Click *Save Selection to AutoText Gallery*.

**Save Content to the *Quick Part* Gallery**
1. Select content.
2. Click INSERT tab.
3. Click Quick Parts button.
4. Click *Save Selection to Quick Part Gallery*.

---

**Exercise 21.2A**  Saving Content to the *Text Box, Footer, AutoText,*  Part 1 of 3
and *Quick Part* Galleries

---

1. Press Ctrl + N to display a blank document and then save the document as a template by completing the following steps:
   a. Press the F12 function key on your keyboard to display the Save As dialog box.
   b. At the Save As dialog box, click the down-pointing arrow at the right side of the *Save as type* option box and then click *Word Template (*.dotx)* at the drop-down list.
   c. Select the text in the *File name* text box and then type **XXX-WWTTemplate** (replacing the *XXX* with your initials).
   d. Click the Save button.
2. Close the **XXX-WWTTemplate.dotx** template.
3. Create a document based on your template **XXX-WWTTemplate.dotx** by completing the following steps:
   a. Click the FILE tab and then click the *New* option.
   b. At the New backstage area, click the *PERSONAL* option that displays below the search text box (and below the suggested searches).

c. Click the thumbnail representing your template **XXX-WWTTemplate** (the template that displays with your initials in place of the *XXX*).

4. Insert **WWTContent.docx** into the current document. (Do this with the Object button arrow on the INSERT tab. This document is located in your Chapter21 folder.)

5. Save the text box as a building block in the *Text Box* gallery by completing the following steps:

   a. Select the text box by clicking the text box and then clicking the text box border.

   b. From the INSERT tab, click the Text Box button and then click *Save Selection to Text Box Gallery* at the drop-down list.

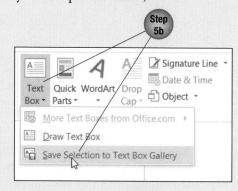

   c. At the Create New Building Block dialog box, delete the existing text and type **WWTTextBox** in the *Name* text box.

   d. Click the down-pointing arrow at the right side of the *Save in* option box and then click **XXX-WWTTemplate.dotx** at the drop-down list. (This saves the building block in the **XXX-WWTTemplate.dotx** rather than the default **Building Block.dotx** template.)

   e. Click OK to close the Create New Building Block dialog box.

6. Save content as a building block in the *Footer* gallery by completing the following steps:

   a. Select the text *"Making your travel dreams a reality"* located below the text box. (Make sure you select the paragraph mark at the end of the text. If necessary, click the Show/Hide ¶ button in the Paragraph group on the HOME tab to display the paragraph mark.)

   b. Click the Footer button in the Header & Footer group on the INSERT tab and then click *Save Selection to Footer Gallery* at the drop-down list.

   c. At the Create New Building Block dialog box, type **WWTFooter** in the *Name* text box.

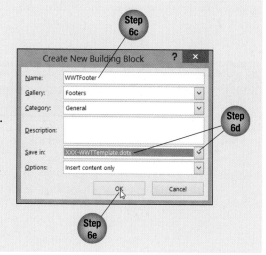

   d. Click the down-pointing arrow at the right side of the *Save in* option box and then click **XXX-WWTTemplate.dotx** at the drop-down list.

   e. Click OK to close the Create New Building Block dialog box.

7.  Save the company name *Pacific Sky Cruise Lines* and the address below it as a building block in the *AutoText* gallery by completing the following steps:

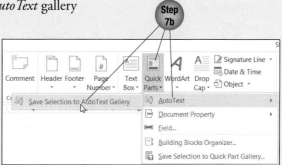

a.  Select the company name and address. Make sure you include the paragraph mark at the end of the last line of the address.
b.  Click the Quick Parts button in the Text group on the INSERT tab, point to *AutoText*, and then click *Save Selection to AutoText Gallery* at the side menu.
c.  At the Create New Building Block dialog box, type **PacificSky**.
d.  Click the down-pointing arrow at the right side of the *Save in* option box and then click **XXX-WWTTemplate.dotx** at the drop-down list.
e.  Click OK to close the Create New Building Block dialog box.

8.  Type your name and company title and then save the text as a building block in the *AutoText* gallery by completing the following steps:

a.  Move the insertion point to a blank line a double space below the Pacific Sky Cruise Lines address.
b.  Type your first and last names.
c.  Press the Enter key and then type **Travel Consultant**. (Do not press the Enter key.)
d.  Select your first and last names and the title *Travel Consultant*. (Include the paragraph mark at the end of the title.)
e.  Press Alt + F3.
f.  At the Create New Building Block dialog box, type **Title**.
g.  Click the down-pointing arrow at the right side of the *Save in* option box and then click **XXX-WWTTemplate.dotx** at the drop-down list.
h.  Click OK to close the Create New Building Block dialog box

9.  Save the letterhead as a building block in the *Quick Part* gallery by completing the following steps:

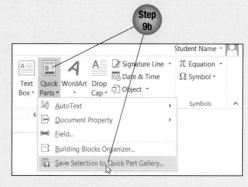

a.  Select the letterhead text (from *WORLD WIDE TRAVEL* through *www.emcp.net/worldwide*), including the paragraph mark at the end of the text.
b.  Click the Quick Parts button on the INSERT tab and then click *Save Selection to Quick Part Gallery* at the drop-down list.
c.  At the Create New Building Block dialog box, type **WWT**.
d.  Click the down-pointing arrow at the right side of the *Save in* option box and then click **XXX-WWTTemplate.dotx** at the drop-down list.
e.  Click OK to close the Create New Building Block dialog box.

10. Close the document without saving it.
11. At the message that displays telling you that you have modified styles, building blocks, or other content that is stored in **XXX-WWTTemplate.dotx** and asking if you want to save changes, click the Save button.

## Editing Building Block Properties

**Edit a Building Block**
1. Click INSERT tab.
2. Click Quick Parts button.
3. Click *Building Blocks Organizer.*
4. Click desired building block.
5. Click Edit Properties button.
6. Make desired changes.
7. Click OK.
**OR**
1. Click desired button.
2. Right-click custom building block.
3. Click *Edit Properties.*
4. Make desired changes.
5. Click OK.

You can make changes to the properties of a building block with options at the Modify Building Blocks dialog box. This dialog box contains the same options as the Create New Building Block dialog box.

Display the Modify Building Blocks dialog box by opening the Building Blocks Organizer dialog box, clicking the desired building block in the list box, and then clicking the Edit Properties button. You can also display this dialog box for a building block that displays in the drop-down gallery. To do this, click the Quick Parts button, right-click the building block that displays in the drop-down gallery, and then click *Edit Properties* at the shortcut menu. Make desired changes to the Modify Building Block dialog box and then click OK. At the message asking if you want to redefine the building block entry, click Yes.

You can also display this dialog box for a custom building block in a button drop-down gallery by clicking the button, right-clicking the custom building block, and then clicking *Edit Properties* at the shortcut menu. For example, to modify a custom text box building block, click the INSERT tab, click the Text Box button, and then scroll down the drop-down list to display the custom text box building block. Right-click the building block and then click *Edit Properties* at the shortcut menu.

## Exercise 21.2B   Editing Building Block Properties                    Part 2 of 3

1. Open a blank document based on your template **XXX-WWTTemplate.dotx** by completing the following steps:
   a. Click the FILE tab and then click the *New* option.
   b. At the New backstage area, click the *PERSONAL* option.
   c. Click the thumbnail that represents your template **XXX-WWTTemplate** (where your initials display in place of the *XXX*).
2. Edit the *WWT* letterhead building block by completing the following steps:
   a. Click the INSERT tab.
   b. Click the Quick Parts button, right-click the *WWT* building block, and then click *Edit Properties* at the shortcut menu.

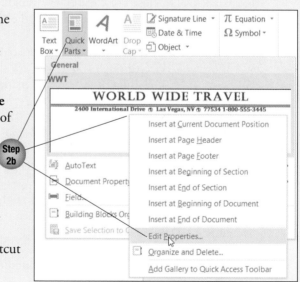

Step 2b

c. At the Modify Building Block dialog box, click in the *Name* text box and then type **Letterhead** at the end of the name.
   d. Click in the *Description* text box and then type **Inserts the World Wide Travel letterhead including the company name and address.**
   e. Click OK to close the dialog box.
   f. At the message asking if you want to redefine the building block entry, click Yes.

3. Edit the *PacificSky* building block by completing the following steps:
   a. Click the INSERT tab, click the Quick Parts button, and then click *Building Blocks Organizer* at the drop-down list.
   b. At the Building Blocks Organizer dialog box, click the *Gallery* heading to sort the building blocks by gallery. (This displays the *AutoText* galleries at the beginning of the list.)
   c. Using the horizontal scroll bar that displays at the bottom of the *Building blocks* list box, scroll to the right and notice that the *PacificSky* building block does not contain a description.
   d. Click the *PacificSky* building block in the list box.
   e. Click the Edit Properties button located at the bottom of the dialog box.
   f. At the Modify Building Block dialog box, click in the *Name* text box and then type **Address** at the end of the name.
   g. Click in the *Description* text box and then type **Inserts the Pacific Sky name and address.**
   h. Click OK to close the dialog box.
   i. At the message asking if you want to redefine the building block entry, click Yes.
   j. Close the Building Blocks Organizer dialog box.

4. Close the document.

5. At the message that displays telling you that you have modified styles, building blocks, or other content that is stored in **XXX-WWTTemplate.dotx** (where your initials display in place of the *XXX*) and asking if you want to save changes, click the Save button.

## Inserting Custom Building Blocks

Any content that you save as a building block can be inserted into a document at the Building Blocks Organizer dialog box. Some content can also be inserted at specific drop-down galleries. For example, insert a custom text box building block by clicking the Text Box button on the INSERT tab and then clicking the desired text box building block at the drop-down gallery. Insert a custom header at the Header button drop-down gallery, a custom footer at the Footer button drop-down gallery, a custom cover page at the Cover Page button drop-down gallery, and so on.

You can specify where you want custom building block content inserted within a document at the button drop-down gallery. To do this, display the button drop-down gallery, right-click the custom building block, and then click the desired location at the shortcut menu. For example, if you click the INSERT tab, click the Quick Parts button, and then right-click the *WWTLetterhead* building block, a shortcut menu displays, as shown in Figure 21.3.

**Figure 21.3 Quick Parts Button Drop-down Gallery Shortcut Menu**

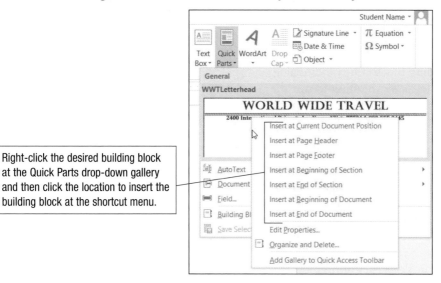

Right-click the desired building block at the Quick Parts drop-down gallery and then click the location to insert the building block at the shortcut menu.

---

**Exercise 21.2C**  **Inserting Custom Building Blocks**                    Part 3 of 3

1. Open a blank document based on your template **XXX-WWTTemplate.dotx** by completing the following steps:
   a. Click the FILE tab and then click the *New* option.
   b. At the New backstage area, click the *PERSONAL* option.
   c. Click the thumbnail representing your template **XXX-WWTTemplate** (where your initials display in place of the *XXX*).
2. Apply the No Spacing style and then change the font to Candara.
3. Insert the letterhead building block as a header by completing the following steps:
   a. Click the INSERT tab.
   b. Click the Quick Parts button, right-click **WWTLetterhead**, and then click the *Insert at Page Header* option at the shortcut menu.
4. Press the Enter key twice, type the current date, and then press the Enter key four times.

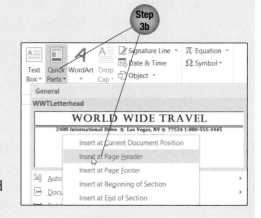

5. Type **Mrs. Jody Lancaster** and then press the Enter key.
6. Insert the Pacific Sky Cruise Lines name and address building block by clicking the Quick Parts button, pointing to *AutoText*, and then clicking the *PacificSkyAddress* building block at the side menu.

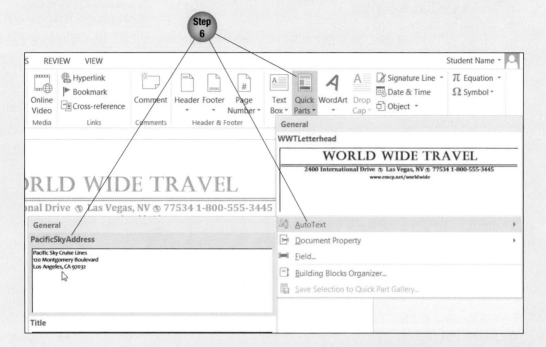

7. Press the Enter key once and then insert a letter document by completing the following steps:
    a. Click the Object button arrow on the INSERT tab and then click *Text from File* at the drop-down list.
    b. At the Insert File dialog box, navigate to your Chapter21 folder and then double-click *PacificSkyLetter01.docx*.
8. With the insertion point positioned a double space below the last paragraph of text in the body of the letter, type **Sincerely,** and then press the Enter key four times.
9. Insert your name and title building block by clicking the Quick Parts button, pointing to *AutoText*, and then clicking your name and title at the side menu.
10. Press the Enter key and then type **C21-E02-PSLtr.docx**.

11. Press the Enter key three times and then insert the custom text box you saved as a building block by completing the following steps:
    a. Click the Text Box button.
    b. Scroll to the end of the drop-down gallery and then click the *WWTTextBox* text box. (Your custom text box will display in the *General* section of the drop-down gallery.)
    c. Click in the document to deselect the text box.

12. Insert the custom footer you created by completing the following steps:
    a. Click the INSERT tab.
    b. Click the Footer button.
    c. Scroll to the end of the drop-down gallery and then click the *WWTFooter* footer. (Your custom footer will display in the *General* section of the drop-down gallery.)
    d. Close the footer pane by double-clicking in the document.

13. Save the completed letter and name it **C21-E02-PSLtr**.

14. Print and then close **C21-E02-PSLtr.docx**.

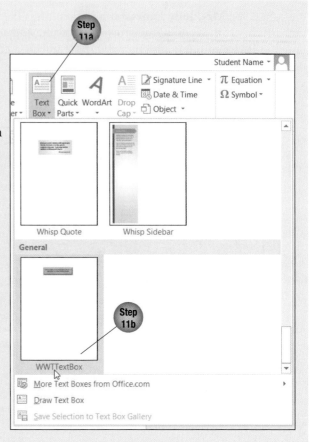

Step 11a

Student Name

Whisp Quote    Whisp Sidebar

General

Step 11b

WWTTextBox

More Text Boxes from Office.com
Draw Text Box
Save Selection to Text Box Gallery

## Modifying Building Blocks

You can insert a building block in a document, make corrections or changes to it, and then save it with the same name or a different name. Save a building block with the same name if you want to update it later to reflect any changes. Save the building block with a new name if you want to use an existing building block as a basis for creating a new one. When you save a modified building block with the original name, a message displays asking if you want to redefine the building block entry. At this message, click Yes.

QUICK
STEPS

## Inserting a Building Block Gallery as a Button on the Quick Access Toolbar

**Insert a Gallery Button on the Quick Access Toolbar**
1. Click desired button.
2. Right-click existing building block.
3. Click *Add Gallery to Quick Access Toolbar*.

To make building blocks more accessible, insert a building block gallery as a button on the Quick Access toolbar. To do this, click the desired button, right-click an existing building block, and then click the *Add Gallery to Quick Access Toolbar* option at the shortcut menu. For example, to add the *Quick Part* gallery to the Quick Access toolbar, click the Quick Parts button on the INSERT tab, right-click a building block at the drop-down gallery, and then click *Add Gallery to Quick Access Toolbar*.

To remove a button from the Quick Access toolbar, right-click the button and then click *Remove from Quick Access Toolbar* at the shortcut menu. Removing a button containing a building block gallery does not delete the building blocks.

1. Open a blank document based on your template **XXX-WWTTemplate.dotx** by completing the following steps:
   a. Click the FILE tab and then click the *New* option.
   b. At the New backstage area, click the *PERSONAL* option.
   c. Click your template **XXX-WWTTemplate** (where your initials display in place of the *XXX*).
2. At World Wide Travel, you have been promoted from travel consultant to senior travel consultant. You decide to modify your name and title building block by completing the following steps:
   a. Click the INSERT tab, click the Quick Parts button, point to *AutoText*, and then click your name and title building block at the side menu.
   b. Edit your title so it displays as **Senior Travel Consultant**.
   c. Select your name and title, click the Quick Parts button, point to *AutoText*, and then click *Save Selection to AutoText Gallery* at the side menu.
   d. At the Create New Building Block dialog box, type **Title** (the original name) in the *Name* text box.
   e. Click the down-pointing arrow at the right side of the *Save in* option box and then click **XXX-WWTTemplate.dotx** at the drop-down list.
   f. Click OK to close the Create New Building Block dialog box.
   g. At the message asking if you want to redefine the building block entry, click Yes.

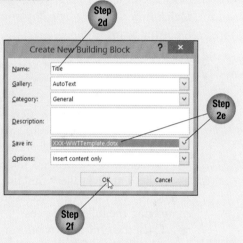

3. Because most of the correspondence you send to Pacific Sky Cruise Lines is addressed to Jody Lancaster, you decide to include her name before the company name and address by completing the following steps:
   a. Click the Quick Parts button, point to *AutoText*, and then click the *PacificSkyAddress* building block at the side menu.
   b. Position the insertion point at the beginning of the company name *Pacific Sky Cruise Lines*, type **Mrs. Jody Lancaster**, and then press the Enter key.
   c. Select the name, company name, and address.
   d. Click the Quick Parts button, point to *AutoText*, and then click *Save Selection to AutoText Gallery* at the side menu.
   e. At the Create New Building Block dialog box, type **PacificSkyAddress** (the original name) in the *Name* text box.
   f. Click the down-pointing arrow at the right side of the *Save in* option box and then click **XXX-WWTTemplate.dotx** at the drop-down list.
   g. Click OK to close the Create New Building Block dialog box.
   h. At the message asking if you want to redefine the building block entry, click Yes.

4. You decide that you want the *WWT* footer to be available in the *Quick Part* gallery. Save the *WWT* footer in the *Quick Part* gallery by completing the following steps:
   a. Click the Footer button on the INSERT tab, scroll through the drop-down gallery, and then click the *WWTFooter* custom footer building block.
   b. Press Ctrl + A to select the footer.
   c. Click the INSERT tab, click the Quick Parts button, and then click *Save Selection to Quick Part Gallery*.
   d. At the Create New Building Block dialog box, type **WWTFooter** in the *Name* text box.
   e. Click the down-pointing arrow at the right side of the *Save in* option box and then click **XXX-WWTTemplate.dotx** at the drop-down list.
   f. Click OK to close the Create New Building Block dialog box. (You now have the footer saved in the *Footer* gallery and *Quick Part* gallery.)
   g. Double-click in the document.

5. Insert the *Quick Part* gallery building blocks as a Quick Parts button on the Quick Access toolbar by completing the following steps:
   a. Click the Quick Parts button and then right-click one of your custom building blocks.
   b. At the shortcut menu that displays, click the *Add Gallery to Quick Access Toolbar* option. (Notice the Quick Parts button that appears at the right side of the Quick Access toolbar.)

6. Insert the *AutoText* gallery building blocks as a button on the Quick Access toolbar by completing the following steps:
   a. Click the Quick Parts button, point to *AutoText*, and then right-click one of your custom building blocks.
   b. At the shortcut menu that displays, click the *Add Gallery to Quick Access Toolbar* option. (Notice the AutoText button that appears at the right side of the Quick Access toolbar.)

7. Close the document without saving it.

8. At the message that displays telling you that you have modified styles, building blocks, or other content that is stored in **XXX-WWTTemplate.dotx** and asking if you want to save changes, click the Save button.

9. Open a blank document based on your template **WWTTemplate.dotx**. (If necessary, refer to Step 1 of this exercise for assistance.)

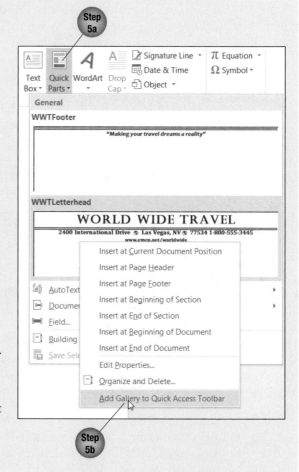

10. Insert the World Wide Travel letterhead building block you created by clicking the Quick Parts button on the Quick Access toolbar, right-clicking the *WWTLetterhead* building block, and then clicking *Insert at Page Header* at the shortcut menu.

11. Click the *No Spacing* style in the Styles group on the HOME tab.

12. Change the font to Candara.

13. Press the Enter key twice, type today's date, and then press the Enter key four times.

14. Insert the building block that includes Jody Lancaster's name, as well as the cruise line name and address, by clicking the AutoText button on the Quick Access toolbar and then clicking the building block at the drop-down list.

15. Press the Enter key and then insert the file named **PacificSkyLetter02.docx**, located in your Chapter21 folder. ***Hint: Do this with the Object button in the Text group on the INSERT tab.***

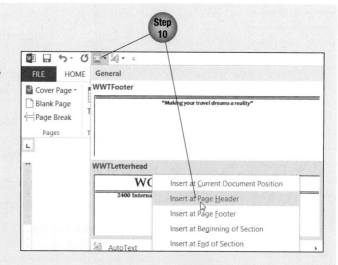

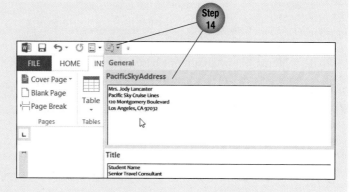

16. Type **Sincerely,** and then press the Enter key four times.

17. Click the AutoText button on the Quick Access toolbar and then click the building block that inserts your name and title.

18. Press the Enter key and then type **C21-E03-PSLtr.docx**.

19. Insert the footer building block you created by clicking the Quick Parts button on the Quick Access toolbar, right-clicking the footer building block, and then clicking *Insert at Page Footer* in the shortcut menu.

20. Save the completed letter and name it **C21-E03-PSLtr**.

21. Print and then close **C21-E03-PSLtr.docx**.

22. Open a blank document based on your template **XXX-WWTTemplate**.

23. Click the AutoText button on the Quick Access toolbar, press the Print Screen button on your keyboard, and then click in the document to remove the drop-down list.

24. At the blank document, click the Paste button. (This pastes the screen capture in your document.)

25. Print the document and then close it without saving it.

26. Remove the Quick Parts button you added to the Quick Access toolbar by right-clicking the Quick Parts button and then clicking *Remove from Quick Access Toolbar* at the shortcut menu. Complete similar steps to remove the AutoText button from the Quick Access toolbar. (The buttons will display dimmed if no documents are open.)

## Saving Building Blocks in a Different Template

After you save the building blocks you created in your own template, they are available only when you use your template to create a document. If you want your building blocks to be available for all documents, save them in the Building Block.dotx template or Normal.dotm template. Use the *Save in* option at the Create New Building Block or Modify Building Block dialog box to save building blocks to one of these two templates.

If you modify an existing building block that you saved in your template and specify that you want it saved in the Normal.dotm or Building Blocks.dotx template, the building block is no longer available in your template. It is available only in documents based on the default Normal.dotm template. If you want to keep a building block in your template and also make it available for other documents, insert the building block content in the document, select the content, and then create a new building block.

---

**Exercise 21.3B**   Saving Building Blocks to a Different Template          Part 2 of 3

---

1. Open a blank document based on your template **XXX-WWTTemplate.dotx** (where your initials display in place of the *XXX*).
2. Create a new *WWTLetterhead* building block and save it in the Building Block.dotx template so it is available for all documents by completing the following steps:
   a. Click the INSERT tab.
   b. Click the Quick Parts button and then click the *WWTLetterhead* building block to insert the content in the document.
   c. Select the letterhead text (from *WORLD WIDE TRAVEL* through *www.emcp.net/worldwide*) including the paragraph mark at the end of the text.
   d. Click the Quick Parts button on the INSERT tab and then click *Save Selection to Quick Part Gallery* at the drop-down list.
   e. At the Create New Building Block dialog box, type **XXX-WWTLetterhead**. (Type your initials in place of the *XXX*.)
   f. Make sure *Building Blocks.dotx* displays in the *Save in* option box and then click OK. (The *WWTLetterhead* building block is still available in your template **XXX-WWTTemplate.dotx** and the new *XXX-WWTLetterhead* building block is available in all documents, including documents based on the **XXX-WWTTemplate.dotx** template.)
   g. Delete the selected letterhead text.

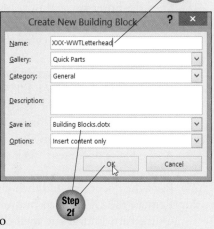

3. Create a new *WWTFooter* building block and then save it in the **Building Blocks.dotx** template so it is available for all documents by completing the following steps:
   a. Click the Quick Parts button on the INSERT tab and then click the *WWTFooter* building block to insert the content in the document.
   b. Select the footer text *"Making your travel dreams a reality"* and make sure you select the paragraph mark at the end of the text.
   c. Click the Quick Parts button on the INSERT tab and then click *Save Selection to Quick Part Gallery* at the drop-down list.

d. At the Create New Building Block dialog box, type **XXX-WWTFooter**. (Type your initials in place of the *XXX*.)

e. Make sure *Building Blocks.dotx* displays in the *Save in* option box and then click OK.

4. Close the document without saving it.

5. Open **WWTContent.docx**.

6. Create a new *WWTTextBox* building block and save it in the **Building Blocks.dotx** template so it is available for all documents by completing the following steps:

a. Select the text box by clicking the text box and then clicking the text box border.

b. Click the INSERT tab, click the Text Box button, and then click *Save Selection to Text Box Gallery* at the drop-down list.

c. At the Create New Building Block dialog box, type **XXX-WWTTextBox**. (Type your initials in place of the *XXX*.)

d. Make sure *Building Blocks.dotx* displays in the *Save in* option box and then click OK.

7. Close **WWTContent.docx** without saving it.

8. Insert the building blocks you created in a document by completing the following steps:

a. Open **PacificSkyAnnounce.docx**, located in your Chapter21 folder.

b. Save the document and name it **C21-E03-PacificSkyAnnounce**.

c. Insert the *XXX-WWTLetterhead* building block by clicking the INSERT tab, clicking the Quick Parts button, right-clicking the *XXX-WWTLetterhead* building block (where your initials display in place of the *XXX*), and then clicking *Insert at Page Header* at the shortcut menu.

d. Insert the *XXX-WWTFooter* building block by clicking the Quick Parts button, right-clicking the *XXX-WWTFooter* building block (where your initials display in place of the *XXX*), and then clicking *Insert at Page Footer* at the shortcut menu.

e. Press Ctrl + End to move the insertion point to the end of the document.

f. Insert the *XXX-WWTTextBox* building block by clicking the Text Box button and then clicking the *XXX-WWTTextBox* building block (where your initials display in place of the *XXX*).

g. Horizontally align the text box by clicking the Align button in the Arrange group on the DRAWING TOOLS FORMAT tab and then clicking *Distribute Horizontally* at the drop-down list.

9. Save, print, and then close **C21-E03-PacificSkyAnnounce.docx**.

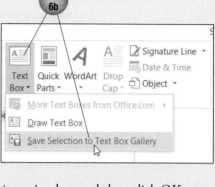

## Deleting Building Blocks

**Delete a Building Block**
1. Display Building Blocks Organizer dialog box.
2. Click desired building block.
3. Click Delete button.
4. Click Yes.
5. Close dialog box.
OR
1. Display desired button drop-down gallery.
2. Right-click desired building block.
3. Click *Organize and Delete* option.
4. Click Delete button.
5. Click Yes.
6. Close dialog box.

When you no longer use a building block you created, consider deleting it. To do this, display the Building Blocks Organizer dialog box, click the building block you want to delete, and then click the Delete button. At the message asking if you are sure you want to delete the selected building block, click Yes.

You can also delete a custom building block by right-clicking the building block at the drop-down gallery and then clicking the *Organize and Delete* option at the shortcut menu. This displays the Building Blocks Organizer dialog box with the building block selected. Click the Delete button that displays at the bottom of the dialog box and then click Yes at the confirmation question. For example, to delete a custom footer, click the INSERT tab, click the Footer button, scroll through the drop-down gallery, right-click the custom footer, and then click *Organize and Delete*. This displays the Building Blocks Organizer dialog box with the custom footer building block selected. Click the Delete button and then click Yes at the confirmation question.

To delete building blocks from a specific template, open a document based on the template and then complete the steps to delete the building blocks. Close the document without saving it and when the message displays telling you that you have modified building blocks and asking if you want to save the changes, click the Save button.

Deleting the entire template you created will also delete the building blocks in the template. To delete a template, display the Open dialog box, click the *Documents* folder in the Navigation pane, and then double-click the *Custom Office Templates* folder in the Content pane. Click your template in the Content pane, click the Organize button, click the *Delete* option, and then close the Open dialog box.

---

## Exercise 21.3C   Deleting Building Blocks and a Template                Part 3 of 3

1. Delete the *XXX-WWTLetterhead* building block by completing the following steps:
   a. Press Ctrl + N to open a blank document.
   b. Click the INSERT tab and then click the Quick Parts button.
   c. Right-click the **XXX-WWTLetterhead** building block and then click *Organize and Delete* at the shortcut menu.
   d. At the Building Blocks Organizer dialog box with the building block selected, click the Delete button.
   e. At the message that displays asking if you are sure you want to delete the selected building block, click Yes.
   f. Close the Building Blocks Organizer dialog box.

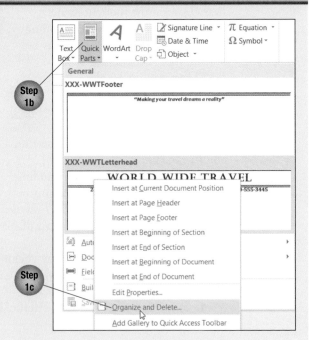

2. Complete steps similar to those in Steps 1b through 1f to delete the *XXX-WWTFooter* building block.

3. Delete the *XXX-WWTTextBox* building block (located in the *Text Box* gallery) by completing the following steps:

   a. Click the Text Box button on the INSERT tab.

   b. Scroll through the drop-down gallery to display your custom text box.

   c. Right-click your text box and then click *Organize and Delete* at the shortcut menu.

   d. At the Building Blocks Organizer dialog box with the building block selected, click the Delete button.

   e. At the message asking if you are sure you want to delete the selected building block, click Yes.

   f. Close the Building Blocks Organizer dialog box.

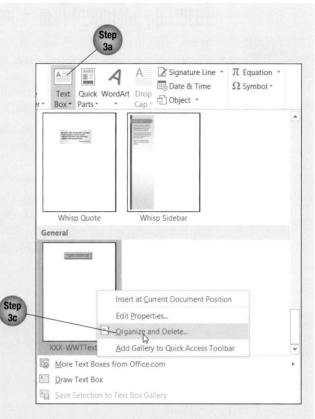

4. Close the document.

5. Delete your **XXX-WWTTemplate.dotx** template by completing the following steps:

   a. Press Ctrl + F12 to display the Open dialog box.

   b. Click the *Documents* folder in the Navigation pane.

   c. Double-click the *Custom Office Templates* folder in the Open dialog box Content pane.

   d. Click **XXX-WTTemplate.dotx** in the Content pane.

   e. Click the Organize button and then click *Delete* at the drop-down list.

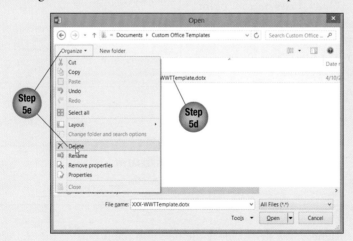

   f. Close the Open dialog box.

# Inserting Document Properties

**QUICK STEPS**

**Insert a Document Property Placeholder**
1. Click INSERT tab.
2. Click Quick Parts button.
3. Point to *Document Property*.
4. Click desired option at side menu.

If you click the Quick Parts button on the INSERT tab and then point to *Document Property* at the drop-down list, a side menu displays with document property options. Click an option at this side menu and a document property placeholder is inserted into the document. Type the desired text in the placeholder.

If you insert the same document property placeholder in multiple locations in a document, updating one of the placeholders will automatically update all occurrences of that placeholder. For example, in Exercise 21.4A, you will insert a *[Company]* document property placeholder in six locations in a document. You will then update the first occurrence of the placeholder and the remaining placeholders will update, as well.

When you click the FILE tab, the Info backstage area displays containing information about the document. Document properties display at the right side of the Info backstage area and include information such as the document size, number of pages, title, and comments. Document properties that you insert with the Quick Parts button sometimes display at the Info backstage area.

---

## Exercise 21.4A  Inserting Document Property Placeholders  Part 1 of 2

1. Open **SEBetaAgrmnt.docx** and save the document with the name **C21-E04-SEBetaAgrmnt**.
2. Select the first occurrence of *SE* in the document (located in the first line of text after the title) and then insert a document property placeholder by completing the following steps:
   a. Click the INSERT tab.
   b. Click the Quick Parts button, point to *Document Property*, and then click *Company* at the side menu.
   c. Type **Stylus Enterprises** in the *[Company]* placeholder.

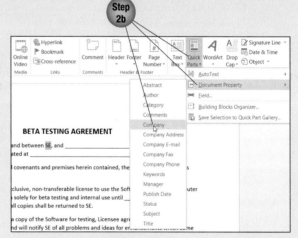

   d. Press the Right Arrow key to move the insertion point outside the *[Company]* placeholder.

3. Select each remaining occurence of *SE* in the document (appears five more times) and insert the *[Company]* document property placeholder. (The company name, *Stylus Enterprises*, will automatically be inserted into the *[Company]* placeholder.)

4. Press Ctrl + End to move the insertion point to the end of the document and then insert a *[Comments]* document property placeholder by completing the following steps:
   a. Click the Quick Parts button, point to *Document Property*, and then click *Comments* at the side menu.
   b. Click the *[Comments]* placeholder tab and then type **First Draft**.
   c. Press the Right Arrow key.
   d. Press Shift + Enter.

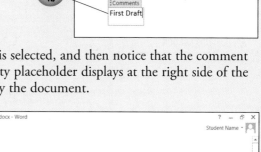

5. Click the FILE tab, make sure the *Info* option is selected, and then notice that the comment you typed in the *[Comments]* document property placeholder displays at the right side of the backstage area. Click the Back button to display the document.

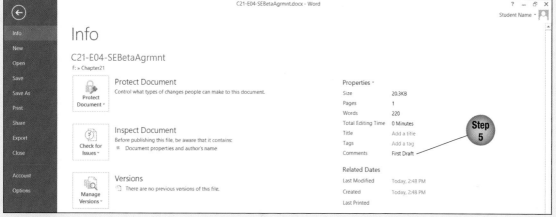

6. Save and then print **C21-E04-SEBetaAgrmnt.docx**.
7. Click in the first occurrence of the company name *Stylus Enterprises*. (This selects the *[Company]* document property placeholder.)
8. Click the *[Company]* placeholder tab, type **Stylus Software Enterprises**, and then press the Right Arrow key. (Notice that the other occurrences of the *[Company]* document property placeholder automatically updated to reflect the new name.)
9. Save **C21-E04-SEBetaAgrmnt.docx**.

# Inserting Fields

Fields are placeholders for data that varies. You inserted fields in documents when you merged main documents with data source files, inserted the date and time in a document, and inserted page numbers in a document. Word provides buttons for inserting many of the types of fields you may want to insert into a document, as well as options at the Field dialog box, as shown in Figure 21.4 on the next page. This dialog box contains a list of all available fields. Just as the Building Blocks Organizer dialog box is a single location for accessing all building blocks, the Field dialog box is a single location for accessing fields. To display the Field dialog box, click the INSERT tab, click the Quick Parts button in the Text group, and then click *Field* at the drop-down list. At the Field dialog box, click the desired field in the *Field names* list box and then click OK.

**Insert a Field**
1. Click INSERT tab.
2. Click Quick Parts button.
3. Click *Field* at drop-down list.
4. Click desired field.
5. Click OK.

**Figure 21.4 Field Dialog Box**

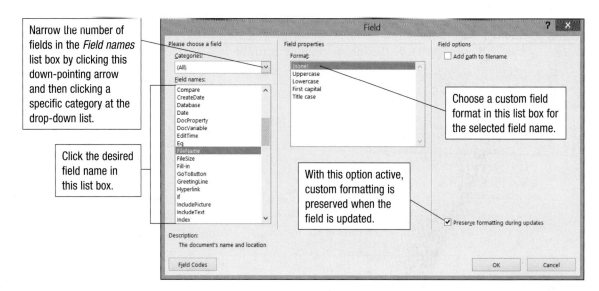

Narrow the number of fields in the *Field names* list box by clicking this down-pointing arrow and then clicking a specific category at the drop-down list.

Click the desired field name in this list box.

Choose a custom field format in this list box for the selected field name.

With this option active, custom formatting is preserved when the field is updated.

## Choosing Field Categories

All available fields display in the *Field names* list box at the Field dialog box. Narrow the list of fields to a specific category by clicking the down-pointing arrow at the right side of the *Categories* option box and then clicking the desired category at the drop-down list. For example, to display only date and time fields, click the *Date and Time* category at the drop-down list.

## Creating Custom Field Formats

Click a field in the *Field names* list box and a description of the field displays below the list box. Field properties related to the selected field also display in the dialog box. You can create custom field formats for some fields. For example, if you click the *FileName* field in the *Field names* list box, you can choose a custom format in the *Format* list box in the *Field Properties* section, such as uppercase, lowercase, first capital, or title capital letters for the file name. If you click the *NumWords* field in the *Field names* list box, you can choose a custom format in the *Format* list box and the *Numeric format* list box.

By default, the *Preserve formatting during updates* check box contains a check mark. With this option active, the custom formatting you choose for a field will be preserved if the field is updated.

## Updating Fields

Some fields, such as the date and time field, update automatically when you open the document. Other fields can be updated manually. You can manually update a field three ways: by clicking the field and then clicking the Update tab; by clicking the field and then pressing the F9 key; and by right-clicking the field and then clicking *Update* at the shortcut menu. You can also update all of the fields in a document (except headers, footers, and text boxes) by pressing Ctrl + A to select the document and then pressing the F9 key.

1. With **C21-E04-SEBetaAgrmnt.docx** open, press Ctrl + End to move the insertion point to the end of the document.
2. Type **Current date and time:**, press the spacebar, and then insert a field that inserts the current date and time by completing the following steps:
   a. Click the INSERT tab.
   b. Click the Quick Parts button and then click *Field* at the drop-down list.
   c. At the Field dialog box, click the down-pointing arrow at the right side of the *Categories* option box and then click *Date and Time* at the drop-down list. (This displays only fields in the Date and Time category in the *Field names* list box.)
   d. Click *Date* in the *Field names* list box.
   e. Click the twelfth option in the *Date formats* list box (the option that will insert the date in figures followed by the time [hours and minutes]).

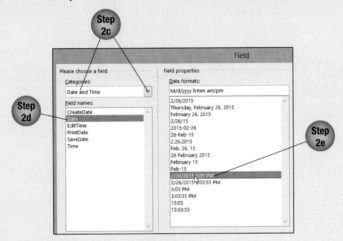

   f. Click OK to close the dialog box.
3. Press Shift + Enter, type **File name and path:**, press the spacebar, and then insert a field for the current file name with custom field formatting by completing the following steps:
   a. Click the INSERT tab.
   b. Click the Quick Parts button and then click *Field* at the drop-down list.
   c. At the Field dialog box, click the down-pointing arrow at the right side of the *Categories* option box and then click *Document Information* at the drop-down list.
   d. Click *FileName* in the *Field names* list box.
   e. Click the *Uppercase* option in the *Format* list box.
   f. Click the *Add path to filename* check box to insert a check mark.

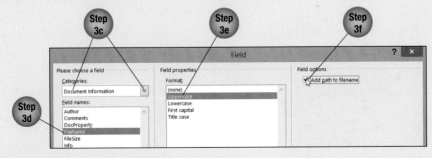

   g. Click OK. (This inserts the current file name in uppercase letters in the document, including the path to the file name.)

4. Insert a header and then insert a custom field in the header by completing the following steps:
   a. Click the Header button in the Header & Footer group and then click *Edit Header* at the drop-down list.
   b. In the header pane, press the Tab key twice. (This moves the insertion point to the right tab at the right margin.)
   c. Click the Quick Parts button in the Insert group on the HEADER & FOOTER TOOLS DESIGN tab and then click *Field* at the drop-down list.
   d. At the Field dialog box, click the down-pointing arrow at the right side of the *Categories* option box and then click *Date and Time* at the drop-down list.
   e. Click in the *Date formats* text box and then type **MMMM yyyy**. (This tells Word to insert the month as text followed by the four-digit year.)

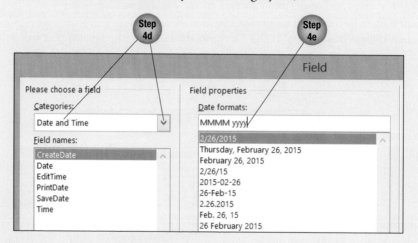

   f. Click OK to close the dialog box.
   g. Double-click in the document.
5. Update the time in the date and time field by clicking the date and time and then clicking the Update tab.
6. Save, print, and then close **C21-E04-SEBetaAgrmnt.docx**.

# Chapter Summary

➤ Word provides a number of predesigned building blocks that you can use to help build a document.

➤ Insert building blocks at the Building Blocks Organizer dialog box. Display this dialog box by clicking the Quick Parts button on the INSERT tab and then clicking *Building Blocks Organizer* at the drop-down list.

➤ The Building Blocks Organizer dialog box provides a single location where you can view all of the available predesigned and custom designed building blocks.

➤ Sort building blocks at the Building Blocks Organizer dialog box by clicking the desired column heading.

➤ You can save content as a building block to specific galleries, such as the *Text Box, Header, Footer,* and *Cover Page* galleries. To save content to a specific gallery, select the content, click the desired button, and then click the option at the drop-down gallery specifying that you want to save the selection to the specific gallery. At the Create New Building Blocks dialog box, specify a name and make any other desired changes and then click OK.

➤ Save content to the *AutoText* gallery by selecting the content, clicking the INSERT tab, clicking the Quick Parts button, pointing to *AutoText,* and then clicking the *Save Selection to AutoText Gallery* option. This displays the Create New Building Blocks dialog box.

➤ Save content to the *Quick Part* gallery by selecting the content, clicking the INSERT tab, clicking the Quick Parts button, and then clicking *Save Selection to Quick Part Gallery* at the drop-down gallery. This displays the Create New Building Blocks dialog box.

➤ Insert a building block at the Building Blocks Organizer dialog box by displaying the dialog box, clicking the desired building block in the *Building blocks* list box, and then clicking the Insert button.

➤ Insert a custom building block from a gallery using a button by clicking the specific button (such as the Text Box, Header, Footer, or Cover Page button), scrolling through the drop-down gallery, and then clicking the custom building block that displays near the end of the drop-down gallery.

➤ Insert a custom building block saved to the *AutoText* gallery by clicking the INSERT tab, clicking the Quick Parts button, pointing to *AutoText,* and then clicking the desired building block at the side menu.

➤ Insert a custom building block saved to the *Quick Part* gallery by clicking the INSERT tab, clicking the Quick Parts button, and then clicking the desired building block at the drop-down list.

➤ Edit a building block with options at the Modify Building Block dialog box. Display this dialog box by displaying the Building Blocks Organizer dialog box, clicking the desired building block, and then clicking the Edit Properties button. You can also display this dialog box by right-clicking a building block at a button drop-down gallery and then clicking the *Edit Properties* option at the shortcut menu.

➤ You can insert a building block gallery as a button on the Quick Access toolbar by clicking the desired button, right-clicking an existing building block, and then clicking the *Add Gallery to Quick Access Toolbar* option at the shortcut menu.

➤ Delete a building block at the Building Blocks Organizer dialog box by clicking the building block in the *Building blocks* list box, clicking the Delete key, and then clicking Yes at the confirmation question.

➤ Another method for deleting a building block is to click the button containing the desired building blocks gallery, right-click the building block, and then click the *Organize and Delete* option at the shortcut menu. This displays the Building Blocks Organizer dialog box with the building block selected. Click the Delete key and then click Yes at the confirmation question.

➤ Insert a document property placeholder by clicking the INSERT tab, clicking the Quick Parts button, pointing to *Document Property,* and then clicking the desired option at the side menu. If a document property placeholder appears in more than one location in a document, editing one placeholder automatically updates the other placeholders in the document.

➤ Fields are placeholders for data and can be inserted with options at the Field dialog box, which is a central location for all of the fields provided by Word. Display the Field dialog box by clicking the Quick Parts button on the INSERT tab and then clicking *Field* at the drop-down list.

➤ Some fields update automatically when you open the document. You can also manually update a field by clicking the field and then clicking the Update tab, pressing the F9 key, or right-clicking the field and then clicking *Update Field*.

# Commands *Review*

| FEATURE | RIBBON TAB, GROUP | BUTTON, OPTION | KEYBOARD SHORTCUT |
|---|---|---|---|
| Building Blocks Organizer dialog box | INSERT, Text | 🗔 , *Building Blocks Organizer* | |
| Create New Building Block dialog box (AutoText gallery) | INSERT, Text | Select text, 🗔 , *AutoText, Save Selection to AutoText Gallery* | Alt + F3 |
| Create New Building Block dialog box (Quick Part gallery) | INSERT, Text | Select text, 🗔 , *Save Selection to Quick Part Gallery* | |
| Document Property side menu | INSERT, Text | 🗔 , *Document Property* | |
| Field dialog box | INSERT, Text | 🗔 , *Field* | |

# Key Points *Review*

**Completion:** In the space provided at the right, indicate the correct term, symbol, or command.

1. The Quick Parts button is located in the Text group on this tab. _____

2. This dialog box provides a single location where you can view all of the predesigned and custom building blocks. _____

3. View custom building blocks saved to the Auto Text gallery by clicking this button on the INSERT tab and then pointing to *Auto Text*. _____

4. With the Quick Parts button, you can save a custom building block in the *AutoText* gallery or this gallery. _____

5. Make changes to the properties of a building block with options at this dialog box. _____

6. To make building blocks more accessible, you can insert a building block gallery as a button on this toolbar _____

7. Delete a building block at this dialog box. _____

8. Insert a document property placeholder by clicking the Quick Parts button on the INSERT tab, pointing to this option, and then clicking the desired option at the side menu. _____

9. Complete these steps to display the Field dialog box. _____

10. To manually update a field, press this key on the keyboard. _____

# Chapter *Assessments*

## Applying Your Skills

Demonstrate your knowledge of features learned in this chapter by completing the following assessments.

### Assessment 21.1  Insert Building Blocks and Fields in a Report

1. Open **PropProIssues.docx** and save the document with the name **C21-A01-PropProIssues**.
2. Make the following changes to the document:
   a. Select the entire document and then change the spacing after paragraphs to 6 points.
   b. Press Ctrl + Home to move the insertion point to the beginning of the document and then press Ctrl + Enter to insert a page break.
   c. Apply the Heading 1 style to the two titles: *PROPERTY PROTECTION ISSUES* and *REFERENCES*.
   d. Apply the Heading 2 style to the three headings in the document.
   e. Apply the Banded theme.
   f. Apply the Red theme colors.
   g. Format the paragraphs of text below the title *REFERENCES* using a hanging indent.
   h. Indent the second paragraph in the *Fair Use* section 0.5 inch from the left and right margins.
3. Press Ctrl + Home to move the insertion point to the beginning of the document and then insert the *Automatic Table 2* table of contents building block.
4. Make sure the Heading 1 style is applied to the title *TABLE OF CONTENTS*.
5. Insert the *Banded* header building block, click the *[DOCUMENT TITLE]* placeholder, and then type **property protection issues**.
6. Insert the *Banded* footer building block.
7. Double-click in the document.
8. Press Ctrl + Home and then insert the *Banded* cover page with the following specifications:
   a. Select the title *PROPERTY PROTECTION ISSUES* and then change the font size to 28 points.
   b. Select the name that displays near the bottom of the cover page above the *[COMPANY NAME]* placeholder and then type your first and last names.
   c. Click the *[COMPANY NAME]* placeholder and then type **barrington & gates**.
   d. Select and then delete the *[Company address]* placeholder.
9. Press Ctrl + End to move the insertion point to the end of the document, press the Enter key, and then insert a field that will insert the file name.
10. Save, print, and then close **C21-A01-PropProIssues.docx**.

## Assessment 21.2 Create Building Blocks and Prepare an Agreement

1. Press Ctrl + N to display a blank document and then save the document as a template named **XXX-BGTemplate.dotx**. (Use your initials in place of the *XXX*.) ***Hint: At the Save As dialog box, change the* Save as type *option to* Word Template (*.dotx).**

2. Close the **XXX-BGTemplate.dotx** template.

3. Create a document based on your template **XXX-BGTemplate** (where your initials display in place of the *XXX*). ***Hint: Display the New backstage area and then click the* PERSONAL *option to display template thumbnails.***

4. Insert the **BGRRFooter.docx** document into the current document. (Do this with the Object button arrow on the INSERT tab. This document is located in your Chapter21 folder.)

5. Select the footer text and then save the selected text as a custom building block in the *Footer* gallery. (Use the Footer button to save the content to the *Footer* gallery.) Name the building block *BGRRFooter* and change the *Save in* option to *XXX-BGTemplate.dotx*.

6. Click the Undo button on the Quick Access toolbar to remove the *BGRRFooter* document. (You may need to click the Undo button more than once.)

7. Insert the **BGRRHeading.docx** document into the current document. (Do this with the Object button arrow on the INSERT tab. This document is located in your Chapter21 folder.)

8. Select the entire document and then save the selected text as a custom building block in the *Quick Part* gallery. Name the building block *BGRRHeading* and change the *Save in* option to *XXX-BGTemplate.dotx*.

9. Click the Undo button on the Quick Access toolbar to remove the *BGRRHeading* document. (You may need to click the Undo button more than once.)

10. Type the following paragraph of text (Bold *Fees* and the colon that follows, turn off bold formatting, and then type the remaining text.):

    **Fees: My hourly rate is \$350, billed in one-sixth (1/6ᵗʰ) of an hour increments. All time spent on work performed, including meetings, telephone calls, correspondences, and emails, will be billed at the hourly rate set forth in this paragraph. Additional expenses, such as out-of-pocket expenses for postage, courier fees, photocopying charges, long distance telephone charges, and search fees, will be charged at the hourly rate set forth in this paragraph.**

11. Select the entire document and then save the selected text as a custom building block in the *AutoText* gallery. Name the building block *BGRRFeesPara* and change the *Save in* option to *XXX-BGTemplate.dotx*.

12. Insert the *Quick Part* gallery as a Quick Parts button on the Quick Access toolbar.

13. Insert the *AutoText* gallery as an AutoText button on the Quick Access toolbar.

14. Close the document without saving it. At the message that displays telling you that you have modified styles, building blocks, or other content and asking if you want to save the changes, click the Save button.

15. Create a document based on your template **XXX-BGTemplate** (where your initials display in place of the *XXX*). ***Hint: Display the New backstage area and then click the* PERSONAL *option to display template thumbnails.***

16. Create the agreement shown in Figure 21.5 on the next page with the following specifications:

    a. Insert the *BGRRHeading* custom building block. ***Hint: Do this with the Quick Parts button on the Quick Access toolbar.***

    b. Insert the *BGRRFeesPara* custom building block. ***Hint: Do this with the AutoText button on the Quick Access toolbar.***

    c. Insert the file named **BGRepAgrmnt.docx**, located in your Chapter21 folder. ***Hint: Use the Text from File option from the Object button arrow drop-down list.***

    d. Insert the *BGRRFooter* footer custom building block. ***Hint: Do this with the Footer button.*** Close the footer pane.

17. Save the completed agreement and name it **C21-A02-BGRRAgrmnt**.
18. Print and then close **C21-A02-BGRRAgmnt.docx**.
19. Open a blank document based on your template **XXX-BGTemplate**.
20. Click the AutoText button on the Quick Access toolbar, press the Print Screen button on your keyboard, and then click in the document to remove the drop-down list.
21. At the blank document, click the Paste button. (This pastes the screen capture in your document.)
22. Print the document and then close it without saving it.
23. Remove the Quick Parts button and AutoText button you added to the Quick Access toolbar.

**Figure 21.5 Assessment 21.2**

## REPRESENTATION AGREEMENT

Rachel Rasmussen, Attorney at Law

**Fees:** My hourly rate is $350, billed in one-sixth (1/6th) of an hour increments. All time spent on work performed, including meetings, telephone calls, correspondences, and emails, will be billed at the hourly rate set forth in this paragraph. Additional expenses, such as out-of-pocket expenses for postage, courier fees, photocopying charges, long distance telephone charges, and search fees, will be charged at the hourly rate set forth in this paragraph.

**Retainer:** I reserve the right to require a retainer for legal services. The retainer funds will be deposited in the Barrington & Gates law firm trust account and will be applied against fees and other charges as incurred. Any unused retainer funds will be returned to you immediately upon the conclusion of my legal representation of you.

**Payment:** Invoices are prepared for all services rendered through the last day of the month. All payments are due within thirty (30) days of the date of the invoice. If you fail to pay any invoice within this time period, I reserve the right to terminate my representation of you and to pursue other remedies available under law.

**Terms:** This Representation Agreement sets forth all of the terms, conditions, and understandings pertaining to my representation. This Agreement does not obligate you to use me or the firm of Barrington & Gates for all of your legal matters, and you may refer matters to another attorney at any time or withdraw from this Agreement at any time. If you withdraw, you will remain obligated to pay the full amount of all fees and expenses outstanding.

Your signature constitutes your agreement to enter into this contract as permitted under Texas Statutes. If the terms in this Agreement are acceptable to you, please date and sign below, and print your name on the line indicated.

Dated: _____

_____     Printed name: _____
Signature

200 TENTH STREET ◆ SUITE 100 ◆ AUSTIN TX 73341 ◆ 512-555-2355

# Expanding Your Skills

Explore additional feature options or use Help to learn a new skill in creating this document.

### Assessment 21.3    Insert Document Properties and Fields in a Report

1. In this chapter, you learned to insert fields in a document from the Field dialog box. Display the Field dialog box by clicking the INSERT tab, clicking the Quick Parts button, and then clicking *Field* at the drop-down list.
2. Experiment with the various options at the Field dialog box. Click the down-pointing arrow at the right of the *Categories* option box and notice how you can choose to display only fields in a specific category. Experiment with other options in the dialog box, such as clicking on a field and reading the information that displays about it in the dialog box.
3. Open **C21-A01-PropProIssues.docx** and then save the document with the name **C21-A03-PropProIssues**.
4. Move the insertion point to the end of the document, press Shift + Enter, and then insert fields by completing the following steps:
   a. Display the Field dialog box.
   b. At the dialog box, change the *Categories* option to *Date and Time*.
   c. Click *Date* in the *Field names* list box.
   d. Click the option in the *Field properties* section of the dialog box that will insert the date as numbers followed by the time (hours and minutes) and *AM* or *PM* (depending on the time of day).
   e. Click OK.
   f. At the document, press Shift + Enter, type **File size:**, and then press the spacebar once.
   g. Display the Field dialog box and then change the *Categories* option to *Document Information*.
   h. Click *FileSize* in the *Field names* list box and then click OK.
   i. At the document, press Shift + Enter, type **Number of words:**, and then press the spacebar once.
   j. Display the Field dialog box, make sure the *Categories* option is *Document Information*, and then click *NumWords* in the *Field names* list box.
   k. Click OK.
5. Print only the last page of the document.
6. Select and then delete the third reference in the *REFERENCES* section (the reference that begins with *Patterson, M. &*).
7. Move the insertion point to the end of the document, click in the numbers that display after *File size:* and press the F9 key. (This updates the file size numbers.)
8. Click in the numbers that display after *Number of words:* and then press the F9 key.
9. Print only the last page of the document.
10. Save and then close **C21-A03-PropProIssues.docx**.

### Assessment 21.4    Insert an Equation Building Block

1. The Building Blocks Organizer dialog box contains a number of predesigned equations that you can insert in a document. At a blank document, display the Building Blocks Organizer dialog box and then insert one of the predesigned equations.
2. Select the equation and then click the EQUATION TOOLS DESIGN tab. Notice that several groups of commands are available for editing an equation.
3. Delete the equation and then type the steps you followed to insert it in the document. Also type a list of the groups available in the EQUATION TOOLS DESIGN tab.
4. Save the document and name it **C21-A04-Equations**.
5. Print and then close the document.

# Achieving Signature Status

Take your skills to the next level by completing this more challenging assessment.

## Assessment 21.5    Create Custom Building Blocks

1. Open a blank document based on your template **XXX-BGTemplate** (where your initials display in place of the *XXX*) that you created in Assessment 21.2. ***Hint: Display the New backstage area and then click the* PERSONAL *option to display template thumbnails.***

2. Insert the **BGRRLtrhd.docx** document into the current document. (Do this with the Object button arrow on the INSERT tab. This document is located in your Chapter21 folder.)

3. Select the entire document and then save the selected text as a custom building block in the *Quick Part* gallery. Name the building block *BGRRLetterhead* and change the *Save in* option to *XXX-BGTemplate.dotx*.

4. Click the Undo button on the Quick Access toolbar to remove the *BGRRLtrhd* document. (You may need to click the Undo button more than once.)

5. Click the HOME tab and then click the *No Spacing* style in the Styles group.

6. Type **Very truly yours,** and then press the Enter key four times.

7. Type **Rachel Rasmussen** and then press the Enter key.

8. Type **Attorney at Law** and then press the Enter key.

9. Press Ctrl + A to select the entire document and then save the selected text as a custom building block in the *AutoText* gallery. Name the building block *BGRRClose* and change the *Save in* option to *XXX-BGTemplate.dotx*.

10. With the entire document selected, press the Delete key.

11. Click the *No Spacing* style in the Styles group on the HOME tab and then type the following paragraph of text:

   > **Thank you for your interest in hiring me as your attorney and in having the firm of Barrington & Gates represent you. At Barrington & Gates, we pride ourselves on providing the highest-quality legal counsel and advice to our clients. Please read the enclosed *Representation Agreement*, sign in the appropriate location, and then return the agreement to me by fax, as an email attachment, or by mail to the address listed below.**

12. Select the entire document and then save the selected text as a custom building block in the *AutoText* gallery. Name the building block *BGRRIntroPara* and change the *Save in* option to *XXX-BGTemplate.dotx*.

13. Close the document without saving it. At the message that displays asking if you want to save the changes to **XXX-BGTemplate.dotx**, click the Save button.

14. Open a blank document based on the **XXX-BGTemplate.dotx** template.

15. Click the *No Spacing* style in the Styles group on the HOME tab and then create the business letter shown in Figure 21.6 on page 747. Use the building blocks you created to insert the letterhead (insert as a header), footer (insert as a footer), first paragraph of text, and complimentary close (the text that begins *Very truly yours,*). Type the additional text shown in the figure. (Type your initials in place of the *XX* located near the end of the letter.)

16. Save the completed letter and name it **C21-A05-ClientLtr**.

17. Print and then close **C21-A05-ClientLtr.docx**.

18. Open a blank document based on your template **XXX-BGTemplate**.

19. Click the INSERT tab, click the Quick Parts button, point to *AutoText* (to display the side menu with your custom building block), and then press the Print Screen button on your keyboard.

20. Click in the document to remove the side menu and then click the Paste button. (This pastes the screen capture of your document with the AutoText side menu displayed.)

21. Print the document and then close it without saving it.

22. Delete your template **XXX-BGTemplate.dotx** by completing the following steps:
   a. Press Ctrl + F12 to display the Open dialog box.
   b. Click the *Documents* folder in the Navigation pane.
   c. Double-click the *Custom Office Templates* folder in the Open dialog box Content pane.
   d. Click **XXX-BGTemplate.dotx** (where your initials display in place of the *XXX*).
   e. Click the Organize button and then click *Delete* at the drop-down list.
   f. Close the Open dialog box.

**Figure 21.6  Assessment 21.5**

**BARRINGTON & GATES**

Rachel Rasmussen, Associate

February 26, 2015

Mr. Evan Markham
310 South 44th Street
Austin, TX 73348

Dear Mr. Markham:

Thank you for your interest in hiring me as your attorney and in having the firm of Barrington & Gates represent you. At Barrington & Gates, we pride ourselves on providing the highest-quality legal counsel and advice to our clients. Please read the enclosed *Representation Agreement*, sign in the appropriate location, and then return the agreement to me by fax, as an email attachment, or by mail to the address listed below.

As I mentioned during our telephone conversation, I will review the information you are returning and then send my responses, suggestions, and questions to you in an email. After reading my email, please call me so we can schedule a meeting to further discuss your legal concerns.

Very truly yours,

Rachel Rasmussen
Attorney at Law

XX
C21-A05-ClientLtr.docx

Enclosure

# Chapter 22

# Customizing AutoCorrect and Word Options

## Performance Objectives

Upon successful completion of Chapter 22, you will be able to:

- Control what kinds of corrections are made by the AutoCorrect feature
- Customize the Quick Access toolbar
- Customize the ribbon
- Import and export Quick Access toolbar and ribbon customizations
- Customize Word options

Microsoft Word offers a number of features to help you customize documents and streamline the formatting of documents. In this chapter, you will learn how to customize the AutoCorrect feature by inserting and deleting characters at the AutoCorrect dialog box. You will also learn how to use the AutoCorrect Options button, customize the Quick Access toolbar and ribbon, and customize Word options.

*Note: Before beginning computer exercises for this chapter copy to your storage medium the Chapter22 folder from the CD that accompanies this textbook and then make Chapter22 the active folder.*

In this chapter, students will produce the following documents:

Exercise 22.1. C22-E01-BT-FAV.docx
Exercise 22.2. C22-E02-InterfaceApps.docx
Exercise 22.3. C22-E03-BTAdventures.docx

Model answers for these exercises are shown on the following pages.

**CHINA, KYRGYZSTAN, TAJIKISTAN, UZBEKISTAN**

**Old Silk Road Adventure**

Bayside Travel is partnering with Family Adventure Vacations to provide adventurous and thrilling family vacations. Our first joint adventure is an exotic trip along the Old Silk Road that includes stunning landscapes in China, Kyrgyzstan, Tajikistan, and Uzbekistan. The Old Silk Road is one of the most fascinating destinations in Asia. Sign up for the Old Silk Road Adventure and experience delicious food, comfortable facilities, cultural interactions, abundant wildlife, and a wide variety of activities of interest to people of all ages.

During the twenty-day trip, you and your family will travel across Kyrgyzstan through majestic mountains and open plains. You will drive the Old Silk Road of Tash Rabat through one of the most spectacular regions of Tien Shan. You will travel through parts of China, Tajikistan, and Uzbekistan visiting museums and local bazaars, witness the Tien Shan Mountains at their most beautiful, and experience the sights of Samarkand and sleepy Bukhara.

Contact one of our college travel adventure consultants to learn more about the newest Student Travel package titled "STudent STyle" that offers a variety of student discounts, rebates, and free travel accessories for qualifying participants.

Through the sponsorship of Ameria Resorts®, we are able to offer you a ➔15 percent discount← for groups of twenty or more people.

**Individual price:**
$3,299 (US)
£1,999 (UK)

**Individual price for groups of twenty or more:**
$3,099 (US)
£1,599 (UK)

For additional information on the Old Silk Road Adventure as well as other exciting vacation specials, please visit our website at www.emcp.net/bayside, or visit www.emcp.net/famadvac to read about other joint ventures between Bayside Travel and Family Adventure Vacations.

5530 Bayside Drive ❖ San Francisco CA 94320 ❖ 1-888-555-8890 ❖ www.emcp.net/bayside

**Exercise 22.1** C22-E01-BT-FAV.docx

---

## NATURAL INTERFACE APPLICATIONS

A major area of artificial intelligence has the goal of creating a more natural interface between human and machine. Currently, computer users are restricted in most instances to using a mouse and keyboard for input. For output, they must gaze at a fairly static, two-dimensional screen. Speakers are used for sound, and a printer for hard copy. The user interface consists of typing, pointing, and clicking. New speech recognition and natural-language technologies promise to change that soon.

### NATURAL-LANGUAGE INTERFACE

Computers that are able to communicate using spoken English, Japanese, or any of the hundreds of other languages currently in use around the world, would certainly be helpful. In the not-so-distant future, computers will most likely be able to read, write, speak, and understand many human languages. Language translators already exist, and they are getting better all the time.

Programmers can look forward to a human-language computer interface. With better interfaces, programmers may be able to describe what they want using natural (human) languages, rather than writing programs in the highly restrictive and rather alien programming languages in use today. Natural-language interfaces are an area of artificial intelligence that is broader in scope than simple speech recognition. The goal is to have a machine that can read a set of news articles on any topic and understand what it has read. Ideally, it could then write its own report summarizing what it has learned.

### SPEECH RECOGNITION

One of the most immediately applicable improvements comes in the area of speech recognition. Rather than typing information into the computer, users can direct it with voice commands. A computer that can take dictation and perform requested actions is a real step forward in convenience and potential. Speech recognition has developed rather slowly, mainly because the typical PC did not have the necessary speed and capacity until very recently.

### VIRTUAL REALITY

Virtual reality (VR) describes the concept of creating a realistic world within the computer. Online games with thousands of interacting players already exist. In these games people can take on a persona and move about a virtual landscape, adventuring and chatting with

STUDENT NAME 1

other players. The quality of a virtual reality system is typically characterized in terms of its immersiveness, which measures how real the simulated world feels and how well it can make users accept the simulated world as their own and forget about reality. With each passing year, systems are able to provide increasing levels of immersion. Called by some the "ultimate in escapism," VR is becoming increasingly common—and increasingly realistic.

### MENTAL INTERFACE

Although still in the experimental phase, a number of interfaces take things a bit further than VR, and they don't require users to click a mouse, speak a word, or even lift a finger. Mental interfaces use sensors mounted around the skull to read the alpha waves given off by our brains. Thinking of the color blue could be used to move the mouse cursor to the right, or thinking of the number seven could move it to the left. The computer measures brain activity and interprets it as a command, eliminating the need to physically manipulate a mouse to move the screen cursor. While this technology has obvious applications for assisting people with disabilities, military researchers are also using it to produce a superior form of interface for pilots.

STUDENT NAME 2

**Exercise 22.2** C22-E02-InterfaceApps.docx
Page 1
Page 2

## Exercise 22.3

C22-E03-BTAdventures.docx

"Travel is fatal to prejudice, bigotry and narrow-mindedness."
Mark Twain

## African Study Adventure

The African Study Adventure program provides travelers with a unique opportunity to travel to African countries and make connections with local people, visit cultural institutions, and travel with knowledgeable tour guides who will provide insightful information about the countries, peoples, and customs.

### Small Groups

The size of each group is limited so that African Study Adventure tour guides can deliver personal service and ensure that you feel comfortable in your surroundings. All tours are limited to a maximum of 25 participants.

### Comprehensive Itineraries

Each program in the African Study Adventure program offers comprehensive sightseeing, exciting activities, and direct encounters with the people of the area you are visiting. Tour guides have developed a range of tours, each with its own principal theme and special highlights.

### Custom Groups

For those who cannot fit African Study Adventure program scheduled departures into their calendars or who prefer to travel with their own friends and family, Bayside Travel has developed custom programs to suit your specific needs.

### Accommodations and Meals

Accommodations will vary with the particular trip. However, Bayside Travel staff has selected accommodations with great care to make sure you will be as comfortable as local conditions allow and that you will enjoy the unique atmosphere of each destination. Most meals are included in the tour package.

## Vacation Adventures

Hurry and book now for one of our special vacation packages. Book within the next two weeks and you will be eligible for our special discount savings as well as earn a complimentary $100 gift card you can use at any of the resorts in our vacation adventures.

### Disneyland Adventure

- Roundtrip airfare into Los Angeles, California
- Three-night hotel accommodations and hotel taxes
- Three-day Resort Ticket
- 24-hour traveler assistance

### Florida Adventure

- Roundtrip airfare to Orlando, Florida
- Seven-night hotel accommodations and hotel taxes
- Four-day Resort Ticket
- Two-day Bonus Ticket
- ome sites

### Cancun Adventure

- Roundtrip airfare to Cancun, Mexico
- Five-night hotel accommodations and hotel taxes
- Free shuttle to and from the airport
- Two excursion tickets

Book a complete air/hotel vacation package and SAVE on fall travel! Bookings must be made by October 14, 2015, for travel January 1 through June 30, 2016 (blackout dates apply). Take advantage of these fantastic savings!

Sylvia Porter

# Customizing AutoCorrect

The AutoCorrect feature in Word corrects certain text automatically as you type. Control what types of corrections are made with options at the AutoCorrect dialog box with the AutoCorrect tab selected, as shown in Figure 22.1. Display this dialog box by clicking the FILE tab, and then clicking *Options*. At the Word Options dialog box, click *Proofing* in the left panel, click the AutoCorrect Options button, and then click the AutoCorrect tab. At the dialog box, you can turn autocorrect features on and off by inserting and removing check marks from the appropriate check boxes, specify AutoCorrect exceptions, replace frequently misspelled words with the correct spellings, add frequently used words, and specify keys to insert the words quickly in a document.

**Figure 22.1 AutoCorrect Dialog Box with AutoCorrect Tab Selected**

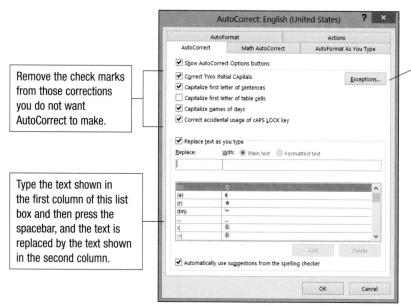

Remove the check marks from those corrections you do not want AutoCorrect to make.

Click this button to display a dialog box with AutoCorrect exceptions to which you can add your own exceptions.

Type the text shown in the first column of this list box and then press the spacebar, and the text is replaced by the text shown in the second column.

## Specifying AutoCorrect Exceptions

### QUICK STEPS

**Display the AutoCorrect Exceptions Dialog Box**
1. Click FILE tab.
2. Click *Options*.
3. Click *Proofing*.
4. Click AutoCorrect Options button.
5. Click AutoCorrect tab.
6. Click Exceptions button.

The check box options at the AutoCorrect dialog box with the AutoCorrect tab selected identify the types of corrections made by AutoCorrect. You can make exceptions to the corrections with options at the AutoCorrect Exceptions dialog box, as shown in Figure 22.2 on the next page. Display this dialog box by clicking the Exceptions button at the AutoCorrect dialog box with the AutoCorrect tab selected.

AutoCorrect will usually capitalize a word that comes after an abbreviation that ends in a period because a period usually ends a sentence. Exceptions to this general practice display in the AutoCorrect Exceptions dialog box with the First Letter tab selected. Many exceptions already display in the dialog box but you can add additional exceptions by typing each desired exception in the *Don't capitalize after* text box and then clicking the Add button.

By default, the AutoCorrect feature corrects the use of two initial capital letters in a word. If you do not want AutoCorrect to correct the capitalizing of two initial capitals in a word, display the AutoCorrect Exceptions dialog box with the INitial CAps tab selected and then type the exception text in the *Don't correct* text box. At the AutoCorrect Exceptions dialog box with the Other Corrections tab selected, type text that you do not want corrected in the *Don't correct* text box. Delete exceptions from the dialog box with any of the tabs selected by clicking the desired text in the list box and then clicking the Delete button.

**Figure 22.2 AutoCorrect Exceptions Dialog Box**

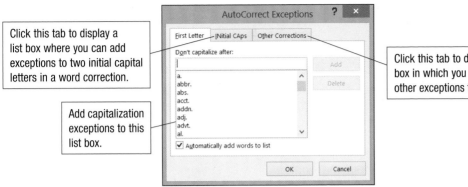

Click this tab to display a list box where you can add exceptions to two initial capital letters in a word correction.

Click this tab to display a list box in which you can add any other exceptions to corrections.

Add capitalization exceptions to this list box.

**QUICK STEPS**

**Add a Word to AutoCorrect**
1. Click FILE tab.
2. Click *Options*.
3. Click *Proofing*.
4. Click AutoCorrect Options button.
5. Click AutoCorrect tab.
6. Type misspelled or abbreviated word.
7. Press Tab.
8. Type correctly spelled word or complete word(s).
9. Click Add button.
10. Click OK.

## Adding Words to AutoCorrect

You can add commonly misspelled words and/or frequently made typographical errors to AutoCorrect. For example, if you consistently type *relavent* instead of *relevant*, you can add *relavent* to AutoCorrect and tell AutoCorrect to correct it as *relevant*. You can also add an abbreviation to AutoCorrect that, when typed, is automatically replaced with the entire word (or words). For example, in Exercise 22.1A, you will add *fav* and the replacement text *Family Adventure Vacations* to AutoCorrect. Subsequently, when you type *fav* and then press the spacebar, AutoCorrect inserts *Family Adventure Vacations*. Control the capitalization of the word (or words) AutoCorrect inserts by controlling the capitalization of the abbreviation. For example, in Exercise 22.1A, you will add *Ky* to AutoCorrect. When you type *Ky* and then press the spacebar, AutoCorrect inserts *Kyrgyzstan*. If you want to insert *KYRGYZSTAN* in the document, you type *KY* and then press the spacebar.

---

**Exercise 22.1A**  Adding Exceptions and Text to AutoCorrect  **Part 1 of 4**

1. At a blank document, click the FILE tab and then click *Options*.
2. At the Word Options dialog box, click *Proofing* in the left panel.
3. Click the AutoCorrect Options button in the *AutoCorrect options* section.
4. At the AutoCorrect dialog box with the AutoCorrect tab selected, add an exception to AutoCorrect by completing the following steps:
    a. Click the Exceptions button.
    b. At the AutoCorrect Exceptions dialog box, click the INitial CAps tab.
    c. Type **STudent** in the *Don't correct* text box and then click the Add button.
    d. Click in the *Don't correct* text box, type **STyle**, and then click the Add button.
    e. Click the OK button.
5. At the AutoCorrect dialog box with the AutoCorrect tab selected, click in the *Replace* text box.

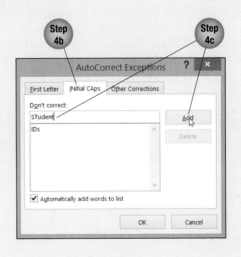

Step 4b

Step 4c

---

6. Type **fav.**
7. Press the Tab key (which moves the insertion point to the *With* text box) and then type **Family Adventure Vacations.**
8. Click the Add button. (This adds *fav* and *Family Adventure Vacations* to AutoCorrect and selects *fav* in the *Replace* text box.)

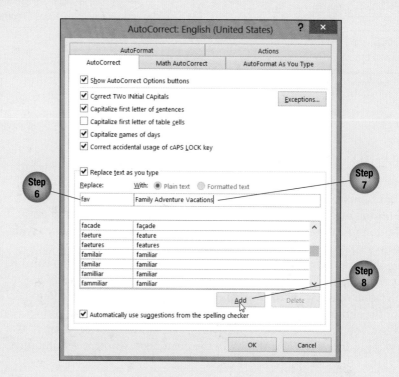

9. Type **Ky** in the *Replace* text box. (The text *fav* is removed automatically when you begin typing *Ky*.)
10. Press the Tab key, type **Kyrgyzstan**, and then click the Add button.
11. With the insertion point positioned in the *Replace* text box, type **Tj**.
12. Press the Tab key, type **Tajikistan**, and then click the Add button.
13. With the insertion point positioned in the *Replace* text box, type **Uz**.
14. Press the Tab key, type **Uzbekistan**, and then click the Add button.
15. With the insertion point positioned in the *Replace* text box, type **bt**.
16. Press the Tab key, type **Bayside Travel**, and then click the Add button.
17. With the insertion point positioned in the *Replace* text box, type **osr**.
18. Press the Tab key, type **Old Silk Road**, and then click the Add button.
19. Click OK to close the AutoCorrect dialog box and then click OK to close the Word Options dialog box.
20. Open **BTLtrhd.docx** and save the document with the name **C22-E01-BT-FAV**.
21. Type the text shown in Figure 22.3 on the next page exactly as shown. AutoCorrect will correct words as you type and not correct the words *STudent* and *STyle*.
22. Save **C22-E01-BT-FAV.docx.**

**Figure 22.3  Exercise 22.1A**

**CHINA, KY, TJ, UZ**

**osr Adventure**

bt is partnering with fav to provide adventurous and thrilling family vacations. Our first joint adventure is an exotic trip along the osr that includes stunning landscapes in China, Ky, Tj, and Uz. The osr is one of the most fascinating destinations in Asia. Sign up for the osr Adventure and experience delicious food, comfortable facilities, cultural interactions, abundant wildlife, and a wide variety of activities of interest to people of all ages.

During the twenty-day trip, you and your family will travel across Ky through majestic mountains and open plains. You will drive the osr of Tash Rabat through one of the most spectacular regions of Tien Shan. You will travel through parts of China, Tj, and Uz visiting museums and local bazaars, witness the Tien Shan Mountains at their most beautiful, and experience the sights of Samarkand and sleepy Bukhara.

Contact one of our college travel adventure consultants to learn more about the newest Student Travel package titled "STudent STyle" that offers a variety of student discounts, rebates, and free travel accessories for qualifying participants.

bt and fav are offering a 15 percent discount if you sign up for this once-in-a-lifetime trip to travel the osr. This exciting adventure is limited to thirty people so don't wait to sign up!

## Using the AutoCorrect Options Button

If you rest the mouse pointer near text that AutoCorrect has just corrected, a small blue box displays below the corrected text. Move the mouse pointer to this blue box and the AutoCorrect Options button displays. Click this button to display a drop-down list with options to change back to the original version, stop automatically correcting the specific text, and display the AutoCorrect dialog box. If the AutoCorrect Options button does not display, turn on the feature. To do this, display the AutoCorrect dialog box with the AutoCorrect tab selected, click the *Show AutoCorrect Options buttons* check box to insert a check mark, and then click OK to close the dialog box.

AutoCorrect
Options

**Exercise 22.1B**  Using the AutoCorrect Options Button                    Part 2 of 4

1. With **C22-E01-BT-FAV.docx** open, select and then delete the last paragraph.
2. Position the insertion point a double-space below the last paragraph of text (you may need to press the Enter key) and type the following text: (AutoCorrect will automatically change *Ameria* to *America*, which you will change in the next step.) **Through the sponsorship of Ameria Resorts, we are able to offer you a 15 percent discount for groups of twenty or more people.**

3. Change the spelling of *America* back to *Ameria* by completing the following steps:
   a. Position the mouse pointer over *America* until a blue box displays below the word.
   b. Position the mouse pointer on the blue box until the AutoCorrect Options button displays.
   c. Click the AutoCorrect Options button and then click the *Change back to "Ameria"* option.

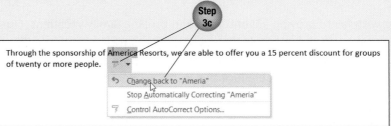

Step 3c

Through the sponsorship of America Resorts, we are able to offer you a 15 percent discount for groups of twenty or more people.

↺  Change back to "Ameria"
   Stop Automatically Correcting "Ameria"
⊤  Control AutoCorrect Options...

4. Save and then print **C22-E01-BT-FAV.docx**.

## Inserting Symbols Automatically

**QUICK STEPS**

**Insert a Symbol to AutoCorrect**
1. Click INSERT tab.
2. Click Symbol button.
3. Click *More Symbols*.
4. Click desired symbol.
5. Click AutoCorrect button.
6. Type text used to insert symbol.
7. Click Add button.
8. Click OK.
9. Click Close button.

AutoCorrect recognizes and replaces symbols as well as text. Several symbols included in AutoCorrect display in the AutoCorrect dialog box and are listed first in the *Replace* text box. Table 22.1 lists these symbols along with the characters you type to insert them.

Along with the symbols provided by Word, other symbols can be inserted in the AutoCorrect dialog box with the AutoCorrect button in the Symbol dialog box. To insert a symbol in the AutoCorrect dialog box, click the INSERT tab, click the Symbol button in the Symbols group, and then click *More Symbols* at the drop-down list. At the Symbol dialog box, click the desired symbol and then click the AutoCorrect button that displays in the lower left corner of the dialog box. This displays the AutoCorrect dialog box with the symbol inserted in the *With* text box and the insertion point positioned in the

**Table 22.1  AutoCorrect Symbols Available at the AutoCorrect Dialog Box**

| Type | To Insert |
|------|-----------|
| (c) | © |
| (r) | ® |
| (tm) | ™ |
| ... | . . . |
| :) or :-) | ☺ |
| :\| or :-\| | ☺ |
| :( or :-( | ☹ |
| --> | → |
| <-- | ← |
| ==> | ➔ |
| <== | ⬅ |
| <=> | ⇔ |

*Replace* text box. Type the text you will use to insert the symbol, click the Add button, and then click OK to close the AutoCorrect dialog box. Click the Close button to close the Symbol dialog box.

1. With **C22-E01-BT-FAV.docx** open, move the insertion point so it is positioned immediately right of the last *s* in *Resorts* (located in the last paragraph) and then type **(r)**. (This inserts the registered trademark symbol.)
2. Move the insertion point immediately left of the *1* in *15* and then type ==>. (This inserts the → symbol.)
3. Move the insertion point immediately right of the *t* in *discount* and then type <==. (This inserts the ← symbol.)
4. Insert the pound (£) currency unit symbol in AutoCorrect by completing the following steps:

   a. Click the INSERT tab.
   b. Click the Symbol button and then click *More Symbols* at the drop-down list.
   c. At the Symbol dialog box, make sure that *(normal text)* displays in the *Font* option box. If it does not, click the down-pointing arrow at the right of the *Font* option box and then click *(normal text)* at the drop-down list (first option in the list).
   d. Scroll through the list of symbols and then click the pound (£) currency unit symbol (located in approximately the sixth or seventh row).
   e. Click the AutoCorrect button located in the lower left corner of the dialog box.
   f. At the AutoCorrect dialog box, type **pcu** in the *Replace* text box and then click the Add button.
   g. Click OK to close the AutoCorrect dialog box and then click the Close button to close the Symbol dialog box.

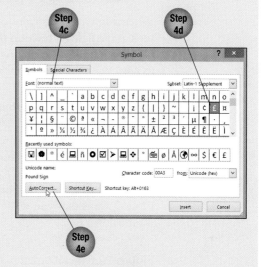

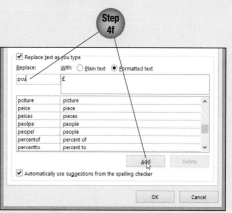

5. Press Ctrl + End to move the insertion point to the end of the document and then press the Enter key twice. (The insertion point should be positioned a double space below the last paragraph of text.)
6. Type the text shown in Figure 22.4 on the next page. Create the pound currency unit symbol by typing **pcu** and then pressing the spacebar. Press the Backspace key once and then type **1,999**. (Complete similar steps when typing **£1,599 (UK)**.)
7. Save **C22-E01-BT-FAV.docx**.

Figure 22.4  Exercise 22.1C

**Individual price:**
$3,299 (US)
£1,999 (UK)

**Individual price for groups of twenty or more:**
$3,099 (US)
£1,599 (UK)

## Customizing AutoFormatting

When you type text, Word provides options to apply some formatting automatically, such as changing a fraction to a fraction character (*1/2* to ½), changing numbers to ordinals (*1st* to *1ˢᵗ*), changing an Internet or network path to a hyperlink (*www.emcp.net* to *www.emcp.net*), and applying bullets or numbers to text. (You learned about this feature in Chapter 3.)

The AutoFormatting options display in the AutoCorrect dialog box with the AutoFormat As You Type tab selected, as shown in Figure 22.5. Display this dialog box by clicking the FILE tab and then clicking *Options*. At the Word Options dialog box, click *Proofing* in the left panel and then click the AutoCorrect Options button. At the AutoCorrect dialog box, click the AutoFormat As You Type tab. At the AutoCorrect dialog box with the AutoFormat As You Type tab selected, remove check marks from those options that you want to turn off and insert check marks for those options that you want to turn on.

**Figure 22.5  AutoCorrect Dialog Box with AutoFormat As You Type Tab Selected**

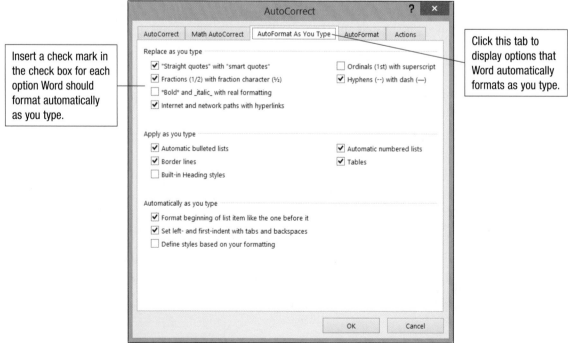

# Deleting AutoCorrect Text

You can delete text from the AutoCorrect dialog box. To do this, display the AutoCorrect dialog box with the AutoCorrect tab selected, click the desired word or words in the list box, and then click the Delete button. Complete similar steps to delete text from the AutoCorrect Exceptions dialog box.

---

**Exercise 22.1D**    **Changing AutoFormatting and Deleting Text**      **Part 4 of 4**
**from AutoCorrect**

1. Make sure **C22-E01-BT-FAV.docx** is open.
2. Suppose that you need to add a couple of web addresses to a document and do not want the addresses automatically formatted as hyperlinks (since you are sending the document as hard copy rather than electronically). Turn off the autoformatting of web addresses by completing the following steps:
   a. Click the FILE tab and then click *Options*.
   b. At the Word Options dialog box, click *Proofing* in the left panel.
   c. Click the AutoCorrect Options button.
   d. At the AutoCorrect dialog box, click the AutoFormat As You Type tab.
   e. Click the *Internet and network paths with hyperlinks* check box to remove the check mark.

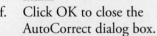

   f. Click OK to close the AutoCorrect dialog box.
   g. Click OK to close the Word Options dialog box.
3. Press Ctrl + End to move the insertion point to the end of the document and then press the Enter key twice.
4. Type the text shown in Figure 22.6 on the next page.
5. Turn on the AutoFormat feature that you turned off in Step 2 by completing Steps 2a through 2g (except in Step 2e, insert the check mark rather than remove it).
6. Delete *bt* from AutoCorrect by completing the following steps:
   a. Click the FILE tab and then click *Options*.
   b. At the Word Options dialog box, click *Proofing* in the left panel.
   c. Click the AutoCorrect Options button in the *AutoCorrect options* section.
   d. At the AutoCorrect dialog box, click the AutoCorrect tab.
   e. At the AutoCorrect dialog box, type **bt** in the *Replace* text box. (This selects the entry in the list box.)
   f. Click the Delete button.

7. Complete steps similar to those in Step 6 to delete the following AutoCorrect entries: *fav, Ky, osr, pcu, Tj,* and *Uz.*
8. Delete the exceptions that you added to the AutoCorrect Exceptions dialog box by completing the following steps:
   a. At the AutoCorrect dialog box with the AutoCorrect tab selected, click the Exceptions button.
   b. At the AutoCorrect Exceptions dialog box, click the INitial CAps tab.
   c. Click *STudent* in the list box and then click the Delete button.
   d. Click *STyle* in the list box and then click the Delete button.
   e. Click OK to close the AutoCorrect Exceptions dialog box.
9. Click OK to close the AutoCorrect dialog box.
10. Click OK to close the Word Options dialog box.
11. Save, print, and then close **C22-E01-BT-FAV.docx**.

**Figure 22.6 Exercise 22.1D**

For additional information on the osr Adventure as well as other exciting vacation specials, please visit our website at www.emcp.net/bayside, or visit www.emcp.net/famadvac to read about other joint ventures between bt and fav.

QUICK
STEPS

**Customize the Quick Access Toolbar**
1. Click Customize Quick Access Toolbar button.
2. Insert check mark(s) before desired button(s).
3. Remove check mark(s) before undesired button(s).

**Add Buttons to the Quick Access Toolbar from Tabs**
1. Right-click desired button on tab.
2. Click *Add to Quick Access Toolbar* at shortcut menu.

Customize Quick Access Toolbar

# Customizing the Quick Access Toolbar

The Quick Access toolbar, by default, contains the Save, Undo, and Redo buttons. You can easily add or remove buttons for basic functions to and from the Quick Access toolbar with options at the Customize Quick Access Toolbar drop-down list, as shown in Figure 22.7 on the next page. Display this list by clicking the Customize Quick Access Toolbar button that displays at the right of the toolbar. Insert a check mark before each button that you want displayed on the toolbar and remove the check mark from each button that you do not want displayed.

The Customize Quick Access Toolbar button drop-down list includes an option for moving the location of the Quick Access toolbar. By default, the Quick Access toolbar is positioned above the ribbon. To move the toolbar below the ribbon, click the *Show Below the Ribbon* option at the drop-down list.

## Adding Buttons from Tabs

You can add buttons or commands from a tab to the Quick Access toolbar. To do this, click the tab, right-click on the desired button or command, and then click *Add to Quick Access Toolbar* at the shortcut menu.

**Figure 22.7 Customize Quick Access Toolbar Button Drop-down List**

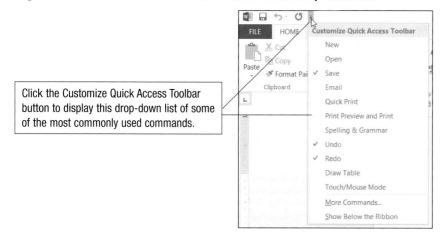

Click the Customize Quick Access Toolbar button to display this drop-down list of some of the most commonly used commands.

**Exercise 22.2A** Customizing the Quick Access Toolbar                 Part 1 of 4

1. Open **InterfaceApps.docx** and save the document with the name **C22-E02-InterfaceApps**.
2. Add a New button to the Quick Access toolbar by clicking the Customize Quick Access Toolbar button that displays at the right of the toolbar and then clicking *New* at the drop-down list.
3. Add an Open button to the Quick Access toolbar by clicking the Customize Quick Access Toolbar button that displays at the right of the toolbar and then clicking *Open* at the drop-down list.
4. Click the New button on the Quick Access toolbar. (This displays a new blank document.)

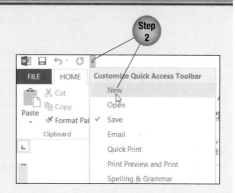

5. Close the document without saving it.
6. Click the Open button on the Quick Access toolbar to display the Open backstage area.
7. Press the Esc key to return to the document.
8. Move the Quick Access toolbar by clicking the Customize Quick Access Toolbar button and then clicking *Show Below the Ribbon* at the drop-down list.
9. Move the Quick Access toolbar back to the default position by clicking the Customize Quick Access Toolbar button and then clicking *Show Above the Ribbon* at the drop-down list.

10. Add the Margins button and Themes button to the Quick Access toolbar by completing the following steps:
    a. Click the PAGE LAYOUT tab.
    b. Right-click the Margins button in the Page Setup group and then click *Add to Quick Access Toolbar* at the shortcut menu.

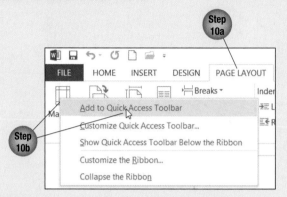

    c. Click the DESIGN tab, right-click the Themes button in the Themes group, and then click *Add to Quick Access Toolbar* at the shortcut menu.
11. Change the top margin by completing the following steps:
    a. Click the Margins button on the Quick Access toolbar and then click *Custom Margins* at the drop-down gallery.
    b. At the Page Setup dialog box, change the top margin to 1.5 inches and then click OK.
12. Change the theme by clicking the Themes button on the Quick Access toolbar and then clicking *View* at the drop-down gallery.
13. Create a screenshot of the Quick Access toolbar by completing the following steps:
    a. Click the New button on the Quick Access toolbar. (This displays a new blank document.)
    b. Click the INSERT tab, click the Screenshot button in the Illustrations group, and then click *Screen Clipping* at the drop-down list.
    c. In a few moments, the **C22-E02-InterfaceApps.docx** document displays in a dimmed manner. Using the mouse, drag from the upper left corner of the screen down and to the right to capture the Quick Access toolbar, and then release the mouse.
    d. With the screenshot image inserted in the document, print the document and then close the document without saving it.
14. Save **C22-E02-InterfaceApps.docx**.

# Customizing the Quick Access Toolbar with Options at the Word Options Dialog Box

The Customize Quick Access Toolbar button drop-down list contains 11 of the most commonly used buttons. However, you can insert many other buttons on the toolbar. To display the buttons available, click the Customize Quick Access Toolbar button and then click *More Commands* at the drop-down list. This displays the Word Options dialog box with *Quick Access Toolbar* selected in the left panel, as shown in Figure 22.8. Another method for displaying this dialog box is to click the FILE tab, click *Options*, and then click *Quick Access Toolbar* in the left panel of the Word Options dialog box.

To reset the Quick Access toolbar to the default (Save, Undo, and Redo buttons), click the Reset button that displays near the bottom of the dialog box. At the message asking if you are sure you want to restore the Quick Access toolbar shared between all documents to its default contents, click Yes.

**Figure 22.8  Word Options Dialog Box with Quick Access Toolbar Selected**

Click the desired command in the list box at the left and then click the Add button and the command displays in the list box at the right.

Click the Reset button to reset the Quick Access toolbar to the default buttons.

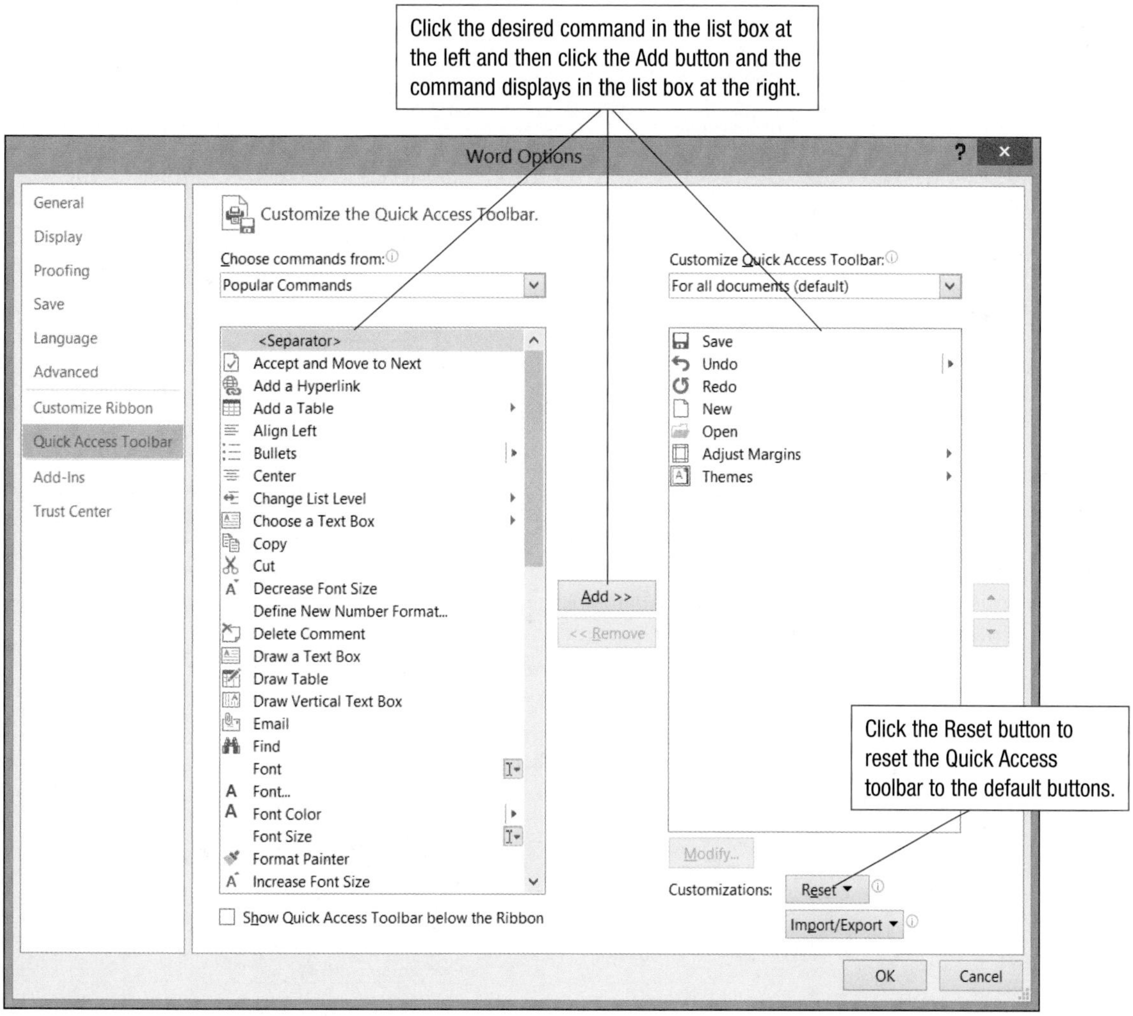

**Add a Button to
the Quick Access
Toolbar from the
Word Options Dialog
Box**
1. Click Customize
   Quick Access
   Toolbar button.
2. Click *More
   Commands* at
   drop-down list.
3. Click desired
   command in left
   list box.
4. Click Add button.
5. Click OK.

You can customize the Quick Access toolbar for all documents or for a specific document. To customize the toolbar for the document currently open, display the Word Options dialog box with *Quick Access Toolbar* selected, click the down pointing arrow at the right of the *Customize Quick Access Toolbar* option, and then click the *For (document name)* option, where the name of the currently open document displays.

The *Choose commands from* option at the Word Options dialog box has a default setting of *Popular Commands*. At this setting, the list box below the option displays only some of the commands available to insert as a button on the Quick Access toolbar. To display all of the commands available, click the down-pointing arrow at the right of the *Choose commands from* option box and then click *All Commands*. The drop-down list also contains options for specifying commands that are not currently available on the ribbon, as well as commands on the FILE tab and various other tabs.

To add a button, click the desired command in the list box at the left side of the commands list box and then click the Add button that displays between the two list boxes. Continue adding all of the desired buttons and then click OK to close the dialog box.

---

## Exercise 22.2B  Inserting and Removing Buttons from the Quick Access Toolbar

Part 2 of 4

1. With **C22-E02-InterfaceApps.docx** open, reset the Quick Access toolbar by completing the following steps:
   a. Click the Customize Quick Access Toolbar button that displays at the right of the Quick Access toolbar and then click *More Commands* at the drop-down list.
   b. At the Word Options dialog box, click the Reset button that displays near the bottom of the dialog box and then click *Reset only Quick Access Toolbar* at the drop-down list.
   c. At the message asking if you are sure you want to restore the Quick Access toolbar shared between all documents to its default contents, click Yes.
   d. Click OK to close the dialog box.
2. Insert buttons on the Quick Access toolbar for the currently open document by completing the following steps:
   a. Click the Customize Quick Access Toolbar button and then click *More Commands*.
   b. At the Word Options dialog box, click the down-pointing arrow at the right of the *Customize Quick Access Toolbar* option and then click *For C22-E02-InterfaceApps.docx* at the drop-down list.

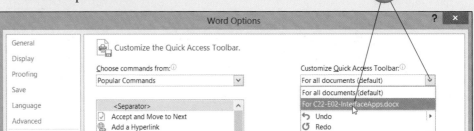

c. Click the down-pointing arrow at the right of the *Choose commands from* option box and then click *All Commands*.

d. Scroll down the list box and then click the second *Close* command (the option preceded by a close icon). (Commands are listed in alphabetical order.)

e. Click the Add button that displays between the two list boxes.

f. Scroll up the list box and then click *Add a Footer*.

g. Click the Add button.

h. Click OK to close the dialog box.

i. Check the Quick Access toolbar and notice that two buttons now display along with the default buttons.

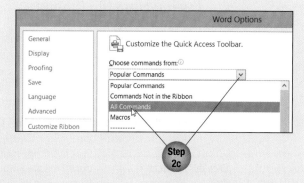

3. Insert a footer by completing the following steps:
   a. Click the Footer button on the Quick Access toolbar.
   b. Click *Integral* at the drop-down list.

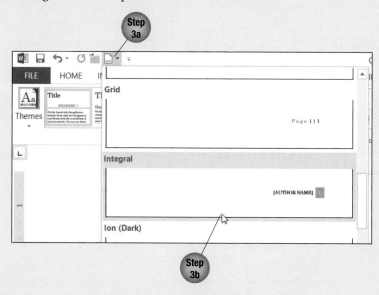

c. Select the name that displays in the footer and then type your first and last names.

d. Double-click in the document.

4. Save and then print **C22-E02-InterfaceApps.docx**.

5. Close **C22-E02-InterfaceApps.docx** by clicking the Close button on the Quick Access toolbar.

# Customizing the Ribbon

In addition to customizing the Quick Access toolbar, you can customize the ribbon by creating a new tab and inserting groups with buttons in the new tab. To customize the ribbon, click the FILE tab and then click *Options*. At the Word Options dialog box, click *Customize Ribbon* in the left panel and the dialog box displays, as shown in Figure 22.9.

**Figure 22.9 Word Options Dialog Box with Customize Ribbon Selected**

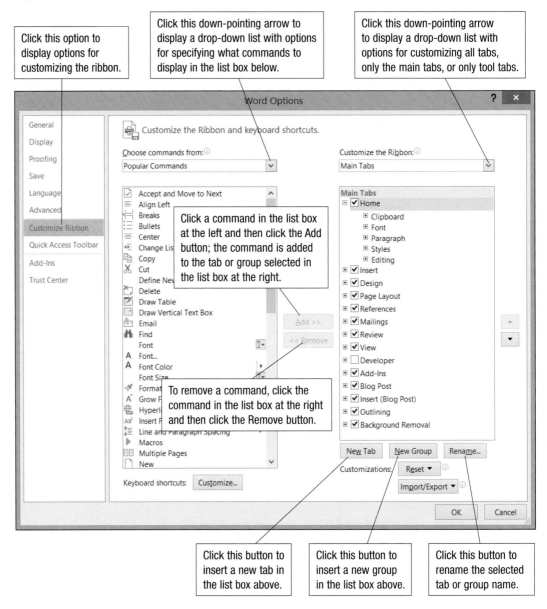

Click this option to display options for customizing the ribbon.

Click this down-pointing arrow to display a drop-down list with options for specifying what commands to display in the list box below.

Click this down-pointing arrow to display a drop-down list with options for customizing all tabs, only the main tabs, or only tool tabs.

Click a command in the list box at the left and then click the Add button; the command is added to the tab or group selected in the list box at the right.

To remove a command, click the command in the list box at the right and then click the Remove button.

Click this button to insert a new tab in the list box above.

Click this button to insert a new group in the list box above.

Click this button to rename the selected tab or group name.

At the *Choose commands from* drop-down list, you can choose to display only popular commands, which is the default, or choose to display all commands, commands not on the ribbon, and all tabs or commands in the FILE tab, main tabs, tool tabs, and custom tabs and groups. The commands in the list box vary depending on the option you select at the *Choose commands from* option drop-down list. Click the down-pointing arrow at the right of the *Customize the Ribbon* option and a drop-down list displays with options for customizing all tabs, only the main tabs, or only tool tabs. By default, *Main Tabs* is selected.

# Creating a New Tab

Add a command to an existing tab or create a new tab and then add commands in groups in the new tab. To create a new tab, click the tab name in the list box at the right side of the dialog box that you want to precede the new tab and then click the New Tab button that displays at the bottom of the list box. This inserts a new tab in the list box along with a new group below the new tab, as shown in Figure 22.10. You can move a new tab up and down in the list box by clicking the tab and then clicking the Move Up and Move Down buttons, respectively, which display at the right of the list box.

**Figure 22.10  Word Options Dialog Box with New Tab Inserted**

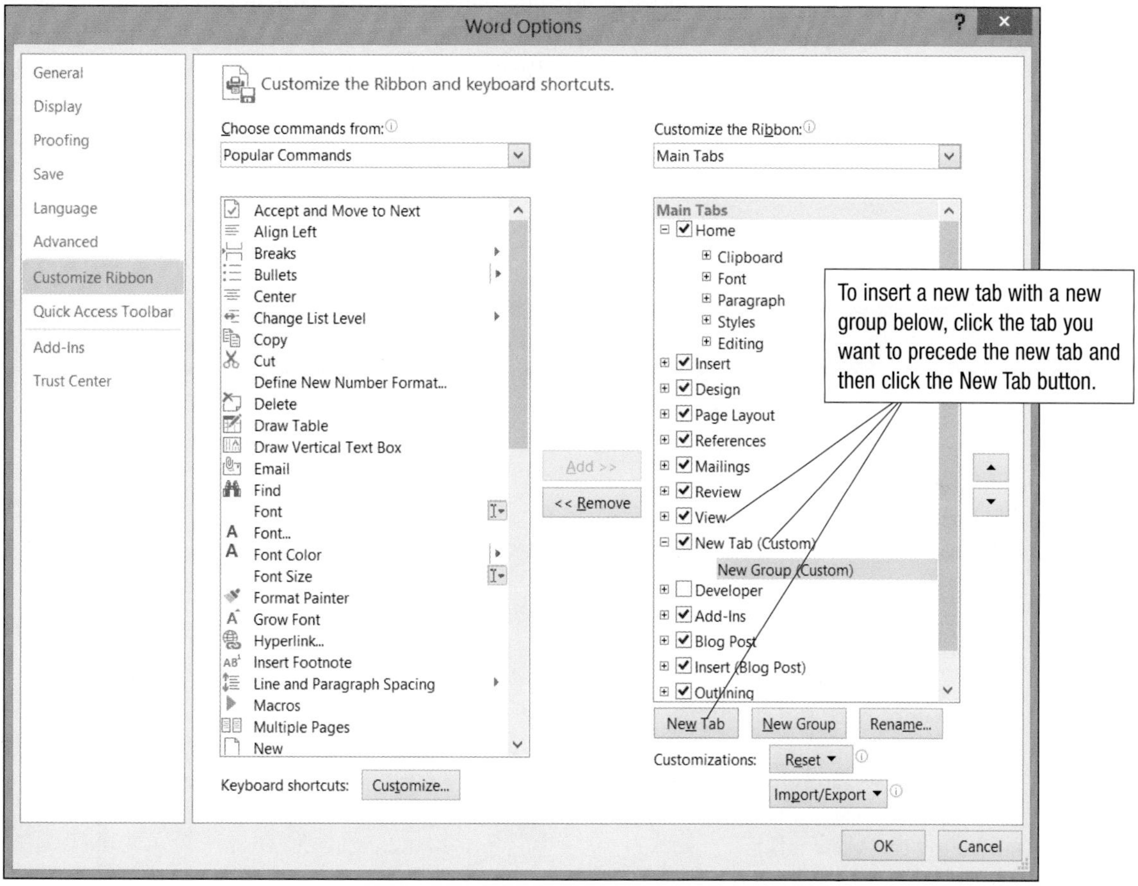

## Renaming a Tab and Group

Rename a tab by clicking the tab in the list box and then clicking the Rename button that displays below the list box at the right. At the Rename dialog box, type the desired name for the tab and then click OK. You can also display the Rename dialog box by right-clicking the tab name and then clicking *Rename* at the shortcut menu.

Complete similar steps to rename the group name. When you click the group name and then click the Rename button (or right-click the group name and then click *Rename* at the shortcut menu), a Rename dialog box displays that contains a variety of symbols. Use the symbols to identify new buttons in the group rather than the group name.

## Adding Commands to a Tab Group

Add commands to a tab by clicking the group name on the tab, clicking the desired command in the list box at the left, and then clicking the Add button that displays between the two list boxes. Remove commands in a similar manner. Click the command that you want to remove from the tab group and then click the Remove button that displays between the two list boxes.

## Resetting the Ribbon

If you customized the ribbon by adding tabs and groups, you can remove all of the customizations and return to the original ribbon by clicking the Reset button that displays below the list box at the right side of the dialog box. When you click the Reset button, a drop-down list displays with two options: *Reset only selected Ribbon tab* and *Reset all customizations*. If you click the *Reset all customizations* option, a message displays asking if you want to delete all ribbon and Quick Access toolbar customizations for this program. At this message, click Yes.

---

### Exercise 22.2C  Customizing the Ribbon                    Part 3 of 4

1. Open **C22-E02-InterfaceApps.docx**.
2. Add a new tab and group by completing the following steps:
   a. Click the FILE tab and then click *Options*.
   b. At the Word Options dialog box, click *Customize Ribbon* in the left panel.
   c. Click the View tab that displays in the list box at the right side of the dialog box. (Do not click the check box before the View tab.)
   d. Click the New Tab button located below the list box. (This inserts a new tab below the View tab.)
   e. With *New Group (Custom)* selected below the new tab, click the New Group button that displays below the list box. (This inserts another new group below the new tab.)
3. Rename the tab and the groups by completing the following steps:
   a. Click the New Tab (Custom) tab.
   b. Click the Rename button that displays below the list box.

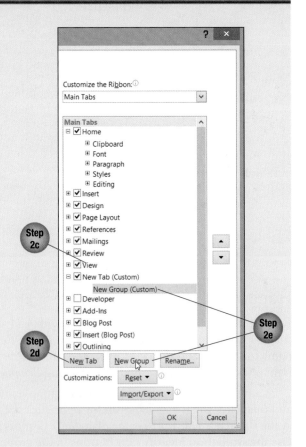

c. At the Rename dialog box, type your initials and then click OK.

d. Click the *New Group (Custom)* group name that displays below your initials tab.

e. Click the Rename button.

f. At the Rename dialog box, type **IP Movement** (*IP* indicates *insertion point*) and then click OK.

g. Click the *New Group (Custom)* group name that displays below the IP Movement (Custom) group and then click the Rename button.

h. At the Rename dialog box, type **Image Editing** and then click OK.

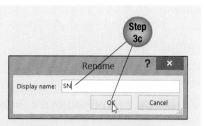

4. Add buttons to the IP Movement (Custom) group by completing the following steps:

a. Click the *IP Movement (Custom)* group in the list box at the right side.

b. Click the down-pointing arrow at the right of the *Choose commands from* option box and then click *Commands Not in the Ribbon* at the drop-down list.

c. Scroll down the list box at the left side of the dialog box (the list displays alphabetically), click the *End of Document* command, and then click the Add button that displays between the two list boxes. (This inserts the command below the *IP Movement (Custom)* group name.)

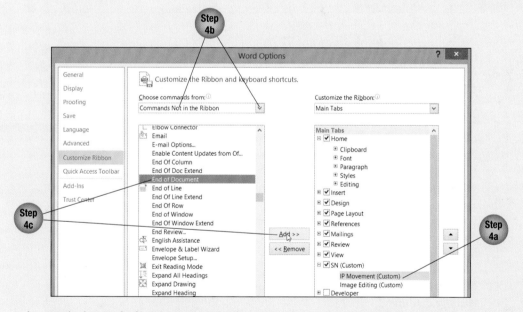

d. With the *End of Line* command selected in the list box at the left side of the dialog box, click the Add button.

e. Scroll down the list box at the left side of the dialog box, click the *Page Down* command, and then click the Add button.

f. Click the *Page Up* command in the list box and then click the Add button.

g. Scroll down the list box, click the *Start of Document* command, and then click the Add button.

h. With the *Start of Line* command selected in the list box, click the Add button.

5. Add buttons to the Image Editing (Custom) group by completing the following steps:
    a. Click the *Image Editing (Custom)* group (below the *IP Movement (Custom)* group).
    b. Click the down-pointing arrow at the right of the *Choose commands from* option box and then click *All Commands* at the drop-down list.
    c. Scroll down the list box at the left side of the dialog box, click the *Online Pictures* command in the list box, and then click the Add button.

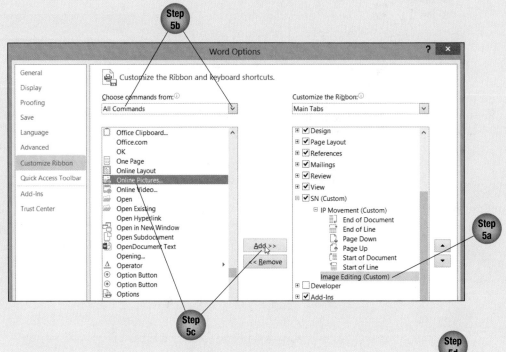

d. Click the down-pointing arrow at the right of the *Choose commands from* option box and then click *All Tabs* at the drop-down list.
    e. In the list box at the left side of the dialog box, click the plus (+) symbol that displays before the *Format* option below the *Picture Tools* heading. (This expands the *Format* option.)
    f. Click the plus symbol that displays before the *Adjust* command.
    g. Click the *Corrections* command and then click the Add button.
    h. With the *Color* command selected, click the Add button.
    i. Click the plus symbol that displays before the *Arrange* command.
    j. Click the *Position* command and then click the Add button.
    k. Click the *Size* command and then click the Add button. (This adds the Crop button and the *Shape Height* and *Shape Width* measurement boxes in a new Size group to the tab.)

6. Click OK to close the Word Options dialog box.
7. Move the insertion point in the document by completing the following steps:
   a. Click the tab containing your initials.
   b. Click the End of Document button in the IP Movement group on the tab.
   c. Click the Start of Document button in the IP Movement group.
   d. Click the End of Line button.
   e. Click the Start of Line button.

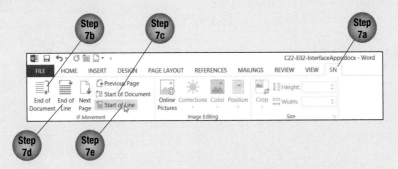

8. Insert an image and then recolor the image by completing the following steps:
   a. Click the Online Pictures button in the Image Editing group on the tab containing your initials.
   b. At the Insert Pictures window, type **computer, talk** in the search text box and then press the Enter key.
   c. Double-click the image shown below. (If this image is not available, choose a similar image.)

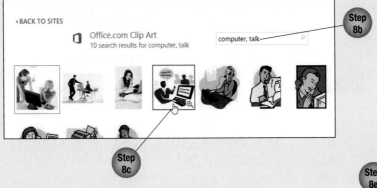

   d. With the image selected in the document, click the tab containing your initials.
   e. Click the *Shape Height* measurement box in the Size group on the new tab, type **1.5**, and then press Enter.
   f. Click the Position button on the new tab and then click the *Position in Middle Right with Square Text Wrapping* option (third column, second row in the *With Text Wrapping* section).
   g. Scroll down to the middle of the first page and make sure the image is still selected.

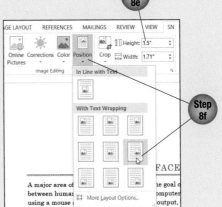

h. Click the Color button in the Image Editing group and then click the *Blue-Gray, Accent color 2 Dark* option (third column, second row in the *Recolor* section).

i. Click the Corrections button and then click the *Brightness: -20% Contrast: +20%* option (second column, fourth row).

9. Create a screenshot of the ribbon with the tab containing your initials by completing the following steps:

a. Click the tab containing your initials.

b. Make sure the computer image is still selected. (This makes all of the buttons active in the Edit Imaging group and Size group on the new tab.)

c. Press Ctrl + N to display a new blank document.

d. Click the INSERT tab, click the Screenshot button in the Illustrations group, and then click *Screen Clipping* at the drop-down list.

e. In a few moments, the **C22-E02-InterfaceApps.docx** document will display in a dimmed manner. Using the mouse, drag from the upper left corner of the screen down and to the right to capture the Quick Access toolbar and the buttons on the tab containing your initials, and then release the mouse.

f. With the screenshot image inserted in the document, print the document and then close it without saving it.

10. Save **C22-E02-InterfaceApps.docx**.

# Importing/Exporting Customizations

If you customize the ribbon and/or Quick Access toolbar, you can export the customizations to a file and then use that file on other computers. To export the customized ribbon and/or Quick Access toolbar, display the Word Options dialog box with *Customize Ribbon* or *Quick Access Toolbar* selected in the left panel, click the Import/Export button that displays below the list box at the right side of the dialog box, and then click *Export all customizations* at the drop-down list. At the File Save dialog box that displays, navigate to the desired folder, type a name for the file in the *File name* text box, and then press the Enter key or click the Save button. By default, Word saves the file type as *Exported Office UI file (\*.exportedUI)* with the *.exportedUI* file extension.

To import a ribbon and Quick Access toolbar customization file, display the Word Options dialog box with *Customize Ribbon* or *Quick Access Toolbar* selected in the left panel, click the Import/Export button, and then click *Import customization file* at the drop-down list. At the File Open dialog box, navigate to the folder containing the customization file and then double-click the file. (The file name will display with the *.exportedUI* file extension.) At the message that displays asking if you want to replace all existing ribbon and Quick Access toolbar customizations for this program, click Yes.

1. With **C22-E02-InterfaceApps.docx** open, export your ribbon and Quick Access toolbar customizations to a file by completing the following steps:
   a. Click the FILE tab and then click *Options*.
   b. Click *Customize Ribbon* in the left panel at the Word Options dialog box.
   c. Click the Import/Export button that displays below the list box at the right side of the dialog box and then click *Export all customizations* at the drop-down list.

   d. At the File Save dialog box, navigate to your Chapter22 folder.
   e. Click in the *File name* text box. (This selects the file name.)
   f. Type **CustomRibbon&QAT** and then press the Enter key.
2. Reset the Quick Access toolbar and ribbon by completing the following steps:
   a. Click the Reset button that displays below the list box at the right side of the dialog box and then click *Reset all customizations* at the drop-down list.

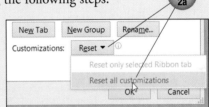

   b. At the message asking if you want to delete all ribbon and Quick Access toolbar customizations, click Yes.
   c. Click OK to close the Word Options dialog box.
3. Save, print, and then close **C22-E02-InterfaceApps.docx**.

# Customizing Word Options

Throughout the chapters in this book, you have made changes to some of the options available at the Word Options dialog box. By default, the Word Options dialog box displays with *General* selected in the left panel, as shown in Figure 22.11 on the next page. Use options in the Word Options dialog box with *General* selected in the left panel to turn the Mini toolbar and live preview feature on or off, specify the ScreenTip style, change user information, choose a different Office background and theme, and specify start up options.

When you open Word 2013, the Word start screen displays by default. This screen contains a *Recent* list as well as templates for creating a document. If you want Word to open directly to a blank document, remove the check mark from the *Show the Start screen when this application starts* option.

**QUICK STEPS**

**Customize Word Options**
1. Click FILE tab.
2. Click *Options*.
3. Click desired option in left panel.
4. Make desired customization choices.
5. Click OK to close Word Options dialog box.

**Figure 22.11 Word Options Dialog Box with *General* Selected**

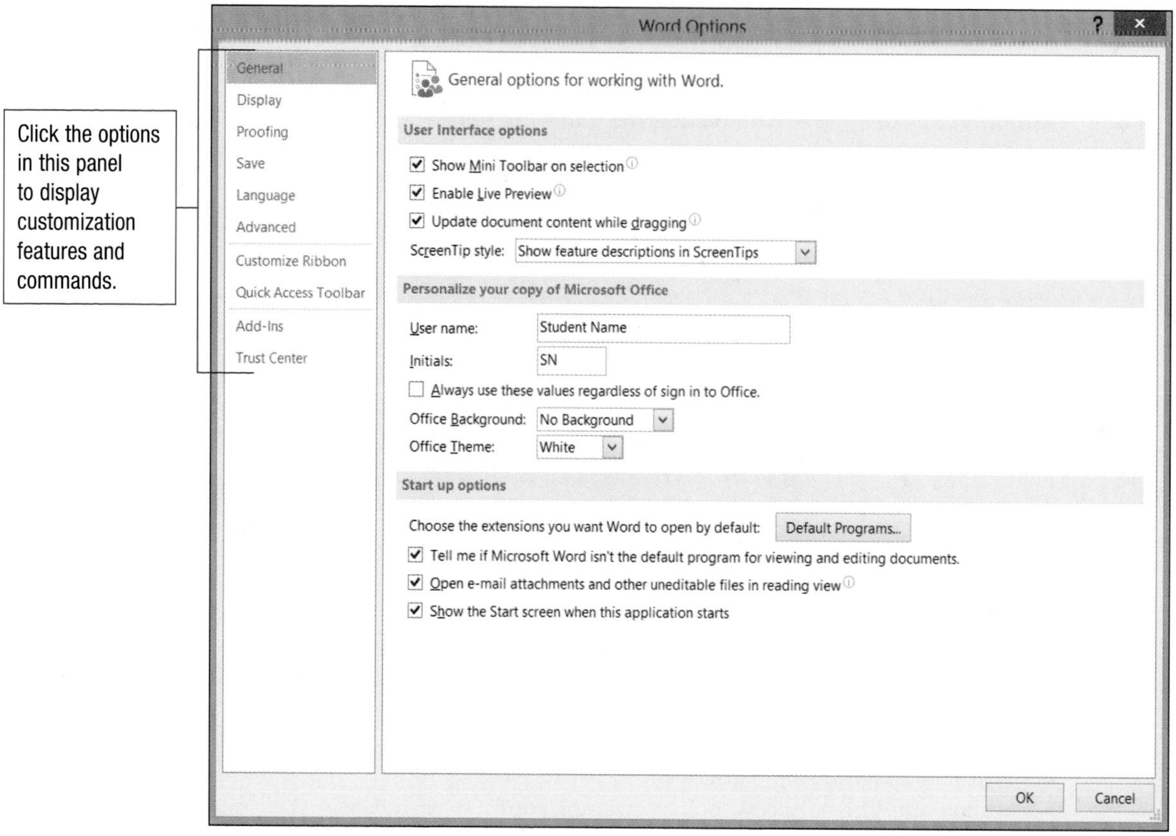

Click the options in this panel to display customization features and commands.

The Word Options dialog box, like many other dialog boxes in Word, contains a Help button in the upper right corner. Click this Help button and the Word Help window displays with information about the options in the dialog box.

1. Customize Word options by completing the following steps:
   a. Click the FILE tab and then click *Options*.
   b. At the Word Options dialog box with *General* selected in the left panel, click the *Show Mini Toolbar on selection* check box to remove the check mark.
   c. Click the *Enable Live Preview* check box to remove the check mark.
   d. Select the current name in the *User name* text box and then type **Sylvia Porter**.
   e. Select the current initials in the *Initials* text box and then type **SP**.
   f. Click the *Always use these values regardless of sign in to Office.* check box to insert a check mark.
   g. Click the *Show the Start screen when this application starts* check box to remove the check mark.

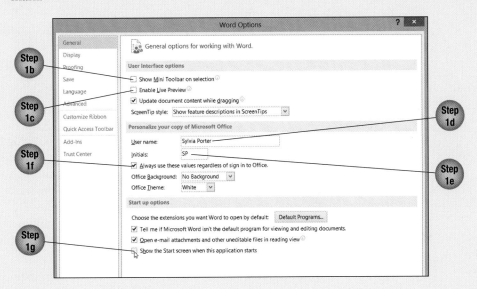

   h. Click OK to close the dialog box.
2. Close Word and then open Word. Notice that a blank document displays rather than the Word Start screen.
3. Open **BTAdventures.docx** and save the document with the name **C22-E03-BTAdventures**.
4. Select text in the document and notice that the Mini toolbar does not display because you turned off the feature.
5. With the text still selected, click the Font button arrow and then hover the mouse pointer over the font options that display at the drop-down gallery. Because you turned off the live preview feature, the text in your document does not display the font over which your mouse pointer is hovering.

6. Insert a user name field by completing the
   following steps:
   a. Press Ctrl + End to move the insertion
      point to the end of the document.
   b. Click the INSERT tab.
   c. Click the Quick Parts button in the Text
      group and then click *Field* at the drop-
      down list.
   d. At the Field dialog box, scroll to the
      bottom of the *Field names* list box and
      then double-click *UserName*.
7. Save **C22-E03-BTAdventures.docx**.

Click the *Display* option in the left panel and the Word Options dialog box displays options for specifying how document content appears on the screen and when it is printed. In a previous chapter, you learned how to turn on and off the display of white space that separates pages in Print Layout view by double-clicking the white space or the line separating the pages. You can also turn on and off the display of white space between pages with the *Show white space between pages in Print Layout view* option at the dialog box. Likewise, you can turn on and off the display of highlighting and ScreenTips that display when you hover the mouse over an option or button.

Click the *Proofing* option in the left panel and the Word Options dialog box displays options for customizing AutoCorrect and the spelling and grammar checker. Again, you used some of these options in previous chapters.

Click the *Save* option in the left panel and the Word Options dialog box displays options for customizing how and where documents are saved. You can change the format in which files are saved from the default *Word Document (\*.docx)* to another format, such as a previous version of Word, Word template, web page, or plain text. You can also change the default locations for where documents and AutoRecover files are saved. These save options are also available with the *Save as type* option at the Save As dialog box. The difference is that changing the file save format with the *Save files in this format* option at the Word Options dialog box with *Save* selected changes the default for all future documents saved.

1. With **C22-E03-BTAdventures.docx** open, click the FILE tab and then click *Options*.
2. At the Word Options dialog box, click the *Display* option in the left panel and then look at the options available.
3. Click the *Proofing* option that displays in the left panel and then look at the options available.
4. Click the *Save* option that displays in the left panel.
5. Change the default local file location by completing the following steps:
   a. Make note of the current default local file location.
   b. Click the Browse button that displays at the right of the *Default local file location* option box.

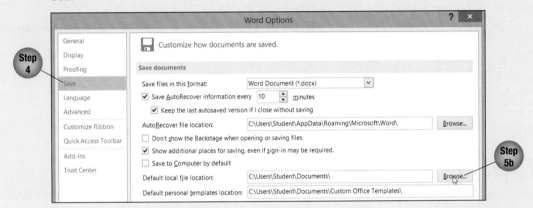

   c. At the Modify Location dialog box, navigate to the Desktop.
   d. Click OK.
6. Click OK to close the Word Options dialog box.
7. Save, print, and then close **C22-E03-BTAdventures.docx**.
8. Close Word and then open Word.
9. At a blank document, press the F12 key to display the Save As dialog box. (Notice that the default save location is the Desktop.)
10. Click the Cancel button to remove the Save As dialog box.

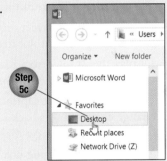

With the *Advanced* option selected, the Word Options dialog box displays a number of sections that identify ways to customize Word, including sections for changing editing options; for specifying how you want text cut, copied, and pasted in a document; for specifying what document content to show; and for customizing the display and printing of a document, among others.

Click the *Add-Ins* option and the Word Options dialog box displays add-ins, which are supplemental options that add custom commands and specialized features to Office 2013 applications.

With the *Trust Center* option selected in the left panel of the Word Options dialog box, hyperlinks display that provide navigation to privacy and security information, including the Word privacy statement, the Office.com privacy statement, and the Customer Experience Improvement Program.

1. At a blank document, click the FILE tab and then click *Options*.
2. At the Word Options dialog box with *General* selected in the left panel, click the *Show Mini Toolbar on selection* check box to insert a check mark.
3. Click the *Enable Live Preview* check box to insert a check mark.
4. Click the *Show the Start screen when this application starts* check box to insert a check mark.
5. Select the current name in the *User name* text box and then type the original name.
6. Select the current initials in the *Initials* text box and then type the original initials.
7. Click the *Always use these values regardless of sign in to Office.* check box to remove the check mark.
8. Change the default file location back to the original setting by completing the following steps:
   a. Click the *Save* option in the left panel of the Word Options dialog box.
   b. Click the Browse button that displays at the right of the *Default local file location* option box.
   c. At the Modify Location dialog box, navigate to the original location.
   d. Click OK.
9. Close the Word Options dialog box.

# Chapter Summary

➤ You can add words to AutoCorrect during a spelling check and at the AutoCorrect dialog box.

➤ Display the AutoCorrect dialog box by clicking the FILE tab, clicking *Options*, clicking *Proofing*, and then clicking the AutoCorrect Options button.

➤ Display the AutoCorrect Exceptions dialog box by clicking the Exceptions button at the AutoCorrect dialog box with the AutoCorrect tab selected. Specify autocorrect exceptions at this dialog box, as well.

➤ Use the AutoCorrect Options button that displays when you hover the mouse over corrected text to change corrected text back to the original spelling, stop the automatic correction of specific text, and display the AutoCorrect dialog box.

➤ The AutoCorrect dialog box contains several symbols that you can insert in a document by typing specific text or characters.

➤ You can insert a symbol from the Symbol dialog box into the AutoCorrect dialog box. To do this, display the Symbol dialog box, click the desired symbol, and then click the AutoCorrect button.

➤ When typing text, control what Word automatically formats with options at the AutoCorrect dialog box with the AutoFormat As You Type tab selected.

➤ Customize the Quick Access toolbar with options from the Customize Quick Access Toolbar button drop-down list.

➤ Use options at the Customize Quick Access Toolbar button drop-down list to change the location of the Quick Access toolbar.

➤ Add a button or command to the Quick Access toolbar by right-clicking the desired button or command and then clicking *Add to Quick Access Toolbar* at the shortcut menu.

➤ You can customize the Quick Access toolbar with options at the Word Options dialog box with *Quick Access Toolbar* selected.

➤ Reset the Quick Access toolbar to the default by clicking the Reset button at the Word Options dialog box with *Quick Access Toolbar* selected and then clicking Yes at the message that displays.

- You can customize the Quick Access toolbar for all documents or for a specific document.
- The *Choose commands from* option at the Word Options dialog box with *Quick Access Toolbar* selected has a default setting of *Popular Commands*. Change this option to *All Commands* to display all of the buttons and options that can be added to the Quick Access toolbar.
- Customize the ribbon with options at the Word Options dialog box with *Customize Ribbon* selected.
- At the Word Options dialog box with *Customize Ribbon* selected, add a new tab by clicking the tab name in the list box at the right side of the dialog box that you want to precede the new tab and then clicking the New Tab button. Adding a new tab also adds a new group.
- Rename a tab or group at the Word options dialog box with *Customize Ribbon* selected by clicking the tab or group, clicking the Rename button, typing the new name in the Rename dialog box, and then clicking OK.
- Add a command to a new tab group by clicking the desired tab group in the list box at the right side of the Word Options dialog box with *Customize Ribbon* selected, clicking the desired command in the list box at the left, and then clicking the Add button.
- To remove a command from a tab group at the Word Options dialog box with *Customize Ribbon* selected, click the command and then click the Remove button that displays between the two list boxes.
- Reset the ribbon by clicking the Reset button at the Word Options dialog box with *Customize Ribbon* selected and then clicking *Reset only selected Ribbon tab* or *Reset all customizations*.
- Export a file containing customizations to the ribbon and/or Quick Access toolbar with the Import/Export button at the Word Options dialog box with *Customize Ribbon* or *Quick Access Toolbar* selected, respectively.
- Customize Word options at the Word Options dialog box.

# Commands *Review*

| FEATURE | RIBBON TAB, GROUP | BUTTON, OPTION |
|---|---|---|
| AutoCorrect dialog box | FILE, *Options* | *Proofing*, AutoCorrect |
| Symbol dialog box | INSERT, Symbols | $\Omega$ , *More Symbols* |
| Word Options dialog box | FILE, *Options* | |

# Key Points *Review*

**Completion:** In the space provided at the right, indicate the correct term, symbol, or command.

1. This feature corrects certain words automatically as you type them. _____

2. Use this button, which displays when you hover the mouse over corrected text, to change corrected text back to the original spelling. _____

3. Type these characters to insert the ☺ symbol in a document. _____

4. Type these characters to insert the ➔ symbol. _____

5. When typing text, control what Word automatically formats with options at the AutoCorrect dialog box with this tab selected. _____

6. Add and remove basic buttons to and from the Quick Access toolbar with options at this drop-down list. _____

7. Add a button to the Quick Access toolbar by right-clicking the desired button and then clicking this option at the shortcut menu. _____

8. If you click the Customize Quick Access Toolbar button and then click *More Commands*, this dialog box displays. _____

9. This is the default setting for the *Choose commands from* option at the Word Options dialog box. _____

10. At the Word Options dialog box with this option selected in the left panel, add a new tab by clicking the tab name in the list box that you want to precede the new tab and then clicking the New Tab button. _____

11. Export a file containing customizations to the ribbon and/or Quick Access toolbar with this button in the Word Options dialog box with *Customize Ribbon* or *Quick Access Toolbar* selected, respectively. _____

12. Change the user name and initials at the Word Options dialog box with this option selected in the left panel. _____

# Chapter Assessments

## Applying Your Skills

Demonstrate your knowledge of features learned in this chapter by completing the following assessments.

### Assessment 22.1 Insert and Format Text in a Medical Plan Document

1. Open **KLHPlan.docx** and save the document with the name **C22-A01-KLHPlan**.
2. Add the following text to AutoCorrect:
   a. Insert *kl* in the *Replace* text box and insert *Key Life Health Plan* in the *With* text box.
   b. Insert *m* in the *Replace* text box and insert *medical* in the *With* text box.
3. With the insertion point positioned at the beginning of the document, type the text shown in Figure 22.12 on the next page.
4. Make the following changes to the document:
   a. Apply the Heading 1 style to the title *Key Life Health Plan*.
   b. Apply the Heading 2 style to the four headings in the document.
   c. Apply the Lines (Simple) style set.
   d. Apply the Frame theme.
5. Insert the *Ion (Dark)* header building block.
6. Insert the *Ion (Dark)* footer building block. Click the *[DOCUMENT TITLE]* placeholder and then type **Key Life Health Plan**. Select the name that displays at the right side of the footer and then type your first and last names.

7. Decrease the value in the *Footer from Bottom* measurement box to 0.3 inch.
8. Double-click in the document.
9. Press Ctrl + End to move the insertion point to the end of the document, press the Enter key, and then insert the *FileName* field.
10. Press Shift + Enter and then insert the *PrintDate* field. (You choose the date format.)
11. Save and then print **C22-A01-KLHPlan.docx**.
12. Delete the two entries you made at the AutoCorrect dialog box.
13. Close **C22-A01-KLHPlan.docx**.

**Figure 22.12  Assessment 22.1**

**kl**

**How the Plan Works**

When you enroll in kl, you and each eligible family member selects a plan option. A kl option includes a main m clinic, any affiliated satellite clinics, and designated hospitals. Family members may choose different m plan options and can easily change options.

Some m plan options do not require you to choose a primary care physician. This means a member may self-refer for specialty care within that m plan option. However, kl encourages members to establish an ongoing relationship with a primary care physician and develop a valuable partnership in the management of their m care.

kl provides coverage for emergency m services outside the service area. If the m emergency is not life threatening, call your primary care physician to arrange for care before going to an emergency facility. If you have a life-threatening emergency, go directly to the nearest appropriate facility. Any follow-up care to emergency m services must be coordinated within your plan option.

## Assessment 22.2    Create a Vacation Document with AutoCorrect and Special Symbols

1. At a blank document, add the following text to AutoCorrect:
   a. Insert *Pt* in the *Replace* text box and insert *Patagonia* in the *With* text box.
   b. Insert *Ft* in the *Replace* text box and insert *Futaleufu* in the *With* text box.
   c. Insert the euro (€) currency symbol in the *With* text box (using the Symbol dialog box) and type **eu** in the *Replace* text box. (The euro currency symbol is located near the bottom of the Symbol dialog box list box with *(normal text)* selected.)
2. Type the text shown in Figure 22.13. Create the smiley face icon by typing **:)** and then pressing the spacebar. (To insert the euro currency symbol, type **eu** and then press the spacebar. Press the Backspace key once and then type the amount.)
3. Save the document with the name **C22-A02-FAV**.
4. Print and then close **C22-A02-FAV.docx**.
5. Delete the *eu*, *Ft*, and *Pt* AutoCorrect entries.

**Figure 22.13  Assessment 22.2**

### LUXURY FAMILY ADVENTURE VACATIONS

Sign up today for one of our exciting luxury family adventure vacations, created for families who enjoy a multitude of outdoor activities and a bit of luxury. Our Chile luxury vacation combines whitewater rafting, hiking, kayaking, and horseback riding into one fun-filled week of adventure travel in beautiful Pt, Chile.

More than a family rafting trip, we'll make sure you are exposed to all that the Ft Valley has to offer including whitewater rafting on the Ft River, which contains sections for all levels of ability and experience; hiking up some of the beautiful tributaries of the Ft River; and horseback riding across beautiful valleys at the base of snow-peaked mountains.

Pt, Chile, provides a wide variety of opportunities for active travel that the whole family can enjoy. You can feel confident that we will take care of all of the details so that your experience is a mix of fun, comfort, and relaxation. ☺

Price for single occupancy:
$2,899
€2,675

Price for double occupancy:
$2,699
€2,450

Price for triple occupancy:
$2,499
€2,100

## Assessment 22.3    Create a Custom Tab and Group

1. At the blank screen, create a new tab with the following specifications:
   a. Insert the new tab after the View tab in the list box at the Word Options dialog box with *Customize Ribbon* selected.
   b. Rename the tab *C22* followed by your initials.
   c. Rename the custom group below your new tab *File Management*.
   d. Change the *Choose commands from* option to *File Tab*.
   e. From the list box at the left side of the dialog box, add the following commands to the *File Management* group: *Close, Open, Quick Print, Save As*, and *Save As Other Format*.
   f. Change the *Choose commands from* option to *Popular Commands*.
   g. From the list box at the left side of the dialog box, add the New command.
   h. Click OK to close the Word Options dialog box.
2. At the blank screen, click your new tab (which begins with *C22* and is followed by your initials).
3. Click the Open button in the File Management group on your new tab.
4. At the Open backstage area, click **C22-A02-FAV.docx**, which displays at the beginning of the *Recent Documents* list.
5. With **C22-A02-FAV.docx** open, save the document in the Word 97-2003 format by completing the following steps:
   a. Click the new tab (which begins with *C22* and is followed by your initials).
   b. Click the Save As button arrow. (This is the second Save As button in the File Management group on your new tab.)
   c. Click *Word 97-2003 Document* at the drop-down list.
   d. At the Save As dialog box with *Word 97-2003 Document (\*.doc)* selected in the *Save as type* option box, type **C22-A03-FAV-Word97-2003Format** and then press the Enter key.
   e. Close **C22-A03-FAV-Word97-2003Format.doc** by clicking the Close button in the File Management group on your new tab.
6. Click the Open button on your new tab and then click **C22-A02-FAV.docx** in the *Recent Documents* list.
7. Send the document to the printer by clicking your new tab and then clicking the Quick Print button in the File Management group.
8. Close the document by clicking the Close button in the File Management group on your new tab.
9. Click the New Blank Document button in the File Management group on your new tab.
10. At the blank document, click your new tab and then click the New Blank Document button. (You now have two blank documents open.)
11. Click the INSERT tab, click the Screenshot button, and then click *Screen Clipping* at the drop-down list.
12. When the first blank document displays in a dimmed manner, use the mouse to select the Quick Access toolbar and ribbon, including the new tab you created with the File Management group buttons.
13. Print the document containing the screen clipping and then close the document without saving it.
14. Display the Word Options dialog box with *Customize Ribbon* selected and then reset the ribbon back to the default.

# Expanding Your Skills

Explore additional feature options or use Help to learn a new skill in creating this document.

## Assessment 22.4  Create a Report on Word Options and Customization Features

1. Display the Word Options dialog box and determine how to do the following:
   a. Change the Office theme. (General)
   b. Change the number of minutes for saving AutoRecover information. (Save)
   c. Change the number of recent documents that display in the *Recent Documents* list at the Open backstage area. (Advanced)
2. At a blank document, create a report that describes how to do the following:
   a. Steps to change the Office theme to Dark Gray.
   b. Steps to change the minutes for saving AutoRecover information to 5 minutes.
   c. Steps to change the number of recent documents that display in the *Recent Documents* list at the Open backstage area to 15.
3. Right-click on a blank location on the Status bar and then look at the options that display in the shortcut menu. Determine how to add the Track Changes feature and caps lock notification to the Status bar, and then add to your report steps that describe how to add these functions.
4. Format your document to improve its appearance.
5. Save the document with the name **C22-A04-Options**.
6. Print and then close **C22-A04-Options.docx**.

# Achieving Signature Status

Take your skills to the next level by completing this more challenging assessment.

## Assessment 22.5  Create a Resume Document with AutoCorrect Text

1. At a blank document, create the document shown in Figure 22.14 on page 786 with the following specifications:
   a. Create AutoCorrect entries for *chronological resume, functional resume,* and *hybrid resume.* You determine the replacement text. **Hint: When typing the headings, type the replacement text in all caps and Word will insert the AutoCorrect text in all capital letters.**
   b. Set the body text in 11-point Constantia and the title in 26-point Constantia. Change the font color to Dark Blue.
   c. Insert the page border, paragraph border, and paragraph shading as shown in Figure 22.14. Make sure you change the paragraph and page border color to Dark Blue and change the page border width to 1½ pt.
   d. Insert the clip art image shown in the figure. **Hint: Look for this clip art image by typing document office papers in the search text box at the Insert Pictures window. If this clip art image is not available, choose a similar image.**
   e. Format the clip art by changing the text wrapping to Tight, flipping the image horizontally, and changing the color to Blue, Accent color 1 Light. (If you did not use the clip art image shown in Figure 22.14, choose your own formatting for the clip art image you insert in the document.) Size and position the clip art image as shown in the figure.
   f. Insert the five symbols at the end of the document as shown in the figure. (The symbol is located in the Wingdings font.) Change the color of the symbols to Dark Blue.
2. Save the completed document and name it **C22-A05-ResumeStyles**.
3. Print and then close **C22-A05-ResumeStyles.docx**.

4. Open a blank document, display the AutoCorrect dialog box, and then display the first entry you made for *chronological resume*. Hold down the Alt key and then press the Print Screen button. Close the dialog box, close the Word Options dialog box, and then click the Paste button at the blank document. (This inserts an image of the AutoCorrect dialog box.)
5. Press Ctrl + End and then press the Enter key.
6. Complete steps similar to those in Step 4 to make a screen capture of the AutoCorrect dialog box with the *functional resume* entry displayed and then insert the screen capture image in the document (below the first screen capture image).
7. Press Ctrl + End and then press the Enter key.
8. Complete steps similar to those in Step 4 to make a screen capture of the AutoCorrect dialog box with the *hybrid resume* entry displayed and then insert the screen capture image in the document (below the second screen capture image).
9. Decrease the sizes of the screen capture images to make them all fit on one page.
10. Save the document and name it **C22-A05-ScreenCaps**.
11. Print and then close **C22-A05-ScreenCaps.docx**.

**Figure 22.14 Assessment 22.5**

# RESUME STYLES

You can write a resume in a variety of ways since different approaches work for different people. The three most popular resume styles include: chronological resume, functional resume, and hybrid resume.

## CHRONOLOGICAL RESUME

The chronological resume is the one many people use without thinking. It lists your training and jobs in order of the dates you started each of them. Typically, people list their most recent training and jobs first and proceed backwards to the first things they did in the past. This is called reverse chronological order. The components of this resume include:

- Personal contact information
- Employment history, including employers, dates of employment, positions held, and achievements
- Educational qualifications
- Professional development

## FUNCTIONAL RESUME

The functional resume emphasizes the skills of the individual and his or her achievements. It is often used when the applicant lacks formal education, or his or her educational qualifications are judged obsolete or irrelevant. If you have had many different jobs with no clear pattern or progression, or a lot of gaps in your work history, some people recommend this approach.

## HYBRID RESUME

The hybrid resume is an increasingly popular resume style that combines the best of both the chronological resume and the functional resume. A hybrid resume retains much of the fixed order of the chronological resume, but more emphasis is placed on skills and achievements – sometimes in a separate section. The hybrid resume is the one that we recommend to most people, in that it produces an excellent clear structure but requires the person to really think hard about his or her achievements and what he or she has to offer. If you decide to use a hybrid resume, you may wish to leave out the detailed responsibilities section and just emphasize the skills, knowledge, and abilities you have.

# Chapter 23

**Tutorial 23.1**
Creating Custom Theme Colors
and Theme Fonts
**Tutorial 23.2**
Saving a Document Theme
**Tutorial 23.3**
Applying, Editing, and Deleting a
Custom Theme

# Customizing Themes

## Performance Objectives

Upon successful completion of Chapter 23, you will be able to:

- Create custom themes, theme colors, and theme fonts
  and apply theme effects
- Save a custom theme
- Edit custom themes
- Reset a theme to the template default
- Delete custom themes and custom theme colors and fonts
- Change the default settings for the style set and theme

The Microsoft Office suite provides themes to ensure consistent formatting both within and across documents and thus help you create documents with a professional, polished look. You can use the themes provided by Office or create your own custom themes. In this chapter, you will learn how to customize theme colors and fonts and save custom themes. You will also learn how to edit and delete custom themes and then reset options to the default template theme.

*Note: Before beginning computer exercises for this chapter, copy to your storage medium the Chapter23 folder from the CD that accompanies this textbook and then make Chapter23 the active folder.*

In this chapter, students will produce the following documents:

Exercise 23.1. C23-E01-Viruses.docx
Exercise 23.2. C23-E02-NSSServices.docx
Exercise 23.3. C23-E03-NSSSecurity.docx

Model answers for these exercises are shown on the following pages.

## Exercise 23.1

C23-E01-Viruses.docx

### COMPUTER VIRUSES

One of the most familiar forms of risk to computer security is the computer virus. A computer virus is a program written by a hacker or a cracker, designed to perform some kind of trick upon an unsuspecting victim's computer. In some cases, the trick performed is mild, such as drawing an offensive image on the victim's screen or changing all of the characters in a document to another language. Sometimes the trick is much more severe, such as reformatting the hard drive and erasing all the data or damaging the motherboard so that it cannot operate properly.

#### Types of Viruses

Viruses can be categorized by their effects, which include being a nuisance, destroying data, facilitating espionage, and destroying hardware. A nuisance virus usually does no real damage but is an inconvenience. The most difficult part of a computer to replace is the data on the hard drive. The installed programs, documents, databases, and saved emails form the heart of a personal computer. A data-destructive virus is designed to destroy this data. Some viruses are designed to create a backdoor into a system to bypass security. Called espionage viruses, they do no damage but allow a hacker or cracker to enter the system later for the purpose of stealing data or spying on the work of the competitor. Very rarely, a virus is created to damage the hardware of the computer system itself. Called hardware-destructive viruses, these bits of programming can weaken or destroy chips, drives, and other components.

#### Methods of Virus Operation

Viruses operate and are transmitted in a variety of ways. An email virus is normally transmitted as an attachment to a message sent over the Internet. Email viruses require the victim to click on the attachment, which causes the virus to execute. Another common form of virus transmission is via a macro, a small subprogram that

> "Viruses can create effects that range from minor and annoying to highly destructive..."

allows users to customize and automate certain functions. A macro virus is written specifically for one program, which then becomes infected when it opens a file with the virus stored in its macros. The boot sector of a floppy disk or hard disk contains a variety of information, including how the disk is organized and whether it is capable of loading an operating system. When a disk is left in a drive and the computer reboots, the operating system automatically reads the boot sector to learn about that disk and to attempt to start any operating system on it. A boot sector virus is designed to alter the boot sector of a disk so that whenever the operating system reads the boot sector, the computer will automatically become infected.

Other types of viruses and methods of infection include the Trojan horse virus, which hides inside another legitimate program or data file, and the stealth virus, which is designed to hide itself from detection software. Polymorphic viruses alter themselves to prevent detection by antivirus software, which operates by examining familiar patterns. Polymorphic viruses alter themselves randomly as they move from computer to computer, making detection more difficult. Multipartite viruses alter their form of attack. Their name reflects their ability to attack in several different ways. They may first infect the boot sector and then later act like a Trojan horse type by infecting a disk file. These viruses are more sophisticated and therefore more difficult to guard against. Another type of virus is the logic bomb, which generally sits quietly dormant waiting for a specific event or set of conditions to occur. A well-known example of a logic bomb was the widely publicized Michelangelo virus, which infected personal computers and caused them to display a message on the artist's birthday.

# Northland Security Systems

## Northland Security Systems Mission

We are a full-service computer information security management and consulting firm offering a comprehensive range of services to help businesses protect electronic data.

## Security Services

Northland Security Systems is dedicated to helping businesses, private and public, protect vital company data through on-site consultation, product installation and training, and 24-hour telephone support services. We show you how computer systems can be compromised, and we walk you through the steps you can take to protect your company's computer system.

## Security Software

We offer a range of security management software to protect your business against viruses, spyware, adware, intrusion, spam, and policy abuse.

## Exercise 23.2

C23-E02-NSSServices.docx

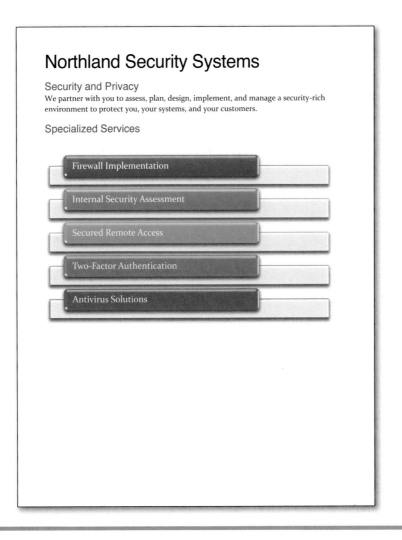

# Creating Custom Themes

A document that you create in Word is based on the Normal.dotm template. This template provides your document with default layout, formatting, styles, and theme formatting. The default template provides a number of built-in or predesigned themes. You have used some of these built-in themes to apply colors, fonts, and effects to content in documents. The same built-in themes are available in Microsoft Word, Excel, Access, PowerPoint, and Outlook. Having these themes available across applications allows you to brand business files—such as documents, workbooks, databases, and presentations—with a consistent and uniform appearance.

A theme is a stylized combination of colors, fonts, and effects. Within a theme, you can change one or all of these elements with buttons in the Document Formatting group on the DESIGN tab. You can switch from the default theme (called *Office*) to one of the built-in themes or you can create your own custom theme. A theme you create will display in the *Themes* drop-down gallery in the *Custom* section. To create a custom theme, select a set of colors, fonts, and/or effects that will give your documents the appropriate style or appearance—perhaps bold or sophisticated.

Themes

Theme    Theme
Colors    Fonts

The Themes, Theme Colors, and Theme Fonts buttons in the Document Formatting group on the DESIGN tab display visual representations of the current theme. For example, the Themes button displays uppercase and lowercase *A*'s with a row of small colored squares below them. If you change the theme colors, the change is reflected in these squares on the Themes button and in the four squares on the Theme Colors button. If you change the theme fonts, the *A*'s on the Themes button and the uppercase *A* on the Theme Fonts button reflect the change.

## Creating Custom Theme Colors

**QUICK STEPS**

**Create Custom Theme Colors**
1. Click DESIGN tab.
2. Click Theme Colors button.
3. Click *Customize Colors*.
4. Select new background, accent, or hyperlink colors.
5. Type name for custom theme colors.
6. Click Save button.

To create custom theme colors, click the DESIGN tab, click the Theme Colors button, and then click *Customize Colors* at the drop-down gallery. This displays the Create New Theme Colors dialog box, as shown in Figure 23.1. Theme colors contain four text and background colors, six accent colors, and two hyperlink colors, as shown in the *Theme colors* section of the dialog box. Change a color in the list box by clicking the color button at the right side of the color option and then clicking the desired color in the color palette.

### Figure 23.1  Create New Theme Colors Dialog Box

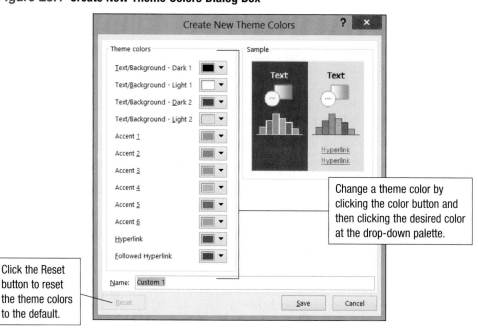

Change a theme color by clicking the color button and then clicking the desired color at the drop-down palette.

Click the Reset button to reset the theme colors to the default.

After you have made all of the desired changes to the theme colors, click in the *Name* text box, type a name for the set of custom theme colors, and then click the Save button. This saves the custom theme colors and also applies the color changes to the active document. Display the custom theme colors by clicking the Theme Colors button in the Document Formatting group on the DESIGN tab. Your custom theme colors will display near the top of the drop-down gallery in the *Custom* section, as shown in Figure 23.2 on the next page.

**Figure 23.2 Theme Colors Button Drop-down Gallery with Custom Theme**

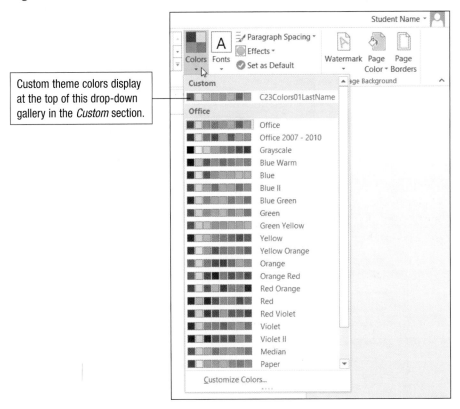

Custom theme colors display at the top of this drop-down gallery in the *Custom* section.

## Resetting Custom Theme Colors

If you change the colors at the Create New Theme Colors dialog box and then decide you do not like the changes, click the Reset button located in the lower left corner of the dialog box. Clicking this button resets the colors back to the default Office theme colors.

---

**Exercise 23.1A**    **Creating Custom Theme Colors**       Part 1 of 3

*Note: If you are running Word 2013 on a computer connected to a network in a public environment, such as a school, you may not be able to save themes to the hard drive. If you are able to save themes to the hard drive, you may need to complete all of the parts of Project 1 during the same session because network system software may delete your custom themes when you close Word. Check with your instructor before beginning Exercise 23.1A.*

1. At a blank document, create custom theme colors by completing the following steps:
   a. Click the DESIGN tab.
   b. Click the Theme Colors button in the Document Formatting group and then click *Customize Colors* at the drop-down gallery.

---

c.  At the Create New Theme
    Colors dialog box, click the
    color button that displays
    to the right of the *Text/
    Background - Light 1* option
    and then click the *Dark Red*
    color in the color palette
    (first color in the *Standard
    Colors* section).

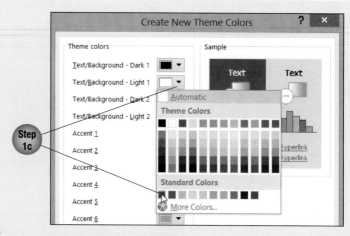

d.  Click the color button that
    displays to the right of the
    *Accent 1* option and then
    click the *Yellow* color in the
    color palette (fourth color in
    the *Standard Colors* section).

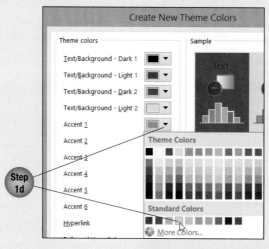

2.  After viewing the colors you have
    chosen in the *Sample* section at the
    right side of the dialog box, start
    over by completing the following
    steps:

    a.  Click the Reset button
        located in the lower left
        corner of the dialog box.

    b.  Click the color button that
        displays to the right of the
        *Text/Background - Dark 2*
        option and then click the
        *Blue* color in the color palette
        (eighth color in the *Standard
        Colors* section).

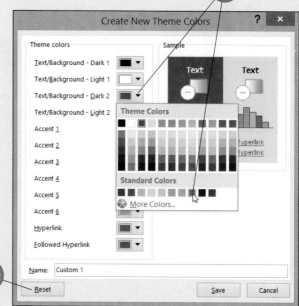

c. Click the color button that displays to the right of the *Accent 1* option and then click the *Purple, Followed Hyperlink, Lighter 60%* in the color palette (last column, third row in the *Theme Colors* section).

d. Click the color button that displays at the right of the *Accent 2* option and then click *Blue, Accent 5, Lighter 40%* in the color palette (ninth column, fourth row in the *Theme Colors* section).

3. Save the custom colors by completing the following steps:

   a. Select the current text in the *Name* text box.

   b. Type **C23Colors01** and then type your last name.

   c. Click the Save button.

4. Close the document without saving it.

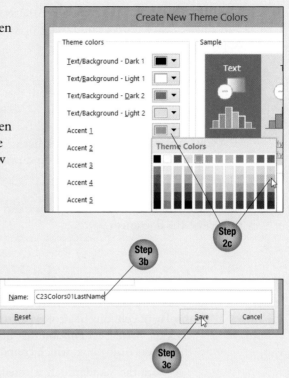

## Applying Custom Theme Colors

After you create custom theme colors, you can apply them to your document by clicking the Theme Colors button in the Themes group in the DESIGN tab and then clicking the custom theme colors that display near the top of the drop-down gallery in the *Custom* section.

---

**Exercise 23.1B**  **Applying Custom Theme Colors**                    **Part 2 of 3**

1. Open **Viruses.docx** and save the document with the name **C23-E01-Viruses**.
2. Apply the Lines (Stylish) style set and then center the title *COMPUTER VIRUSES*.
3. Insert a text box pull quote by completing the following steps:
   a. Click the INSERT tab.
   b. Click the Quick Parts button and then click *Building Blocks Organizer*.
   c. At the Building Blocks Organizer dialog box, click the *Name* column heading to alphabetize the building blocks by name.
   d. Scroll down the list box and then click the *Retrospect Quote*. (You will not see the entire name. Click the first *Retrospect* building block in the *Text Box* gallery).
   e. Click the Insert button.
   f. With the insertion point positioned in the pull quote text box, type "**Viruses can create effects that range from minor and annoying to highly destructive . . .** ".
   g. Select the quote text that you just typed and then change the font size to 10 points.
   h. Click the DRAWING TOOLS FORMAT tab, click in the *Shape Width* measurement box, type **2.7**, and then press the Enter key.

   i.   Click the Position button in the Arrange group and then click *Position in Middle Right with Square Text Wrapping* (third column, second row in the *With Text Wrapping* section).

4. Apply your custom theme colors by completing the following steps:

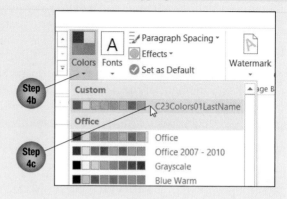

   a.   Click the DESIGN tab.

   b.   Click the Theme Colors button in the Themes group.

   c.   Click the *C23Colors01* (followed by your last name) custom theme that displays near the top of the drop-down gallery in the *Custom* group.

5. Save **C23-E01-Viruses.docx**.

6. Print page 1 of **C23-E01-Viruses.docx** and then close the document.

## Choosing Colors at the Colors Dialog Box

When you click a color button in the Create New Theme Colors dialog box, color sets display in columns in a color palette. If you want more control over what colors display, click the *More Colors* option that displays at the bottom of the color palette. This displays the Colors dialog box, which contains two tabs: a Standard tab and a Custom tab.

With the Standard tab selected, click the desired color option that displays in the multicolored "honeycomb" figure. With the Custom tab selected, click the desired color in the color square and fine-tune the color by dragging the slider button (left-pointing arrow) on the vertical slider bar that displays at the right side of the color square. You can also enter number values in the *Red*, *Green*, and *Blue* text boxes in the dialog box. Each value for a particular color is represented by a number range of 0 - 255. This number range indicates how much red, green, and blue are combined to form a specific color.

---

**Exercise 23.1C**   **Choosing Custom Colors**                     **Part 3 of 3**

---

1. At a blank document, create custom theme colors by completing the following steps:

   a.   Click the DESIGN tab.

   b.   Click the Theme Colors button in the Themes group and then click the *Customize Colors* option at the drop-down gallery.

   c.   At the Create New Theme Colors dialog box, change the Text/Background - Dark 1 color by completing the following steps:

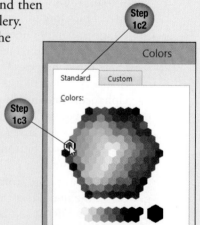

      1)   Click the color button that displays to the right of the *Text/Background - Dark 1* option and then click the *More Colors* option at the bottom of the color palette.

      2)   At the Colors dialog box, click the Standard tab if necessary.

      3)   Click the *Dark Green* color at the left edge of the honeycomb, as shown at the right.

      4)   Click OK to close the Colors dialog box.

d.  Change the Text/Background - Light 2 color by completing the following steps:
   1)  Click the color button for the *Text/Background - Light 2* option and then click the *More Colors* option.
   2)  At the Colors dialog box, click the Standard tab if necessary.
   3)  Click the *Yellow* color in the lower portion of the honeycomb, as shown at the right.
   4)  Click OK to close the Colors dialog box.
e.  Change the Accent 2 color by completing the following steps:
   1)  Click the color button for the *Accent 2* option and then click the *More Colors* option.
   2)  At the Colors dialog box, click the Custom tab if necessary.
   3)  Select the number in the *Red* text box and then type **0**.
   4)  Select the number in the *Green* text box and then type **168**.
   5)  Select the number in the *Blue* text box and then type **0**.
   6)  Click OK to close the Colors dialog box.

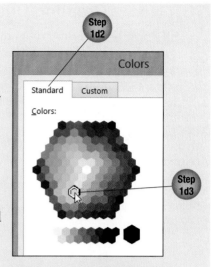

2.  Save the custom theme colors by completing the following steps:
   a.  Select the text in the *Name* text box.
   b.  Type **C23Colors02** and then type your last name.
   c.  Click the Save button.
3.  Close the document without saving it.
4.  Open **C23-E01-Viruses.docx**.

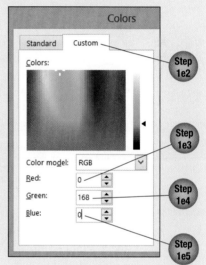

5.  Apply the custom theme colors by completing the following steps:
   a.  Click the DESIGN tab.
   b.  Click the Theme Colors button in the Themes group.
   c.  Click the *C23Colors02* (followed by your last name) custom theme that displays near the top of the drop-down gallery in the *Custom* group.
6.  Save **C23-E01-Viruses.docx**.
7.  Print page 1 of **C23-E01-Viruses.docx** and then close the document.

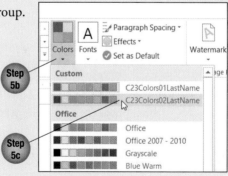

## Creating Custom Theme Fonts

**QUICK STEPS**

**Create Custom Theme Fonts**
1. Click DESIGN tab.
2. Click Theme Fonts button.
3. Click *Customize Fonts*.
4. Choose desired fonts.
5. Type name for custom theme fonts.
6. Click Save button.

To create custom theme fonts, click the DESIGN tab, click the Theme Fonts button, and then click *Customize Fonts* at the drop-down gallery. This displays the Create New Theme Fonts dialog box, as shown in Figure 23.3. At this dialog box, choose a heading font and body font. Type a name for the set of custom theme fonts in the *Name* box and then click the Save button.

**Figure 23.3 Create New Theme Fonts Dialog Box**

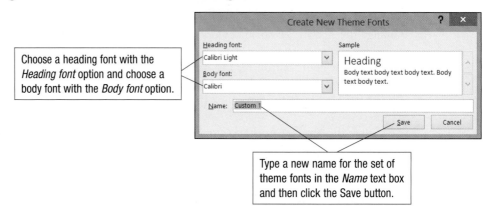

Choose a heading font with the *Heading font* option and choose a body font with the *Body font* option.

Type a new name for the set of theme fonts in the *Name* text box and then click the Save button.

---

**Exercise 23.2A  Creating Custom Theme Fonts**                    **Part 1 of 3**

1. At a blank document, create custom theme fonts by completing the following steps:
   a. Click the DESIGN tab.
   b. Click the Theme Fonts button in the Themes group and then click the *Customize Fonts* option at the drop-down gallery.
   c. At the Create New Theme Fonts dialog box, click the down-pointing arrow at the right of the *Heading font* option box, scroll up the drop-down list, and then click *Arial*.

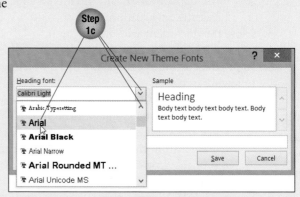

Step 1c

   d. Click the down-pointing arrow at the right of the *Body font* option box, scroll down the drop-down list, and then click *Times New Roman*.
2. Save the custom theme fonts by completing the following steps:
   a. Select the text in the *Name* text box.
   b. Type **C23Fonts01** and then type your last name.
   c. Click the Save button.
3. Close the document without saving it.

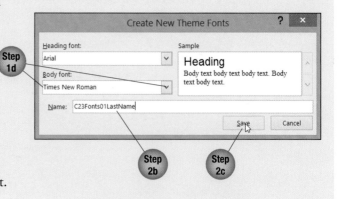

Step 1d

Step 2b

Step 2c

# Applying Theme Effects

The options available in the Theme Effects button drop-down gallery apply sets of line and fill effects to graphics in a document. You cannot create your own theme effects but you can apply a theme effect and then save the formatting as your own custom theme.

Theme Effects

# Saving a Custom Theme

When you have customized theme colors and fonts and applied theme effects to a document, you can save them as a custom theme. To do this, click the Themes button in the Document Formatting group on the DESIGN tab and then click *Save Current Theme* at the drop-down gallery. This displays the Save Current Theme dialog box, which has many of the same options that are available in the Save As dialog box. Type a name for your custom theme in the *File name* text box and then click the Save button.

**QUICK STEPS**

**Save a Custom Theme**
1. Click DESIGN tab.
2. Click Themes button.
3. Click *Save Current Theme.*
4. Type name for custom theme.
5. Click Save button.

---

**Exercise 23.2B**   Applying Theme Effects and Saving a              Part 2 of 3
                     Custom Theme

---

1. At a blank document, create custom theme colors by completing the following steps:

   a. Click the DESIGN tab.

   b. Click the Theme Colors button and then click *Customize Colors* at the bottom of the drop-down gallery.

   c. At the Create New Theme Colors dialog box, click the color button for the *Text/Background - Dark 2* option and then click the *Blue* color (eighth color option in the *Standard Colors* section).

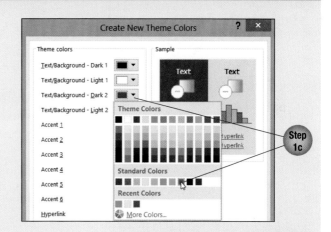

   d. Change the Accent 1 color by completing the following steps:

      1) Click the color button that displays at the right of the *Accent 1* option.

      2) Click the *More Colors* option at the bottom of the color palette.

      3) At the Colors dialog box, click the Standard tab if necessary.

      4) Click the dark green color at the left of the honeycomb, as shown at the right.

      5) Click OK to close the dialog box.

   e. Save the custom theme colors with the name *C23Colors03* (followed by your last name).

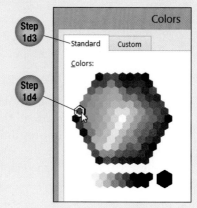

2. Close the document without saving it.
3. Open **NSSServices.docx** and save the document with the name **C23-E02-NSSServices**.
4. Make the following changes to the document:
   a. Apply the Title style to the company name *Northland Security Systems*.
   b. Apply the Heading 1 style to the heading *Northland Security Systems Mission*.
   c. Apply the Heading 2 style to the headings *Security Services* and *Security Software*.
5. Apply the custom theme colors you saved by completing the following steps:
   a. Click the DESIGN tab.
   b. Click the Theme Colors button in the Themes group.
   c. Click the *C23Colors03* (followed by your last name) custom theme that displays near the top of the drop-down gallery in the *Custom* group.

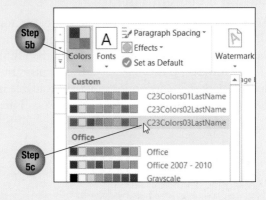

6. Apply the custom theme fonts you saved by clicking the Theme Fonts button in the Themes group and then clicking the *C23Fonts01* (followed by your last name) custom theme that displays near the top of the drop-down gallery in the *Custom* group.
7. Apply a theme effect by clicking the Theme Effects button in the Document Formatting group and then clicking *Glossy* at the drop-down gallery.

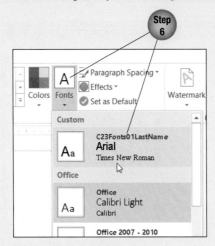

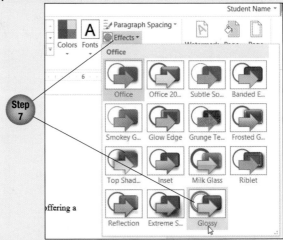

8. Make the following changes to the SmartArt graphic:
   a. Click near the graphic to select it. (When the graphic is selected, a border displays around it.)
   b. Click the SMARTART TOOLS DESIGN tab.
   c. Click the Change Colors button and then click *Colorful Range - Accent Colors 5 to 6* (last color option in the *Colorful* section).
   d. Click the More button at the right of the SmartArt Styles group and then click *Cartoon* (third column, first row in the *3-D* section).
   e. Click outside the graphic to deselect it.

9. Save the custom theme colors and fonts, as well as the Glossy theme effect, as a custom theme by completing the following steps:
   a. Click the DESIGN tab.
   b. Click the Themes button in the Document Formatting group.
   c. Click the *Save Current Theme* option that displays at the bottom of the drop-down gallery.
   d. At the Save Current Theme dialog box, type **C23Theme01** and then type your last name in the *File name* text box.
   e. Click the Save button.

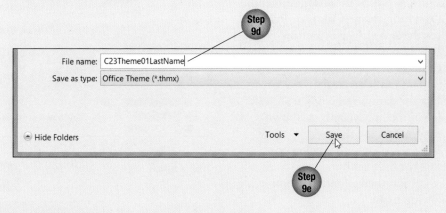

10. Save and then print **C23-E02-NSSServices.docx**.

# Editing Custom Themes

Custom theme colors and custom theme fonts can be edited. To edit custom theme colors, click the DESIGN tab and then click the Theme Colors button in the Document Formatting group. At the drop-down gallery of custom and built-in themes, right-click your custom theme and then click *Edit* at the shortcut menu. This displays the Edit Theme Colors dialog box, which contains the same options that are available at the Create New Theme Colors dialog box, as shown in Figure 23.1 on page 790. Make the desired changes to the theme colors and then click the Save button.

To edit custom theme fonts, click the Theme Fonts button in the Document Formatting group on the DESIGN tab, right-click your custom theme, and then click *Edit* at the shortcut menu. This displays the Edit Theme Fonts dialog box, which contains the same options that are available at the Create New Theme Fonts dialog box, as shown in Figure 23.3 on page 796. Make the desired changes to the theme fonts and then click the Save button.

**QUICK STEPS**

**Edit Custom Theme Colors or Fonts**
1. Click DESIGN tab.
2. Click Theme Colors button or Theme Fonts button.
3. Right-click desired custom theme colors or fonts.
4. Click *Edit*.
5. Make desired changes.
6. Click Save button.

1.  With **C23-E02-NSSServices.docx** open, edit the custom theme colors by completing the following steps:
    a.  Click the DESIGN tab.
    b.  Click the Theme Colors button.
    c.  Right-click the *C23Colors03* (followed by your last name) custom theme and then click *Edit* at the shortcut menu.
    d.  At the Edit Theme Colors dialog box, click the *Accent 6* color button.
    e.  Click *More Colors* at the color palette.
    f.  At the Colors dialog box, click the Standard tab if necessary.
    g.  Click the dark green color at the left edge of the honeycomb, as shown below and to the right.
    h.  Click OK to close the dialog box.
    i.  Click the Save button.

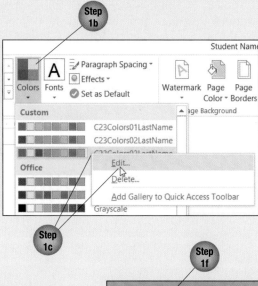

2.  Edit the custom theme fonts by completing the following steps:
    a.  Click the Theme Fonts button in the Document Formatting group.
    b.  Right-click the *C23Fonts01* (followed by your last name) custom theme and then click *Edit* at the shortcut menu.
    c.  At the Edit Theme Fonts dialog box, click the down-pointing arrow at the right of the *Body font* option box, scroll up the drop-down list, and then click *Constantia*.
    d.  Click the Save button.
3.  Apply a different theme effect by clicking the Theme Effects button in the Document Formatting group and then clicking *Extreme Shadow* at the drop-down gallery. (This effect applies a shadow behind each shape.)
4.  Save the changes to the custom theme by completing the following steps:
    a.  Click the Themes button and then click *Save Current Theme* at the drop-down gallery.
    b.  At the Save Current Theme dialog box, click the *C23Theme01LastName.thmx* theme document (where your last name displays in place of *LastName*).
    c.  Click the Save button.
    d.  At the replace question, click Yes.
5.  Save, print, and then close **C23-E02-NSSServices.docx**.

# Resetting a Template Theme

If you apply a built-in theme other than the Office default theme or if you apply a custom theme, you can reset the theme back to the template default. To do this, click the Themes button and then click *Reset to Theme from Template* at the drop-down gallery. If you are working in the default template provided by Word, clicking this option resets the theme to the Office default theme.

## Exercise 23.3A  Applying Themes and Resetting to the Template Theme

Part 1 of 2

1. Open **NSSSecurity.docx** and save the document with the name **C23-E03-NSSSecurity**.
2. Apply the Title style to the company name and the Heading 1 style to the two headings in the document.
3. Apply your custom theme by completing the following steps:
   a. Click the DESIGN tab.
   b. Click the Themes button.
   c. Click the *C23CustomTheme01LastName* custom theme that displays at the top of the drop-down gallery in the *Custom* section.
4. Save and then print **C23-E03-NSSSecurity.docx**.
5. Reset the theme to the Office default by clicking the Themes button and then clicking *Reset to Theme from Template* at the drop-down gallery. (This returns the default to the Office theme.)
6. Save and then close **C23-E03-NSSSecurity.docx**.

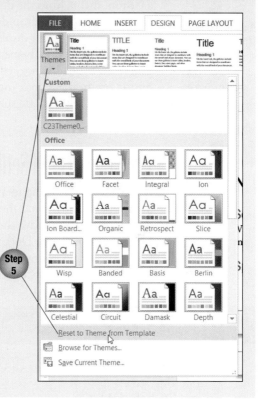

# Deleting Custom Themes

**QUICK STEPS**

**Delete Custom Theme Colors or Fonts**
1. Click DESIGN tab.
2. Click Theme Colors or Theme Fonts button.
3. Right-click desired custom theme.
4. Click *Delete*.
5. Click Yes.

**Delete a Custom Theme**
1. Click DESIGN tab.
2. Click Themes button.
3. Right-click custom theme.
4. Click *Delete*.
5. Click Yes.

Delete custom theme colors from the Theme Colors button drop-down gallery, custom theme fonts from the Theme Fonts button drop-down gallery, and custom themes from the Save Current Theme dialog box.

To delete custom theme colors, click the Theme Colors button, right-click the theme you want to delete, and then click *Delete* at the shortcut menu. At the message asking if you want to delete the theme colors, click Yes.

To delete custom theme fonts, click the Theme Fonts button, right-click the theme you want to delete, and then click *Delete* at the shortcut menu. At the message asking if you want to delete the theme fonts, click Yes.

Delete a custom theme (which includes custom colors, fonts, and effects) at the Themes button drop-down gallery or at the Save Current Theme dialog box. To delete a custom theme from the drop-down gallery, click the Themes button, right-click the custom theme in the drop-down gallery, click *Delete* at the shortcut menu, and then click Yes at the message that displays. To delete a custom theme from the Save Current Theme dialog box, click the Themes button and then click *Save Current Theme* at the drop-down gallery. At the dialog box, click the custom theme document name, click the Organize button on the dialog box toolbar, and then click *Delete* at the drop-down list. At the message asking if you are sure you want to send the theme to the Recycle Bin, click Yes.

# Changing Default Settings

If you apply formatting to a document—such as a specific style set, theme, and paragraph spacing—and then decide that you want the formatting available for future documents, you can save the formatting as the default theme. To do this, click the Set as Default button in the Document Formatting group on the DESIGN tab. At the message box that displays asking if you want the current style set and theme as the default and telling you that the settings will be applied to new documents, click the Yes button.

---

**Exercise 23.3B** Applying and Deleting Custom Themes      Part 2 of 2

1. At a blank document, delete the custom theme colors you created by completing the following steps:
   a. Click the DESIGN tab.
   b. Click the Theme Colors button in the Document Formatting group.
   c. Right-click the C23Colors01 (followed by your last name) custom theme.
   d. Click *Delete* at the shortcut menu.
   e. At the question asking if you want to delete the theme colors, click Yes.

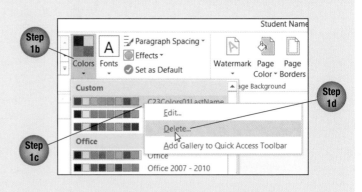

2. Complete steps similar to those in Step 1 to delete the *C23Colors02* (followed by your last name) custom theme colors and *C23Colors03* (followed by your last name) custom theme colors.
3. Delete the custom theme fonts you created by completing the following steps:
   a. Click the Theme Fonts button in the Document Formatting group.
   b. Right-click the *C23Fonts01* (followed by your last name) custom theme.
   c. Click *Delete* at the shortcut menu.
   d. At the question asking if you want to delete the theme fonts, click Yes.
4. Delete the custom theme you created by completing the following steps:
   a. Click the Themes button.
   b. Right-click the *C23Theme01LastName* custom theme.
   c. Click *Delete* at the shortcut menu that displays.

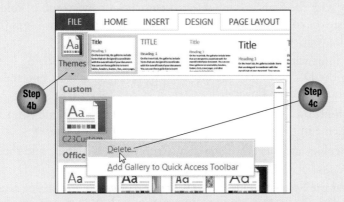

   d. At the message asking if you want to delete the theme, click Yes.
5. Close the document without saving it.

# Chapter Summary

- Create custom theme colors with options at the Create New Theme Colors dialog box.
- Click the Reset button in the Create New Theme Colors dialog box to reset the colors to the default Office theme colors.
- Apply custom theme colors by clicking the DESIGN tab, clicking the Theme Colors button, and then clicking the custom theme in the *Custom* section of the drop-down gallery.
- Additional color options are available at the Colors dialog box with the Standard tab or Custom tab selected. Display this dialog box by clicking a color button in the Create New Theme Colors dialog box and then clicking the *More Colors* option.
- The Colors dialog box with the Standard tab selected contains a honeycomb of colors. Click the Custom tab and a square of color displays with a vertical slider bar and text boxes for specifying number values for red, green, and blue.
- Create custom theme fonts with options at the Create New Theme Fonts dialog box. Display this dialog box by clicking the DESIGN tab, clicking the Theme Fonts button, and then clicking the *Customize Fonts* option at the drop-down gallery.
- Apply custom theme fonts by clicking the DESIGN tab, clicking the Theme Fonts button, and then clicking the custom theme in the *Custom* section of the drop-down gallery.
- Create custom theme colors and custom theme fonts, apply a theme effect, and then save the changes in a custom theme.
- Save a custom theme at the Save Current Theme dialog box. Display this dialog box by clicking the Themes button in the Document Formatting group and then clicking *Save Current Theme* at the drop-down gallery.
- Edit custom theme colors with options at the Edit Theme Colors dialog box. Display this dialog box by clicking the Theme Colors button, right-clicking the custom theme, and then clicking the *Edit* option.
- Edit custom theme fonts with options at the Edit Theme Fonts dialog box. Display this dialog box by clicking the Theme Fonts button, right-clicking the custom theme, and then clicking the *Edit* option.
- Reset the theme to the template default by clicking the *Reset to Theme from Template* at the Themes button drop-down gallery.
- Delete custom theme colors by clicking the Theme Colors button, right-clicking the custom theme, and then clicking the *Delete* option.
- Delete custom theme fonts by clicking the Theme Fonts button, right-clicking the custom theme, and then clicking the *Delete* option.
- Delete a custom theme by right-clicking the theme at the Themes button drop-down gallery and then clicking *Delete* at the shortcut menu. A custom theme can also be deleted at the Save Current Theme dialog box. Display this dialog box by clicking the Themes button and then clicking *Save Current Theme* at the drop-down gallery. Click the custom theme document name, click the Organize button, and then click *Delete* at the drop-down list.

# *Commands* Review

| FEATURE | RIBBON TAB, GROUP | BUTTON, OPTION |
|---|---|---|
| Create New Theme Colors dialog box | DESIGN, Document Formatting | , *Customize Colors* |
| Create New Theme Fonts dialog box | DESIGN, Document Formatting | A , *Customize Fonts* |
| Save Current Theme dialog box | DESIGN, Document Formatting | Aa , *Save Current Theme* |
| Theme effects | DESIGN, Document Formatting | ◉ |

# *Key Points* Review

**SNAP**

**Completion:** In the space provided at the right, indicate the correct term, symbol, or command.

1. This is the name of the default theme. _____

2. The Themes button is located on this tab. _____

3. Create custom theme colors with options at this dialog box. _____

4. Custom theme colors that you create display in this section of the Theme Colors button drop-down gallery. _____

5. With this tab selected, the Colors dialog box displays a honeycomb of color options. _____

6. With this tab selected, the Colors dialog box displays the *Red*, *Green*, and *Blue* text boxes. _____

7. Create custom theme fonts with options at this dialog box. _____

8. To edit custom theme fonts, click the Theme Fonts button, do this to the custom theme, and then click *Edit* at the shortcut menu. _____

9. Click this option at the Themes button drop-down gallery to set the theme back to the template default. _____

10. Delete a custom theme by right-clicking the custom theme at the Themes button drop-down gallery and then clicking *Delete*. _____

# Chapter *Assessments*

## Applying Your Skills

Demonstrate your knowledge of features learned in this chapter by completing the following assessments.

### Assessment 23.1    Create and Apply Custom Themes to a Medical Plans Document

1.  At a blank document, create a set of custom theme colors named *C23Colors01* followed by your initials that makes the following color changes:
    a.  Change the Accent 1 color to Dark Red (first option in the *Standard Colors* section).
    b.  Change the Accent 5 color to Gold, Accent 4, Darker 50% (eighth column, bottom row in the *Theme Colors* section).
2.  Create custom theme fonts named *C23Fonts01* followed by your initials that change the heading font to Corbel and the body font to Garamond.
3.  Click the Theme Effects button and then click *Top Shadow* at the drop-down gallery (first column, third row).
4.  Save the custom theme and name it *C23Theme01* followed by your initials. ***Hint: Do this with the Save Current Theme option at the Themes button drop-down gallery.***
5.  Close the document without saving the changes.
6.  Open **KLHPlan.docx** and save the document with the name **C23-A01-KLHPlan**.
7.  Make the following changes to the document:
    a.  Apply the Lines (Simple) style set.
    b.  With the insertion point positioned at the beginning of the document, type the title **Key Life Health Plan**.
    c.  Apply the Heading 1 style to the title.
    d.  Apply the Heading 2 style to the three headings in the document.
8.  Move the insertion point to the end of the document, press Ctrl + Enter to insert a page break, and then insert the document **KLHPlanGraphic.docx**. ***Hint: Do this with the Object button arrow on the INSERT tab.***
9.  Apply the custom theme you created by clicking the DESIGN tab, clicking the Themes button, and then clicking the custom theme named *C23Theme01* followed by your initials.
10. Save, print, and then close **C23-A01-KLHPlan.docx**.

### Assessment 23.2    Create and Apply Custom Themes to a Real Photography Document

1.  At a blank document, create a set of custom theme colors named *C23Colors02* followed by your initials that makes the following color changes:
    a.  Change the Text/Background - Dark 2 color to Orange, Accent 2, Darker 50%.
    b.  Change the Accent 1 color to a custom color at the Colors dialog box with the Custom tab selected. Type **0** in the *Red* text box, **140** in the *Green* text box, and **0** in the *Blue* text box.
2.  Create a set of custom theme fonts named *C23Fonts02* followed by your initials that changes the heading font to Harrington.
3.  Click the Theme Effects button and then click *Grunge Texture* at the drop-down gallery (third column, second row).
4.  Save the custom theme and name it *C23Theme02* followed by your initials. ***Hint: Do this with the Save Current Theme option at the Themes button drop-down gallery.***
5.  Close the document without saving the changes.

6. Open **RPServices.docx** and save the document with the name **C23-A02-RPServices**.
7. Apply your *C23 Theme02(initials)* theme to the document.
8. Save, print, and then close **C23-A02-RPServices.docx**.

# Expanding Your Skills

Explore additional feature options or use Help to learn a new skill in creating this document.

## Assessment 23.3    Explore and Apply Themes

1. Open **DevelopSoftware.docx** and save the document with the name **C23-A03-DevelopSoftware**.
2. The Themes button drop-down gallery contains a number of available themes. Hover your mouse pointer over some of the themes in the Themes button drop-down gallery to see how each theme changes the document formatting. Apply the Droplet theme to the document.
3. Determine the heading font and body font used by the theme by clicking on any character in the title *Application Software*, clicking the HOME tab, and then clicking the Font button arrow. The heading font and body font are listed at the beginning of the drop-down list. Make note of these fonts.
4. With the insertion point positioned on the title *Application Software*, determine the font color by clicking the Font Color button arrow and then checking the color palette to determine which color option is selected. (The selected option is surrounded by an orange border.)
5. Position the insertion point on the heading *Developing Software* and then determine the font color.
6. After determining the Droplet theme heading and body fonts and font colors, make the following changes:
    a.   Press Ctrl + End to move the insertion point to the end of the document.
    b.   Type **Theme name:**, press the spacebar, and then type **Droplet**.
    c.   Press Shift + Enter to move the insertion point to the next line.
    d.   Type **Heading and body font:**, press the spacebar, and then type the name of the font.
    e.   Press Shift + Enter.
    f.   Type **Title font color:**, press the spacebar, and then type the title font color name.
    g.   Type **Heading font color:**, press the spacebar, and then type heading font color name.
7. Save and then print **C23-A03-DevelopSoftware.docx**.
8. Apply the Organic theme to the document and then determine the heading and body font, the title font color, and the heading font color. Change the information that displays at the bottom of the document to reflect the new theme.
9. Save, print, and then close **C23-A03-DevelopSoftware.docx**.

# Achieving Signature Status

Take your skills to the next level by completing this more challenging assessment.

## Assessment 23.4    Create and Apply a Custom Theme

1. Open **TECRevenues.docx** and save the document and name it **C23-A04-TECRevenues**.
2. Create the following custom theme colors named *C23ColorsTEC* followed by your initials with the following changes:
   a. Change the Text/Background - Dark 2 color to Orange, Accent 2, Darker 50% (sixth column, last row in the *Theme Colors* section).
   b. Change the Accent 1 color to Green, Accent 6, Darker 50% (tenth column, last row in the *Theme Colors* section)
   c. Change the Accent 4 color to Orange, Accent 2, Darker 50%.
   d. Change the Accent 6 color to Green, Accent 6, Darker 25%.
3. Create the following custom theme fonts named *C23FontsTEC* followed by your initials with the following changes:
   a. Change the heading font to Copperplate Gothic Bold.
   b. Change the body font to Constantia.
4. Apply the Riblet theme effect (last column, third row).
5. Save the custom theme and name it *C23ThemeTEC* followed by your initials. ***Hint: Do this with the Save Current Theme option at the Themes button drop-down gallery.***
6. Save, print, and then close **C23-A04-TECRevenues.docx**.
7. Open **TECCorporate.docx** and then save the document with Save As and name it **C23-A04-TECCorporate**.
8. Apply the *C23ThemeTEC* (followed by your initials) custom theme to the document.
9. Save, print, and then close **C23-A04-TECCorporate.docx**.
10. At a blank document, use the Print Screen button to make a screen capture of the Theme Colors button drop-down gallery (make sure your custom theme colors display), a screen capture of the Theme Fonts button drop-down gallery (make sure your custom theme fonts display), and a screen capture of the Save Current Theme dialog box (make sure your custom themes are visible). Insert all three screen capture images on the same page. (You will need to size the images.)
11. Save the document and name it **C23-A04-ScreenImages**.
12. Print and then close **C23-A04-ScreenImages.docx**.
13. At a blank document, delete the custom color themes, custom font themes, and custom themes that you created in this chapter.

# Chapter 24

# Creating and Managing Styles

## Performance Objectives

Upon successful completion of Chapter 24, you will be able to:

- Apply styles
- Create new styles from existing formatting and styles
- Assign a keyboard shortcut to a style
- Modify styles and save styles in a template
- Display all styles
- Reveal style formatting
- Save and delete a custom style set
- Create and modify styles for multilevel lists and tables
- Investigate document styles using the Style Inspector
- Manage and organize styles

In addition to the themes discussed in Chapter 23, Word provides a number of predesigned styles, which are grouped into style sets, that you can use to apply consistent formatting in documents. If none of the predesigned styles provides the formatting you want, you can create your own styles. In this chapter, you will learn how to apply, create, modify, delete, manage, and organize styles, as well as how to save and delete a custom style set.

*Note: Before beginning computer exercises for this chapter, copy to your storage medium the Chapter24 folder from the CD that accompanies this textbook and then make Chapter24 the active folder.*

In this chapter, students will produce the following documents:

Exercise 24.1. C24-E01-AfricanAdventure.docx
Exercise 24.2H. C24-E02-BTZenith.docx
Exercise 24.2I. C24-E02-BTVacations.docx
Exercise 24.3A. C24-E03-BTTours.docx
Exercise 24.3B. C24-E03-BTTables.docx
Exercise 24.3C. C24-E03-BTTablesModified.docx
Exercise 24.3E. C24-E03-BTZenith.docx
Exercise 24.3F. C24-E03-BTEastAdventures.docx

Model answers for these exercises are shown on the following pages.

"Travel is fatal to prejudice, bigotry and narrow-mindedness."
Mark Twain

## African Study Adventure

The African Study Adventure program provide travelers with a unique opportunity to travel to African countries and make connections with local people, visit cultural institutions, and travel with knowledgeable tour guides who will provide insightful information about the countries, peoples, and customs.

### Small Groups

The size of each group is limited so that African Study Adventure tour guides can deliver personal service and ensure that you feel comfortable in your surroundings. All tours are limited to a maximum of 25 participants.

### Comprehensive Itineraries

Each program in the African Study Adventure program offers comprehensive sightseeing, exciting activities, and direct encounters with the people of the area you are visiting. Tour guides have developed a range of tours, each with its own principal theme and special highlights.

### Custom Groups

For those who cannot fit African Study Adventure program scheduled departures into their calendars or who prefer to travel with their own friends and family, Bayside Travel has developed custom programs to suit your specific needs.

### Accommodations and Meals

Accommodations will vary with the particular trip. However, Bayside Travel staff has selected accommodations with great care to make sure you will be as comfortable as local conditions allow and that you will enjoy the unique atmosphere of each destination. Most meals are included in the tour package.

**Exercise 24.1**  C24-E01-AfricanAdventure.docx

---

# Bayside Travel

## *Extreme Adventures*

We are excited to announce that Bayside Travel has teamed with ZENITH ADVENTURES to provide our clients with thrilling, adrenaline-producing, extreme outdoor adventures. You can choose from a variety of exciting adventures including Antarctic expedition cruises, tall-ship sailing, and bicycling tours. Many of our trips are appropriate for beginners, so get out and enjoy an amazing outdoor adventure with family and friends!

### Antarctic Adventures

Travel with our Antarctic experts, cruise on our state-of-the-art ships, and experience Antarctica in all of its grandeur. We use ice-rated expedition ships custom designed for your comfort and safety. Each ship can carry up to 100 passengers, provides excellent viewing for watching whales, seabirds, and icebergs, and includes facilities for educational presentations by our Antarctic experts.  For our more adventurous clients, we offer additional activities such as snowshoeing, sea-kayaking, and camping on the Antarctic ice. Plan on a shore excursion where you can view penguin rookeries, seal colonies, and places of historical and scientific interest. To carry you to the Antarctic shore, we use inflatable boats that can carry 12 to 15 people.  After a thrilling day on shore, we will take you back to the ship where you can enjoy a delicious meal prepared by our gourmet chefs. Our Antarctic travel experts are naturalists, historians, and adventurers committed to providing you with a fabulous Antarctic adventure.

*Antarctic Exploration, $4399*

*Weddell Sea Adventure, $6899*

*Falkland Islands Journey, $7699*

*Sailing Spectacular, $8999*

### Tall-Ship Adventures

Visit exotic and spectacular locations in the South Pacific aboard the Laura Devon, a luxurious tall ship. On your tall-ship adventure, seek out the hidden Pacific by sailing the trade winds to discover the undisturbed cultures and beauty of remote islands and communities.  Our tall-ship sailing adventure combines exotic exploration and timeless romance. You can sign on for the challenge of an ocean voyage with blue water sailing or a more leisurely island voyage sailing through tropical paradises. For many, tall-ship sailing is the ultimate in escapist adventuring. Sailing on the magnificent Laura Devon, combined with the sparkling beauty of the South Pacific, makes for the adventure of a lifetime.

**Exercise 24.2H**  C24-E02-BTZenith.docx

---

*Vanuatu Exploration, $1599*

*Tahiti to Cook Islands, $2899*

*Fiji to Vanuatu, $2999*

*Tonga to Fiji, $3999*

### Bicycling Adventures

A bicycle is the perfect form of transportation for a travel adventure. Sign up for one of our bicycle tours and travel at your own pace, interact with village residents, stay healthy and fit, and know that your adventure has a minimal effect on the environment. We offer bicycle tours ranging from a leisurely trip through the Loire Valley of France to a mountain-bike expedition in the Atlas Mountains in Morocco. Our Zenith Adventure bicycle guides provide you with historical and educational information about the region in which you are traveling. They also take care of luggage and transportation needs and maintain your bicycle.  We are confident that we can provide the bicycle adventure of a lifetime!

*Loire Valley Tour, $2399*

*Tuscan Village Tour, $2499*

*Atlas Trek Extreme, $2899*

*Great Wall of China, $3299*

## *Volunteer Adventures*

Beginning next year, ZENITH ADVENTURES, together with Bayside Travel, will offer volunteer vacation opportunities. Tentative volunteer adventures include building village and mountain paths, building homes, and helping the families of trail porters improve village facilities. Our volunteer adventures will provide you with an exciting vacation and a rewarding volunteer experience. The group size will be limited to a maximum of 15, and participants will be required to raise a minimum amount of money to contribute to the program and local charities. All charities have been carefully screened to ensure that funds are well managed and distributed fairly. Look for more information in our next newsletter and consider a rewarding volunteer adventure.

---

# Bayside Travel

## *Vacation Adventures*

Hurry and book now for one of our special vacation packages. Book within the next two weeks and you will be eligible for our special discount savings as well as earn a complimentary $100 gift card you can use at any of the resorts in our vacation adventures.

### Disneyland Adventure

ROUNDTRIP AIR FARE INTO LOS ANGELES, CALIFORNIA

THREE-NIGHT HOTEL ACCOMMODATIONS AND HOTEL TAXES

THREE-DAY RESORT TICKET

24-HOUR TRAVELER ASSISTANCE

### Florida Adventure

ROUNDTRIP AIRFARE TO ORLANDO, FLORIDA

SEVEN-NIGHT HOTEL ACCOMMODATIONS AND HOTEL TAXES

FOUR-DAY RESORT TICKET

TWO-DAY BONUS TICKET

FREE TRANSPORTATION TO SOME SITES

### Cancun Adventure

ROUNDTRIP AIRFARE TO CANCUN, MEXICO

FIVE-NIGHT HOTEL ACCOMMODATIONS AND HOTEL TAXES

FREE SHUTTLE TO AND FROM THE AIRPORT

TWO EXCURSION TICKETS

Book a complete air/hotel vacation package and SAVE on fall travel! Bookings must be made by October 14, 2015, for travel January 1 through June 30, 2016 (blackout dates apply). Take advantage of these fantastic savings!

**Exercise 24.2I**  C24-E02-BTVacations.docx

---

# Bayside Travel

A) African Study Adventure

  ❋ Small groups

  ❋ Comprehensive itineraries

  ❋ Custom groups

  ❋ Accommodations and meals

  ❋ Rates

    ✓ Single-occupancy rate: $2,975

    ✓ Double-occupancy rate

B) Southwest Sun Adventure

  ❋ Small groups

  ❋ Guided day trips

  ❋ Grand Canyon vistas

  ❋ Bilingual tour guides

  ❋ Rates

    ✓ Single-occupancy rate

    ✓ Double-occupancy rate

*5530 Bayside Drive* ❖ *Sa*

**Exercise 24.3A**

C24-E03-BTTours.docx

# Bayside Travel

| Antarctic Adventures | | |
|---|---|---|
| Adventure | Duration | Price |
| Antarctic Exploration | 8 days, 7 nights | $4,399 |
| Weddell Sea Adventure | 10 days, 9 nights | $6,899 |
| Falkland Islands Journey | 14 days, 13 nights | $7,699 |
| Sailing Spectacular | 14 days, 13 nights | $8,999 |

| Tall-Ship Adventures | | |
|---|---|---|
| Adventure | Duration | Price |
| Vanuatu Exploration | 5 days, 4 nights | $1,599 |
| Tahiti to Cook Islands | 7 days, 6 nights | $2,899 |
| Fiji To Vanuatu | 7 days, 6 nights | $2,999 |
| Tonga to Fiji | 10 d |  |

| Bicycling Adv | | |
|---|---|---|
| Adventure | Dura |  |
| Loire Valley Tour | 6 day |  |
| Tuscan Village Tour | 7 day |  |
| Atlas Trek Extreme | 7 day |  |
| Great Wall of China | 10 da |  |

*5530 Bayside Drive* ❖ *Sa*

**Exercise 24.3B**

C24-E03-BTTables.docx

# Bayside Travel

| Antarctic Adventures | | |
|---|---|---|
| **Adventure** | **Duration** | **Price** |
| Antarctic Exploration | 8 days, 7 nights | $4,399 |
| Weddell Sea Adventure | 10 days, 9 nights | $6,899 |
| Falkland Islands Journey | 14 days, 13 nights | $7,699 |
| Sailing Spectacular | 14 days, 13 nights | $8,999 |

| Tall-Ship Adventures | | |
|---|---|---|
| **Adventure** | **Duration** | **Price** |
| Vanuatu Exploration | 5 days, 4 nights | $1,599 |
| Tahiti to Cook Islands | 7 days, 6 nights | $2,899 |
| Fiji To Vanuatu | 7 days, 6 nights | $2,999 |
| Tonga to Fiji | 10 days, 9 nights | $3,999 |

| Bicycling Adventures | | |
|---|---|---|
| **Adventure** | **Duration** | **Price** |
| Loire Valley Tour | 6 days, 5 nights | $2,399 |
| Tuscan Village Tour | 7 days, 6 nights | $2,499 |
| Atlas Trek Extreme | 7 days, 6 nights | $2,899 |
| Great Wall of China | 10 days, 9 nights | $3,299 |

*5530 Bayside Drive* ❖ *San Francisco CA 94320* ❖ *1-888-555-8890* ❖ *www.emcp.net/bayside*

**Exercise 24.3C**

C24-E03-BTTablesModified.docx

**Exercise 24.3E**

C24-E03-BTZenith.docx

## Bayside Travel

### Extreme Adventures

We are excited to announce that *Bayside Travel* has teamed with ZENITH ADVENTURES to provide our clients with thrilling, adrenaline-producing, extreme outdoor adventures. You can choose from a variety of exciting adventures including Antarctic expedition cruises, tall-ship sailing, and bicycling tours. Many of our trips are appropriate for beginners, so get out and enjoy an amazing outdoor adventure with family and friends!

### Antarctic Adventures

Travel with our Antarctic experts, cruise on our state-of-the-art ships, and experience Antarctica in all of its grandeur. We use ice-rated expedition ships custom designed for your comfort and safety. Each ship can carry up to 100 passengers, provides excellent viewing for watching whales, seabirds, and icebergs, and includes facilities for educational presentations by our Antarctic experts. For our more adventurous clients, we offer additional activities such as snowshoeing, sea-kayaking, and camping on the Antarctic ice. Plan on a shore excursion where you can view penguin rookeries, seal colonies, and places of historical and scientific interest. To carry you to the Antarctic shore, we use inflatable boats that can carry 12 to 15 people. After a thrilling day on shore, we will take you back to the ship where you can enjoy a delicious meal prepared by our gourmet chefs. Our Antarctic travel experts are naturalists, historians, and adventurers committed to providing you with a fabulous Antarctic adventure.

> Antarctic Exploration, $4399
>
> Weddell Sea Adventure, $6899
>
> Falkland Islands Journey, $7699
>
> Sailing Spectacular, $8999

### Tall-Ship Adventures

Visit exotic and spectacular locations in the South Pacific aboard the Laura Devon, a luxurious tall ship. On your tall-ship adventure, seek out the hidden Pacific by sailing the trade winds to discover the ...of remote islands and communities. Our tall-ship sailing adventure ...timeless romance. You can sign on for the challenge of an ocean ...r a more leisurely island voyage sailing through tropical paradises. For

...n Francisco CA 94320 ❖ 1-888-555-8890 ❖ www.emcp.net/bayside

many, tall-ship sailing is the ultimate in escapist adventuring. Sailing on the magnificent Laura Devon, combined with the sparkling beauty of the South Pacific, makes for the adventure of a lifetime.

> Vanuatu Exploration, $1599
>
> Tahiti to Cook Islands, $2899
>
> Fiji to Vanuatu, $2999
>
> Tonga to Fiji, $3999

### Bicycling Adventures

A bicycle is the perfect form of transportation for a travel adventure. Sign up for one of our bicycle tours and travel at your own pace, interact with village residents, stay healthy and fit, and know that your adventure has a minimal effect on the environment. We offer bicycle tours ranging from a leisurely trip through the Loire Valley of France to a mountain-bike expedition in the Atlas Mountains in Morocco. Our Zenith Adventure bicycle guides provide you with historical and educational information about the region in which you are traveling. They also take care of luggage and transportation needs and maintain your bicycle. We are confident that we can provide the bicycle adventure of a lifetime!

> Loire Valley Tour, $2399
>
> Tuscan Village Tour, $2499
>
> Atlas Trek Extreme, $2899
>
> Great Wall of China, $3299

### Volunteer Adventures

Beginning next year, ZENITH ADVENTURES, together with *Bayside Travel*, will offer volunteer vacation opportunities. Tentative volunteer adventures include building village and mountain paths, building homes, and helping the families of trail porters improve village facilities. Our volunteer adventures will provide you with an exciting vacation and a rewarding volunteer experience. The group size will be limited to a maximum of 15, and participants will be required to raise a minimum amount of money to contribute to the program and local charities. All charities have been carefully screened to ensure that funds are well managed and distributed fairly. Look for more information in our next newsletter and consider a rewarding volunteer adventure.

## Eastern Adventures

Join Bayside Travel in a joint adventure with Lifetime Tours in experiencing the beauty and splendor of the East. Upcoming adventure tours include the beauty and majesty of Japan and the cultural and natural marvels of China.

### Japan Adventures

Japan is a country of unique contrasts from the neon lights and bustling activity of Tokyo to the sweeping vistas of the Japanese Alps. Join Bayside Travel in a joint adventure with Maruyama Tours in experiencing the beauty and splendor of Japan. Choose from one of three adventure tours to experience the sights and sounds of Japan from the urban centers of Tokyo and Kyoto to the breathtaking views of Japan's mountain ranges and coastlines.

| Adventure | Duration | Price |
|---|---|---|
| Japan Extravaganza | 14 days, 13 nights | $9,799 |
| Treasures of Japan | 12 days, 11 nights | $8,299 |
| Northern Exploration | 10 days, 9 nights | $7,599 |

### China Adventures

The 2008 Olympics hosted by China provided the world the opportunity to see a nation of ancient riches complemented by amazing modern marvels of architecture and engineering. China is a land of natural and cultural beauty from the Great Wall of China and the Forbidden City of Beijing to the Xi'an's Terracotta Army, Suzhou gardens, and the majestic peaks of Huangshan.

| Adventure | Duration | Price |
|---|---|---|
| Cultural China | 14 days, 13 nights | $11,359 |
| China & Yangtze Experience | 14 days, 13 nights | $10,759 |
| China Village Experience | 10 days, 9 nights | $8,299 |

5530 Bayside Drive ❖ San Francisco CA 94320 ❖ 1-888-555-8890 ❖ www.emcp.net/bayside

**Exercise 24.3F**

C24-E03-BTEastAdventures.docx

# Applying Styles

A *style* is a set of formatting instructions that you can apply to text. Word provides a number of predesigned styles and groups styles that apply similar formatting into sets called *style sets*. Whereas a theme changes the overall colors, fonts, and effects used in a document, a style set changes how the colors, fonts, and effects are combined and which color, font, and effect is dominant. Using the styles within a style set, you can apply formatting that gives your document a uniform and professional appearance.

A variety of methods is available for applying styles to text in a document. You can apply a style by clicking the style thumbnail in the Styles group on the HOME tab or by clicking the More button and then clicking the desired style at the drop-down gallery.

The Styles task pane provides another method for applying a style. Display the Styles task pane, as shown in Figure 24.1 on the next page, by clicking the Styles group task pane launcher or pressing Alt + Ctrl + Shift + S. The styles in the currently selected style set display in the task pane followed by a paragraph symbol (¶), indicating that the style applies paragraph formatting, or a character symbol (**a**), indicating that the style applies character formatting. If both characters display to the right of a style, the style applies both paragraph and character formatting. In addition to displaying styles that apply formatting, the Styles task pane also displays a *Clear All* style that clears all formatting from the selected text.

**Figure 24.1 Styles Task Pane**

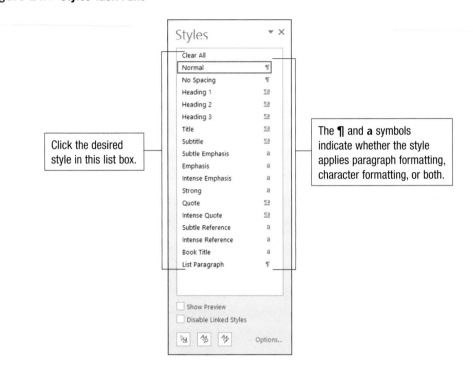

Click the desired style in this list box.

The ¶ and **a** symbols indicate whether the style applies paragraph formatting, character formatting, or both.

**QUICK STEPS**

**Apply a Style**
Click desired style in Styles group.
OR
1. Click More button in Styles group on HOME tab.
2. Click desired style.
OR
1. Display Styles task pane.
2. Click desired style in task pane.
OR
1. Click More button in Styles group.
2. Click *Apply Styles* at drop-down gallery.
3. Click down-pointing arrow at right of *Style Name* option box.
4. Click desired style at drop-down list.

If you hover the mouse pointer on a style in the Styles task pane, a ScreenTip displays with information about the formatting applied by the style. Apply a style in the Styles task pane by clicking the style. Close the Styles task pane by clicking the Close button located in the upper right corner of the task pane.

Styles can also be applied at the Apply Styles window, as shown in Figure 24.2. Display this window by clicking the More button at the right of the thumbnails in the Styles group and then clicking *Apply Styles* at the drop-down gallery or by pressing Ctrl + Shift + S. Like the Styles task pane, the Apply Styles window contains the styles of the currently selected style set. Click the down-pointing arrow at the right of the *Style Name* option box and then click the desired style at the drop-down list. You can also type the name of the style in the *Style Name* option box and then press the Enter key.

**Figure 24.2 Apply Styles Window**

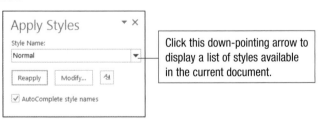

Click this down-pointing arrow to display a list of styles available in the current document.

1. Open **AfricanAdventure.docx** and save the document with the name **C24-E01-AfricanAdventure**.

2. Apply styles using the Styles task pane by completing the following steps:
   a. Select the heading *Small Groups*.
   b. Click the Styles group task pane launcher on the HOME tab. (This displays the Styles task pane.)
   c. Click the *Intense Emphasis* style in the Styles task pane. (Notice that the style is followed by the character symbol [**a**], indicating that the style applies character formatting.)

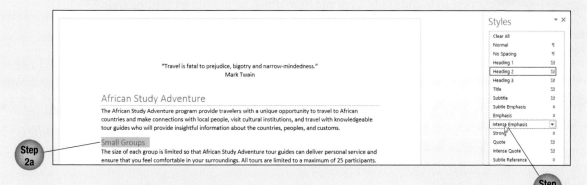

   d. Select the heading *Comprehensive Itineraries*.
   e. Click the *Intense Emphasis* style in the Styles task pane.
   f. Complete steps similar to those in Steps 1d and 1e to apply the Intense Emphasis style to the remaining headings (*Custom Groups* and *Accommodations and Meals*).
   g. Select the Mark Twain quote (including the name *Mark Twain*) that displays at the beginning of the document and then click the *Quote* style in the Styles task pane.
   h. Remove the formatting from the quote text by making sure the text is selected and then clicking the *Clear All* style located near the top of the Styles task pane.
   i. Click anywhere in the heading *Small Groups* and notice that the Intense Emphasis style is selected in the Styles task pane. Hover the mouse pointer over the Intense Emphasis style and read the information in the ScreenTip about the formatting applied by the style.
   j. Close the Styles task pane by clicking the Close button located in the upper right corner of the task pane.

3. Display the Apply Styles window by clicking the More button at the right of the style thumbnails in the Styles group and then clicking *Apply Styles* at the drop-down gallery.

4. Select the Mark Twain quote (including the name) located at the beginning of the document, click the down-pointing arrow at the right of the *Style Name* option box, and then click *Intense Quote* at the drop-down list. (You will need to scroll down the list box to display this option.)

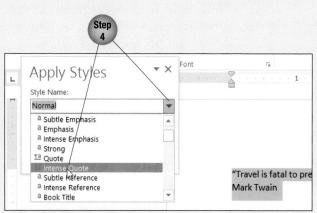

5. Close the Apply Styles window by clicking the Close button located in the upper right corner of the window.
6. Save, print, and then close **C24-E01-AfricanAdventure.docx**.

# Creating Styles

QUICK
STEPS

**Create a Style Based on Existing Formatting**
1. Apply desired formatting to text.
2. Select text.
3. Click More button in Styles group.
4. Click *Create a Style*.
5. Type name for new style.
6. Click OK.

**Create a Style Based on an Existing Style**
1. Apply style to text.
2. Make desired formatting changes.
3. Select text.
4. Click More button in Styles group.
5. Click *Create a Style*.
6. Type name for new style.
7. Click OK.

If none of the predesigned styles provided by Word contains the formatting you want, you can create your own style. You can create a style based on existing formatting, create a new style and apply all of the formatting, or modify an existing style.

## Creating a Style Based on Existing Formatting

To create a style based on existing formatting, apply the desired formatting to text in a document and then select the text. Click the More button at the right of the thumbnails in the Styles group and then click *Create a Style* at the drop-down gallery. At the Create New Style from Formatting dialog box, as shown in Figure 24.3, type a name for the new style in the *Name* text box and then click OK. The style is inserted in the *Styles* gallery and is available for use in the current document.

**Figure 24.3  Create New Style from Formatting Dialog Box**

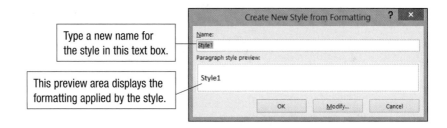

Type a new name for the style in this text box.

This preview area displays the formatting applied by the style.

## Creating a Style Based on an Existing Style

To create a style based on an existing style, apply the style to text, make the desired formatting changes, and then select the text. Click the More button at the right of the thumbnails in the Styles group and then click *Create a Style* at the drop-down gallery. At the Create New Style from Formatting dialog box, type a name for the new style in the *Name* text box and then click OK.

1. Open **BTStyles.docx** and save the document with the name **C24-E02-BTStyles**.
2. Create a style based on the formatting of the *CustomTitle* text by completing the following steps:
   a. Click the Show/Hide ¶ button in the Paragraph group on the HOME tab to turn on the display of nonprinting characters.
   b. Select the text *CustomTitle*. (Make sure you select the paragraph mark [¶] after *Title*.)
   c. Click the More button at the right of the thumbnails in the Styles group.
   d. Click the *Create a Style* option.
   e. At the Create New Style from Formatting dialog box, type **CustomTitle**.
   f. Click OK.
   g. Click the Show/Hide ¶ button to turn off the display of nonprinting characters.
3. Save **C24-E02-BTStyles.docx**.

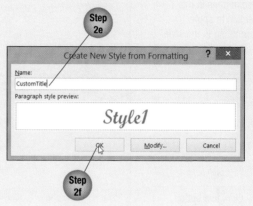

## Creating a New Style

You can also create a style without first applying formatting to text. To do this, click the More button at the right of the thumbnails in the Styles group and then click *Create a Style* at the drop-down gallery. At the Create New Style from Formatting dialog box, click the Modify button. This displays an expanded Create New Style from Formatting dialog box, as shown in Figure 24.4 on the next page. At this dialog box, type a new name for the style in the *Name* text box and then use the *Style type* option box to specify the type of style you are creating. Click the down-pointing arrow at the right of the option and a drop-down list displays with options for creating a paragraph style, character style, linked style (both a paragraph and character style), table style, or list style. Choose the option that identifies the type of style you are creating.

The *Style based on* option has a default setting of ¶ *Normal*. You can base a new style on an existing style. To do this, click the down-pointing arrow at the right of the *Style based on* option box and then click the desired style at the drop-down list. For example, you can base a new style on a predesigned style such as the Heading 1 style. Click the *Heading 1* style at the drop-down list and the formatting settings of Heading 1 display in the Create New Style from Formatting dialog box. Apply additional formatting at the dialog box to modify the formatting of the Heading 1 style. If a predesigned style contains some of the formatting you want for your new style, choosing the predesigned style at the *Style based on* option drop-down list saves you formatting time.

Use the *Style for following paragraph* option to tell Word what style to use for the next paragraph in the document when you press the Enter key. For example, you can create a style that formats a caption heading and have it followed by a style that applies paragraph formatting to the text that follows the caption heading (such as italic formatting or a specific font and font size). In this situation, you would create the style that applies the desired paragraph formatting to the text that follows a caption heading. You would then create the caption heading style and then use the *Style for following paragraph* option to

**QUICK STEPS**

**Create a New Style**
1. Click More button in Styles group.
2. Click *Create a Style*.
3. Click Modify button.
4. Type new name for style.
5. Apply desired formatting.
6. Click OK.

**Figure 24.4 Expanded Create New Style from Formatting Dialog Box**

Type a name for the style in this text box.

Choose a style type in this option box, such as paragraph, character (or both), table, or list.

Use buttons in this section to apply formatting to the style.

Choose a style in this option box on which to base the new style.

Click this button to display a list of formatting options.

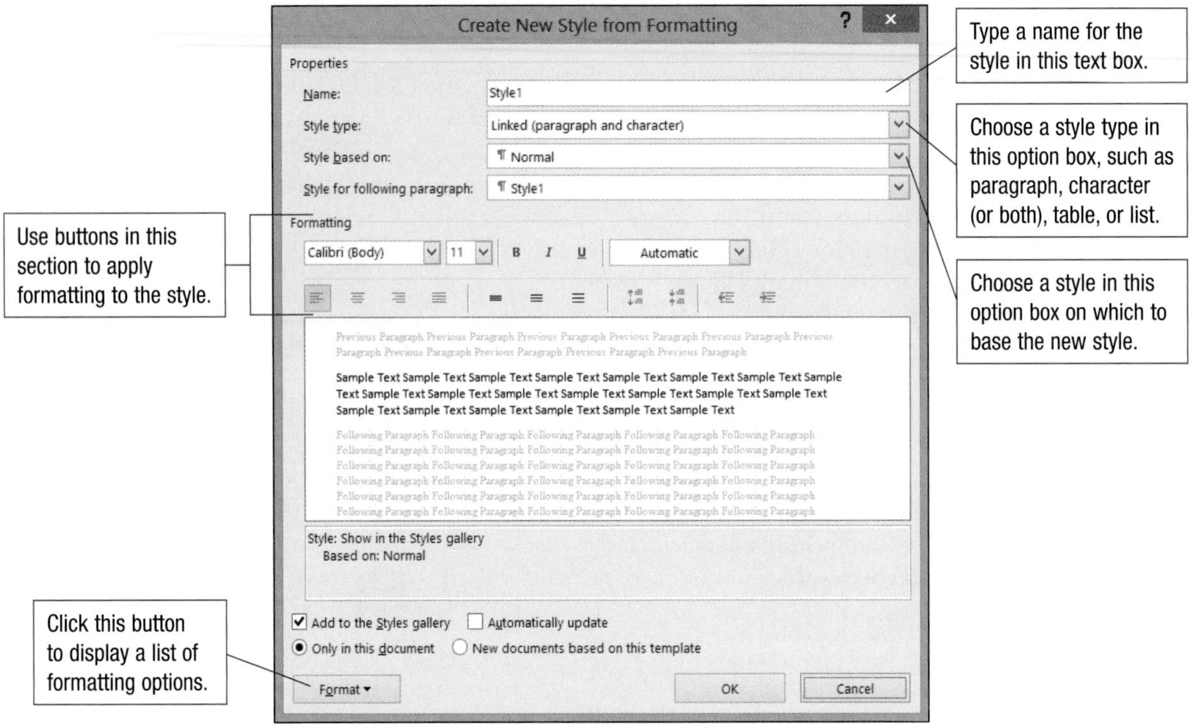

specify that the paragraph style you created is applied when you press the Enter key after applying the caption heading style.

The Create New Style from Formatting dialog box contains a number of options for specifying formatting for the new style. Use options in the *Formatting* section to apply character and paragraph formatting, such as changing the font, font size, font color, and font effects and changing paragraph alignment, spacing, and indenting. Click the Format button that displays in the lower left corner of the dialog box and a drop-down list displays with a number of formatting options. Use options at this drop-down list, to specify formatting for the style with options in dialog boxes such as the Font, Paragraph, Tabs, Borders, Language, and Frame dialog boxes.

Unless the Create New Style from Formatting dialog has been customized, the *Add to the Styles gallery* check box located in the lower left corner of the dialog box contains a check mark. With this option active, the style you create will display in the Styles group on the HOME tab. Additionally, the *Only in this document* option is active. With this option active, the style is saved only with the current document. If you want the style available for new documents based on the Normal template (or any other template on which the current document is based), click the *New documents based on this template* option. The *Automatically update* check box is empty by default. Insert a check mark in this option if you want every change you make to text with a style applied to update that style. Keep this option inactive if you want the style formatting to remain as you defined it.

# Assigning a Keyboard Shortcut to a Style

Consider assigning a keyboard shortcut to a style that you apply on a regular basis. A keyboard shortcut can be assigned to a style with any of the following combinations:

Alt + letter

Alt + Ctrl + letter

Alt + Shift + letter

Ctrl + Shift + letter

Alt + Ctrl + Shift + letter

Word already uses many combinations for Word functions. For example, pressing Ctrl + Shift + F displays the Font dialog box.

Assign a keyboard shortcut to a style at the expanded Create New Style from Formatting dialog box by clicking the Format button and then clicking *Shortcut key* at the drop-down list. This displays the Customize Keyboard dialog box, as shown in Figure 24.5. With the insertion point positioned in the *Press new shortcut key* text box, press the desired keys. Word inserts the message *Currently assigned to* below the *Current keys* list box. If the keyboard shortcut is already assigned to a command, the command is indicated after the *Currently assigned to* message. If Word is not already using the keyboard shortcut, *[unassigned]* displays after the *Currently assigned to* message. When assigning a keyboard shortcut, make sure you use an unassigned combination of keystrokes.

**Figure 24.5  Customize Keyboard Dialog Box**

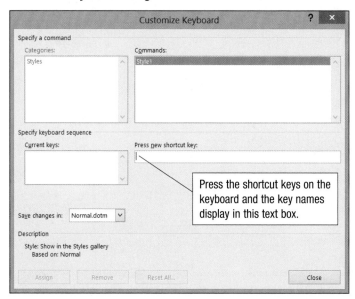

1. With **C24-E02-BTStyles.docx** open, press Ctrl + End to move the insertion point to the end of the document.
2. Click the More button at the right of the thumbnails in the Styles group.
3. Click *Create a Style*.
4. At the Create New Style from Formatting dialog box, type **CustomEmphasis**.
5. Click the Modify button.

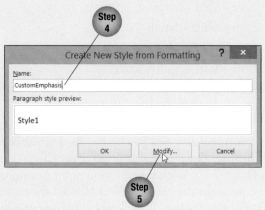

6. At the Create New Style from Formatting expanded dialog box, make the following changes:
   a. Click the down-pointing arrow at the right of the *Font Size* option and then click *12* at the drop-down list.
   b. Click the down-pointing arrow at the right of the *Font Color* option.
   c. Click the *Dark Blue* color (ninth option in the *Standard Colors* section).
   d. Click the Format button located near the bottom of the Create New Style from Formatting dialog box and then click *Font* at the drop-down list.

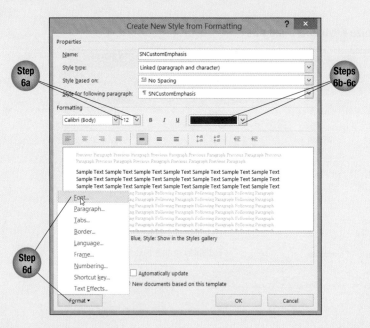

   e. At the Font dialog box, click the *Small caps* check box to insert a check mark and then click OK to close the dialog box.
   f. Click the Format button and then click *Paragraph* at the drop-down list.
   g. At the Paragraph dialog box with the Indents and Spacing tab selected, click the up-pointing arrow at the right of the *Left* measurement box in the *Indentation* section until *0.3"* displays.
   h. Select the current measurement in the *After* measurement box in the *Spacing* section and then type **3**.

i.   Click OK to close the Paragraph dialog box.
j.   Click OK to close the Create New Style from Formatting dialog box.
7.  Create a character style and assign a keyboard shortcut to it by completing the following steps:
    a.   Click the *No Spacing* style in the Styles group on the HOME tab.
    b.   Click the More button at the right side of the thumbnails in the Styles group and then click *Create a Style* at the drop-down gallery.
    c.   At the Create New Style from Formatting dialog box, type **Zenith** in the *Name* text box.
    d.   Click the Modify button.
    e.   At the Create New Style from Formatting dialog box, click the down-pointing arrow at the right side of the *Style type* option box and then click *Character* at the drop-down list.
    f.   Click the down-pointing arrow at the right of the *Font* option, scroll down the drop-down list, and then click *Imprint MT Shadow*.
    g.   Click the Format button located near the bottom of the dialog box and then click *Font* at the drop-down list.

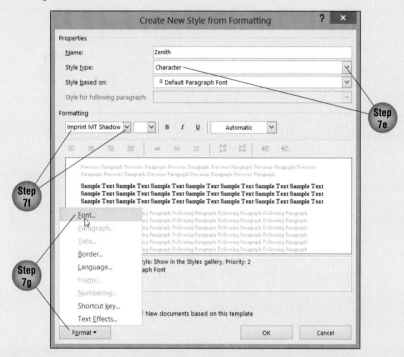

    h.   At the Font dialog box, click the *Small caps* check box to insert a check mark and then click OK to close the dialog box.
    i.   Click the Format button and then click *Shortcut key* at the drop-down list.

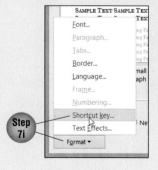

j.  At the Customize Keyboard dialog box with the insertion point positioned in the *Press new shortcut key* text box, press the keys Alt + Z.

k.  Check to make sure *[unassigned]* displays after *Currently assigned to*.

l.  Click the Assign button.

m.  Click the Close button to close the Customize Keyboard dialog box.

n.  Click OK to close the Create New Style from Formatting dialog box.

8.  Save **C24-E02-BTStyles.docx**.

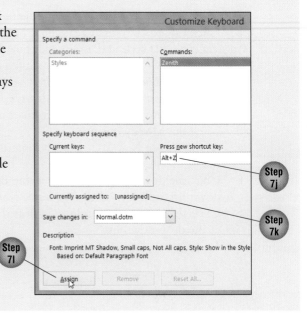

## Modifying a Style

**QUICK STEPS**

**Modify a Style**
1. Right-click desired style in Styles group or Styles drop-down gallery.
2. Click *Modify*.
3. Type new name for style.
4. Make desired changes.
5. Click OK.

If a predesigned style contains most of the formatting you want, you can modify it to create a new style. To do this, right-click the style in the Styles group and then click *Modify* at the shortcut menu. This displays the Modify Style dialog box, which contains the same options that are available at the Create New Style from Formatting dialog box. Type a new name in the *Name* text box, make the desired changes, and then click OK.

Another method for modifying an existing style is to update the style to match selected text. To do this, apply a predesigned style to text, such as the Heading 1 style. Apply additional formatting to the text and then select the text. Right-click the *Heading 1* style in the Styles group and then click the *Update Heading 1 to Match Selection* option at the shortcut menu.

**Exercise 24.2C** Modifying an Existing Style                                         Part 3 of 9

1.  With **C24-E02-BTStyles.docx** open, modify the Heading 2 style by completing the following steps:

a.  Right-click the *Heading 2* style in the Styles group on the HOME tab and then click *Modify* at the shortcut menu.

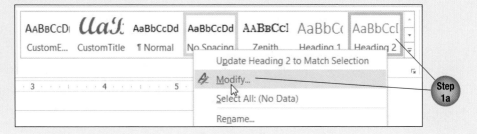

b. At the Modify Style dialog box, type **CustomHeading** in the *Name* text box.
c. Click the down-pointing arrow at the right of the *Font* option and then click *Candara* at the drop-down list.
d. Click the Italic button.
e. Click the down-pointing arrow at the right of the *Font Color* option and then click *Dark Blue* (ninth option in the *Standard Colors* section).

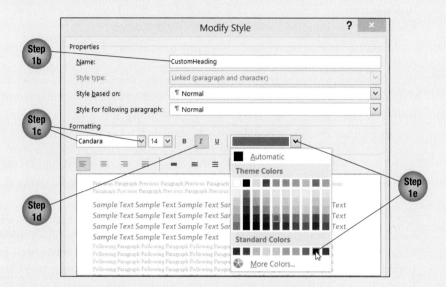

f. Click the Format button located near the bottom of the dialog box and then click *Paragraph* at the drop-down list.
g. At the Paragraph dialog box with the Indents and Spacing tab selected, select the current measurement in the *After* measurement box in the *Spacing* section and then type **6**.
h. Click OK to close the Paragraph dialog box.
i. Click the Format button located near the bottom of the dialog box and then click *Border* at the drop-down list.
j. At the Borders and Shading dialog box, click the Shading tab.
k. Click the down-pointing arrow at the right of the *Fill* option and then click the *Blue, Accent 1, Lighter 80%* color at the drop-down list (fifth column, second row in the *Theme Colors* section).
l. Click OK to close the Borders and Shading dialog box.
m. Click OK to close the Modify Style dialog box.

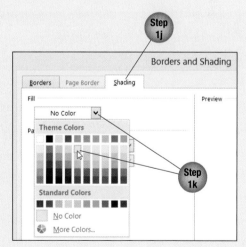

2. Save **C24-E02-BTStyles.docx**.

## Saving Styles in a Template

**Create Document Based on Template**
1. Click FILE tab.
2. Click *New* option.
3. Click PERSONAL option.
4. Click template thumbnail.

The styles you created in C24-E02-BTStyles.docx are saved only in that document. If you want the styles available for future Bayside Travel documents, save the document containing the styles as a template. With the styles saved in a template document, you can create documents based on the template and use the styles to format text.

Save a document as a template by changing the *Save as type* option at the Save As dialog box to *Word Template (*.dotx)*. By default, Word saves a template document in the Custom Office Templates folder on the local hard drive.

To create a document based on a template, click the FILE tab and then click the *New* option. At the New backstage area, click the *PERSONAL* option to display thumbnails of the templates saved in the Custom Office Templates folder and then click the desired template thumbnail. The styles created and saved with the template will display in the Styles group on the HOME tab.

In Exercise 24.2D, you will save a document as a template in the Custom Office Templates folder on the local hard drive. In a school or other public environment, templates saved in the Custom Office Templates folder may be deleted if the computers are reset on a regular basis. Resetting computers deletes any templates saved in the Custom Office Templates folder.

If you are working on a computer in a public environment, you may want to save a backup of your template on your storage medium (such as a USB flash drive). To do this, display the Open dialog box, click the *Documents* folder in the Navigation pane, and then double-click the *Custom Office Templates* folder that displays in the Content pane. Right-click the template you want to copy and then click *Copy* at the shortcut menu. Click the drive representing your USB flash drive (or other storage device) and then double-click the *Chapter24* folder. Right-click in a blank area of the Content pane and then click *Paste* at the shortcut menu. Complete similar steps to copy a template from your storage device to the Custom Office Templates folder on the local hard drive.

---

### Exercise 24.2D    Saving Styles in a Template and Applying    Part 4 of 9
### Custom Styles

1. With **C24-E02-BTStyles.docx** open, press Ctrl + A to select all of the text (except the header and footer) in the document and then press the Delete key.
2. Click the *No Spacing* style in the Styles group on the HOME tab.
3. Save the document as a template by completing the following steps:
   a. Press the F12 key to display the Save As dialog box.
   b. Click the *Save as type* option box and then click *Word Template (*.dotx)* at the drop-down list.
   c. Click in the *File name* text box, type your three initials followed by a hyphen and then type **BTTemplate**.
   d. Click the Save button. (This saves the template in the Custom Office Templates folder.)
4. Save the **XXX-BTTemplate.dotx** template to your Chapter24 folder by pressing the F12 key to display the Save As dialog box, navigating to the Chapter24 folder on your storage medium, and then clicking the Save button.
5. Close the **XXX-BTTemplate.dotx** template (where your initials display in place of the XXX).

6. Open a document based on the **XXX-BTTemplate.dotx** template by completing the following steps:
   a. Click the FILE tab and then click the *New* option.
   b. Click the *PERSONAL* option.
   c. Click the **XXX-BTTemplate.dotx** template thumbnail (where your initials display in place of the *XXX*).
7. Insert a document into the existing document by completing the following steps:
   a. Press the Enter key once, click the INSERT tab, and then click the Object button arrow.
   b. Click *Text from File* at the drop-down list.
   c. Navigate to your Chapter24 folder and then double-click **BTZenith.docx**.
8. Apply the CustomTitle style by completing the following steps:
   a. Click anywhere in the title *Extreme Adventures*.
   b. Click the HOME tab and then click the *CustomTitle* style in the Styles group.
   c. Scroll to the end of the document, click anywhere in the title *Volunteer Adventures*, and then click the *CustomTitle* style.
9. Apply the CustomHeading style by completing the following steps:
   a. Press Ctrl + Home to move the insertion point to the beginning of the document.
   b. Click anywhere in the heading *Antarctic Adventures*.
   c. Click the *CustomHeading* style in the Styles group. (Note that the style name begins with *Heading2* when you hover your mouse over the style thumbnail.)

   d. Apply the CustomHeading style to the headings *Tall-Ship Adventures* and *Bicycling Adventures*.
10. Apply the CustomEmphasis style by completing the following steps:
    a. Select the lines of text in the *Antarctic Adventures* section that contain money amounts.
    b. Click the *CustomEmphasis* style in the Styles group.
    c. Apply the CustomEmphasis style to the lines of text in the *Tall-Ship Adventures* section that contain money amounts.
    d. Apply the CustomEmphasis style to the lines of text in the *Bicycling Adventures* section that contain money amounts.
11. Select the text *Zenith Adventures* that displays in the first sentence in the first paragraph of text below the *Extreme Adventures* title and then press Alt + Z. (This applies the Zenith style.)
12. Press Ctrl + End to move the insertion point to the end of the document. Select the text *Zenith Adventures* that displays in the first sentence of the last paragraph of text and then press Alt + Z to apply the Zenith style.
13. Save the document and name it **C24-E02-BTZenith.docx**.

## Modifying an Applied Style

One of the advantages of applying styles in a document is that if you modify the style formatting, all of the text in the document to which that style has been applied automatically updates. Using styles streamlines formatting and maintains consistency in your documents.

1. With **C24-E02-BTZenith.docx** open, edit the CustomTitle style to change the font size and alignment by completing the following steps:
   a. Right-click the *CustomTitle* style in the *Styles* gallery in the Styles group on the HOME tab.
   b. Click *Modify* at the shortcut menu.
   c. At the Modify Style dialog box, change the font size to 22 points.
   d. Click the Align Left button that displays in the *Formatting* section.
   e. Click OK to close the Modify Style dialog box.
2. Scroll through the document and notice that the custom title style is applied to both titles in the document.
3. Save **C24-E02-BTZenith.docx**.

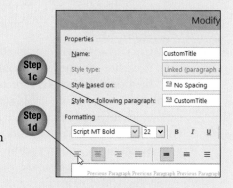

# Displaying All Styles

Each style set contains a title style and body text style, a number of heading level styles, and other styles that are designed to work together in a single document. Only the styles for the currently selected style set display in the *Styles* drop-down gallery or Styles task pane. You can display all available styles with options at the Style Pane Options dialog box, as shown in Figure 24.6. Display this dialog box by clicking the Styles group task pane launcher and then clicking the <u>Options</u> hyperlink that displays in the lower right corner of the Styles task pane.

**Figure 24.6  Style Pane Options Dialog Box**

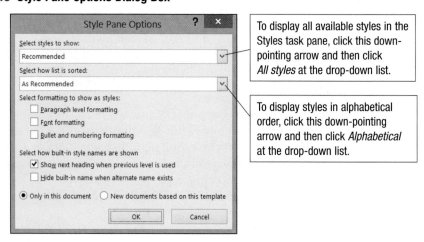

To display all available styles in the Styles task pane, click this down-pointing arrow and then click *All styles* at the drop-down list.

To display styles in alphabetical order, click this down-pointing arrow and then click *Alphabetical* at the drop-down list.

To display all available styles, click the down-pointing arrow at the right of the *Select styles to show* option box and then click *All styles* at the drop-down list. Specify how you want the styles sorted in the Styles task pane with the *Select how list is sorted* option.

1. With **C24-E02-BTZenith.docx** open, display all available styles in the Styles task pane by completing the following steps:
   a. Click the Styles group task pane launcher.
   b. Click the <u>Options</u> hyperlink that displays in the lower right corner of the Styles task pane.
   c. At the Style Pane Options dialog box, click the down-pointing arrow at the right of the *Select styles to show* option and then click *All styles* at the drop-down list.
   d. Click the down-pointing arrow at the right of the *Select how list is sorted* option and then click *Alphabetical* at the drop-down list.
   e. Click OK to close the dialog box.
2. Apply styles by completing the following steps:
   a. Select the lines of text in the *Antarctic Adventures* section that contain money amounts.
   b. Click the *Body Text Indent* style.
   c. Click the *Book Title* style.
   d. Apply the Body Text Indent and Book Title styles to the two other occurrences of lines of text containing money amounts.
3. Save and then print **C24-E02-BTZenith.docx**.

*Step 1c*

**Style Pane Options**  ?  ×

Select styles to show:
All styles

Select how list is sorted:
As Recommended

Alphabetical
As Recommended
Font
Based on
By type

☐ bullet and numbering formatting

*Step 1d*

Select how built-in style names are shown
☑ Show next heading when previous level is used
☐ Hide built-in name when alternate name exists

◉ Only in this document   ○ New documents based on this template

OK   Cancel

*Step 1e*

# Revealing Style Formatting

As you learned earlier, if you hover the mouse pointer over a style in the Styles task pane, a ScreenTip displays with information about the formatting applied by the style. The styles in the *Styles* gallery display with a visual representation of the formatting applied by the style.

You can also display a visual representation of styles by clicking the *Show Preview* check box in the Styles task pane. Another method for displaying the formatting applied by a style is to display the Reveal Formatting task pane by pressing Shift + F1.

1. With **C24-E02-BTZenith.docx** open, view the styles in the Styles task pane by completing the following steps:
   a. With the Styles task pane open, click the *Show Preview* check box to insert a check mark.
   b. Scroll through the list box to see how styles display with the preview feature turned on.
   c. Click the *Show Preview* check box to remove the check mark.
   d. Close the Styles task pane by clicking the Close button in the upper right corner of the task pane.
2. Display style formatting in the Reveal Formatting task pane by completing the following steps:
   a. Press Shift + F1 to turn on the display of the Reveal Formatting task pane.
   b. Click the *Distinguish style source* check box to insert a check mark.
   c. Click anywhere in the title *Extreme Adventures* and notice in the Reveal Formatting task pane the formatting applied by the style.
   d. Click anywhere in the heading *Antarctic Adventures* and notice in the Reveal Formatting task pane the formatting applied by the style.
   e. Click other text in the document and view the formatting.
   f. Click the *Distinguish style source* check box to remove the check mark.
   g. Press Shift + F1 to turn off the display of the Reveal Formatting task pane.

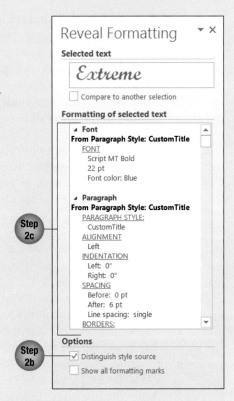

Step 2c

Step 2b

## Saving a Custom Style Set

Word provides a number of predesigned styles and groups styles that apply similar formatting into style sets. In Chapter 2, you learned how to apply styles in the Styles group on the HOME tab and how to apply a style set in the Document Formatting group on the DESIGN tab. In addition to using the style sets provided by Word, you can create and/or modify styles and then save those styles into a custom style set. For example, you can save the styles in the XXX-BTTemplate.dotx template as a custom style set. The advantage to creating a custom style set is that set is saved in the Normal.dotm template and is available for all documents, not just documents based on a specific template.

To save styles in a custom style set, click the DESIGN tab, click the More button at the right side of the style set thumbnails, and then click *Save as a New Style Set* at the drop-down gallery. This displays the Save as a New Style Set dialog box and makes the QuickStyles subfolder on the local hard drive the active folder. The *Save as type* option at the dialog box is set at *Word Template (*.dotx)*. The custom style set you create is saved as a template that is available with the Normal.dotm template, which is the default template on which most documents are based. Type a name for the style set in the *File name* text box and then press Enter or click the Save button. The custom style set will be available in the style set gallery in the Document Formatting group on the DESIGN tab for all documents.

## Changing Default Settings

If you apply a predesigned or custom style set to most documents, you can set that style set as the default and it will be available for all future documents. Change the default style set with the Set as Default button in the Document Formatting group on the DESIGN tab. In addition to changing the default style set, making changes to the theme, theme colors, theme fonts, theme effects, and paragraph spacing will make them default settings, as well. When you click the Set as Default button, a message displays asking if you want the current style set and theme as the default and telling you that the settings will be applied to new documents. At this message, click the Yes button.

When you set the current style set, themes, theme colors, theme fonts, theme effects, and paragraph spacing as the default style set, the changes are made to the Normal.dotm template. If you want to return to the original default settings, open a previous document that was created before you changed the default settings, click the Set as Default button in the Document Formatting group on the DESIGN tab, and then click Yes at the message that displays.

---

**Exercise 24.2H**    **Saving Styles in a Custom Style Set**          Part 8 of 9

1. With **C24-E02-BTZenith.docx** open, save the styles in a custom style set by completing the following steps:
   a. Click the DESIGN tab.
   b. Click the More button at the right side of the style set thumbnails.
   c. Click the *Save as a New Style Set* option at the drop-down gallery.

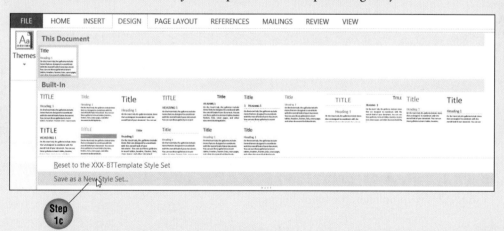

Step 1c

   d. At the Save as a New Style Set dialog box, type **XXX-BTStyles** (replacing the *XXX* with your initials) and then press Enter.
2. Save, print, and then close **C24-E02-BTZenith.docx**.
3. Open **BTVacations.docx** and then save the document and name it **C24-E02-BTVacations**.

---

4.  Apply the XXX-BTStyles custom style (where your initials display in place of the *XXX*) by completing the following steps:

    a.  Click the DESIGN tab.

    b.  Click the More button at the right side of the style set thumbnails.

    c.  Click the *XXX-BTStyles* custom style set (where your initials display in place of the *XXX*) located in the *Custom* section of the drop-down gallery.

5.  Click the HOME tab and then apply the following styles to the specified text:

    a.  Apply the CustomTitle style to the title *Vacation Adventures*.

    b.  Apply the CustomHeading style to the headings *Disneyland Adventure*, *Florida Adventure*, and *Cancun Adventure*.

    c.  Apply the CustomEmphasis style to the bulleted text below the *Disneyland Adventure* heading, *Florida Adventure* heading, and *Cancun Adventure* heading.

6.  Save and then print **C24-E02-BTVacations.docx**.

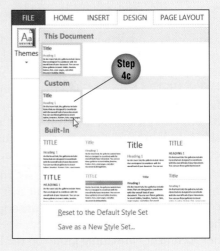

## QUICK STEPS

**Delete a Custom Style Set**

1. Click DESIGN tab.
2. Click More button at right side of style set thumbnails.
3. Right-click custom style set in *Custom* section.
4. Click *Delete*.
5. Click Yes.

## Deleting a Custom Style Set

If you no longer need a custom style set that you have saved, delete it at the style set drop-down gallery. To do this, click the DESIGN tab and then click the More button at the right side of the style set thumbnails. At the drop-down gallery, right-click your custom style set in the *Custom* section and then click *Delete* at the shortcut menu. At the message that displays asking if you want to delete the style set, click the Yes button.

---

**Exercise 24.2I**    Deleting a Custom Style Set      Part 9 of 9

1.  With **C24-E02-BTVacations.docx** open, delete the XXX-BTStyles custom style set (where your initials display in place of the *XXX*) by completing the following steps:

    a.  Click the DESIGN tab.

    b.  Click the More button at the right side of the style set thumbnails.

    c.  Right-click the *XXX-BTStyles* custom style set (where your initials display in place of the *XXX*) located in the *Custom* section of the drop-down gallery.

    d.  Click *Delete* at the drop-down gallery.

    e.  At the message that displays, click Yes.

2.  Save and then close **C24-E02-BTVacations.docx**.

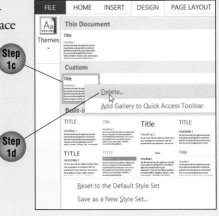

# Creating Multilevel List and Table Styles

In this chapter, you have learned how to create styles that are available in the Styles group on the HOME tab and also how to save styles in a custom style set. You can save character and paragraph styles and custom style sets in the Styles group but you cannot save list styles and table styles. However, you can save list styles and table styles in the current document or a template document.

## Creating a Multilevel List Style

Word provides a number of predesigned list styles that you can apply to text in a document. These styles are generally paragraph styles that apply formatting to text such as paragraph indenting and spacing. These list styles apply formatting only to one level of the list. If you want to create a multilevel list style that applies formatting to more than one level of a list, create the style at the Define New List Style dialog box, as shown in Figure 24.7. Display this dialog box by clicking the Multilevel List button in the Paragraph group on the HOME tab and then clicking *Define New List Style* at the drop-down list. You can also create a multilevel list style at the Create New Style from Formatting dialog box by changing the *Style type* to *List*.

The Define New List Style dialog box (and the Create New Style from Formatting dialog box with *List* selected in the *Style type* option) contains the same options as the Create New Style from Formatting dialog box with *Paragraph*, *Character*, or *Linked (paragraph and character)* selected along with some additional options, such as the *Start at* and *Apply formatting to* options. By default, the *Apply formatting to* option is set at *1st level*. With this option selected, apply the desired formatting for the letter, number, or symbol that begins the first level of your list. (The formatting you apply affects only the letter, number, or symbol—not the following text.)

**Figure 24.7  Define New List Style Dialog Box**

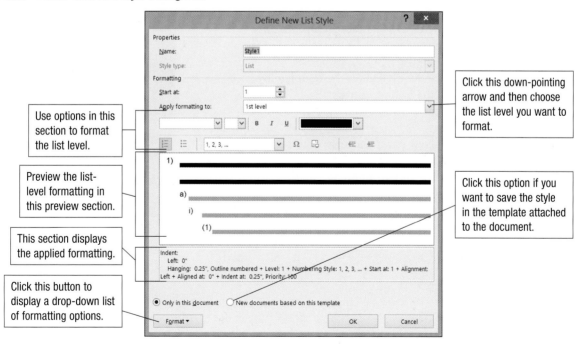

After specifying formatting for the first level, click the down-pointing arrow at the right of the *Apply formatting to* option box, click *2nd level*, and then apply the desired formatting for the second level. Continue in this manner until you have specified formatting for the desired number of levels.

## Updating a Template in an Existing Document

If you open a document based on a template and then create a style, you can specify that you want the style saved in the template and available for any future documents created with the template. A document based on a template is attached to the template. To save a style in a template, open a document based on the template, create a style, and then click the *New documents based on this template* option at the Create New Style dialog box. When you save the document, a message displays asking if you want to update the attached document template. At this message, click Yes.

---

**Exercise 24.3A**  **Saving a Document as a Template and Creating and Applying a Multilevel List Style**    Part 1 of 6

1. Open **BTListTableTemplate.docx** and then save it as a template by completing the following steps:
   a. Press the F12 key to display the Save As dialog box.
   b. At the Save As dialog box, click the *Save as type* option box and then click *Word Template (*.dotx)* at the drop-down list.
   c. Click in the *File name* text box, type your three initials followed by a hyphen, type **BTListTableTemplate**, and then press the Enter key.
   d. Close **XXX-BTListTableTemplate.dotx** (where your initials display in place of the *XXX*).
2. Open a document based on the template by completing the following steps:
   a. Click the FILE tab and then click the *New* option.
   b. At the New backstage area, click the *PERSONAL* option.
   c. Click the *XXX-BTListTableTemplate* thumbnail (where your initials display in place of the *XXX*).

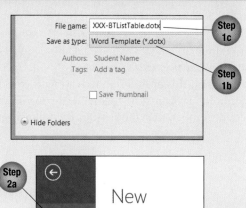

3. At the document based on the **XXX-BTListTableTemplate.dotx** template, create a multilevel list style by completing the following steps:

   a. Click the Multilevel List button in the Paragraph group on the HOME tab.

   b. Click the *Define New List Style* option that displays at the bottom of the drop-down list.

   c. At the Define New List Style dialog box, type **BTMultilevelList** in the *Name* text box.

   d. Click the down-pointing arrow at the right of the option box containing the text *1, 2, 3, ...* and then click *A, B, C, ...* at the drop-down list.

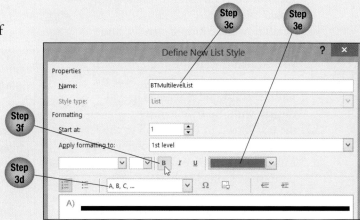

   e. Click the down-pointing arrow at the right of the *Font Color* option and then click the *Blue* color (eighth option in the *Standard Colors* section).

   f. Click the Bold button.

   g. Click the down-pointing arrow at the right of the *Apply formatting to* option box and then click *2nd level* at the drop-down list.

   h. Click the Symbol button that displays below the *Font Color* option.

   i. At the Symbol dialog box, change the font to Wingdings; scroll to the end of the list box; click the sun symbol (☀), which is located in approximately the fifth row from the bottom of the list box; and then click OK.

   j. At the Define New List Style dialog box, click the Bold button and then change the font color to Blue.

   k. Click the down-pointing arrow at the right of the *Apply formatting to* option box and then click *3rd level* at the drop-down list.

   l. Click the Symbol button.

   m. At the Symbol dialog box, make sure that Wingdings is selected as the font; scroll to the end of the list box; click the check mark symbol (✓), which is located in approximately the last row; and then click OK.

   n. At the Define New List Style dialog box, click the Bold button and then make sure the font color is Blue.

   o. Click the *New documents based on this template* option located near the bottom of the dialog box.

   p. Click OK to close the Define New List Style dialog box.

4. Close the document without saving it. At the message that displays asking if you want to save changes to **XXX-BTListTableTemplate.dotx**, click the Save button.

5. Open a document based on the template by completing the following steps:

   a. Click the FILE tab and then click the *New* option.

   b. At the New backstage area, click the *PERSONAL* option.

   c. Click the *XXX-BTListTableTemplate* thumbnail.

6. Insert a document into the current document by completing the following steps:

   a. Click the INSERT tab.

   b. Click the Object button arrow and then click *Text from File* at the drop-down list.

   c. Navigate to your Chapter24 folder and then double-click **BTTourList.docx**.

7. Apply the multilevel style you created by completing the following steps:
    a. Select the text you just inserted.
    b. Click the HOME tab and then click the Multilevel List button in the Paragraph group.
    c. Scroll down the drop-down list and then click the multilevel list style you created (located in the *List Styles* section). (Hover your mouse over the multilevel list and a ScreenTip will display with the style name.)

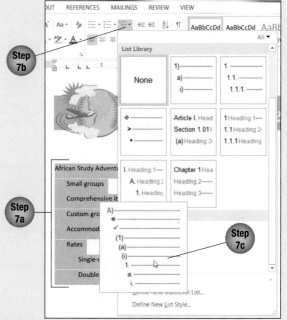

8. Add the text shown in Figure 24.8 to the document by completing the following steps:
    a. Move the insertion point so it is positioned immediately right of the text *Double-occupancy rate: $2,755* and then press the Enter key. (This moves the insertion point down to the next line and inserts a check mark bullet.)
    b. Click twice on the Decrease Indent button in the Paragraph group on the HOME tab to move the insertion point to the left margin. (This inserts *B)* in the document.)
    c. Type the text shown in Figure 24.8. (When typing the text, click the Increase Indent button to move the insertion point to the next level or click the Decrease Indent button to move the insertion point to the previous level.)
9. Click the DESIGN tab, click the Paragraph Spacing button in the Document Formatting group, and then click *Double* at the drop-down gallery.
10. Save the document in your Chapter24 folder and name it **C24-E03-BTTours**.
11. Print and then close **C24-E03-BTTours.docx**.
12. If you are working on a computer in a public environment such as a school, make a backup of **XXX-BTListTableTemplate.dotx** by copying **XXX-BTListTableTemplate.dotx** from the Custom Office Templates folder in the Documents folder on the local hard drive to your Chapter24 folder.

**Figure 24.8 Exercise 24.3A**

Southwest Sun Adventure
    Small groups
    Guided day trips
    Grand Canyon vistas
    Bilingual tour guides
    Rates
        Single-occupancy rate: $1,450
        Double-occupancy rate: $1,249

# Creating a Table Style

The TABLE TOOLS DESIGN tab contains a number of predesigned styles you can apply to a table. If none of these styles applies the desired formatting to a table, create your own table style.

Create a table style at the Create New Style from Formatting dialog box with *Table* selected in the *Style type* option box, as shown in Figure 24.9. Display this dialog box by clicking the More button at the right of the thumbnails in the Styles group on the HOME tab and then clicking *Create a Style*. At the Create New Style from Formatting dialog box, click the Modify button. Click the down-pointing arrow at the right of the *Style type* option and then click *Table* at the drop-down list. You can also display this dialog box by inserting a table in the document, clicking the More button that displays at the right of the thumbnails in the Table Styles group on the TABLE TOOLS DESIGN tab, and then clicking *New Table Style* at the drop-down list.

The Create New Style from Formatting dialog box with *Table* selected as the style type contains options for formatting the entire table or specific portions of the table. By default, *Whole table* is selected in the *Apply formatting to* option. With this option selected, any formatting options you choose will affect the entire table. To format a specific portion of the table, click the down-pointing arrow at the right of the *Apply formatting to* option and then click the desired option at the drop-down list. Using options at this drop-down list, you can specify that you want to apply formatting to sections in the table, such as the header row, total row, first column, last column, odd banded rows, even banded rows, and so on.

**Figure 24.9  Create New Style from Formatting Dialog Box with the Table Style Type Selected**

Use options in this section to format the whole table or specific portions of the table.

Click this down-pointing arrow and then choose the portion of the table to format.

Preview the table formatting in this section.

This section displays the applied formatting.

Click this button to display a drop-down list of formatting options.

1. Open **XXX-BTListTableTemplate.dotx** from the Custom Office Templates folder in the Documents folder on the local hard drive. If your template does not appear in the Custom Office Templates folder, open the template from your Chapter24 folder. (Open the template as a normal document at the Open dialog box [not through the New backstage area].)

2. Create a table style by completing the following steps:

   a. Click the More button at the right of the thumbnails in the Styles group on the HOME tab and then click *Create a Style* at the drop-down list.

   b. At the Create New Style from Formatting dialog box, type **BTTable** in the *Name* text box.

   c. Click the Modify button.

   d. At the Create New Style from Formatting dialog box, click the down-pointing arrow at the right of the *Style type* option box and then click *Table* at the drop-down list.

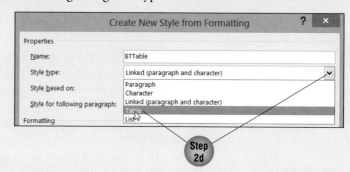

   e. Make sure *Whole table* is selected in the *Apply formatting to* option.

   f. Click the down-pointing arrow at the right of the *Font* option and then click *Constantia* at the drop-down list.

   g. Click the down-pointing arrow at the right of the *Font Size* option and then click *12* at the drop-down list.

   h. Click the down-pointing arrow at the right of the *Font Color* option and then click the *Dark Blue* color (ninth color option in the *Standard Colors* section).

   i. Click the Border button arrow and then click *All Borders* at the drop-down list. (See the image below to locate the button.)

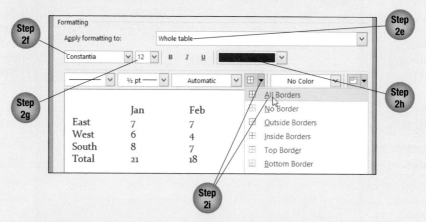

   j. Click the down-pointing arrow at the right of the *Apply formatting to* option and then click *Header row* at the drop-down list.

   k. Click the down-pointing arrow at the right of the *Font Size* option and then click *14* at the drop-down list.

   l. Click the Bold button.

   m. Click the down-pointing arrow at the right of the *Fill Color* option and then click *Orange, Accent 2, Lighter 40%* (sixth column, fourth row in the *Theme Colors* section).

n.  Click the Alignment button arrow located immediately right of the *Fill Color* option and then click *Align Center* at the drop-down list.

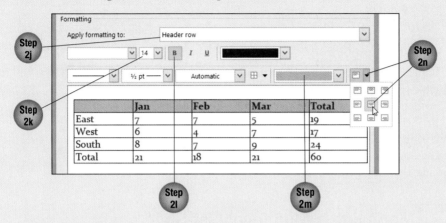

o.  Click the down-pointing arrow at the right of the *Apply formatting to* option and then click *Even banded rows* at the drop-down list.
p.  Click the *Fill Color* option and then click *Orange, Accent 2, Lighter 60%* (sixth column, third row in the *Theme Colors* section).
q.  Click OK to close the Create New Style from Formatting dialog box.
3.  If you opened the template from your Chapter24 folder, click the Save button on the Quick Access toolbar.
4.  Save the template to the Custom Office Templates folder by completing the following steps:
    a.  Press the F12 key to display the Save As dialog box.
    b.  Click the *Save as type* option box and then click *Word Document (*.docx)*.
    c.  Click the *Save as type* option box again and then click *Word Template (*.dotx)*. (This ensures that the Custom Office Templates folder is active.)
    d.  Click the Save button and then click Yes if a message displays asking if you want to replace the existing template.
    e.  Close **XXX-BTListTableTemplate.dotx**.
5.  Open a document based on the template by completing the following steps:
    a.  Click the FILE tab and then click the *New* option.
    b.  At the New backstage area, click the *PERSONAL* option.
    c.  Click the ***XXX-BTListTableTemplate.dotx*** template thumbnail (where your initials display in place of the *XXX*).
6.  Insert a document into the current document by completing the following steps:
    a.  Press the Enter key twice and then click the INSERT tab.
    b.  Click the Object button arrow and then click *Text from File* at the drop-down list.
    c.  Navigate to your Chapter24 folder and then double-click ***BTAdvTables.docx***.
7.  Apply the table style you created by completing the following steps:
    a.  Click in any cell in the top table.
    b.  Click the TABLE TOOLS DESIGN tab.

c. In the Table Styles group, click the table style you created. (Your table style should be the first thumbnail in the group. If it is not, click the More button at the right of the thumbnails and then click your table style at the drop-down gallery. To find your table style, hover the mouse pointer over a table and wait for the ScreenTip to display the style name.)

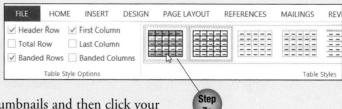

8. Apply your table style to the two other tables in the document.
9. Save the document and name it **C24-E03-BTTables.docx**.
10. Print and then close the document.

## Modifying a Multilevel List Style

Like other styles, a multilevel list style can be modified. To do this, click the Multilevel List button, scroll down the drop-down list to display the style you want to modify, right-click the style, and then click *Modify* at the shortcut menu. This displays the Modify Style dialog box, which contains the same formatting options as the Create New Style from Formatting dialog box.

## Modifying a Table Style

You can modify a table style that you created or modify one of the predesigned table styles. To modify a table style, open the document containing the desired table style you want to modify. Click in a table with that style applied or insert a new table in the document. Click the TABLE TOOLS DESIGN tab, right-click the table style, and then click *Modify Table Style* at the shortcut menu. (If the desired table style is not visible, click the More button that displays at the right of the table styles.) This displays the Modify Style dialog box, which contains the same formatting options as the Create New Style from Formatting dialog box.

**Exercise 24.3C**  Modifying a Table Style                          Part 3 of 6

1. Open **C24-E03-BTTables.docx** and then save the document with the name **C24-E03-BTTablesModified**.
2. Modify the table style you created by completing the following steps:
    a. Click in any cell in the top table.
    b. Click the TABLE TOOLS DESIGN tab.
    c. Your table style should be the first thumbnail in the Table Styles group. (If your table style is not visible, click the More button at the right of the thumbnails and then locate your table style.)
    d. Right-click your table style and then click *Modify Table Style* at the shortcut menu.
    e. At the Modify Style dialog box, click the Format button that displays in the lower left corner of the dialog box and then click *Table Properties* at the drop-down list.

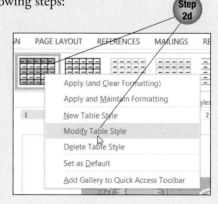

f.  At the Table Properties dialog box with the Table tab selected, click the *Center* option in the *Alignment* section.

g.  Click OK to close the Table Properties dialog box.

h.  Click the down-pointing arrow at the right of the *Apply formatting to* option and then click *Odd banded rows* at the drop-down list.

i.  Click the *Fill Color* option and then click *Blue, Accent 1, Lighter 80%* (fifth column, second row in the *Theme Colors* section).

j.  Click the *New document based on this template* option (located near the bottom of the dialog box).

k.  Click OK to close the Modify Style dialog box. (Notice that the formatting changes for the three tables in the document because the table style is applied to each table.)

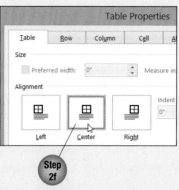

Step 2f

3.  Select the second row in the top table of the document, press Ctrl + B to apply bold formatting, and then press Ctrl + E to center the text in the cells.

4.  Apply bold formatting to and center-align the second row in the middle table and the second row in the bottom table.

5.  Save and then print **C24-E03-BTTablesModified.docx**. (At the message asking if you want to save the changes to the template, click the Yes button.)

6.  Close **C24-E03-BTTablesModified.docx**.

7.  If you are working on a public computer, copy the **XXX-BTListTableTemplate.dotx** template from the Custom Office Templates folder in the Documents folder on the local hard drive to your Chapter24 folder.

# Using the Style Inspector

As you continue working with styles and creating and applying styles to documents, situations may arise in which you have applied multiple styles to text. If multiple styles are applied to text and the formatting applied is not what you intended, you can investigate the document styles using the Style Inspector. Turn on the Style Inspector by clicking the Styles group task pane launcher to display the Styles task pane and then clicking the Style Inspector button that displays at the bottom of the task pane. The Style Inspector displays paragraph- and text-level formatting for the paragraph where the insertion point is positioned. Figure 24.9 displays the Style Inspector with the insertion point positioned in the title in the C24-E03-BTZenith.docx document.

**Figure 24.9  Style Inspector**

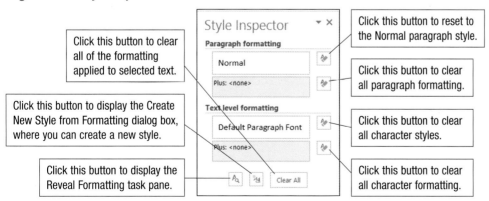

The *Paragraph formatting* option box and the *Text level formatting* option box display style formatting applied to the selected text or character where the insertion point is positioned. A box displays below each option that contains the word *Plus:* followed by any additional formatting that is not specific to the style formatting.

Hover your mouse over the *Paragraph formatting* option box or *Text level formatting* option box and a down-pointing arrow displays. Click the arrow and a drop-down list displays with options for clearing the formatting applied to the text, applying a new style, and displaying the Reveal Formatting task pane. Click the New Style button, which displays to the right of the Reveal Formatting button, and the Create New Style from Formatting dialog box displays.

Use the buttons that display at the right of the *Paragraph formatting* option box to return the paragraph style back to the Normal style and clear any paragraph formatting applied to the text. Use the buttons at the right of the *Text level formatting* option box to clear character formatting applied to text.

---

## Exercise 24.3D   Using the Style Inspector                          Part 4 of 6

1. Open **C24-E02-BTZenith.docx** and then save the document with the name **C24-E03-BTZenith**.
2. Click anywhere in the title *Extreme Adventures*.
3. Click the Styles group task pane launcher. (This displays the Styles task pane.)
4. Turn on the Style Inspector by clicking the Style Inspector button that displays at the bottom of the Styles task pane.

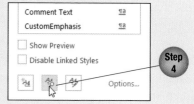

5. At the Style Inspector, hover the mouse pointer over the *Paragraph formatting* option box and then look at the information about the custom title style that displays in the ScreenTip.
6. Click anywhere in the heading *Antarctic Adventures*.
7. Hover the mouse pointer over the *Paragraph formatting* option and then look at the information that displays about the custom heading.

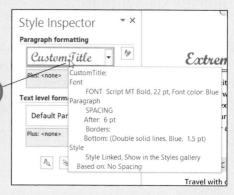

8. Remove paragraph and character styles and apply a style to text in the document by completing the following steps:
   a. Select the lines of text in the *Antarctic Adventures* section that contain money amounts.
   b. Remove the paragraph style from the text by clicking the Reset to Normal Paragraph Style button that displays at the right of the *Paragraph formatting* option box.
   c. Remove the character style from the text by clicking the Clear Character Style button that displays at the right of the *Text level formatting* option box.
   d. Click the *Block Text* style that displays in the Styles task pane.

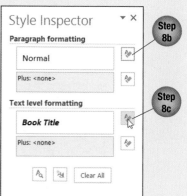

9. Select the lines of text in the *Tall-Ship Adventures* section that contain money amounts and then complete Steps 8b through 8d to remove styles and apply a style.

10. Select the lines of text in the *Bicycling Adventures* section that contain money amounts and then complete Steps 8b through 8d to remove styles and apply a style.

11. Close the Style Inspector by clicking the Close button (contains an *X*) that displays in the upper right corner of the Style Inspector.

12. Save **C24-E03-BTZenith.docx**.

# Managing Styles

The Manage Styles dialog box provides one location for managing your styles. Display this dialog box, as shown in Figure 24.10, by clicking the Manage Styles button that displays at the bottom of the Styles task pane. You can also display the Manage Styles dialog box by clicking the Paragraph Spacing button in the Document Formatting group on the DESIGN tab and then clicking *Custom Paragraph Spacing* at the drop-down gallery.

**Figure 24.10 Manage Styles Dialog Box**

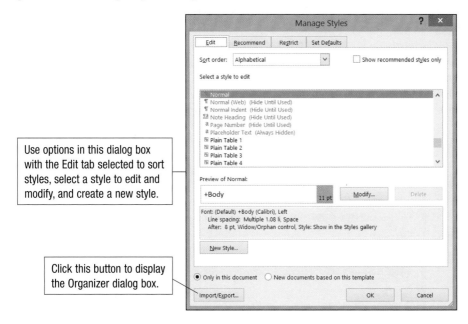

Use options in this dialog box with the Edit tab selected to sort styles, select a style to edit and modify, and create a new style.

Click this button to display the Organizer dialog box.

The options available in the Manage Styles dialog box vary depending on which tab is selected. Select the Edit tab and you have options to sort styles, select a style to edit and modify, and create a new style.

Click the Recommend tab and options display for specifying which styles you want to display in the Styles pane and in what order. With the Recommend tab selected, styles display in the list box preceded by priority numbers. Styles display in ascending order, with the styles preceded by the lowest numbers displaying first. You can change the priority of a style by clicking the style in the list box and then clicking the Move Up button, Move Down button, or Move Last button, or you can assign a value number with the Assign Value button.

With the Restrict tab selected, you can permit or restrict access to styles. This allows you to control which styles other individuals can apply or modify in a document.

Click the Set Defaults tab to display character and formatting options. You can specify whether changes made in this dialog box will affect the current document or all documents based on the current document. If you are using the default document, changes will affect the Normal.dotm template.

1. With **C24-E03-BTZenith.docx** open, make sure the Styles task pane displays. (If not, click the Styles group task pane launcher.)
2. Click anywhere in the first paragraph of text. (Do not click a title or heading.)
3. Click the Manage Styles button that displays at the bottom of the Styles task pane.
4. At the Manage Styles dialog box, make sure the Edit tab is active. (If not, click the Edit tab.)
5. Click the *Show recommended styles only* check box to insert a check mark. (This causes only the styles recommended by Word [along with your custom styles] to display in the *Select a style to edit* list box.)
6. Make sure *As Recommended* is selected in the *Sort order* option box. (If it is not, click the down-pointing arrow at the right of the *Sort order* option box and then click *As Recommended* at the drop-down list.)
7. Create a new style by completing the following steps:
    a. Click the New Style button that displays near the lower left corner of the dialog box.

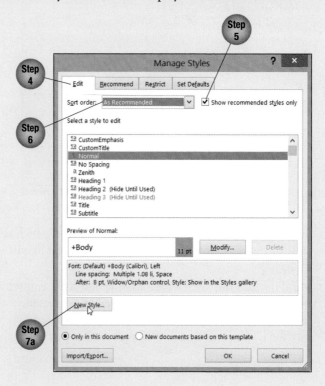

b. At the Create New Style from Formatting dialog box, type your two initials in the *Name* text box followed by **CoNameEmphasis**.
c. Click the down-pointing arrow at the right of the *Style type* list box and then click *Character* at the drop-down list.
d. Click the Bold button in the *Formatting* section of the dialog box.
e. Click the Italic button.
f. Click the down-pointing arrow at the right of the *Font Color* option and then click the *Dark Blue* color (ninth option in the *Standard Colors* section).
g. Click the *Add to the Styles gallery* check box located near the lower left corner of the dialog box to insert a check mark. (Skip this step if the check box already contains a check mark.)
h. Click OK to close the Create New Style from Formatting dialog box.

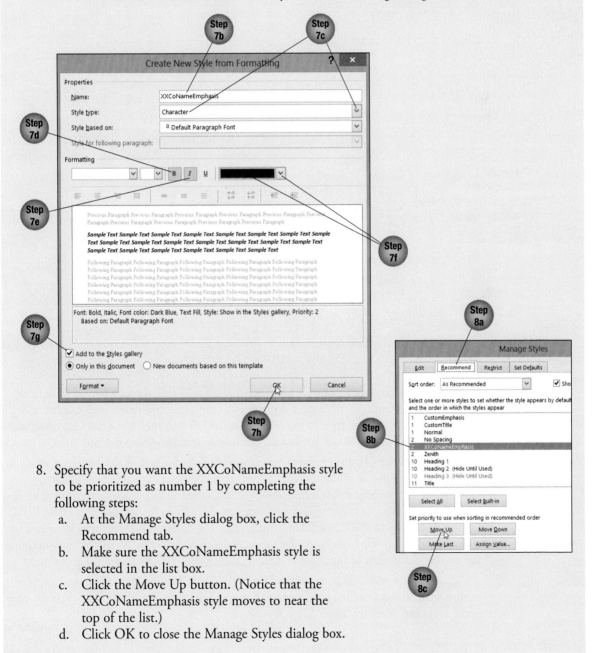

8. Specify that you want the XXCoNameEmphasis style to be prioritized as number 1 by completing the following steps:
   a. At the Manage Styles dialog box, click the Recommend tab.
   b. Make sure the XXCoNameEmphasis style is selected in the list box.
   c. Click the Move Up button. (Notice that the XXCoNameEmphasis style moves to near the top of the list.)
   d. Click OK to close the Manage Styles dialog box.

9. Select the company name *Bayside Travel* in the first paragraph of the document and then apply the XXCoNameEmphasis style (where your initials display in place of the *XX*).
10. Select the company name *Bayside Travel* in the last paragraph of the document and then apply the XXCoNameEmphasis style (where your initials display in place of the *XX*).
11. Close the Styles task pane.
12. Save and then print **C24-E03-BTZenith.docx**.

If you create a style (or styles) for a specific document or template and then decide that you want to copy the style to the default template, Normal.dotm, or another template, copy the style using the Organizer dialog box with the Styles tab selected, as shown in Figure 24.11. Display this dialog box by clicking the Import/Export button at the Manage Styles dialog box.

**Figure 24.11  Organizer Dialog Box**

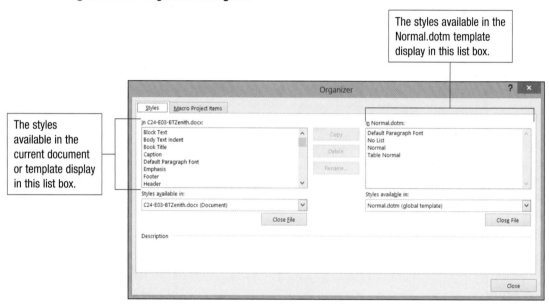

The styles available in the Normal.dotm template display in this list box.

The styles available in the current document or template display in this list box.

At the Organizer dialog box with the Styles tab selected, you can copy a style from a document or template to another document or template and delete and rename styles. To copy a style, click the style in the list box at the left and then click the Copy button that displays between the two list boxes. Complete similar steps to delete a style.

By default, the Organizer dialog box displays in the list box at the left templates available in the open document and the list box at the right displays the templates available in the Normal.dotm template. Choose a different document or template by clicking the Close File button. This removes the styles from the list box and changes the Close File button to the Open File button. Choose a different document or template by clicking the Open File button. At the Open dialog box, navigate to the folder containing the desired document or template and then double-click the document or template.

To rename a style, click the desired style in the list box and then click the Rename button that displays between the two list boxes. At the Rename dialog box, type the new name and then press the Enter key.

1. The **XXX-BTTemplate.dotx** and **XXX-BTListTableTemplate.dotx** templates both contain styles for formatting Bayside Travel documents. Copy the Bayside Travel styles in **XXX-BTListTableTemplate.dotx** to **XXX-BTTemplate.dotx** by completing the following steps:
   a. Press Ctrl + N to display a blank document.
   b. Display the Styles task pane.
   c. Click the Manage Styles button located near the bottom of the Styles task pane.
   d. At the Manage Styles dialog box, click the Import/Export button located in the lower left corner of the dialog box.
   e. At the Organizer dialog box, click the Close File button located below the left list box.
   f. Click the Open File button (previously the Close File button).
   g. At the Open dialog box, click the *Documents* folder in the Navigation pane and then double-click the *Custom Office Templates* folder in the Content pane. (Make sure you click the *Documents* folder to display the *Custom Office Templates* folder.)
   h. Double-click **XXX-BTListTableTemplate.dotx** in the Content pane (where your initials display in place of the *XXX*). (If your template is not available in the Custom Office Templates folder, navigate to your Chapter24 folder and then double-click **XXX-BTListTableTemplate.dotx**.)
   i. Click the Close File button located below the right list box.
   j. Click the Open File button (previously the Close File button).
   k. At the Open dialog box, click the *Documents* folder in the Navigation pane and then double-click the *Custom Office Templates* folder in the Content pane.
   l. Double-click **XXX-BTTemplate.dotx** in the Content pane (where your initials display in place of the *XXX*). (If your template is not available in the Custom Office Templates folder, navigate to your Chapter24 folder and then double-click **XXX-BTTemplate.dotx**.)
   m. Click the *BTTable* style in the left list box.
   n. Click the Copy button that displays between the two list boxes.

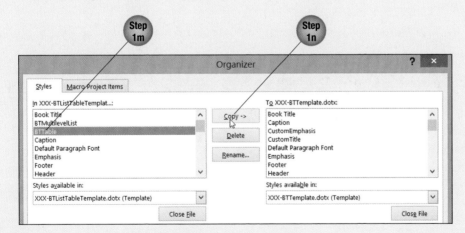

   o. Click the *BTMultiLevelList* style in the left list box.
   p. Click the Copy button that displays between the two list boxes.
   q. Click the Close button to close the Organizer dialog box.
   r. If a message asking if you want to save the changes made to **XXX-BTTemplate.dotx**, click the Save button.

2. If you copied styles from templates from your Chapter24 folder, copy the **XXX-BTTemplate.dotx** template from your Chapter24 folder to the Custom Office Templates folder in the Documents folder on the local hard drive.

3. Open a document based on **XXX-BTTemplate.dotx** by completing the following steps:
   a. Click the FILE tab and then click the *New* option.
   b. Click the *PERSONAL* option.
   c. Click the **XXX-BTTemplate.dotx** template thumbnail (where your initials display in place of the *XXX*).

4. Insert a document into the existing document by completing the following steps:
   a. Click the INSERT tab.
   b. Click the Object button arrow and then click *Text from File* at the drop-down list.
   c. Navigate to your Chapter24 folder and then double-click ***BTEastAdventures.docx***.

5. Apply the following styles to the document:
   a. Apply the CustomTitle style to the title *Eastern Adventures*.
   b. Apply the CustomHeading style to the two headings in the document.
   c. Apply the BTTables style to the two tables in the document.

6. Save the document and name it **C24-E03-BTEastAdventures**. If a message displays asking if you want to save changes to the document template, click Yes.

7. Print and then close **C24-E03-BTEastAdventures.docx**.

8. Delete any templates you have saved in the Custom Office Templates folder by completing the following steps:
   a. Press Ctrl + F12 to display the Open dialog box.
   b. Click the *Documents* folder in the Navigation pane.
   c. Double-click the *Custom Office Templates* folder in the Content pane.
   d. Click the first template in the Content pane that begins with your initials.
   e. Hold down the Ctrl key and then click any other templates that begin with your initials.
   f. Click the Organize button on the toolbar.
   g. Click *Delete* at the drop-down list.
   h. Click the Cancel button to close the Open dialog box.
   i. If necessary, close the Styles task pane.

# Chapter Summary

- A style is a set of formatting instructions that can be applied to text. Word provides a number of predesigned styles that are grouped into style sets.

- You can apply styles in four ways: click the style thumbnail in the Styles group, click the More button at the right of the thumbnails in the Styles group and then click the style at the drop-down gallery, use options at the Styles task pane, or use options at the Apply Styles window.

- Click the Styles group task pane launcher to display the Styles task pane.

- Display the Apply Styles window by clicking the More button at the right of the thumbnails in the Styles group and then clicking *Apply Style* at the drop-down gallery.

- You can create a style based on existing formatting or style formatting or by modifying an existing style. You can also create a new style without first applying formatting to text.

- Create a style at the Create New Style from Formatting dialog box. Display this dialog box by clicking the More button at the right of the thumbnails in the Styles group on the HOME tab and then clicking *Create a Style* at the drop-down gallery.

- Use options at the expanded Create New Style from Formatting dialog box to name the style and specify the style type and style formatting.

- A keyboard shortcut can be assigned to a style with options at the Customize Keyboard dialog box. Display this dialog box by clicking the Format button at the expanded Create New Style from Formatting dialog box and then clicking *Shortcut key* at the drop-down list.

- An advantage of applying styles is that when you modify a style, all of the text in the document to which that style has been applied updates automatically.

- To make the styles in a document available for future documents, save the document as a template. Do this by displaying the Save As dialog box, changing the *Save as type* option to *Word Template (*.dotx)*, and then clicking the Save button.

- Open a document based on a template by clicking the FILE tab and then clicking the *New* option. At the New backstage area, click the *PERSONAL* option and then click the template thumbnail.

- Reveal style formatting by hovering the mouse over a style in the Styles task pane and then clicking the *Show Preview* check box in the Styles task pane or by pressing Shift + F1 to turn on the display of the Reveal Formatting task pane.

- Save custom styles in a style set by clicking the DESIGN tab, clicking the More button at the right side of the style set thumbnails, and then clicking *Save as a New Style Set* at the drop-down gallery. At the Save as a New Style Set dialog box, type a name for the new style set and then click the Save button. The custom style set will be available for all future documents based on the Normal.dotm template.

- Delete a custom style set by clicking the More button at the right side of the style set thumbnails in the Document Formatting group on the DESIGN tab, right-clicking the custom style set, and then clicking *Delete* at the shortcut menu.

- Change default settings by choosing a style set, theme, theme colors, theme fonts, theme effects, and/or paragraph spacing and then clicking the Set as Default button in the Document Formatting group on the DESIGN tab.

- Create a multilevel list style at the Define New List Style dialog box. Display this dialog box by clicking the Multilevel List button in the Paragraph group on the HOME tab and then clicking *Define New Style List*.

- You can also create a multilevel list style at the Create New Style from Formatting dialog box with the *Style type* option changed to *List*. Specify formatting for each desired level in the list.

- ➤ A multilevel list style displays in the *List Styles* section of the Multilevel List button drop-down list.
- ➤ Create a table style at the Create New Style from Formatting dialog box with *Table* selected in the *Style type* option box. Specify formatting for the entire table or specific portions of the table.
- ➤ A table style that you create displays in the Table Styles group on the TABLE TOOLS DESIGN tab.
- ➤ Modify a multilevel list style by clicking the Multilevel List button, right-clicking the desired style, and then clicking *Modify* at the shortcut menu. This displays the Modify Style dialog box, where you can specify the desired changes.
- ➤ Modify a table style by clicking in a table, clicking the TABLE TOOLS DESIGN tab, right-clicking the desired table style, and then clicking *Modify Table Style* at the shortcut menu. This displays the Modify Style dialog box, where you can specify the desired changes.
- ➤ Use the Style Inspector to investigate the styles applied to text in a document. Display the Style Inspector by displaying the Styles task pane and then clicking the Style Inspector button that displays at the bottom of the task pane.
- ➤ The Manage Styles dialog box provides one location for managing styles. Display this dialog box by clicking the Manage Styles button that displays at the bottom of the Styles task pane.
- ➤ Copy styles from a template or document to another template or document with options at the Organizer dialog box. Display this dialog box by clicking the Import/Export button that displays in the bottom left corner of the Manage Styles dialog box. You can also delete and rename styles at the Organizer dialog box.

# *Commands* Review

| FEATURE | RIBBON TAB, GROUP | BUTTON, OPTION | KEYBOARD SHORTCUT |
|---|---|---|---|
| Apply Styles window | HOME, Styles | ⊽, *Apply Styles* | Ctrl + Shift + S |
| Create New Style from Formatting dialog box | HOME, Styles | ⊽, *Create a Style* | |
| Manage Styles dialog box | HOME, Styles | ▣, 🖳 | |
| Organizer dialog box | HOME, Styles | ▣, 🖳, Import/Export... | |
| Reveal Formatting task pane | | | Shift + F1 |
| Style Inspector | HOME, Styles | ▣, 🖳 | |
| Style Pane Options dialog box | HOME, Styles | ▣, Options | |
| Styles task pane | HOME, Styles | ▣ | Alt + Ctrl + Shift + S |

# Key Points Review

**Completion:** In the space provided at the right, indicate the correct term, symbol, or command.

1. Use this keyboard shortcut to display the Styles task pane. _____

2. Character styles display in the Styles task pane followed by this symbol. _____

3. If you hover the mouse pointer over a style in the Styles task pane, this displays with information about the formatting applied. _____

4. To create a style based on text with existing formatting, select the text, click the More button, and then click this option at the drop-down gallery. _____

5. Assign a keyboard shortcut to a style with options at this dialog box. _____

6. To modify an existing style, do this to the style in the Styles group and then click *Modify* at the shortcut menu. _____

7. At the Save As dialog box, save a document as a template by changing the *Save as type* option to this. _____

8. By default, Word saves a template document in this folder on the local hard drive. _____

9. Use this keyboard shortcut to display the Reveal Formatting task pane. _____

10. Create a multilevel list style with options at the Create New Style from Formatting dialog box with the *Style type* changed to *List* or with options at this dialog box. _____

11. To modify a table style, click in a table, click the TABLE TOOLS DESIGN tab, right-click the table style, and then click this option at the shortcut menu. _____

12. Use this feature to investigate the styles applied to text in a document. _____

13. Use options at the Manage Styles dialog box with this tab selected to sort styles, select a style to edit and modify, and create a new style. _____

14. Copy a style from one template to another at this dialog box. _____

# Chapter Assessments

## Applying Your Skills

Demonstrate your knowledge of features learned in this chapter by completing the following assessments.

### Assessment 24.1    Create and Apply Styles to a Committee Report

1. Open **KMStyles.docx** and save the document with the name **C24-A01-KMStyles**.
2. Create a style based on the formatting of the *KodiakTitle* text and name it *KodiakTitle*. (Make sure you select the paragraph symbol with the text.)
3. Press Ctrl + End to move the insertion point to the end of the document and then create a new style named *KodiakQuote*. Apply the following formatting at the Create New Style from Formatting expanded dialog box:
   a. Change the left and right indents to 0.5 inch and the spacing after paragraphs to 12 points. ***Hint: Display these formatting options by clicking the Format button in the lower left corner of the dialog box and then clicking*** **Paragraph.**
   b. Click the Italic button.
   c. Change the font color to Dark Blue.
   d. Insert a blue, single-line top border and a blue, single-line bottom border. ***Hint: Display these formatting options by clicking the Format button and then clicking*** **Border.**
4. At the document, press the Up Arrow key once and then create a style named *KodiakHeading* and apply the following formatting:
   a. Change the font to Copperplate Gothic Bold.
   b. Change the font color to Blue.
5. Save the styles you created in a style set named with your three initials followed by *Kodiak*.
6. Save and then close **C24-A01-KMStyles.docx**.
7. Open **KMReport.docx** and then save the document with the name **C24-A01-KMReport**.
8. Change to the style set named with your initials followed by *Kodiak*.
9. Apply the KodiakTitle style to the two titles in the document: *Audit Committee Report* and *Compensation Committee Report*.
10. Apply the KodiakHeading style to the four headings in the report: *Committee Responsibilities, Fees to Independent Auditor, Compensation Philosophy*, and *Competitive Compensation*.
11. Apply the KodiakQuote style to the second paragraph of text in the document (the paragraph that begins *Assist the company's board of directors*).
12. Edit the KodiakTitle style by changing the font color to Dark Blue and underlining the text.
13. Edit the KodiakHeading style by changing the font color to Dark Blue.
14. Turn on the display of the Styles task pane and then display all of the styles in alphabetical order. ***Hint: Do this at the Style Pane Options dialog box.***
15. Select the bulleted text in the *Committee Responsibilities* section and then apply the Block Text style. With the text still selected, click the Font Color button on the HOME tab and then click the *Dark Blue* color.
16. Select the bulleted text in the *Compensation Philosophy* section, apply the Block Text style, and then change the font color to Dark Blue.
17. Save the modified styles as a style set with the same name (your initials followed by *Kodiak*). (At the Save as a New Style Set dialog box, click your style set name in the Content pane and then click the Save button. At the message asking if you want to replace the existing file, click Yes.)
18. Save and then print **C24-A01-KMReport.docx**.
19. Select and then delete the contents of the document (except the header).

20. Save the document as a template (in the Custom Office Templates folder) and name it **XXX-KMStyles** (using your initials in place of the *XXX*).
21. Close the template.

## Assessment 24.2    Create and Apply Multilevel List and Table Styles

1. Open **KMListTable.docx**.
2. Click the Multilevel List button in the Paragraph group on the HOME tab, click *Define New List Style*, and then create a style named *KMList*. Apply the following formatting at the Define New List Style dialog box:
   a. For the first level numbering, change the font to Cambria, apply bold formatting, and change the font color to Dark Blue.
   b. For the second level numbering, specify the snowflake symbol (❈) as the bullet, apply bold formatting, and change the font color to Dark Blue. *Note: The snowflake symbol is located in approximately the third or fourth row in the Symbol dialog box with the Wingdings font selected.*
3. At the document, select and then delete the contents of the document (except the header).
4. Save the document as a template and name the template **XXX-KMListTable.dotx** (using your initials in place of the *XXX*).
5. Close the template.
6. Open a document based on your **XXX-KMListTable.dotx** template. *Hint: Do this at the New backstage area.*
7. Insert the document named **KMAgendas.docx** into the current document.
8. Change to the style set named with your initials followed by *Kodiak*.
9. Apply the KodiakTitle style to the title *Kodiak Annual Meeting*.
10. Apply the KodiakHeading style to the two headings in the document: *Finance Department Agenda* and *Research Department Agenda*.
11. Select the text below the *Finance Department Agenda* heading and then apply the KMList multilevel list style. *Hint: Do this with the Multilevel List button in the Paragraph group on the HOME tab.*
12. Select the text below the *Research Department Agenda* heading and then apply the KMList multilevel list style.
13. Save the document and name it **C24-A02-KMAgendas.docx**.
14. Print and then close **C24-A02-KMAgendas.docx**.
15. In Word, open the template **XXX-KMListTable.dotx** from the Custom Office Templates folder in the Documents folder on your local hard drive.
16. Create a table style at the Create New Style from Formatting dialog box with the following specifications:
   a. Type **KMTable** in the *Name* text box.
   b. At the expanded Create New Style from Formatting dialog box, change the *Style type* to *Table*.
   c. For the whole table, change the font to Cambria and the color to Dark Blue, click the Border button arrow and then click *All Borders*, and then, if necessary, change the border color to Blue.
   d. For the header row, change the font size to 12 points; apply bold formatting; change the font color to White, Background 1; and apply the Blue, Accent 1, Darker 25% fill color (fifth column, fifth row in the *Theme Colors* section).
   e. For the odd banded rows, apply a fill color of Blue, Accent 1, Lighter 80% (fifth column, second row in the *Theme Colors* setion).
17. Save and then close **XXX-KMListTable.dotx**.
18. Press Ctrl + N to display a blank document and then delete the XXXKodiak style set (where your initials display in place of the *XXX*).

## Assessment 24.3    Organize Styles

1. With a blank document open, display the Organizer dialog box. *Hint: Click the Styles group task pane launcher, click the Manage Styles button, and then click the Import/Export button.*
2. At the Organizer dialog box, click the Close File button located below the left list box and then click the Open File button. At the Open dialog box, click the *Documents* folder in the Navigation pane, double-click the *Custom Office Templates* folder in the Content pane, and then double-click **XXX-KMListTable.dotx**.
3. Click the Close File button located below the right list box and then click the Open File button. At the Open dialog box, click the *Documents* folder in the Navigation pane, double-click the *Custom Office Templates* folder in the Content pane, and then double-click **XXX-KMStyles.dotx**.
4. Copy the KMList and KMTable styles from the left list box in the Organizer dialog box to the right list box and then close the dialog box. At the message that displays asking if you want to save the changes to XXX-KMStyles.dotx, click the Save button.
5. Open a document based on the **XXX-KMStyles.dotx** template. *Hint: Do this at the New backstage area.*
6. Insert the file named **KMSales.docx** and then save the document with the name **C24-A03-KMSales**.
7. Apply the KodiakTitle style to the title *Quarterly Sales*.
8. Apply the KodiakHeading style to the four headings in the document.
9. Apply the KMTable style to the four tables in the document.
10. Save, print, and then close **C24-A03-KMSales.docx**.
11. Close the Styles task pane and then close the blank document without saving changes.

# Expanding Your Skills

Explore additional feature options or use Help to learn a new skill in creating this document.

## Assessment 24.4    Modify a Predesigned Table Style

1. In this chapter, you learned how to create a table style and apply all of the formatting to the style. You can also create a style based on an existing predesigned table style. At a blank document, insert a table with a couple of rows and columns and then determine how to modify an existing table style. After experimenting with modifying a table style, close the document without saving it.
2. Open **NSSTables.docx** and save the document with the name **C24-A04-NSSTables**.
3. Click in any cell in the top table and then click the TABLE TOOLS DESIGN tab.
4. Modify the List Table 1 Light - Accent 1 table style (second column, first row in *List Tables* section) by changing the name to *NSSTable* and then apply the following formatting:
   a. For the whole table, change the font to Candara and change the alignment to Align Center. *Hint: The alignment button is located to the right of the Fill Color button.*
   b. For the whole table, change the table alignment to Center. *Hint: Do this at the Table Properties dialog box with the Table tab selected. Display this dialog box by clicking the Format button and then clicking* Table Properties.
   c. For the header row, change the fill color to Blue, Accent 1, Lighter 60% (fifth column, third row in *Theme Colors* section).
   d. For the first column, change the alignment to Align Center Left and remove the bold formatting.
   e. For odd banded rows, change the fill color to Green, Accent 6, Lighter 80% (last column, second row in *Theme Colors* section).
   f. For even banded rows, change the fill color to Blue, Accent 1, Lighter 80% (fifth column, second row in *Theme Colors* section).

5. After modifying the table style, apply the table style to the four tables in the document. (The NSSTable style is located in the *List Tables* section of the drop-down gallery.)
6. Save, print, and then close **C24-A04-NSSTables.docx**.

# Achieving Signature Status

Take your skills to the next level by completing this more challenging assessment.

## Assessment 24.5    Design, Apply, and Organize Styles

1. Open **RPLtrhd.docx** and save the document with the name **C24-A05-RPStyles**.
2. Looking at the letterhead font and colors, create a title style, heading style, and quote style. You determine the formatting and names of the styles.
3. Save the styles in a style set and name it *XXXRPhoto* (using your initials in place of the *XXX*).
4. Save and then close **C24-A05-RPStyles.docx**.
5. Open **RPReport.docx** and save the document with the name **C24-A05-RPReport**.
6. Apply the XXXRPhoto style set.
7. Apply the title style you created to the text *Photography*, *Camera Basics*, and *Digital Cameras*.
8. Apply the heading style you created to the text *Pixels*, *Aspect Ratio*, and *White Balance*.
9. Apply the quote style you created to the first paragraph and last paragraph of the document.
10. Save and then print **C24-A05-RPReport.docx** and then select all of the report content and delete it.
11. Save **C24-A05-RPReport.docx** as a template in the Custom Office Templates folder and name it **XXX-RPStyles** (using your initials in place of the *XXX*).
12. Close the template.
13. At a blank document, write a memo to your instructor that describes the three styles you created, including the name of each style and the formatting you applied to it. Save the completed document and name it **C24-A05-MemotoInstructor**. Print and then close **C24-A05-MemotoInstructor.docx**.

14. At a blank document, create a table style for Real Photography. (You determine the name and formatting.) Save the document and name it **C24-A05-TableStyle**.
15. Open the Manage Styles dialog box from the Styles task pane and display the Organizer dialog box. Copy the table style you created to the **XXX-RPStyles.dotx** template and then close the document.
16. Create a document based on the **XXX-RPStyles.dotx** template.
17. Insert the document named **RPTables.docx**.
18. Apply your title style to the text *July Weekly Invoices*, apply your heading style to the four headings, and apply your table style to the four tables.
19. Save the document and name it **C24-A05-RPTables**.
20. Make sure all of the tables display on one page. You may need to delete blank lines between headings and tables or remove blank lines at the end of the document.
21. Print and then close **C24-A05-RPTables.docx**.
22. At a blank document, delete the style set you created.

# Chapter 25

# Protecting, Preparing, and Sharing Documents

## Performance Objectives

Upon successful completion of Chapter 25, you will be able to:

- Protect a document by restricting formatting and editing and by controlling access and viewing
- Modify document properties by viewing and modifying document information
- Restrict access to a document and verify its authenticity
- Inspect a document for accessibility and compatibility issues and manage versions of a document
- Share documents between programs, computers, and websites and as email attachments

In Chapter 20, you learned to perform workgroup activities such as inserting comments into a document, tracking changes made by other users, comparing documents, and combining documents from multiple users. In this chapter, you will learn how to protect the integrity of shared documents, limit formatting and editing by other users, prepare documents for distribution, and share and present documents online.

*Note: Before beginning computer exercises for this chapter, copy to your storage medium the Chapter25 folder from the CD that accompanies this textbook and then make Chapter25 the active folder.*

In this chapter, students will produce the following documents:

Exercise 25.1. C25-E01-TECAnnualReport.docx
Exercise 25.3. C25-E03-REAgrmnt.docx
Exercise 25.4. C25-E04-Lease.docx
Exercise 25.5. C25-E05-BTZTAdventures.docx
Exercise 25.6. C25-E06-BTZTAdv.docx

Model answers for these exercises are shown on the following pages.

**Exercise 25.1**

C25-E01-TECAnnualReport.docx

## TERRA ENERGY CORPORATION

### Overview

Terra Energy Corporation is a development stage company that was incorporated on May 1, 2009. The corporation and its subsidiary (collectively referred to as the "Company") designs, develops, configures, and offers for sale power systems that provide highly reliable, high-quality, environmentally friendly power. The Company has segmented the potential markets for its products into two broad categories: high-energy, high-power, uninterruptible power system (UPS), and high-power distributed generation and utility power-grid energy storage system. We have available for sale several high-energy products that deliver a low level of power over a long period of time (typically measured in hours). These products are tailored to the telecommunications, cable systems, computer networks, and Internet markets.

We are developing a new high-energy product for potential applications in the renewable energy market for both photovoltaic and wind turbine uses. As part of exploring these markets, we have committed to invest $2 million in Clear Sun Energies and we have purchased the inverter electronics technology of Technology Pacific[SN1].

We have taken significant actions over the last eighteen months to reduce our expenditures for product development, infrastructure, and production readiness. Our headcount, development spending, and capital expenditures have been significantly reduced. We have continued the preliminary design and development of potential products for markets under consideration and with specific approval by the Company's board of directors.

### Research and Development

We believe that our research and development efforts are essential to our ability to successfully design and deliver our products to our targeted customers, as well as to modify and improve them to reflect the evolution of markets and customer needs. Our research and development team has worked closely with potential customers to define product features and performance to address specific needs. Our research and development expenses, including engineering expenses, were approximately $8,250,000 in 2014, $15,525,000 in 2013, and $7,675,000 in 2012. We expect research and development expenses in 2015 to be lower than in 2014. As we determine market opportunities, we may need to make research and development expenditures in the future. As of December 31, 2014, we employed twenty-five engineers and technicians who were engaged in research and development.

### Manufacturing

Historically, our manufacturing has consisted of the welding and assembly of our products. We have previously contracted out the manufacture of our high-energy flywheel components, using our design drawings and processes to facilitate more rapid growth by taking advantage of third-party installed manufacturing capacity. For a limited number of non-proprietary components, we generate performance specifications and obtain either standard or custom components.

Our facility is underutilized as a result of reductions in development work and customer orders for production. We are maintaining a limited manufacturing staff, many of whom are skilled in quality-control techniques. We expect to continue to utilize contract manufacturing and outside suppliers in the future based on our estimate of product demand from potential customers. The suppliers of the mechanical flywheel and the control electronics for our high-power UPS product are both single-source suppliers, and the

Page 1

---

C25-E01-TECAnnualReport.docx

**Main document changes and comments**

| Page 1: Commented | Student Name | 3/4/2015 11:43:00 AM |
|---|---|---|

Include additional information on the impact of this purchase.

**Header and footer changes**

**Text Box changes**

**Header and footer text box changes**

**Footnote changes**

**Endnote changes**

Comments

**Exercise 25.3**  C25-E03-REAgrmnt.docx

---

**Page 1**

1

## REAL ESTATE SALE AGREEMENT

The Buyer, BUYER, and Seller, SELLER, hereby agree that SELLER will sell and BUYER will buy the following property, with such improvements as are located thereon, and is described as follows: All that tract of land lying and being in Land Lot _____ of the _____ District, Section _____ of _____ County, and being known as Address: _____
City:_____ State: _____ Zip:_____, together with all light fixtures, electrical, mechanical, plumbing, air-conditioning, and any other systems or fixtures as are attached thereto; all plants, trees, and shrubbery now a part thereof, together with all the improvements thereon, and all appurtenances thereto, all being hereinafter collectively referred to as the "Property." The full legal description of said Property is the same as is recorded with the Clerk of the Superior Court of the County in which the Property is located and is made a part of this Agreement by reference.

SELLER will sell and BUYER will buy upon the following terms and conditions, as completed or marked. On any conflict of terms or conditions, that which is added will supersede that which is printed or marked. It is understood that the Property will be bought by Warranty Deed, with covenants, restrictions, and easements of record.

**Financing:** The balance due to SELLER will be evidenced by a negotiable Promissory Note of Borrower, secured by a Mortgage or Deed to Secure Debt on the Property and delivered by BUYER to SELLER dated the date of closing.

**New financing:** If BUYER does not obtain the required financing, the earnest money deposit shall be forfeited to SELLER as liquidated damages. BUYER will make application for financing within five days of the date of acceptance of the Agreement and in a timely manner furnish any and all credit, employment, financial, and other information required by the lender.

**Closing costs:** BUYER will pay all closing costs to include: Recording Fees, Intangibles Tax, Credit Reports, Funding Fees, Loan Origination Fee, Document Preparation Fee, Loan Insurance Premium, Title Insurance Policy, Attorney's Fees, Courier Fees, Overnight Fee, Appraisal Fee, Survey, Transfer Tax, Satisfaction and Recording Fees, Wood Destroying Organism Report, and any other costs associated with the funding or closing of this Agreement.

**Prorations:** All taxes, rentals, condominium or association fees, monthly mortgage insurance premiums, and interest on loans will be prorated as of the date of closing.

**Title insurance:** Within five (5) days of this Agreement SELLER will deliver to BUYER or closing attorney: Title insurance commitment for an owner's policy in the amount of the purchase price. Any expense of securing title, including but not limited to legal fees, discharge of liens, and recording fees will be paid by SELLER.

C25-E03-REAgrmnt.docx

---

**Page 2**

2

**Survey:** Within ten (10) days of acceptance of this Agreement, BUYER or closing attorney, may, at BUYER's expense, obtain a new staked survey showing any improvements now existing thereon and certified to BUYER, lender, and the title insurer.

**Default and attorney's fees:** Should BUYER elect not to fulfill obligations under this Agreement, all earnest monies will be retained by SELLER as liquidated damages and fund settlement of any claim, whereupon BUYER and SELLER will be relieved of all obligations under this Agreement. If SELLER defaults under this agreement, the BUYER may seek specific performance in return of the earnest money deposit. In connection with any litigation arising out of this Agreement, the prevailing party shall be entitled to recover all costs including reasonable attorney's fees.

IN WITNESS WHEREOF, all of the parties hereto affix their hands and seals this _____ day of _____, 20_____.

C25-E03-REAgrmnt.docx

---

**Exercise 25.4**  C25-E04-Lease.docx

---

1

## LEASE AGREEMENT

THIS LEASE AGREEMENT (hereinafter referred to as the "Agreement") made and entered into this DAY of MONTH, YEAR, by and between Lessor and Lessee.

WITNESSETH:

WHEREAS, Lessor is the owner of real property and is desirous of leasing the Premises to Lessee upon the terms and conditions as contained herein.

NOW, THEREFORE, for and in consideration of the covenants and obligations contained herein and other good and valuable consideration, the receipt and sufficiency of which is hereby acknowledged, the parties hereto agree as follows:

1. TERM. Lessor leases to Lessee and Lessee leases from Lessor the described Premises.
2. RENT. The total rent for the premise is RENT due on the fifteenth day of each month less any set off for approved repairs.
3. DAMAGE DEPOSIT. Upon the due execution of this Agreement, Lessee shall deposit with Lessor the sum of DEPOSIT receipt of which is hereby acknowledged by Lessor, as security for any damage caused to the Premises during the term hereof. Such deposit shall be returned to Lessee, without interest, and less any set off for damages to the Premises upon the termination of this Agreement.
4. USE OF PREMISES. The Premises shall be used and occupied by Lessee and Lessee's immediate family, exclusively, as a private single family dwelling, and no part of the Premises shall be used at any time during the term of this Agreement by Lessee for the purpose of carrying on any business, profession, or trade of any kind, or for any purpose other than as a private single family dwelling. Lessee shall not allow any other person, other than Lessee's immediate family, to occupy the Premises.
5. CONDITION OF PREMISES. Lessee stipulates, represents, and warrants that Lessee has examined the Premises, and that they are in good order, repair, and in a safe, clean, and tenantable condition.
6. ALTERATIONS AND IMPROVEMENTS. Lessee shall make no alterations or improvements on the Premises or construct any building or make any other improvements on the Premises without the prior written consent of Lessor.
7. NON-DELIVERY OF POSSESSION. In the event Lessor cannot deliver possession of the Premises to Lessee upon the commencement of the term, through no fault of Lessor or its agents, then Lessor or its agents shall have no liability, but the rental herein provided shall abate until possession is given. Lessor or its agents shall have thirty (30) days in which to give possession, and if possession is tendered within such time, Lessee agrees to accept the demised Premises and pay the rental herein provided from that date. In the event possession cannot be delivered within such time, through no fault of Lessor or its agents, then this Agreement and all rights hereunder shall terminate.

Lease Agreement

---

**Page 2**

2

8. UTILITIES. Lessee shall be responsible for arranging for and paying for all utility services required on the Premises.

IN WITNESS WHEREOF the parties have reviewed the information above and certify, to the best of their knowledge, that the information provided by the signatory is true and accurate.

Lease Agreement

## BAYSIDE TRAVEL

### Antarctic Zenith Adventures

Travel with our Antarctic experts, cruise on our state-of-the-art ships, and experience Antarctica in all of its grandeur. We use ice-rated expedition ships custom-designed for your comfort and safety. Each ship can carry up to 100 passengers and provides excellent viewing for watching whales, seabirds, and icebergs as well as facilities for educational presentations by our Antarctic experts. For our more adventurous clients, we offer additional activities such as snowshoeing, sea-kayaking, and camping on the Antarctic ice. Plan on a shore excursion where you can view penguin rookeries, seal colonies, and places of historical and scientific interest. To carry you to the Antarctic shore, we use inflatable boats that can carry 12 to 15 people. After a thrilling day on shore, we will take you back to the ship where you can enjoy a delicious meal prepared by our gourmet chefs. Our Antarctic travel experts are naturalists, historians, and adventurers committed to providing you with a fabulous Antarctic adventure.

| Zenith Adventures | Length | Price |
|---|---|---|
| Antarctic Exploration | 7 days | $4,399 |
| Weddell Sea Adventure | 10 days | $6,899 |
| Falkland Islands | 14 days | $7,699 |
| Sailing Spectacular | 14 days | $8,999 |

### Upcoming Adventures

Beginning next year, Zenith Adventures, together with Bayside Travel, will offer volunteer vacation opportunities. Tentative volunteer adventures include building village and mountain paths, building homes, and helping the families of trail porters improve village facilities. Our volunteer adventures will provide you with

**Exercise 25.5**  C25-E05-BTZTAdventures.docx

Page 1

---

an exciting vacation and a rewarding volunteer experience. The group size will be limited to a maximum of 15 and participants will be required to raise a minimum amount of money to contribute to the program and local charities. All charities have been carefully screened to ensure that funds are well-managed and distributed fairly. Look for more information in our next newsletter and consider a rewarding volunteer adventure.

### Bicycling Adventure

A bicycle is the perfect form of transportation for a travel adventure. Sign up for one or our bicycle tours and travel at your own pace, interact with village residents, stay healthy and fit, and know that your adventure has a minimal effect on the environment. We offer bicycle tours ranging from a leisurely trip through the Loire Valley of France to a mountain-bike expedition in the Atlas Mountains in Morocco. Our Zenith Adventures bicycle guides provide you with historical and educational information about the region in which you are traveling. They also take care of luggage and transportation needs and maintain your bicycle. We are confident that we can provide the bicycle adventure of a lifetime!

Student Name

Page 2

---

## BAYSIDE TRAVEL

### Antarctic Zenith Adventures

Travel with our Antarctic experts, cruise on our state-of-the-art ships, and experience Antarctica in all of its grandeur. We use ice-rated expedition ships custom-designed for your comfort and safety. Each ship can carry up to 100 passengers and provides excellent viewing for watching whales, seabirds, and icebergs as well as facilities for educational presentations by our Antarctic experts. For our more adventurous clients, we offer additional activities such as snowshoeing, sea-kayaking, and camping on the Antarctic ice. Plan on a shore excursion where you can view penguin rookeries, seal colonies, and places of historical and scientific interest. To carry you to the Antarctic shore, we use inflatable boats that can carry 12 to 15 people. After a thrilling day on shore, we will take you back to the ship where you can enjoy a delicious meal prepared by our gourmet chefs. Our Antarctic travel experts are naturalists, historians, and adventurers committed to providing you with a fabulous Antarctic adventure.

| Zenith Adventures | Length | Price |
|---|---|---|
| Antarctic Exploration | 7 days | $3,500 |
| Weddell Sea Adventure | 10 days | $6,899 |
| Falkland Islands | 14 days | $7,699 |
| Sailing Spectacular | 14 days | $8,999 |

### Upcoming Adventures

Beginning next year, Zenith Adventures, together with Bayside Travel, will offer volunteer vacation opportunities. Tentative volunteer adventures include building village and mountain paths, building homes, and helping the families of trail porters improve village facilities. Our volunteer adventures will provide you with

**Exercise 25.6**  C25-E06-BTZTAdv.docx

---

an exciting vacation and a rewarding volunteer experience. The group size will be limited to a maximum of 15 and participants will be required to raise a minimum amount of money to contribute to the program and local charities. All charities have been carefully screened to ensure that funds are well-managed and distributed fairly. Look for more information in our next newsletter and consider a rewarding volunteer adventure.

### Bicycling Adventure

A bicycle is the perfect form of transportation for a travel adventure. Sign up for one or our bicycle tours and travel at your own pace, interact with village residents, stay healthy and fit, and know that your adventure has a minimal effect on the environment. We offer bicycle tours ranging from a leisurely trip through the Loire Valley of France to a mountain-bike expedition in the Atlas Mountains in Morocco. Our Zenith Adventures bicycle guides provide you with historical and educational information about the region in which you are traveling. They also take care of luggage and transportation needs and maintain your bicycle. We are confident that we can provide the bicycle adventure of a lifetime!

Student Name

Page 2

# Protecting Documents

Within your company or organization, you may want to distribute copies of documents you create among members of a group. In some situations, however, you may want to protect a document and limit the changes that can be made to it. If you create a document that contains sensitive, restricted, or private information, consider protecting it by saving it as a read-only document or securing it with a password.

With options at the Restrict Editing task pane, you can limit what formatting and editing users can perform on the text in a document. Limiting the changes others can make is especially useful when a number of people in an organization will be reviewing and editing the same document. For example, suppose you are responsible for preparing the yearly corporate report for your company. This report contains information from a variety of departments, such as finance, human resources, and sales and marketing. You can prepare the report and then specify what sections given individuals are allowed to edit. For example, you can specify that a person from the finance department can edit only financial information and that a person from human resources can edit only data pertinent to the human resources department. By setting these limits, you can protect the integrity of the document.

To protect a document, display the Restrict Editing task pane, as shown in Figure 25.1, by clicking the REVIEW tab and then clicking the Restrict Editing button in the Protect group. Use options in the *Formatting restrictions* section to limit formatting to specific styles and use options in the *Editing restrictions* section to specify the type of editing allowed in the document.

Restrict Editing

## Figure 25.1 Restrict Editing Task Pane

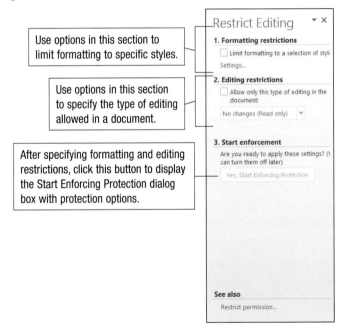

Use options in this section to limit formatting to specific styles.

Use options in this section to specify the type of editing allowed in a document.

After specifying formatting and editing restrictions, click this button to display the Start Enforcing Protection dialog box with protection options.

## Restricting Formatting

**QUICK STEPS**

**Display the Formatting Restrictions Dialog Box**
1. Click REVIEW tab.
2. Click Restrict Editing button.
3. Click Settings hyperlink in Restrict Editing task pane.

With options in the *Formatting restrictions* section of the Restrict Editing task pane, you can lock specific styles used in a document, thus allowing the use of only those styles and prohibiting users from making other formatting changes. Click the Settings hyperlink in the *Formatting restrictions* section and the Formatting Restrictions dialog box displays, as shown in Figure 25.2.

**Figure 25.2 Formatting Restrictions Dialog Box**

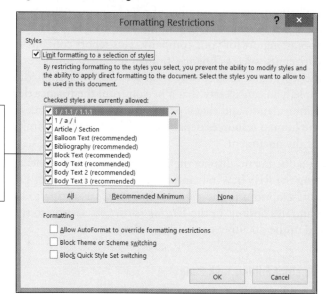

Insert check marks in the check boxes preceding those styles you want to allow and remove check marks from the check boxes preceding styles you do not want to allow.

If you insert a check mark in the *Limit formatting to a selection of styles* check box, a list of styles becomes available in the *Checked styles are currently allowed* list box. In this list box, insert check marks from the check boxes that precede styles you want to allow and remove check marks in the check boxes that precede styles you do not want to allow. Limit formatting to a minimum number of styles by clicking the Recommended Minimum button. This allows formatting with styles that Word uses for certain features, such as bulleted and numbered lists. Click the None button to remove all of the check marks and allow no styles to be used in the document. Click the All button to insert check marks in all of the check boxes and allow all of the styles to be used in the document. Use options in the *Formatting* section of the dialog box to allow or not allow AutoFormat to make changes in a document and to allow or not allow users to switch themes or style sets.

1. Open **TECAnnualReport.docx** and save the document with the name **C25-E01-TECAnnualReport**.
2. Restrict formatting to the Heading 1 and Heading 2 styles by completing the following steps:
   a. Click the REVIEW tab.
   b. Click the Restrict Editing button in the Protect group.

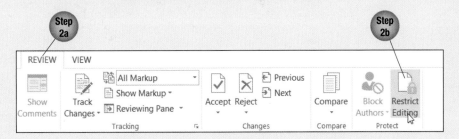

   c. At the Restrict Editing task pane, click the *Limit formatting to a selection of styles* check box to insert a check mark. (Skip this step if the check box already contains a check mark.)
   d. Click the <u>Settings</u> hyperlink.
   e. At the Formatting Restrictions dialog box, click the None button.
   f. Scroll down the list box and then insert check marks in the *Heading 1* and *Heading 2* check boxes.
   g. Click OK.

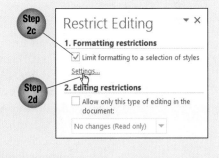

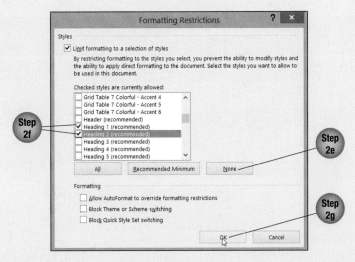

   h. At the message telling you that the document may contain formatting or styles that are not allowed and asking if you want to remove them, click Yes.
3. Save **C25-E01-TECAnnualReport.docx**.

## Enforcing Restrictions

**QUICK STEPS**

**Display the Start Enforcing Protection Dialog Box**
1. Click REVIEW tab.
2. Click Restrict Editing button.
3. Specify formatting and/or editing options.
4. Click Yes, Start Enforcing Protection button.

Specifying formatting and editing restrictions, as well as any exceptions to those restrictions, is the first step in protecting your document. The next step is to start enforcing the restrictions you have specified. Click the Yes, Start Enforcing Protection button in the task pane to display the Start Enforcing Protection dialog box, as shown in Figure 25.3.

**Figure 25.3 Start Enforcing Protection Dialog Box**

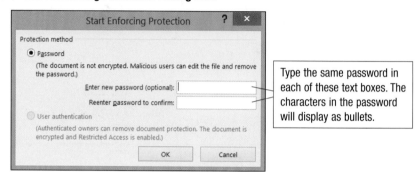

Type the same password in each of these text boxes. The characters in the password will display as bullets.

At the Start Enforcing Protection dialog box, the *Password* option is selected automatically. To create a password, type what you want to use in the *Enter new password (optional)* text box. (A password is case sensitive. Use a combination of lower- and uppercase letters, as well as symbols and numbers, to make the password more secure.) Click in the *Reenter password to confirm* text box and then type the same password again. Choose the *User authentication* option if you want to use encryption to prevent any unauthorized changes. If Word does not recognize the password, check to make sure Caps Lock is turned off and then try typing the password again.

---

## Exercise 25.1B   Protecting a Document                                    Part 2 of 3

1. With **C25-E01-TECAnnualReport.docx** open, click the Yes, Start Enforcing Protection button in the Restrict Editing task pane.
2. At the Start Enforcing Protection dialog box, type **formatting** in the *Enter new password (optional)* text box. (Bullets will display in the text box, rather than the letters you type.)
3. Press the Tab key (which moves the insertion point to the *Reenter password to confirm* text box) and then type **formatting**. (Bullets will display in the text box, rather than the letters you type.)
4. Click OK to close the dialog box.

---

5. Read the information that displays in the task pane telling you that the document is protected, special restrictions are in effect, and text can be formatted only with certain styles. Click the <u>Available styles</u> hyperlink. (This displays the Styles task pane with only four styles in the *Pick formatting to apply* list box: *Clear All, Normal, Heading 1,* and *Heading 2.*)

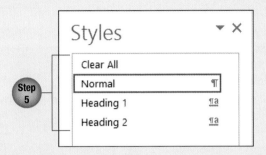

6. Apply the Heading 1 style to the title *TERRA ENERGY CORPORATION* and apply the Heading 2 style to the following headings: *Overview, Research and Development, Manufacturing,* and *Sales and Marketing.*
7. Close the Styles task pane.
8. Apply the Lines (Simple) style set.
9. If a message displays indicating that some of the styles could not be updated, click OK.
10. Save the document.
11. Remove password protection from the document by completing the following steps:
    a. Click the Stop Protection button located near the bottom of the task pane.
    b. At the Unprotect Document dialog box, type **formatting** in the text box.
    c. Click OK.

12. Save **C25-E01-TECAnnualReport.docx**.

## Restricting Editing

Use the *Editing restrictions* option at the Restrict Editing task pane to limit the types of changes a user can make to a document. Insert a check mark in the *Allow only this type of editing in the document* check box and the drop-down list below the option becomes active. Click the down-pointing arrow at the right of the option box and the following options become available: *Tracked changes, Comments, Filling in forms,* and *No changes (Read only).*

If you do not want users to be able to make any changes to a document, choose the *No changes (Read only)* option. If you want users to be able to make changes that are tracked in the document, choose the *Tracked changes* option. If you want users to be able to make comments in a document, choose the *Comments* option. The *Tracked Changes* and *Comments* options are useful in a workgroup environment in which documents are routed to various members of a group for review. If you choose the *Filling in forms* option, users will be able to fill in the fields in a form but will not be able to make any changes to the form text.

1. With **C25-E01-TECAnnualReport.docx** open, restrict editing to adding comments by completing the following steps:

   a. Make sure the Restrict Editing task pane displays.

   b. Click the *Allow only this type of editing in the document* check box to insert a check mark.

   c. Click the down-pointing arrow at the right of the option box below the *Allow only this type of editing in the document* and then click *Comments* at the drop-down list.

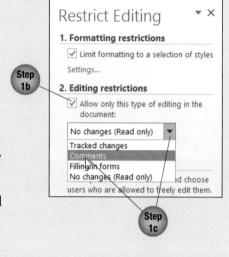

2. Click the Yes, Start Enforcing Protection button located near the bottom of the task pane.

3. At the Start Enforcing Protection dialog box, click OK. (Adding a password is optional.)

4. Read the information in the task pane that tells you the document is protected and the only editing allowed is to insert comments.

5. Click each ribbon tab and notice the buttons and options that are dimmed and unavailable.

6. Insert a comment by completing the following steps:

   a. Move the insertion point immediately right of the period that ends the last sentence in the second paragraph of the *Overview* section.

   b. Click the REVIEW tab (if necessary), click the Show Markup button in the Tracking group, point to *Balloons*, and then click the *Show All Revisions Inline* option.

   c. Click the Reviewing Pane button to turn on the display of the Reviewing pane.

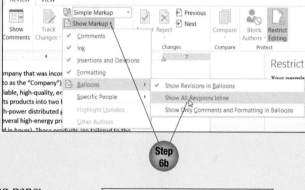

   d. Click the New Comment button in the Comments group on the REVIEW tab.

   e. Type the following in the Reviewing pane: **Include additional information on the impact of this purchase.**

   f. Close the Reviewing pane.

   g. Click the Stop Protection button located near the bottom of the Restrict Editing task pane.

   h. Close the Restrict Editing task pane.

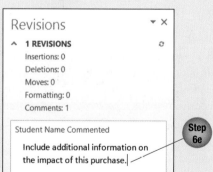

7. Save the document and then print only page 1.

8. Print only the comment. (To do this, display the Print backstage area, click the first gallery in the *Settings* category, click the *List of Markup* option, and then click the Print button.)

9. Close **C25-E01-TECAnnualReport.docx**.

# Protecting a Document with a Password

In a previous section of this chapter, you learned how to protect a document with a password by using options at the Start Enforcing Protection dialog box. You can also protect a document with a password by using options at the General Options dialog box, as shown in Figure 25.4. To display this dialog box, press the F12 key to display the Save As dialog box, click the Tools button located near the bottom of the dialog box next to the Save button, and then click *General Options* at the drop-down list.

At the General Options dialog box, you can assign a password to open the document, modify the document, or both. To insert a password to open the document, click in the *Password to open* text box and then type the password. (As noted earlier, a password must be 8 to 15 characters—including lowercase and uppercase letters, as well as numbers and symbols—and is case sensitive.) Use the *Password to modify* option to create a password that a user must enter before making edits to the document.

At the General Options dialog box, insert a check mark in the *Read-only recommended* check box to save a document as a read-only document. If a user opens a document that is saved as read-only and then makes changes to it, he or she must save the document with a new name to keep the edited version. Use this option if you do not want users to be able to change the original document.

**QUICK STEPS**

**Add a Password to a Document**
1. Press the F12 key.
2. Click Tools button.
3. Click *General Options.*
4. Type password in *Password to open* text box.
5. Press Enter.
6. Type same password again.
7. Press Enter.

**Figure 25.4 General Options Dialog Box**

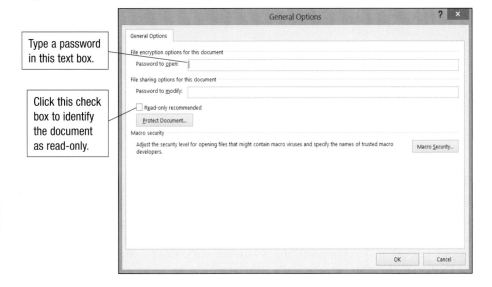

Type a password in this text box.

Click this check box to identify the document as read-only.

1. Open **TECContract.docx** and save the document with the name **C25-E02-TECContract**.
2. Save the document and protect it with a password by completing the following steps:
   a. Press the F12 key to display the Save As dialog box.
   b. Click the Tools button located near the bottom of the dialog box (next to the Save button) and then click *General Options* at the drop-down list.

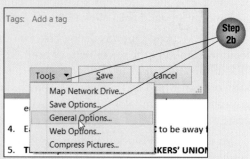

   c. At the General Options dialog box, type your first name in the *Password to open* text box. (If your name is longer than 15 characters, abbreviate it. You will not see your name; Word displays the letters as bullets.)
   d. After typing your name, press the Enter key.
   e. At the Confirm Password dialog box, type your name again and then press the Enter key. (Be sure to type it exactly as you did in the *Password to open* text box, including uppercase and lowercase letters.)

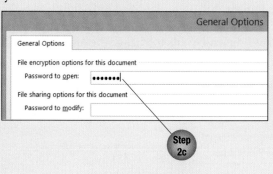

   f. Click the Save button at the Save As dialog box.
3. Close **C25-E02-TECContract.docx**.
4. Open **C25-E02-TECContract.docx** and type your password when prompted.
5. Close **C25-E02-TECContract.docx**.

## Opening a Document in Different Views

Use the Open button in the Open dialog box to open a document in different views. At the Open dialog box, click the Open button arrow and a drop-down list of options displays. Click the *Open Read-Only* option and the document opens in read-only mode. In this mode, you can make changes to the document but cannot save it with the same name. Click the *Open as Copy* option and a copy of the document opens and the text *Copy (1)* displays at the beginning of the document name in the Title bar. If you click the *Open in Protected View* option, the document opens in Read Mode view and the text *(Protected View)* displays after the document name in the Title bar. Also, a message bar displays telling you that the file was opened in Protected view. To edit the document, press the Esc key to exit Read Mode view and return to Print Layout view and then click the Enable Editing button in the message bar. Open a document with the *Open and Repair* option and Word opens a new version and attempts to repair any issues with the document.

1. Open **TECTraining.docx** and then save the document and name it **C25-E02-TECTraining**.
2. Close **C25-E02-TECTraining.docx**.
3. Open a document as a read-only document by completing the following steps:
   a. Press Ctrl + F12 to display the Open dialog box and then navigate to your Chapter25 folder.
   b. Click once on the document name *C25-E02-TECTraining.docx*.
   c. Click the Open button arrow (located near the bottom right corner of the dialog box) and then click *Open Read-Only* at the drop-down list. (The document opens in Read Mode and the text *Read-Only* displays after the name in the Title bar.)

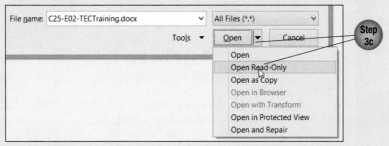

   d. Close the document.
4. Open a document in Protected view by completing the following steps:
   a. Press Ctrl + F12 to display the Open dialog box.
   b. Click once on the document name *PremPro.docx* located in your Chapter25 folder.
   c. Click the Open button arrow and then click *Open in Protected View* at the drop-down list.
   d. Press the Esc key to exit Read Mode view and display the document in Print Layout view. Notice the message bar that displays with information telling you that the file was opened in Protected view.
   e. Click each ribbon tab and notice that most formatting options are dimmed.
   f. Click in the document and then click the Enable Editing button in the message bar. This removes *(Protected View)* after the document name in the Title bar and makes available the options on the tabs.

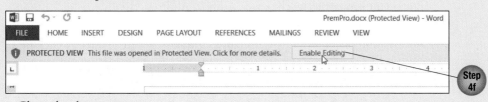

   g. Close the document.

# Managing Document Properties

Each document you create has properties associated with it, such as the type of document, where it is located, and when it was created, modified, and accessed. You can view and modify document properties at the Info backstage area and modify document properties at the document information panel. To display information about the document, click the FILE tab. Document property information displays at the right side of the Info backstage area, as shown in Figure 25.5 on the next page.

**Figure 25.5  Info Backstage Area**

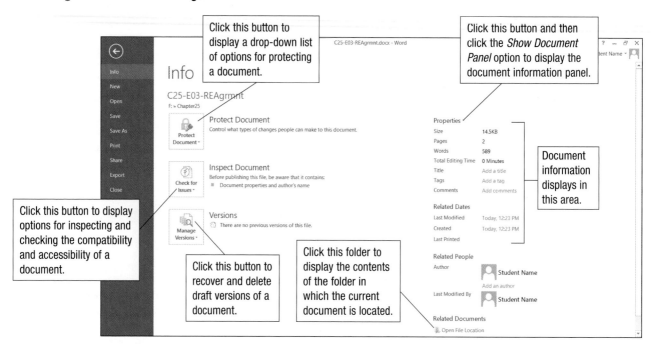

Click this button to display a drop-down list of options for protecting a document.

Click this button and then click the *Show Document Panel* option to display the document information panel.

Document information displays in this area.

Click this button to display options for inspecting and checking the compatibility and accessibility of a document.

Click this button to recover and delete draft versions of a document.

Click this folder to display the contents of the folder in which the current document is located.

The document property information that displays in the Info backstage area includes the file size, number of pages and words, total editing time, and any tags or comments that have been added. Add or update a document property by hovering your mouse over the information that displays at the right of the property (a rectangle text box with a light blue border displays), clicking in the text box, and then typing the desired information. In the *Related Dates* section, dates display for when the document was created and when it was last modified and printed. The *Related People* section displays the name of the author of the document and the name of the person who last modified it. This section also contains options for adding additional author names. The *Related Documents* section displays the Open File Location folder that, when clicked, will display the contents of the folder in which the current document is located. Display additional document properties by clicking the <u>Show All Properties</u> hyperlink.

You can also add information to a document's properties at the document information panel, as shown in Figure 25.6. Display this panel by clicking the Properties button that displays above the document property information at the Info backstage area and then clicking *Show Document Panel* at the drop-down list.

**Figure 25.6  Document Information Panel**

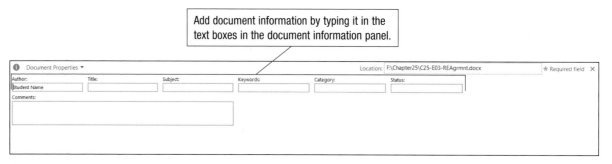

Add document information by typing it in the text boxes in the document information panel.

By typing specific information in each text box in the document information panel, you can describe a document. Adding text in even some of the boxes can help you organize and identify your documents. For example, if you insert specific words contained in the document in the *Keywords* text box, you can search for all documents containing those keywords. The text you type in the document information panel is saved with the document. You can print the document properties for a document by displaying the Print backstage area, clicking the first gallery in the *Settings* category, clicking *Document Info* at the drop-down list, and then clicking the Print button.

In addition to inserting information about a document in the document information panel, you can insert specific information with options at the Properties dialog box, as shown in Figure 25.7. The name of the dialog box reflects the currently open document. Display this dialog box by clicking the Document Properties button that displays in the upper left corner of the document information panel and then clicking *Advanced Properties* at the drop-down list. You can also display this dialog box by displaying the Info backstage area, clicking the Properties button, and then clicking *Advanced Properties* at the drop-down list. Another method for displaying the Properties dialog box is to display the Open dialog box, click the desired document, click the Organize button, and then click *Properties* at the drop-down list. You can also right-click the desired file name and then click *Properties* at the shortcut menu.

**QUICK STEPS**

**Display the Document Information Panel**
1. Click FILE tab.
2. Click Properties button at Info backstage area.
3. Click *Show Document Panel*.

**Display the Properties Dialog Box**
1. Click FILE tab.
2. Click Properties button.
3. Click *Advanced Properties*.

**Figure 25.7  Properties Dialog Box with General Tab Selected**

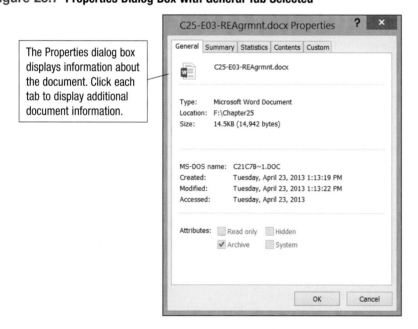

The Properties dialog box displays information about the document. Click each tab to display additional document information.

The Properties dialog box with the General tab selected displays information about the document type, size, and location. Click the Summary tab to view fields such as title, subject, author, company, category, keywords, and comments. Some fields may contain data and others may be blank. You can insert, edit, or delete text in the fields. With the Statistics tab selected, information displays such as the number of pages, paragraphs, lines, words, and characters. View the document without opening it by clicking the Contents tab. This displays a portion of the document in the viewing window. Click the Custom tab and the Properties dialog box displays, as shown in Figure 25.8 on the next page.

**Figure 25.8  Properties Dialog Box with Custom Tab Selected**

Click the desired option in the *Name* list box, specify the type of property, and then enter the data in the *Value* text box.

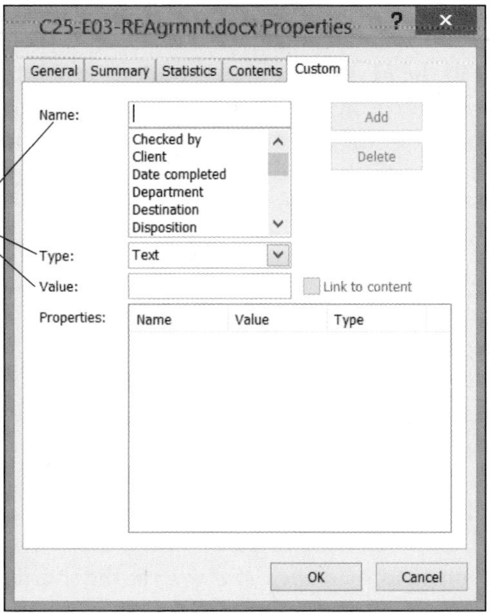

Use the options at the Properties dialog box with the Custom tab selected to add custom properties to the document. For example, you can add properties that display the date the document was completed, information on the department in which the document was created, and much more. The list box below the *Name* option box displays the predesigned properties provided by Word. You can choose a predesigned property or create your own.

To choose a predesigned property, select the desired property in the list box, specify what type of property it is (text, value, date, number, yes/no), and then type a value. For example, to specify the department in which the document was created, click *Department* in the list box, make sure *Text* displays in the *Type* list box, click in the *Value* text box, and then type the name of the department.

---

**Exercise 25.3A   Inserting Document Properties**                    Part 1 of 3

1. Open **REAgrmnt.docx** and save the document with the name **C25-E03-REAgrmnt**.
2. Make the following changes to the document:
   a.  Insert page numbers that print at the tops of all pages at the right margin.
   b.  Insert the footer **C25-E03-REAgrmnt.docx** centered on each page.
3. Add document properties by completing the following steps:
   a.  Click the FILE tab. (Make sure the Info backstage area displays.)

b. Hover your mouse over the text *Add a title* that displays at the right of the *Title* document property, click in the text box that displays, and then type **Real Estate Sale Agreement**.

c. Display the document information panel by clicking the Properties button that displays above the document property information and then clicking *Show Document Panel* at the drop-down list.

d. Select any text that appears in the *Author* text box and then type your first and last names.

e. Press the Tab key twice (which makes the *Subject* text box active) and then type **Real Estate Sale Agreement**.

f. Press the Tab key and then type the following words in the *Keywords* text box: **real estate, agreement, contract, purchasing**.

g. Press the Tab key and then type **Agreement** in the *Category* text box.

h. Press the Tab key twice and then type the following text in the *Comments* text box: **This is a real estate sale agreement between two parties.**

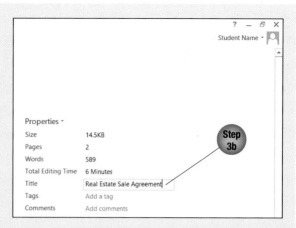

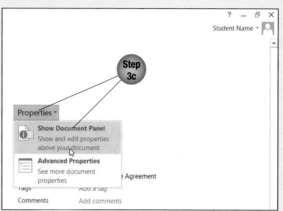

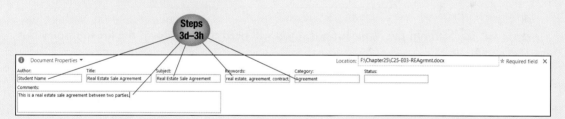

4. Add custom information by completing the following steps:

a. Click the Document Properties button that displays in the upper left corner of the document information panel and then click *Advanced Properties* at the drop-down list.

b. At the Properties dialog box, click the Summary tab, select the current title in the *Title* text box, and then type **C25-E03-REAgrmnt.docx**.

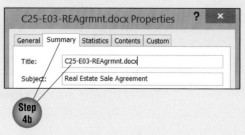

c. Click the Custom tab.

d. Click *Checked by* in the *Name* list box.

e. Make sure *Text* displays in the *Type* list box.

f. Click in the *Value* text box and then type your first and last names.

g. Click the Add button.

h. Click *Date completed* in the *Name* list box.

i. Click the down-pointing arrow at the right of the *Type* option box and then click *Date*.

j. Click in the *Value* text box and then type today's date in this form: ##/##/####.

k. Click the Add button.

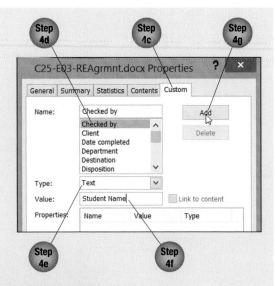

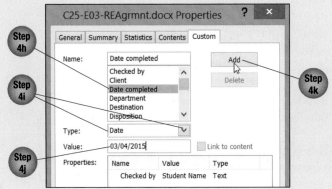

l. Click *Status* in the *Name* list box. (You will need to scroll down the list to display this option.)

m. Click the down-pointing arrow at the right of the *Type* option box and then click *Text*.

n. Click in the *Value* text box and then type **First Draft**.

o. Click the Add button.

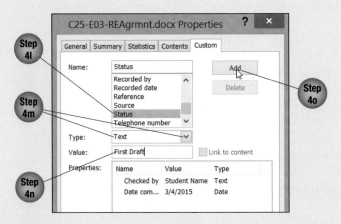

p. Click OK to close the Properties dialog box.

5. Click the Close button that displays in the upper right corner of the document information panel.
6. Save **C25-E03-REAgrmnt.docx** and then print only the document properties by completing the following steps:
   a. Click the FILE tab and then click the *Print* option.
   b. At the Print backstage area, click the first gallery in the *Settings* category and then click *Document Info* at the drop-down list.

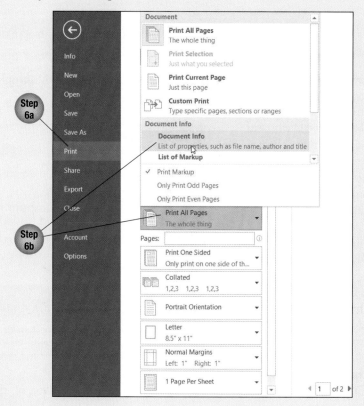

   c. Click the Print button.
7. Save **C25-E03-REAgrmnt.docx**.

# Restricting Documents

The middle panel at the Info backstage area contains buttons that provide options for protecting a document, checking for issues in a document, and managing versions of a document. Click the Protect Document button in the middle panel and a drop-down list displays with the following options: *Mark as Final, Encrypt with Password, Restrict Editing, Restrict Access,* and *Add a Digital Signature.*

## Marking a Document as Final

Click the *Mark as Final* option to save the document as a read-only document. When you click this option, a message displays telling you that the document will be marked and then saved. At this message, click OK. This displays another message telling you that the document has been marked as final to indicate that editing is complete and that it is

**QUICK STEPS**

**Mark a Document as Final**
1. Click FILE tab.
2. Click Protect Document button at Info backstage area.
3. Click *Mark as Final*.

the final version of the document. The message further indicates that when a document is marked as final, the status property is set to *Final*; typing, editing commands, and proofing marks are turned off; and the document can be identified by the Mark as Final icon, which displays near the left side of the Status bar. At this message, click OK. After a document is marked as final, the message *This document has been marked as final to discourage editing.* displays to the right of the Protect Document button at the Info backstage area.

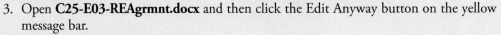

**Exercise 25.3B**   Marking a Document as Final                                         Part 2 of 3

1. With **C25-E03-REAgrmnt.docx** open, mark the document as final by completing the following steps:
   a. Click the FILE tab.
   b. Click the Protect Document button at the Info backstage area and then click *Mark as Final* at the drop-down list.
   c. At the message telling you that the document will be marked and saved, click OK.
   d. At the next message that displays, click OK. (Notice the message that displays to the right of the Protect Document button.)
   e. Click the Back button to return to the document.
2. At the document, notice the message bar that displays near the top of the screen and then close the document.
3. Open **C25-E03-REAgrmnt.docx** and then click the Edit Anyway button on the yellow message bar.
4. Save **C25-E03-REAgrmnt.docx**.

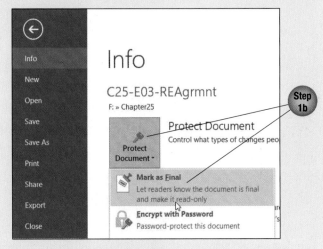

## Encrypting a Document

Word provides a number of methods for protecting a document with a password. Previously in this chapter, you learned how to protect a document with a password using options at the Start Enforcing Protection dialog box and using options at the General Options dialog box. In addition to these two methods, you can protect a document with a password by clicking the Protect Document button at the Info backstage area and then clicking the *Encrypt with Password* option at the drop-down list. At the Encrypt Document dialog box that displays, type your password in the text box (the characters will display as round bullets) and then press the Enter key or click OK. At the Confirm Password dialog box, type your password again (the characters will display as round bullets) and then press the Enter key or click OK. When you apply a password, the message *A password is required to open this document.* displays to the right of the Protect Document button.

## Restricting Editing

Click the Protect Document button at the Info backstage area and then click the *Restrict Editing* option at the drop-down list and the document displays with the Restrict Editing task pane. This is the same task pane you learned about previously in this chapter.

## Adding a Digital Signature

Select the *Add a Digital Signature* option at the Protect Document button drop-down list to insert an invisible digital signature in a document. A *digital signature* is an electronic stamp that vertifies a document's authenticity. Before adding a digital signature, you must obtain one. You can obtain a digital signature from a commercial certification authority.

## Inserting a Signature Line

If you have obtained a signing certificate or if your company provides a signing certificate, you can insert a signature line in a document that specifies who should sign it. The signature line can include information about the intended signer, such as the person's name, title, and email address. It can also provide instructions for the intended signer. If you send an electronic copy of a document to the intended signer, the person sees the signature line and the instructions. Insert a signature line with the Signature Line button in the Text group on the INSERT tab.

Signature Line

---

**Exercise 25.3C**  Encrypting a Document with a Password                      Part 3 of 3

---

1. With **C25-E03-REAgrmnt.docx** open, encrypt the document with a password by completing the following steps:
   a. Click the FILE tab, click the Protect Document button at the Info backstage area, and then click *Encrypt with Password* at the drop-down list.

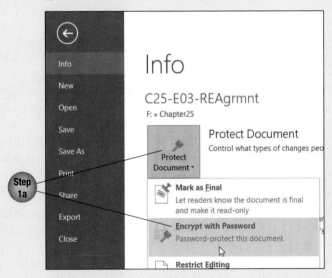

b. At the Encrypt Document dialog box, type your initials in uppercase letters. (The characters will display as bullets).
c. Press the Enter key.
d. At the Confirm Password dialog box, type your initials again in uppercase letters in the *Reenter password* text box (the characters will display as bullets) and then press the Enter key.
2. Click the Back button to return to the document.
3. Save and then close **C25-E03-REAgrmnt.docx**.
4. Open **C25-E03-REAgrmnt.docx**. At the Password dialog box, type your initials in uppercase letters in the *Enter password to open file text box* and then press the Enter key.
5. Save, print, and then close **C25-E03-REAgrmnt.docx**.

# Inspecting a Document

Use options from the Check for Issues button drop-down list at the Info backstage area to inspect a document for personal and hidden data and to check a document for compatibility and accessibility issues. When you click the Check for Issues button, a drop-down list displays with the following options: *Inspect Document, Check Accessibility,* and *Check Compatibility.*

## Using the Document Inspector

Word includes a document inspector that will inspect your document for personal data, hidden data, and metadata. *Metadata* is data that describes other data, such as document properties.

You may want to remove some personal or hidden data before you share a document with other people. To check your document for personal or hidden data, click the FILE tab, click the Check for Issues button at the Info backstage area, and then click the *Inspect Document* option at the drop-down list. This displays the Document Inspector dialog box, as shown in Figure 25.9 on the next page.

By default, the document inspector checks all of the items listed in the dialog box. If you do not want the inspector to check a specific item in your document, remove the check mark preceding the item. For example, if you know your document has headers and footers that you do not need to check, click the *Headers, Footers, and Watermarks* check box to remove the check mark. To scan the document to identify information, click the Inspect button located near the bottom of the dialog box.

When the inspection is complete, the results display in the dialog box. A check mark before an item indicates that the inspector did not find the specific items included in that option. If an exclamation point displays before an item, it means the inspector found items and a list of the items is displayed. If you want to remove the found items, click the Remove All button that displays at the right of the corresponding item. Click the Reinspect button to ensure that the specific items were removed and then click the Close button.

**Figure 25.9  Document Inspector Dialog Box**

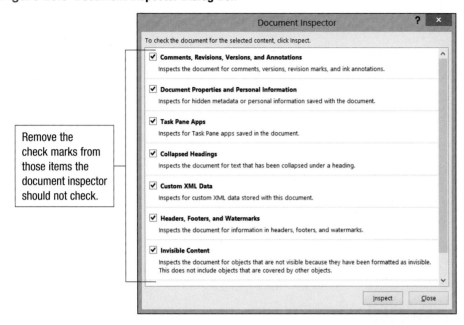

Remove the check marks from those items the document inspector should not check.

---

# Exercise 25.4  Inspecting a Document                              Part 1 of 1

1. Open **Lease.docx** and save the document with the name **C25-E04-Lease**.
2. Make the following changes to the document:
   a. Turn on Track Changes.
   b. Select the title *LEASE AGREEMENT* and then change the font size to 14 points.
   c. Delete the word *first* that displays in the second numbered paragraph (the *RENT* paragraph) and then type **fifteenth**.
   d. Move the insertion point to the beginning of the text *IN WITNESS WHEREOF* (located on page 2) and then press the Tab key.
   e. Turn off Track Changes.
3. Hide text by completing the following steps:
   a. Move the insertion point to the end of the first paragraph of text in the document (one space after the period at the end of the sentence).
   b. Type **The entire legal description of the property is required for this agreement to be valid.**
   c. Select the text you just typed, being careful not to include the paragraph symbol at the end of the sentence.
   d. Click the HOME tab.
   e. Click the Font group dialog box launcher.
   f. At the Font dialog box, click the *Hidden* option in the *Effects* section.
   g. Click OK to close the dialog box.

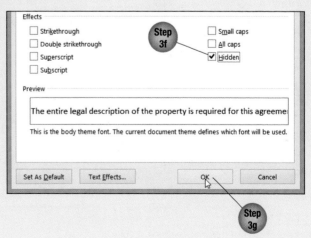

4. Click the Save button on the Quick Access toolbar.
5. Inspect the document by completing the following steps:
   a. Click the FILE tab.
   b. Click the Check for Issues button at the Info backstage area and then click *Inspect Document* at the drop-down list.

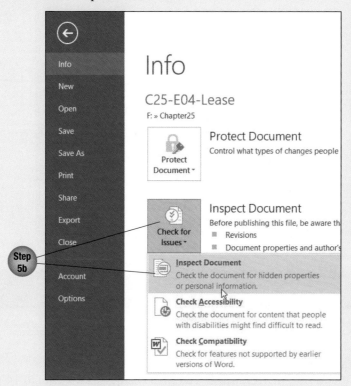

   c. At the Document Inspector dialog box, indicate not to check the document for XML data by clicking the *Custom XML Data* check box to remove the check mark.
   d. Click the Inspect button.

e.  Read through the inspection results and then remove all of the hidden text by clicking the Remove All button that displays at the right side of the *Hidden Text* section. (Make sure that a message displays below *Hidden Text* indicating that the text was successfully removed.)

f.  Click the Reinspect button.
g.  To keep the header and footer text in the document, click the *Headers, Footers, and Watermarks* check box to remove the check mark.
h.  Click the Inspect button.
i.  Read through the inspection results and then remove all of the revisions by clicking the Remove All button that displays at the right side of the *Comments, Revisions, Versions, and Annotations* section.
j.  Click the Reinspect button.
k.  To leave the remaining items in the document, click the Close button.
6.  Click the Back button to return to the document and then save the document.
7.  Print and then close **C25-E04-Lease.docx**.

## Checking the Accessibility of a Document

Word provides the accessibility checker feature to check documents for content that someone with a disability, such as a visual impairment, might find difficult to read. Check the accessibility of a document by clicking the Check for Issues button at the Info backstage area and then clicking *Check Accessibility*. The accessibility checker examines the document for the most common accessibility problems in Word documents and groups the problems into three categories: errors—content that is very difficult or impossible for people with disabilities to understand; warnings—content that makes a file difficult for people with disabilities to understand; tips—content that people with disabilities can understand but that can be better organized. Examples of these three types of accessibility issues are provided in Table 25.1 on the next page.

The accessibility checker examines the document, closes the Info backstage area, and displays the Accessibility Checker task pane. At the Accessibility Checker task pane, unreadable errors are grouped in the *ERRORS* section, content that is difficult to read is grouped in the *WARNINGS* section, and content that may or may not be difficult to read is grouped in the *TIPS* section. When you select an issue in one of the sections, an explanation of how to fix the issue and why the issue should be fixed displays at the bottom of the task pane. The accessibility checker examines a document for issues in each of the three categories shown in Table 25.1.

**Table 25.1 Accessibility Checker Issues**

### ERRORS

**Alt text:** All objects have alternate text. Objects include pictures, clip art images, tables, SmartArt, shapes, charts, embedded objects, and video and audio files. Providing alternate text for an object helps readers understand the information presented by the object.

**Table headers:** Tables specify column header information. A table header row provides context and helps readers navigate the data in a table.

**Document structure:** Long documents use styles to provide structure. Headings and/or a table of contents are used to help organize the content. Creating a structure helps readers find information in the document.

### WARNINGS

**Meaningful hyperlink text:** Hyperlink text includes a ScreenTip and matches the hyperlink target. Hyperlink text should provide a description of the destination, not just the URL.

**Simple table structure:** Tables have a simple structure that does not include nested tables or merged or split cells. Tables should have a simple two-dimensional structure to be easily navigated and understood by readers.

**Blank cells:** Tables do not use blank cells for formatting or contain entirely blank rows or columns. Encountering blank cells may lead readers to think they have reached the end of the table.

**Blank characters:** Repeated blank characters (such as a series of blank spaces, tabs, or paragraphs) are avoided. Blank characters may lead readers to think they have reached the end of the document. Paragraphs of text should be separated by paragraph styles instead of blank lines.

**Heading length:** Headings do not contain too much information. Keep headings short (fewer than 20 words). Short and concise headings help readers navigate the document more easily.

**Floating objects:** The use of floating objects is avoided. Specify that objects have text wrapping set to *Inline with Text*, *Square*, or *Top and Bottom*. Documents with floating objects are difficult to navigate.

### TIPS

**Closed captions:** Closed captions are included for inserted audio and video files. Without closed captions, important information in audio or video files may not be available to people with disabilities.

**Table layout:** Tables are structured for easy navigation and use the appropriate reading order. For English, data in a table is read from left to right and top to bottom. Tab through the cells in a table to ensure that the information is presented in a logical order.

**Watermarks:** No watermark images are used in the document. Watermark images may not be understood by people with visual disabilities.

**Heading order:** All headings appear in the correct order. Use correct heading levels so readers can find information and navigate easily in the document.

The first item in the *ERRORS* section, *Alt text*, refers to a text-based representation of an image. For example, if your document contains a picture, you may want to include alternate text that describes the picture. To create alternate text for an image, right-click the image in the document and then click *Format Picture* at the shortcut menu. At the Format Picture task pane, click the Layout & Properties icon and then click *ALT TEXT* to expand the options. Type a title for the image in the *Title* text box and type a description for the image in the *Description* text box.

Create alternate text for a table by right-clicking the table in the document and then clicking *Table Properties* at the shortcut menu. At the Table Properties dialog box, click the Alt Text tab. Type a title for the table in the *Title* text box and a description in the *Description* text box.

When creating alternate text for an object, describe the object accurately and succinctly and avoid phrases such as "Image of. . ." and "This is. . .". The alternate text that you create for an image will display when a screen reader is used to view the document or save the document in a file format such as HTML (hypertext markup language) or DAISY (digital accessible information system). If you save a document in a format that is easy to share or publish, such as PDF (portable document format) or XML (extensible markup language), then all the changes you made to the document to make it accessible are included.

When preparing accessible documents, use the built-in heading styles to identify headings. Screen readers used by people with visual impairments recognize text with a heading style applied as a heading. Text with direct formatting applied, such as a larger font size or bold formatting, is not recognized as a heading by screen readers. Another advantage to applying built-in heading styles is that the font size of the heading text can be increased by modifying the heading style and changing the size of the heading font.

In addition to applying heading styles to make documents more accessible, apply body text styles. As you can with headings, you can modify the size of the body font in the style and all of the text in the document with that style applied will increase in size. Increasing the font size of text in a document makes the text easier to read for people with visual impairments.

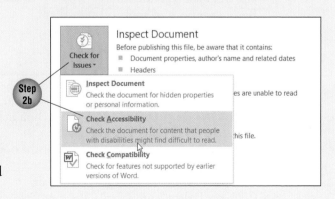

## Exercise 25.5A  Checking the Accessibility of a Document  Part 1 of 3

1. Open **BTZTAdventures.docx** and save the document with the name **C25-E05-BTZTAdventures**.
2. Check the accessibility of the document by completing the following steps:
   a. Click the FILE tab.
   b. At the Info backstage area, click the Check for Issues button and then click *Check Accessibility* at the drop-down list.
   c. Notice the Accessibility Checker task pane that displays at the right side of the screen. The task pane displays an *ERRORS, WARNINGS,* and *TIPS* section.

3. Add alternate text to the picture by completing the following steps:
   a. Click *Picture 3* in the *ERRORS* section in the Accessibility Checker task pane. (This selects the picture in the document.)
   b. Read the information that displays near the bottom of the task pane describing why you should fix the error and how to fix it.
   c. Right-click the picture in the document and then click *Format Picture* at the shortcut menu.
   d. At the Format Picture task pane, click the Layout & Properties icon.
   e. Click *ALT TEXT* to expand the options.
   f. Click in the *Title* text box and then type **Penguins in Antarctica**.
   g. Click in the *Description* text box and then type **Adelie penguins on an iceberg in Antarctica.**
   h. Click the Close button in the upper right corner of the Format Picture task pane.

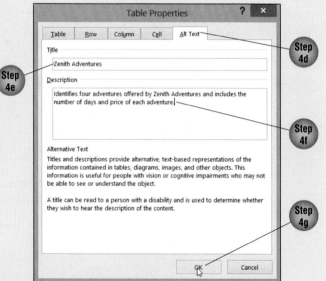

4. Add alternate text to the table in the document by completing the following steps:
   a. Click *Table* in the *ERRORS* section of the Accessibility Checker task pane. (This selects the table in the document.)
   b. Read the information that displays near the bottom of the task pane describing why you should fix the error and how to fix it.
   c. Right-click the table in the document and then click *Table Properties* at the shortcut menu.
   d. At the Table Properties dialog box, click the Alt Text tab.
   e. Click in the *Title* text box and then type **Zenith Adventures**.
   f. Click in the *Description* text box and then type **Identifies four adventures offered by Zenith Adventures and includes the number of days and price of each adventure.**
   g. Click the OK button.
5. Delete the blank row in the table by completing the following steps:
   a. Click *Table Row* in the *WARNINGS* section in the Accessibility Checker task pane. (This selects the blank row in the table.)
   b. Read the information that displays near the bottom of the task pane describing why you should fix the issue and how to fix it.
   c. Click the TABLE TOOLS LAYOUT tab.
   d. Click the Delete button in the Rows & Columns group and then click *Delete Rows* at the drop-down list.

6. Specify that you want the picture in line with the text by completing the following steps:
   a. Click *Picture 3* in the *WARNINGS* section of the Accessibility Checker task pane. (This selects the picture in the document.)
   b. Read the information that displays near the bottom of the task pane describing why you should fix the issue and how to fix it.
   c. Click the Layout Options button that displays outside the upper right corner of the picture.
   d. Click the *In Line with Text* option.
7. Remove blank spaces in the *Upcoming Adventures* heading by completing the following steps:
   a. Click *4 Characters* in the *WARNINGS* section of the Accessibility Checker task pane. (This selects the four blank spaces between *Upcoming* and *Adventures*.)
   b. Read the information that displays near the bottom of the task pane describing why you should fix the issue and how to fix it.
   c. Press the Delete key to delete the four spaces and then press the spacebar once.
8. The last item in the Accessibility Checker task pane is *Using Image Watermark*, which displays in the *TIPS* section. Remove the watermark in the document by completing the following steps:
   a. Click the DESIGN tab.
   b. Click the Watermark button in the Page Background group.
   c. Click *Remove Watermark* at the drop-down list.
9. Notice that the Accessibility Checker task pane now displays a message indicating that no accessibility issues were found. Close the Accessibility Checker task pane.
10. The headings in the document have heading styles applied and the text has the Body Text style applied. Increase the size of the heading fonts in the heading styles by completing the following steps:
    a. Click the HOME tab.
    b. Right-click the *Heading 1* style in the Styles group and then click *Modify* at the shortcut menu.
    c. At the Modify Style dialog box, click the down-pointing arrow at the right side of the *Font Size* option box and then click *26* at the drop-down list.
    d. Click OK to close the Modify Style dialog box. (If the title *BAYSIDE TRAVEL* does not display in 26 point size, reapply the Heading 1 style to the title.)
    e. Right-click the *Heading 2* style in the Styles group and then click *Modify* at the shortcut menu.
    f. At the Modify Style dialog box, click the down-pointing arrow at the right side of the *Font Size* option box and then click *20* at the drop-down list.
    g. Click OK to close the Modify Style dialog box.
11. Increase the size of the body font in the text style by completing the following steps:
    a. Click anywhere in the paragraph of text below the heading *Antarctic Zenith Adventures*.
    b. Click the More button at the right side of the Styles group and then click *Apply Styles* at the drop-down gallery.
    c. At the Apply Styles window, make sure *Body Text* displays in the *Style Name* text box. If not, select the text in the *Style Name* text box, type **Body Text**, and then press Enter. (This identifies the font in the Body Text style that was applied to the text in the document.)

Step 11c

Step 11d

    d. Click the Modify button in the Apply Styles window.
    e. At the Modify Style dialog box, make sure that *Body Text* displays in the *Name* text box.
    f. Click the down-pointing arrow at the right side of the *Font Size* option box and then click *14* at the drop-down list.
    g. Click OK to close the Modify Style dialog box.
    h. Close the Apply Styles window.
12. Save and then print **C25-E05-BTZTAdventures.docx**.

## Checking the Compatibility of a Document

**QUICK STEPS**

**Check Compatibility**
1. Click FILE tab.
2. Click Check for Issues button.
3. Click *Check Compatibility*.
4. Click OK.

Word includes a compatibility checker that checks documents to identify elements that are not supported or will act differently in previous versions of Word (from Word 97 through Word 2010). To run the compatibility checker, open the desired document, click the FILE tab, click the Check for Issues button at the Info backstage area, and then click *Check Compatibility* at the drop-down list. This displays the Microsoft Word Compatibility Checker dialog box, as shown in Figure 25.10. The dialog box displays a summary of the elements in the document that are not compatible with previous versions of Word. The dialog box also indicates what will happen when the document is saved and then opened in a previous version.

**Figure 25.10  Microsoft Word Compatibility Checker Dialog Box**

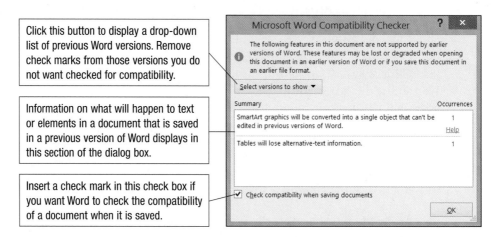

Click this button to display a drop-down list of previous Word versions. Remove check marks from those versions you do not want checked for compatibility.

Information on what will happen to text or elements in a document that is saved in a previous version of Word displays in this section of the dialog box.

Insert a check mark in this check box if you want Word to check the compatibility of a document when it is saved.

Click the Select versions to show button and a drop-down list displays with three options: *Word 97-2003*, *Word 2007*, and *Word 2010*. If you are sending the document to someone who will be opening it in Word 2010, click the *Word 97-2003* option at the drop-down list to remove the check mark. Click the Select versions to show button again and then click the *Word 2007* option at the drop-down list. With this option selected, only compatibility issues between Word 2013 and Word 2010 will display in the Microsoft Word Compatibility Checker dialog box. If you want to check compatibility issues with versions 97 through 2003, remove the check mark from the *Word 2007* and *Word 2010* options. If you want the compatibility checker to check a document each time you save it, insert a check mark in the *Check compatibility when saving documents* check box.

1. With **C25-E05-BTZTAdventures.docx** open, check the compatibility of elements in the document by completing the following steps:

    a. Press Ctrl + End to move the insertion point to the end of the document and then press the Enter key two times.

    b. Insert **BTZTGraphic.docx** from your Chapter25 folder.

    c. Click the FILE tab, click the Check for Issues button at the Info backstage area, and then click *Check Compatibility* at the drop-down list.

    d. At the Microsoft Word Compatibility Checker dialog box, read the information that displays in the *Summary* list box.

    e. Click the Select versions to show button and then click *Word 97-2003* at the drop-down list. (This removes the check mark from the option.) Notice that the information about SmartArt graphics being converted to static objects disappears from the *Summary* list box. This is because Word 2007 and Word 2010 support SmartArt graphics.

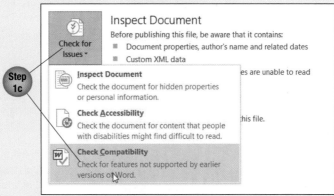

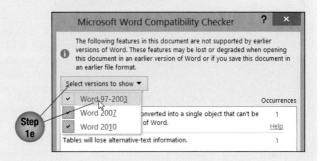

    f. Click OK to close the dialog box.

2. Save **C25-E05-BTZTAdventures.docx**.

3. Save the document in Word 2003 format by completing the following steps:

    a. Press the F12 key to display the Save As dialog box.

    b. At the Save As dialog box, click the *Save as type* option box and then click *Word 97-2003 Document (*.doc)* at the drop-down list.

    c. Select the text in the *File name* text box and then type **C25-E05-BTZTAdv-2003format**.

    d. Click the Save button.

    e. Click the Continue button.

4. Close **C25-E05-BTZTAdv-2003format.doc**.

## Managing Versions

As you work in a document, Word automatically saves the document every 10 minutes. This automatic backup feature can be helpful if you accidentally close your document without saving it or if the power to your computer is disrupted while you are working in the document. The backup versions of your document that Word automatically saves are listed to the right of the Manage Versions button at the Info backstage area, as shown in Figure 25.11 on the next page. Each autosave document displays with *Today* followed by the time and *(autosave)*. When you save and then close your document, the autosave backup documents are deleted.

**Figure 25.11  Autosave Documents at Info Backstage Area**

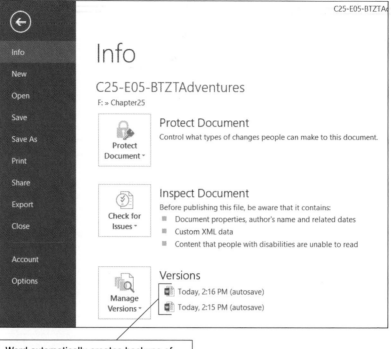

Word automatically creates backups of your document and lists them in this section. The backup documents are deleted when you save the document. To open a backup, click the desired version.

**QUICK STEPS**

**Open an Autosave Backup Document**
1. Click FILE tab.
2. Click document name at right of Manage Versions button.
3. Display UnsavedFiles folder.
OR
1. Click FILE tab.
2. Click Manage Versions button.
3. Click *Recover Unsaved Documents*.
OR
1. Click FILE tab.
2. Click *Open* option.
3. Click Recover Unsaved Documents button.

To open an autosave backup document, click the FILE tab and then click the backup document that you want to open, which displays to the right of the Manage Versions button. The document opens as a read-only document and a yellow message bar displays with a Compare button and Restore button. Click the Compare button and the autosave document is compared to the original document. You can then decide which changes to accept and reject. Click the Restore button and a message displays indicating that you are about to overwrite the last saved version with the selected version. At this message, click OK.

When you save a document, the autosave backup documents are deleted. However, if you close a document without saving it (after 10 minutes) or the power is disrupted while you are working, Word keeps the backup file in the UnsavedFiles folder on the hard drive. Access this folder by clicking the Manage Versions button at the Info backstage area and then clicking *Recover Unsaved Documents*. At the Open dialog box that displays, double-click the backup file that you want to open. You can also display the UnsavedFiles folder by clicking the FILE tab, clicking the *Open* option, and then clicking the Recover Unsaved Documents button that displays near the *Recent Documents* list.

Files in the UnsavedFiles folder are kept for four days after the creation of the document. After that, they are automatically deleted.

Manage a backup file by right-clicking the backup file. At the shortcut menu that displays, click the *Open Version* option to open the backup file, click the *Delete This Version* option to delete the backup file, or click the *Compare with Current* option to compare the backup file with the currently open file. If you want to delete all of the unsaved files, open a blank document, click the FILE tab, click the Manage Versions button, and then click the *Delete All Unsaved Documents* option. At the message asking if you are sure you want to delete the unsaved documents, click Yes.

As mentioned previously, Word automatically saves a backup of your unsaved document every 10 minutes by default. To change this default setting, click the FILE tab and then click *Options*. At the Word Options dialog box, click *Save* in the left panel. Notice that the *Save AutoRecover information every* measurement box is set at 10 minutes. To change this number, click the up-pointing arrow to the right of *10* to increase the number of minutes between autosaves or click the down-pointing arrow to decrease the number of minutes between autosaves.

**QUICK STEPS**

**Delete a Backup File**
1. Click FILE tab.
2. Right-click backup file.
3. Click *Delete This Version*.

**Delete All Unsaved Versions**
1. Click FILE tab.
2. Click Manage Versions button.
3. Click *Delete All Unsaved Documents*.
4. Click Yes.

**Change the AutoRecover Time**
1. Click FILE tab.
2. Click *Options*.
3. Click *Save*.
4. Type desired minutes in *Save AutoRecover information every* measurement box.
5. Click OK.

**Exercise 25.5C**   Opening an Autosave Document                      Part 3 of 3

1. Decrease the autosave time by completing the following steps:
   a. Click the FILE tab and then click *Options*.
   b. At the Word Options dialog box, click *Save* in the left panel.
   c. Click the down-pointing arrow at the right of the *Save AutoRecover information every* measurement box until *1* displays.

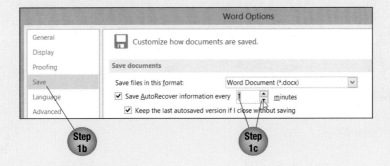

2. Open **C25-E05-BTZTAdventures.docx**.
3. Press Ctrl + End to move the insertion point to the end of the document and then type your first and last names.

4. Leave the document open for more than one minute without making any changes. After at least one minute has passed, click the FILE tab and then check to see if an autosave document displays to the right of the Manage Versions button. (If not, click the Back button to return to the document and wait a few more minutes.)

5. When an autosave document displays at the Info backstage area, click the Back button to return to the document.

6. Select the SmartArt and then delete the SmartArt.

7. Click the FILE tab and then click the autosave document that displays to the right of the Manage Versions button. If more than one autosave document displays, click the one at the top of the list. This opens the autosave document as read-only.

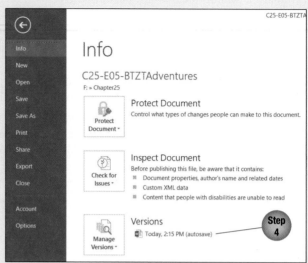

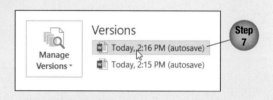

8. Restore the document to the autosave document by clicking the Restore button that displays in the yellow message bar.

9. At the message that displays indicating you are about to overwrite the last saved version with the selected version, click OK. (This saves the document with the SmartArt.)

10. Press the Esc key to display the document in Normal view.

11. Check to see what versions of previous documents Word has saved by completing the following steps:
    a. Click the FILE tab.
    b. Click the Manage Versions button and then click *Recover Unsaved Documents* at the drop-down list.
    c. At the Open dialog box that displays draft documents in the UnsavedFiles folder on your hard drive, check the documents that display in the Content pane.
    d. Click the Cancel button to close the Open dialog box.

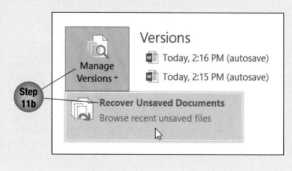

12. Delete a backup file by completing the following steps:
    a. Click the FILE tab.
    b. Right-click the first autosave backup file name that displays to the right of the Manage Versions button.
    c. Click *Delete This Version* at the shortcut menu.
    d. At the message that displays asking if you are sure you want to delete the selected version, click the Yes button.
13. Return the autosave time back to 10 minutes by completing the following steps:
    a. At the backstage area, click *Options.*
    b. At the Word Options dialog box, click *Save* in the left panel.
    c. Click the up-pointing arrow at the right of the *Save AutoRecover information every* measurement box until *10* displays.
    d. Click OK to close the dialog box.
14. Save, print, and then close **C25-E05-BTZTAdventures.docx**.
15. Delete all of the unsaved backup files by completing the following steps:
    a. Press Ctrl + N to display a blank document.
    b. Click the FILE tab.
    c. Click the Manage Versions button and then click *Delete All Unsaved Documents*.
    d. At the message that displays, click Yes.
16. Click the Back button to return to the blank document.

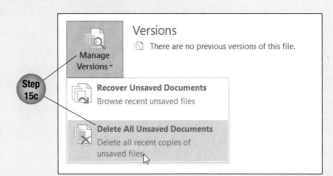

# Sharing Documents

Word provides a number of options for sharing documents between programs, websites, and other computers and as email attachments. Options for sending and sharing documents are available at the Share backstage area. Display this area by clicking the FILE tab and then clicking the *Share* option.

## Inviting People to View a Document

Invite people to view your document at the *Invite People* option at the Share backstage area. To use this feature, you must first save your Word document to your SkyDrive or a shared location, such as a website or SharePoint library. (Microsoft SharePoint is a collection of products and software that includes a number of components. If your company or organization uses SharePoint, you and your colleagues can save documents in a library on your organization's SharePoint site and have a central location for accessing documents.)

If you have a Word document open from your SkyDrive folder (or another shared location), the Share backstage area with the *Invite People* option selected will display, as shown in Figure 25.12 on the next page. If you have a document open that is not saved to your SkyDrive, the information at the right side of the backstage area will tell you to save your document. To do this, click the Save To Cloud button and at the Save As backstage area, click your SkyDrive and then click the Browse button. At the Save

As dialog box, navigate to your SkyDrive folder and then click the Save button. In a few moments, the Share backstage area will redisplay with the options shown in Figure 25.12.

When you click the *Invite People* option at the Share backstage area, options display for typing the names or email addresses of the people that you want to view and/or edit the document. If you want to invite several people, separate the names or email addresses with semicolons.

The option box to the right of the *Type names or e-mail addresses* text box contains the default setting *Can edit*. At this setting, the people you invite can edit the document. If you want the people you invite only to view the document, change this option to *Can View*.

When all of the names or email addresses are entered, click the Share button. An email is sent to each email address you typed, and in a few moments, the name or names display in the backstage area below the *Shared with* heading. Any time you open the document in the future and display the Share backstage area, the names of the people you shared the document with will display below the *Shared with* heading. If you want to stop sharing the document with someone, right-click the person's name below the *Shared with* heading and then click *Remove User* at the shortcut menu.

**Figure 25.12 Share Backstage Area**

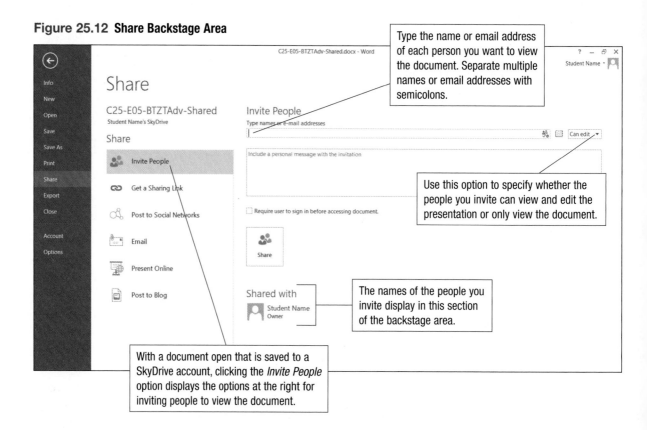

*Note: To complete this exercise, you must have a SkyDrive account.*

1. Open **C25-E05-BTZTAdventures.docx** and save the document with the name **C25-E06-BTZTAdv**.
2. Save **C25-E06-BTZTAdv.docx** to your SkyDrive folder and name it **C25-E06-BTZTAdv-Shared**.
3. With **C25-E06-BTZTAdv-Shared.docx** open, click the FILE tab and then click the *Share* option.
4. At the Share backstage area, click in the *Type names or e-mail addresses* text box.
5. Type the email address for your instructor and/or the email address of a classmate or friend.
6. Click the down-pointing arrow at the right side of the option box containing the text *Can edit* and then click *Can view* at the drop-down list.
7. Click the Share button.

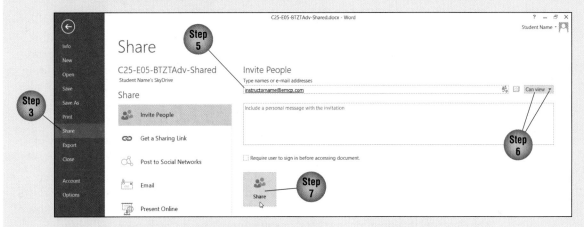

8. After a few moments, notice the name or names that display below the *Shared with* heading in the Share backstage area.
9. Check with your instructor and/or classmate or friend to see if they were able to open the emails containing the links to your document.
10. Remove the name (or one of the names) that displays below the *Shared with* heading by right-clicking the name and then clicking *Remove User* at the shortcut menu.
11. If you have **C25-E06-BTZTAdv.docx** saved on a removable device, close **C25-E06-BTZT Adv-Shared.docx** saved to your SkyDrive and then reopen **C25-E06-BTZTAdv.docx** from your removable device.

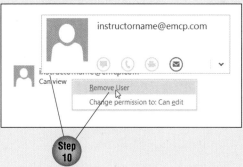

If you open a document that is saved to your SkyDrive, the Share backstage area displays additional options, including *Get a Sharing Link* and *Post to Social Networks*. Click *Get a Sharing Link* and options display for creating a link for viewing or for editing. Click the Create Link button that displays to the right of the *View Link* text box and a link displays for viewing the document. Click the Create Link button to the right of the *Edit Link* text box and a link displays for viewing and editing the document. If you want to paste a link for viewing your document but not editing it, select the link that displays in the *View Link* text box and then paste it in an email, instant message, or social media site. If you want to paste a link for viewing and editing, click the Create Link button to the right of the *Edit Link* text box and then copy the link that displays.

Click the *Post to Social Networks* options to connect to and post your document to a social network, such as Facebook or Twitter. Before being able to post, you must connect to the desired social network(s). If you are not connected, click the *Post to Social Networks* option and then click the <u>Click here to connect social networks</u> hyperlink.

## Sending a Document as an Email Attachment

If you click the *Email* option at the Share backstage area, options display for sending a copy of the document as an attachment to an email, sending a link to the document, attaching a PDF or XPS copy of the open document to an email address, and sending an email as an Internet fax.

To send a document as an email attachment, you must have an Outlook email account. If you want to create an email that contains a link to the document, the document must be saved to your SkyDrive or a shared location, such as a website or SharePoint library.

Click the Send as PDF button and your document is converted to PDF format and attached to the email. As noted earlier, the acronym *PDF* stands stand for *portable document format*, which is a file format developed by Adobe Systems that captures all of the elements in a document as an electronic image. Click the Send as XPS button and your document is converted to XPS format and attached to the email. XPS is a Microsoft file format for publishing content in an easily viewable format. The acronym *XPS* stands stand for *XML paper specification*. The acronym *XML* stands for *extensible markup language*, which is a set of rules for encoding documents electronically. Information displays to the right of each button and provides a brief description of the format.

Click the Send as Internet Fax button to fax the current document without using a fax machine. To use this button, you must be signed up with a fax service provider. If you have not previously signed up for a service, you will be prompted to do so.

*Note: Before completing this optional exercise, check with your instructor to determine if Outlook is your email provider.*

1. With **C25-E06-BTZTAdv.docx** open, click the FILE tab and then click the *Share* option.
2. At the Share backstage area, click the *Email* option and then click the Send as Attachment button.

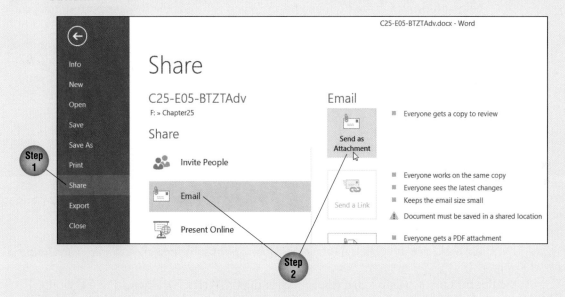

3. At the Outlook window, type your instructor's email address in the *To* text box.
4. Click the Send button.

## Presenting a Document Online

With the Present Online feature, you can share a Word document with others over the Internet. Send links to the people you want to view the document and then they can view the document using their own browsers. To use this feature, you must have a network service to host the document. You can use the Office Document Service, which is available to anyone with a Windows Live ID (such as a SkyDrive account) and Microsoft Office 2013. You can view an online document in Internet Explorer, Firefox, and Safari.

To present a document online, click the *Present Online* option at the Share backstage area and then click the Present Online button. At the Present Online window that displays, click the CONNECT button, and, if necessary, enter your Windows Live ID user name and password. When Word has connected to your account and prepared your document, the Present Online window will display with a unique link that Word created for your document. Click the Copy Link hyperlink in the Present Online window to copy the unique link and then paste the link into an email you will send to the people you want to view your document. If you have an Outlook account, you can also click the Send in Email hyperlink to open Outlook and then paste the link in a message window.

After everyone has opened the document link in a web browser, click the START PRESENTATION button in the Present Online window. The people viewing your document do not need to have Word installed on their computers to view the document because the document will display through their web browsers.

When presenting your document online, the PRESENT ONLINE tab displays with options for sharing the document through OneNote, displaying the unique link to send to more people, editing the document, and ending the document presentation. When presenting your document online, you can make edits to the document by clicking the Edit button in the Present Online group on the PRESENT ONLINE tab. A yellow message bar will display telling you that the presentation is paused. Make the desired edits and then click the Resume button. When you click the Resume button, the people viewing your document will see the edited version.

When you are finished presenting your document, click the End Online Presentation button in the Present Online group on the PRESENT ONLINE tab. At the message that displays telling you that all of the people will be disconnected and asking if you want to end the online presentation, click the End Online Presentation button.

## Exercise 25.6C  Optional: Presenting Online                     Part 3 of 3

*Note: To complete this project, you must have a Windows Live ID account. Depending on your system configuration and what services are available, these steps will vary.*

1. With **C25-E06-BTZTAdv.docx** open, click the FILE tab and then click the *Share* option.
2. At the Share backstage area, click the *Present Online* option and then click the Present Online button.
3. At the Present Online window that displays, click the CONNECT button. (If a CONNECT button does not appear, skip to Step 5.)
4. Type your user name and password into the Windows Security dialog box.
5. At the Present Online window with the unique link selected, click the Copy Link hyperlink.
6. Send the link to colleagues by opening the desired email account, pasting the link into a new message window, and then sending the email to the viewers. If you are using Microsoft Outlook, click the Send in Email hyperlink and Microsoft Outlook opens in a new message window with the link inserted in the message. In Outlook, send the link to the people you want to view the document.
7. When everyone has received the link, click the START PRESENTATION button at the Present Online window.
8. Edit one of the prices in the table by completing the following steps:
   a. Click the Edit button in the Present Online group on the PRESENT ONLINE tab.
   b. Scroll through the document to display the table.
   c. Edit the Antarctic Exploration adventure price from *$4,399* to *$3,500*. (You may need to increase the zoom of the document.)
   d. Click the Resume button on the yellow message bar.
9. Click the End Online Presentation button on the PRESENT ONLINE tab.
10. At the message that displays telling you that all remote viewers will be disconnected if you continue, click the End Online Presentation button.
11. If necessary, increase the zoom of the document back to 100%.
12. Save, print, and then close **C25-E05-BTZTAdv.docx**.

# Chapter *Summary*

➤ Restrict formatting and editing in a document and apply a password to it with options at the Restrict Editing task pane. Display this task pane by clicking the REVIEW tab and then clicking the Restrict Editing button in the Protect group.

➤ Restrict formatting by specifying styles that are and are not allowed in a document. Do this at the Formatting Restrictions dialog box. Display this dialog box by clicking the <u>Settings</u> hyperlink in the Restrict Editing task pane.

➤ To restrict editing in a document, click the *Allow only this type of editing in the document* option at the Restrict Editing task pane, click the down-pointing arrow at the right of the option box, and then click the desired option.

➤ Enforce editing and formatting restrictions by clicking the Yes, Start Enforcing Protection button in the Restrict Editing task pane and then create a password at the Start Enforcing Protection dialog box.

➤ Protect a document with a password using options at the Start Enforcing Protection dialog box or General Options dialog box.

➤ Open a document in different views with options at the Open button drop-down list in the Open dialog box.

➤ The Info backstage area displays document properties information.

➤ Display the document information panel by clicking the Properties button at the Info backstage area and then clicking *Show Document Panel* at the drop-down list. Describe the document by typing information in the text boxes at the document information panel.

➤ Document information can also be added at the Properties dialog box. Display this dialog box by clicking the Properties button at the Info backstage area and then clicking *Advanced Properties* or by clicking the Document Properties button at the document information panel and then clicking *Advanced Properties*.

➤ When a document is marked as final, it is saved as a read-only document. Mark a document as final by clicking the Protect Document button at the Info backstage area and then clicking *Mark as Final* at the drop-down list. Typing, editing commands, and proofing marks are turned off when a document is marked as final.

➤ Protect a document with a password by clicking the Protect Document button at the Info backstage area and then clicking *Encrypt with Password*. At the Encrypt Document dialog box, type the password and then press the Enter key. Type the password again at the Confirm Password dialog box and then press the Enter key.

➤ Another method for displaying the Restrict Editing task pane is to click the Protect Document button at the Info backstage area and then click *Restrict Editing* at the drop-down list.

➤ Inspect a document for personal data, hidden data, and metadata with options at the Document Inspector dialog box. Display this dialog box by clicking the Check for Issues button at the Info backstage area and then clicking *Inspect Document* at the drop-down list.

➤ The accessibility checker reviews a document to identify content that people with disabilities might find difficult to read. Run the accessibility checker by clicking the Check for Issues button at the Info backstage area and then clicking *Check Accessibility* at the drop-down list.

➤ Run the compatibility checker to review your document and identify elements that are not supported or will act differently in previous versions of Word. To determine the compatibility of the features in your document, click the Check for Issues button at the Info backstage area and then click *Check Compatibility* at the drop-down list.

- By default, Word automatically saves a backup of an unsaved document every 10 minutes and the backup documents display to the right of the Manage Versions button at the Info backstage area. Open a backup document by clicking the document name.
- When you save a document, Word automatically deletes the backup documents. However, if you close a document without saving it or if the power to your computer is disrupted while you are working, Word keeps the backup document in the UnsavedFiles folder on the hard drive. Display this folder by clicking the Manage Versions button at the Info backstage area and then clicking *Recover Unsaved Documents* at the drop-down list.
- Delete an autosave backup file by displaying the Info backstage area, right-clicking the desired autosave backup file, and then clicking *Delete This Version* at the shortcut menu. Delete all of the unsaved documents by displaying a blank document, clicking the FILE tab, clicking the Manage Versions button, and then clicking *Delete All Unsaved Documents*.
- You can change the 10-minute autosave default setting with the *Save AutoRecover information every* measurement box at the Word Options dialog box with *Save* selected. Display this dialog box by clicking the FILE tab, clicking *Options*, and then clicking *Save* in the left panel.
- With options at the Share backstage area, you can invite people to view and/or edit a document, send a document as an email attachment in PDF or XPS format, send a document as a fax, and present a document online.
- Use the Present Online feature to share a document with others over the Internet. Send links to the people you want to view the document and then they can view the document in their own browsers.

# *Commands* Review

| FEATURE | RIBBON TAB, GROUP | BUTTON, OPTION |
|---|---|---|
| accessibility checker | FILE | , *Check Accessibility* |
| compatibility checker | FILE | , *Check Compatibility* |
| document information panel | FILE | Properties ▾ , *Show Document Panel* |
| Document Inspector dialog box | File | , *Inspect Document* |
| Encrypt Document dialog box | FILE | , *Encrypt with Password* |
| Formatting Restrictions dialog box | REVIEW, Protect | , <u>Settings</u> |
| General Options dialog box | | **F12, Tools,** *General Options* |
| Properties dialog box | FILE | Properties ▾ , *Advanced Properties* |
| Restrict Editing task pane | REVIEW, Protect | |
| Share backstage area | FILE | *Share* |
| UnsavedFiles folder | FILE | , *Recover Unsaved Documents* |

# Key Points *Review*

**Completion:** In the space provided at the right, indicate the correct term, command, or number.

1. Use options in this section of the Restrict Editing task pane to limit how users can format the text in a document. _____

2. Use options in this section of the Restrict Editing task pane to limit how users can revise the text in a document. _____

3. Click this button in the Restrict Editing task pane to display the Start Enforcing Protection dialog box. _____

4. Protect a document with a password using options at the Start Enforcing Protection dialog box or with options at this dialog box. _____

5. You can add information about a document's properties at this panel. _____

6. Display the Properties dialog box by clicking the Document Properties button at the Info backstage area and then clicking this option at the drop-down list. _____

7. Mark a document as final by clicking this button at the Info backstage area and then clicking *Mark as Final* at the drop-down list. _____

8. Use this feature to inspect a document for personal data, hidden data, and metadata. _____

9. This feature checks a document for content that people with disabilities might find difficult to read. _____

10. Use this feature to check a document and identify elements that are not supported in previous versions of Word. _____

11. By default, Word automatically saves a document after this number of minutes. _____

12. Word keeps backup files of unsaved documents in this folder on the hard drive. _____

13. The *Invite People* option is available at this backstage area. _____

14. With this feature, you can share a Word document with others over the Internet. _____

# *Chapter Assessments*

## Applying Your Skills

Demonstrate your knowledge of features learned in this chapter by completing the following assessments.

### Assessment 25.1    Restrict Formatting and Editing of a Writing Report

1. Open **WritingProcess.docx** and save the document with the name **C25-A01-WritingProcess**.
2. Display the Restrict Editing task pane and then restrict formatting to Heading 2 and Heading 3 styles. (At the message that displays asking if you want to remove formatting or styles that are not allowed, click No.)
3. Enforce the protection and provide the password *writing*.
4. Click the <u>Available styles</u> hyperlink in the Restrict Editing task pane.
5. Apply the Heading 2 style to the two titles: *THE WRITING PROCESS* and *REFERENCES*.
6. Apply the Heading 3 style to the seven remaining headings in the document. (The Heading 3 style may not display until you apply the Heading 2 style to the first title.)
7. Close the Styles task pane and then close the Restrict Editing task pane.
8. Save the document and then print only page 1.
9. Close **C25-A01-WritingProcess.docx**.

### Assessment 25.2    Restrict Editing to Comments in a Software Life Cycle Document

1. Open **CommCycle.docx** and save the document with the name **C25-A02-CommCycle**.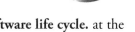
2. Display the Restrict Editing task pane, restrict editing to comments only, and then start enforcing the protection. (Do not provide a password.)
3. Type the comment **Create a SmartArt graphic that illustrates the software life cycle.** at the end of the first paragraph of text in the document.
4. Type the comment **Include the problem-solving steps.** at the end of the paragraph in the *Design* section.
5. Type the comment **Describe a typical beta testing cycle.** at the end of the paragraph in the *Testing* section.
6. Close the Restrict Editing task pane and, if necessary, close the Reviewing pane.
7. Print only the comments.
8. Save and then close **C25-A02-CommCycle.docx**.

### Assessment 25.3    Insert Document Properties, Check Accessibility and Compatibility, and Save a Presentation Document in a Different Format

1. Open **Presentation.docx** and save the document with the name **C25-A03-Presentation**.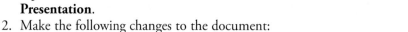
2. Make the following changes to the document:
   a. Apply the Heading 1 style to the title *Delivering a How-To Presentation*.
   b. Apply the Heading 2 style to the three headings in the document.
   c. Change the style set to Centered.
   d. Apply the View theme and apply the Green theme colors.
   e. Change the color of the clip art image to Green, Accent color 1 Light.
3. Display the document information panel and then type the following in the specified text boxes:
      Author: (type your first and last names)
      Title: **Delivering a How-To Presentation**
      Subject: **Presentations**

Keywords: **presentation, how-to, delivering, topics**
Comments: **This document describes the three steps involved in developing a how-to presentation.**

4. Display the Properties dialog box (by clicking the Document Properties button in the upper left corner of the document information panel and then clicking *Advanced Properties*) and then create the following custom properties (with the Custom tab selected):
   a. Click *Checked by* in the *Name* list box, leave the *Type* option set at *Text*, type your first and last names in the *Value* text box, and then click the Add button.
   b. Click *Date completed* in the *Name* list box, change the *Type* option to *Date*, type today's date in the *Value* text box, and then click the Add button.
   c. Click *Project* in the *Name* list box, change the *Type* option to *Text*, type **Preparing and Delivering Presentations** in the *Value* text box, and then click the Add button.
   d. With the Properties dialog box open, press Alt + Print Screen button on your keyboard to capture an image of the dialog box.
   e. Click OK to close the Properties dialog box.
5. At the document, complete the following steps:
   a. Close the document information panel.
   b. Press Ctrl + N to open a blank document.
   c. Click the Paste button to insert the screen capture image.
   d. Print the document.
   e. Close the document without saving it.
6. Save **C25-A03-Presentation.docx** and then print only the document properties. (The custom properties do not print.)
7. Run the accessibility checker on the document and then create alternate text for the clip art image and the SmartArt graphic. Close the accessibility checker.
8. Save and then print **C25-A03-Presentation.docx**.
9. Run the compatibility checker to determine what features are not supported by earlier versions of Word.
10. Save the document in the *Word 97-2003 Document (*.doc)* format and name it **C25-A03-Presentation-2003format**.
11. Save, print, and then close **C25-A03-Presentation-2003format.doc**.

# Expanding Your Skills

Explore additional feature options or use Help to learn a new skill in creating this document.

## Assessment 25.4    Create a Document on Inserting and Removing a Signature

1. The Text group on the INSERT tab contains a Signature Line button for inserting a signature in a document. Use Word's Help feature to learn about inserting and removing a signature by typing **add or remove a digital signature** at the Word Help window and then clicking the Add or remove a digital signature in Office files hyperlink. Read the information in the article and then prepare a Word document with the following information:
   • An appropriate title
   • How to create a signature line in Word
   • How to sign a signature line in Word
   • How to remove a signature from Word
   • How to add an invisible digital signature in Word
2. Apply formatting to enhance the appearance of the document.
3. Save the document and name it **C25-A04-Signature**.
4. Print and then close **C25-A04-Signature.docx**.

# Achieving Signature Status

Take your skills to the next level by completing this more challenging assessment.

## Assessment 25.5 — Format, Insert Document Properties, Check Compatibility, and Save a Document in a Different Format

1. Open **InfoSystem.docx** and save the document with the name **C25-A05-InfoSystem**.
2. Format the document so it appears as shown in Figure 25.13 on the next page with the following specifications:
   a. Apply the Lines (Stylish) style set and then apply the Dividend theme.
   b. Insert the Integral footer and type your name as the author.
   c. Insert the SmartArt Continuous Cycle graphic and apply the Colorful - Accent Colors color and the Metallic Scene style.
   d. Recolor the clip art image as shown in the figure.
   e. Make any other changes necessary so your document displays as shown in Figure 25.13.
3. Display the document information panel and then type the following in the specified text boxes:
   Author: (type your first and last names)
   Title: **Developing an Information System**
   Subject: **Software Development**
   Keywords: **software, design, plan**
   Category: **Software**
   Status: **Draft**
   Comments: **This document describes the four steps involved in developing an information system.**
4. Display the Properties dialog box with the Custom tab selected and then add the following properties:
   a. Add the *Client* property with the text **Stylus Enterprises**.
   b. Add the *Department* property with the text **Development Department**.
   c. Add the *Document number* property with the number **24**.
   d. Press Alt + Print Screen key to make a screen capture image of the dialog box.
   e. Close the Properties dialog box.
   f. At the document, close the document information panel, press Ctrl + N to insert a blank document, and then paste your screen capture image. Print the document and then close it without saving it.
5. At the **C25-A05-InfoSystem.docx** document, save the document and then print only the document properties.
6. Inspect the document and remove any hidden text.
7. Run the accessibility checker and then create alternate text for the clip art image.
8. Save **C25-A05-InfoSystem.docx**.
9. Run the compatibility checker to determine what features are not supported by earlier versions of Word.
10. Save the document in the *Word 97-2003 Document (*.doc)* format and name it **C25-A05-InfoSystem-2003format**.
11. Save, print, and then close **C25-A05-InfoSystem-2003format.docx**.

**Figure 25.13  Assessment 25.5**

## Developing an Information System

Identifying and assembling a team of employees with the required skills and expertise is a necessary first step in developing a new in-house information system. A management group may be involved in answering questions and providing information in the early planning phases of the project, but programmers and/or software engineers handle the design and implementation of any new system.

Programmers specialize in the development of new software, while software engineers are highly skilled professionals with programming and teamwork training. Their organized, professional application of the software development process is called software engineering.

### Project Plan

The first step in the system development life cycle is planning. The planning step involves preparing a needs analysis and conducting feasibility studies. During this step, a company usually establishes a project team, and the team creates a project plan. The project plan includes an estimate of how long the project will take to complete, an outline of the steps involved, and a list of deliverables. Deliverables are documents, services, hardware, and software that must be finished and delivered by a certain time and date.

### Project Team

Because of their large size, information systems require the creation of a project team. A project team usually includes a project manager, who acts as the team leader. Sometimes the project manager also functions as a systems analyst, responsible for completing the systems analysis and making design recommendations. Other project team members include software engineers and technicians. The software engineers deal with programming software, while technicians handle hardware issues. The comprehensive process software engineers initiate is called the system development life cycle (SDLC), a series of steps culminating in a completed information system.

### Designing the System

A project is ready to move into the design stage once the project team has approved the plan, including the budget. The design process begins with the writing of the documentation, which covers functional and design specifications. In most cases, the project team creates the functional specifications, describing what the system must be able to do.

ext phase, implementation, once the development team and the systems ation and approve the plans. This step is where the actual work of putting , including creating a prototype and completing the programming. In most em is the longest, most difficult step in the process.

STUDENT NAME   1

### Support Stage

A system goes into the support stage after it has been accepted and approved. A support contract normally allows users to contact the systems house for technical support, training, and sometimes on-site troubleshooting. Even if the system was designed in-house, the responsible department often operates as an independent entity—sometimes even charging the department acquiring the system. The support stage continues until a new information system is proposed and developed, usually years later. At that point, the existing system is retired and no longer used.

STUDENT NAME   2

# *Performance Assessments*

U N I T **5**

## Customizing Documents and Features

## ASSESSING PROFICIENCIES

In this unit, you learned how to insert, modify, and delete building blocks and how to customize AutoCorrect, Word options, themes, and style sets. You also learned how to create, edit, and modify styles; apply styles to text in documents; and protect and prepare documents for distribution.

*Note: Before beginning computer assessments, copy to your storage medium the Unit05PA folder from the CD that accompanies this textbook and then make Unit05PA the active folder.*

**Assessment U5.1**    **Format and Insert Fields in a Report**

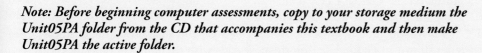

1. Open **Singapore.docx** and save the document with the name **U5-PA01-Singapore**.
2. With the insertion point positioned at the beginning of the document, press Ctrl + Enter to insert a page break.
3. Apply the Heading 1 style to the title *SINGAPORE*.
4. Apply the Heading 2 style to the seven headings in the document.
5. Apply the Lines (Stylish) style set and change the theme colors to Blue Warm.
6. Use the Paragraph Spacing button on the DESIGN tab to change the paragraph spacing to Double.
7. Move the *Population* chart so it is positioned below the paragraph of text in the *Population* section.
8. Insert the *Filigree* footer building block and then make the document active.
9. Press Ctrl + Home to move the insertion point to the beginning of the document.
10. Insert the *Automatic Table 1* table of contents building block.
11. Press Ctrl + End to move the insertion point to the end of the document and then insert a field that will insert the file name. Press Enter and then insert a field that will insert the current date and time.
12. Save, print, and then close **U5-PA01-Singapore.docx**.

**Assessment U5.2**    **Create Building Blocks and Prepare a Business Letter**

1. Open **TRC-CBFooter.docx**.
2. Select the entire document, save the selected text in a custom building block in the *Quick Part* gallery, and name the building block with your initials followed by *TRC-CBFooter*.
3. Close **TRC-CBFooter.docx**.
4. Open **TRC-CBLtrhd.docx**.
5. Select the entire document, save the selected text in a custom building block in the *Quick Part* gallery, and name the building block with your initials followed by *TRC-CBLtrhd*.
6. Close **TRC-CBLtrhd.docx**.

7. At a blank document, click the *No Spacing* style in the Styles group on the HOME tab and then type the following text:

> **We carry a variety of earth-moving equipment for heavy construction including backhoes, dozers, excavators (including hydraulic excavators and mini-excavators), skid-steer loaders (including compact skid-steer, track skid-steer, and wheeled skid-steer loaders), tractors, cable locators, trenchers (including ride-on and walk-behind trenchers), and wheel loaders.**

8. Select the entire document, save the selected text in a custom building block in the *Quick Part* gallery, and name the building block with your initials followed by *TRC-CBEquipPara*.
9. Save each custom building block in the *Quick Part* gallery as a Quick Parts button on the Quick Access toolbar.
10. Close the document without saving it.
11. At a blank document, click the *No Spacing* style and then create the business letter shown in Figure U5.1 on the next page with the following specifications:
    a. Insert as a page header the custom building block that is named with your initials followed by *TRC-CBLtrhd*. **Hint: To do this, click the Quick Parts button on the Quick Access toolbar,** right-click *the custom building block, and then click the* **Insert at Page Header** *option.*
    b. Type the date, inside address, and first paragraph of text as shown in Figure U5.1.
    c. Insert the custom building block that is named with your initials followed by *TRC-CBEquipPara*.
    d. Type the remaining text in the letter.
    e. Insert as a page footer the custom building block that is named with your initials followed by *TRCC-CBFooter*. **Hint: Refer to Step 11a.**
12. Save the completed letter and name it **U5-PA02-TRC-CBLtr**.
13. Print and then close **U5-PA02-TRC-CBLtr.docx**.
14. Press Ctrl + N to open a new blank document.
15. Click the Quick Parts button on the Quick Access toolbar, press the Print Screen button on your keyboard, and then click in the document.
16. At the blank document, click the Paste button. (This pastes the screen capture into your document.)
17. Print the document and then close it without saving it.
18. Remove the Quick Parts button from the Quick Access toolbar and then delete your custom building blocks.

**Assessment U5.3**    **Create and Apply Custom Themes and AutoCorrect Entries to a Rental Form**

 **Grade It**

1. At a blank document, create custom theme colors named with your initials that make the following color changes:
   a. Change the Text/Background - Dark 2 color to Orange, Accent 2, Darker 50% (sixth column, last row in the *Theme Colors* section).
   b. Change the Accent 1 color to Green, Accent 6, Darker 25% (tenth column, fifth row in the *Theme Colors* section).
2. Create custom theme fonts named with your initials that apply the Verdana font to headings and the Cambria font to body text.
3. Save the custom theme and name it with your initials. **Hint: Do this with the Save Current Theme** *option at the* **Themes** *drop-down gallery.*
4. Close the document without saving the changes.

**Tennison Rental Company**

*Council Bluffs Location*

Current Date

Mr. Harold Nesbitt
Nesbitt Construction
3102 South 32nd Street
Council Bluffs, IA 51053

Dear Mr. Nesbitt:

Thank you for your interest in renting equipment from our company, Tennison Rental Company. We pride ourselves on maintaining the most extensive and well-maintained equipment in the greater Nebraska-Iowa region.

We carry a variety of earth-moving equipment for heavy construction including backhoes, dozers, excavators (including hydraulic excavators and mini-excavators), skid-steer loaders (including compact skid-steer, track skid-steer, and wheeled skid-steer loaders), tractors, cable locators, trenchers (including ride-on and walk-behind trenchers), and wheel loaders.

Come to our Council Bluffs site or visit our Omaha location and check out our inventory of earth-moving equipment. We are confident that we have the machinery you need.

Sincerely,

Kelsey Sanderson
General Manager

XX
U5-PA02-TRC-CBLtr.docx

**4410 West Broadway ✗ Council Bluffs, IA 51052 ✗ 712.555.8800**

5. Open **TRCRentalForm.docx** and save the document with the name **U5-PA03-TRCRentalForm**.
6. Search for all occurrences of *trc* and replace them with *Tennison Rental Company*.
7. Add the following text to AutoCorrect:
   a. Insert *trc* in the *Replace* text box and insert *Tennison Rental Company* in the *With* text box.
   b. Insert *cera* in the *Replace* text box and insert *Construction Equipment Rental Agreement* in the *With* text box.

8. Move the insertion point to the blank line above the heading *Further Assurances* (located at the bottom of the second page) and then type the text shown in Figure U5.2. Use the numbering feature to number each paragraph with a lowercase letter followed by a right parenthesis. (If the AutoCorrect feature capitalizes the first word after the letter and right parenthesis, use the AutoCorrect Options button to return the letter to lowercase.)

9. Apply the Heading 1 style to the title *Construction Equipment Rental Agreement* and apply the Heading 2 style to the headings in the document (*Lease, Rent, Use and Operation of Equipment, Insurance, Risk of Loss, Maintenance, Return of Equipment, Warranties of Lessee, Default,* and *Further Assurances*).

10. Apply your custom theme to the document.

11. Insert a building block that inserts the word *SAMPLE* as a watermark.

12. Insert the Semaphore footer.

13. Center the title and change the spacing after the title to 12 points.

14. Save, print, and then close **U5-PA03-TRCRentalForm.docx**.

15. At a blank screen, complete the following steps:
    a. Click the DESIGN tab, click the Themes button, and then click *Save Current Theme*.
    b. With the Save Current Theme dialog box open, press Alt + Print Screen.
    c. Click the Cancel button to close the dialog box.
    d. At the blank document, click the HOME tab and then click the Paste button. (This pastes the screen capture into the document.)
    e. Print and then close the document without saving it.

16. At a blank screen, delete your custom theme, custom theme colors, and custom theme fonts. Also delete the *trc* and *cera* AutoCorrect entries.

**Figure U5.2  Assessment U5.3**

Default

Upon the occurrence of default, trc may without any further notice exercise any one or more of the following remedies:

a) declare all unpaid Rentals under this cera to be immediately due and payable;

b) terminate this cera as to any or all items of Equipment;

c) take possession of the Equipment, and for this purpose enter upon any premises of Lessee and remove the Equipment, without any liability, suit, action, or other proceeding by Lessee;

d) cause Lessee at his/her expense to promptly return the Equipment to trc in the condition set forth in this cera;

e) use, hold, sell, lease, or otherwise dispose of the Equipment or any item of it on the premises of Lessee or any other location without affecting the obligations of Lessee as provided in this cera;

f) proceed by appropriate action either at law or in equity to enforce performance by Lessee of the applicable covenants of this cera or to recover damages for the breach of them; or

g) exercise any other rights accruing to trc under any applicable law upon a default by a lessee.

**Create and Apply Building Blocks and Styles to a Business Conduct Report**  **Grade It**

1. Open **TRCStyles.docx**.
2. Select the clip art image, the text *Tennison Rental Company*, and the text *Omaha Location*; save the selected text in a custom building block in the *Quick Part* gallery; and name the building block with your initials followed by *TRCHeader*.
3. Select the horizontal line and the address and telephone number below, save the selected text in a custom building block in the *Quick Part* gallery, and name the building block with your initials followed by *TRCFooter*.
4. Insert each custom building block in the *Quick Part* gallery as a Quick Parts button on the Quick Access toolbar.
5. Select the *Title* text (including the paragraph mark after the text) and then create a style named with your initials followed by *TRCTitle*. **Hint: Make sure you create a style and not a building block.**
6. Select the *Heading 1* text and then create a style named with your initials followed by *TRCHeading1*.
7. Select the *Heading 2* text and then create a style named with your initials followed by *TRCHeading2*.
8. Save the styles you created as a style set named with your initials followed by *Tennison*.
9. Close **TRCStyles.docx** without saving the changes.
10. Open **TRCBusCode.docx** and save the document with the name **U5-PA04-TRCBusCode**.
11. Change to the style set named *Tennison* (preceded by your initials).
12. Apply your custom title style to the title *Business Conduct Code*; apply your custom Heading 1 style to the headings in all uppercase letters; and apply your custom Heading 2 style to the headings with only the first letter in uppercase.
13. Insert the *TRCHeader* building block (preceded by your initials) as a header.
14. Insert the *TRCFooter* building block (preceded by your initials) as a footer.
15. Save, print, and then close **U5-PA04-TRCBusCode.docx**.
16. Make screen captures by completing the following steps:
    a. Press Ctrl + N to display a blank document.
    b. Click the DESIGN tab and then click the More button at the right side of the style set thumbnails. At the drop-down gallery, hover the mouse over your custom style set and then press the Print Screen key on your keyboard.
    c. Click in the document to remove the style set gallery and then click the Paste button.
    d. Click the Quick Parts button on the Quick Access toolbar.
    e. Press the Print Screen key on your keyboard.
    f. Click in the document and then press Ctrl + End.
    g. Press the Enter key once and then click the Paste button.
    h. Make sure the two screen captures display on one page. If necessary, decrease the sizes of the screen captures.
    i. Print the document and then close it without saving it.
17. Delete the building blocks you created and remove the Quick Parts button from the Quick Access toolbar.
18. Delete the custom style set you created that is named *Tennison* (preceded by your initials).

1. At a blank screen, create a new tab with the following specifications:
   a. Insert the new tab after the View tab in the list box in the Word Options dialog box with the *Customize Ribbon* option selected.
   b. Rename the tab *NSS* followed by your initials.
   c. Rename the custom group below your new tab as *Building Blocks*.
   d. Change the *Choose commands from* option to *All Commands*.
   e. From the list box at the left side of the dialog box, add the following commands to the Building Blocks group in the new tab: *Building Blocks Organizer*, *Document Property*, *Field*, and *Organizer*.
   f. Click OK to close the Word Options dialog box.
2. Close the document without saving it.
3. Open the document named **NSSStyles.docx**.
4. Copy styles by completing the following steps:
   a. Click your new NSS tab (the one that begins with *NSS* followed by your initials).
   b. Click the Organizer button in the Building Blocks group.
   c. At the Organizer dialog box, click the Close File button located below the right list box and then click the Open File button. (Make sure you click the Close File button below the right list box and not the left list box.)
   d. At the Open dialog box, display all file types. (Do this with the option box that displays to the right of the *File name* text box.)
   e. Navigate to your Unit05PA folder and then double-click ***NSSWebRpt.docx***.
   f. Copy from the left list box to the right list box the following styles: NSSHeading1, NSSTable, and NSSTitle.
   g. Close the Organizer dialog box. At the message that displays asking if you want to save the changes to **NSSWebRpt.docx**, click the Save button.
5. Close **NSSStyles.docx**.
6. Open **NSSWebRpt.docx** and save the document with the name **U5-PA05-NSSWebRpt**.
7. Apply the following styles:
   a. Apply the NSSTitle style to the title *Navigating and Searching the Web*.
   b. Apply the NSSHeading1 style to the three headings in the document.
   c. Apply the NSSTable style to the three tables in the document. ***Hint: Do this at the TABLE TOOLS DESIGN tab.***
8. Insert a document property by completing the following steps:
   a. Move the insertion point to the end of the document.
   b. Click the Document Property button in the Building Blocks group on your tab and then click *Title* at the drop-down list.
   c. Type **Navigating and Searching the Web** in the *[Title]* placeholder and then press the Right Arrow key to deselect the placeholder.
   d. Press Shift + Enter and then insert the *Author* document property.
   e. Select the name that appears in the *[Author]* placeholder, type your first and last names, and then press the Right Arrow key to deselect the placeholder.
9. Insert a footer by completing the following steps:
   a. Click the Building Blocks Organizer button in the Building Blocks group on your tab.
   b. At the Building Blocks Organizer, click the *Name* column heading to sort the building blocks by name.
   c. Insert the *Blank* footer. (Make sure you insert the *Blank* footer and not the *Blank (Three Columns)* footer.)
   d. Select and then delete the *[Type here]* placeholder in the footer pane.

e. Insert the *Title* document property using the Document Property button on your custom tab. (When you insert the document property, it automatically inserts the title you typed earlier.)

f. Double-click in the document to make it active.

10. Save and then print **U5-PA05-NSSWebRpt.docx**.

11. Make the following modifications to the styles:

a. Modify the font color of the NSSHeading1 style to Dark Blue.

b. Modify the NSSTable style so it aligns the entire table data at the left margin and applies Blue, Accent 1, Lighter 80% shading to the even banded rows.

12. Save, print, and then close **U5-PA05-NSSWebRpt.docx**.

13. At the blank document, reset your ribbon. ***Hint: Do this at the Word Options dialog box with* Customize Ribbon *selected in the left panel*.

14. Close the document without saving it.

## Assessment U5.6    Restrict Formatting in a Report

 **Grade It**

1. Open **InterfaceApps.docx** and save the document with the name **U5-PA06-InterfaceApps**.

2. Display the Restrict Editing task pane and then restrict formatting to the Heading 1 and Heading 2 styles. (At the message that displays asking if you want to remove formatting or styles that are not allowed, click No.)

3. Enforce the protection and provide the password *report*.

4. Save and then close **U5-PA06-InterfaceApps.docx**.

5. Open **U5-PA06-InterfaceApps.docx**.

6. Make sure the Restrict Editing task pane displays and then click the <u>Available styles</u> hyperlink.

7. Apply the Heading 1 style to the title of the report and apply the Heading 2 style to the four headings in the report.

8. Close the Styles task pane.

9. Close the Restrict Editing task pane.

10. Save the document and then print only page 1.

11. Close **U5-PA06-InterfaceApps.docx**.

## Assessment U5.7    Insert Document Properties and Save a Document in a Previous Version of Word

 **Grade It**

1. Open **KLHHighlights.docx** and save the document with the name **U5-PA07-KLHHighlights**.

2. Make the following changes to the document:

a. Apply the Heading 1 style to the three headings in the document (*Plan Highlights*, *Quality Assessment*, and *Provider Network*).

b. Change the style set to Centered.

c. Apply the Blue II theme colors.

3. Move the insertion point to the end of the document and then insert the document named **KLHPlanGraphic.docx**.

4. Display the document information panel and then type the following information in the specified text boxes:

Author: (Type your first and last names.)

Title: **Key Life Health Plan**

Subject: **Company Health Plan**

Keywords: **health, plan, network**

Category: **Health Plan**
Comments: **This document describes highlights of the Key Life Health Plan.**

5. Close the document information panel.
6. Save the document and then print only the document properties.
7. Inspect the document and remove any hidden text.
8. Save and then print **U5-PA07-KLHHighlights.docx**.
9. Assume that the document will be read by a colleague with Word 2003. Run the compatibility checker to determine what features are not supported by earlier versions of Word.
10. Save the document in the *Word 97-2003 Document (\*.doc)* format and name it **U5-PA07-KLHHighlights-2003format**.
11. Save, print, and then close **U5-PA07-KLHHighlights-2003format.doc**.

# CREATING ORIGINAL DOCUMENTS

The activities in Assessment U5.8 and Assessment U5.9 give you the opportunity to practice your writing skills as well as demonstrate your mastery of some of the important Word features presented in this unit. When you compose each document, use correct grammar, precise word choices, and clear sentence construction.

### Assessment U5.8  Design and Apply Building Blocks

**Situation:** You have been hired as the office manager for Highland Construction Company. The address of the company is 9025 Palmer Park Boulevard, Colorado Springs, CO 80904 and the telephone number is (719) 555-4575. You are responsible for designing business documents that maintain a common appearance and formatting. You decide that your first task is to create a letterhead document using the company name, address, and telephone number, as well as a clip art image and other elements to add visual interest. Save the completed letterhead document with the name **HCCLetterhead**. Using the text and elements in the letterhead document, create a building block and name it with your initials followed by *HCCLetterhead*. Save, print, and then close **HCCLetterhead.docx**.

Create the following additional building blocks for your company. (You choose the building block names but use your initials in each one.)

- Create a building block footer that contains a border line (in a color matching the colors in the letterhead) and the company slogan: "Building Dreams Since 1985."

- Create the following complimentary close building block:

  Sincerely,


  Your Name
  Office Manager

- Create the following client name and address building block:

  Mr. Jake Montoya
  Roswell Industries
  1020 Wasatch Street
  Colorado Springs, CO 80902

- Create the following client name and address building block:

  > Ms. Claudia Sanborn
  > S & S Supplies
  > 537 Constitution Avenue
  > Colorado Springs, CO 80911

At a blank document, create a letter to Jake Montoya by inserting the company letterhead (the building block that begins with your initials followed by *HCCLetterhead*). (Refer to Appendix D for information about formatting a business letter using the default Microsoft spacing.) Press the Enter key, type today's date, press the Enter key twice, and then insert the *Jake Montoya* building block. Type **Dear Mr. Montoya:**, and then press the Enter key. Insert the file named **HCCLetter01.docx** and then insert your complimentary close building block. Finally, insert the footer building block you created for the company. Save the letter with the name **U5-PA08-HCCLtr01.** Print and then close the letter. Complete similar steps to create a letter to Claudia Sanborn. Save the completed letter with the name **U5-PA08-HCCLtr02.** Print and then close the letter.

## Assessment U5.9   Create AutoCorrect Entries and Format an Agreement Document

**Situation:** As the office manager at Highland Construction Company, you are responsible for preparing construction agreements. Create an AutoCorrect entry that will replace *hcc* with *Highland Construction Company* and *bca* with *Building Construction Agreement*. Open **HCCAgreement.docx** and then type the text shown in Figure U5.3 at the beginning of the document.

Insert the following in the document:

- Insert at the end of the document a *PrintDate* field and *FileName* field.
- Insert your footer building block as a footer.
- Insert a cover page.

Add or apply any other elements or formats to improve the appearance of the document and then save the document with the name **U5-PA09-HCCAgreement.docx**. Print and then close the document.

Delete the building blocks you created and then delete the AutoCorrect entries *hcc* and *bca*.

**Figure U5.3** **Assessment U5.9**

**bca**

**THIS bca** made this _____ day of _____, 20___, by and between hcc and _____, hereinafter referred to as "owner," for the considerations hereinafter named, hcc and owner agree as follows:

**Financing Arrangements:** The owner will obtain a construction loan to finance construction under this bca. If adequate financing has not been arranged within thirty days of the date of this bca, or the owner cannot provide evidence to hcc of other financial ability to pay the full amount, then hcc may treat this bca as null and void and retain the down payment made on the execution of this bca.

# UNIT 6

## Referencing Data

# Chapter 26

# Inserting Endnotes, Footnotes, and References

## Performance Objectives

Upon successful completion of Chapter 26, you will be able to:

- Insert and modify footnotes and endnotes
- Insert and modify citations and bibliographies

When you write a research paper or report, you may need to include references to identify the sources of information you used. Word provides a variety of methods for citing references, including footnotes, endnotes, in-text citations, and bibliographies. You will learn how to cite sources with these reference features and how to edit, modify, and delete references.

*Note: Before beginning computer exercises for this chapter, copy to your storage medium the Chapter26 folder from the CD that accompanies this textbook and then make Chapter26 the active folder.*

In this chapter, students will produce the following documents:

Exercise 26.1A. C26-E01-InterfaceApps.docx
Exercise 26.1C. C26-E01-InternetFuture.docx
Exercise 26.2. C26-E02-DevelopDTP.docx

Model answers for these exercises are shown on the following pages.

**Exercise 26.1A**

C26-E01-InterfaceApps.docx

---

**NATURAL INTERFACE APPLICATIONS**

Creating a more natural interface between human and machine is the goal in a major area of artificial intelligence. Currently, computer users are restricted in most instances to using a mouse and keyboard for input. For output, they must gaze at a fairly static, two-dimensional screen. Speakers are used for sound, and a printer for hard copy. The user interface consists of typing, pointing, and clicking. New speech recognition and natural-language technologies promise to change that soon.[1]

**Speech Recognition**

One of the most immediately applicable improvements in technology comes in the area of speech recognition. Rather than typing information in the computer, users can direct the computer with voice commands. A computer that can take dictation and perform requested actions is a real step forward in convenience and potential. Speech recognition technology has developed rather slowly, mainly because the typical PC did not have the necessary speed and capacity until very recently.[2]

**Natural-Language Interface**

Computers that are able communicate using spoken English or Japanese, or any of the hundreds of other languages currently in use around the world, would certainly be helpful. Computers, in the not-so-distant future, will most likely be able to read, write, speak, and understand many human languages. Language translators already exist, and they are getting better all the time.

Programmers can look forward to a human-language computer interface. With better interfaces, programmers may be able to describe what they want using natural (human) language, rather than writing programs in the highly restrictive and rather alien programming languages in use today. Natural-language interfaces are an area of artificial intelligence that is broader in scope than simple speech recognition. The goal is to have a machine that can read a set of news articles on any

---

[1] Ray Curtis, *Artificial Intelligence* (Chicago: Home Town Publishing, 2015), 45-51.
[2] Heather Clemens and Nicolas Reyes, "Integrating Speech Recognition," *Design Technologies* (2014): 24-26.

---

topic and understand what it has read. Ideally, it could then write its ov [...] has learned.[3]

**Virtual Reality**

Virtual reality (VR) describes the concept of creating a realistic world within the computer. Online games with thousands of interacting players already exist. In these games people can take on a persona and move about a virtual landscape, adventuring and chatting with other players. The quality of a virtual reality system is typically characterized in terms of its *immersiveness*, which measures how real the simulated world feels and how well it can make users accept the simulated world as their own and forget about reality. With each passing year, systems are able to provide increasing levels of immersion. Called by some the "ultimate in escapism," VR is becoming increasingly common—and increasingly real.[4]

**Mental Interface**

Although still in the experimental phase, a number of interfaces take things a bit further than VR, and they don't require users to click a mouse, speak a word, or even lift a finger. Mental interfaces use sensors mounted around the skull to read the alpha waves given off by our brains. Thinking of the color blue could be used to move the mouse cursor to the right, or thinking of the number seven could move it to the left. The computer measures brain activity and interprets it as a command, eliminating the need to physically manipulate a mouse to move the screen cursor. While this technology has obvious applications for assisting people with disabilities, military researchers are also using it to produce a superior form of interface for pilots.[5]

---

[3] Daniel Glenovich, "Language Interfaces," *Corporate Computing* (2015): 8-12.
[4] William Novak, *Virtual Reality Worlds* (San Francisco: Lilly Harris Publishers, 2013), 53-68.
[5] Kathleen Beal, "Challenges of Artificial Intelligence," *Interface Design* (2015): 10-18.

**FUTURE OF THE INTERNET**

The Internet is having trouble keeping up with the rapid increase in users and the increased workload created by the popularity of bandwidth-intensive applications such as music and video files. The broadband connections needed to enjoy these new applications are not evenly distributed. Several ongoing projects promise to provide solutions for these problems in the future. Once these connectivity problems are dealt with, people around the world will be able to enjoy the new web services that are only a few short years away.[1]

**Satellite Internet Connections**

Many people living in remote or sparsely populated areas are not served by broadband Internet connections. Cable or optical fiber networks are very expensive to install and maintain, and ISPs are not interested in providing service to areas or individuals unless they think it will be profitable. One hope for people without broadband connections is provided by satellite TV networks. Remote ISPs connect to the satellite network using antennae attached to their servers. Data is relayed to and from ISP servers to satellites, which are in turn connected to an Internet backbone access point. While the connection speeds might not be as fast as those offered by regular land-based broadband access, they are faster than the service twisted-pair cable can offer and much better than no access at all.[2]

**Second Internet**

A remedy for the traffic clogging the information highway is **Internet2**, a revolutionary new type of Internet currently under development. When fully operational, Internet2 will enable large research universities in the United States to collaborate and share huge amounts of complex scientific information at amazing speeds. Led by over 170 universities working in partnership with industry and government, the Internet2 consortium is developing and deploying advanced network technologies and applications.

Internet2 is a testing ground for universities to work together and develop advanced Internet technologies such as telemedicine, digital libraries, and virtual laboratories. Internet2 universities will be connected to an ultrahigh-speed network called the Abilene backbone. Each university will use state-of-the-art equipment to take advantage of transfer speeds provided by the network.

---

[1] Joshua Abrahamson, *Future Trends in Computing* (Los Angeles: Gleason-Rutherford Publishing, 2014), 5-9.
[2] Aileen Dossa, *Satellite Systems* (Boston: Robison Publishing House, 2015), 15-38.

Page 1

**Internet Services for a Fee**

Industry observers predict that large portals such as AOL, MSN, and Y... effective structures and marketing strategies to get consumers to pay ... market, called bring-your-own-access (BYOA), will combine essential ... weather, with *services,* such as search, directory, email, IM, and online shopping, into a new product with monthly access charges. But to entice current and potential customers into the BYOA market, ISP and telecom companies must offer improvements in the area of security, privacy, and ease-of-use. Additionally, they are expected to develop new ways to personalize content and add value to the current range of Internet services.[3]

**Internet in 2030**

Ray Kurzweil, a computer futurist, has looked ahead to the year 2030 and visualized a Web that offers no clear distinctions between real and simulated environments and people. Among the applications he sees as very possible are computerized displays in eyeglasses that could offer simultaneous translations of foreign language conversations, nanobots (microscopic robots) that would work with our brains to extend our mental capabilities, and more sophisticated avatars (simulated persons on-screen) that people will interact with online. Technologies that allow people to protect their feelings as well as their images and voices may usher in a period when people could "be" with another person even though they are physically hundreds or even thousands of miles apart.

---

[3] Jolene Fuzak, "Fee-Based Internet Services," *Connections* (2014): 2-6.

Page 2

Model Answers

Student Name

Instructor Name

Course Title

Current Date

Development of Desktop Publishing

Since the 1970s, microcomputers have been an integral part of the business

environment. Businesses use microcomputers and software packages to perform a variety

of tasks. In the 1980s, the three most popular types of software purchased for

microcomputers were word processing, spreadsheets, and databases (Schueller).

During the early 1990s, the introduction of software programs called desktop publishing

gained popularity among mic

and its ability to produce hig

fastest growing microcompu

today (Wesson).

Until the mid-1980s, g

professionals. However, desk

into the office and home. Fas

supply of clip art, increased s

desktop publishing (Nakamu

created, and produced at a co

In traditional publishi

publication project, which ma

desktop publishing software,

Page 1

complete a project, greatly reducing the costs of publishing documents (Nakamura). The

two approaches have a great deal in common. "Both approaches involve setting goals,

planning and organizing content, analyzing layout and design, arranging design elements,

typesetting, printing, and distributing the project" (Corsini 28).

Page 2

Works Cited

Corsini, Elena. *Computers in the Education World*. Houston: Rio Grande Publishing, 2015.

Nakamura, Janet. "Computer Applications and Publishing." *Current Technology Times* VI

(2014): 20-28.

Schueller, Barbara. *The Past, Present and Future of Desktop Publishing*. 18 April 2014. 3

March 2015. <www.emcp.org/publishing>.

Wesson, Scott. "The History of Popular Computer Software." *Computer Education* (2015):

10-18.

Page 3

Model Answers

# Creating Footnotes and Endnotes

Research papers and reports generally contain information from a variety of sources. To acknowledge and credit these sources, you can insert footnotes or endnotes in a document formatted in a specific reference style, such as MLA style. (You will learn more about different reference styles in the next section.) A *footnote* is an explanatory note or reference that is placed at the bottom of the page on which a source is referenced. An *endnote* is also an explanatory note or reference, but it is placed at the end of the paper or report.

Two steps are involved in creating a footnote or an endnote. The first step is to insert a reference number for the footnote or endnote in the text where the source is referenced. The second step is to type the bibliographic information about the source. In Word, footnotes and endnotes are created in a similar manner.

To create a footnote, position the insertion point where you want the reference number to appear, click the REFERENCES tab, and then click the Insert Footnote button in the Footnotes group. This inserts a superscript number in the document and a separator line at the bottom of the page with a superscript number below it. With the insertion point positioned immediately right of the superscript number beneath the separator line, type the text for the footnote entry. Word automatically numbers footnotes with superscript arabic numbers and endnotes with superscript lowercase roman numerals.

**QUICK STEPS**

**Insert a Footnote**
1. Click REFERENCES tab.
2. Click Insert Footnote button.
3. Type footnote text.

**Insert an Endnote**
1. Click REFERENCES tab.
2. Click Insert Endnote button.
3. Type endnote text.

Insert Footnote

Insert Endnote

---

## Exercise 26.1A  Creating Footnotes                               Part 1 of 3

1. Open **InterfaceApps.docx** and save the document with the name **C26-E01-InterfaceApps**.
2. Create the first footnote shown in Figure 26.1 on the next page by completing the following steps:
   a. Position the insertion point at the end of the first paragraph of text in the document.
   b. Click the REFERENCES tab.
   c. Click the Insert Footnote button in the Footnotes group.
   d. With the insertion point positioned at the bottom of the page immediately following the superscript number, type the first footnote shown in Figure 26.1.

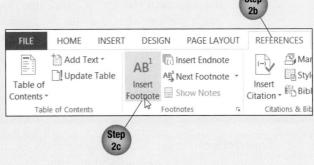

3. Move the insertion point to the end of the paragraph in the *Speech Recognition* section and then create the second footnote shown in Figure 26.1.

4. Move the insertion point to the end of the second paragraph in the *Natural-Language Interface* section and then create the third footnote shown in Figure 26.1.
5. Move the insertion point to the end of the paragraph in the *Virtual Reality* section and then create the fourth footnote shown in Figure 26.1.
6. Move the insertion point to the end of the last paragraph in the document and then create the fifth footnote shown in Figure 26.1.
7. Save, print, and then close **C26-E01-InterfaceApps.docx**.

**Figure 26.1 Exercise 26.1A**

Ray Curtis, *Artificial Intelligence* (Chicago: Home Town Publishing, 2015), 45-51.

Heather Clemens and Nicolas Reyes, "Integrating Speech Recognition," *Design Technologies* (2014): 24-26.

Daniel Glenovich, "Language Interfaces," *Corporate Computing* (2015): 8-12.

William Novak, *Virtual Reality Worlds* (San Francisco: Lilly Harris Publishers, 2013), 53-68.

Kathleen Beal, "Challenges of Artificial Intelligence," *Interface Design* (2015): 10-18.

## Printing Footnotes and Endnotes

When you print a document that contains footnotes, Word automatically reduces the number of text lines on the page to create space for the footnote(s) and the line separating the footnote(s) from the document text. Word separates the footnote(s) from the document text with a 2-inch line that begins at the left margin. If the page does not contain enough space for the footnote(s), the note number(s) and reference text are moved to the next page. When endnotes are created in a document, Word prints all of the notes at the end of the document, separated from the text by a 2-inch line.

**Exercise 26.1B  Creating Endnotes**                          Part 2 of 3

1. Open **InternetFuture.docx** and save the document with the name **C26-E01-InternetFuture**.
2. Change the style set to Lines (Simple) and change the paragraph spacing to Relaxed.
3. Create the first endnote shown in Figure 26.2 on the next page by completing the following steps:
   a. Position the insertion point at the end of the first paragraph of text in the document.
   b. Click the REFERENCES tab.
   c. Click the Insert Endnote button.
   d. Type the first endnote shown in Figure 26.2.

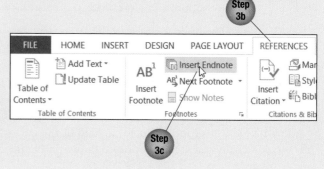

4. Move the insertion point to the end of the paragraph in the *Satellite Internet Connections* section and then create the second endnote shown in Figure 26.2.
5. Move the insertion point to the end of the second paragraph in the *Second Internet* section and then create the third endnote shown in Figure 26.2.
6. Move the insertion point to the end of the paragraph in the *Internet Services for a Fee* section and then create the fourth endnote shown in Figure 26.2.
7. Save and then print **C26-E01-InternetFuture.docx**.

**Figure 26.2 Exercise 26.1B**

Joshua Abrahamson, *Future Trends in Computing* (Los Angeles: Gleason-Rutherford Publishing, 2014), 8-12.

Aileen Dossa, *Satellite Systems* (Boston: Robison Publishing House, 2015), 15-38.

Terry Ventrella, "Future of the Internet," *Computing Today* (2015): 33-44.

Jolene Fuzak, "Fee-Based Internet Services," *Connections* (2014): 2-6.

## Viewing and Editing Footnotes and Endnotes

To view footnotes in a document, click the Next Footnote button in the Footnotes group on the REFERENCES tab. This moves the insertion point to the location of the first footnote reference number following the location of the insertion point. To view endnotes in a document, click the Next Footnote button arrow and then click *Next Endnote* at the drop-down list. With other options at the Next Footnote button drop-down list, you can view the next footnote, previous footnote, or previous endnote.

Next Footnote

Show Notes

With the Show Notes button, you can move the insertion point to specific footnote text. Click the Next Footnote button to move the insertion point to the next footnote reference number and then click the Show Notes button. This moves the insertion point to the specific footnote text at the bottom of the page. Click the Show Notes button again and the insertion point is moved back to the footnote reference number.

When you move, copy, or delete a footnote or endnote reference number, all of the remaining footnotes or endnotes renumber automatically. To move a footnote or endnote, select the reference number and then click the Cut button in the Clipboard group on the HOME tab. Position the insertion point at the location that you want the footnote or endnote inserted and then click the Paste button. To delete a footnote or endnote, select the reference number and then press the Delete key. This deletes the reference number as well as the footnote or endnote text.

Click the Footnotes group dialog box launcher and the Footnote and Endnote dialog box displays, as shown in Figure 26.3 on the next page. At this dialog box, you can convert footnotes to endnotes and endnotes to footnotes; change the location of footnotes or endnotes; change the number formatting; start footnote or endnote numbering with a specific number, letter, or symbol; and change the note numbering within sections in a document.

**Figure 26.3 Footnote and Endnote Dialog box**

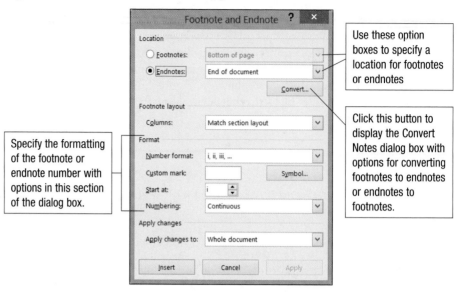

Use these option boxes to specify a location for footnotes or endnotes

Click this button to display the Convert Notes dialog box with options for converting footnotes to endnotes or endnotes to footnotes.

Specify the formatting of the footnote or endnote number with options in this section of the dialog box.

**Exercise 26.1C** Formatting Endnotes and Converting Endnotes to Footnotes — **Part 3 of 3**

1. With **C26-E01-InternetFuture.docx** open, move the insertion point to the beginning of the document and then edit the endnotes by completing the following steps:
   a. Click the REFERENCES tab.
   b. Click the Next Footnote button arrow and then click *Next Endnote* at the drop-down list.
   c. Click the Show Notes button. (This displays the endnote text.)
   d. Change the page numbers for the *Joshua Abrahamson* entry from *8-12* to *5-9*.
   e. Click the Show Notes button again to return to the reference number in the document.
2. Press Ctrl + A to select the document and then change the font to Constantia. (Note that selecting the document does not select the endnote text.)
3. Change the font for the endnotes by completing the following steps:
   a. Press Ctrl + End to move the insertion point to the end of the document.
   b. Click on any endnote entry and then press Ctrl + A to select all of the endnote entries.
   c. Change the font to Constantia.
   d. Press Ctrl + Home.
4. Convert the endnotes to footnotes by completing the following steps:
   a. Click the REFERENCES tab and then click the Footnotes group dialog box launcher.
   b. At the Footnote and Endnote dialog box, click the Convert button.

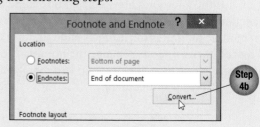

Step 1b

Step 4b

   c.   At the Convert Notes dialog box with the *Convert all endnotes to footnotes* option selected, click OK.

   d.   Click the Close button to close the dialog box.

5.  Change the footnote numbers by completing the following steps:

   a.   Click the Footnotes group dialog box launcher.

   b.   At the Footnote and Endnote dialog box, click the *Footnotes* option in the *Location* section.

   c.   Click the down-pointing arrow at the right side of the *Footnotes* option and then click *Below text* at the drop-down list.

   d.   Click the down-pointing arrow at the right side of the *Number format* option box and then click *a, b, c, . . .* at the drop-down list.

   e.   Change the starting number (letter) by clicking the up-pointing arrow at the right side of the *Start at* option until *d* displays in the option box.

   f.   Click the Apply button and then scroll through the document and notice the number format.

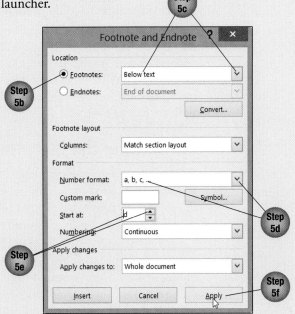

6.  Change the footnote number format back to arabic numbers by completing the following steps:

   a.   With the REFERENCES tab active, click the Footnotes group dialog box launcher.

   b.   At the Footnote and Endnote dialog box, click the *Footnotes* option in the *Location* section.

   c.   Click the down-pointing arrow at the right side of the *Number Format* option box and then click *1, 2, 3, . . .* at the drop-down list.

   d.   Change the starting number back to 1 by clicking the down-pointing arrow at the right side of the *Start at* option until *1* displays in the option box.

   e.   Click the Apply button.

7.  Delete the third footnote by completing the following steps:

   a.   Press Ctrl + Home.

   b.   Make sure the REFERENCES tab is active and then click three times on the Next Footnote button in the Footnotes group.

   c.   Select the third footnote reference number (superscript number) and then press the Delete key.

8.  Save, print, and then close **C26-E01-InternetFuture.docx**.

# Creating Citations and Bibliographies

In addition to using footnotes and endnotes to credit sources in a research paper or report, consider inserting in-text citations and a page listing the references to identify sources of quotations, facts, ideas, and summarized material. An in-text citation acknowledges that you are borrowing information from a source rather than plagiarizing (stealing) the words or ideas of another.

Word provides three commonly used editorial styles for citing references in research papers and reports: the American Psychological Association (APA) reference style, which is generally used in the social sciences and research fields; the Modern Language Association (MLA) style, which is generally used in the humanities and English composition; and *The Chicago Manual of Style* (CMS), which is used in both the humanities and social sciences and considered more complex than APA or MLA style.

If you prepare a research paper or report in APA or MLA style, format your document according to the following general guidelines: Use standard-sized paper (8.5 × 11 inches); set 1-inch top, bottom, left, and right margins; set the text in a 12-point serif typeface (such as Cambria or Times New Roman); double-space the text; indent the first line of each paragraph 0.5 inch; and insert page numbers in the upper right corners of pages.

## Formatting the First Page of a Research Paper or Report

When formatting a research paper or report according to MLA or APA standards, you will need to follow certain guidelines for properly formatting the first page of the document. Each style has specific requirements for the information that is provided and how it is formatted within a document.

When using MLA style, in the upper left corner of the first page of the document, insert your name, your instructor's name, the course title, and the current date, all double-spaced. Double-space after the date and then type the title of the document centered on the page. Double-space after the title and then type the first line of text. Finally, insert a header in the upper right corner that includes your last name followed by the current page number on each page.

When using APA style, create a title page that is separate from the text of the paper. On this page, include the title of your paper, your name, and your school's name, all double-spaced, centered, and positioned on the upper half of the page. The title page also includes a header with the text *Running Head:* followed by the title of your paper in uppercase letters at the left margin and the page number at the right margin.

---

**Exercise 26.2A**   **Formatting the First Page of a Research Paper**                     Part 1 of 8

1. Open **DevelopDTP.docx** and save the document with the name **C26-E02-DevelopDTP**.
2. Format the first page of the document by completing the following steps:
   a. Press Ctrl + A to select the entire document.
   b. Change the font to Cambria and the font size to 12 points.
   c. Change the line spacing to 2.0.
   d. Remove the spacing after paragraphs by clicking the PAGE LAYOUT tab, clicking in the *After* measurement box in the *Spacing* section, typing **0**, and then pressing the Enter key.

e. Press Ctrl + Home to position the insertion point at the beginning of the document, type your first and last names, and then press the Enter key.

f. Type your instructor's name and then press the Enter key.

g. Type the title of your course and then press the Enter key.

h. Type the current date and then press the Enter key.

i. Type and then center the document title: **Development of Desktop Publishing**.

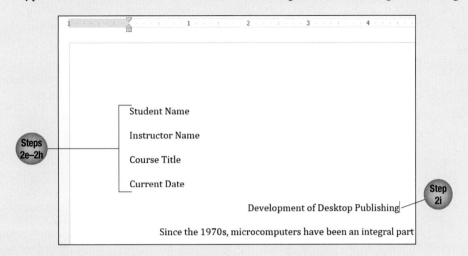

3. Insert a header in the document by completing the following steps:

   a. Click the INSERT tab.

   b. Click the Header button in the Header & Footer group and then click *Edit Header* at the drop-down list.

   c. Press the Tab key twice to move the insertion point to the right margin in the Header pane.

   d. Type your last name and then press the spacebar.

   e. Click the Page Number button in the Header & Footer group on the HEADER & FOOTER TOOLS DESIGN tab, point to *Current Position*, and then click the *Plain Number* option.

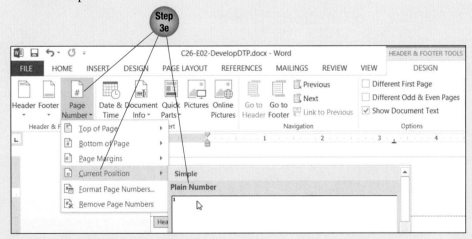

   f. Select the header text and change the font to 12-point Cambria.

   g. Double-click in the body of the document.

4. Save **C26-E02-DevelopDTP.docx**.

## Inserting Sources and Citations

**Insert a New Citation**
1. Click REFERENCES tab.
2. Click Insert Citation button.
3. Click *Add New Source* at drop-down list.
4. Type required source information.
5. Click OK.

When you create an in-text citation, Word requires you to enter information about the source in fields at the Create Source dialog box. To insert a citation in a document, click the REFERENCES tab, click the Insert Citation button in the Citations & Bibliography group, and then click *Add New Source* at the drop-down list. At the Create Source dialog box, shown in Figure 26.4, select the type of reference you want to cite—such as a book, journal article, or report—and then type the bibliographic information in the required fields. If you want to include more information than is required in the displayed fields, click the *Show All Bibliography Fields* check box to insert a check mark and then type additional bibliographic information in the extra fields.

After filling in the necessary source information, click OK. The citation is automatically placed in the document at the location of the insertion point.

**Figure 26.4  Create Source Dialog Box**

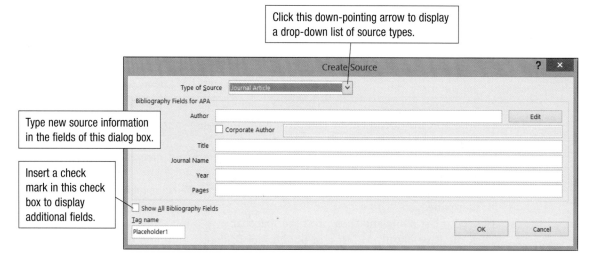

Click this down-pointing arrow to display a drop-down list of source types.

Type new source information in the fields of this dialog box.

Insert a check mark in this check box to display additional fields.

## Inserting Citation Placeholders

Insert Citation

If you want to insert the information for an in-text source citation later, insert a citation placeholder. To do this, click the Insert Citation button in the Citations & Bibliography group and then click *Add New Placeholder* at the drop-down list. At the Placeholder Name dialog box, type a name for the citation placeholder and then press Enter or click the OK button. Insert the citation text later at the Edit Source dialog box, which contains the same options as the Create Source dialog box.

1. With **C26-E02-DevelopDTP.docx** open, press Ctrl + End to move the insertion point to the end of the document and then type the text shown in Figure 26.5 on page 929 up to the first citation (the text *(Weston)*). To insert the citation, complete these steps:
   a. Press the spacebar once after typing the text *today*.
   b. Click the REFERENCES tab.
   c. Make sure the *Style* option is set at *MLA*. If it is not, click the down-pointing arrow at the right of the *Style* option and then click *MLA* at the drop-down list.

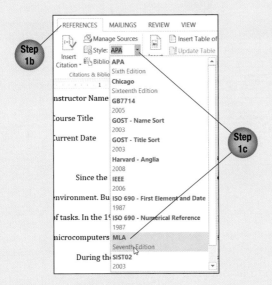

   d. Click the Insert Citation button in the Citations & Bibliography group and then click *Add New Source* at the drop-down list.

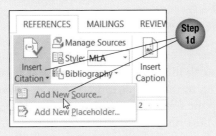

e. At the Create Source dialog box, click the down-pointing arrow at the right of the *Type of Source* option and then click *Journal Article* at the drop down list.

f. Click in the *Author* text box, type **Scott Weston**, and then press the Tab key three times.

g. Type **The History of Popular Computer Software** in the *Title* text box and then press the Tab key.

h. Type **Computer Education** in the *Journal Name* text box and then press the Tab key.

i. Type **2015** in the *Year* text box and then press the Tab key.

j. Type **10-18** in the *Pages* text box.

k. Click OK.

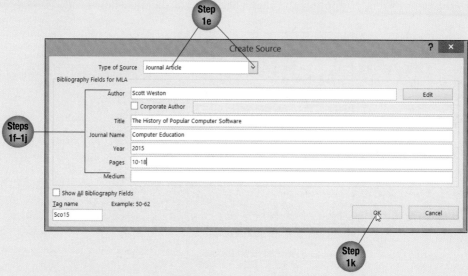

l. Type the period to end the sentence.

2. Continue typing the text up to the next citation (the text *(Prasad)*) and insert the following source information from a book. (Click the down-pointing arrow at the right of the *Type of Source* option and then click *Book* at the drop-down list.)

    *Author:* **Allen Prasad**
    *Title:* **Desktop Publishing in Education**
    *Year:* **2015**
    *City:* **Chicago**
    *Publisher:* **Great Lakes Publishing House**

3. Continue typing the text up to the next citation (the text *(Nakamura)*) and insert a citation placeholder by completing the following steps. (You will create the citation and fill in the source information in the next project.)

a. Click the Insert Citation button in the Citations & Bibliography group.

b. Click *Add New Placeholder* at the drop-down list.

c. At the Placeholder Name dialog box, type **Nakamura** and then press Enter.

4. Type the remaining text in Figure 26.5 on the next page.

5. Save **C26-E02-DevelopDTP.docx**.

**Figure 26.5 Exercise 26.2B**

During the early 1990s, another type of software program called desktop

publishing gained popularity among microcomputer users. With the introduction of

the laser printer and its ability to produce high quality documents, desktop

publishing software became the fastest growing microcomputer application of the

1990s, and its widespread use continues today (Weston). Desktop publishing

involves using desktop publishing software or word processing software with

desktop publishing capabilities, a computer system, and a printer to produce

professional-looking documents (Prasad).

Until the mid-1980s, graphic design depended almost exclusively on design

professionals. However, desktop publishing changed all that by bringing graphic

design into the office and home. Faster microprocessors, improved printer

capabilities, increased supply of clip art, increased storage capacity, and the like

continue to expand the role of desktop publishing (Nakamura). Everything from a

flyer to a newsletter can be designed, created, and produced at a computer.

## Editing a Source

After inserting information about a source into a document, you may need to edit
the information to correct errors or change data. One method for editing a source is
to click the citation in the document, click the *Citation Options* arrow that displays at
the right side of the selected citation, and then click *Edit Source* at the drop-down list.
This displays the Edit Source dialog box, which contains the same options as the Create
Source dialog box. Make the desired changes at this dialog box and then click OK.

## Inserting a Citation with an Existing Source

Once you insert source information at the Create Source dialog box, Word automatically
saves it. To insert a citation in a document with source information that has already been
saved, click the Insert Citation button in the Citations & Bibliography group and then
click the desired source at the drop-down list.

**QUICK STEPS**

**Insert a Citation
with an Existing
Source**
1. Click REFERENCES
   tab.
2. Click Insert Citation
   button.
3. Click desired source
   at drop-down list.

1. With **C26-E02-DevelopDTP.docx** open, add the *Nakamura* source information by completing the following steps:
   a. Click the *Nakamura* citation in the document.
   b. Click the *Citation Options* arrow that displays at the right side of the selected citation.
   c. Click *Edit Source* at the drop-down list.
   d. At the Edit Source dialog box, click the *Type of Source* option box arrow and then click *Journal Article*.
   e. Type the following information in the specified text boxes:
      *Author:* **Janet Nakamura**
      *Title:* **Computer Applications and Publishing**
      *Journal Name:* **Current Technology Times**
      *Year:* **2014**
      *Pages:* **20-28**
      *Volume:* **VI** (Display the *Volume* field by clicking the *Show All Bibliography Fields* check box and then scroll down the options list.)
   f. Click the OK button to close the Edit Source dialog box.
2. Press Ctrl + End to move the insertion point to the end of the document and then press Enter. Type the text in Figure 26.6 up to the citation text *(Weston)* and then insert a citation from an existing source by completing the following steps:
   a. If necessary, click the REFERENCES tab.
   b. Click the Insert Citation button in the Citations & Bibliography group.
   c. Click the *Scott Weston* reference at the drop-down list.
3. Type the remaining text in Figure 26.6 and complete steps similar to those in Step 2 to insert a citation for the existing source by Janet Nakamura.
4. Save and then print **C26-E02-DevelopDTP.docx**.

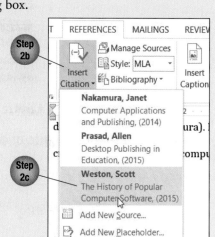

**Figure 26.6  Exercise 26.2C**

In traditional publishing, several people may be involved in completing the publication project, which may be costly and time-consuming (Weston). With the use of desktop publishing software, one person may be performing all of the tasks necessary to complete a project, greatly reducing the costs of publishing documents (Nakamura). The two approaches have a great deal in common.

## Modifying Source Information

After you have inserted information about a source into a document, you may need to edit the information to correct errors or change data. To modify source information, click the REFERENCES tab and then click the Manage Sources button in the Citations & Bibliography group. This displays the Source Manager dialog box, as shown in Figure 26.7. In the *Master List* section, the Source Manager dialog box displays all of the citations you have created in Word (except any citation that was initially inserted as a placeholder, such as *Nakamura*). The *Current List* section of the dialog box displays all of the citations included in the document that is currently open.

At the Source Manager dialog box, click the desired source in the *Current List* section. Click the Edit button that displays between the list boxes and then make any desired changes at the Edit Source dialog box. The Edit Source dialog box contains the same options as the Create Source dialog box. You can also edit a source by clicking the desired citation in the document to select the citation placeholder, clicking the *Citation Options* arrow, and then clicking *Edit Source* at the drop-down list.

You may also want to add new sources or delete existing sources in a document. To insert a new source, click the New button at the Source Manager dialog box and then insert the source information in the required fields. To delete a source from a document, click the source in the *Current List* section and then click the Delete button.

**Modify Source Information**
1. Click REFERENCES tab.
2. Click Manage Sources button.
3. Edit, add, and/or delete sources.
4. Click Close.

Manage Sources

**Figure 26.7 Source Manager Dialog Box**

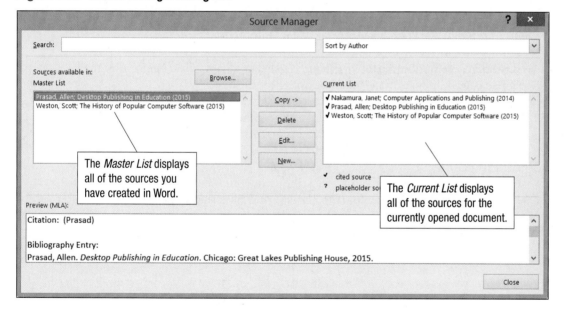

## Inserting Page Numbers in a Citation

If you include a direct quote from a source, be sure to add quotation marks around all of the text used from that source and provide the page number(s) of the quoted material in the citation. To insert specific page numbers into a citation, click the citation in the document to select the citation placeholder. Click the *Citation Options* arrow and then click *Edit Citation* at the drop-down list. At the Edit Citation dialog box, type in the page number or numbers of the source containing the quote and then click OK.

**Insert a Page Number in a Citation**
1. Click citation to display placeholder.
2. Click *Citation Options* arrow.
3. Click *Edit Citation*.
4. Type page number(s).
5. Click OK.

1. With **C26-E02-DevelopDTP.docx** open, edit a source by completing the following steps:
   a. Click the REFERENCES tab.
   b. Click the Manage Sources button in the Citations & Bibliography group.
   c. At the Source Manager dialog box, click the *Weston, Scott* source entry in the *Master List* section.
   d. Click the Edit button.

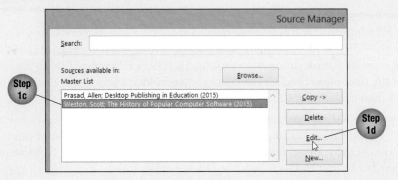

   e. At the Edit Source dialog box, delete the text in the *Author* text box and then type **Scott Wesson**.
   f. Click OK to close the Edit Source dialog box.
   g. At the message asking if you want to update both the *Master List* and *Current List* sections with the changes, click Yes.
   h. Click the Close button to close the Source Manager dialog box. (Notice that the last name changed in both *Weston* citations to reflect the edit.)
2. Delete a source by completing the following steps:
   a. Select and then delete the last sentence in the second paragraph in the document, including the citation (the sentence that begins *Desktop publishing involves using*).
   b. Click the Manage Sources button in the Citations & Bibliography group on the REFERENCES tab.
   c. At the Source Manager dialog box, click the *Prasad, Allen* entry in the *Current List* section. (This entry does not contain a check mark because you deleted the citation from the document.)
   d. Click the Delete button.

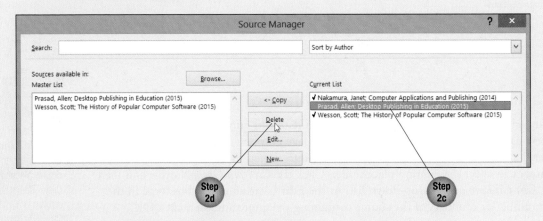

   e. Click the Close button to close the Source Manager dialog box.

3. Create and insert a new source in the document by completing the following steps:
   a. Click the Manage Sources button in the Citations & Bibliography group on the REFERENCES tab.
   b. Click the New button in the Source Manager dialog box.
   c. Type the following book information in the Create Source dialog box. (First change the *Type of Source* option to *Book*.)
      *Author:* **Elena Corsini**
      *Title:* **Computers in the Education World**
      *Year:* **2015**
      *City:* **Houston**
      *Publisher:* **Rio Grande Publishing**
   d. Click OK to close the Create Source dialog box.
   e. Click the Close button to close the Source Manager dialog box.
   f. Position the insertion point one space after the period that ends the last sentence in the document and then type this sentence: **"Both approaches involve setting goals, planning and organizing content, analyzing layout and design, arranging design elements, typesetting, printing, and distributing the project"** (Press the spacebar once after typing the quotation mark after *project*.)

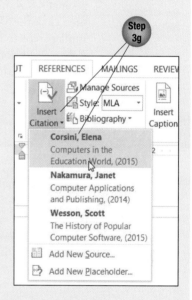

   g. Insert a citation at the end of the sentence for Elena Corsini by clicking the Insert Citation button in the Citations & Bibliography group and then clicking the *Corsini, Elena* reference at the drop-down list.
   h. Type the period to end the sentence.
4. Because you inserted a direct quote from Elena Corsini, you need to include the page number of the book in which you found the quote. Insert the page number within the citation by completing the following steps:
   a. Click anywhere in the *Corsini* citation. (This displays the citation placeholder.)
   b. Click the Citation Options arrow that displays at the right of the citation placeholder and then click *Edit Citation* at the drop-down list.
   c. At the Edit Citation dialog box, type **28** in the *Pages* text box.
   d. Click OK.

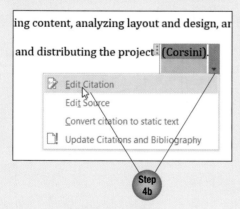

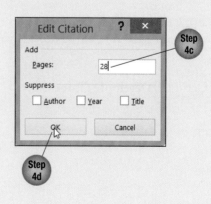

5. Save **C26-E02-DevelopDTP.docx**.

## Inserting a Sources List

**Insert a Sources List**

1. Insert new page at end of document.
2. Click REFERENCES tab.
3. Click Bibliography button.
4. Click desired option for predesigned works cited, reference, or bibliography page.

Bibliography

If you include citations in a report or research paper, you need to insert a sources list as a separate page at the end of the document. A sources list is an alphabetical list of the books, journal articles, reports, and other sources referenced in the report or paper. Depending on the reference style used in the report or paper, a sources list may be a bibliography, references page, or works cited page.

When you type source information for citations, Word automatically saves the information from all of the fields and compiles a sources list, alphabetized by the authors' last names and/or the titles of the sources. Insert a works cited page for a document formatted in MLA style, insert a references page for a document formatted in APA style, and insert a bibliography for a document formatted in Chicago style.

To insert a works cited page, move the insertion point to the end of the document and then insert a new page. Click the REFERENCES tab and make sure the *Style* option is set at *MLA*. Click the Bibliography button in the Citations & Bibliography group and then click the *Works Cited* option in the *Built-In* section of the drop-down list. Complete similar steps to insert a references page in an APA-style document except click the *References* option instead, or click the *Bibliography* option to insert a bibliography into a Chicago-style document.

---

**Exercise 26.2E   Inserting a Works Cited Page**                    **Part 5 of 8**

1. With **C26-E02-DevelopDTP.docx** open, insert a works cited page at the end of the document by completing these steps:
   a. Press Ctrl + End to move the insertion point to the end of the document.
   b. Press Ctrl + Enter to insert a page break.
   c. Click the REFERENCES tab.
   d. Click the Bibliography button in the Citations & Bibliography group.
   e. Click the *Works Cited* option in the *Built-In* section of the drop-down list.
2. Save and then print **C26-E02-DevelopDTP.docx**.

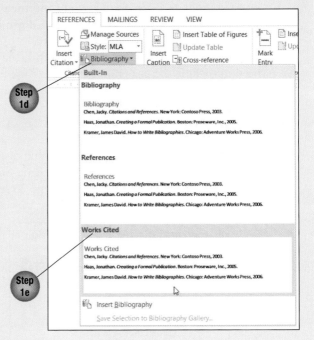

## Modifying and Updating a Sources List

If you insert a new source or modify an existing source at the Source Manager dialog box, Word automatically inserts the source information into the sources list. However, if you insert a new citation, which requires you to add a new source, Word will not automatically update the sources list. To update the sources list, click anywhere in the list and then click the Update Citations and Bibliography tab. The updated sources list will reflect any changes made to the citations and source information in the document.

**QUICK STEPS**

**Update a Sources List**
1. Click anywhere in sources list.
2. Click Update Citations and Bibliography tab.

---

**Exercise 26.2F**  **Modifying and Updating a Works Cited Page**  **Part 6 of 8**

1. With **C26-E02-DevelopDTP.docx** open, create a new source and citation by completing the following steps:
   a. Position the insertion point immediately left of the period that ends the last sentence in the first paragraph of the document (after the word *databases*).
   b. Press the spacebar once.
   c. Click the REFERENCES tab.
   d. Click the Insert Citation button in the Citations & Bibliography group and then click *Add New Source* at the drop-down list.
   e. At the Create Source dialog box, type the following source information from a website. (Change the *Type of Source* option to *Web site* and click the *Show All Bibliography Fields* check box to display all of the fields.)
      *Author:* **Barbara Schueller**
      *Name of Web Page:* **The Past, Present and Future of Desktop Publishing**
      *Year:* **2014**
      *Month:* **April**
      *Day:* **18**
      *Year Accessed:* (type current year in numbers)
      *Month Accessed:* (type current month in letters)
      *Day Accessed:* (type current day in numbers)
      *URL:* **www.emcp.org/publishing**
   f. Click OK to close the Create Source dialog box.
2. Update the works cited page to include the new source by completing the following steps:
   a. Click anywhere in the sources list text.
   b. Click the Update Citations and Bibliography tab. (Notice that the updated sources list includes the *Schueller* reference.)
3. Save **C26-E02-DevelopDTP.docx**.

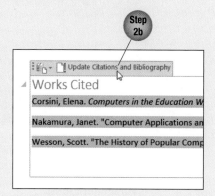

Step 2b

---

## Formatting a Sources List

The different reference styles have specific formatting guidelines. The formatting applied by Word to the sources list may need to be changed to meet the specific guidelines of the MLA, APA, or Chicago style. For example, MLA and APA styles require the following formatting guidelines for the sources list:

- Begin the sources list on a separate page after the last page of text in the report.
- Include the title *Works Cited*, *References*, or *Bibliography* at the top of the page and center it on the width of the page.
- Double-space between and within entries.
- Begin each entry at the left margin and format second and subsequent lines in each entry with a hanging indent.
- Alphabetize the entries by the authors' names.

The general formatting requirements for the Chicago style are similar except for the spacing of entries. Single-space within entries and double-space between entries.

1. With **C26-E02-DevelopDTP.docx** open, make the following formatting changes to the works cited page:
   a. Select the *Works Cited* heading and the entries below the heading.
   b. Click the *No Spacing* style in the Styles group on the HOME tab.
   c. With the text still selected, change the font to Cambria, the font size to 12 points, and the line spacing to 2.0.

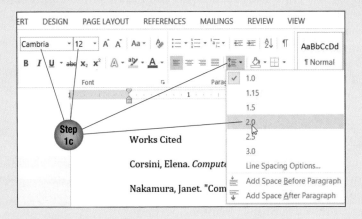

   d. Click anywhere in the title *Works Cited* and then click the Center button in the Paragraph group.
   e. Select only the works cited entries and then press Ctrl + T. (This formats the entries with a hanging indent.)
2. Press Ctrl + Home to move the insertion point to the beginning of the document.
3. Save and then print **C26-E02-DevelopDTP.docx**.

## Changing the Citation Style

Various subjects and instructors or professors may require different forms of citation or reference styles. You can change the citation or reference style before beginning a new document or in an existing document. To do this, click the REFERENCES tab, click the down-pointing arrow at the right of the *Style* option, and then click the desired style at the drop-down list.

**QUICK STEPS**

**Change the Citation Style**
1. Click REFERENCES tab.
2. Click down-pointing arrow at right of *Style* option.
3. Click desired style.

**Exercise 26.2H**    **Changing Citation Styles**      Part 8 of 8

1. With **C26-E02-DevelopDTP.docx** open, change the in-text citations and works cited page from MLA style to APA style by completing the following steps:
   a. With the insertion point positioned at the beginning of the document, click the REFERENCES tab.
   b. Click the down-pointing arrow at the right of the *Style* option in the Citations & Bibliography group and then click *APA* at the drop-down list.

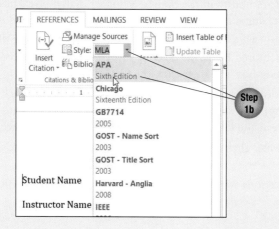

   c. Scroll through the document and notice the changes in the style of the citations and sources list page.
2. Display the last page of the document and then format the sources list by completing the following steps:
   a. Change the title *Works Cited* to *References*.
   b. Select the four references, change the font to 12-point Cambria, change the spacing after paragraphs to 0, and then change the line spacing to 2.0.
3. Save **C26-E02-DevelopDTP.docx** and then print only the references page.
4. Change the citation and bibliography style to Chicago style by clicking the down-pointing arrow at the right of the *Style* option and then clicking *Chicago* at the drop-down list.
5. Scroll to the last page in the document, change the title *References* to *Bibliography*, select the four references, and then change the font to 12-point Cambria.
6. Print page 3 of **C26-E02-DevelopDTP.docx**.
7. Save and then close the document.
8. Display a blank document, click the REFERENCES tab, change the style to *MLA*, and then close the document without saving it.

# Chapter Summary

➤ Footnotes and endnotes are explanatory notes or references. Footnotes are inserted and printed at the bottom of the page and endnotes are printed at the end of the document. Type the text for footnotes or endnotes at the footnote or endnote pane.

➤ By default, Word numbers footnotes with arabic numbers and endnotes with lowercase roman numerals.

➤ If you move, copy, or delete a reference number in a document, all of the other footnotes or endnotes renumber automatically.

➤ Delete a footnote or endnote by selecting the reference number and then pressing the Delete key.

➤ Consider using in-text citations to acknowledge sources in a paper. Commonly used citation and reference styles include the American Psychological Association (APA), Modern Language Association (MLA), and *The Chicago Manual of Style* (Chicago).

➤ Insert a citation using the Insert Citation button in the Citations & Bibliography group on the REFERENCES tab. Specify source information at the Create Source dialog box.

➤ Insert a citation placeholder in a document if you want to type the source information at a later time.

➤ Modify a source by clicking the REFERENCES tab, clicking the Manage Sources button, clicking the source you want to modify in the Source Manager dialog box, clicking the Edit button, and then making the desired changes at the Edit Source dialog box.

➤ To insert a new source, click the New button at the Source Manager dialog box and then insert the information in the required fields. To delete a source, click the source in the *Current List* section in the Source Manager dialog box and then click the Delete button.

➤ After including citations in a report or paper, insert a sources list (such as a works cited page, references page, or bibliography) on a separate page at the end of the document. Insert a sources list with the Bibliography button in the Citations & Bibliography group on the REFERENCES tab.

➤ To update a sources list, click anywhere in the list text and then click the Update Citations and Bibliography tab.

➤ Change the reference style with the *Style* option in the Citations & Bibliography group on the REFERENCES tab.

# Commands Review

| FEATURE | RIBBON TAB, GROUP | BUTTON | KEYBOARD SHORTCUT |
|---|---|---|---|
| bibliography | REFERENCES, Citations & Bibliography | | |
| Create Source dialog box | REFERENCES, Citations & Bibliography | | |
| endnote | REFERENCES, Footnotes | | Alt + Ctrl + D |
| footnote | REFERENCES, Footnotes | | Alt + Ctrl + F |
| next footnote | REFERENCES, Footnotes | | |

| FEATURE | RIBBON TAB, GROUP | BUTTON | KEYBOARD SHORTCUT |
|---|---|---|---|
| show notes | REFERENCES, Footnotes |  | |
| Source Manager dialog box | REFERENCES, Citations & Bibliography | | |
| style | REFERENCES, Citations & Bibliography | | |

# Key Points *Review*

**Completion:** In the space provided at the right, indicate the correct term, symbol, or command.

1. Footnotes are inserted at the bottoms of pages, whereas endnotes are inserted here.  _____

2. Word numbers footnotes with this type of number.  _____

3. Word numbers endnotes with this type of number.  _____

4. View footnotes in a document by clicking this button in the Footnotes group.  _____

5. Three commonly used styles for providing references in a report are APA (American Psychological Association), CMS (*The Chicago Manual of Style*), and this.  _____

6. Insert a new citation in a document with options at this dialog box.  _____

7. Click this tab to display the Citations & Bibliography group.  _____

8. To modify a source, click this button in the Citations & Bibliography group.  _____

9. To update a works cited page, click anywhere on the page and then click this tab.  _____

10. Change the citation or reference style with this option.  _____

# Chapter *Assessments*

## Applying Your Skills

Demonstrate your knowledge of features learned in this chapter by completing the following assessments.

### Assessment 26.1    Insert Footnotes in a Designing Newsletters Report

1. Open **DesignNwsltr.docx** and save the document with the name **C26-A01-DesignNwsltr**.
2. Create the first footnote shown in Figure 26.8 on the next page at the end of the first paragraph in the *Applying Guidelines* section.
3. Create the second footnote shown in Figure 26.8 at the end of the third paragraph in the *Applying Guidelines* section.

4. Create the third footnote shown in Figure 26.8 at the end of the last paragraph in the *Applying Guidelines* section.
5. Create the fourth footnote shown in Figure 26.8 at the end of the only paragraph in the *Choose Paper Size and Type* section.
6. Create the fifth footnote shown in Figure 26.8 at the end of the only paragraph in the *Choosing Paper Weight* section.
7. Save and then print **C26-A01-DesignNwsltr.docx**.
8. Select the entire document and then change the font to Constantia.
9. Select all of the footnotes and change the font to Constantia.
10. Delete the third footnote.
11. Save, print, and then close **C26-A01-DesignNwsltr.docx**.

**Figure 26.8 Assessment 26.1**

James Habermann, "Designing a Newsletter," *Desktop Designs* (2015): 23-29.

Shirley G. Pilante, "Adding Pizzazz to Your Newsletter," *Desktop Publisher* (2014): 32-37.

Arlita S. Maddock, "Guidelines for a Better Newsletter," *Business Computing* (2015): 9-14.

Monica Alverso, "Paper Styles for Newsletters," *Design Technologies* (2014): 45-51.

Keith Sutton, "Choosing Paper Styles," *Design Techniques* (2014): 8-11.

**Assessment 26.2  Insert Sources and Citations in a Privacy Rights Report**

SNAP Grade It

1. Open **PrivRights.docx** and save the document with the name **C26-A02-PrivRights**.
2. Make sure that MLA style is selected in the Citations & Bibliography group on the REFERENCES tab.
3. Format the first page to meet MLA requirements by making the following changes:
   a. Select the entire document, change the font to 12-point Cambria, change the line spacing to 2.0, and remove the spacing after paragraphs.
   b. Move the insertion point to the beginning of the document, type your name, press the Enter key, type your instructor's name, press the Enter key, type the title of your course, press the Enter key, type the current date, and then press the Enter key.
   c. Type the title **Privacy Rights** and then center it on the page.
   d. Insert a header that displays your last name and the page number at the right margin and change the font to 12-point Cambria.
4. Press Ctrl + End to move the insertion point to the end of the document and then type the text shown in Figure 26.9 on page 944 up to the first citation (the text *(Hartley)*). Insert the source information for a journal article written by Kenneth Hartley using the following information:
   *Author:* **Kenneth Hartley**
   *Title:* **Privacy Laws**
   *Journal Name:* **Business World**
   *Year:* **2014**
   *Pages:* **24-46**
   *Volume:* **XII**

5. Continue typing the text up to the next citation (the text *(Ferraro)*) and insert the following source information for a book:

    *Author:* **Ramona Ferraro**
    *Title:* **Business Employee Rights**
    *Year:* **2015**
    *City:* **Tallahassee**
    *Publisher:* **Everglades Publishing House**

6. Continue typing the text up to the next citation (the text *(Aldrich)*) and insert the following information for an article in a periodical:

    *Author:* **Kelly Aldrich**
    *Title:* **What Rights Do Employees Have?**
    *Periodical Title:* **Great Plains Times**
    *Year:* **2013**
    *Month:* **May**
    *Day:* **6**
    *Pages:* **18-22**

7. Insert a page number in the citation for Kelly Aldrich using the Edit Citation dialog box.
8. Type the remaining text in Figure 26.9.
9. In the *Master List* section of the Source Manager dialog box, edit the title of the Kenneth Hartley source to read *Small Business Privacy Laws*.
10. Select and delete the last two sentences in the second paragraph and then delete the Ramona Ferraro source in the *Current List* section of the Source Manager dialog box.
11. Insert a works cited page on a separate page at the end of the document.
12. Create a new source in the document using the Source Manager dialog box and include the following source information for a website:

    *Author:* **Harold Jefferson**
    *Name of Web Page:* **Small Business Policies and Procedures**
    *Year:* **2014**
    *Month:* **December**
    *Day:* **12**
    *Year Accessed:* (type current year)
    *Month Accessed:* (type current month)
    *Day Accessed:* (type current day)
    *URL:* **www.emcp.net/policies**

13. Insert a citation for the Harold Jefferson source at the end of the last sentence in the first paragraph.
14. Update the works cited page.
15. Format the works cited page to meet MLA requirements with the following changes:
    a. Select the *Works Cited* heading and all of the entries and then click the *No Spacing* style.
    b. Change the font to 12-point Cambria and change the spacing to 2.0.
    c. Center the title *Works Cited*.
    d. Format the works cited entries with a hanging indent.
16. Save and then print **C26-A02-PrivRights.docx**.
17. Change the document and sources list from MLA to APA style.
18. Format the sources list to meet APA requirements by changing the title to *References*, selecting the references, and formatting the references using these specifications: change the font to 12-point Cambria, change the spacing after paragraphs to 0, and change the line spacing to 2.0.
19. Save the document, print page 2, and then close **C26-A02-PrivRights.docx**.

**Figure 26.9 Assessment 26.2**

An exception to the ability of companies to monitor their employees does exist. If the company has pledged to respect any aspect of employee privacy, it must keep that pledge. For example, if a business states that it will not monitor employee email or phone calls, by law, it must follow this stated policy (Hartley). However, no legal requirement exists mandating that companies notify their employees when and if monitoring takes place (Ferraro). Therefore, employees should assume they are always monitored and act accordingly.

Privacy advocates are calling for this situation to change. "They acknowledge that employers have the right to ensure that their employees are doing their jobs, but they question the need to monitor employees without warning and without limit" (Aldrich 20). The American Civil Liberties Union has, in fact, proposed a Fair Electronic Monitoring Policy to prevent abuses of employee privacy.

# Expanding Your Skills

Explore additional feature options or use Help to learn a new skill in creating this document.

### Assessment 26.3    Customize Footnotes/Endnotes

1.  As you learned in this chapter, you can convert endnotes to footnotes. You can also convert footnotes to endnotes. Open **C26-E01-InterfaceApps.docx** and save the document with the name **C26-A03-InterfaceApps**.
2.  Using options at the Footnote and Endnote dialog box, make the following changes:
    a.  Convert the footnotes to endnotes. (After converting the footnotes to endnotes, make sure to click the *Endnotes* option at the top of the Endnote and Footnote dialog box.)
    b.  Change the number format to arabic numbers (1, 2, 3, . . .).
    c.  Change the starting number to 5.
3.  Save, print, and then close **C26-A03-InterfaceApps.docx**.

# Achieving Signature Status

Take your skills to the next level by completing this more challenging assessment.

## Assessment 26.4    Format a Report in MLA Style

1. Open **DevelopSystem.docx** and save the document with the name **C26-A04-DevelopSystem**.
2. Format the document so it displays as shown in Figure 26.10 with the following specifications:
   a. Format the document in MLA style. (For help, refer to Exercise 26.2, which includes eight parts.) Change the document font to 12-point Cambria.
   b. Use the information from the works cited page to insert citations into the document. The *Janowski* citation is for a journal article, the *Mendoza* citation is for a book, and the *Yamashita* citation is for a website.
   c. Format the works cited page to meet MLA requirements.
3. Save, print, and then close **C26-A04-DevelopSystem.docx**.

**Figure 26.10  Assessment 26.4**

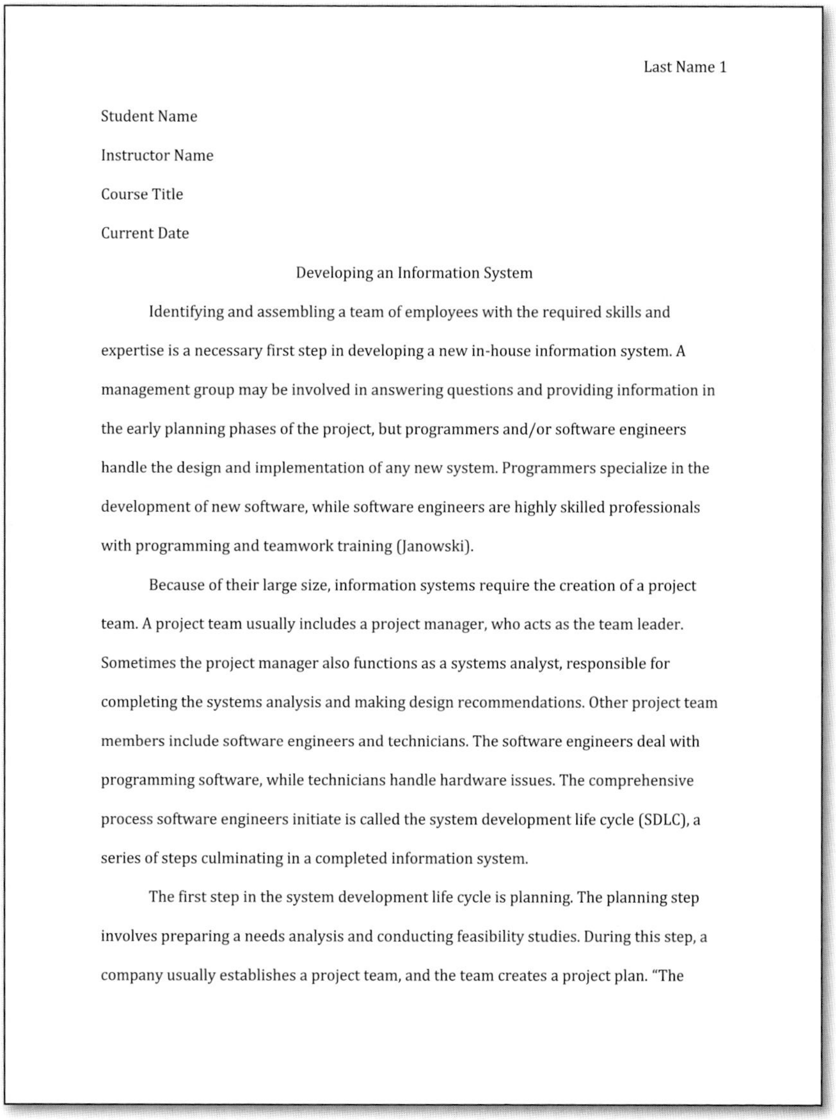

Last Name 1

Student Name

Instructor Name

Course Title

Current Date

Developing an Information System

Identifying and assembling a team of employees with the required skills and expertise is a necessary first step in developing a new in-house information system. A management group may be involved in answering questions and providing information in the early planning phases of the project, but programmers and/or software engineers handle the design and implementation of any new system. Programmers specialize in the development of new software, while software engineers are highly skilled professionals with programming and teamwork training (Janowski).

Because of their large size, information systems require the creation of a project team. A project team usually includes a project manager, who acts as the team leader. Sometimes the project manager also functions as a systems analyst, responsible for completing the systems analysis and making design recommendations. Other project team members include software engineers and technicians. The software engineers deal with programming software, while technicians handle hardware issues. The comprehensive process software engineers initiate is called the system development life cycle (SDLC), a series of steps culminating in a completed information system.

The first step in the system development life cycle is planning. The planning step involves preparing a needs analysis and conducting feasibility studies. During this step, a company usually establishes a project team, and the team creates a project plan. "The

Page 1

**Figure 26.10  Assessment 26.4 (continued)**

project plan includes an estimate of how long the project will take to complete, an outline of the steps involved, and a list of deliverables" (Mendoza 42). Deliverables are documents, services, hardware, and software that must be finished and delivered by a certain time and date.

A project is ready to move into the design stage once the project team has approved the plan, including the budget. The design process begins with the writing of the documentation, which covers functional and design specifications. In most cases, the project team creates the functional specifications, describing what the system must be able to do (Yamashita).

The project can move into the next phase, implementation, once the development team and the systems house develop the design specification and approve the plans. This step is where the actual work of putting the system together is completed, including creating a prototype and completing the programming. In most cases, implementing the new system is the longest, most difficult step in the process.

A system goes into the support stage after it has been accepted and approved. A support contract normally allows users to contact the systems house for technical support, training, and sometimes on-site troubleshooting. Even if the system was designed in-house, the responsible department often operates as an independent entity—sometimes even charging the department acquiring the system. The support stage continues until a new information system is proposed and developed, usually years later. At that point, the existing system is retired and no longer used.

Page 2

**Figure 26.10 Assessment 26.4 (continued)**

Last Name 3

Works Cited

Janowski, Robert. "Information System Management." *Technology: Computer Networking* (2014): 35-41.

Mendoza, Carla. *Building Computer Networks.* Oklahoma City: Blue Field Publishing House, 2015.

Yamashita, Paul. *How is an Information System Designed?* 19 October 2013. 20 February 2015. <www.emcp.net/systemdesign>.

Page 3

# Chapter 27

**Tutorial 27.1**
Marking Index Entries and
Inserting an Index
**Tutorial 27.2**
Creating a Concordance File
**Tutorial 27.3**
Updating and Deleting an Index

# Creating Indexes

## Performance Objectives

Upon successful completion of Chapter 27, you will be able to:

- Create an index and insert it in the document
- Mark entries and subentries for an index, including cross-references
- Create a concordance file and use it to create an index
- Update and delete an index

An *index* is a list of topics contained in a publication and the pages on which those topics are discussed. Creating an index manually can be tedious but using Word, you can automate the process. In this chapter, you will learn how to create an index and insert it into a document, as well as how to update and delete an index.

*Note: Before beginning computer exercises for this chapter, copy to your storage medium the Chapter27 folder from the CD that accompanies this textbook and then make Chapter27 the active folder.*

In this chapter, students will produce the following documents:

Exercise 27.1. C27-E01-DTP.docx
Exercise 27.2. C27-E02-Computers.docx
Exercise 27.3. C27-E03-PlanNwsltr.docx

Model answers for these exercises are shown on the following pages.

INDEX

3

**Exercise 27.1**

C27-E01-DTP.docx

(Page 3)

INDEX

**Exercise 27.2**

C27-E02-Computers.docx

(Page 4)

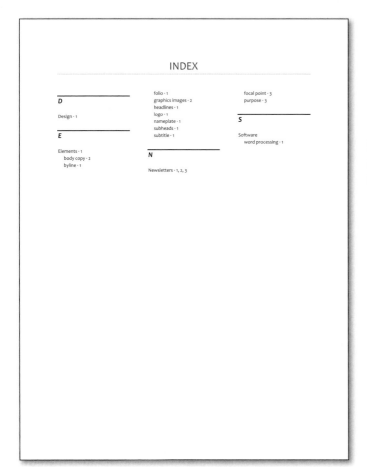

INDEX

D

Design · 1

E

Elements · 1
 body copy · 2
 byline · 1

folio · 1
graphics images · 2
headlines · 1
logo · 1
nameplate · 1
subheads · 1
subtitle · 1

N

Newsletters · 1, 2, 3

focal point · 3
purpose · 3

S

Software
 word processing · 1

**Exercise 27.3**

C27-E03-PlanNwsltr.docx
(Page 4)

# Creating an Index

Word automates the process of creating an index and, as you will learn in the next chapter, a table of contents—both in a similar manner. Although Word automates the process, creating an index still takes thought and consideration. The author of a book, manuscript, or report must determine which topics should be listed as main entries and which topics should be listed as subentries under a main entry. An index may include such topics as the main idea of a document, the main subject of a chapter or section, variations of a heading or subheading, and abbreviations. Figure 27.1 on the next page shows an example of an index.

## Marking Text for an Index

When you create an index in Word, you electronically mark the words that you want to include as entries. Before marking the words, however, you need to determine what main entries and subentries to include. Options for marking text as index entries are available at the Mark Index Entry dialog box.

To mark text for inclusion in an index, select the word or words, click the REFERENCES tab, and then click the Mark Entry button in the Index group. You can also press Alt + Shift + X. At the Mark Index Entry dialog box, as shown in Figure 27.2 on the next page, the selected word(s) appears in the *Main entry* text box. If you want the text to be listed as a main entry, leave it as displayed and then click the Mark button.

**QUICK STEPS**

**Mark Text for an Index**
1. Select text.
2. Click REFERENCES tab.
3. Click Mark Entry button.
4. Make desired changes.
5. Click Mark button.
6. Click Close button.

**OR**
1. Select text.
2. Press Alt + Shift + X.
3. Make desired changes.
4. Click Mark button.
5. Click Close button.

Mark Entry

**Figure 27.1 Sample Index**

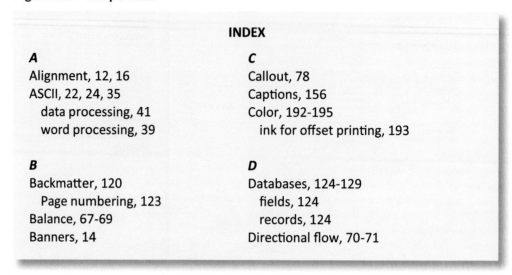

**INDEX**

**A**
Alignment, 12, 16
ASCII, 22, 24, 35
   data processing, 41
   word processing, 39

**B**
Backmatter, 120
   Page numbering, 123
Balance, 67-69
Banners, 14

**C**
Callout, 78
Captions, 156
Color, 192-195
   ink for offset printing, 193

**D**
Databases, 124-129
   fields, 124
   records, 124
Directional flow, 70-71

**Figure 27.2 Mark Index Entry Dialog Box**

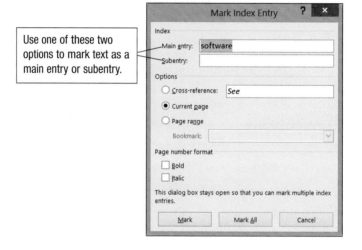

This turns on the display of nonprinting characters in the document and inserts a field code immediately after the selected text.

For example, in Exercise 27.1A, when you mark the word *software* for inclusion in an index, Word inserts the code *{XE "software"}* immediately after the word. When you mark the words *word processing* as a subentry and *software* as the main entry, Word inserts the code *{XE "software:word processing"}* immediately after the words. Click the Close button to close the Mark Index Entry dialog box.

If you want the text you selected to be listed as a subentry, make the following changes at the Mark Index Entry dialog box: type the main entry in the *Main entry* text box, click in the *Subentry* text box, and then type the selected text. For example, suppose a publication includes the terms *Page layout* and *Portrait*. The words *Page layout* are to be marked as a main entry for the index and *Portrait* is to be marked as a subentry under *Page layout*. To mark these words for inclusion in an index, you would complete the following steps:

1. Select *Page layout*.
2. Click the REFERENCES tab and then click the Mark Entry button or press Alt + Shift + X.

3. At the Mark Index Entry dialog box, click the Mark button or Mark All button. (This turns on the display of nonprinting symbols.)

4. With the Mark Index Entry dialog box still displayed on the screen, click in the document to make it active and then select *Portrait*.

5. Click the Mark Index Entry dialog box title bar to make it active.

6. Select *Portrait* in the *Main entry* text box and then type **Page layout**.

7. Click in the *Subentry* text box and then type **Portrait**.

8. Click the Mark button.

9. Click the Close button.

The main entry or subentry does not have to be the same as the selected text. You can select text for an index, type the text you want to display in the *Main entry* or *Subentry* text box, and then click the Mark button.

At the Mark Index Entry dialog box, you can also apply bold and/or italic formatting to the page numbers that will appear in the index. To apply formatting, click *Bold* and/or *Italic* to insert check marks in the appropriate check boxes.

The *Options* section of the Mark Index Entry dialog box contains three options for adding page numbers and cross-references. The *Current page* option is the default. At this setting, the current page number is provided for the main entry or subentry displayed. Select the *Page range* option to mark entries that span multiple pages. Click the *Cross-reference* option to cross-reference the main entry or subentry. Type the text to be used as a cross-reference for that entry in the *Cross-reference* text box. For example, you could mark the word *Serif* and cross-reference it to *Typefaces*.

Click the Mark All button at the Mark Index Entry dialog box to mark the first occurrence of the text in each paragraph as an index entry. Word marks occurrences of the text only if the use of uppercase and lowercase letters is exactly the same as in the index entry.

## Exercise 27.1A  Marking Words for an Index                    Part 1 of 2

1. Open **DTP.docx** and save the document with the name **C27-E01-DTP**.

2. Insert page numbers centered at the bottom of each page.

3. In the first paragraph, mark the word *software* as a main entry for the index and mark the words *word processing* as a subentry below *software* by completing the following steps:

   a. Select *software* (located in the second sentence of the first paragraph).

   b. Click the REFERENCES tab and then click the Mark Entry button in the Index group.

   c. At the Mark Index Entry dialog box, click the Mark All button. (This turns on the display of nonprinting symbols.)

d. With the Mark Index Entry dialog box still displayed, click in the document to make it active and then select the words *word processing*, located in the last sentence of the first paragraph. (You may want to drag the dialog box down the screen so more of the document text is visible.)

e. Click the Mark Index Entry dialog box title bar to make the dialog box active.

f. Select *word processing* in the *Main entry* text box and then type **software**.

g. Click in the *Subentry* text box and then type **word processing**.

h. Click the Mark All button.

i. With the Mark Index Entry dialog box still displayed, complete steps similar to those in Steps 3d through 3h to mark the *first* occurrences of the following words as main entries or subentries for the index:

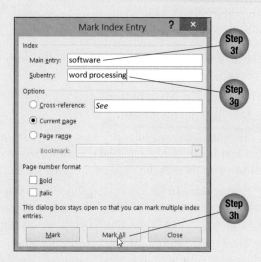

In the first paragraph in the *Defining Desktop Publishing* section:
> *spreadsheets:* subentry (main entry: *software*)
> *database:* subentry (main entry: *software*)

In the second paragraph in the *Defining Desktop Publishing* section:
> *publishing:* main entry
> *desktop:* subentry (main entry: *publishing*)
> *printer:* main entry
> *laser:* subentry (main entry: *printer*)

In the third paragraph in the *Defining Desktop Publishing* section:
> *design:* main entry

In the fourth paragraph in the *Defining Desktop Publishing* section:
> *traditional:* subentry (main entry: *publishing*)

In the first paragraph in the *Initiating the Process* section:
> *publication:* main entry
> *planning:* subentry (main entry: *publication*)
> *creating:* subentry (main entry: *publication*)
> *content:* subentry (main entry: *publication*)
> *intended audience:* subentry (main entry: *publication*)

In the third paragraph in the *Planning the Publication* section:
> *message:* main entry

j. Click the Close button to close the Mark Index Entry dialog box.

4. Turn off the display of nonprinting characters.

5. Save **C27-E01-DTP.docx**.

# Inserting an Index

After you have marked all of the words that you want to include in an index as main entries or subentries, the next step is to insert the index in the document. An index generally appears at the end of a document and begins on a new page.

To insert the index, position the insertion point at the end of the document and then insert a page break. With the insertion point positioned below the page break, type *INDEX* and then press the Enter key. With the insertion point positioned at the left margin, click the REFERENCES tab and then click the Insert Index button in the Index group. At the Index dialog box, as shown in Figure 27.3, select the desired formatting and then click OK. Word inserts the index with the formatting you selected at the location of the insertion point. Word also inserts section breaks above and below the index text.

**Insert an Index**
1. Click REFERENCES tab.
2. Click Insert Index button.
3. Select desired format.
4. Click OK.

Insert Index

**Figure 27.3 Index Dialog Box**

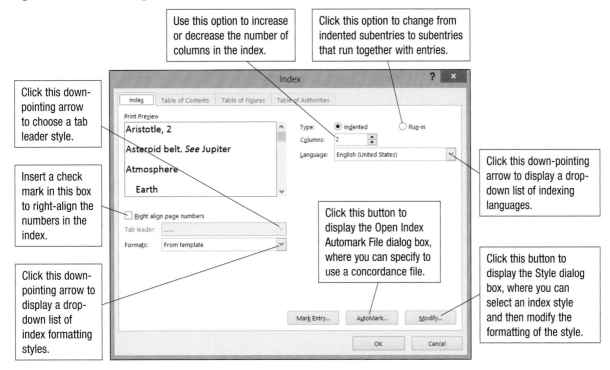

At the Index dialog box, you can customize the format of the index, specifying how the entries and subentries will appear. The *Print Preview* section shows how the index will display in the document. If you want the numbers right-aligned in the index, insert a check mark in the *Right align page numbers* check box. (This makes the *Tab leader* option active.) Click the down-pointing arrow at the right side of the *Formats* option box and a drop-down list of formatting options displays. Select the *Formal* option and the *Tab leader* option becomes available. The default tab leader character is a period. To change to a different character, click the down-pointing arrow at the right side of the *Tab leader* option box and then click the desired character at the drop-down list.

In the *Type* section, the *Indented* option is the default, which means subentries appear indented below main entries. If you click *Run-in*, subentries display on the same line as main entries. By default, Word inserts an index in two columns. You can increase or decrease the number of columns with the *Columns* option. If your document contains text in a language other than English, you can create an index using the other language's alphabet. To use another language for an index, the language must be added to the Word Options dialog box with *Language* selected. (For more information, refer to Assessment 27.4.)

You can create a concordance file for an index (covered later in this chapter) and then identify the file by clicking the AutoMark button and then double-clicking the file name in the Open Index Automark File dialog box. You can modify the formatting of an index by clicking the Modify button. At the Style dialog box that displays, click the style in the *Styles* list box that you want to modify and then click the Modify button. At the Modify Style dialog box, apply the desired formatting and then click OK. The Modify Style dialog box that displays is the same dialog box that you used to modify styles in Chapter 24.

## Exercise 27.1B    Inserting an Index                                    Part 2 of 2

1. With **C27-E01-DTP.docx** open, position the insertion point at the end of the document and then press Ctrl + Enter to insert a page break.
2. Type **INDEX** and then press the Enter key.
3. Click the REFERENCES tab and then click the Insert Index button in the Index group.
4. At the Index dialog box, click the Modify button that displays in the lower right corner.
5. At the Style dialog box with *Index 1* selected in the *Styles* list box, click the Modify button.
6. At the Modify Style dialog box, click the Bold button.
7. Click OK to close the Modify Style dialog box.
8. At the Style dialog box, click *Index 2* in the *Styles* list box and then click the Modify button.
9. At the Modify Style dialog box, click the Italic button and then click OK.
10. Click OK at the Style dialog box.
11. At the Index dialog box, click the up-pointing arrow at the right of the *Columns* option to change the number to 3.
12. Click the *Right align page numbers* check box to insert a check mark. (This makes the *Tab leader* option active.)
13. Click the down-pointing arrow at the right side of the *Tab leader* option box and then click the hyphen leader at the drop-down list.

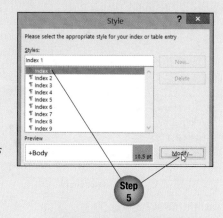

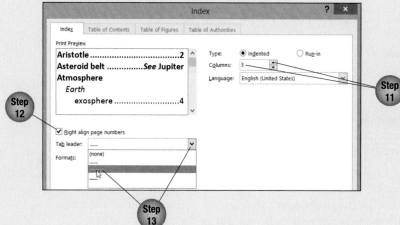

14. Click OK to close the Index dialog box.
15. Apply the Heading 1 style to the title *INDEX* and then center the title.
16. Save and then print the last page (the index page) of the document.
17. Close **C27-E01-DTP.docx**.

# Marking Index Entry Options

The *Options* section of the Mark Index Entry dialog box provides additional options for marking text for an index. You can mark a bookmark as an index entry or you can mark text that refers readers to another index entry.

## Marking Text That Spans a Range of Pages

If you want to use more than a few words as a single index entry, consider identifying the text as a bookmark and then marking the bookmark as an index entry. This option is especially useful when the text for an entry spans a range of pages. To mark text that you have identified as a bookmark, position the insertion point at the end of the text, click the REFERENCES tab, and then click the Mark Entry button in the Index group. At the Mark Index Entry dialog box, type the index entry for the text and then click the *Page range* option in the *Options* section. Click the down-pointing arrow at the right of the *Bookmark* option box and then click the bookmark name at the drop-down list. Click the Mark button to mark the bookmark text and then close the dialog box.

## Marking an Entry as a Cross-Reference

In some situations, you may want to mark for inclusion in an index text that refers readers to another entry. For example, if you use the acronym *MIS* in a document to refer to *Management Information Systems*, you can mark *MIS* as an index entry that refers readers to the entry for *Management Information Systems*. To do this, select *MIS*, click the REFERENCES tab, and then click the Mark Entry button in the Index group. At the Mark Index Entry dialog box, click *Cross-reference* in the *Options* section of the dialog box (to move the insertion point inside the text box), type *Management Information Systems*, and then click the Mark button.

---

**Exercise 27.** **Marking Entries and Inserting an Index**                    **Part 1 of 1**

---

1. Open **Computers.docx** and save the document with the name **C27-E02-Computers**.
2. Make the following changes to the document:
   a. Apply the Heading 1 style to the title *COMPUTERS*.
   b. Apply the Heading 2 style to the five headings in the document (*Speed*, *Accuracy*, *Versatility*, *Storage*, and *Communications*).
   c. Change the style set to Lines (Stylish).
   d. Change the theme colors to Blue.
   e. Change the theme fonts to Candara.
3. Create a bookmark for the *Speed* section of the document by completing the following steps:
   a. Select text from the beginning of the heading *Speed* through the paragraph of text that follows the heading.

b. Click the INSERT tab.
c. Click the Bookmark button in the Links group.
d. At the Bookmark dialog box, type **Speed** in the *Bookmark name* text box.
e. Click the Add button.

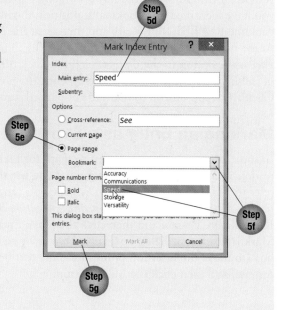

4. Complete steps similar to those in Step 3 to create the following bookmarks:
a. Select text from the beginning of the *Accuracy* heading through the paragraph of text that follows the heading and then create a bookmark named *Accuracy*.
b. Select text from the beginning of the *Versatility* heading through the paragraph of text that follows the heading and then create a bookmark named *Versatility*.
c. Select text from the beginning of the *Storage* heading through the paragraph of text that follows the heading and then create a bookmark named *Storage*.
d. Select text from the beginning of the *Communications* heading through the two paragraphs of text that follow the heading and then create a bookmark named *Communications*.

5. Mark the *Speed* bookmark as an index entry that spans multiple pages by completing the following steps:
a. Move the insertion point so it is positioned immediately following the only paragraph of text in the *Speed* section.
b. Click the REFERENCES tab.
c. Click the Mark Entry button in the Index group.
d. At the Mark Index Entry dialog box, type **Speed** in the *Main entry* text box.
e. Click the *Page range* option.
f. Click the down-pointing arrow at the right of the *Bookmark* option box and then click *Speed* at the drop-down list.
g. Click the Mark button.

6. Complete steps similar to those in Step 5 to mark the following bookmarks as index entries: *Accuracy, Versatility, Storage,* and *Communications*.

7. With the Mark Index Entry dialog box open, mark the *first* occurrences of the following words (click the Mark All button) as main entries or subentries for the index:
a. Mark *computers*, located in the first sentence of the first paragraph of text in the document as a main entry.
b. Mark *personal computers*, located in the second paragraph of text in the document, as a main entry.
c. Mark *supercomputers*, located in the *Speed* section of the document, as a main entry.
d. Mark *GIGO*, located in the *Accuracy* section of the document, as a main entry.
e. Mark the following text located in the *Versatility* section:
   *Human Genome Project:* main entry
   *DNA:* main entry

f.  Mark the following text located in the *Communications* section:
    *wireless devices:* main entry
    *personal digital assistants:* subentry (main entry: *wireless devices*)
    *notebook computers:* subentry (main entry: *wireless devices*)
    *cell phones:* subentry (main entry: *wireless devices*)
    *local area network:* main entry
    *wide area network:* main entry
g.  Click the Close button to close the Mark Index Entry dialog box.

8.  Mark *microcomputers* as a cross-reference by completing the following steps:
a.  Press Ctrl + Home to move the insertion point to the beginning of the document.
b.  Select the word *microcomputers* that is located in the first sentence of the second paragraph of text.
c.  If necessary, click the REFERENCES tab.
d.  Click the Mark Entry button in the Index group.
e.  At the Mark Index Entry dialog box, click the *Cross-reference* option in the *Options* section (after the word *See*) and then type **personal computers**.
f.  Click the Mark button.
g.  Click the Close button to close the Mark Index Entry dialog box.

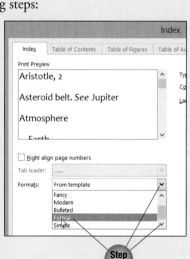

9.  Complete steps similar to those in Step 8 to mark the following text as cross-references:
a.  Select *LAN* in the second paragraph of text in the *Communications* section and cross-reference it to *local area network*.
b.  Select *WAN* in the second paragraph of text in the *Communications* section and cross-reference it to *wide area network*.

10. Close the Mark Index Entry dialog box and then turn off the display of nonprinting characters.

11. Insert the index in the document by completing the following steps:
a.  Position the insertion point at the end of the document.
b.  Insert a page break.
c.  With the insertion point positioned below the page break, type **INDEX**, and then press the Enter key.
d.  Click the REFERENCES tab.
e.  Click the Insert Index button in the Index group.
f.  At the Index dialog box, click the down-pointing arrow at the right of the *Formats* option box, scroll down the drop-down list, and then click *Formal*.
g.  Make sure *3* displays in the *Columns* measurement box.
h.  Click OK to close the dialog box.
i.  Apply the Heading 1 style to the title *INDEX*.

12. Save and then print the last page (the index page) of the document.

13. Close **C27-E02-Computers.docx**.

# Creating a Concordance File

**Create a Concordance File**
1. Click INSERT tab.
2. Click Table button and drag to create table.
3. In first column, type words to include in index.
4. In second column, type main entry and subentry (separated by colon plus space).
5. Save document.

Save words that appear frequently in a document as a concordance file. Doing this will spare you from having to mark all of these words as entries or subentries in a document. A *concordance file* is a Word document that contains a two-column table and no text outside the table. In the first column of the table, you enter the words that you want to appear in the index. In the second column, you enter the main entry and subentry (if there is one) that should appear for each word in the first column. To indicate a subentry, add a colon (plus a space) after the main entry and then type the subentry.

Figure 27.4 shows an example of a completed concordance file. The first column lists words as they appear in the document (for example, *World War I*, *technology*, and *television*). The second column lists words as they should appear in the index, specifying whether each word is a main entry or subentry. For example, the text *motion pictures* in the first column will appear in the index as a subentry under the main entry *Technology*, as specified in the second column.

After you have created a concordance file, you can use it to quickly mark text in a document for inclusion in an index. To do this, open the document containing the text you want marked for an index, display the Index dialog box, and then click the AutoMark button. At the Open Index AutoMark File dialog box, double-click the concordance file name in the list box. When you double-click the file name, Word turns on the display of nonprinting symbols, searches the document for text that matches the words in the first column of the concordance file, and then marks each occurrence of each word as specified in the second column. After marking the text for the index, insert the index in the document as described earlier.

**Figure 27.4  Concordance File**

| | |
|---|---|
| World War I | World War I |
| technology | Technology |
| teletypewriters | Technology: teletypewriters |
| motion pictures | Technology: motion pictures |
| television | Technology: television |
| Radio Corporation of America | Radio Corporation of America |
| coaxial cable | Coaxial cable |
| telephone | Technology: telephone |
| Communications Act of 1934 | Communications Act of 1934 |
| World War II | World War II |
| radar system | Technology: radar system |
| computer | Computer |
| Atanasoff Berry Computer | Computer: Atanasoff Berry Computer |
| Korean War | Korean War |
| Columbia Broadcasting System | Columbia Broadcasting System |
| Cold War | Cold War |
| Vietnam | Vietnam |
| artificial satellite | Technology: artificial satellite |
| Communications Satellite Act of 1962 | Communications Satellite Act of 1962 |

As you create the concordance file in Exercise 27.3A, the AutoCorrect feature in Word will automatically capitalize the first letter of the first word entered within each cell. In Figure 27.4, you can see that several of the first words in the first column do not begin with capital letters. Before you begin the exercise, consider turning off this AutoCorrect capitalization feature. To do this, click the FILE tab and then click *Options*. At the Word Options dialog box, click *Proofing* in the left panel of the dialog box and then click the AutoCorrect Options button. At the AutoCorrect dialog box with the AutoCorrect tab selected, click the *Capitalize first letter of table cells* check box to remove the check mark. Click OK to close the dialog box and then click OK to close the Word Options dialog box.

1. At a blank document, create the text shown in Figure 27.5 on the next page as a concordance file by completing the following steps:
   a. Click the INSERT tab.
   b. Click the Table button in the Tables group.
   c. Drag down and to the right until *2 × 1 Table* displays at the top of the grid and then click the left mouse button.

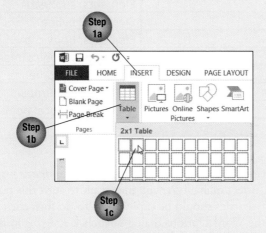

   d. Type the text in the cells as shown in Figure 27.5 on the next page. Press the Tab key to move to the next cell. (If you did not remove the check mark before the *Capitalize first letter of table cells* option at the AutoCorrect dialog box, the *n* in the first word in the first cell *newsletters* is automatically capitalized. Hover the mouse over the capital *N* until the blue rectangle displays, click the AutoCorrect Options button that displays, and then click *Stop Auto-capitalizing First Letter of Table Cells* at the drop-down list.)
2. Save the document with the name **C27-E03-CFile**.
3. Close **C27-E03-CFile.docx**.

Figure 27.5 Exercise 27.3A

| newsletters | Newsletters |
|---|---|
| Newsletters | Newsletters |
| Software | Software |
| Desktop publishing | Software: desktop publishing |
| word processing | Software: word processing |
| Printers | Printers |
| Laser | Printers: laser |
| Design | Design |
| Communication | Communication |
| Consistency | Design: consistency |
| Elements | Elements |
| Nameplate | Elements: nameplate |
| Logo | Elements: logo |
| Subtitle | Elements: subtitle |
| Folio | Elements: folio |
| Headlines | Elements: headlines |
| Subheads | Elements: subheads |
| Byline | Elements: byline |
| Body Copy | Elements: body copy |
| Graphics Images | Elements: graphics images |
| Audience | Newsletters: audience |
| Purpose | Newsletters: purpose |
| focal point | Newsletters: focal point |

If you removed the check mark before the *Capitalize first letter of table cells* option at the AutoCorrect dialog box, you may want to turn this feature back on, depending on how many entries should be capitalized. To do this, click the FILE tab and then click *Options*. At the Word Options dialog box, click *Proofing* in the left panel of the dialog box and then click the AutoCorrect Options button. At the AutoCorrect dialog box with the AutoCorrect tab selected, click the *Capitalize first letter of table cells* check box to insert the check mark. Click OK to close the dialog box and then click OK to close the Word Options dialog box.

---

**Exercise 27.3B**    **Inserting an Index Using a Concordance File**    Part 2 of 3

1. Open **PlanNwsltr.docx** and save the document with the name **C27-E03-PlanNwsltr**.
2. Mark the text to include in the index using the concordance file by completing the following steps:
   a. Click the REFERENCES tab.
   b. Click the Insert Index button in the Index group.
   c. At the Index dialog box, click the AutoMark button.

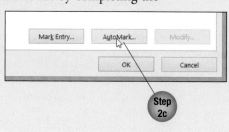

Step 2c

    d. At the Open Index AutoMark File dialog box, if necessary, click the file type button to the right of the *File name* text box and then click *All Files (\*.\*)* at the drop-down list.

    e. Double-click ***C27-E03-CFile.docx*** in the Content pane. (This turns on the display of nonprinting symbols.)

3. Insert the index in the document by completing the following steps:
    a. Position the insertion point at the end of the document.
    b. Insert a page break.
    c. Type **INDEX**.
    d. Press the Enter key.
    e. Click the Insert Index button in the Index group.
    f. At the Index dialog box, click the down-pointing arrow at the right of the *Formats* option box and then click *Modern* at the drop-down list.
    g. Make sure *3* displays in the *Columns* measurement box.
    h. Click OK to close the dialog box.

4. Apply the Heading 1 style to the *INDEX* title and then center it on the page.
5. Turn off the display of nonprinting characters.
6. Save **C27-E03-PlanNwsltr.docx** and then print only the index page.

# Updating and Deleting an Index

If you make changes to a document after you have inserted the index, be sure to update the index. To do this, click anywhere within the index and then click the Update Index button in the Index group or press the F9 key.

You can also delete the index after inserting it in the document. To delete the index, select the index using either the mouse or keyboard and then press the Delete key.

**QUICK STEPS**

**Update an Index**
1. Click in index.
2. Click Update Index button or press F9 key.

**Delete an Index**
1. Select entire index.
2. Press Delete key.

Update Index

## Exercise 27.3C   Updating an Index   Part 3 of 3

1. With **C27-E03-PlanNwsltr.docx** open, insert a page break at the beginning of the title *PLANNING A NEWSLETTER*.

2. Update the index by clicking anywhere in the index, clicking the REFERENCES tab, and then clicking the Update Index button in the Index group.

3. Save **C27-E03-PlanNwsltr. docx** and then print only the index page.

4. Close **C27-E03-PlanNwsltr. docx**.

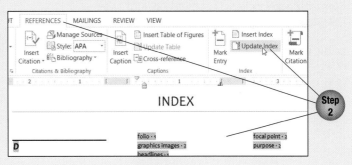

# Chapter Summary

➤ Mark text for inclusion in an index at the Mark Index Entry dialog box. Display this dialog box by clicking the Mark Entry button on the REFERENCES tab or pressing Alt + Shift + X.

➤ At the Mark Index Entry dialog box, specify whether the selected text is a main entry or subentry. The main entry or subentry does not have to be the same as the selected text.

➤ Click the Mark button at the Mark Index Entry dialog box to mark the currently selected text or click the Mark All button to mark all occurrences of the selected text in the document.

➤ After marking all of the relevant text as a main entry or subentry for the index, insert the index in the document. Place the index at the end of the document beginning on a new page.

➤ Apply formatting and customize the appearance of the index with options at the Index dialog box.

➤ Word provides seven formatting options for an index at the *Formats* option box in the Index dialog box.

➤ You can identify text as a bookmark and then mark the bookmark as an index entry. Doing this is especially useful when the text for an entry spans a range of pages.

➤ Mark text as a cross-reference if you want it to refer readers to another index entry.

➤ Words that appear frequently in a document can be saved as a concordance file, which eliminates the need to mark individual entries and subentries. A concordance file is a Word document that contains only a two-column table.

➤ Use a concordance file to mark text to include in the index by displaying the Index dialog box and then clicking the AutoMark button. At the Open Index AutoMark File dialog box, double-click the concordance file name.

➤ Update an index by clicking the index and then clicking the Update Index button in the Index group or by pressing the F9 key.

# Commands Review

| FEATURE | RIBBON TAB, GROUP | BUTTON, OPTION | KEYBOARD SHORTCUT |
|---|---|---|---|
| Index dialog box | REFERENCES, Index | 📄 | |
| Mark Index Entry dialog box | REFERENCES, Index | 📄 | Alt + Shift + X |
| Open Index AutoMark File dialog box | REFERENCES, Index | 📄 , AutoMark | |
| update index | REFERENCES, Index | 📄 | F9 |

# Key Points Review

**Completion:** In the space provided at the right, indicate the correct term, symbol, or command.

1. Use this keyboard shortcut to display the Mark Index Entry dialog box.

2. When you mark a word to include in the index, the selected word displays in this text box in the Mark Index Entry dialog box.

3. Click this button at the Mark Index Entry dialog box to mark the first occurrence of the text in each paragraph in the document.

4. An index generally appears at this location in a document.

5. If you want to mark more than a few words as a single index entry, consider identifying the text as this.

6. The Mark Entry button is located in the Index group on this tab.

7. If you want the text for an index entry to refer readers to another index entry, mark it as this.

8. Save time when marking text for an index by creating and using this type of file.

9. Click this button at the Index dialog box to display the Open Index AutoMark File dialog box.

10. Use this keyboard shortcut to update an index.

# Chapter Assessments

## Applying Your Skills

Demonstrate your knowledge of features learned in this chapter by completing the following assessments.

### Assessment 27.1    Create an Index for a Natural Interface Report

1. Open **NIApps.docx** and save the document with the name **C27-A01-NIApps**.
2. Create the following bookmarks:
    a. Create a bookmark for the *SPEECH RECOGNITION* section and name the bookmark *Speech*.
    b. Create a bookmark for the *NATURAL-LANGUAGE INTERFACE* section and name the bookmark *NLInterface*.
    c. Create a bookmark for the *VIRTUAL REALITY* section and name the bookmark *VReality*.
    d. Create a bookmark for the *MENTAL INTERFACE* section and name the bookmark *MInterface*.
3. Mark the following bookmarks as index entries that span multiple pages:
    a. Mark the *Speech* bookmark as a multipage index entry and type **Speech recognition** in the *Main entry* text box.
    b. Mark the *NLInterface* bookmark as a multipage index entry and type **Natural-language interface** in the *Main entry* text box.

    c.   Mark the *VReality* bookmark as a multipage index entry and type **Virtual reality** in the *Main entry* text box.

    d.   Mark the *MInterface* bookmark as a multipage index entry and type **Mental interface** in the *Main entry* text box.

  4.  Mark *VR* (located in the *VIRTUAL REALITY* section) as an index entry and cross-reference it to *Virtual reality*.

  5.  Mark the first occurrences of the following words as main entries or subentries for the index:

    a.   Mark *artificial intelligence*, located in the first sentence of the first paragraph of text in the document, as a main entry.

    b.   Mark the following text located in the *SPEECH RECOGNITION* section:

        *computer:* main entry

        *voice commands:* main entry

        *speed:* subentry (main entry: *computer*)

        *capacity:* subentry (main entry: *computer*)

    c.   Mark the following text located in the *NATURAL-LANGUAGE INTERFACE* section:

        *languages:* main entry

        *translators:* subentry (main entry: *languages*)

  6.  Insert the index at the end of the document on a new page, change the *Formats* option at the Index dialog box to *Modern* and, if necessary, change the number of columns to *2*.

  7.  Apply the Heading 1 style to the *INDEX* heading, change the type size to 14 points, apply bold formatting, and then center the heading.

  8.  Select all of the index entries and then change the font to *Cambria*.

  9.  Save and then print the last page of the document.

10.  Close **C27-A01-NIApps.docx**.

## Assessment 27.2    Create an Index Using a Concordance File

  1.  At a blank document, create the text shown in Figure 27.6 on the next page as a concordance file.

  2.  Save the document with the name **C27-A02-CFile**.

  3.  Print and then close **C27-A02-CFile.docx**.

  4.  Open **DesignNwsltr.docx** and save the document with the name **C27-A02-DesignNwsltr**.

  5.  Make the following changes to the document:

    a.   Mark the text for an index using the concordance file **C27-A02-CFile.docx**.

    b.   Insert the index at the end of the document. Use the *From template* format and make sure *2* displays in the *Columns* measurement box.

    c.   Apply the Heading 1 style to the *Index* title.

  6.  Insert page numbering at the bottom center of each page.

  7.  Change the line spacing to 2.0 for the entire document (including the index).

  8.  Insert a page break at the beginning of the title *CREATING NEWSLETTER LAYOUT*.

  9.  Update the index. (Note that the Index will return to the default line spacing.)

10.  Save the document again, print the index, and then close **C27-A02-DesignNwsltr.docx**.

**Figure 27.6  Assessment 27.2**

| NEWSLETTER | Newsletter |
|---|---|
| newsletter | Newsletter |
| consistency | Newsletter: consistency |
| element | Elements |
| margins | Elements: margins |
| column layout | Elements: column layout |
| nameplate | Elements: nameplate |
| location | Elements: location |
| logos | Elements: logos |
| color | Elements: color |
| ruled lines | Elements: ruled lines |
| Focus | Elements: focus |
| balance | Elements: balance |
| graphics | Graphics |
| images | Images |
| photos | Photos |
| Headlines | Newsletter: headlines |
| subheads | Newsletter: subheads |
| White space | White space |
| directional flow | Newsletter: directional flow |
| paper | Paper |
| Size | Paper: size |
| type | Paper: type |
| weight | Paper: weight |
| stock | Paper: stock |
| margin size | Newsletter: margin size |

# Expanding Your Skills

Explore additional feature options or use Help to learn a new skill in creating this document.

### Assessment 27.3    Customize an Index

1. Open **C27-A02-DesignNwsltr.docx** and save the document with the name **C27-A03-DesignNwsltr**.
2. Apply the Slice theme.
3. Display the Index dialog box, specify that you want run-in entries in one column in the *From template* format, and then close the Index dialog box. At the message asking if you want to replace the selected index, click OK.
4. Save **C27-A03-DesignNwsltr.docx**.
5. Print only the index and then close the document.

## Assessment 27.4    Create an Index for a Spanish Document

Before completing this assessment, check to make sure that the *Spanish (Spain)* language option is available at the Index dialog box. If it is not available, install the language. To do this, click the REVIEW tab, click the Language button in the Language group, and then click *Language Preferences* at the drop-down list. At the Word Options dialog box with *Language* selected in the left panel, click the down-pointing arrow at the right side of the *[Add additional editing languages]* option box, scroll down the drop-down list, and then click *Spanish (Spain)*. Click the Add button located to the right of the *[Add additional editing languages]* option box and then click OK to close the Word Options dialog box. (You will be instructed to restart Office.)

1. Using the *Language* option in the Index dialog box, you can create an index for a document written in Spanish. The steps for creating an index for a document written in Spanish are the same as the steps for creating a document written in English except that you need to change the *Language* option to *Spanish (Spain)*. Open **SpanishDoc.docx** and save the document with the name **C27-A04-SpanishDoc**.
2. Mark the text to include in the index using the concordance file named **SpanishCFile.docx** by completing the following steps:
   a. Click the REFERENCES tab and then click the Insert Index button in the Index group.
   b. At the Index dialog box, click the AutoMark button.
   c. At the Open Index AutoMark File dialog box, make sure your Chapter27 folder is active and then double-click **SpanishCFile.docx** in the Content pane. (This turns on the display of nonprinting characters.)
3. Insert the index in the document by completing the following steps:
   a. Position the insertion point at the end of the document and then insert a page break.
   b. Type **INDICE** and then press the Enter key. (*Indice* is the Spanish translation of the English word *Index*.)
   c. Click the Insert Index button in the Index group.
   d. At the Index dialog box, click the down-pointing arrow at the right of the *Language* option box and then click *Spanish (Spain)* at the drop-down list.
   e. Click the down-pointing arrow at the right of the *Formats* option box and then click *Formal* at the drop-down list.
   f. Make sure *3* displays in the *Columns* measurement box.
   g. Click OK to close the dialog box.
4. Apply the Heading 1 style to the *INDICE* title and change the font to Cambria.
5. Turn off the display of nonprinting characters.
6. Save **C27-A04-SpanishDoc.docx** and then print only the index page.

## Achieving Signature Status

Take your skills to the next level by completing this more challenging assessment.

## Assessment 27.5    Format a Report and Create an Index

START From Scratch

1. At a blank document, type the text in a table as shown in Figure 27.7 on the next page. (You will use this information as a concordance file to create an index for a report.) After typing the text, open **CompSystems.docx** (you may want to print the document), identify at least five additional entries for the index, and then type the entries in the table. Close **CompSystems.docx**.
2. Save the table document and name it **C27-A05-CFile**.
3. Print and then close **C27-A05-CFile.docx**.
4. Open **BMCStyles.docx**.
5. Display the Organizer dialog box. *Hint: Click the Styles group task pane launcher, click the Manage Styles button, and then click the Import/Export button.*

6. Copy the *BMCHeading*, *BMCTable*, and *BMCTitle* styles from the left list box of the Organizer dialog box to the right list box.
7. Close **BMCStyles.docx**.
8. At a blank document, insert the file named **CompSystems.docx** and then save the document with the name **C27-A05-CompSystems**. (Make sure that you insert the file using the Object button arrow.)
9. Format the document so it appears as shown in Figure 27.8 on the next page with the following specifications:
   a. Apply the BMCTitle style to the two titles in the document.
   b. Apply the BMCHeading style to the headings in the document.
   c. Apply the BMCTable style to the two tables in the document.
   d. Change the paragraph spacing to Relaxed.
   e. Insert bullets, a header, and a footer as shown in the figure. (Change the font color for the header and footer text to Dark Blue and apply bold formatting.)
   f. Insert an index at the end of the document using the **C27-A05-CFile.docx** concordance file. (You determine the formatting of the index.)
10. Save and then print **C27-A05-CompSystems.docx**.
11. Display the Organizer dialog box and then delete the following styles from the right list box: *BMCHeading*, *BMCTable*, and *BMCTitle*.
12. Close **C27-A05-CompSystems.docx**.

**Figure 27.7 Assessment 27.5**

| network | Network |
| communications | Communications |
| medium | Communications: medium |
| wireless signal | Communications: wireless signal |
| internal | Network: internal |
| global | Network: global |
| sharing | Network: sharing |
| functionality | Network: functionality |
| hardware | Communications: hardware |
| relay systems | Communications: relay systems |
| protocols | Network: protocols |
| transmission | Transmission |
| speeds | Transmission: speeds |
| binary | Binary |
| converter | Converter |
| television | Television |

**Figure 27.8  Assessment 27.5**

Page 1

1

## Computer Networks

A computer network consists of two or more computing or other devices connected by a communications medium, such as a wireless signal or a cable. A computer network provides a way to connect with others and share files and resources such as printers or an Internet connection.

In business settings, networks allow you to communicate with employees, suppliers, vendors, customers, and government agencies. Many companies have their own network, called an intranet, which is essentially a private Internet within the company's corporate "walls." Some companies also offer an extension of their internal network, called an extranet, to suppliers and customers. For example, a supplier might be allowed to access inventory information on a company's internal network to make sure the company does not run short of a vital part for its manufacturing process. In your home, networks are useful for sharing resources among members of your family. For example, using a home network, you might share one printer or fax machine among three or four computers.

The Internet is a global network made up of several networks linked together. If you consider all the applications, services, and tools the Internet allows you to access, you can begin to understand the power of networking and how it opens up a new world of sharing and functionality.

## Communications Systems

A computer network is one kind of communications system. This system includes sending and receiving hardware, transmission and relay systems, common sets of standards so all the equipment can "talk" to each other, and communications software.

You use such a networked communications system whenever you send/receive IM or email messages, pay a bill online, shop at an Internet store, send a document to a shared printer at work or at home, or download a file.

The world of computer network communications systems is made up of:

- Transmission media upon which the data travels to/from its destination.
- A set of standards and network protocols (rules for how data is handled as it travels along a communications channel). Devices use these to send and receive data to and from each other.
- Hardware and software to connect to a communications pathway from the sending and receiving ends.

**Blue Mountain Computer Services and Training**

Page 2

2

The first step in understanding a communications system is to learn the basics about transmission signals and transmission speeds when communicating over a network.

### Types of Signals

Two types of signals are used to transmit voices and other sounds over a computer network: analog and digital. An analog signal is formed by continuous sound waves that fluctuate from high to low. Your voice is transmitted as an analog signal over traditional telephone lines at a certain frequency. A digital signal uses a discrete signal that is either high or low. In computer terms, high represents the digital bit 1, and low represents the digital bit 0. These are the only two states for digital data.

Telephone lines carry your voice using an analog signal. However, computers don't "speak" analog; rather, they use a binary system of 1s and 0s to turn analog data into digital signals. If you send data between computers using an analog medium such as a phone line, the signal has to be transformed from digital to analog (modulated) and back again to digital (demodulated) to be understood by the computer on the receiving end. The piece of hardware that sends and receives data from a transmission source such as your telephone line or cable television connection is a modem. The word modem comes from the combination of the words *modulate* and *demodulate*.

Today, most new communications technologies simply use a digital signal, saving the trouble of converting transmissions. An example of this trend is the demise in 2009 of analog television transmissions as the industry switched to digital signals. Many people were sent scrambling to either buy a more recent television set or buy a converter to convert digital transmissions back to analog to work with their older equipment. More recent computer networks, too, use a pure digital signal method of sending and receiving data over a network.

### Transmission Speed

If you've ever been frustrated with how long it takes to download a file from a website, you are familiar with the fact that, in a communications system, data moves from one computer to another at different speeds. The speed of transmission is determined by a few key factors.

The first factor is the speed at which a signal can change from high to low, which is called frequency. A signal sent at a faster frequency provides faster transmission (Table 1). The other factor contributing to the speed of data transmission is bandwidth. On a computer network, the term bandwidth refers to the number of bits (pieces of data) per second that can be transmitted over a communications medium. Think of bandwidth as being like a highway. At rush hour, with the same amount of cars, a two-lane

**Blue Mountain Computer Services and Training**

Page 3

3

highway accommodates less traffic and everybody moves at a slower speed than on a four-lane highway, where much more traffic can travel at a faster speed.

**Table 1: Bandwidth Measurements**

| Term | Abbreviation | Meaning |
|---|---|---|
| 1 kilobit per second | 1 Kbps | 1 thousand bits per second |
| 1 megabit per second | 1 Mbps | 1 million bits per second |
| 1 gigabit per second | 1 Gbps | 1 billion bits per second |
| 1 terabit per second | 1 Tbps | 1 trillion bits per second |
| 1 petabit per second | 1 Pbps | 1 quadrillion bits per second |

If you have plenty of bandwidth and your data is transmitted at a high frequency, you get faster transmission speeds. Any communications medium that is capable of carrying a large amount of data at a fast speed is known as broadband.

Though transmission speeds at any moment in time may vary depending on network traffic and other factors, each of the common communications media has a typical speed (Table 2). These speeds are constantly being improved upon. In fact, some very high-powered connections provide transmission speeds of as much as 100 gigabits (one billion bits) per second, which allows you to download a high-definition DVD movie in two seconds.

**Table 2: Average Network Connection Speeds**

| Type of Connection | Typical Speed |
|---|---|
| 56 K dial-up | 56 Kbps |
| satellite | 1.5 Mbps |
| DSL | 7 Mbps |
| fiber-optic | 25 Mbps |
| cable TV | 50 Mbps |

**Blue Mountain Computer Services and Training**

Page 4

4

## INDEX

**Blue Mountain Computer Service and Training**

# Chapter 28

# Creating Specialized Tables

**Performance Objectives**

Upon successful completion of Chapter 28, you will be able to:

- Create, insert, and update a table of contents
- Create, insert, and update a table of figures
- Create, insert, and update a table of authorities

**Tutorial 28.1**
Inserting a Table of Contents
**Tutorial 28.2**
Customizing and Updating
a Table of Contents
**Tutorial 28.3**
Assigning Levels to Table
of Contents Entries
**Tutorial 28.4**
Creating and Customizing
Captions
**Tutorial 28.5**
Inserting a Table of Figures
**Tutorial 28.6**
Inserting and Updating
a Table of Authorities

Books, textbooks, reports, and manuscripts often include specialized tables, such as a table of contents, table of figures, or table of authorities. Creating these tables manually can be tedious. However, with Word, the steps and tasks required—like those required to create an index—are automated, allowing you to create specialized tables quickly and easily. In this chapter, you will learn the steps to mark text for inclusion in a table of contents, table of figures, or table of authorities and the steps to insert the table in the document.

*Note: Before beginning computer exercises for this chapter, copy to your storage medium the Chapter28 folder from the CD that accompanies this textbook and then make Chapter28 the active folder.*

In this chapter, students will produce the following documents:

Exercise 28.1. C28-E01-AIReport.docx
Exercise 28.2. C28-E02-CompEval.docx
Exercise 28.3B. C28-E03-TechRpt.docx
Exercise 28.3C. C28-E03-TTSAdventures.docx
Exercise 28.4. C28-E04-LarsenBrief.docx

Model answers for these exercises are shown on the following pages.

**Exercise 28.1**

C28-E01-AIReport.docx

## CONTENTS

i

## TABLE OF CONTENTS

i

**Exercise 28.2**

C28-E02-CompEval.docx

Model Answers

i

**Exercise 28.3B**  C28-E03-TechRpt.docx

Page 1

---

## Productivity Software

Productivity software includes software that people typically use to complete work, such as word processing software (working with words), spreadsheet software (working with data, numbers, and calculations), database software (organizing and retrieving data records), or presentation software (creating slide shows with text and graphics).

### WORD PROCESSING SOFTWARE

With word processing software, you can create documents that include sophisticated formatting; change text fonts; add special effects such as bold, italics, and underlining; add shadows, background colors, and other effects to text and objects; and include tables, photos, drawings, and links to online content. With a mail merge feature, you can take a list of names and addresses and print personalized letters and envelopes or labels. Figure 1 shows the application of some of the word processing features and tools Microsoft Word offers.

Figure 1 Word Document

### SPREADSHEET SOFTWARE

Using spreadsheet software, such as Microsoft Excel, you can perform calculations that range from simple (adding, averaging, and multiplying) to complex (estimating standard deviations based on a range of numbers, for example). In addition, spreadsheet software offers sophisticated charting and graphing capabilities. Formatting tools help you create polished looking documents such as budgets, invoices, schedules, attendance records, and purchase orders. Figure 2 shows a typical Excel spreadsheet making use of several key features.

Figure 2 Excel Worksheet

1

Page 2

---

## Output Devices

To get information into a computer, a person uses an input device. To get information out, a person uses an output device. Some common output devices include monitors and printers.

### MONITOR

A monitor, or screen, is the most common output device used with a personal computer. The most common monitors use either a thin film transistor (TFT) active matrix liquid crystal display (LCD) or a plasma display. Plasma displays have a true level of color reproduction compared with LCDs. Emerging display technologies include surface-conduction electron-emitter displays (SED) and organic light emitting diodes (OLED).

Figure 3 Monitor

### PRINTERS

After monitors, printers are the most important output devices. The print quality produced by these devices is measured in dpi, or dots per inch. As with screen resolution, the greater the number of dots per inch, the better the quality. The earliest printers for personal computers were dot matrix printers that used perforated computer paper. These impact printers worked something like typewriters, transferring the image of a character by using pins to strike a ribbon.

A laser printer uses a laser beam to create points of electrical charge on a cylindrical drum. Toner, composed of particles of ink with a negative electrical charge, sticks to the charged points on the positively charged drum. As the page moves past the drum, heat and pressure fuse the toner to the page. Inkjet printers use a print head that moves across the page that sprays a fine mist of ink when an electrical charge moves through the print cartridge.

Figure 4 Laser Printer

2

Page 3

---

An inkjet printer can use color cartridges and so provides affordable color printing suitable for home and small office use.

## Developing Software

Through the years, some software products have become incredibly sophisticated as new features are added in each version. The *software development life cycle* (SDLC) has evolved over time. This procedure dictates the general flow of creating a new software product as shown in the figure below. The SDLC involves performing market research to ensure that a need or demand for the product exists; completing a business analysis to match the solution to the need; creating a plan for implementing the software, which involves creating a budget and schedule for the project; writing the software program; testing the software; deploying the software to the public, either by selling the product in a package or online; and performing maintenance and bug fixes to keep the product functioning optimally.

Figure 5 Software Life Cycle

3

Page 4

**Exercise 28.3C**

C28-E03-TTSAdventures.docx

Page 1

---

**TERRA TRAVEL SERVICES**

**Antarctic Zenith Adventures**

Travel with our Antarctic experts, cruise on our state-of-the-art ships, and experience Antarctica in all of its grandeur. We use ice-rated expedition ships custom-designed for your comfort and safety. Each ship can carry up to 100 passengers and provides excellent viewing for watching whales, seabirds, and icebergs as well as facilities for educational presentations by our Antarctic experts. For our more adventurous clients, we offer additional activities such as snowshoeing, sea-kayaking, and camping on the Antarctic ice. Plan on a shore excursion where you can view penguin rookeries, seal colonies, and places of historical and scientific interest. To carry you to the Antarctic shore, we use inflatable boats that can carry 12 to 15 people. After a thrilling day on shore, we will take you back to the ship where you can enjoy a delicious meal prepared by our g[...] historians, and adventurers committed t[...]

*Adventure 1 Antarctic Zenith Adventures*

| Zenith Adventures | Length | |
|---|---|---|
| Antarctic Exploration | 7 days | |
| Weddell Sea Adventure | 10 days | |
| Falkland Islands | 14 days | |
| Sailing Spectacular | 14 days | |

**Upcoming Adventures**

Beginning next year, Zenith Adventures, [...] opportunities. Tentative volunteer adven[...] homes, and helping the families of trail p[...] provide you with an exciting vacation an[...] limited to a maximum of 15 and particip[...] contribute to the program and local char[...] funds are well-managed and distributed [...] consider a rewarding volunteer adventu[...]

Page 2

---

**Bicycling Adventure**

A bicycle is the perfect form of transportation for a travel adventure. Sign up for one or our bicycle tours and travel at your own pace, interact with village residents, stay healthy and fit, and know that your adventure has a minimal effect on the environment. We offer bicycle tours ranging from a leisurely trip through the Loire Valley of France to a mountain-bike expedition in the Atlas Mountains in Morocco. Our Zenith Adventures bicycle guides provide you with historical and educational information about the region in which you are traveling. They also take care of luggage and transportation needs and maintain your bicycle. We are confident that we can provide the bicycle adventure of a lifetime!

*Adventure 2 Tall-Ship Adventures*

| Zenith Adventure | Length | Price |
|---|---|---|
| Loire Valley Tour | 7 days | $1,999 |
| Tuscan Village Tour | 8 days | $2,499 |
| Atlas Trek Extreme | 9 days | $2,899 |
| Great Wall of Chin | 14 days | $3,299 |

Page 3

**TABLE OF AUTHORITIES**

*Cases*

State v. Bertelli, 63 W.2d 77, 542 P.2d 751 (1971) --------------------------------------------2

State v. Connors, 73 W.2d 743, 430 P.2d 199 (1974)------------------------------------- 2, 3

State v. Landers, 103 W.2d 432, 893 P.2d 2 (1984) ----------------------------------- 2, 3

*Statutes*

RCW 7.42A.429(1)--------------------------------------------------------------------------2

RCW 7.53.443 ------------------------------------------------------------------------------2

RCW 7.72A.432(2)--------------------------------------------------------------------------2

RCW 7.89.321 ------------------------------------------------------------------------------2

i

**Exercise 28.4**

C28-E04-LarsenBrief.docx

# Creating a Table of Contents

A table of contents typically appears at the beginning of a book, manuscript, or report and contains headings and subheadings with page numbers. In Chapter 21, you created a table of contents using the Quick Parts button in the Text group on the INSERT tab. You can also create a table of contents using the Table of Contents button in the Table of Contents group on the REFERENCES tab. Identify the text to be included in a table of contents by applying built-in or custom heading styles, assigning levels, or marking text.

## Applying Styles

To create a table of contents by applying built-in heading styles, open the document and then apply the styles you want to use. Word uses text with the Heading 1 style applied as the first level of contents text, text with the Heading 2 style applied for the second level, and so on. Apply built-in styles with options in the Styles group on the HOME tab.

## Inserting a Table of Contents

After you have applied styles to the headings in the document, insert the table of contents. To do this, position the insertion point where you want the table to appear in the document, click the REFERENCES tab, click the Table of Contents button, and then click the desired option at the drop-down list.

**QUICK STEPS**

**Insert a Table of Contents**
1. Apply heading styles.
2. Click REFERENCES tab.
3. Click Table of Contents button.
4. Click desired options at drop-down list.

Table of Contents

## Numbering Table of Contents Pages

**Number the Table of Contents Pages**
1. Click INSERT tab.
2. Click Page Number button.
3. Click *Format Page Numbers* at drop-down list.
4. Change number format to lowercase roman numerals.
5. Click OK.

Page Number

Generally, the pages in a table of contents are numbered with lowercase roman numerals (*i, ii, iii*). You can change the page number format to lowercase roman numerals at the Page Number Format dialog box, as shown in Figure 28.1. Display this dialog box by clicking the INSERT tab, clicking the Page Number button in the Header & Footer group, and then clicking *Format Page Numbers* at the drop-down list.

Numbering on the first page of the document, excluding the table of contents page(s), should begin with the arabic number 1. To insert two page numbering formats, separate the table of contents from the beginning of the document with a section break that begins a new page.

**Figure 28.1  Page Number Format Dialog Box**

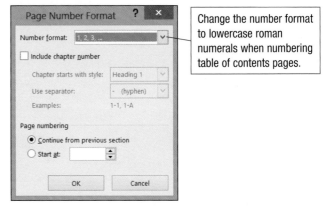

Change the number format to lowercase roman numerals when numbering table of contents pages.

## Navigating Using a Table of Contents

When a Word-generated table of contents is included in a document, readers can use the table of contents headings to navigate within the document. Table of contents headings are hyperlinks that are connected to the headings in the document.

To navigate in a document using the table of contents headings, click in the table of contents to select it. Position the mouse pointer over the desired heading and a box displays with the path and file name, as well as the text *Ctrl+Click to follow link*. Hold down the Ctrl key and then click the left mouse button and the insertion point is moved to the location of the heading.

1. Open **AIReport.docx** and save the document with the name **C28-E01-AIReport**.
2. Position the insertion point immediately left of the first *N* in *NATURAL INTERFACE APPLICATIONS* and then insert a section break by completing the following steps:
   a. Click the PAGE LAYOUT tab.
   b. Click the Breaks button in the Page Setup group.
   c. Click the *Next Page* option in the *Section Breaks* section.

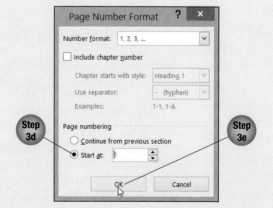

3. With the insertion point positioned below the section break, insert page numbers in the section and change the beginning number to 1 by completing the following steps:
   a. Click the INSERT tab.
   b. Click the Page Number button in the Header & Footer group, point to *Bottom of Page*, and then click *Plain Number 2*.
   c. Click the Page Number button in the Header & Footer group on the HEADER & FOOTER TOOLS DESIGN tab and then click *Format Page Numbers* at the drop-down list.
   d. At the Page Number Format dialog box, click *Start at* in the *Page numbering* section. (This inserts a *1* in the *Start at* text box.)
   e. Click OK to close the Page Number Format dialog box.

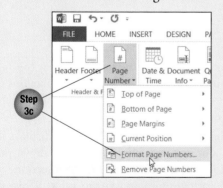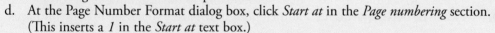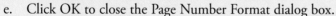

   f. Double-click in the document to make it active.
4. Insert a table of contents at the beginning of the document by completing the following steps:
   a. Press Ctrl + Home to move the insertion point to the beginning of the document.

b. Click the REFERENCES tab.
c. Click the Table of Contents button in the Table of Contents group and then click the *Automatic Table 1* option in the *Built-In* section of the drop-down list.

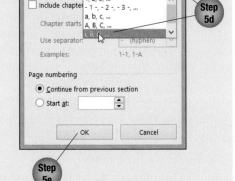

5. Insert a page number on the table of contents page by completing the following steps:
   a. Scroll up the document and then click any character in the *CONTENTS* heading
   b. Click the INSERT tab.
   c. Click the Page Number button and then click *Format Page Numbers* at the drop-down list.
   d. At the Page Number Format dialog box, click the down-pointing arrow at the right of the *Number format* option box and then click *i, ii, iii, . . .* at the drop-down list.
   e. Click OK to close the dialog box.

6. Navigate within the document using the table of contents by completing the following steps:
   a. Click on any character in the table of contents.
   b. Position the mouse pointer on the *Virtual Reality* heading, hold down the Ctrl key, click the left mouse button, and then release the Ctrl key. (This moves the insertion point to the beginning of the *Virtual Reality* heading in the document.
   c. Press Ctrl + Home to move the insertion point to the beginning of the document.

7. Save **C28-E01-AIReport.docx** and then print only page 1 (the table of contents page).

## Customizing the Table of Contents

Customize an existing table of contents in a document with options at the Table of Contents dialog box, as shown in Figure 28.2 on the next page. Display this dialog box by clicking the Table of Contents button on the REFERENCES tab and then clicking *Custom Table of Contents* at the drop-down list.

At the Table of Contents dialog box, a sample table of contents displays in the *Print Preview* section. Change the table of contents format by clicking the down-pointing arrow at the right of the *Formats* option box (located in the *General* section). At the drop-down list that displays, click the format that you want to apply. When you select a different format, that format displays in the *Print Preview* section.

Page numbers in a table of contents display immediately after the headings or aligned at the right margin, depending on what option is selected. The number of levels of headings that displays depends on the number of heading levels that are specified in the document. Specify the number of levels in the *Show levels* measurement box.

**Figure 28.2 Table of Contents Dialog Box**

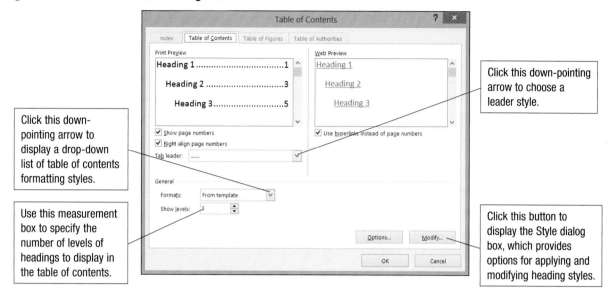

Click this down-pointing arrow to display a drop-down list of table of contents formatting styles.

Use this measurement box to specify the number of levels of headings to display in the table of contents.

Click this down-pointing arrow to choose a leader style.

Click this button to display the Style dialog box, which provides options for applying and modifying heading styles.

Consider using a tab leader to guide readers' eyes from the table of contents heading to the corresponding page number. The default tab leader is a period. To choose a different leader, click the down-pointing arrow at the right of the *Tab leader* option box and then click the desired leader character from the drop-down list.

Word automatically identifies headings in a table of contents as hyperlinks and inserts page numbers. You can use these hyperlinks to move the insertion point to a specific heading in the document. To move the insertion point to a specific heading, position the mouse pointer on the corresponding heading in the table of contents, hold down the Ctrl key (the mouse pointer turns into a hand), and then click the left mouse button. If you will post your document to the Web, consider removing the page numbers because readers will need only to click the hyperlink to view a specific page. Remove the page numbers by removing the check mark from the *Show page numbers* check box in the Table of Contents dialog box.

You can modify the formatting of a heading level style by clicking the Modify button. At the Style dialog box that displays, click the level in the *Styles* list box that you want to modify and then click the Modify button. At the Modify Style dialog box, apply the desired formatting and then click OK. The Modify Style dialog box that displays is the same dialog box that you used to modify styles in Chapter 24.

If you change options at the Table of Contents dialog box and then click OK, a message will display asking if you want to replace the selected table of contents. At this message, click Yes.

## Updating a Table of Contents

If you add, delete, move, or edit headings or other text in a document after you have inserted a table of contents, be sure to update the table. To do this, click anywhere in the table of contents and then click the Update Table button or press the F9 key (the Update Field key). At the Update Table of Contents dialog box, as shown in Figure 28.3 on the next page, click *Update page numbers only* if changes occurred only to the page numbers and click *Update entire table* if changes were made to headings within the document. Click OK or press the Enter key to close the dialog box.

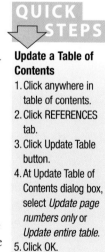

**QUICK STEPS**

**Update a Table of Contents**
1. Click anywhere in table of contents.
2. Click REFERENCES tab.
3. Click Update Table button.
4. At Update Table of Contents dialog box, select *Update page numbers only* or *Update entire table*.
5. Click OK.

Update Table

Figure 28.3 **Update Table of Contents Dialog Box**

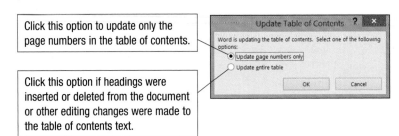

**Remove a Table of Contents**
1. Click REFERENCES tab.
2. Click Table of Contents button.
3. Click *Remove Table of Contents* at drop-down list.
**OR**
1. Click on any character in table of contents.
2. Click Table of Contents tab.
3. Click *Remove Table of Contents* at drop-down list.

Click this option to update only the page numbers in the table of contents.

Click this option if headings were inserted or deleted from the document or other editing changes were made to the table of contents text.

# Removing a Table of Contents

You can remove a table of contents from a document by clicking the Table of Contents button on the REFERENCES tab and then clicking *Remove Table of Contents* at the drop-down list. You can also remove a table of contents by clicking on any character in the table; clicking the Table of Contents tab, located in the upper left corner of the table of contents (immediately left of the Update Table tab); and then clicking *Remove Table of Contents* at the drop-down list.

---

**Exercise 28.** Modifying, Customizing, and Updating the Table of Contents                    Part 2 of 2

1. With **C28-E01-AIReport.docx** open, modify the level 1 and level 2 styles by completing the following steps:
   a. Click the REFERENCES tab, click the Table of Contents button, and then click *Custom Table of Contents* at the drop-down list.
   b. At the Table of Contents dialog box, click the Modify button that displays in the lower right corner of the dialog box.
   c. At the Style dialog box with *TOC 1* selected in the *Styles* list box, click the Modify button.
   d. At the Modify Style dialog box, change the font size to 12 points and then click the Italic button.
   e. Click OK to close the Modify Style dialog box.
   f. At the Style dialog box, click *TOC 2* in the *Styles* list box and then click the Modify button.
   g. At the Modify Style dialog box, change the font size to 11 points, click the Italic button, and then click OK.
   h. Click OK at the Style dialog box.

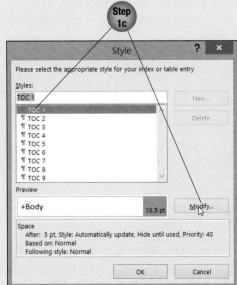

i. At the Table of Contents dialog box, click the down-pointing arrow at the right side of the *Show levels* option box until *1* displays.

j. Click OK to close the Table of Contents dialog box.

k. At the message asking if you want to replace the selected table of contents, click Yes.

2. After looking at the modified table of contents, you decide to apply a different formatting style and display two levels of headings. With the insertion point positioned in the table of contents, complete the following steps:

a. With the REFERENCES tab selected, click the Table of Contents button and then click *Custom Table of Contents* at the drop-down list.

b. At the Table of Contents dialog box, click the down-pointing arrow at the right of the *Formats* option in the *General* section and then click *Formal* at the drop-down list.

c. Click the down-pointing arrow at the right of the *Tab leader* option box and then click the solid line option (bottom option) at the drop-down list.

d. Click the up-pointing arrow at the right side of the *Show Levels* option box to display *2* in the option box.

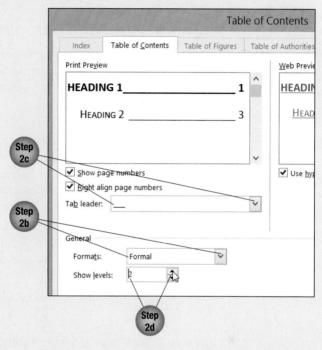

e. Click OK to close the dialog box.

f. At the message asking if you want to replace the selected table of contents, click OK.

3. Use the table of contents to move the insertion point to the *NAVIGATION* heading, which is located near the bottom of page 3.

4. Press Ctrl + Enter to insert a page break.

5. Update the table of contents by completing the following steps:

a. Click on any character in the table.

b. Click the Update Table tab.

c. At the Update Table of Contents dialog box, make sure *Update page numbers only* is selected and then click OK.

6. Save the document, print only the table of contents page, and then close **C28-E01-AIReport.docx**.

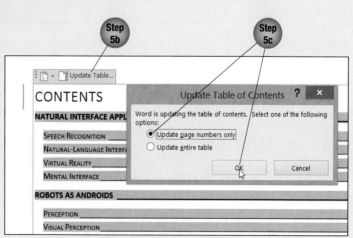

## Assigning Levels to Table of Contents Entries

**Add Text**

Another method for creating a table of contents is to assign levels to headings to be included using the Add Text button in the Table of Contents group on the REFERENCES tab. Click this button and a drop-down list of level options displays. Click a level option to assign it to the text you have selected. After assigning levels to all of the headings, insert the table of contents by clicking the Table of Contents button and then clicking the desired option at the drop-down list.

## Marking Table of Contents Entries as Fields

Applying styles to text applies specific formatting. If you want to identify headings to include in a table of contents but do not want to apply style formatting, mark the headings as field entries. To do this, select the text you want to include in the table of contents and then press Alt + Shift + O. This displays the Mark Table of Contents Entry dialog box, as shown in Figure 28.4.

In the dialog box, the text you selected displays in the *Entry* text box. Specify the level for the selected text with the *Level* measurement box and then click the Mark button. This turns on the display of nonprinting characters in the document and inserts a field code immediately after the selected text. As you will see in Exercise 28.2A, when you select the first title, Word inserts the following code immediately after the title:

TC "COMPENSATION" \f C \l "1" }

The Mark Table of Contents Entry dialog box remains open. To mark the next entry for the table of contents, select the text and then click the title bar of the Mark Table of Contents Entry dialog box. Specify the level and then click the Mark button. Continue in this manner until you have marked all of the table of contents entries.

**Figure 28.4  Mark Table of Contents Entry Dialog Box**

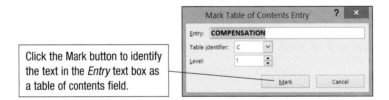

Click the Mark button to identify the text in the *Entry* text box as a table of contents field.

If you mark table of contents entries as fields, you will need to activate the *Table entry fields* option when inserting the table of contents in the document. To do this, display the Table of Contents dialog box and then click the Options button. At the Table of Contents Options dialog box, as shown in Figure 28.5 on the next page, click the *Table entry fields* check box to insert a check mark and then click OK.

**Figure 28.5** **Table of Contents Options Dialog Box**

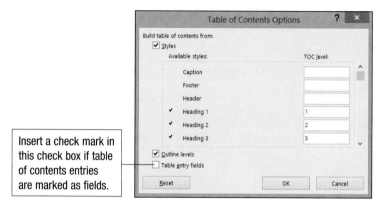

Insert a check mark in this check box if table of contents entries are marked as fields.

## Exercise 28.2A    Marking Headings as Fields                Part 1 of 2

1. Open **CompEval.docx** and save the document with the name **C28-E02-CompEval**.
2. Position the insertion point immediately left of the *C* in the title *COMPENSATION* and then insert a section break that begins a new page.
3. Mark the titles and headings as fields for insertion in a table of contents by completing the following steps:
   a. Select the title *COMPENSATION*.
   b. Press Alt + Shift + O.
   c. At the Mark Table of Contents Entry dialog box, make sure the *Level* is set at *1* and then click the Mark button. (This turns on the display of nonprinting characters.)
   d. Click in the document, scroll down, and then select the title *EVALUATION*.
   e. Click the dialog box title bar and then click the Mark button.
   f. Click in the document, scroll up, and then select the heading *Rate of Pay*.
   g. Click the dialog box title bar and then click the up-pointing arrow at the right of the *Level* measurement box until *2* displays.
   h. Click the Mark button.
   i. Mark the following headings as level 2:
      *Direct Deposit Option*
      *Pay Progression*
      *Overtime*
      *Work Performance Standards*
      *Performance Evaluation*
      *Employment Records*
   j. Click the Close button to close the Mark Table of Contents Entry dialog box.

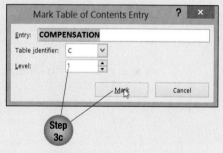

Step
3c

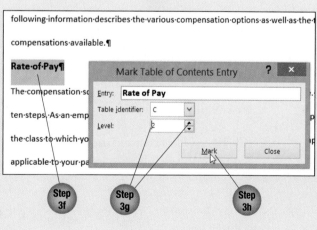

Step
3f

Step
3g

Step
3h

4. Position the insertion point at the beginning of the title *COMPENSATION* and then insert page numbers at the bottom center of each page and change the starting number to 1. **Hint: Refer to Exercise 28.1A, Step 3.**

5. Double-click in the document.

6. Insert a table of contents at the beginning of the document by completing the following steps:

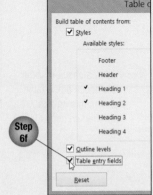

   a. Position the insertion point at the beginning of the document (on the new page).

   b. Type the title **TABLE OF CONTENTS** and then press the Enter key.

   c. Click the REFERENCES tab.

   d. Click the Table of Contents button and then click *Custom Table of Contents* at the drop-down list.

   e. At the Table of Contents dialog box, click the Options button.

   f. At the Table of Contents Options dialog box, click the *Table entry fields* check box to insert a check mark.

   g. Click OK to close the Table of Contents Options dialog box.

   h. Click OK to close the Table of Contents dialog box.

   i. For the *TABLE OF CONTENTS* heading, change the font size to 14 points, apply bold formatting, and then center the heading.

7. Insert a lowercase roman numeral page number on the table of contents page. **Hint: Refer to Exercise 28.1A, Step 5.**

8. Turn off the display of nonprinting characters.

9. Save **C28-E02-CompEval.docx** and then print only page 1 (the table of contents page).

If you insert additional information in a document, you can easily update the table of contents. To do this, insert the text and then mark the text with options at the Mark Table of Contents Entry dialog box. Click anywhere in the table of contents and then click the Update Table tab. At the Update Table of Contents dialog box, click the *Update entire table* option and then click OK.

---

## Exercise 28.2B  Updating the Entire Table of Contents                Part 2 of 2

1. With **C28-E02-CompEval.docx** open, insert a file into the document by completing the following steps:

   a. Press Ctrl + End to move the insertion point to the end of the document.

   b. Press Ctrl + Enter to insert a page break.

   c. Click the INSERT tab.

   d. Click the Object button arrow in the Text group and then click *Text from File* at the drop-down list.

   e. At the Insert File dialog box, navigate to your Chapter28 folder and then double-click **PosClassification.docx**.

2. Select and then mark text for inclusion in the table of contents by completing the following steps:

   a. Select the title *POSITION CLASSIFICATION*.

   b. Press Alt + Shift + O.

   c. At the Mark Table of Contents Entry dialog box, make sure that *1* displays in the *Level* measurement box and then click the Mark button.

   d. Click the Close button to close the Mark Table of Contents Entry dialog box.

3. Update the table of contents by completing the following steps:
   a. Select the entire table of contents (excluding the title).
   b. Click the REFERENCES tab.
   c. Click the Update Table button in the Table of Contents group.
   d. At the Update Table of Contents dialog box, click the *Update entire table* option.
   e. Click OK.

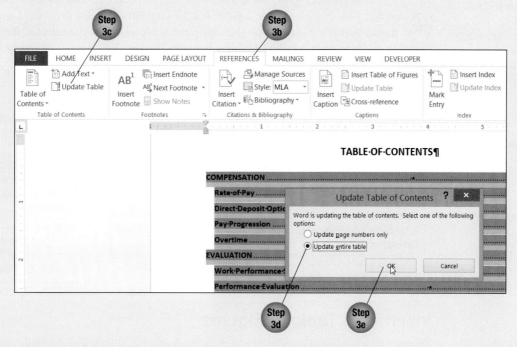

4. Turn off the display of nonprinting characters.
5. Save the document, print only page 1 (the table of contents page), and then close **C28-E02-CompEval.docx**.

# Creating a Table of Figures

A document that contains figures should include a table of figures so readers can quickly locate specific information. Figure 28.6 shows an example of a table of figures. You can create a table of figures by marking figures or images with captions and then using the caption names to create the table.

**Figure 28.6 Table of Figures**

**TABLE OF FIGURES**

## Creating Captions

QUICK
STEPS

**Create a Caption**
1. Select text or image.
2. Click REFERENCES tab.
3. Click Insert Caption button.
4. Type caption name.
5. Click OK.

A *caption* is text that describes an item such as an image, table, equation, or chart. A caption generally displays below the item. Create a caption by selecting the item, clicking the REFERENCES tab, and then clicking the Insert Caption button in the Captions group. This displays the Caption dialog box, as shown in Figure 28.7.

At the dialog box, *Figure 1* displays in the *Caption* text box and the insertion point is positioned after *Figure 1*. Type a name for the caption and then press the Enter key. Word inserts *Figure 1* followed by the caption you typed below the selected item. If the insertion point is positioned in a table when you display the Caption dialog box, *Table 1* displays in the *Caption* text box instead of *Figure 1*.

**Figure 28.7  Caption Dialog Box**

Insert Caption

Type a caption in this text box after *Figure 1*.

Insert a check mark in this check box to exclude the label from the caption.

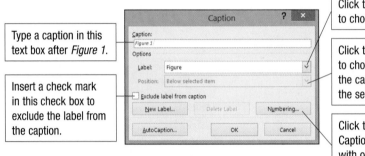

Click this down-pointing arrow to choose a different label.

Click this down-pointing arrow to choose whether to position the caption above or below the selected item.

Click this button to display the Caption Numbering dialog box with options for changing the numbering style.

## Inserting a Table of Figures

QUICK
STEPS

**Insert a Table of Figures**
1. Click REFERENCES tab.
2. Click Insert Table of Figures button.
3. Select desired format.
4. Click OK.

After you have marked each item in a document as a caption, insert the table of figures. A table of figures is generally placed at the beginning of a document—after the table of contents and on a separate page. To insert the table of figures, click the Insert Table of Figures button in the Captions group on the REFERENCES tab. At the Table of Figures dialog box, as shown in Figure 28.8, make any necessary changes and then click OK.

Insert Table of Figures

**Figure 28.8  Table of Figures Dialog Box**

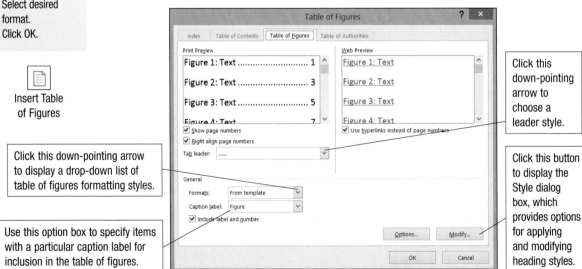

Click this down-pointing arrow to display a drop-down list of table of figures formatting styles.

Use this option box to specify items with a particular caption label for inclusion in the table of figures.

Click this down-pointing arrow to choose a leader style.

Click this button to display the Style dialog box, which provides options for applying and modifying heading styles.

The options available at the Table of Figures dialog box are similar to those available at the Table of Contents dialog box. From the drop-down list at the *Formats* option box, you can choose a format for the table of figures, change the alignment of the page numbers, and add leaders before page numbers.

If a document contains captioned figures as well as tables, equations, or other items, create a table of figures for each type of captioned item. For example, if a document contains both captioned figures and captioned tables, insert the figures in the table of figures by clicking the Insert Table of Figures button in the Captions group on the REFERENCES tab and then clicking OK at the Table of Figures dialog box. Insert the tables in the table of figures by completing similar steps except at the Table of Figures dialog box change the *Caption labels* option to *Table*.

---

**Exercise 28.3A    Creating a List of Figures**                                     **Part 1 of 3**

1. Open **TechRpt.docx** and save the document with the name **C28-E03-TechRpt**.
2. Add the caption *Figure 1 Word Document* to an image by completing the following steps:
   a. Click the screen image that displays in the *WORD PROCESSING SOFTWARE* section.
   b. Click the REFERENCES tab.
   c. Click the Insert Caption button in the Captions group.
   d. At the Caption dialog box with the insertion point positioned after *Figure 1* in the *Caption* text box, press the spacebar once and then type **Word Document**.
   e. Click OK or press the Enter key.

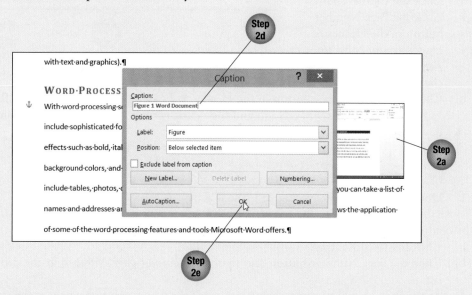

   f. Press Ctrl + E to center the caption in the text box.
3. Complete steps similar to those in Step 2 to create the caption *Figure 2 Excel Worksheet* for the image in the *SPREADSHEET SOFTWARE* section.
4. Complete steps similar to those in Step 2 to create the caption *Figure 3 Monitor* for the image in the *MONITOR* section.
5. Complete steps similar to those in Step 2 to create the caption *Figure 4 Software Life Cycle* for the SmartArt graphic in the *Developing Software* section.

6. Insert a table of figures at the beginning of the document by completing the following steps:
    a. Press Ctrl + Home to move the insertion point to the beginning of the document.
    b. Insert a section break that begins a new page.
    c. Press Ctrl + Home to move the insertion point back to the beginning of the document.
    d. Type **TABLE OF FIGURES** and then apply bold formatting and center the heading.
    e. Press the Enter key, turn off bold formatting, and then change the paragraph alignment back to left alignment. (The insertion point may not move down to the next line.)
    f. If necessary, click the REFERENCES tab.
    g. Click the Insert Table of Figures button in the Captions group.
    h. At the Table of Figures dialog box, click the down-pointing arrow at the right of the *Formats* option box and then click *Formal* at the drop-down list.
    i. Click OK.

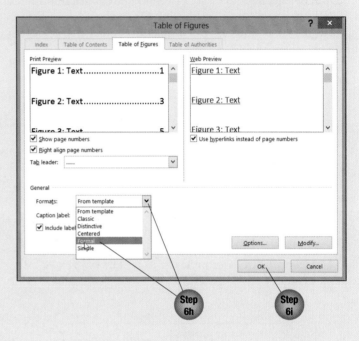

7. Move the insertion point to the title *Productivity Software* and then insert page numbering by completing the following steps:
    a. Click the INSERT tab.
    b. Click the Page Number button in the Header & Footer group, point to *Bottom of Page*, and then click *Plain Number 2*.
    c. Click the Page Number button in the Header & Footer group on the HEADER & FOOTER TOOLS DESIGN tab and then click *Format Page Numbers* at the drop-down list.
    d. At the Page Number Format dialog box, click *Start at* in the *Page numbering* section. (This inserts *1* in the *Start at* text box.)
    e. Click OK to close the dialog box.
    f. Double-click in the document to make it active.
8. Move the insertion point to the title *TABLE OF FIGURES* and then format page numbering by completing the following steps:
    a. Click the INSERT tab.
    b. Click the Page Number button and then click *Format Page Numbers* at the drop-down list.
    c. At the Page Number Format dialog box, click the down-pointing arrow at the right of the *Number format* option box and then click *i, ii, iii, . . .* at the drop-down list.
    d. Click OK to close the dialog box.
9. Save **C28-E03-TechRpt.docx**.

## Updating or Deleting a Table of Figures

If you make changes to a document after inserting a table of figures, make sure you update the table of figures. To do this, click anywhere within the table of figures and then click the Update Table button in the Captions group on the REFERENCES tab or press the F9 key. At the Update Table of Figures dialog box, click *Update page numbers only* if the changes you made were to the page numbers only or click *Update entire table* if you made changes to the caption text. Click OK or press the Enter key to close the dialog box. To delete a table of figures, select the entire table using the mouse or the keyboard and then press the Delete key.

**Update the Table of Figures**
1. Click in table of figures.
2. Click REFERENCES tab.
3. Click Update Table button or press the F9 key.
4. Click OK.

**Delete the Table of Figures**
1. Select entire table of figures.
2. Press Delete key.

Update Table

---

## Exercise 28.3B  Updating the Table of Figures  Part 2 of 3

1. With **C28-E03-TechRpt.docx** open, insert an image of a laser printer by completing the following steps:
   a. Move the insertion point to the beginning of the second paragraph of text in the *Printers* section.
   b. Click the INSERT tab and then click the Pictures button in the Illustrations group.
   c. At the Insert Picture dialog box, navigate to your Chapter28 folder and then double-click the file named *LaserPrinter.png*.
   d. Change the height of the clip art image to 1.4 inches.
   e. Change the text wrapping to Square.
2. Add the caption *Figure 4 Laser Printer* to the printer image and then center the caption.
3. Click on any character in the table of figures.
4. Press the F9 key on your keyboard.
5. At the Update Table of Figures dialog box, click the *Update entire table* option and then click OK.
6. Save, print, and then close **C28-E03-TechRpt.docx**.

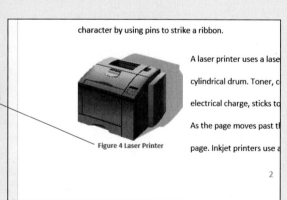

Step 2

character by using pins to strike a ribbon.

A laser printer uses a lase

cylindrical drum. Toner, c

electrical charge, sticks to

As the page moves past th

Figure 4 Laser Printer

page. Inkjet printers use a

2

## Customizing Captions

The Caption dialog box contains a number of options for customizing captions (see Figure 28.7). Click the down-pointing arrow at the right of the *Label* option to specify the type of label. The default is *Figure*, which you can change to *Equation* or *Table*. With the *Position* option, you can change the position of the caption so it appears above the selected item. By default, a caption is positioned below the item. If you want the caption to include only a number and not a label, insert a check mark in the *Exclude label from caption* check box. This will prevent the label *Figure*, *Table*, or *Equation* from appearing with the caption.

Click the New Label button and the Label dialog box displays. At this dialog box, type a custom label for the caption. Word automatically inserts an arabic number (*1, 2, 3*, and so on) after the caption label. If you want to change the caption numbering style, click the Numbering button. At the Caption Numbering dialog box that displays, click the down-pointing arrow at the right side of the *Format* option box and then click the desired numbering style at the drop-down list. For example, you can change caption numbering to uppercase or lowercase letters or roman numerals.

If you insert items such as tables in a document on a regular basis, you can specify that you want a caption inserted automatically with each item. To do this, click the AutoCaption button. At the AutoCaption dialog box, insert a check mark before the item (such as *Microsoft Word Table*) in the *Add caption when inserting* list box and then click OK. Each time you insert a table in a document, Word inserts a caption above the table.

---

**Exercise 28 3C**    **Creating and Customizing Captions and Inserting a Table of Figures**      **Part 3 of 3**

---

1. Open Word, open **TTSAdventures.docx**, and then save the document and name it **C28-E03-TTSAdventures**.
2. Insert a custom caption for the first table by completing the following steps:
   a. Click in any cell in the first table.
   b. Click the REFERENCES tab.
   c. Click the Insert Caption button.
   d. At the Caption dialog box, press the spacebar once and then type **Antarctic Zenith Adventures** in the *Caption* text box.
   e. Remove the label (*Figure*) from the caption by clicking the *Exclude label from caption* check box to insert a check mark.
   f. Click the Numbering button.

g. At the Caption Numbering dialog box, click the down-pointing arrow at the right side of the *Format* option box and then click the *A, B, C, . . .* option at the drop-down list.

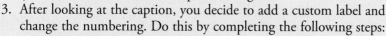

h. Click OK to close the Caption Numbering dialog box.

i. At the Caption dialog box, click the down-pointing arrow at the right side of the *Position* option and then click *Above selected item* at the drop-down list.

j. Click OK to close the Caption dialog box.

3. After looking at the caption, you decide to add a custom label and change the numbering. Do this by completing the following steps:
   a. Select the *Antarctic Zenith Adventures* caption.
   b. Click the Insert Caption button in the Captions group on the REFERENCES tab.
   c. At the Caption dialog box, click the *Exclude label from caption* check box to remove the check mark.
   d. Click the New Label button.
   e. At the New Label dialog box, type **Adventure** and then click OK.
   f. Click OK to close the Caption dialog box.

4. Format the caption by completing the following steps:
   a. Select the *Adventure 1 Antarctic Zenith Adventures* caption.
   b. Click the HOME tab.
   c. Click the Font Color button arrow.
   d. Click the *Dark Blue* color (ninth color in the *Standard Colors* section).
   e. Click the Bold button.

5. Insert a custom caption for the second table by completing the following steps:
   a. Click in any cell in the second table.
   b. Click the REFERENCES tab and then click the Insert Caption button.
   c. At the Caption dialog box, press the spacebar and then type **Tall-Ship Adventures**.
   d. If necessary, click the down-pointing arrow at the right side of the *Position* option and then click *Above selected item* at the drop-down list
   e. Click OK to close the Caption dialog box.

6. Select the *Adventure 2 Tall-Ship Adventures* caption, apply the Dark Blue font color, and apply bold formatting.

7. Insert a table of figures by completing the following steps:
   a. Press Ctrl + Home and then press Ctrl + Enter to insert a page break.
   b. Press Ctrl + Home to move the insertion point above the page break.
   c. Turn on bold formatting, type **TABLES**, turn off bold formatting, and then press the Enter key.
   d. Click the REFERENCES tab and then click the Insert Table of Figures button in the Captions group.
   e. At the Table of Figures dialog box, click OK.

8. Save, print, and then close **C28-E03-TSSAdventures.docx**.

# Creating a Table of Authorities

A *table of authorities* is a list of citations that appears in a legal brief or other legal document as well as the page numbers on which the citations appear. Word provides many common categories under which citations can be organized: Cases, Statutes, Other

Authorities, Rules, Treatises, Regulations, and Constitutional Provisions. Within each category, Word alphabetizes the citations. Figure 28.9 shows an example of a table of authorities.

**Figure 28.9  Table of Authorities**

**TABLE OF AUTHORITIES**

CASES

Mansfield v. Rydell, 72 Wn.2d 200, 433 P.2d 723 (1993) ................................................ 3
State v. Fletcher, 73 Wn.2d 332, 124 P.2d 503 (2006) ................................................ 5
Yang v. Buchwald, 21 Wn.2d 385, 233 P.2d 609 (2012) ................................................ 7

STATUTES

RCW 8.12.230(2) ................................................................................................ 4
RCW 6.23.590 .................................................................................................. 7
RCW 5.23.103(3) ............................................................................................. 10

**Mark Citations for a Table of Authorities**
1. Select first occurrence of citation.
2. Press Alt + Shift + I.
3. At Mark Citation dialog box, edit and format text.
4. Specify category.
5. Click Mark All button.

Mark Citation

Creating a table of authorities requires thought and planning. Before you mark any text in a legal document for inclusion in such a table, first determine what section headings to use and what listings to include within each section. When you mark the text for the table, you need to find the first occurrence of each citation, mark it as a full citation with the complete name, and then specify a short citation. To mark a citation for a table of authorities, complete the following steps:

1. Select the first occurrence of the citation.
2. Click the REFERENCES tab and then click the Mark Citation button or press Alt + Shift + I.
3. At the Mark Citation dialog box, as shown in Figure 28.10 on the next page, edit and format the text in the *Selected text* text box as you want it to appear in the table of authorities. Edit and format the text in the *Short citation* text box so it matches the short citation that you want Word to search for in the document.
4. Click the down-pointing arrow at the right of the *Category* text box and then click the category from the drop-down list that applies to the citation.
5. Click the Mark button to mark the selected citation or click the Mark All button if you want Word to mark all of the long and short citations in the document that match those displayed in the Mark Citation dialog box.
6. The Mark Citation dialog box remains open so that you can mark other citations. To find the next citation in a document, click the Next Citation button. (This prompts Word to search the document for the next occurrence of text commonly found in a citation, such as *in re* or *v.*)
7. Select the text for the next citation and then complete Steps 3 through 5.
8. After marking all of the citations, click the Close button to close the Mark Citations dialog box.

**Figure 28.10 Mark Citation Dialog Box**

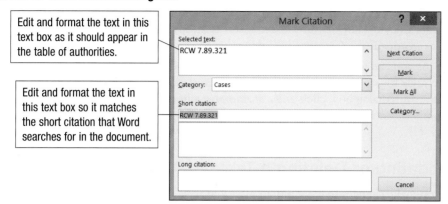

Edit and format the text in this text box as it should appear in the table of authorities.

Edit and format the text in this text box so it matches the short citation that Word searches for in the document.

## Inserting a Table of Authorities

Once you have marked the citations in a document, you can insert the table of authorities. A table of authorities is inserted in a document in a manner similar to that used to insert a table of contents or figures. A table of authorities generally appears at the beginning of a document on a separate page. To insert a table of authorities in a document that contains text marked as citations, click the REFERENCES tab and then click the Insert Table of Authorities button. This displays the Table of Authorities dialog box, as shown in Figure 28.11. At this dialog box, make any necessary changes and then click OK to close the dialog box.

**QUICK STEPS**

**Insert a Table of Authorities**
1. Click REFERENCES tab.
2. Click Insert Table of Authorities button.
3. Select desired format.
4. Click OK.

Insert Table of Authorities

**Figure 28.11 Table of Authorities Dialog Box**

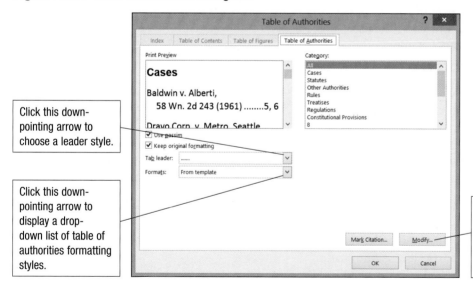

Click this down-pointing arrow to choose a leader style.

Click this down-pointing arrow to display a drop-down list of table of authorities formatting styles.

Click this button to display the Style dialog box where you can select a level style and then modify the formatting of the level style.

Like the Table of Contents dialog box and Table of Figures dialog box, the Table of Authorities dialog box contains options for formatting a table of authorities. The *Use passim* option is active by default (the check box contains a check mark), which tells Word to replace five or more page references to the same authority with *passim*. With the *Keep original formatting* check box active, Word retains the formatting of the citation as it appears in the document. Click the *Tab leader* option to change the leader character. When you insert a table of authorities, Word includes a heading for each of the seven categories by default. If you want to insert citations for only a specific category, select that category at the *Category* drop-down list.

As you can for a table of contents, you can modify the formatting of a heading level style for a table of authorities. To do this, click the Modify button in the Table of Authorities dialog box, click *Table of Authorities* in the *Styles* list box, and then click the Modify button. At the Modify Style dialog box, apply the desired formatting and then click OK.

## Updating or Deleting a Table of Authorities

If you make changes to a document after you have inserted a table of authorities, be sure to update the table. To do this, click anywhere in the table and then click the Update Table button or press the F9 key. If you need to edit a citation, edit it in the document and not in the table of authorities. If you edit a citation in the table of authorities, your changes will be lost the next time you update the table. To delete a table of authorities, select the entire table using the mouse or keyboard and then press the Delete key.

QUICK STEPS

**Update a Table of Authorities**
1. Click anywhere in table of authorities.
2. Click REFERENCES tab.
3. Click Update Table of Authorities button or press F9 key.

Update Table

---

**Exercise 28.4**  Inserting a Table of Authorities                               Part 1 of 1

1. Open **LarsenBrief.docx** and save the document with the name **C28-E04-LarsenBrief**.
2. Mark *RCW 7.89.321* as a statute citation by completing the following steps:
   a. Select *RCW 7.89.321*. (This citation is located near the middle of the second page.) ***Hint: Use the Find feature to help you locate this citation.***
   b. Click the REFERENCES tab.
   c. Click the Mark Citation button in the Table of Authorities group.
   d. At the Mark Citation dialog box, click the down-pointing arrow at the right of the *Category* text box and then click *Statutes* at the drop-down list.
   e. Click the Mark All button. (This turns on the display of nonprinting characters.)
   f. Click the Close button to close the Mark Citation dialog box.

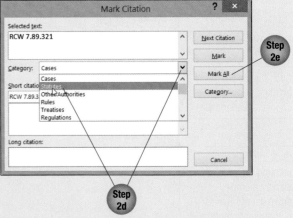

3. Complete steps similar to those in Step 2 to mark *RCW 7.53.443* as a statute citation. (This citation is located near the middle of the second page.)
4. Complete steps similar to those in Step 2 to mark *RCW 7.72A.432(2)* as a statute citation. (This citation is located near the bottom of the second page.)
5. Complete steps similar to those in Step 2 to mark *RCW 7.42A.429(1)* as a statute citation. (This citation is located near the bottom of the second page.)

6. Mark *State v. Connors, 73 W.2d 743, 430 P.2d 199 (1974)* as a case citation by completing the following steps:

   a. Select *State v. Connors, 73 W.2d 743, 430 P.2d 199 (1974)*. (This citation is located near the middle of the second page.) ***Hint: Use the Find feature to help you locate this citation.***

   b. Press Alt + Shift + I.

   c. At the Mark Citation dialog box, type **State v. Connors** in the *Short citation* text box.

   d. Click the down-pointing arrow at the right of the *Category* text box and then click *Cases* at the drop-down list.

   e. Click the Mark All button.

   f. Click the Close button to close the Mark Citation dialog box.

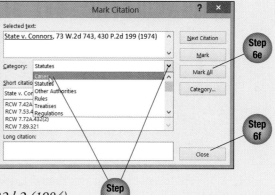

7. Complete steps similar to those in Step 6 to mark *State v. Bertelli, 63 W.2d 77, 542 P.2d 751 (1971)*. Enter **State v. Bertelli** as the short citation. (This citation is located near the middle of the second page.)

8. Complete steps similar to those in Step 6 to mark *State v. Landers, 103 W.2d 432, 893 P.2d 2 (1984)*. Enter **State v. Landers** as the short citation. (This citation is located near the bottom of the second page.)

9. Insert page numbering by completing the following steps:

   a. Position the insertion point at the beginning of the document and then press the Enter key once.

   b. Position the insertion point immediately left of the *S* in *STATEMENT OF CASE* and then insert a section break that begins a new page.

   c. With the insertion point positioned below the section break, insert a page number at the bottom center of each page and change the starting number to 1.

10. Double-click in the document to make it active and press Ctrl + Home to move the insertion point to the beginning of the document. Type **TABLE OF AUTHORITIES** and then center it and apply bold formatting.

11. Press the Enter key, turn off bold formatting, and then change the paragraph alignment back to left.

12. Modify and insert the table of authorities by completing the following steps:

    a. Click the REFERENCES tab.

    b. Click the Insert Table of Authorities button in the Table of Authorities group.

    c. At the Table of Authorities dialog box, make sure *All* is selected in the *Categories* list box and then click the Modify button.

    d. At the Style dialog box, click *Table of Authorities* in the *Styles* list box and then click the Modify button.

    e. At the Modify Style dialog box, click the Italic button.

    f. Click the down-pointing arrow at the right side of the Font Color option box and then click *Dark Blue* at the drop-down color palette (ninth option in the *Standard Colors* section).

    g. Click OK to close the Modify Style dialog box, click OK to close the Style dialog box, and click OK to close the Table of Authorities dialog box.

13. Apply different formatting to the table of authorities by completing the following steps:

    a. Click the Undo button on the Quick Access toolbar to remove the table of authorities. (If this does not remove the table of authorities, select the *Cases* entries and *Statutes* entries and then press the Delete key.)

    b. Click the Insert Table of Authorities button.

    c. At the Table of Authorities dialog box, click the down-pointing arrow at the right of the *Formats* option box and then click *Distinctive* at the drop-down list.

    d. Click the down-pointing arrow at the right side of the *Tab leader* option box and then click the hyphens at the drop-down list (second option from the bottom of the list).

    e. Click OK to close the Table of Authorities dialog box.

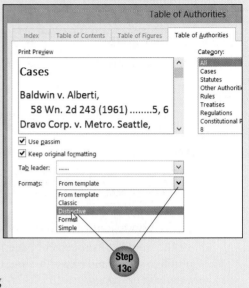

Step 13c

14. With the insertion point positioned anywhere in the table of authorities, change the page numbering format to lowercase roman numerals.

15. Turn off the display of nonprinting characters.

16. Make sure the table of authorities displays the correct page numbers by selecting all the entries in the *Cases* section and the *Statutes* section, and then clicking the Update Table button in the Table of Authorities group.

17. Save **C28-E04-LarsenBrief.docx** and then print the table of authorities page.

18. Close **C28-E04-LarsenBrief.docx**.

# Chapter Summary

➤ Word provides options for automating the creation of a table of contents, table of figures, and table of authorities.

➤ Text to be included in a table of contents can be identified three ways: by applying a heading style, assigning a level, or marking text as a field entry.

➤ Mark text as a field entry at the Mark Table of Contents dialog box. Display this dialog box by pressing Alt + Shift + O.

➤ Creating a table of contents involves two steps: applying the appropriate styles to or marking text that will be included and inserting the table of contents in the document.

➤ To insert a table of contents, position the insertion point where you want the table to appear, click the REFERENCES tab, click the Table of Contents button, and then click the desired option at the drop-down list.

➤ If you want the table of contents to print on a page separate from the document text, insert a section break that begins a new page between the table of contents and title of the document.

➤ If you make changes to a document after inserting a table of contents, update the table by clicking anywhere in it and then clicking the Update Table button on the REFERENCES tab or by pressing the F9 key. Update a table of figures or table of authorities in a similar manner.

➤ Remove a table of contents by clicking the Table of Contents button on the REFERENCES tab and then clicking *Remove Table of Contents* at the drop-down list.

- Create a table of figures by marking specific items in a document with captions and then using the caption names to create the table. Mark captions at the Caption dialog box. Display this dialog box by clicking the Insert Caption button on the REFERENCES tab.

- The Caption dialog box contains options for specifying the caption label, position, and numbering; excluding the label from the caption; creating a new label; and creating captions automatically.

- Insert a table of figures in a document in a manner similar to that used to insert a table of contents. A table of figures generally appears at the beginning of a document—on the page following the table of contents.

- A table of authorities is a list of the citations in a legal brief or other legal document and the pages on which the citations appear.

- When you mark text for a table of authorities, find the first occurrence of a citation, mark it as a full citation with the complete name, and then specify a short citation at the Mark Citation dialog box. Display this dialog box by clicking the Mark Citation button on the REFERENCES tab or pressing Alt + Shift + I.

- Insert a table of authorities in a document in a manner similar to that used to insert a table of contents or figures. A table of authorities generally appears at the beginning of a document.

- Delete a table of figures or table of authorities by selecting the entire table and then pressing the Delete key.

# *Commands* Review

| FEATURE | RIBBON TAB, GROUP | BUTTON, OPTION | KEYBOARD SHORTCUT |
|---------|-------------------|----------------|-------------------|
| Caption dialog box | REFERENCES, Captions | 🖼 | |
| Mark Citation dialog box | REFERENCES, Table of Authorities | 🖹 | Alt + Shift + I |
| Mark Table of Contents Entry dialog box | | | Alt + Shift + O |
| Page Number Format dialog box | INSERT, Header & Footer | #️, *Format Page Numbers* | |
| Table of Authorities dialog box | REFERENCES, Table of Authorities | 🖹 | |
| Table of Contents dialog box | REFERENCES, Table of Contents | 🖹, *Custom Table of Contents* | |
| Table of Contents Options dialog box | REFERENCES, Table of Contents | 🖹, *Custom Table of Contents, Options* | |
| Table of Figures dialog box | REFERENCES, Captions | 🖹 | |
| update table of authorities | REFERENCES, Table of Authorities | 🗎 | |
| update table of contents | REFERENCES, Table of Contents | 🗎 | F9 |
| update table of figures | REFERENCES, CAPTIONS | 🗎 | F9 |

**Completion:** In the space provided at the right, indicate the correct term, symbol, or command.

1. A table of contents generally appears in this location in the document.

_____

2. In a built-in table of contents, Word uses text with this heading style applied as the first level.

_____

3. A table of contents is typically numbered with this type of numbers.

_____

4. Use this keyboard shortcut to update a table of contents.

_____

5. Delete a table of contents by clicking the Table of Contents button on the REFERENCES tab and then clicking this option.

_____

6. Use this keyboard shortcut to display the Mark Table of Contents Entry dialog box.

_____

7. If you mark table of contents entries as fields, you will need to activate this option at the Table of Contents Options dialog box when inserting the table into the document.

_____

8. Create a table of figures with items marked with these.

_____

9. This list identifies the pages on which citations appear in a legal brief or other legal document.

_____

10. Use this keyboard shortcut to display the Mark Citation dialog box.

_____

# Chapter Assessments

## Applying Your Skills

Demonstrate your knowledge of features learned in this chapter by completing the following assessments.

**Assessment 28.1   Create and Update a Table of Contents for a Photography Report**

1. Open **PhotoRpt.docx** and save the document with the name **C28-A01-PhotoRpt**.
2. Move the insertion point to the beginning of the heading *Photography* and then insert a section break that begins a new page.
3. With the insertion point positioned below the section break, insert page numbers at the bottom center of pages and change the beginning page number to 1.
4. Press Ctrl + Home to move the insertion point to the beginning of the document (on the blank page) and then create a table of contents with the *Automatic Table 1* option at the Table of Contents button drop-down list.
5. Display the Table of Contents dialog box, select *Distinctive* at the *Formats* option box, and make sure *3* displays in the *Show levels* measurement box.
6. Change the page numbering format on the table of contents page to lowercase roman numerals.
7. Save the document and then print only the table of contents page.

8. Insert a page break at the beginning of the heading *Camera Basics*.
9. Update the table of contents.
10. Save the document and then print only the table of contents page.
11. Close **C28-A01-PhotoRpt.docx**.

## Assessment 28.2    Insert Captions and a Table of Figures in a Report

 **Grade It**

1. Open **InputDevices.docx** and save the document with the name **C28-A02-InputDevices**.
2. Insert a caption for each of the three images in the document that uses *Figure* as the label, uses numbers (*1, 2, 3,* and so on) as the figure numbers, and displays centered below the image. Use *Keyboard* for the first figure caption, *Mouse* for the second, and *Laptop* for the third.
3. Move the insertion point to the beginning of the title COMPUTER INPUT DEVICES and then insert a section break that begins a new page.
4. Press Ctrl + Home, type **Table of Figures**, press the Enter key, and then insert a table of figures with the Formal format.
5. Apply the Heading 1 style to the title *Table of Figures*.
6. Move the insertion point to the title COMPUTER INPUT DEVICES and then insert a page number at the bottom center of each page and change the starting number to 1.
7. Move the insertion point to the title TABLE OF FIGURES and then change the page numbering style to lowercase roman numerals.
8. Insert a page break at the beginning of the MOUSE heading.
9. Update the table of figures.
10. Save, print, and then close **C28-A02-InputDevices.docx**.

## Assessment 28.3    Create a Table of Authorities for a Legal Brief

 **Grade It**

1. Open **SilversBrief.docx** and save the document with the name **C28-A03-SilversBrief**.
2. Mark the following as case citations with the specified short citations. ***Hint: Use the Find feature to help you locate each citation.***
   a. *Richmond Newspapers, Inc. v. Virginia*, 448 U.S. 555 (1980)
      Short citation: Richmond Newspapers, Inc. v. Virginia
   b. *Globe Newspaper Co. v. Superior Court*, 457 U.S. 596 (1982)
      Short citation: Globe Newspaper Co. v. Superior Court
   c. *Naucke v. City of Park Hills*, 284 F. 3d 923, 927 (2d Cir. 2002)
      Short citation: Naucke v. City of Park Hills
   d. *Singer v. Fulton County Sheriff*, 63 F. 3d 110, 120 (2d Cir. 1995)
      Short citation: Singer v. Fulton County Sheriff
   e. *Bowden v. Keane*, 237 F. 3d 125, 129 (2d Cir. 2001)
      Short citation: Bowden v. Keane
   f. *Cf. Guzman v. Scully*, 80 F. 3d 772, 775-76 (2d Cir. 1996)
      Short citation: Cf. Guzman v. Scully
3. Press Ctrl + Home to move the insertion point to the beginning of the document and then press the Enter key once.
4. With the insertion point positioned at the beginning of *STATEMENT OF CASE*, insert a section break that begins a new page.
5. With the insertion point positioned below the section break, insert a page number at the bottom center of each page and change the starting number to 1.
6. Move the insertion point to the beginning of the document, type **TABLE OF AUTHORITIES**, and center and apply bold formatting to the head.
7. Press the Enter key, turn off bold formatting, and change the paragraph alignment back to left.
8. Insert a table of authorities. (You determine the format style.)

9. With the insertion point positioned anywhere in the table of authorities, change the numbering format to lowercase roman numerals.
10. Save, print, and then close **C28-A03-SilversBrief.docx**.

## Expanding Your Skills

Explore additional feature options or use Help to learn a new skill in creating this document.

### Assessment 28.4    Create a Table of Contents and a Table of Figures

1. Open **NavigateWeb.docx** and save the document with the name **C28-A04-NavigateWeb**.
2. Move the insertion point to the beginning of the title *Navigating the Web* and then insert a section break that begins a new page.
3. With the insertion point below the section break, number the pages at the bottom right of each page and change the starting number to 1.
4. Click in any cell in the first table in the document and then use the caption feature to create the caption *Table A: Common Top-Level Domain Suffixes* and position it above the table.
5. Click in any cell in the second table and then create the caption *Table B: Common Search Tools* and position it above the table.
6. Click in any cell in the third table and then create the caption *Table C: Advanced Search Parameters* and position it above the table.
7. Move the insertion point to the beginning of the document and then insert the Automatic Table 2 table of contents. Make sure the table of contents displays with hyphen (---) leaders. If the leaders are not hyphens, display the Table of Contents dialog box and change the tab leader format to hyphens.
8. Press Ctrl + Enter to insert a page break.
9. Type **Table of Figures**, press the Enter key, and then insert the table of figures using the Formal format with hyphen (---) leaders.
10. Apply the Heading 1 style to the title *Table of Figures*.
11. Move the insertion point to the beginning of the document and then change the numbering format to lowercase roman numerals.
12. Insert a page break at the beginning of the title *Searching the Web*.
13. Update the entire table of contents and then update the table of figures.
14. Save, print, and then close **C28-A04-NavigateWeb.docx**.

## Achieving Signature Status

Take your skills to the next level by completing this more challenging assessment.

### Assessment 28.5    Create a Table of Contents, a Table of Figures, and a Table of Tables

1. Open **Networks.docx** and save the document with the name **C28-A05-Networks**.
2. Format the document so it appears as shown in Figure 28.12 on the next page with the following specifications:
   a. Insert the captions for the figures and tables as shown in Figure 28.12.
   b. Insert the table of contents as shown in Figure 28.12.
   c. Insert the tables of figures and tables as shown on the second page of Figure 28.12. (You will need to create two different tables of figures: one for the figures and one for the tables. Use the *Caption label* option at the Table of Figures dialog box to specify figures and then tables when creating each table of figures.)
   d. Insert page numbers as shown. (Change the page numbering format to lowercase roman numerals for the table of contents page and table of figures and tables page.)
3. Save, print, and then close **C28-A05-Networks.docx**.

# Figure 28.12 Assessment 28.5

### COMMUNICATIONS SYSTEMS

A computer network is one kind of communications system. This system includes sending and receiving hardware, transmission and relay systems, common sets of standards so all the equipment can "talk" to each other, and communications software.

#### NETWORK COMMUNICATIONS

You use such a networked communications system whenever you send/receive IM or email messages, pay a bill online, shop at an Internet store, send a document to a shared printer at work or at home, or download a file.

The world of computer network communications systems is made up of:

- Transmission media upon which the data travels to/from its destination.
- A set of standards and network protocols (rules for how data is handled as it travels along a communications channel). Devices use these to send and receive data to and from each other.
- Hardware and software to connect to a communications pathway from the sending and receiving ends.

Figure 1: Wireless Network Base

The first step in understanding a communications system is to learn the basics about transmission signals and transmission speeds when communicating over a network.

#### TYPES OF SIGNALS

Two types of signals are used to transmit voices and other sounds over a computer network: analog and digital. An analog signal is formed by continuous sound waves that fluctuate from high to low. Your voice is transmitted as an analog signal over traditional telephone lines at a certain frequency. A digital signal uses a discrete signal that is either high or low. In computer terms, high represents the digital bit 1, and low represents the digital bit 0. These are the only two states for digital data.

Telephone lines carry your voice using an analog signal. However, computers don't "speak" analog; rather, they use a binary system of 1s and 0s to turn analog data into digital signals. If you send data between computers using an analog medium such as a phone line, the signal has to be transformed from digital to analog (modulated) and back again to digital (demodulated) to be

Figure 2: Wireless Modem

1

# Figure 28.12  Assessment 28.5 (continued)

understood by the computer on the receiving end. The piece of hardware that sends and receives data from a transmission source such as your telephone line or cable television connection is a modem. The word modem comes from the combination of the words *modu*late and *demo*dulate.

Today, most new communications technologies simply use a digital signal, saving the trouble of converting transmissions. An example of this trend is the demise in 2009 of analog television transmissions as the industry switched to digital signals. Many people were sent scrambling to either buy a newer television set or buy a converter to convert digital transmissions back to analog to work with their older equipment. Newer computer networks, too, use a pure digital signal method of sending and receiving data over a network.

## TRANSMISSION SPEED

If you've ever been frustrated with how long it takes to download a file from a website, you are familiar with the fact that, in a communications system, data moves from one computer to another at different speeds. The speed of transmission is determined by a few key factors.

The first factor is the speed at which a signal can change from high to low, which is called frequency. A signal sent at a faster frequency provides faster transmission (Figure 1). The other factor contributing to the speed of data transmission is bandwidth. On a computer network, the term bandwidth refers to the number of bits (pieces of data) per second that can be transmitted over a communications medium. Think of bandwidth as being like a highway. At rush hour, with the same amount of cars, a two-lane highway accommodates less traffic and everybody moves at a slower speed than on a four-lane highway, where much more traffic can travel at a faster speed.

Table 1: Bandwidth

| Term | Abbreviation | Meaning |
|---|---|---|
| 1 kilobit per second | 1 Kbps | 1 thousand bits per second |
| 1 megabit per second | 1 Mbps | 1 million bits per second |
| 1 gigabit per second | 1 Gbps | 1 billion bits per second |
| 1 terabit per second | 1 Tbps | 1 trillion bits per second |
| 1 petabit per second | 1 Pbps | 1 quadrillion bits per second |

If you have plenty of bandwidth and your data is transmitted at a high frequency, you get faster transmission speeds. Any communications medium that is capable of carrying a large amount of data at a fast speed is known as broadband.

Though transmission speeds at any moment in time may vary depending on network traffic and other factors, each of the common communications media has a typical speed (Figure 2). These speeds are constantly being improved upon. In fact, some very high-powered connections provide transmission speeds of as much as 100 gigabits (one billion bits) per second, which allows you to download a high-definition DVD movie in two seconds.

Table 2: Average Network Connection Speeds

| Type of Connection | Typical Speed |
|---|---|
| 56 K dial-up | 56 Kbps |
| satellite | 1.5 Mbps |
| DSL | 7 Mbps |
| fiber-optic | 25 Mbps |
| cable TV | 50 Mbps |

3

# Chapter 29

## Creating Forms

**Performance Objectives**

Upon successful completion of Chapter 29, you will be able to:

- Design a form and create and protect a form template
- Insert text controls
- Fill in a form
- Edit a form template
- Insert instructional text
- Create a form using a table and insert picture and date picker content controls
- Insert a drop-down list from a data field
- Set properties for content controls
- Create a form using legacy tools
- Print a form or only the data in the form
- Customize form field options

Many businesses use preprinted forms that respondents fill in by hand or with a computer. Preprinted forms cost a company money to print and require space for storage. With Word, you can create your own forms and eliminate the need to buy and store preprinted forms. In this chapter, you will learn how to use ***content controls***—including plain text, picture, date picker, and drop-down list content controls—to create basic forms. You will also learn how to create forms with legacy tools, including text, check box, and drop-down list form fields. In addition, you will save forms as protected documents, create documents from the forms, and enter the requested information.

*Note: Before beginning computer exercises for this chapter, copy to your storage medium the Chapter29 folder from the CD that accompanies this textbook and then make Chapter29 the active folder.*

In this chapter, students will produce the following documents:

Exercise 29.1B. C29-E01-DesmondML.docx
Exercise 29.1D. C29-E01-PierobonML.docx
Exercise 29.2. C29-E02-SBFax.docx
Exercise 29.3. C29-E03-SBSurvey.docx
Exercise 29.4. C29-E04-TrevierApp.docx
Exercise 29.5. C29-E05-ReynoldsApp.docx
Exercise 29.6. C29-E06-MurciaApp.docx
Exercise 29.7. C29-E07-LAAppHarris.docm

Model answers for these exercises are shown on the following pages.

STORYTELLER BOOKS
Mailing List Request

**First Name:** Holly     **Last Name:** Desmond

**Address:** 1542 Windett Lane

**City:** Geneva     **State:** IL     **Zip Code:** 60123

**Telephone:** 630-555-1443     **Birthday:** October 23

All information provided will be used by Storyteller Books only to provide you with information regarding upcoming sales and events.

**Exercise 29.1B**  C29-E01-DesmondML.docx

---

STORYTELLER BOOKS
Mailing List Request

**First Name:** Val     **Last Name:** Pierobon

**Address:** 1550 South Meridian Street

**City:** St. Charles     **State:** IL     **Zip Code:** 60123

**Home Phone:** 630-555-0098     **Cell Phone:** 630-555-3423

**Email Address:** vpierobon@emcp.net

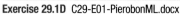

All information provided will be used by Storyteller Books only to provide you with information regarding upcoming sales and events.

**Exercise 29.1D**  C29-E01-PierobonML.docx

---

# STORYTELLER BOOKS

**4350 Jenkins Boulevard**
**Glen Ellyn, IL 60137**
**(630) 555-7998**

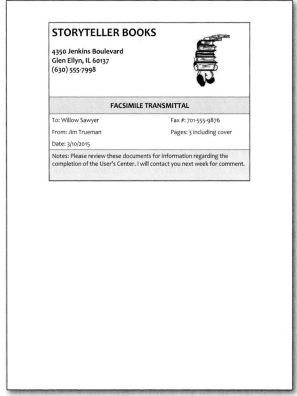

### FACSIMILE TRANSMITTAL

| | |
|---|---|
| To: Willow Sawyer | Fax #: 701-555-9876 |
| From: Jim Trueman | Pages: 3 including cover |
| Date: 3/10/2015 | |

Notes: Please review these documents for information regarding the completion of the User's Center. I will contact you next week for comment.

**Exercise 29.2**  C29-E02-SBFax.docx

---

# STORYTELLER BOOKS

**4350 Jenkins Boulevard**
**Glen Ellyn, IL 60137**
**(630) 555-7998**

### READER SURVEY

*To help us serve you better, please take a moment to complete this survey.*

| | |
|---|---|
| Today's date | March 10, 2015 |
| How often do you read? | Daily |
| Do you read for work? | Yes |
| Do you read for pleasure or entertainment? | Yes |
| What do you prefer to read for work? | Trade publications |
| What do you prefer to read for entertainment? | Books |
| Where do you prefer to shop? | In store |

Comments: I do most of my shopping in the store, but I am going to start ordering online in the near future.

**Exercise 29.3**  C29-E03-SBSurvey.docx

**Exercise 29.4**

C29-E04-TrevierApp.docx

## LIFETIME ANNUITY COMPANY
3310 CUSHMAN STREET ✧ FAIRBANKS, AK 99705 ✧ 907-555-8875

### INSURANCE APPLICATION

| FIRST APPLICANT | SECOND APPLICANT |
|---|---|
| Name: Sara Trevier | Name: Chris Trevier |
| Address: 1762 32nd Street, Fairbanks, AK 99702 | Address: 1762 32nd Street, Fairbanks, AK 99702 |
| Date of Birth: 03/28/1978 | Date of Birth: 10/02/1977 |
| Occupation: Engineer Technician | Occupation: Police Officer |

1. During the past three years, have you for any reason consulted a doctor or been hospitalized?

First Applicant: Yes ☐ No ☒     Second Applicant: Yes ☐ No ☒

2. Have you ever been treated for or advised that you have any of the following: heart, lung, kidney, or liver disorder; high blood pressure; drug abuse, including alcohol; cancer or tumor; diabetes; or any disorder of your immune system?

First Applicant: Yes ☒ No ☐     Second Applicant: Yes ☐ No ☒

3. During the past three years, have you for any reason been denied life insurance by any other insurance company?

First Applicant: Yes ☐ No ☒     Second Applicant: Yes ☐ No ☒

FIRST APPLICANT'S SIGNATURE          SECOND APPLICANT'S SIGNATURE

_____          _____

## LIFETIME ANNUITY COMPANY
3310 CUSHMAN STREET ✧ FAIRBANKS, AK 99705 ✧ 907-555-8875

### PREFERRED INSURANCE APPLICATION

| Name: Jennifer Reynolds | | Date: 03/10/2015 |
|---|---|---|
| Address: 2309 North Ridge Drive, Fairbanks, AK 99708 | | |
| Date of Birth: 12/18/1971 | Client #: 210-322 | Gender: Female ☒ Male ☐ |
| Nonprofit Employer: Public School | Premium Payments: Quarterly | |

1. Will this insurance replace any existing insurance or annuity?
Yes ☒ No ☐

2. Within the past three years has your driver's license been suspended or revoked, or have you been convicted for driving under the influence of alcohol or drugs?
Yes ☐ No ☒

3. Do you have any intention of traveling or residing outside the United States or Canada within the next twelve months?
Yes ☐ No ☒

| APPLICANT'S SIGNATURE: | DATE: |
|---|---|
| _____ | _____ |

**Exercise 29.5**

C29-E05-ReynoldsApp.docx

Exercise 29.6

C29-E06-MurciaApp.docx

## LIFETIME ANNUITY COMPANY
### 3310 CUSHMAN STREET ✦ FAIRBANKS, AK 99705 ✦ 907-555-8875

### APPLICATION FOR BENEFITS CHANGE

| Date: 03/10/2015 | Policy #: 411-38 | | Type of Program: Family | |
|---|---|---|---|---|
| First Name: Chad | Middle Name: Richard | | Last Name: Murcia | |
| Address: 512 South 142nd Street | City: Fairbanks | State: AK | | Zip Code: 99702 |

Method of Payment:
☐ Direct Payment
☒ Monthly Deductions

Payment Period:
☐ Monthly      ☐ Semi-Annually
☒ Quarterly    ☐ Annually

1. Are you currently working?
   Yes ☒     No ☐

2. Do you work full time?
   Yes ☒     No ☐

3. Do you wish to add the total disability income provision?     Yes ☐ No ☒

4. In which program are you currently enrolled?  Premium

5. In which program do you want to enroll?  Platinum

SIGNATURE:                                    DATE:

## LIFETIME ANNUITY COMPANY
### 3310 CUSHMAN STREET ✦ FAIRBANKS, AK 99705 ✦ 907-555-8875

| **Policy Number: 10-A-321** | |
|---|---|
| First Name: Lindsay | Date of Birth: 11/03/1985 |
| Last Name: Harris | Occupation: Physical Therapist |
| Address: 3002 N. 42nd St., Fairbanks, AK 99703 | Phone Number: (907) 555-3175 |

Exercise 29.7

C29-E07-LAAppHarris.docm

# Creating a Form

In Word, a *form* is a protected document that includes user-defined sections into which a respondent enters information. These user-defined sections are made up of *content controls* and *form fields*. Content controls limit response options to ensure the collection of desired data. Three types of content controls are available: drop-down boxes, check boxes, and date pickers. Form fields are spaces allotted for a respondent to enter specific text.

The DEVELOPER tab, as shown in Figure 29.1, contains options for inserting content controls. The DEVELOPER tab also contains options for creating forms with legacy tools, which are tools for developing forms that were available in previous versions of Word. These tools also include options called *form fields*.

**Figure 29.1 DEVELOPER Tab**

## Designing a Form

The goals in creating a form are twofold: to gather all of the information necessary to meet a specific objective and to gather information that is useful and accurate. Thus, the first step in creating a form is to determine its purpose. Make a list of all of the information you need to meet your objective. Be careful not to include unnecessary or redundant information, which will clutter the appearance of the form and frustrate the person who is completing it.

The next step is to plan the layout of the form. The simplest way to design a form is to find an existing form that requests similar information or serves a similar purpose and then mimic it. Finding a similar form is not always easy, however, and in many cases you will need to design your form from scratch. If you need to start the design from scratch, first sketch out your form on paper. This will give you a guide to follow as you create the form in Word.

Here are some other points to consider when designing your form:

- Group like items in the form. This makes providing complete and accurate information easier for the respondent.

- Place the most important information at the top of the form to increase the likelihood of obtaining the information you desire most. Many respondents fail to complete a form entirely before submitting it.

- Use fonts, colors, lines, and graphics purposefully and sparingly. Overusing such design elements tends to clutter a form and make it difficult to read.

- Use white space, lines, and shading to separate sections of the form. Each section should be clearly defined.

## Creating a Form Template

**QUICK STEPS**

**Create a Form Template**
1. Open blank document.
2. Display Save As dialog box.
3. Change *Save as type* option to *Word Template (*.dotx)*.
4. Click Save button.

**Display the DEVELOPER Tab**
1. Click FILE tab.
2. Click *Options*.
3. Click *Customize Ribbon*.
4. Click DEVELOPER tab check box to insert check mark.
5. Click OK.

**Protect the Template**
1. Click DEVELOPER tab.
2. Click Restrict Editing button.
3. Click *Allow only this type of editing in the document* check box.
4. Click *Filling in forms* at drop-down list in *Editing Restrictions* section.
5. Click Yes, Start Enforcing Protection button.

A form is created as a template, so a respondent who fills in a form is working in a copy of the form rather than the original. The original is the form template document, which is saved as a protected document. That way, a form can be used again and again without changing the original. When a form is created from a protected form template document, information can be typed only into the fields designated when the form was created.

Figure 29.2 shows an example of a form template document created with the form feature. (You will create this form in Exercise 29.1A.) You can create forms that contain data fields for text, such as the fields *First Name:*, *Last Name:*, *Address:*, and so on. You can also create forms that contain drop-down lists, date pickers, and pictures.

**Figure 29.2  Exercise 29.1A**

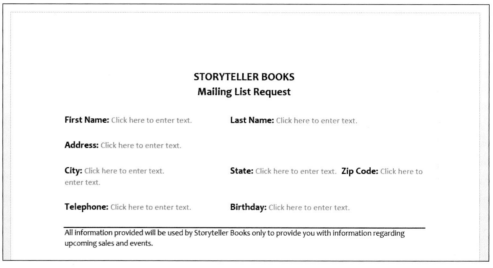

Create a new form template by opening a blank document, displaying the Save As dialog box, changing the *Save as type* option to *Word Template (*.dotx)*, and then clicking the Save button. This saves the blank template in the Custom Office Templates folder in the Documents folder on the computer's hard drive. To use the template, display the New backstage area, click the *PERSONAL* option, and then click the template thumbnail.

As mentioned in Chapter 24, if you are working on computers in a public environment, you should save a backup of your template on your storage medium (such as a USB flash drive). That way, if the computers are reset on a regular basis, you can copy your template back to the Custom Office Templates folder.

Another option for managing templates is to change the default location that templates are saved from the Custom Office Templates folder to another location, such as a disk drive. To change the default location for templates, display the Word Options dialog box, click *Save* in the left panel, and then specify the folder or drive in which to save templates with the *Default personal templates folder* option. The folder or drive you specify at this option will be the folder or drive that displays when you click the *PERSONAL* option at the New backstage area.

The exercises in this chapter are written based on the assumption that you are saving to the default Custom Office Templates folder. Please check with your instructor to determine if you will be saving templates to a different location. Also determine if you need to make backup copies of your templates.

## Displaying the DEVELOPER Tab

To display the DEVELOPER tab, click the FILE tab and then click *Options*. At the Word Options dialog box, click *Customize Ribbon* in the left panel. In the list box at the right, click the Developer tab check box to insert a check mark and then click OK to close the dialog box. The DEVELOPER tab is positioned to the right of the VIEW tab.

## Protecting a Template

If you want users to enter information in a template but not edit the template itself, protect the template. To do this, click the Restrict Editing button in the Protect group on the DEVELOPER tab. This displays the Restrict Editing task pane, as shown in Figure 29.3.

At this task pane, click in the *Allow only this type of editing in the document* check box to insert a check mark. Click the down-pointing arrow at the right of the option box in the *Editing restrictions* section and then click *Filling in forms* at the drop-down list. Click the Yes, Start Enforcing Protection button in the task pane. At the Start Enforcing Protection dialog box, type a password, confirm the password, and then close the dialog box. A password is not required to protect a form. If you do not want to password-protect the template, click OK at the Start Enforcing Protection dialog box without entering a password.

**Figure 29.3 Restrict Editing Task Pane**

To protect a fill-in form, click this check box and then select *Filling in forms* from the drop-down list.

Click this button to enforce the restrictions specified in this task pane.

1.  Display the DEVELOPER tab by completing the following steps:
    a.  Click the FILE tab and then click *Options*.
    b.  At the Word Options dialog box, click *Customize Ribbon* in the left panel.
    c.  Click the Developer tab check box in the list box at the right to insert a check mark.

   d.  Click OK to close the dialog box.
2.  Create the form shown in Figure 29.2 on page 1008. To begin, create a template by completing the following steps:
    a.  Press Ctrl + N to display a blank document.
    b.  Press the F12 key to display the Save As dialog box.
    c.  At the Save As dialog box, type **XXXMailingListTemplate** in the *File name* text box (typing your initials in place of the *XXX*).
    d.  Click the *Save as type* option box and then click *Word Template (*.dotx)* at the drop-down list.
    e.  Click the Save button.
3.  At the new template, type the beginning portion of the form shown in Figure 29.2 up to the colon after *First Name:* by completing the following steps:
    a.  Click the PAGE LAYOUT tab and then click the down-pointing arrow at the right of the *Spacing After* option in the Paragraph group until *0 pt* displays in the measurement box.
    b.  Click the HOME tab, turn on bold formatting, and then change the font to Candara and the font size to 14 points.
    c.  Click the Center button in the Paragraph group, type **STORYTELLER BOOKS**, and then press the Enter key.
    d.  Type **Mailing List Request** and then press the Enter key twice.
    e.  Click the Align Left button in the Paragraph group and change the font size to 12 points.
    f.  Set left tabs at the 3-inch mark and 4.5-inch mark on the horizontal ruler.
    g.  Type **First Name:** and then turn off bold formatting.
    h.  Press the spacebar once.

4. Insert a text content control by completing the following steps:
   a. Click the DEVELOPER tab.
   b. Click the Plain Text Content Control button in the Controls group. (This inserts a plain text content control in the document.)

c. Press the Right Arrow key to deselect the control.
5. Press the Tab key to move the insertion point to the tab at the 3-inch mark.
6. Turn on bold formatting, type **Last Name:**, and then turn off bold formatting.
7. Press the spacebar once and then click the Plain Text Content Control button in the Controls group.
8. Press the Right Arrow key to deselect the control.
9. Press the Enter key twice.
10. Continue to enter the text and content controls as displayed in Figure 29.2. Remember to turn off bold formatting before inserting the plain text content control. (When you enter the line that contains *City:*, *State:*, and *Zip Code:*, press Tab to align each item at the correct tab setting. As you type, content controls and text appear crowded and wrap to the next line. The content controls will not print when you create a document from this template.)
11. Position the insertion point a double space below the last line of the form.
12. Insert the horizontal line by pressing Shift + - (the hyphen key) three times and then pressing the Enter key. (AutoFormat will automatically change the hyphens into a vertical line.)
13. Change the font to 10-point Candara and then type the paragraph of text below the horizontal line as shown in Figure 29.2.

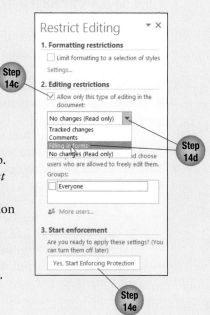

14. Protect the template by completing the following steps:
    a. Click the DEVELOPER tab.
    b. Click the Restrict Editing button in the Protect group.
    c. Click the *Allow only this type of editing in the document* check box in the Restrict Editing task pane.
    d. Click the down-pointing arrow at the right of the option box in the *Editing restrictions* section of the task pane and then click *Filling in forms* at the drop-down list.
    e. Click the Yes, Start Enforcing Protection button.
    f. At the Start Enforcing Protection dialog box, click OK. (Creating a password is optional.)
    g. Close the Restrict Editing task pane.
15. Save and then close **XXXMailingListTemplate.dotx**.

## Inserting Text Controls

**Plain Text
Content Control**

The Controls group on the DEVELOPER tab contains two text control buttons: the Rich Text Content Control button and the Plain Text Content Control button. The Plain Text Content Control button inserts a control that takes on the format of the text that surrounds it. The Rich Text Content Control button inserts a control that allows users to apply formatting to text and type multiple paragraphs of text. In this chapter, you will use only plain text content controls.

**QUICK STEPS**

**Opening a Protected Form Template**
1. Click FILE tab.
2. Click *New* option.
3. Click *PERSONAL* option.
4. Click desired template thumbnail.

## Opening and Filling in a Form Document

After you create, protect, and save a form template, you can use the template to create a personalized form document that allows easy data entry. To begin, open the protected form template by clicking the FILE tab and then clicking the *New* option. At the New backstage area, click the *PERSONAL* option and then click the thumbnail representing your template.

When you open a protected form template, the insertion point is automatically inserted in the first data field. To fill in the form, type the information for that data field. Click in a data field to make it active, and then type your response. Press the Tab key to move the insertion point to the next data field or press Shift + Tab to move the insertion point to the preceding data field.

---

**Exercise 29.1B**   **Filling in the Mailing List Form**                              **Part 2 of 4**

1. Create a form document from the **XXXMailingListTemplate** template. To begin, click the FILE tab and then click the *New* option.
2. At the New backstage area, click the *PERSONAL* option.
3. Click the **XXXMailingListTemplate** thumbnail.
4. With the first text content control selected (the one that displays after *First Name:*), type **Holly**.
5. Press the Tab key to advance to the next data field and continue entering the information as displayed in Figure 29.4 on the next page. Make sure the labels are bold but not the data field text.
6. Save the document by completing the following steps:
   a. Press the F12 key.
   b. At the Save As dialog box, navigate to your Chapter29 folder.
   c. Type **C29-E01-DesmondML** in the *File name* text box and then press the Enter key.
7. Print and then close **C29-E01-DesmondML.docx**.

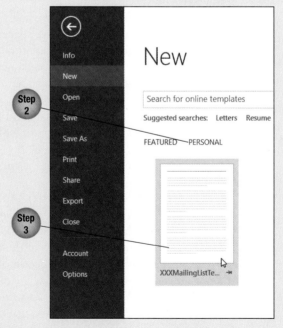

**Figure 29.4  Exercise 29.1B**

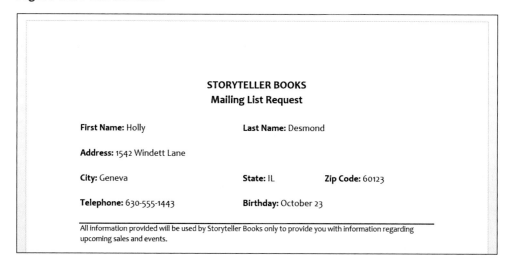

**STORYTELLER BOOKS**
**Mailing List Request**

First Name: Holly                    Last Name: Desmond

Address: 1542 Windett Lane

City: Geneva                    State: IL              Zip Code: 60123

Telephone: 630-555-1443              Birthday: October 23

All information provided will be used by Storyteller Books only to provide you with information regarding upcoming sales and events.

# Editing a Form Template

When you create and then protect a form template, the text in the template cannot be changed. If you want to make changes to a form template, you must open the template, turn off the protection, and then make the changes. After making the changes, be sure to protect the template again before you save it.

To turn off the protection of a template document, click the Restrict Editing button in the Protect group on the DEVELOPER tab. At the Restrict Editing task pane, click the Stop Protection button. Make any necessary changes to the template and then protect it again by clicking the Yes, Start Enforcing Protection button.

By default, Word saves a template in the Custom Office Templates folder. To open a template for editing, display the Open dialog box, click the *Documents* folder in the Navigation pane, and then double-click the *Custom Office Templates* folder in the Content pane.

**QUICK STEPS**

**Edit a Form Template**
1. Click DEVELOPER tab.
2. Click Restrict Editing button.
3. Click Stop Protection button in Restrict Editing task pane.
4. Make desired changes.
5. Click Yes, Start Enforcing Protection button.

**Exercise 29.1C  Editing the Mailing List Form Template**                    Part 3 of 4

1. Edit the **XXXMailingListTemplate.dotx** as shown in Figure 29.5 on the next page. To begin, press Ctrl + F12 to display the Open dialog box.
2. At the Open dialog box, click the *Documents* folder (if necessary) in the Navigation pane and then double-click the *Custom Office Templates* folder in the Content pane.
3. Double-click the document name *XXXMailingListTemplate.dotx* in the Content pane.

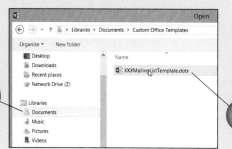

4. Unprotect the template by completing the following steps:
   a. Click the DEVELOPER tab.
   b. Click the Restrict Editing button in the Protect group.
   c. At the Restrict Editing task pane, click the Stop Protection button located near the bottom of the task pane.
   d. Close the Restrict Editing task pane.

5. Delete, edit, and insert a content control by completing the following steps:
   a. Select the word *Birthday*, the colon, and the content control *Click here to enter text.* and then press the Delete key.
   b. Edit the word *Telephone*, changing it to **Home Phone**.
   c. Move the insertion point to the right of *the Home Phone:* content control.
   d. Press the Tab key.
   e. Turn on bold formatting, type **Cell Phone:**, turn off bold formatting, and then press the spacebar.
   f. Click the Plain Text Content Control button in the Controls group.
   g. Move the insertion point so it is positioned at the right side of the *Cell Phone:* content control.
   h. Press the Enter key twice.
   i. Turn on bold formatting, type **Email Address:**, turn off bold formatting, and then press the spacebar.
   j. Click the Plain Text Content Control button in the Controls group.
6. Protect the document by completing the following steps:
   a. With the DEVELOPER tab selected, click the Restrict Editing button in the Protect group.
   b. Click the Yes, Start Enforcing Protection button.
   c. At the Start Enforcing Protection dialog box, click OK.
   d. Close the Restrict Editing task pane.
7. Save and then close **XXXMailingListTemplate.dotx**.

**Figure 29.5 Exercise 29.1C**

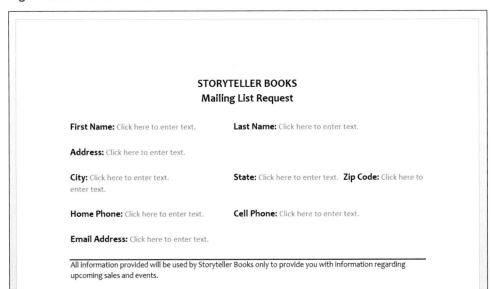

1. Create a form document from the **XXXMailingListTemplate.dotx** template by completing the following steps:
   a. Click the FILE tab and then click the *New* option.
   b. At the New backstage area, click the *PERSONAL* option.
   c. Click the ***XXXMailingListTemplate*** thumbnail.
   d. Type the following text in the specified data fields:
      *First Name:* **Val**
      *Last Name:* **Pierobon**
      *Address:* **1550 South Meridian Street**
      *City:* **St. Charles**
      *State:* **IL**
      *Zip Code:* **60123**
      *Home Phone:* **630-555-0098**
      *Cell Phone:* **630-555-3423**
      *Email Address:* **vpierobon@emcp.net**

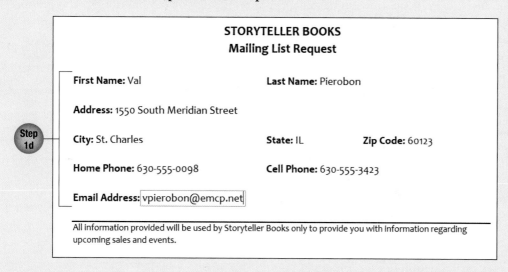

**STORYTELLER BOOKS**
**Mailing List Request**

First Name: Val          Last Name: Pierobon

Address: 1550 South Meridian Street

City: St. Charles     State: IL     Zip Code: 60123

Home Phone: 630-555-0098     Cell Phone: 630-555-3423

Email Address: vpierobon@emcp.net

All information provided will be used by Storyteller Books only to provide you with information regarding upcoming sales and events.

Step 1d

2. Save the document in your Chapter29 folder with the name **C29-E01-PierobonML**.
3. Print and then close **C29-E01-PierobonML.docx**.

# Inserting Instructional Text

Providing instructional text for respondents who are filling in a form can aid in obtaining accurate information. When you create a form, add text to each data field that provides specific directions on what information to enter. The instructional text is replaced with the data entered by the respondent.

To insert instructional text, click the Plain Text Content Control button in the Controls group on the DEVELOPER tab and then type the instructional text. You can also type the instructional text at the location where you will insert the text content control, select the text, and then click the Plain Text Content Control button.

**QUICK STEPS**

**Insert Instructional Text**
1. Click DEVELOPER tab.
2. Click Plain Text Content Control button.
3. Type instructional text.

# Creating Forms Using Tables

The table feature in Word is an efficient tool for designing and creating forms. Using a table allows you to set up the framework for your form and provides spaces to enter data fields. Using a table also allows for easy alignment and placement of the elements of the form.

---

**Exercise 29.2A** — **Inserting Controls in a Fax Template** — **Part 1 of 3**

---

1. Open **SBFax.docx** and then save it as a template by completing the following:
   a. Press the F12 key to display the Save As dialog box.
   b. At the Save As dialog box, type **XXXFaxTemplate** in the *File name* text box (typing your initials in place of the *XXX*).
   c. Click the *Save as type* option and then click *Word Template (*.dotx)* at the drop-down list.
   d. Click the Save button.
2. If the table does not contain gray dashed gridlines between the two cells in the first row (and between other cells and rows in the table), turn on the display of nonprinting table gridlines by completing the following steps:
   a. Click in any cell in the table.
   b. Click the TABLE TOOLS LAYOUT tab.
   c. Click the View Gridlines button in the Table group.
3. Insert in the *To:* cell instructional text and a text content control by completing the following steps:
   a. Click the DEVELOPER tab.
   b. Click in the *To:* text box and position the insertion point one space to the right of the colon.
   c. Click the Plain Text Content Control button in the Controls group.
   d. Type **Receiver's name**.

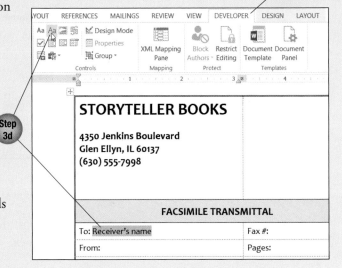

4. Complete steps similar to those in Step 3 to insert the text content control and instructional text in the *Fax #:*, *From:*, *Pages:*, and *Notes:* cells, as shown in Figure 29.6 on the next page. (You will insert a field for the date in the next exercise.)
5. Click the Save button on the Quick Access toolbar to save the template.

**Figure 29.6 Exercise 29.2A**

# STORYTELLER BOOKS

**4350 Jenkins Boulevard**
**Glen Ellyn, IL 60137**
**(630) 555-7998**

| **FACSIMILE TRANSMITTAL** | |
|---|---|
| To: Receiver's name | Fax #: Fax number |
| From: Sender's name | Pages: # of pages |
| Date: | |
| Notes: Enter notes | |

## Inserting Pictures

A picture content control can be inserted in a template that displays a picture, clip art image, drawing, shape, chart, table, or SmartArt graphic. Insert a picture or other visual element in a form using the Picture Content Control button in the Controls group on the DEVELOPER tab. Click this button and a picture frame containing a picture icon is inserted where the insertion point is located. Click the picture icon and the Insert Picture dialog box displays. At this dialog box, navigate to the folder containing the picture you want to insert and then double-click the picture file. The picture image fills the picture content control.

## Using the Date Picker

A date picker content control can be inserted in a template that displays a calendar when the respondent clicks the down-pointing arrow at the right of the control. The respondent can navigate to the desired month and year and then click the date. To insert a date picker content control, click the Date Picker Content Control button in the Controls group on the DEVELOPER tab.

**QUICK STEPS**

**Insert a Picture**
1. Click DEVELOPER tab.
2. Click Picture Content Control button.
3. Click picture icon.
4. Navigate to desired folder and double-click desired picture file.

**Insert a Date Content Control**
1. Click DEVELOPER tab.
2. Click Date Picker Content Control button.

Picture      Date
Content    Picker
Control   Content
          Control

1. With **XXXFaxTemplate.dotx** open, insert a picture content control by completing the following steps:

    a. Click in the cell at the right in the top row, click the TABLE TOOLS LAYOUT tab, and then click the Align Center button in the Alignment group.

    b. Click the DEVELOPER tab.

    c. Click the Picture Content Control button in the Controls group.

    d. Click the picture icon that displays in the middle of the picture content control in the cell.

    e. At the Insert Pictures window, click the Browse button, navigate to your Chapter29 folder, and then double-click *Books.jpg*.

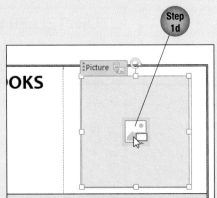

2. Insert a date picker content control by completing the following steps:

    a. Click in the *Date:* cell and then position the insertion point one space to the right of the colon.

    b. Click the Date Picker Content Control button in the Controls group.

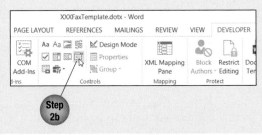

3. Protect the template and only allow filling in the form. (Refer to Exercise 29.1A, Step 14.)

4. Save and then close **XXXFaxTemplate.dotx**.

1. Create a form document from the **XXXFaxTemplate.dotx** template by completing the following steps:

    a. Click the FILE tab and then click the *New* option.

    b. At the New backstage area, click the *PERSONAL* option.

    c. Click the **XXXFaxTemplate** template (where your initials display in place of the *XXX*).

    d. Click on the word *To:*. (This selects the *To:* content control.)

    e. Type **Willow Sawyer** and then press the Tab key.

    f. Type **701-555-9876** and then press the Tab key.

    g. Type **Jim Trueman** and then press the Tab key.

    h. Type **3 including cover** and then press the Tab key.

    i. With the *Date:* content control text selected, click the down-pointing arrow at the right of the content control and then click the Today button that displays below the calendar.

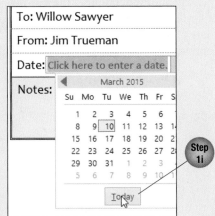

    j. Press the Tab key.

    k. Type **Please review these documents for information regarding the completion of the User's Center. I will contact you next week for comment.**

2. Save the document in the Chapter29 folder on your storage medium and name it **C29-E02-SBFax**.
3. Print and then close **C29-E02-SBFax.docx**.

# Creating Drop-down Lists

When you create a form, you may want the respondent to choose from specific options rather than type data into a data field. To make only specific options available, create a data field with a drop-down list. To create a drop-down list, create a form template document, type the field label, and then click the Drop-Down List Content Control button in the Controls group on the DEVELOPER tab.

# Setting Properties for Content Controls

You can customize a content control with options at a properties dialog box. The options at the dialog box vary depending on the selected content control. For example, you can add a list of items for a drop-down list content control, lock a picture content control, and specify formatting for inserting a date with a date picker content control.

## Specifying Drop-down List Properties

To create the list of items from which a respondent will choose, select the control and then click the Properties button in the Controls group on the DEVELOPER tab. This displays the Content Control Properties dialog box, as shown in Figure 29.7. Each content control includes properties that you can change with options at the Content Control Properties dialog box. The content of the dialog box varies depending on the control selected.

**Figure 29.7  Content Control Properties Dialog Box for Drop-down List Content Control**

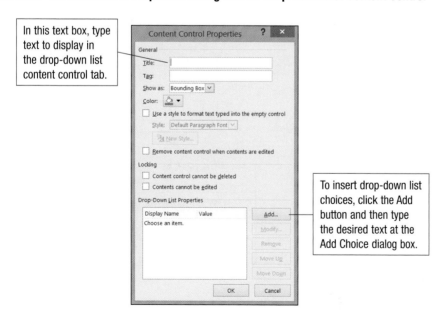

In this text box, type text to display in the drop-down list content control tab.

To insert drop-down list choices, click the Add button and then type the desired text at the Add Choice dialog box.

**QUICK STEPS**

**Create a Drop-down List**
1. Create template form document.
2. Type field label.
3. Click DEVELOPER tab.
4. Click Drop-Down List Content Control button.

**Specify Drop-down List Properties**
1. Select drop-down list content control.
2. Click DEVELOPER tab.
3. Click Properties button.
4. Click Add button.
5. Type desired choice.
6. Click OK.
7. Continue clicking Add button and typing desired choices.
8. Click OK to close Content Control Properties dialog box.

Drop-Down List Content Control

Control Properties

To add drop-down list choices, click the Add button in the dialog box. At the Add Choice dialog box, type the first choice in the *Display Name* text box and then click OK. At the Content Control Properties dialog box, click the Add button and then continue until you have entered all of the choices.

Create a title for the drop-down list content control with the *Title* option in the Content Control Properties dialog box. Type the desired text in the *Title* text box and the text you type displays in the content control tab at the template. Having a content control title is not necessary but it can provide additional information for the person filling in the form.

You can modify the list by clicking the desired option in the *Drop-Down List Properties* section and then clicking the Modify button. You can also change the position of an item in the list by selecting the desired item and then clicking the Move Up or Move Down button. To remove an item from the list, select the item and then click the Remove button.

To fill in a form with a drop-down list data field, select the drop-down list content control, click the down-pointing arrow at the right of the data field, and then click the desired option. You can also hold down the Alt key, press the Down Arrow key until the desired option is selected, and then press the Enter key.

In addition to these options, Word provides the Combo Box Content Control button in the Controls group on the DEVELOPER tab. A combo box is similar to a drop-down list but allows the respondent to edit or change the choices in the list.

---

**Exercise 29.3A**  **Inserting Controls in a Survey Template**  **Part 1 of 3**

1. Open **SBSurvey.docx** and then save it as a template by completing the following:
   a. Press the F12 key to display the Save As dialog box.
   b. At the Save As dialog box, type **XXXSurveyTemplate** in the *File name* text box (typing your initials in place of the *XXX*).
   c. Click the *Save as type* option box and then click *Word Template (*.dotx)* at the drop-down list.
   d. Click the Save button.
2. Click in the cell immediately right of the *How often do you read?* cell and then insert a drop-down list by completing the following steps:
   a. Click the DEVELOPER tab.
   b. Click the Drop-Down List Content Control button in the Controls group.
   c. With the content control selected, click the Properties button in the Controls group.

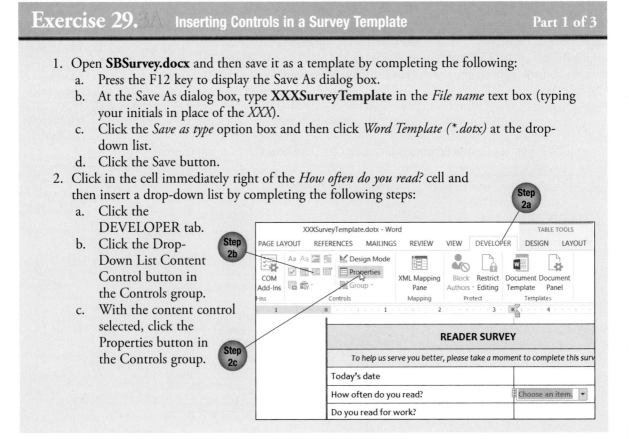

d.  At the Content Control Properties dialog box, click the Add button.

e.  At the Add Choice dialog box, type **Daily** in the *Display Name* text box and then click OK.

3.  Complete steps similar to those in Steps 2d and 2e to expand the drop-down list, typing the following additional choices:

    **Weekly**
    **Monthly**
    **I don't read.**

4.  Click in the *Title* text box and then type **Frequency**.

5.  Click OK to close the Content Control Properties dialog box.

6.  Click in the cell immediately right of the *Do you read for work?* cell and then insert a drop-down list, typing the following choices:

    **Yes**
    **No**
    **Sometimes**

7.  Click in the cell immediately right of the *Do you read for pleasure or entertainment?* cell and then insert a drop-down list, typing the following choices:

    **Yes**
    **No**
    **Sometimes**

8.  Click in the cell immediately right of the *What do you prefer to read for work?* cell and then click the Combo Box Content Control button in the Controls group. With the content control selected, click the Properties button and then type the following choices. (Make sure you use the Combo Box Content Control button and not the Drop-Down List Content Control button.)

    **Manuals**
    **Journals**
    **Textbooks**

9.  Click in the cell immediately right of the *What do you prefer to read for entertainment?* cell and then insert a combo box content control, typing the following choices (make sure you use the Combo Box Content Control button):

    **Books**
    **Magazines**
    **Newspapers**

10. Click in the cell immediately right of the *Where do you prefer to shop?* cell and then insert a drop-down list, typing the following choices:

    **In store**
    **Online**

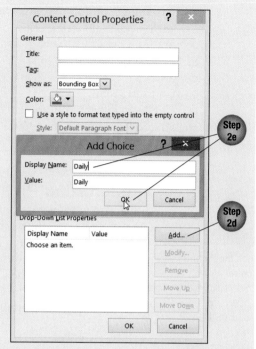

11. Insert a content control in the *Comments:* cell by completing the following steps:
    a. Click in the *Comments:* cell and then position the insertion point one space to the right of the colon.
    b. Type **Type comments here.**
    c. Select *Type comments here.* and then click the Plain Text Content Control button in the Controls group.
    d. Click in a different cell to deselect the content control.
12. Click the Save button on the Quick Access toolbar to save the template.

## Customizing Picture Content Control Properties

**Lock the Picture Control**
1. Select picture data field.
2. Click DEVELOPER tab.
3. Click Properties button.
4. Insert check mark in *Contents cannot be edited* check box.
5. Click OK.

When you use a picture control in a form template, consider locking the picture. With the picture locked, the insertion point does not stop at the picture data field when the respondent presses the Tab key to move to the next data field. To lock a picture, select the picture data field and then click the Properties button in the Controls group on the DEVELOPER tab. At the Content Control Properties dialog box, as shown in Figure 29.8, insert a check mark in the *Contents cannot be edited* check box. If you do not want the picture content control to be deleted, insert a check mark in the *Content control cannot be deleted* check box.

**Figure 29.8  Content Control Properties Dialog Box for Picture Content Control**

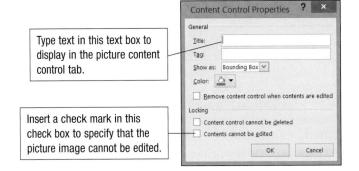

Type text in this text box to display in the picture content control tab.

Insert a check mark in this check box to specify that the picture image cannot be edited.

## Customizing Date Picker Content Control Properties

The date picker content control has a default format of *m/d/yyyy* for inserting the date. This date format can be customized with options at the Content Control Properties dialog box, as shown in Figure 29.9 on the next page. Choose the desired date format in the list box in the *Date Picker Properties* section of the dialog box and then click OK.

**Figure 29.9 Content Control Properties Dialog Box for Date Picker Content Control**

Type text in this text box to specify that you want to display in the date picker content control tab.

Specify the date format by choosing an option in this list box.

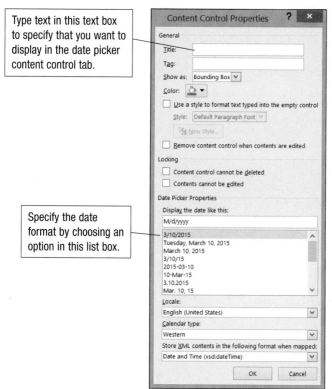

Exercise 29.3B   **Customizing Picture and Date Picker Content Control Properties**   Part 2 of 3

1. With **XXXSurveyTemplate.dotx** open, insert a picture content control and lock the control by completing the following steps:
   a. Click in the cell at the right in the top row of the table, click the TABLE TOOLS LAYOUT tab, and then click the Align Center button in the Alignment group.
   b. Click the DEVELOPER tab.
   c. Click the Picture Content Control button in the Controls group.
   d. Click the picture icon that displays in the middle of the picture content control in the cell.
   e. At the Insert Pictures window, click the Browse button, navigate to your Chapter29 folder, and then double-click *Books.jpg*.
   f. Click the Properties button in the Controls group.
   g. At the Content Control Properties dialog box, type **Books Image** in the *Title* text box.
   h. Click the *Contents cannot be edited* check box to insert a check mark.
   i. Click OK to close the dialog box.

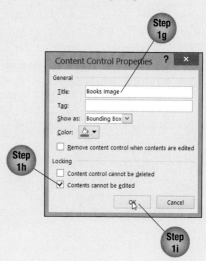

2. Insert a date picker content control and customize the control by completing the following steps:
   a. Click in the cell immediately right of the *Today's date* cell.
   b. If necessary, click the DEVELOPER tab.
   c. Click the Date Picker Content Control button in the Controls group.
   d. Click the Properties button in the Controls group.
   e. Type **Date** in the *Title* text box.
   f. Click the third option from the top in the list box in the *Date Picker Properties* section of the Content Control Properties dialog box.
   g. Click OK to close the dialog box.
3. Protect the template and only allow filling in the form. (Refer to Exercise 29.1A, Step 14 on page 1010.)
4. Save and then close **XXXSurveyTemplate.dotx**.

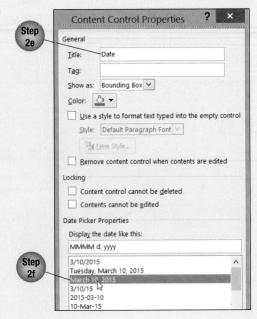

**Step 2e**

**Step 2f**

---

## Exercise 29.3C   Filling in the Survey Form                                   Part 3 of 3

1. Create a form document from the **XXXSurveyTemplate.dotx** template by completing the following steps:
   a. Click the FILE tab and then click the *New* option.
   b. At the New backstage area, click the *PERSONAL* option.
   c. Click the *XXXSurveyTemplate* thumbnail (where your initials display in place of the *XXX*).
2. With the *Date:* content control text selected, click the down-pointing arrow at the right of the content control and then click the Today button that displays below the calendar.
3. Press the Tab key. (This selects the drop-down list content control in the cell immediately right of *How often do you read?*)
4. Choose an option from the drop-down list by clicking the down-pointing arrow at the right of the drop-down list content control and then clicking *Daily*.
5. Continue filling in the form with options as shown in Figure 29.10 on the next page. Since the combo box for *What do you prefer to read for work?* does not contain the option *Trade publications*, type the entry in the content control.

| READER SURVEY | |
|---|---|
| To help us serve you better, please take a moment to complete this survey. | |
| Today's date | March 10, 2015 |
| How often do you read? | Frequency — Choose an item. |
| Do you read for work? | Choose an item. |
| Do you read for pleasure or entertainment? | Daily / Weekly / Monthly |
| What do you prefer to read for work? | I don't read. |

**Step 4**

6. Save the document in your Chapter29 folder with the name **C29-E03-SBSurvey**.
7. Print and then close **C29-E03-SBSurvey.docx**.

**Figure 29.10 Exercise 29.3C**

# STORYTELLER BOOKS

4350 Jenkins Boulevard
Glen Ellyn, IL 60137
(630) 555-7998

### READER SURVEY

*To help us serve you better, please take a moment to complete this survey.*

| | |
|---|---|
| Today's date | March 10, 2015 |
| How often do you read? | Daily |
| Do you read for work? | Yes |
| Do you read for pleasure or entertainment? | Yes |
| What do you prefer to read for work? | Trade publications |
| What do you prefer to read for entertainment? | Books |
| Where do you prefer to shop? | In store |
| Comments: I do most of my shopping in the store, but I am going to start ordering online in the near future. | |

# Creating a Form with Legacy Tools

Click the Legacy Tools button in the Controls group on the DEVELOPER tab and a drop-down list displays with a number of form fields that you can insert into a form. You can insert a text, check box, or drop-down list form field.

Legacy Tools

## Inserting a Text Form Field

The text form field in the Legacy Tools drop-down list is similar to the plain text content control. To insert a text form field, position the insertion point in the desired location, click the Legacy Tools button in the Controls group on the DEVELOPER tab, and then click the Text Form Field button. This inserts a gray shaded box in the form. This shaded box is where the respondent enters data when filling in the form. (If the form is printed, the shading does not print.) You can turn off the gray shading by clicking the Form Field Shading button in the Legacy Tools drop-down list. If the gray shading is turned off, click the button again to turn it back on.

**Insert a Text Form Field**
1. Click DEVELOPER tab.
2. Click Legacy Tools button.
3. Click Text Form Field button.

1. Open **LAApp01.docx** and then save it as a template by completing the following:
   a. Press the F12 key to display the Save As dialog box.
   b. At the Save As dialog box, type **XXXLAApp01Template** in the *File name* text box (typing your initials in place of the *XXX*).
   c. Click the *Save as type* option box and then click *Word Template (*.dotx)* at the drop-down list.
   d. Click the Save button.
2. Insert a text form field by completing the followng steps. (Figure 29.11 on the next page shows the filled-in form.)
   a. Click the DEVELOPER tab.
   b. Position the insertion point one space to the right of the colon after the *Name:* field below the heading *FIRST APPLICANT*.
   c. Click the Legacy Tools button in the Controls group on the DEVELOPER tab and then click the Text Form Field button.

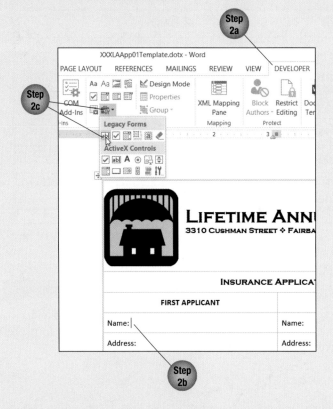

3. Complete steps similar to those in Steps 2b and 2c to insert a text form field one space to the right of the colon in each of the following data fields in the *FIRST APPLICANT* and *SECOND APPLICANT* sections: *Name:*, *Address:*, *Date of Birth:*, and *Occupation:*.
4. Click the Save button on the Quick Access toolbar to save the template.

**Figure 29.11 Exercises 29.4B and 29.4C**

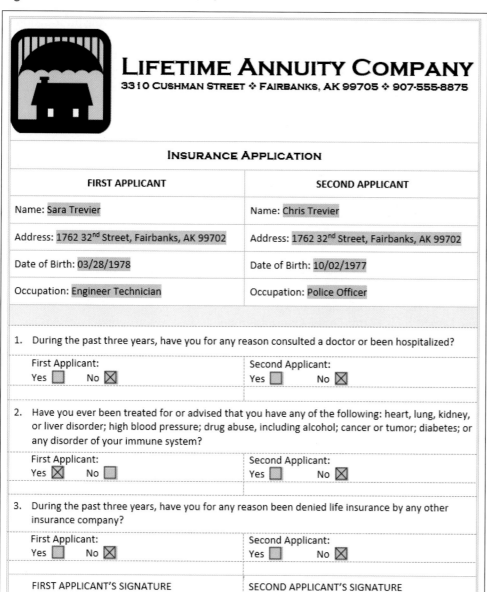

# LIFETIME ANNUITY COMPANY
### 3310 CUSHMAN STREET ❖ FAIRBANKS, AK 99705 ❖ 907-555-8875

### INSURANCE APPLICATION

| FIRST APPLICANT | SECOND APPLICANT |
|---|---|
| Name: Sara Trevier | Name: Chris Trevier |
| Address: 1762 32nd Street, Fairbanks, AK 99702 | Address: 1762 32nd Street, Fairbanks, AK 99702 |
| Date of Birth: 03/28/1978 | Date of Birth: 10/02/1977 |
| Occupation: Engineer Technician | Occupation: Police Officer |

1. During the past three years, have you for any reason consulted a doctor or been hospitalized?

   First Applicant: Yes ☐  No ☒   |   Second Applicant: Yes ☐  No ☒

2. Have you ever been treated for or advised that you have any of the following: heart, lung, kidney, or liver disorder; high blood pressure; drug abuse, including alcohol; cancer or tumor; diabetes; or any disorder of your immune system?

   First Applicant: Yes ☒  No ☐   |   Second Applicant: Yes ☐  No ☒

3. During the past three years, have you for any reason been denied life insurance by any other insurance company?

   First Applicant: Yes ☐  No ☒   |   Second Applicant: Yes ☐  No ☒

| FIRST APPLICANT'S SIGNATURE | SECOND APPLICANT'S SIGNATURE |
|---|---|
| | |

**Insert a Check Box
Form Field**
1. Click DEVELOPER
tab.
2. Click Legacy Tools
button.
3. Click Check Box
Form Field button.

# Inserting a Check Box Form Field

You can insert a check box form field where you want the person entering information to insert a check mark (*X*) or leave the check box blank. Check boxes are useful in forms for indicating *Yes* and *No* and for inserting options where the respondent inserts check marks for specific options. To insert a check box form field, click the Legacy Tools button in the Controls group on the DEVELOPER tab and then click the Check Box Form Field button at the drop-down list.

---

**Exercise 29.** 1B    Inserting Check Box Form Fields                                 Part 2 of 4

1. With **XXXLAApp01Template.dotx** open, insert a check box by completing the following steps:
   a. Move the insertion point so it is positioned two spaces to the right of the *Yes* with the heading *First Applicant* below the first question.
   b. Make sure the DEVELOPER tab is active.
   c. Click the Legacy Tools button in the Controls group.
   d. Click the Check Box Form Field button at the drop-down list.

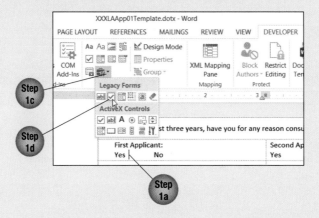

2. Complete steps similar to those in Steps 1c and 1d to insert the remaining check boxes for the *Yes* and *No* responses below questions 1, 2, and 3 (refer to Figure 29.11 on the previous page).
3. Protect the template and only allow filling in the form. (Refer to Exercise 29.1A, Step 14 on page 1010.)
4. Save and then close **XXXLAApp01Template.dotx**.

---

Fill in a form with text and check box form fields in the same manner as filling in a form with content controls. To fill in the form, open a document based on the template and type the information in the data field. Press the Tab key to move to the next field or press Shift + Tab to move to the previous field. You can also click in the desired data field and then type the information. To insert a check mark in a check box, press the spacebar or use the mouse to click in the desired field.

1. Create a form document from the **XXXLAApp01Template.dotx** template as shown in Figure 29.11. To begin, click the FILE tab and then click the *New* option.
2. At the New backstage area, click the *PERSONAL* option.
3. Click the *XXXLAApp01Template* thumbnail.
4. Word displays the form document with the insertion point positioned in the first form field after *Name:*. Type the name **Sara Trevier**.

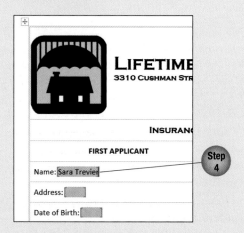

5. Press the Tab key to move to the next form field.
6. Fill in the remaining text and check box form fields as shown in Figure 29.11. Press the Tab key to move to the next data field or press Shift + Tab to move to the previous data field. To insert an *X* in a check box, make the check box active and then press the spacebar.
7. When the form is completed, save the document in your Chapter29 folder with the name **C29-E04-TrevierApp**.
8. Print **C29-E04-TrevierApp.docx**.

# Printing a Form

After filling in a form document, you can print the document in the normal manner. In some situations, you may want to print only the data (not the entire form) or print the form without the filled-in data.

If you are using a preprinted form that is inserted in the printer, you will want to print only the data. Word will print the data in the same location on the page as it appears in the form document. To print only the data in a form, display the Word Options dialog box and then click the *Advanced* option in the left panel. Scroll down the dialog box and then click the *Print only the data from a form* option in the *When printing this document* section.

When you print the form data in Exercise 29.4D, the table gridlines will print as well as the shading and clip art image. If you do not want these elements to print, remove them from the form.

1. With **C29-E04-TrevierApp.docx** open, specify that you want to print only the data by completing the following steps:
   a. Click the FILE tab and then click *Options.*
   b. At the Word Options dialog box, click *Advanced* in the left panel.
   c. Scroll down the dialog box to the *When printing this document* section and then click the *Print only the data from a form* option.
   d. Click OK to close the Word Options dialog box.

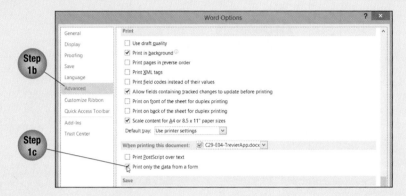

   e. Click the FILE tab, click the *Print* option, and then click the Print button at the Print backstage area.
2. Remove the check mark from the *Print only the data from a form* option by completing the following steps:
   a. Click the FILE tab and then click *Options.*
   b. At the Word Options dialog box, click *Advanced* in the left panel.
   c. Scroll down the dialog box to the *When printing this document* section and then click the *Print only the data from a form* option to remove the check mark.
   d. Click OK to close the Word Options dialog box.
3. Save and then close **C29-E04-TrevierApp.docx**.

# Customizing Form Field Options

A text form field contains default settings and some of these defaults can be changed with options at the Text Form Field Options dialog box. You can also change some of the default settings for a check box form field with options at the Check Box Form Field Options dialog box. Previously in this chapter, you learned how to insert a drop-down list content control. You can also insert a drop-down list form field and then change default settings with options at the Drop-Down Form Field Options dialog box.

## Creating a Drop-down List Form Field

If you want a field to provide a number of options from which a respondent can choose when filling in the form, insert a drop-down list form field. To do this, click the Legacy Tools button in the Controls group on the DEVELOPER tab and then click the Drop-Down Form Field button at the drop-down list. To insert the choices, click the Properties button in the Controls group. This displays the Drop-Down Form Field Options dialog box, as shown in Figure 29.12 on the next page.

**Figure 29.12 Drop-down Form Field Options Dialog Box**

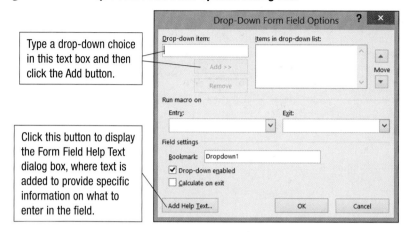

Type a drop-down choice in this text box and then click the Add button.

Click this button to display the Form Field Help Text dialog box, where text is added to provide specific information on what to enter in the field.

At the dialog box, type the first option in the *Drop-down item* text box and then click the Add button. This inserts the item in the *Items in drop-down list* list box. Continue in this manner until you have inserted all of the drop-down list items. You can remove drop-down list items from the *Items in drop-down list* list box by clicking the item and then clicking the Remove button. When all of the items you want to include display in the list box, click OK to close the dialog box.

If you want to provide instructional text for respondents who are filling in the form, click the Add Help Text button located in the lower left corner of the Drop-Down Form Field Options dialog box. This displays the Form Field Help Text dialog box with the Status Bar tab selected. At the dialog box, click the *Type your own* option and then type the text you want to display when the field is active. The text you type displays in the Status bar when the respondent is filling in the form.

To fill in a drop-down list form field, click the down-pointing arrow at the right of the field and then click the desired option at the drop-down list. You can also display the drop-down list by pressing the F4 key or holding down the Alt key and then pressing the Down Arrow key.

**QUICK STEPS**

**Create a Drop-down Form Field**
1. Click DEVELOPER tab.
2. Click Legacy Tools button.
3. Click Drop-Down Form Field button.
4. Click Properties button.
5. Type first list option.
6. Click Add button.
7. Continue typing desired choices and clicking Add button.
8. Click OK.

**Exercise 29.5    Inserting Drop-down Form Fields and Filling in a Form    Part 1 of 1**

1. Open **LAApp02.docx** and then save the document as a template named **XXXLAApp02Template. dotx** in the Custom Office Templates folder.
2. Insert a drop-down form field. (Figure 29.13 on page 1033 shows the filled-in form.)
   a. Position the insertion point one space to the right of the colon after *Nonprofit Employer:*.
   b. Click the DEVELOPER tab.
   c. Click the Legacy Tools button in the Controls group and then click the Drop-Down Form Field button.

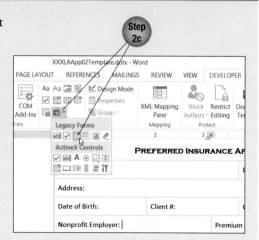

Step 2c

3. Insert the drop-down list choices and create instructional text by completing the following steps:

   a. With the insertion point positioned immediately right of the drop-down form field, click the Properties button in the Controls group on the DEVELOPER tab.

   b. At the Drop-Down Form Field Options dialog box, type **College** in the *Drop-down item* text box.

   c. Click the Add button.

   d. Type **Public School** in the *Drop-down item* text box.

   e. Click the Add button.

   f. Type **Private School** in the *Drop-down item* text box.

   g. Click the Add button.

   h. Click the Add Help Text button that displays in the lower left corner of the dialog box.

   i. At the Form Field Help Text dialog box with the Status Bar tab selected, click the *Type your own* option.

   j. Type the text **Click the down-pointing arrow at the right side of the Nonprofit Employer form field and then click the employer at the drop-down list.** in the text box.

   k. Click OK to close the Form Field Help Text dialog box.

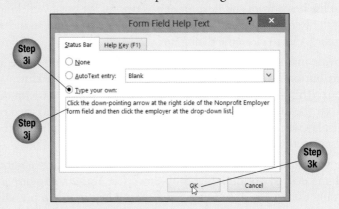

   l. Click OK to close the Drop-Down Form Field Options dialog box.

4. Insert a drop-down form field one space after the colon that follows *Premium Payments:* and complete steps similar to those in Step 3 to insert the following items at the Drop-Down Form Field Options dialog box: *Annually*, *Semiannually*, and *Quarterly*.

5. Insert text form fields (using the Text Form Field button from the Legacy Tools drop-down list) one space following the colon after each of the following: *Name:*, *Date:*, *Address:*, *Date of Birth:*, and *Client #:*.

6. Insert check box form fields two spaces to the right of *Female* and *Male* following *Gender:* and to the right of *Yes* and *No* in the questions.

7. Protect the template and allow filling in the form. (Refer to Exercise 29.1A, Step 14 on page 1010.)

8. Save and then close **XXXLAApp02Template.dotx**.

9. Create a form document from the **XXXLAApp02Template.dotx** template and fill in the form as shown in Figure 29.13 on the next page. To begin, click the FILE tab and then click the *New* option.

10. At the New backstage area, click the *PERSONAL* option.

11. Click the *XXXLAApp02Template* thumbnail.

12. Enter the data in the data fields as shown in Figure 29.13. (To insert *Public School* in the *Nonprofit Employer* drop-down form field, click the down-pointing arrow at the right of the field and then click *Public School* at the drop-down list. [Notice the instructional text that displays in the Status bar.] Complete similar steps to insert *Quarterly* in the *Premium Payments* drop-down form field.)

13. When the form is completed, save the document with the name **C29-E05-ReynoldsApp**.

14. Print and then close **C29-E05-ReynoldsApp.docx**.

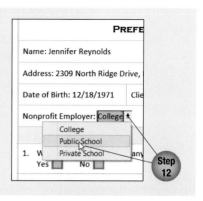

**Figure 29.13 Exercise 29.5**

# LIFETIME ANNUITY COMPANY
### 3310 CUSHMAN STREET ✦ FAIRBANKS, AK 99705 ✦ 907-555-8875

### PREFERRED INSURANCE APPLICATION

| | |
|---|---|
| Name: Jennifer Reynolds | Date: 03/10/2015 |

Address: 2309 North Ridge Drive, Fairbanks, AK 99708

| | | |
|---|---|---|
| Date of Birth: 12/18/1971 | Client #: 210-322 | Gender:  Female ☒   Male ☐ |

| | |
|---|---|
| Nonprofit Employer: Public School | Premium Payments: Quarterly |

1. Will this insurance replace any existing insurance or annuity?
   Yes ☒    No ☐

2. Within the past three years has your driver's license been suspended or revoked, or have you been convicted for driving under the influence of alcohol or drugs?
   Yes ☐    No ☒

3. Do you have any intention of traveling or residing outside the United States or Canada within the next twelve months?
   Yes ☐    No ☒

APPLICANT'S SIGNATURE: _____    DATE: _____

## Customizing Check Box Form Field Options

You can change check box form field options at the Check Box Form Field Options dialog box. Display this dialog box by selecting a check box form field and then clicking the Properties button in the Controls group on the DEVELOPER tab. By default, Word inserts a check box in a form template document in the same size as the adjacent text. You can change the default setting of *Auto* to *Exactly* and then type the desired point size in the text box. A check box form field is empty by default. If you want the check box to be checked by default, click the *Checked* option in the *Default value* section of the dialog box. You can also select and then apply formatting to a check box.

---

**Exercise 29.6A**    **Inserting and Customizing Check Box Form Fields**        Part 1 of 2

1. Open **LAApp03.docx** and then save the document as a template named **XXXLAApp03Template.dotx**.
2. Insert a check box that contains a check mark by completing the following steps. (Figure 29.14 on page 1036 shows the filled-in form.)
   a. Position the insertion point two spaces to the right of the *Yes* located below the *Are you currently working?* question.
   b. Click the DEVELOPER tab, click the Legacy Tools button in the Controls group, and then click the Check Box Form Field button at the drop-down list.
   c. With the insertion point positioned immediately right of the check box form field, click the Properties button in the Controls group.
   d. At the Check Box Form Field Options dialog box, click the *Checked* option in the *Default value* section.
   e. Click OK.
3. Complete steps similar to those in Step 2 to insert to the right of *Yes* below the *Do you work full time?* question a check box that contains a check mark.
4. Insert the remaining check boxes for questions 1, 2, and 3 (without check marks).
5. Insert a drop-down field two spaces after the question mark that ends question 4 and insert the following items at the Drop-Down Form Field Options dialog box: *Standard*, *Premium*, *Gold*, and *Platinum*.
6. Insert a drop-down field two spaces after the question mark that ends question 5 and insert the following items at the Drop-Down Form Field Options dialog box: *Standard*, *Premium*, *Gold*, and *Platinum*.
7. Save the template.

---

## Customizing Text Form Fields

To change options for a text form field, select the form field (or position the insertion point immediately right of the form field) and then click the Properties button in the Controls group on the DEVELOPER tab. This displays the Text Form Field Options dialog box. At this dialog box, you can change the type of text you want inserted in the field. The default setting at the *Type* option box is *Regular text*. You can change this to *Number*, *Date*, *Current date*, *Current time*, or *Calculation*.

If you change the *Type* option, Word displays an error message if the correct type of information is not entered in the form field. For example, if you change the *Type* option to *Number*, a respondent filling in the form can only enter a number. If the respondent tries to enter something other than a number, Word displays an error message and selects the entry, and the insertion point stays in the form field until a number is entered. If a particular text form field generally requires the same information, type that information in the *Default text* box and that text will always display in the form field. When the form is filled in, the respondent can leave the default text in the form field or type over the text. Use the *Maximum length* option at the dialog box to specify an exact number of characters for the form field. This option has a default setting of *Unlimited*.

Apply formatting to text in a form field with options in the *Text format* option box. For example, if you want to display text in all uppercase letters, click the down-pointing arrow at the right of the *Text format* option box and then click *Uppercase* at the drop-down list. When the respondent has typed text in the form field, that text is automatically converted to uppercase letters as soon as the respondent presses the Tab key or the Enter key. The *Text format* options vary depending on what is selected in the *Type* option box. You can also select a form field, apply formatting, and then use Format Painter to apply the same formatting to other form fields.

---

## Exercise 29.6B  Customizing Text Form Fields  Part 2 of 2

1. With **XXXLAApp03Template.dotx** open, create a custom text form field by completing the following steps:
   a. Position the insertion point one space to the right of the colon after *Type of Program:*.
   b. Insert a text box form field by clicking the Legacy Tools button in the Controls group and then clicking the Text Form Field button at the drop-down list.
   c. Most employees are enrolled in a family insurance program. Reflect this by making *Family* the default setting for the text form field. To do this, make sure the insertion point is positioned immediately right of the text form field and then click the Properties button.
   d. At the Text Form Field Options dialog box, type **Family** in the *Default text* box.
   e. Click OK to close the dialog box.
2. Create a custom text form field for the *State:* form field that specifies the field must contain two uppercase letters. Do this by completing the following steps:
   a. Position the insertion point one space to the right of the colon after *State:*.
   b. Insert a text box form field by clicking the Legacy Tools button in the Controls group and then clicking the Text Form Field button at the drop-down list.
   c. Click the Properties button.
   d. At the Text Form Field Options dialog box, click the up-pointing arrow at the right of the *Maximum length* measurement box until *2* displays.
   e. Click the down-pointing arrow at the right of the *Text format* option box and then click *Uppercase*.

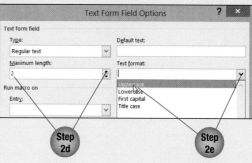

f.  Click OK to close the Text Form Field Options dialog box.
3.  Complete steps similar to those in Step 2 to create a custom text form field for the *Zip Code:* form field that specifies a maximum length of 5 characters for the field.
4.  Complete steps similar to those in Step 2 to create a custom text form field for the *Policy #:* form field that specifies a maximum length of 6 characters for the field.
5.  Protect the template and only allow filling in the form.
6.  Save and then close **XXXLAApp03Template.dotx**.
7.  Create a form document from the **XXXLAApp03Template.dotx** template and fill in the form as shown in Figure 29.14. (Type **ak** in the *State:* data field and then press the Tab key. This changes the text to uppercase letters.)
8.  When the form is completed, save the document with the name **C29-E06-MurciaApp**.
9.  Print and then close **C29-E06-MurciaApp.docx**.

**Figure 29.14  Exercise 29.6B**

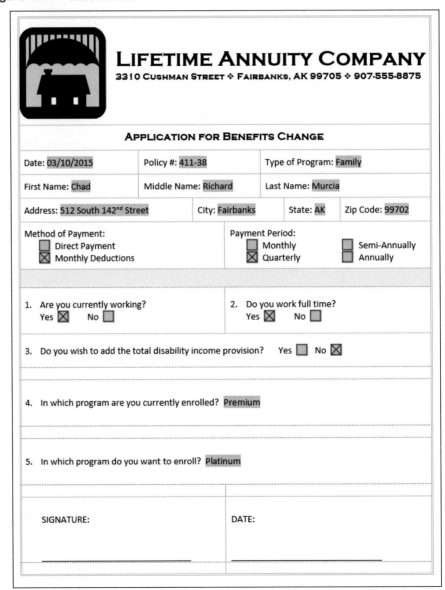

# Modifying Tab Order

Tabbing in a fill-in form moves to fields from left to right because that is the normal way an English-language speaking person reads a document. In some forms, you may want to change the tab order so that pressing the Tab key in a fill-in form makes active the next field down instead of the field to the right. Changing tab order is useful for forms in which a person will read down the page instead of across, for forms that may be translated into a language that reads from top to bottom instead of left to right, and for forms that will be read by a reading program for someone who is visually impaired.

When you press the Tab key in a fill-in form, Word automatically makes the next field to the right active. To change the tab order, you need to specify a macro that will run when exiting the field. The macros for the fields in the form in Exercise 29.7 have been written and are included in the LAApp04.docm document. You will use these macros to specify the tab order in the document. Specify a macro to run when exiting a field by displaying the options dialog box for the field, clicking the down-pointing arrow at the right of the *Exit* option box, and then clicking the macro at the drop-down list.

*Note: If you want to view the macro VBA (visual basic for applications) coding, open the LAApp04.docm macro-enabled document, click the VIEW tab, and then click the Macros button in the Macros group. At the Macros dialog box, click the macro name in the list box and then click the Edit button. This displays the macro in the Microsoft Visual Basic for Applications window. After viewing the macro code, close the window by clicking the Close button in the upper right corner of the window.*

| Exercise 29. | Modifying Tab Order in a Form | Part 1 of 1 |
| --- | --- | --- |

1. Open **LAApp04.docm**, which is a macro-enabled document, by completing the following steps:
   a. Press Ctrl + F12 to display the Open dialog box.
   b. Make sure the option box to the right of the *File name* text box displays with *All Files (*.*)*. If it does not, click the option box and then click *All Files (*.*)* at the drop-down list.
   c. Navigate to your Chapter29 folder and then double-click ***LAApp04.docm***.
   d. When the document opens, click the Enable Content button that displays in the yellow message bar below the ribbon.
   e. If a message displays asking if you want to make the document a trusted document, click the Yes button.
2. Save the document with Save As and name it **C29-E07-LAApp04**. (The document will be saved as a macro-enabled document with the file extension *.docm*.)

3. Specify the exit macro for the *First Name* field by completing the following steps:
   a. Double-click the *First Name* field to display the Text Form Field Options dialog box.
   b. At the Text Form Field Options dialog box, click the down-pointing arrow at the right side of the *Exit* option box and then click *TabtoLastName* at the drop-down list. (This macro tells Word to make the *Last Name* field active when the Tab key is pressed rather than the *Date of Birth* field.)

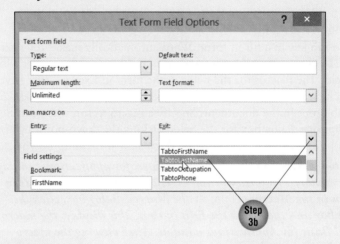

   c. Click the OK button.
4. Double-click the *Last Name* field and then specify the *TabtoAddress* macro as the exit macro.
5. Double-click the *Address* field and then specify the *TabtoDOB* macro as the exit macro.
6. Double-click the *Date of Birth* field and then specify the *TabtoOccupation* macro as the exit macro.
7. Double-click the *Occupation* field and then specify the *TabtoPhone* macro as the exit macro.
8. Protect the document and allow filling in the form.
9. Save and then close **C29-E07-LAApp04.docm**.
10. Create a form with the **C29-E07-LAApp04.docm** document by completing the following steps:
    a. Open **C29-E07-LAApp04.docm**. (Make sure the Open dialog box displays all of the files.)
    b. When the document opens in Read mode, click the Enable Content button that displays in the yellow message bar below the ribbon.
    c. Click the VIEW tab in Read mode and then click the *Edit Document* option.
    d. Type the following data in the specified field in the form:
       *Policy Number:* **10-A-321**
       *First Name:* **Lindsay**
       *Last Name:* **Harris**
       *Address:* **3002 N. 42nd St., Fairbanks, AK 99703**
       *Date of Birth:* **11/03/1985**
       *Occupation:* **Physical Therapist**
       *Phone Number:* **(907) 555-3175**
11. Save the document with Save As and name it **C29-E07-LAAppHarris**.
12. Print and then close **C29-E07-LAAppHarris.docm**.

# Chapter *Summary*

- A form is created as a template document with data fields that can be filled in with different information each time the template document is used.

- Three basic steps are involved in creating a form: designing the form document based on a template and building the structure of the form; inserting data fields in which information will be entered with the keyboard; and saving the form as a protected document.

- Save a form as a template at the Save As dialog box by changing the *Save as type* option to *Word Template (*.dotx)*. A template is automatically saved in the Custom Office Templates folder in the Documents folder on the computer's hard drive.

- Insert content controls with buttons on the DEVELOPER tab. Display this tab by displaying the Word Options dialog box, clicking *Customize Ribbon* in the left panel, clicking the Developer tab check box in the list box at the right, and then clicking OK.

- The Plain Text Content Control button on the DEVELOPER tab inserts a control that takes on the format of the text that surrounds it.

- Use options at the Restrict Editing task pane to protect a template. You can protect a template so respondents can enter information in the form but cannot edit the form. Display the task pane by clicking the Restrict Editing button in the Protect group on the DEVELOPER tab.

- To open a template for editing, display the Open dialog box, click the *Documents* folder in the Navigation pane, double-click the *Custom Office Templates* folder in Content pane and then double-click the form template.

- To edit a form template, stop protection of the template, make the desired changes, and then protect the template.

- Include instructional text in a content control by clicking the Plain Text Content Control button on the DEVELOPER tab and then typing the instructional text.

- Use the Picture Content Control button on the DEVELOPER tab to insert a picture content control in a form, use the Date Picker Content Control button to insert a date picker content control, and use the Drop-Down List Content Control button to insert a drop-down list of choices for a data field.

- Insert a combo box content control if you want to provide a drop-down list of choices and let respondents enter their own data.

- Click the Properties button on the DEVELOPER tab to change the properties of the selected content control. This displays the Content Control Properties dialog box. The contents of this dialog box vary depending on what content control is selected.

- The Legacy Tools button in the Controls group on the DEVELOPER tab contains buttons for inserting text, check box, and drop-down list form fields into a form.

- A text form field is similar to a plain text content control. Insert a text form field by clicking the Legacy Tools button on the DEVELOPER tab and then clicking the Text Form Field button at the drop-down list.

- Insert a check box form field in a form in which you want the respondent to choose an option by inserting an *X* in the check box.

- Print a filled-in form in the normal manner or print only the data. To print only the data, display the Word Options dialog box with *Advanced* selected and then insert a check mark in the *Print only the data from a form* check box in the *When printing this document* section.

- Create a drop-down list of choices by inserting a drop-down list form field and then typing choices in the Drop-Down Form Field Options dialog box. Display this dialog box by inserting a drop-down list form field and then clicking the Properties button on the DEVELOPER tab.

- To fill in a form with a drop-down list form field, the respondent clicks the down-pointing arrow at the right of the form field and then clicks the desired option at the drop-down list. Another way to display the drop-down list is to press the F4 key or hold down the Alt key and then press the Down Arrow key.
- Customize check box form field options at the Check Box Form Field Options dialog box. Display this dialog box by inserting a check box form field and then clicking the Properties button on the DEVELOPER tab.
- Customize text form field options at the Text Form Field Options dialog box. Display this dialog box by inserting a text form field and then clicking the Properties button on the DEVELOPER tab.

# *Commands* Review

| FEATURE | RIBBON TAB, GROUP | BUTTON, OPTION | KEYBOARD SHORTCUT |
|---|---|---|---|
| check box form field | DEVELOPER, Controls | , Check Box Form Field | |
| Check Box Form Field Options dialog box | DEVELOPER, Controls | , Check Box Form Field, | |
| content control properties | DEVELOPER, Controls | | |
| date picker content control | DEVELOPER, Controls | | |
| drop-down list content control | DEVELOPER, Controls | | |
| drop-down list form field | DEVELOPER, Controls | , Drop-Down Form Field | |
| Drop-Down List Form Field Options dialog box | DEVELOPER, Controls | , Drop-Down Form Field, | |
| Legacy Tools drop-down list | DEVELOPER, Controls | | |
| New backstage area | FILE | *New* | |
| next data field | | | Tab |
| picture content control | DEVELOPER, Controls | | |
| plain text content control | DEVELOPER, Controls | Aa | |
| previous data field | | | Shift + Tab |
| Restrict Editing task pane | DEVELOPER, Protect | | |
| text form field | DEVELOPER, Controls | , Text Form Field | |
| Text Form Field Options dialog box | DEVELOPER, Controls | , Text Form Field, | |
| Word Options dialog box | FILE | *Options* | |

# Key Points Review

**Completion:** In the space provided at the right, indicate the correct term, symbol, or command.

1. By default, a template is saved in this folder in the Documents folder.

2. Click the Restrict Editing button on the DEVELOPER tab and this task pane displays.  _____

3. This group on the DEVELOPER tab contains content control buttons.  _____

4. When filling in a form, press this key to move to the next data field.  _____

5. Click this button on the DEVELOPER tab to insert a picture frame containing a picture icon.  _____

6. Click this button on the DEVELOPER tab to insert a date content control.  _____

7. Insert this type of content control in a form if you want the respondent to choose from a specific list of options.  _____

8. Customize a date picker content control with options at this dialog box.  _____

9. The Legacy Tools button is located in this group on the DEVELOPER tab.  _____

10. When you insert a text form field, this is inserted in the form.  _____

11. Insert this type of form field if you want the respondent to choose an option by inserting an *X*.  _____

12. To print only the form data, display the Word Options dialog box with this option selected and then insert a check mark in the *Print only the data from a form* check box.  _____

13. If you want the respondent to insert data in a data field by choosing from a list, insert this type of form field.  _____

14. To display a check box in a form with an *X* automatically inserted in the form field, click this option at the Check Box Form Field Options dialog box.  _____

15. With the insertion point positioned immediately right of a text form field, click this button on the DEVELOPER tab to display the Text Form Field Options dialog box.  _____

# Chapter Assessments

## Applying Your Skills

Demonstrate your knowledge of features learned in this chapter by completing the following assessments.

### Assessment 29.1    Create and Fill in a Book Order Form

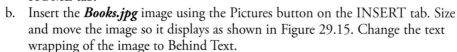

1. Create the form shown in Figure 29.15 with the following specifications:
   a. At a blank document, click the *No Spacing* style in the Styles group on the HOME tab.
   b. Insert the ***Books.jpg*** image using the Pictures button on the INSERT tab. Size and move the image so it displays as shown in Figure 29.15. Change the text wrapping of the image to Behind Text.
   c. Set the company name, *STORYTELLER BOOKS*, in 22-point Candara and apply bold formatting. Set the remainder of the text in 11-point Candara and apply bold formatting. Insert the book symbol at the Symbol dialog box with the *Wingdings* font selected. (The book symbol is in the first row of the symbol list box.)
   d. Insert a plain text content control one space after the colon for each of the following: *Name:*, *Book Title:*, *Author:*, *Email:*, *Telephone:*, and *Notes:*.
   e. Insert the horizontal line by holding down the Shift key, pressing the hyphen key three times, and then pressing the Enter key.
2. Protect the document and only allow filling in the form. (Do not enter a password.)
3. Save the document as a template in the Custom Office Templates folder and name it **XXXBookRequestTemplate** (using your initials in place of the *XXX*).
4. Close **XXXBookRequestTemplate.dotx**.

**Figure 29.15  Assessment 29.1**

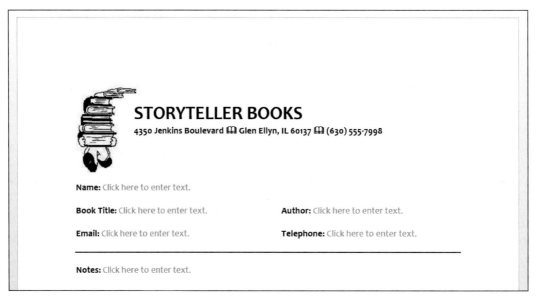

5. Create a form document from the **XXXBookRequestTemplate** template by completing the following steps:
   a. Click the FILE tab and then click the *New* option. At the New backstage area, click the *PERSONAL* option and then click the *XXXBookRequestTemplate* thumbnail (where your initials display in place of the *XXX*).
   b. Insert the following data in the specified fields:
      *Name:* **Chris Felder**
      *Book Title:* **I Know Why the Caged Bird Sings**
      *Author:* **Maya Angelou**
      *Email:* **cfelder@emcp.net**
      *Telephone:* **(630) 555-8965**
      *Notes:* **I am interested in purchasing a paperback version either new or used.**
6. Save the document with the name **C29-A01-SBRequest**.
7. Print and then close **C29-A01-SBRequest.docx**.

## Assessment 29.2    Create and Fill in a Catalog Request Form

1. Open **SBCatRequest.docx** and then save the document as a template in the Custom Office Templates folder and name it **XXXCatalogRequestTemplate.dotx** (typing your initials in place of the *XXX*).
2. Create the form shown in Figure 29.16 with the following specifications:
   a. Insert a picture content control in the cell in the upper right corner of the table and then insert the image named **Books.jpg**. (Make sure you center-align the picture content control in the cell and specify that the picture content cannot be edited.)
   b. Insert plain text content controls for *Name:*, *Address:*, *City:*, *State:*, *Zip Code:*, *Email:*, and *Telephone:*.
   c. Insert a date picker content control for *Date:* that inserts the date with the month spelled out followed by the day and year in numbers.
   d. Insert a drop-down list content control for *Preferred Shipping Method:* that offers the following choices: *USPS Standard*, *USPS Priority*, *FedEx Standard*, and *FedEx Overnight*.

**Figure 29.16  Assessment 29.2**

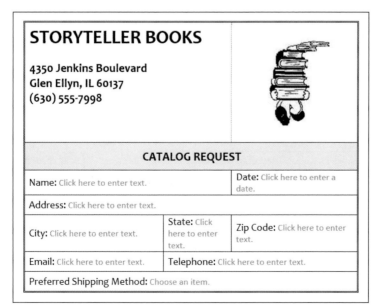

3. Protect the template. (You do not need to enter a password.)
4. Save and then close **XXXCatalogRequestTemplate.dotx**.
5. Create a form document from the **XXXCatalogRequestTemplate** template and insert the following data in the specified fields:

   *Name:* **Donna Hendrix**
   *Date: Insert the current date.*
   *Address:* **2123 North Myers**
   *City:* **St. Charles**
   *State:* **IL**
   *Zip Code:* **60125**
   *Email:* **dhendrix@emcp.net**
   *Telephone:* **(630) 555-3204**
   *Preferred Shipping Method: Choose* USPS Priority *from the drop-down list.*
6. Save the document with the name **C29-A02-SBHendrixCatReq**.
7. Print and then close **C29-A02-SBHendrixCatReq.docx**.

## Assessment 29.3   Create and Fill in an Application Form

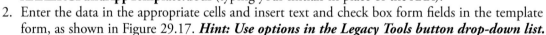

1. Open **ERCFundingApp.docx** and then save the document as a template in the Custom Office Templates folder and name it **XXXERCFundAppTemplate.dotx** (typing your initials in place of the *XXX*).
2. Enter the data in the appropriate cells and insert text and check box form fields in the template form, as shown in Figure 29.17. ***Hint: Use options in the Legacy Tools button drop-down list.***
3. Protect the template and only allow filling in the form. (You do not need to enter a password.)
4. Save and then close **XXXERCFundAppTemplate.dotx**.

**Figure 29.17 Assessment 29.3**

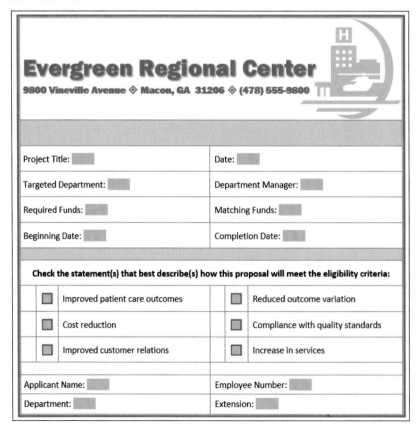

5. Create a form document from the **XXXERCFundAppTemplate.dotx** template and insert the following data in the specified fields:

> *Project Title:* **Quality Improvement Project**
> *Date:* (*Insert current date*)
> *Targeted Department:* **Pediatrics**
> *Department Manager:* **Angela Gilmore**
> *Required Funds:* **$50,000**
> *Matching Funds:* **$25,000**
> *Beginning Date:* **07/01/2015**
> *Completion Date:* **06/30/2016**
> *Insert an "X" in each of the check boxes* except *Cost reduction*
> *Applicant Name:* **Maria Alvarez**
> *Employee Number:* **321-4890**
> *Department:* **Pediatrics**
> *Extension:* **4539**

6. Save the document with the name **C29-A03-FundApp**.
7. Print and then close **C29-A03-FundApp.docx**.

## Assessment 29.4    Create and Fill in a Patient Update Form

1. Open **WCDSForm.docx** and then save the document as a template in the Custom Office Templates folder and name it **XXXWCDSFormTemplate.dotx** (typing your initials in place of the *XXX*).
2. Enter the data in the appropriate cells and insert form fields in the form shown in Figure 29.18 on the next page with the following specifications:
   a. Insert a text form field for *Patient Number:* that specifies a maximum length of 4 characters.
   b. Insert a text form field for *State:* that specifies a maximum length of 2 characters and a text format of Uppercase.
   c. Insert a text form field for *Zip Code:* that specifies a maximum length of 5 characters.
   d. Insert a text form field for *Medical Insurance:* that specifies *Premiere Group* as the default text.
   e. Insert a check box form field in the cell immediately left of *Both parents* that is checked by default.
   f. Insert a text form field for the first *Relationship:* data field that specifies *Mother* as the default text.
   g. Insert a text form field for the second *Relationship:* data field that specifies *Father* as the default text.
   h. Insert the remaining text and check box form fields as shown in Figure 29.18.
3. Protect the template and only allow filling in the form.
4. Save and then close **XXXWCDSFormTemplate.dotx**.
5. Create a form document from the **XXXWCDSFormTemplate.dotx** template and insert the following data in the specified fields:

> *Patient Name:* **Ethan Mark Springer**
> *Patient Number:* **4221**
> *Address:* **345 Jackson Court**
> *City:* **Bismarck**
> *State:* **nd** (This text will change to uppercase when you press Tab.)
> *Zip Code:* **58506**
> *Telephone:* **(701) 555-3481**
> *Medical Insurance:* (*Leave the default* Premiere Group.)
> (*Leave the check mark in the* Both parents *check box.*)
> *Relationship:* (*Leave the default* Mother.)
> *Relationship:* (*Leave the default* Father.)

*Name:* **Elizabeth Springer**
*Name:* **Chris Springer**
*Address:* **345 Jackson Court, Bismarck, ND 58506**
*Address:* **345 Jackson Court, Bismarck, ND 58506**
*Home Telephone:* **(701) 555-3481**
*Home Telephone:* **(701) 555-3481**
*Work Telephone:* **(701) 555-8711**
*Work Telephone:* **(701) 555-0075**

6. Save the document with the name **C29-A04-ESpringer**.
7. Print and then close **C29-A04-ESpringer.docx**.

**Figure 29.18 Assessment 29.4**

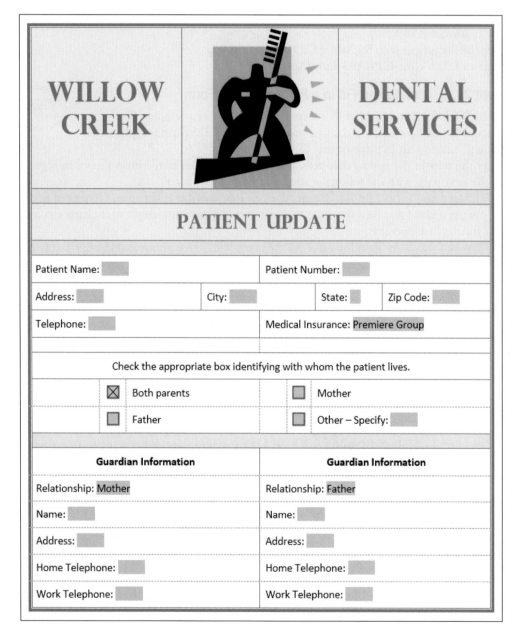

# Expanding Your Skills

Explore additional feature options or use Help to learn a new skill in creating this document.

**Assessment 29.5**  **Create a Client Information Form That Includes *Building Block* Gallery Content Controls**

1. The Controls group on the DEVELOPER tab contains additional buttons you can use when creating a form. In addition to the Legacy Tools check box form field, you can insert a check box with the Check Box Content Control. Use the Building Block Gallery Content Control button to insert a content control for inserting building blocks in a form. Experiment with the Check Box Content Control button and Building Block Gallery Content Control button to determine how to use them in a form and then open **BGBuildingBlocks.docx** and create the following building blocks:
   a. Select the name *Barrington & Gates*, the line below, and the text *Rachel Rasmussen, Associate* and then save the selected text in a custom building block in the *Quick Part* gallery named with your initials followed by *BGRR*.
   b. Select the name *Barrington & Gates*, the line below, and the text *Gerald Castello, Associate* and then save the selected text in a custom building block in the *Quick Part* gallery named with your initials followed by *BGGC*.
   c. Close **BGBuildingBlocks.docx**.
2. Open **BGClientInfo.docx** and then save the document as a template in the Custom Office Templates folder with the name **XXXBGClientInfo.dotx** (typing your initials in place of the *XXX*).
3. Add the following form fields to the form:
   a. Make the top cell active and then insert the building block gallery content control.
   b. Insert a check box (using the Check Box Content Control button) in the cell immediately left of each of the following cell entries: *Employee, Friend, Lawyer referral service, Yellow Pages, Internet,* and *Other*.
4. Because your template contains the building block gallery content control, you cannot protect it and only allow filling in the form. Doing this would keep you from being able to use the building block content control. Save and then close **XXXBGClientInfo.dotx**.
5. Create a form document from the **XXXBGClientInfo.dotx** template with the following specifications:
   a. Click the building block content control in the top cell, click the Quick Parts button that displays at the right of the content control tab, and then click the *BGGC* building block that is preceded by your initials.
   b. Fill in each text content control by clicking the text *Click here to enter text* and then typing text of your choosing. Click only one of the check box content controls in the *Referred by* section.
6. Save the completed form document with the name **C29-A05-GC-Client**.
7. Print and then close **C29-A05-GC-Client.docx**.
8. Create a form document from the **XXXBGClientInfo.dotx** template with the following specifications:
   a. Click the building block content control in the top cell, click the Quick Parts button that displays at the right of the content control tab, and then click the *BGRR* building block that is preceded by your initials.
   b. Fill in each text content control by clicking the text *Click here to enter text* and then typing text of your choosing. Click only one of the check box content controls in the *Referred by* section.
9. Save the completed form document with the name **C29-A05-RR-Client**.
10. Print and then close **C29-A05-RR-Client.docx**.

# Achieving Signature Status

Take your skills to the next level by completing these more challenging assessments.

## Assessment 29.6    Create and Fill in an Application Form

1. Create the form shown in Figure 29.19 as a template and use the table feature to create the columns and rows. Apply border and shading formatting as shown in the figure. Set the company name in the font Magneto and set the remaining text in Candara.
2. Insert a picture content control and insert the **SSAviation.jpg** image. Insert a date picker content control and plain text content controls in the appropriate cells. Insert drop-down list content controls for the two bottom rows in the table. Add the following options for the *Desired license:* drop-down list content control: *Private, Commercial, Instrument,* and *Certified Flight Instructor.* Add the following options for the *How did you hear about South Sound Aviation?* drop-down list content control: *Internet, Business card, Referral, Brochure,* and *Other.*
3. Protect the template and only allow filling in the form. Do not set a password.
4. Save the document as a template in your Chapter29 folder, name the template **XXXApplicationTemplate.dotx**, and then close the document.
5. Create a form document from the **XXXApplicationTemplate** template. You determine the data to enter in each data field.
6. Save the document with the name **C29-A06-FlightApp**.
7. Print and then close **C29-A06-FlightApp.docx**.

**Figure 29.19  Assessment 29.6**

| | | |
|---|---|---|
| *South Sound Aviation* 8994 Airport Boulevard Auburn, WA 98022 (425) 555-3311 OR (206) 555-9075 southsoundaviation@emcp.net | | |
| **FLIGHT TRAINING APPLICATION** | | |
| Name: | | Date: |
| Address: | | |
| City: | State: | Zip Code: |
| Email: | Home Phone: | Cell Phone: |
| Desired license: | | |
| How did you hear about South Sound Aviation? | | |

## Assessment 29.7    Create and Fill in a Secondary Payer Form

1. Create the form template and form fields shown in Figure 29.20 with the following specifications:
   a. Consider using **ERCFundingApp.docx** to help you create the form shown in Figure 29.20. (Make sure the gridlines display.)
   b. Create data fields, cells, shading, and other formatting as shown in Figure 29.20.
   c. Consider specifying text form field options for the *State:* and *Zip Code:* data fields.
2. Save the document as a template in your Chapter29 folder and name the template **XXXERCInsFormTemplate.dotx**.
3. Protect the template and only allow filling in the form without setting a password.
4. Save and then close **XXXERCInsFormTemplate.dotx**.
5. Create a form document from the **XXXERCInsFormTemplate.dotx** template and insert data of your choosing in each data field.
6. Save the document with the name **C29-A07-InsForm**.
7. Print and then close **C29-A07-InsForm.docx**.

**Figure 29.20  Assessment 29.7**

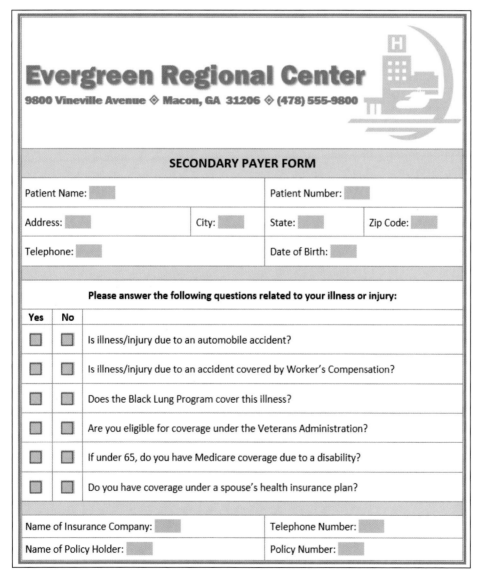

# Using Outline View and Formatting with Macros

## Performance Objectives

Upon successful completion of Chapter 30, you will be able to:

- Create an outline by assigning levels to titles, headings, and so on
- Create a master document and subdocuments
- Record, store, and name macros
- Run, pause, and delete macros
- Assign macros to keyboard commands or toolbars

- Specify macro security settings
- Save a macro-enabled document or template
- Record and run a macro with Fill-in fields

Use the outline feature in Word to view specific titles, headings, and body text in a document. With this feature, you can quickly see an overview of a document by collapsing parts of it so only specific titles and headings display. With the titles and headings collapsed, you can perform editing functions including moving and deleting sections of a document. For some documents, such as books and procedures manuals, consider creating master documents and subdocuments.

Word includes a time-saving feature called a *macro*, which automates the formatting of a document. The word *macro* was coined by computer programmers to label a collection of commands used to make a large programming job easier and faster.

*Note: Before beginning computer exercises, copy to your storage medium the Chapter30 folder located on the CD that accompanies this textbook and then make Chapter30 the active folder.*

In this chapter, students will produce the following documents:

Exercise 30.1. C30-E01-InternetSecurity.docx
Exercise 30.2. C30-E02-CompViruses.docx
Exercise 30.3A (Step 11). C30-E03-Newsletters.docx
Exercise 30.3B (Step 9). C30-E03-Newsletters.docx
Exercise 30.4B. C30-E04-WriteResume.docx
Exercise 30.4C. C30-E04-ResumeStandards.docx
Exercise 30.5. C30-E05-GSHLtr.docx
Exercise 30.6. C30-E06-TofC.docx
Exercise 30.7. C30-E07-Affidavit.docx

Model answers for these exercises are shown on the following pages.

UNAUTHORIZED ACCESS
    User IDs and Passwords
    System Backdoors
    Spyware
INFORMATION THEFT
    Device Security
    Data Browsing

**Exercise 30.1**

C30-E01-InternetSecurity.docx

HARDWARE AND SOFTWARE SECURITY RISKS
    Cracking Software for Copying
    Systems Failure
COMPUTER VIRUSES
    Types of Viruses
    Methods of Virus Operation

**Exercise 30.2**

C30-E02-CompViruses.docx

Model Answers

SECTION A: NEWSLETTERS

Preparing a newsletter requires a number of preliminary steps. Before determining the contents of the newsletter, determine the basic elements to be included in the newsletter, study newsletter design, and determine the purpose of the newsletter.

F:\Chapter30\MODULE 1.docx

F:\Chapter30\MODULE 2.docx

F:\Chapter30\MODULE 3.docx

F:\Chapter30\MODULE 4.docx

**Exercise 30.3A (Step 11)**

C30-E03-Newsletters.docx

SECTION A: NEWSLETTERS

Preparing a newsletter requires a number of preliminary steps. Before determining the contents of the newsletter, determine the basic elements to be included in the newsletter, study newsletter design, and determine the purpose of the newsletter.

One of the biggest challenges in creating a newsletter is balancing change with consistency. A newsletter is a document that is typically reproduced on a regular basis, whether monthly, bimonthly, or quarterly. With each issue, new ideas can be presented, new text created, and new graphics or photos used. However, for your newsletter to be effective, each issue must also maintain a consistent appearance. Consistency contributes to your publication's identity and gives your readers a feeling of familiarity.

F:\Chapter30\MODULE 1.docx

F:\Chapter30\MODULE 5.docx

F:\Chapter30\MODULE 3.docx

F:\Chapter30\MODULE 4.docx

**Exercise 30.3B (Step 9)**

C30-E03-Newsletters.docx

Model Answers

**RESUME PRESENTATION STANDARDS**

Presentation focuses on the way your resume looks. It relates to the fonts you use, the paper you print it on, any graphics you might include, and how many pages your resume should be.

*Typestyle*

Use a typestyle (font) that is clean, conservative, and easy to read. Stay away from anything that is too fancy, glitzy, curly, and the like. Your goal is to create a competitive-distinctive document and, to achieve that, we recommend an alternative typestyle. Your choice of typestyle should be dictated by the content, format, and length of your resume. Some fonts look better than others at smaller or larger sizes; some have "bolder" boldface type; some require more white space to make them readable. Once you have written your resume, experiment with a few different typestyles to see which one best enhances your document.

*Type Size*

Readability is everything! If the type size is too small, your resume will be difficult to read and difficult to skim for essential information. Interestingly, a too-large type size, particularly for senior-level professionals, can also give a negative impression by conveying a juvenile or unprofessional image. As a general rule, select type from 10 to 12 points in size. However, there is no hard-and-fast rule, and a lot depends on the typestyle you choose.

*Type Enhancements*

Bold, italics, underlining, and capitalization are ideal to highlight certain words, phrases, achievements, projects, numbers, and other information to which you want to draw special attention. However, do not overuse these enhancements. If your resume becomes too cluttered with special formatting, nothing stands out.

*Page Length*

For most industries and professions, the "one- to to-page rule" for resume writing still holds true. Keep it short and succinct, giving just enough information to pique your reader's interest. However, there are many instances when a resume can be longer than two pages.

> *You have an extensive list of technical qualifications that are relevant to the position for which you are applying.*
>
> *You have extensive educational training and numerous credential/certifications, all of which are important to include.*
>
> *You have an extensive list of special projects, task forces, and committees to include that are important to your current career objectives.*
>
> *You have an extensive list of professional honors, awards, and commendations.*

**Exercise 30.4**   C30-E04-ResumeStandards.docx

---

*Paper Color*

Be conservative with your paper color choice. White, ivory, and light gray are ideal. Other "flashier" colors are inappropriate for most individuals unless you are in a highly creative industry and your paper choice is part of the overall design and presentation of a creative resume.

*Graphics*

An attractive, relevant graphic can really enhance your resume. Just be sure not to get carried away; be tasteful and relatively conservative.

*White Space*

Readability in a resume is everything. If people have to struggle to read your resume, they simply won't make the effort. Therefore, be sure to leave plenty of white space. It really does make a difference.

---

*Resume Strategies*

Following are core strategies for writing an effective and successful resume:

1. Who are you and how do you want to be perceived?
2. Sell it to me ... don't tell it to me.
3. Use keywords.
4. Use the "big" and save the "little."
5. Make your resume "interviewable."
6. Eliminate confusion with structure and content.
7. Use function to demonstrate achievement.
8. Remain in the realm of reality.
9. Be confident.

*Writing Style*

Always write in the first person, dropping the word "I" from the front of each sentence. This style gives your resume a more aggressive and more professional tone than the passive, third-person voice. Here are some examples:

*First Person:*

> *Manage 22-person team responsible for design and marketing of a new portfolio of PC-based applications for Landmark's consumer-sales division.*

*Third Person:*

> *Ms. Sanderson manages a 22-person team responsible for design and marketing of a new portfolio of PC-based application for Landmark's consumer-sales division.*

*Phrases to Avoid*

Try *not* to use phrases such as "responsible for" and "duties included." These words create a passive tone and style. Instead, use active verbs to describe what you did. Compare these two ways of conveying the same information:

> *Responsible for all marketing and special events for the store, including direct mailing, in-store fashion shows, and new-product introductions and promotions.*
>
> *Orchestrated a series of marketing and special-event programs for McGregor's, one of the company's largest and most profitable operating locations. Managed direct-mail campaigns, in-store fashion shows, and new-product introductions and promotions.*

**Exercise 30.4**   C30-E04-WriteResume.docx

---

# ST. FRANCIS HOSPITAL

May 12, 2015

Mr. Victor Durham
Good Samaritan Hospital
1201 James Street
St. Louis, MO 62033

Dear Victor:

Congratulations on obtaining eight new registered nurse positions at your hospital. The attached registered nurse job description is generic. Depending on the specialty, you may want to include additional responsibilities:

*Procedural*

- Uses the nursing process to prescribe, coordinate, and delegate patient care from admission through discharge.
- Analyzes the patient's condition and reports changes to the appropriate health care provider.
- Observes patient for signs and symptoms, collects data on patient, and reports and documents results.

*Teaching*

- Teaches patient, family, staff, and students.
- Assumes responsibility for patient and family teaching and discharge planning.
- Participates in orientation of new staff and/or acts as preceptor.

I am interested in hearing about your recruitment plan. We are hiring additional medical personnel in the fall at St. Francis, and I need to begin formulating a recruitment plan.

Sincerely,

Marcus Knowles

XX
C30-E05-GSHLtr.docx

3500 MEEKER BOULEVARD or REDFIELD, NE 68304 or 308-555-5000

**Exercise 30.5**   C30-E05-GSHLtr.docx

**COMPUTER CONCEPTS**

**Exercise 30.6**

C30-E06-TofC.docx

---

**AFFIDAVIT OF TRUST**

1. The name of the currently acting Trustee is LOREN HOUSTON.

2. The address of the currently acting Trustee is 102 Marine Drive, Los Angeles, CA.

3. The trust is currently in full force and effect.

4. Attached to this Affidavit and incorporated in it are selected provisions of the trust evidencing the following:
   a. Article One: Creation of the trust and initial Trustee
   b. Article Four: Statement of revocability of the trust
   c. Article Fifteen: Successor Trustees
   d. Article Seventeen: Powers of the Trustee

5. The trust provisions, which are not attached to this Affidavit, are of a personal nature and set forth the distribution of trust property. They do not modify the powers of the Trustee.

6. The signatory of this Affidavit is currently the acting Trustee of the trust and declares that the foregoing statements and the attached trust provisions are true and correct, under penalty of perjury.

_____
LOREN HOUSTON

STATE OF CALIFORNIA      )
                         ) ss.
COUNTY OF LOS ANGELES  )

     On this day personally appeared before me LOREN HOUSTON, known to me to be the individual described in and who executed the aforesaid instrument, and acknowledged that he/she signed as his/her free and voluntary act and deed for the uses and purposes therein mentioned.
     Given under my hand and official seal this 9th day of March, 2015.

_____
NOTARY PUBLIC in and for the State of California
My appointment expires 12/31/2016

**Exercise 30.7**

C30-E07-Affidavit.docx

# Creating an Outline

**Display a Document in Outline View**
1. Click VIEW tab.
2. Click Outline button.

To create an outline, you identify titles, headings, and subheadings within a document as particular levels. Use Outline view to assign these levels to types of text. You can also enter text and edit text while working in Outline view. To switch to Outline view, click the VIEW tab and then click the Outline button in the Views group. Figure 30.1 shows a document in Outline view that has levels assigned to the title and headings. The figure also identifies the OUTLINING tab that contains options and buttons for working in Outline view.

**Figure 30.1  Document in Outline View**

**Apply Level Formatting**
1. Display document in Outline view.
2. Click desired heading.
3. Click Promote button or Demote button.

In Figure 30.1, the title *UNAUTHORIZED ACCESS* is identified as a level 1 heading, the heading *User IDs and Passwords* is identified as a level 2 heading, and the paragraphs that follow the title and heading are identified as body text. The title and headings shown in Figure 30.1 display preceded by a selection symbol (round button containing a plus [+] symbol). Click this symbol to select text in that particular heading.

## Assigning Headings

Text in Outline view is identified as body text except for text with a heading style applied. If the Heading 1 style is applied to text, the text is identified as level 1 text in Outline view, text with the Heading 2 style applied is identified as level 2 text, and so on. In Outline view, you can assign levels to different types of text in a document using buttons in the Outline Tools group on the OUTLINING tab. These buttons are described in Table 30.1 on the next page.

**Table 30.1  OUTLINING Tab Buttons**

| Button | Name | Action |
|---|---|---|
| [«] | Promote to Heading 1 | Promotes text to highest level of outline. |
| [←] | Promote | Promotes heading (and its body text) by one level; promotes body text to heading level of preceding heading. |
| Level 1 [▾] | Outline Level | Assigns and displays current level of text. |
| [→] | Demote | Demotes heading by one level; demotes body text to heading level below preceding heading. |
| [»] | Demote to Body Text | Demotes heading to body text. |
| [▲] | Move Up | Moves selected item up within outline. |
| [▼] | Move Down | Moves selected item down within outline. |
| [+] | Expand | Expands first heading level below currently selected heading. |
| [−] | Collapse | Collapses body text into heading and then collapses lowest heading levels into higher heading levels. |
| Show Level: All Levels [▾] | Show Level | Displays all headings through lowest level chosen. |
| ☑ Show Text Formatting | Show Text Formatting | Displays outline with or without character formatting. |
| ☐ Show First Line Only | Show First Line Only | Switches between displaying all body text or only first line of each paragraph. |

To change a heading that is identified as normal text to a level 1 heading, position the insertion point on any character in the heading and then click the Promote to Heading 1 button in the Outline Tools group on the OUTLINING tab. This applies the Heading 1 style to the heading. To change a paragraph to a level 2 heading, position the insertion point anywhere within the text and then click the Demote button. This applies the Heading 2 style to the text.

1. Open **InternetSecurity.docx** and save the document with the name **C30-E01-InternetSecurity**.
2. Change to Outline view by clicking the VIEW tab and then clicking the Outline button in the Views group.

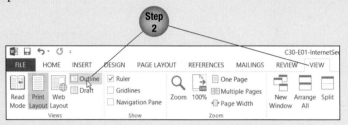

3. Promote and demote heading levels by completing the following steps:
   a. Position the insertion point anywhere in the title *UNAUTHORIZED ACCESS* and then click the Promote to Heading 1 button in the Outline Tools group on the OUTLINING tab. (This displays *Level 1* in the Outline Level button.)
   b. Position the insertion point anywhere in the heading *User IDs and Passwords* and then click the Demote button in the Outline Tools group. (This displays *Level 2* in the Outline Level button.)
   c. Position the insertion point anywhere in the heading *System Backdoors* and then click the Promote button in the Outline Tools group.
   d. Position the insertion point anywhere in the heading *Spoofing* and then click the Promote button in the Outline Tools group.
   e. Position the insertion point anywhere in the heading *Spyware* and then click the Promote button.
4. Save **C30-E01-InternetSecurity.docx**.

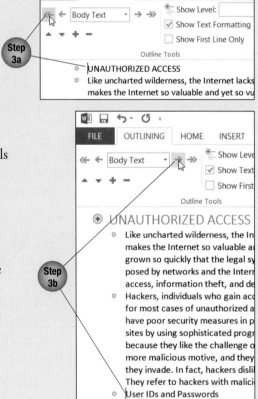

A heading can also be promoted or demoted in Outline view by dragging the selection symbol that displays before the heading 0.5 inch to the left or right. The selection symbol for a level heading displays as a circle containing a plus symbol, and the selection symbol for body text displays as a circle. For example, to demote text identified as level 1 to level 2, position the arrow pointer on the selection symbol (circle containing a plus symbol) that displays before the level 1 text until the pointer turns into a four-headed arrow. Hold down the left mouse button, drag the mouse to the right until a gray vertical line displays down the screen, and then release the mouse button. Complete similar steps to promote a heading. You can also promote a heading with the keyboard shortcut Alt + Shift + Left Arrow key and demote a heading with Alt + Shift + Right Arrow key.

1. With **C30-E01-InternetSecurity.docx** open and displayed in Outline view, promote the section 2 title to level 1 by completing the following steps:
    a. Position the mouse pointer on the selection symbol (small gray circle) that displays before the title *INFORMATION THEFT* until the mouse pointer turns into a four-headed arrow.
    b. Hold down the left mouse button, drag the mouse to the left until a gray vertical line displays near the left side of the page (as shown in the image below), and then release the mouse button. (When you release the mouse button, check to make sure *Level 1* displays in the Outline Level button.)

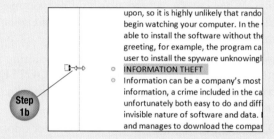

2. Promote the *Device Security* heading to level 2 by completing the following steps:
    a. Position the mouse pointer on the selection symbol (small gray circle) that displays before the *Device Security* heading until the mouse pointer turns into a four-headed arrow.
    b. Hold down the left mouse button, drag the mouse to the right until a gray vertical line displays, and then release the mouse button. (Check to make sure *Level 2* displays in the Outline Level button.)

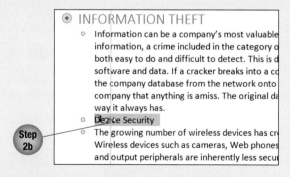

3. Promote the heading *Data Browsing* to level 2 by positioning the insertion point anywhere in the heading and then pressing Alt + Shift + Left Arrow key.
4. Save **C30-E01-InternetSecurity.docx**.

# Collapsing and Expanding a Document

One of the major advantages of working in Outline view is being able to see a condensed outline of your document without all of the text between the titles, headings, and subheadings displaying. Word lets you "collapse" a level in an outline so that any text or subsequent lower levels disappear temporarily. When you collapse levels, viewing the outline of a document is much easier. For example, when an outline is collapsed, you can see an overview of the entire document and move easily to different locations within it. You can also move titles and headings and their subheadings to new locations in the outline.

Being able to collapse and expand headings in an outline provides flexibility in using the outline feature. One popular use of this feature is to move quickly from one part of a document to another. For example, suppose you are working at the beginning of a lengthy document and want to move to a particular section but cannot remember the heading of that section or the page on which it is located. To move quickly to that section, you can switch to Outline view, collapse the entire outline, position the insertion point in the desired heading, and then expand the outline.

Another popular use of the outline feature is in maintaining consistency between various headings. When creating a particular heading, you may need to refer to the previous heading. To do this, switch to Outline view and collapse the outline; the previous heading is visible.

To collapse the entire document, click the down-pointing arrow at the right of the Show Level button in the Outline Tools group on the OUTLINING tab and then click the desired level at the drop-down list. For example, if the document contains three levels, click *Level 3* at the drop-down list.

Figure 30.2 shows the C30-E01-InternetSecurity.docx document collapsed so that only the titles and headings display. When a title or heading that is followed by text is collapsed, a gray horizontal line displays beneath the title or heading, as shown in Figure 30.2.

**Figure 30.2  Collapsed Document**

1. With **C30-E01-InternetSecurity.docx** open, make sure the document displays in Outline view and then press Ctrl + Home to move the insertion point to the beginning of the document.
2. Click the down-pointing arrow at the right of the Show Level button in the Outline Tools group and then click *Level 2* at the drop-down list.

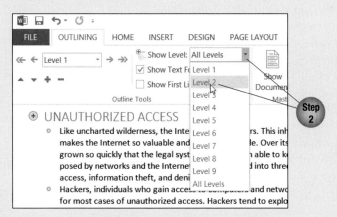

3. With the outline collapsed, click the selection symbol that displays before *Spoofing* and then press the Delete key. (This deletes the heading and the text below the heading.)
4. Save and then print **C30-E01-InternetSecurity.docx**. (This will print the collapsed outline, not the entire document.)
5. Click the Close Outline View button.
6. Close **C30-E01-InternetSecurity.docx**.

To collapse all of the text beneath a particular heading (including the text following any subsequent headings), position the insertion point within the heading and then click the Collapse button in the Outline Tools group on the OUTLINING tab. To make the text appear again, click the Expand button in the Outline Tools group.

1. Open **CompViruses.docx** and save the document with the name **C30-E02-CompViruses**.
2. Click the VIEW tab and then click the Outline button in the Views group.
3. Promote and demote the headings in the document as follows:
    a. Promote the title *COMPUTER VIRUSES* to level 1.
    b. Demote the heading *Types of Viruses* to level 2.
    c. Promote the heading *Methods of Virus Operation* to level 2.
    d. Promote the title *HARDWARE AND SOFTWARE SECURITY RISKS* to level 1.
    e. Demote the heading *Systems Failure* to level 2.
    f. Promote the heading *Employee Theft* to level 2.
    g. Promote the heading *Cracking Software for Copying* to level 2.

4. Make sure the two titles, *COMPUTER VIRUSES* and *HARDWARE AND SOFTWARE SECURITY RISKS*, display with bold formatting applied. If not, apply bold formatting to the two titles while still in Outline view.

5. Collapse and expand the document by completing the following steps:

   a. Position the insertion point anywhere in the title *COMPUTER VIRUSES* and then click the Collapse button in the Outline Tools group on the OUTLINING tab. (This collapses the text in the first section so that only the title and headings display.)

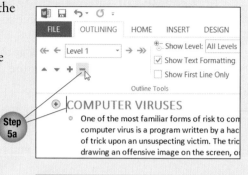

Step 5a

   b. Click the Expand button to expand the display of the text in the first section.

   c. With the insertion point still positioned in the title *COMPUTER VIRUSES*, click the down-pointing arrow at the right of the Show Level button and then click *Level 1* at the drop-down list. (This displays only the two titles.)

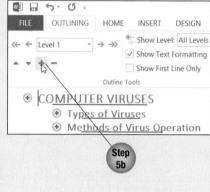

Step 5b

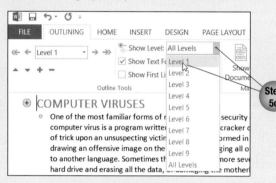

Step 5c

   d. Click the down-pointing arrow at the right of the Show Level button and then click *Level 2* at the drop-down list. (This displays the titles and headings.)

   e. Click the Expand button in the Outline Tools group. (This expands the *COMPUTER VIRUSES* section.)

   f. Click the *Show First Line Only* check box in the Outline Tools group to insert a check mark. (This displays the level 2 headings and the first line of each paragraph in the *COMPUTER VIRUSES* section.)

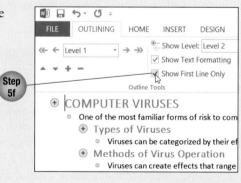

Step 5f

   g. Click the *Show First Line Only* check box to remove the check mark.

   h. Click the down-pointing arrow at the right of the Show Level button and then click *Level 2* at the drop-down list. (This displays the titles and headings.)

   i. Click the selection symbol that precedes *Employee Theft*.

   j. With the heading selected, press the Delete key.

   k. Save and then print **C30-E02-CompViruses.docx**.

   l. Click the down-pointing arrow at the right of the Show Level button and then click *All Levels* at the drop-down list. (This displays the entire document.)

6. Save **C30-E02-CompViruses.docx**.

## Organizing an Outline

Collapsing and expanding headings within an outline is only part of the versatility that the outline feature offers. This feature also allows you to rearrange an entire document by reorganizing the outline. Whole sections of a document can be quickly rearranged by moving the headings at the beginnings of those sections. The text that is collapsed beneath the headings is moved at the same time.

For example, to move a level 2 heading below other level 2 headings, collapse the outline, select the level 2 heading to be moved, and then click the Move Down button in the Outline Tools group until the level 2 heading is in the desired position. If the headings are collapsed, you only need to select the heading and move it to the desired location. Any subsequent text that is hidden is moved automatically.

You can also move headings in a document by positioning the mouse pointer on the selection symbol that displays before the desired heading until the pointer turns into a four-headed arrow. Hold down the mouse, drag the heading to the desired location, and then release the mouse button. As you drag the mouse, a gray horizontal line displays in the document with an arrow attached. Use this horizontal line to help you move the heading to the desired location.

---

**Exercise 30.2B   Moving Headings in a Document**                                    Part 2 of 2

1. With **C30-E02-CompViruses.docx** open, make sure the document displays in Outline view and then press Ctrl + Home to move the insertion point to the beginning of the document.
2. Click the down-pointing arrow at the right of the Show Level button and then click *Level 1* at the drop-down list.
3. Move the section *HARDWARE AND SOFTWARE SECURITY RISKS* to the beginning of the document by completing the following steps:
   a. Click any character in the title *HARDWARE AND SOFTWARE SECURITY RISKS*.
   b. Click the Move Up button in the Outline Tools group on the OUTLINING tab.

4. Move the heading *Systems Failure* below the heading *Cracking Software for Copying* by completing the following steps:
   a. Click the down-pointing arrow at the right of the Show Level button and then click *Level 2* at the drop-down list.
   b. Position the mouse pointer on the selection symbol that precedes the heading *Systems Failure* until the pointer turns into a four-headed arrow.

c. Hold down the left mouse button, drag the mouse down until the gray horizontal line with the arrow attached is positioned below *Cracking Software for Copying*, and then release the mouse button.

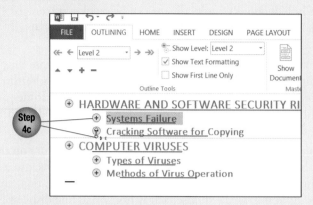

d. Deselect the text.
5. Save and then print **C30-E02-CompViruses.docx**. (This will print the collapsed outline, not the entire document.)
6. Click the down-pointing arrow at the right of the Show Level button and then click *All Levels* at the drop-down list.
7. Click the Close Outline View button.
8. Delete the blank line above the heading *Systems Failure*.
9. Save and then close **C30-E02-CompViruses.docx**.

# Creating a Master Document and Subdocuments

**Create a Master Document**
1. Display document in Outline view.
2. Assign heading levels to titles and headings.
3. Click Show Document button.
4. Select headings and text to be divided into subdocument.
5. Click Create button.

For a project that contains many parts or sections, such as a reference guide or book, consider using a *master document*. A master document contains a number of separate documents referred to as *subdocuments*.

A master document is useful in a situation in which several people are working on one project. Each person prepares a document for part of the project and then all of the documents are combined in a master document. A master document also allows for easier editing. Rather than work in one large document, you can make changes in several subdocuments and then see all of your edits reflected in the master document. You can create a new master document or format an existing document as a master with buttons in the Master Document group on the OUTLINING tab.

## Creating a Master Document

To create a master document, switch to Outline view, assign heading levels to titles and headings within the document, and then click the Show Document button in the Master Document group. Select the headings and text to be divided into a subdocument and then click the Create button in the Master Document group. Text specified as a subdocument is enclosed within a box formed by thin gray lines and a subdocument icon displays in the upper left corner of the border.

Word creates a subdocument for each heading at the top level within the selected text. For example, if the selected text begins with Heading 1 text, Word creates a new subdocument at each Heading 1 in the selected text.

Save the master document in the same manner as a normal document. Word automatically assigns a document name to each subdocument using the first characters in the subdocument heading.

## Opening and Closing a Master Document and its Subdocuments

Open a master document at the Open dialog box in the same manner as a normal document. Subdocuments in a master document display collapsed in the master document, as shown in Figure 30.3. This figure displays the master document C30-E03-Newsletters.docx that you will create in Exercise 30.3A.

Notice that Word automatically converts subdocument names into hyperlinks. To open a subdocument, hold down the Ctrl key and then click the subdocument hyperlink.

**Figure 30.3 Master Document**

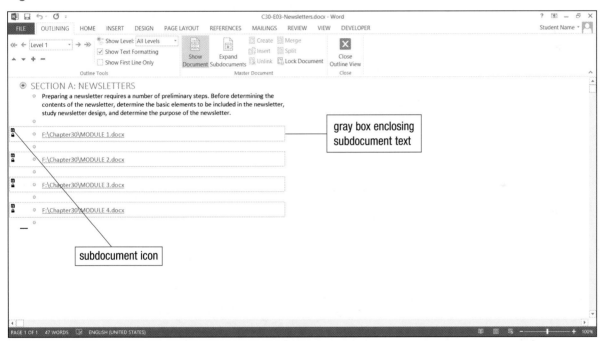

Close a subdocument in the normal manner and, if you made any changes, you will be asked if you want to save the changes. Closing a subdocument redisplays the master document and the subdocument hyperlink displays in a different color (identifying that the hyperlink has been used).

## Expanding and Collapsing Subdocuments

Open a master document and its subdocuments automatically collapse. To expand the subdocuments, click the Expand Subdocuments button in the Master Document group on the OUTLINING tab. This expands the subdocuments and also changes the Expand Subdocuments button to the Collapse Subdocuments button.

1. At a blank document, type the text shown in Figure 30.4 on the next page. (Press the Enter key after typing the text.)
2. With the insertion point positioned at the end of the document, insert the document **NewsletterElements.docx**. (Do this with the Object button on the INSERT tab.)
3. With the insertion point positioned at the end of the document, insert the document **NewsletterDesign.docx**. (Do this with the Object button on the INSERT tab.)
4. Move the insertion point to the beginning of the document.
5. Change to Outline view.
6. Promote and demote the headings in the document as follows:
   *SECTION A: NEWSLETTERS*: Level 1
   *MODULE 1: DEFINING NEWSLETTER ELEMENTS*: Level 2
   *Designing a Newsletter*: Level 3
   *Defining Basic Newsletter Elements*: Level 3
   *MODULE 2: PLANNING A NEWSLETTER*: Level 2
   *Defining the Purpose of a Newsletter*: Level 3
   *MODULE 3: DESIGNING A NEWSLETTER*: Level 2
   *Applying Desktop Publishing Guidelines*: Level 3
   *MODULE 4: CREATING NEWSLETTER LAYOUT*: Level 2
   *Choosing Paper Size and Type*: Level 3
   *Choosing Paper Weight*: Level 3
   *Creating Margins for Newsletters*: Level 3
7. Save the document and name it **C30-E03-Newsletters**.
8. Create subdocuments with the module text by completing the following steps:
   a. Select the entire first module by clicking on the selection symbol that displays immediately left of the heading *MODULE 1: DEFINING NEWSLETTER ELEMENTS*.

   b. Scroll through the document to the heading *MODULE 4: CREATING NEWSLETTER LAYOUT*.
   c. Hold down the Shift key and then click the selection symbol immediately left of the heading. (This selects all of the text in Modules 1, 2, 3, and 4.)

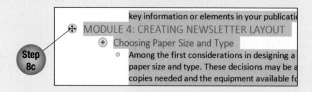

d. With the text selected, click the Show Document button in the Master Document group on the OUTLINING tab.

e. Click the Create button in the Master Document group.

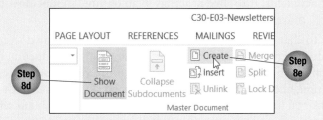

9. Save and then close **C30-E03-Newsletters.docx**.

10. Open **C30-E03-Newsletters.docx**.

11. Print **C30-E03-Newsletters.docx**. At the question asking if you want to open the subdocuments, click No. (The document will print collapsed, as displayed on the screen.)

12. Edit the Module 1 subdocument by completing the following steps:

   a. Hold down the Ctrl key and then click the F:\Chapter30\MODULE 1.docx hyperlink.

   b. With the **MODULE 1.docx** document displayed, edit the title so it reads *MODULE 1: DEFINING ELEMENTS*.

   c. Change the heading *Designing a Newsletter* so it displays as *Designing*.

   d. Change the heading *Defining Basic Newsletter Elements* so it displays as *Defining Basic Elements*.

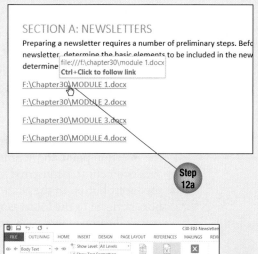

13. Save the subdocument by clicking the Save button on the Quick Access toolbar.

14. Close the subdocument.

15. Click the VIEW tab and then click the Outline button in the Views group.

16. Expand the subdocuments by clicking the Expand Subdocuments button in the Master Document group on the OUTLINING tab.

17. Print page 1 of the master document.

18. Collapse the subdocuments by clicking the Collapse Subdocuments button in the Master Document group on the OUTLINING tab.

19. Save and then close **C30-E03-Newsletters.docx**.

**Figure 30.4 Exercise 30.3A**

SECTION A: NEWSLETTERS

Preparing a newsletter requires a number of preliminary steps. Before determining the contents of the newsletter, determine the basic elements to be included in the newsletter, study newsletter design, and determine the purpose of the newsletter.

## Rearranging Subdocuments

Many of the features of a master document are similar to the features of an outline. For example, expanding and collapsing an outline is very similar to expanding and collapsing subdocuments. Also, like headings in an outline, subdocuments in a master document can be moved and rearranged.

To change the position of a subdocument, show the document and collapse the subdocuments. Position the mouse pointer on the subdocument icon, hold down the left mouse button (mouse pointer turns into a four-headed arrow), drag to the desired location, and then release the mouse button. As you drag with the mouse, a dark gray, horizontal line displays, identifying where the subdocument will be inserted.

When moving a collapsed subdocument, the dark gray, horizontal line must be positioned above the gray circle that displays above the subdocument. If you position the line between the gray circle and the top border of a collapsed subdocument, Word will display a message telling you that you cannot change a locked subdocument or master document. With the line positioned immediately above the subdocument border, Word assumes that you want to insert the selected subdocument into the subdocument. Word will not allow this because the subdocuments are locked.

## Inserting a Subdocument

A document can be inserted into an existing master document as a subdocument. To insert a document as a subdocument, make sure that the subdocuments in the master document are expanded and then position the insertion point where you want the document to be inserted.

To insert a document into an existing master document as a subdocument, position the insertion point above or below the subdocument heading where you want the new subdocument to be inserted. A subdocument cannot be inserted within body text. Click the Insert button in the Master Document group. At the Insert Subdocument dialog box, navigate to the folder containing the document that you want to insert in the master document and then double-click the document.

## Unlinking a Subdocument

Subdocuments are linked to the master document. Subdocuments and the master document can be unlinked, making the subdocument text become part of the master document. To unlink a subdocument from the master document, expand the subdocuments, click anywhere in the subdocument that you want to unlink, and then click the Unlink button in the Master Documents group.

## Splitting or Combining Subdocuments

A subdocument can be split into smaller subdocuments or several subdocuments can be combined into one. To split a subdocument, expand the subdocuments, select the specific text within the subdocument, and then click the Split button in the Master Document group on the OUTLINING tab. Word assigns a document name based on the first characters in the subdocument heading.

To combine subdocuments, expand the subdocuments and then click the subdocument icon of the first subdocument to be combined. Hold down the Shift key and then click the subdocument icon of the last subdocument. (The subdocuments must be adjacent.) With the subdocuments selected, click the Merge button in the Master Document group. Word saves the combined subdocuments with the name of the first subdocument.

1. Open **C30-E03-Newsletters.docx** and then display the document in Outline view.
2. Click the Show Document button in the Master Document group (Make sure the subdocuments are collapsed.)

   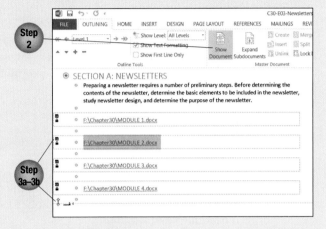
   Step 2

3. Move the Module 2 subdocument below the Module 4 subdocument by completing the following steps:
   a. Position the arrow pointer on the subdocument icon that displays to the left of the Module 2 subdocument. (The pointer turns into an arrow up and to the right.)

      Step 3a–3b

   b. Hold down the left mouse button, drag down so that the dark gray, horizontal line displays below the last small gray circle (below the Module 4 subdocument) and then release the mouse button.
4. Insert a subdocument into the master document by completing the following steps:
   a. Click the Expand Subdocuments button.
   b. Position the insertion point on the blank line below the paragraph of text below the heading *SECTION A: NEWSLETTERS*.

      Step 4b    Step 4c
      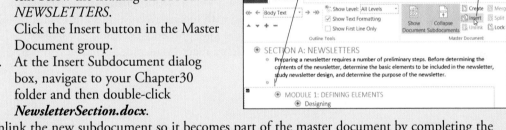

   c. Click the Insert button in the Master Document group.
   d. At the Insert Subdocument dialog box, navigate to your Chapter30 folder and then double-click *NewsletterSection.docx*.
5. Unlink the new subdocument so it becomes part of the master document by completing the following steps:
   a. Click in the paragraph of text below the heading *SECTION B: MAINTAINING CONSISTENCY*.
   b. Click the Unlink button in the Master Document group.
   c. Select and then delete the heading *SECTION B: MAINTAINING CONSISTENCY*. (The paragraphs should be separated by only one blank line.)
6. Delete the Module 2 subdocument by completing the following steps:
   a. Click the selection symbol that displays to the left of the subdocument *MODULE 2: PLANNING A NEWSLETTER*.

      Step 6a
      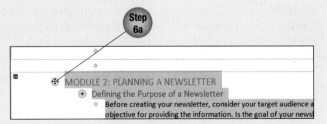

   b. Press the Delete key.

7. Split the Module 1 subdocument by completing the following steps:
   a. In the Module 1 subdocument, edit the heading *Defining Basic Elements* so that it displays as *MODULE 2: DEFINING BASIC ELEMENTS*.
   b. Click in the heading *MODULE 2: DEFINING BASIC ELEMENTS* and then click the Promote button to change the heading from level 3 to level 2.
   c. Position the mouse pointer on the selection symbol that displays immediately left of the heading *MODULE 2: DEFINING BASIC ELEMENTS* until the pointer turns into a four-headed arrow and then click the left mouse button.
   d. With the text selected, click the Split button in the Master Document group on the OUTLINING tab.
   e. Click the Collapse Subdocuments button in the Master Document group. At the question asking if you want to save the changes to the master document, click OK.

8. Click the Show Document button and delete the next page section break between the two paragraphs in *SECTION A: NEWSLETTERS*. Delete one of the continuous section breaks between Module 5 and Module 3.
9. Save and then print **C30-E03-Newsletters.docx**. (The master document will print with the subdocuments collapsed.)
10. Close **C30-E03-Newsletters.docx**.

# Creating Macros

***Macros*** are time-saving tools that automate the formatting of Word documents. Two basic steps are involved in working with macros: recording a macro and running a macro. When you record a macro, all of the keys pressed and dialog boxes displayed are recorded and become part of the macro. After a macro is recorded you can run it to carry out the recorded actions.

## Recording a Macro

**Record a Macro**
1. Click VIEW tab.
2. Click Macros button arrow.
3. Click *Record Macro* at drop-down list.
4. At Record Macro dialog box, type name and description and specify where to store macro.
5. Click OK.
6. Perform actions to be recorded.
7. Click macro icon on Status bar to stop recording.

Recording a macro involves turning on the macro recorder, performing the steps to be recorded, and then turning off the recorder. Both the VIEW tab and DEVELOPER tab contain buttons for recording a macro. If the DEVELOPER tab does not appear on the ribbon, turn on the display by opening the Word Options dialog box, inserting a check mark in the *Developer* check box in the list box at the right, and then clicking OK to close the dialog box.

To record a macro, click the Record Macro button in the Code group on the DEVELOPER tab. You can also click the VIEW tab, click the Macros button arrow in the Macros group, and then click *Record Macro* at the drop-down list. This displays the Record Macro dialog box, as shown in Figure 30.5 on the next page. At the Record Macro dialog box, type a name for the macro in the *Macro name* text box. A macro name must begin with a letter and can contain only letters and numbers. Type a description of the macro in the *Description* text box located at the bottom of the dialog box. A macro description can contain a maximum of 255 characters including spaces.

By default, Word stores a macro in the Normal template. Macros stored in this template are available for any document based on the Normal template. In a company or school setting, where computers may be networked, consider storing macros in

**Figure 30.5  Record Macro Dialog Box**

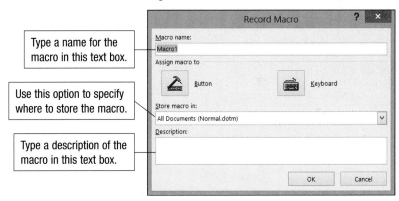

Type a name for the macro in this text box.

Use this option to specify where to store the macro.

Type a description of the macro in this text box.

personalized documents or templates. Specify the location for macros with the *Store macro in* option at the Record Macro dialog box.

After typing the macro name, specifying where the macro is to be stored, and typing a description, click OK or press the Enter key to close the Record Macro dialog box. At the open document, a macro icon displays near the left side of the Status bar and the mouse displays with a cassette icon attached. In the document, perform the actions to be recorded and after you have finished, click the Stop Recording button (previously the Record Macro button) located in the Code group on the DEVELOPER tab or click the macro icon that displays toward the left side of the Status bar.

When you record macros in the exercises for this chapter, you will name the macros beginning with your initials. An exercise step may instruct you, for example, to "record a macro named XXXInd01." Insert your initials in the macro name instead of the *XXX*.

Recorded macros are stored in the Normal template by default and display at the Macros dialog box. If the computer you use is networked, macros recorded by other students will also display at the dialog box. Naming a macro with your initials will help you distinguish your macros from those of other users.

## Exercise 30.4A  Recording Macros                        Part 1 of 4

1. Turn on the display of the DEVELOPER tab by completing the following steps. (Skip these steps if the DEVELOPER tab is visible.)
   a. Click the FILE tab and then click *Options*.
   b. At the Word Options dialog box, click *Customize Ribbon* in the left panel.
   c. In the list box at the right, click the *Developer* check box to insert a check mark.

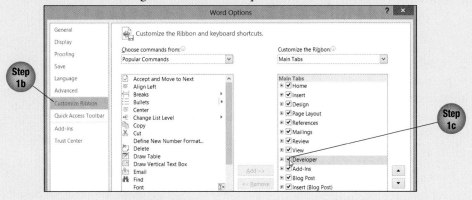

   d. Click OK to close the dialog box.

2. Record a macro that selects text and then indents a paragraph of text and applies italic formatting by completing the following steps:

   a. Open **MacroText.docx** and then position the insertion point at the left margin of the paragraph that begins with *This is text to use for creating macros.*

   b. Click the DEVELOPER tab.

   c. Click the Record Macro button in the Code group on the DEVELOPER tab.

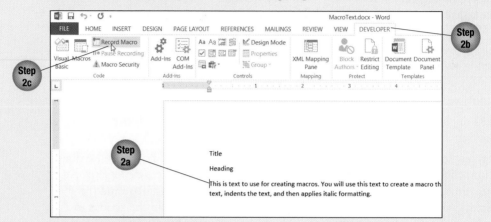

   d. At the Record Macro dialog box, type **XXXIndentItalics** in the *Macro name* text box (typing your initials in place of the *XXX*).

   e. Click inside the *Description* text box and then type **Select text, indent text, and apply italic formatting.** (If text displays in the *Description* text box, select the text and then type the description.)

   f. Click OK.

   g. At the document, press the F8 key to turn on the Extend mode.

   h. Hold down the Shift key and Ctrl key and then press the Down Arrow key. (Shift + Ctrl + Down Arrow is the keyboard shortcut to select a paragraph.)

   i. Click the HOME tab.

   j. Click the Paragraph group dialog box launcher.

   k. At the Paragraph dialog box, click the up-pointing arrow at the right of the *Left* option until *0.5"* displays.

   l. Click the up-pointing arrow at the right of the *Right* option until *0.5"* displays.

   m. Click OK.

   n. Press Ctrl + I to apply italic formatting.

   o. Press the Esc key on the keyboard and then press the Left Arrow key. (This deselects the text.)

   p. Click the macro icon on the Status bar to turn off the macro recording.

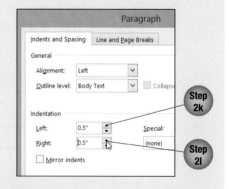

3. Record a macro that applies formatting to a heading by completing the following steps:
   a. Move the insertion point to the beginning of the text *Heading*.
   b. Click the DEVELOPER tab and then click the Record Macro button in the Code group.
   c. At the Record Macro dialog box, type **XXXHeading** in the *Macro name* text box (typing your initials in place of the *XXX*).
   d. Click inside the *Description* text box and then type **Select text, change font size, turn on bold and italic, and insert bottom border line.** (If text displays in the *Description* text box, select the text and then type the description.)
   e. Click OK.
   f. At the document, press the F8 key and then press the End key.
   g. Click the HOME tab.
   h. Click the Bold button in the Font group.
   i. Click the Italic button in the Font group.
   j. Click the Font Size button arrow and then click *12* at the drop-down gallery.
   k. Click the Border button arrow and then click *Bottom Border* at the drop-down list.
   l. Press the Home key. (This moves the insertion point back to the beginning of the heading and deselects the text.)
   m. Click the macro icon on the Status bar to turn off the macro recording.
4. Close the document without saving it.

## Running a Macro

To run a recorded macro, click the Macros button in the Code group on the DEVELOPER tab or click the Macros button on the VIEW tab. This displays the Macros dialog box, as shown in Figure 30.6. At this dialog box, double-click the desired macro in the list box or click the macro and then click the Run button.

**Run a Macro**
1. Click VIEW tab.
2. Click Macros button.
3. At Macros dialog box, double-click desired macro.

**Figure 30.6  Macros Dialog Box**

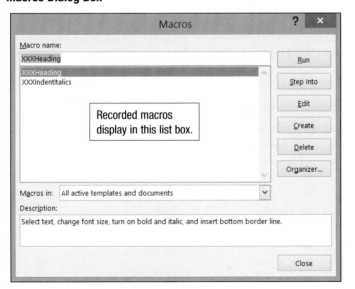

1. Open **WriteResume.docx** and save the document with the name **C30-E04-WriteResume**.
2. With the insertion point positioned at the beginning of the heading *Resume Strategies*, run the XXXHeading macro by completing the following steps:
   a. Click the VIEW tab.
   b. Click the Macros button in the Macros group.

   c. At the Macros dialog box, click *XXXHeading* in the list box.
   d. Click the Run button.

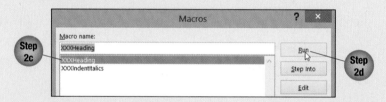

3. Complete steps similar to those in Steps 2a through 2d to run the macro for the two other headings in the document: *Writing Style* and *Phrases to Avoid*.
4. With the insertion point positioned at the left margin of the paragraph below *First Person:*, complete the following steps to run the XXXIndentItalics macro:
   a. Click the DEVELOPER tab.
   b. Click the Macros button in the Code group.
   c. At the Macros dialog box, double-click *XXXIndentItalics* in the list box.
5. Complete steps similar to those in Steps 4a through 4c to run the XXXIndentItalics macro for the paragraph below *Third Person:*, the paragraph that begins *Responsible for all marketing and special events*, and the paragraph that begins *Orchestrated a series of marketing and special-event programs*.
6. Save, print, and then close **C30-E04-WriteResume.docx**.

### Running a Macro Automatically

You can create a macro that starts automatically when you perform a certain action, such as opening, closing, or closing Word. To use a macro that starts automatically, the macro must be saved in the Normal template and contain one of the names listed below:

| **Automatic Macro Name** | **Action** |
| --- | --- |
| AutoExec | Runs when Word is opened. |
| AutoOpen | Runs when a document is opened. |
| AutoNew | Runs when a new document is opened. |
| AutoClose | Runs when a document is closed. |
| AutoExit | Runs when Word is closed. |

To create a macro that runs automatically, display the Record Macro dialog box, type the desired macro name from the list on the previous page in the *Macro name* text box, and then click OK. Complete the desired steps for the macro and then end the recording.

1. At a blank document, create a macro that changes the font and view and runs automatically when you open a new document by completing the following steps:
   a. Click the VIEW tab.
   b. Click the Macros button arrow in the Macros group and then click *Record Macro* at the drop-down list.
   c. At the Record Macro dialog box, type **AutoNew** in the *Macro name* text box.
   d. Click inside the *Description* text box and then type **Runs automatically when a new document is opened and changes the font and document view.** (If text displays in the *Description* text box, select the text and then type the description.)
   e. Click OK.
   f. Click the HOME tab, click the Font button arrow, and then click *Constantia* at the drop-down gallery.

   **Step 1c**

   **Record Macro**    ?  ×

   Macro name:

   AutoNew

   Assign macro to

   Button          Keyboard

   Store macro in:

   All Documents (Normal.dotm)    ▼

   Description:

   Runs automatically when a new document is opened and changes the font and document view.    **Step 1d**

   OK          Cancel

   **Step 1e**

   g. Click the VIEW tab and then click the Draft button in the Views group.
   h. Press the spacebar and then press the Backspace key. (To save the document in Draft view, an action must appear in the *Undo* drop-down list. Pressing the spacebar and then pressing the Backspace key will create the action in the *Undo* list.)
   i. Click the macro icon on the Status bar to turn off the macro recording.
2. Close the document without saving it and then close Word.
3. Open Word and then open a blank document. Notice that the blank document contains the new settings (11-point Constantia and Draft view) because the *AutoNew* macro ran automatically.
4. Insert into the current document the document named **ResumeStandards.docx** located in your Chapter30 folder. (Do this with the Object button arrow on the INSERT tab.)
5. Position the insertion point at the beginning of the heading *Typestyle* and then run the XXXHeading macro.
6. Position the insertion point at the beginning of each remaining heading and run the XXXHeading macro. (The remaining headings include *Type Size*, *Type Enhancements*, *Page Length*, *Paper Color*, *Graphics*, and *White Space*.)
7. Select the second through fifth paragraphs in the *Page Length* section and then run the XXXIndentItalics macro. (Do not select the paragraph symbol after the last word in the fifth paragraph.)
8. Keep the heading *Paper Color* with the paragraph of text that follows.
9. Save the document and name it **C30-E04-ResumeStandards**.
10. Print and then close **C30-E04-ResumeStandards.docx**.

## Pausing and Resuming a Macro

When recording a macro, you can temporarily suspend the recording, perform actions that are not recorded, and then resume recording the macro. To pause the recording of a macro, click the Pause Recording button in the Code group on the DEVELOPER tab. To resume recording the macro, click the Resume Recorder button (previously the Pause Recording button).

## Deleting a Macro

If you no longer need a macro that has been recorded, you can delete it. To delete a macro, display the Macros dialog box, click the macro name in the list box, and then click the Delete button. At the message asking if you want to delete the macro, click Yes. Click the Close button to close the Macros dialog box.

---

### Exercise 30.4D    Deleting a Macro                                        Part 4 of 4

1. At a blank document, delete the XXXIndentItalics macro by completing the following steps:
   a. Click the DEVELOPER tab and then click the Macros button in the Code group.
   b. At the Macros dialog box, click *XXXIndentItalics* in the list box.
   c. Click the Delete button.
   d. At the message asking if you want to delete the macro, click Yes.
   e. Click the Close button to close the Macros dialog box.
2. Complete steps similar to those in Step 1 to delete the *AutoNew* macro.
3. Close the document without saving it.

---

## Assigning a Macro

Consider assigning macros that you use regularly to a keyboard command or toolbar. To run a macro that is assigned to a keyboard command, press the assigned keys. To run a macro that is assigned to a toolbar, click the button.

### Assigning a Macro to a Keyboard Command

Consider assigning macros that you use regularly to keyboard commands. To run a macro that has been assigned to a keyboard command, simply press the assigned keys. A macro can be assigned to a keyboard command with the following combinations:

    Alt + letter
    Ctrl + letter
    Alt + Ctrl + letter
    Alt + Shift + letter
    Ctrl + Shift + letter
    Alt + Ctrl + Shift + letter

**Figure 30.7 Customize Keyboard Dialog Box**

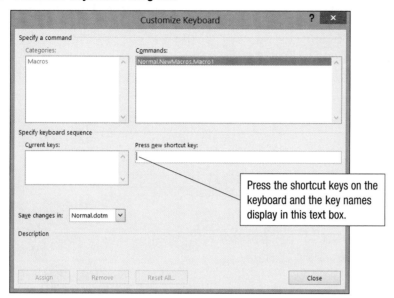

Press the shortcut keys on the keyboard and the key names display in this text box.

Word already uses many combinations for Word functions. For example, pressing Alt + Ctrl + C inserts the copyright symbol. Assign a macro to a keyboard command at the Customize Keyboard dialog box, as shown in Figure 30.7. Specify the keyboard command by pressing the desired keys, such as Alt + D. The keyboard command you enter displays in the *Press new shortcut key text* box. Word inserts the message *Currently assigned to:* below the *Current keys* list box. If the keyboard command is already assigned to a command, the command is listed after the *Currently assigned to:* message. If Word has not used the keyboard command, *[unassigned]* displays after the *Currently assigned to:* message. When assigning a keyboard command to a macro, make sure you use an unassigned keyboard command.

In Exercise 30.5, you will record a macro and then assign it to a keyboard command. If you delete the macro, the keyboard command is also deleted. This allows you to use the key combination again.

**Exercise 30.5**    **Assigning a Macro to a Keyboard Command**       **Part 1 of 1**

1. Record a macro named XXXFont that selects text and applies font formatting and assign it the keyboard command Alt + Ctrl + A by completing the following steps:
   a. At a blank document, click the DEVELOPER tab and then click the Record Macro button in the Code group.
   b. At the Record Macro dialog box, type **XXXFont** in the *Macro name* text box.
   c. Click inside the *Description* text box and then type **Select text and change the font and font color.**
   d. Click the Keyboard button.

e. At the Customize Keyboard dialog box with the insertion point positioned in the *Press new shortcut key* text box, press Alt + Ctrl + A.
f. Click the Assign button.
g. Click the Close button.

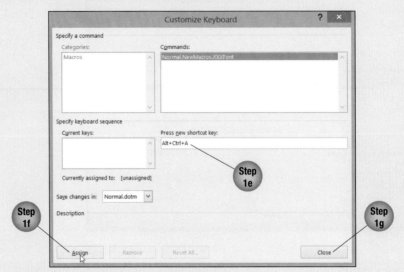

h. At the document, click the HOME tab.
i. Press Ctrl + A.
j. Click the Font group dialog box launcher.
k. At the Font dialog box, select *Cambria* in the *Font* list box and change the *Font color* option to Dark Blue.
l. Click OK to close the Font dialog box.
m. At the document, press the Down Arrow on the keyboard.
n. Click the macro icon on the Status bar to turn off the macro recording.
2. Close the document without saving it.
3. Open **GSHLtr.docx** and save the document with the name **C30-E05-GSHLtr**.
4. Run the XXXFont macro by pressing Alt + Ctrl + A.
5. Run the XXXHeading macro for the headings *Procedural* and *Teaching*.
6. Save, print, and then close **C30-E05-GSHLtr.docx**.

## Assigning a Macro to the Quick Access Toolbar

Add a macro that you use regularly to the Quick Access toolbar. To run a macro from the Quick Access toolbar, just click the button. To assign a macro to the toolbar, click the Button button at the Record Macro dialog box. This displays the Word Options dialog box with the *Quick Access Toolbar* option selected in the left panel. Click the macro name in the left list box and then click the Add button that displays between the two list boxes. This adds the macro name in the right list box.

Specify a button icon by clicking the Modify button, clicking the desired icon at the Modify Button dialog box, and then clicking OK. Click OK to close the Word Options dialog box and a Macro button is inserted on the Quick Access toolbar. To remove a Macro button from the Quick Access toolbar, right-click the button on the toolbar and then click *Remove from Quick Access Toolbar* at the shortcut menu.

1. At a blank document, create a macro named XXXTab and assign it to the Quick Access toolbar by completing the following steps:

   a. Click the macro icon on the Status bar.

   b. At the Record Macro dialog box, type **XXXTab** in the *Macro name* text box.

   c. Click in the *Description* text box and then type **Set left tabs at 0.5 and 1.0 and right tab with leaders at 5.5.**

   d. Click the Button button.

   e. At the Word Options dialog box, click the macro named *Normal.NewMacros.XXXTab* in the left list box.

   f. Click the Add button located between the two list boxes.

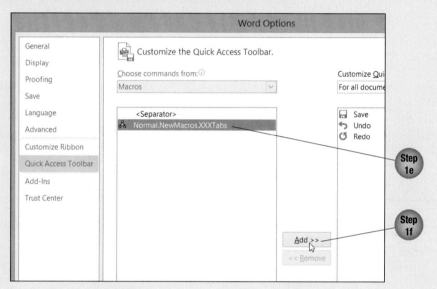

   g. Click the Modify button located in the lower right corner of the dialog box.

   h. At the Modify Button dialog box, click the fourth button from the left in the top row.

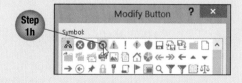

   i. Click OK to close the Modify Button dialog box.

   j. Click OK to close the Word Options dialog box.

   k. At the blank document, click the HOME tab and then click the Paragraph group dialog box launcher.

   l. At the Paragraph dialog box, click the Tabs button located in the lower left corner of the dialog box.

   m. At the Tabs dialog box, type **0.5** and then click the Set button.

   n. Type **1** and then click the Set button.

o.  Type **5.5**, click the *Right* option in the *Alignment* section, click *2 .......* in the *Leader* section, and then click the Set button.

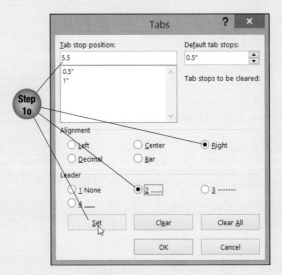

p.  Click OK to close the dialog box.
q.  At the blank document, click the macro icon on the Status bar to turn off recording.
2.  Close the document without saving it.
3.  At a blank document, create the document shown in Figure 30.8 on the next page by completing the following steps:
    a.  Click the Macro button on the Quick Access toolbar.

    b.  Type the text as shown in Figure 30.8. (Type the first column of text at the first tab stop, not the left margin.)
4.  After typing the text, run the XXXFont macro by pressing Alt + Ctrl + A.
5.  Select the title *COMPUTER CONCEPTS* and apply bold formatting.
6.  Save the document and name it **C30-E06-TofC**.
7.  Print and then close **C30-E06-TofC.docx**.
8.  Remove the Macro button from the Quick Access toolbar by right-clicking the button and then clicking *Remove from Quick Access Toolbar* at the shortcut menu.

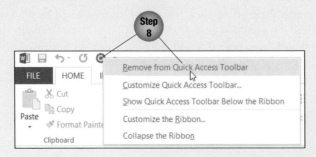

**Figure 30.8 Exercise 30.6**

**COMPUTER CONCEPTS**

Computer Hardware .......................................................................3

Types of Computers ..............................................................4

Hardware Components ..........................................................8

Computer Software ......................................................................14

Operating Systems ...............................................................16

Application Software ...........................................................20

Networking ...................................................................................25

Types of Networks ...............................................................27

Uses of Networks .................................................................30

Network Topologies .............................................................34

## Specifying Macro Security Settings

Some macros can pose a potential security risk, introducing and spreading viruses on your computer or network. For this reason, Microsoft Word provides macro security settings that you can use to specify what actions you want to occur with macros in a document. To display the macro security settings, click the DEVELOPER tab and then click the Macro Security button in the Code group. This displays the Trust Center with *Macro Settings* selected in the left panel, as shown in Figure 30.9 on the next page.

Choose the first option, *Disable all macros without notification*, and all macros and security alerts are disabled. The second option, *Disable all macros with notification,* is the default setting. At this setting, a security alert appears if a macro is present and you are asked if you want to enable the macro. Choose the third option, *Disable all macros except digitally signed macros,* and a digitally signed macro by a trusted publisher will automatically run. (However, you will still need to enable a digitally signed macro by a publisher that is not trusted.) The last option, *Enable all macros (not recommended; potentially dangerous code can run),* allows all macros to run but, as the option implies, this is not recommended.

The changes that you make to the macro security settings in Word only apply to Word. The macro security settings are not changed in the other programs in the Office suite.

**Figure 30.9** **Trust Center**

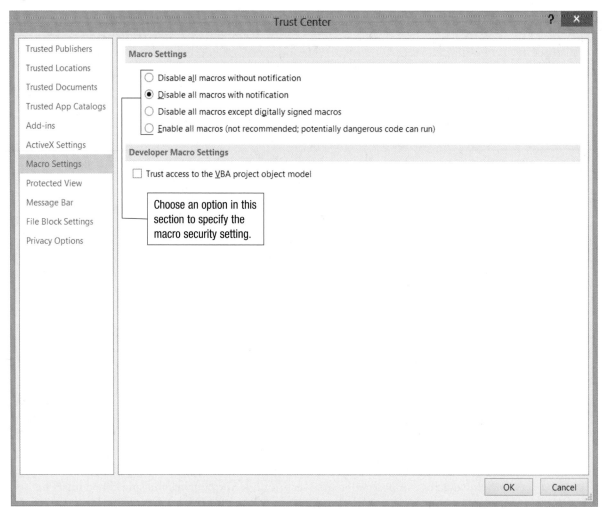

## Saving a Macro-Enabled Document or Template

By default, the macros you create are saved in the *Normal.dotm* template. The extension *.dotm* identifies the template as "macro-enabled." A template or document must be macro-enabled for a macro to be saved in it.

In addition to the *Normal.dotm* template, you can save macros in a specific document or template to make them available when you open that document or template. To specify a location for saving a macro, display the Record Macro dialog box, click the down-pointing arrow at the right side of the *Store macro in* option box, and then click the desired document or template.

Save a document containing macros as a macro-enabled document. To do this, display the Save As dialog box and then change the *Save as type* option to *Word Macro-Enabled Document (\*.docm)*. Save a template containing macros as a macro-enabled template by changing the *Save as type* option at the Save As dialog box to *Word Macro-Enabled Template (\*.dotm)*.

## Copying Macros between Documents and Templates

Macros saved in a document can be copied to other documents or templates at the Organizer dialog box with the Macro Project Items tab selected. Display this dialog box by clicking the Macros button in the Code group on the DEVELOPER tab and then clicking the Organizer button at the Macros dialog box. You can also display the Macros dialog box by clicking the Macros button on the VIEW tab.

Macros created in a document or template are saved in the NewMacros project. At the Organizer dialog box with the Macro Project Items tab selected, copy the NewMacros project from a document or template to another document or template. To copy the NewMacro project, click *NewMacro* in the list box at the left or right and then click the Copy button that displays between the two list boxes.

By default, the Organizer dialog box displays the NewMacro project for the open document in the list box at the left and the NewMacro project for the Normal.dotm template in the list box at the right. Choose a different document or template by clicking the Close File button. This changes the Close File button to the Open File button. Choose a different document or template by clicking the Open File button. At the Open dialog box, navigate to the folder containing the desired document or template and then double-click the document or template.

The Organizer dialog box contains buttons for renaming and deleting macro projects. To rename the NewMacro project, click *NewMacro* in the list box and then click the Rename button that displays between the two list boxes. At the Rename dialog box, type the new name and then press the Enter key. Delete a macro project by clicking the project name in the list box and then clicking the Delete button that displays between the two list boxes.

---

**Exercise 30.7A**  **Changing Macro Security Settings, Copying Macros, and Saving a Macro-Enabled Document**  **Part 1 of 3**

1. At a blank screen, change macro security settings by completing the following steps:
   a. Click the DEVELOPER tab and then click the Macro Security button in the Code group.
   b. At the Trust Center, click the *Enable all macros (not recommended; potentially dangerous code can run)* option.

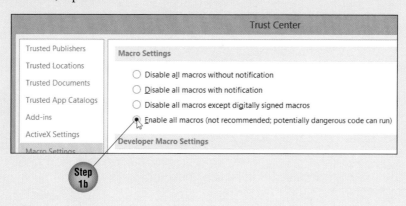

   c. Click OK.

2. Press Ctrl + N to display a blank document.
3. Save the document as a macro-enabled document in your Chapter 30 folder by completing the following steps:
   a. Press the F12 key to display the Save As dialog box.
   b. Type **C30-E07-LegalMacros** in the *File name* text box.
   c. Click the *Save as type* option box and then click *Word Macro-Enabled Document (\*.docm)* at the drop-down list.

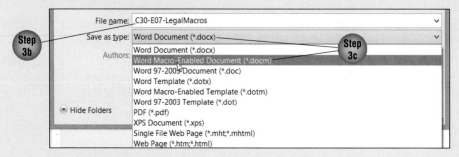

   d. Click the Save button.
4. The Chapter30 folder on your storage medium contains a macro-enabled document named **MacroDocument.docm** that contains two macros. Copy the macros from the **MacroDocument.docm** document to the current document by completing the following steps:
   a. Make sure the DEVELOPER tab is active and then click the Macros button in the Code group.
   b. At the Macros dialog box, click the Organizer button.
   c. At the Organizer dialog box with the Macro Project Items tab selected, click the Close File button located below the right list box (the list box containing *NewMacros*).
   d. Click the Open File button (previously the Close File button).
   e. At the Open dialog box, click the option box that displays to the right of the *File name* text box and then click *All Files (\*.\*)* at the drop-down list.
   f. Navigate to your Chapter30 folder and then double-click ***MacroDocument.docm***.

g. At the Organizer dialog box with *NewMacros* selected in the list box at the right, click the Copy button that displays between the list boxes.

h. Click the Close button to close the Organizer dialog box.

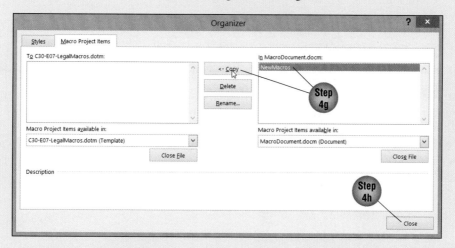

5. Save **C30-E07-LegalMacros.docm**.

## Recording a Macro with Fill-in Fields

In Chapter 16, you inserted a Fill-in field in a document that prompted the operator to insert information at the keyboard during a merge. You can also insert a Fill-in field in a macro that requires input from the keyboard.

To insert a Fill-in field in a macro, begin the recording of the macro. At the point when the Fill-in field is to be inserted, click the INSERT tab, click the Quick Parts button in the Text group, and then click *Field* at the drop-down list. At the Field dialog box with *(All)* selected in the *Categories* list box, as shown in Figure 30.10, scroll down

**Figure 30.10 Field Dialog Box**

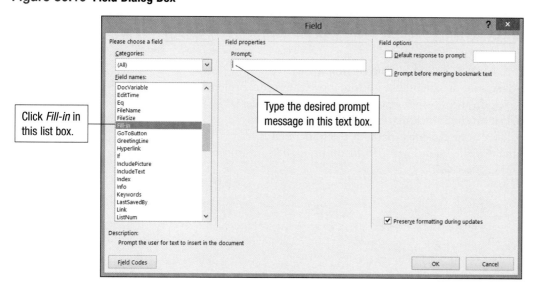

the *Field names* and then click the *Fill-in* field. Add information telling the operator what text to enter at the keyboard by clicking in the *Prompt:* text box and then typing the desired message. When you run the macro, type the desired text specified by the prompt message.

1. With **C30-E07-LegalMacros.docm** open, create a macro that is saved in the current document. Begin by clicking the VIEW tab, clicking the Macros button arrow, and then clicking *Record Macro* at the drop-down list.
2. At the Record Macro dialog box, type **Notary** in the *Macro name* text box.
3. Click the down-pointing arrow at the right side of the *Store macro in* option box and then click *C30-E07-LegalMacros.docm (document)* at the drop-down list.

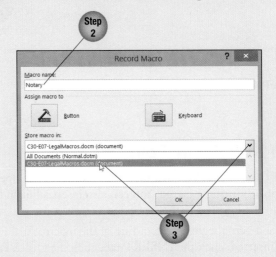

Step 2

Step 3

4. Click in the *Description* text box and then type **Notary signature information.**
5. Click the Keyboard button.
6. At the Customize Keyboard dialog box with the insertion point positioned in the *Press new shortcut key* text box, press Alt + Shift + S.
7. Click the Assign button.
8. Click the Close button.
9. At the document, click the HOME tab and then click the *No Spacing* style in the Styles group.
10. Set three left tabs by completing the following steps:
    a. Make sure the alignment button above the vertical ruler displays with the left tab icon.
    b. Click on the 0.5-inch mark on the horizontal ruler.
    c. Click on the 2-inch mark on the horizontal ruler.
    d. Click on the 2.5-inch mark on the horizontal ruler.
11. Type the text shown in Figure 30.11 on page 1088 up to *(name of person).* (Do not type the text *(name of person).*)

12. Insert a Fill-in field by completing the following steps:
    a. Click the INSERT tab.
    b. Click the Quick Parts button in the Text group and then click *Field* at the drop-down list.
    c. At the Field dialog box with *(All)* selected in the *Categories* list box, scroll down the list and then click *Fill-in*.
    d. Click in the *Prompt:* text box and then type **Type name of person signing.**
    e. Click the OK button.

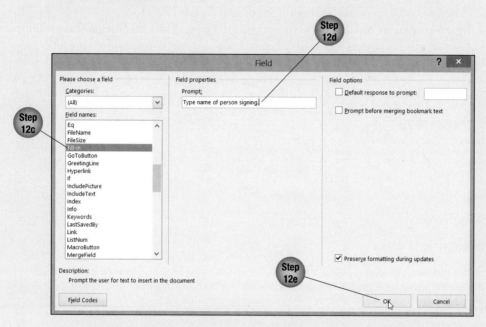

f. At the Microsoft Word dialog box, type **(name of person)** in the text box and then click OK.

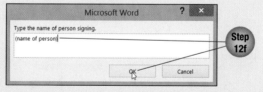

13. Continue typing the notary signature information shown in Figure 30.11 up to the text *(day)* and then insert a Fill-in field, by completing steps similar to those in Step 12, that prompts the operator to type the current day.
14. Continue typing the notary signature information shown in Figure 30.11 up to the text *(month)* and then, by completing steps similar to those in Step 12, insert a Fill-in field that prompts the operator to type the current month.
15. Continue typing the notary signature information shown in Figure 30.11 up to the text *(expiration date)* and then, by completing steps similar to those in Step 12, insert a Fill-in field that prompts the operator to type the expiration date.
16. After inserting the expiration date information, press the Enter key once.
17. End the recording by clicking the macro icon on the Status bar.
18. Click the Save button on the Quick Access toolbar to save the document.
19. Press Ctrl + A to select the entire document and then press the Delete key. (The document should not contain any text.)

20. Save the document as a macro-enabled template by completing the following steps:
    a.  Press the F12 key to display the Save As dialog box.
    b.  At the Save As dialog box, click the *Save as type* option box and then click *Word Macro-Enabled Template (*.dotm)* at the drop-down list.
    c.  Select the text in the *File name* text box and then type **XXX-C30-E07-LegalMacrosTemplate** (typing your initials in place of the *XXX*).
    d.  Click the Save button. (The template will be saved in the Custom Office Templates folder in the Documents folder on the computer's hard drive.)
21. Save the template in your Chapter30 folder with the name **C30-E07-LegalMacrosTemplate**. (Make sure it is saved as a macro-enabled template).
22. Close the **C30-E07-LegalMacrosTemplate.dotm** template.

**Figure 30.11 Exercise 30.7B**

STATE OF CALIFORNIA          )
                             ) ss.
COUNTY OF LOS ANGELES        )

On this day personally appeared before me (name of person), known to me to be the individual described in and who executed the aforesaid instrument, and acknowledged that he/she signed as his/her free and voluntary act and deed for the uses and purposes therein mentioned.
Given under my hand and official seal this (day) day of (month), 2015.

_____
NOTARY PUBLIC in and for the State of California
My appointment expires (expiration date)

## Opening a Template in File Explorer

When you save a document as a template, Word saves it in the Custom Office Templates folder. If you save a template in another folder or location, the template will not display when you click the *PERSONAL* option at the New backstage area. You can, however, open a document based on a template saved in a location other than the Custom Office Templates folder by opening the template in File Explorer. To do this, click the File Explorer icon on the Taskbar, navigate to the folder containing the template, and then double-click the template. Instead of the template opening, a blank document opens that is based on the template.

In Exercise 30.7B, you saved the legal macros template in the Custom Office Templates folder and also your Chapter30 folder. In the next exercise, you will use File Explorer to open a blank document based on the legal macros template you saved to your Chapter30 folder.

1. Open a document based on the *C30-E07-LegalMacrosTemplate.dotm* template in your Chapter30 folder using File Explorer by completing the following steps:
   a. Click the File Explorer icon on the Taskbar. (The Taskbar displays along the bottom of the screen.)
   b. Navigate to your Chapter30 folder and then double-click **C30-E07-LegalMacrosTemplate.dotm**.
2. Use the Object button on the INSERT tab to insert the document named **Affidavit.docx**, located in your Chapter30 folder, into the current document.
3. Position the insertion point at the beginning of the title *AFFIDAVIT OF TRUST* and then run the Title macro.
4. Select the numbered paragraphs of text (paragraphs 1 through 6) and then run the Indent macro.
5. Complete the following finds and replaces:
   a. Find all occurrences of *NAME* and replace them with *LOREN HOUSTON*. (Be sure to replace only the occurrences of *NAME* in all uppercase letters.) ***Hint: Expand the Find and Replace dialog box and insert a check mark in the* Match case *option.***
   b. Find the one occurrence of *ADDRESS* and replace it with *102 Marine Drive, Los Angeles, CA*. (Be sure to replace only the occurrence of *ADDRESS* in all uppercase letters.)
6. Move the insertion point to the end of the document a double space below the text and then run the Notary macro by completing the following steps:
   a. Press Alt + Shift + S.
   b. When the macro stops and prompts you for the name of a person, type **LOREN HOUSTON** and then click OK.
   c. When the macro stops and prompts you for the day, type **9th** and then click OK.
   d. When the macro stops and prompts you for the month, type **March** and then click OK.
   e. When the macro stops and prompts you for the expiration date, type **12/31/2016** and then click OK.

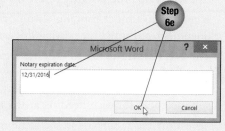

7. Save the document and name it **C30-E07-Affidavit**.
8. Print and then close **C30-E07-Affidavit.docx**.
9. At a blank screen, change the macro security settings by completing the following steps:
   a. Click the DEVELOPER tab and then click the Macro Security button in the Code group.
   b. At the Trust Center, click the *Disable all macros with notification* option.
   c. Click OK.

# Chapter Summary

- Use the outline feature in Word to format headings within a document; view formatted titles, headings, and body text in a document; and edit text.

- Display a document in Outline view by clicking the VIEW tab and then clicking the Outline button in the Document Views group.

- In Outline view, identify particular titles, headings, and subheadings within a document as certain levels.

- When a document displays in Outline view, the OUTLINING tab contains buttons for assigning levels and expanding and collapsing an outline.

- When a paragraph is identified as a level 1 heading, the Heading 1 style is applied to it. The Heading 2 style is applied to a paragraph identified as a level 2 heading.

- Promote or demote a heading in Outline view by dragging the selection symbol that displays before a title or heading.

- One of the advantages of working in Outline view is being able to see a condensed outline of your document without all of the text between titles, headings, and subheadings displaying. Another advantage of working in Outline view is being able to maintain consistency between titles and headings.

- To collapse all of the text beneath a particular heading, click the Collapse button in the Outline Tools group on the OUTLINING tab. Click the Expand button to display all of the text.

- In Outline view, you can rearrange the contents of a document. To move a heading and the body text below it, select the heading and then click the Move Down or Move Up button in the Outline Tools group. You can also move a heading and the body text below it by dragging the selection symbol that displays before the heading to the desired position.

- A master document contains a number of separate documents called subdocuments. Create a master document or format an existing document as a master document in Outline view.

- The OUTLINING tab in Outline view contains buttons for working with master documents and subdocuments. Clicking the Show Document button and then clicking the Create button—both located in the Master Document group on the OUTLINING tab—causes Word to create a subdocument for each heading at the top level within the selected text.

- Save a master document in the same manner as a normal document. Word automatically assigns a document name to each subdocument using the first characters in the subdocument heading.

- Move a subdocument within a master document by dragging the subdocument icon to the desired position.

- Use buttons in the Master Document group on the OUTLINING tab to create, insert, unlink, expand, collapse, merge, and split subdocuments.

- Use the macro feature to record and then execute a series of commands or apply formatting.

- Recording a macro involves turning on the macro recorder, performing the steps to be recorded, and then turning off the recorder.

- Run a macro by displaying the Macros dialog box and then double-clicking the desired macro name.

- You can create a macro that starts automatically when Word opens, when a document opens, when a new document opens, when a document is closed, or when Word is closed.

- You can temporarily suspend the recording of a macro by clicking the Pause Recording button in the Code group on the DEVELOPER tab.

- Delete a macro by displaying the Macros dialog box, clicking the macro name to be deleted, and then clicking the Delete button.

- Assign a macro to a keyboard command at the Record Macro dialog box.

➤ To run a macro that has been assigned a keyboard command, press the keys assigned to the macro.

➤ You can add a macro to the Quick Access toolbar and then run the macro by clicking the macro button on the toolbar.

➤ Specify macro security settings at the Trust Center with *Macro Settings* selected in the left panel. Display the Trust Center by clicking the Macro Security button in the Code group on the DEVELOPER tab.

➤ Save a document as a macro-enabled document or a template as a macro-enabled template with the *Save as type* option at the Save As dialog box.

➤ When a Fill-in field is inserted in a macro, keyboard entry is required while the macro runs.

# Commands *Review*

| FEATURE | RIBBON TAB, GROUP | BUTTON, OPTION | KEYBOARD SHORTCUT |
|---|---|---|---|
| collapse outline | OUTLINING, Outline Tools | ▬ | Alt + Shift + _ |
| collapse subdocuments | OUTLINING, Master Document | ⬆ | |
| expand outline | OUTLINING, Outline Tools | ✚ | Alt + Shift + + |
| expand subdocuments | OUTLINING, Master Document | ⬇ | |
| Field dialog box | INSERT, Text | ▦ , *Field* | |
| Macros dialog box | DEVELOPER, Code OR View, Macros | ▤ | Alt + F8 |
| move down outline level | OUTLINING, Outline Tools | ▼ | Alt + Shift + Down |
| move up outline level | OUTLINING, Outline Tools | ▲ | Alt + Shift + Up |
| outline view | VIEW, Views | ▣ | Alt + Ctrl + O |
| Record Macro dialog box | DEVELOPER, Code OR View, Macros | ▤ | |
| show document | OUTLINING, Master Document | ▤ | |
| Trust Center dialog box | DEVELOPER, Code | ⚠ | |

# Key Points *Review*

**Completion:** In the space provided at the right, indicate the correct term, command, or number.

1. The Outline button is located on this tab. _____

2. Click this button to promote a title or heading to level 1. _____

3. Promote or demote a heading in Outline view by dragging this symbol, which displays before a heading. _____

4. Click this button on the OUTLINING tab to collapse all of the text beneath a particular heading. _____

5. The Show Document button is located in this group in the OUTLINING tab. _____

6. Click the Expand Subdocuments button and the name of the button changes to this. _____

7. The Record Macro button is included in the Code group on this tab. _____

8. A macro name must begin with a letter and can contain only letters and these. _____

9. When macro recording is turned on, a macro icon displays on this. _____

10. Delete a macro at this dialog box. _____

11. Assign a macro to a keyboard command at this dialog box. _____

12. You can add a button to this toolbar to run a recorded macro. _____

13. Click this button in the Code group on the DEVELOPER tab to display the Trust Center. _____

14. Inserting this type of field in a macro requires input from the keyboard. _____

# Chapter *Assessments*

## Applying Your Skills

Demonstrate your knowledge of features learned in this chapter by completing the following assessments.

### Assessment 30.1    Assign Levels in Outline View

1. Open **EmpComp.docx** and save the document with the name **C30-A01-EmpComp**.
2. Change to Outline view and then promote or demote titles and headings as follows:

   *COMPENSATION*: Level 1
   *Rate of Pay*: Level 2
   *Pay Progression*: Level 2
   *Overtime*: Level 2
   *Shift Differential*: Level 2
   *EMPLOYEE PERFORMANCE*: Level 1
   *Work Performance Standards*: Level 2
   *Performance Evaluation*: Level 2
   *Employment Records*: Level 2

3. Collapse the outline so only the two levels of titles and headings display.
4. Save and then print **C30-A01-EmpComp.docx**. (This will print the collapsed outline, not the entire document.)

## Assessment 30.2    Move and Delete Headings in a Collapsed Outline

1. With **C30-A01-EmpComp.docx** open, make sure the document displays in Outline view and then save the document with Save As and name it **C30-A02-EmpComp**.
2. Make the following changes:
    a. Change the Show Level button to Level 1.
    b. Move the title *COMPENSATION* below the title *EMPLOYEE PERFORMANCE*.
    c. Change the Show Level button to Level 2.
    d. Move the heading *Pay Progression* below the heading *Overtime*.
    e. Delete the *Shift Differential* heading.
3. Save and then print **C30-A02-EmpComp.docx**.
4. Display the entire document and then close Outline view.
5. Save and then close **C30-A02-EmpComp.docx**.

## Assessment 30.3    Create and Arrange a Master Document

1. Open **WebContent.docx** and save the document with the name **C30-A03-WebContent**.
2. Change to Outline view.
3. Assign to Level 1 the following headings:
    *Browsing Web Pages*
    *Searching Online Content*
    *Evaluating Web Content*
    *Intellectual Property*
4. Click the Show Document button in the Master Document group on the OUTLINING tab.
5. Create subdocuments by selecting the entire document and then clicking the Create button in the Master Document group.
6. Save and then close **C30-A03-WebContent.docx**.
7. Open **C30-A03-WebContent.docx** and then print the document. (The subdocuments will be collapsed.)
8. Display the document in Outline view and then make the following changes to it:
    a. Click the Show Document button in the Master Document group on the OUTLINING tab.
    b. Move the *Evaluating Web Content* subdocument above the *Searching Online Content* subdocument. (Before you release the mouse button, make sure the dark gray, horizontal line is positioned above the gray circle above the *Searching Online Content* subdocument.)
    c. Delete the Intellectual Property subdocument.
9. Save, print, and then close **C30-A03-WebContent.docx**.

## Assessment 30.4    Record and Run Formatting Macros

1. Open **MacroText.docx** and then create a macro named XXXTitle with the following specifications:
    a. Position the insertion point at the beginning of the word *Title* and then turn on the macro recorder.
    b. Press the F8 key and then press the End key.
    c. Click the Center button and then click the Bold button.
    d. Change the font size to 14 points.
    e. Click the Shading button arrow and then click *Green, Accent 6, Lighter 40%* (last column, fourth row).
    f. Click the *Bottom Border* option.
    g. Turn off the macro recorder.
2. Create a macro named XXXDocFont that selects the entire document and then changes the font to Cambria. Assign the macro to the Quick Access toolbar.
3. Close **MacroText.docx** without saving it.

4. Open **DesignNwsltr.docx** and save the document with the name **C30-A04-DesignNwsltr**.
5. Click the button on the Quick Access toolbar that represents the XXXDocFont macro.
6. With the insertion point positioned at the left margin of the title *DESIGNING A NEWSLETTER*, run the XXXTitle macro.
7. Move the insertion point to the beginning of the title *CREATING NEWSLETTER LAYOUT* and then run the XXXTitle macro.
8. Run the XXXHeading macro (created in Exercise 30.4A) for the four headings in the document: *Applying Guidelines*, *Choosing Paper Size and Type*, *Choosing Paper Weight*, and *Creating Margins*.
9. Save, print, and then close **C30-A04-DesignNwsltr.docx**.
10. Remove the XXXDocFont button from the Quick Access toolbar.

## Assessmt 30.5      Record and Run a Macro That Sets Tabs

1. At a blank document, run the XXXTab macro and then create the document shown in Figure 30.12. (Type the text in the first column at the second tab stop [the tab stop at 1 inch], not the left margin.)
2. Save the completed document and name it **C30-A05-PRDept**.
3. Print and then close **C30-A05-PRDept.docx**.

**Figure 30.12  Assessment 30.5**

---

### McCORMACK FUNDS CORPORATION

#### Public Relations Department, Extension Numbers


Roger Maldon .................................................................................. 129

Kimberly Holland.............................................................................. 143

Richard Perez ................................................................................... 317

Sharon Rawlins................................................................................. 211

Earl Warnberg.................................................................................. 339

Susan Fanning .................................................................................. 122

## Assessment 30.6    Record and Run a Macro with Fill-in Fields

1. At a blank document, record a macro named XXXNotSig that includes the information shown in Figure 30.13. Click the *No Spacing* style and then set left tabs at the 0.5-inch mark, 1.5-inch mark, and 3-inch mark on the horizontal ruler. Include Fill-in fields in the macro at the three places the text is in parentheses. After inserting the *(county)* Fill-in field, press the Enter key and then end the macro recording.
2. Close the document without saving it.
3. Open **Agreement.docx** and save the document with the name **C30-A06-Agreement**.
4. Move the insertion point to the end of the document and then run the XXXNotSig macro and insert the following information when prompted:
   *(name 1)*: **LLOYD KOVICH**
   *(name 2)*: **JOANNE MILNER**
   *(county)*: **Ramsey County**
5. Save, print, and then close **C30-A06-Agreement.docx**.

**Figure 30.13  Assessment 30.6**

STATE OF MINNESOTA    )
                      ) ss.
COUNTY OF RAMSEY      )

    I certify that I know or have satisfactory evidence that (name 1) and (name 2) are the persons who appeared before me, and said persons acknowledge that they signed the foregoing Contract and acknowledged it to be their free and voluntary act for the uses and purposes therein mentioned.

                                   _____

                                   NOTARY PUBLIC in and for the State of
                                   Minnesota residing in (county)

# Expanding Your Skills

Explore additional feature options or use Help to learn a new skill in creating this document.

## Assessment 30.7    Create and Run a Macro with Fields

1. Open **SFHMacroText.docx** and then use the document to create the following macros for St. Francis Hospital:
   a. Create a macro named XXXSFHDocFormat that selects the entire document (use Ctrl + A), applies the No Spacing style (click the *No Spacing* style in the Styles group), changes the line spacing to double (press Ctrl + 2), and changes the font to Constantia.
   b. Create a macro named XXXSFHMargins that changes the top margin to 1.5 inches and the left and right margins to 1.25 inches.
   c. Create a macro named XXXSFHTitle that selects a line of text (at the beginning of the line, press the F8 key and then press the End key), changes the font size to 14 points, applies bold formatting to the text, centers the text, and then deselects the text.
   d. Create a macro named XXXSFHHeading that selects a line of text, changes the font size to 12 points, applies bold formatting to the text, applies underlining to the text, and deselects the text.

2. In this chapter, you learned how to create macros using Fill-in fields. You can also create macros using other fields from the Fields dialog box. With **SFHMacroText.docx** open, press Ctrl + End to move the insertion point to the end of the document and then create a macro named XXXSFHEnd that completes the following steps:
   a. Change the line spacing to single (press Ctrl + 1).
   b. Insert the *FileName* field.
   c. Press the Enter key and insert the *Date* field.
   d. Press the Enter key, type **Number of Pages:**, press the spacebar, and then insert the *NumPages* field.
   e. Press the Enter key and then insert a Fill-in field that prompts the user to type his or her name.
3. Close **SFHMacroText.docx** without saving it.
4. Open **PropProtectIssues.docx** and save the document with the name **C30-A07-PropProtectIssues**.
5. Run the XXXSFHDocFormat macro and then run the XXXSFHMargins macro.
6. Run the XXXSFHTitle macro for the title of the document and run the XXXSFHHeading macro for the three headings in the document (*Intellectual Property*, *Fair Use*, and *Intellectual Property Protection*).
7. Press Ctrl + End to move the insertion point to the end of the document and then run the XXXSFHEnd macro. At the prompt asking for your name, type your first and last names.
8. Save, print, and then close **C30-A07-PropProtectIssues.docx**.
9. Open **InterfaceApplications.docx** and save the document with the name **C30-A07-InterfaceApplications**.
10. Run macros in the document by completing steps similar to those in Steps 5 through 7.
11. Save, print, and then close **C30-A07-InterfaceApplications.docx**.

## Achieving Signature Status

Take your skills to the next level by completing this more challenging assessment.

### Assessment 30.8    Create and Run a Menu Formatting Macro

1. Open **MacroText.docx**.
2. Create a macro with the following specifications:
   a. Name the macro XXXMenu and assign the macro to the Quick Access toolbar. (You determine the description.)
   b. With insertion point at the beginning of the document, create a Fill-in field with the prompt *Type the current date.*
   c. Select the entire document and then apply the following formatting:
      • Change the font to 14-point Monotype Corsiva and apply bold formatting.
      • Center the text.
      • Apply Green, Accent 6, Lighter 60% paragraph shading.
      • Display the Borders and Shading dialog box with the Borders tab selected, scroll down the *Style* list box and then click the third line option from the end, change the color to Purple, click the *Box* option in the *Setting* section, and then close the dialog box.
   d. End the recording of the macro.
3. Close **MacroText.docx** without saving it.
4. Open **Menu.docx** and save the document with the name **C30-A08-Menu**.
5. Press the Down Arrow key once and then apply the XXXMenu macro by clicking the button on the Quick Access toolbar that represents the macro. Type the date **August 6, 2015** at the fill-in prompt. Your document should appear as shown in Figure 30.14 on the next page.
6. Save, print, and then close **C30-A08-Menu.docx**.

7. Open **ChefMenu01.docx** and save the document with the name **C30-A08-ChefMenu01**.
8. Press the Down Arrow key once, apply the XXXMenu macro, and type **August 11, 2015** at the fill-in prompt.
9. Save, print, and then close **C30-A08-ChefMenu01.docx**.
10. Open **ChefMenu02.docx** and save the document with the name **C30-A08-ChefMenu02**.
11. Press the Down Arrow key once, apply the XXXMenu macro, and type **August 12, 2015** at the fill-in prompt.
12. Save, print, and then close **C30-A08-ChefMenu02.docx**.
13. Remove the XXXMenu button from the Quick Access toolbar.

**Figure 30.14 Assessment 30.8**

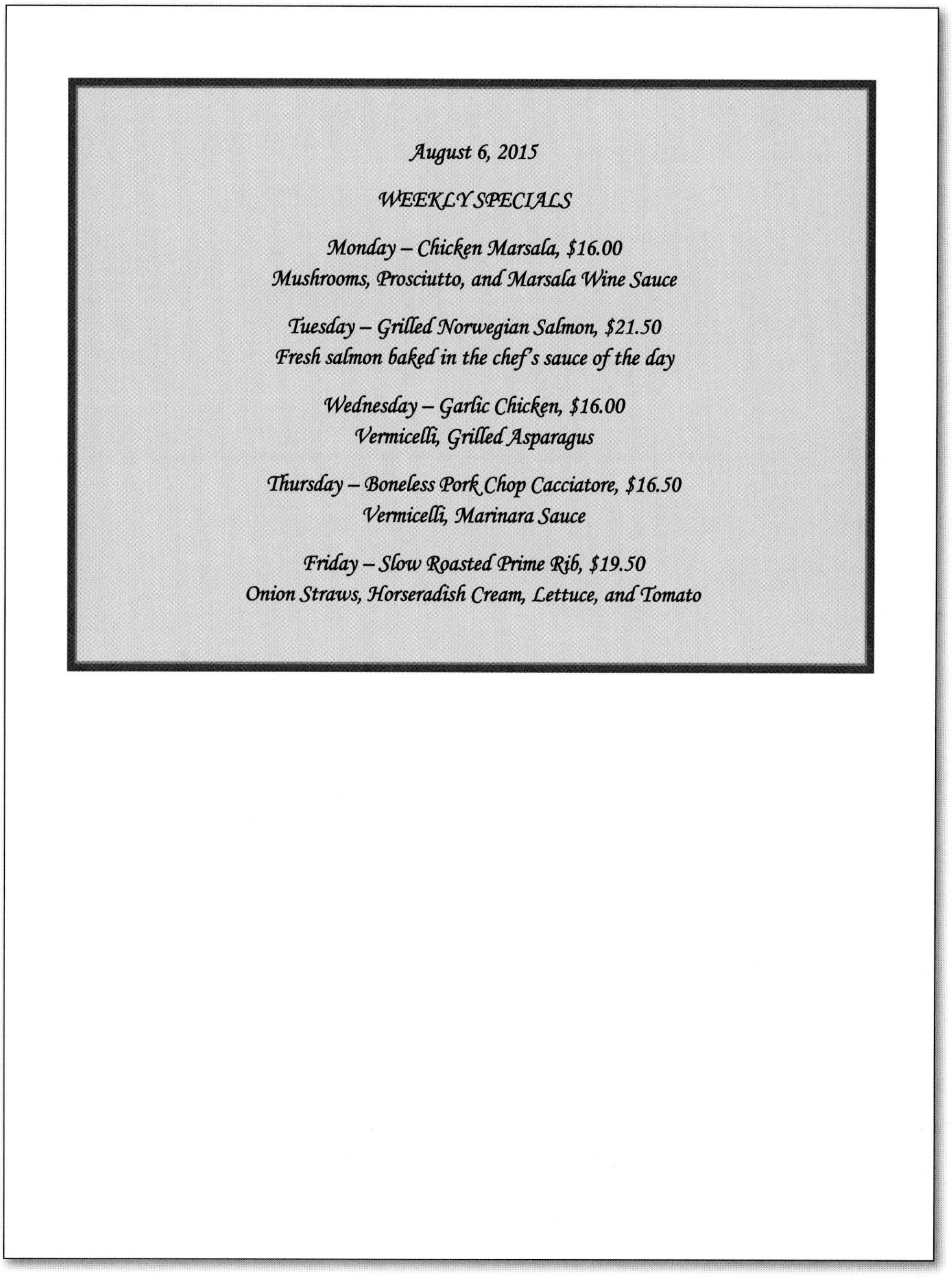

*August 6, 2015*

*WEEKLY SPECIALS*

*Monday – Chicken Marsala, $16.00*
*Mushrooms, Prosciutto, and Marsala Wine Sauce*

*Tuesday – Grilled Norwegian Salmon, $21.50*
*Fresh salmon baked in the chef's sauce of the day*

*Wednesday – Garlic Chicken, $16.00*
*Vermicelli, Grilled Asparagus*

*Thursday – Boneless Pork Chop Cacciatore, $16.50*
*Vermicelli, Marinara Sauce*

*Friday – Slow Roasted Prime Rib, $19.50*
*Onion Straws, Horseradish Cream, Lettuce, and Tomato*

## Referencing Data

# ASSESSING PROFICIENCIES

In this unit, you have learned how to reference data with footnotes, endnotes, citations, and bibliographies. You have also learned to create an index, table of contents, table of figures, and table of authorities, and you have learned to create forms with content controls and form fields, use the outline view, create a master and subdocument, and format a document with macros. The following assessments address these skills.

*Note: Before beginning computer assessments, copy to your storage medium the Unit06PA folder from the CD that accompanies this textbook and then make Unit06PA the active folder.*

**Assessment U6.1**     **Insert Footnotes in a Report**

1. Open **InterfaceApps.docx** and save the document with the name **U6-PA01-InterfaceApps**.
2. Create the first footnote shown in Figure U6.1 on the next page at the end of the first paragraph in the document.
3. Create the second footnote shown in Figure U6.1 at the end of the paragraph in the *Speech Recognition* section.
4. Create the third footnote shown in Figure U6.1 at the end of the paragraph in the *Virtual Reality* section.
5. Create the fourth footnote shown in Figure U6.1 at the end of the last paragraph in the document.
6. Save and then print **U6-PA01-InterfaceApps.docx**.
7. Select the entire document and then change the font to Constantia.
8. Select all of the footnotes and change the font to Constantia.
9. Delete the third footnote.
10. Save, print, and then close **U6-PA01-InterfaceApps.docx**.

**Assessment U6.2**     **Create Citations and Prepare a Works Cited Page for a Report**

1. Open **BuildWebsite.docx** and save the document with the name **U6-PA02-BuildWebsite**.
2. Format the title page to meet MLA (Modern Language Association) requirements with the following changes:
    a.  Select the entire document, change the font to 12-point Cambria, change the line spacing to 2.0, and remove the extra space after paragraphs.
    b.  Move the insertion point to the beginning of the document, type your name, press the Enter key, type your instructor's name, press the Enter key, type the title of your course, press the Enter key, and then type the current date.
    c.  Insert a header that displays your last name and the page number at the right margin and then change the font to 12-point Cambria.
3. Press Ctrl + End to move the insertion point to the end of the document and then type the text shown in Figure U6.2 on page 1101 (in MLA style) up to the

Charles Raines and Saul Silverstein, *Computers: Natural-Language Technologies* (Newark: Mansfield & Nassen Publishing, 2015), 67-72.

Theodore M. Sutton, *Computers and Communicating* (Los Angeles: Southwest Publishing House, 2014), 10-14.

Jin Chun and Mariah Anderson, *Natural-Language Computing* (Cleveland: Hammermaster Publishing, 2015), 45-51.

Cecilia Castillo, *Computers and the Art of Virtual Reality* (Philadelphia: Old Town Press and Publishing House, 2014), 2-6.

first citation (the text *(Mercado)*). Insert the source information from a journal article written by Claudia Mercado using the following information:

> *Author:* **Claudia Mercado**
> *Title:* **Connecting a Web Page**
> *Journal Name:* **Connections**
> *Year:* **2015**
> *Pages:* **12-21**
> *Volume:* **IV**

4. Continue typing the text up to the next citation (the text *(Holmes)*) and insert the following source information from a website:

> *Author:* **Brent Holmes**
> *Name of Web Page:* **Hosting Your Web Page**
> *Year:* **2014**
> *Month:* **September**
> *Day:* **28**
> *Year Accessed:* (*type current year*)
> *Month Accessed:* (*type current month*)
> *Day Accessed:* (*type current day*)
> *URL:* **www.emcp.net/hosting**

5. Continue typing the text up to the next citation (the text *(Vukovich)*) and insert the following information from a book:

> *Author:* **Ivan Vukovich**
> *Title:* **Computer Technology in the Business Environment**
> *Year:* **2014**
> *City:* **San Francisco**
> *Publisher:* **Gold Coast Publishing**

6. Insert the page number in the citation by Ivan Vukovich using the Edit Citation dialog box.
7. Type the remaining text in Figure U6.2.
8. Edit the *Ivan Vukovich* source by changing the last name to *Vulkovich* in the *Master List* section of the Source Manager dialog box.
9. Create a new source in the document using the Source Manager dialog box and include the following source information for a journal article:

> *Author:* **Sonia Jaquez**
> *Title:* **Organizing a Web Page**

*Journal Name:* **Design Techniques**
*Year:* **2015**
*Pages:* **32-44**
*Volume:* **IX**

10. Type the following sentence at the end of the last paragraph in the document:
    **Browsers look for pages with these names first when a specific file at a website is requested, and index pages display by default if no other page is specified.**
11. Insert a citation for Sonia Jaquez at the end of the sentence you just typed.
12. Insert a citation for Claudia Mercado following the second sentence in the first paragraph of the document.
13. Insert a works cited page at the end of the document on a separate page.
14. Format the works cited page to meet MLA requirements with the following changes:
    a. Select the *Works Cited* title and all of the entries and click the *No Spacing* style.
    b. Change the font to 12-point Cambria and change the spacing to 2.0.
    c. Center the title *Works Cited.*
    d. Format the works cited entries with a hanging indent.
15. Save and then print **U6-PA02-BuildWebsite.docx**.
16. Change the document and works cited page from MLA style to APA (American Psychological Association) style. Make sure you change the title of the sources list to *References*. Select the references in the list and then change the spacing after paragraphs to 0, the line spacing to 2.0, and the font to 12-point Cambria.
17. Save **U6-PA02-BuildWebsite.docx**, print page 3, and then close the document.

Figure U6.2 **Assessment U6.2**

One of the first tasks in website development is finding a good host for the site.

Essentially, a web host lets you store a copy of your web pages on the hard drive of a

powerful computer connected to the Internet with a fast connection that can handle

thousands of users (Mercado). Hosting your own website is possible but is only feasible if

you own an extra computer that can be dedicated to the role of a web server, have a

high-speed Internet connection, and feel confident about handling the job of network

security and routing (Holmes). Most people's situations do not fit those criteria. Fortunately,

several free and fee-based web hosting services are available.

As you plan a website, decide what types of content you will include and think about

how all of the pages should link together. Most websites have a home page that provides the

starting point for users entering the site. "Like the top of a pyramid or the table of contents of

a book, the home page leads to other web pages via hyperlinks" (Vukovich 26). Most home

pages have the default name of index.html (or sometimes index.htm).

**Assessment U6.3** **Create an Index and Table of Contents for a Report**

1. At a blank document, create the text shown in Figure U6.3 as a concordance file.
2. Save the document with the name **U6-PA03-CFile**.
3. Print and then close **U6-PA03-CFile.docx**.
4. Open **DTPDesign.docx** and save the document with the name **U6-PA03-DTPDesign**.
5. Make the following changes to the document:
   a. Apply the Heading 1 style to the title and apply the Heading 2 style to the two headings in the report.
   b. Change the style set to Basic (Simple).
   c. Mark text for an index using the concordance file **U6-PA03-CFile.docx**.
   d. Insert the index at the end of the document on a separate page.
   e. Apply the Heading 1 style to the title of the index.
   f. Insert a table of contents at the beginning of the document.
   g. Number the table of contents page with a lowercase roman numeral.
   h. Number the other pages in the report with arabic numbers and start the numbering with 1 on the page containing the report title.

**Figure U6.3** **Assessment U6.3**

| | |
|---|---|
| message | Message |
| publication | Publication |
| Design | Design |
| flyer | Flyer |
| letterhead | Letterhead |
| newsletter | Newsletter |
| intent | Design: intent |
| audience | Design: audience |
| layout | Design: layout |
| thumbnail | Thumbnail |
| principles | Design: principles |
| Focus | Design: focus |
| focus | Design: focus |
| balance | Design: balance |
| proportion | Design: proportion |
| contrast | Design: contrast |
| directional flow | Design: directional flow |
| consistency | Design: consistency |
| color | Design: color |
| White space | White space |
| white space | White space |
| Legibility | Legibility |
| headline | Headline |
| Subheads | Subheads |
| subheads | Subheads |

6. Change the format of the title heading *Table of Contents* to all caps.
7. Make sure that the table of contents displays the correct page numbers. If not, update the table of contents.
8. Save, print, and then close **U6-PA03-DTPDesign.docx**.

**Create Captions and Insert a Table of Figures in a Report**

1. Open **SoftwareCareers.docx** and save the document with the name **U6-PA04-SoftwareCareers**.
2. Position the insertion point in a cell in the first table and create the caption *Table 1: Software Development Careers* above the table. (Change the paragraph spacing after to 0 points.)
3. Position the insertion point in a cell in the second table and create the caption *Table 2: Application Development Careers* above the table. (Change the paragraph spacing after to 0 points.)
4. Move the insertion point to the beginning of the document and then insert a section break that begins a new page.
5. With the insertion point positioned below the section break, number the pages at the bottom center of each page and change the starting page number to 1.
6. Move the insertion point to the beginning of the document and then insert the Automatic Table 2 table of contents.
7. Press Ctrl + Enter to insert a page break. (If your insertion point does not move to the new page, continue to Step 8. The insertion point will move to the new page when you start typing *Tables*.)
8. Type **Tables**, press the Enter key (your insertion point may not move down to the next line), and then insert the table of figures using the Formal format.
9. Apply the Heading 1 style to the title *Tables*.
10. Move the insertion point to the beginning of the document and then change the numbering format to lowercase roman numerals.
11. Update the entire table of contents.
12. Save, print, and then close **U6-PA04-SoftwareCareers.docx**.

**Create and Fill in a Purchase Order Form**

1. Create the form shown in Figure U6.4 on the next page as a template and use a table to create the columns and rows. Include the following elements:
   a. Apply border and shading formatting as shown in the figure.
   b. Insert a picture content control, a date picker content control, and plain text content controls in the appropriate cells. Lock the picture content control so it cannot be edited.
   c. Insert a drop-down list content control for *Company Status* with the following choices: *Bronze*, *Silver*, and *Gold*.
2. Protect the template.
3. Save the template with the name **XXX-SBPOTemplate**. (Replace the *XXX* with your initials.)
4. Print and then close **XXX-SBPOTemplate.dotx**.
5. Create a form document from the **XXX-SBPOTemplate** template with the following information:
   *Company Name:* **John's Corner Market**
   *Date:* (*Insert current date.*)
   *Company Status: Choose the* Gold *option.*
   *Description:* **Sales Insight**
   *Quantity:* **5**
   *Cost:* **$20.50**

*Description:* **Strategic Marketing**
*Quantity:* **2**
*Cost:* **$134.50**
*Description:* **Advertising**
*Quantity:* **3**
*Cost:* **$201.00**

6. Save the document with the name **U6-PA05-SB-JCM**.
7. Print and then close **U6-PA05-SB-JCM.docx**.

Figure U6.4  **Assessment U6.5**

# STORYTELLER BOOKS

4350 Jenkins Boulevard
Glen Ellyn, IL 60137
(630) 555-7998

| PURCHASE ORDER | | |
|---|---|---|
| **Company Name:** Enter company name | **Date:** Click here to enter a date. | |
| **Company Status:** Choose an item. | | |
| **Description** | **Quantity** | **Cost** |
| Item description | Enter quantity | Enter cost |
| Item description | Enter quantity | Enter cost |
| Item description | Enter quantity | Enter cost |

**Assessment U6.6**    **Create and Fill in an Insurance Application Form**

1. Open **LAApp05.docx** and then save the document as a template and name it **XXXLAProfAppTemplate**. (Type your initials in place of the *XXX*).
2. Insert form fields in the template as shown in Figure U6.5 on the next page with the following specifications:
   a. Insert a text form field for *Client Number:* that specifies a maximum length of 6 characters.
   b. Insert a text form field for *Type of Deduction:* that specifies *Flat* as the default text.
   c. Insert a drop-down list form field for *Deduction Amount:* that includes the following four choices: *None, $1,000, $2,500,* and *$5,000*.
   d. Insert four check boxes in the cell in the middle of the form table as shown in Figure U6.5. ***Hint: You can move the insertion point to a tab stop within a cell by pressing Ctrl + Tab.*** Insert a check box form field in the cell immediately left of *AANA* that is checked by default.
   e. Insert the remaining text and check box form fields as shown in Figure U6.5.
3. Protect the template.
4. Save, print, and then close **XXXLAProfAppTemplate.dotx**.

5. Create a form document from the **XXXLAProfAppTemplate.dotx** template and then insert the following information in the specified data fields:

   *First Name:* **Rachel**
   *Middle Name:* **Brianne**
   *Last Name:* **Hayward**
   *Address:* **12091 South 234th Street, Fairbanks, AK 99704**
   *Date of Birth:* **01/18/1982**
   *Client Number:* **10-541**
   *Current Date:* (*Insert the current date.*)
   *Type of Deduction:* **Flat**
   *Deduction Amount:* **$5,000**
   (*Leave the check mark in the* AANA *check box and also insert a check mark in the* APTA-PPS *check box.*)
   (*Insert a check mark in the* Occupational Therapist *check box.*)

6. Save the document with the name **U6-PA06-ProfAppHayward**.

7. Print and then close **U6-PA06-ProfAppHayward.docx**.

Figure U6.5  **Assessment U6.6**

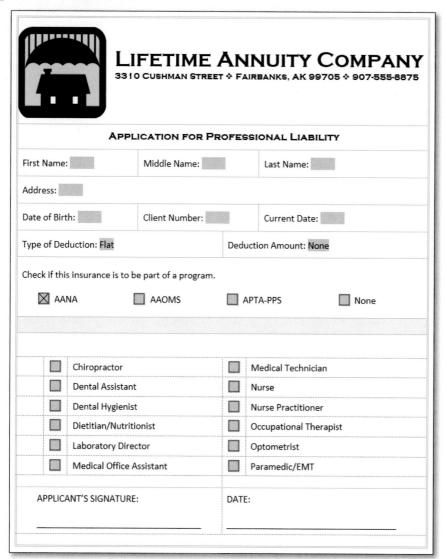

**Create Subdocuments**

1. Open **CommSoftware.docx** and save the document with the name **U6-PA07-CommSoftware**.
2. Display the document in Outline view and assign to level 1 the following headings:
   *Electronic Mail*
   *Instant Messaging Software*
   *Groupware*
   *Web Browsers*
   *Webconferencing*
3. Click the Show Document button in the Master Document group on the OUTLINING tab.
4. Create subdocuments by selecting the entire document and then clicking the Create button in the Master Document group.
5. Save and then close **U6-PA07-CommSoftware.docx**.
6. Open **U6-PA07-CommSoftware.docx** and then print the document. (The subdocuments will be collapsed.)
7. Make the following changes to the document:
   a. Move the Web Browsers subdocument above the Instant Messaging Software subdocument. (Before you release the mouse button, make sure the dark gray, horizontal line is positioned above the gray circle above the Instant Messaging Software subdocument.)
   b. Delete the Groupware subdocument.
8. Save, print, and then close **U6-PA07-CommSoftware.docx**.

**Create and Run Macros**

1. At a blank document, create the following macros:
   a. Create a macro named XXXAPMFormat (using your initials in place of the *XXX*) that selects the entire document, changes the font to Constantia, and changes the font color to Dark Blue.
   b. Create a macro named XXXAPMTitle that changes the font size to 14 points, applies bold formatting, centers the text, and applies Blue, Accent 1, Lighter 60% paragraph shading.
2. At a new blank document, create a macro named XXXAPMInfo that includes the information shown in Figure U6.6. Insert Fill-in fields in the macro where the text is in parentheses.
3. After recording the macros, close the documents without saving them.
4. Open **Lease.docx** and save the document with the name **U6-PA08-Lease**.
5. Run the XXXAPMFormat macro.
6. With the insertion point positioned at the beginning of the title *LEASE AGREEMENT*, run the XXXAPMTitle macro.
7. Move the insertion point to the end of the document and then run the XXXAPMInfo macro. Insert the following information when prompted:
   *(name)*: Grace Hillstrand
   *(date):* May 22, 2015
8. Save, print, and then close **U6-PA08-Lease.docx**.
9. Open **REAgrmnt.docx** and save the document with the name **U6-PA08-REAgrmnt**.
10. Run the XXXAPMFormat macro.
11. With the insertion point positioned at the beginning of the title *REAL ESTATE SALE AGREEMENT*, run the XXXAPMTitle macro.

12. Move the insertion point to the end of the document and then run the XXXAPMInfo macro. Insert the following information when prompted:
    *(name)*: Grace Hillstrand
    *(date):* May 29, 2015
13. Save, print, and then close **U6-PA08-REAgrmnt.docx**.

Figure U6.6 **Assessment U6.8**

This document is the sole property of Azure Property Management and may not be reproduced, copied, or sold without express written consent of a legal representative of Azure Property Management. *(press Enter once)*

Prepared by: (name)  *(press Shift + Enter)*
Date: (date)

# CREATING ORIGINAL DOCUMENTS

The activities in Assessment U6.9 and Assessment U6.10 give you the opportunity to practice your writing skills as well as demonstrate your mastery of some of the important Word features presented in this unit. When you compose the documents, use correct grammar, precise word choices, and clear sentence construction.

## Assessment U6.9    Format an Employee Handbook

**Situation:** You work in the human resources department at Brennan Distributors and are responsible for preparing an employee handbook. Open **BDHandbook.docx** and save it with the name **U6-PA09-BDHandbook**. Make the following changes to the document:

- Insert a page break before each centered title (except the first title, *Introduction*).
- Apply heading styles to the titles and headings.
- Change to a style set of your choosing.
- Apply a theme that makes the handbook easy to read.
- Insert a table of contents.
- Create a concordance file and then insert an index.
- Insert appropriate page numbering in the document.
- Add elements to improve the appearance of the document.

Save, print, and then close **U6-PA09-BDHandbook.docx**.

## Assessment U6.10    Create a Contact Information Form

**Situation:** You work for the Evergreen Regional Center and are responsible for creating fill-in forms for the records department. Your supervisor has asked you to create a template for a fill-in form. Use **ERCFunding.docx** as a reference (for the clip art image, font face, and colors) and create a form that includes the following specifications. (You determine the layout of the form and the types of form fields used.)

- Use the information in the first cell in the **ERCFunding.docx** document for the first cell in the template you design.
- Add this title to the form: *Contact Information*.
- Include the following fields:
    - *Name*
    - *Birth date*
    - *Marital status*
    - *Gender*
    - *Address*
    - *Phone*
    - *Email address*
    - *Occupation*
    - *Emergency contact*
    - *Emergency phone*

After creating the form template, save the template document with the name **U6-PA10-ERCContact**. Use the **U6-PA10-ERCContact.dotx** form template to create a filled-in form. You make up the information to insert in the form. Save the completed form document with the name **U6-PA10-ERCContactInfo**. Print and then close **U6-PA10-ERCContactInfo.docx**.

# Appendix A

## Proofreader Marks

| Proofreader Mark | Example | Revised |
|---|---|---|
| # Insert space | letter#tothe | letter to the |
| ℘ Delete | the command𝔰 is | the command is |
| lc / Lowercase | lc he is Branch Manager | he is branch manager |
| cap or uc ≡ Uppercase | cap Margaret simpson | Margaret Simpson |
| ¶ New paragraph | ¶ The new product | The new product |
| no ¶ No paragraph | the meeting. no ¶ Bring the | the meeting. Bring the |
| ∧ Insert | pens, and clips | pens, and clips |
| ⊙ Insert period | a global search ⊙ | a global search. |
| ⊐ Move right | ⊐ With the papers | With the papers |
| ⊏ Move left | ⊏ access the code | access the code |
| ⊐⊏ Center | ⊐ Chapter Six ⊏ | Chapter Six |
| ∽ Transpose | It is raesonable | It is reasonable |
| sp Spell out | sp 475 Mill Ave. | 475 Mill Avenue |
| ... Stet (do not delete) | I am very pleased | I am very pleased |
| ⌒ Close up | regret fully | regretfully |
| ss Single-space | The margin top ss is 1 inch. | The margin top is 1 inch. |
| ds Double-space | ds Paper length is set for 11 inches. | Paper length is set for 11 inches. |
| ts Triple-space | ts The F8 function key turns on Extend | The F8 function key turns on Extend |
| bf Boldface | bf Boldface type provides emphasis. | **Boldface** type provides emphasis. |
| ital Italics | ital Use italics for terms to be defined. | Use *italics* for terms to be defined. |

# Formatting a Personal Business Letter

A variety of options is available for formatting a personal business letter—a letter from you as an individual, rather than you representing a company. One of the most commonly used formats is the *block style*. In block style format, all elements of the letter align at the left margin. You can create a personal business letter with the default Microsoft Word 2013 line and paragraph spacing, or you can remove the spacing and then create the letter.

## Formatting with Microsoft Word Default Spacing

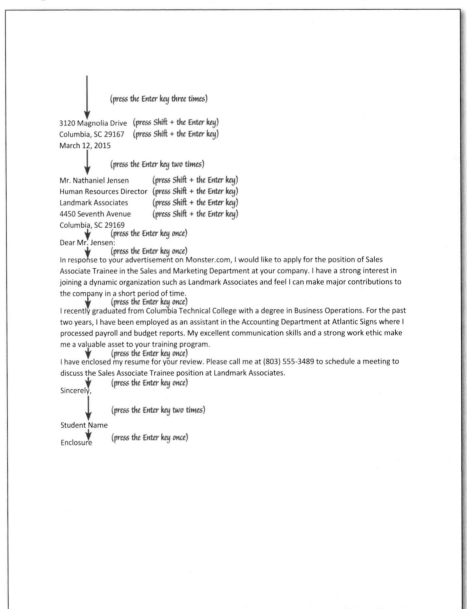

The Word default line spacing is 1.08 and the default spacing after paragraphs is 8 points. You can remove this formatting by clicking the *No Spacing* style in the Styles group on the HOME tab. Applying this style changes the line spacing to 1 and the spacing after paragraphs to 0 points. To format a personal business letter without the Word default spacing, click the *No Spacing* style and then type the letter as shown below.

## Formatting with No Spacing Style Applied

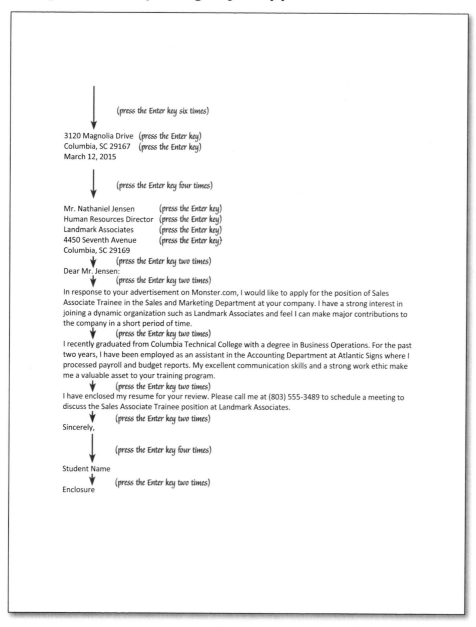

# Formatting a Memo

The formatting of an interoffice correspondence, referred to as a *memo* (short for *memorandum*), varies from company to company. However, the content of a memo should be brief and to the point, and the format should support quick reading, easy distribution, and efficient filing.

In some of the exercises in this textbook, you will be required to type and format a memo. You can create a memo with the default Microsoft Word 2013 line and paragraph spacing, or you can remove the spacing and then create the memo. Include your reference initials at the end of the memo, as shown in the following example (where the *XX* indicates your initials). You can also include the document name below the initials, although this is optional.

In the examples below and on the next page, the reference initials display in uppercase letters. Usually, reference initials are typed in lowercase letters. However, Word automatically formats some text as you type it. When you type a lowercase letter at the beginning of a line, Word automatically corrects it to an uppercase letter. If your instructor wants you to type lowercase initials, turn off the automatic correction. To do this, complete the following steps:

1. Click the FILE tab and then click *Options*.
2. At the Word Options dialog box, click *Proofing* in the left panel and then click the AutoCorrect Options button.

## Formatting with Microsoft Word Default Spacing

TO: ⎯⎯▶ Jim Everson, Resources Coordinator *(press the Enter key)*
   *Tab twice*

FROM: ⎯▶ Isabelle Brown, Training Coordinator *(press the Enter key)*
   *Tab twice*

DATE: ⎯⎯▶ February 16, 2015 *(press the Enter key)*
   *Tab twice*

SUBJECT: ⎯▶ Network and Internet Books *(press the Enter key)*
   *Tab once*

While attending the Southern Computer Technology Conference earlier this month, I discovered several excellent network and internet security reference books. Two of these reference books, *Managing Network Security* by Douglas Baker (published by Evergreen Publishing House) and *Network Management* by Geraldine Kingston (published by Bonari & Jenkins), I would like you to order and make available in the business section of the library. Both books retail for approximately $55. If you have enough in your budget, please order two copies of each book. *(press the Enter key)*

Two other reference books, *Internet Security* by Jeong Pak (published by Meridian Publishers) and *Protecting and Securing Data* by Glenn Rowan (published by Canon Beach Publishing), I would like you to order for the technical support team training that will take place in April. I will need 15 copies of *Internet Security* and 20 copies of *Protecting and Securing Data*. *(press the Enter key)*

XX *(press Shift + the Enter key)*
BookMemo.docx

3. At the AutoCorrect dialog box, click the AutoCorrect tab and then click the *Capitalize first letter of sentences* check box to remove the check mark.

4. Click OK to close the AutoCorrect dialog box and then click OK to close the Word Options dialog box.

After typing your initials, press Shift + Enter (the New Line command) to move the insertion point to the next line without adding paragraph spacing and then type the document name.

The Word default line spacing is 1.08 and the default spacing after paragraphs is 8 points. You can remove this formatting by clicking the *No Spacing* style in the Styles group on the HOME tab. Applying this style changes the line spacing to 1 and the spacing after paragraphs to 0 points. To format a memo without the Word default spacing, click the *No Spacing* style and then type the memo as shown below.

## Formatting with No Spacing Style Applied

TO:————➤Jim Everson, Resources Coordinator *(press the Enter key two times)*
    *Tab twice*

FROM:———➤Isabelle Brown, Training Coordinator *(press the Enter key two times)*
     *Tab twice*

DATE:———➤February 16, 2015 *(press the Enter key two times)*
    *Tab twice*

SUBJECT:——➤ Network and Internet Books *(press the Enter key three times)*
    *Tab once*

While attending the Southern Computer Technology Conference earlier this month, I discovered several excellent network and internet security reference books. Two of these reference books, *Managing Network Security* by Douglas Baker (published by Evergreen Publishing House) and *Network Management* by Geraldine Kingston (pubished by Bonari & Jenkins), I would like you to order and make available in the business section of the library. Both books retail for approximately $55. If you have enough in your budget, please order two copies of each book. *(press the Enter key twice)*

Two other reference books, *Internet Security* by Jeong Pak (published by Meridian Publishers) and *Protecting and Securing Data* by Glenn Rowan (published by Canon Beach Publishing), I would like you to order for the technical support team training that will take place in April. I will need 15 copies of *Internet Security* and 20 copies of *Protecting and Securing Data*. *(press the Enter key twice)*

XX *(press the Enter key once)*
BookMemo.docx

# Formatting a Business Letter

Like a personal business letter, a business letter can be created with a variety of formatting options. One of the most common is the ***block style***. In block style format, all elements of the letter align at the left margin. You can create a business letter with the default Microsoft Word 2013 line and paragraph spacing, or you can remove the spacing and then create the letter. Include your reference initials at the end of the letter, as shown below (where the *XX* indicates your initials). If you want to type your reference initials in lowercase letters, refer to the information in Appendix C.

The business letters in this appendix use standard punctuation, which includes a colon after the salutation (*Dear Mrs. Cardoza*:) and a comma after the complimentary close (*Sincerely,*).

## Formatting with Microsoft Word Default Spacing

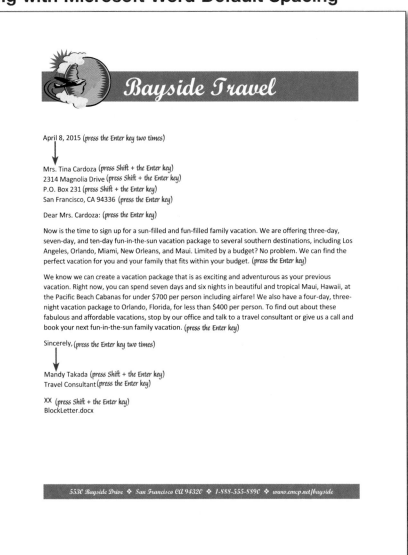

The Word default line spacing is 1.08 and the default spacing after paragraphs is 8 points. You can remove this formatting by clicking the *No Spacing* style in the Styles group on the HOME tab. Applying this style changes the line spacing to 1 and the spacing after paragraphs to 0 points. To format a business letter without the Word default spacing, click the *No Spacing* style and then type the letter as shown in the following example.

## Formatting with No Spacing Style Applied

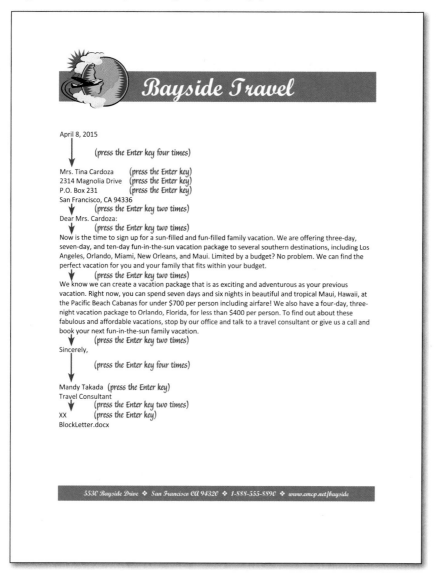

# Index

Boldface page numbers indicate figures and tables.

# F

# M

| Feature | Ribbon Tab, Group | Button, Option | Option | Quick Access Toolbar | Keyboard Shortcut |
|---|---|---|---|---|---|
| Align text center | HOME, Paragraph |  |  |  | Ctrl + E |
| Align text left | HOME, Paragraph |  |  |  | Ctrl + L |
| Align text right | HOME, Paragraph |  |  |  | Ctrl + R |
| AutoCorrect | FILE | Options | Proofing |  |  |
| Bibliography | REFERENCES, Citations & Bibliography |  |  |  |  |
| Bold text | HOME, Font | B |  |  | Ctrl + B |
| Borders | HOME, Paragraph |  |  |  |  |
| Building Blocks Organizer | INSERT, Text |  | Building Blocks Organizer |  |  |
| Bullets | HOME, Paragraph |  |  |  |  |
| Change case of text | HOME, Font | Aa |  |  | Shift + F3 |
| Change style sets | DESIGN, Document Formatting |  |  |  |  |
| Chart | INSERT, Illustrations |  |  |  |  |
| Clear all formatting | HOME, Font |  |  |  |  |
| Clip Art | INSERT, Illustrations |  |  |  |  |
| Close Word |  | X |  |  | Alt + F4 |
| Close document | FILE | Close |  |  | Ctrl + F4 |
| Columns | PAGE LAYOUT, Page Setup |  |  |  |  |
| Combine documents | REVIEW, Compare |  | Combine |  |  |
| Compare documents | REVIEW, Compare |  | Compare |  |  |
| Copy text | HOME, Clipboard |  |  |  | Ctrl + C |
| Cover page | INSERT, Pages |  |  |  |  |
| Cut text | HOME, Clipboard |  |  |  | Ctrl + X |
| Date and time | INSERT, Text |  |  |  | Alt + Shift + T (time) <br> Alt + Shift + D (date) |
| Decrease font size | HOME, Font | A |  |  | Ctrl + Shift + < |
| Display nonprinting characters | HOME, Paragraph | ¶ |  |  | Ctrl + Shift +* |
| Drop cap | INSERT, Text | A |  |  |  |
| Endnote | REFERENCES, Footnotes |  |  |  | Alt + Ctrl + D |
| Envelopes | MAILINGS, Create |  |  |  |  |
| Font dialog box | HOME, Font |  |  |  | Ctrl + Shift + F |
| Footer | INSERT, Header & Footer |  |  |  |  |
| Footnote | REFERENCES, Footnotes | AB |  |  | Alt + Ctrl + F |
| Format painter | HOME, Clipboard |  |  |  | Ctrl + Shift + C |
| Header | INSERT, Header & Footer |  |  |  |  |
| Help |  | ? |  |  | F1 |
| Highlight text | HOME, Font | aby |  |  |  |
| Hyperlink | INSERT, Links |  |  |  | Ctrl + K |
| Hyphenate | PAGE LAYOUT, Page Setup | a bc |  |  |  |
| Increase font size | HOME, Font | A |  |  | Ctrl + Shift + > |
| Index | REFERENCES, Index |  |  |  |  |
| Insert file | INSERT, Text |  | Text from File |  |  |
| Italicize text | HOME, Font | I |  |  | Ctrl + I |
| Justify text | HOME, Paragraph |  |  |  | Ctrl + J |
| Labels | MAILINGS, Create |  |  |  |  |
| Line spacing | HOME, Paragraph |  |  |  | Ctrl + 1 (single) <br> Ctrl + 2 (double) <br> Ctrl + 5 (1.5) |
| Mail merge | MAILINGS, Start Mail Merge |  |  |  |  |

| Feature | Ribbon Tab, Group | Button, Option | Option | Quick Access Toolbar | Keyboard Shortcut |
|---|---|---|---|---|---|
| Margins | PAGE LAYOUT, Page Setup | [icon] | | | |
| Mark index entry | REFERENCES, Index | [icon] | | | Alt + Shift + X |
| Mark table of contents entry | | | | | Alt + Shift + O |
| Multilevel List | HOME, Paragraph | [icon] | | | |
| Navigation pane | VIEW, Show | | Navigation Pane | | Ctrl + F |
| New document | FILE | New | Blank document | | Ctrl + N |
| New Line command | | | | | Shift + Enter |
| Nonbreaking space | | | | | Ctrl + Shift + Spacebar |
| Numbering | HOME, Paragraph | [icon] | | | |
| Open backstage area | FILE | Open | | | Ctrl + O |
| Orientation | PAGE LAYOUT, Page Setup | [icon] | | | |
| Page borders | DESIGN, Page Background | [icon] | | | |
| Page break | INSERT, Pages | [icon] | | | Ctrl + Enter |
| Page numbering | INSERT, Header & Footer | [icon] | | | |
| Page size | PAGE LAYOUT, Page Setup | [icon] | | | |
| Paste text | HOME, Clipboard | [icon] | | | Ctrl + V |
| Picture | INSERT, Illustrations | [icon] | | | |
| Print backstage area | FILE | Print | | | Ctrl + P |
| Redo | | | | [icon] | Ctrl + Y |
| Repeat last action | | | | | F4 or Ctrl + Y |
| Replace | HOME, Editing | [icon] | | | Ctrl + H |
| Reveal formatting task pane | | | | | Shift + F1 |
| Save | FILE | Save | | [icon] | Ctrl + S |
| Save As | FILE | Save As | | | F12 |
| Screenshot | INSERT, Illustrations | [icon] | | | |
| Shading | HOME, Paragraph | [icon] | | | |
| Shapes | INSERT, Illustrations | [icon] | | | |
| SmartArt | INSERT, Illustrations | [icon] | | | |
| Sort text dialog box | HOME, Paragraph | [icon] | | | |
| Spelling and grammar checking | REVIEW, Proofing | [icon] | | | F7 |
| Strikethrough text | HOME, Font | [icon] | | | |
| Subscript text | HOME, Font | $x_2$ | | | Ctrl + = |
| Superscript text | HOME, Font | $x^2$ | | | Ctrl + Shift + + |
| Symbol dialog box | INSERT, Symbols | $\Omega$ | More Symbols | | |
| Table | INSERT, Tables | [icon] | | | |
| Table of Contents | REFERENCES, Table of Contents | [icon] | | | |
| Table of Figures | REFERENCES, Captions | [icon] | | | |
| Tabs dialog box | HOME, Paragraph | [icon] | Tabs | | |
| Text box | INSERT, Text | [icon] | Draw Text Box | | |
| Themes | DESIGN, Document Formatting | [icon] | | | |
| Thesaurus task pane | REVIEW, Proofing | [icon] | | | Shift + F7 |
| Track changes | REVIEW, Tracking | [icon] | | | Ctrl + Shift + E |
| Underline text | HOME, Font | [icon] | | | Ctrl + U |
| Undo | | | | [icon] | Ctrl + Z |
| Watermark | DESIGN, Page Background | [icon] | | | |
| Word Count dialog box | REVIEW, Proofing | [icon] | | | |
| WordArt | INSERT, Text | [icon] | | | |